CLASSICS OF PHILOSOPHY

VOLUME II

Modern and Contemporary

CLASSICS OF PHILOSOPHY

VOLUME II
Modern and Contemporary

Louis P. Pojman

New York Oxford
OXFORD UNIVERSITY PRESS
1998

OXFORD UNIVERSITY PRESS

Oxford New York
Athens Auckland Bangkok Bogotá Bombay Buenos Aires
Calcutta Cape Town Dar es Salaam Delhi Florence Hong Kong
Istanbul Karachi Kuala Lumpur Madras Madrid Melbourne
Mexico City Nairobi Paris Singapore Taipei Tokyo Toronto

and associated companies in

Berlin Ibadan

Published by Oxford University Press, Inc.
198 Madison Avenue, New York, New York 10016

Library of Congress Cataloging-in-Publication Data
Philosophy: the classics/[edited by] Louis P. Pojman.
p. cm.
Includes bibliographical references.
Contents: v. 1. Ancient and medieval—v. 2. Modern and contemporary
ISBN 978-0-19-511645-8 (v. 1).—ISBN 978-0-19-511646-5 (v. 2)
1. Philosophy. I. Pojman, Louis P.
BD21.P476 1997
100–dc21 97-1134
CIP

Printing (last digit): 9 8 7 6 5

Printed in the United States of America
on acid-free paper

Dedicated to
William Lawhead and Wallace Matson
whose love of the classics
has inspired me

Contents

Preface *ix*

Time Line *xi*

PART III: THE MODERN PERIOD

15. Rene Descartes 463
* Meditations on First Philosophy, 465

16. Thomas Hobbes 491
Leviathan or The Matter, Form, & Power of a Commonwealth Ecclesiastical and Civil, 493

17. Blaise Pascal 529
Pensees, 530

18. Baruch Spinoza 533
Ethic, 534

19. Gottfried Wilhelm Leibniz 578
* Discourse on Metaphysics, 581
* The Monadology, 602
* Theodicy: Abridgement of the Argument Reduced to Syllogistic Form, 609

20. John Locke 614
An Essay Concerning Human Understanding, 615

21. George Berkeley 644
Three Dialogues Between Hylas and Philonous in Opposition to Sceptics and Atheists, 646

22. William Paley 667
Natural Theology, or Evidences of the Existence and Attributes of the Deity Collected from the Appearances of Nature, 667

23. David Hume 670
* An Enquiry Concerning Human Understanding, 672
* Dialogues Concerning Natural Religion, 728

24. Immanuel Kant 771
Prolegomena to Any Future Metaphysics, 774
Foundation for the Metaphysic of Morals, 820

25. Georg Wilhelm Friedrich Hegel 857
Phenomenology of Spirit, 859

26. Arthur Schopenhauer 864
The World as Will and Representation, 865
Essay on the Freedom of the Will, 888

27. Soren Kierkegaard 901
Readings, 902
Concluding Unscientific Postscript, 905

28. John Stuart Mill 913
* Utilitarianism, 914
On Liberty, 945
The Subjection of Women, 981

29. Karl Marx 995
Towards a Critique of Hegel's *Philosophy of Right*, 996
Economic and Philosophical Manuscripts, 997
The German Ideology, 1011

30. Friedrich Nietzsche 1014
Aphorisms, 1015
Joyful Wisdom, 1016
Beyond Good and Evil, 1017
Twilight of the Idols, 1022
The Anti-Christ, 1034

PART IV: THE CONTEMPORARY PERIOD

31. W. K. Clifford 1047
The Ethics of Belief, 1048

32. Charles Sanders Peirce 1052
* The Fixation of Belief, 1053

33. William James 1062
* The Will to Believe, 1063
Pragmatism, 1070

34. Bertrand Russell 1085
* The Problems of Philosophy, 1086
* A Free Man's Worship, 1134

35. G. E. Moore 1139
Philosophical Papers, 1140

36. Ludwig Wittgenstein 1147
Tractatus Logico-Philosophicus, 1148
Philosophical Investigations, 1156

37. Edmund Husserl 1165
Ideas: General Introduction to Pure Phenomenology, 1166

38. Martin Heidegger 1180
* The Fundamental Question of Metaphysics, 1181

39. Jean-Paul Sartre 1201
Being and Nothingness, 1202
* Existentialism and Humanism, 1213

40. A. J. Ayer 1218
Language, Truth and Logic, 1219

41. W. V. O. Quine 1226
* Two Dogmas of Empiricism, 1227

42. Nelson Goodman 1240
Fact, Fiction and Forecast, 1240

43. John Rawls 1245
* Justice as Fairness, 1247

*** Selection reprinted in its entirety**

Preface

This volume contains the last two parts, "The Modern Period" and "The Contemporary Period," of the four-part volume *Classics of Philosophy*.

Part III, "The Modern Period," begins with the whole of Descartes' *Meditations*, then a large selection from Hobbes's *Leviathan*. I have included Pascal's The Wager from his *Pensees*. Next we have a sizable portion of Spinoza's *Ethic*, followed by three works of G. W. Leibniz. After this comes four works of British Empiricists: Locke's theory of knowledge, Berkeley's *Three Dialogues*, Paley's Watch Argument for the Existence of God, and two complete works of Hume: *An Enquiry Concerning Human Understanding* and *Dialogues Concerning Natural Religion*. Next come Immanuel Kant's *Prolegomena to Any Future Metaphysics* and his *Foundation for the Metaphysic of Morals*, both complete. These are followed by selections from Hegel, Schopenhauer, and Kierkegaard. John Stuart Mill's *Utilitarianism* is reprinted in its entirety, and *On Liberty* and *The Subjection of Women* in part. Selections from the work of Karl Marx on alienation, property, communism, and money round out this part of our work.

Part IV deals with the Contemporary Period. I have begun with W. K. Clifford's rationalist essay "The Ethics of Belief," followed by two American works on the same subject, belief: Peirce's "The Fixation of Belief" and William James's "The Will to Believe." I have also included two chapters from James's *Pragmatism*, "What Pragmatism Means" and "Pragmatism's Conception of Truth." This is followed by Bertrand Russell's *The Problems of Philosophy*, which includes classic expressions of the representational theory of perception, the problem of induction, and the correspondence theory of truth. Russell's famous *A Free Man's Worship* is also included. Next comes G. E. Moore's defense of common sense, followed by selections from Wittgenstein's *Tractatus Logico-Philosophicus* and *Philosophical Investigations* (sections dealing with Language Games and Forms of Life).

The next section deals with writings in Phenomenology and Existentialism and includes the writings of Edmund Husserl (the general theory of phenomenology), Martin Heidegger (on Metaphysics), and Jean-Paul Sartre, especially his *Existentialism and Humanism*. I have included a selection from A. J. Ayer's *Language, Truth and Logic* as a representation of logical positivism. The last three essays have already been judged as classics: W. V. O. Quine's "Two Dogmas of Empiricism" (1953), Nelson Goodman's "New Riddle of Induction" (1955), and John Rawls's "Justice as Fairness" (1958).

Brief introductions on each philosopher, including a bibliography, precede his works.

I have included complete works or, at least, complete sections of works, wherever possible, given the constraints on a book like this. With regard to works in other languages, I have chosen the best translations in terms of accuracy and accessibility.

Beginning on page xi I have included a time line in order to place the philosophers in this collection in chronological context with other major figures and events.

Several people gave me constructive advice on this project: Brian Magee, James Allard, Daniel Frank, Stanley Obitts, and Wayne Pomerleau. I especially want to thank Wallace Matson who provided special help, allowing me to use his translation of Epictetus's *Encheiridion* and correcting an earlier draft of my introductions. To him and my long time friend and former colleague Bill Lawhead, both of whom have contributed to my knowledge of the history of philosophy, this work is dedicated. My editor, Robert Miller, was a strong support, providing encouragement at every step of the way. My wife, Trudy, with her love and devotion, as always was the force that enabled me to accomplish this task with exhilarating joy.

United States Military Academy
West Point, N.Y.

L.P.P.

Time Line

Philosophers		Major Figures and Events
THE MODERN PERIOD		Johann Gutenberg invents the printing press, 1445 Leonardo Da Vinci, 1452–1517
Rene Descartes	1596–1650	The reign of Louis XIV in France, 1643–1715
Blaise Pascal	1623–1662	
Benedict (Baruch) Spinoza	1632–1677	Johann Sebastian Bach, 1685–1750
John Locke	1632–1704	*Two Treatises on Government*, 1689
Sir Issaac Newton	1642–1727	Publication of *Principia Mathematica*, 1687
Gottfried Leibniz	1646–1716	
George Berkeley	1685–1753	Wolfgang Amadeus Mozart, 1756–1791
Voltaire	1694–1778	*Candide*, 1759
David Hume	1711–1776	Ludwig von Beethoven, 1770–1827
Jean Jacques Rousseau	1712–1778	American Revolution, 1775–1783
Adam Smith	1723–1790	*The Wealth of Nations*, 1776
Immanuel Kant	1724–1804	*Critique of Pure Reason*, 1781
Edmund Burke	1729–1797	French Revolution, 1789–92
Jeremy Bentham	1748–1832	Industrial Revolution in England, c. 1790 Napoleon crowns himself Emperor of France, 1804
Mary Wollstonecraft	1759–1797	Charles Darwin, 1809–1882 Richard Wagner, 1813–1883
George W. F. Hegel	1770–1831	Fyodor Dostoevsky, 1821–1881 Leo Tolstoy, 1828–1910
Arthur Schopenhauer	1788–1860	Second French Revolution, 1830 Opium War in China, 1839

* Philosophers whose names appear in **boldface** appear in this volume.

Auguste Comte	1798–1857	The Italian Revolution, 1848
John Stuart Mill	1806–1873	*On Liberty*, 1859 Darwin's *Origin of the Species*, 1859
Soren Kierkegaard	1813–1855	*Fear and Trembling*, 1841
Karl Marx	1818–1883	*The Communist Manifesto*, 1848 Sigmund Freud, 1856–1939
Friedrich Engels	1820–1895	American Civil War, 1861–1865 Bismark unites Germany, 1870 C. G. Jung, 1875–1961
Friedrich Nietzsche	1844–1900	Pablo Picasso, 1881–1973 James Joyce, 1882–1941 Virginia Woolf, 1882–1941 The Dreyfus Affair (France), 1899

THE CONTEMPORARY PERIOD

Charles S. Peirce	1839–1914	Albert Einstein presents theory of relativity, 1905
William James	1842–1910	
Gottlob Frege	1848–1925	First World War, 1914–1918
Edmund Husserl	1859–1938	
Henri Bergson	1859–1941	Russian Communist Revolution, 1917
John Dewey	1859–1952	Gandhi begins his crusade for Indian Independence, 1919
Alfred North Whitehead	1861–1947	Joseph Stalin becomes General Secretary of the Communist Party, 1922
Bertrand Russell	1872–1970	The Great Depression, 1929 Spanish Civil War, 1936–1939
Ludwig Wittgenstein	1889–1951	Second World War, 1939–1945
Martin Heidegger	1889–1976	Dropping of the Atomic Bomb on Hiroshima Aug. 6, 1945
Rudolph Carnap	1891–1970	India gains Independence, 1947
Gilbert Ryle	1900–1976	Israel becomes a Nation, 1949
Karl Popper	1902–1994	The People's Republic of China under Mao Tse-tung established, 1949 Crick & Watson identify the structure of DNA, 1953
John Wisdom	1904–1993	Korean War, 1950–52
Jean-Paul Sartre	1905–1980	Cuban Missile Crisis, 1962
Nelson Goodman	1906	Assassination of John F. Kennedy, 1963
Simone d'Beauvoir	1908–1986	

Willard V. O. Quine	1908–	War in Viet Nam, 1963–1972
A. J. Ayer	1910–1989	Assassination of Martin Luther King, 1968
John Rawls	1921–	*A Theory of Justice*, 1971
Thomas Kuhn	1922–1996	The Fall of the Soviet Union, 1991
Michel Foucault	1926–1984	Apartheid ends in South Africa, 1994

PART III

THE MODERN PERIOD

Chapter 15

Rene Descartes

There was once a young man who was troubled because he discovered that many of the things he believed, many of which he had been taught by his elders and in school, were false or, at least, were unsupported by the evidence. Despite having the best education available, he found it filled with error. For some years he resolved that were he to obtain leisure time, he would use it not for entertainment or professional purposes but in order to rework his entire system of knowledge. He writes:

> I had been nourished on the humanities since childhood, and since I was given to believe that by their means a clear and certain knowledge could be obtained of all that is useful in life, I was extremely eager to learn them. But as soon as I had finished my course of study at the end of which one is normally admitted among the ranks of the learned, I completely altered my view on the matter. For I found myself embarrassed by so many doubts and errors, that it seemed to me that the only profit I had had from my efforts to acquire knowledge was the progressive discovery of my own ignorance. And yet I was in one of the most prestigious schools in Europe, and if knowledge existed anywhere, it must be in the scholars there. I had learned everything that the others were learning there, and, not content with the studies in which we were instructed, I had even perused all the books that came into my hands, treating of subjects considered advanced and esoteric. At the same time I knew that others regarded me with respect, even though some of these were as brilliant as any age has produced.
>
> Having studied with the best, and learned from them, I was confident that I should seek knowledge in myself, or at least in the great book of the world. I employed the rest of my youth in travel, in seeing courts and armies, in conversation with men of diverse temperaments and conditions, in collecting varied experiences, in testing myself in the various predicaments in which I was placed by fortune. In all circumstances I sought to bring my mind to bear on the things that came before it so that I might derive some profit from my experience. I had a passion to learn to distinguish truth from falsehood in order to have clear insight into my actions and how to live my life.
>
> So for nine years I did nothing but roam hither and thither, trying to be a spectator rather than an actor in all the comedies which the world displays. I considered the manners and customs of other men, and found nothing to give me settled convictions. I noticed in people's beliefs and customs as much diversity as I had earlier noticed in the views of philosophers. So much was this so, that I learned not to believe too firmly anything that I had been convinced of only by example and custom. I thus gradually freed myself from many errors that may obscure the light of nature

> in us and make us less capable of hearing reason. But after spending these years in the study of the book of the world and in trying to gain experience, the day came when I resolved to make my studies within myself, and use all of the powers of my mind to choose the path that I must follow.[1]

These are the words of the man considered to be the father of modern philosophy, Rene Descartes. Descartes was born in France in 1596 and educated by the Jesuits, an intellectually elite order in the Roman Catholic Church, in La Fleche. At seventeen he left school for Paris where he plunged into a fast-moving social life. After a few years of high society, he withdrew to a more contemplative life. In 1618 he became a soldier, serving in three different European armies. After four years he retired from the army and resumed his travels to Switzerland, Italy, and, finally Holland, where he settled and became a writer of philosophy. He reputedly did most of his research and writing, especially in winter, sitting up in bed. He became famous, and even the rulers of Europe wrote to him for advice. One of the rules who admired him was Queen Christina of Sweden. She invited Descartes to visit her in Stockholm and teach her philosophy. Against the advice of friends he moved to Stockholm. The queen insisted that the lessons be given three times a week at 5 A.M. in spite of his being a late night owl. He was not happy in Sweden and hated the cold weather, and a few months after he arrived he caught pneumonia from which he died on February 11, 1650.

Descartes' classic work in the theory of knowledge is his *Meditations on First Philosophy* written in Holland in November 1640. It is a short but tightly written set of six philosophical meditations, one for each day of the week (even philosophers should rest on the Sabbath). Each meditation is to occupy the mind in reflection for an entire day. He begins by admitting that he has painfully discovered that many of his former beliefs were false. How can he be sure that his present beliefs won't suffer the same fate? He is revolted by the thought that he may be deceived in his beliefs and desires to know the truth. How shall he separate the true beliefs from the false? He decides that there is only one way. He must destroy his tottering, unstable house of "knowledge" and lay a new foundation upon which to construct an indestructible edifice. The method consists of doubting everything that can be doubted, and then, upon the pure remainder of certain truth, beginning the process of constructing an indubitable system of knowledge. The result is a type of rationalism in which the only certainties are discovered by the mind through self-evident insight or reason.

FOR FURTHER READING:

Curley, E. M. *Descartes Against the Skeptics.* (Harvard University Press, 1978).
Dicker, George. *Descartes.* (Oxford University Press, 1992). A comprehensive treatment.
Doney, Willis, ed. *Descartes: A Collection of Critical Essays.* (Doubleday, 1967).
Hooker, Michael, ed. *Descartes, Critical and Interpretative Essays.* (Johns Hopkins Press, 1978).
Kenny, Anthony. *Descartes: A Study of His Philosophy.* (Doubleday, 1967).
Markie, Peter. *Descartes' Gambit.* (Cornell University Press, 1986).

1. Rene Descartes, *Discourse on Method* in *The Philosophical Works of Descartes* vol I, trans. Elizabeth Haldane and G. R. T. Ross (Dover Publications, 1911).

Meditations on First Philosophy

in which are demonstrated the existence of God and the distinction between the human soul and the body

FIRST MEDITATION

What Can Be Called Into Doubt

Some years ago I was struck by the large number of falsehoods that I had accepted as true in my childhood, and by the highly doubtful nature of the whole edifice that I had subsequently based on them. I realized that it was necessary, once in the course of my life, to demolish everything completely and start again right from the foundations if I wanted to establish anything at all in the sciences that was stable and likely to last. But the task looked an enormous one, and I began to wait until I should reach a mature enough age to ensure that no subsequent time of life would be more suitable for tackling such inquiries. This led me to put the project off for so long that I would now be to blame if by pondering over it any further I wasted the time still left for carrying it out. So today I have expressly rid my mind of all worries and arranged for myself a clear stretch of free time. I am here quite alone, and at last I will devote myself sincerely and without reservation to the general demolition of my opinions.

But to accomplish this, it will not be necessary for me to show that all my opinions are false, which is something I could perhaps never manage. Reason now leads me to think that I should hold back my assent from opinions which are not completely certain and indubitable just as carefully as I do from those which are patently false. So, for the purpose of rejecting all my opinions, it will be enough if I find in each of them at least some reason for doubt. And to do this I will not need to run through them all individually, which would be an endless task. Once the foundations of a building are undermined, anything built on them collapses of its own accord; so I will go straight for the basic principles on which all my former beliefs rested.

Whatever I have up till now accepted as most true I have acquired either from the senses or through the senses. But from time to time I have found that the senses deceive, and it is prudent never to trust completely those who have deceived us even once.

Yet although the senses occasionally deceive us with respect to objects which are very small or in the distance, there are many other beliefs about which doubt is quite impossible, even though they are derived from the senses—for example, that I am here, sitting by the fire, wearing a winter dressing-gown, holding this piece of paper in my hands, and so on. Again, how could it be denied that these hands or this whole body are mine? Unless perhaps I were to liken myself to madmen, whose brains are so damaged by the persistent vapours of melancholia that they firmly maintain they are kings when they are paupers, or say they are dressed in purple when they are naked, or that their heads are made of earthenware, or that they are pumpkins, or made of glass. But such people are insane, and I would be thought equally mad if I took anything from them as a model for myself.

A brilliant piece of reasoning! As if I were not a man who sleeps at night, and regularly has all the same experiences while asleep as madmen do when awake—indeed sometimes even more improbable ones. How often, asleep at night, am I convinced of just such familiar events—that I am here in my dressing-gown, sitting by the fire—when in fact I am lying undressed in bed! Yet at the moment my eyes are certainly wide awake when I look at this piece of paper; I shake my head and it is not asleep; as I stretch out and feel my hand I do so deliberately, and I known what I am doing. All this would not happen with such distinctness to someone asleep. Indeed! As if I did not remember other occasions when I have been tricked by exactly similar thoughts while asleep! As I think about this more carefully, I see plainly that there are never any sure signs by means of which being awake can be distinguished from being asleep. The result is that I begin to feel dazed, and this very feeling only reinforces the notion that I may be asleep.

Suppose then that I am dreaming, and that these particulars—that my eyes are open, that I am moving my head and stretching out my hands—are not true. Perhaps, indeed, I do not even have such hands or such a body at all. Nonetheless, it must surely be admitted that the visions which come in sleep are like paintings, which must have been fashioned in the likeness of things that are real, and hence that at least these general kinds of things—eyes, head, hands and the body as a whole—are things which are not imaginary but are real and exist. For even when painters try to create sirens and satyrs with the most extraordinary bodies, they cannot give them natures which are new in all respects; they simply jumble up the limbs of different animals. Or if perhaps they manage to think up something so new that nothing remotely similar has ever been seen before—something which is therefore completely fictitious and unreal—at least the colours used in the composition must be real. By similar reasoning, although these general kinds of things—eyes, head, hands and so on—could be imaginary, it must at least be admitted that certain other even simpler and more universal things are real. These are as it were the real colours from which we form all the images of things, whether true or false, that occur in our thought.

This class appears to include corporeal nature in general, and its extension; the shape of extended things; the quantity, or size and number of these things; the place in which they may exist, the time through which they may endure, and so on.

So a reasonable conclusion from this might be that physics, astronomy, medicine, and all other disciplines which depend on the study of composite things, are doubtful; while arithmetic, geometry and other subjects of this kinds, which deal only with the simplest and most general things, regardless of whether they really exist in nature or not, contain something certain and indubitable. For whether I am awake or asleep, two and three added together are five, and a square has no more than four sides. It seems impossible that such transparent truths should incur any suspicion of being false.

And yet firmly rooted in my mind is the long-standing opinion that there is an omnipotent God who made me the kind of creature that I am. How do I know that he has not brought it about that there is no earth, no sky, no extended thing, no shape, no size, no place, while at the same time ensuring that all these things appear to me to exist just as they do now? What is more, since I sometimes believe that others go astray in cases where they think they have the most perfect knowledge, may I not similarly go wrong every time I add two and three or count the sides of a square, or in some even simpler matter, if that is imaginable? But perhaps God would not have allowed me to be deceived in this way, since he is said to be supremely good. But if it were inconsistent with his goodness to have created me such that I am deceived all the time, it would seem equally foreign to his goodness to allow me to be deceived even occasionally; yet this last assertion cannot be made.

Perhaps there may be some who would prefer to deny the existence of so powerful a God rather than believe that everything else is uncertain. Let us not argue with them, but grant them that everything said about God is a fiction. According to their supposition, then, I have arrived at my present state by fate or chance or a continuous chain of events, or by some other means; yet since deception and error seem to be imperfections, the less powerful they make my original cause, the more likely it is that I am so imperfect as to be deceived all the time. I have no answer to these arguments, but am finally compelled to admit that there is not one of my former beliefs about which a doubt may not properly be raised; and this is not flippant or ill-considered conclusion, but is based on powerful and well thought-out reasons. So in future I must withhold my assent from these former beliefs just as carefully as I would from obvious falsehoods, if I want to discover any certainty.

But it is not enough merely to have noticed this; I must make an effort to remember it. My habitual opinions keep coming back, and, despite my wishes, they capture my belief, which is as it were bound over to them as a result of long occupation and the law of custom. I shall never get out of the habit of confidently assenting to these opinions, so long as I suppose them to be what in fact they are, namely highly probable opinions—opinions which, despite the fact that they are in a sense doubtful, as has just been shown, it is still much more reasonable to believe than to deny. In view of this, I think it will be a good plan to turn my will in completely the opposite direction and deceive myself, by pretending for a time that these former opinions are utterly false and imaginary. I shall do this until the weight of preconceived opinion is counter-balanced and the distorting influence of habit no longer prevents my judgement from perceiving things correctly. In the meantime, I know that no danger or error will result from my plan, and that I cannot possibly go too far in my distrustful attitude. This is because the task now in hand does not involve action but merely the acquisition of knowledge.

I will suppose therefore that not God, who is supremely good and the source of truth, but rather some malicious demon of the utmost power and cunning has employed all his energies in order to deceive me. I shall think that the sky, the air, the earth, colours, shapes, sounds and all external things are merely the delusions of dreams which he has devised to ensnare my judgement. I shall consider myself as not having hands or eyes, or flesh, or blood or senses, but as falsely believing that I have all these things. I shall stubbornly and firmly persist in this mediation; and, even if it is not in my power to know any truth, I shall at least do what is in my power, that is, resolutely guard against assenting to any falsehoods, so that the deceiver, however powerful and cunning he may be, will be unable to impose on me in the slightest degree. But this is an arduous undertaking, and a kind of laziness brings me back to normal life. I am like a prisoner who is enjoying an imaginary freedom while asleep; as he begins to suspect that he is asleep, he dreads being woken up, and goes along with the pleasant illusion as long as he can. In the same way, I happily slide back into my old opinions and dread being shaken out of them, for fear that my peaceful sleep may be followed by hard labour when I wake, and that I shall have to toil not in the light, but amid the inextricable darkness of the problems I have now raised.

SECOND MEDITATION

The Nature of the Human Mind, and How It Is Better Known Than the Body

So serious are the doubts into which I have been thrown as a result of yesterday's meditation that I can neither put them out of my mind nor see any way of resolving them. It feels as if I have fallen unexpectedly into a deep whirlpool which tumbles me around so that I can neither stand on the bottom nor swim up to the top. Nevertheless I will make an effort and once more attempt the same path which I started on yesterday. Anything which admits of the slightest doubt I will set aside just as if I had found it to be wholly false; and I will proceed in this way until I recognize something certain, or, if nothing else, until I at least recognize for certain that there is no certainty. Archimedes used to demand just one firm and immovable point in order to shift the entire earth; so I too can hope for great things if I manage to find just one thing, however slight, that is certain and unshakeable.

I will suppose then, that everything I see is spurious. I will believe that my memory tells me lies, and that none of the things that it reports ever happened. I have no senses. Body, shape, extension, movement and place are chimeras. So what remains true? Perhaps just the one fact that nothing is certain.

Yet apart from everything I have just listed, how do I know that there is not something else which does not allow even the slightest occasion for doubt? Is there not a God, or whatever I may call him, who puts into me the thoughts I am now having? But why do I think this, since I myself may perhaps be the author of these thoughts? In that case am not I, at least, something? But I have just said that I have no senses and no body. This is the sticking point: what follows from this? Am I not so bound up with a body and with senses that I cannot exist without them? But I have convinced myself that there is absolutely nothing in the world, no sky, no earth, no minds, no bodies. Does it now follow that I too do not exist? No: if I convinced myself of something then I certainly existed. But there is a deceiver of supreme power and cunning who is deliberately and constantly deceiving me. In that case I too undoubtedly exist, if he is deceiving me; and let him deceive me as much as he can, he will never bring it about that I am nothing so long as I think that I am something. So after considering everything very thoroughly, I must finally conclude that this proposition, I am, I exist, is necessarily true whenever it is put forward by me or conceived in my mind.

But I do not yet have a sufficient understanding of what this 'I' is, that now necessarily exists. So I must be on my guard against carelessly taking something else to be this 'I,' and so making a mistake in the very item of knowledge that I maintain is the most certain and evident of all. I will therefore go back and meditate on what I originally believed myself to be, before I embarked on this present train of thought. I will then subtract anything capable of being weakened, even minimally, by the arguments now introduced, so that what is left at the end may be exactly and only what is certain and unshakeable.

What then did I formerly think I was? A man. But what is a man? Shall I say 'a rational animal'? No; for then I should have to inquire what an animal is, what rationality is, and in this way one question would lead me down the slope to other harder ones, and I do not now have the time to waste on subtleties of this kind. Instead I propose to concentrate on what came into my thoughts spontaneously and quite naturally whenever I used to consider what I was. Well, the first thought to come to mind was that I had a face, hands, arms and the whole mechanical structure of limbs which can be seen in a corpse, and which I called the body. The next thought was that I was nourished, that I moved about, that I engaged in sense-perception and thinking; and these actions I attributed to the soul. But as to the nature of this soul, either I did not think about this or else I imagined it to be something tenuous, like a wind or fire or ether, which permeated my more solid parts. As to the body, however, I had no doubts about it, but thought I knew its nature distinctly. If I had tried to describe the mental conception I had of it, I would have expressed it as follows: by a body I understand whatever has a determinable shape and a definable location and can occupy a space in such a way as to exclude any other body; it can be perceived by touch, sight, hearing, taste or smell, and can be moved in various ways, not by itself but by whatever else comes into contact with it. For, according to my judgement, the power of self-movement, like the power of sensation or of thought, was quite foreign to the nature of a body; indeed, it was a source of wonder to me that certain bodies were found to contain faculties of this kind.

But what shall I now say that I am, when I am supposing that there is some supremely powerful and, if it is permissible to say so, malicious deceiver, who is deliberately trying to trick me in every way he can? Can I now assert that I possess even the most insignificant of all the attributes which I have just said belong to the nature of a body? I scrutinize them, think about them, go over them again, but nothing suggests itself; it is tiresome and pointless to go through the list once more. But what about the attributes I assigned to the soul? Nutrition or movement? Since now I do not have a body, these are mere fabrications. Sense-perception? This surely does not occur without a body, and besides, when asleep I have appeared to perceive through the senses many things which I afterwards realized I did not perceive through the senses at all. Thinking? At last I have discovered it—thought; this alone is inseparable from me. I am, I exist—that is certain. But for how long? For as long as I am thinking. For it could be that were I totally to cease from thinking, I should totally cease to exist. At present I am not admitting anything except what is necessarily true. I am, then, in the strict sense only a thing that thinks; that is, I am a mind, or intelligence, or intellect, or reason—words whose meaning I have been ignorant of until now. But for all that I am a thing which is real and which truly exists. But what kind of a thing? As I have just said—a thinking thing.

What else am I? I will use my imagination. I am not that structure of limbs which is called a human body, I am not even some thin vapour which permeates the limbs—a wind, fire, air, breath, or whatever I depict in my imagination; for these are things which I have supposed to be nothing. Let this supposition stand; for all that I am still something. And yet may it not perhaps be the case that these very things which I am supposing to be nothing, because they are unknown to me, are in reality identical with the 'I' of which I am aware? I do not know, and for the moment I shall not argue the point, since I can make judgements only about things which are known to me. I know that I exist; the question is, what is this 'I' that I know? If the 'I' is understood strictly as we have been taking it, then it is quite certain that knowledge of it does not depend on things of whose existence I am as yet unaware; so it cannot depend on any of the things which I invent in my imagination. And this very word 'invent' shows me my mistake. It would indeed be a case of fictitious invention if I used my imagination to establish that I was something or other; for imagining is simply contemplating the shape or image of a corporeal thing. Yet now I know for certain both that I exist and at the same time that all such images and, in general, everything relating to the nature of body, could be mere dreams and chimeras. Once this point has been grasped, to say 'I will use my imagination to get to know more distinctly what I am' would seem to be as silly as saying 'I am now awake, and see some truth; but since my vision is not yet clear enough, I will deliberately fall asleep so that my dreams may provide a truer and clearer representation.' I thus realize that none of the things that the imagination enables me to grasp is at all relevant to this knowledge of myself which I possess, and that the mind must therefore be most carefully diverted from such things if it is to perceive its own nature as distinctly as possible.

But what then am I? A thing that thinks. What is that? A thing that doubts, understands, affirms, denies, is willing, is unwilling, and also imagines and has sensory perceptions.

This is a considerable list, if everything on it belongs to me. But does it? Is it not one and the same 'I' who is now doubting almost everything, who nonetheless understands some things, who affirms that this one thing is true, denies everything else, desires to know more, is unwilling to be deceived, imagines many things even involuntarily, and is aware of many things which apparently come from the senses? Are not all these things just as true as the fact that I exist, even if I am asleep all the time, and even if he who created me is doing all he can to deceive me? Which of all these activities is distinct from my thinking? Which of them can be said to be separate from myself? The fact that it is I who am doubting and understanding and willing is so evident that I see no way of making it any clearer. But it is also the case that the 'I' who imagines is the same 'I'. For even if, as I have supposed, none of the objects of imagination are real, the power of imagination is something which really exists and is part of my thinking. Lastly, it is also the same 'I' who has sensory perceptions, or is aware of bodily things as it were through the senses. For example, I am now seeing light, hearing a noise, feeling heat. But I am asleep, so all this is false. Yet I certainly seem to see, to hear, and to be warmed. This cannot be false; what is called 'having a sensory perception' is strictly just this, and in this restricted sense of the term it is simply thinking.

From all this I am beginning to have a rather better understanding of what I am. But it still appears—and I cannot stop thinking this—that the corporeal things of which images are formed in my thought, and which the senses investigate, are known with much more distinctness than this puzzling 'I' which cannot be pictured in the imagination. And yet it is surely surprising that I should have a more distinct grasp of things which I realize are doubtful, unknown and foreign to me, than I have of that which is true and known—my own self. But I see what it is: my mind enjoys wandering off and will not yet submit to being restrained within the bounds of truth. Very well then; just this once let us give it a completely free rein, so that after a while, when it is time to tighten the reins, it may more readily submit to being curbed.

Let us consider the things which people commonly think they understand most distinctly of all; that is, the bodies which we touch and see. I do not mean bodies in general—for general perceptions are apt to be somewhat more confused—but one particular body. Let us take, for example, this piece of wax. It has just been taken from the honeycomb; it has not yet quite lost the taste of the honey; it retains some of the scent of the flowers from which it was gathered; its colour, shape and size are plain to see; it is hard, cold and can be handled without difficulty; if you rap it with your knuckle it makes a sound. In short, it has everything which appears necessary to enable a body to be known as distinctly as possible. But even as I speak, I put the wax by the fire, and look: the residual taste is eliminated, the smell goes away, the colour changes, the shape is lost, the size increases; it becomes a liquid and hot; you can hardly touch it, and if you strike it, it no longer makes a sound. But does the same wax remain? It must be admitted that it does; no one denies it, no one thinks otherwise. So what was it in the wax that I understood with such distinctness? Evidently one of the features which I arrived at by means of the senses; for whatever came under taste, smell, sight, touch or hearing has now altered—yet the wax remains.

Perhaps the answer lies in the thought which now comes to mind; namely, the wax was not after all the sweetness of the honey, or the fragrance of the flowers, or the whiteness, or the shape, or the sound, but was rather a body which presented itself to me in these various forms a little while ago, but which now exhibits different ones. But what exactly is it that I am now imagining? Let us concentrate, take away everything which does not belong to the wax, and see what is left: merely something extended, flexible and changeable. But what is meant here by 'flexible' and 'changeable'? Is it what I picture in my imagination: that this piece of wax is capable of changing from a round shape to a square shape, or from a square shape to a triangular shape? Not at all; for I can grasp that the wax is capable of countless changes of this kind, yet I am unable to run through this immeasurable number of changes in my imagination, from which it follows that it is not the faculty of imagination that gives me my grasp of the wax as flexible and changeable. And what is meant by 'extended'? Is the extension of the wax also unknown? For it increases if the wax melts, increases again if it boils, and is greater still if the heat is increased. I would not be making a correct judgement about the nature of wax unless I believed it capable of being extended in many more different ways than

I will ever encompass in my imagination. I must therefore admit that the nature of this piece of wax is in no way revealed by my imagination, but is perceived by the mind alone. (I am speaking of this particular piece of wax; the point is even clearer with regard to wax in general.) But what is this wax which is perceived by the mind alone? It is of course the same wax which I see, which I touch, which I picture in my imagination, in short the same wax which I thought it to be from the start. And yet, and here is the point, the perception I have of it is a case not of vision or touch or imagination—nor has it ever been, despite previous appearances—but of purely mental scrutiny; and this can be imperfect and confused, as it was before, or clear and distinct as it is now, depending on how carefully I concentrate on what the wax consists in.

But as I reach this conclusion I am amazed at how weak and prone to error my mind is. For although I am thinking about these matters within myself, silently and without speaking, nonetheless, the actual words bring me up short, and I am almost tricked by ordinary ways of talking. We say that we see the wax itself, if it is there before us, not that we judge it to be there from its colour or shape; and this might lead me to conclude without more ado that knowledge of the wax comes from what the eye sees, and not from the scrutiny of the mind alone. But then if I look out of the window and see men crossing the square, as I just happen to have done, I normally say that I see the men themselves, just as I say that I see the wax. Yet do I see any more than hats and coats which could conceal automatons? I judge that they are men. And so something which I thought I was seeing with my eyes is in fact grasped solely by the faculty of judgement which is in my mind.

However, one who wants to achieve knowledge above the ordinary level should feel ashamed at having taken ordinary ways of talking as a basis for doubt. So let us proceed, and consider on which occasion my perception of the nature of the wax was more perfect and evident. Was it when I first looked at it, and believed I knew it by my external senses, or at least by what they call the 'common' sense—that is, the power of imagination? Or is my knowledge more perfect now, after a more careful investigation of the nature of the wax and of the means by which it is known? Any doubt on this issue would clearly be foolish; for what distinctness was there in my earlier perception? Was there anything in it which an animal could not possess? But when I distinguish the wax from its outward forms—take the clothes off, as it were, and consider it naked—then although my judgement may still contain errors, at least my perception now requires a human mind.

But what am I to say about this mind, or about myself? (So far, remember, I am not admitting that there is anything else in me except a mind.) What, I ask, is this 'I' which seems to perceive the wax so distinctly? Surely my awareness of my own self is not merely much truer and more certain than my awareness of the wax, but also much more distinct and evident. For if I judge that the wax exists from the fact that I see it, clearly this same fact entails much more evidently that I myself also exist. It is possible that what I see is not really the wax; it is possible that I do not even have eyes with which to see anything. But when I see, or think I see (I am not here distinguishing the two), it is simply not possible that I who am now thinking am not something. By the same token, if I judge that the wax exists from the fact that I touch it, the same result follows, namely that I exist. If I judge that it exists from the fact that I imagine it, or for any other reason, exactly the same thing follows. And the result that I have grasped in the case of the wax may be applied to everything else located outside me. Moreover, if my perception of the wax seemed more distinct after it was established not just by sight or touch but by many other considerations, it must be admitted that I now know myself even more distinctly. This is because every consideration whatsoever which contributes to my perception of the wax, or of any other body cannot but establish even more effectively the nature of my own mind. But besides this, there is so much else in the mind itself which can serve to make my knowledge of it more distinct, that it scarcely seems worth going through the contributions made by considering bodily things.

I see that without any effort I have now finally got back to where I wanted. I now know that even bodies are not strictly perceived by the senses or the faculty of imagination but by the intellect alone, and that this perception derives not from their being touched or seen but from their being understood; and in view of this I know plainly that I can achieve an easier and more evident perception of my own mind than of anything else. But since the habit of holding on to old opinions cannot be set aside so quickly, I should like to stop here and meditate for some time on this new knowledge I have gained, so as to fix it more deeply in my memory.

THIRD MEDITATION

The Existence of God

I will now shut my eyes, stop my ears, and withdraw all my senses. I will eliminate from my thoughts all images of bodily things, or rather, since this is hardly possible, I will regard all such images as vacuous, false and worthless. I will converse with myself and scrutinize myself more deeply; and in this way I will attempt to achieve, little by little, a more intimate knowledge of myself. I am a thing that thinks: that is, a thing that doubts, affirms, denies, understands a few things, is ignorant of many things, is willing, is unwilling, and also which imagines and has sensory perceptions; for as I have noted before, even though the objects of my sensory experience and imagination may have no existence outside me, nonetheless the modes of thinking which I refer to as cases of sensory perception and imagination, in so far as they are simply modes of thinking, do exist within me—of that I am certain.

In this brief list I have gone through everything I truly know, or at least everything I have so far discovered that I know. Now I will cast around more carefully to see whether there may be other things within me which I have not yet noticed. I am certain that I am a thinking thing. Do I not therefore also know what is required for my being certain about anything? In this first item of knowledge there is simply a clear and distinct perception of what I am asserting; this would not be enough to make me certain of the truth of the matter if it could ever turn out that something which I perceived with such clarity and distinctness was false. So I now seem to be able to lay it down as a general rule that whatever I perceive very clearly and distinctly is true.

Yet I previously accepted as wholly certain and evident many things which I afterwards realized were doubtful. What were these? The earth, sky, stars, and everything else that I apprehended with the senses. But what was it about them that I perceived clearly? Just that the ideas, or thoughts, of such things appeared before my mind. Yet even now I am not denying that these ideas occur within me. But there was something else which I used to assert, and which through habitual belief I thought I perceived clearly, although I did not in fact do so. This was that there were things outside me which were the sources of my ideas and which resembled them in all respects. Here was my mistake; or at any rate, if my judgement was true, it was not thanks to the strength of my perception.

But what about when I was considering something very simple and straightforward in arithmetic or geometry, for example that two and three added together make five, and so on? Did I not see at least these things clearly enough to affirm their truth? Indeed, the only reason for my later judgement that they were open to doubt was that it occurred to me that perhaps some God could have given me a nature such that I was deceived even in matters which seemed most evident. And whenever my preconceived belief in the supreme power of God comes to mind, I cannot but admit that it would be easy for him, if he so desired, to bring it about that I go wrong even in those matters which I think I see utterly clearly with my mind's eye. Yet when I turn to the things themselves which I think I perceive very clearly, I am so convinced by them that I spontaneously declare: let whoever can do so deceive me, he will never bring it about that I am nothing, so long as I continue to think I am something; or make it true at some future time that I have never existed, since it is now true that I exist; or bring it about that two and three added together are more or less than five, or anything of this kind in which I see a manifest contradiction. And since I have no cause to think that there is a deceiving God, and I do not yet even know for sure whether there is a God at all, any reason for doubt which depends simply on this supposition is a very slight and, so to speak, metaphysical one. But in order to remove even this slight reason for doubt, as soon as the opportunity arises I must examine whether there is a God, and, if there is, whether he can be a deceiver. For if I do not know this, it seems that I can never be quite certain about anything else.

First, however, considerations of order appear to dictate that I now classify my thoughts into definite kinds, and ask which of them can properly be said to be the bearers of truth and falsity. Some of my thoughts are as it were the images of things, and it is only in these cases that the term 'idea' is strictly appropriate—for example, when I think of a man, or a chimera, or the sky, or an angel, or God. Other thoughts have various additional forms: thus when I will, or am afraid, or affirm, or deny, there is always a particular thing which I take as the object of my thought, but my thought includes something more than the likeness of that thing. Some thoughts in this category are called volitions or emotions, while others are called judgements.

Now as far as ideas are concerned, provided they are considered solely in themselves and I do not refer them to anything else, they cannot strictly speaking be false; for whether it is a goat or a chimera that I am imagining, it is just as true that I imagine the former as the latter. As for the will and the emotions, here too one need not worry about falsity; for even if the things which I may desire are wicked or even non-existent, that does not make it any less true that I desire them. Thus the only remaining thoughts where I must be on my guard against making a mistake are judgements. And the chief and most common mistake which is to be found here consists in my judging that the ideas which are in me resemble, or conform to, things located outside me. Of course, if I considered just the ideas themselves simply as modes of my thought, without referring them to anything else, they could scarcely give me any material for error.

Among my ideas, some appear to be innate, some to be adventitious, and others to have been invented by me. My understanding of what a thing is, what truth is, and what thought is, seems to derive simply from my own nature. But my hearing a noise, as I do now, or seeing the sun, or feeling the fire, comes from things which are located outside me, or so I have hitherto judged. Lastly, sirens, hippogriffs and the like are my own invention. But perhaps all my ideas may be thought of as adventitious, or they may all be innate, or all made up; for as yet I have not clearly perceived their true origin.

But the chief question at this point concerns the ideas which I take to be derived from things existing outside me: what is my reason for thinking that they resemble these things? Nature has apparently taught me to think this. But in addition I know by experience that these ideas do not depend on my will, and hence that they do not depend simply on me. Frequently I notice them even when I do not want to: now, for example, I feel the heat whether I want to or not, and this is why I think that this sensation or idea of heat comes to me from something other than myself, namely the heat of the fire by which I am sitting. And the most obvious judgement for me to make is that the thing in question transmits to me its own likeness rather than something else.

I will now see if these arguments are strong enough. When I say 'Nature taught me to think this', all I mean is that a spontaneous impulse leads me to believe it, not that its truth has been revealed to me by some natural light. There is a big difference here. Whatever is revealed to me by the natural light—for example that from the fact that I am doubting it follows that I exist, and so on—cannot in any way be open to doubt. This is because there cannot be another faculty both as trustworthy as the natural light and also capable of showing me that such things are not true. But as for my natural impulses, I have often judged in the past that they were pushing me in the wrong direction when it was a question of choosing the good, and I do not see why I should place any greater confidence in them in other matters.

Then again, although these ideas do not depend on my will, it does not follow that they must come from things located outside me. Just as the impulses which I was speaking of a moment ago seem opposed to my will even though they are within me, so there may be some other faculty not yet fully known to me, which produces these ideas without any assistance from external things; this is, after all, just how I have always thought ideas are produced in me when I was dreaming.

And finally, even if these ideas did come from things other than myself, it would not follow that they must resemble those things. Indeed, I think I have often discovered a great disparity between an object and its idea in many cases. For example, there are two different ideas of the sun which I find within me. One of them, which is acquired as it were from the senses and which is a prime example of an idea which I reckon to come from an external source, makes the sun appear very small. The other idea is based on astronomical reasoning, that is, it is derived from certain notions which are innate in me (or else it is constructed by me in some other way), and this idea shows the sun to be several times larger than the earth. Obviously both these ideas cannot resemble the sun which exists outside me; and reason persuades me that the idea which seems to have emanated most directly from the sun itself has in fact no resemblance to it at all.

All these considerations are enough to establish that it is not reliable judgement but merely some blind impulse that has made me believe up till now that there exist things distinct from myself which transmit to me ideas or images of themselves through the sense organs or in some other way.

But it now occurs to me that there is another way of investigating whether some of the things of which I possess ideas exist outside me. In so far as the ideas are considered simply as modes of thought, there is no recognizable inequality among them: they all appear to come from within me in the same fashion. But in so far as different ideas are considered as images which represent different things, it is clear that they differ widely. Undoubtedly, the ideas which represent substances to me amount to something more and, so to speak, contain within themselves more objective reality than the ideas which merely represent modes or accidents. Again, the idea that gives me my understanding of a supreme God, eternal, infinite, immutable, omniscient, omnipotent and the creator of all things that exist apart from him, certainly has in it more objective reality than the ideas that represent finite substances.

Now it is manifest by the natural light that there must be at least as much reality in the efficient and total cause as in the effect of that cause. For where, I ask, could the effect get its reality from, if not from the cause? And how could the cause give it to the effect unless it possessed it? It follows from this both that something cannot arise from nothing, and also that what is more perfect—that is, contains in itself more reality—cannot arise from what is less perfect. And this is transparently true not only in the case of effects which possess what the philosophers call actual or formal reality, but also in the case of ideas, where one is considering only what they call objective reality. A stone, for example, which previously did not exist, cannot begin to exist unless it is produced by something which contains, either formally or eminently, everything to be found in the stone; similarly, heat cannot be produced in an object which was not previously hot, except by something of at least the same order, degree, or kind, of perfection as heat, and so on. But it is also true that the idea of heat, or of a stone, cannot exist in me unless it is put there by some cause which contains at least as much reality as I conceive to be in the heat or in the stone. For although this cause does not transfer any of its actual or formal reality to my idea, it should not on that account be supposed that it must be less real. The nature of an idea is such that of itself it requires no formal reality except what it derives from my thought, of which it is a mode. But in order for a given idea to contain such and such objective reality, it must surely derive it from some cause which contains at least as much formal reality as there is objective reality in the idea. For if we suppose that an idea contains something which was not in its cause, it must have got this from nothing; yet the mode of being by which a thing exists objective or representatively in the intellect by way of an idea, imperfect though it may be, is certainly not nothing, and so it cannot come from nothing.

And although the reality which I am considering in my ideas is merely objective reality, I must not on that account suppose that the same reality need not exist formally in the causes of my ideas, but that it is enough for it to be present in them objectively. For just as the objective mode of beings belongs to ideas by their very nature, so the formal mode of being belongs to the causes of ideas—or at least the first and most important ones—by their very nature. And although one idea may perhaps originate from another, there cannot be an infinite regress here; eventually one must reach a primary idea, the cause of which will be like an archetype which contains formally and in fact all the reality or perfection which is present only objectively or representatively in the idea. So it is clear to me, by the natural light, that the ideas in me are like pictures, or images which can easily fall short of the perfection of the things from which they are taken, but which cannot contain anything greater or more perfect.

The longer and more carefully I examine all these points, the more clearly and distinctly I recognize their truth. But what is my conclusion to be? If the objective reality of any of my ideas turns out to be so great that I am sure the same reality does not reside in me, either formally or eminently, and hence that I myself cannot be its cause, it will necessarily follow that I am not alone in the world, but that some other thing which is the cause of this idea also exists. But if no such idea is to be found in me, I shall have no argument to convince me of the existence of anything apart from myself. For despite a most careful and comprehensive survey, this is the only argument I have so far been able to find.

Among my ideas, apart from the idea which gives me a representation of myself, which cannot present any difficulty in this context, there are ideas which variously represent God, corporeal and inanimate things, angels, animals and finally other men like myself.

As far as concerns the ideas which represent other men, or animals, or angels, I have no difficulty in understanding that they could be put together from the ideas I have of myself, of corporeal things and of God, even if the world contained no men besides me, no animals and no angels.

As to my ideas of corporeal things, I can see nothing in them which is so great or excellent as to make it seem impossible that it originated in myself. For if I scrutinize them thoroughly and examine them one by one, in the way in which I examined the idea of the wax yesterday, I notice that the things which I perceive clearly and distinctly in them are very few in number. The list comprises size, or extension in length, breadth and depth; shape, which is a function of the boundaries of this extension; position, which is a relation between various items possessing shape; and motion, or change in position; to these may be added substance, duration and number. But as for all the rest, including light and colours, sounds, smells, tastes, heat and cold and the other tactile qualities, I think of these only in a very confused and obscure way, to the extent that I do not even know whether they are true or false, that is, whether the ideas I have of them are ideas of real things or of non-things. For although, as I have noted before, falsity in the strict sense, or formal falsity, can occur only in judgements, there is another kind of falsity, material falsity, which occurs in ideas, when they represent non-things as things. For example, the ideas which I have of heat and cold contain so little clarity and distinctness that they do not enable me to tell whether cold is merely the absence of heat or vice versa, or whether both of them are real qualities, or neither is. And since there can be no ideas which are not as it were of things, if it is true that cold is nothing but the absence of heat, the idea which represents it to me as something real and positive deserves to be called false; and the same goes for other ideas of this kind.

Such ideas obviously do not require me to posit a source distinct from myself. For on the one hand, if they are false, that is, represent non-things, I know by the natural light that they arise from nothing—that is, they are in me only because of a deficiency and lack of perfection in my nature. If on the other hand they are true, then since the reality which they represent is so extremely slight that I cannot even distinguish it from a non-thing, I do not see why they cannot originate from myself.

With regard to the clear and distinct elements in my ideas of corporeal things, it appears that I could have borrowed some of these from my idea of myself, namely substance, duration, number and anything else of this kind. For example, I think that a stone is a substance, or is a thing capable of existing independently, and I also think that I am a substance. Admittedly I conceive of myself as a thing that thinks and is not extended, whereas I conceive of the stone as a thing that is extended and does not think, so that the two conceptions differ enormously; but they seem to agree with respect to the classification 'substance'. Again, I perceive that I now exist, and remember that I have existed for some time; moreover, I have various thoughts which I can count; it is in these ways that I acquire the ideas of duration and number which I can then transfer to other things. As for all the other elements which make up the ideas of corporeal things, namely extension, shape position and movement, these are not formally contained in me, since I am nothing but a thinking thing; but since they are merely modes of a substance, and I am a substance, it seems possible that they are contained in me eminently.

So there remains only the idea of God; and I must consider whether there is anything in the idea which could not have originated in myself. By the word 'God' I understand a substance that is infinite, eternal, immutable, independent, supremely intelligent, supremely powerful, and which created both myself and everything else (if anything else there be) that exists. All these attributes are such that, the more carefully I concentrate on them, the less possible it seems that they could have originated from me alone. So from what has been said it must be concluded that God necessarily exists.

It is true that I have the idea of substance in me in virtue of the fact that I am a substance; but this would not account for my having the idea of an infinite substance, when I am finite, unless this idea proceeded from some substance which really was infinite.

And I must not think that, just as my conceptions of rest and darkness are arrived at by negating movement and light, so my perception of the infinite is arrived at not by means of a true idea but merely by negating the finite. On the contrary, I clearly understand that there is more reality in an infinite substance than in a finite one, and hence that my perception of the infinite, that is God, is in some way prior to my perception of the finite, that is myself. For how could I understand that I doubted or desired—that is, lacked something—and that I was not wholly perfect, unless there were in me some idea of a more perfect being which enabled me to recognize my own defects by comparison?

Nor can it be said that this idea of God is perhaps materially false and so could have come from nothing, which is what I observed just a moment ago in the case of the ideas of heat and cold, and so on. On the contrary, it is utterly clear and distinct, and contains in itself more objective reality than any other idea; hence there is no idea which is in itself truer or less liable to be suspected of falsehood. This idea of a supremely perfect and infinite being is, I say, true in the highest degree; for although perhaps one may imagine that such a being does not exist, it cannot be supposed that the idea of such a being represents something unreal, as I said with regard to the idea of cold. The idea is, moreover, utterly clear and distinct; for whatever I clearly and distinctly perceive as being real and true, and implying any perfection, is wholly contained in it. It does not matter that I do not grasp the infinite, or that there are countless additional attributes of God which I cannot in any way grasp,and perhaps cannot even reach in my thought; for it is in the nature of the infinite not to be grasped by a finite being like myself. It is enough that I understand the infinite, and that I judge that all the attributes which I clearly perceive and know to imply some perfection—and perhaps countless others of which I am ignorant—are present in God either formally or eminently. This is enough to make the idea that I have of God the truest and most clear and distinct of all my ideas.

But perhaps I am something greater than I myself understand, and all the perfections which I attribute to God are somehow in me potentially, though not yet emerging or actualized. For I am now experiencing a gradual increase in my knowledge, and I see nothing to prevent its increasing more and more to infinity. Further, I see no reason why I should not be able to use this increased knowledge to acquire all the other perfections of God. And finally, if the potentiality for these perfections is already within me, why should not this be enough to generate the idea of such perfections?

But all this is impossible. First, though it is true that there is a gradual increase in my knowledge, and that I have many potentialities which are not yet actual, this is all quite irrelevant to the idea of God, which contains absolutely nothing that is potential; indeed, this gradual increase in knowledge is itself the surest sign of imperfection. What is more, even if my knowledge always increases more and more, I recognize that it will never actually be infinite, since it will never reach the point where it is not capable of a further increase; God, on the other hand, I take to be actually infinite, so that nothing can be added to his perfection. And finally, I perceive that the objective being of an idea cannot be produced merely by potential being, which strictly speaking is nothing, but only by actual or formal being.

If one concentrates carefully, all this is quite evident by the natural light. But when I relax my concentration, and my mental vision is blinded by the images of things perceived by the senses, it is not so easy for me to remember why the idea of a being more perfect than myself must necessarily proceed from some being which is in reality more perfect. I should therefore like to go further and inquire whether I myself, who have this idea, could exist if no such being existed.

From whom, in that case, would I derive my existence? From myself presumably, or from my parents, or from some other beings less perfect than God; for nothing more perfect than God, or even as perfect, can be thought of or imagined.

Yet if I derived my existence from myself, then I should neither doubt nor want, nor lack anything at all; for I should have given myself all the perfections of which I have any idea, and thus I should myself be God. I must not suppose that the items I lack would be more difficult to acquire than those I now have. On the contrary, it is clear that, since I am a thinking thing or substance, it would have been far more difficult for me to emerge out of nothing than merely to acquire knowledge of the many things of which I am ignorant—such knowledge being merely an accident of that substance. And if I had derived my existence from myself, which is a greater achievement, I should certainly not have denied myself the knowledge in question, which is something much easier to acquire, or indeed any of the attributes which I perceive to be contained in the idea of God; for none of them seem any harder to achieve. And if any of them were harder to achieve, they would certainly appear so to me, if I had indeed got all my other attributes from myself, since I should experience a limitation of my power in this respect.

I do not escape the force of these arguments by supposing that I have always existed as I do now, as if it followed from this that there was no need to look for any author of my existence. For a lifespan can be divided into countless parts, each completely independent of the others, so that it does not follow from the fact that I existed a little while ago that I must exist now, unless there is some cause which as it were creates me afresh at this moment—that is, which preserves me. For it is quite clear to anyone who attentively considers the nature of time that the same power and action are needed to preserve anything at each individual moment of its duration as would be required to create that thing anew if it were not yet in existence. Hence the distinction between preservation and creation is only a conceptual one, and this is one of the things that are evident by the natural light.

I must therefore now ask myself whether I possess some power enabling me to bring it about that I who now exist will still exist a little while from now. For since I am nothing but a thinking thing—or at least since I am now concerned only and precisely with that part of me which is a thinking thing—if there were such a power in me, I should undoubtedly be aware of it. But I experience no such power, and this very fact makes me recognize most clearly that I depend on some being distinct from myself.

But perhaps this being is not God, and perhaps I was produced either by my parents or by other causes less perfect than God. No; for as I have said before, it is quite clear that there must be at least as much in the cause as in the effect. And therefore whatever kind of cause is eventually proposed, since I am a thinking thing and have within me some idea of God, it must be admitted that what caused me is itself a thinking thing and possesses the idea of all the perfections which I attribute to God. In respect of this cause one may again inquire whether it derives its existence from itself or from another cause. If from itself, then it is clear from what has been said that it is itself God, since if it has the power of existing through its own might, then undoubtedly it also has the power of actually possessing all the perfections of which it has an idea—that is, all the perfections which I conceive to be in God. If, on the other hand, it derives its existence from another cause, then the same question may be repeated concerning this further cause, namely whether it derives its existence from itself or from another cause, until eventually the ultimate cause is reached, and this will be God.

It is clear enough that an infinite regress is impossible here, especially since I am dealing not just with the cause that produced me in the past, but also and most importantly with the cause that preserves me at the present moment.

Nor can it be supposed that several partial causes contributed to my creation, or that I received the idea of one of the perfections which I attribute to God from one cause and the idea of another from another—the supposition here being that all the perfections are to be found somewhere in the universe but not joined together in a single being, God. On the contrary, the unity, the simplicity, or the inseparability of all the attributes of God is one of the most important of the perfections which I understand him to have. And surely the idea of the unity of all his perfections could not have been placed in me by any cause which did not also provide me with the ideas of the other perfections; for no cause could have made me understand the interconnection and inseparability of the perfections without at the same time making me recognize what they were.

Lastly, as regards my parents, even if everything I have ever believed about them is true, it is certainly not they who preserve me; and in so far as I am a thinking thing, they did not even make me; they merely placed certain dispositions in the matter which I have always regarded as containing me, or rather in my mind, for that is all I now take myself to be. So there can be no difficulty regarding my parents in this context. Altogether then, it must be concluded that the mere fact that I exist and have within me an idea of a most perfect being, that is, God, provides a very clear proof that God indeed exists.

It only remains for me to examine how I received this idea from God. For I did not acquire it from the senses; it has never come to me unexpectedly, as usually happens with the ideas of things that are perceivable by the senses, when these things present themselves to the external sense organs—or seem to do so. And it was not invented by me either; for I am plainly unable either to take away anything from it or to add anything to it. The only remaining alternative is that it is innate in me, just as the idea of myself is innate in me.

And indeed it is no surprise that God, in creating me, should have placed this idea in men to be, as it were, the mark of the craftsman stamped on his work—not that the mark need be anything distinct from the work itself. But the mere fact that God created me is a very strong basis for believing that I am somehow made in his image and likeness, and that I perceive that likeness, which includes the idea of God, by the same faculty which enables me to perceive myself. That is, when I turn my mind's eye upon myself, I understand that I am a thing which is incomplete and dependent on another and which aspires without limit to ever greater and better things; but I also understand at the same time that he on whom I depend has within him all those greater things, not just indefinitely and potentially but actually and infinitely, and hence that he is God. The whole force of the argument lies in this: I recognize that it would be impossible for me to exist with the kind of nature I have—that is, having within me the idea of God—were it not the case that God really existed. By 'God' I mean the very being the idea of whom is within me, that is, the possessor of all the perfections which I cannot grasp, but can somehow reach in my thought, who is subject to no defects whatsoever. It is clear enough from this that he cannot be a deceiver, since it is manifest by the natural light that all fraud and deception depend on some defect.

But before examining this point more carefully and investigating other truths which may be derived from it, I should like to pause here and spend some time in the contemplation of God; to reflect on his attributes, and to gaze with wonder and adoration on the beauty of this immense light, so far as the eye of my darkened intellect can bear it. For just as we believe through faith that the supreme happiness of the next life consists solely in the contemplation of the divine majesty, so experience tells us that this same contemplation, albeit much less perfect, enables us to know the greatest joy of which we are capable in this life.

FOURTH MEDITATION

Truth and Falsity

During these past few days I have accustomed myself to leading my mind away from the senses; and I have taken careful note of the fact that there is very little about corporeal things that is truly perceived, whereas much more is known about the human mind, and still more about God. The result is that I now have no difficulty in turning my mind away from imaginable things and towards things which are objects of the intellect alone and are totally separate from matter. And indeed the idea I have of the human mind, in so far as it is a thinking thing, which is not extended in length, breadth or height and has no other bodily characteristics, is much more distinct than the idea of any corporeal thing. And when I consider the fact that I have doubts, or that I am a thing that is incomplete and dependent, then there arises in me a clear and distinct idea of a being who is independent and complete, that is, an idea of God. And from the mere fact that there is such an idea within me, or that I who possess this idea exist, I clearly infer that God also exists, and that every single moment of my entire existence depends on him. So clear is this conclusion that I am confident that the human intellect cannot know anything that is more evident or more certain. And now, from this contemplation of the true God, in whom all the treasures of wisdom and the sciences lie hidden, I think I can see a way forward to the knowledge of other things.

To being with, I recognize that it is impossible that God should ever deceive me. For in every case of trickery or deception some imperfection is to be found; and although the ability to deceive appears to be an indication of cleverness or power, the will to deceive is undoubtedly evidence of malice or weakness, and so cannot apply to God.

Next, I know by experience that there is in me a faculty of judgement which, like everything else which is in me, I certainly received from God. And since God does not wish to deceive me, he surely did not give me the kind of faculty which would ever enable me to go wrong while using it correctly.

There would be no further doubt on this issue were it not that what I have just said appears to imply that I am incapable of ever going wrong. For if everything that is in me comes from God, and he did not endow me with a faculty for making mistakes, it appears that I can never go wrong. And certainly, so long as I think only of God, and turn my whole attention to him, I can find no cause of error or falsity. But when I turn back to myself, I know by experience that I am prone to countless errors. On looking for the cause of these errors, I find that I possess not only a real and positive idea of God, or a being who is supremely perfect, but also what may be described as a negative idea of nothingness, or of that which is farthest removed from all perfection. I realize that I am, as it were, something intermediate between God and nothingness, or between supreme being and non-being: my nature is such that in so far as I was created by the supreme being, there is nothing in me to enable me to go wrong or lead me astray; but in so far as I participate in nonthingness or non-being, that is, in so far as I am not myself the supreme being and am lacking in countless respects, it is no wonder that I make mistakes. I understand, then, that error as such is not something real which depends on God, but merely a defect. Hence my going wrong does not require me to have a faculty specially bestowed on me by God; it simply happens as a result of the fact that the faculty of true judgement which I have from God is in my case not infinite.

But this is still not entirely satisfactory. For error is not a pure negation, but rather a privation or lack of some knowledge which somehow should be in me. And when I concentrate on the nature of God, it seems impossible that he should have placed in me a faculty which is not perfect of its kind, or which lacks some perfection which it ought to have. The more skilled the craftsman the more perfect the work produced by him; if this is so, how can anything produced by the supreme creator of all things not be complete and perfect in all respects? There is, moreover, no doubt that God could have given me a nature such that I was never mistaken; again, there is no doubt that he always wills what is best. Is it then better that I should make mistakes than that I should not do so?

As I reflect on these matters more attentively, it occurs to me first of all that it is no cause for surprise if I do not understand the reasons for some of God's actions; and there is no call to doubt his existence if I happen to find that there are other instances where I do not grasp why or how certain things were made by him. For since I now know that my own nature is very weak and limited, whereas the nature of God is immense, incomprehensible and infinite, I also know without more ado that he is capable of countless things whose causes are beyond my knowledge. And for this reason alone I consider the customary search for final causes to be totally useless in physics; there is considerable rashness in thinking myself capable of investigating the impenetrable purposes of God.

It also occurs to me that whenever we are inquiring whether the works of God are perfect, we ought to look at the whole universe, not just at one created thing on its own. For what would perhaps rightly appear very imperfect if it existed on its own is quite perfect when its function as a part of the universe is considered. It is true that, since my decision to doubt everything, it is so far only myself and God whose existence I have been able to know with certainty; but after considering the immense power of God, I cannot deny that many other things have been made by him, or at least could have been made, and hence that I may have a place in the universal scheme of things.

Next, when I look more closely at myself and inquire into the nature of my errors (for these are the only evidence of some imperfection in me), I notice that they depend on two concurrent causes, namely on the faculty of knowledge which is in me, and on the faculty of choice or freedom of the will; that is, they depend on both the intellect and the will simultaneously. Now all that the intellect does is to enable me to perceive the ideas which are subjects for possible judgement; and when regarded strictly in this light, it turns out to contain no error in the proper sense of that term. For although countless things may exist without there being any corresponding ideas in me, it should not, strictly speaking, be said that I am deprived of these ideas, but merely that I lack them, in a negative sense. This is because I cannot produce any reason to prove that God ought to have given me a greater faculty of knowledge than he did; and no matter how skilled I understand a craftsman to be, this does not make me think he ought to have put into every one of his works all the perfections which he is able to put into some of them. Besides, I cannot complain that the will or freedom of choice which I received from God is not sufficiently extensive or perfect, since I know by experience that it is not restricted in any way. Indeed, I think it is very noteworthy that there is nothing else in me which is so perfect and so great that the possibility of a further increase in its perfection or greatness is beyond my understanding. If, for example, I consider the faculty of understanding, I immediately recognize that in my case it is extremely slight and very finite, and I at once form the idea of an understanding which is much greater—indeed supremely great and infinite; and from the very fact that I can form an idea of it, I perceive that it belongs to the nature of God. Similarly, if I examine the faculties or imagination, or any others, I discover that in my case each one of these faculties is weak and limited, while in the case of God it is immeasurable. It is only the will, or freedom of choice, which I experience within me to be so great that the idea of any greater faculty is beyond my grasp; so much so that it is above all in virtue of the will that I understand myself to bear in some way the image and likeness of God. For although God's will is incomparably greater than mine, both in virtue of the knowledge and power that accompany it and make it more firm and efficacious, and also in virtue of its object, in that it ranges over a greater number of items, nevertheless it does not seem any greater than mine when considered as will in the essential and strict sense. This is because the will simply consists in our ability to do or not do something (that is, to affirm or deny, to pursue or avoid); or rather, it consists simply in the fact that when the intellect puts something forward for affirmation or denial or for pursuit or avoidance, our inclinations are such that we do not feel we are determined by any external force. In order to be free, there is no need for me to be inclined both ways; on the contrary, the more I incline in one direction—either because I clearly understand that reasons of truth and goodness point that way, or because of a divinely produced disposition of my inmost thoughts—the freer is my choice. Neither divine grace nor natural knowledge ever diminishes freedom; on the contrary, they increase and strengthen it. But the indifference I feel when there is no reason pushing me in one direction rather than another is the lowest grade of freedom; it is evidence not of any perfection of freedom, but rather of a defect in knowledge or a kind of negation. For if I always saw clearly what was true and good, I should never have to deliberate about the right judgement or choice; in that case, although I should be wholly free, it would be impossible for me ever to be in a state of indifference.

From these considerations I perceive that the power of willing which I received from God is not, when considered in itself, the cause of my mistakes; for it is both extremely ample and also perfect of its kind. Nor is my power of understanding to blame; for since my understanding comes from God, everything that I understand I undoubtedly understand correctly, and any error here is impossible. So what then is the source of my mistakes? It must be simply this: the scope of the will is wider than that of the intellect; but instead of restricting it within the same limits, I extend its use to matters which I do not understand. Since the will is indifferent in such cases, it easily turns aside from what is true and good, and this is the source of my error and sin.

For example, during the past few days I have been asking whether anything in the world exists, and I have realized that from the very fact of my raising this question it follows quite evidently that I exist. I could not but judge that something which I understood so clearly was true; but this was not because I was compelled so to judge by any external force, but because a great light in the intellect was followed by a great inclination in the will, and thus the spontaneity and freedom of my belief was all the greater in proportion to my lack of indifference. But now, besides the knowledge that I exist, in so far as I am a thinking thing, an idea of corporeal nature comes into my mind; and I happen to be in doubt as to whether the thinking nature which is in me, or rather which I am, is distinct from this corporeal nature or identical with it. I am making the further supposition that my intellect has not yet come upon any persuasive reason in favour of one alternative rather than the other. This obviously implies that I am indifferent as to whether I should assert or deny either alternative, or indeed refrain from making any judgement on the matter.

What is more, this indifference does not merely apply to cases where the intellect is wholly ignorant, but extends in general to every case where the intellect does not have sufficiently clear knowledge at the time when the will deliberates. For although probable conjectures may pull me in one direction, the mere knowledge that they are simply conjectures, and not certain and indubitable reasons, is itself quite enough to push my assent the other way. My experience in the last few days confirms this: the mere fact that I found that all my previous beliefs were in some sense open to doubt was enough to turn my absolutely confident belief in their truth into the supposition that they were wholly false.

If, however, I simply refrain from making a judgement in cases where I do not perceive the truth with sufficient clarity and distinctness, then it is clear that I am behaving correctly and avoiding error. But if in such cases I either affirm or deny, then I am not using my free will correctly. If I go for the alternative which is false, then obviously I shall be in error; if I take the other side, then it is by pure chance that I arrive at the truth, and I shall still be at fault since it is clear by the natural light that the perception of the intellect should always precede the determination of the will. In this incorrect use of free will may be found the privation which constitutes the essence of error. The privation, I say, lies in the operation of the will in so far as it proceeds from me, but not in the faculty of will which I received from God, nor even in its operation, in so far as it depends on him.

And I have no cause for complaint on the grounds that the power of understanding or the natural light which God gave me is no greater than it is; for it is in the nature of a finite intellect to lack understanding of many things, and it is in the nature of a created intellect to be finite. Indeed, I have reason to give thanks to him who has never owed me anything for the great bounty that he has shown me, rather than thinking myself deprived or robbed of any gifts he did not bestow.

Nor do I have any cause for complaint on the grounds that God gave me a will which extends more widely than my intellect. For since the will consists simply of one thing which is, as it were, indivisible, it seems that its nature rules out the possibility of anything being taken away from it. And surely, the more widely my will extends, then the greater thanks I owe to him who gave it to me.

Finally, I must not complain that the forming of those acts of will or judgements in which I go wrong happens with God's concurrence. For in so far as these acts depend on God, they are wholly true and good; and my ability to perform them means that there is in a sense more perfection in men than would be the case if I lacked this ability. As for the privation involved—which is all that the essential definition of falsity and wrong consists in—this does not in any way require the concurrence of God, since it is not a thing; indeed, when it is referred to God as its cause, it should be called not a privation but simply a negation. For it is surely no imperfection in God that he has given me the freedom to assent or not to assent in those cases where he did not endow my intellect with a clear and distinct perception; but it is undoubtedly an imperfection in me to misuse that freedom and make judgements about matters which I do not fully understand. I can see, however, that God could easily have brought it about that without losing my freedom, and despite the limitations in my knowledge, I should nonetheless never make a mistake. He could, for example, have endowed my intellect with a clear and distinct perception of everything about which I was ever likely to deliberate; or he could simply have impressed it unforgettably on my memory that I should never make a judgement about anything which I did not clearly and distinctly understand. Had God made me this way, then I can easily understand that, considered as a totality, I would have been more perfect than I am now. But I cannot therefore deny that there may in some way be more perfection in the universe as a whole because some of its parts are not immune from error, while others are immune, than there would be if all the parts were exactly alike. And I have no right to complain that the role God wished me to undertake in the world is not the principal one or the most perfect of all.

What is more, even if I have no power to avoid error in the first way just mentioned, which requires a clear perception of everything I have to deliberate on, I can avoid error in the second way, which depends merely on my remembering to withhold judgement on any occasion when the truth of the matter is not clear. Admittedly, I am aware of a certain weakness in me, in that I am unable to keep my attention fixed on one and the same item of knowledge at all times; but by attentive and repeated meditation I am nevertheless able to make myself remember it as often as the need arises, and thus get into the habit of avoiding error.

It is here that man's greatest and most important perfection is to be found, and I therefore think that today's meditation, involving an investigation into the cause of error and falsity, has been very profitable. The cause of error must surely be the one I have explained; for if, whenever I have to make a judgement, I restrain my will so that it extends to what the intellect clearly and distinctly reveals, and no further, then it is quite impossible for me to go wrong. This is because every clear and distinct perception is undoubtedly something, and hence cannot come from nothing, but must necessarily have God for its author. Its author, I say, is God, who is supremely perfect, and who cannot be a deceiver on pain of contradiction; hence the perception is undoubtedly true. So today I have learned not only what precautions to take to avoid ever going wrong, but also what to do to arrive at the truth. For I shall unquestionably reach the truth, if only I give sufficient attention to all the things which I perfectly understand, and separate these from all the other cases where my apprehension is more confused and obscure. And this is just what I shall take good care to do from now on.

FIFTH MEDITATION

The Essence of Material Things, and the Existence of God Considered a Second Time

There are many matters which remain to be investigated concerning the attributes of God and the nature of myself, or my mind; and perhaps I shall take these up at another time. But now that I have seen what to do and what to avoid in order to reach the truth, the most pressing task seems to be to try to escape from the doubts into which I fell a few days ago, and see whether any certainty can be achieved regarding material objects.

But before I inquire whether any such things exist outside me, I must consider the ideas of these things, in so far as they exist in my thought, and see which of them are distinct, and which confused.

Quantity, for example, or 'continuous' quantity as the philosophers commonly call it, is something I distinctly imagine. That is, I distinctly imagine the extension of the quantity (or rather of the thing which is quantified) in length, breadth and depth. I also enumerate various parts of the thin, and to these parts I assign various sizes, shapes, positions and local motions; and to the motions I assign various durations.

Not only are all these things very well known and transparent to me when regarded in this general way, but in addition there are countless particular features regarding shape, number, motion and so on, which I perceive when I give them my attention. And the truth of these matters is so open and so much in harmony with my nature, that on first discovering them it seems that I am not so much learning something new as remembering what I knew before; or it seems like noticing for the first time things which were long present within me although I had never turned my mental gaze on them before.

But I think the most important consideration at this point is that I find within me countless ideas of things which even though they may not exist anywhere outside me still cannot be called nothing; for although in a sense they can be thought of at will, they are not my invention but have their own true and immutable natures. When, for example, I imagine a triangle, even if perhaps no such figure exists, or has ever existed, anywhere outside my thought, there is still a determinate nature, or essence, or form of the triangle which is immutable and eternal, and not invented by me or dependent on my mind. This is clear from the fact that various properties can be demonstrated of the triangle, for example that its three angles equal two right angles, that its greatest side subtends its greatest angle, and the like; and since these properties are ones which I now clearly recognize whether I want to or not, even if I never thought of them at all when I previously imagined the triangle, it follows that they cannot have been invented by me.

It would be beside the point for me to say that since I have from time to time seen bodies of triangular shape, the idea of the triangle may have come to me from external things by means of the sense organs. For I can think up countless other shapes which there can be no suspicion of my ever having encountered through the senses, and yet I can demonstrate various properties of these shapes, just as I can with the triangle. All these properties are certainly true, since I am clearly aware of them, and therefore they are something, and not merely nothing; for it is obvious that whatever is true is something; and I have already amply demonstrated that everything of which I am clearly aware is true. And even if I had not demonstrated this, the nature of my mind is such that I cannot but assent to these things, at least so long as I clearly perceive them. I also remember that even before, when I was completely preoccupied with the objects of the senses, I always held that the most certain truths of all were the kind which I recognized clearly in connection with shapes, or numbers or other items relating to arithmetic or geometry, or in general to pure and abstract mathematics.

But if the mere fact that I can produce from my thought the idea of something entails that everything which I clearly and distinctly perceive to belong to that thing really does belong to it, is not this a possible basis for another argument to prove the existence of God? Certainly, the idea of God, or a supremely perfect being, is one which I find within me just as surely as the idea of any shape or number. And my understanding that it belongs to his nature that he always exists is no less clear and distinct than is the case when I prove of any shape or number that some property belongs to its nature. Hence, even if it turned out that not everything on which I have meditated in these past days is true, I ought still to regard the existence of God as having at least the same level of certainty as I have hitherto attributed to the truths of mathematics.

At first sight, however, this is not transparently clear, but has some appearance of being a sophism. Since I have been accustomed to distinguish between existence and essence in everything else, I find it easy to persuade myself that existence can also be separated from the essence of God, and hence that God can be thought of as not existing. But when I concentrate more carefully, it is quite evident that existence can no more be separated from the essence of God than the fact that its three angles equal two right angles can be separated from the essence of a triangle, or than the idea of a mountain can be separated from the idea of a valley. Hence it is just as much of a contradiction to think of God (that is, a supremely perfect being) lacking existence (that is, lacking a perfection), as it is to think of a mountain without a valley.

However, even granted that I cannot think of God except as existing, just as I cannot think of a mountain without a valley, it certainly does not follow from the fact that I think of a mountain with a valley that there is any mountain in the world; and similarly, it does not seem to follow from the fact that I think of God as existing that he does exist. For my thought does not impose any necessity on things; and just as I may imagine a winged horse even though no horse has wings, so I may be able to attach existence to God even though no God exists.

But there is a sophism concealed here. From the fact that I cannot think of a mountain without a valley, it does not follow that a mountain and valley exist anywhere, but simply that a mountain and a valley, whether they exist or not, are mutually inseparable. But from the fact that I cannot think of God except as existing, it follows that existence is inseparable from God, and hence that he really exists. It is not that my thought makes it so, or imposes any necessity on any thing; on the contrary, it is the necessity of the thing itself, namely the existence of God, which determines my thinking in this respect. For I am not free to think of God without existence (that is, a supremely perfect without a supreme perfection) as I am free to imagine a horse with or without wings.

And it must not be objected at this point that while it is indeed necessary for me to suppose God exists, once I have made the supposition that he has all perfections (since existence is one of the perfections), nevertheless the original supposition was not necessary. Similarly, the objection would run, it is not necessary for me to think that all quadrilaterals can be inscribed in a circle; but given this supposition, it will be necessary for me to admit that a rhombus can be inscribed in a circle—which is patently false. Now admittedly, it is not necessary that I ever light upon any thought of God; but whenever I do choose to think of the first and supreme being, and bring forth the idea of god from the treasure house of my mind as it were, it is necessary that I attribute all perfections to him, even if I do not at that time enumerate them or attend to them individually. And this necessity plainly guarantees that, when I later realize that existence is a perfection, I am correct in inferring that the first and supreme being exists. In the same way, it is not necessary for me ever to imagine a triangle; but whenever I do wish to consider a rectilinear figure having just three angles, it is necessary that I attribute to it the properties which license the inference that its three angles equal no more than two right angles, even if I do not notice this at the time. By contrast, when I examine what figures can be inscribed in a circle, it is in no way necessary for me to think that this class includes all quadrilaterals. Indeed, I cannot even imagine this, so long as I am willing to admit only what I clearly and distinctly understand. So there is a great difference between this kind of false supposition and the true ideas which are innate in me, of which the first and most important is the idea of God. There are many ways in which I understand that this idea is not something fictitious which is dependent on my thought, but is an image of a true and immutable nature. First of all, there is the fact that, apart from God, there is nothing else of which I am capable of thinking such that existence belongs to its essence. Second, I cannot understand how there could be two or more Gods of this kind; and after supposing that one God exists, I plainly see that it is necessary that he has existed from eternity and will abide for eternity. And finally, I perceive many other attributes of God, none of which I can remove or alter.

But whatever method of proof I use, I am always brought back to the fact that it is only what I clearly and distinctly perceive that completely convinces me. Some of the things I clearly and distinctly perceive are obvious to everyone, while others are discovered only by those who look more closely and investigate more carefully; but once they have been discovered, the latter are judged to be just as certain as the former. In the case of a right-angled triangle, for example, the fact that the square on the hypotenuse is equal to the square on the other two sides is not so readily apparent as the fact that the hypotenuse subtends the largest angle; but once one has seen it, one believes it just as strongly. But as regards God, if I were not overwhelmed by preconceived opinions, and if the images of things perceived by the senses did not besiege my thought on every side, I would certainly acknowledge him sooner and more easily than anything else. For what is more self-evident than the fact that the supreme being exists, or that God, to whose essence alone existence belongs exists?

Although it needed close attention for me to perceive this, I am now just as certain of it as I am of everything else which appears most certain. And what is more, I see that the certainty of all other things depends on this, so that without it nothing can ever be perfectly known.

Admittedly my nature is such that so long as I perceive something very clearly and distinctly I cannot but believe it to be true. But my nature is also such that I cannot fix my mental vision continually on the same thing, so as to keep perceiving it clearly; and often the memory of a previously made judgement may come back, when I am no longer attending to the arguments which led me to make it. And so other arguments can now occur to me which might easily undermine my opinion, if I were unaware of God; and I should thus never have true and certain knowledge about anything, but only shifting and changeable opinions. For example, when I consider the nature of a triangle, it appears most evident to me, steeped as I am in the principles of geometry, that its three angles are equal to two right angles; and so long as I attend to the proof, I cannot but believe this to be true. But as soon as I turn my mind's eye away from the proof, then in spite of still remembering that I perceived it very clearly, I can easily fall into doubt about its truth, if I am unaware of God. For I can convince myself that I have a natural disposition to go wrong from time to time in matters which I think I perceive as evidently as can be. This will seem even more likely when I remember that there have been frequent cases where I have regarded things as true and certain, but have later been led by other arguments to judge them to be false.

Now, however, I have perceived that God exists, and at the same time I have understood that everything else depends on him, and that he is no deceiver; and I have drawn the conclusion that everything which I clearly and distinctly perceive is of necessity true. Accordingly, even if I am no longer attending to the arguments which led me to judge that this is true, as long as I remember that I clearly and distinctly perceived it, there are no counter-arguments which can be adduced to make me doubt it, but on the contrary I have true and certain knowledge about it. And I have knowledge not just of this matter, but of all matters which I remember ever having demonstrated, in geometry and so on. For what objections can now be raised? That the way I am made makes me prone to frequent error? But I now know that I am incapable of error in those cases where my understanding is transparently clear. Or can it be objected that I have in the past regarded as true certain many things which I afterwards recognized to be false? But none of these were things which I clearly and distinctly perceived: I was ignorant of this rule for establishing the truth, and believed these things for other reasons which I later discovered to be less reliable. So what is left to say? Can one raise the objection I put to myself a while ago, that I may be dreaming, or that everything which I am now thinking has a little truth as what comes to the mind of one who is asleep? Yet even this does not change anything. For even though I might be dreaming, if there is anything which is evident to my intellect, then it is wholly true.

Thus I see plainly that the certainty and truth of all knowledge depends uniquely on my awareness of the true God, to such an extent that I was incapable of perfect knowledge about anything else until I became aware of him. And now it is possible for me to achieve full and certain knowledge of countless matters, both concerning God himself and other things whose nature is intellectual, and also concerning the whole of that corporeal nature which is the subject-matter of pure mathematics.

SIXTH MEDITATION

The Existence of Material Things, and the Real Distinction Between Mind and Body

It remains for me to examine whether material things exist. And at least I now know they are capable of existing, in so far as they are the subject-matter of pure mathematics, since I perceive them clearly and distinctly. For there is no doubt that God is capable of creating everything that I am capable of perceiving in this manner; and I have never judged that something could not be made by him except on the grounds that there would be a contradiction in my perceiving it distinctly. The conclusion that material things exist is also suggested by the faculty of imagination, which I am aware of using when I turn my mind to material things. For when I give more attentive consideration to what imagination is, it seems to be nothing else but an application of the cognitive faculty to a body which is intimately present to it, and which therefore exists.

To make this clear, I will first examine the difference between imagination and pure understanding. When I imagine a triangle, for example, I do not merely understand that it is a figure bounded by three lines, but at the same time I also see the three lines with my mind's eye as if they were present before me; and this is what I call imagining. But if I want to think of a chiliagon, although I understand that it is a figure consisting of a thousand sides just as well as I understand the triangle to be a three-sided figure, I do not in the same way imagine the thousand sides or see them as if they were present before me. It is true that since I am in the habit of imagining something whenever I think of a corporeal thing, I may construct in my mind a confused representation of some figure; but it is clear that this is not a chiliagon. For it differs in no way from the representation I should form if I were thinking of a myriagon, or any figure with very many sides. Moreover, such a representation is useless for recognizing the properties which distinguish a chiliagon from other polygons. But suppose I am dealing with a pentagon: I can of course understand the figure of a pentagon, just as I can the figure of a chiliagon, without the help of the imagination; but I can also imagine a pentagon, by applying my mind's eye to its five sides and the area contained within them. And in doing this I notice quite clearly that imagination requires a peculiar effort of mind which is not required for understanding; this additional effort of mind clearly shows the difference between imagination and pure understanding.

Besides this, I consider that this power of imagining which is in me, differing as it does form the power of understanding, is not a necessary constituent of my own essence, that is, of the essence of my mind. For if I lacked it, I should undoubtedly remain the same individual as I now am; from which it seems to follow that it depends on something distinct from myself. And I can easily understand that, if there does exist some body to which the mind is so joined that it can apply itself to contemplate it, as it were, whenever it pleases, then it may possibly be this very body that enables me to imagine corporeal things. So the difference between this mode of thinking and pure understanding may simply be this: when the mind understands, it in some way turns towards itself and inspects one of the ideas which are within it; but when it imagines, it turns towards the body and looks at something in the body which conforms to an idea understood by the mind or perceived by the senses. I can, as I say, easily understand that this is how imagination comes about, if the body exists; and since there is no other equally suitable way of explaining imagination that comes to mind, I can make a probable conjecture that the body exists. But this is only a probability; and despite a careful and comprehensive investigation, I do not yet see how the distinct idea of corporeal nature which I find in my imagination can provide any basis for a necessary inference that some body exists.

But besides that corporeal nature which is the subject-matter of pure mathematics, there is much else that I habitually imagine, such as colours, sounds, tastes, pain and so on—though not so distinctly. Now I perceive these things much better by means of the senses, which is how, with the assistance of memory, they appear to have reached the imagination. So in order to deal with them more fully, I must pay equal attention to the senses, and see whether the things which are perceived by means of that mode of thinking which I call 'sensory perception' provide me with any sure argument for the existence of corporeal things.

To begin with, I will go back over all the things which I previously took to be perceived by the senses, and reckoned to be true; and I will go over my reasons for thinking this. Next, I will set out my reasons for subsequently calling these things into doubt. And finally I will consider what I should now believe about them.

First of all then, I perceived by my senses that I had a head, hands, feet and other limbs making up the body which I regarded as part of myself, or perhaps even as my whole self. I also perceived by my senses that this body was situated among many other bodies which could affect it in various favourable or unfavourable ways; and I gauged the favourable effects by a sensation of pleasure, and the unfavourable ones by a sensation of pain. In addition to pain and pleasure, I also had sensations within me of hunger, thirst, and other such appetites, and also of physical propensities towards cheerfulness, sadness, anger and similar emotions. And outside me, besides the extension, shapes and movements of bodies, I also had sensations of their hardness and heat, and of the other tactile qualities. In addition, I had sensations of light, colours, smells, tastes and sounds, the variety of which enabled me to distinguish the sky, the earth, the seas, and all other bodies, one from another. Considering the ideas of all these qualities which presented themselves to my thought, although the ideas were, strictly speaking, the only immediate objects of my sensory awareness, it was not unreasonable for me to think that the items which I was perceiving through the senses were things quite distinct from my thought, namely bodies which produced the ideas. For my experience was that these ideas came to me quite without my consent, so that I could not have sensory awareness of any object, even if I wanted to, unless it was present to my sense organs; and I could not avoid having sensory awareness of it when it was present. And since the ideas perceived by the senses were much more lively and vivid and even, in their own way, more distinct than any of those which I deliberately formed through meditating or which I found impressed on my memory, it seemed impossible that they should have come from within me; so the only alternative was that they came from other things. Since the sole source of my knowledge of these things was the ideas themselves, the supposition that the things resembled the ideas was bound to occur to me. In addition, I remembered that the use of my senses had come first, while the use of my reason came only later; and I saw that the ideas which I formed myself were less vivid than those which I perceived with the senses and were, for the most part, made up of elements of sensory ideas. In this way I easily convinced myself that I had nothing at all in the intellect which I had not previously had in sensation. As for the body which by some special right I called 'mine', my belief that this body, more than any other, belonged to me had some justification. For I could never be separated from it, as I could from other bodies; and I felt all my appetites and emotions in, and on account of, this body; and finally, I was aware of pain and pleasurable ticklings in parts of this body, but not in other bodies external to it. But why should that curious sensation of pain give rise to a particular distress of mind; or why should a certain kind of delight follow on a tickling sensation? Again, why should that curious tugging in the stomach which I call hunger tell me that I should eat, or a dryness of the throat tell me to drink, and so on? I was not able to give any explanation of all this, except that nature taught me so. For there is absolutely no connection (at least that I can understand) between the tugging sensation and the decision to take food, or between the sensation of something causing pain and the mental apprehension of distress that arises from that sensation. These and other judgements that I made concerning sensory objects, I was apparently taught to make by nature; for I had already made up my mind that this was how things were, before working out any arguments to prove it.

Later on, however, I had many experiences which gradually undermined all the faith I had had in the senses. Sometimes towers which had looked round from a distance appeared square from close up; and enormous statues standing on their pediments did not seem large when observed from the ground. In these and countless other such cases, I found that the judgements of the external senses were mistaken. And this applied not just to the external senses but to the internal senses as well. For what can be more internal than pain? And yet I had heard that those who had had a leg or an arm amputated sometimes still seemed to feel pain intermittently in the missing part of the body. So even in my own case it was apparently not quite certain that a particular limb was hurting, even if I felt pain in it. To these reasons for doubting, I recently added two very general ones. The first was that every sensory experience I have ever thought I was having while awake I can also think of myself as sometimes having while asleep; and since I do not believe that what I seem to perceive in sleep comes from things located outside me, I did not see why I should be any more inclined to believe this of what I think I perceive while awake. The second reason for doubt was that since I did not know the author of my being (or at least was pretending not to), I saw nothing to rule out the possibility that my natural constitution made me prone to error even in matters which seemed to me most true. As for the reasons for my previous confident belief in the truth of the things perceived by the senses, I had no trouble in refuting them. For since I apparently had natural impulses towards many things which reason told me to avoid, I reckoned that a great deal of confidence should not be placed in what I was taught by nature. And despite the fact that the perceptions of the senses were not dependent on my will, I did not think that I should on that account infer that they proceeded from things distinct from myself, since I might perhaps have a faculty not yet known to me which produced them.

But now, when I am beginning to achieve a better knowledge of myself and the author of my being, although I do not think I should heedlessly accept everything I seem to have acquired from the senses, neither do I think that everything should be called into doubt.

First, I know that everything which I clearly and distinctly understand is capable of being created by God so as to correspond exactly with my understanding of it. Hence the fact that I can clearly and distinctly understand one thing apart from another is enough to make me certain that the two things are distinct, since they are capable of being separated, at least by God. The question of what kind of power is required to being about such a separation does not affect the judgement that the two things are distinct. Thus, simply by knowing that I exist and seeing at the same time that absolutely nothing else belongs to my nature or essence except that I am a thinking thing, I can infer correctly that my essence consists solely in the fact that I am a thinking thing. It is true that I may have (or, to anticipate, that I certainly have) a body that is very closely joined to me. But nevertheless, on the one hand I have a clear and distinct idea of myself, in so far as I am simply a thinking, non-extended thing; and on the other hand I have a distinct idea of body, in so far as this is simply an extended, non-thinking thing. And accordingly, it is certain that I am really distinct from my body, and can exist without it.

Besides this, I find in myself faculties for certain special modes of thinking, namely imagination and sensory perception. Now I can clearly and distinctly understand myself as a whole without these faculties; but I cannot, conversely, understand these faculties without me, that is, without an intellectual substance to inhere in. This is because there is an intellectual act included in their essential definition; and hence I perceive that the distinction between them and myself corresponds to the distinction between the modes of a thing and the thing itself. Of course I also recognize that there are other faculties (like those of changing position, of taking on various shapes, and so on) which, like sensory perception and imagination, cannot be understood apart from some substance for them to inhere in, and hence cannot exist without it. But it is clear that these other faculties, if they exist, must be in a corporeal or extended substance and not an intellectual one; for the clear and distinct conception of them includes extension, but does not include any intellectual act whatsoever. Now there is in me a passive faculty of sensory perception, that is, a faculty for receiving and recognizing the ideas of sensible objects; but I could not make use of it unless there was also an active faculty, either in me or in something else, which produced or brought about these ideas. But this faculty cannot be in me, since clearly it presupposes no intellectual act on my part, and the ideas in question are produced without my cooperation and often even against my will. So the only alternative is that it is in another substance distinct from me—a substance which contains either formally or eminently all the reality which exists objectively in the ideas produced by this faculty (as I have just noted). This substance is either a body, that is, a corporeal nature, in which case it will contain formally and in fact everything which is to be found objective or representatively in the ideas; or else it is God, or some creature more noble than a body, in which case it will contain eminently whatever is to be found in the ideas. But since God is not a deceiver, it is quite clear that he does not transmit the ideas to me either directly from himself, or indirectly, via some create which contains the objective reality of the ideas not formally but only eminently. For God has given me no faculty at all for recognizing any such source for these ideas; on the contrary, he has given me a great propensity to believe that they are produced by corporeal things. So I do not see how God could be understood to be anything but a deceiver if the ideas were transmitted from a source other than corporeal things. It follows that corporeal things exist. They may not all exist in a way that exactly corresponds with my sensory grasp of them, for in many cases the grasp of the senses is very obscure and confused. But at least they possess all the properties which I clearly and distinctly understand, that is, all those which, viewed in general terms, are comprised within the subject-matter of pure mathematics.

What of the other aspects of corporeal things which are either particular (for example that the sun is of such and such a size or shape), or less clearly understood, such as light or sound or pain, and so on? Despite the high degree of doubt and uncertainty involved here, the very fact that God is not a deceiver, and the consequent impossibility of there being any falsity in my opinions which cannot be corrected by some other faculty supplied by God, offers me a sure hope that I can attain the truth even in these matters. Indeed, there is no doubt that everything that I am taught by nature contains some truth. For if nature is considered in its general aspect, then I understand by the term nothing other than God himself, or the ordered system of created things established by God. And by my own nature in particular I understand nothing other than the totality of things bestowed on me by God.

There is nothing that my own nature teaches me more vividly than that I have a body, and that when I feel pain there is something wrong with the body, and that when I am hungry or thirsty the body needs food and drink, and so on. So I should not doubt that there is some truth in this.

Nature also teaches me, by these sensations of

pain, hunger, thirst and so on, that I am not merely present in my body as a sailor is present in a ship, but that I am very closely joined and, as it were, intermingled with it, so that I and the body form a unit. If this were not so, I, who am nothing but a thinking thing, would not feel pain when the body was hurt, but would perceive the damage purely by the intellect, just as a sailor perceives by sight if anything in his ship is broken. Similarly, when the body needed food or drink, I should have an explicit understanding of the fact, instead of having confused sensations of hunger and thirst. For these sensations of hunger, thirst, pain and so on are nothing but confused modes of thinking which arise from the union and, as it were, intermingling of the mind with the body.

I am also taught by nature that various other bodies exist in the vicinity of my body, and that some of these are to be sought out and others avoided. And from the fact that I perceive by my senses a great variety of colours, sounds, smells and tastes, as well as differences in heat, hardness and the like, I am correct in inferring that the bodies which are the source of these various sensory perceptions possess differences corresponding to them, though perhaps not resembling them. Also, the fact that some of the perceptions are agreeable to me while others are disagreeable makes it quite certain that my body, or rather my whole self, in so far as I am a combination of body and mind, can be affected by the various beneficial or harmful bodies which surround it.

There are, however, many other things which I may appear to have been taught by nature, but which in reality I acquired not from nature but from a habit of making ill-considered judgements; and it is therefore quite possible that these are false. Cases in point are the belief that any space in which nothing is occurring to stimulate my senses must be empty; or that the heat in a body is something exactly resembling the idea of heat which is in me; or that when a body is white or green, the selfsame whiteness or greeness which I perceive through my senses is present in the body; or that in a body which is bitter or sweet there is the selfsame taste which I experience, and so on; or, finally, that stars and towers and other distinct bodies have the same size and shape which they present to my senses, and other examples of this kind. But to make sure that my perceptions in this matter are sufficiently distinct, I must more accurately define exactly what I mean when I say that I am taught something by nature. In this context I am taking nature to be something more limited than the totality of things bestowed on me by God. For this includes many things that belong to the mind alone—for example my perception that what is done cannot be undone, and all other things that are known by the natural light; but at this stage I am not speaking of these matters. It also includes much that relates to the body alone, like the tendency to move in a downward direction, and so on; but I am not speaking of these matters either. My sole concern here is with what God has bestowed on me as a combination of mind and body. My nature, then, in this limited sense, does indeed teach me to avoid what induces a feeling of pain and to seek out what induces feelings of pleasure, and so on. But it does not appear to teach us to draw any conclusions from these sensory perceptions about things located outside us without waiting until the intellect has examined the matter. For knowledge of the truth about such things seems to belong to the mind alone, not to the combination of mind and body. Hence, although a star has no greater effect on my eye than the flame of a small light, that does not mean that there is any real or positive inclination in me to believe that the star is no bigger than the light; I have simply made this judgement from childhood onwards without any rational basis. Similarly, although I feel heat when I go near a fire and feel pain when I go too near, there is no convincing argument for supposing that there is something in the fire which resembles the heat, any more than for supposing that there is something which resembles the pain. There is simply reason to suppose that there is something in the fire, whatever it may eventually turn out to be, which produces in us the feelings of heat or pain. And likewise, even though there is nothing in any given space that stimulates the senses, it does not follow that there is no body there. In these cases and many others I see that I have been in the habit of misusing the order of nature. For the proper purpose of the sensory perceptions given me by nature is simply to inform the mind of what is beneficial or harmful for the composite of which the mind is a part; and to this extent they are sufficiently clear and distinct. But I misuse them by treating them as reliable touchstones for immediate judgements about the essential nature of the bodies located outside us; yet this is an area where they provide only very obscure information.

I have already looked in sufficient detail at how, notwithstanding the goodness of God, it may happen that my judgements are false. But a further problem now comes to mind regarding those very things which nature presents to me as objects which I should seek out or avoid, and also regarding the internal sensations, where I seem to have detected errors—e.g., when someone is tricked by the pleasant taste of some food into eating the poison concealed inside it. Yet in this case, what the man's nature urges him to go for is simply what is responsible for the pleasant taste, and not the poison, which his nature knows nothing about. The only inference that can be drawn from this is that his nature is not omniscient. And this is not surprising, since man is a limited thing, and so it is only fitting that his perfection should be limited.

And yet it is not unusual for us to go wrong even in cases where nature does urge us towards something. Those who are ill, for example, may desire food or drink that will shortly afterwards turn out to be bad for them. Perhaps it may be said that they go wrong because their nature is disordered, but this does not remove the difficulty. A sick man is no less one of God's creatures than a healthy one, and it seems no less a contradiction to suppose that he has received from God a nature which deceives him. Yet a clock constructed with wheels and weights observes all the laws of its nature just as closely when it is badly made and tells the wrong time as when it completely fulfils the wishes of the clockmaker. In the same way, I might consider the body of a man as a kind of machine equipped with and made up of bones, nerves, muscles, veins, blood and skin in such a way that, even if there were no mind in it, it would still perform all the same movements as it now does in those cases where movement is not under the control of the will or, consequently, of the mind. I can easily see that if such a body suffers from dropsy, for example, and is affected by the dryness of the throat which normally produces in the mind the sensation of thirst, the resulting condition of the nerves and other parts will dispose the body to take a drink, with the result that the disease will be aggravated. Yet this is just as natural as the body's being stimulated by a similar dryness of the throat to take a drink when there is no such illness and the drink is beneficial. Admittedly, when I consider the purpose of the clock, I may say that it is departing from its nature when it does not tell the right time; and similarly when I consider the mechanism of the human body, I may think that, in relation to the movements which normally occur in it, it too is deviating from its nature if the throat is dry at a time when drinking is not beneficial to its continued health. But I am well aware that 'nature' as I have just used it has a very different significance from 'nature' in the other sense. As I have just used it, 'nature' is simply a label which depends on my thought; it is quite extraneous to the things to which it is applied, and depends simply on my comparison between the idea of a sick man and a badly-made clock, and the idea of a healthy man and a well-made clock. But by 'nature' in the other sense I understand something which is really to be found in the things themselves; in this sense, therefore, the term contains something of the truth.

When we say, then, with respect to the body suffering from dropsy, that it has a disordered nature because it has a dry throat and yet does not need drink, the term 'nature' is here used merely as an extraneous label. However, with respect to the composite, that is, the mind united with this body, what is involved is not a mere label, but a true error of nature, namely that it is thirsty at a time when drink is going to cause it harm. It thus remains to inquire how it is that the goodness of God does not prevent nature, in this sense, from deceiving us.

The first observation I make at this point is that there is a great difference between the mind and the body, inasmuch as the body is by its very nature always divisible, while the mind is utterly indivisible. For when I consider the mind, or myself in so far as I am merely a thinking thing, I am unable to distinguish any parts within myself; I understand myself to be something quite single and complete. Although the whole mind seems to be united to the whole body, I recognize that if a foot or arm or any other part of the body is cut off, nothing has thereby been taken away from the mind. As for the faculties of willing, of understanding, of sensory perception and so on, these cannot be termed parts of the mind, since it is one and the same mind that wills, and understands and has sensory perceptions. By contrast, there is no corporeal or extended thing that I can think of which in my thought I cannot easily divide into parts; and this very fact makes me understand that it is divisible. This one argument would be enough to show me that the mind is completely different from the body, even if I did not already know as much from other considerations.

My next observation is that the mind is not immediately affected by all parts of the body, but only by the brain, or perhaps just by one small part of the brain, namely the part which is said to contain the 'common' sense. Every time this part of the brain is in a given state, it presents the same signals to the mind, even though the other parts of the body may be in a different condition at the time. This is established by countless observations, which there is no need to review here.

I observe, in addition, that the nature of the body is such that whenever any part of it is moved by another part which is some distance away, it can always be moved in the same fashion by any of the parts which lie in between, even if the more distant part does nothing. For example, in a cord ABCD, if one end D is pulled so that the other end A moves, the exact same movement could have been brought about if one of the intermediate points B or C had been pulled, and D had not moved at all. In similar fashion, when I feel a pain in my foot, physiology tells me that this happens by means of nerves distributed throughout the foot, and that these nerves are like cords which go from the foot right up to the brain. When the nerves are pulled in the foot, they in turn pull on inner parts of the brain to which they are attached, and produce a certain motion in them; and nature has laid it down that this motion should produce in the mind a sensation of pain, as occurring in the foot. But since these nerves, in passing from the foot to the brain, must pass through the calf, the thigh, the lumbar region, the back and the neck, it can happen that, even if it is not the part in the foot but one of the intermediate parts which is being pulled, the same motion will occur in the brain as occurs when the foot is hurt, and so it will necessarily come about that the mind feels the same sensation of pain. And we must suppose the same thing happens with regard to any other sensation.

My final observation is that any given movement occurring in the part of the brain that immediately affects the mind produces just one corresponding sensation; and hence the best system that could be devised is that it should produce the one sensation which, of all possible sensations, is most especially and most frequently conducive to the preservation of the healthy man. And experience shows that the sensations which nature has given us are all of this kind; and so there is absolutely nothing to be found in them that does not bear witness to the power and goodness of God. For example, when the nerves in the foot are set in motion in a violent and unusual manner, this motion, by way of the spinal cord, reaches the inner parts of the brain, and there gives the mind its signal for having a certain sensation, namely the sensation of a pain as occurring in the foot. This stimulates the mind to do its best to get rid of the cause of the pain, which it takes to be harmful to the foot. It is true that God could have made the nature of man such that this particular motion in the brain indicated something else to the mind; it might, for example, have made the mind aware of the actual motion occurring in the brain, or in the foot, or in any of the intermediate regions; or it might have indicated something else entirely. But there is nothing else which would have been so conducive to the continued well-being of the body. In the same way, when we need drink, there arises a certain dryness in the throat; this sets in motion the nerves of the throat, which in turn move the inner parts of the brain. This motion produces in the mind a sensation of thirst, because the most useful thing for us to know about the whole business is that we need drink in order to stay healthy. And so it is in the other cases.

It is quite clear from all this that, notwithstanding the immense goodness of God, the nature of man as a combination of mind and body is such that it is bound to mislead him from time to time. For there may be some occurrence, not in the foot but in one of the other areas through which the nerves travel in their route from the foot to the brain, or even in the brain itself; and if this cause produces the same motion which is generally produced by injury to the foot, then pain will be felt as if it were in the foot. This deception of the senses is natural, because a given motion in the brain must always produce the same sensation in the mind; and the origin of the motion in question is much more often going to be something which is hurting the foot, rather than something existing elsewhere. So it is reasonable that this motion should always indicate to the mind a pain in the foot rather than in any other part of the body. Again, dryness of the throat may sometimes arise not, as it normally does, from the fact that a drink is necessary to the health of the body, but from some quite opposite cause, as happens in the case of the man with dropsy. Yet it is much better that it should mislead on this occasion than that it should always mislead when the body is in good health. And the same goes for the other cases.

This consideration is the greatest help to me, not only for noticing all the errors to which my nature is liable, but also for enabling me to correct or avoid them without difficulty. For I know that in matters regarding the well-being of the body, all my senses report the truth much more frequently than not. Also, I can almost always make use of more than one sense to investigate the same thing; and in addition, I can use both my memory, which connects present experiences with preceding ones, and my intellect, which has by now examined all the causes of error. Accordingly, I should not have any further fears about the falsity of what my senses tell me every day; on the contrary, the exaggerated doubts of the last few days should be dismissed as laughable. This applies especially to the principle reason for doubt, namely my inability to distinguish between being asleep and being awake. For I now notice that there is a vast difference between the two, in that dreams are never linked by memory with all the other actions of life as waking experiences are. If, while I am awake, anyone were suddenly to appear to me and then disappear immediately, as happens in sleep, so that I could not see where he had come from or where he had gone to, it would not be unreasonable for me to judge that he was a ghost, or a vision created in my brain, rather than a real man. But when I distinctly see where things come from and where and when they come to me, and when I can connect my perceptions of them with the whole of the rest of my life without a break, then I am quite certain that when I encounter these things I am not asleep but awake. And I ought not to have even the slightest doubt of their reality if, after calling upon all the senses as well as my memory and my intellect in order to check them, I receive no conflicting reports from any of these sources. For from the fact that God is not a deceiver it follows that in cases like these I am completely free from error. But since the pressure or things to be done does not always allow us to stop and make such a meticulous check, it must be admitted that in this human life we are often liable to make mistakes about particular things, and we must acknowledge the weakness of our nature.

Chapter 16

THOMAS HOBBES

Thomas Hobbes (1588–1679) is the greatest English political philosopher, who gave classic expression to the idea that morality and politics arise out of a social contract. He was born on Good Friday, April 5, 1588, in Westbury, England, the son of an eccentric vicar. On the day of his birth the Spanish Armada, the greatest naval fleet the world had seen up to that time, was spotted off the coast of southern England. The chronicler John Aubrey reports that Hobbes's mother, only seven months pregnant, startled by the news, fell into labor with Hobbes and delivered him. Hobbes wrote of this experience, "Unbeknownst to my mother at that time she gave birth to twins, myself and fear. And fear has been my constant companion throughout life." Hobbes's lifetime was filled with the dangers of war, the invading Spanish Armada, the religious wars of Europe, the Civil War in England. His political philosophy may be read as a cure against the fear and insecurity of people desperately in need of peace and tranquility.

Hobbes was educated at Oxford University, and lived through an era of political revolutions as a scholar and tutor (he was tutor to Prince Charles II of England). He was widely traveled and was in communication with most of the intellectual luminaries of his day, both on the Continent (Galileo, Gassendi, and Descartes) and in England (Francis Bacon, Ben Johnson, and William Harvey), and was regarded as a brilliant, if somewhat unorthodox and controversial, intellectual.

Hobbes is known today primarily for his masterpiece in political theory, *Leviathan* (1651), a book written during the English civil wars (1642–1646), sometimes referred to as "The Great Rebellion," which pitted the forces of monarchy (the Royalists) under Charles I against those of Parliament under Oliver Cromwell. Hobbes's work was intended to support the Royalists, as he believed that the monarchy was the best guarantee for orderly and stable government. Yet the Royalists misconstrued his interpretation as supporting the rebels, no doubt because Hobbes rejected the usual grounds for the monarchy, the divine right of kings. For this reason, and because the book conveyed a materialist view of human nature, thought to be dangerous to religion, it was suppressed or violently attacked throughout Hobbes's lifetime.

What are the doctrines which his contemporaries found so controversial? First of all, Hobbes breaks from the medieval notion that the State is a natural organism, based on natural devotion and interdependence. He develops a moral and political theory based not on natural affection but on psychological egoism. Hobbes argues that people are all egoists who always act in their own self-interest, to obtain gratification and avoid harm. However, we cannot obtain any of the basic goods because of the inherent fear of harm and death, the insecurity in an unregulated "state of nature," in which life is "solitary, poor, nasty, brutish and short." We cannot relax our guard, for everyone is constantly in fear of everyone else. In this state of anarchy the prudent person concludes that it really is in all our self-interest to make a contract to keep to a minimal morality of respecting human life, keeping covenants made, and obeying the laws of the society. This minimal morality, which Hobbes refers to as "The Laws of Nature," is nothing more than a set of maxims of prudence. In order to ensure that we all obey this covenant Hobbes proposes a strong sovereign or "Leviathan" to impose severe penalties on those who disobey the laws, for "covenants without sword are but words." The term "Leviathan" refers to the sea monster (or whale) referred to in the Book of Job:

> Let those curse the day who are skilled to rouse up Leviathan (3:8).
> Can you draw out Leviathan with a fishhook or press down his tongue with a cord?
> Can you put a rope in his nose or pierce his jaw with a hook?
> Will he make a covenant with you to take him for your servant for ever?
> His sneezings flash forth light, and his eyes are like the eyelids of the dawn.
> Out of his mouth go flaming torches; sparks of fire leap forth.
> Out of his nostrils comes forth smoke, as from a boiling pot and burning rushes.
> His breath kindles coals, and flame comes forth from his mouth.
> When he raises himself up the mighty are afraid; at the crashing they are beside them selves.
> Upon earth there is not his like, a creature without fear.
> He beholds everything that is high; he is king over all the sons of pride (Job 41).

The State is the great Leviathan, awesome and powerful, inspiring fear, but offering protection from violence and harm. We begin with Hobbes's discussion of human nature in Part I of *Leviathan* and move on through Part II on the Commonwealth.

FOR FURTHER READING:

Gauthier, David. *The Logic of Leviathan: The Moral and Political Thought of Thomas Hobbes.* (Clarendon Press, 1969)

Hampton, Jean. *Hobbes and the Social Contract.* (Cambridge University Press, 1986).

Hobbes, Thomas. *Leviathan.* (Penguin, 1986). Introduction by C. B. MacPherson. A useful introduction together with an inexpensive edition.

Kavka, Gregory. *Hobbesian Moral and Political Theory.* (Princeton University Press, 1986). An advanced, thorough work.

Oakshott, Michael. *Hobbes on Civil Association.* (University of California Press, 1975).

Peters, Richard. *Hobbes.* (Penguin, 1956). A clear exposition of Hobbes's ideas.

Rogers, G. A. J. and Alan Ryan, eds. *Perspectives on Thomas Hobbes.* (Oxford University Press, 1989).

Turnbull, Colin. *The Mountain People.* (Simon & Schuster, 1972). A poignant account of a displaced people in northern Uganda whose social conditions reflect a Hobbesian state of nature.

Wolin, Sheldon S. *Politics and Vision.* (Little, Brown, 1960). A perceptive history of Western political thought with a good chapter on Hobbes.

Leviathan or The Matter, Form, & Power of a Commonwealth Ecclesiastical and Civil

PART 1. OF MAN

Chapter 1. Of Sense

Concerning the thoughts of man, I will consider them first singly, and afterwards in train, or dependence upon one another. Singly, they are every one a representation or appearance, of some quality, or other accident of a body without us; which is commonly called an object. Which object works on the eyes, ears, and other parts of a man's body; and by diversity of working, produces diversity of appearances.

The original of them all, is that which we call SENSE; (For there is no conception in a man's mind, which hath not at first, totally, or by parts, been begotten upon the organs of sense.) The rest are derived from that original.

To know the natural cause of sense, is not very necessary to the business now in hand; and I have elsewhere written of the same at large. Nevertheless, to fill each part of my present method, I will briefly deliver the same in this place.

The cause of sense, is the external body, or object, which presses the organ proper to each sense, either immediately, as in the taste and touch; or mediately, as in seeing, hearing, and smelling: which pressure, by the mediation of nerves, and other strings and membranes of the body, continued inwards to the brain and heart, causes there a resistance, or counter-pressure, or endeavour of the heart, to deliver it self: which endeavour, because outward, seems to be some matter without. And this seeming, or, fancy, is that which men call sense; and consists, as to the eye, in a light, or colour figured; to the ear, in a sound; to the nostril, in an odour; to the tongue and palate, in a savour; and to the rest of the body, in heat, cold, hardness, softness, and such other qualities as we discern by feeling. All which qualities called sensible, are in the object, that causes them, but so many several motions of the matter, by which it presses our organs diversely. Neither in us that are pressed, are they any thing else, but divers motions (for motion produces nothing but motion). But their appearance to us is fancy, the same waking, that dreaming. And as pressing, rubbing, or striking the eye, makes us fancy a light; and pressing the ear, produces a din; so do the bodies also we see, or hear, produce the same by their strong, though unobserved action. For if those colours and sounds were in the bodies, or objects that cause them, they could not be severed from them, as by glasses, and in echoes by reflection, we see they are; where we know the thing we see, is in one place; the appearance in another. And though at some certain distance, the real and very object seem invested with the fancy it begets in us; yet still the object is one thing, the image or fancy is another. So that sense in all cases, is nothing else but original fancy, caused (as I have said) by the pressure, that is, by the motion, of external things upon our eyes, ears, and other organs thereunto ordained.

But the philosophy-schools, through all the universities of Christendom, grounded upon certain texts of Aristotle, teach another doctrine; and say, for the cause of vision, that the thing seen, sends forth on every side a visible species (in English) a visible show, apparition, or aspect, or a being seen; the receiving whereof into the eye, is seeing. And for the cause of hearing, that the thing heard, sends forth an audible species, that is, an audible aspect, or audible being seen; which entering at the ear, maketh hearing. Nay for the cause of understanding also, they say the thing understood, sends forth intelligible species, that is, an intelligible being seen; which coming into the understanding, makes us understand. I say not this, as disapproving the use of universities: but because I am to speak hereafter of their office in a commonwealth, I must let you see on all occasions by the way, what things would be amended in them; amongst which the frequency of insignificant speech is one.

Chapter 2. Of Imagination

That when a thing lies still, unless somewhat else stir it, it will lie still for ever, is a truth that no man doubts of. But that when a thing is in motion, it will eternally be in motion, unless somewhat else stay it, though the reason be the same (namely, that nothing can change it self) is not so easily assented to. For men measure, not only other men, but all other things, by themselves: and because they find themselves subject after motion to pain, and lassitude, think every thing else grows weary of motion, and seeks repose of its own accord; little considering, whether it be not some other motion, wherein that desire of rest they find in themselves, consists. From hence it is, that the schools say, heavy bodies fall downwards, out of an appetite to rest, and to conserve their nature in that place which is most proper for them; ascribing appetite and knowledge of what is good for their conservation (which is more than man has) to things inanimate, absurdly.

When a body is once in motion, it moves (unless something else hinder it) eternally; and whatsoever hinders it, cannot in an instant, but in time, and by degrees quite extinguish it: And as we see in the water, though the wind cease, the waves give not over rolling for a long time after; so also it happens in that motion, which is made in the internal parts of a man, then, when he sees, dreams &c. For after the object is removed, or the eye shut, we still retain an image of the thing seen, though more obscure then when we see it. And this is it, the Latins call imagination, from the image made in seeing; and apply the same, though improperly, to all the other senses. But the Greeks call it fancy; which signifies appearance, and is as proper to one sense, as to another. IMAGINATION therefore is nothing but decaying sense; and is found in men, and many other living creatures, as well sleeping, as waking.

The decay of sense in men waking, is not the decay of the motion made in sense; but an obscuring of it, in such manner as the light of the sun obscures the light of the stars; which stars do no less exercise their virtue, by which they are visible, in the day, than in the night. But because amongst many strokes, which our eyes, ears, and other organs receive from external bodies, the predominant only is sensible; therefore the light of the sun being predominant, we are not affected with the action of the stars. And any object being removed from our eyes, though the impression it made in us remain; yet other objects more present succeeding, and working on us, the imagination of the past is obscured, and made weak, as the voice of a man is in the noise of the day. From whence it followeth, that the longer the time is, after the sight or sense of any object, the weaker is the imagination. For the continual change of man's body destroys in time the parts which in sense were moved: so that distance of time, and of place, hath one and the same effect in us. For as at a great distance of place, that which we look at appears dim, and without distinction of the smaller parts; and as voices grow weak, and inarticulate; so also, after great distance of time, our imagination of the past is weak; and we lose (for example) of cities we have seen, many particular streets, and of actions, many particular circumstances. This decaying sense, when we would express the thing it self (I mean fancy it self), we call imagination, as I said before; but when we would express the decay, and signify that the sense is fading, old, and past, it is called memory. So that imagination and memory are but one thing, which for divers considerations hath divers names.

Much memory, or memory of many things, is called experience. Again, imagination being only of those things which have been formerly perceived by sense, either all at once, or by parts at several times; the former (which is the imagining the whole object, as it was presented to the sense) is simple imagination; as when one imagines a man, or horse, which he hath seen before. The other is compounded; as when from the sight of a man at one time, and of a horse at another, we conceive in our mind a Centaur. So when a man compounds the image of his own person, with the image of the actions of another man; as when a man imagines himself a Hercules or an Alexander (which happens often to them that are much taken with reading of romances) it is a compound imagination, and properly but a fiction of the mind. There be also other imaginations that rise in men (though waking) from the great impression made in sense: as from gazing upon the sun, the impression leaves an image of the sun before our eyes a long time after; and from being long and vehemently attent upon geometrical figures, a man shall in the dark (though awake) have the images of lines and angles before his eyes: which kind of fancy hath no particular name; as being a thing that doth not commonly fall into men's discourse.

The imaginations of them that sleep are those we call dreams. And these also (as all other imaginations) have been before, either totally or by parcels in the sense. And because in sense, the brain and nerves, which are the necessary organs of sense, are so benumbed in sleep, as not easily to be moved by the action of external objects, there can happen in sleep no imagination; and therefore no dream, but what proceeds from the agitation of the inward parts of man's body; which inward parts, for the connexion they have with the brain, and other organs, when they be distempered, do keep the same in motion; whereby the imaginations there formerly made, appear as if a man were waking; saving that the organs of sense being now benumbed, so as there is no new object, which can master and obscure them with a more vigorous impression, a dream must needs be more clear, in this silence of sense, than are our a waking thoughts. And hence it comes to pass, that it is a hard matter, and by many thought impossible to distinguish exactly between sense and dreaming. For my part, when I consider that in dreams, I do not often, nor constantly think of the same persons, places, objects, and actions that I do waking; nor remember so long a train of coherent thoughts, dreaming, as at other times; and because waking I often observe the absurdity of dreams, but never dream of the absurdities of my waking thoughts; I am well satisfied, that being awake, I know I dream not; though when I dream I think myself awake.

And seeing dreams are caused by the distemper of some of the inward parts of the body; divers distempers must needs cause different dreams. And hence it is, that lying cold breeds dreams of fear, and raises the thought and image of some fearful object (the motion from the brain to the inner parts, and from the inner parts to the brain being reciprocal;) and that as anger causes heat in some parts of the body, when we are awake; so when we sleep the over heating of the same parts causes anger, and raiseth up in the brain the imagination of an enemy. In the same manner, as natural kindness, when we are awake, causes desire; and desire makes heat in certain other parts of the body; so also, too much heat in those parts, while we sleep, raiseth in the brain an imagination of some kindness shown. In sum, our dreams are the reverse of our waking imaginations; the motion when we are awake, beginning at one end; and when we dream, at another.

The most difficult discerning of a man's dream, from his waking thoughts, is then, when by some accident we observe not that we have slept: which is easy to happen to a man full of fearful thoughts; and whose conscience is much troubled; and that sleeps, without the circumstances, of going to bed, or putting off his clothes, as one that noddeth in a chair. For he that taketh pains, and industriously lays himself to sleep, in case any uncouth and exorbitant fancy come unto him, cannot easily think it other than a dream. We read of Marcus Brutus (one that had his life given him by Julius Caesar, and was also his favourite, and notwithstanding murdered him), how at Philippi, the night before he gave battle to Augustus Caesar, he saw a fearful apparition, which is commonly related by historians as a vision; but considering the circumstances, one may easily judge to have been but a short dream. For sitting in his tent, pensive and troubled with the horror of his rash act, it was not hard for him, slumbering in the cold, to dream of that which most affrighted him; which fear, as by degrees it made him wake; so also it must needs make the apparition by degrees to vanish; and having no assurance that he slept, he could have no cause to think it a dream, or any thing but a vision. And this is no very rare accident; for even they that be perfectly awake, if they be timorous, and superstitious, possessed with fearful tales, and alone in the dark, are subject to the like fancies; and believe they see spirits and dead men's ghosts walking in churchyards; whereas it is either their fancy only, or else the knavery of such persons, as make use of such superstitious fear, to pass disguised in the night, to places they would not be known to haunt.

From this ignorance of how to distinguish dreams, and other strong fancies, from vision and sense, did arise the greatest part of the religion of the Gentiles in time past, that worshipped satyrs, fawns, nymphs, and the like; and now-a-days the opinion that rude people have of fairies, ghosts, and goblins, and of the power of witches. For as for witches, I think not that their witchcraft is any real power; but yet that they are justly punished, for the false belief they have, that they can do such mischief, joined with their purpose to do it if they can: their trade being nearer to a new religion than to a craft or science. And for fairies, and walking ghosts, the opinion of them has I think been on purpose, either taught, or not confuted, to keep in credit the use of exorcism, of crosses, of holy water, and other such inventions of ghostly men. Nevertheless, there is no doubt, but God can make unnatural apparitions: But that he does it so often, as men need to fear such things, more than they fear the stay, or change, of the course of nature, which he also can stay, and change, is no point of Christian faith. But evil men under pretext that God can do any thing, are so bold as to say any thing when it serves their turn, though they think it untrue; it is the part of a wise man, to believe them no further, than right reason makes that which they say, appear credible. If this superstitious fear of spirits were taken away, and with it, prognostics from-dreams, false prophecies, and many other things depending thereon, by which, crafty ambitious persons abuse the simple people, men would be much more fitted than they are for civil obedience.

And this ought to be the work of the schools: but they rather nourish such doctrine. For (not knowing what imagination, or the senses are), what they receive, they teach: some saying, that imaginations rise of themselves, and have no cause; others, that they rise most commonly from the will; and that good thoughts are blown (inspired) into a man by God, and evil thoughts by the Devil; or that good thoughts are poured (infused) into a man by God, and evil ones by the Devil. Some say the senses receive the species of things, and deliver them to the common sense; and the common sense delivers them over to the fancy, and the fancy to the memory, and the memory to the judgment, like handing of things from one to another, with many words making nothing understood.

The imagination that is raised in man (or any other creature endued with the faculty of imagining) by words, or other voluntary signs, is that we generally call understanding; and is common to man and beast. For a dog by custom will understand the call, or the rating of his master; and so will many other beasts. That understanding which is peculiar to man, is the understanding not only his will, but his conceptions and thoughts, by the sequel and contexture of the names of things into affirmations, negations, and other forms of speech; and of this kind of understanding I shall speak hereafter.

Chapter 3. Of the Consequence or Train of Imaginations

By Consequence, or train of thoughts, I understand that succession of one thought to another, which is called (to distinguish it from discourse in words) mental discourse.

When a man thinks on any thing whatsoever, his next thought after, is not altogether so casual as it seems to be. Not every thought to every thought succeeds indifferently. But as we have no imagination, whereof we have not formerly had sense, in whole, or in parts; so we have no transition from one imagination to another, whereof we never had the like before in our senses. The reason whereof is this. All fancies are motions within us, relics of those made in the sense: and those motions that immediately succeeded one another in the sense, continue also together after sense: insomuch as the former coming again to take place, and be predominant, the latter followeth, by coherence of the matter moved, in such manner, as water upon a plain table is drawn which way any one part of it is guided by the finger. But because in sense, to one and the same thing perceived, sometimes one thing, sometimes another succeeds, it comes to pass in time, that in the imagining of any thing, there is no certainty what we shall imagine next; only this is certain, it shall be something that succeeded the same before, at one time or another.

This train of thoughts, or mental discourse, is of two sorts. The first is unguided, without design, and inconstant; wherein there is no passionate thought, to govern and direct those that follow, to it self, as the end and scope of some desire, or other passion: in which case the thoughts are said to wander, and seem impertinent one to another, as in a dream. Such are commonly the thoughts of men, that are not only without company, but also without care of any thing; though even then their thoughts are as busy as at other times, but without harmony; as the sound which a lute out of tune would yield to any man; or in tune, to one that could not play. And yet in this wild ranging of the mind, a man may oft-times perceive the way of it, and the dependance of one thought upon another. For in a discourse of our present civil war, what could seem more impertinent, than to ask (as one did) what was the value of a Roman penny? Yet the coherence to me was manifest enough. For the thought of the war, introduced the thought of the delivering up the king to his enemies; the thought of that, brought in the thought of the delivering up of Christ; and that again the thought of the 30 pence, which was the price of that treason; and thence easily followed that malicious question, and all this in a moment of time; for thought is quick.

The second is more constant; as being regulated by some desire, and design. For the impression made by such things as we desire, or fear, is strong, and permanent, or (if it cease for a time), of quick return: so strong it is sometimes, as to hinder and break our sleep. From desire, arises the thought of some means we have seen produce the like of that which we aim at; and from the thought of that, the thought of means to that mean; and so continually, till we come to some beginning within our own power. And because the end, by the greatness of the impression, comes often to mind, in case our thoughts begin to wander, they are quickly again reduced into the way: which observed by one of the seven wise men, made him give men this precept, which is now worn out, *Respice finem*; that is to say, in all your actions, look often upon what you would have, as the thing that directs all your thoughts in the way to attain it.

The train of regulated thoughts is of two kinds; one, when of an effect imagined, we seek the causes, or means that produce it: and this is common to man and beast. The other is, when imagining any thing whatsoever, we seek all the possible effects, that can by it be produced; that is to say, we imagine what we can do with it, when we have it. Of which I have not at any time seen any sign, but in man only; for this is a curiosity hardly incident to the nature of any living creature that has no other passion but sensual, such as are hunger, thirst, lust, and anger. In sum, the discourse of the mind, when it is governed by design, is nothing but seeking, or the faculty of invention, which the Latins called *sagacitas*, and *solertia*; a hunting out of the causes, of some effect, present or past; or of the effects, of some present or past cause. Sometimes a man seeks what he hath lost; and from that place, and time, wherein he misses it, his minds runs back, from place to place, and time to time, to find where, and when he had it; that is to say, to find some certain, and limited time and place, in which to being a method of seeking. Again, from thence, his thoughts run over the same places and times, to find what action, or other occasion might make him lose it. This we call remembrance, or calling to mind: the Latins call it *reminiscentia*, as it were a re-conning of our former actions.

Sometimes a man knows a place determinate, within the compass whereof he is to seek; and then his thoughts run over all the parts thereof, in the same manner as one would sweep a room, to find a jewel; or as a spaniel ranges the field, till he find a scent; or as a man should run over the alphabet, to start a rhyme.

Sometimes a man desires to know the event of an action; and then he thinks of some like action past, and the events thereof one after another; supposing like events will follow like actions. As he that foresees what will become of a criminal, reckons what he has seen follow on the like crime before; having this order of thoughts, the crime, the officer, the prison, the judge, and the gallows. Which kind of thoughts, is called foresight, and prudence, or providence; and sometimes wisdom; though such conjecture, through the difficulty of observing all circumstances, be very fallacious. But this is certain; by how much one man has more experience of things past, than another; by so much also he is more prudent, and his expectations the seldomer fail him. The present only has a being in nature; things past have a being in the memory only, but things to come have no being at all; the future being but a fiction of the mind, applying the sequels of actions past, to the actions that are present; which with most certainty is done by him that has most experience; but not with certainty enough. And though it be called prudence, when the event answers our expectation; yet in its own nature, it is but presumption. For the foresight of things to come, which is providence, belongs only to him by whose will they are to come. From him only, and supernaturally, proceeds prophecy. The best prophet naturally is the best guesser; and the best guesser, he that is most versed and studied in the matters he guesses at: for he hath most signs to guess by. . . .

Chapter 6. Of the Interior Beginnings of Voluntary Motions; Commonly Called the Passions; and the Speeches by which They are Expressed

There be in animals, two sorts of motions peculiar to them: one called vital; begun in generation, and continued without interruption through their whole life; such as are the course of the blood, the pulse, the breathing, the concoction, nutrition, excretion, &c; to which motions there needs no help of imagination: the other is animal motion, otherwise called voluntary motion; as to go, to speak, to move any of our limbs, in such manner as is first fancied in our minds. That sense is motion in the organs and interior parts of man's body, caused by the action of the things we see, hear, &c.; and that fancy is but the relics of the same motion, remaining after sense, has been already said in the first and second chapters. And because going, speaking, and the like voluntary motions, depend always upon a precedent thought of whither, which way, and what; it is evident, that the imagination is the first internal beginning of all voluntary motion. And although unstudied men do not conceive any motion at all to be there, where the thing moved is invisible; or the space it is moved in, is (for the shortness of it) insensible; yet that doth not hinder, but that such motions are. For let a space be never so little, that which is moved over a greater space, whereof that little one is part, must first be moved over that. These small beginnings of motion, within the body of man, before they appear in walking, speaking, striking, and other visible actions, are commonly called ENDEAVOR.

This endeavor, when it is toward something which causes it, is called APPETITE, or DESIRE; the latter, being the general name; and the other, oftentimes restrained to signify the desire of food, namely hunger and thirst. And when the endeavor is fromward something, it is generally called AVERSION. These words, appetite and aversion, we have from the Latins; and they both of them signify the motions, one of approaching, the other of retiring. So also do the Greek words for the same, which are [*orme*] and [*aphorme*]. For nature itself does often press upon men those truths, which afterwards, when they look for somewhat beyond nature, the stumble at. For the Schools find in mere appetite to go, or move, no actual motion at all: but because some motion they must acknowledge, they call it metaphorical motion; which is but an absurd speech: for though words may be called metaphorical; bodies and motions cannot.

That which men desire, they are also said to LOVE: and to HATE those things for which they have aversion. So that desire and love are the same thing; save that by desire, we always signify the absence of the object; by love, most commonly the presence of the same. So also by aversion, we signify the absence; and by hate, the presence of the object.

Of appetites and aversions, some are born with men; as appetite of food, appetite of excretion, and exoneration (which may also and more properly be called aversions, from somewhat they feel in their bodies); and some other appetites, not many. The rest, which are appetites of particular things, proceed from experience, and trial of their effects upon themselves or other men. For of things we know not at all, or believe not to be, we can have no further desire, than to taste and try. But aversion we have for things, not only which we know have hurt us, but also that we do not know whether they will hurt us, or not.

Those things which we neither desire, nor hate, we are said to contemn; CONTEMPT being nothing else but an immobility, or contumacy of the heart, in resisting the action of certain things; and proceeding from that the heart is already moved otherwise, by other more potent objects; or from want of experience of them.

And because the constitution of a man's body is in continual mutation, it is impossible that all the same things should always cause in him the same appetites, and aversions: much less can all men consent, in the desire of almost any one and the same object.

But whatsoever is the object of any man's appetite or desire, that is it which he for his part calls good: and the object of his hate and aversion, evil; and of his contempt, vile and inconsiderable. For these words of good, evil, and contemptible, are ever used with relation to the person that uses them: there being nothing simply and absolutely so; nor any common rule of good and evil, to be taken from the nature of the objects themselves; but from the person of the man (where there is no commonwealth); or (in a commonwealth) from the person that represents it; or from an arbitrator or judge, whom men disagreeing shall by consent set up, and make his sentence the rule thereof.

The Latin tongue has two words, whose significations approach to those of good and evil; but are not precisely the same; and those are pulchrum and turpe. Whereof the former signifies that, which by some apparent signs promises good; and the latter, that which promises evil. But in our tongue we have not so general names to express them by. But for pulchrum we say in some things, fair; in others, beautiful, or handsome, or gallant, or honorable, or comely, or amiable; and for turpe, foul, deformed, ugly, base, nauseous, and the like, as the subject shall require; all which words, in their proper places, signify nothing else but the mien, or countenance, that promises good and evil. So that of good there be three kinds; good in the promise, that is pulchrum; good in effect, as the end desired, which is called jucundum, delightful; and good as the means, which is called utile, profitable; and as many of evil: for evil in promise, is that they call turpe; evil in effect, and end, is molestum, unpleasant, troublesome; and evil in the means, inutile, unprofitable, hurtful.

As, in sense, that which is really within us, is, (as I have said before,) only motion, caused by the action of external objects, but in appearance; to the sight, light and colour; to the ear, sound; to the nostril, odor, &c.: so, when the action of the same object is continued from the eyes, ears, and other organs to the heart, the real effect there is nothing but motion, or endeavor; which consists in appetite, or aversion, to or from the object moving. But the appearance, or sense of that motion, is that we either call delight, or trouble of mind.

This motion, which is called appetite, and for the appearance of it delight, and pleasure, seems to be a corroboration of vital motion, and a help thereunto; and therefore such things as caused delight, were not improperly called jucunda, from helping or fortifying; and the contrary, molesta, offensive, from hindering, and troubling the motion vital.

Pleasure therefore (or delight), is the appearance, or sense of good; and molestation or displeasure, the appearance, or sense of evil. And consequently all appetite, desire, and love, is accompanied with some delight more or less; and all hatred and aversion, with more or less displeasure and offence.

Of pleasures or delights, some arise from the sense of an object present; and those may be called pleasures of sense (the word sensual, as it is used by those only that condemn them, having no place till there be laws). Of this kind are all onerations and exonerations of the body; as also all that is pleasant, in the sight, hearing, smell, taste, or touch. Others arise from the expectation, that proceeds from foresight of the end, or consequence of things; whether those things in the sense please or displease. And these are pleasures of the mind of him that draws those consequences, and are generally called JOY. In the like manner, displeasures are some in the sense, and called PAIN; others in the expectation of consequences, and are called GRIEF.

These simple passions called appetite, desire, love, aversion, hate, joy, and grief, have their names for divers considerations diversified. As first, when they one succeed another, they are diversely called from the opinion men have of the likelihood of attaining what they desire. Secondly, from the object loved or hated. Thirdly, from the consideration of many of them together. Fourthly, from the alteration or succession it self.

For appetite, with an opinion of attaining, is called HOPE.

The same, without such opinion, DESPAIR.

Aversion, with opinion of hurt from the object, FEAR.

The same, with hope of avoiding that hurt by resistance, COURAGE.

Sudden courage, ANGER.

Constant hope, CONFIDENCE of ourselves.

Constant despair, DIFFIDENCE of ourselves.

Anger for great hurt done to another, when we conceive the same to be done by injury, INDIGNATION.

Desire of good to another, BENEVOLENCE, GOOD WILL, CHARITY. If to man generally, GOOD NATURE.

Desire of riches, COVETOUSNESS: a name used always in signification of blame; because men contending for them, are displeased with one another's attaining them; though the desire in itself, be to be blamed, or allowed, according to the means by which those riches are sought.

Desire of office, or precedence, AMBITION: a name used also in the worse sense, for the reason before mentioned.

Desire of things that conduce but a little to our ends, and fear of things that are but of little hindrance, PUSILLANIMITY.

Contempt of little helps and hindrances, MAGNANIMITY.

Magnanimity, in danger of death or wounds, VALOR, FORTITUDE.

Magnanimity, in the use of riches, LIBERALITY.

Pusillanimity, in the same, WRETCHEDNESS, MISERABLENESS, or PARSIMONY; as it is liked or disliked.

Love of persons for society, KINDNESS.

Love of persons for pleasing the sense only, NATURAL LUST.

Love of the same, acquired from rumination, that is, imagination of pleasure past, LUXURY.

Love of one singularly, with desire to be singularly beloved, THE PASSION OF LOVE. The same, with fear that the love is not mutual, JEALOUSY.

Desire, by doing hurt to another, to make him condemn some fact of his own, REVENGEFULNESS.

Desire to know why, and how, CURIOSITY; such as is in no living creature but man: so that man is distinguished, not only by his reason, but also by this singular passion from other animals; in whom the appetite of food, and other pleasures of sense, by predominance, take away the care of knowing causes; which is a lust of the mind, that by a perseverance of delight in the continual and indefatigable generation of knowledge, exceedeth the short vehemence of any carnal pleasure.

Fear of power invisible, feigned by the mind, or imagined from tales publicly allowed, RELIGION; not allowed, SUPERSTITION. And when the power imagined, is truly such as we imagine, TRUE RELIGION.

Fear, without the apprehension of why, or what,

PANIC TERROR, called so from the fables, that make Pan the author of them; whereas in truth, there is always in him that so feareth, first, some apprehension of the cause, though the rest run away by example, every one supposing his fellow to know why. And there this passion happens to none but in a throng, or multitude of people.

Joy, from apprehension of novelty, ADMIRATION; proper to man, because it excites the appetite of knowing the cause.

Joy, arising from imagination of a man's own power and ability, is that exultation of the mind which is called GLORYING: which if grounded upon the experience of his own former actions, is the same with confidence: but if grounded on the flattery of others; or only supposed by himself, for delight in the consequences of it, is called VAINGLORY: which name is properly given; because a well grounded confidence begetteth attempt; whereas the supposing of power does not, and is therefore rightly called vain.

Grief, from opinion of want of power, is called DEJECTION of mind.

The vain-glory which consists in the feigning or supposing of abilities in ourselves, which we know are not, is most incident to young men, and nourished by the histories, or fictions of gallant persons; and is corrected oftentimes by age, and employment.

Sudden glory, is the passion which maketh those grimaces called LAUGHTER; and is caused either by some sudden act of their own, that pleases them; or by the apprehension of some deformed thing in another, by comparison whereof they suddenly applaud themselves. And it is incident most to them, that are conscious of the fewest abilities in themselves; who are forced to keep themselves in their own favour, by observing the imperfections of other men. And therefore much laughter at the defects of others, is a sign of pusillanimity. For of great minds, one of the proper works is, to help and free others from scorn; and compare themselves only with the most able.

On the contrary, sudden dejection, is the passion that causes WEEPING; and is caused by such accidents, as suddenly take away some vehement hope, or some prop of their power: and they are most subject to it, that rely principally on helps external, such as are women, and children. Therefore some weep for the loss of friends; others for their unkindness; others for the sudden stop made to their thoughts of revenge, by reconciliation. But in all cases, both laughter, and weeping, are sudden motions; custom taking them both away. For no man laughs at old jests; or weeps for an old calamity.

Grief, for the discovery of some defect of ability, is SHAME, or the passion that discovers itself in BLUSHING; and consists in the apprehension of some thing dishonorable; and in young men, is a sign of the love of good reputation, and commendable: in old men it is a sign of the same; but because it comes too late, not commendable.

The contempt of good reputation is called IMPUDENCE.

Grief, for the calamity of another, is PITY; and arises from the imagination that the like calamity may befall himself; and therefore is called also COMPASSION, and in the phrase of this present time a FELLOW-FEELING: and therefore for calamity arriving from great wickedness, the best men have the least pity; and for the same calamity, those have least pity, that think themselves least obnoxious to the same.

Contempt, or little sense of the calamity of others, is that which men call CRUELTY; proceeding from security of their own fortune. For, that any man should take pleasure in other men's great harms, without other end of his own, I do not conceive it possible.

Grief, for the success of a competitor in wealth, honour, or other good, if it be joined with endeavor to enforce our own abilities to equal or exceed him, is called EMULATION: but joined with endeavor to supplant, or hinder a competitor, ENVY.

When in the mind of man, appetites, and aversions, hopes, and fears, concerning one and the same thing, arise alternatively; and divers good and evil consequences of the doing, or omitting the thing propounded, come successively into our thoughts; so that sometimes we have an appetite to it; sometimes an aversion from it; sometimes hope to be able to do it; sometimes despair, or fear to attempt it; the whole sum of desires, aversions, hopes and fears continued till the thing be either done, or thought impossible, is that we call DELIBERATION.

Therefore of things past, there is no deliberation; because manifestly impossible to be changed: nor of things known to be impossible, or thought so; because men know, or think such deliberation vain. But of things impossible, which we think possible, we may deliberate; not knowing it is in vain. And it is called deliberation; because it is a putting an end to the liberty we had of doing, or omitting, according to our own appetite, or aversion.

This alternate succession of appetites, aversions, hopes and fears, is no less in other living creatures than in man: and therefore beasts also deliberate.

Early deliberation is then said to end, when that whereof they deliberate, is either done, or thought impossible; because till then we retain the liberty of doing, or omitting, according to our appetite, or aversion.

In deliberation, the last appetite, or aversion, immediately adhering to the action, or to the omission thereof, is that we call the WILL; the act (not the faculty) of willing. And beasts that have deliberation, must necessarily also have will. The definition of the will, given commonly by the Schools, that it is a rational appetite, is not good. For if it were, then could there be no voluntary act against reason. For a voluntary act is that, which proceeds from the will, and no other. But if instead of a rational appetite, we shall say an appetite resulting from a precedent deliberation, then the definition is the same that I have given here. Will therefore is the last appetite in deliberating. And though we say in common discourse, a man had a will once to do a thing, that nevertheless he forbore to do; yet that is properly but an inclination, which makes no action voluntary; because the action depends not of it, but of the last inclination, or appetite. For if the intervenient appetites, make any action voluntary; then by the same reason all intervenient aversions, should make the same action involuntary; and so one and the same action, should be both voluntary and involuntary.

By this it is manifest, that not only actions that have their beginning from covetousness, ambition, lust, or other appetites to the thing propounded; but also those that have their beginning from aversion, or fear of those consequences that follow the omission, are voluntary actions.

The forms of speech by which the passions are expressed, are partly the same, and partly different from those, by which we express our thoughts. And first, generally all passions may be expressed indicatively; as I love, I fear, I joy, I deliberate, I will, I command: but some of them have particular expressions by themselves, which nevertheless are not affirmations, unless it be when they serve to make other inferences, besides that of the passion they proceed from. Deliberation is expressed subjunctively; which is a speech proper to signify suppositions, with their consequences; as, if this be done, then this will follow; and differs not from the language of reasoning, save that reasoning is in general words; but deliberation for the most part is of particulars. The language of desire, and aversion, is imperative; as do this, forbear that; which when the party is obliged to do, or forbear, is command; otherwise prayer; or else counsel. The language of vain-glory, of indignation, pity and revengefulness, optative: but of the desire to know, there is a peculiar expression, called interrogative; as, what is it, when shall it, how is it done, and why so? other language of the passions I find none: for cursing, swearing, reviling, and the like, do not signify as speech; but as the actions of a tongue accustomed.

These forms of speech, I say, are expressions, or voluntary significations of our passions: but certain signs they be not; because they may be used arbitrarily, whether they that use them, have such passions or not. The best signs of passions present, are either in the countenance, motions of the body, actions, and ends, or aims, which we otherwise know the man to have.

And because in deliberation, the appetites, and aversions, are raised by foresight of the good and evil consequences, and sequels of the action whereof we deliberate; the good or evil effect thereof depends on the foresight of a long chain of consequences, of which very seldom any man is able to see to the end. But for so far as a man seeth, if the good in those consequences be greater than the evil, the whole chain is that which writers call apparent, or seeming good. And contrarily, when the evil exceeds the good, the whole is apparent, or seeming evil: so that he who hath by experience, or reason, the greatest and surest prospect of consequences, deliberates best himself; and is able when he will, to give the best counsel unto others.

Continual success in obtaining those things which a man from time to time desires, that is to say, continual prospering, is that men call FELICITY; I mean the felicity of this life. For there is no such thing as perpetual tranquillity of mind, while we live here; because life itself is but motion, and can never be without desire, nor without fear, no more than without sense. What kind of felicity God hath ordained to them that devoutly honour Him, a man shall no sooner know, than enjoy; being joys, that now are as incomprehensible, as the word of schoolmen beatifical vision is unintelligible.

The form of speech whereby men signify their opinion of the goodness of any thing, is PRAISE.

That whereby they signify the power and greatness of any thing, is MAGNIFYING. And that whereby they signify the opinion they have of a man's felicity, is by the Greeks called for which we have no name in our tongue. And thus much is sufficient for the present purpose, to have been said of the PASSIONS.

Chapter 10. Of Power, Worth, Dignity, Honour, and Worthiness

The power of a man (to take it universally) is his present means, to obtain some future apparent good; and is either original or instrumental.

Natural power, is the eminence of the faculties of body, or mind: as extraordinary strength, form, prudence, arts, eloquence, liberality, nobility. Instrumental are those powers, which acquired by these, or by fortune, are means and instruments to acquire more: as riches, reputation, friends, and the secret working of God, which men call good luck. For the nature of power, is in this point, like to fame, increasing as it proceeds; or like the motion of heavy bodies, which the further they go, make still the more haste.

The greatest of human powers, is that which is compounded of the powers of most men, united by consent, in one person, natural, or civil, that has the use of all their powers depending on his will; such as is the power of a common-wealth: or depending on the will of each particular; such as is the power of a faction or of divers factions leagued. Therefore to have servants, is power; to have friends, is power: for they are strengths united.

Also riches joined with liberality, is power; because it procureth friends, and servants: without liberality, not so; because in this case they defend not; but expose men to envy, as a prey.

Reputation of power, is power; because it draweth with it the adherence of those that need protection.

So is reputation of love of man's country (called popularity) for the same reason.

Also, what quality soever maketh a man beloved, or feared of many; or the reputation of such quality, is power; because it is a means to have the assistance, and service of many.

Good success is power; because it maketh reputation of wisdom, or good fortune; which makes men either fear him, or rely on him.

Affability of men already in power, is increase of power; because it gaineth love.

Reputation of prudence in the conduct of peace or war, is power; because to prudent men, we commit the government of ourselves, more willingly than to others.

Nobility is power, not in all places, but only in those commonwealths, where it has privileges: for in such privileges consists their power.

Eloquence is power, because it is seeming prudence.

Form is power; because being a promise of good, it recommendeth men to the favour of women and strangers.

The sciences, are small power; because not eminent; and therefore, not acknowledged in any man; nor are at all, but in a few, and in them, but of a few things. For science is of that nature, as none can understand it to be, but such as in a good measure have attained it.

Arts of public use, as fortification, making of engines, and other instruments of war; because they confer to defence, and victory, are power: and though the true mother of them, be science, namely the mathematics; yet, because they are brought into the light, by the hand of the artificer, they be esteemed (the midwife passing with the vulgar for the mother) as his issue.

The value, or WORTH of a man, is as of all other things, his price; that is to say, so much as would be given for the use of his power: and therefore is not absolute; but a thing dependant on the need and judgment of another. An able conductor of soldiers, is of great price in time of war present, or imminent; but in peace not so. A learned and uncorrupt judge, is much worth in time of peace; but not so much in war. And as in other things, so in men, not the seller, but the buyer determines the price. For let a man (as most men do) rate themselves at the highest value they can; yet their true value is no more than it is esteemed by others.

The manifestation of the value we set on one another, is that which is commonly called honoring, and dishonoring. To value a man at a high rate, is to honour him; at a low rate, is to dishonor him. But high, and low, in this case, is to be understood by comparison to the rate that each man setteth on himself.

The public worth of a man, which is the value set on him by the commonwealth, is that which men commonly call DIGNITY. And this value of him by the commonwealth, is understood, by offices of command, judicature, public employment; or by names and titles, introduced for distinction of such value.

To pray to another, for aid of any kind, is to HONOUR; because a sign we have an opinion he has power to help; and the more difficult the aid is, the more is the honour.

To obey, is to honour, because no man obeys them, whom they think have no power to help, or hurt them. And consequently to disobey, is to dishonor.

To give great gifts to a man, is to honour him; because it is buying of protection, and acknowledging of power. To give little gifts, is to dishonor; because it is but alms, and signifies an opinion of the need of small helps.

Chapter 11. Of the Difference of Manners

By manners I mean not decency of behavior; as how one man should salute another, or how a man should wash his mouth, or pick his teeth before company, and such other points of the small morals; but those qualities of mankind, that concern their living together in peace, and unity. To which end we are to consider, that the felicity of this life, consists not in the repose of a mind satisfied. For there is no such (utmost aim) nor summum bonum (greatest good) as is spoken of in the books of the old moral philosophers. Nor can a man any more live, whose desires are at an end, than he, whose senses and imaginations are at a stand. Felicity is a continual progress of the desire, from one object to another; the attaining of the former, being still but the way to the latter. The cause whereof is, that the object of man's desire, is not to enjoy once only, and for one instant of time; but to assure for every, the way of his future desire. And therefore the voluntary actions, and inclinations of all men, tend, not only to the procuring, but also to the assuring of a contented life; and differ only in the way: which arises partly from the diversity of passions, in divers men; and partly from the difference of the knowledge, or opinion each one has of the causes, which produce the effect desired.

So that in the first place, I put for a general inclination of all mankind, a perpetual and restless desire of power after power, that ceases only in death. And the cause of this, is not always that a man hopes for a more intensive delight, than he has already attained to; or that he cannot be content with a moderate power: but because he cannot assure the power and means to live well, which he hath present, without the acquisition of more. And from hence it is, that kings, whose power is greatest, turn their endeavors to the assuring it at home by laws, or abroad by wars: and when that is done, there succeeds a new desire; in some, of fame from new conquest; in others, ease and sensual pleasure; in others, of admiration, or being flattered for excellence in some art, or other ability of the mind.

Competition of riches, honour, command, or other power, inclines to contention, enmity, and war: because the way of one competitor, to the attaining of his desire, is to kill, subdue, supplant, or repel the other. Particularly, competition of praise, inclines to a reverence of antiquity. For men contend with the living, not with the dead; to these ascribing more than due, that they may obscure the glory of the other.

Desire of ease, and sensual delight, disposes men to obey a common power: because by such desires, a man doth abandon the protection might be hoped for from his own industry, and labour. Fear of death, and wounds, disposes to the same; and for the same reason. On the contrary, needy men, and hardy, not contented with their present condition; as also, all men that are ambitious of military command, are inclined to continue the causes of war; and to stir up trouble and sedition: for there is no honour military but by war; nor any such hope to mend an ill game, as by causing a new shuffle.

Desire of knowledge, and arts of peace, inclines men to obey a common power: For such desire, contains a desire of leisure; and consequently protection from some other power than their own.

Desire of praise, disposes to laudable actions, such as please them whose judgment they value; for of those men whom we contemn [despise], we contemn also the praises. Desire of fame after death does the same. And though after death, there be no sense of the praise given us on earth, as being joys, that are either swallowed up in the unspeakable joys of Heaven, or extinguished in the extreme torments of hell: yet is not such fame vain; because men have a present delight therein, from the foresight of it, and of the benefit that may redound thereby to their posterity: which though they now see not, yet they imagine; and any thing that is pleasure to the sense, the same also is pleasure in the imagination.

To have received from one, to whom we think ourselves equal, greater benefits than there is hope to requite, disposes to counterfeit love; but really secret hatred; and puts a man into the estate of a desperate debtor, that in declining the sight of his creditor, tacitly wishes him there, where he might never see him more. For benefits oblige, and obligation is thraldom; and unrequitable obligation, perpetual thraldom; which is to one's equal, hateful. But to have received benefits from one, whom we acknowledge for superior, inclines to love; because the obligation is no new depression: and cheerful acceptation (which men call gratitude) is such an honour done to the obliger, as is taken generally for retribution. Also to receive benefits, though from an equal, or inferior, as long as there is hope of requital, disposes to love: for in the intention of the receiver, the obligation is of aid, and service mutual; from whence proceeds an emulation of who shall exceed in benefiting; the most noble and profitable contention possible; wherein the victor is placed with his victory, and the other revenged by confessing it.

To have done more hurt to a man, than he can, or is willing to expiate, inclines the doer to hate the sufferer. For he must expect revenge, or forgiveness; both which are hateful.

Fear of oppression, disposes a man to anticipate, or to seek aid by society: for there is no other way by which a man can secure his life and liberty.

Men that distrust their own subtlety, are in tumult and sedition, better disposed for victory, than they that suppose themselves wise, or crafty. For these love to consult, the other (fearing to be circumvented) to strike first. And in sedition, men being always in the precincts of battle, to hold together, and use all advantages of force, is a better stratagem, than any that can proceed from subtlety of wit.

Vain-glorious men, such as without being conscious to themselves of great sufficiency, delight in supposing themselves gallant men, are inclined only to ostentation; but not to attempt: because when danger or difficulty appears, they look for nothing but to have their insufficiency discovered.

Vain-glorious men, such as estimate their sufficiency by the flattery of other men, or the fortune of some precedent action, without assured ground of hope from the true knowledge of themselves, are inclined to rash engaging; and in the approach of danger, or difficulty, to retire if they can: because not seeing the way of safety, they will rather hazard their honour, which may be salved with an excuse; than their lives, for which no salve is sufficient.

Men that have a strong opinion of their own wisdom in matter of government, are disposed to ambition. Because without public employment in council or magistracy, the honour of their wisdom is lost. And therefore eloquent speakers are inclined to ambition; for eloquence seems wisdom, both to themselves and others.

Pusillanimity disposes men to irresolution, and consequently to lose the occasions, and fittest opportunities of action. For after men have been in deliberation till the time of action approach, if it be not then manifest what is best to be done, it is a sign, the difference of motives, the one way and the other, are not great: therefore not to resolve then, is to lose the occasion by weighing of trifles; which is pusillanimity.

Frugality (though in poor men a virtue) maketh a man unapt to achieve such actions, as require the strength of many men at once: for it weakeneth their endeavor, which is to be nourished and kept in vigor by reward.

Eloquence, with flattery, disposes men to confide in them that have it; because the former is seeming wisdom, the latter seeming kindness. Add to them military reputation, and it disposes men to adhere, and subject themselves to those men that have them. The two former, having given them caution against danger from him; the latter gives them caution against danger from others.

Want of science, that is, ignorance of causes, disposes, or rather constrains a man to rely on the advice, and authority of others. For all men whom the truth concerns, if they rely not on their own, must rely on the opinion of some other, whom they think wiser than themselves, and see not why he should deceive them.

Chapter 12. Of Religion

Seeing there are no signs, nor fruit of religion, but in many only; there is no cause to doubt, but that the seed of religion, is also only in man; and consists in some peculiar quality, or at least in some eminent degree thereof, not to be found in other living creatures.

And first, it is peculiar to the nature of man, to be inquisitive into the causes of the events they see, some more, some less; but all men so much, as to be curious in the search of the causes of their own good and evil fortune.

Secondly, upon the sight of any thing that hath a beginning, to think also it had a cause, which determined the same to begin, then when it did, rather than sooner or later.

Thirdly, whereas there is no other felicity of beasts, but the enjoying of their quotidian food, ease, and lusts; as having little or no foresight of the time to come, for want of observation, and memory of the order, consequence, and dependence of the things they see; man observes how one event hath been produced by another; and remembers in them antecedence and consequence; and when he cannot assure himself of the true causes of things (for the causes of good and evil fortune for the most part are invisible), he supposes causes of them, either such as his own fancy suggests; or trusts to the authority of other men, such as he thinks to be his friends, and wiser than himself.

The two first, make anxiety. For being assured that there be causes of all things that have arrived hitherto, or shall arrive hereafter; it is impossible for a man, who continually endeavors to secure himself against the evil he fears, and procure the good he desires, not to be in a perpetual solicitude of the time to come; so that every man, especially those that are over provident, are in an estate like to that of Prometheus. For as Prometheus (which interpreted, is, the prudent man) was bound to the hill Caucasus, a place of large prospect, where, an eagle feeding on his liver, devoured in the day, as much as was repaired in the night: so that man, which looks too far before him, in the care of future time, has his heart all the day long, gnawed on by fear of death, poverty, or other calamity; and has no repose, nor pause of his anxiety, but in sleep.

This perpetual fear, always accompanying mankind in the ignorance of causes, as it were in the dark, must needs have for object something. And therefore when there is nothing to be seen, there is nothing to accuse, either of their good, or evil fortune, but some power, or agent invisible: in which sense perhaps it was, that some of the old poets said, that the gods were at first created by human fear: which spoken of the gods (that is to say, of the many gods of the Gentiles) is very true. But the acknowledging of one God, eternal, infinite, and omnipotent, may more easily be derived, from the desire men have to know the causes of natural bodies, and their several virtues, and operations; than from the fear of what was to befall them in time to come. For he that from any effect he seeth come to pass, should reason to the next and immediate cause thereof, and from thence to the cause of that cause, and plunge himself profoundly in the pursuit of causes; shall at last come to this, that there must be (as even the heathen philosophers confessed) one first mover; that is, a first, and an eternal cause of all things; which is that which men mean by the name of God: and all this without thought of their fortune; the solicitude whereof, both inclines to fear, and hinders them from the search of the causes of other things; and thereby gives occasion of feigning of as many gods, as there be men that feign them.

And for the matter, or substance of the invisible agents, so fancied; they could not by natural cogitation, fall upon any other conceit, but that it was the same with that of the soul of man; and that the soul of man, was of the same substance, with that which appears in a dream, to one that sleeps; or in a looking-glass, to one that is awake; which, men not knowing that such apparitions are nothing else but creatures of fancy, think to be real, and external substances; and therefore call them ghosts; as the Latins called them *imagines*, and *umbrae*, and thought them spirits, that is, thin aerial bodies; and this invisible agents, which they feared, to be like them; save that they appear, and vanish when they please. But the opinion that such spirits were incorporeal, or immaterial, could never enter into the mind of any man by nature; because, though men may put together words of contradictory signification, as spirit, and incorporeal; yet they can never have the imagination of any thing answering to them: and therefore, men that by their own meditation, arrive to the acknowledgment of one infinite, omnipotent, and eternal God, choose rather to confess he is incomprehensible, and above their understanding, than to define his nature by spirit incorporeal, and then confess their definition to be unintelligible: or if they give him such a title, it is not dogmatically, with intention to make the divine nature understood; but piously, to honour him with attributes, of significations, as remote as they can from the grossness of bodies visible.

Then, for the way by which they think these invisible agents wrought their effects; that is to say, what immediate causes they used, in bringing to pass, men that know not what it is that we call causing (that is, almost all men) have no other rule to guess by, but by observing, and remembering what they have seen to precede the like effect at some other time, or times before, without seeing between the antecedent and subsequent event, any dependence or connexion at all: and therefore from the like things past, they expect the like things to come; and hope for good or evil luck, superstitiously, from things that have no part at all in the causing of it: as the Athenians did for their war at Lepanto, demand another Phormio; the Pompeian faction for their war in Africa, another Scipio; and others have done in divers other occasions since. In like manner they attribute their fortune to a bystander, to a lucky or unlucky place, to words spoken, especially if the name of God be amongst them; as charming and conjuring (the liturgy of witches); insomuch as to believe, they have power to turn a stone into bread, bread into a man, or any thing into any thing.

Thirdly, for the worship which naturally men exhibit to powers invisible, it can be no other, but such expressions of their reverence, as they would use towards men; gifts, petitions, thanks, submission of body, considerate addresses, sober behavior, premeditated words, swearing (that is, assuring one another of their promises), by invoking them. Beyond that reason suggesteth nothing; but leaves them either to rest there; or for further ceremonies, to rely on those they believe to be wiser than themselves.

Lastly, concerning how these invisible powers declare to men the things which shall hereafter come to pass, especially concerning their good or evil fortune in general, or good or ill success in any particular undertaking, men are naturally at a stand; save that using to conjecture of the time to come, by the time past, they are very apt, not only to take casual things, after one or two encounters, for prognostics of the like encounter ever after, but also to believe the like prognostics from other men, of whom they have once conceived a good opinion.

And in these four things, opinion of ghosts, ignorance of second causes, devotion towards what men fear, and taking of things casual for prognostics, consists the natural seed of religion, which by reason of the different fancies, judgments, and passions of several men, hath grown up into ceremonies so different, that those which are used by one man, are for the most part ridiculous to another.

For these seeds have received culture from two sorts of men. One sort have been they, that have nourished, and ordered them, according to their own invention. The other have done it, by God's commandment, and direction: but both sorts have done it, with a purpose to make those men that relied on them, the more apt to obedience, laws, peace, charity, and civil society. So that the religion of the former sort, is a part of human politics; and teaches part of the duty which earthly kings require of their subjects. And the religion of the latter sort is divine politics; and contains precepts to those that have yielded themselves subjects in the kingdom of God. Of the former sort, were all the founders of commonwealths, and the lawgivers of the Gentiles: of the latter sort, were Abraham, Moses, and our blessed Savior; by whom have been derived unto us the laws of the kingdom of God.

And for that part of religion, which consists in opinions concerning the nature of powers invisible, there is almost nothing that has a name, that has not been esteemed amongst the Gentiles, in one place or another, a god, or devil; or by their poets feigned to be inanimated, inhabited, or possessed by some spirit or other.

The unformed matter of the world, was a god, by the name of Chaos.

The heaven, the ocean, the planets, the fire, the earth, the winds, were so many gods.

Men, women, a bird, a crocodile, a calf, a dog, a snake, an onion, a leek, deified. Besides that, they filled almost all places, with spirits called demons: the plains, with Pan, and Panises, or Satyrs; the woods, with Fawns, and Nymphs: the sea, with Tritons, and other Nymphs; every river, and fountain, with a ghost of his name, and with Nymphs; every house with its Lares or familiars; every man with his Genius; hell with ghosts, and spiritual officers, as Charon, Cerberus, and the Furies; and in the night time, all places with larvae, lemures, ghosts of men deceased, and a whole kingdom of fairies and bugbears. They have also ascribed divinity, and built temples to mere accidents, and qualities; such as are time, night, day, peace, concord, love, contention, virtue, honour, health, rust, fever, and the like; which when they prayed for, or against, they prayed to, as if there were ghosts of those names hanging over their heads, and letting fall, or withholding that good, or evil, for, or against which they prayed. They invoked also their own wit, by the name of Muses; their own ignorance, by the name of Fortune; their own lust, by the name of Cupid; their own rage, by the name Furies; their own privy members, by the name of Priapus, and attributed their pollutions, to Incubi, and Succubae: insomuch as there was nothing, which a poet could introduce as a person in his poem, which they did not make either a god, or a devil. . . .

Chapter 13. Of the Natural Condition of Mankind as Concerning Their Felicity, and Misery

Nature hath made men so equal, in the faculties of body, and mind; as that though there be found one man sometimes manifestly stronger in body, or of quicker mind than another; yet when all is reckoned together, the difference between man, and man, is not so considerable, as that one man can thereupon claim to himself any benefit, to which another may not pretend, as well as he. For as to the strength of body, the weakest has strength enough to kill the strongest, either by secret machination, or by confederacy with others, that are in the same danger with himself.

And as to the faculties of the mind (setting aside the arts grounded upon words, and especially that skill of proceeding upon general, and infallible rules, called science; which very few have, and but in few things; as being not a native faculty, born with us; nor attained, [as prudence], while we look after somewhat else), I find yet a greater equality amongst men, than that of strength. For prudence, is but experience; which equal time, equally bestows on all men, in those things they equally apply themselves unto. That which may perhaps make such equality incredible, is but a vain conceit of one's own wisdom, which almost all men think they have in a greater degree, than the vulgar; that is, than all men but themselves, and a few others, whom by fame, or for concurring with themselves, they approve. For such is the nature of men, that howsoever they may acknowledge many others to be more witty, or more eloquent, or more learned; yet they will hardly believe there be many so wise as themselves: For they see their own wit at hand, and other men's at a distance. But this proves rather that men are in that point equal, than unequal. For there is not ordinarily a greater sign of the equal distribution of any thing, than that every man is contented with his share.

From this equality of ability, arises equality of hope in the attaining of our ends. And therefore if any two men desire the same thing, which nevertheless they cannot both enjoy, they become enemies; and in the way to their end (which is principally their own conservation, and sometimes their delectation only), endeavor to destroy, or subdue one another. And from hence it comes to pass, that where an invader hath no more to fear, than another man's single power; if one plant, sow, build, or possess a convenient seat, others may probably be expected to come prepared with forces united, to dispossess, and deprive him, not only of the fruit of his labour, but also of his life, or liberty. And the invader again is in the like danger of another.

And from this diffidence of one another, there is no way for any man to secure himself, so reasonable, as anticipation; that is, by force, or wiles, to master the persons of all men he can, so long, till he see no other power great enough to endanger him: and this is no more than his own conservation requires, and is generally allowed. Also because there be some, that taking pleasure in contemplating their own power in the acts of conquest, which they pursue farther than their security requires; if others, that otherwise would be glad to be at ease within modest bounds, should not by invasion increase their power, they would not be able, long time, by standing only on their defence, to subsist. And by consequence, such augmentation of dominion over men, being necessary to a man's conservation, it ought to be allowed him.

Again, men have no pleasure (but on the contrary a great deal of grief) in keeping company, where there is no power able to over-awe them all. For every man looks that his companion should value him, at the same rate he sets upon himself: and upon all signs of contempt, or undervaluing, naturally endeavors, as far as he dares (which amongst them that have no common power to keep them in quiet, is far enough to make them destroy each other), to extort a greater value from his condemners, by damage; and from others, by the example.

So that in the nature of man, we find three principal causes of quarrel. First, competition; secondly, diffidence; thirdly, glory.

The first, maketh men invade for gain; the second, for safety; and the third, for reputation. The first use violence, to make themselves masters of other men's persons, wives, children, and cattle; the second to defend them; the third, for trifles, as a word, a smile, a different opinion, and any other sign of undervalue, either direct in their persons, or by reflection in their kindred, their friends, their nation, their profession, or their name.

Hereby it is manifest, that during the time men live without a common power to keep them all in awe, they are in that condition which is called war; and such a war, as is of every man, against every man. For WAR, consists not in battle only, or the act of fighting; but in a tract of time, wherein the will to contend by battle is sufficiently known: and therefore the notion of time, is to be considered in the nature of war; as it is in the nature of weather. For as the nature of foul weather, lies not in a shower or two of rain; but in an inclination thereto of many days together: so the nature of war, consists not in actual fighting; but in the known disposition thereto, during all the time there is no assurance to the contrary. All other time is PEACE.

Whatsoever therefore is consequent to a time of war, where every man is enemy to every man; the same is consequent to the time; wherein men live without other security, than what their own strength, and their own invention shall furnish them withal. In such condition, there is no place for industry; because the fruit thereof is uncertain: and consequently no culture of the earth; no navigation, nor use of the commodities that may be imported by sea; no commodious building; no instruments of moving, and removing such things as require much force; no knowledge of the face of the earth; no account of time; no arts; no letters; no society; and which is worst of all, continual fear, and danger of violent death; and the life of man, solitary, poor, nasty, brutish, and short.

It may seem strange to some man, that has not well weighed these things; that nature should thus dissociate, and render men apt to invade, and destroy one another: and he may therefore, not trusting to this inference, made from the passions, desire perhaps to have the same confirmed by experience. Let him therefore consider with himself, when taking a journey, he arms himself, and seeks to go well accompanied; when going to sleep, he locks his doors; when even in his house he locks his chests; and this when he knows there be laws, and public officers, armed, to revenge all injuries shall be done him; what opinion he has of his fellow subjects, when he rides armed; of his fellow citizens, when he locks his doors; and of his children, and servants, when he locks his chests. Does he not there as much accuse mankind by his actions, as I do by my words? But neither of us accuse man's nature in it. The desires, and other passions of man, are in themselves no sin. No more are the actions, that proceed from those passions, till they know a law that forbids them: which till laws be made they cannot know: nor can any law be made, till they have agreed upon the person that shall make it.

It may peradventure be thought, there was never such a time, nor condition of war as this; and I believe it was never generally so, over all the world: but there are many places, where they live so now. For the savage people in many places of America, except the government of small families, the concord whereof depends on natural lust, have no government at all; and live at this day in that brutish manner, as I said before. Howsoever, it may be perceived what manner of life there would be, where there were no common power to fear; by the manner of life, which men that have formerly lived under a peaceful government, use to degenerate into, in a civil war.

But though there had never been any time, wherein particular men were in a condition of war one against another; yet in all times, kings, and persons of sovereign authority, because of their independency, are in continual jealousies, and in the state and posture of gladiators; having their weapons pointing, and their eyes fixed on one another; that is, their forts, garrisons, and guns upon the frontiers of their kingdoms; and continual spies upon their neighbours; which is a posture war. But because they uphold thereby, the industry of their subjects; there does not follow from it, that misery, which accompanies the liberty of particular men.

To this war of every man against every man, this also is consequent; that nothing can be unjust. The notions of right and wrong, justice and injustice have there no place. Where there is no common power, there is no law: where no law no injustice. Force, and fraud, are in war the two cardinal virtues. Justice, and injustice are none of the faculties neither of the body, nor mind. If they were, they might be in a man that were alone in the world, as well as his senses, and passions. They are qualities, that relate to men in society, not in solitude. It is consequent also to the same condition, that there be no propriety, no dominion, no mine and thine distinct; but only that to be every man's, that he can get; and for so long, as he can keep it. And thus much for the ill condition, which man by mere nature is actually placed in; though with a possibility to come out of it, consisting partly in the passions, partly in his reason.

The passions that incline men to peace, are fear of death; desire of such things as are necessary to commodious living; and a hope by their industry to obtain them. And reason suggests convenient articles of peace, upon which men may be drawn to agreement. These articles, are they, which otherwise are called the Laws of Nature: whereof I shall speak more particularly, in the two following chapters.

Chapter 14. Of the First and Second Natural Laws, and of Contracts

The RIGHT OF NATURE, which writers commonly call *jus naturale*, is the liberty each man hath, to use his own power, as he will himself, for the preservation of his own nature; that is to say, of his own life; and consequently, of doing any thing, which in his own judgment, and reason, he shall conceive to be the aptest means thereunto.

By LIBERTY, is understood, according to the proper signification of the word, the absence of external impediments: which impediments, may oft take away part of a man's power to do what he would; but cannot hinder him from using the power left him, according as his judgment,and reason shall dictate to him.

A LAW OF NATURE (*lex naturalis*), is a precept, or general rule, found out by reason, by which a man is forbidden to do that, which is destructive of his life, or taketh away the means of preserving the same; and to omit that, by which he thinks it may be best preserved. For though they that speak of this subject, use to confound jus, and lex, right and law; yet they ought to be distinguished; because RIGHT, consists in liberty to do, or to forbear; whereas LAW, determines, and binds to one of them: so that law, and right, differ as much, as obligation, and liberty; which in one and the same matter are inconsistent.

And because the condition of man (as hath been declared in the precedent chapter) is a condition of war of every one against every one; in which case every one is governed by his own reason; and there is nothing he can make use of that may not be a help unto him, in preserving his life against his enemies; it followeth, that in such a condition, every man has a right to every thing; even to one another's body. And therefore, as long as this natural right of every man to every thing endures, there can be no security to any man (how strong or wise soever he be) of living out the time, which nature ordinarily allows men to live. And consequently it is a precept, or general rule of reason, that every man, ought to endeavor peace, as far as he has hope of obtaining it; and when he cannot obtain it, that he may seek, and use, all helps, and advantages of war. The first branch of which rule, containeth the first, and fundamental law of nature; which is, to seek peace, and follow it. The second, the sum of the right of nature; which is, by all means we can, to defend ourselves.

From this fundamental law of nature, by which men are commanded to endeavor peace, is derived this second law; that a man be willing, when others are so too, as far-forth, as for peace, and defence of himself he shall think it necessary, to lay down this right to all things; and be contented with so much liberty against other men, as he would allow other men against himself. For as long as every man holds this right, of doing any thing he likes; so long are all men in the condition of war. But if other men will not lay down their right, as well as he; then there is no reason for any one, to divest himself of his: for that were to expose himself to prey (which no man is bound to) rather than to dispose himself to peace. This is that law of the Gospel; whatsoever you require that others should do to you, that do ye to them. And that law of all men, [what you would not have done to you, do not do to others].

To lay down a man's right to any thing, is to divest himself of the liberty, of hindering another of the benefit of his own right to the same. For he that renounces or passeth away his right, giveth not to any other man a right which he had not before; because there is nothing to which every man had not right by nature: but only stands out of his way, that he may enjoy his own original right, without hindrance from him; not without hindrance from another. So that the effect which redounds to one man, by another man's defect of right, is but so much diminution of impediments to the use of his own right original.

Right is laid aside, either by simply renouncing it; or by transferring it to another. By simply RENOUNCING; when he cares not to whom the benefit thereof redounds. By TRANSFERRING; when he intends the benefit thereof to some certain person, or persons. And when a man hath in either manner abandoned, or granted away his right; then is he said to be OBLIGED, or BOUND, not to hinder those, to whom such right is granted, or abandoned, from the benefit of it: and that he ought, and it is his DUTY, not to make void that voluntary act of his own: and that such hindrance is INJUSTICE, and INJURY, as being sine jure; the right being before renounced, or transferred. So that injury, or injustice, in the controversies of the world, is somewhat like to that, which in the disputations of scholars is called absurdity. For as it is there called an absurdity, to contradict what one maintained in the beginning: so in the world, it is called injustice, and injury, voluntarily to undo that, which from the beginning he had voluntarily done. The way by which a man either simply renounces, or transfers his right, is a declaration, or signification, by some voluntary and sufficient sign, or signs, that he doth so renounce, or transfer; or hath so renounced, or transferred the same, to him that accepts it. And these signs are either words only, or actions only; (as it happens most often) both words, and actions. And the same are the BONDS, by which men are bound, and obliged: bonds, that have their strength, not from their own nature (for nothing is more easily broken than a man's word), but from fear of some evil consequence upon the rupture.

Whensoever a man transfers his right, or renounces it; it is either in consideration of some right reciprocally transferred to himself; or for some other good he hopes for thereby. For it is a voluntary act: and of the voluntary acts of every man, the object is some good to himself. And therefore there be some rights, which no man can be understood by any words, or other signs, to have abandoned, or transferred. As first a man cannot lay down the right of resisting them, that assault him by force, to take away his life; because he cannot be understood to aim thereby, at any good to himself. The same may be said of wounds, and chains, and imprisonment; both because there is no benefit consequent to such patience; as there is to the patience of suffering another to be wounded, or imprisoned: as also because a man cannot tell, when he sees men proceed against him by violence, whether they intend his death or not. And lastly the motive, and end for which this renouncing, and transferring of right is introduced, is nothing else but the security of a man's person, in his life, and in the means of so preserving life, as not to be weary of it. And therefore if a man by words, or other signs, seem to despoil himself of the end, for which those signs were intended; he is not to be understood as if he meant it, or that it was his will; but that he was ignorant of how such words and actions were to be interpreted.

The mutual transferring of right, is that which men call CONTRACT.

There is difference between transferring of right to the thing; and transferring, or tradition, that is, delivery of the thing it self. For the thing may be delivered together with the translation of the right; as in buying and selling with ready money; or exchange of goods, or lands: and it may be delivered some time after.

Again, one of the contractors, may deliver the thing contracted for on his part, and leave the other to perform his part at some determinate time after, and in the mean time be trusted; and then the contract on his part, is called PACT, or COVENANT: or both parts may contract now, to perform hereafter: in which cases, he that is to perform in time to come, being trusted, his performance is called keeping of promise, or faith; and the failing of performance (if it be voluntary) violation of faith.

When the transferring of right, is not mutual; but one of the parties transfers, in hope to gain thereby friendship, or service from another, or from his friends; or in hope to gain the reputation of charity, or magnanimity; or to deliver his mind from the pain of compassion; or in hope or reward in heaven; this is not contract, but GIFT, FREE-GIFT, GRACE: which words signify one and the same thing.

Signs of contract, are either express, or by inference. Express, are words spoken with understanding of what they signify: and such words are either of the time present, or past; as, I give, I grant, I have given, I have granted, I will that this be yours: or of the future; as, I will give, I will grant: which words of the future are called PROMISE.

Signs by inference, are sometimes the consequence of words; sometimes the consequence of silence; sometimes the consequences of actions; sometimes the consequence of forbearing an action: and generally a sign by inference, of any contract, is whatsoever sufficiently argues the will of the contractor.

Words alone, if they be of the time to come, and contain a bare promise, are an insufficient sign of a free-gift and therefore not obligatory. For if they be of the time to come, as, tomorrow I will give, they are a sign I have not given yet, and consequently that my right is not transferred, but remains till I transfer it by some other act. But if the words be of the time present, or past, as, I have given, or do give to be delivered tomorrow, then is my tomorrow's right given away to day; and that by the virtue of the words, though there were no other argument of my will. And there is a great difference in the signification of these words, volo hoc tuum esse cras, and cras dabo; that is, between I will that this be thine tomorrow, and, I will give it thee tomorrow: for the word I will, in the former manner of speech, signifies an act of the will present; but in the latter, it signifies a promise of an act of the will to come: and therefore the former words, being of the present, transfer a future right; the latter, that be of the future, transfer nothing. But if there be other signs of the will to transfer a right, besides words; then, though the gift be free, yet may the right be understood to pass by words of the future: as if a man propound a prize to him that comes first to the end of a race, the gift is free: and though the words be of the future, yet the right passeth: for if he would not have his words so be understood, he should not have let them run.

In contracts, the right passeth, not only where the words are of the time present, or past, but also where they are of the future: because all contract is mutual translation, or change of right; and therefore he that promises only, because he hath already received the benefit for which he promises, is to be understood as if he intended the right should pass: for unless he had been content to have his words so understood, the other would not have performed his part first. And for that cause, in buying, and selling, and other acts of contract, a promise is equivalent to a covenant; and therefore obligatory.

He that performs first in the case of a contract, is said to MERIT that which he is to receive by the performance of the other; and he hath it as due. Also when a prize is propounded to many, which is to be given to him only that wins; or money is thrown amongst many, to be enjoyed by them that catch it; though this be a free gift; yet so to win, or so to catch, is to merit, and to have it as DUE. For the right is transferred in the propounding of the prize, and in throwing down the money; though it be not determined to whom, but by the event of the contention. But there is between these two sorts of merit, this difference, that in contract, I merit by virtue of my own power, and the contractor's need; but in this case of free gift, I am enabled to merit only by the benignity of the giver: in contract, I merit at the contractor's hand that he should depart with his right; in this case of gift, I merit not that the giver should part with his right; but that when he has parted with it, it should be mine, rather than another's. . . .

If a covenant be made, wherein neither of the parties perform presently, but trust one another; in the condition of mere nature (which is a condition of war of every man against every man), upon an reasonable suspicion, it is void: but if there be a common power set over them both, with right and force sufficient to compel performance, it is not void. For he that performs first, has no assurance the other will perform after; because the bonds of words are too weak to bridle men's ambition, avarice, anger, and other passions, without the fear of some coercive power; which in the condition of mere nature, where all men are equal, and judges of the justness of their own fears, cannot possibly be supposed. And therefore he which performs first, does but betray himself to his enemy; contrary to the right (he can never abandon) of defending his life, and means of living.

But in a civil estate, where there is a power set up to constrain those that would otherwise violate their faith, that fear is no more reasonable; and for that cause, he which by the covenant is to perform first, is obliged so to do.

The cause of fear, which maketh such a covenant invalid, must be always something arising after the covenant made; as some new fact, or other sign of the will not to perform: else it cannot make the covenant void. For that which could not hinder a man from promising, ought not to be admitted as a hindrance of performing.

He that transfers any right, transfers the means of enjoying it, as far as lies in his power. As he that sells land, is understood to transfer the herbage, and whatsoever grows upon it; nor can he that sells a mill turn away the stream that drives it. And they that give to a man the right of government in sovereignty, are understood to give him the right of levying money to maintain soldiers; and of appointing magistrates for the administration of justice.

To make covenants with brute beasts, is impossible; because not understanding our speech, they understand not, nor accept of any translation of right; nor can translate any right to another: and without mutual acceptation, there is no covenant.

To make covenant with God, is impossible, but by mediation of such as God speaks to, either by revelation supernatural, or by his lieutenants that govern under him, and in his name: for otherwise we know not whether our covenants be accepted, or not. And therefore they that vow any thing contrary to any law of nature, vow in vain; as being a thing unjust to pay such vow. And if it be a thing commanded by the law of nature, it is not the vow, but the law that binds them.

The matter, or subject of a covenant, is always something that falls under deliberation (for to covenant, is an act of the will; that is to say an act, and the last act, of deliberation) and is therefore always understood to be something to come; and which is judged possible for him that covenants, to perform.

And therefore, to promise that which is known to be impossible, is no covenant. But if that prove impossible afterwards, which before was thought possible, the covenant is valid, and bind (though not to the thing it self), yet to the value; or, if that also be impossible, to the unfeigned endeavor of performing as much as is possible: for to more no man can be obliged.

Men are freed of their covenants two ways; by performing; or by being forgiven. For performance, is the natural end of obligation; and forgiveness, the restitution of liberty; as being a retransferring of that right, in which the obligation consisted.

Covenants entered into by fear, in the condition of mere nature, are obligatory. For example, if I covenant to pay a ransom, or service for my life, to an enemy; I am bound by it. For it is a contract, wherein one receives the benefit of life; the other is to receive money, or service for it; and consequently, where no other law (as in the condition, of mere nature) forbids the performance, the covenant is valid. Therefore prisoners of war, if trusted with the payment of their ransom, are obliged to pay it: and if a weaker prince, make a disadvantageous peace with a stronger, for fear; he is bound to keep it; unless (as hath been said before) there arises some new, and just cause of fear, to renew the war. And even in commonwealths, if I be forced to redeem myself from a thief by promising him money, I am bound to pay it, till the civil law discharge me. For whatsoever I may lawfully do without obligation, the same I may lawfully covenant to do through fear: and what I lawfully covenant, I cannot lawfully break.

A former covenant, makes void a later. For a man that hath passed away his right to one man today, hath it not to pass tomorrow to another: and therefore the later promise passeth no right, but is null.

A covenant not to defend myself from force, by force, is always void. For (as I have showed before) no man can transfer, or lay down his right to save himself from death, wounds, and imprisonment, (the avoiding whereof is the only end of laying down any right, and therefore the promise of not resisting force, in no covenant transfers any right; nor is obliging. For though a man may covenant thus, unless I do so, or so, kill me; he cannot covenant thus, unless I do so, or so, I will not resist you, when you come to kill me. For man by nature chooses the lesser evil, which is danger of death in resisting; rather than the greater, which is certain and present death in not resisting. And this is granted to be true by all men, in that they lead criminals to execution, and prison, with armed men, notwithstanding that such criminals have consented to the law, by which they are condemned.

A covenant to accuse one self, without assurance of pardon, is likewise invalid. For in the condition of nature, where every man is judge, there is no place for accusation: and in the civil state, the accusation is followed with punishment; which being force, a man is not obliged not to resist. The same is also true, of the accusation of those, by whose condemnation a man falls into misery; as of a father, wife, or benefactor. For the testimony of such an accuser, if it be not willingly given, is presumed to be corrupted by nature; and therefore not to be received: and where a man's testimony is not to be credited, he is not bound to give it. Also accusations upon torture, are not to be reputed as testimonies. For torture is to be used but as means of conjecture, and light, in the further examination, and search of truth: and what is in that case confessed, tends to the ease of him that is tortured, not to the informing of the torturers: and therefore ought not to have the credit of a sufficient testimony: for whether he deliver himself by true, or false accusation, he does it by the right of preserving his own life.

The force of words, being (as I have formerly noted) too weak to hold men to the performance of their covenants; there are in man's nature, but two imaginable helps to strengthen it. And those are either a fear of the consequence of breaking their word; or a glory, or pride in appearing not to need to break it. This latter is a generosity too rarely found to be presumed on, especially in the pursuers of wealth, command, or sensual pleasure; which are the greatest part of mankind. The passion to be reckoned upon, is fear; whereof there be two very general objects: one, the power of spirits invisible; the other, the power of those men they shall therein offend. Of these two, though the former be the greater power, yet the fear of the latter is commonly the greater fear. The fear of the former is in every man, his own religion: which hath place in the nature of man before civil society. The latter hath not so; at least not place enough, to keep men to their promises; because in the condition of mere nature, the inequality of power is not discerned, but by the event of battle. So that before the time of civil society, or in the interruption thereof by war, there is nothing can strengthen a covenant of peace agreed on, against the temptations of avarice, ambition, lust, or other strong desire, but the fear of that invisible power, which they every one worship as God; and fear as a revenger of their perfidy. All therefore that can be done between two men not subject to civil power, is to put one another to swear by the God he fears: which swearing, or OATH, is a form of speech, added to a promise; by which he that promises, signifies, that unless he perform, he renounces the mercy of his God, or calleth to him for vengeance on himself. Such was the heathen form, Let Jupiter kill me else, as I kill this beast. So is our form, I shall do thus, and thus, so help me God. And this, with the rites and ceremonies, which every one uses in his own religion, that the fear of breaking faith might be the greater.

By this it appears, that an oath taken according to any other form, or rite, than his, that swears, is in vain; and no oath: and that there is no swearing by any thing which the swearer thinks not God. For though men have sometimes used to swear by their kings, for fear, or flattery; yet they would have it thereby understood, they attributed to them divine honour. And that swearing unnecessarily by God, is but profaning of his name: and swearing by other things, as men do in common discourse, is not swearing, but an impious custom, gotten by too much vehemence of talking.

It appears also, that the oath adds nothing to the obligation. For a covenant, if lawful, binds in the sight of God, without the oath, as much as with it: if unlawful, binds not at all; though it be confirmed with an oath.

Chapter 15. Of Other Laws of Nature

From that law of nature, by which we are obliged to transfer to another, such rights, as being retained, hinder the peace of mankind, there followeth a third; which is this, that men perform their covenants made: without which, covenants are in vain, and but empty words; and the right of all men to all things remaining, we are still in the condition of war.

And in this law of nature, consists the fountain and original of JUSTICE. For where no covenant hath proceeded, there hath no right been transferred, and every man has right to every thing; and consequently, no action can be unjust. But when a covenant is made, then to break it is unjust: and the definition of INJUSTICE, is no other than the not performance of covenant. And whatsoever is not unjust, is just.

But because covenants of mutual trust, where there is a fear of not performance on either part (as hath been said in the former chapter), are invalid; though the original of justice be the making of covenants; yet injustice actually there can be none, till the cause of such fear be taken away; which while men are in the natural condition of war, cannot be done. Therefore before the names of just, and unjust can have place, there must be some coercive power, to compel men equally to the performance of their covenants, by the terror of some punishment, greater than the benefit they expect by the breach of their covenant; and to make good that propriety, which by mutual contract men acquire, in recompense of the universal right they abandon: and such power there is none before the erection of a commonwealth. And this is also to be gathered out of the ordinary definition of justice in the Schools: for they say, that justice is the constant will of giving to every man his own. And therefore where there is no own, that is, no propriety, there is no injustice; and where there is no coercive power erected, that is, where there is no commonwealth, there is no propriety; all men having right to all things: therefore where there is no commonwealth, there nothing is unjust. So that the nature of justice, consists in keeping of valid covenants: but the validity of covenants begins not but with the constitution of a civil power, sufficient to compel men to keep them: and then it is also that propriety begins.

The fool hath said in his heart, there is no such thing as justice; and sometimes also with his tongue; seriously alleging, that every man's conservation, and contentment, being committed to his own care, there could be no reason, why every man might not do what he thought conduced thereunto: and therefore also to make, or not make; keep, or not keep covenants, was not against reason, when it conduced to one's benefit. He does not therein deny, that there be covenants; and that they are sometimes broken, sometimes kept; and that such breach of them may be called injustice, and the observance of them justice: but he questions, whether injustice, taking away the fear of God (for the same fool hath said in his heart there is no God), may not sometimes stand with that reason, which dictates to every man his own good; and particularly then, when it conduces to such a benefit, as shall put a man in a condition, to neglect not only the dispraise, and revilings, but also the power of other men. The kingdom of God is gotten by violence: but what if it could be gotten by unjust violence? were it against reason so to get it, when it is impossible to receive hurt by it? and if it be not against reason, it is not against justice; or else justice is not to be approved for good. From such reasoning as this, successful wickedness hath obtained the name of virtue: and some that in all other things have disallowed the violation of faith; yet have allowed it, when it is for the getting of a kingdom. And the heathen that believed, that Saturn was deposed by his son Jupiter, believed nevertheless the same Jupiter to be the avenger of injustice: somewhat like a piece of law in Coke's *Commentaries on Littleton*;[1] where he says, if the right heir of the crown be attainted of treason; yet the crown shall descend to him, and eo instante the attender be void: from which instances a man will be very prone to infer; that when the heir apparent of a kingdom, shall kill him that is in possession, though his father; you man call it injustice, or by what other name you will; yet it can never be against reason, seeing all the voluntary actions of men tend to the benefit of themselves; and those actions are most reasonable, that conduce most to their ends. This specious reasoning is nevertheless false.

For the question is not of promises mutual, where there is no security of performance on either side; as when there is no civil power erected over the parties promising; for such promises are no covenants: but either where one of the parties has performed already; or where there is a power to make him perform; there is the question whether it be against reason, that is, against the benefit of the other to perform, or not. And I say it is not against reason. For the manifestation whereof, we are to consider; first, that when a man doth a thing, which notwithstanding any thing can be foreseen, and reckoned on, tends to his own destruction, howsoever some accident which he could not expect, arriving may turn it to his benefit; yet such events do not make it reasonably or wisely done. Secondly, that in a condition of war, wherein every man to every man, for want of a common power to keep them all in awe, is an enemy, there is no man can hope by his own strength, or wit, to defend himself from destruction, without the help of confederates; where every one expects the same defence by the confederation, that any one else does: and therefore he which declares he thinks it reason to deceive those that help him, can in reason expect no other means of safety, than what can be had from his own single power. He therefore that breaks his covenant, and consequently declares that he thinks he may with reason do so, cannot be received into any society, that unite themselves for peace and defence, but by the error of them that receive him; nor when he is received, be retained in it, without seeing the danger of their error; which errors a man cannot reasonably reckon upon as the means of his security: and therefore if he be left, or cast out of society, he perishes; and if he live in society, it is by the errors of other men, which he could not foresee, nor reckon upon; and consequently against the reason of his preservation; and so, as all men that contribute not to his destruction, forbear him only out of ignorance of what is good for themselves.

As for the instance of gaining the secure and perpetual felicity of heaven, by any way; it is frivolous: there being but one way imaginable; and that is not breaking, but keeping of covenant.

And for the other instance of attaining sovereignty by rebellion; it is manifest, that though the event follow, yet because it cannot reasonably be expected, but rather the contrary; and because by gaining it so, others are taught to gain the same in like manner, the attempt thereof is against reason. Justice therefore, that is to say, keeping of covenant, is a rule of reason, by which we are forbidden to do any thing destructive to our life; and consequently a law of nature.

There be some that proceed further; and will not have the law of nature, to be those rules which conduce to the preservation of man's life on earth; but to the attaining of an eternal felicity after death; to which they think the breach of covenant may conduce; and consequently be just and reasonable (such are they that think it a work of merit to kill, or depose, or rebel against, the sovereign power constituted over them by their own consent). But because there is no natural knowledge of man's estate after death; much less of the reward that is then to be given to breach of faith; but only a belief grounded upon other men's saying, that they know it supernaturally, or that they know those, that knew them, that knew others, that knew it supernaturally; breach of faith cannot be called a precept of reason, or nature.

Others, that allow for a law of nature, the keeping of faith, do nevertheless make exception of certain persons; as heretics, and such as use not to perform their covenant to others: and this also is against reason. For if any fault of a man, be sufficient to discharge our covenant made; the same ought in rea-

1. Sir Edward Coke (1552–1634) was the first Lord Chief Justice of England. His *Commentaries on Littleton*, refers to Sir Thomas de Littleton's (1407–1481) *Treatise on Tenures.*

son to have been sufficient to have hindered the making of it.

The names of just, and unjust, when they are attributed to men, signify one thing; and when they are attributed to actions, another. When they are attributed to men, they signify conformity, or inconformity of manners, to reason. But when they are attributed to actions, they signify the conformity, or inconformity to reason, not of manners, or manner of life, but of particular actions. A just man therefore, is he that taketh all the care he can, that his actions may be all just: and an unjust man, is he that neglects it. And such men are more often in our language styled by the names of righteous, and unrighteous; than just, and unjust; though the meaning be the same. Therefore a righteous man, does not lose that title, by one, or a few unjust actions, that proceed from sudden passion, or mistake of things, or persons: nor does an unrighteous man, lose his character, for such actions, as he does, or forbears to do for fear: because his will is not framed by the justice, but by the apparent benefit of what he is to do. That which gives to human actions the relish of justice, is a certain nobleness or gallantness of courage (rarely found), by which a man scorns to be beholding for the contentment of his life, to fraud, or breach of promise. This justice of the manners, is that which is meant, where justice is called a virtue; and injustice a vice.

But the justice of actions denominates men, not just, but guiltless: and the injustice of the same (which is also called injury), gives them but the name of guilty.

Again, the injustice of manners, is the disposition, or aptitude to do injury; and is injustice before it proceed to act; and without supposing any individual person injured. But the injustice of an action (that is to say injury), supposes an individual person injured; namely him, to whom the covenant was made: and therefore many times the injury is received by one man, when the damage redounds to another. As when the master commands his servant to give money to a stranger; if it be not done, the injury is done to the master, whom he had before covenanted to obey; but the damage redounds to the stranger, to whom he had no obligation; and therefore could not injure him. And so also in commonwealths, private men may remit to one another their debts; but not robberies or other violences, whereby they are damaged; because the detaining of debt, is an injury to themselves; but robbery and violence, are injuries to the person of the commonwealth.

Whatsoever is done to a man, conformable to his own will signified to the doer, is no injury to him. For if he that doeth it, hath not passed away his original right to do what he please, by some antecedent covenant, there is no breach of covenant; and therefore no injury done him. And if he have; then his will to have it done being signified, is a release of that covenant: and so again there is no injury done him.

Justice of actions, is by writers divided into commutative, and distributive: and the former they say consists in proportion arithmetical; the latter in proportion geometrical. Commutative therefore, they place in the equality of value of the things contracted for; and distributive, in the distribution of equal benefit, to men of equal merit. As if it were injustice to sell dearer than we buy; or to give more to a man than he merits. The value of all things contracted for, is measured by the appetite of the contractors: and therefore the just value, is that which they be contented to give. And merit (besides that which is by covenant, where the performance on one part, merits the performance of the other part, and falls under justice commutative, not distributive) is not due by justice; but is rewarded of grace only. And therefore this distinction, in the sense wherein it uses to be expounded, is not right. To speak properly commutative justice, is the justice of a contractor; that is, a performance of covenant, in buying, and selling; hiring, and letting to hire; lending, and borrowing; exchanging, bartering, and other acts of contract.

And distributive justice, the justice of an arbitrator; that is to say, the act of defining what is just. Wherein (being trusted by them that make him arbitrator) if he perform his trust, he is said to distribute to every man his own: and his is indeed just distribution, and may be called (though improperly) distributive justice; but more properly equity; which also is a law of nature, as shall be shown in due place.

As justice depends on antecedent covenant; so does GRATITUDE depend on antecedent grace; that is to say, antecedent free-gift: and is the fourth law of nature; which may be conceived in this form, that a man which receives benefit from another of mere grace, endeavor that he which giveth it, have no reasonable cause to repent him of his good will. For no man giveth, but with intention of good to himself; because gift is voluntary; and of all voluntary acts, the object is to every man his own good; of which if men see they shall be frustrated, there will be no beginning of benevolence, or trust; nor consequently of mutual help nor of reconciliation of one man to another; and therefore they are to remain still in the condition of war; which is contrary to the first and fundamental law of nature, which commands men to seek peace. The breach of this law, is called ingratitude; and hath the same relation to grace, that injustice hath to obligation by covenant.

A fifth law of nature, is COMPLAISANCE; that is to say, that every man strive to accommodate himself to the rest. For the understanding whereof, we may consider, that there is in men's aptness to society, a diversity of nature, rising from their diversity of affections; not unlike to that we see in stones brought together for building of an edifice. For as that stone which by the asperity, and irregularity of figure, takes more room from others, than itself fills; and for the hardness, cannot be easily made plain, and thereby hinders the building, is by the builders cast away as unprofitable, and troublesome: so also, a man that by asperity of nature, will strive to retain those things which to himself are superfluous, and to others necessary; and for the stubbornness of his passions, cannot be corrected, is to be left, or cast out of society, as cumbersome thereunto. For seeing every man, not only by right, but also by necessity of nature, is supposed to endeavor all he can, to obtain that which is necessary for his conservation; he that shall oppose himself against it, for things superfluous, is guilty of the war that thereupon is to follow; and therefore doth that, which is contrary to the fundamental law of nature, which commands to seek peace. The observers of this law, may be called SOCIABLE (the Latins call them *commodi*); the contrary, stubborn, unsociable, froward, intractable.

A sixth law of nature, is this, that upon caution of the future time, a man ought to pardon the offences past of them that repenting, desire it. For PARDON, is nothing but granting of peace; which though granted to them that persevere in their hostility, be not peace, but fear; yet not granted to them that give caution of the future time, is sign of an aversion to peace; and therefore contrary to the law of nature.

A seventh is, that in revenges (that is, retribution of evil for evil), men look not at the greatness of the evil past, but the greatness of the good to follow. Whereby we are forbidden to inflict punishment with any other design, than for correction of the offender, or direction of others. For this law is consequent to the next before it, that commands pardon, upon security of the future time. Besides, revenge without respect to the example, and profit to come, is a triumph, or glorying in the hurt of another, tending to no end (for the end is always somewhat to come); and glorying to no end, is vain-glory, and contrary to reason; and to hurt without reason, tends to the introduction of war; which is against the law of nature; and is commonly styled by the name of cruelty.

And because all signs of hatred, or contempt, provoke to fight; insomuch as most men choose rather to hazard their life, than not to be revenged; we may in the eighth place, for a law of nature, set down this precept, that no man by deed, word, countenance, or gesture, declare hatred, or contempt of another. The breach of which law, is commonly called contumely.

The question who is the better man, has no place in the condition of mere nature; where (as has been shewn before) all men are equal. The inequality that now is, has been introduced by the laws civil. I know that Aristotle in the first book of his *Politics*, for a foundation of his doctrine, maketh men by nature, some more worthy to command, meaning the wiser sort (such as he thought himself to be for his philosophy); others to serve (meaning those that had strong bodies, but were not philosophers as he); as if master and servant were not introduced by consent of men, but by difference of wit: which is not only against reason; but also against experience. For there are very few so foolish, that had not rather govern themselves, than be governed by others: nor when the wise in their own conceit, contend by force, with them who distrust their own wisdom, do they always, or often, or almost at any time, get the victory. If nature therefore have made men equal, that equality is to be acknowledged: or if nature have made men unequal; yet because men that think themselves equal, will not enter into conditions of peace, but upon equal terms, such as equality must be admitted. And therefore the ninth law of nature, I put this, that every man acknowledge other for his equal by nature. The breach of this precept is pride.

On this law, depends another, that at the entrance into conditions of peace, no man require to reserve to himself any right, which he is not content should be reserved to every one of the rest. As it is necessary for all men that seek peace, to lay down certain rights of nature; that is to say, not to have liberty to do all they list: so it is necessary for man's life, to retain some; as right to govern their own bodies; enjoy air, water, motion, ways to go from place to place; and all things else without which a man cannot live, or not live well. If in this case, at the making of peace, men require for themselves that which they would not have to be granted to others, they do contrary to the precedent law, that commands the acknowledgment of natural equality, and therefore also against the law of nature. The observers of this law are those we call modest, and the breakers arrogant men. The Greeks call the violation of this law [*pleonexia*]; that is, a desire of more than their share.

Also if a man be trusted to judge between man and man, it is a precept of the law of nature, that he deal equally between them. For without that, the controversies of men cannot be determined but by war. He therefore that is partial in judgment, doth what in him lies, to deter men from the use of judges, and arbitrators; and consequently (against the fundamental law of nature) is the cause of war.

The observance of this law, from the equal distribution to each man, of that which in reason belongs to him, is called EQUITY, and (as I have said before) distributive justice: the violation, acception of persons.

And from this followeth another law, that such things as cannot be divided, be enjoyed in common, if it can be; and if the quantity of the thing permit, without stint; otherwise proportionably to the number of them that have right. For otherwise the distribution is unequal, and contrary to equity.

But some things there be, that can neither be divided, nor enjoyed in common. Then, the law of nature, which prescribes equity, requires, that the entire right; or else (making the use alternate) the first possession, be determined by lot. For equal distribution, is of the law of nature; and other means of equal distribution cannot be imagined.

Of lots there be two sorts, arbitrary, and natural. Arbitrary, is that which is agreed on by the competitors: natural, is either primogeniture (which the Greek calls [*kleronomia*], which signifies, given by lot); or first seizure.

And therefore those things which cannot be enjoyed in common, nor divided, ought to be adjudged to the first possessor; and in some cases to the first-born, as acquired by lot.

It is also a law of nature, that all men that mediate peace, be allowed safe conduct. For the law that commands peace, as the end, commands intercession, as the means; and to intercession the means is safe conduct.

And because, though men be never so willing to observe these laws, there may nevertheless arise questions concerning a man's action; first, whether it were done, or not done; secondly (if done), whether against the law, or not against the law; the former whereof, is called a question of fact; the latter a question of right; therefore unless the parties to the question, covenant mutually to stand to the sentence of another, they are as far from peace as ever. This other, to whose sentence they submit, is called an ARBITRATOR. And therefore it is of the law of nature, that they that are at controversy, submit their right to the judgment of an arbitrator.

And seeing every man is presumed to do all things in order to his own benefit, no man is a fit arbitrator in his own cause: and if he were never so fit; yet equity allowing to each party equal benefit, if one be admitted to be judge, the other is to be admitted also; and so the controversy, that is, the cause of war, remains, against the law of nature.

For the same reason no man in any cause ought to be received for arbitrator, to whom greater profit, or honour, or pleasure apparently arises out of the victory of one party, than of the other: for he hath taken (though an unavoidable bribe, yet) a bribe; and no man can be obliged to trust him. And thus also the controversy, and the condition of war remains, contrary to the law of nature.

And in a controversy of fact, the judge being to give no more credit to one, than to the other (if there be no other arguments), must give credit to a third; or to a third and fourth; or more: for else the question is undecided, and left to force, contrary to the law of nature.

These are the laws of nature, dictating peace, for a means of the conservation of men in multitudes; and which only concern the doctrine of civil society. There be other things tending to the destruction of particular men; as drunkenness, and all other parts of intemperance; which may therefore also be reckoned amongst those things which the law of nature hath forbidden; but are not necessary to be mentioned, nor are pertinent enough to this place.

And though this may seem too subtle a deduction of the laws of nature, to be taken notice of by all men; whereof the most part are too busy in getting food, and the rest too negligent to understand; yet to leave all men inexcusable, they have been contracted into one easy sum, intelligible, even to the meanest capacity; and that is, Do not that to another, which thou wouldest not have done to thyself; which shows him, that he has no more to do in learning the laws of nature, but, when weighing the actions of other men with his own, they seem too heavy, to put them into the other part of the balance, and his own into their place, that his own passions, and self-love, may add nothing to the weight; and then there is none of these laws of nature that will not appear unto him very reasonable.

The laws of nature oblige *in foro interno* [in conscience]; that is to say, they bind to a desire they should take place: but *in foro externo* [in civil law]; that is, to the putting them in act, not always. For he that should be modest, and tractable, and perform all he promises, in such time, and place, where no man else should do so, should but make himself a prey to others, and procure his own certain ruin, contrary to the ground of all laws of nature, which tend to nature's preservation. And again, he that having sufficient security, that others shall observe the same laws towards him, observes them not himself, seeks not peace, but war; and consequently the destruction of his nature by violence.

And whatsoever laws bind *in foro interno*, may be broken, not only by a fact contrary to the law, but also by a fact according to it, in case a man think it contrary. For though his action in this case, be according to the law; yet his purpose was against the law; which, where the obligations is in foro interno, is a breach.

The laws of nature are immutable and eternal; for injustice, ingratitude, arrogance, pride, iniquity, acception of persons, and the rest, can never be made lawful. For it can never be that war shall preserve life, and peace destroy it.

The same laws, because they oblige only to a desire, and endeavor, I mean an unfeigned and constant endeavor, are easy to be observed. For in that they require nothing but endeavor; he that endeavors their performance, fulfills them; and he that fulfills the law, is just.

And the science of them, is the true and only moral philosophy. For moral philosophy is nothing else but the science of what is good, and evil, in the conversation, and society of mankind. Good, and evil, are names that signify our appetites, and aversions; which in different tempers, customs, and doctrines of men, are different: and divers men, differ not only in their judgment, on the senses of what is pleasant, and unpleasant to the taste, smell, hearing, touch, and sight; but also of what is conformable, or disagreeable to reason, in the actions of common life. Nay, the same man, in divers times, differs from himself; and one time praises, that is, calleth good, what another time he dispraises, and calleth evil: from whence arise disputes, controversies, and at last war. And therefore so long a man is in the condition of mere nature (which is a condition of war), as private appetite is the measure of good, and evil: and consequently all men agree on this, that peace is good, and therefore also the way, or means of peace, which (as I have shewed before) are justice, gratitude, modesty, equity, mercy, and the rest of the laws of nature, are good; that is to say, moral virtues; and their contrary vices, evil. Now the science of virtue and vice, is moral philosophy; and therefore the true doctrine of the laws of nature, is the true moral philosophy. But the writers of moral philosophy, though they acknowledge the same virtues and vices; yet not seeing wherein consisted their goodness; nor that they come to be praised, as the means of peaceable, sociable, and comfortable living; place them in a mediocrity of passions: as if not the cause, but the degree of daring, made fortitude; or not the cause, but the quantity of a gift, made liberality.

These dictates of reason, men use to call by the name of laws; but improperly: for they are but conclusions, or theorems concerning what conduces to the conversion and defence of themselves; whereas law, properly, is the word of him, that by right hath command over others. But yet if we consider the same theorems, as delivered in the word of God, that by right commands all things; then are they properly called laws.

PART 2. OF COMMONWEALTH

Chapter 17. Of the Causes, Generation, and Definition of a Commonwealth

The final cause, end, or design of men (who naturally love liberty, and dominion over others), in the introduction of that restraint upon themselves (in which we see them live in commonwealths), is the foresight of their own preservation, and of a more contented life thereby; that is to say, of getting themselves out from that miserable condition of war, which is necessarily consequent (as hath been shown), to the natural passions of men, when there is no visible power to keep them in awe, and tie them by fear of punishment to the performance of their covenants, and observation of those laws of nature set down in the fourteenth and fifteenth chapters.

For the laws of nature (as justice, equity, modesty, mercy, and [in sum] doing to others, as we would be done to), of themselves, without the terror of some power to cause them to be observed, are contrary to our natural passions, that carry us to partiality pride, revenge, and the like. And covenants without the sword are but words, and of no strength to secure a man at all. Therefore notwithstanding the laws of nature (which every one hath then kept, when he has the will to keep them, when he can do it safely), if there be no power erected, or not great enough for our security; every man will, and may lawfully, rely on his own strength and art for caution against all other men. And in all places, where men have lived by small families, to rob and spoil one another, has been a trade, and so far from being reputed against the law of nature, that the greater spoils they gained, the greater was their honour; and men observed no other laws therein, but the laws of honour; that is, to abstain from cruelty, leaving to men their lives, and instruments of husbandry. And as small families did then; so now do cities and kingdoms which are but greater families (for their own security) enlarge their dominions, upon all pretenses of danger, and fear of invasion, or assistance that may be given to invaders, endeavor as much as they can, to subdue, or weaken their neighbors, by open force, and secret arts, for want of other caution, justly; and are remembered for it in after ages with honour.

Nor is it the joining together of a small number of men, that gives them this security; because in small numbers, small additions on the one side or the other, make the advantage of strength so great, as is sufficient to carry the victory; and therefore gives encouragement to an invasion. The multitude sufficient to confide in for our security, is not determined by any certain number, but by comparison with the enemy we fear; and is then sufficient, when the odds of the enemy is not of so visible and conspicuous moment, to determine the event of war, as to move him to attempt.

And be there never so great a multitude; yet if their actions be directed according to their particular judgments, and particular appetites, they can expect thereby no defence, nor protection, neither against a common enemy, nor against the injuries of one another. For being distracted in opinions concerning the best use and application of their strength, they do not help, but hinder one another; and reduce their strength by mutual opposition to nothing: whereby they are easily, not only subdued by a very few that agree together; but also when there is no common enemy, they make war upon each other, for their particular interests. For if we could suppose a great multitude of men to consent in the observation of justice, and other laws of nature, without a common power to keep them all in awe; we might as well suppose all mankind to do the same; and then there neither would be, nor need to be any civil government, or commonwealth at all; because there would be peace without subjection.

Nor is it enough for the security, which men desire should last all the time of their life, that they be governed, and directed by one judgment, for a limited time; as in one battle, or one war. For though they obtain a victory by their unanimous endeavor against a foreign enemy; yet afterwards, when either they have no common enemy, or he that by one part is held for an enemy, is by another part held for a friend, they must needs by the difference of their interests dissolve, and fall again into a war amongst themselves.

It is true, that certain living creatures, as bees and ants, live sociably one with another (which are therefore by Aristotle numbered amongst political creatures); and yet have no other direction, than their particular judgments and appetites; nor speech, whereby one of them can signify to another, what he thinks expedient for the common benefit: and therefore some man may perhaps desire to know, why mankind cannot do the same. To which I answer,

First, that men are continually in competition for honour and dignity, which these creatures are not; and consequently amongst men there arises on that ground, envy and hatred, and finally war; but amongst these not so.

Secondly, that amongst these creatures, the common good differs not from the private; and being by nature inclined to their private, they procure thereby the common benefit. But man, whose joy consists in comparing himself with other men, can relish nothing but what is eminent.

Thirdly, that these creatures, having not (as man) the use of reason, do not see, nor think they see any fault, in the administration of their common business; whereas amongst men, there are very many, that think themselves wiser, and abler to govern the public, better than the rest; and these strive to reform and innovate, one this way, another that way; and thereby bring it into distraction and civil war.

Fourthly, that these creatures, though they have some use of voice, in making known to one another their desires, and other affections; yet they want that art of words, by which some men can represent to others, that which is good, in the likeness of evil; and evil, in the likeness of good; and augment, or diminish the apparent greatness of good and evil; discontenting men, and troubling their peace at their pleasure.

Fifthly, irrational creatures cannot distinguish between injury, and damage; and therefore as long as they be at ease, they are not offended with their fellows: whereas man is then most troublesome, when he is most at ease: for then it is that he loves to shew his wisdom, and control the actions of them that govern the commonwealth.

Lastly, the agreement of these creatures is natural; that of men, is by covenant only, which is artificial: and therefore it is no wonder if there be somewhat else required (besides covenant) to make their agreement constant and lasting; which is a common power, to keep them in awe, and to direct their actions to the common benefit.

The only way to erect such a common power, as may be able to defend them from the invasion of foreigners, and the injuries of one another, and thereby to secure them in such sort, as that by their own industry, and by the fruits of the earth, they may nourish themselves and live contentedly; is, to confer all their power and strength upon one man, or upon one assembly of men,that may reduce all their wills, by plurality of voices, unto one will: which is as much as to say, to appoint one man, or assembly of men, to bear their person; and every one to own, and acknowledge himself to be author of whatsoever he that so beareth their person, shall act, or cause to be acted, in those things which concern the common peace and safety; and therein to submit their wills, every one to his will, and their judgments, to his judgment. This is more than consent, or concord; it is a real unity of them all, in one and the same person, made by covenant of every man with every man, in such manner, as if every man should say to every man, I authorize and give up my right of governing myself, to this man, or to this assembly of men, on this condition, that thou give up thy right to him, and authorize all his actions in like manner. This done, the multitude so united in one person, is called a COMMONWEALTH, in Latin CIVITAS. This is the generation of that great LEVIATHAN, or rather (to speak more reverently) of that mortal god, to which we owe under the immortal God, our peace and defence. For by this authority, given him by every particular man in the commonwealth, he hath the use of so much power and strength conferred on him, that by terror thereof, he is enabled to form the wills of them all, to peace at home, and mutual aid against their enemies abroad. And in him consists the essence of the commonwealth; which (to define it) is one person, of whose acts a great multitude, by mutual covenants one with another, have made themselves every one the author, to the end he may use the strength and means of them all, as he shall think expedient, for their peace and common defence.

And he that carries this person, is called SOVEREIGN, and said to have sovereign power; and every one besides, his SUBJECT.

The attaining to this sovereign power, is by two ways. One, by natural force; as when a man maketh his children, to submit themselves, and their children to his government, as being able to destroy them if they refuse; or by war subdues his enemies to his will, giving them their lives on that condition. The other, is when men agree amongst themselves, to submit to some man, or assembly of men, voluntarily, on confidence to be protected by him against all others. This latter, may be called a political commonwealth, or commonwealth by institution; and the former, a commonwealth by acquisition. And first, I shall speak of a commonwealth by institution.

Chapter 18. Of the Rights of Sovereigns by Institution

A commonwealth is said to be instituted, when a multitude of men do agree, and covenant, every one, with every one, that to whatsoever man, or assembly of men, shall be given by the major part, the right to present the person of them all (that is to say, to be their representative); every one, as well he that voted for it, as he that voted against it, shall authorize all the actions and judgments, of that man, or assembly of men, in the same manner, as if they were his own, to the end, to live peaceably amongst themselves, and be protected against other men.

From this institution of a commonwealth are derived all the rights, and faculties of him, or them, on whom the sovereign power is conferred by the consent of the people assembled.

First, because they covenant, it is to be understood, they are not obliged by former covenant to any thing repugnant hereunto. And consequently they that have already instituted a commonwealth, being thereby bound by covenant, to own the actions, and judgments of one, cannot lawfully make a new covenant, amongst themselves, to be obedient to any other, in any thing whatsoever, without his permission. And therefore, they that are subjects to a monarch, cannot without his leave cast off monarchy, and return to the confusion of a disunited multitude; nor transfer their person from him that beareth it, to another man, or other assembly of men: for they are bound, every man to every man, to own, and be reputed author of all, that he that already is their sovereign, shall do, and judge fit to be done: so that any one man dissenting, all the rest should break their covenant made to that man, which is injustice: and they have also every man given the sovereignty to him that beareth their person; and therefore if they depose him, they take from him that which is his own, and so again it is injustice. Besides, if he that attempts to depose his sovereign, be killed, or punished by him for such attempt, he is author of his own punishment, as being by the institution, author of all his sovereign shall do: and because it is injustice for a man to do any thing, for which he may be punished by his own authority, he is also upon that title, unjust. And whereas some men have pretended for their disobedience to their sovereign, a new covenant, made, not with men, but with God; this also is unjust: for there is no covenant with God, but by mediation of somebody that represents God's person; which none doth but God's lieutenant, who hath the sovereignty under God. But this pretence of covenant with God, is so evident a lie, even in the pretenders' own consciences, that it is not only an act of an unjust, but also a vile, and unmanly disposition.

Secondly, because the right of bearing the person of them all, is given to him they make sovereign, by covenant only of one to another, and not of him to any of them; there can happen no breach of covenant on the part of the sovereign; and consequently none of his subjects, by any pretence of forfeiture, can be freed from his subjection. That he which is made sovereign maketh no covenant with his subjects beforehand, is manifest; because either he must make it with the whole multitude, as one party to the covenant; or he must make a several covenant with every man. With the whole, as one party, it is impossible; because as yet they are not one person: and if he make so many several covenants as there be men, those covenants after he hath the sovereignty are void, because what act soever can be pretended by any one of them for breach thereof, is the act both of himself, and of all the rest, because done in the person, and by the right of every one of them in particular. Besides, if any one, or more of them, pretend a breach of the covenant made by the sovereign at his institution; and others, or one other of his subjects, or himself alone, pretend there was no such breach, there is in this case, no judge to decide the controversy; it returns therefore to the sword again; and every man recovers the right of protecting himself by his own strength, contrary to the design they had in the institution. It is therefore in vain to grant sovereignty by way of precedent covenant. The opinion that any monarch receives his power by covenant, that is to say, on condition, proceeds from want of understanding this easy truth, that covenants being but words and breath, have no force to oblige, contain, constrain, or protect any man, but what it has from the public sword; that is, from the untied hands of that man, or assembly of men that hath the sovereignty, and whose actions are avouched by them all, and performed by the strength of them all, in him united. But when an assembly of men is made sovereign; then no man imagines any such covenant to have passed in the institution; for no man is so dull as to say, for example, the people of Rome made a covenant with the Romans, to hold the sovereignty on such or such conditions; which not performed, the Romans might lawfully depose the Roman people. That men see not the reason to be alike in a monarchy, and in a popular government, proceeds from the ambition of some, that are kinder to the government of an assembly, whereof they may hope to participate, than of monarchy, which they despair to enjoy.

Thirdly, because the major part hath by consenting voices declared a sovereign; he that dissented must now consent with the rest; that is, be contented to avow all the actions he shall do, or else justly be destroyed by the rest. For if he voluntarily entered into the congregation of them that were assembled, he sufficiently declared thereby his will, (and therefore tacitly covenanted) to stand to what the major part should ordain: and therefore if he refuse to stand thereto, or make protestation against any of their decrees, he does contrary to his covenant, and therefore unjustly. And whether he be of the congregation, or not; and whether his consent be asked, or not, he must either submit to their decrees, or be left in the condition of war he was in before; wherein he might without injustice be destroyed by any man whatsoever.

Fourthly, because every subject is by this institution author of all the actions, and judgments of the sovereign instituted; it follows, that whatsoever he doth, it can be no injury to any of his subjects; nor ought he to be by any of them accused of injustice. For he that doth any thing by authority from another, doth therein no injury to him by whose authority he acts: but by this institution of a commonwealth, every particular man is author of all the sovereign doth; and consequently he that complains of injury from his sovereign, complains of that whereof he himself is author; and therefore ought not to accuse any man but himself; no nor himself of injury; because to do injury to one's self, is impossible. It is true that they that have sovereign power, may commit iniquity; but not injustice, or injury in the proper signification.

Fifthly, and consequently to that which was said last, no man that hath sovereign power can justly be put to death, or otherwise in any manner by his subjects punished. For seeing every subject is author of the actions of his sovereign; he punishes another, for the actions committed by himself.

And because the end of this institution, is the peace and defence of them all; and whosoever has right to the end, has right to the means; it belongs of right, to whatsoever man, or assembly that hath the sovereignty, to be judge of both of the means of peace and defence; and also of the hindrances, and disturbances of the same; and to do whatsoever he shall think necessary to be done, both beforehand, for the preserving of peace and security, by prevention of discord at home, and hostility from abroad; and, when peace and security are lost, for the recovery of the same. And therefore,

Sixthly, it is annexed to the sovereignty, to be judge of what opinions and doctrines are averse, and what conducing to peace; and consequently on what occasions, how far, and what, men are to be trusted withal, in speaking to multitudes of people; and who shall examine the doctrines of all books before they be published. For the actions of men proceed from their opinions; and in the well-governing of opinions, consists the well-governing of men's actions, in order to their peace, and concord. And though in matter of doctrine, nothing ought to be regarded but the truth; yet this is not repugnant to regulating of the same by peace. For doctrine repugnant to peace, can no more be true, than peace and concord can be against the law of nature. It is true, that in a commonwealth, where by the negligence, or unskillfulness of governors, and teachers, false doctrines are by time generally received; the contrary truths may be generally offensive: Yet the most sudden, and rough bustling in of a new truth, that can be, does never break the peace, but only sometimes awake the war. For those men that are so remissly governed, that they dare take up arms, to defend, or introduce an opinion, are still in war; and their condition not peace, but only a cessation of arms for fear of one another; and they live as it were, in the precincts of battle continually. It belongs therefore to him that hath the sovereign power, to be judge, or constitute all judges of opinions and doctrines, as a thing necessary to peace; thereby to prevent discord and civil war.

Seventhly, is annexed to the sovereignty, the whole power of prescribing the rules, whereby every man may know, what goods he may enjoy, and what actions he may do, without being molested by any of his fellow-subjects; and this is it men call propriety. For before constitution of sovereign power (as hath already been shown) all men had right to all things; which necessarily causes war: and therefore this propriety, being necessary to peace, and depending on sovereign power, is the act of that power, in order to the public peace. These rules of propriety (or *meum* and *tuum* [mine and thine]) and of good, evil, lawful, and unlawful in the actions of subjects, are the civil laws; that is to say, the laws of each commonwealth in particular; though the name of civil law be now restrained to the ancient civil laws of the city of Rome; which being the head of a great part of the world, her laws at that time were in these parts the civil law.

Eighthly, is annexed to the sovereignty, the right of judicature; that is to say, of hearing and deciding all controversies, which may arise concerning law, either civil, or natural; or concerning fact. For without the decision of controversies, there is no protection of one subject, against the injuries of another; the laws concerning meum and tuum are in vain; and to every man remains, from the natural and necessary appetite of his own conservation, the right of protecting himself by his private strength, which is the condition of war; and contrary to the end for which every commonwealth is instituted.

Ninthly, is annexed to the sovereignty, the right of making war and peace with other nations, and commonwealths; that is to say, of judging when it is for the public good, and how great forces are to be assembled, armed, and paid for that end; and to levy money upon the subjects, to defray the expenses thereof. For the power by which the people are to be defended, consists in their armies; and the strength of an army, in the union of their strength under one command; which command the sovereign instituted, therefore hath; because the command of the militia, without other institution, maketh him that hath it sovereign. And therefore whosoever is made general of an army, he that hath the sovereign power is always generalissimo.

Tenthly, is annexed to the sovereignty, the choosing of all counsellors, ministers, magistrates, and officers, both in peace, and war. For seeing the sovereign is charged with the end, which is the common peace and defence, he is understood to have power to use such means, as he shall think most fit for his discharge.

Eleventhly, to the sovereign is committed the power of rewarding with riches, or honour; and of punishing with corporal, or pecuniary punishment, or with ignominy every subject according to the law he hath formerly made; or if there be no law made, according as he shall judge most to conduce to the encouraging of men to serve the commonwealth, or deterring of them from doing disservice to the same.

Lastly, considering what values men are naturally apt to set upon themselves; what respect they look for from others; and how little they value other men; from whence continually arise amongst them, emulation, quarrels, factions, and at last war, to the destroying of one another, and diminution of their strength against a common enemy; it is necessary that there be laws of honour, and a public rate of the worth of such men as have deserved, or are able to deserve well of the commonwealth; and that there be force in the hands of some or other, to put those laws in execution. But it hath already been shown, that not only the whole militia, or forces of the commonwealth; but also the judicature of all controversies, is annexed to the sovereignty. To the sovereign therefore it belongs also to give titles of honour; and to appoint what order of place, and dignity, each man shall hold; and what signs of respect, in public or private meetings, they shall give to one another.

These are the rights, which make the essence of sovereignty; and which are the marks, whereby a man may discern in what man, or assembly of men, the sovereign power is placed, and resides. For these are incommunicable, and inseparable. The power to coin money; to dispose of the estate and persons of infant heirs; to have preemption in markets; and all other statute prerogatives, may be transferred to the sovereign; and yet the power to protect his subjects be retained. But if he transfer the militia, he retains the judicature in vain, for want of execution of the laws: or if he grant away the power of raising money; the militia is in vain: or if he give away the government of doctrines, men will be frightened into rebellion with the fear of spirits. And so if we consider any one of the said rights, we shall presently see, that the holding of all the rest will produce no effect, in the conservation of peace and justice, the end for which all commonwealths are instituted. And this division is it, whereof it is said, a kingdom divided in itself cannot stand: for unless this division precede, division into opposite armies can never happen. If there had not first been an opinion received of the greatest part of England, that these powers were divided between the King, and the Lords, and the House of Commons, the people had never been divided and fallen into this civil war; first between those that disagreed in politics; and after between the dissenters about the liberty of religion; which have so instructed men in this point of sovereign right, that there be few now (in England) that do not see, that these rights are inseparable, and will be so generally acknowledged at the next return of peace;[2] and so continue, till their miseries are forgotten; and no longer, except the vulgar be better taught than they have hitherto been.

And because they are essential and inseparable rights, it follows necessarily, that in whatsoever words any of them seem to be granted away, yet if the sovereign power itself be not in direct terms renounced, and the name of sovereign no more given by the grantees to him that grants them, the grant is void: for when he has granted all he can, if we grant back the sovereignty, all is restored, as inseparably annexed thereunto.

This great authority being indivisible, and inseparably annexed to the sovereignty, there is little ground for the opinion of them, that say of sovereign kings, though they be singulis majores, of greater power than every one of their subjects, yet they be universis minores, of less power than them

2. Hobbes wrote this work in the midst of the English civil war (1641–1646; 1648–1652) in which Parliament fought King Charles I (the Royalists), which Parliament won.

all together. For if by all together, they mean not the collective body as one person, then all together, and every one, signify the same; and the speech is absurd. But if by all together, they understand them as one person (which person the sovereign bears), then the power of all together, is the same with the sovereign's power; and so again the speech is absurd: which absurdity they see well enough, when the sovereignty is in an assembly of the people; but in a monarch they see it not; and yet the power of sovereignty is the same in whomsoever it be placed.

And as the power, so also the honour of the sovereign, ought to be greater, than that of any, or all the subjects. For in the sovereignty is the fountain of honour. The dignities of lord, earl, duke, and prince are his creatures. As in the presence of the master, the servants are equal, and without any honour at all; so are the subjects, in the presence of the sovereign. And though they shine some more, some less, when they are out of his sight; yet in his presence, they shine no more than the stars in the presence of the sun.

But a man may here object, that the condition of subjects is very miserable; as being obnoxious to the lusts, and other irregular passions of him, or them that have so unlimited a power in their hands. And commonly they that live under a monarch, think it the fault of monarchy; and they that live under the government of democracy, or other sovereign assembly, attribute all the inconvenience to that form of commonwealth; whereas the power in all forms, if they be perfect enough to protect them, is the same; not considering that the estate of man can never be without some incommodity or other; and that the greatest, that in any form of government can possibly happen to the people in general, is scarce sensible, in respect of the miseries, and horrible calamities, that accompany a civil war, or that dissolute condition of masterless men, without subjection to laws, and a coercive power to tie their hands from rapine and revenge: nor considering that the greatest pressure of sovereign governors, proceeds not from any delight, or profit they can expect in the damage or weakening of their subjects, in whose vigor, consists their own strength and glory; but in the restiveness of themselves, that unwillingly contributing to their own defence, make it necessary for their governors to draw from them what they can in time of peace, that they may have means on any emergent occasion, or sudden need, to resist, or take advantage on their enemies. For all men are by nature provided of notable multiplying glasses (that is their passions and self-love), through which, every little payment appears a great grievance; but are destitute of those prospective glasses (namely moral and civil science), to see afar off the miseries that hang over them, and cannot without such payments be avoided. . . .

Chapter 21. Of the Liberty of Subjects

LIBERTY, or FREEDOM, signifies (properly) the absence of opposition (by opposition, I mean external impediments of motion); and may be applied no less to irrational, and inanimate creatures, than to rational. For whatsoever is so tied, or environed, as it cannot move, but within a certain space, which space is determined by the opposition of some external body, we say it hath not liberty to go further. And so of all living creatures, whilst they are imprisoned, or restrained, with walls, or chains; and of the water whilst it is kept in by banks, or vessels, that otherwise would spread itself into a larger space, we use to say, they are not at liberty, to move in such manner, as without those external impediments they would. But when the impediment of motion, is in the constitution of the thing itself, we use not to say, it wants the liberty; but the power to move; as when a stone lies still, or a man is fastened to his bed by sickness.

And according to this proper, and generally received meaning of the word, a FREEMAN, is he, that in those things, which by his strength and wit he is able to do, is not hindered to do what he has a will to. But when the words free, and liberty, are applied to any thing but bodies, they are abused; for that which is not subject to motion, is not subject to impediment: and therefore, when it is said (for example) the way is free, no liberty of the way is signified, but of those that walk in it without stop. And when we say a gift is free, there is not meant any liberty of the gift, but of the giver, that was not bound by any law, or covenant to give it. So when we speak freely, it is not the liberty of voice, or pronunciation, but of the man, whom no law hath obliged to speak otherwise than he did. Lastly, from the use of the word free-will, no liberty can be inferred of the will, desire, or inclination, but the liberty of the man; which consists in this, that he finds no stop, in doing what he has the will, desire, or inclination to do.

Fear, and liberty are consistent; as when a man throws his goods into the sea for fear the ship should sink, he doth it nevertheless very willingly, and may refuse to do it if he will: it is therefore the action of one that was free: so a man sometimes pays his debt, only for fear of imprisonment, which because nobody hindered him from detaining, was the action of a man at liberty. And generally all actions which men do in commonwealths, for fear of the law, are actions, which the doers had liberty to omit.

Liberty, and necessity are consistent: as in the water, that hath not only liberty, but a necessity of descending by the channel; so likewise in the actions which men voluntarily do: which, because they proceed from their will, proceed from liberty; and yet, because every act of man's will, and every desire, and inclination proceeds from some cause, and that from another cause, in a continual chain (whose first link is in the hand of God the first of all causes), they proceed from necessity. So that to him that could see the connexion of those causes, the necessity of all men's voluntary actions, would appear manifest. And therefore God, that sees, and disposes all things, sees also that the liberty of man in doing what he will, is accompanied with the necessity of doing that which God will, and no more, nor less. For though men may do many things, which God does not command, nor is therefore author of them; yet they can have no passion, nor appetite to any thing, of which appetite God's will is not the cause. And did not his will assure the necessity of man's will, and consequently of all that on man's will depends, the liberty of men would be a contradiction, and impediment to the omnipotence and liberty of God. And this shall suffice (as to the matter in hand) of that natural liberty, which only is properly called liberty.

But as men, for the attaining of peace, and conservation of themselves thereby, have made an artificial man, which we call a commonwealth; so also have they made artificial chains, called civil laws, which they themselves, by mutual covenants, have fastened at one end, to the lips of that man, or assembly, to whom they have given the sovereign power; and at the other end to their own ears. These bonds in their own nature but weak, may nevertheless be made to hold, by the danger, though not by the difficulty of breaking them.

In relation to these bonds only it is, that I am to speak now, of the liberty of subjects. For seeing there is no commonwealth in the world, wherein there be rules enough set down, for the regulating of all the actions, and words of men (as being a thing impossible): it followeth necessarily, that in all kinds of actions, but the laws pretermitted, men have the liberty, of doing what their own reasons shall suggest, for the most profitable to themselves. For if we take liberty in the proper sense, for corporal liberty; that is to say, freedom from chains, and prison, it were very absurd for men to clamor as they do, for the liberty they so manifestly enjoy. Again, if we take liberty, for an exemption from laws, it is no less absurd, for men to demand as they do, that liberty, by which all other men may be masters of their lives. And yet as absurd as it is, this is it they demand; not knowing that the laws are of no power to protect them, without a sword in the hands of a man, or men, to cause those laws to be put in execution. The liberty of a subject, lies therefore only in those things, which in regulating their actions, the sovereign hath pretermitted: such as is the liberty to buy, and sell, and otherwise contract with one another; to choose their own abode, their own diet, their own trade of life, and institute their children as they themselves think fit; and the like.

Nevertheless we are not to understand, that by such liberty, the sovereign power of life and death, is either abolished, or limited. For it has been already shown, that nothing the sovereign representative can do to a subject, on what pretence soever, can properly be called injustice, or injury; because every subject is author of every act the sovereign doth; so that he never wants right to any thing, otherwise, than as he himself is the subject of God, and bound thereby to observe the laws of nature. And therefore it may, and doth often happen in commonwealths, that a subject may be put to death, by the command of the sovereign power; and yet neither do the other wrong: as when Jephtha caused his daughter to be sacrificed: in which, and the like cases, he that so dies, had liberty to do the action, for which he is nevertheless, without injury put to death. And the same holds also in a sovereign prince, that puts to death an innocent subject. For though the action be against the law of nature, as being contrary to equity (as was the killing of Uriah, by David); yet it was not an injury to Uriah; but to God. Not to Uriah, because the right to do what he pleased, was given him by Uriah himself: and yet to God, because David was God's subject; and prohibited all iniquity by the law of nature. Which distinction, David himself, when he repented the fact, evidently confirmed, saying, To thee only have I sinned. In the same manner, the people of Athens, when they banished the most potent of their commonwealth for ten years, thought they committed no injustice; and yet they never questioned what crime he had done; but what hurt he would do; nay they commanded the banishment of they knew not whom; and every citizen bringing his oystershell into market place, written with the name of him he desired should be banished, without actual accusing him, sometimes banished an Aristides, for his reputation of justice; and sometimes a scurrilous jester, as Hyperbolus, to make a jest of it. And yet a man cannot say, the sovereign people of Athens wanted right to banish them; or an Athenian the liberty to jest, or to be just.[3]

The liberty, whereof there is so frequent and honorable mention, in the histories, and philosophy of the ancient Greeks, and Romans, and in the writings, and discourse of those that from them have received all their learning in the politics, is not the liberty of particular men; but the liberty of the commonwealth: which is the same with that, which every man then should have, if there were no civil laws, nor commonwealth at all. And the effects of it also be the same. For as amongst masterless men, there is perpetual war, of every man against his neighbor; no inheritance, to transmit to the son, nor to expect from the father; no propriety of goods, or lands; no security; but a full and absolute liberty in every particular man: so in states, and commonwealths not dependent on one another, every commonwealth (not every man) has an absolute liberty, to do what it shall judge (that is to say, what that man, or assembly that represents it, shall judge) most conducing to their benefit. But withall, they live in the condition of a perpetual war, and upon the confines of battle, with their frontiers armed, and cannons planted against their neighbors round about. The Athenians, and Romans were free; that is, free commonwealths: not that any particular men had the liberty to resist their own representative; but that their representative had the liberty to resist, or invade other people. There is written on the turrets of the city of Lucca in great characters at this day, the word LIBERTAS; yet no man can thence infer, that a particular man has more liberty, or immunity from the service of the commonwealth there, than in Constantinople. Whether a commonwealth be monarchical, or popular, the freedom is still the same.

But it is an easy thing, for men to be deceived, by the specious name of liberty, and for want of judgment to distinguish, mistake that for their private inheritance, and birth right, which is the right of the public only. And when the same error is confirmed by the authority of men in reputation for their writings in this subject, it is no wonder if it produce sedition, and change of government. In these western parts of the world, we are made to receive our opinions concerning the institution, and rights of commonwealths, from Aristotle, Cicero, and other men, Greeks and Romans, that living under popular states, derived those rights, not from the principles of nature, but transcribed them into their books, out of the practice of their own commonwealths, which were popular; as the grammarians describe the rules of language, out of the practice of the time; or the rules of poetry, out of the poems of Homer and Virgil. And because the Athenians were taught (to keep them from desire of changing their government), that they were freemen, and all that lived under monarchy were slaves; therefore Aristotle puts it down in his *Politics*. In democracy, Liberty is to be supposed: for it is commonly held, that no man is Free in any other government. And as Aristotle; so Cicero, and other writers have ground their civil doctrine, on the opinions of the Romans, who were taught to hate monarchy, at first, by them that having deposed their sovereign, shared amongst them the sovereignty of Rome; and afterwards by their successors. And by reading of these Greek, and Latin authors, men from their childhood have gotten a habit (under a false show of liberty), of favoring tumults, and of licentious controlling the actions of their sovereigns; and again of controlling those controllers, with the effusion of so much blood; as I think I may truly say, there was never any thing so dearly bought, as these western parts have brought the learning of the Greek and Latin tongues.

To come now to the particulars of the true liberty of a subject; that is to say, what are the things, which though commanded by the sovereign, he may nevertheless, without injustice, refuse to do; we are to consider, what rights we pass away, when we make a commonwealth; or (which is all one), what liberty we deny ourselves, by owning all the actions (without exception) of the man, or assembly we make our sovereign. For in the act of our submission, consists both our obligation, and our liberty; which must therefore be inferred by arguments taken from thence; there being no obligation on any man, which arises not from some act of his own; for all men equally, are by nature free. And because such arguments, must either be drawn from the express words, I authorize all his actions, or from the intention of

3. The Athenians in the fifth century B.C. expelled innocent men thought to be dangerous to the state. The names of the men deemed dangerous were written on pieces of broken pottery. The famous general Aristides was expelled in 483 B.C. but recalled a few years later. The demagogue Hyperbolus was expelled in 417 B.C.

him that submits himself to his power (which intention is to be understood by the end for which he so submits); the obligation, and liberty of the subject, is to be derived, either from those words (or others equivalent); or else from the end of the institution of sovereignty, namely, the peace of the subjects within themselves, and their defence against a common enemy.

First therefore, seeing sovereignty by institution, is by covenant of every one to every one; and sovereignty by acquisition, by covenants of the vanquished to the victor, or child to the parent; it is manifest, that every subject has liberty in all those things, the right whereof cannot by covenant be transferred. I have shewn before the 14th chapter, that covenants, not to defend a man's own body, are void. Therefore, If the sovereign command a man (though justly condemned) to kill, wound, or maim himself; or not to resist those that assault him; or to abstain from the use of food, air, medicine, or any other thing, without which he cannot live; yet hath that man the liberty to disobey.

If a man be interrogated by the sovereign, or his authority, concerning a crime done by himself, he is not bound (without assurance of pardon) to confess it; because no man (as I have shown in the same chapter) can be obliged by covenant to accuse himself.

Again, the consent of a subject to sovereign power, is contained in these words, I authorize, or take upon me, all his actions; in which there is no restriction at all, of his own former natural liberty: for by allowing him to kill me, I am not bound to kill myself when he commands me. It is one thing to say, kill me, or my fellow, if you please; another thing to say, I will kill myself, or my fellow. It followeth therefore, that No man is bound by the words themselves, either to kill himself, or any other man; and consequently, that the obligation a man may sometimes have, upon the command of the sovereign to execute any dangerous, or dishonorable office, depends not on the words of our submission; but on the intention, which is to be understood by the end thereof. When therefore our refusal to obey, frustrates the end for which the sovereignty was ordained; then there is no liberty to refuse: otherwise there is.

Upon this ground, a man that is commanded as a soldier to fight against the enemy, though his sovereign have right enough to punish his refusal with death, may nevertheless in many cases refuse, without injustice; as when he substitutes a sufficient soldier in his place: for in this case he deserts not the service of the commonwealth. And there is allowance to be made for natural timorousness; not only to women (of whom no such dangerous duty is expected), but also to men of feminine courage. When armies fight, there is on one side, or both, a running away; yet when they do it not out of treachery, but fear, they are not esteemed to do it unjustly, but dishonorably. For the same reason, to avoid battle, is not injustice, but cowardice. But he that enrolls himself a soldier, or taketh imprest money, taketh away the excuse of a timorous nature; and is obliged, not only to go to the battle, but also not to run from it, without his captain's leave. And when the defence of the commonwealth, requires at once the help of all that are able to bear arms, every one is obliged; because otherwise the institution of the commonwealth, which they have not the purpose, or courage to preserve, was in vain.

To resist the sword of the commonwealth, in defence of another man, guilty, or innocent, no man hath liberty; because such liberty, takes away from the sovereign, the means of protecting us; and is therefore destructive of the very essence of government. But in case a great many men together, have already resisted the sovereign power unjustly, or committed some capital crime, for which every one of them expects death, whether have they not the liberty then to join together, and assist, and defend one another? Certainly they have: for they but defend their lives, which the guilty man may as well do, as the innocent. There was indeed injustice in the first breach of their duty; their bearing of arms subsequent to it, though it be to maintain what they have done, is no new unjust act. And if it be only to defend their persons, it is not unjust at all. But the offer of pardon taketh from them, to whom it is offered, the plea of self-defence, and maketh their perseverance in assisting, or defending the rest, unlawful.

As for other liberties, they depend on the silence of the law. In cases where the sovereign has prescribed no rule, there the subject hath the liberty to do, or forbear, according to his own discretion. And therefore such liberty is in some places more, and in some less; and in some times more, in other times less, according as they that have the sovereignty shall think most convenient. As for example, there was a time, when in England a man might enter into his own land (and dispossess such as wrongfully possessed it), by force. But in aftertimes, that liberty of forcible entry, was taken away by a statute made (by the king) in parliament. And in some places of the world, men have the liberty of many wives: in other places, such liberty is not allowed.

If a subject have a controversy with his sovereign, of debt, or of right of possession of lands or goods, or concerning any service required at his hands, or concerning any penalty, corporal, or pecuniary, grounded on a precedent law; he hath the same liberty to sue for his right, as if it were against a subject; and before such judges, as are appointed by the sovereign. For seeing the sovereign demands by force of a former law, and not by virtue of his power; he declares thereby, that he requires no more, than shall appear to be due by that law. The suit therefore is not contrary to the will of the sovereign; and consequently the subject hath the liberty to demand the hearing of his cause; and sentence, according to that law. But if he demand, or take any thing by pretence of his power; there lies, in that case, no action of law: for all that is done by him in virtue of his power, is done by the authority of every subject, and consequently, he that brings an action against the sovereign, brings it against himself.

If a monarch, or sovereign assembly, grant a liberty to all, or any of his subjects, which grant standing, he is disabled to provide for their safety, the grant is void; unless he directly renounce, or transfer the sovereignty to another. For in that he might openly (if it had been his will), and in plain terms, have renounced, or transferred it, and did not; it is to be understood it was not his will; but that the grant proceeded from ignorance of the repugnancy between such a liberty and the sovereign power: and therefore the sovereignty is still retained; and consequently all those powers, which are necessary to the exercising thereof; such as are the power of war, and peace, of judicature, of appointing officers, and councilors, of levying money, and the rest named in the 18th chapter.

The obligation of subjects to the sovereign, is understood to last as long, and no longer, than the power lasts, by which he is able to protect them. For the right men have by nature to protect themselves, when none else can protect them, can by no covenant be relinquished. The sovereignty is the soul of the commonwealth; which once departed from the body, the members do no more receive their motion from it. The end of obedience is protection; which, wheresoever a man sees it, either in his own, or in another's sword, nature applies his obedience to it, and his endeavor to maintain it. And though sovereignty, in the intention of them that make it, be immortal; yet is it in its own nature, not only subject to violent death, by foreign war; but also through the ignorance, and passions of men, it hath in it, from the very institution, many seeds of a natural mortality, by intestine discord.

If a subject be taken prisoner in war; or his person, or his means of life be within the guards of the enemy, and hath his life and corporal liberty given him, on condition to be subject to the victor, he hath liberty to accept the condition; and having accepted it, is the subject of him that took him; because he had no other way to preserve himself. The case is the same, if he be detained on the same terms, in a foreign country. But if a man be held in prison, or bonds, or is not trusted with the liberty of his body; he cannot be understood to be bound by covenant to subjection; and therefore may, if he can, make his escape by any means whatsoever.

If a monarch shall relinquish the sovereignty, both for himself, and his heirs; his subjects return to the absolute liberty of nature; because, though nature may declare who are his sons, and who are the nearest of his kin; yet it depends on his own will (as hath been said in the precedent chapter), who shall be his heir. If therefore he will have no heir, there is no sovereignty, nor subjection. The case is the same, if he die without known kindred, and without declaration of his heir. For then there can no heir be known, and consequently no subjection be due.

If the sovereign banish his subject; during the banishment, he is not subject. But he that is sent on a message, or hath leave to travel, is still subject; but it is, by contract between sovereigns, not by virtue of the covenant of subjection. For whosoever enters into another's dominion, is subject to all the laws thereof; unless he have a privilege by the amity of the sovereigns, or by special license.

If a monarch subdued by war, render himself subject to the victor; his subjects are delivered from their former obligation, and become obliged to the victor. But if he be held prisoner, or have not the liberty of his own body; he is not understood to have given away the right of sovereignty; and therefore his subjects are obliged to yield obedience to the magistrates formerly placed, governing not in their own name, but in his. For, his right remaining, the question is only of the administration; that is to say, of the magistrates and officers; which, if he have not means to name, he is supposed to approve those, which he himself had formerly appointed.

Chapter 17

BLAISE PASCAL

Blaise Pascal (1623–1662), scientist, philosopher, and mathematician, was born in Clermont in Auvergne, France, the son of a nobleman who was a government official. A child prodigy, he learned Latin, Greek, mathematics, and science under his father's supervision. As a child he discovered Pythagoras's theorem. At sixteen he published a treatise on conic sections (projective geometry) and at eighteen invented a calculating machine. In 1646 he began work on the problem of the vacuum, which later led to his inventing the barometer. He made discoveries on the nature of probability, which, since his work was used to enhance gambling, troubled his soul.

Suddenly, on the night of November 23, 1654, he had a deeply religious experience. He calls it "The night of fire" and speaks of "joy, joy, joy, tears of joy!" and exhalts the "God of Abraham, God of Isaac, God of Jacob, not the God of the philosophers and scholars." From that time forward he devoted his entire energies to his faith. Eight years earlier he had already joined the Jansenists, a radical Catholic movement, seeking to purify the Church (for example, they proposed three yearly Lents, each consisting of forty days of fasting). Now he devoted his life to carrying out their ideals.

Pascal was struck with the insignificance of human life. Man is a creature of contradictions, a creature occupying a middle position in the universe between the infinitesimal and the infinite. He is an All in relation to Nothing, a Nothing in relation to the All. Man's condition is "inconstancy, boredom, anxiety . . . Man is only a reed, the weakest in nature, but he is a thinking reed."

> What kind of chimera then is man? What novelty, what monster, what chaos, what subject of contradictions, what prodigy? Judge of all things, imbecile worm of the earth, depository of truth, sink of uncertainty and error, glory and scum of the universe.
>
> When I consider the short duration of my life, swallowed up in the eternity before and after, the little space which I fill, and even can see, engulfed in the infinite immensity of space of which I am ignorant, and which knows me not, I am frightened, and am astonished being here rather than there, why now rather than then.

He held that faith was the appropriate mode for apprehending God, announcing that "the heart has reasons of its own which the mind knows nothing of."

> Know, then, proud man, what a paradox you are to yourself. Humble yourself, weak reason. Silence yourself, foolish nature, learn that man infinitely surpasses man, and hear from your master your real state which you do not know . . . Hear God.

Reprinted from Blaise Pascal, *Thoughts,* translated by W. F. Trotter (New York: Collier & Son, 1910).

In the famous section from his *Pensees* (Thoughts) Pascal argues that if we do a cost-benefit analysis of the matter, it turns out that it is eminently reasonable to get ourselves to believe that God exists, regardless of whether we have good evidence for that belief. The argument goes something like this: Regarding the proposition "God exists," reason is neutral. It can neither prove or disprove it. But we must make a choice on the matter, for not to choose for God is in effect to choose against him and lose the possible benefits that belief would bring. Since these benefits of faith promise to be infinite and the loss equally infinite, we must take a gamble on faith.

William James in his *Will to Believe* (see chapter 33) asserts that he is following Pascal in his advocacy of the Will over Reason with regard to faith.

FOR FURTHER READING:

Adams, A. *Grandeur and Illusion.* (Weidenfeld, 1972).
Broome, J. H. *Pascal.* (Arnold, 1965).
Krailsheimer, Alban. *Pascal.* (Hill & Wang, 1980).
Mensard, J. *Pascal, His Life and Works.* (Boivin, 1952).
Pascal, Blaise. *Pensees*, trans. A. J. Krailsheimer. (Penguin, 1966).
Pascal, Blaise. *Thoughts*, trans. W. F. Trotter. (Collier & Son, 1910).
Pascal, Blaise. *The Provincial Letters*, trans. A. J. Krailsheimer. (Penguin, 1967).

Pensees

THE WAGER

Infinite—Nothing.—Our soul is cast into a body, where it finds number, time, dimension. Thereupon it reasons, calls this nature, necessity, and can believe nothing else.

Unity joined to infinity adds nothing to it, no more than one foot to an infinite measure. The finite is annihilated in the presence of the infinite, and becomes a pure nothing. So our spirit before God, so our justice before divine justice. There is not so great disproportion between our justice and that of God, as between unity and infinity.

The justice of God must be vast like His compassion. Now, justice to the outcast is less vast, and ought to offend our feelings less than mercy towards the elect.

We know that there is an infinite, and are ignorant of its nature. As we know it to be false that numbers are finite, it is therefore true that there is an infinity in number. But we do not know what it is. It is false that it is even, it is false that it is odd; for the addition of a unit can make no change in its nature. Yet it is a number, and every number is odd or even (this is certainly true of every finite number). So we may well know that there is a God without knowing what He is. Is there not one substantial truth, seeing there are so many things which are not the truth itself?

We know then the existence and nature of the finite, because we also are finite and have extension. We know the existence of the infinite, and are ignorant of its nature, because it has extension like us, but not limits like us. But we know neither the existence nor the nature of God, because He has neither extension nor limits.

But by faith we know His existence; in glory we shall know His nature. Now, I have already shown that we may well know the existence of a thing, without knowing its nature.

Let us now speak according to natural lights.

If there is a God, He is infinitely incomprehensible, since, having neither parts nor limits, He has no affinity to us. We are then incapable of knowing either what He is or if He is. This being so, who will dare to undertake the decision of the question? Not we, who have no affinity to Him.

Who then will blame Christians for not being able to give a reason for their belief, since they profess a religion for which they cannot give a reason? They declare, in expounding it to the world, that it is a foolishness, *stultitiam*; and then you complain that they do not prove it! If they proved it, they would not keep their words; it is in lacking proofs, that they are not lacking in sense. "Yes, but although this excuses those who offer it as such, and take away from them the blame of putting it forward without reason, it does not excuse those who receive it." Let us then examine this point, and say, "God is, or He is not." But to which side shall we incline? Reason can decide nothing here. There is an infinite chaos which separates us. A game is being played at the extremity of this infinite distance where heads or tails will turn up. What will you wager? According to reason, you can do neither the one thing nor the other; according to reason, you can defend neither of the propositions.

Do not then reprove for error those who have made a choice; for you know nothing about it. "No, but I blame them for having made, not this choice, but a choice; for again both he who chooses heads and he who chooses tails are equally at fault, they are both in the wrong. The true course is not to wager at all."

—Yes; but you must wager. It is not optional. You are embarked. Which will you choose then; Let us see. Since you must choose, let us see which interests you least. You have two things to lose, the true and the good; and two things to stake, your reason and your will, your knowledge and your happiness; and your nature has two things to shun, error and misery. Your reason is no more shocked in choosing one rather than the other, since you must of necessity choose. This is one point settled. But your happiness? Let us weigh the gain and the loss in wagering that God is. Let us estimate these two chances. If you gain, you gain all; if you lose, you lose nothing. Wager then without hesitation that He is.—"That is very fine. Yes, I must wager; but I may perhaps wager too much."—Let us see. Since there is an equal risk of gain and of loss, if you had only to gain two lives, instead of one, you might still wager. But if there were three lives to gain, you would have to play (since you are under the necessity of playing), and you would be imprudent, when you are forced to play, not to chance your life to gain three at a game where there is an equal risk of loss and gain. But there is an eternity of life and happiness. And this being so, if there were an infinity of chances, of which one only would be for you, you would still be right in wagering one to win two, and you would act stupidly, being obliged to play, by refusing to stake one life against three at a game in which you had an infinity of an infinitely happy life to gain. But there is here an infinity of an infinitely happy life to gain, a chance of gain against a finite number of chances of loss, and what you stake is finite. It is all divided; wherever the infinite is and there is not an infinity of chances of loss against that of gain, there is no time to hesitate, you must give all. And thus, when one is forced to play, he must renounce reason to preserve his life, rather than risk it for infinite gain, as likely to happen as the loss of nothingness.

For it is no use to say it is uncertain if we will gain, and it is certain that we risk, and that the infinite distance between the *certainty* of what is staked and the *uncertainty* of what will be gained, equals the finite good which is certainly staked against the uncertain infinite. It is not so, as every player stakes a certainty to gain an uncertainty, and yet he stakes a finite certainty to gain a finite uncertainty, without transgressing against reason. There is not an infinite distance between the certainty staked and the uncertainty of the gain; that is untrue. In truth, there is an infinity between the certainty of gain and the certainty of loss. But the uncertainty of the gain is proportioned to the certainty of the stake according to the proportion of the chances of gain and loss. Hence it comes that, if there are as many risks on one side as on the other, the course is to play even; and then the certainty of the stake is equal of the uncertainty of the gain, so far is it from the fact that there is an infinite distance between them. And so our proposition is of infinite force, when there is the finite to stake in a game where there are equal risks of gain and of loss, and the infinite to gain. This is demonstrable; and if men are capable of any truths, this is one.

"I confess it, I admit it. But still is there no means of seeing the faces of the cards?"—Yes, Scripture and the rest, &c.—"Yes, but I have my hands tied and my mouth closed; I am forced to wager, and am not free. I am not released, and am so made that I cannot believe. What then would you have me do?"

"True. But at least learn your inability to believe,

since reason brings you to this, and yet you cannot believe. Endeavour then to convince yourself, not by increase of proofs of God, but by the abatement of your passions. You would like to attain faith, and do not know the way; you would like to cure yourself of unbelief, and ask the remedy for it. Learn of those who have been bound like you, and who now stake all their possessions. These are people who know the way which you would follow, and who are cured of an ill of which you would be cured. Follow the way by which they began; by acting as if they believe, taking the holy water, having masses said, &c. Even this will naturally make you believe, and deaden your acuteness.—"But this is what I am afraid of."—And why? What have you to lose?

But to show you that this leads you there, it is this which will lessen the passions, which are your stumbling-blocks.

The end of this discourse.—Now what harm will befall you in taking this side? You will be faithful, honest, humble, grateful, generous, a sincere friend, truthful. Certainly you will not have those poisonous pleasures, glory and luxury; but will you not have others? I will tell you that you will thereby gain in this life, and that, at each step you take on this road, you will see so great certainty of gain, so much nothingness in what you risk, that you will at last recognize that you have wagered for something certain and infinite, for which you have given nothing.

"Ah! This discourse transports me, charms me," &c.

If this discourse pleases you and seems impressive, know that it is made by a man who has knelt, both before and after it, in prayer to that Being, infinite and without parts, before whom he lays all he has, for you also to lay before Him all you have for your own good and for His glory, so that strength may be given to lowliness.

Chapter 18

Baruch Spinoza

Baruch Spinoza (1632–1677) was born in Amsterdam, Holland, of a prosperous merchant family, Jews who had fled Portugal because of religious persecution. After an education in the Jewish tradition (the Hebrew Bible, The Talmud and Jewish codes, the works of Maimonides), as well as in Latin, Spinoza showed an inclination toward independent and heretical thinking. He fell into disfavor with the synagogue authorities for arguing that there is nothing in the Hebrew Bible to support the views that God has no body, that there are angels, or that the soul is immortal. He also maintained that Moses, alleged author of the first five books, was no guide to science, nor a final guide to theology. The authorities, after trying in vain to silence him with bribes and threats, excommunicated him in July 1656. Befriended by Christians, Spinoza left Amsterdam and eventually settled in the town of Voorburg and later in The Hague, where he worked as a lens grinder. During this period of his life he encountered and was deeply influenced by the philosophies of Descartes and Hobbes.

In his major work, Spinoza sought to bring to philosophy the certainty of mathematical reasoning by beginning with absolutely certain truths and reasoning carefully and explicitly from them. Like Euclid's *Elements*, each of its five parts opens with definitions, axioms, and postulates, and is followed by theorems proved from them. Informal remarks elaborating on the implications of the theorems follow in Scholia (Notes) and Appendices.

Spinoza published only two works during his lifetime, the *Principles of Descartes's Philosophy* and the *Theologico-Political Treatise*, but his genius was known to scholars in all parts of Europe. He was also respected as a man of unimpeachable character. On February 20, 1677, he died of pulmonary disease aggravated by inhaling glass dust from his lens grinding. He was buried in the New Church on the Spuy. The *Ethic* was published—at some risk—by Spinoza's friends a year after his death. A sizable selection from it is set forth below.

Spinoza concurred with Hobbes and Descartes in holding that all matter is governed by deterministic laws, while rejecting (as did Hobbes) dualism, the notion of a soul which is somehow a different kind of reality from matter. Most significantly, he rejected the common Judeo-Christian notion of God as creating and ruling the material world from outside—"transitive cause." Rather, he maintained, God is the *immanent* cause of all things—the world's inherent energy, which he also designated as Substance. In Part 1 (here reprinted complete) Spinoza demonstrates that, rather than the two ultimate realities of Descartes, thought and extension, only one substance exists. This is God or Nature, which exists *necessarily*, not caused by anything prior to itself. Thought and extension are real, but not really distinct: they are two of the infinite *attributes* of God. All finite things are *modes* of God, not separate substances but depending on the one substance, somewhat as a wave depends on the ocean. Spinoza is thus a pantheist ("all-God-ist"). God, however, is not a person. Nor is He (or "It") providential; He *is* the deterministic way things go; free will—if it implies the possibility of altering the natural order—is an illusion. While we should love God, as the perfect (complete) being, God cannot love us or providentially take an interest in our lives.

In Part 2, "Of the Nature and Origin of the Mind," Spinoza demonstrates that the *mental* and the *physical* (thought and extension) are "one and the same, expressed in two ways": mind and body differ only conceptually. Parts 3 and 4 (not included in this work) deal with the nature of human affects (emotions, passions) and "human bondage" to them. Finally, Part 5 (part of which is reprinted below) deals with the power of the intellect to free us from this bondage. Here Spinoza argues that just as God is free from passions, we should be too (to the limited extent that this is possible for us); when we are, we may experience the "intellectual love of God," which, "manifested through the human mind, considered under the form of eternity," is "part of the infinite love with which God loves Himself," and is not "destroyed with the body."

FOR FURTHER READING

Allison, Henry, *Benedict de Spinoza*. (Yale University Press, 1987).

Bennett, Jonathan. *A Study of Spinoza's Ethics*. (Hackett, 1984).

Curley, E. M. *Spinoza's Metaphysics: An Essay in Interpretation*. (Harvard University Press, 1969).

Curley, E. M. *Behind the Geometrical Method: A Reading of Spinoza's Ethics*. (Princeton University Press, 1988).

Donagan, Alan. *Spinoza*. (University of Chicago, 1989).

Kashhap, Paul, ed. *Studies in Spinoza*. (University of California Press, 1972).

Hampshire, Stuart. *Spinoza*. (Penguin Books, 1952).

Mandelbaum, Maurice and Eugene Freeman, eds. *Spinoza: Essays in Interpretation*. (Open Court Press, 1975).

Matson, Wallace. "Spinoza's Theory of Mind," *The Monist* vol 55 (1971). Reprinted in Mandelbaum & Freeman.

Wolfson, Harry. *The Philosophy of Spinoza: Unfolding the Latent Processes of His Reasoning*. (Schocken, 1969).

Ethic

PART 1 OF GOD

Definitions

I. By cause of itself, I understand that, whose essence involves existence; or that, whose nature cannot be conceived unless existing.

II. That thing is called finite in its own kind which can be limited by another thing of the same nature. For example, a body is called finite, because we always conceive another which is greater. So a thought is limited by another thought; but a body is not limited by a thought, nor a thought by a body.

III. By substance, I understand that which is in itself and is conceived through itself; in other words, that, the conception of which does not need the conception of another thing from which it must be formed.

IV. By attribute, I understand that which the intellect perceives of substance, as if constituting its essence.

V. By mode, I understand the affections of substance, or that which is in another thing through which also it is conceived.

VI. By God, I understand Being absolutely infinite, that is to say, substance consisting of infinite

Reprinted by permission from Spinoza, *Ethics*, selected with an Introduction by Wallace I. Matson.

attributes, each one of which expresses eternal and infinite essence.

Explanation I say absolutely infinite but not infinite in its own kind; for of whatever is infinite only in its kind, we can deny infinite attributes; but to the essence of that which is absolutely infinite pertains whatever expresses essence and involves no negation.

VII. That thing is called free which exists from the necessity of its own nature alone, and is determined to action by itself alone. That thing, on the other hand, is called necessary, or rather compelled, which by another is determined to existence and action in a fixed and prescribed manner.

VIII. By eternity, I understand existence itself, so far as it is conceived necessarily to follow from the definition alone of the eternal thing.

Explanation For such existence, like the essence of the thing, is conceived as an eternal truth. It cannot therefore be explained by duration or time, even if the duration be conceived without beginning or end.

Axioms

I. Everything which is, is either in itself or in another.

II. That which cannot be conceived through another must be conceived through itself.

III. From a given determinate cause an effect necessarily follows; and, on the other hand, if no determinate cause be given, it is impossible that an effect can follow.

IV. The knowledge of an effect depends upon and involves the knowledge of the cause.

V. Those things which have nothing mutually in common with one another cannot through one another can be mutually understood, that is to say, the conception of the one does not involve the conception of the other.

VI. A true idea must agree with that of which it is the idea (*cum suo ideato*).

VII. The essence of that thing which can be conceived as not existing does not involve existence.

Prop. I.—Substance is by its nature prior to its affections

Demonst.—This is evident from Defs. 3 and 5.

Prop. II.—Two substances having different attributes have nothing in common with one another

Demonst.—This is also evident from Def. 3. For each substance must be in itself and must be conceived through itself, that is to say, the conception of one does not involve the conception of the other.—Q.E.D.

Prop. III.—If two things have nothing in common with one another, one cannot be the cause of the other

Demonst.—If they have nothing mutually in common with one another, they cannot (Ax. 5) through one another be mutually understood, and therefore (Ax. 4) one cannot be the cause of the other.—Q.E.D.

Prop. IV.—Two or more distinct things are distinguished from another, either by the difference of the attributes of the substances, or by the difference of their affections

Demonst.—Everything which is, is either in itself or in another (Ax. 1), that is to say (Defs. 3 and 5), outside the intellect there is nothing but substances and their affections. There is nothing therefore outside the intellect by which a number of things can be distinguished one from another, but substances or (which is the same thing by Def. 4) their attributes and their affections.—Q.E.D.

Prop. V.—In nature there cannot be two or more substances of the same nature or attribute

Demonst.—If there were two or more distinct substances, they must be distinguished one from the other by difference of attributes or difference of affections (Prop. 4). If they are distinguished only by difference of attributes, it will be granted that there is but one substance of the same attribute. But if they are distinguished by difference of affections, since substance is prior by nature to its affections (Prop. 1), the affections therefore being placed on one side, and the substance being considered in itself, or, in other words (Def. 3 and Ax. 6), truly considered, it cannot be conceived as distinguished from another substance, that is to say (Prop. 4), there cannot be two or more substances, but only one possessing the same nature or attribute.—Q.E.D.

Prop. VI.—One substance cannot be produced by another substance

Demonst.—There cannot in nature be two substances of the same attribute (Prop. 5), that is to say (Prop. 2), two which have anything in common with one another. And therefore (Prop. 2) one cannot be the cause of the other, that is to say, one cannot be produced by the other.—Q.E.D.

Corol.—Hence it follows that there is nothing by which substance can be produced, for in nature there is nothing but substances and their affections (as is evident from Ax. 1 and Defs. 3 and 5). But substance cannot be produced by substance (Prop. 6). Therefore absolutely there is nothing by which substance can be produced.—Q.E.D.

Another Demonst.—This corollary is demonstrated more easily by the *reductio ad absurdum.* For if there were anything by which substance could be produced, the knowledge of substance would be dependent upon the knowledge of its cause (Ax. 4), and therefore (Def. 3) it would not be substance.

Prop. VII.—It pertains to the nature of substance to exist

Demonst.—There is nothing by which substance can be produced (Corol. Prop. 6). It will therefore be the cause of itself, that is to say (Def. 1), its essence necessarily involves existence, or in other words it pertains to its nature to exist.—Q.E.D.

Prop. VIII.—Every substance is necessarily infinite

Demonst.—Substance which has only one attribute cannot exist except as one substance (Prop. 5), and to the nature of this one substance it pertains to exist (Prop. 7). It must therefore from its nature exist as finite or infinite. But it cannot exist as finite substance, for (Def. 2) it must (if finite) be limited by another substance of the same nature, which also must necessarily exist (Prop. 7), and therefore there would be two substances of the same attribute, which is absurd (Prop. 5). It exists therefore as infinite substance.—Q.E.D.

Schol. 1.—Since finiteness is in truth partly negation, and infinitude absolute affirmation of existence of some kind, it follows from Prop. 7 alone that all substance must be infinite.

Schol 2.—I fully expect that those who judge things confusedly, and who have not been accustomed to cognise things through their first causes, will find it difficult to comprehend the demonstration of the 7th Proposition, since they do not distinguish between the modifications of substances and substances themselves, and are ignorant of the manner in which things are produced. Hence it comes to pass that they erroneously ascribe to substances a beginning like that which they see belongs to natural things; for those who are ignorant of the true causes of things confound every thing, and without any mental repugnance represent trees speaking like men, or imagine that men are made out of stones as well as begotten from seed, and that all forms can be changed the one into the other. So also those who confound human nature with the divine, readily attribute to God human affects, especially so long as they are ignorant of the manner in which affects are produced in the mind. But if men would attend to the nature of substance, they could not entertain a single doubt of the truth of Proposition 7; indeed this proposition would be considered by all to be axiomatic, and reckoned amongst common notions. For by "substance" would be understood that which is in itself and is conceived through itself, or, in other words, that, the knowledge of which does not need the knowledge of another thing. But by "modifications" would be understood those things which are in another thing—those things, the conception of which is formed from the conception of the thing in which they are. Hence, we can have true ideas of non-existent modifications, since although they may not actually exist outside the intellect, their essence nevertheless is so comprehended in something else, that they may be conceived through it. But the truth of substances is not outside the intellect unless in the substances themselves, because they are conceived through themselves. If any one, therefore, were to say that he possessed a clear and distinct, that is to say, a true idea of substance, and that he nevertheless doubted whether such a substance exists, he would forsooth be in the same position as if he were to say that he had a true idea and nevertheless doubted whether or not it was false (as is evident to any one who pays a little attention). Similarly if any one were to affirm that substance is created, he would affirm at the same time that a false idea had become true, and this is a greater absurdity than can be conceived. It is therefore necessary to admit that the existence of substance, like its essence, is an eternal truth. Hence a demonstration (which I have thought worth while to append) by a different method is possible, showing that there are not two substances possessing the same nature. But in order to prove this methodically it is to be noted: 1. That the true definition of any one thing neither involves nor expresses anything except the nature of the thing defined. From which it follows, 2. That a definition does not involve or express any certain number of individuals, since it expresses nothing but the nature of the thing defined. For example, the definition of a triangle expresses nothing but the simple nature of a triangle, and not any certain number of triangles. 3. It is to be observed that of every existing thing there is some certain cause by reason of which it exists. 4. Finally, it is to be observed that this cause, by reason of which a thing exists, must either be contained in the nature itself and definition of the existing thing (simply because it pertains to the nature of the thing to exist), or it must exist outside the thing. This being granted, it follows that if a certain number of individuals exist in nature, there must necessarily be a cause why those individuals, and neither more nor fewer, exist. If, for example, there are twenty men in existence (whom, for the sake of greater clearness, I suppose existing at the same time, and that no others existed before them), it will not be sufficient, in order that we may give a reason why twenty men exist, to give a cause for human nature generally; but it will be necessary, in addition, to give a reason why neither more nor fewer than twenty exist, since, as we have already observed under the third head, there must necessarily be a cause why each exists. But this cause (as we have shown under the second and third heads) cannot be contained in human nature itself, since the true definition of a man does not involve the number twenty, and therefore (by the fourth head) the cause why these twenty men exist, and consequently the cause why each exists, must necessarily lie outside each one; and therefore we must conclude generally that whenever it is possible for several individuals of the same nature to exist, there must necessarily be an external cause for their existence.

Since now it pertains to the nature of substance to exist (as we have shown in this scholium), its definition must involve necessary existence, and consequently from its definition alone its existence must be concluded. But from its definition (as we have already shown under the second and third heads) the existence of more substances than one cannot be deduced. It follows, therefore, from this definition necessarily that there cannot be two substances possessing the same nature.

Prop. IX.—The more reality or being a thing possesses, the more attributes belong to it

Demonst.—This is evident from Def. 4.

Prop. X.—Each attribute of a substance must be conceived through itself

Demonst.—For an attribute is that which the intellect perceives of substance, as if constituting its essence (Def. 4), and therefore (Def. 3) it must be conceived through itself.—Q.E.D.

Schol.—From this it is apparent that although two attributes may be conceived as really distinct—that is to say, one without the assistance of the other—we cannot nevertheless thence conclude that they constitute two beings or two different substances; for this is the nature of substances, that each of its attributes is conceived through itself, since all the attributes which substance possesses were always in it together, nor could one be produced by another; but each expresses the reality or being of substance. It is very far from being absurd, therefore, to ascribe to one substance a number of attributes, since nothing in nature is clearer than that each being must be conceived under some attribute, and the more reality or being it has, the more attributes it possesses expressing necessity or eternity and infinity. Nothing consequently is clearer than that Being absolutely infinite is necessarily defined, as we have shown (Def. 6), as Being which consists of infinite attributes, each one of which expresses a certain essence, eternal and infinite. But if any one now asks by what sign, therefore, we may distinguish between substances, let him read the following propositions, which show that in nature only one substance exists, and that it is absolutely infinite. For this reason that sign would be sought for in vain.

Prop. XI.—God, or substance consisting of infinite attributes, each one of which expresses eternal and infinite essence, necessarily exists

Demonst.—If this be denied, conceive, if it be possible, that God does not exist. Then it follows (Ax. 7) that His essence does not involve existence. But this (Prop. 7) is absurd. Therefore God necessarily exists.—Q.E.D.

Another proof.—For the existence of non-existence of everything there must be a reason or cause.

For example, if a triangle exists, there must be a reason or cause why it exists; and if it does not exist, there must be a reason or cause which hinders its existence or which negates it. But this reason or cause must either be contained in the nature of the thing or lie outside it. For example, the nature of the thing itself shows the reason why a square circle does not exist, the reason being that a square circle involves a contradiction. And the reason, on the other hand, why substance exists follows from its nature alone, which involves existence (see Prop. 7). But the reason why a circle or triangle exists or does not exist is not drawn from their nature, but from the order of corporeal nature generally; for from that it must follow, either that a triangle necessarily exists, or that it is impossible for it to exist. But this is self-evident. Therefore it follows that if there be no cause nor reason which hinders a thing from existing, it exists necessarily. If, therefore, there be no reason nor cause which hinders God from existing, or which negates His existence, we must conclude absolutely that He necessarily exists. But if there be such a reason or cause, it must be either in the nature itself of God or must lie outside it, that is to say, in another substance of another nature. For if the reason lay in a substance of the same nature, the existence of God would be by this very fact admitted. But substance possessing another nature could have nothing in common with God (Prop. 2), and therefore could not give Him existence nor negate it. Since, therefore, the reason or cause which could negate the divine existence cannot be outside the divine nature, it will necessarily, supposing that the divine nature does not exist, be in His Nature itself, which would therefore involve a contradiction. But to affirm this of the Being absolutely infinite and consummately perfect is absurd. Therefore neither in God nor outside God is there any cause or reason which can negate His existence, and therefore God necessarily exists.—Q.E.D.

Another proof.—Inability to exist is impotence, and, on the other hand, ability to exist is power, as is self-evident. If, therefore, there is nothing which necessarily exists excepting things finite, it follows that things finite are more powerful than the absolutely infinite Being, and this (as is self-evident) is absurd; therefore either nothing exists or Being absolutely infinite also necessarily exists. But we ourselves exist, either in ourselves or in something else which necessarily exists (Ax. 1 and Prop. 7). Therefore the Being absolutely infinite, that is to say (Def. 6), God, necessarily exists.—Q.E.D.

Schol.—In this last demonstration I wished to prove the existence of God *a posteriori*, in order that the demonstration might be the more easily understood, and not because the existence of God does not follow *a priori* from the same grounds. For since ability to exist is power, it follows that the more reality belongs to the nature of anything, the greater is the power for existence it derives from itself; and it also follows, therefore, that the Being absolutely infinite, or God, has from Himself an absolutely infinite power of existence, and that He therefore necessarily exists. Many persons, nevertheless, will perhaps not be able easily to see the force of this demonstration, because they have been accustomed to contemplate those things alone which flow from external causes, and they see also that those things which are quickly produced from these causes, that is to say, which easily exist, easily perish, whilst, on the other hand, they adjudge those things to be more difficult to produce, that is to say, not so easy to bring into existence, to which they conceive more properties pertain. In order that these prejudices may be removed, I do not need here to show in what respect this saying, "What is quickly made quickly perishes," is true, nor to inquire whether, looking at the whole of nature, all things are or are not equally easy. But this only it will be sufficient for me to observe, that I do not speak of things which are produced by external causes, but that I speak of substances alone which (Prop. 6) can be produced by no external cause. For whatever perfection or reality those things may have which are produced by external causes, whether they consist of many parts or of few, they owe it all to the virtue of an external cause, and therefore their existence springs from the perfection of an external cause alone and not from their own. On the other hand, whatever perfection substance has is due to no external cause. Therefore its existence must follow from its nature alone, and is therefore nothing else than its essence. Perfection consequently does not prevent the existence of a thing, but establishes it; imperfection, on the other hand, prevents existence, and so of no existence can we be more sure than of the existence of the Being absolutely infinite or perfect, that is to say, God. For since His essence shuts out all imperfection and involves absolute perfection, for this very reason all cause of doubt concerning His existence is taken away, and the highest certainty concerning it is given,—a truth which I trust will be evident to any one who bestows only moderate attention.

Prop. XII.—No attribute of substance can be truly conceived from which it follows that substance can be divided

Demonst. For the parts into which substance thus conceived would be divided will or will not retain the nature of substance. If they retain it, then (Prop. 8) each part will be infinite, and (Prop. 6) the cause of itself, and will consist of an attribute differing from that of any other part (Prop. 5), so that from one substance more substances could be formed, which (Prop. 6) is absurd. Moreover the parts (Prop. 2) would have nothing in common with their whole, and the whole (Def. 4 and Prop. 10) could be, and could be conceived without its parts, which no one will doubt to be an absurdity. But if the second case be supposed, namely, that the parts will not retain the nature of substance, then, since the whole substance might be divided into equal parts, it would lose the nature of substance and cease to be, which (Prop. 7) is absurd.

Prop. XIII.—Substance absolutely infinite is indivisible

Demonst.—For if it were divisible, the parts into which it would be divided will or will not retain the nature of substance absolutely infinite. If they retain it, there will be a plurality of substances possessing the same nature, which (Prop. 5) is absurd. If the second case be supposed, then (as above), substance absolutely infinite can cease to be, which (Prop. 11) is also absurd.

Corol.—Hence it follows that no substance, and consequently no bodily substance in so far as it is substance, is divisible.

Schol.—That substance is indivisible is more easily to be understood from this consideration alone, that the nature of substance cannot be conceived unless as infinite, and that by a part of substance nothing else can be understood than finite substance, which (Prop. 8) involves a manifest contradiction.

Prop. XIV.—Besides God, no substance can be nor can be conceived

Demonst.—Since God is Being absolutely infinite, of whom no attribute can be denied which expresses the essence of substance (Def. 6), and since He necessarily exists (Prop. 11), it follows that if there were any substance besides God, it would have to be explained by some attribute of God, and thus two substances would exist possessing the same attribute, which (Prop. 5) is absurd; and therefore there cannot be any substance excepting God, and consequently none other can be conceived. For if any other could be conceived, it would necessarily be conceived as existing, and this (by the first part of this demonstration) is absurd. Therefore besides God no substance can be, nor can be conceived.—Q.E.D.

Corol. 1.—Hence it follows with the greatest clearness, firstly, that God is one, that is to say (Def. 6), in nature there is but one substance, and it is absolutely infinite, as (Schol. Prop. 10) we have already intimated.

Corol. 2.—It follows, secondly, that the thing extended (*rem extensam*) and the thing thinking (*rem cogitantem*) are either attributes of God or (Ax. 1) affections of the attributes of God.

Prop. XV.—Whatever is, is in God, and nothing can either be or be conceived without God

Demonst.—Besides God there is no substance, nor can any be conceived (Prop. 14), that is to say (Def. 3), nothing which is in itself and is conceived through itself. But modes (Def. 5) can neither be nor be conceived without substance; therefore in the divine nature only can they be, and through it alone can they be conceived. But besides substances and modes nothing is assumed (Ax. 1). Therefore nothing can be or be conceived without God.—Q.E.D.

Schol.—There are those who imagine God to be like a man, composed of body and soul and subject to passions; but it is clear enough from what has already been demonstrated how far off men who believe this are from the true knowledge of God. But this I dismiss, for all men who have in any way looked into the divine nature deny that God is corporeal. That He cannot be so they conclusively prove by showing that by "body" we understand a certain quantity possessing length, breadth, and depth, limited by some fixed form; and that to attribute these to God, a being absolutely infinite, is the greatest absurdity. But yet at the same time, from other arguments by which they endeavour to confirm their proof, they clearly show that they remove altogether from the divine nature substance itself corporeal or extended, affirming that it was created by God. By what divine power, however, it could have been created they are altogether ignorant, so that it is clear they do not understand what they themselves say. But I have demonstrated, at least in my own opinion, with sufficient clearness (see Corol. Prop. 6 and Schol. 2, Prop. 8), that no substance can be produced or created by another being (*ab alio*). Moreover (Prop. 14), we have shown that besides God no substance can be nor can be conceived; and hence we have concluded that extended substance is one of the infinite attributes of God. But for the sake of a fuller explanation, I will refute my adversaries' arguments, which, taken altogether, come to this. First, that corporeal substance, in so far as it is substance, consists, as they suppose, of parts, and therefore they deny that it can be infinite, and consequently that it can pertain to God. This they illustrate by many ex-

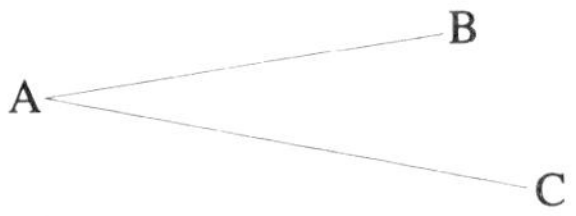

amples, one or two of which I will adduce. If corporeal substance, they say, be infinite, let us conceive it to be divided into two parts; each part, therefore, will be either finite or infinite. If each part be finite, then the infinite is composed of two finite parts, which is absurd. If each part be infinite, there is then an infinite twice as great as another infinite, which is also absurd. Again, if finite quantity be measured by equal parts of a foot each, it must contain an infinite number of such parts, and similarly if it be measured by equal parts of an inch each; and therefore one infinite number will be twelve times greater than another infinite number. Lastly, if from one point of any infinite quantity it be imagined that two lines, AB, AC, which at first are at a certain and determinate distance from one another, be infinitely extended, it is plain that the distance between B and C will be continually increased, and at length from being determinate will be indeterminable. Since therefore these absurdities follow, as they think, from supposing quantity to be infinite, they conclude that corporeal substance must be finite, and consequently cannot pertain to the essence of God. A second argument is assumed from the absolute perfection of God. For God, they say, since He is a being absolutely perfect, cannot suffer; but corporeal substance, since it is divisible, can suffer: it follows, therefore, that it does not pertain to God's essence. These are the arguments which I find in authors, by which they endeavour to show that corporeal substance is unworthy of the divine nature, and cannot pertain to it. But any one who will properly attend will discover that I have already answered these arguments, since the sole foundation of them is the supposition that bodily substance consists of parts, a supposition which (Prop. 12 and Corol. Prop. 13) I have shown to be absurd. Moreover, if any one will rightly consider the matter, he will see that all these absurdities (supposing that they are all absurdities, a point which I will now take for granted), from which these authors attempt to draw the conclusion that substance extended is finite, do not by any means follow from the supposition that quantity is infinite, but from the supposition that infinite quantity is measurable, and that it is made up of finite parts. Therefore, from the absurdities to which this leads nothing can be concluded, excepting that infinite quantity is not measurable, and that it cannot be composed of finite parts. But this is what we have already demonstrated (Prop. 12, &c.), and the shaft therefore which is aimed at us turns against those who cast it. If, therefore, from these absurdities any one should attempt to conclude that substance extended must be finite, he would, forsooth, be in the position of the man who supposes a circle to have the properties of a square, and then concludes that it has no centre, such that all the lines drawn from it to the circumference are equal. For corporeal substance, which cannot be conceived except as infinite, one and indivisible (Props. 8, 5, and 12), is conceived by those against whom I argue to be composed of finite parts, and to be multiplex and divisible, in order that they may prove it finite. Just in the same way others, after they have imagined a line to consist of points, know how to discover many arguments, by which they show that a line cannot be divided *ad infinitum*; and indeed it is not less absurd to suppose that corporeal substance is composed of bodies or parts than to suppose that a body is composed of surfaces, surfaces of lines, and that lines, finally, are composed of points. Every one who knows that clear reason is infallible ought to admit this, and especially those who deny that a vacuum can exist. For if corporeal substance could be so divided that its parts could be really distinct, why could not one part be annihilated, the rest remaining, as before, connected with one another? And why must all be so fitted together that there can be no vacuum? For of things which are really distinct the one from the other, one can be and remain in its own position without the other. Since, therefore, it is supposed that there is no vacuum in nature (about which I will speak at another time), but that all the parts must be united, so that no vacuum can exist, it follows that they cannot be really separated; that is to say, that corporeal substance, in so far as it is substance, cannot be divided. If, nevertheless, any one should now ask why there is a natural tendency to consider quantity as capable of division, I reply that quantity is conceived by us in two ways: either abstractly or superficially; that is to say, as we imagine it, or else as substance, in which way it is conceived by the intellect alone. If, therefore, we regard quantity (as we do very often and easily) as it exists in the imagination, we find it to be finite, divisible, and composed of parts; but if we regard it as it exists in the intellect, and conceive it in so far as it is substance, which is very difficult, then, as we have already sufficiently demonstrated, we find it to be infinite, one, and indivisible. This will be plain enough to all who know how to distinguish between the imagination and the intellect, and more especially if we remember that matter is everywhere the same, and that, except in so far as we regard it as affected in different ways, parts are not distinguished in it; that is to say, they are distinguished with regard to mode, but not with regard to reality. For example, we conceive water as being divided, in so far as it is water, and that its parts are separated from one another; but in so far as it is corporeal substance we cannot thus conceive it, for as such it is neither separated nor divided. Moreover, water, in so far as it is water, is originated and destroyed; but in so far as it is substance, it is neither originated nor destroyed. By this reasoning I think that I have also answered the second argument, since that too is based upon the assumption that matter, considered as substance, is divisible and composed of parts. And even if what I have urged were not true, I do not know why matter should be unworthy of the divine nature, since (Prop. 14) outside God no substance can exist from which the divine nature could suffer. All things, I say, are in God, and everything which takes place takes place by the laws alone of the infinite nature of God, and follows (as I shall presently show) from the necessity of His essence. Therefore in no way whatever can it be asserted that God suffers from anything, or that substance extended, even if it be supposed divisible, is unworthy of the divine nature, provided only it be allowed that it is eternal and infinite. But enough on this point for the present.

Prop. XVI.—From the necessity of the divine nature infinite numbers of things in infinite ways (that is to say, all things which can be conceived by the infinite intellect) must follow

Demonst.—This proposition must be plain to every one who considers that from the given definition of anything a number of properties necessarily following from it (that is to say, following from the essence of the thing itself) are inferred by the intellect, and just in proportion as the definition of the thing expresses a greater reality, that is to say, just in proportion as the essence of the thing defined involves a greater reality, will more properties be inferred. But the divine nature possesses absolutely infinite attributes (Def. 6), each one of which expresses infinite essence in its own kind (*in suo genere*), and therefore, from the necessity of the divine nature, infinite numbers of things in infinite ways (that is to say, all things which can be conceived by the infinite intellect) must necessarily follow.—Q.E.D.

Corol. 1.—Hence it follows that God is the efficient cause of all things which can fall under the infinite intellect.

Corol. 2.—It follows, secondly, that God is cause through Himself, and not through that which is contingent (*per accidens*).

Corol. 3.—It follows, thirdly, that God is absolutely the first cause.

Prop. XVII.—God acts from the laws of His own nature only, and is compelled by no one

Demonst.—We have just shown (Prop. 16) that from the necessity, or (which is the same thing) from the laws only of the divine nature, infinite numbers of things absolutely follow; and we have demonstrated (Prop. 15) that nothing can be, nor can be conceived, without God, but that all things are in God. Therefore, outside Himself, there can be nothing by which He may be determined or compelled to act; and therefore He acts from the laws of His own nature only, and is compelled by no one.—Q.E.D.

Corol. 1.—Hence it follows, firstly, that there is no cause, either external to God or within Him, which can excite Him to act except the perfection of His own nature.

Corol. 2.—It follows, secondly, that God alone is a free cause; for God alone exists from the necessity alone of His own nature (Prop. 11, and Corol. 1, Prop. 14), and acts from the necessity alone of His own nature (Prop. 17). Therefore (Def. 7) He alone is a free cause.—Q.E.D.

Schol. There are some who think that God is a free cause because He can, as they think, bring about that those things which we have said follow from His nature—that is to say, those things which are in His power—should not be, or should not be produced by Him. But this is simply saying that God could bring about that it should not follow from the nature of a triangle that its three angles should be equal to two right angles, or that from a given cause an effect should not follow, which is absurd. But I shall show farther on, without the help of this proposition, that neither intellect nor will pertain to the nature of God.

I know, indeed, that there are many who think themselves able to demonstrate that intellect of the highest order and freedom of will both pertain to the nature of God, for they say that they know nothing more perfect which they can attribute to Him than that which is the chief perfection in ourselves. But although they conceive God as actually possessing the highest intellect, they nevertheless do not believe that He can bring about that all those things should exist which are actually in His intellect, for they think that by such a supposition they would destroy His power. If He had treated, they say, all things which are in His intellect, He could have created nothing more, and this, they believe, does not accord with God's omnipotence so then they prefer to consider God as indifferent to all things, and creating nothing excepting that which He has decreed to create by a certain absolute will. But I think that I have shown with sufficient clearness (Prop. 16) that from the supreme power of God, or from His infinite nature, infinite things in infinite ways, that is to say, all things, have necessarily flowed, or continually follow by the same necessity, in the same way as it follows from the nature of a triangle, from eternity and to eternity, that its three angles are equal to two right angles. The omnipotence of God has therefore been actual from eternity, and in the same actuality will remain to eternity. In this way the omnipotence of God, in my opinion, is far more firmly established. My adversaries, indeed (if I may be permitted to speak plainly), seem to deny the omnipotence of God, inasmuch as they are forced to admit that He has in His mind an infinite number of things which might be created, but which, nevertheless, He will never be able to create, for if He were to create all things which He has in His mind, He would according to them, exhaust His omnipotence and make Himself imperfect. Therefore, in order to make a perfect God, they are compelled to make Him incapable of doing all those things to which His power extends, and anything more absurd than this, or more opposed to God's omnipotence, I do not think can be imagined. Moreover—to say a word, too, here about the intellect and will which we commonly attribute to God—if intellect and will pertain to His eternal essence, these attributes cannot be understood in the sense in which men generally use them, for the intellect and will which could constitute His essence would have to differ entirely from our intellect and will, and could resemble ours in nothing except in name. There could be no further likeness than that between the celestial constellation of the Dog and the animal which barks. This I will demonstrate as follows. If intellect pertains to the divine nature, it cannot, like our intellect, follow the things which are its object (as many suppose), nor can it be simultaneous in its nature with them, since God is prior to all things in causality (Corol. 1, Prop. 16); but, on the contrary, the truth and formal essence of things is what it is, because as such it exists objectively in God's intellect. Therefore the intellect of God, in so far as it is conceived to constitute His essence, is in truth the cause of things, both of their essence and of their existence,—a truth which seems to have been understood by those who have maintained that God's intellect, will, and power are one and the same thing. Since, therefore, God's intellect is the sole cause of things, both of their essence and of their existence (as we have already shown), it must necessarily differ from them with regard both to its essence and existence; for an effect differs from its cause precisely in that which it has from its cause. For example, one man is the cause of the existence but not of the essence of another, for the essence is an eternal truth; and therefore with regard to essence the two men may exactly resemble one another, but with regard to existence they must differ. Consequently if the existence of one should perish, that of the other will not therefore perish; but if the essence of one could be destroyed and become false, the essence of the other would be likewise destroyed. Therefore a thing which is the cause both of the essence and of the existence of any effect must differ from that effect both with regard to its essence and with regard to its existence. But the intellect of God is the cause both of the essence and existence of our intellect; therefore the intellect of God, so far as it is conceived to constitute the divine essence, differs from our intellect both with regard to its essence and its existence, nor can it coincide with our intellect in anything except the name, which is what we essayed to prove. The same demonstration may be applied to the will, as anyone may easily see for himself.

Prop. XVIII.—God is the immanent, and not the transitive cause of all things

Demonst.—All things which are, are in God and must be conceived through Him (Prop. 15), and therefore (Corol. 1, Prop. 16) He is the cause of the things which are in Himself. This is the first thing which was to be proved. Moreover, outside God there can be no substance (Prop. 14), that is to say (Def. 3), outside Him nothing can exist which is in itself. This was the second thing to be proved. God, therefore, is the immanent, but not the transitive cause of all things.—Q.E.D.

Prop. XIX.—God is eternal, or, in other words, all His attributes are eternal

Demonst.—For God (Def. 6) is substance, which (Prop. 11) necessarily exists, that is to say (Prop. 7), a substance to whose nature it pertains to exist, or (which is the same thing) a substance from the definition of which it follows that it exists, and therefore (Def. 8) He is eternal. Again, by the attributes of God is to be understood that which (Def. 4) expresses the essence of the divine substance, that is to say, that which pertains to substance. It is this, I say, which the attributes themselves must involve. But eternity pertains to the nature of substance (Prop. 7). Therefore each of the attributes must involve eternity, and therefore all are eternal.—Q.E.D.

Schol.—This proposition is as clear as possible, too, from the manner in which (Prop. 11) I have demonstrated the existence of God. From that demonstration I say it is plain that the existence of God, like His essence, is an eternal truth. Moreover (Prop. 19 of the "Principles of the Cartesian Philosophy"), I have demonstrated by another method the eternity of God, and there is no need to repeat the demonstration here.

Prop. XX.—The existence of God and His essence are one and the same thing

God (Prop. 19) and all His attributes are eternal, that is to say (Def. 8), each one of His attributes expresses existence. The same attributes of God, therefore, which (Def. 4) manifest the eternal essence of God, at the same time manifest His eternal existence; that is to say, the very same thing which constitutes the essence of God constitutes at the same time His existence, and therefore His existence and His essence are one and the same thing.—Q.E.D.

Corol. 1.—Hence it follows, 1. That the existence of God, like His essence, is an eternal truth.

Corol. 2.—It follows, 2. That God is immutable, or (which is the same thing) all His attributes are immutable; for if they were changed as regards their existence, they must be changed also as regards their essence (Prop. 20); that is to say (as is self-evident), from being true, they would become false, which is absurd.

Prop. XXI.—All things which follow from the absolute nature of any attribute of God must for ever exist, and must be infinite; that is to say, through that same attribute they are eternal and infinite

Demonst.—Conceive, if possible (supposing that the truth of the proposition is denied), that in some attribute of God something which is finite and has a determinate existence or duration follows from the absolute nature of that attribute; for example, an idea of God in thought. But thought, since it is admitted to be an attribute of God, is necessarily (Prop. 11) in its nature infinite. But so far as it has the idea of God it is by supposition finite. But (Def. 2) it cannot be conceived as finite unless it be determined by thought itself. But it cannot be determined by thought itself so far as it constitutes the idea of God, for so far by supposition it is finite. Therefore it must be determined by thought so far as it does not constitute the idea of God, but which, nevertheless (Prop. 11), necessarily exists. Thought, therefore, exists which does not form the idea of God, and therefore from its nature, in so far as it is absolute thought, the idea of God does not necessarily follow (for it is conceived as forming and as not forming the idea of God), which is contrary to the hypothesis. Therefore, if an idea of God in thought, or anything else in any attribute of God, follow from the necessity of the absolute nature of that attribute (for the demonstration being universal will apply in every case), that thing must necessarily be infinite, which was the first thing to be proved.

Again, that which thus follows from the necessity of the nature of any attribute cannot have a determinate duration. For, if the truth of this be denied, let it be supposed that in some attribute of God a thing exists which follows from the necessity of the nature of the attribute—for example, an idea of God in thought—and let it be supposed that at some time it has either not existed or will not exist. But since thought is supposed to be an attribute of God, it must exist both necessarily and unchangeably (Prop. 11, and Corol. 2, Prop. 20). Therefore, beyond the limits of the duration of the idea of God (for it is supposed that at some time it has either not existed or will not exist), thought must exist without the idea of God; but this is contrary to hypothesis, for the supposition is that thought being given, the idea of God necessarily follows. Therefore neither an idea of God in thought, nor anything else which necessarily follows from the absolute nature of any attribute of God, can have a determinate duration, but through the same attribute is eternal; which was the second thing to be proved. Observe that what we have affirmed here is true of everything which in any attribute of God necessarily follows from the absolute nature of God.

Prop. XXII.—Whatever follows from any attribute of God, in so far as it is modified by a modification which through the same attribute exists necessarily and infinitely, must also exist necessarily and infinitely

Demonst.—This proposition is demonstrated in the same manner as the preceding proposition.

Prop. XXIII.—Every mode which exists necessarily and infinitely must necessarily follow either from the absolute nature of some attribute of God, or from some attribute modified by a modification which exists necessarily and infinitely

Demonst.—Mode is that which is in something else through which it must be conceived (Def. 5), that is to say (Prop. 15), it is in God alone and through God alone can be conceived. If a mode, therefore, be conceived to exist necessarily and to be infinite, its necessary existence and infinitude must be concluded from some attribute of God or perceived through it, in so far as it is conceived to express infinitude and necessity of existence, that is to say (Def. 8), eternity, or, in other words (Def. 6 and Prop. 19), in so far as it is considered absolutely. A mode, therefore, which exists necessarily and infinitely must follow from the absolute nature of some attribute of God, either immediately (Prop. 21), or mediately through some modification following from His absolute nature, that is to say (Prop. 22), a modification which necessarily and infinitely exists.—Q.E.D.

Prop. XXIV.—The essence of things produced by God does not involve existence

This is evident from the first Definition; for that thing whose nature (considered, that is to say, in itself) involves existence, is the cause of itself and exists from the necessity of its own nature alone.

Corol.—Hence it follows that God is not only the cause of the commencement of the existence of things, but also of their continuance in existence, or, in other words (to use scholastic phraseology), God is the *causa essendi rerum*. For if we consider the essence of things, whether existing or non-existing, we discover that it neither involves existence nor duration, and therefore the essence of existing things cannot be the cause of their existence nor of their duration, but God only is the cause, to whose nature alone existence pertains (Carol. 1, Prop. 14).

Prop. XXV.—God is not only the efficient cause of existence of things, but also of their essence

Demonst.—Suppose that God is not the cause of the essence of things; then (Ax. 4) the essence of things can be conceived without God, which (Prop. 15) is absurd. Therefore God is the cause of the essence of things.—Q.E.D.

Schol.—This proposition more clearly follows from Prop. 16. For from this proposition it follows that, from the existence of the divine nature, both the essence of things and their existence must necessarily be concluded, or, in a word, in the same sense in which God is said to be the cause of Himself He must be called the cause of all things. This will appear still more clearly from the following corollary.

Corol.—Individual things are nothing but affections or modes of God's attributes, expressing those attributes in a certain and determinate manner. This is evident from Prop. 15 and Def. 5.

Prop. XXVI.—A thing which has been determined to any action was necessarily so determined by God, and that which has not been thus determined by God cannot determine itself to action

Demonst.—That by which things are said to be determined to any action is necessarily something positive (as is self-evident); and therefore God, from the necessity of His nature, is the efficient cause both of its essence and of its existence (Props. 25 and 16), which was the first thing to be proved. From this also the second part of the proposition follows most clearly. For if a thing which has not been determined by God could determine itself, the first part of the proposition would be false, and to suppose this possible is an absurdity, as we have shown.

Prop. XXVII.—A thing which has been determined by God to any action cannot render itself indeterminate

Demonst.—This proposition is evident from the third Axiom.

Prop. XXVIII.—An individual thing, or a thing which is finite and which as a determinate existence, cannot exist nor be determined to action unless it be determined to existence and action by another cause which is also finite and has a determinate existence; and again, this cause cannot exist nor be determined to action unless by another cause which is also finite and determined to existence and action, and so on ad infinitum

Demonst.—Whatever is determined to existence and action is thus determined by God (Prop. 26 and Corol. Prop. 24). But that which is finite and which has a determinate existence could not be produced by the absolute nature of any attribute of God, for whatever follows from the absolute nature of any attribute of God is infinite and eternal (Prop. 21). The finite and determinate must therefore follow from God, or from some attribute of God, in so far as the latter is considered to be affected by some mode, for besides substance and modes nothing exists (Ax. 1, and Defs. 3 and 5), and modes (Corol. Prop. 25) are nothing but affections of God's attributes. But the finite and determinate could not follow from God, or from any one of His attributes, so far as that attribute is affected with a modification which is eternal and infinite (Prop. 22). It must, therefore, follow or be determined to existence and action by God, or by some attribute of God, in so far as the attribute is modified by a modification which is finite, and which has a determinate existence. This was the first thing to be proved. Again, this cause or this mode (by the same reasoning by which we have already demonstrated the first part of this proposition) must be determined by another cause, which is also finite, and which has a determinate existence, and this last cause (by the same reasoning) must, in its turn, be determined by another cause, and so on continually (by the same reasoning) *ad infinitum*.

Schol.—Since certain things must have been immediately produced by God, that is to say, those which necessarily follow from His absolute nature; these primary products being the mediating cause for things which, nevertheless, without God can neither be nor can be conceived; it follows, firstly, that of things immediately produced by God He is the proximate cause absolutely, and not in their own kind (*in suo genere*), as we say; for effects of God can neither be nor be conceived without their cause (Pro. 15, and Corol. Prop. 24).

It follows, secondly, that God cannot be properly called the remote cause of individual things, unless for the sake of distinguishing them from the other things which He has immediately produced, or rather which follow from His absolute nature. For by a remote cause we understand that which is in no way joined to its effect. But all things which are, are in

God, and so depend upon Him that without Him they can neither be nor be conceived.

Prop. XXIX.—In nature there is nothing contingent, but all things are determined from the necessity of the divine nature to exist and act in a certain manner

Demonst.—Whatever is, is in God (Prop. 15); but God cannot be called a contingent thing, for (Prop. 11) He exists necessarily and not contingently. Moreover, the modes of the divine nature have followed from it necessarily and not contingently (Prop. 16), and that, too, whether it be considered absolutely (Prop. 21), or as determined to action in a certain manner (Prop. 27). But God is the cause of these modes, not only in so far as they simply exist (Corol. Prop. 24), but also (Prop. 26) in so far as they are considered as determined to any action. And if they are not determined by God (by the same proposition), it is an impossibility and not a contingency that they should determine themselves; and, on the other hand (Prop. 27), if they are determined by God, it is an impossibility and not a contingency that they should render themselves indeterminate. Wherefore all things are determined from a necessity of the divine nature, not only to exist, but to exist and act in a certain manner, and there is nothing contingent.—Q.E.D.

Schol.—Before I go any farther, I wish here to explain, or rather to recall to recollection, what we mean by *natura naturans* and what by *natura naturata*. For, from what has gone before, I think it is plain that by *natura naturans* we are to understand that which is in itself and is conceived through itself, or those attributes of substance which express eternal and infinite essence, that is to say (Corol. 1, Prop. 14, and Corol. 2, Prop. 17), God in so far as He is considered as a free cause. But by *natura naturata* I understand everything which follows from the necessity of the nature of God, or of any one of God's attributes, that is to say, all the modes of God's attributes in so far as they are considered as things which are in God, and which without God can neither be nor can be conceived.

Prop. XXX.—The actual intellect, whether finite or infinite, must comprehend the attributes of God and the affections of God, and nothing else

Demonst.—A true idea must agree with that of which it is the idea (Ax. 6), that is to say (as is self-evident), that which is objectively contained in the intellect must necessarily exist in nature. But in nature (Corol. 1, Prop. 14) only one substance exists, namely, God, and no affections (Prop. 15) excepting those which are in God, and which (by the same proposition) can neither be nor be conceived without God. Therefore the actual intellect, whether finite or infinite, must comprehend the attributes of God and the affections of God, and nothing else.—Q.E.D.

Prop. XXXI.—The actual intellect, whether it be finite or infinite, together with the will, desire, love, &c., must be referred to the natura naturata *and not to the* natura naturans

Demonst.—For by the intellect (as is self-evident) we do not understand absolute thought, but only a certain mode of thought, which mode differs from other modes, such as desire, love, &c., and therefore (Def. 5) must be conceived through absolute thought, that is to say (Prop. 15 and Def. 6), it must be conceived through some attribute of God which expresses the eternal and infinite essence of thought in such a manner that without that attribute it can neither be nor can be conceived. Therefore (Schol. Prop. 29) the actual intellect, &c., must be referred to the *natura naturata*, and not to the *natura naturans*, in the same manner as all other modes of thought.—Q.E.D.

Schol.—I do not here speak of the *actual* intellect because I admit that any intellect *potentially* exists, but because I wish, in order that there may be no confusion, to speak of nothing excepting of that which we perceive with the utmost clearness, that is to say, the understanding itself, which we perceive as clearly as we perceive anything. For we can understand nothing through the intellect which does not lead to a more perfect knowledge of the understanding.

Prop. XXXII.—The will cannot be called a free cause, but can only be called necessary

Demonst.—The will is only a certain mode of thought, like the intellect, and therefore (Prop. 28) no volition can exist or be determined to action unless it be determined by another cause, and this again by another, and so on *ad infinitum*. And if the will be supposed infinite, it must be determined to existence and action by God, no in so far as He is substance absolutely infinite, but in so far as He possesses an attribute which expresses the infinite and eternal essence of thought (Prop. 23). In whatever way, therefore, the will be conceived, whether finite or infinite, it requires a cause by which it may be determined to existence and action, and therefore (Def. 7) it cannot be called a free cause but only necessary or compelled.—Q.E.D.

Corol. 1.—Hence it follows, firstly, that God does not act from freedom of the will.

Corol. 2.—It follows, secondly, that will and intellect are related to the nature of God as motion and rest, and absolutely as all natural things, which (Prop. 29) must be determined by God to existence and action in a certain manner. For the will, like all other things, needs a cause by which it may be determined to existence and action in a certain manner, and although from a given will or intellect infinite things may follow, God cannot on this account be said to act from freedom of will, any more than He can be said to act from freedom of motion and rest by reason of the things which follow from motion and rest (for from motion and rest infinite numbers of things follow). Therefore, will does not appertain to the nature of God more than other natural things, but is related to it as motion and rest and all other things are related to it; these all following, as we have shown, from the necessity of the divine nature, and being determined to existence and action in a certain manner.

Prop. XXXIII.—Things could have been produced by God in no other manner and in no other order than that in which they have been produced

Demonst.—All things have necessarily followed from the given nature of God (Prop. 16), and from the necessity of His nature have been determined to existence and action in a certain manner (Prop. 29). If, therefore, things could have been of another nature, or could have been determined in another manner to action, so that the order of nature would have been different, the nature of God might then be different to that which it now is, and hence (Prop. 11) that different nature would necessarily exist, and there might consequently be two or more Gods, which (Corol. 1, Prop. 14) is absurd. Therefore, things could be produced by God in no other manner and in no other order than that in which they have been produced.—Q.E.D.

Schol. 1.—Since I have thus shown, with greater clearness than that of noonday light, that in things there is absolutely nothing by virtue of which they can be called contingent, I wish now to explain in a few words what is to be understood by *contingent*, but firstly, what is to be understood by *necessary* and *impossible*. A thing is called necessary either in reference to its essence or its cause. For the existence of a thing necessarily follows either from the essence and definition of the thing itself, or from a given efficient cause. In the same way a thing is said to be impossible either because the essence of the thing itself or its definition involves a contradiction, or because no external cause exists determinate to the production of such a thing. But a thing cannot be called contingent unless with reference to a deficiency in our knowledge. For if we do not know that the essence of a thing involves a contradiction, or if we actually know that it involves no contradiction, and nevertheless we can affirm nothing with certainty about its existence because the order of causes is concealed from us, that thing can never appear to us either as necessary or impossible, and therefore we call it either contingent or possible.

Schol. 2.—From what has gone before it clearly follows that things have been produced by God in the highest degree of perfection, since they have necessarily followed from the existence of a most perfect nature. Nor does this doctrine accuse God of any imperfection, but, on the contrary, His perfection has compelled us to affirm it. Indeed, from its contrary would clearly follow, as I have shown above, that God is not absolutely perfect, since, if things had been produced in any other fashion another nature would have had to be assigned to Him, different from that which the consideration of the most perfect Being compels us to assign to Him. I do not doubt that many will reject this opinion as ridiculous, nor will they care to apply themselves to its consideration, and this from no other reason than that they have been in the habit of assigning to God another liberty widely different from that absolute will which (Def. 7) we have taught. On the other hand, I do not doubt, if they were willing to study the matter and properly to consider the series of our demonstrations, that they would altogether reject this liberty which they now assign to God, not only as of no value, but as a great obstacle to knowledge. Neither is there any need that I should here repeat those things which are said in the scholium to Prop. 17. But for the sake of those who differ from me, I will here show that although it be granted that will pertains to God's essence, it follows nevertheless from His perfection that things could be created in no other mode or order by Him. This it will be easy to show if we first consider that which my opponents themselves admit, that it depends upon the decree and will of God alone that each thing should be what it is, for otherwise God would not be the cause of all things. It is also admitted that all God's decrees were decreed by God Himself from all eternity, for otherwise imperfection and inconstancy would be proved against Him. But since in eternity there is no *when* nor *before* nor *after*, it follows from the perfection of God alone that He neither can decree nor could ever have decreed anything else than that which He has decreed; that is to say, God has not existed before His decrees, and can never exist without them. But it is said that although it be supposed that God had made the nature of things different from that which it is, or that from eternity He had decreed something else about nature and her order, it would not thence follow that any imperfection exists in God. But if this be said, it must at the same time be allowed that God can change His decrees. For if God had decreed something about nature and her order other than that which He has decreed—that is to say, if He had willed and conceived something else about nature—He would necessarily have had an intellect and a will different from those which He now has. And if it be allowed to assign to God another intellect and another will without any change of His essence and of His perfections, what is the reason why He cannot now change His decrees about creation and nevertheless remain equally perfect? For His intellect and will regarding created things and their order remain the same in relationship to His essence and perfection in whatever manner His intellect and will are conceived. Moreover, all the philosophers whom I have seen admit that there is no such thing as an intellect existing potentially in God, but only an intellect existing actually. But since His intellect and His will are not distinguishable from His essence, as all admit, it follows from this also that if God had had another intellect actually and another will, His essence would have been necessarily different, and hence, as I showed at the beginning, if things had been produced by God in a manner different from that in which they now exist, God's intellect and will, that is to say, His essence (as has been granted), must have been different, which is absurd.

Since, therefore, things could have been produced by God in no other manner or order, this being a truth which follows from His absolute perfection, there is no sound reasoning which can persuade us to believe that God was unwilling to create all things which are in His intellect with the same perfection as that in which they exist in His intellect. But we shall be told that there is no perfection nor imperfection in things, but that that which is in them by reason of which they are perfect or imperfect and are said to be good or evil depends upon the will of God alone, and therefore if God had willed He could have effected that that which is now perfection should have been the extreme of imperfection, and *vice versa*. But what else would this be than openly to affirm that God, who necessarily understands what He wills, is able by His will to understand things in a manner different from that in which He understands them, which, as I have just shown, is a great absurdity? I can therefore turn the argument on my opponents in this way. All things depend upon the power of God. In order that things may be differently constituted, it would be necessary that God's will should be differently constituted; but God's will cannot be other than it is, as we have lately most clearly deduced from His perfection. Things therefore cannot be differently constituted. I confess that this opinion, which subjects all things to a certain indifferent God's will, and affirms that all things depend upon God's good pleasure, is at a less distance from the truth than the opinion of those who affirm that God does everything for the sake of the Good. For these seem to place something outside of God which is independent of Him, to which He looks while He is at work as to a model, or at which He aims as if at a certain mark. This is indeed nothing else than to subject God to fate, the most absurd thing which can be affirmed of Him whom we have shown to be the first and only free cause of the essence of all things as well as of their existence. Therefore it is not worth while that I should waste time in refuting this absurdity.

Prop. XXXIV.—The power of God is His essence itself

Demonst.—From the necessity alone of the essence of God it follows that God is the cause of

Himself (Prop. 11), and (Prop. 16 and its Corol.) the cause of all things. Therefore the power of God, by which He Himself and all things are and act, is His essence itself.—Q.E.D.

Prop. XXXV.—Whatever we conceive to be in God's power necessarily exists

Demonst.—For whatever is in God's power must (Prop. 34) be so comprehended in His essence that it necessarily follows from it, and consequently exists necessarily.—Q.E.D.

Prop. XXXVI.—Nothing exists from whose nature an effect does not follow

Demonst.—Whatever exists expresses the nature or the essence of God in a certain and determinate manner (Corol. Prop. 25); that is to say (Prop. 34), whatever exists expresses the power of God, which is the cause of all things, in a certain and determinate manner, and therefore (Prop. 16) some effect must follow from it.

APPENDIX

I have now explained the nature of God and its properties. I have shown that He necessarily exists; that He is one God; that from the necessity alone of His own nature He is and acts; that He is, and in what way He is, the free cause of all things; that all things are in Him, and so depend upon Him that without Him they can neither be nor can be conceived; and, finally, that all things have been predetermined by Him, not indeed from freedom of will or from absolute good pleasure, but from His absolute nature or infinite power.

Moreover, wherever an opportunity was afforded, I have endeavored to remove prejudices which might hinder the perception of the truth of what I have demonstrated; but because not a few still remain which have been and are now sufficient to prove a very great hindrance to the comprehension of the connection of things in the manner in which I have explained it, I have thought it worth while to call them up to be examined by reason. But all these prejudices which I here undertake to point out depend upon this solely: that it is commonly supposed that all things in nature, like men, work to some end; and indeed it is thought to be certain that God Himself directs all things to some sure end, for it is said that God has made all things for man, and man that he may worship God. This, therefore, I will first investigate by inquiring, firstly, why so many rest in this prejudice, and why all are so naturally inclined to embrace it? I shall then show its falsity, and, finally, the manner in which there have arisen from it prejudices concerning *good* and *evil, merit* and *sin, praise* and *blame, order* and *disorder, beauty* and *deformity*, and so forth. This, however, is not the place to deduce these things from the nature of the human mind. It will be sufficient if I here take as an axiom that which no one ought to dispute, namely, that man is born ignorant of the causes of things, and that he has a desire, of which he is conscious, to seek that which is profitable to him. From this it follows, firstly, that he thinks himself free because he is conscious of his wishes and appetites, whilst at the same time he is ignorant of the causes by which he is led to wish and desire, not dreaming what they are; and, secondly, it follows that man does everything for an end, namely, for that which is profitable to him, which is what he seeks. Hence it happens that he attempts to discover merely the final causes of that which has happened; and when he has heard them he is satisfied, because there is no longer any cause for further uncertainty. But if he cannot hear from another what these final causes are, nothing remains but to turn to himself and reflect upon the ends which usually determine him to the like actions, and thus by his own mind he necessarily judges that of another. Moreover, since he discovers, both within and without himself, a multitude of means which contribute not a little to the attainment of what is profitable to himself—for example, the eyes, which are useful for seeing, the teeth for mastication, plants and animals for nourishment, the sun for giving light, the sea for feeding fish, &c.—it comes to pass that all natural objects are considered as means for obtaining what is profitable. These too being evidently discovered and not created by man, hence he has a cause for believing that some other person exists, who has prepared them for man's use. For having considered them as means it was impossible to believe that they had created themselves, and so he was obliged to infer from the means which he was in the habit of providing for himself that some ruler or rulers of nature exist, endowed with human liberty, who have taken care of all things for him, and have made all things for his use. Since he never heard anything about the mind of these rulers, he was compelled to judge of it from his own, and hence he affirmed that the gods direct everything for his advantage, in order that he may be bound to them and hold them in the highest honour. This is the reason why each man has devised for himself, out of his own brain, a different mode of worshipping God, so that God might love him above others, and direct all nature to the service of his blind cupidity and insatiable avarice.

Thus has this prejudice been turned into a superstition and has driven deep roots into the mind—a prejudice which was the reason why every one has so eagerly tried to discover and explain the final causes of things. The attempt, however, to show that nature does nothing in vain (that is to say, nothing which is not profitable to man), seems to end in showing that nature, the gods, and man are alike mad.

Do but see, I pray, to what all this has led. Amidst so much in nature that is beneficial, not a few things must have been observed which are injurious, such as storms, earthquakes, diseases, and it was affirmed that these things happened either because the gods were angry because of wrongs which had been inflicted on them by man, or because of sins committed in the method of worshipping them; and although experience daily contradicted this, and showed by an infinity of examples that both the beneficial and the injurious were indiscriminately bestowed on the pious and the impious, the inveterate prejudices on this point have not therefore been abandoned. For it was much easier for a man to place these things aside with others of the use of which he was ignorant, and thus retain his present and inborn state of ignorance, than to destroy the whole superstructure and think out a new one. Hence it was looked upon as indisputable that the judgments of the gods far surpass our comprehension; and this opinion alone would have been sufficient to keep the human race in darkness to all eternity, if mathematics, which does not deal with ends, but with the essences and properties of forms, had not placed before us another rule of truth. In addition to mathematics, other causes also might be assigned, which it is superfluous here to enumerate, tending to make men reflect upon these universal prejudices, and leading them to a true knowledge of things.

I have thus sufficiently explained what I promised in the first place to explain. There will now be no need of many words to show that nature has set no end before herself, and that all final causes are nothing but human fictions. For I believe that this is sufficiently evident both from the foundations and causes of this prejudice, and from Prop. 16 and Corol. Prop. 32, as well as from all those propositions in which I have shown that all things are begotten by a certain eternal necessity of nature and in absolute perfection. Thus much, nevertheless, I will add, that this doctrine concerning an end altogether overturns nature. For that which is in truth the cause it considers as the effect, and *vice versa*. Again, that which is first in nature it puts last; and, finally, that which is supreme and most perfect it makes the most imperfect. For (passing by the first two assertions as self-evident) it is plain from Props. 21, 22, and 23, that that effect is the most perfect which is immediately produced by God, and in proportion as intermediate causes are necessary for the production of a thing is it imperfect. But if things which are immediately produced by God were made in order that He might obtain the end He had in view, then the last things for the sake of which the first exist, must be the most perfect of all. Again, this doctrine does away with God's perfection. For if God works to obtain an end, He necessarily seeks something of which he stands in need. And although theologians and metaphysicians distinguish between the end of want and the end of assimilation (*finem indegentiœ et finem assimilationis*), they confess that God has done all things for His own sake, and not for the sake of the things to be created, because before the creation they can assign nothing excepting God for the sake of which God could do anything; and therefore they are necessarily compelled to admit that God stood in need of and desired those things for which He determined to prepare means. This is self-evident. Nor is it here to be overlooked that the adherents of this doctrine, who have found a pleasure in displaying their ingenuity in assigning the ends of things, have introduced a new species of argument, not the *reductio ad impossibile*, but the *reductio ad ignorantiam*, to prove their position, which shows that it had no other method of defence left. For, by way of example, if a stone has fallen from some roof on somebody's head and killed him, they will demonstrate in this manner that the stone has fallen in order to kill the man. For if it did not fall for that purpose by the will of God, how could so many circumstances concur through chance (and a number often simultaneously do concur)? You will answer, perhaps, that the event happened because the wind blew and the man was passing that way. But, they will urge, why did the wind blow at that time, and why did the man pass that way precisely at the same moment? If you again reply that the wind rose then because the sea on the preceding day began to be stormy, the weather hitherto having been calm, and that the man had been invited by a friend, they will urge again—because there is no end of questioning—But why was the sea agitated? why was the man invited at that time? And so they will not cease from asking the causes of causes, until at last you fly to the will of God, the refuge for ignorance.

So, also, when they behold the structure of the human body, they are amazed; and because they are ignorant of the causes of such art, they conclude that the body was made not by mechanical but by a supernatural or divine art, and has been formed in such a way so that the one part may not injure the other. Hence it happens that the man who endeavours to find out the true causes of miracles, and who desires as a wise man to understand nature, and not to gape at it like a fool, is generally considered and proclaimed to be a heretic and impious by those whom the vulgar worship as the interpreters both of nature and the gods. For these know that if ignorance be removed, amazed stupidity, the sole ground on which they rely in arguing or in defending their authority, is taken away also. But these things I leave and pass on to that which I determined to do in the third place.

After man has persuaded himself that all things which exist are made for him, he must in everything adjudge that to be of the greatest importance which is most useful to him, and he must esteem that to be of surpassing worth by which he is most beneficially affected. In this way he is compelled to form those notions by which he explains nature; such, for instance, as *good, evil, order, confusion, heat, cold beauty*, and *deformity*, &c.; and because he supposes himself to be free, notions like those of *praise* and *blame, sin* and *merit*, have arisen. These latter I shall hereafter explain when I have treated of human nature; the former I will here briefly unfold.

It is to be observed that man has given the name *good* to everything which leads to health and the worship of God; on the contrary, everything which does not lead thereto he calls *evil*. But because those who do not understand nature affirm nothing about things themselves, but only imagine them, and take the imagination to be understanding, they therefore, ignorant of things and their nature, firmly believe an *order* to be in things; for when things are so placed that, if they are represented to us through the senses, we can easily imagine them, and consequently easily remember them, we call them well arranged; but if they are not placed so that we can imagine and remember them, we call them badly arranged or *confused*. Moreover, since those things are more especially pleasing to us which we can easily imagine, men therefore prefer order to confusion, as if order were something in nature apart from our own imagination; and they say that God has created everything in order, and in this manner they ignorantly attribute imagination to God, unless they mean perhaps that God, out of consideration for the human imagination, has disposed things in the manner in which they can most easily be imagined. No hesitation either seems to be caused by the fact that an infinite number of things are discovered which far surpass our imagination, and very many which confound it through its weakness. But enough of this. The other notions which I have mentioned are nothing but modes in which the imagination is affected in different ways, and nevertheless they are regarded by the ignorant as being specially attributes of things, because, as we have remarked, men consider all things as made for themselves, and call the nature of a thing good, evil, sound, putrid, or corrupt, just as they are affected by it. For example, if the motion by which the nerves are affected by means of objects represented to the eye conduces to well-being, the objects by which it is caused are called *beautiful*; while those exciting a contrary motion are called *deformed*. Those things, too, which stimulate the senses through the nostrils are called sweet-smelling or thinking; those which act through the taste are called sweet or bitter, full-flavoured or insipid; those which act through the touch, hard or soft, heavy or light; those, lastly, which act through the ears are said to make a noise, sound, or harmony, the last having caused men to lose their senses to such a degree that they have believed that God even is delighted with it. Indeed, philosophers may be found who have persuaded themselves that the celestial motions beget a harmony. All these things sufficiently show that every one judges things by the constitution of his brain, or rather accepts the affections of his imagination in the place of things. It is not, therefore, to be wondered at, as we may observe in passing, that all those controversies which we see have arisen amongst men, so that at last scepticism has been the result. For although human bodies agree in many things, they differ in more, and therefore that which to one person is good will appear to another evil, that which to one is well arranged to another is confused, that which pleases one will displease another, and so on in other cases which I pass by both because we cannot notice them at length here, and because they are within the experience of every one. For every one has heard the expressions: So many heads, so many ways of thinking; Every one is satisfied with his own way of thinking; Differences of brains are not less common than differences of taste;—all which maxims show that men decide upon matters according to the constitution of their brains, and imagine rather than understand things. If men understood things, they would, as mathematics prove, at least be all alike convinced if they were not all alike attracted. We see, therefore, that all those methods by which the common people are in the habit of explaining nature are only different sorts of imaginations, and do not reveal the nature of anything in itself, but only the constitution of the imagination; and because they have names as if they were entities existing apart from the imagination, I call them entities not of the reason but of the imagination. All argument, therefore, urged against us based upon such notions can be easily refuted. Many people, for instance, are accustomed to argue thus:—If all things have followed from the necessity of the most perfect nature of God, how is it that so many imperfections have arisen in nature—corruption, for instance, of things till they stink; deformity, exciting disgust; confusion, evil, crime, &c.? But, as I have just observed, all this is easily answered. For the perfection of things is to be judged by their nature and power alone; nor are they more or less perfect because they delight or offend the human senses, or because they are beneficial or prejudicial to human nature. But to those who ask why God has not created all men in such a manner that they might be controlled by the dictates of reason alone, I give but this answer: Because to Him material was not wanting for the creation of everything, from the highest down to the very lowest grade of perfection; or, to speak more properly, because the laws of his nature were so ample that they sufficed for the production of everything which can be conceived by an infinite intellect, as I have demonstrated in Prop. 16.

These are the prejudices which I undertook to notice here. If any others of a similar character remain, they can easily be rectified with a little thought by any one.

PART 2 OF THE NATURE AND ORIGIN OF THE MIND

I pass on now to explain those things which must necessarily follow from the essence of God or the Being eternal and infinite; not indeed to explain all these things, for we have demonstrated (Prop. 16, pt. 1) that an infinitude of things must follow in an infinite number of ways,—but to consider those things only which may conduct us as it were by the hand to a knowledge of the human mind and its highest happiness.

Definitions

I. By body, I understand a mode which expresses in a certain and determinate manner the essence of God in so far as He is considered as the thing extended. (See Corol. Prop. 25, pt. 1.)

II. I say that to the essence of anything pertains that, which being given, the thing itself is necessarily posited, and being taken away, the thing is necessarily taken; or, in other words, that, without which the thing can neither be nor be conceived, and which in its turn cannot be nor be conceived without the thing.

III. By idea, I understand a conception of the mind which the mind forms because it is a thinking thing.

Explanation.—I use the word conception rather than perception because the name perception seems to indicate that the mind is passive in its relation to the object. But the word conception seems to express the action of the mind.

IV. By adequate idea, I understand an idea which, in so far as it is considered in itself, without reference to the object, has all the properties or internal signs of a true idea.

Explanation.—I say internal, so as to exclude that which is external, the agreement, namely, of the idea with its object.

V. Duration is the indefinite continuation of existence.

Explanation.—I call it indefinite because it cannot be determined by the nature itself of the existing thing nor by the efficient cause, which necessarily posits the existence of the thing but does not take it away.

VI. By reality and perfection I understand the same thing.

VII. By individual things I understand things which are finite and which have a determinate existence; and if a number of individuals so unite in one action that they are all simultaneously the cause of one effect, I consider them all, so far, as a one individual thing.

Axioms

I. The essence of man does not involve necessary existence; that is to say, the existence as well as the non-existence of this or that man many or may not follow from the order of nature.

II. Man thinks.

III. Modes of thought, such as love, desire, or the affections of the mind, by whatever name they may be called, do not exist, unless in the same individual the idea exist of a thing loved, desired, &c. But the idea may exist although no other mode of thinking exist.

IV. We perceive that a certain body is affected in many ways.

V. No individual things are felt or perceived by us excepting bodies and modes of thought.

The postulates will be found after Proposition 13.

Prop. I.—Thought is an attribute of God, or God is a thinking thing

Demonst.—Individual thoughts, or this and that thought, are modes which express the nature of God in a certain and determinate manner (Corol. Prop. 25, pt. 1). God therefore possesses an attribute (Def. 5, pt. 1), the conception of which is involved in all individual thoughts, and through which they are conceived. Thought, therefore, is one of the infinite attributes of God which expresses the eternal and infinite essence of God (Def. 6, pt. 1), or, in other words, God is a thinking thing.—Q.E.D.

Prop. II.—Extension is an attribute of God, or God is an extended thing

Demonst.—The demonstration of this proposition is of the same character as that of the last.

Prop. III.—In God there necessarily exists the idea of His essence, and of all things which necessarily follow from His essence

Demonst.—For God (Prop. 1, pt. 2) can think an infinitude of things in infinite ways, or (which is the same thing, by Prop. 16, pt. 1) can form an idea of His essence and of all the things which necessarily follow from it. But everything which is in the power of God is necessary (Prop. 35, pt. 1), and therefore this idea necessarily exists, and (Prop. 15, pt. 1) it cannot exist unless in God.

Schol.—The common people understand by God's power His free will and right over all existing things, which are therefore commonly looked upon as contingent; for they say that God has the power of destroying everything and reducing it to nothing. They very frequently, too, compare God's power with the power of kings. That there is any similarity between the two we have disproved in the first and second Corollaries of Prop. 32, pt. 1, and in Prop. 16, pt. 1, we have shown that God does everything with that necessity with which He understands Himself; that is to say, as it follows from the necessity of the divine nature that God understands Himself (a truth admitted by all), so by the same necessity it follows that God does an infinitude of things in infinite ways. Moreover, in Prop. 34, pt. 1, we have shown that the power of God is nothing but the active essence of God, and therefore it is as impossible for us to conceive that God does not act as that He does not exist. If it pleased me to go farther, I should show besides that the power which the common people ascribe to God is not only a human power (which shows that they look upon God as a man, or as being like a man), but that it also involves a weakness. But I do not care to talk so much upon the same subject. Again and again I ask the reader to consider and reconsider what is said upon this subject in the first part, from Prop. 16 to the end. For it is not possible for any one properly to understand the things which I wish to prove unless he takes great care not to confound the power of God with the human power and right of kings. . . .

Prop. VI.—The modes of any attribute have God for a cause only in so far as He is considered under that attribute of which they are modes, and not in so far as He is considered under any other attribute

Demonst.—Each attribute is conceived by itself and without any other (Prop. 10, pt. 1). Therefore the modes of any attribute involve the conception of that attribute and of no other, and therefore (Ax. 4, pt. 1) have God for a cause in so far as He is considered under that attribute of which they are modes, and not so far as He is considered under any other attribute.—Q.E.D.

Prop. VII.—The order and connection of ideas is the same as the order and connection of things

This is evident from Ax. 4, pt. 1. For the idea of anything caused depends upon a knowledge of the cause of which the thing caused is the effect.

Corol.—Hence it follows that God's power of thinking is equal to His actual power of acting; that is to say, whatever follows *formally* from the infinite nature of God, follows from the idea of God [idea Dei], in the same order and in the same connection *objectively* in God.

Schol.—Before we go any farther, we must here recall to our memory what we have already demonstrated, that everything which can be perceived by the infinite intellect as constituting the essence of substance pertains entirely to the one sole substance only, and consequently that substance thinking and substance extended are one and the same substance, which is now comprehended under this attribute and now under that. Thus, also, a mode of extension and the idea of that mode are one and the same thing expressed in two different ways—a truth which some of the Hebrews appear to have seen as if through a cloud, since they say that God, the intellect of God, and the things which are the objects of that intellect are one and the same thing. For example, the circle existing in nature and the idea that is in God of an existing circle are one and the same thing, which is manifested through different attributes; and, therefore, whether we think of nature under the attribute of extension, or under the attribute of thought, or under any other attribute whatever, we shall discover one and the same order, or one and the same connection of causes; that is to say, in every case the same sequence of things. Nor have I had any other reason for saying that God is the cause of the idea, for example, of the circle in so far only as He is a thinking thing, but this, that the formal Being of the idea of a circle can only be perceived through another mode of thought, as its proximate cause, and this again must be perceived through another, and so on *ad infinitum*. So that when things are considered as modes of thought, we must explain the order of the whole of nature or the connection of causes by the attribute of thought alone, and when things are considered as modes of extension, the order of the whole of nature must be explained through the attribute of extension alone, and so with other attributes. Therefore God is in truth the cause of things as they are in themselves in so far as He consists of infinite attributes, nor for the present can I explain the matter more clearly.

Prop. VIII.—The ideas of non-existent individual things or modes are comprehended in the infinite idea of God, in the same way that the formal essences of individual things or modes are contained in the attributes of God

Demonst.—This proposition is evident from the preceding proposition, but it is to be understood more clearly from the preceding scholium.

Corol.—Hence it follows that when individual things do not exist unless in so far as they are comprehended in the attributes of God, their objective Being or ideas do not exist unless in so far as the infinite idea of God exists; and when individual things are said to exist, not only in so far as they are included in God's attributes, but in so far as they are said to have duration, their ideas involve the existence through which they are said to have duration.

Schol.—If any one desires an instance in order that what I have said may be more fully understood, I cannot give one which will adequately explain what I have been saying, since an exact parallel deos not exist: nevertheless, I will endeavour to give as good an illustration as can be found.

The circle, for example, possess this property, that the rectangles contained by the segments of all straight lines cutting one another in the same circle are equal; therefore in a circle there is contained an infinite number of rectangles equal to one another, but none of them can be said to exist unless in so far as the circle exists, nor can the idea of any one of these rectangles be said to exist unless in so far as it is comprehended in the idea of the circle. Out of this infinite number of rectangles, let two only, E and D, be conceived to exist. The ideas of these two rectangles do not now exist merely in so far as they are comprehended in the idea of the circle, but because they involve the existence of their rectangles, and it is this which distinguishes them from the other ideas of the other rectangles.

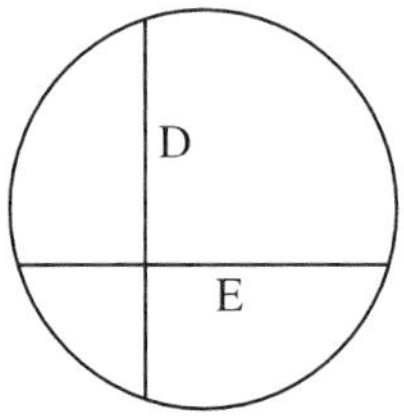

Prop. IX.—The idea of an individual thing actually existing has God for a cause, not in so far as He is infinite, but in so far as He is considered to be affected by another idea of an individual thing actually existing, of which idea also He is the cause in so far as He is affected by a third, and so on ad infinitum

Demonst.—The idea of any individual thing actually existing is an individual mode of thought, and is distinct from other modes of thought (Corol. and Schol. Prop. 8, pt. 2), and therefore (Prop. 6, pt. 2) has God for a cause in so far only as He is a thinking thing; not indeed as a thinking thing absolutely (Prop. 28, pt. 1), but in so far as He is considered as affected by another mode of thought. Again, He is the cause of this latter mode of thought in so far as He is considered as affected by another, and so on *ad infinitum*. But the order and connection of ideas (Prop. 7, pt. 2) is the same as the order and connection of causes; therefore every individual idea has for its cause another idea, that is to say, God in so far as He is affected by another idea; while of this second idea God is again the cause in the same way, and so on *ad infinitum*.—Q.E.D.

Corol.—A knowledge of everything which happens in the individual object of any idea exists in God in so far only as He possesses the idea of that object.

Demonst.—The idea of everything which happens in the object of any idea exists in God (Prop. 3, pt. 2), not in so far as He is infinite, but in so far as He is considered as affected by another idea of an individual thing (Prop. 9, pt. 2); but (Prop. 7, pt. 2) the order and connection of ideas is the same as the order and connection of things, and therefore the knowledge of that which happens in any individual object will exist in God in so far only as He has the idea of that object.

Prop. X.—The Being of substance does not pertain to the essence of man, or, in other words, substance does not constitute the form of man

Demonst.—The Being of substance involves necessary existence (Prop. 7, pt. 1). If, therefore, the Being of substance pertained to the essence of man, the existence of man would necessarily follow from the existence of substance (Def. 2, pt. 2), and consequently he would necessarily exist, which (Ax. 1, pt. 2) is an absurdity. Therefore the Being of substance does not pertain, &c.—Q.E.D.

Corol.—Hence it follows that the essence of man consists of certain modifications of the attributes of God; for the Being of substance does not pertain to the essence of man (Prop. 10, pt. 2). It is therefore something (Prop. 15, pt. 1) which is in God, and which without God can neither be nor be conceived, or (Corol. Prop. 25, pt. 1) an affection or mode which expresses the nature of God in a certain and determinate manner.

Schol.—Every one must admit that without God nothing can be nor be conceived; for every one admits that God is the sole cause both of the essence and of the existence of all things; that is to say, God is not only the cause of things, to use a common expression, *secundum fieri*, but also *secundum esse*. But many people say that that pertains to the essence of a thing without which the thing can neither be nor can be conceived, and they therefore believe either that the nature of God belongs to the essence of created things, or that created things can be or can be conceived without God; or, which is more probable, there is no consistency in their thought. I believe that the cause of this confusion is that they have not observed a proper order of philosophic study. For although the divine nature ought to be studied first, because it is first in the order of knowledge and in the order of things, they think it last; while, on the other hand, those things which are called objects of the senses are believed to stand before everything else. Hence it has come to pass that there was nothing of which men thought less than the divine nature while they have been studying natural objects, and when they afterwards applied themselves to think about God, there was nothing of which they could think less than those prior fictions upon which they had built their knowledge of natural things, for these fictions could in no way help to the knowledge of the divine nature. It is no wonder, therefore, if we find them continually contradicting themselves. But this I pass by. For my only purpose was to give a reason why I did not say that that pertains to the essence of a thing without which the thing can neither be nor can be conceived; and my reason is, that individual things cannot be nor be conceived without God, and yet God does not pertain to their essence. I have rather, therefore, said that the essence of a thing is necessarily that which being given, the thing is posited, and being taken away, the thing is taken away, or that without which the thing can neither be nor be conceived, and which in its turn cannot be or be conceived without the thing.

Prop. XI.—The first thing which forms the actual Being of the human mind is nothing else than the idea of an individual thing actually existing

Demonst.—The essence of man is formed (Corol. Prop. 10, pt. 2) by certain modes of the attributes of God, that is to say (Ax. 2, pt. 2), modes of thought, the idea of all of them being prior by nature to the modes of thought themselves (Ax. 3, pt. 2); and if this idea exists, other modes (which also have an idea in nature prior to them) must exist in the same individual likewise (Ax. 3, pt. 2). Therefore an idea is the first thing which forms the Being of the human mind. But it is not the idea of a non-existent thing, for then the idea itself (Corol. Prop. 8, pt. 2) could not be said to exist. It will, therefore, be the idea of something actually existing. Neither will it be the idea of an infinite thing, for an infinite thing must always necessarily exist (Props. 21 and 22, pt. 1), and this (Ax. 1, pt. 2) is absurd. Therefore the first thing which forms the actual Being of the human mind is the idea of an individual thing actually existing.—Q.E.D.

Corol.—Hence it follows that the human mind is a part of the infinite intellect of God, and therefore, when we say that the human mind perceives this or that thing, we say nothing else than that God has this or that idea; not indeed in so far as He is infinite, but in so far as He is manifested through the nature of the human mind, or in so far as He forms the essence of the human mind; and when we say that God has this or that idea, not merely in so far as He forms the nature of the human mind, but in so far as He has at the same time with the human mind the idea also of another thing, then we say that the human mind perceives the thing partially or inadequately.

Schol.—At this point many of my readers will no doubt stick fast, and will think of many things which will cause delay; and I therefore beg of them to advance slowly, step by step, with men, and not to pronounce judgment until they shall have read everything which I have to say.

Prop. XII.—Whatever happens in the object of the idea constituting the human mind must be perceived by the human mind; or, in other words, an idea of that thing will necessarily exist in the human mind. That is to say, if the object of the idea constituting the human mind be a body, nothing can happen in that body which is not perceived by the mind

Schol.—This proposition is plainly deducible and more easily to be understood from Schol. Prop. 7, pt. 2, to which the reader is referred.

Prop. XIII.—The object of the idea constituting the human mind is a body, or a certain mode of extension actually existing, and nothing else

Demonst.—For if the body were not the object of the human mind, the ideas of the affections of the body would not be in God (Corol. Prop. 9, pt. 2) in so far as He has formed our mind, but would be in Him in so far as He has formed the mind of another thing; that is to say (Corol. Prop. 11, pt. 2), the ideas of the affections of the body would not be in our mind. But (Ax. 4, pt. 2) we have ideas of the affections of a body; therefore the object of the idea constituting the human mind is a body, and that too (Prop. 11, pt. 2) actually existing. Again, if there were also any other object of the mind besides a body, since nothing exists from which some effect does not follow (Prop. 36, pt. 1), the idea of some effect produced by this object would necessarily exist in our mind (Prop. 11, pt. 2). But (Ax. 5, pt. 2) there is no such idea, and therefore the object of our mind is a body existing, and nothing else.—Q.E.D.

Corol.—Hence it follows that man is composed of mind and body, and that the human body exists as we perceive it.

Schol.—Hence we see not only that the human mind is united to the body, but also what is to be understood by the union of the mind and body. But no one can understand it adequately or distinctly without knowing adequately beforehand the nature of our body; for those things which we have proved hitherto are altogether general, nor do they refer more to man than to other individuals, all of which are animate, although in different degrees. For of everything there necessarily exists in God an idea of which He is the cause, in the same way as the idea of the human body exists in Him; and therefore everything that we have said of the idea of the human body is necessarily true of the idea of any other thing. We cannot, however, deny that ideas, like objects themselves, differ from one another, and that one is more excellent and contains more reality than another, just as the object of one idea is more excellent and contains more reality than another. Therefore, in order to determine the difference between the human mind and other things and its superiority over them, we must first know, as we have said, the nature of its object, that is to say, the nature of the human body. I am not able to explain it here, nor is such an explanation necessary for what I wish to demonstrate.

This much, nevertheless, I will say generally, that in proportion as one body is better adapted than another to do or suffer many things, in the same proportion will the mind at the same time be better adapted to perceive many things, and the more the actions of a body depend upon itself alone, and the less other bodies co-operate with it in action, the better adapted will the mind be for distinctly understanding. We can thus determine the superiority of one mind to another; we can also see the reason why we have only a very confused knowledge of our body, together with many other things which I shall deduce in what follows.

Postulate 1.—The human body is composed of a number of individuals of diverse nature, each of which is composite to a high degree.

Postulate 2.—Of the individuals of which the human body is composed, some are fluid, some soft, and some hard.

Postulate 3.—The individuals composing the human body, and consequently the human body itself, are affected by external bodies in many ways.

Postulate 4.—The human body needs for its preservation many other bodies by which it is, as it were, continually regenerated.

Postulate 5.—When a fluid part of the body is determined by an external body, so that it often strikes upon another which is soft, the fluid part changes the plane of the soft part, and leaves upon it, as it were, some traces of the impelling external body.

Postulate 6.—The human body can move and arrange external bodies in many ways.

Prop. XIV.—The human mind is adapted to the perception of many things, and its aptitude increases in proportion to the number of ways in which its body can be disposed

Demonst.—The human body is affected (Post. 3 and 6) in many ways by external bodies, and is so disposed as to affect external bodies in many ways. But the human mind must perceive (Prop. 12, pt. 2) everything which happens in the human body. The human mind is therefore adapted, &c.—Q.E.D.

Prop. XV.—The idea which constitutes the formal Being of the human mind is not simple, but is composed of a number of ideas

Demonst.— The idea which constitutes the formal Being of the human mind is the idea of a body (Prop. 13, pt. 2) which (Post. 1) is composed of a number of individuals composite to a high degree. But an idea of each individual composing the body must necessarily exist in God (Corol. Prop. 8, pt. 2); therefore (Prop. 7, pt. 2) the idea of the human body is composed of these several ideas of the component parts.—Q.E.D.

Prop. XVI.—The idea of every way in which the human body is affected by external bodies must involve the nature of the human body, and at the same time the nature of the external body

Demonst.—All the ways in which any body is affected follow at the same time from the nature of the affected body, and from the nature of the affecting body (Ax. 1, pt. 2); therefore the idea of these affections (Ax. 4, pt. 1) necessarily involves the nature of each body, and therefore the idea of each way in which the human body is affected by an external body involves the nature of the human body and of the external body.—Q.E.D.

Corol. 1.—Hence it follows, in the first place, that the human mind perceives the nature of many bodies together with that of its own body.

Corol. 2.—It follows, secondly, that the ideas we have of external bodies indicate the constitution of our own body rather than the nature of external body.

This I have explained in the Appendix of the First Part by many examples.

Prop. XVII.—If the human body be affected in a way which involves the nature of any external body, the human mind will contemplate that external body as actually existing or as present, until the human body be affected by an affect which excludes the existence or presence of the external body

Demonst.—This is evident. For so long as the human body is thus affected, so long will the human mind (Prop. 12, pt. 2) contemplate this affect of the external body, that is to say (Prop. 16, pt. 2), it will have an idea of a mode actually existing which involves the nature of the external body, that is to say, an idea which does not exclude the existence or presence of the nature of the external body, but posits it; and therefore the mind (Corol. 1, Prop. 16, pt. 2) will contemplate the external body as actually existing, &c.—Q.E.D.

Corol.—The mind is able to contemplate external things by which the human body was once affected as if they were present, although they are not present and do not exist.

Schol.—We see, therefore, how it is possible for us to contemplate things which do not exist as if they were actually present. This may indeed be produced by other causes, but I am satisfied with having here shown one cause through which I could explain it, just as if I had explained it through the true cause. I do not think however, that I am far from the truth, since no postulate which I have assumed contains anything which is not confirmed by an experience that we cannot mistrust after we have proved the existence of the human body as we perceive it (Corol. following Prop. 13, pt. 2). Moreover (Corol. Prop. 17, pt. 2, and Corol. 2, Prop. 16, pt. 2), we clearly see what is the difference between the idea, for example, of Peter, which constitutes the essence of the mind itself of Peter, and the idea of Peter himself which is in another man; for example, in Paul. For the former directly manifests the essence of the body of Peter himself, nor does it involve existence unless so long as Peter exists; the latter, on the other hand, indicates rather the constitution of the body of Paul than the nature of Peter; and therefore so long as Paul's body exists with that constitution, so long will Paul's mind contemplate Peter as present, although he does not exist. But in order that we may retain the customary phraseology, we will give to those affections of the human body, the ideas of which represent to us external bodies as if they were present, the name of *images of things*, although they do not actually reproduce the forms of the things. When the mind contemplates bodies in this way, we will say that it imagines. Here I wish it to be observed, in order that I may begin to show what *error* is, that these imaginations of the mind, regarded by themselves, contain no error, and that the mind is not in error because it imagines, but only in so far as it is considered as wanting in an idea which excludes the existence of those things which it imagines as present. For if the mind, when it imagines non-existent things to be present, could at the same time know that those things did not really exist, it would think its power of imagination to be a virtue of its nature and not a defect, especially if this faculty of imagining depended upon its own nature alone, that is to say (Def. 7, pt. 1), if this faculty of the mind were free.

Prop. XVIII.—If the human body has at any time been simultaneously affected by two or more bodies, whenever the mind afterwards imagines one of them, it will also remember the others

Demonst.—The mind imagines a body (Corol. Prop. 17, pt. 2) because the human body is affected and disposed by the impressions of an external body, just as it was affected when certain of its parts received an impulse from the external body itself. But by hypothesis, the body was at that time disposed in such a manner that the mind imagined two bodies at once; therefore it will imagine two at once now, and whenever it imagines one, it will immediately recollect the other.—Q.E.D.

Schol.—We clearly understand by this what memory is. It is nothing else than a certain concatenation of ideas, involving the nature of things which are outside the human body, a concatenation which corresponds in the mind to the order and concatenation of the affections of the human body. I say, firstly, that it is a concatenation of those ideas only which involve the nature of things which are outside the human body, and not of those ideas which explain the nature of those things, for there are in truth (Prop. 16, pt. 2) ideas of the affections of the human body, which involve its nature as well as the nature of external bodies. I say, in the second place, that this concatenation takes place according to the order and concatenation of the affections of the human body, that I may distinguish it from the concatenation of ideas which takes place according to the order of the intellect, and enables the mind to perceive things through their first causes, and is the same in all men. Hence we can clearly understand how it is that the mind from the thought of one thing at once turns to the thought of another thing which is not in any way like the first. For example, from the thought of the word *pomum* a Roman immediately turned to the thought of the fruit, which has no resemblance to the articulate sound *pomum*, nor anything in common with it, excepting this, that the body of that man was often affected by the thing and the sound; that is to say, he often heard the word *pomum* when he saw the fruit. In this manner each person will turn from one thought to another according to the manner in which the habit of each has arranged the images of things in the body. The soldier, for instance, if he sees the footsteps of a horse in the sand, will immediately turn from the thought of a horse to the thought of a horseman, and so to the thought of war. The countryman, on the other hand, from the thought of a horse will turn to the thought of his plough, his field, &c.; and thus each person will turn from one thought to this or that thought, according to the manner in which he has been accustomed to connect and bind together the images of things in his mind.

Prop. XXIII.—The mind does not know itself except in so far as it perceives the ideas of the affections of the body

Prop. XXIV.—The human mind does not involve an adequate knowledge of the parts composing the human body

Prop. XXV.—The idea of each affection of the human body does not involve an adequate knowledge of an external body

Demonst.—We have shown that the idea of an affection of the human body involves the nature of an external body so far as (Prop. 16, pt. 2) the external body determines the human body in some certain manner. But in so far as the external body is an individual which is not related to the human body, its idea or knowledge is in God (Prop. 9, pt. 2) in so far as He is considered as affected by the idea of another thing, which idea (Prop. 7, pt. 2) is prior by nature to the external body itself. Therefore the adequate knowledge of an external body is not in God in so far as He has the idea of the affection of the human body, or, in other words, the idea of the affection of the human body does not involve an adequate knowledge of an external body.—Q.E.D.

Prop. XXVI.—The human mind perceives no external body as actually existing, unless through the ideas of the affections of its body

Demonst.—If the human body is in no way affected by an external body, then (Prop. 7, pt. 2) the idea of the human body, that is to say (Prop. 13, pt. 2), the human mind, is not affected in any way by the idea of the existence of that body, nor does it in any way perceive the existence of that external body. But in so far as the human body is affected in any way by any external body, so far (Prop. 16, pt. 2, with its Corol.) does it perceive the external body.—Q.E.D.

Corol.—In so far as the human mind imagines an external body, so far it has not an adequate knowledge of it.

Demonst.—When the human mind through the ideas of the affections of its body contemplates external bodies, we say that it then imagines (Schol. Prop. 17, pt. 2), nor can the mind (Prop. 26, pt. 2) in any other way imagine external bodies as actually existing. Therefore (Prop. 25, pt. 2) in so far as the mind imagines external bodies it does not possess an adequate knowledge of them.—Q.E.D.

Prop. XXVII.—The idea of any affection of the human body does not involve an adequate knowledge of the human body itself

Demonst.—Every idea of any affection of the human body involves the nature of the human body in so far as the human body itself is considered as affected in a certain manner (Prop. 16, pt. 2). But in so far as the human body is an individual which can be affected in a multitude of other ways, its idea, &c. (See Demonst. Prop. 25, pt. 2.)

Prop. XXVIII.—The ideas of the affections of the human body, in so far as they are related only to the human mind, are not clear and distinct, but confused

Prop. XXIX.—The idea of the idea of any affection of the human body does not involve an adequate knowledge of the human mind

Demonst.—The idea of an affection of the human body (Prop. 27, pt. 2) does not involve an adequate knowledge of the body itself, or, in other words, does not adequately express its nature, that is to say (Prop. 13, pt. 2), it does not correspond adequately with the nature of the human mind, and therefore (Ax. 6, pt. 1) the idea of this idea does not adequately express the nature of the human mind, nor involve an adequate knowledge of it.—Q.E.D.

Corol.—From this it is evident that the human mind, when it perceives thing in the common order of nature, has no adequate knowledge of itself nor of its own body, nor of external bodies, but only a confused and mutilated knowledge; for the mind does not know itself unless in so far as it perceives the ideas of the affections of the body (Prop. 23, pt. 2). Moreover (Prop. 19, pt. 2), it does not perceive its body unless through those same ideas of the affections by means of which alone (Prop. 26, pt. 2) it perceives external bodies. Therefore in so far as it possesses these ideas it possesses an adequate knowledge neither of itself (Prop. 29, pt. 2), nor of its body (Prop. 27, pt. 2), nor of external bodies (Prop. 25, pt. 2), but merely (Prop. 28, pt. 2, together with the scholium) a mutilated and confused knowledge.—Q.E.D.

Schol.—I say expressly that the mind has no adequate knowledge of itself, nor of its body, nor of external bodies, but only a confused knowledge, as often as it perceives things in the common order of nature, that is to say, as often as it is determined to the contemplation of this or that *externally*—namely, by a chance coincidence, and not as often as it is determined *internally*—for the reason that it contemplates several things at once, and is determined to understand in what they differ, agree, or oppose one another; for whenever it is internally disposed in this or in any other way, it then contemplates things clearly and distinctly, as I shall show presently.

Prop. XXX.—About the duration of our body we can have but a very inadequate knowledge

Demonst.—The duration of our body does not depend upon its essence (Ax. 1, pt. 2), nor upon the absolute nature of God (Prop. 21, pt. 1), but (Prop. 28, pt. 1) the body is determined to existence and action by causes which also are determined by others to existence and action in a certain and determinate manner, whilst these, again, are determined by others, and so on *ad infinitum.* The duration, therefore, of our body depends upon the common order of nature and the constitution of things. But an adequate knowledge of the way in which things are constituted, exists in God in so far as He possesses the ideas of all things, and not in so far as He possesses only the idea of the human body (Corol. Prop. 9, pt. 2). Therefore the knowledge of the duration of our body is altogether inadequate in God, in so far as He is only considered as constituting the nature of the human mind, that is to say (Corol. Prop. 11, pt. 2), this knowledge in our mind is altogether inadequate.—Q.E.D.

Prop. XXXI.—About the duration of individual things which are outside us we can have but a very inadequate knowledge

Demonst.—Each individual thing, like the human body, must be determined to existence and action by another individual thing in certain and determinate manner, and this again by another, and so on *ad infinitum* (Prop. 28, pt. 1). But we have demonstrated in the preceding proposition, from this common property of individual things, that we have but a very inadequate knowledge of the duration of our own body; therefore the same conclusion is to be drawn about the duration of individual things, that is to say, that we can have but a very inadequate knowledge of it.—Q.E.D.

Corol.—Hence it follows that all individual things are contingent and corruptible, for we can have no adequate knowledge concerning their duration (Prop. 31, pt. 2), and this is what is to be understood by us as their contingency and capability of corruption (Schol. 1, Prop. 33, pt. 1); for (Prop. 29, pt. 1) there is no other contingency but this.

Prop. XXXII.—All ideas, in so far as they are related to God, are true

Demonst.—All the ideas which are in God always agree with those things of which they are the ideas (Corol. Prop. 7, pt. 2), and therefore (Ax. 6, pt. 1) they are all true.—Q.E.D.

Prop. XXXIII.—In ideas there is nothing positive on account of which they are called false

Demonst.—If the contrary be asserted, conceive, if it be possible, a positive mode of thought which shall constitute the form or error of falsity. This mode of thought cannot be in God (Prop. 32, pt. 2), but outside God it can neither be nor be conceived (Prop. 15, pt. 1), and therefore in ideas there is nothing positive on account of which they are called false.—Q.E.D.

Prop. XXXIV.—Every idea which in us is absolute, that is to say, adequate and perfect, is true

Demonst.—When we say that an adequate and perfect idea is in us, we say nothing else than (Corol. Prop. 11, pt. 2) that an adequate and perfect idea exists in God in so far as He constitutes the essence of the human mind, and consequently (Prop. 32, pt. 2) we say nothing else than that this idea is true.—Q.E.D.

Prop. XXXV.—Falsity consists in the privation of knowledge, which inadequate, that is to say, mutilated and confused ideas involve

Demonst.—There is nothing positive in ideas which can constitute a form of falsity (Prop. 33, pt. 2). But falsity cannot consist in absolute privation (for we say that minds and not bodies err and are mistaken); nor can it consist in absolute ignorance, for to be ignorant and to be in error are different. Falsehood, therefore, consists in the privation of knowledge which is involved by inadequate knowledge of things or by inadequate and confused ideas.—Q.E.D.

Schol.—In the scholium of Prop. 17, pt. 2, I have explained how error consists in the privation of knowledge; but for the sake of fuller explanation, I will give an example. For instance, men are deceived because they think themselves free, and the sole reason for thinking so is that they are conscious of their own actions, and ignorant of the causes by which those actions are determined. Their idea of liberty therefore is this—that they know no cause for their own actions; for as to saying that their actions depend upon their will, these are words to which no idea is attached. What the will is, and in what manner it moves the body, every one is ignorant, for those who pretend otherwise, and devise seats and dwelling-places of the soul, usually excite our laughter or disgust. Just in the same manner, when we look at the sun, we imagine his distance from us to be about 200 feet; the error not consisting solely in the imagination, but arising from our not knowing what the true distance is when we imagine, and what the causes of our imagination. For although we may afterwards know that the sun is more than 600 diameters of the earth distant from us, we still imagine it near us, since we imagine it to be so near, not because we are ignorant of its true distance, but because of an affection of our body involves the essence of the sun, in so far as our body itself is affected by it.

Prop. XXXVI.—Inadequate and confused ideas follow by the same necessity as adequate or clear and distinct ideas

Prop. XXXVII.—That which is common to everything, and which is equally in the part and in the whole, forms the essence of no individual thing

Demonst.—For if this be denied, let that which is common be conceived, if possible, to constitute the essence of some individual thing,—the essence, for example, of B. Without B, therefore (Def. 2, pt. 2), that which is common can neither be nor be conceived. But this is contrary to the hypothesis. Therefore that which is common does not pertain to the essence of B, nor does it form the essence of any other individual thing.

Prop. XXXVIII.—Those things which are common to everything, and which are equally in the part and in the whole, can only be adequately conceived

Demonst.—Let there be something A, which is common to all bodies, and which is equally in the part of each body and in the whole. I say that A can only be adequately conceived. For the idea of A (Corol. Prop. 7, pt. 2) will necessarily be adequate in God, both in so far as He has the idea of the human body and in so far as He has the idea of its affections, which (Props. 16, 25, and 27, pt. 2) involve the nature of the human body, and partly also the nature of external bodies; that is to say (Props. 12 and 13, pt. 2), this idea will necessarily be adequate in God in so far as He constitutes the human mind, or in so far as He has ideas which are in the human mind. The mind, therefore (Corol. Prop. 11, pt. 2), necessarily perceives A adequately, both in so far as it perceives itself or its own or any external body; nor can A be conceived in any other manner.—Q.E.D.

Corol.—Hence it follows that some ideas or notions exist which are common to all men, for (Lem. 2) all bodies agree in some things, which (Prop. 38, pt. 2) must be adequately, that is to say, clearly and distinctly, perceived by all.

Prop. XXXIX.—There will exist in the human mind an adequate idea of that which is common and proper to the human body, and to any external bodies by which the human body is generally affected—of that which equally in the part of each of these external bodies and in the whole is common and proper

Demonst.—Let A be something which is common and proper to the human body and certain external bodies; let it exist equally in the human body and in those external bodies, and let it exist equally in the part of each external body and in the whole. An adequate idea of A itself will exist in God (Corol. Prop. 7, pt. 2), both in so far as He has the idea of the human body and in so far as He has the idea of the given external bodies. Let it be supposed that the human body is affected by an external body through that which it has in common with the external body, that is to say, by A. The idea of this affection will involve the property of A (Prop. 16, pt. 2), and therefore (Corol. Prop. 7, pt. 2) the idea of this affection, in so far as it involves the property of A, will exist adequately in God in so far as He is affected by the idea of the human body, that is to say (Prop. 13, pt. 2), in so far as He constitutes the nature of the human mind. Therefore (Corol. Prop. 11, pt. 2) this idea is also adequate in the human mind.—Q.E.D.

Corol.—Hence it follows that the more things the body has in common with other bodies, the more things will the mind be adapted to perceive.

Prop. XL.—Those ideas are also adequate which follow in the mind from ideas which are adequate in it

Demonst.—This is evident. For when we say that an idea follows in the human mind from ideas which are adequate in it, we do but say (Corol. Prop. 11, pt. 2) that in the divine intellect itself an idea exists of which God is the cause, not in so far as He is infinite, nor in so far as He is affected by the ideas of a multitude of individual things, but in so far only as He constitutes the essence of the human mind.

Schol. 1.—I have thus explained the origin of those notions which are called common, and which are the foundations of our reasoning; but of some axioms or notions other causes exist which it would be advantageous to explain by our method, for we should thus be able to distinguish those notions which are more useful than others, and those which are scarcely of any use; those which are common; those which are clear and distinct only to those persons who do not suffer from prejudice; and, finally, those which are ill-founded. Moreover, it would be manifest whence these notions which are called *second*, and consequently the axioms founded upon them, have taken their origin, and other things, too, would be explained which I have thought about these matters at different times. Since, however, I have set apart this subject for another treatise, and because I do not wish to create disgust with excessive prolixity, I have determined to pass by this matter here. But not to omit anything which is necessary for us to know, I will briefly give the causes from which terms called *Transcendental*, such as *Being, Thing, Something*, have taken their origin. These terms have arisen because the human body, inasmuch as it is limited, can form distinctly in itself a certain number only of images at once. (For the explanation of the word *image*, see Schol. Prop. 17, pt. 2.) If this number be exceeded, the images will become confused; and if the number of images which the body is able to form distinctly be greatly exceeded, they will all run one into another. Since this is so, it is clear (Corol. Prop. 17, and Prop. 18, pt. 2) that in proportion to the number of images which can be formed at the same time in the body will be the number of bodies which the human mind can imagine at the same time. If the images in the body, therefore, are all confused, the mind will confusedly imagine all the bodies without distinguishing the one from the other, and will include them all, as it were, under one attribute, that of being or thing. The same confusion may also be caused by lack of uniform force in the images and from other analogous causes, which there is no need to discuss here, the consideration of one cause being sufficient for the purpose we have in view. For it all comes to this, that these terms signify ideas in the highest degree confused.

It is in this way that those notions have arisen which are called *Universal*, such as *Man, Horse, Dog*, &c.; that is to say, so many images of men, for instance, are formed in the human body at once, that they exceed the power of the imagination, not entirely, but to such a degree that the mind has no power to imagine the determinate number of men and the small differences of each, such as colour and size, &c. It will therefore distinctly imagine that only in which all of them agree in so far as the body is affected by them, for by that the body was chiefly affected, that is to say, by each individual, and this it will express by the name *man*, covering thereby an infinite number of individuals; to imagine a determinate number of individuals being out of its power. But we must observe that these notions are not formed by all persons in the same way, but that they vary in each case according to the thing by which the body is more frequently affected, and which the mind more easily imagines or recollects. For example, those who have more frequently looked with admiration upon the stature of men, by the name *man* will understand an animal of erect stature, while those who have been in the habit of fixing their thoughts on something else, will form another common image of men, describing man, for instance, as an animal capable of laughter, a biped without feathers, a rational animal, and so on; each person forming universal images of things according to the temperament of his own body. It is not therefore to be wondered at that so many controversies have arisen amongst those philosophers who have endeavoured to explain natural objects by the images of things alone.

Schol. 2.—From what has been already said, it clearly appears that we perceive many things and form universal ideas:

1. From individual things, represented by the senses to us in a mutilated and confused manner, and without order to the intellect (Corol. Prop. 29, pt. 2). These perceptions I have therefore been in the habit of calling knowledge from vague experience.

2. From signs; as, for example, when we hear or read certain words, we recollect things and form certain ideas of them similar to them, through which ideas we imagine things (Schol. Prop. 18, pt. 2). These two ways of looking at things I shall hereafter call knowledge of the first kind, opinion or imagination.

3. From our possessing common notions and adequate ideas of the properties of things (Corol. Prop. 38, Prop. 39, with Corol. and Prop. 40, pt. 2). This I shall call reason and knowledge of the second kind.

Besides these two kinds of knowledge, there is a third, as I shall hereafter show, which we shall call intuitive science. This kind of knowing advances from an adequate idea of the formal essence of certain attributes of God to the adequate knowledge of the essence of things. All this I will explain by one example. Let there be three numbers given through which it is required to discover a fourth which shall be to the third as the second is to the first. A merchant does not hesitate to multiply the second and third together and divide the product by the first, either because he has not yet forgotten the things which he heard without any demonstration from his schoolmaster, or because he has seen the truth of the rule with the more simple numbers, or because from the 19th Prop. in the 7th book of Euclid he understands the common property of all proportionals.

But with the simplest numbers there is no need of all this. If the numbers 1, 2, 3, for instance, be given, every one can see that the fourth proportional is 6 much more clearly than by any demonstration, because from the ratio in which we see by one intuition that the first stands to the second we conclude the fourth.

Prop. XLI.—Knowledge of the first kind alone is the cause of falsity; knowledge of the second and third orders is necessarily true

Demonst.—To knowledge of the first kind we have said, in the preceding scholium, that all those ideas belong which are inadequate and confused, and, therefore (Prop. 35, pt. 2), this knowledge alone is the cause of falsity. Moreover, to knowledge of the second and third kind we have said that those ideas belong which are adequate, and therefore this knowledge (Prop. 34, pt. 2) is necessarily true.

Prop. XLII.—It is the knowledge of the second and third, and not that of the first kind, which teaches us to distinguish the true from the false

Demonst.—This proposition is self-evident. For he who knows how to distinguish between the true and the false must have an adequate idea of the true and the false, that is to say (Schol. 2, Prop. 40, pt. 2), he must know the true and the false by the second or third kind of knowledge.

Prop. XLIII.—He who has a true idea knows at the same time that he has a true idea, nor can he doubt the truth of the thing

Schol.—In the scholium to Prop. 21, pt. 2, I have explained what is the idea of an idea, but it is to be observed that the preceding proposition is evident by itself. For no one who has a true idea is ignorant that a true idea involves the highest certitude; to have a true idea signifying just this, to know a thing perfectly or as well as possible. No one, in fact, can doubt this, unless he supposes an idea to be something dumb, like a picture on a tablet, instead of being a mode of thought, that is to say, intelligence itself. Moreover, I ask who can know that he understands a thing unless he first of all understands that thing? that is to say, who can know that he is certain of anything unless he is first of all certain of that thing? Then, again, what can be clearer or more certain than a true idea as the standard of truth? Just as light reveals both itself and the darkness, so truth is the standard of itself and of the false. I consider what has been said to be a sufficient answer to the objection that if a true idea is distinguished from a false idea only in so far as it is said to agree with that of which it is the idea, the true idea therefore has no reality nor perfection above the false idea (since they are distinguished by an external sign alone), and consequently the man who has true ideas will have no greater reality or perfection than he who has false ideas only. I consider, too, that I have already replied to those who inquire why men have false ideas, and how a man can certainly know that he has ideas which agree with those things of which they are the ideas. For with regard to the difference between a true and a false idea, it is evident from Prop. 35, pt. 2, that the former is related to the latter as being is to non-being. The causes of falsity, too, I have most clearly shown in Props. 19–35, including the sholium to the last. From what has there been said, the nature of the difference between a man who has true ideas and one who has only false ideas is clear. With regard to the last-mentioned point—how a man can know that he has an idea which agrees with that of which it is the idea—I have shown almost more times than enough that he knows it simply because he has an idea which agrees with that of which it is the idea, that is to say, because truth is its own standard. We must remember, besides, that our mind, in so far as it truly perceives things, is a part of the infinite intellect of God (Corol. Prop. 11, pt. 2), and therefore it must be that the clear and distinct ideas of the mind are as true as those of God.

Prop. XLIV.—It is not of the nature of reason to consider things as contingent but as necessary

Demonst.—It is in the nature of reason to perceive things truly (Prop. 41, pt. 2), that is to say (Ax. 6, pt. 1), as they are in themselves, that is to say (Prop. 29, pt. 1), not as contingent but as necessary.—Q.E.D.

Corol. 1.—Hence it follows that it is through the imagination alone that we look upon things as contingent both with reference to the past and the future.

Schol.—How this happens I will explain in a few words. We have shown above (Prop. 17, pt. 2, with Corol.) that unless causes occur preventing the present existence of things, the mind always imagines them present before it, even if they do not exist. Again (Prop. 18, pt. 2), we have shown that if the human body has once been simultaneously affected by two external bodies, whenever the mind afterwards imagines one it will immediately remember the other; that is to say, it will look upon both as present before it, unless causes occur which prevent the present existence of the things. No one doubts, too, that we imagine time because we imagine some bodies to move with a velocity less, or greater than, or equal to that of others. Let us therefore suppose a boy who yesterday, for the first time, in the morning saw Peter, at midday Paul, in the evening Simeon, and to-day in the morning again sees Peter. It is plain from Prop. 18, pt. 2, that as soon as he sees the morning light he will imagine the sun passing through the same part of the sky as on the day preceding; that is to say, he will imagine the whole day, and at the same time Peter will be connected in his imagination with the morning, Paul with midday, and Simeon with the evening. In the morning, therefore, the existence of Paul and Simeon will be imagined in relation to future time, while in the evening, if the boy should see Simeon, he will refer Peter and Paul to the past, since they will be connected with the past in his imagination. This process will be constant in proportion to the regularity with which he sees Peter, Paul, and Simeon in this order. If it should by some means happen that on some other evening, in the place of Simeon, he should see James, on the following morning he will connect in his imagination with the evening at one time Simeon and at another James, but not both together. For he is supposed to have seen one and then the other in the evening, but not both together. His imagination will therefore fluctuate, and he will connect with a future evening first one and then the other; that is to say, he will consider neither as certain, but both as a contingency in the future.

This fluctuation of the imagination will take place in the same way if the imagination is dealing with things which we contemplate in the same way with reference to past or present time, and consequently we imagine things related to time past, present, or future as contingent.

Corol. 2.—It is of the nature of reason to perceive things under a certain form of eternity.

Demonst.—It is of the nature of reason to consider things as necessary and not as contingent (Prop. 44, pt. 2). This necessity of things it perceives truly (Prop. 41, pt. 2); that is to say (Ax. 6, pt. 1), as it is in itself. But (Prop. 16, pt. 1) this necessity of things is the necessity itself of the eternal nature of God. Therefore it is of the nature of reason to consider things under this form of eternity. Moreover, the foundations of reason are notions which explain those things which are common to all (Prop. 38, pt. 2), and these things explain the essence of no individual thing (Prop. 37, pt. 2), and must therefore be conceived without any relation to time, but under a certain form of eternity.—Q.E.D.

Prop. XLV.—Every idea of any body or actually existing individual thing necessarily involves the eternal and infinite essence of God

Demonst.—The idea of an individual thing actually existing necessarily involves both the essence and existence of the thing itself (Corol. Prop. 8, pt. 2). But individual things (Prop. 15, pt. 1) cannot be conceived without God, and since (Prop. 6, pt. 2) God is their cause in so far as He is considered under that attribute of which they are modes, their ideas (Ax. 4, pt. 1) must necessarily involve the conception of that attribute, or, in other words (Def. 6, pt. 1), must involve the eternal and infinite essence of God.—Q.E.D.

Schol.—By existence is to be understood here not duration, that is, existence considered in the abstract, as if it were a certain kind of quantity, but I speak of the nature itself of the existence which is assigned to individual things, because from the eternal necessity of the nature of God infinite numbers of things follow in infinite ways (Prop. 16, pt. 1). I repeat, that I speak of the existence itself of individual things in so far as they are in God. For although each individual thing is determined by another individual thing to existence in a certain way, the force nevertheless by which each thing perseveres in its existence follows from the eternal necessity of the nature of God (see Corol. Prop. 24, pt. 1).

Prop. XLVI.—The knowledge of the eternal and infinite essence of God which each idea involves is adequate and perfect

Demonst.—The demonstration of the preceding proposition is universal, and whether a thing be considered as a part of as a whole, its idea, whether it be of a part or whole, will involve the eternal and infinite essence of God (Prop. 45, pt. 2). Therefore that which gives a knowledge of the eternal and infinite essence of God is common to all, and is equally in the part and in the whole. This knowledge therefore (Prop. 38, pt. 2) will be adequate.—Q.E.D.

Prop. XLVII.—The human mind possesses an adequate knowledge of the eternal and infinite essence of God

Demonst.—The human mind possesses ideas by which (Prop. 23, pt. 2) it perceives itself and its own body (Prop. 19, pt. 2), together with (Corol. 1, Prop. 16, and Prop. 17, pt. 2) external bodies, as actually existing. Therefore (Props. 45 and 46, pt. 2) it possesses an adequate knowledge of the eternal and infinite essence of God.—Q.E.D.

Schol.—Hence we see that the infinite essence and the eternity of God are known to all; and since all things are in God and are conceived through Him, it follows that we can deduce from this knowledge many things which we can know adequately, and that we can thus form that third sort of knowledge mentioned in Schol. 2, Prop. 40, pt. 2, of whose excellence and value the Fifth Part will be the place to speak. The reason why we do not possess a knowledge of God as distinct as that which we have of common notions is, that we cannot imagine God as we can bodies; and because we have attached the name God to the images of things which we are in the habit of seeing, an error we can hardly avoid, inasmuch as we are continually affected by external bodies. Many errors, of a truth, consist merely in the application of the wrong names to things. For if a man says that the lines which are drawn from the centre of the circle to the circumference are not equal, he understands by the circle, at all events for the time, something else than mathematicians understand by it. So when men make errors in calculation, the numbers which are in their minds are not those which are upon the paper. As far as their mind is concerned there is no error, although it seems as if there were, because we think that the numbers in their minds are those which are upon the paper. If we did not think so, we should not believe them to be in error. For example, when I lately heard a man complaining that his court had flown into one of his neighbour's fowls, I understood what he meant, and therefore did not imagine him to be in error. This is the source from which so many controversies arise—that men either do not properly explain their own thoughts, or do not properly interpret those of other people; for, in truth, when they most contradict one another, they either think the same things or something different, so that those things which they suppose to be errors and absurdities in another person are not so.

Prop. XLVIII.—In the mind there is no absolute or free will, but the mind is determined to this or that volition by a cause, which is also determined by another cause, and this again by another, and so on ad infinitum

Demonst.—The mind is a certain and determinate mode of thought (Prop. 11, pt. 2), and therefore (Corol. 2, Prop. 17, pt. 1) it cannot be the free cause of its own actions, or have an absolute faculty of willing or not willing, but must be determined to this or that volition (Prop. 28, pt. 1) by a cause which is also determined by another cause, and this again by another, and so on *ad infinitum*.—Q.E.D.

Schol.—In the same manner it is demonstrated that in the mind there exists no absolute faculty of understanding, desiring, loving, &c. These and the like faculties, therefore, are either altogether fictitious, or else are nothing but metaphysical or universal entities, which we are in the habit of forming from individual cases. The intellect and will, therefore, are related to this or that idea or volition as rockiness is related to this or that rock, or as man is related to Peter or Paul. The reason why men imagine themselves to be free we have explained in the Appendix to the First Part. Before, however, I advance any farther, I must observe that by the will I understand a faculty of affirming or denying, but not a desire; a faculty, I say, by which the mind affirms or denies that which is true or false, and not a desire by which the mind seeks a thing or turns away from it. But now that we have demonstrated that these faculties are universal notions which are not distinguishable from the individual notions from which they are formed, we must now inquire whether the volitions themselves are anything more than the idea of things. We must inquire, I say, whether in the mind there exists any other affirmation or negation than that which the idea involves in so far as it is an idea. For this purpose see the following proposition, together with Def. 3, pt. 2, so that thought may not fall into pictures. For by ideas I do not understand the images which are formed at the back of the eye, or, if you please, in the middle of the brain, but rather the conceptions of thought.

Prop. XLIX.—In the mind there is no volition or affirmation and negation excepting that which the idea, in so far as it is an idea, involves

Demonst.—In the mind there exists (Prop. 48, pt. 2) no absolute faculty of willing or not willing. Only individual volitions exist, that is to say, this and that affirmation and this and that negation. Let us conceive therefore, any individual volition, that is, any mode of thought, by which the mind affirms that the three angles of a triangle are equal to two right angles. This affirmation involves the conception or idea of the triangle, that is to say, without it the affirmation cannot be conceived. For to say that A must involve the conception B, is the same as saying that A cannot be conceived without B. But this idea of the triangle must involve this same affirmation that its three angles are equal to two right angles. Therefore also, *vice versa*, this idea of the triangle without this affirmation can neither be nor be conceived. Therefore (Def. 2, pt. 2) this affirmation pertains to the essence of the idea of the triangle, nor is it anything else besides this. Whatever too we have said of this volition (since it has been taken arbitrarily) applies to all other volitions, that is to say, they are nothing but ideas.—Q.E.D.

Corol.—The will and the intellect are one and the same.

Demonst.—The will and the intellect are nothing but the individual volitions and ideas themselves

(Prop. 48, pt. 2, and its Schol.) But the individual volition and idea (Prop. 49, pt. 2) are one and the same. Therefore the will and the intellect are one and the same.—Q.E.D.

Schol.—I have thus removed what is commonly thought to be the cause of error. It has been proved above that falsity consists solely in the privation which mutilated and confused ideas involve. A false idea, therefore, in so far as it is false, does not involve certitude. Consequently, when we say that a man assents to what is false and does not doubt it, we do not say that he is certain, but merely that he does not doubt, that is to say, that he assents to what is false, because there are no causes sufficient to make his imagination waver (Schol. Prop. 44, pt. 2). Although, therefore, a man may be supposed to adhere to what is false, we shall never on that account say that he is certain. For by certitude we understand something positive (Prop. 43, pt. 2, with the Schol.), and not the privation of doubt; but by the privation of certitude we understand falsity. If the preceding proposition, however, is to be more clearly comprehended, a word or two must be added; it yet remains also that I should answer the objections which may be brought against our doctrine, and finally, in order to remove all scruples, I have thought it worth while to indicate some of its advantages. I say some, as the principal advantages will be better understood when we come to the Fifth Part. I begin, therefore, with the first, and I warn my readers carefully to distinguish between an idea or conception of the mind and the images of things formed by our imagination. Secondly, it is necessary that we should distinguish between ideas and the words by which things are signified. For it is because these three things, images, words, and ideas, are by many people either altogether confounded or not distinguished with sufficient accuracy and care that such ignorance exists about this doctrine of the will, so necessary to be known both for the purposes of speculation and for the wise government of life. Those who think that ideas consist of images, which are formed in us by meeting with external bodies, persuade themselves that those ideas of things of which we can form no similar image are not ideas, but mere fancies constructed by the free power of the will. They look upon ideas, therefore, as dumb pictures on a tablet, and being prepossessed with this prejudice, they do not see that an idea, in so far as it is an idea, involves affirmation or negation. Again, those who confound words with the idea, or with they affirmation itself which the idea involves, think that they can will contrary to their perception, because they affirm or deny something in words alone contrary to their perception. It will be easy for us, however, to divest ourselves of these prejudices if we attend to the nature of thought, which in no way involves the conception of extension, and by doing this we clearly see that an idea, since it is a mode of thought, is not an image of anything, nor does it consist of words. For the essence of words and images is formed of bodily motions alone, which involve in no way whatever the conception of thought.

Let thus much suffice under this head. I pass on now to the objections to which I have already alluded.

The first is, that it is supposed to be certain that the will extends itself more widely than the intellect, and is therefore different from it. The reason why men suppose that the will extends itself more widely than the intellect is because they say they have discovered that they do not need a larger faculty of assent—that is to say, of affirmation—and denial than that which they now have for the purpose of assenting to an infinite number of other things which we do not perceive, but that they do need a greater faculty for understanding them. The will, therefore, is distinguished from the intellect, the latter being finite, the former infinite. The second objection which can be made is that there is nothing which experience seems to teach more clearly than the possibility of suspending our judgment, so as not to assent to the things we perceive; and we are strengthened in this opinion because no one is said to be deceived in so far as he perceives a thing, but only in so far as he assents to it or dissents from it. For example, a man who imagines a winged horse does not therefore admit the existence of a winged horse; that is to say, he is not necessarily deceived, unless he grants at the same time that a winged horse exists. Experience, therefore, seems to show nothing more plainly than that the will or faculty of assent is free, and different from the faculty of the intellect.

Thirdly, it may be objected that one affirmation does not seem to contain more reality than another; that is to say, it does not appear that we need a greater power for affirming a thing to be true which is true than for affirming a thing to be true which is false. Nevertheless, we observe that one idea contains more reality or perfection than another, for as some objects are nobler than others, in the same proportion are their ideas more perfect. It appears indisputable, therefore, that there is a difference between the will and the intellect.

Fourthly, it may be objected that if a man does not act from freedom of the will, what would he do if he were in a state of equilibrium, like the ass of Buridanus? Would he not perish from hunger and thirst? and if this is granted, do we not seem to conceive him as a statue of a man or as an ass? If I deny that he would thus perish, he will consequently determine himself and possess the power of going where he likes and doing what he likes.

There may be other objections besides these, but as I am not bound to discuss what every one may dream, I shall therefore make it my business to answer as briefly as possible those only which I have mentioned. In reply to the first objection, I grant that the will extends itself more widely than the intellect, if by the intellect we understand only clear and distinct ideas; but I deny that the will extends itself more widely than the perceptions or the faculty of conception; nor, indeed, do I see why the faculty of will should be said to be infinite any more than the faculty of feeling; for as by the same faculty of will we can affirm an infinite number of things (one after the other, for we cannot affirm an infinite number of things at once), so also by the same faculty of feeling we can feel or perceive (one after another) an infinite number of bodies. If it be said that there are an infinite number of things which we cannot perceive, I reply that such things as these we can reach by no thought, and consequently by no faculty of will. But it is said that if God wished us to perceive those things, it would be necessary for Him to give us a larger faculty of perception, but not a larger faculty of will than He has already given us, which is the same thing as saying that if God wished us to understand an infinite number of other beings, it would be necessary for Him to give us a greater intellect, but not a more universal idea of being (in order to embrace that infinite number of beings), than He has given us. For we have shown that the will is a Universal, or the idea by which we explain all individual volitions, that is to say, that which is common to them all. It is not to be wondered at, therefore, that those who believe this common or universal idea of all the volitions to be a faculty should say that it extends itself infinitely beyond the limits of the intellect. For the universal is predicated of one or of many, or of an infinite number of individuals.

The second objection I answer by denying that we have free power of suspending judgment. For when we say that a person suspends judgment, we only say in other words that he sees that he does not perceive the thing adequately. The suspension of the judgment, therefore, is in truth a perception and not free will. In order that this may be clearly understood, let us take the case of a boy who imagines a horse and perceives nothing else. Since this imagination involves the existence of the horse (Corol. Prop. 17, pt. 2), and the boy does not perceive anything which negates its existence, he will necessarily contemplate it as present, nor will he be able to doubt its existence although he may not be certain of it. This is a thing which we daily experience in dreams, nor do I believe that there is any one who thinks that he has the free power during dreams of suspending his judgment upon those things which he dreams, and of causing himself not to dream those things which he dreams that he sees; and yet in dreams it nevertheless happens that we suspend our judgment, for we dream that we dream.

I grant, it is true, that no man is deceived in so far as he perceives; that is to say, I grant that mental images considered in themselves involve no error (Schol. Prop. 17, pt. 2); but I deny that a man in so far as he perceives affirms nothing. For what else is it to perceive a winged horse than to affirm of the horse that it has wings? For if the mind perceived nothing else but this winged horse, it would regard it as present, nor would it have any reason for doubting its existence, nor any power of refusing assent to it, unless the image of the winged horse be joined to an idea which negates its existence, or the mind perceives that the idea of the winged horse which it has is inadequate. In either of the two latter cases it will necessarily deny or doubt the existence of the horse.

With regard to the third objection, what has been said will perhaps be a sufficient answer,—namely, that the will is something universal, which is predicated of all ideas, and that it signifies that only which is common to them all, that is to say, affirmation. Its adequate essence, therefore, in so far as it is thus considered in the abstract, must be in every idea, and in this sense only must it be the same in all; but not in so far as it is considered as constituting the essence of an idea, for so far, the individual affirmations differ just as the ideas differ. For example, the affirmation which the idea of a circle involves differs from that which the idea of a triangle involves, just as the idea of a circle differs from the idea of a triangle. Again, I absolutely deny that we need a power of thinking in order to affirm that to be true which is true, equal to that which we need in order to affirm that to be true which is false. For these two affirmations, if we look to the mind, are related to one another as being and non-being, for there is nothing positive in ideas which constitutes a form of falsity (Prop. 35, pt. 2, with its Schol., and Schol. to Prop. 47, pt. 2).

Here therefore particularly is it to be observed how easily we are deceived when we confuse universals with individuals, and the entities of reason and abstractions with realities.

With regard to the fourth objection, I say that I entirely grant that if a man were placed in such a state of equilibrium he would perish of hunger and thirst, supposing he perceived nothing but hunger and thirst, and the food and drink which were equidistant from him. If you ask me whether such a man would not be thought an ass rather than a man, I reply that I do not know; nor do I know what ought to be thought of a man who hangs himself, or of children, fools, and madmen.

It remains for me now to show what service to our own lives a knowledge of this doctrine is. This we shall easily understand from the remarks which follow. Notice—

1. It is of service in so far as it teaches us that we do everything by the will of God alone, and that we are partakers of the divine nature in proportion as our actions become more and more perfect and we more and more understand God. This doctrine, therefore, besides giving repose in every way to the soul, has also this advantage, that it teaches us in what our highest happiness or blessedness consists, namely, in the knowledge of God alone, by which we are drawn to do those things only which love and piety persuade. Hence we clearly see how greatly those stray from the true estimation of virtue who expect to be distinguished by God with the highest regards for virtue and the noblest actions as if for the completest servitude, just as if virtue itself and the service of God were not happiness itself and the highest liberty.

2. It is of service to us in so far as it teaches us how we ought to behave with regard to the things of fortune, or those which are not in our power, that is to say, which do not follow from our own nature; for it teaches us with equal mind to wait for and bear each form of fortune, because we know that all things follow from the eternal decree of God, according to that same necessity by which it follows from the essence of a triangle that its three angles are equal to two right angles.

3. This doctrine contributes to the welfare of our social existence, since it teaches us to hate no one, to despise no one, to mock no one, to be angry with no one, and to envy no one. It teaches every one, moreover, to be content with his own, and to be helpful to his neighbour, not from any womanish pity, from partiality, or superstition, but by the guidance of reason alone, according to the demand of time and circumstance, as I shall show in the Third Part.

4. This doctrine contributes not a little to the advantage of common society, in so far as it teaches us by what means citizens are to be governed and led; not in order that they may be slaves, but that they may freely do those things which are best.

Thus I have discharged the obligation laid upon me in this scholium, and with it I make an end of the Second Part, in which I think that I have explained the nature of the human mind and its propensities at sufficient length, and, considering the difficulties of the subject, with sufficient clearness. I think, too, that certain truths have been established, from which much that is noble, most useful, and necessary to be known can be deduced, as we shall partly see from what follows.

FROM PART FIVE

Prop. XIV.—The mind can cause all the affections of the body or the images of things to be related to the idea of God (ideam Dei)

Demonst.—There is no affection of the body of which the mind cannot form some clear and distinct conception (Prop. 4, pt. 5), and therefore (Prop. 15, pt. 1) it can cause all the affections of the body to be related to the idea of God.—Q.E.D.

Prop. XV.—He who clearly and distinctly understands himself and his affects loves God, and loves Him better the better he understands himself and his affects

Demonst.—He who clearly and distinctly understands himself and his affects rejoices (Prop. 53, pt. 3), and his joy is attended with the idea of God (Prop. 14, pt. 5), therefore (Def. 6 of the Affects) he loves God, and (by the same reasoning) loves Him better the better he understands himself and his affects.—Q.E.D.

Prop. XVI.—This love to God above everything else ought to occupy the mind

Demonst.—For this love is connected with all the affections of the body (Prop. 14, pt. 5), by all of which it is cherished (Prop. 15, pt. 5), and therefore (Prop. 11, pt. 5) above everything else ought to occupy the mind.—Q.E.D.

Prop. XVII.—God is free from passions, nor is He affected with any affect of joy or sorrow

Demonst.—All ideas, in so far as they are related to God, are true (Prop. 32, pt. 2); that is to say (Def. 4, pt. 2), are adequate, and therefore (by the general definition of the Affects) God is free from passions. Again, God can neither pass to a greater nor to a less perfection (Corol. 2, Prop. 20, pt. 1), and therefore (Defs. 2 and 3 of the Affects) He cannot be affected with any affect of joy or sorrow.—Q.E.D.

Corol. Properly speaking, God loves no one and hates no one; for God (Prop. 17, pt. 5) is not affected with any affect of joy or sorrow, and consequently (Defs. 6 and 7 of the Affects) He neither loves nor hates any one.

Prop. XVIII.—No one can hate God

Demonst.—The idea of God which is in us is adequate and perfect (Props. 46 and 47, pt. 3), and therefore in so far as we contemplate God do we act (Prop. 3, pt. 3), and consequently (Prop. 59, pt. 3) no sorrow can exist with the accompanying idea of God; that is to say (Def. 7 of the Affects), no one can hate God.—Q.E.D.

Corol.—Love to God cannot be turned into hatred.

Schol.—But some may object, that if we understand God to be the cause of all things, we do for that very reason consider Him to be the cause of sorrow. But I reply, that in so far as we understand the causes of sorrow, it ceases to be a passion (Prop. 3, pt. 5), that is to say (Prop. 59, pt. 3), it ceases to be sorrow; and therefore in so far as we understand God to be the cause of sorrow do we rejoice.

Prop. XIX.—He who loves God cannot strive that God should love him in return

Demonst.—If a man were to strive after this, he would desire (Corol. Prop. 17, pt. 5) that God, whom he loves, should not be God, and consequently (Prop. 19, pt. 3) he would desire to be sad, which (Prop. 28, pt. 3) is absurd. Therefore he who loves God, &c.—Q.E.D.

Prop. XX.—This love to God cannot be defiled either by the affect of envy or jealousy, but is the more strengthened the more people we imagine to be connected with God by the same bond of love

Demonst.—This love to God is the highest good which we can seek according to the dictate of reason (Prop. 28, pt. 4); is common to all men (Prop. 36, pt. 4); and we desire that all may enjoy it (Prop. 37, pt. 4). It cannot, therefore (Def. 23 of the Affects), be sullied by the affect of envy, nor (Prop. 18, pt. 5, and Def. of Jealousy in Schol. Prop. 35, pt. 3) by that of jealousy, but, on the contrary (Prop. 31, pt. 3), it must be the more strengthened the more people we imagine to rejoice in it.—Q.E.D.

Schol.—It is possible to show in the same manner that there is no affect directly contrary to this love and able to destroy it, and so we may conclude that this love to God is the most constant of all the affects, and that, in so far as it is related to the body, it cannot be destroyed unless with the body itself. What its nature is, in so far as it is related to the mind alone, we shall see hereafter.

I have, in what has preceded, included all the remedies for the affects, that is to say, everything which the mind, considered in itself alone, can do against them. It appears therefrom that the power of the mind over the affects consists—

1. In the knowledge itself of the affects. (See Schol. Prop. 4, pt. 5.)
2. In the separation by the mind of the affects from the thought of an external cause, which we imagine confusedly. (See Prop. 2, pt. 5, and Schol. Prop. 4, pt. 5.)
3. In duration, in which the affections which are related to objects we understand surpass those related to objects conceived in a mutilated or confused manner. (Prop. 7, pt. 5.)
4. In the multitude of causes by which the affections which are related to the common properties of things or to God are nourished. (Prop. 11, pt. 5.)
5. In the order in which the mind can arrange its affects and connect them one with the other. (Schol.

Prop. 10, pt. 5, and see also Props. 12, 13, and 14, pt. 5.)

But that this power of the mind over the affects may be better understood, it is to be carefully observed that we call the affects great when we compare the affect of one man with that of another, and see that one man is agitated more than another by the same affect, or when we compare the affects of one and the same man with one another, and discover that he is affected or moved more by one affect than by another.

For (Prop. 5, pt. 4) the power of any affect is limited by the power of the external cause as compared with our own power. But the power of the mind is limited solely by knowledge, whilst impotence or passion is estimated solely by privation of knowledge, or, in other words, by that through which ideas are called inadequate; and it therefore follows that that mind suffers the most whose largest part consists of inadequate ideas, so that it is distinguished rather by what it suffers than by what it does, while, on the contrary, that mind acts the most whose largest part consists of adequate ideas, so that although it may possess as many inadequate ideas as the first, it is nevertheless distinguished rather by those which belong to human virtue than by those which are a sign of human impotence. Again, it is to be observed that our sorrows and misfortunes mainly proceed from too much love towards an object which is subject to many changes, and which we can never possess. For no one is troubled or anxious about any object he does not love, neither do wrongs, suspicions, hatreds, &c., arise except from love towards objects of which no one can be truly the possessor.

From all this we easily conceive what is the power which clear and distinct knowledge, and especially that third kind of knowledge (see Schol. Prop. 47, pt. 2) whose foundation is the knowledge itself of God, possesses over the affects; the power, namely, by which it is able, in so far as they are passions, if not actually to destroy them (see Prop. 3, pt. 5, with the Schol. to Prop. 4, pt. 5), at least to make them constitute the smallest part of the mind (see Prop. 14, pt. 5). Moreover, it begets a love towards an immutable and eternal object (see Prop. 15, pt. 5) of which we are really partakers (see Prop. 45, pt. 2); a love which therefore cannot be vitiated by the defects which are in common love, but which can always become greater and greater (Prop. 15, pt. 5), occupy the largest part of the mind (Prop. 16, pt. 5), and thoroughly affect it.

I have now concluded all that I had to say relating to this present life. For any one who will attend to what has been urged in this scholium, and to the definition of the mind and its affects, and to Props. 1 and 3, pt. 3, will easily be able to see the truth of what I said in the beginning of the scholium, that in these few words all the remedies for the affects are comprehended. It is time, therefore, that I should now pass to the consideration of those matters which appertain to the duration of the mind without relation to the body.

Prop. XXI.—The mind can imagine nothing, nor can it recollect anything that is past, except while the body exists

Demonst.—The mind does not express the actual existence of its body, nor does it conceive as actual the affections of the body, except while the body exists (Corol. Prop. 8, pt. 2), and consequently (Prop. 26, pt. 2) it conceives no body as actually existing except while its own body exists. It can therefore imagine nothing (see the definition of Imagination in Schol. Prop. 17, pt. 2), nor can it recollect anything that is past, except while the body exists (see the definition of Memory in Schol. Prop. 18, pt. 2).—Q.E.D.

Prop. XXII.—In God, nevertheless, there necessarily exists an idea which expresses the essence of this or that human body under the form of eternity

Demonst.—God is not only the cause of the existence of this or that human body, but also of its essence (Prop. 25, pt. 1), which therefore must necessarily be conceived through the essence of God itself (Ax. 4, pt. 1) and by a certain eternal necessity (Prop. 16, pt. 1). This conception, moreover, must necessarily exist in God (Prop. 3, pt. 2).—Q.E.D.

Prop. XXIII.—The human mind cannot be absolutely destroyed with the body, but something of it remains which is eternal

Demonst.—In God there necessarily exists a conception or idea which expresses the essence of the human body (Prop. 22, pt. 5). This conception or idea is therefore necessarily something which pertains to the essence of the human mind (Prop. 13, pt. 2). But we ascribe to the human mind no duration which can be limited by time, unless in so far as it expresses the actual existence of the body, which is manifested through duration, and which can be limited by time, that is to say (Corol. Prop. 8, pt. 2), we cannot ascribe duration to the mind except while the body exists.

But nevertheless, since this something is that which is conceived by a certain eternal necessity through the essence itself of God (Prop. 22, pt. 5), this something which pertains to the essence of the mind will necessarily be eternal.—Q.E.D.

Schol.—This idea which expresses the essence of the body under the form of eternity is, as we have said, a certain mode of thought which pertains to the essence of the mind and is necessarily eternal. It is impossible, nevertheless, that we should recollect that we existed before the body, because there are no traces of any such existence in the body, and also because eternity cannot be defined by time, or have any relationship to it. Nevertheless we feel and know by experience that we are eternal. For the mind is no less sensible of those things which it conceives through intelligence than of those which it remembers, for demonstrations are the eyes of the mind by which it sees and observes things.

Although, therefore, we do not recollect that we existed before the body, we feel that our mind, in so far as it involves the essence of the body under the form of eternity, is eternal, and that this existence of the mind cannot be limited by time nor manifested through duration. Only in so far, therefore, as it involves the actual existence of the body can the mind be said to possess duration, and its existence be limited by a fixed time, and so far only has it the power of determining the existence of things in time, and of conceiving them under the form of duration.

Prop. XXIV.—The more we understand individual objects, the more we understand God

Demonst.—This is evident from Corol. Prop. 25, pt. 1.

Prop. XXV.—The highest effort of the mind and its highest virtue is to understand things by the third kind of knowledge

Demonst.—The third kind of knowledge proceeds from an adequate idea of certain attributes of God to an adequate knowledge of the essence of things (see its definition in Schol. 2, Prop. 40, pt. 2); and the more we understand things in this manner (Prop. 24, pt. 5), the more we understand God; and therefore (Prop. 28, pt. 4) the highest virtue of the mind, that is to say (Def. 8, pt. 4), the power or nature of the mind, or (Prop. 7, pt. 3) its highest effort, is to understand things by the third kind of knowledge.—Q.E.D.

Prop. XXVI.—The better the mind is adapted to understand things by the third kind of knowledge, the more it desires to understand them by this kind of knowledge

Prop. XXVII.—From this third kind of knowledge arises the highest possible peace of mind

Prop. XXVIII.—The effort or the desire to know things by the third kind of knowledge cannot arise from the first kind but may arise from the second kind of knowledge

Demonst.—This proposition is self-evident; for everything that we clearly and distinctly understand, we understand either through itself or through something which is conceived through itself; or, in other words, ideas which are clear and distinct in us, or which are related to the third kind of knowledge (Schol. 2, Prop. 40, pt. 2), cannot follow from mutilated and confused ideas, which (by the same scholium) are related to the first kind of knowledge, but from adequate ideas, that is to say (by the same scholium), from the second and third kinds of knowledge. Therefore (Def. 1 of the Affects) the desire of knowing things by the third kind of knowledge cannot arise from the first kind, but may arise from the second.—Q.E.D.

Prop. XXIX.—Everything which the mind understands under the form of eternity, it understands not because it conceives the present actual existence of the body, but because it conceives the essence of the body under the form of eternity

Demonst.—In so far as the mind conceives the present existence of its body does it conceive duration which can be determined in time, and so far only has it the power of conceiving things in relation to time (Prop. 21, pt. 5, and Prop. 26, pt. 2). But eternity cannot be manifested through duration (Def. 8, pt. 1, and its explanation), therefore the mind so far has not the power of conceiving things under the form of eternity: but because it is the nature of reason to conceive things under the form of eternity (Corol. 2, Prop. 44, pt. 2), and because it also pertains to the nature of the mind to conceive the essence of the body under the form of eternity (Prop. 23, pt. 5), and excepting these two things nothing else pertains to the nature of the mind (Prop. 13, pt. 2), therefore this power of conceiving things under the form of eternity does not pertain to the mind except in so far as it conceives the essence of the body under the form of eternity.—Q.E.D.

Schol.—Things are conceived by us as actual in two ways; either in so far as we conceive them to exist with relation to a fixed time and place, or in so far as we conceive them to be contained in God, and to follow from the necessity of the divine nature. But those things which are conceived in this second way as true or real we conceive under the form of eternity, and their ideas involve the eternal and infinite essence of God, as we have shown in Prop. 45, pt. 2, to the scholium of which proposition the reader is also referred.

Prop. XXX.—Our mind, in so far as it knows itself and the body under the form of eternity, necessarily has a knowledge of God, and knows that it is in God and is conceived through Him

Demonst.—Eternity is the very essence of God, in so far as that essence involves necessary existence (Def. 8, pt. 1). To conceive things therefore under the form of eternity, is to conceive them in so far as they are conceived through the essence of God as actually existing things, or in so far as through the essence of God they involve existence. Therefore our mind, in so far as it conceives itself and its body under the form of eternity, necessarily has a knowledge of God, and knows, &c.—Q.E.D.

Prop. XXXI.—The third kind of knowledge depends upon the mind as its formal cause, in so far as the mind itself is eternal

Schol.—As each person therefore becomes stronger in this kind of knowledge, the more is he conscious of himself and of God; that is to say, the more perfect and the happier he is, a truth which will still more clearly appear from what follows. Here, however, it is to be observed, that although we are now certain that the mind is eternal in so far as it conceives things under the form of eternity, yet, in order that we wish to prove may be more easily explained and better understood, we shall consider the mind, as we have hitherto done, as if it had just begun to be, and had just begun to understand things under the form of eternity. This we can do without any risk of error, provided only we are careful to conclude nothing except from clear premisses.

Prop. XXXII.—We delight in whatever we understand by the third kind of knowledge, and our delight is accompanied with the idea of God as its cause

Corol.—From the third kind of knowledge necessarily springs the intellectual love of God.—For from this kind of knowledge arises (Prop. 32, pt. 5) joy attended with the idea of God as its cause, that is to say (Def. 6 of the Affects), the love of God, not in so far as we imagine Him as present (Prop. 29, pt. 5), but in so far as we understand that He is eternal; and that is what I call the intellectual love of God.

Prop. XXXIII.—The intellectual love of God which arises from the third kind of knowledge is eternal

Demonst.—The third kind of knowledge (Prop. 31, pt. 5, and Ax. 3, pt. 1) is eternal, and therefore (by the same axiom) the love which springs from it is necessarily eternal.—Q.E.D.

Schol.—Although this love to God has no beginning (Prop. 33, pt. 5), it nevertheless has all the perfections of love, just as if it had originated;—as we supposed in the corollary of Prop. 32, pt. 5. Nor is there here any difference, excepting that the mind has eternally possessed these same perfections which we imagined as now accruing to it, and has possessed them with the accompanying idea of God as the eternal cause. And if joy consist in the passage to a greater perfection, blessedness must indeed consist in this, that the mind is endowed with perfection itself.

Prop. XXXIV.—The mind is subject to affects which are related to passions only so long as the body exists

Demonst.—An imagination is an idea by which the mind contemplates any object as present (see its definition in Schol. Prop. 17, pt. 2). This idea nevertheless indicates the present constitution of the human body rather than the nature of the external object (Corol. 2, Prop. 16, pt. 2). An affect, therefore (by the general definition of the Affects), is an imagination in so far as it indicates the present constitution of the body, and therefore (Prop. 21, pt. 5) the mind, only so long as the body exists, is subject to affects which are related to passions.—Q.E.D.

Corol.—Hence it follows that no love except intellectual love is eternal.

Schol.—If we look at the common opinion of men, we shall see that they are indeed conscious of the eternity of their minds, but they confound it with duration, and attribute it to imagination or memory, which they believe remain after death.

Prop. XXXV.—God loves Himself with an infinite intellectual love

God is absolutely infinite (Def. 6, pt. 1), that is to say (Def. 6, pt. 2), the nature of God delights in infinite perfection accompanied (Prop. 3, pt. 2) with the idea of Himself, that is to say (Prop. 11, and Def. 1, pt. 1), with the idea of Himself as cause, and this is what, in Corol. Prop. 32, pt. 5, we have called intellectual love.

Prop. XXXVI.—The intellectual love of the mind towards God is the very love with which He loves Himself, not in so far as He is infinite, but in so far as He can be manifested through the essence of the human mind, considered under the form of eternity; that is to say, the intellectual love of the mind towards God is part of the infinite love with which God loves Himself

Demonst.—This love of the mind must be related to the actions of the mind (Corol. Prop. 32, pt. 5, and Prop. 3, pt. 3), and it is therefore an action by which the mind contemplates itself; and which is accompanied with the idea of God as cause (Prop. 32, pt. 5, with the Corol.); that is to say (Corol. Prop. 25, pt. 1, and Corol. Prop. 11, pt. 2), it is an action by which God, in so far as He can be manifested through the human mind, contemplates Himself, the action being accompanied with the idea of Himself; and therefore (Prop. 35, pt. 5), this love of the mind is part of the infinite love with which God loves Himself.—Q.E.D.

Corol.—Hence it follows that God, in so far as He loves Himself, loves men, and consequently that the love of God towards men and the intellectual love of the mind towards God are one and the same thing.

Schol.—Hence we clearly understand that our salvation, or blessedness, or liberty consists in a constant and eternal love towards God, or in the love of God towards men. This love or blessedness is called Glory in the sacred writings, and not without reason. For whether it be related to God or to the mind, it may properly be called repose of mind, which is, in truth, not distinguished from glory. For in so far as it is related to God, it is (Prop. 35, pt. 5) joy (granting that it is allowable to use this word), accompanied with the idea of Himself, and it is the same thing when it is related to the mind (Prop. 27, pt. 5). Again, since the essence of our mind consists in knowledge alone, whose beginning and foundation is God (Prop. 15, pt. 1, and Schol. Prop. 47, pt. 2), it is clear to us in what manner and by what method our mind, with regard both to essence and existence, follows from the divine nature, and continually depends upon God. I thought it worth while for me to notice this here, in order that I might show, by this example, what that knowledge of individual objects which I have called intuitive or of the third kind (Schol. 2, Prop. 40, pt. 2) is able to do, and how much more potent it is than the universal knowledge, which I have called knowledge of the second kind. For although I have shown generally in the First Part that all things, and consequently also the human mind, depend upon God both with regard to existence and essence, yet that demonstration, although legitimate, and placed beyond the possibility of a doubt, does not, nevertheless, so affect our mind as a proof from the essence itself of any individual object which we say depends upon God.

Prop. XXXVII.—There is nothing in nature which is contrary to this intellectual love, or which can negate it

This intellectual love necessarily follows from the nature of the mind, in so far as it is considered, through the nature of god, as an eternal truth (Props. 33 and 29, pt. 5). If there were anything, therefore, contrary to this love, it would be contrary to the truth, and consequently whatever might be able to negate this love would be able to make the true false, which (as is self-evident) is absurd. There exists, therefore, nothing in nature, &c.—Q.E.D.

Schol.—The axiom of the Fourth Part refers only to individual objects, in so far as they are considered in relation to a fixed time and place. This, I believe, no one can doubt.

Prop. XXXVIII.—The more objects the mind understands by the second and third kinds of knowledge, the less it suffers from those affects which are evil, and the less it fears death

Demonst.—The essence of the mind consists in knowledge (Prop. 11, pt. 2). The more things, therefore, the mind knows by the second and third kinds of knowledge, the greater is that part which abides (Props. 29 and 23, pt. 5), and consequently (Prop. 37, pt. 5) the greater is that part which is not touched by affects which are contrary to our nature, that is to say (Prop. 30, pt. 4), which are evil. The more things, therefore, the mind understands by the second and third kinds of knowledge, the greater is that part which remains unharmed, and the less consequently does it suffer from the affects.

Schol. We are thus enabled to understand that which I touched upon in Schol. Prop. 39, pt. 4, and which I promised to explain in this part, namely that death is by so much the less injurious to us as the clear and distinct knowledge of the mind is greater, and consequently as the mind loves God more. Again, since (Prop. 27, pt. 5) from the third kind of knowledge there arises the highest possible peace, it follows that it is possible for the human mind to be of such a nature that that part of it which we have shown perishes with its body (Prop. 21, pt. 5), in comparison with the part of it which remains, is of no consequence. But more fully upon this subject presently.

Prop. XXXIX.—He who possesses a body fit for many things possesses a mind of which the greater part is eternal

Demonst.—He who possesses a body fitted for doing many things is least of all agitated by those affects which are evil (Prop. 38, pt. 4), that is to say (Prop. 30, pt. 4), by affects which are contrary to our nature, and therefore (Prop. 10, pt. 5) he possesses the power of arranging and connecting the affections of the body according to the order of the intellect, and consequently (Prop. 14, pt. 5) of causing all the affections of the body to be related to the idea of God (Prop. 15, pt. 5); in consequence of which he is affected with a love to God, which (Prop. 16, pt. 5) must occupy or form the greatest part of his mind, and therefore (Prop. 33, pt. 5) he possesses a mind of which the greatest part is eternal.

Schol. Inasmuch as human bodies are fit for many things, we cannot doubt the possibility of their possessing such a nature that they may be related to minds which have a large knowledge of themselves and of God, and whose greatest or principal part is eternal, so that they scarcely fear death. To understand this more clearly, it is to be here considered that we live in constant change, and that according as we change for the better or the worse we are called happy or unhappy. For he who passes from infancy or childhood to death is called unhappy, and, on the other hand, we consider ourselves happy if we can pass through the whole period of life with a sound mind in a sound body. Moreover, he who, like an infant or child, possesses a body fit for very few things, and almost altogether dependent on external causes, has a mind which, considered in itself alone, is almost entirely unconscious of itself, of God, and of objects. On the other hand, he who possesses a body fit for many things possesses a mind which, considered in itself alone, is largely conscious of itself, of God, and of objects. In this life, therefore, it is our chief endeavour to change the body of infancy, so far as its nature permits and is conducive thereto, into another body which is fitted for many things, and which is related to a mind conscious as much as possible of itself, of God, and of objects; so that everything which is related to its memory or imagination, in comparison with the intellect is scarcely of any moment, as I have already said in the scholium of the preceding proposition.

Prop. XL.—The more perfection a thing possesses, the more it acts and the less it suffers, and conversely the more it acts the more perfect it is

Demonst.—The more perfect a thing is, the more reality it possesses (Def. 6, pt. 2), and consequently (Prop. 3, pt. 3, with the Schol.) the more it acts and the less it suffers. Inversely also it may be demonstrated in the same way that the more a thing acts the more perfect it is.—Q.E.D.

Corol.—Hence it follows that that part of the mind which abides, whether great or small, is more perfect than the other part. For the part of the mind which is eternal (Props. 23 and 29, pt. 5) is the intellect, through which alone we are said to act (Prop. 3, pt. 3), but that part which, as we have shown, perishes, is the imagination itself (Prop. 21, pt. 5), through which alone we are said to suffer (Prop. 3, pt. 3, and the general definition of the affects). Therefore (Prop. 40, pt. 5) that part which abides, whether great or small, is more perfect than the latter.—Q.E.D.

Schol.—These are the things I proposed to prove concerning the mind, in so far as it is considered without relation to the existence of the body, and from these, taken together with Prop. 21, pt. 1, and other propositions, it is evident that our mind, in so far as it understands, is an eternal mode of thought, which is determined by another eternal mode of thought, and this again by another, and so on *ad infinitum*, so that all taken together form the eternal and infinite intellect of God.

Prop. XLI.—Even if we did not know that our mind is eternal, we should still consider as of primary importance Piety and Religion, and absolutely everything which in the Fourth Part we have shown to be related to strength of mind and generosity

Demonst.—The primary and sole foundation of virtue or of the proper conduct of life (by Corol. Prop. 22, and Prop. 24, pt. 4) is to seek our own profit. But in order to determine what reason prescribes as profitable, we had no regard to the eternity of the mind, which we did not recognise tile we came to the Fifth Part. Therefore, although we were at that time ignorant that the mind is eternal, we considered as of primary importance those things which we have shown are related to strength of mind and generosity; and therefore, even if we were now ignorant of the eternity of the mind, we should consider those commands of reason as of primary importance.—Q.E.D.

Schol.—The creed of the multitude seems to be different from this; for most persons seem to believe that they are free in so far as it is allowed them to obey their lusts, and that they give up a portion of their rights, in so far as they are bound to live according to the commands of divine law. Piety, therefore, and religion, and absolutely all those things that are related to greatness of soul, they believe to be burdens which they hope to be able to lay aside after death; hoping also to receive some reward for their bondage, that is to say, for their piety and religion. It is not merely this hope, however, but also and chiefly fear of dreadful punishments after death, by which they are induced to live according to the commands of divine law, that is to say, as far as their feebleness and impotent mind will permit; and if this hope and fear were not present to them, but if they, on the contrary, believed that minds perish with the body, and that there is no prolongation of life for miserable creatures exhausted with the burden of their piety, they would return to ways of their own liking; they would prefer to let everything be controlled by their own passions, and to obey fortune rather than themselves.

This seems to me as absurd as if a man, because he does not believe that he will be able to feed his body with good food to all eternity, should desire to satiate himself with poisonous and deadly drugs; or as if, because he sees that the mind is not eternal or immortal, he should therefore prefer to be mad and to live without reason,—absurdities so great that they scarcely deserve to be repeated.

Prop. XLII.—Blessedness is not the reward of virtue, but is virtue itself; nor do we delight in blessedness because we restrain our lusts; but, on the contrary, because we delight in it, therefore are we able to restrain them

Demonst.—Blessedness consists in love towards God (Prop. 36, pt. 5, and its Schol.), which arises from the third kind of knowledge (Corol. Prop. 32, pt. 5), and this love, therefore (Props. 59 and 3, pt. 3), must be related to the mind in so far as it acts. Blessedness, therefore (Def. 8, pt. 4), is virtue itself, which was the first thing to be proved. Again, the more the mind delights in this divine love or blessedness, the more it understands (Prop. 32, pt. 5), that is to say (Corol. Prop. 3, pt. 5), the greater is the power it has over its affects which are evil. Therefore, it is because the mind delights in this divine love or blessedness that it possesses the power of restraining the lusts; and because the power of man to restrain the affects is in the intellect alone, no one, therefore, delights in blessedness because he has restrained his affects, but, on the contrary, the power of restraining his lusts springs from blessedness itself.—Q.E.D.

Schol.—I have finished everything I wished to explain concerning the power of the mind over the affects and concerning its liberty. From what has been said we see what is the strength of the wise man, and how much he surpasses the ignorant who is driven forward by lust alone. For the ignorant man is not only agitated by external causes in many ways, and never enjoys true peace of soul, but lives also ignorant, as it were, both of God and of things, and as soon as he ceases to suffer ceases also to be. On the other hand, the wise man, in so far as he is considered as such, is scarcely ever moved in his mind, but, being conscious by a certain eternal necessity of himself, of God, and of things, never ceases to be, and always enjoys true peace of soul. If the way which, as I have shown, leads hither seem very difficult, it can nevertheless be found. It must indeed be difficult since it is so seldom discovered; for if salvation lay ready to hand and could be discovered without great labour, how could it be possible that it should be neglected almost by everybody? But all noble things are as difficult as they are rare.

Chapter 19

Gottfried Wilhelm Leibniz

G. W. Leibniz was born on July 1, 1646, in Leipzig. His father, a scholar and a Professor of Moral Philosophy at the University of Leipzig, who apparently began to teach Leibniz as a small child, died when Leibniz was only six years old. Leibniz seems to have been largely self-taught, teaching himself Latin at the age of seven. Gaining admittance to his late father's library, he concentrated especially in the Church Fathers and in the Latin classics. Leibniz attended university from age fourteen to age twenty-one, first at the University of Leibzig and then the University of Altdorf, graduating with degrees in law and in philosophy. He was soon recognized as a talented young man of great promise and was offered a position on the faculty at the University of Altdorf. He declined the offer, choosing instead public service. Under the patronage of Baron Johann Christian von Boineburg, Leibniz entered the service of the Elector of Mainz and occupied a number of positions in Mainz and nearby Nuremburg. There he stayed until he was sent to Paris in spring 1672 on diplomatic business, a trip that deeply affected his intellectual development.

In Paris from 1672 to 1676 Leibniz made the acquaintance of such intellectual luminaries as Christian Huygens, who became his teacher and introduced him to other philosophers and scientists, such as Arnauld and Malebranche. It was in Paris that he laid the foundations for his work in calculus. Before Leibniz returned to Germany, in December 1676, he stopped in England and in Holland, where he met Spinoza. Both Boineburg and the Elector of Mainz had died while he was in Paris. Leibniz returned to the court of Hanover as a counselor, where he settled for the rest of his life.

Although recognized today as one of the leading philosophers of all time and one of two founders of calculus (with Newton), Leibniz was not popular in his own time. Newton accused him of stealing his invention of calculus (we know now that the two geniuses invented it independently, Leibniz publishing his work first in 1684, Newton in 1687), and many of his contemporaries (including the prestigious Royal Society) belittled his work. Bertrand Russell has written the following in this regard:

> Leibniz was one of the supreme intellects of all time, but as a human being he was not admirable. He had, it is true, the virtues that one would wish to find mentioned in a testimonial to a prospective employee: he was industrious, frugal, temperate, and financially honest. But he was wholly destitute of those higher philosophic virtues that are so notable in Spinoza. His best thought was not such as would win him popularity, and he left his records of it unpublished in his desk. . . . It was the popular Leibniz who invented the doctrine that this is the best of all possible worlds (to which F. H. Bradley added the sardonic comment, "and everything in it is a necessary evil"); it was this Leibniz that Voltaire caricatured as Doctor Pangloss.[1]

1. Bertrand Russell, *A History of Western Philosophy* (Simon & Schuster, 1945), p. 581.

Regarding his stinginess, it is reported that when any young woman at the court of Hanover married, he used to give her a "wedding present," consisting of useful maxims, ending up with the advice not to give up washing now that she had secured a husband.

Leibniz published very little in his lifetime. A major work on Locke's *Essay* was withheld from publication when Locke died in 1704. His only systematic work is *Theodicy* (1710), whose thesis: "this is the best of all possible worlds" was satirized by Voltaire's *Candide*. In metaphysics, the "Discourse on Metaphysics," which I have included in this section, was written in 1686 but left unpublished. Themes from the "Discourse," however appeared, somewhat transformed, in the "New System of Nature," which Leibniz published in 1695—the first public exposition of his metaphysical system. These themes appear further developed in later summaries of his doctrines, the unpublished "Principles of Nature and Grace" and "Monadology" (included below). He did extensive work in physics, writing "A Specimen of Dynamics" (1695) and invented a calculating machine that could add, subtract, multiply, divide, and extract square roots. He was passionately interested in theology and sought to reconcile Catholicism with his own Protestant faith. He went even farther, seeking to reconcile Cartesian dualism with Hobbesian materialism—and these with the major ideas of the medieval schoolmen.

Leibniz died in Hanover on November 14, 1716.

What were Leibniz's main ideas? They center on the idea of *substance*, on ultimate reality. Whereas Descartes thought there were three substances, God, mind (thought), and matter (extension); and Spinoza thought that there was only one, God or Nature (both thought and extension are attributes of God); Leibniz held that extension cannot be an attribute of a substance. For extension implies plurality and, so, can only apply to the aggregate of substances. Each single substance must be unextended. He held that there must be an infinite number of substances, which he called *monads*: simple, indivisible, substances that make up all of reality. The monad is without parts, windowless, and eternal. In a letter to Burcher de Volder, Leibniz describes them thus:

> Considering matters accurately, it must be said that there is nothing in things except simple substances, and, in them, nothing but perception and appetite. Moreover, matter and motion are not so much substances or things as they are the phenomena of permanent beings, the reality of which is located in the harmony of each percipient with itself (with respect to different times) and with different percipients.

In this passage Leibniz says the monad is immaterial, lacking spatial extension, containing only perception and desire (appetite). In fact, the monad is a soul. There are an infinite number of these entities, which are windowless in the sense that each one mirrors the entire universe from a particular point of view, some more clearly and distinctly than others, in hierarchical order. The monads never interact but function like an infinite set of clocks which keep perfect time, arranged by God in a preestablished harmony, so that each of us can communicate with the thoughts of other monads. A human body is composed entirely of monads, each of which is a soul, and as such, immortal, but there is a dominant monad (*soul*) which rules over the soulish monads.

Matter and space, as they appear to the senses, are unreal, but they are reflections of the arrangements of monads in an order that mirrors real but abstract relations.

Although this seems to lend itself to a deterministic world view, Leibniz was a theist, who recognized the need to explain how a good God could permit evil. He set forth the idea of a *theodicy*, or idea of the best of all worlds, in which God is thought to have contemplated an infinite set of worlds and chosen one with the best ratio of good over evil. It was not possible for God to create a better world than this one, so long as humans have free will—something of very high value.

> Let us suppose that the current of one and the same river carries along with it various boats, which differ among themselves only in cargo, some being laden with wood,

> others with stone, and some more, the others less. That being so, it will come about that the boats most heavily laden will go more slowly than the others, provided it be assumed that the wind or the oar, or some other similar means, assist them not at all . . . Let us now compare the force which the current exercises on boats, and communicates to them, with the action of God, who produces and conserves whatever is positive in creatures, . . . let us compare the inertia of matter with the natural imperfection of creatures, and the slowness of the laden boat with the defects to be found in the qualities and the action of the creature; and we shall find that there is nothing so just as this comparison. The current is the cause of the boat's movement, but not of its retardation; God is the cause of perfection in the nature and the actions of the creature, but the limitation of the receptivity of the creature is the cause of the defects there are in its action . . . God is no more the cause of sin than the river's current is the cause of the retardation of the boat.[2]

So although our nature may incline us one way or the other, an ineliminable input of choice, not God or circumstances, causes us to act in one way or another, for good or evil.

Our final reading, *The Theodicy: An Abridgement of the Argument Reduced to Syllogistic Form* (1710), schematizes Leibniz's central arguments justifying the ways of God in the light of evil. God permitted evil in order to bring about greater good, and Adam's fall was a *felix culpa* (a happy sin) because it led to the incarnation of the Son of God, raising humanity to a higher destiny than would otherwise have been the case. He argues that although God can foresee the future, humans are still free in that they act voluntarily. If so, then the idea of preestablished harmony is not deterministic but compatible with free will.

FOR FURTHER READING

Broad, C. D. *Leibniz: An Introduction.* (Cambridge University Press, 1975).

Brown, Stuart. *Leibniz.* (University of Minnesota Press, 1984).

Costabel, Pierre. *Leibniz and Dynamics.* (Cornell University Press, 1973).

Frankfurt, Harry, ed. *Leibniz.* (Doubleday, 1972).

Hick, John. *Evil and the God of Love.* (Harper & Row, 1966).

Hooker, Michael, ed. *Leibniz: Critical and Interpretative Essays* (University of Minnesota Press, 1982).

Ishiguro, Hidé. *Leibniz's Philosophy of Logic and Language.* (Cornell University Press, 1972).

Jolley, Nicholas. *Leibniz and Locke.* (Oxford University Press, 1984).

Mates, Benson. *The Philosophy of Leibniz: Metaphysics and Language.* (Oxford University Press, 1986).

Parkinson, G. H. R. *Logic and Reality in Leibniz's Metaphysics.* (Oxford University Press, 1965).

Rescher, Nicholas. *The Philosophy of Leibniz.* (Prentice-Hall, 1967).

Russell, Bertrand. *A Critical Exposition of the Philosophy of Leibniz.* (George Allen & Unwin, 1900).

Woolhouse, R. S., ed. *Leibniz: Metaphysics and Philosophy of Science.* (Oxford University Press, 1981).

---

2. Leibniz, *Theodicy* Part I, Para 30.

Discourse on Metaphysics

I. CONCERNING THE DIVINE PERFECTION AND THAT GOD DOES EVERYTHING IN THE MOST DESIRABLE WAY

The conception of God which is the most common and the most full of meaning is expressed well enough in the words: God is an absolutely perfect being. The implications, however, of these words fail to receive sufficient consideration. For instance, there are many different kinds of perfection, all of which God possesses, and each one of them pertains to him in the highest degree.

We must also know what perfection is. One thing which can surely be affirmed about it is that those forms or natures which are not susceptible of it to the highest degree, say the nature of numbers or of figures, do not permit of perfection. This is because the number which is the greatest of all (that is, the sum of all the numbers), and likewise the greatest of all figures, imply contradictions. The greatest knowledge, however, and omnipotence contain no impossibility. Consequently power and knowledge do admit of perfection, and in so far as they pertain to God they have no limits.

Whence it follows that God who possesses supreme and infinite wisdom acts in the most perfect manner not only metaphysically, but also from the moral standpoint. And with respect to ourselves it can be said that the more we are enlightened and informed in regard to the work of God the more will we be disposed to find them excellent and conforming entirely to that which we might desire.

II. AGAINST THOSE WHO HOLD THAT THERE IS IN THE WORKS OF GOD NO GOODNESS, OR THAT THE PRINCIPLES OF GOODNESS AND BEAUTY ARE ARBITRARY

Therefore I am far removed from the opinion of those who maintain that there are no principles of goodness or perfection in the nature of things, or in the ideas which God has about them, and who say that the works of God are good only through the formal reason that God has made them. If this position were true, God, knowing that he is the author of things, would not have to regard them afterwards and find them good, as the Holy Scripture witnesses. Such anthropological expressions are used only to let us know that excellence is recognized in regarding the works themselves, even if we do not consider their evident dependence on their author. This is confirmed by the fact that it is in reflecting upon the works that we are able to discover the one who wrought. They must therefore bear in themselves his character. I confess that the contrary opinion seems to me extremely dangerous and closely approaches that of recent innovators who hold that the beauty of the universe and the goodness which we attribute to the works of God are chimeras of human beings who think of God in human terms. In saying, therefore, that things are not good according to any standard of goodness, but simply by the will of God, it seems to me that one destroys, without realizing it, all the love of God and all his glory; for why praise him for what he has done, if he would be equally praiseworthy in doing the contrary? Where will be his justice and his wisdom if he has only a certain despotic power, if arbitrary will takes the place of reasonableness, and if in accord with the definition of tyrants, justice consists in that which is pleasing to the most powerful? Besides it seems that every act of willing supposes some reason for the willing and this reason, of course, must precede the act. This is why, accordingly, I find so strange those expressions of certain philosophers who say that the eternal truths of metaphysics and Geometry, and consequently the principles of goodness, of justice, and of perfection, are effects only of the will of God. To me it seems that all these follow from his understanding, which does not depend upon his will any more than does his essence.

III. AGAINST THOSE WHO THINK THAT GOD MIGHT HAVE MADE THINGS BETTER THAN HE HAS

No more am I able to approve of the opinion of certain modern writers who boldly maintain that that which God has made is not perfect in the highest degree, and that he might have done better. It seems to me that the consequences of such an opinion are wholly inconsistent with the glory of God. *Uti minus malum habet rationem boni, ita minus bonum habet rationem mali.* I think that one acts imperfectly if he acts with less perfection than he is capable of. To show that an architect could have done better is to find fault with his work. Furthermore this opinion is contrary to the Holy Scriptures when they assure us of the goodness of God's work. For if comparative perfection were sufficient, then in whatever way God had accomplished this work, since there is an infinitude of possible imperfections, it would always have been good in comparison with the less perfect; but a thing is little praiseworthy when it can be praised only in this way.

I believe that a great many passages from the divine writings and from the holy fathers will be found favoring my position, while hardly any will be found in favor of that of these modern thinkers. Their opinion is, in my judgment, unknown to the writers of antiquity and is a deduction based upon the too slight acquaintaince which we have with the general harmony of the universe and with the hidden reasons for God's conduct. In our ignorance, therefore, we are tempted to decide audaciously that many things might have been done better.

These modern thinkers insist upon certain hardly tenable subtleties, for they imagine that nothing is so perfect that there might not have been something more perfect. This is an error. They think, indeed, that they are thus safeguarding the liberty of God. As if it were not the highest liberty to act in perfection according to the sovereign reason. For to think that God acts in anything without having any reason for his willing, even if we overlook the fact that such action seems impossible, is an opinion which conforms little to God's glory. For example, let us suppose that God chooses between A and B, and that he takes A without any reason for preferring it to B. I say that this action on the part of God is at least not praiseworthy, for all praise ought to be founded upon reason which *ex hypothesi* is not present here. My opinion is that God does nothing for which he does not deserve to be glorified.

IV. THAT LOVE FOR GOD DEMANDS ON OUR PART COMPLETE SATISFACTION WITH AND ACQUIESCENCE IN THAT WHICH HE HAS DONE

The general knowledge of this great truth that God acts always in the most perfect and most desirable manner possible, is in my opinion the basis of the love which we owe to God in all things; for he who loves seeks his satisfaction in the felicity or perfection of the object loved and in the perfection of his actions. *Idem velle et idem nolle vera amicitia est.* I believe that it is difficult to love God truly when one, having the power to change his disposition, is not disposed to wish for that which God desires. In fact those who are not satisfied with what God does seem to me like dissatisfied subjects whose attitude is not very different from that of rebels. I hold therefore, that on these principles, to act conformably to the love of God it is not sufficient to force oneself to be patient, we must be really satisfied with all that comes to us according to his will. I mean this acquiescence in regard to the past; for as regards the future one should not be a quietist with the arms folded, open to ridicule, awaiting that which God will do; according to the sophism which the ancients called λόγου ἄεργου, the lazy reason. It is necessary to act conformably to the presumptive will of God as far as we are able to judge of it, trying with all our might to contribute to the general welfare and particularly to the ornamentation and the perfection of that which touches us, or of that which is nigh and so to speak at our hand. For if the future shall perhaps show that God has not wished our good intention to have its way, it does not follow that he has not wished us to act as we have; on the contrary, since he is the best of all masters, he ever demands only the right intentions, and it is for him to know the hour and the proper place to let good designs succeed.

V. IN WHAT THE PRINCIPLES OF THE DIVINE PERFECTION CONSIST, AND THAT THE SIMPLICITY OF THE MEANS COUNTER-BALANCES THE RICHNESS OF THE EFFECTS

It is sufficient therefore to have this confidence in God, that he has done everything for the best and that nothing will be able to injure those who love him. To know in particular, however, the reasons which have moved him to choose this order of the universe, to permit sin, to dispense his salutary grace in a certain manner,—this passes the capacity of a finite mind, above all when such a mind has not come into the joy of the vision of God. Yet it is possible to make some general remarks touching the course of providence in the government of things. One is able to say, therefore, that he who acts perfectly is like an excellent Geometer who knows how to find the best construction for a problem; like a good architect who utilizes his location and the funds destined for the building in the most advantageous manner, leaving nothing which shocks or which does not display that beauty of which it is capable; like a good householder who employs his property in such a way that there shall be nothing uncultivated or sterile; like a clever machinist who makes his production in the least difficult way possible; and like an intelligent author who encloses the most of reality in the least possible compass.

Of all beings those which are the most perfect and occupy the least possible space, that is to say those which interfere with one another the least, are the spirits whose perfections are the virtues. That is why we may not doubt that the felicity of the spirits is the principal aim of God and that he puts this purpose into execution, as far as the general harmony will permit. We will recur to this subject again.

When the simplicity of God's way is spoken of, reference is specially made to the means which he employs, and on the other hand when the variety, richness and abundance are referred to, the ends or effects are had in mind. Thus one ought to be proportioned to the other, just as the cost of a building should balance the beauty and grandeur which is expected. It is true that nothing costs God anything, just as there is not cost for a philosopher who makes hypotheses in constructing his imaginary world, because God has only to make decrees in order that a real world come into being; but in matters of wisdom the decrees or hypotheses meet the expenditure in proportion as they are more independent of one another. The reason wishes to avoid multiplicity in hypotheses or principles very much as the simplest system is preferred in Astronomy.

VI. THAT GOD DOES NOTHING WHICH IS NOT ORDERLY, AND THAT IT IS NOT EVEN POSSIBLE TO CONCEIVE OF EVENTS WHICH ARE NOT REGULAR

The activities or the acts of will of God are commonly divided into ordinary and extraordinary. But it is well to bear in mind that God does nothing out of order. Therefore, that which passes for extraordinary is so only with regard to a particular order established among the created things, for as regards the universal order, everything conforms to it. This is so true that not only does nothing occur in this world which is absolutely irregular, but it is even impossible to conceive of such an occurrence. Because, let us suppose for example that some one jots down a quantity of points upon a sheet of paper helter skelter, as do those who exercise the ridiculous art of Geomancy; now I say that it is possible to find a geometrical line whose concept shall be uniform and constant, that is, in accordance with a certain formula, and which line at the same time shall pass through all of those points, and in the same order in which the hand jotted them down; also if a continuous line be traced, which is now straight, now circular, and now of any other description, it is possible to find a mental equivalent, a formula or an equation common to all the points of this line by virtue of which formula the changes in the direction of the line must occur. There is no instance of a face whose contour does not form part of a geometric line and which can not be traced entire by a certain mathematical motion. But when the formula is very complex, that which conforms to it passes for irregular. Thus we may say that in whatever manner God might have created the world, it would always have been regular and in a certain order. God, however, has chosen the most perfect, that is to say the one which is at the same time the simplest in hypotheses and the richest in phenomena, as might be the case with a geometric line, whose construction was easy, but whose properties and effects were extremely remarkable and of great significance. I use these comparisons to picture a certain imperfect resemblance to the divine wisdom, and to point out that which may at least raise our minds to conceive in some sort what cannot otherwise be expressed. I do not pretend at all to explain thus the great mystery upon which depends the whole universe.

VII. THAT MIRACLES CONFORM TO THE REGULAR ORDER ALTHOUGH THEY GO AGAINST THE SUBORDINATE REGULATIONS; CONCERNING THAT WHICH GOD DESIRES OR PERMITS AND CONCERNING GENERAL AND PARTICULAR INTENTIONS

Now since nothing is done which is not orderly, we may say that miracles are quite within the order of natural operations. We use the term natural of these operations because they conform to certain subordinate regulations which we call the nature of things. For it can be said that this nature is only a custom of God's which he can change on the occasion of a stronger reason than that which moved him to use these regulations. As regards general and particular intentions, according to the way in which we understand the matter, it may be said on the one hand that everything is in accordance with his most general intention, or that which best conforms to the most perfect order he has chosen; on the other hand, however, it is also possible to say that he has particular intentions which are exceptions to the subordinate regulations above mentioned. Of God's laws, however, the most universal, i.e., that which rules the whole course of the universe, is without exceptions.

It is possible to say that God desires everything which is an object of his particular intention. When we consider the objects of his general intentions, however, such as are the modes of activities of created things and especially of the reasoning creatures with whom God wishes to co-operate, we must make a distinction; for if the action is good in itself, we may say that God wishes it and at times commands it, even though it does not take place; but if it is bad in itself and becomes good only by accident through the course of events and especially after chastisement and satisfaction have corrected its malignity and rewarded the ill with interest in such a way that more perfection results in the whole train of circumstances than would have come if that ill had not occurred,—if all this takes place we must say that God permits the evil, and not that he desired it, although he has co-operated by means of the laws of nature which he has established. He knows how to produce the greatest good from them.

VIII. IN ORDER TO DISTINGUISH BETWEEN THE ACTIVITIES OF GOD AND THE ACTIVITIES OF CREATED THINGS WE MUST EXPLAIN THE CONCEPTION OF AN INDIVIDUAL SUBSTANCE

It is quite difficult to distinguish God's actions from those of his creatures. Some think that God does everything; others image that he only conserves the force that he has given to created things. How far can we say either of these opinions is right?

In the first place since activity and passivity pertain properly to individual substances (*actiones sunt suppositorum*) it will be necessary to explain what such a substance is. It is indeed true that when several predicates are attributes of a single subject and this subject is not an attribute of another, we speak of it as an individual substance, but this is not enough, and such an explanation is merely nominal. We must therefore inquire what it is to be an attribute in reality of a certain subject. Now it is evident that every true predication has some basis in the nature of things, and even when a proposition is not identical, that is, when the predicate is not expressly contained in the subject, it is still necessary that it be virtually contained in it, and this is what the philosophers call *in-esse*, saying thereby that the predicate is in the subject. Thus the content of the subject must always include that of the predicate in such a way that if one understands perfectly the concept of the subject, he will know that the predicate appertains to it also. This being so, we are able to say that this is the nature of an individual substance or of a complete being, namely, to afford a conception so complete that the concept shall be sufficient for the understanding of it and for the deduction of all the predicates of which the substance is or may become the subject. Thus the quality of king, which belonged to Alexander the Great, an abstraction from the subject, is not sufficiently determined to constitute an individual, and does not contain the other qualities of the same subject, nor everything which the idea of this prince includes. God, however, seeing the individual concept, or haecceity, of Alexander, sees there at the same time the basis and the reason of all the predicates which can be truly uttered regarding him; for instance that he will conquer Darius and Porus, even to the point of knowing *a priori* (and not by experience) whether he died a natural death or by poison,—facts which we can learn only through history. When we carefully consider the connection of things we see also the possibility of saying that there was always in the soul of Alexander marks of all that had happened to him and evidences of all that would happen to him and trace even of everything which occurs in the universe, although God alone could recognize them all.

IX. THAT EVERY INDIVIDUAL SUBSTANCE EXPRESSES THE WHOLE UNIVERSE IN ITS OWN MANNER AND THAT IN ITS FULL CONCEPT IS INCLUDED ALL ITS EXPERIENCES TOGETHER WITH ALL THE ATTENDANT CIRCUMSTANCES AND THE WHOLE SEQUENCE OF EXTERIOR EVENTS

There follow from these considerations several noticeable paradoxes; among others that it is not true that two substances may be exactly alike and differ only numerically, *solo numero*, and that what St. Thomas says on this point regarding angels and intelligences (*quod ibi omne individuum sit species infima*) is true of all substances, provided that the specific difference is understood as Geometers understand it in the case of figures; again that a substance will be able to commence only through creation and perish only through annihilation; that a substance cannot be divided into two nor can one be made out of two, and that thus the number of substances neither augments nor diminishes through natural means, although they are frequently transformed. Furthermore every substance is like an entire world and like a mirror of God, or indeed of the whole world which it portrays, each one in its own fashion; almost as the same city is variously represented according to the various situations of him who is regarding it. Thus the universe is multiplied in some sort as many times as there are substances, and the glory of God is multiplied in the same way by as many wholly different representations of his works. It can indeed be said that every substance bears in some sort the character of God's infinite wisdom and omnipotence, and imitates him as much as it is able to; for it expresses, although confusedly, all that happens in the universe, past, present and future, deriving thus a certain resemblance to an infinite perception or power of knowing. And since all other substances express this particular substance and accommodate themselves to it, we can say that it exerts its power upon all the others in imitation of the omnipotence of the creator.

X. THAT THE BELIEF IN SUBSTANTIAL FORMS HAS A CERTAIN BASIS IN FACT, BUT THAT THESE FORMS EFFECT NO CHANGES IN THE PHENOMENA AND MUST NOT BE EMPLOYED FOR THE EXPLANATION OF PARTICULAR EVENTS

It seems that the ancients, able men, who were accustomed to profound meditations and taught theology and philosophy for several centuries and some of whom recommend themselves to us on account of their piety, had some knowledge of that which we have just said and this is why they introduced and maintained the substantial forms so much decried to-day. But they were not so far from the truth nor so open to ridicule as the common run of our new philosophers imagine. I grant that the consideration of these forms is of no service in the details of physics and ought not to be employed in the explanation of particular phenomena. In regard to this last point, the schoolmen were at fault, as were also the physicians of times past who followed their example, thinking they had given the reason for the properties of a body in mentioning the forms and qualities without going to the trouble of examining the manner of operation; as if one should be content to say that a clock had a certain amount of clockness derived from its form, and should not inquire in what that clockness consisted. This is indeed enough for the man who buys it, provided he surrenders the care of it to someone else. The fact, however, that there was this misunderstanding and misuse of the substantial forms should not bring us to throw away something whose recognition is so necessary in metaphysics. Since without these we will not be able, I hold, to know the ultimate principles nor to lift our minds to the knowledge of the incorporeal natures and of the marvels of God. Yet as the geometer does not need to encumber his mind with the famous puzzle of the composition of the continuum, and as no moralist, and still less a jurist or a statesman has need to trouble himself with the great difficulties which arise in conciliating free will with the providential activity of God, (since the geometer is able to make all his demonstrations and the statesman can complete all his deliberations without entering into these discussions which are so necessary and important in Philosophy and Theology), so in the same way the physicist can explain his experiments, now using simpler experiments already made, now employing geometrical and mechanical demonstrations without any need of the general considerations which belong to another sphere, and if he employs the co-operation of God, or perhaps of some soul or animating force, or something else of a similar nature, he goes out of his path quite as much as that man who, when facing an important practical question would wish to enter into profound argumentations regarding the nature of destiny and of our liberty; a fault which men quite frequently commit without realizing it when they cumber their minds with considerations regarding fate, and thus they are even sometimes turned from a good resolution or from some necessary provision.

XI. THAT THE OPINIONS OF THE THEOLOGIANS AND OF THE SO-CALLED SCHOLASTIC PHILOSOPHERS ARE NOT TO BE WHOLLY DESPISED

I know that I am advancing a great paradox in pretending to resuscitate in some sort the ancient philosophy, and to recall *postliminio* the substantial forms almost banished from our modern thought. But perhaps I will not be condemned lightly when it is known that I have long meditated over the modern philosophy and that I have denoted much time to experiments in physics and to the demonstrations of geometry and that I, too, for a long time was persuaded of the baselessness of those "beings" which, however, I was finally obliged to take up again in spite of myself and as though by force. The many investigations which I carried on compelled me to recognize that our moderns do not do sufficient justice to Saint Thomas and to the other great men of that period and that there is in the theories of the scholastic philosophers and theologians far more solidity than is imagined, provided that these theories are employed *à propos* and in their place. I am persuaded that if some careful and meditative mind were to take the trouble to clarify and direct their thoughts in the manner of analytic geometers, he would find a great treasure of very important truths, wholly demonstrable.

XII. THAT THE CONCEPTION OF THE EXTENSION OF A BODY IS IN A WAY IMAGINARY AND DOES NOT CONSTITUTE THE SUBSTANCE OF THE BODY

But to resume the thread of our discussion, I believe that he who will meditate upon the nature of substance, as I have explained it above, will find that the whole nature of bodies is not exhausted in their extension, that is to say, in their size, figure and motion, but that we must recognize something which corresponds to soul, something which is commonly called substantial form, although these forms effect no change in the phenomena, any more than do the souls of beasts, that is if they have souls. It is even possible to demonstrate that the ideas of size, figure and motion are not so distinctive as is imagined, and that they stand for something imaginary relative to our preceptions as do, although to a greater extent, the ideas of color, heat, and the other similar qualities in regard to which we may doubt whether they are actually to be found in the nature of the things outside of us. This is why these latter qualities are unable to constitute "substance" and if there is no other principle of identity in bodies than that which has just been referred to a body would not subsist more than for a moment.

The souls and the substance-forms of other bodies are entirely different from intelligent souls which alone know their actions, and not only do not perish through natural means but indeed always retain the knowledge of what they are; a fact which makes them alone open to chastisement or recompense, and makes them citizens of the republic of the universe whose monarch is God. Hence it follows that all the other creatures should serve them, a point which we shall discuss more amply later.

XIII. AS THE INDIVIDUAL CONCEPT OF EACH PERSON INCLUDES ONCE FOR ALL EVERYTHING WHICH CAN EVER HAPPEN TO HIM, IN IT CAN BE SEEN, *A PRIORI* THE EVIDENCES OR THE REASONS FOR THE REALITY OF EACH EVENT, AND WHY ONE HAPPENED SOONER THAN THE OTHER. BUT THESE EVENTS, HOWEVER CERTAIN, ARE NEVERTHELESS CONTINGENT, BEING BASED ON THE FREE CHOICE OF GOD AND OF HIS CREATURES. IT IS TRUE THAT THEIR CHOICES ALWAYS HAVE THEIR REASONS, BUT THEY INCLINE TO THE CHOICES UNDER NO COMPULSION OF NECESSITY

But before going further it is necessary to meet a difficulty which may arise regarding the principles which we have set forth in the preceding. We have said that the concept of an individual substance includes once for all everything which can ever happen to it and that in considering this concept one will be able to see everything which can truly be said concerning the individual, just as we are able to see in the nature of a circle all the properties which can be derived from it. But does it not seem that in this way the difference between contingent and necessary truths will be destroyed, that there will be no place for human liberty, and that an absolute fatality will rule as well over all our actions as over all the rest of the events of the world? To this I reply that a distinction must be made between that which is certain and that which is necessary. Every one grants that future contingencies are assured since God foresees them, but we do not say just because of that that they are necessary. But it will be objected, that if any conclusion can be deduced infallibly from some definition or concept, it is necessary; and now since we have maintained that everything which is to happen to anyone is already virtually included in his nature or concept, as all the properties are contained in the definition of a circle, therefore, the difficulty still remains. In order to meet the objection completely, I say that the connection or sequence is of two kinds; the one, absolutely necessary, whose contrary implies contradiction, occurs in the eternal verities like the truths of geometry; the other is necessary only *ex hypothesi*, and so to speak by accident, and in itself it is contingent since the contrary is not implied. This latter sequence is not founded upon ideas wholly pure and upon the pure understanding of God, but upon his free decrees and upon the processes of the universe. Let us given an example. Since Julius Caesar will become perpetual Dictator and master of the Republic and will overthrow the liberty of Rome, this action is contained in his concept, for we have supposed that it is the nature of such a perfect concept of a subject to involve everything, in fact so that the predicate may be included in the subject *ut possit inesse subjecto*. We may say that it is not in virtue of this concept or idea that he is obliged to perform this action, since it pertains to him only because God knows everything. But it will be insisted in reply that his nature or form responds to this concept, and since God imposes upon him this personality, he is compelled henceforth to live up to it. I could reply by instancing the similar case of the future contingencies which as yet have no reality save in the understanding and will of God, and which, because God has given them in advance this form, must needs correspond to it. But I prefer to overcome a difficulty rather than to excuse it by instancing other difficulties, and what I am about to say will serve to clear up the one as well as the other. It is here that must be applied the distinction in the kind of relation, and I say that that which happens conformably to these decrees is assured, but that it is not therefore necessary, and if anyone did the contrary, he would do nothing impossible in itself, although it is impossible *ex hypothesi* that that other happen. For if anyone were capable of carrying out a complete demonstration by virtue of which he could prove this connection of the subject, which is Caesar, with the predicate, which is his successful enterprise, he would bring us to see in fact that the future dictatorship of Caesar had its basis in his concept or nature, so that one would see there a reason why he resolved to cross the Rubicon rather than to stop, and why he gained instead of losing the day at Pharsalus, and that it was reasonable and by consequence assured that this would occur, but one would not prove that it was necessary in itself, nor that the contrary implied a contradiction, almost in the same way in which it is reasonable and assured that God will always do what is best although that which is less perfect is not thereby implied. For it would be found that this demonstration of this predicate as belonging to Caesar is not as absolute as are those of numbers or of geometry, but that this predicate supposes a sequence of things which God has shown by his free will. This sequence is based on the first free decree of God which was to do always that which is the most perfect and upon the decree which God made following the first one, regarding human nature, which is that men should always do, although freely, that which appears to be the best. Now every truth which is founded upon this kind of decree is contingent, although certain, for the decrees of God do not change the possibilities of things and, as I have already said, although God assuredly chooses the best, this does not prevent that which is less perfect from being possible in itself. Although it will never happen, it is not its impossibility but its imperfection which causes him to reject it. Now nothing is necessitated whose opposite is possible. One will then be in a position to satisfy these kinds of difficulties, however great they may appear (and in fact they have not been less vexing to all other thinkers who have ever treated this matter), provided that he considers well that all contingent propositions have reasons why they are thus, rather than otherwise, or indeed (what is the same thing) that they have proof *a priori* of their truth, which render them certain and show that the connection of the subject and predicate in these propositions has its basis in the nature of the one and of the other, but he must further remember that such contingent propositions have not the demonstrations of necessity, since their reasons are founded only on the principle of contingency or of the existence of things, that is to say, upon that which is, or which appears to be the best among several things equally possible. Necessary truths, on the other hand, are founded upon the principle of contradiction, and upon the possibility or impossibility of the essences themselves, without regard here to the free will of God or of creatures.

XIV. GOD PRODUCES DIFFERENT SUBSTANCES ACCORDING TO THE DIFFERENT VIEWS WHICH HE HAS OF THE WORLD, AND BY THE INTERVENTION OF GOD, THE APPROPRIATE NATURE OF EACH SUBSTANCE BRINGS IT ABOUT THAT WHAT HAPPENS TO ONE CORRESPONDS TO WHAT HAPPENS TO ALL THE OTHERS, WITHOUT, HOWEVER, THEIR ACTING UPON ONE ANOTHER DIRECTLY

After having seen, to a certain extent, in what the nature of substances consists, we must try to explain the dependence they have upon one another and their actions and passions. Now it is first of all very evident that created substances depend upon God who preserves them and can produce them continually by a kind of emanation just as we produce our thoughts, for when God turns, so to say, on all sides and in all fashions, the general system of phenomena which he finds it good to produce for the sake of manifesting his glory, and when he regards all the aspects of the world in all possible manners, since there is no relation which escapes his omniscience, the result of each view of the universe as seen from a different position is a substance which expresses the universe conformably to this view, provided God sees fit to render his thought effective and to produce the substance, and since God's vision is always true, our perceptions are always true and that which deceives us are our judgments, which are of us. Now we have said before, and it follows from what we have just said that each substance is a world by itself, independent of everything else excepting God; therefore, all our phenomena that is all things which are ever able to happen to us, are only consequences of our being. Now as the phenomena maintain a certain order conformably to our nature, or so to speak to the world which is in us (from whence it follows that we can, for the regulation of our conduct, make useful observations which are justified by the outcome of the future phenomena) and as we are thus able often to judge the future by the past without deceiving ourselves, we have sufficient grounds for saying that these phenomena are true and we will not be put to the task of inquiring whether they are outside of us, and whether others perceive them also.

Nevertheless it is most true that the perceptions and expressions of all substances intercorrespond, so that each one following independently certain reasons or laws which he has noticed meets others which are doing the same, as when several have agreed to meet together in a certain place on a set day, they are able to carry out the plan if they wish. Now although all express the same phenomena, this does not bring it about that their expressions are exactly alike. It is sufficient if they are proportional. As when several spectators think they see the same thing and are agreed about it, although each one sees or speaks according to the measure of his vision. It is God alone, (from whom all individuals emanate continually, and who sees the universe not only as they see it, but besides in a very different way from them) who is the cause of this correspondence in their phenomena and who brings it about that that which is particular to one, is also common to all, otherwise there would be no relation. In a way, then, we might properly say, although it seems strange, that a particular substance never acts upon another particular substance nor is it acted upon by it. That which happens to each one is only the consequence of its complete idea or concept, since this idea already includes all the predicates and expresses the whole universe. In fact nothing can happen to us except thoughts and perceptions, and all our thoughts and perceptions are but the consequence, contingent it is true, of our precedent thoughts and perceptions, in such a way that were I able to consider directly all that happens or appears to me at the present time, I should be able to see all that will happen to me or that will ever appear to me. This future will not fail me, and will surely appear to me even if all that which is outside of me were destroyed, save only that God and myself were left.

Since, however, we ordinarily attribute to other

things an action upon us which brings us to perceive things in a certain manner, it is necessary to consider the basis of this judgment and to inquire what there is of truth in it.

XV. THE ACTION OF ONE FINITE SUBSTANCE UPON ANOTHER CONSISTS ONLY IN THE INCREASE IN THE DEGREES OF EXPRESSION OF THE FIRST COMBINED WITH A DECREASE IN THAT OF THE SECOND, IN SO FAR AS GOD HAS IN ADVANCE FASHIONED THEM SO THAT THEY SHALL ACT IN ACCORD

Without entering into a long discussion it is sufficient for reconciling the language of metaphysics with that of practical life to remark that we preferably attribute to ourselves, and with reason, the phenomena which we express the most perfectly, and that we attribute to other substances those phenomena which each one expresses the best. Thus a substance, which is of an infinite extension in so far as it expresses all, becomes limited in proportion to its more or less perfect manner of expression. It is thus then that we may conceive of substances as interfering with and limiting one another, and hence we are able to say that in this sense they act upon one another, and that they, so to speak, accommodate themselves to one another. For it can happen that a single change which augments the expression of the one may diminish that of the other. Now the virtue of a particular substance is to express well the glory of God, and the better it expresses it, the less is it limited. Everything when it expresses its virtue or power, that is to say, when it acts, changes to better, and expands just in so far as it acts. When therefore a change occurs by which several substances are affected (in fact every change affects them all) I think we may say that those substance, which by this change pass immediately to a greater degree of perfection, or to a more perfect expression, exert power and act, while those which pass to a lesser degree disclose their weakness and suffer. I also hold that every activity of a substance which has perception implies some pleasure, and every passion some pain, except that it may very well happen that a present advantage will be eventually destroyed by a greater evil, whence it comes that one may sin in acting or exerting his power and in finding pleasure.

XVI. THE EXTRAORDINARY INTERVENTION OF GOD IS NOT EXCLUDED IN THAT WHICH OUR PARTICULAR ESSENCES EXPRESS, BECAUSE THEIR EXPRESSION INCLUDES EVERYTHING. SUCH INTERVENTION, HOWEVER, GOES BEYOND THE POWER OF OUR NATURAL BEING OR OF OUR DISTINCT EXPRESSION, BECAUSE THESE ARE FINITE, AND FOLLOW CERTAIN SUBORDINATE REGULATIONS

There remains for us at present only to explain how it is possible that God has influence at times upon men or upon other substances by an extraordinary or miraculous intervention, since it seems that nothing is able to happen which is extraordinary or supernatural in as much as all the events which occur to the other substances are only the consequences of their natures. We must recall what was said above in regard to the miracles in the universe. These always conform to the universal law of the general order, although they may contravene the subordinate regulations, and since every person or substance is like a little world which expresses the great world, we can say that this extraordinary action of God upon this substance is nevertheless miraculous, although it is comprised in the general order of the universe in so far as it is expressed by the individual essence or concept of this substance. This is why, if we understand in our natures all that they express, nothing is supernatural in them, because they reach out to everything, an effect always expressing its cause, and God being the veritable cause of the substances. But as that which our natures express the most perfectly pertains to them in a particular manner, that being their special power, and since they are limited, as I have just explained, many things there are which surpass the powers of our natures and even of all limited natures. As a consequence, to speak more clearly, I say that the miracles and the extraordinary interventions of God have this peculiarity that they cannot be foreseen by any created mind however enlightened. This is because the distinct comprehension of the fundamental order surpasses them all, while on the other hand, that which is called natural depends upon less fundamental regulations which the creatures are able to understand. In order then that my words may be as irreprehensible as the meaning I am trying to convey, it will be well to associate certain words with certain significations. We may call that which includes everything that we express and which expresses our union with God himself, nothing going beyond it, our essence. But that which is limited in us may be designated as our nature or our power and in accordance with this terminology that which goes beyond the natures of all created substances is supernatural.

XVII. AN EXAMPLE OF A SUBORDINATE REGULATION IN THE LAW OF NATURE WHICH DEMONSTRATES THAT GOD ALWAYS PRESERVES THE SAME AMOUNT OF FORCE BUT NOT THE SAME QUANTITY OF MOTION:—AGAINST THE CARTESIANS AND MANY OTHERS

I have frequently spoken of subordinate regulations, or of the laws of nature, and it seems that it will be well to give an example. Our new philosophers are unanimous in employing that famous law that God always preserves the same amount of motion in the universe. In fact it is a very plausible law, and in times past I held it for indubitable. But since then I have learned in what its fault consists. Monsieur Descartes and many other clever mathematicians have thought that the quantity of motion, that is to say the velocity multiplied by the mass[1] of the moving body, is exactly equivalent to the moving force, or to speak in mathematical terms that the force varies as the velocity multiplied by the mass. Now it is reasonable that the same force is always preserved in the universe. So also, looking to phenomena, it will be readily seen that a mechanical perpetual motion is impossible, because the force in such a machine, being always diminished a little by friction and so ultimately destined to be entirely spent, would necessarily have to recoup its losses, and consequently would keep on increasing of itself without any new impulsion from without; and we see furthermore that the force of a body is diminished only in proportion as it gives up force, either to a contiguous body or to its own parts, in so far as they have a separate movement. The mathematicians to whom I have referred think that what can be said of force can be said of the quantity of motion. In order, however, to show the difference I make two suppositions: in the first place, that a body falling from a certain height acquires a force enabling it to remount to the same height, provided that its direction is turned that way, or provided that there are no hindrances. For instance, a pendulum will rise exactly to the height from which it has fallen, provided the resistance of the air and of certain other small particles do not diminish a little its acquired force.

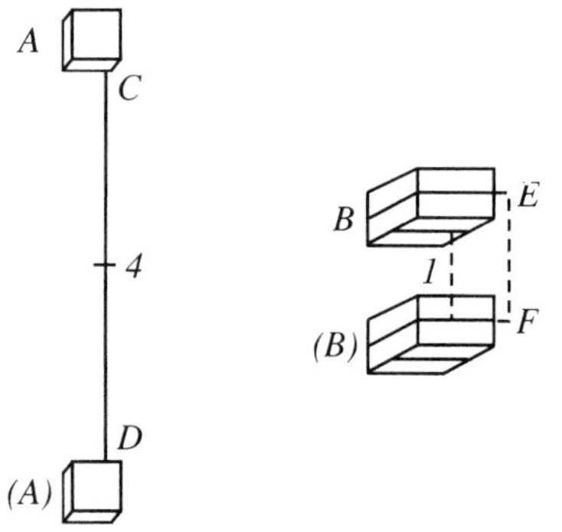

I suppose in the second place that it will take as much force to lift a body A weighing one pound to the height CD, four feet, as to raise a body B weighing four pounds to the height EF, one foot. These two suppositions are granted by our new philosophers. It is therefore manifest that the body A falling from the height CD acquires exactly as much force as the body B falling from the height EF, for the body B at F, having by the first supposition sufficient force to return to E, has therefore the force to carry a body of four pounds to the distance of one foot, EF. And likewise the body A at D, having the force to return to C, has also the force required to carry a body weighing one pound, its own weight, back to C, a distance of four feet. Now by the second supposition the force of these two bodies is equal. Let us now see if the quantity of motion is the same in each case. It is here that we will be surprised to find a very great difference, for it has been proved by Galileo that the velocity acquired by the

1. This term is employed here for the sake of clearness. Leibniz did not possess the concept "mass," which was enunciated by Newton in the same year in which the present treatise was written, 1686. Leibniz uses the terms "body," "magnitude of body," etc. The technical expression "mass" occurs once only in the writings of Leibniz (in a treatise published in 1695), and was there doubtless borrowed from Newton. For the history of the controversy concerning the Cartesian and Leibnizian measure of force, see Mach's *Science of Mechanics*, Chicago, 1893, pp. 272 et seq.—*Trans.*

fall CD is double the velocity acquired by the fall EF, although the height is four times as great. Multiplying, therefore, the body A, whose mass is 1, by its velocity, which is 2 the product or the quantity of movement will be 2, and on the other hand, if we multiply the body B, whose mass is 4, by its velocity, which is 1, the product or quantity of motion will be 4. Hence the quantity of the motion of the body A at the point D is half the quantity of motion of the body B at the point F, yet their forces are equal, and there is therefore a great difference between the quantity of motion and the force. This is what we set out to show. We can see therefore how the force ought to be estimated by the quantity of the effect which it is able to produce, for example by the height to which a body of certain weight can be raised. This is a very different thing from the velocity which can be imparted to it, and in order to impart to it double the velocity we must have double the force. Nothing is simpler than this proof and Monsieur Descartes has fallen into error here, only because he trusted too much to his thoughts even when they had not been ripened by reflection. But it astonishes me that his disciples have not noticed this error, and I am afraid that they are beginning to imitate little by little certain Peripatetics whom they ridicule, and that they are accustoming themselves to consult rather the books of their master, than reason or nature.

XVIII. THE DISTINCTION BETWEEN FORCE AND THE QUANTITY OF MOTION IS, AMONG OTHER REASONS, IMPORTANT AS SHOWING THAT WE MUST HAVE RECOURSE TO METAPHYSICAL CONSIDERATIONS IN ADDITION TO DISCUSSIONS OF EXTENSION IF WE WISH TO EXPLAIN THE PHENOMENA OF MATTER

This consideration of the force, distinguished from the quantity of motion is of importance, not only in physics and mechanics for finding the real laws of nature and the principles of motion, and even for correcting many practical errors which have crept into the writings of certain able mathematicians, but also in metaphysics it is of importance for the better understanding of principles. Because motion, if we regard only its exact and formal meaning, that is, change of place, is not something entirely real, and when several bodies change their places reciprocally, it is not possible to determine by considering the bodies alone to which among them movement or repose is to be attributed, as I could demonstrate geometrically, if I wished to stop for it now. But the force, or the proximate cause of these changes is something more real, and there are sufficient grounds for attributing it to one body rather than to another, and it is only through this latter investigation that we can determine to which one the movement must appertain. Now this force is something different from size, from form or from motion, and it can be seen from this consideration that the whole meaning of a body is not exhausted in its extension together with its modifications as our moderns persuade themselves. We are therefore obliged to restore certain beings or forms which they have banished. It appears more and more clear that although all the particular phenomena of nature can be explained mathematically or mechanically by those who understand them, yet nevertheless, the general principles of corporeal nature and even of mechanics are metaphysical rather than geometric, and belong rather to certain indivisible forms or natures as the causes of the appearances, than to the corporeal mass or to extension. This reflection is able to reconcile the mechanical philosophy of the moderns with the circumspection of those intelligent and well-meaning persons who, with a certain justice, fear that we are becoming too far removed from immaterial beings and that we are thus prejudicing piety.

XIX. THE UTILITY OF FINAL CAUSES IN PHYSICS

As I do not wish to judge people in ill part I bring no accusation against our new philosophers who pretend to banish final causes from physics, but I am nevertheless obliged to avow that the consequences of such a banishment appear to me dangerous, especially when joined to that position which I refuted at the beginning of this treatise. That position seemed to go the length of discarding final causes entirely as though God proposed no end and no good in his activity, or as if good were not to be the object of his will. I hold on the contrary that it is just in this that the principle of all existences and of the laws of nature must be sought, hence God always proposes the best and most perfect. I am quite willing to grant that we are liable to err when we wish to determine the purposes or councils of God, but this is the case only when we try to limit them to some particular design, thinking that he has had in view only a single thing, while in fact he regards everything at once. As for instance, if we think that God has made the world only for us, it is a great blunder, although it may be quite true that he has made it entirely for us, and that there is nothing in the universe which does not touch us and which does not accommodate itself to the regard which he has for us according to the principle laid down above. Therefore when we see some good effect or some perfection which happens or which follows from the works of God we are able to say assuredly that God has purposed it, for he does nothing by chance, and is not like us who sometimes fail to do well. Therefore, far from being able to fall into error in this respect as do the extreme statesmen who postulate too much foresight in the designs of Princes, or as do commentators who seek for too much erudition in their authors, it will be impossible to attribute too much reflection to God's infinite wisdom, and there is no matter in which error is less to be feared provided we confine ourselves to affirmations and provided we avoid negative statements which limit the designs of God. All those who see the admirable structure of animals find themselves led to recognize the wisdom of the author of things and I advise those who have any sentiment of piety and indeed of true philosophy to hold aloof from the expressions of certain pretentious minds who instead of saying that eyes were made for seeing, say that we see because we find ourselves having eyes. When one seriously holds such opinions which hand everything over to material necessity or to a kind of chance (although either alternative ought to appear ridiculous to those who understand what we have explained above) it is difficult to recognize an intelligent author of nature. The effect should correspond to its cause and indeed it is best known through the recognition of its cause, so that it is reasonable to introduce a sovereign intelligence ordering things, and in place of making use of the wisdom of this sovereign being, to employ only the properties of matter to explain phenomena. As if in order to account for the capture of an important place by a prince, the historian should say it was because the particles of powder in the cannon having been touched by a spark of fire expanded with a rapidity capable of pushing a hard solid body against the walls of the place, while the little particles which composed the brass of the cannon were so well interlaced that they did not separate under this impact,—as if he should account for it in this way instead of making us see how the foresight of the conqueror brought him to choose the time and the proper means and how his ability surmounted all obstacles.

XX. A NOTEWORTHY DISQUISITION IN PLATO'S PHAEDO AGAINST THE PHILOSOPHERS WHO WERE TOO MATERIALISTIC

This reminds me of a fine disquisition by Socrates in Plato's Phaedo, which agrees perfectly with my opinion on this subject and seems to have been uttered expressly for our too materialistic philosophers. This agreement has led me to a desire to translate it although it is a little long. Perhaps this example will give some of us an incentive to share in many of the other beautiful and well balanced thoughts which are found in the writings of this famous author.[2]

XXI. IF THE MECHANICAL LAWS DEPENDED UPON GEOMETRY ALONE WITHOUT METAPHYSICAL INFLUENCES, THE PHENOMENA WOULD BE VERY DIFFERENT FROM WHAT THEY ARE

Now since the wisdom of God has always been recognized in the detail of the mechanical structures of certain particular bodies, it should also be shown in the general economy of the world and in the constitution of the laws of nature. This is so true that even in the laws of motion in general, the plans of this wisdom have been noticed. For if bodies were only extended masses, and motion were only a change of place, and if everything ought to be and could be deduced by geometric necessity from these two definitions alone, it would follow, as I have

2. There is a gap here in the MS., intended for the passage from Plato, the translation of which Leibniz did not supply.—*Trans.*

shown elsewhere, that the smallest body on contact with a very large one at rest would impart to it its own velocity, yet without losing any of the velocity that it had. A quantity of other rules wholly contrary to the formation of a system would also have to be admitted. But the decree of the divine wisdom in preserving always the same force and the same total direction has provided for a system. I find indeed that many of the effects of nature can be accounted for in a twofold way, that is to say by a consideration of efficient causes, and again independently by a consideration of final causes. An example of the latter is God's decree to always carry out his plan by the easiest and most determined way. I have shown this elsewhere in accounting for the catoptric and dioptric laws, and I will speak more at length about it in what follows.

XXII. RECONCILIATION OF THE TWO METHODS OF EXPLANATION, THE ONE USING FINAL CAUSES, AND THE OTHER EFFICIENT CAUSES, THUS SATISFYING BOTH THOSE WHO EXPLAIN NATURE MECHANICALLY AND THOSE WHO HAVE RECOURSE TO INCORPOREAL NATURES

It is worth while to make the preceding remark in order to reconcile those who hope to explain mechanically the formation of the first tissue of an animal and all the interrelation of the parts, with those who account for the same structure by referring to final causes. Both explanations are good; both are useful not only for the admiring of the work of a great artificer, but also for the discovery of useful facts in physics and medicine. And writers who take these diverse routes should not speak ill of each other. For I see that those who attempt to explain beauty by the divine anatomy ridicule those who imagine that the apparently fortuitous flow of certain liquids has been able to produce such a beautiful variety and that they regard them as overbold and irreverent. These others on the contrary treat the former as simple and superstitious, and compare them to those ancients who regarded the physicists as impious when they maintained that not Jupiter thundered but some material which is found in the clouds. The best plan would be to join the two ways of thinking. To use a practical comparison, we recognize and praise the ability of a workman not only when we show what designs he had in making the parts of his machine, but also when we explain the instruments which he employed in making each part, above all if these instruments are simple and ingeniously contrived. God is also a workman able enough to produce a machine still a thousand times more ingenious than is our body, by employing only certain quite simple liquids purposely composed in such a way that ordinary laws of nature alone are required to develop them so as to produce such a marvellous effect. But it is also true that this development would not take place if God were not the author of nature. Yet I find that the method of efficient causes, which goes much deeper and is in a measure more immediate and *a priori*, is also more difficult when we come to details, and I think that our philosophers are still very frequently far removed from making the most of this method. The method of final causes, however, is easier and can be frequently employed to find out important and useful truths which we should have to seek for a long time, if we were confined to that other more physical method of which anatomy is able to furnish many examples. It seems to me that Snellius, who was the first discoverer of the laws of refraction would have waited a long time before finding them if he had wished to seek out first how light was formed. But he apparently followed that method which the ancients employed for Catoptrics, that is, the method of final causes. Because, while seeking for the easiest way in which to conduct a ray of light from one given point to another given point by reflection from a given plane (supposing that that was the design of nature) they discovered the equality of the angles of incidence and reflection, as can be seen from a little treatise by Heliodorus of Larissa and also elsewhere. This principle Mons. Snellius, I believe, and afterwards independently of him, M. Fermat, applied most ingeniously to refraction. For since the rays while in the same media always maintain the same proportion of sines, which in turn corresponds to the resistance of the media, it appears that they follow the easiest way, or at least that way which is the most determinate for passing from a given point in one medium to a given point in another medium. That demonstration of this same theorem which M. Descartes has given, using efficient causes, is much less satisfactory. At least we have grounds to think that he would never have found the principle by that means if he had not learned in Holland of the discovery of Snellius.

XXIII. RETURNING TO IMMATERIAL SUBSTANCES WE EXPLAIN HOW GOD ACTS UPON THE UNDERSTANDING OF SPIRITS AND ASK WHETHER ONE ALWAYS KEEPS THE IDEA OF WHAT HE THINKS ABOUT

I have thought it well to insist a little upon final causes, upon incorporeal natures and upon an intelligent cause with respect to bodies so as to show the use of these conceptions in physics and in mathematics. This for two reasons, first to purge from mechanical philosophy the impiety that is imputed to it, second, to elevate to nobler lines of thought the thinking of our philosophers who incline to materialistic considerations alone. Now, however, it will be well to return from corporeal substances to the consideration of immaterial natures and particularly of spirits, and to speak of the methods which God uses to enlighten them and to act upon them. Although we must not forget that there are here at the same time certain laws of nature in regard to which I can speak more amply elsewhere. It will be enough for now to touch upon ideas and to inquire if we see everything in God and how God is our light. First of all it will be in place to remark that the wrong use of ideas occasions many errors. For when one reasons in regard to anything, he imagines that he has an idea of it and this is the foundation upon which certain philosophers, ancient and modern, have constructed a demonstration of God that is extremely imperfect. It must be, they say, that I have an idea of God, or of a perfect being, since I think of him and we cannot think without having ideas; now the idea of this being includes all perfections and since existence is one of these perfections, it follows that he exists. But I reply, inasmuch as we often think of impossible chimeras, for example of the highest degree of swiftness, of the greatest number, of the meeting of the conchoid with its base or determinant, such reasoning is not sufficient. It is therefore in this sense that we can say that there are true and false ideas according as the thing which is in question is possible or not. And it is when he is assured of the possibility of a thing, that one can boast of having an idea of it. Therefore, the aforesaid argument proves that God exists, if he is possible. This is in fact an excellent privilege of the divine nature, to have need only of a possibility or an essence in order to actually exist, and it is just this which is called *ens a se*.

XXIV. WHAT CLEAR AND OBSCURE, DISTINCT AND CONFUSED, ADEQUATE AND INADEQUATE, INTUITIVE AND ASSUMED KNOWLEDGE IS, AND THE DEFINITION OF NOMINAL, REAL, CAUSAL AND ESSENTIAL

In order to understand better the nature of ideas it is necessary to touch somewhat upon the various kinds of knowledge. When I am able to recognize a thing among others, without being able to say in what its differences or characteristics consist, the knowledge is confused. Sometimes indeed we may know clearly, that is without being in the slightest doubt, that a poem or a picture is well or badly done because there is in it an "I know not what" which satisfies or shocks us. Such knowledge is not yet distinct. It is when I am able to explain the peculiarities which a thing has, that the knowledge is called distinct. Such is the knowledge of an assayer who discerns the true gold from the false by means of certain proofs or marks which make up the definition of gold. But distinct knowledge has degrees, because ordinarily the conceptions which enter into the definitions will themselves have need of definition, and are only known confusedly. When at length everything which enters into a definition or into distinct knowledge is known distinctly, even back to the primitive conception, I call that knowledge adequate. When my mind understands at once and distinctly all the primitive ingredients of a conception, then we have intuitive knowledge. This is extremely rare as most human knowledge is only confused or indeed assumed. It is well also to distinguish nominal from real definition. I call a definition nominal when there is doubt whether an exact conception of it is possible; as for instance, when I say that an endless screw is a line in three dimensional space whose parts are congruent or fall one upon another. Now although this is one of the reciprocal properties of an endless screw, he who did not know from elsewhere what an endless screw was could doubt if such a line were possible, because the other lines whose ends are congruent (there are only two: the circumference of a circle and the straight line) are plane figures, that is to say they can be described *in plano*.

This instance enables us to see that any reciprocal property can serve as a nominal definition, but when the property brings us to see the possibility of a thing it makes the definition real, and as long as one has only a nominal definition he cannot be sure of the consequences which he draws, because if it conceals a contradiction or an impossibility he would be able to draw the opposite conclusions. That is why truths do not depend upon names and are not arbitrary, as some of our new philosophers think. There is also a considerable difference among real definitions, for when the possibility proves itself only by experience, as in the definition of quicksilver, whose possibility we know because such a body, which is both an extremely heavy fluid and quite volatile, actually exists, the definition is merely real and nothing more. If, however, the proof of the possibility is *a priori*, the definition is not only real but also causal as for instance when it contains the possible generation of a thing. Finally when the definition, without assuming anything which requires a proof *a priori* of its possibility, carries the analysis clear to the primitive conception, the definition is perfect or essential.

XXV. IN WHAT CASES KNOWLEDGE IS ADDED TO MERE CONTEMPLATION OF THE IDEA

Now it is manifest that we have no idea of a conception when it is impossible. And in case the knowledge, where we have the idea of it, is only assumed, we do not visualize it because such a conception is known only in like manner as conceptions, internally impossible. And if it be in fact possible, it is not by this kind of knowledge that we learn its possibility. For instance, when I am thinking of a thousand or of a chiliagon, I frequently do it without contemplating the idea. Even if I say a thousand is ten times a hundred, I frequently do not trouble to think what ten and a hundred are, because I assume that I know, and I do not consider it necessary to stop just at present to conceive of them. Therefore it may well happen, as it in fact does happen often enough, that I am mistaken in regard to a conception which I assume that I understand, although it is an impossible truth or at least is incompatible with others with which I join it, and whether I am mistaken or not, this way of assuming our knowledge remains the same. It is, then, only when our knowledge is clear in regard to confused conceptions, and when it is intuitive in regard to those which are distinct, that we see its entire idea.

XXVI. IDEAS ARE ALL STORED UP WITHIN US. PLATO'S DOCTRINE OF REMINISCENCE

In order to see clearly what an idea is, we must guard ourselves against a misunderstanding. Many regard the idea as the form or the differentiation of our thinking, and according to this opinion we have the idea in our mind, in so far as we are thinking of it, and each separate time that we think of it anew we have another idea although similar to the preceding one. Some, however, take the idea as the immediate object of thought, or as a permanent form which remains even when we are no longer contemplating it. As a matter of fact our soul has the power of representing to itself any form or nature whenever the occasion comes for thinking about it, and I think that this activity of our soul is, so far as it expresses some nature, form or essence, properly the idea of the thing. This is in us, and is always in us, whether we are thinking of it or no. (Our soul expresses God and the universe and all essences as well as all existences.) This position is in accord with my principles that naturally nothing enters into our minds from outside.

It is a bad habit we have of thinking as though our minds receive certain messengers, as it were, or as if they had doors or windows. We have in our minds all those forms for all periods of time because the mind at every moment expresses all its future thoughts and already thinks confusedly of all that of which it will ever think distinctly. Nothing can be taught us of which we have not already in our minds the idea. This idea is as it were the material out of which the thought will form itself. This is what Plato has excellently brought out in his doctrine of reminiscence, a doctrine which contains a great deal of truth, provided that it is properly understood and purged of the error of pre-existence, and provided that one does not conceive of the soul as having already known and thought at some other time what it learns and thinks now. Plato has also confirmed his position by a beautiful experiment. He introduces a small boy, whom he leads by short steps, to extremely difficult truths of geometry bearing on incommensurables, all this without teaching the boy anything, merely drawing out replies by a well arranged series of questions. This shows that the soul virtually knows those things, and needs only to be reminded (animadverted) to recognize the truths. Consequently it possesses at least the idea upon which those truths depend. We may say even that it already possesses those truths, if we consider them as the relations of the ideas.

XXVII. IN WHAT RESPECT OUR SOULS CAN BE COMPARED TO BLANK TABLETS AND HOW CONCEPTIONS ARE DERIVED FROM THE SENSES

Aristotle preferred to compare our souls to blank tablets prepared for writing, and he maintained that nothing is in the understanding which does not come through the senses. This position is in accord with the popular conceptions as Aristotle's positions usually are. Plato thinks more profoundly. Such tenets or practicologies are nevertheless allowable in ordinary use somewhat in the same way as those who accept the Copernican theory still continue to speak of the rising and setting of the sun. I find indeed that these usages can be given a real meaning containing no error, quite in the same way as I have already pointed out that we may truly say particular substances act upon one another. In this same sense we may say that knowledge is received from without through the medium of the senses because certain exterior things contain or express more particularly the causes which determine us to certain thoughts. Because in the ordinary uses of life we attribute to the soul only that which belongs to it most manifestly and particularly, and there is no advantage in going further. When, however, we are dealing with the exactness of metaphysical truths, it is important to recognize the powers and independence of the soul which extend infinitely further than is commonly supposed. In order, therefore, to avoid misunderstandings it would be well to choose separate terms for the two. These expressions which are in the soul whether one is conceiving of them or not may be called ideas, while those which one conceives of or constructs may be called conceptions, *conceptus*. But whatever terms are used, it is always false to say that all our conceptions come from the so-called external senses, because those conceptions which I have of myself and of my thoughts, and consequently of being, of substance, of action, of identity, and of many others came from an inner experience.

XXVIII. THE ONLY IMMEDIATE OBJECT OF OUR PERCEPTIONS WHICH EXISTS OUTSIDE OF US IS GOD, AND IN HIM ALONE IS OUR LIGHT

In the strictly metaphysical sense no external cause acts upon us excepting God alone, and he is in immediate relation with us only by virtue of our continual dependence upon him. Whence it follows that there is absolutely no other external object which comes into contact with our souls and directly excites perceptions in us. We have in our souls ideas of everything, only because of the continual action of God upon us, that is to say, because every effect expresses its cause and therefore the essences of our souls are certain expressions, imitations or images of the divine essence, divine thought and divine will, including all the ideas which are there contained. We may say, therefore, that God is for us the only immediate external object, and that we see things through him. For example, when we see the sun or the stars, it is God who gives to us and preserves in us the ideas and whenever our senses are affected according to his own laws in a certain manner, it is he, who by his continual concurrence, determines our thinking. God is the sun and the light of souls, *lumen illuminans omnem hominem venientem in hunc mundum*, although this is not the current conception. I think I have already remarked that during the scholastic period many believed God to be the light of the soul, *intellectus agens animae rationalis*, following in this the Holy Scriptures and the fathers who were always more Platonic than Aristotelian in their mode of thinking. The Averroists misused this conception, but others, among whom were several mystic theologians, and William of Saint Amour, also I think, understood this conception in a manner which assured the dignity of God and was able to raise the soul to a knowledge of its welfare.

XXIX. YET WE THINK DIRECTLY BY MEANS OF OUR OWN IDEAS AND NOT THROUGH GOD'S

Nevertheless I cannot approve of the position of certain able philosophers who seem to hold that our ideas themselves are in God and not at all in us. I think that in taking this position they have neither sufficiently considered the nature of substance, which we have just explained, nor the entire extension and independence of the soul which includes all that happens to it, and expresses God, and with him all possible and actual beings in the same way that an effect expresses its cause. It is indeed inconceivable that the soul should think using the ideas of something else. The soul when it thinks of anything must be affected effectively in a certain manner, and it must needs have in itself in advance not only the passive capacity of being thus affected, a capacity already wholly determined, but it must have besides an active power by virtue of which it has always had in its nature the marks of the future production of this thought, and the disposition to produce it at its proper time. All of this shows that the soul already includes the idea which is comprised in any particular thought.

XXX. HOW GOD INCLINES OUR SOULS WITHOUT NECESSITATING THEM; THAT THERE ARE NO GROUNDS FOR COMPLAINT; THAT WE MUST NOT ASK WHY JUDAS SINNED BECAUSE THIS FREE ACT IS CONTAINED IN HIS CONCEPT, THE ONLY QUESTION BEING WHY JUDAS THE SINNER IS ADMITTED TO EXISTENCE, PREFERABLY TO OTHER POSSIBLE PERSONS; CONCERNING THE ORIGINAL IMPERFECTION OR LIMITATION BEFORE THE FALL AND CONCERNING THE DIFFERENT DEGREES OF GRACE

Regarding the action of God upon the human will there are many quite different considerations which it would take too long to investigate here. Nevertheless the following is what can be said in general. God in co-operating with ordinary actions only follows the laws which he has established, that is to say, he continually preserves and produces our being so that the ideas come to us spontaneously or with freedom in that order which the concept of our individual substance carries with itself. In this concept they can be foreseen for all eternity. Furthermore, by virtue of the decree which God has made that the will shall always seek the apparent good in certain particular respects (in regard to which this apparent good always has in it something of reality expressing or imitating God's will), he, without at all necessitating our choice, determines it by that which appears most desirable. For absolutely speaking, our will as contrasted with necessity, is in a state of indifference, being able to act otherwise, or wholly to suspend its action, either alternative being and remaining possible. It therefore devolves upon the soul to be on guard against appearances, by means of a firm will, to reflect and to refuse to act or decide in certain circumstances, except after mature deliberation. It is, however, true and has been assured from all eternity that certain souls will not employ their power upon certain occasions.

But who could do more than God has done, and can such a soul complain of anything except itself? All these complaints after the deed are unjust, inasmuch as they would have been unjust before the deed. Would this soul a little before committing the sin have had the right to complain of God as though he had determined the sin. Since the determinations of God in these matters cannot be foreseen, how would the soul know that it was pre-ordained to sin unless it had already committed the sin? It is merely a question of wishing to or not wishing to, and God could not have set an easier or juster condition. Therefore all judges without asking the reasons which have disposed a man to have an evil will, consider only how far this will is wrong. But, you object, perhaps it is ordained from all eternity that I will sin. Find your own answer. Perhaps it has not been. Now then, without asking for what you are unable to know and in regard to which you can have no light, act according to your duty and your knowledge. But, some one will object; whence comes it then that this man will assuredly do this sin? The reply is easy. It is that otherwise he would not be a man. For God foresees from all time that there will be a certain Judas, and in the concept or idea of him which God has, is contained this future free act. The only question, therefore, which remains is why this certain Judas, the betrayer who is possible only because of the idea of God, actually exists. To this question however, we can expect no answer here on earth excepting to say in general that it is because God has found it good that he should exist notwithstanding that sin which he foresaw. This evil will be more than overbalanced. God will derive a greater good from it, and it will finally turn out that this series of events in which is included the existence of this sinner, is the most perfect among all the possible series of events. An explanation in every case of the admirable economy of this choice cannot be given while we are sojourners on earth. It is enough to know the excellence without understanding it. It is here that must be recognized *altitudinem divitiarum*, the unfathomable depth of the divine wisdom, without hesitating at a detail which involves an infinite number of considerations. It is clear, however, that God is not the cause of ill. For not only after the loss of innocence by men, has original sin possessed the soul, but even before that there was an original limitation or imperfection in the very nature of all creatures, which rendered them open to sin and able to fall. There is, therefore, no more difficulty in the supralapsarian view than there is in the other views of sin. To this also, it seems to me can be reduced the opinion of Saint Augustine and of other authors: that the root of evil is in the negativity, that is to say, in the lack or limitation of creatures which God graciously remedies by whatever degree of perfection it pleases him to give. This grace of God, whether ordinary or extraordinary has its degrees and its measures. It is always efficacious in itself to produce a certain proportionate effect and furthermore it is always sufficient not only to keep one from sin but even to effect his salvation, provided that the man cooperates with that which is in him. It has not always, however, sufficient power to overcome the inclination, for, if it did, it would no longer be limited in any way, and this superiority to limitations is reserved to that unique grace which is absolutely efficacious. This grace is always victorious whether through its own self or through the congruity of circumstances.

XXXI. CONCERNING THE MOTIVES OF ELECTION; CONCERNING FAITH FORESEEN AND THE ABSOLUTE DECREE AND THAT IT ALL REDUCES TO THE QUESTION WHY GOD HAS CHOSEN AND RESOLVED TO ADMIT TO EXISTENCE JUST SUCH A POSSIBLE PERSON, WHOSE CONCEPT INCLUDES JUST SUCH A SEQUENCE OF FREE ACTS AND OF FREE GIFTS OF GRACE. THIS AT ONCE PUTS AN END TO ALL DIFFICULTIES

Finally, the grace of God is wholly unprejudiced and creatures have no claim upon it. Just as it is not sufficient in accounting for God's choice in his dispensations of grace to refer to his absolute or conditional prevision of men's future actions, so it is also wrong to imagine his decrees as absolute with no reasonable motive. As concerns foreseen faith and good works, it is very true that God has elected none but those whose faith and charity he foresees, *quos se fide donaturum praescivit*. The same question, however, arises again as to why God gives to some rather than to others the grace of faith or of good works. As concerns God's ability to foresee not only the faith and good deeds, but also their material and predisposition, or that which a man on his part contributes to them (since there are as truly diversities on the part of men as on the part of grace, and a man although he needs to be aroused to good and needs to become converted, yet acts in accordance with his temperament),—as regards his ability to foresee there are many who say that God, knowing what a particular man will do without grace, that is without his extraordinary assistance, or knowing at least what will be the human contribution, resolves to give grace to those whose natural dispositions are the best, or at any rate are the least imperfect and evil. But if this were the case then the natural dispositions in so far as they were good would be like gifts of grace, since God would have given advantages to some over others; and therefore, since he would well know that the natural advantages which he had given would serve as motives for his grace or for his extraordinary assistance, would not everything be reduced to his mercy? I think, therefore, that since we do not know how much and in what way God regards natural dispositions in the dispensations of his grace, it would be safest and most exact to say, in accordance with our principles and as I have already remarked, that there must needs be among possible beings the person Peter or John whose concept or idea contains all that particular sequence of ordinary and extraordinary manifestations of grace together with the rest of the accompanying events and circumstances, and that it has pleased God to choose him among an infinite number of persons equally possible for actual existence. When we have said this there seems nothing left to ask, and all difficulties vanish. For in regard to that great and ultimate question why it has pleased God to choose him among so great a number of possible persons, it is surely unreasonable to demand more than the general reasons which we have given. The reasons in detail surpass our ken. Therefore, instead of postulating an absolute decree, which being without reason would be unreasonable, and instead of postulating reasons which do not succeed in solving the difficulties and in turn have need themselves of reasons, it will be best to say with St. Paul that there are for God's choice certain great reasons of wisdom and congruity which he follows, which reasons, however, are unknown to mortals and are founded upon the general order, whose goal is the greatest perfection of the world. This is what is meant when the motives of God's glory and of the manifestation of his justice are spoken of, as well as when men speak of his mercy, and his perfection in general; that immense vastness of wealth with which the soul of the same St. Paul was so thrilled.

XXXII. USEFULNESS OF THESE PRINCIPLES IN MATTERS OF PIETY AND OF RELIGION

In addition it seems that the thoughts which we have just explained and particularly the great principle of the perfection of God's operations and the concept of substance which includes all its changes with all its accompanying circumstances, far from injuring, serve rather to confirm religion, serve to dissipate great difficulties, to inflame souls with a divine love and to raise the mind to a knowledge of incorporeal substances much more than the present-day hypotheses. For it appears clearly that all other substances depend upon God just as our thoughts emanate from our own substances; that God is all in all and that he is intimately united to all created things, in proportion however to their perfection; that it is he alone who determines them from without by his influence, and if to act is to determine directly, it may be said in metaphysical language that God alone acts upon me and he alone causes me to do good or ill, other substances contributing only because of his determinations; because God, who takes all things into consideration, distributes his bounties and compels created beings to accommodate themselves to one another. Thus God alone constitutes the relation or communication between substances. It is through him that the phenomena of the one meet and accord with the phenomena of the others, so that there may be a reality in our perceptions. In common parlance, however, an action is attributed to particular causes in the sense that I have explained above because it is not necessary to make continual mention of the universal cause when speaking of particular cases. It can be seen also that every substance has a perfect spontaneity (which becomes liberty with intelligent substances). Everything which happens to it is a consequence of its idea or its being and nothing determines it except God only. It is for this reason that a person of exalted mind and revered saintliness may say that the soul ought often to think as if there were only God and itself in the world. Nothing can make us hold to immortality more firmly than this independence and vastness of the soul which protects it completely against exterior things, since it alone constitutes our universe and together with God is sufficient for itself. It is as impossible for it to perish save through annihilation as it is impossible for the universe to destroy itself, the universe whose animate and perpetual expression it is. Furthermore, the changes in this extended mass which is called our body cannot possibly affect the soul nor can the dissipation of the body destroy that which is indivisible.

XXXIII. EXPLANATION OF THE RELATION BETWEEN THE SOUL AND THE BODY, A MATTER WHICH HAS BEEN REGARDED AS INEXPLICABLE OR ELSE AS MIRACULOUS; CONCERNING THE ORIGIN OF CONFUSED PERCEPTIONS

We can also see the explanation of that great mystery "the union of the soul and the body," that is to say how it comes about that the passions and actions of the one are accompanied by the actions and passions or else the appropriate phenomena of the other. For it is not possible to conceive how one can have an influence upon the other and it is unreasonable to have recourse at once to the extraordinary intervention of the universal cause in an ordinary and particular case. The following, however, is the true explanation. We have said that everything which happens to a soul or to any substance is a consequence of its concept; hence the idea itself or the essence of the soul brings it about that all of its appearances or perceptions should be born out of its nature and precisely in such a way that they correspond of themselves to that which happens in the universe at large, but more particularly and more perfectly to that which happens in the body associated with it, because it is in a particular way and only for a certain time according to the relation of other bodies to its own body that the soul expresses the state of the universe. This last fact enables us to see how our body belongs to us, without, however, being attached to our essence. I believe that those who are careful thinkers will decide favorably for our principles because of this single reason, viz., that they are able to see in what consists the relation between the soul and the body, a parallelism which appears inexplicable in any other way. We can also see that the perceptions of our senses even when they are clear must necessarily contain certain confused elements, for as all the bodies in the universe are in sympathy, ours receives the impressions of all the others, and while our senses respond to everything, our soul cannot pay attention to every particular. That is why our confused sensations are the result of a variety of perceptions. This variety is infinite. It is almost like the confused murmuring which is heard by those who approach the shore of a sea. It comes from the continual beatings of innumerable waves. If now, out of many perceptions which do not at all fit together to make one, no particular one perception surpasses the others, and if they make impressions about equally strong or equally capable of holding the attention of the soul, they can be perceived only confusedly.

XXXIV. CONCERNING THE DIFFERENCE BETWEEN SPIRITS AND OTHER SUBSTANCES, SOULS OR SUBSTANTIAL FORMS; THAT THE IMMORTALITY WHICH MEN DESIRE INCLUDES MEMORY

Supposing that the bodies which constitute a *unum per se*, as human bodies, are substances, and have substantial forms, and supposing that animals have souls, we are obliged to grant that these souls and these substantial forms cannot entirely perish, any more than can the atoms or the ultimate elements of matter, according to the position of other philosophers; for no substance perishes, although it may become very different. Such substances also express the whole universe, although more imperfectly than do spirits. The principal difference, however, is that they do not know that they are, nor what they are. Consequently, not being able to reason, they are unable to discover necessary and universal truths. It is also because they do not reflect regarding themselves that they have no moral qualities, whence it follows that undergoing a thousand transformations, as we see a caterpillar change into a butterfly, the result from a moral or practical standpoint is the same as if we said that they perished in each case, and we can indeed say it from the physical standpoint in the same way that we say bodies perish in their dissolution. But the intelligent soul, knowing that it is and having the ability to say that word "I" so full of meaning, not only continues and exists, metaphysically far more certainly than do the others, but it remains the same from the moral standpoint, and constitutes the same personality, for it is its memory or knowledge of this ego which renders it open to punishment and reward. Also the immortality which is required in morals and in religion does not consist merely in this perpetual existence, which pertains to all substances, for if in addition there were no remembrance of what one had been, immortality would not be at all desirable. Suppose that some individual could suddenly become King of China on condition, however, of forgetting what he had been, as though being born again, would it not amount to the same practically, or as far as the effects could be perceived, as if the individual were annihilated, and a king of China were the same instant created in his place? The individual would have no reason to desire this.

XXXV. THE EXCELLENCE OF SPIRITS; THAT GOD CONSIDERS THEM PREFERABLE TO OTHER CREATURES; THAT THE SPIRITS EXPRESS GOD RATHER THAN THE WORLD, WHILE OTHER SIMPLE SUBSTANCES EXPRESS THE WORLD RATHER THAN GOD

In order, however, to prove by natural reasons that God will preserve forever not only our substance, but also our personality, that is to say the recollection and knowledge of what we are (although the distinct knowledge is sometimes suspended during sleep and in swoons) it is necessary to join metaphysics to moral considerations. God must be considered not only as the principle and the cause of all substances and of all existing things, but also as the chief of all persons or intelligent substances, as the absolute monarch of the most perfect city or republic, such as is constituted by all the spirits together in the universe, God being the most complete of all spirits at the same time that he is greatest of all beings. For assuredly the spirits are the most perfect of substances and best express the divinity. Since all the nature, purpose, virtue and function of substances is, as has been sufficiently explained, to express God and the universe, there is no room for doubting that those substances which give the expression, knowing what they are doing and which are able to understand the great truths about God and the universe, do express God and the universe incomparably better than do those natures which are either brutish and incapable of recognizing truths, or are wholly destitute of sensation and knowledge. The difference between intelligent substances and those which are not intelligent is quite as great as between a mirror and one who sees. As God is himself the greatest and wisest of spirits it is easy to understand that the spirits with which he can, so to speak, enter into conversation and even into social relations by communicating to them in particular ways his feelings and his will so that they are able to know and love their benefactor, must be much nearer to him than the rest of created things which may be regarded as the instruments of spirits. In the same way we see that all wise persons consider far more the condition of a man than of anything else however precious it may be; and it seems that the greatest satisfaction which a soul, satisfied in other respects, can have is to see itself loved by others. However, with respect to God there is this difference that his glory and our worship can add nothing to his satisfaction, the recognition of creatures being nothing but a consequence of his sovereign and perfect felicity and being far from contributing to it or from causing it even in part. Nevertheless, that which is reasonable in finite spirits is found eminently in him and as we praise a king who prefers to preserve the life of a man before that of the most precious and rare of his animals, we should not doubt that the most enlightened and most just of all monarchs has the same preference.

XXXVI. GOD IS THE MONARCH OF THE MOST PERFECT REPUBLIC COMPOSED OF ALL THE SPIRITS, AND THE HAPPINESS OF THIS CITY OF GOD IS HIS PRINCIPAL PURPOSE

Spirits are of all substances the most capable of perfection and their perfections are different in this that they interfere with one another the least, or rather they aid one another the most, for only the most virtuous can be the most perfect friends. Hence it follows that God who in all things has the greatest perfection will have the greatest care for spirits and will give not only to all of them in general, but even to each one in particular the highest perfection which the universal harmony will permit. We can even say that it is because he is a spirit that God is the originator of existences, for if he had lacked the power of will to choose what is best, there would have been no reason why one possible being should exist rather than any other. Therefore God's being a spirit himself dominates all the consideration which he may have toward created things. Spirits alone are made in his image, being as it were of his blood or as children in the family, since they alone are able to serve him of free will, and to act consciously imitating the divine nature. A single spirit is worth a whole world, because it not only expresses the whole world, but it also knows it and governs itself as does God. In this way we may say that though every substance expresses the whole universe, yet the other substances express the world rather than God, while spirits express God rather than the world. This nature of spirits, so noble that it enables them to approach divinity as much as is possible for created things, has as a result that God derives infinitely more glory from them than from the other beings, or rather than other beings furnish to spirits the material for glorifying him. This moral quality of God which constitutes him Lord and Monarch of spirits influences him so to speak personally and in a unique way. It is through this that he humanizes himself, that he is willing to suffer human woes, and that he enters into social relations with us and this consideration is so dear to him that the happy and prosperous condition of his empire which consists in the greatest possible felicity of its inhabitants, becomes supreme among his laws. Happiness is to persons what perfection is to beings. And if the dominant principle in the existence of the physical world is the decree to give it the greatest possible perfection, the primary purpose in the moral world or in the city of God which constitutes the noblest part of the universe ought to be to extend the greatest happiness possible. We must not therefore doubt that God has so ordained everything that spirits not only shall live forever, because this is unavoidable, but that they shall also preserve forever their moral quality, so that his city may never lose a person, quite in the same way that the world never loses a substance. Consequently they will always be conscious of their being, otherwise they would be open to neither reward nor punishment, a condition which is the essence of a republic, and above all of the most perfect republic where nothing can be neglected. In fine, God being at the same time the most just and the most debonnaire of monarchs, and requiring only a good will on the part of men, provided that it be sincere and intentional, his subjects cannot desire a better condition. To render them perfectly happy he desires only that they love him.

XXXVII. JESUS CHRIST HAS REVEALED TO MEN THE MYSTERY AND THE ADMIRABLE LAWS OF THE KINGDOM OF HEAVEN, AND THE GREATNESS OF THE SUPREME HAPPINESS WHICH GOD HAS PREPARED FOR THOSE WHO LOVE HIM

The ancient philosophers knew very little of these important truths. Jesus Christ alone has expressed them divinely well, and in a way so clear and simple that the dullest minds have understood them. His gospel has entirely changed the face of human affairs. It has brought us to know the kingdom of heaven, or that perfect republic of spirits which deserves to be called the city of God. He it is who has discovered to us its wonderful laws. He alone has made us see how much God loves us and with what care everything that concerns us has been provided for; how God, inasmuch as he cares for the sparrows, will not neglect reasoning beings, who are infinitely more dear to him; how all the hairs of our heads are numbered; how heaven and earth may pass away but the word of God and that which belongs to the means of our salvation will not pass away; how God has more regard for the least one among intelligent souls than for the whole machinery of the world; how we ought not to fear those who are able to destroy the body but are unable to destroy the soul, since God alone can render the soul happy or unhappy; and how the souls of the righteous are protected by his hand against all the upheavals of the universe, since God alone is able to act upon them; how none of our acts are forgotten; how everything is to be accounted for; even careless words and even a spoonful of water which is well used; in fact how everything must result in the greatest welfare of the good, for then shall the righteous become like suns and neither our sense nor our minds have ever tasted of anything approaching the joys which God has laid up for those that love him.

The Monadology

1. The Monad, of which we shall here speak, is nothing but a *simple* substance, which enters into *compounds*. By 'simple' is meant 'without parts.'

2. And there must be *simple* substances, since there are *compounds*; for a *compound* is nothing but a collection or aggregatum of *simple* things.

3. Now where there are no parts, there can be neither extension nor form [figure] nor divisibility. These Monads are the real atoms of nature and, in a word, the elements of things.

4. No dissolution of these elements need be feared, and there is no conceivable way in which a *simple* substance can be destroyed by natural means.

5. For the same reason there is no conceivable way in which a *simple* substance can come into being by natural means, since it cannot be formed by the combination of parts [composition].

6. Thus it may be said that a Monad can only come into being or come to an end all at once; that is to say, it can come into being only by creation and come to an end only by annihilation, while that which is *compound* comes into being or comes to an end by parts.

7. Further, there is no way of explaining how a Monad can be altered in *quality* or internally changed by any other created thing; since it is impossible to change the place of anything in it or to conceive in it any internal motion which could be produced, directed, increased or diminished therein, although all this is possible in the case of *compounds*, in which there are changes among the parts. The Monads have no *windows*, through which anything could come in or go out. Accidents cannot sep-

Translated by Robert Latta.

arate themselves from substances nor go about outside of them, as the 'sensible species' of the Scholastics used to do. Thus neither substance nor accident can come into a Monad from outside.

8. Yet the Monads must have some qualities, otherwise they would not even be existing things. And if *simple* substances did not differ in *quality*, there would be absolutely no means of perceiving any change in things. For what is in the *compound* can come only from the *simple* elements it contains, and the Monads, if they had no qualities, would be indistinguishable from one another, since they do not differ in quantity. Consequently, space being a plenum, each part of space would always receive, in any motion, exactly the equivalent of what it already had, and no one state of things would be discernible from another.

9. Indeed, each Monad must be different from every other. For in nature there are never two beings which are perfectly alike and in which it is not possible to find an internal difference, or at least a difference founded upon an intrinsic *quality* [denomination].

10. I assume also as admitted that every created being, and consequently the created Monad, is subject to change, and further that this change is continuous in each.

11. It follows from what has just been said, that the natural changes of the Monads come from an internal principle, since an external cause can have no influence upon their inner being.

12. But, besides the principle of the change, there must be a particular series of changes [un detail de ce qui change], which constitutes, so to speak, the specific nature and variety of the *simple* substances.

13. This particular series of changes should involve a multiplicity in the *unit* [unite] or in that which is *simple*. For, as every natural change takes place gradually, something changes and something remains unchanged; and consequently a *simple* substance must be affected and related in many ways, although it has no parts.

14. The passing condition, which involves and represents a multiplicity in the *unit* [unite] or in the *simple* substance, is nothing but what is called Perception, which is to be distinguished from Apperception or Consciousness, as will afterwards appear. In this matter the Cartesian view is extremely defective, for it treats as non-existent those *perceptions* of which we are not consciously aware. This has also led them to believe that minds [esprits] alone are Monads, and that there are no *souls* of animals nor other Entelechies. Thus, like the crowd, they have failed to distinguish between a prolonged unconsciousness and absolute death, which has made them fall again into the Scholastic prejudice of *souls* entirely separate [from bodies], and has even confirmed ill-balanced minds in the opinion that *souls* are mortal.

15. The activity of the internal principle which produces change or passage from one *perception* to another may be called Appetition. It is true that desire [l'appetit] cannot always fully attain to the whole *perception* at which it aims, but it always obtains some of it and attains to new *perceptions*.

16. We have in ourselves experience of a multiplicity in *simple* substance, when we find that the least thought of which we are conscious involves variety in its object. Thus all those who admit that the *soul* is a *simple* substance should admit this multiplicity in the Monad; and M. Bayle ought not to have found any difficulty in this, as he has done in his Dictionary, article 'Rorarius.'

17. Moreover, it must be confessed that *perception* and that which depends upon it are inexplicable on mechanical grounds, that is to say, by means of figures and motions. And supposing there were a machine, so constructed as to think, feel, and have *perception*, it might be conceived as increased in size, while keeping the same proportions, so that one might go into it as into a mill. That being so, we should, on examining its interior, find only parts which work one upon another, and never anything by which to explain a *perception*. Thus it is in a *simple* substance, and not in a *compound* or in a machine, that *perception* must be sought for. Further, nothing but this (namely, *perceptions* and their changes) can be found in a *simple* substance. It is also in this alone that all the internal activities of *simple* substances can consist.

18. All *simple* substances or created Monads might be called Entelechies, for they have in them a certain perfection (echousi to enteles); they have a certain self-sufficiency (autarkeia) which makes them the sources of their internal activities and, so to speak, incorporeal automata.

19. If we are to give the name of Soul to everything which has *perceptions* and desires [appetits] in the general sense which I have explained, then all *simple* substances or created Monads might be called *souls*; but as feeling [le sentiment] is something more than a bare *perception*, I think it right that the general name of Monads or Entelechies should suffice for *simple* substances which have *perception* only, and that the name of Souls should be given only to those in which *perception* is more distinct, and is accompanied by memory.

20. For we experience in ourselves a condition in which we remember nothing and have no distinguishable *perception*; as when we fall into a swoon or when we are overcome with a profound dreamless sleep. In this state the *soul* does not perceptibly differ from a bare Monad; but as this state is not lasting, and the *soul* comes out of it, the *soul* is something more than a bare Monad.

21. And it does not follow that in this state the *simple* substance is without any *perception*. That, indeed, cannot be, for the reasons already given; for it cannot perish, and it cannot continue to exist without being affected in some way, and this affection is nothing but its *perception*. But when there is a great multitude of little *perceptions*, in which there is nothing distinct, one is stunned; as when one turns continuously round in the same way several times in succession, whence comes a giddiness which may make us swoon, and which keeps us from distinguishing anything. Death can for a time put animals into this condition.

22. And as every present state of a *simple* substance is naturally a consequence of its preceding state, in such a way that its present is big with its future;

23. And as, on waking from stupor, we are conscious of our *perceptions*, we must have had *perceptions* immediately before we awoke, although we were not at all conscious of them; for one *perception* can in a natural way come only from another *perception*, as a motion can in a natural way come only from a motion.

24. It thus appears that if we had in our *perceptions* nothing marked and, so to speak, striking and highly-flavoured, we should always be in a state of stupor. And this is the state in which the bare Monads are.

25. We see also that nature has given heightened *perceptions* to animals, from the care she has taken to provide them with organs, which collect numerous rays of light, or numerous undulations of the air, in order, by *uniting* them, to make them have greater effect. Something similar to this takes place in smell, in taste and in touch, and perhaps in a number of other senses, which are unknown to us. And I will explain presently how that which takes place in the *soul* represents what happens in the bodily organs.

26. Memory provides the *soul* with a kind of consecutiveness, which resembles [imite] reason, but which is to be distinguished from it. Thus we see that when animals have a *perception* of something which strikes them and of which they have formerly had a similar *perception*, they are led, by means of representation in their memory, to expect what was combined with the thing in this previous *perception*, and they come to have feelings similar to those they had on the former occasion. For instance, when a stick is shown to dogs, they remember the pain it has caused them, and howl and run away.

27. And the strength of the mental image which impresses and moves them comes either from the magnitude or the number of the preceding *perceptions*. For often a strong impression produces all at once the same effect as a long-formed habit, or as many and oft-repeated ordinary *perceptions*.

28. In so far as the concatenation of their *perceptions* is due to the principle of memory alone, men act like the lower animals, resembling the empirical physicians, whose methods are those of mere practice without theory. Indeed, in three-fourths of our actions we are nothing but empirics. For instance, when we expect that there will be daylight to-morrow, we do so empirically, because it has always so happened until now. It is only the astronomer who thinks it on *rational* grounds.

29. But it is the knowledge of *necessary* and eternal truths that distinguishes us from the mere animals and gives us Reason and the sciences, raising us to the knowledge of ourselves and of God. And it is this in us that is called the *rational soul* or mind [esprit].

30. It is also through the knowledge of *necessary* truths, and through their abstract expression, that we rise to acts of reflexion, which make us think of what is called I, and observe that this or that is within us: and thus, thinking of ourselves, we think of being, of substance, of the *simple* and the *compound*, of the immaterial, and of God Himself, conceiving that what is limited in us is in Him without limits. And these acts of reflexion furnish the chief objects of our reasonings.

31. Our reasonings are grounded upon two great principles, that of *contradiction*, in virtue of which we judge false that which involves a *contradiction*, and true that which is opposed or contradictory to the false;

32. And that of sufficient reason, in virtue of which we hold that there can be no fact real or existing, no statement true, unless there be a sufficient reason, why it should be so and not otherwise, although these reasons usually cannot be known by us.

33. There are also two kinds of truths, those of reasoning and those of fact. Truths of reasoning are *necessary* and their opposite is impossible: truths of fact are *contingent* and their opposite is possible. When a truth is *necessary*, its reason can be found by analysis, resolving it into more *simple* ideas and truths, until we come to those which are primary.

34. It is thus that in Mathematics speculative Theorems and practical Canons are reduced by analysis to Definitions, Axioms, and Postulates.

35. In short, there are *simple* ideas, of which no definition can be given; there are also *axioms* and *postulates*, in a word, primary principles, which cannot be proved, and indeed have no need of proof; and these are identical propositions, whose opposite involves an express *contradiction*.

36. But there must also be a sufficient reason for *contingent* truths or truths of fact, that is to say, for the sequence or connexion of the things which are dispersed throughout the universe of created beings, in which the analyzing into particular reasons might go on into endless detail, because of the immense variety of things in nature and the infinite division of bodies. There is an infinity of present and past forms and motions which go to make up the efficient cause of my present writing; and there is an infinity of minute tendencies and dispositions of my *soul*, which go to make its final cause.

37. And as all this detail again involves other prior or more detailed *contingent* things, each of which still needs a similar analysis to yield its reason, we are no further forward: and the sufficient or final reason must be outside of the sequence or series of particular *contingent* things, however infinite this series may be.

38. Thus the final reason of things must be in a *necessary* substance, in which the variety of particular changes exists only eminently, as in its source; and this substance we call God.

39. Now as this substance is a sufficient reason of all this variety of particulars, which are also connected together throughout; there is only one God, and this God is sufficient.

40. We may also hold that this supreme substance, which is unique, universal and *necessary*, nothing outside of it being independent of it,—this substance, which is a pure sequence of possible being, must be illimitable and must contain as much reality as is possible.

41. Whence it follows that God is absolutely perfect; for perfection is nothing but amount of positive reality, in the strict sense, leaving out of account the limits or bounds in things which are limited. And where there are no bounds, that is to say in God, perfection is absolutely infinite.

42. It follows also that created beings derive their perfections from the influence of God, but that their imperfections come from their own nature, which is incapable of being without limits. For it is in this that they differ from God. An instance of this original imperfection of created beings may be seen in the natural inertia of bodies.

43. It is farther true that in God there is not only the source of existences but also that of essences, in so far as they are real, that is to say, the source of what is real in the possible. For the understanding of God is the region of eternal truths or of the ideas on which they depend, and without Him there would be nothing real in the possibilities of things, and not only would there be nothing in existence, but nothing would even be possible.

44. For if there is a reality in essences or possibilities, or rather in eternal truths, this reality must needs be founded in something existing and actual, and consequently in the existence of the *necessary* Being, in whom essence involves existence, or in whom to be possible is to be actual.

45. Thus God alone (or the *necessary* Being) has this prerogative that He must necessarily exist, if He is possible. And as nothing can interfere with the possibility of that which involves no limits, no negation and consequently no *contradiction,* this [His possibility] is sufficient of itself to make known the existence of God a priori. We have thus proved it, through the reality of eternal truths. But a little while ago we proved it also a posteriori, since there exist *contingent* beings, which can have their final or sufficient reason only in the *necessary* Being, which has the reason of its existence in itself.

46. We must not, however, imagine, as some do, that eternal truths, being dependent on God, are arbitrary and depend on His will, as Descartes, and afterwards M. Poiret, appear to have held. That is true only of *contingent* truths, of which the principle is fitness [*convenance*] or choice of the best, whereas *necessary* truths depend solely on His understanding and are its inner object.

47. Thus God alone is the primary *unity* or original *simple* substance, of which all created or derivative Monads are products and have their birth, so to speak, through continual fulgurations of the Divinity from moment to moment, limited by the receptivity of the created being, of whose essence it is to have limits.

48. In God there is Power, which is the source of all, also Knowledge, whose content is the variety of the ideas, and finally Will, which makes changes or products according to the principle of the best. These characteristics correspond to what in the created Monads forms the ground or basis, to the faculty of Perception and to the faculty of Appetition. But in God these attributes are absolutely infinite or perfect; and in the created Monads or the Entelechies (or *perfectihabiae*, as Hermolaus Barbarus translated the word) there are only imitations of these attributes, according to the degree of perfection of the Monad.

49. A created thing is said to act outwardly in so far as it has perfection, and to suffer [or be passive] in relation to another, in so far as it is imperfect. Thus activity [action] is attributed to a Monad, in so far as it has distinct *perceptions*, and passivity [passion] in so far as it has *perceptions* are confused.

50. And one created thing is more perfect than another, in this, that there is found in the more perfect that which serves to explain a priori what takes place in the less perfect, and it is on this account that the former is said to act upon the latter.

51. But in *simple* substances the influence of one Monad upon another is only ideal, and it can have its effect only through the mediation of God, in so far as in the ideas of God any Monad rightly claims that God, in regulating the others from the beginning of things, should have regard to it. For since one created Monad cannot have any physical influence upon the inner being of another, it is only by this means that the one can be dependent upon the other.

52. Accordingly, among created things, activities and passivities are mutual. For God, comparing two *simple* substances, finds in each reasons which oblige Him to adapt the other to it, and consequently what is active in certain respects is passive from another point of view; active in so far as what we distinctly know in it serves to explain [*rendre raison de*] what takes place in another, and passive in so far as the explanation [raison] of what takes place in it is to be found in that which is distinctly known in another.

53. Now, as in the Ideas of God there is an infinite number of possible universes, and as only one of them can be actual, there must be a sufficient reason for the choice of God, which leads Him to decide upon one rather than another.

54. And this reason can be found only in the fitness [*convenance*], or in the degrees of perfection, that these worlds possess, since each possible thing has the right to aspire to existence in proportion to the amount of perfection it contains in germ.

55. Thus the actual existence of the best that wisdom makes known to God is due to this, that His goodness makes Him choose it, and His power makes Him produce it.

56. Now this connexion or adaptation of all created things to each and of each to all, means that each *simple* substance has relations which express all the others, and, consequently, that it is a perpetual living mirror of the universe.

57. And as the same town, looked at from various sides, appears quite different and becomes as it were numerous in aspects [perspectivement]; even so, as a result of the infinite number of *simple* substances, it is as if there were so many different universes, which, nevertheless are nothing but aspects [perspectives] of a single universe, according to the special point of view of each Monad.

58. And by this means there is obtained as great variety as possible, along with the greatest possible order; that is to say, it is the way to get as much perfection as possible.

59. Besides, no hypothesis but this (which I venture to called proved) fittingly exalts the greatness of God; and this Monsieur Bayle recognized when, in his Dictionary (article *Rorarius*), he raised objections to it, in which indeed he was inclined to think that I was attributing too much to God—more than it is possible to attribute. But he was unable to give any reason which could show the impossibility of this universal harmony, according to which every substance exactly expresses all others through the relations it has with them.

60. Further, in what I have just said there may be seen the reasons a priori why things could not be otherwise than they are. For God in regulating the whole has had regard to each part, and in particular to each Monad, whose nature being to represent, nothing can confine it to the representing of only one part of things; though it is true that this representation is merely confused as regards the variety of particular things [*le detail*] in the whole universe, and can be distinct only as regards a small part of things, namely, those which are either nearest or greatest in relation to each of the Monads; otherwise each Monad would be a deity. It is not as regards their object, but as regards the different ways in which they have knowledge of their object, that the Monads are limited. In a confused way they all strive after [*vont a*] the infinite, the whole; but they are limited and differentiated through the degrees of their distinct *perceptions*.

61. And *compounds* are in this respect analogous with [*symbolisent avec*] *simple* substances. For all is a plenum (and thus all matter is connected together) and in the plenum every motion has an effect upon distant bodies in proportion to their distance, so that each body not only is affected by those which are in contact with it and in some way feels the effect of everything that happens to them, but also is mediately affected by bodies adjoining those with which it itself is in immediate contact. Wherefore it follows that this inter-communication of things extends to any distance, however great. And consequently every body feels the effect of all that takes place in the universe, so that he who sees all might read in each what is happening everywhere, and even what has happened or shall happen, observing in the present that which is far off as well in time as in place: sympnoia panta, as Hippocrates said. But a *soul* can read in itself only that which is there represented distinctly; it cannot all at once unroll everything that is enfolded in it, for its complexity is infinite.

62. Thus, although each created Monad represents the whole universe, it represents more distinctly the body which specially pertains to it, and of which it is the *entelechy*; and as this body expresses the whole universe through the connexion of all matter in the plenum, the *soul* also represents the whole universe in representing this body, which belongs to it in a special way.

63. The body belonging to a Monad (which is its *entelechy* or its *soul*) constitutes along with the *entelechy* what may be called a living being, and along with the *soul* what is called an animal. Now this body of living being or of an animal is always organic; for, as every Monad is, in its own way, a mirror of the universe, and as the universe is ruled according to a perfect order, there must also be order in that which represents it, i.e. in the *perceptions* of the *soul*, and consequently there must be order in the body, through which the universe is represented in the *soul*.

64. Thus the organic body of each living being is a kind of divine machine or natural automaton, which infinitely surpasses all artificial automata. For a machine made by the skill of man is not a machine in each of its parts. For instance, the tooth of a brass wheel has parts or fragments which for us are not artificial products, and which do not have the special characteristics of the machine, for they give no indication of the use for which the wheel was intended. But the machines of nature, namely, living bodies, are still machines in their smallest parts ad infinitum. It is this that constitutes the difference between nature and art, that is to say, between the divine art and ours.

65. And the Author of nature has been able to employ this divine and infinitely wonderful power of art, because each portion of matter is not only infinitely divisible, as the ancients observed, but is also actually subdivided without end, each part into further parts, of which each has some motion of its own; otherwise it would be impossible for each portion of matter to express the whole universe.

66. Whence it appears that in the smallest particle of matter there is a world of creatures, living beings, animals, entelechies, *souls*.

67. Each portion of matter may be conceived as like a garden full of plants and like a pond full of fishes. But each branch of every plant, each member of every animal, each drop of its liquid parts is also some such garden or pond.

68. And though the earth and the air which are between the plants of the garden, or the water which is between the fish of the pond, be neither plant nor fish; yet they also contain plants and fishes, but mostly so minute as to be imperceptible to us.

69. Thus there is nothing fallow, nothing sterile, nothing dead in the universe, no chaos, no confusion save in appearance, somewhat as it might appear to be in a pond at a distance, in which one would see a confused movement and, as it were, a swarming of fish in the pond, without separately distinguishing the fish themselves.

70. Hence it appears that each living body has a dominant *entelechy*, which in an animal is the *soul*; but the members of this living body are full of other living beings, plants, animals, each of which has also its dominant *entelechy* or *soul*.

71. But it must not be imagined, as has been done by some who have misunderstood my thought, that each *soul* has a quantity or portion of matter belonging exclusively to itself or attached to it for ever, and that it consequently owns other inferior living beings, which are devoted for ever to its service. For all bodies are in a perpetual flux like rivers, and parts are entering into them and passing out of them continually.

72. Thus the *soul* changes its body only by degrees, little by little, so that it is never all at once deprived of all its organs; and there is often metamorphosis in animals, but never metempsychosis or transmigration of *souls*; nor are there *souls* entirely separate [from bodies] nor unembodied spirits [genies sans corps]. God alone is completely without body.

73. It also follows from this that there never is absolute birth [generation] nor complete death, in the strict sense, consisting in the separation of the *soul* from the body. What we call births [generations] are developments and growths, while what we call deaths are envelopments and diminutions.

74. Philosophers have been much perplexed about the origin of forms, entelechies, or *souls*; but nowadays it has become known, through careful studies of plants, insects, and animals, that the organic bodies of nature are never products of chaos or putrefaction, but always come from seeds, in which there was undoubtedly some preformation; and it is held that not only the organic body was already there before conception, but also a *soul* in this body, and, in short, the animal itself; and that by means of conception this animal has merely been prepared for the great transformation involved in its becoming an animal of another kind. Something like this is indeed seen apart from birth [generation], as when worms become flies and caterpillars become butterflies.

75. The animals, of which some are raised by means of conception to the rank of larger animals, may be called spermatic, but those among them which are not so raised but remain in their own kind (that is, the majority) are born, multiply, and are destroyed like the large animals, and it is only a few chosen ones [*elus*] that pass to a greater theatre.

76. But this is only half of the truth, and accordingly I hold that if an animal never comes into being by natural means [*naturellement*], no more does it come to an end by natural means; and that not only will there be no birth [generation], but also no complete destruction or death in the strict sense. And these reasonings, made a posteriori and drawn from experience are in perfect agreement with my principles deduced a priori, as above.

77. Thus it may be said that not only the *soul* (mirror of an indestructible universe) is indestructible, but also the animal itself, though its mechanism [machine] may often perish in part and take off or put on an organic slough [des depouilles organiques].

78. These principles have given me a way of explaining naturally the union or rather the mutual agreement [conformite] of the *soul* and the organic body. The *soul* follows its own laws, and the body likewise follows its own laws; and they agree with each other in virtue of the pre-established harmony between all substances, since they are all representations of one and the same universe.

79. Souls act according to the laws of final causes through *appetitions*, ends, and means. Bodies act according to the laws of efficient causes or motions. And the two realms, that of efficient causes and that of final causes, are in harmony with one another.

80. Descartes recognized that *souls* cannot impart any force to bodies, because there is always the same quantity of force in matter. Nevertheless he was of opinion that the *soul* could change the direction of bodies. But that is because in his time it was not known that there is a law of nature which affirms also the conservation of the same total direction in matter. Had Descartes noticed this he would have come upon my system of pre-established harmony.

81. According to this system bodies act as if (to suppose the impossible) there were no *souls*, and *souls* act as if there were no bodies, and both act as if each influenced the other.

82. As regards minds [*esprits*] or *rational souls*, though I find that what I have just been saying is true of all living beings and animals (namely that animals and *souls* come into being when the world begins and no more come to an end than the world does), yet there is this peculiarity in *rational* animals, that their spermatic animalcules, so long as they are only spermatic, have merely ordinary or sensuous [sensitive] *souls*; but when those which are chosen [*elus*], so to speak, attain to human nature through an actual conception, their sensuous *souls* are raised to the rank of reason and to the prerogative of minds [*esprits*].

83. Among other differences which exist between ordinary *souls* and minds [*esprits*], some of which differences I have already noted, there is also this: that *souls* in general are living mirrors or images of the universe of created things, but that minds are also images of the Deity or Author of nature Himself, capable of knowing the system of the universe, and to some extent of imitating it through architectonic ensamples [*echantillons*], each mind being like a small divinity in its own sphere.

84. It is this that enables spirits [or minds-esprits] to enter into a kind of fellowship with God, and brings it about that in relation to them He is not only what an inventor is to his machine (which is the relation of God to other created things), but also what a prince is to his subjects, and, indeed, what a father is to his children.

85. Whence it is easy to conclude that the totality [*assemblage*] of all spirits [*esprits*] must compose the City of God, that is to say, the most perfect State that is possible, under the most perfect of Monarchs.

86. This City of God, this truly universal monarchy, is a moral world in the natural world, and is the most exalted and most divine among the works of God; and it is in it that the glory of God really consists, for He would have no glory were not His greatness and His goodness known and admired by spirits [*esprits*]. It is also in relation to this divine City that God specially has goodness, while His wisdom and His power are manifested everywhere.

87. As we have shown above that there is a perfect harmony between the two realms in nature, one of efficient, and the other of final causes, we should here notice also another harmony between the physical realm of nature and the moral realm of grace, that is to say, between God, considered as Architect of the mechanism [machine] of the universe and God considered as Monarch of the divine City of spirits.

88. A result of this harmony is that things lead to grace by the very ways of nature, and that this globe, for instance, must be destroyed and renewed by natural means at the very time when the government of spirits requires it, for the punishment of some and the reward of others.

89. It may also be said that God as Architect satisfies in all respects God as Lawgiver, and thus that sins must bear their penalty with them, through the order of nature, and even in virtue of the mechanical structure of things; and similarly that noble actions will attain their rewards by ways which, on the bodily side, are mechanical, although this cannot and ought not always to happen immediately.

90. Finally, under this perfect government no good action would be unrewarded and no bad one unpunished, and all should issue in the well-being of the good, that is to say, of those who are not malcontents in this great state, but who trust in Providence, after having done their duty, and who love and imitate, as is meet, the Author of all good, finding pleasure in the contemplation of His perfections, as is the way of genuine 'pure love,' which takes pleasure in the happiness of the beloved. This it is which leads wise and virtuous people to devote their energies to everything which appears in harmony with the presumptive or antecedent will of God, and yet makes them content with what God actually brings to pass by His secret, consequent and positive [decisive] will, recognizing that if we could sufficiently understand the order of the universe, we should find that it exceeds all the desires of the wisest men, and that it is impossible to make it better than it is, not only as a whole and in general but also for ourselves in particular, if we are attached, as we ought to be, to the Author of all, not only as to the architect and efficient cause of our being, but as to our master and to the final cause, which ought to be the whole aim of our will, and which can alone make our happiness.

Theodicy: Abridgement of the Argument Reduced to Syllogistic Form

Some intelligent persons have desired that this supplement be made [to the Theodicy], and I have the more readily yielded to their wishes as in this way I have an opportunity again to remove certain difficulties and to make some observations which were not sufficiently emphasized in the work itself.

I. Objection. Whoever does not choose the best is lacking in power, or in knowledge, or in goodness.

God did not choose the best in creating this world.

Therefore, God has been lacking in power, or in knowledge, or in goodness.

Answer. I deny the minor, that is, the second premise of this syllogism; and our opponent proves it by this.

Prosyllogism. Whoever makes things in which there is evil, which could have been made without any evil, or the making of which could have been omitted, does not choose the best.

God has made a world in which there is evil; a world, I say, which could have been made without any evil, or the making of which could have been omitted altogether.

Therefore, God has not chosen the best.

Answer. I grant the minor of this prosyllogism; for it must be confessed that there is evil in this world which God has made, and that it was possible to make a world without evil, or even not to create a world at all, for its creation has depended on the free will of God; but I deny the major, that is, the first of the two premises of the prosyllogism, and I might content myself with simply demanding its proof; but in order to make the matter clearer, I have wished to justify this denial by showing that the best plan is not always that which seeks to avoid evil, since it may happen that *the evil is accompanied by a greater good.* For example, a general of an army will prefer a great victory with a slight wound to a condition without wound and without victory. We have proved this more fully in the large work by making it clear, by instances taken from mathematics and elsewhere, that an imperfection in the part may be required for a greater perfection in the whole. In this I have followed the opinion of St. Augustine, who has said a hundred times, that God has permitted evil in order to bring about good, that is, a greater good; and that of Thomas Aquinas (in libr. II. sent. dist. 32, qu. I, art. 1), that the permitting of evil tends to the good of the universe. I have shown that the ancients called Adam's fall *felix cupla*, a happy sin, because it had been retrieved with immense advantage by the incarnation of the Son of God, who has given to the universe something nobler than anything that ever would have been among creatures except for it. For the sake of a clearer understanding, I have added, following many good authors, that it was in accordance with order and the general good that God allowed to certain creatures the opportunity of exercising their liberty, even when he foresaw that they would turn to evil, but which he could so well rectify; because it was not fitting that, in order to hinder sin, God should always act in an extraordinary manner. To overthrow this objection, therefore, it is sufficient to show that a world with evil might be better than a world without evil; but I have gone even farther, in the work, and have even proved that this universe must be in reality better than every other possible universe.

II. Objection. If there is more evil than good in intelligent creatures, then there is more evil than good in the whole work of God.

Now, there is more evil than good in intelligent creatures.

Therefore, there is more evil than good in the whole work of God.

Answer. I deny the major and the minor of this conditional syllogism. As to the major, I do not admit it at all, because this pretended deduction from a part to the whole, from intelligent creatures to all creatures, supposes tacitly and without proof that creatures destitute of reason cannot enter into comparison nor into account with those which possess it. But why may it not be that the surplus of good in the non-intelligent creatures which fill the world, compensates for, and even incomparably surpasses, the surplus of evil in the rational creatures? It is true that the value of the latter is greater; but, in compensation, the others are beyond comparison the more numerous, and it may be that the proportion of number and quantity surpasses that of value and of quality.

As to the minor, that is no more to be admitted; that is, it is not at all to be admitted that there is more evil than good in the intelligent creatures. There is no need even of granting that there is more evil than good in the human race, because it is possible, and in fact very probable, that the glory and the perfection of the blessed are incomparably greater than the misery and the imperfection of the damned, and that here the excellence of the total good in the smaller number exceeds the total evil in the greater number. The blessed approach the Divinity, by means of a Divine Mediator, as near as may suit these creatures, and make such progress in good as is impossible for the damned to make in evil, approach as nearly as they may to the nature of demons. God is infinite, and the devil is limited; the good may and does go to infinity, while evil has its bounds. It is therefore possible, and is credible, that in the comparison of the blessed and the damned, the contrary of that which I have said might happen in the comparison of intelligent and non-intelligent creatures, takes place; namely, it is possible that in the comparison of the happy and the unhappy, the proportion of degree exceeds that of number, and that in the comparison of intelligent and non-intelligent creatures, the proportion of number is greater than that of value. I have the right to suppose that a thing is possible so long as its impossibility is not proved; and indeed that which I have here advanced is more than a supposition.

But in the second place, if I should admit that there is more evil than good in the human race, I have still good grounds for not admitting that there is more evil than good in all intelligent creatures. For there is an inconceivable number of genii, and perhaps of other rational creatures. And an opponent could not prove that in all the City of God, composed as well of genii as of rational animals without number and of an infinity of kinds, evil exceeds good. And although in order to answer an objection, there is no need of proving that a thing is, when its mere possibility suffices; yet, in this work, I have not omitted to show that it is a consequence of the supreme perfection of the Sovereign of the universe, that the kingdom of God is the most perfect of all possible states or governments, and that consequently the little evil there is, is required for the consummation of the immense good which is found there.

III. Objection. If it is always impossible not to sin, it is always unjust to punish.

Now, it is always impossible not to sin; or, in other words, every sin is necessary.

Therefore, it is always unjust to punish.

The minor of this is proved thus:

1. Prosyllogism. All that is predetermined is necessary.

Every event is predetermined.

Therefore, every event (and consequently sin also) is necessary.

Again this second minor is proved thus:

2. Prosyllogism. That which is future, that which is foreseen, that which is involved in the causes, is predetermined.

Every event is such.

Therefore, every event is predetermined.

Answer. I admit in a certain sense the conclusion of the second prosyllogism, which is the minor of the first; but I shall deny the major of the first prosyllogism, namely, that every thing predetermined is necessary; understanding by the *necessity* of sinning, for example, or by the impossibility of not sinning, or of not performing any action, the necessity with which we are here concerned, that is, that which is essential and absolute, and which destroys the morality of an action and the justice of punishments. For if anyone understood another necessity or impossibility, namely, a necessity which should be only moral, or which was only hypothetical (as will be explained shortly); it is clear that I should deny the major of the objection itself. I might content myself with this answer and demand the proof of the proposition denied; but I have again desired to explain my procedure in this work, in order to better elucidate the matter and to throw more light on the whole subject, by explaining the necessity which ought to be rejected and the determination which must take place. That *necessity* which is contrary to morality and which ought to be rejected, and which would render punishment unjust, is an insurmountable necessity which would make all opposition useless, even if we should wish with all our heart to avoid the necessary action, and should make all possible efforts to that end. Now, it is manifest that this is not applicable to voluntary actions, because we would not perform them if we did not choose to. Also their prevision and predetermination are not absolute, but presuppose the will: if it is certain that we shall perform them, it is not less certain that we shall choose to perform them. These voluntary actions and their consequences will not take place no matter what we do or whether we wish them or not; but, *through* that which we shall do and through that which we shall wish to do, which leads to them. And this is involved in prevision and in predetermination, and even constitutes their ground. And the necessity of such an event is called conditional or hypothetical, or the necessity of consequence, because it supposes the will, and the other *requisites*; whereas the necessity which destroys morality and renders punishment unjust and reward useless, exists in things which will be whatever we may do or whatever we may wish to do, and, in a word, is in that which is essential; and this is what is called an absolute necessity. Thus it is to no purpose, as regards what is absolutely necessary, to make prohibitions or commands, to propose penalties or prizes, to praise or to blame; it will be none the less. On the other hand, in voluntary actions and in that which depends upon them, precepts armed with power to punish and to recompense are very often of use and are included in the order of causes which make an action exist. And it is for this reason that not only cares and labors but also prayers are useful; God having had these prayers in view before he regulated things and having had that consideration for them which was proper. This is why the precept which says *ora et labora* (pray and work), holds together good; and not only those who (under the vain pretext of the necessity of events) pretend that the care which business demands may be neglected, but also those who reason against prayer, fall into what the ancients even then called the *lazy sophism*. Thus the predetermination of events by causes is just what contributes to morality instead of destroying it, and causes incline the will, without compelling it. This is why the *determination* in question is not a necessitation—it is certain (to him who knows all) that the effect will follow this inclination; but this effect does not follow by a necessary consequence, that is, one of the contrary of which implies contradiction. It is also by an internal inclination such as this that the will is determined, without there being any necessity. Suppose that one has the greatest passion in the world (a great thirst, for example), you will admit to me that the soul can find some reason for resisting it, if it were only that of showing its power. Thus, although one may never be in a perfect indifference of equilibrium and there may be always a preponderance of inclination for the side taken, it, nevertheless, never renders the resolution taken absolutely necessary.

IV. Objection. Whoever can prevent the sin of another and does not do so, but rather contributes to it although he is well informed of it, is accessory to it.

God can prevent the sin of intelligent creatures; but he does not do so, and rather contributes to it by his concurrence and by the opportunities which he brings about, although he has a perfect knowledge of it.

Hence, etc.

Answer. I deny the major of this syllogism. For it is possible that one could prevent sin, but ought not, because he could not do it without himself committing a sin, or (when God is in question) without performing an unreasonable action. Examples have been given and the application to God himself has been made. It is possible also that we contribute to evil and that sometimes we even open the road to it, in doing things which we are obliged to do; and, when we do our duty or (in speaking of God), when, after thorough consideration, we do that which reason demands, we are not responsible for the results, even when we foresee them. We do not desire these evils; but we are willing to permit them for the sake of a greater good which we cannot reasonably help preferring to other considerations. And this is a *consequent* will, which results from *antecedent* wills by which we will the good. I know that some persons, in speaking of the antecedent and consequent will of God, have understood by the *antecedent* that which wills that all men should be saved; and by the *consequent*, that which wills, in consequence of persistent sin, that some should be damned. But these are merely illustrations of a more general idea, and it may be said for the same reason that God, by his antecedent will, wills that men should not sin; and by his consequent or final and decreeing will (that which is always followed by its effect), he wills to permit them to sin, this permission being the result of superior reasons. And we have the right to say in general that the antecedent will of God tends to the production of good and the prevention of evil, each taken in itself and as if alone (*particulariter et secundum quid*, Thom. I, qu. 19, art. 6), according to the measure of the degree of each good and of each evil; but that the divine consequent or final or total will tends toward the production of as many goods as may be put together, the combination of which becomes in this way determined, and includes also the permission of some evils and the exclusion of some goods, as the best possible plan for the universe demands. Arminius, in his *Anti-perkinsus*, has very well explained that the will of God may be called consequent, not only in relation to the action of the creature considered beforehand in the divine understanding, but also in relation to other anterior divine acts of will. But this consideration of the passage cited from Thomas Aquinas, and that from Scotus (I. dist. 46, qu. XI), is enough to show that they make this distinction as I have done here. Nevertheless, if anyone objects to this use of terms let him substitute *deliberating* will, in place of antecedent, and *final* or decreeing will, in place of consequent. For I do not wish to dispute over words.

V. Objection. Whoever produces all that is real in a thing, is its cause.

God produces all that is real in sin.

Hence, God is the cause of sin.

Answer. I might content myself with denying the major or the minor, since the term *real* admits of interpretations which would render these propositions false. But in order to explain more clearly, I will make a distinction. *Real* signifies either that which is positive only, or, it includes also private beings: in the first case, I deny the major and admit the minor; in the second case, I do the contrary. I might have limited myself to this, but I have chosen to proceed still farther and give the reason for this distinction. I have been very glad therefore to draw attention to the fact that every reality purely positive or absolute is a perfection; and that imperfection comes from limitation, that is, from the privative: for to limit is to refuse progress, or the greatest possible progress. Now God is the cause of all perfections and consequently of all realities considered as purely positive. But limitations or privations result from the original imperfection of creatures, which limits their receptivity. And it is with them as with a loaded vessel, which the river causes to move more or less slowly according to the weight which it carries: thus its speed depends upon the river, but the retardation which limits this speed comes from the load. Thus in the *Theodicy*, we have shown how the creature, in causing sin, is a defective cause; how errors and evil inclinations are born of privation; and how privation is accidentally efficient; and I have justified the opinion of St. Augustine (lib. I. ad Simpl. qu. 2) who explains, for example, how God makes the soul obdurate, not by giving it something evil, but because the effect of his good impression is limited by the soul's resistance and by the circumstances which contribute to this resistance, so that he does not give it all the good which would overcome its evil. *Nec* (inquit) *ab illo erogatur aliquid quo homo fit deterior, sed tantum quo fit melior non erogatur.* But if God had wished to do more, he would have had to make either other natures for creatures or other miracles to change their natures, things which the best plan could not admit. It is as if the current of the river must be more rapid than its fall admitted or that the boats should be loaded more lightly, if it were necessary to make them move more quickly. And the original limitation or imperfection of creatures requires that even the best plan of the universe could not receive more good, and could not be exempt from certain evils, which, however, are to result in a greater good. There are certain disorders in the parts which marvelously enhance the beauty of the whole; just as certain dissonances, when properly used, render harmony more beautiful. But this depends on what has already been said in answer to the first objection. . . .

Chapter 20

JOHN LOCKE

The English philosopher John Locke (1632–1704) was born in Bristol and raised as a Puritan. He was educated at Christ Church, Oxford University, where he became a tutor in Greek rhetoric and philosophy. Later he was a practicing physician and assistant to Lord Ashley, the Earl of Shaftesbury. In 1683, because of the Earl of Shaftesbury's anti-Stuart political views, Locke was forced to flee to the Netherlands. There he wrote his two great masterpieces: *An Essay Concerning Human Understanding* (published in 1689), from which our selection is taken, and *Two Treatises on Civil Government* (published in 1690). He returned to England in 1689, wrote his final work, *The Reasonableness of Christianity,* and died in 1704.

Locke's work in the theory of knowledge is the first systematic assault on Cartesian rationalism, the view that reason alone guarantees knowledge. Locke argued that if our claims to knowledge make any sense, they must be derived from the world. He rejects the rationalist notion that we have *innate ideas* (actual knowledge of metaphysical truths, such as mathematical truths, universals, and the laws of nature) because (1) there is not good deductive argument establishing the existence of such entities; (2) children and idiots do not seem to possess them; and (3) an empirical way of knowing, which seems far more reasonable, has no place for such entities.

According to Locke, the mind at birth is a *tabula rasa,* a blank slate. It is like white paper, devoid of characteristics until it receives sense perceptions. All knowledge begins with sensory experience upon which the powers of the mind operate, developing complex ideas, abstractions, and the like. In place of the absolute certainty that the rationalists sought to find, Locke says that apart from the knowledge of the self, most of what we know we know in degrees of certainty derived from inductive generalizations. For example, we see the sun rise every morning and infer that it is highly probable that it will rise tomorrow, but we cannot be absolutely certain.

Locke holds a Representational Theory of Perception in which objects in the world cause our sense organs to start processes that result in perceptual experience. We are never aware of the thing in itself, the object which is perceived and which causes the idea to arise in our mind, but only the idea or *representation* of the object. We are directly aware of the idea but in as much as the object is the cause of the idea, we may be said to be *indirectly* aware of the object itself.

Locke held a causal theory of perception in which processes in the external world impinge on the perceiver's sense organs, which in turn send messages to the brain, where they are transformed into mental events. We may diagram the Causal Theory of Perception this way:

Objects and Events in the Real World

↓ (Energy coming to sense organs: insensible particles reflected from the object onto the sense organ or contacted with the sense organ)

Sense Organs

↓ (Signals to brain)

Brain Event
↓ (Transformation from physical to mental event)
Perceptual Experience
The mechanical yields the non-mechanical IDEA in the Mind

Although the process is physical and mechanistic, it yields a nonphysical result, a mental event, the perceptual experience, what will later be identified as a *percept* or *sense datum*.

Locke divides our ideas into two types: ideas of primary qualities and ideas of secondary qualities. Primary qualities are inseparable from their objects and so truly represent them. Examples of primary qualities are solidity, extension, figure, movement, and number. These are the building blocks of knowledge. Secondary qualities are not in the things themselves but are caused by primary qualities. They include colors, sounds, tastes, and touch. They are power that objects have to do certain things. Fire has the power to change liquids into gases, sugar is soluble in warm water, and glass is fragile. Solubility, flammability, and fragility are dispositional qualities in bodies, and as such cause changes in the world.

FOR FURTHER READING:

Aaron, Richard I. *John Locke.* (Clarendon Press, 1971).
Ayers, Michael. *Locke.* (Routledge & Kegan Paul, 1991).
Bennett, Jonathan. *Locke, Berkeley, and Hume: Central Themes.* (Oxford University Press, 1971).
Dunn, John. *Locke.* (Oxford University Press, 1984).
Dunn, John, et al., eds. *The British Empiricists.* (Oxford University Press, 1992).
Jolley, Nicholas. *Leibniz and Locke.* (Oxford University Press, 1984).
Mackie, J. L. *Problems from Locke.* (Oxford University Press, 1971).
Martin, C. B. and D. M. Armstrong, eds. *Locke and Berkeley: A Collection of Critical Essays.* (University of Notre Dame Press, 1968).
Woolhouse, R. S. *Locke.* (Harvester Press, 1983).

An Essay Concerning Human Understanding

BOOK I

Chapter 1. Introduction

1. An inquiry into the understanding pleasant and useful. Since it is the understanding, that sets man above the rest of sensible beings, and gives him all the advantage and dominion, which he has over them; it is certainly a subject, even for its nobleness, worth our labour to enquire into. The understanding, like the eye, whilst it makes us see and perceive all other things, takes no notice of itself; and it requires art and pains to set it at a distance and make it its own object. But, whatever be, the difficulties that lie in the way of this enquiry; whatever it be that keeps us so much in the dark to ourselves; sure I am, that all the light we can let in upon our minds, all the acquaintance we can make with our own understandings, will not only be very pleasant, but bring us great advantage, in directing our thoughts in the search of other things.

2. Design. This, therefore, being my purpose, to enquire into the original, certainty, and extent of human knowledge; together with the grounds and degrees of belief, opinion, and assent; I shall not at present meddle with the physical consideration of the mind; or trouble myself to examine, wherein its essence consists, or by what motions of our spirits, or alterations of our bodies, we come to have any sensation by our organs, or any ideas in our understandings; and whether those ideas do in their formation, any, or all of them, depend on matter or no: These are speculations, which, however curious and entertaining, I shall decline, as lying out of my way in the design I am now upon. It shall suffice to my present purpose, to consider the discerning faculties of a man, as they are employed about the objects, which they have to do with: And I shall imagine I have not wholly misemployed myself in the thoughts I shall have on this occasion, if, in this historical, plain method, I can give any account of the ways, whereby our understandings come to attain those notions of things we have, and can set down any measures of the certainty of our knowledge, or the grounds of those persuasions which are to be found amongst men, so various, different, and wholly contradictory; and yet asserted somewhere or other, with such assurance and confidence, that he that shall take a view of the opinions of mankind, observe their Opposition, and at the same time consider the fondness and devotion wherewith they are embraced, the resolution and eagerness wherewith they are maintained, may perhaps have reason to suspect, that either there is no such thing as truth at all; or that mankind hath no sufficient means to attain a certain knowledge of it.

3. Method. It is therefore worth while to search out the bounds between opinion and knowledge; and examine by what measures, in things, whereof we have no certain knowledge, we ought to regulate our assent, and moderate our persuasions. In order whereunto, I shall pursue this following method.

First, I shall enquire into the original of those ideas, notions, or whatever else you please to call them, which a man observes, and is conscious to himself he has in his mind; and the ways whereby the understanding comes to be furnished with them.

Secondly, I shall endeavor to shew what knowledge the understanding hath by those ideas; and the certainty, evidence, and extent of it.

Thirdly, I shall make some enquiry into the nature and grounds of faith, or opinion; whereby I mean that assent, which we give to any proposition as true, of whose truth yet we have no certain knowledge; and here we shall have occasion to examine the reasons and degrees of *assent*.

4. Useful to know the extent of our comprehension. If, by this enquiry into the nature of the understanding, I can discover the powers thereof; how far they reach; to what things they are in any degree proportionate; and where they fail us: I suppose it may be of use to prevail with the busy mind of man, to be more cautious in meddling with things exceeding its comprehension; to stop when it is at the utmost extent of its tether; and to sit down in a quiet ignorance of those things which, upon examination, are found to be beyond the reach of our capacities. We should not then perhaps be so forward, out of an affectation of an universal knowledge, to raise questions, and perplex ourselves and others with disputes about things, to which our understandings are not suited; and of which we cannot frame in our minds any clear or distinct perceptions, or whereof (as it has perhaps too often happened) we have not any notions at all. If we can find out how far the understanding can extend its view, how far it has faculties to attain certainty, and in what cases it can only judge and guess; we may learn to content ourselves with what is attainable by us in this state.

5. Our capacity proportioned to our state and concerns, to discover things useful to us. For, though the comprehension of our understandings comes exceeding short of the vast extent of things; yet we shall have cause enough to magnify the bountiful author of our being, for that proportion and degree of knowledge he has bestowed on us, so far above all the rest of the inhabitants of this our mansion. Men have reason to be well satisfied with what God hath thought fit for them, since he hath given them (as St. Peter says), whatsoever is necessary for the conveniences of life, and information of virtue; and has put within the reach of their discovery the comfortable provision for this life, and the way that leads to a better. How short soever their knowledge may come of an universal or perfect comprehension of whatsoever is, it yet secures their great concernments, that they have light enough to lead them to the knowledge of their maker, and the sight of their own duties. Men may find matter sufficient to busy their heads, and employ their hands with variety, delight, and satisfaction; if they will not boldly quarrel with their own constitution, and throw away the blessings their hands are filled with, because they are not big enough to grasp every thing. We shall not have much reason to complain of the narrowness of our minds, if we will but employ them about what may be of use to us; for of that they are very capable: And it will be an unpardonable, as well as childish peevishness, if we undervalue the advantages of our knowledge, and neglect to improve it to the ends for which it was given us, because there are some things that are set out of the reach of it. It will be no excuse to an idle and untoward servant, who would not attend his business by candle-light, to plead that he had not broad sun-shine. The candle, that is set up in us, shines bright enough for all our purposes. The discoveries we can make with this, ought to satisfy us; and we shall then use our understandings right, when we entertain all objects in that way and proportion that they are suited to our faculties, and upon those grounds they are capable of being proposed to us, and not peremptorily, or intemperately require demonstration, and demand certainty, where probability only is to be had, and which is sufficient to govern all our concernments. If we will disbelieve every thing, because we cannot certainly know all things; we shall do as wisely as he, who would not use his legs, but sit still and perish, because he had no wings to fly. . . .

8. What idea stands for. This much I thought necessary to say concerning the occasion of this enquiry into human understanding. But, before I proceed on to what I have thought on this subject, I must here in the entrance beg pardon of my reader for the frequent use of the word "idea," which he will find in the following treatise. It being that term, which, I think, serves best to stand for whatsoever is the object of the understanding when a man thinks; I have used it to express whatever is meant by phantasm, notion, species, or whatever it is which the mind can be employed about in thinking; and I could not avoid frequently using it.

I presume it will be easily granted me, that there are such ideas in men's minds; every one is conscious of them in himself, and men's words and actions will satisfy him that they are in others. Our first enquiry then shall be, how they come into the mind.

Chapter 2. No Innate Principles in the Mind.

1. The way shown how we come by any knowledge, sufficient to prove it not innate. It is an established opinion amongst some men, that there are in the understanding certain innate principles; some primary notions, characters, as it were, stamped upon the mind of man, which the soul receives in its very first being; and brings into the world with it. It would be sufficient to convince unprejudiced readers of the falseness of this supposition, if I should only shew (as I hope I shall in the following parts of this discourse) how men, barely by the use of their natural faculties, may attain to all the knowledge they have, without the help of any innate impressions; and may arrive at certainty, without any such original notions or principles. For I imagine any one will easily grant, that it would be impertinent to suppose, the ideas of colours innate in a creature, to whom God hath given sight, and a power to receive them by the eyes, from external objects: And no less unreasonable would it be to attribute several truths to the impressions of nature, and innate characters, when we may observe in ourselves faculties, fit to attain as easy and certain knowledge of them, as if they were originally imprinted on the mind.

But because a man is not permitted without censure to follow his own thoughts in the search of truth, when they lead him ever so little out of the common road; I shall set down the reasons that made me doubt of the truth of that opinion, as an excuse for my mistake, if I be in one; which I leave to be considered by those who, with me, dispose themselves to embrace truth, wherever they find it.

2. General assent, the great argument. There is nothing more commonly taken for granted, than that there are certain principles, both speculative and practical, (for they speak of both), universally agreed upon by all mankind: Which therefore, they argue, must needs be the constant impressions, which the souls of men receive in their first beings, and which they bring into the world with them, as necessarily and really as they do any of their inherent faculties.

3. Universal consent proves nothing. This argument, drawn from universal consent, has this misfortune in it, that if it were true in matter of fact, that there were certain truths wherein all mankind agreed, it would not prove them innate, if there can be any other way shewn how men may come to that universal agreement, in the things they do consent in, which I presume may be done.

4. What is, is; and it is impossible for the same thing to be, and not to be; not universally assented to. But, which is worse, this argument of universal consent, which is made use of to prove innate principles, seems to me a demonstration that there are none such; because there are none to which all mankind give an universal assent. I shall begin with the speculative, and instance in those magnified principles of demonstration; "Whatsoever is, is;" and "It is impossible for the same thing to be and not to be;" which, of all others, I think have the most allowed title to innate. These have so settled a reputation of maxims universally received, that it will, no doubt, be thought strange, if any one should seem to question it. But yet I take liberty to say, that these propositions are so far from having an universal assent, that there are a great part of mankind to whom they are not so much as known.

5. Not on the mind naturally imprinted, because not known to children, idiots, etc. For, first, it is evident, that all children and idiots have not the least apprehension or thought of them; and the want of that is enough to destroy that universal assent, which must needs be the necessary concomitant of all innate truths: It seeming to me near a contradiction, to say, that there are truths imprinted on the soul, which it perceives or understands not; imprinting, if it signify any thing, being nothing else, but the making certain truths to be perceived. For to imprint any thing on the mind, without the mind's perceiving it, seems to me hardly intelligible. If therefore children and idiots have souls, have minds, with those impressions upon them, they must unavoidably perceive them, and necessarily know and assent to these truths: Which since they do not, it is evident that there are no such impressions. For if they are not notions naturally imprinted, how can they be innate? and if they are notions imprinted, how can they be unknown? To say a notion is imprinted on the mind, and yet at the same time to say, that the mind is ignorant of it, and never yet took notice of it, is to make this impression nothing. No proposition can be said to be in the mind which it never yet knew, which it was never yet conscious of. For if any one may, then, by the same reason, all propositions that are true, and the mind is capable ever of assenting to, may be said to be in the mind, and to be imprinted: Since, if any one can be said to be in the mind, which it never yet knew, it must be only, because it is capable of knowing it, and so the mind is of all truths it ever shall know. Nay, thus truths may be imprinted on the mind, which it never did, nor ever shall know: For a man may live long, and die at last in ignorance of many truths, which his mind was capable of knowing, and that with certainty. So that if the capacity of knowing, be the natural impression contended for, all the truths a man ever comes to know, will, by this account, be every one of them innate; and this great point will amount to no more, but only to a very improper way of speaking; which, whilst it pretends to assert the contrary, says nothing different from those, who deny innate principles. For nobody, I think, ever denied that the mind was capable of knowing several truths. The capacity, they say, is innate, the knowledge acquired. But then to what end such contest for certain innate maxims? If truths can be imprinted on the understanding without being perceived, I can see no difference there can be, between any truths the mind is capable of knowing in respect of their original: They must all be innate, or all adventitious: In vain shall a man go about to distinguish them. He therefore that talks of innate notions in the understanding, cannot (if he intend thereby any distinct sort of truths) mean such truths to be in the understanding, as it never perceived, and is yet wholly ignorant of. For if these words (to be in the understanding) have any propriety, they signify to be understood: So that to be in the understanding, and not to be understood; to be in the mind, and never to be perceived; is all one, as to say any thing is, and is not, in the mind or understanding. If therefore these two propositions, "Whatsoever is, is," and "It is impossible for the same thing to be and not to be," are by nature imprinted, children cannot be ignorant of them; infants, and all that have souls, must necessarily have them in their understandings, know the truth of them, and assent to it.

6. That men know when they come to the use of reason, answered. To avoid this, it is usually answered, That all men know and assent to them, when they come to the use of reason, and this is enough to prove them innate. I answer,

7. Doubtful expressions, that have scarce any signification, go for clear reasons, to those who, being prepossessed, take not the pains to examine even what they themselves say. For to apply this answer with any tolerable sense to our present purpose, it must signify one of these two things; either, that, as soon as men come to the use of reason, these supposed native inscriptions come to be known, and observed by them: Or else, that the use and exercise of men's reason assists them in the discovery of these principles, and certainly makes them known to them.

8. If reason discovered them, that would not prove them innate. If they mean, that by the use of reason men may discover these principles; and that this is sufficient to prove them innate: Their way of arguing will stand thus, (viz.) that, whatever truths reason can certainly discover to us, and make us firmly assent to, those are all naturally imprinted on the mind; since that universal assent, which is made the mark of them, amounts to no more but this; that by the use of reason, we are capable to come to a certain knowledge of and assent to them, and, by this means, there will be no difference between the maxims of the mathematicians, and theorems they deduce from them; all must be equally allowed innate; they being all discoveries made by the use of reason, and truths that a rational creature may certainly come to know, if he apply his thoughts rightly that way.

9. It is false that reason discovers them. But how can these men think the use of reason necessary, to discover principles that are supposed innate, when reason (if we may believe them) is nothing else but the faculty of deducing unknown truths from principles or propositions, that are already known? That certainly can never be thought innate, which we have need of reason to discover; unless, as I have said, we will have all the certain truths that reason ever teaches us, to be innate. We may as well think the use of reason necessary to make our eyes discover visible objects, as that there should be need of reason, or the exercise thereof, to make the understanding see what is originally engraven on it, and cannot be in the understanding before it be perceived by it. So that to make a reason discover those truths, thus imprinted, is to say, that the use of reason discovers to a man what he knew before: And if men have those innate impressed truths originally, and before the use of reason, and yet are always ignorant of them till they come to the use of reason, it is in effect to say, that men know, and know them not, at the same time.

10. It will here perhaps be said, that mathematical demonstrations, and other truths that are not innate, are not assented to, as soon as proposed, wherein they are distinguished from these maxims and other innate truths. I shall have occasion to speak of assent, upon the first proposing, more particularly by and by. I shall here only, and that very readily, allow, that these maxims and mathematical demonstrations are in this different; that the one have need of reason, using of proofs, to make them out, and to gain our assent; but the other, as soon as understood, are, without any the least reasoning, embraced and assented to. But I withal beg leave to observe, that it lays open the weakness of this subterfuge, which requires the use of reason for the discovery of these general truths: Since it must be confessed, that in their discovery there is no use made of reasoning at all. And I think those, who give this answer, will not be forward to affirm that the knowledge of this maxim, "That it is impossible for the same thing to be and not to be," is a deduction of our reason. For this would be to destroy that bounty of nature they seem so fond of, whilst they make the knowledge of those principles to depend on the labour of our thoughts. For all reasoning is search, and casting about, and requires pains and application. And how can it with any tolerable sense be supposed, that what was imprinted by nature, as the foundation and guide of our reason, should need the use of reason to discover it? . . .

BOOK II

Chapter 1. Of Ideas in General, and Their Original

1. Idea is the object of thinking. Every man being conscious to himself that he thinks, and that which his mind is applied about, whilst thinking, being the ideas that are there, it is past doubt that men have in their minds several ideas, such as are those expressed by the words, Whiteness, Hardness, Sweetness, Thinking, Motion, Man, Elephant, Army, Drunkenness, and others. It is in the first place then to be enquired, how he comes by them. I know it is a received doctrine, that men have native ideas, and original characters, stamped upon their minds, in their very first being. This opinion I have, at large, examined already; and, I suppose, what I have said, in the foregoing book, will be much more easily admitted, when I have shewn, whence the understanding may get all the ideas it has, and by what ways and degrees they may come into the mind for which I shall appeal to every one's own observation and experience.

2. All ideas come from sensations or reflection. Let us then suppose the mind to be, as we say, white paper, void of all characters, without any ideas; how comes it to be furnished? Whence comes it by that vast store which the busy and boundless fancy of man has painted on it with an almost endless variety? Whence has it all the materials of reason and knowledge? To this I answer, in one word, from experience; in all that our knowledge is founded, and from that it ultimately derives itself. Our observation employed either about external sensible objects, or about the internal operations of our minds, perceived and reflected on by ourselves, is that which supplies our understandings with all the materials of thinking. These two are the fountains of knowledge, from whence all the ideas we have, or can naturally have, do spring.

3. The objects of sensation one source of ideas. First, Our senses, conversant about particular sensible objects, do convey into the mind several distinct perceptions of things, according to those various ways wherein those objects do affect them: And thus we come by those ideas we have of Yellow, White, Heat, Cold, Soft, Hard, Bitter, Sweet, and all those which we call sensible qualities; which when I say the senses convey into the mind, I mean, they from external objects convey into the mind what produces there those perceptions. This great source of most of the ideas we have, depending wholly upon our senses, and derived by them to the understanding, I call SENSATION.

4. The operations of our minds the other source of them. Secondly, The other fountain from which experience furnishes the understanding with ideas, is the perception of the operations of our own mind within us, as it is employed about the ideas it has got; which operations, when the soul comes to reflect on and consider, do furnish the understanding with another set of ideas, which could not be had from things without. And such are Perception, Thinking, Doubting, Believing, Reasoning, Knowing, Willing, and all the different actings of our own minds; which we being conscious of and observing in ourselves, do from these receive into our understandings as distinct ideas, as we do from bodies affecting our senses. This source of ideas every man has wholly in himself; and though it be not sense, as having nothing to do with external objects, yet it is very like it, and might properly enough be called internal sense. But as I call the other sensation, so I call this REFLECTION, the ideas it affords being such only as the mind gets by reflecting on its own operations within itself. By reflection then, in the following part of this discourse, I would be understood to mean that notice which the mind takes of its own operations, and the manner of them; by reason whereof there come to be ideas of these operations in the understanding. These two, I say, viz. external material things, as the objects of sensation; and the operations of our own minds within, as the objects of reflection; are to me the only originals from whence all our ideas take their beginnings. The term operations here I use in a large sense, as comprehending not barely the actions of the mind about its ideas, but some sort of passions arising sometimes from them, such as is the satisfaction or uneasiness arising from any thought.

5. All our ideas of the one or the other of these. The understanding seems to me not to have the least glimmering of any ideas, which it doth not receive from one of these two. External objects furnish the mind with the ideas of sensible qualities, which are all those different perceptions they produce in us: And the mind furnishes the understanding with ideas of its own operations.

These, when we have taken a full survey of them, and their several modes, combinations, and relations, we shall find to contain all our whole stock of ideas; and that we have nothing in our minds which did not come in one of these two ways. Let any one examine his own thoughts, and thoroughly search into his understanding; and then let him tell me, whether all the original ideas he has there, are any other than of the objects of his senses, or of the operations of his mind, considered as objects of his reflection; and how great a mass of knowledge soever he imagines to be lodged there, he will, upon taking a strict view, see that he has not any idea in his mind, but what one of these two have imprinted; though perhaps, with infinite variety compounded and enlarged by the understanding, as we shall see hereafter.

6. Observable in children. He that attentively considers the state of a child, at his first coming into the world, will have little reason to think him stored with plenty of ideas, that are to be the matter of his future knowledge: It is by degrees he comes to be furnished with them. And though the ideas of obvious and familiar qualities imprint themselves before the memory begins to keep a register of time or order, yet it is often so late before some unusual qualities come in the way, that there are few men that cannot recollect the beginning of their acquaintance with them: And if it were worth while, no doubt a child might be so ordered as to have but a very few even of the ordinary ideas, till he were grown up to a man. But all that are born into the world being surrounded with bodies that perpetually and diversely affect them; variety of ideas, whether care be taken of it or not, are imprinted on the minds of children. Light and colors are busy at hand every-where, when the eye is but open; sounds and some tangible qualities fail not to solicit their proper senses, and force an entrance to the mind; but yet, I think, it will be granted easily, that if a child were kept in a place where he never saw any other but black and white till he were a man, he would have no more ideas of scarlet or green, than he that from his childhood never tasted an oyster, or a pineapple, has of those particular relishes.

7. Men are differently furnished with these according to the different objects they converse with. Men then come to be furnished with fewer or more simple ideas from without, according as the objects they converse with afford greater or less variety; and from the operations of their minds within, according as they more or less reflect on them. For though he that contemplates the operations of his mind, cannot but have plain and clear ideas of them; yet, unless he turn his thoughts that way, and considers them attentively, he will no more have clear and distinct ideas of all the operations of his mind, and all that may be observed therein, than he will have all the particular ideas of any landscape, or of the parts and motions of a clock, who will not turn his eyes to it, and with attention heed all the parts of it. The picture, or clock may be so placed, that they may come in his way every day; but yet he will have but a confused idea of all the parts they are made up of, till he applies himself with attention to consider them each in particular.

8. Ideas of reflection later, because they need attention. And hence we see the reason why it is pretty late before most children get ideas of the operations of their own minds; and some have not any very clear or perfect ideas of the greatest part of them all their lives: Because, though they pass there continually, yet, like floating visions, they make not deep impressions enough to leave in their mind clear, distinct, lasting ideas, till the understanding turns inward upon itself, reflects on its own operations, and makes them the objects of its own contemplation. Children when they come first into it, are surrounded with a world of new things, which, by a constant solicitation of these senses, draw the mind constantly to them, forward to take notice of new, and apt to be delighted with the variety of changing objects. Thus the first years are usually employed and diverted in looking abroad. Men's business in them is to acquaint themselves with what is to be found without: And so growing up in a constant attention to outward sensation, seldom make any considerable reflection on what passes within them till they come to be of riper years; and some scarce ever at all.

9. The soul begins to have ideas when it begins to perceive. To ask at what time a man has first any ideas, is to ask when he begins to perceive; having ideas, and perception, being the same thing. I know it is an opinion, that the soul always thinks, and that it has the actual perception of ideas in itself constantly as long as it exists; and that actual thinking is as inseparable from the soul, as actual extension is from the body; which if true, to enquire after the beginning of a man's ideas is the same as to enquire after the beginning of his soul. For by this account soul and its ideas, as body and its extension, will begin to exist both at the same time. . . .

Chapter 2. Of Simple Ideas

1. Uncompounded appearances. The better to understand the nature, manner, and extent of our knowledge, one thing is carefully to be observed concerning the ideas we have; and that is, that some of them are simple, and some complex.

Though the qualities that affect our senses are, in the things themselves, so united and blended, that there is no separation, no distance between them; yet it is plain, the ideas they produce in the mind enter by the senses simple and unmixed. For though the sight and touch often take in from the same object, at the same time, different ideas; as a man sees at once motion and color; the hand feels softness and warmth in the same piece of wax; yet the simple ideas, thus united in the same subject, are as perfectly distinct as those that come in by different senses: The coldness and hardness which a man feels in a piece of ice being as distinct ideas in the mind, as the smell and whiteness of a lily; or as the taste of sugar, and smell of a rose. And there is nothing can be plainer to a man, than the clear and distinct perception he has of those simple ideas; which, being each in itself uncompounded, contains in it nothing but one uniform appearance, or conception in the mind, and is not distinguishable into different ideas.

2. The mind can neither make nor destroy them. These simple ideas, the materials of all our knowledge, are suggested and furnished to the mind only by those two ways above-mentioned, viz. sensation and reflection. When the understanding is once stored with these simple ideas, it has the power to repeat, compare, and unite them, even to an almost infinite variety, and so can make at pleasure new complex ideas. But it is not in the power of the most exalted wit, or enlarged understanding, by any quickness or variety of thought, to invent or frame one new simple idea in the mind, not taken in by the ways before mentioned: Nor can any force of the understanding destroy those that are there. The dominion of man, in this little world of his own understanding, being much-what the same as it is in the great world of visible things; wherein his power, however managed by art and skill, reaches no farther than to compound and divide the materials that are made to his hand; but can do nothing towards making the least particle of new matter, or destroying one atom of what is already in being. The same inability will every one find in himself, who shall go about to fashion in his understanding any simple idea, not received in by his senses from external objects, or by reflection from the operations of his own mind about them. I would have any one try to fancy any taste, which had never affected his palate; or frame the idea of a scent he had never smelt: And when he can do this, I will also conclude that a blind man hath ideas of colors, and a deaf man true distinct notions of sounds.

3. Only the qualities that affect the sense are imaginable. This is the reason why, though we cannot believe it impossible to God to make a creature with other organs, and more ways to convey into the understanding the notice of corporeal things than those five, as they are usually counted, which he has given to man: Yet I think, it is not possible for any one to imagine any other qualities in bodies, howsoever constituted, whereby they can be taken notice of, besides sounds, tastes, smells, visible and tangible qualities. And had mankind been made but with four senses, the qualities then, which are the objects of the fifth sense, had been as far from our notice, imagination, and conception, as now any belonging to a sixth, seventh, or eighth sense, can possibly be: Which, whether yet some other creatures, in some other parts of this vast and stupendous universe, may not have, will be a great presumption to deny. He that will not set himself proudly at the top of all things, but will consider the immensity of this fabric, and the great variety that is to be found in this little and inconsiderable part of it which he has to do with, may be apt to think, that in other mansions of it there may be other and different intelligent beings, of whose faculties he has as little knowledge or apprehension, as a worm shut up in one drawer of a cabinet hath of the senses or understanding of a man: Such variety and excellency being suitable to the wisdom and power of the maker. I have here followed the common opinion of man's having but five senses; though, perhaps, there may be justly counted more: But either supposition serves equally to my present purpose.

Chapter 3. Of Ideas of One Sense

1. Division of simple ideas. The better to conceive the ideas we receive from sensation, it may not be amiss for us to consider them, in reference to the different ways whereby they make their approaches to our minds, and make themselves perceivable by us.

First, Then, there are some which come into our minds by one sense only.

Secondly, there are others that convey themselves into the mind by more senses than one.

Thirdly, Others that are had from reflection only.

Fourthly, There are some that make themselves way, and are suggested to the mind by all the ways of sensation and reflection.

We shall consider them apart under these several heads.

First, There are some ideas which have admittance only through one sense, which is peculiarly adapted to receive them. Thus light and colours, as white, red, yellow, blue, with their several degrees or shades and mixtures, as green, scarlet, purple, sea-green, and the rest, come in only by the eyes: All kinds of noises, sounds, and tones, only by the ears: The several tastes and smells, by the nose and palate. And if these organs, or the nerves, which are the conduits to convey them from without to their audience in the brain, the mind's presence-room (as I may so call it) are any of them so disordered, as not to perform their functions, they have no postern to be admitted by; no other way to bring themselves into view, and be perceived by the understanding.

The most considerable of those belonging to the touch are heat and cold, and solidity: All the rest, consisting almost wholly in the sensible configuration, as smooth and rough, or else more or less firm adhesion of the parts, as hard and soft, tough and brittle, are obvious enough.

2. Few simple ideas have names. I think, it will be needless to enumerate all the particular simple ideas, belonging to each sense. Nor indeed is it possible, if we would; there being a great many more of them belonging to most of the senses, than we have names for. The variety of smells, which are as many almost, if not more, than species of bodies in the world, do most of them want names. Sweet and stinking commonly serve our turn for these ideas, which in effect is little more than to call them pleasing or displeasing; though the smell of a rose and violet, both sweet, are certainly very distinct ideas. Nor are the different tastes, that by our palates we receive ideas of, much better provided with names. Sweet, bitter, sour, harsh, and salt, are almost all the epithets we have to denominate that numberless variety of relishes, which are to be found distinct, not only in almost every sort of creatures, but all the different parts of the same plant, fruit, or animal. The same may be said of colours and sounds. I shall therefore, in the account of simple ideas I am here giving, content myself to set down only such, as are most material to our present purpose, or are in themselves less apt to be taken notice of, though they are very frequently the ingredients of our complex ideas, amongst which, I think, I may well account solidity; which therefore I shall treat of in the next chapter.

Chapter 4. Of Solidity

1. We receive this idea from touch. The idea of solidity we receive by our touch: And it arises from the resistance which we find in body, to the entrance of any other body into the place it possesses, till it has left it. There is no idea which we receive more constantly from sensation, than solidity. Whether we move or rest, in what posture soever we are, we always feel some thing under us that supports us, and hinders our farther sinking downwards; and the bodies which we daily handle make us perceive, that, whilst they remain between them, they do by an insurmountable force hinder the approach of the parts of our hands that press them. That which thus hinders the approach of two bodies, when they are moved one towards another, I call solidity. I will not dispute, whether this acceptation of the word solid be nearer to its original signification, than that which mathematicians use it in: It suffices, that I think the common notion of solidity will allow, if not justify, this use of it; but, if any one think it better to call it impenetrability, he has my consent. Only I have thought the term solidity the more proper to express this idea, not only because of its vulgar use in that sense, but also because it carries some thing more of positive in it than impenetrability, which is negative, and is perhaps more a consequence of solidity, than solidity itself. This, of all other, seems the idea most intimately connected with and essential to body, so as no-where else to be found or imagined, but only in matter. And though our senses take no notice of it, but in masses of matter, of a bulk sufficient to cause a sensation in us; yet the mind, having once got this idea from such grosser sensible bodies, traces it farther; and considers it, as well as figure, in the minutest particle of matter that can exist: And finds it inseparably inherent in body, wherever or however modified.

2. Solidity fills space. This is the idea which belongs to body, whereby we conceive it to fill space. The idea of which filling of space is, that, where we imagine any space taken up by a solid substance, we conceive it so to possess it, that it excludes all other solid substances; and will for ever hinder any other two bodies, that move towards one another in a straight line, from coming to touch one another, unless it removes from between them, in a line not parallel to that which they move in. This idea of it the bodies which we ordinarily handle sufficiently furnish us with.

6. What it is. If any one asks me, what this solidity is, I send him to his senses to inform him: Let him put a flint or a foot-ball between his hands, and then endeavor to join them, and he will know. If he thinks this not a sufficient explication of solidity, what it is, and wherein it consists; I promise to tell him what it is, and wherein it consists, when he tells me what thinking is, or wherein it consists; or explains to me what extension or motion is, which perhaps seems much easier. The simple ideas we have are such as experience teaches them us, but if, beyond that, we endeavor by words to make them clearer in the mind, we shall succeed no better, than if we went about to clear up the darkness of a blind man's mind by talking; and to discourse into him the ideas of light and colours. The reason of this I shall shew in another place.

Chapter 5. Of Simple Ideas of Divers Senses

The ideas we get by more than one sense are of space, or extension, figure, rest, and motion; for these make perceivable impressions, both on the eyes and touch: And we can receive and convey into our minds the ideas of the extension, figure, motion, and rest of bodies, both by seeing and feeling. But having occasion to speak more at large of these in another place, I here only enumerate them.

Chapter 6. Of Simple Ideas of Reflection

1. Simple ideas are operations of the mind about its other ideas. The mind, receiving the ideas, mentioned in the foregoing chapters, from without, when it turns its view inward upon itself, and observes its own actions about those ideas it has, takes from thence other ideas, which are as capable to be the objects of its contemplation as any of those it received from foreign things.

2. The idea of perception, and the idea of willing, we have from reflection. The two great and principal actions of the mind, which are most frequently considered, and which are so frequent, that every one that pleases may take notice of them in himself, are these two: Perception or Thinking; and Volition, or Willing. The power of thinking is called the understanding, and the power of volition is called the will; and these two powers or abilities in the mind are denominated faculties. Of some of the modes of these simple ideas of reflection, such as are Remembrance, Discerning, Reasoning, Judging, Knowledge, Faith, &c. I shall have occasion to speak hereafter.

Chapter 7. Of Simple Ideas of Both Sensation and Reflection

1. Ideas of pleasure and pain. There be other simple ideas which convey themselves into the mind by all the ways of sensation and reflection, viz. Pleasure or Delight, and its opposite, Pain or Uneasiness; Power; Existence; Unity.

2. Mix with almost all our other ideas. Delight or uneasiness, one or other of them, join themselves to almost all our ideas, both of sensation and reflection: And there is scarce any affection of our senses from without, any retired thought of our mind within, which is not able to produce in us pleasure or pain. By pleasure and pain I would be understood to signify whatsoever delights or molests us; whether it arises from the thoughts of our minds, or any thing operating on our bodies. For whether we call it satisfaction, delight, pleasure, happiness, &c. on the one side; or uneasiness, trouble, pain, torment, anguish, misery, &c. on the other; they are still but different degrees of the same thing, and belong to the ideas of pleasure and pain, delight or uneasiness; which are the names I shall most commonly use for those two sorts of ideas.

7. Existence and unity. Existence and unity are two other ideas that are suggested to the understanding by every object without, and every idea within. When ideas are in our minds, we consider them as being actually there, as well as we consider things to be actually without us; which is, that they exist, or have existence: And whatever we can consider as one thing, whether a real being or idea, suggests to the understanding the idea of unity.

8. Power. Power also is another of those simple ideas which we receive from sensation and reflection. For observing in ourselves, that we can at pleasure move several parts of our bodies which were at rest; the effects also, that natural bodies are able to produce in one another, occurring every moment to our senses, we both these ways get the idea of power.

9. Succession. Besides these there is another idea, which, though suggested by our senses, yet is more constantly offered to us by what passes in our minds; and that is the idea of succession. For if we look immediately into ourselves, and reflect on what is observable there, we shall find our ideas always, whilst we are awake, or have any thought, passing in train, one going and another coming, without intermission.

10. Simple ideas the materials of all our knowledge. These, if they are not all, are at least (as I think) the most considerable of those simple ideas which the mind has, and out of which is made all its other knowledge: All which it receives only by the two forementioned ways of sensation and reflection.

Nor let any one think these too narrow bounds for the capacious mind of man to expatiate in, which takes its flight farther than the stars, and cannot be confined by the limits of the world; that extends its thoughts often even beyond the utmost expansion of matter, and makes excursions into that incomprehensible inane. I grant all this, but desire any one to assign any simple idea which is not received from one of those inlets before-mentioned, or any complex idea not made out of those simple ones. Nor will it be so strange to think these few simple ideas sufficient to employ the quickest thought, or largest capacity; and to furnish the materials of all that various knowledge, and more various fancies and opinions of all mankind, if we consider how many words may be made out of the various composition of twenty-four letters; or if, going one step farther, we will but reflect on the variety of combinations may be made, with barely one of the above-mentioned ideas, viz. number, whose stock is inexhaustible and truly infinite; and what a large and immense field doth extension alone afford the mathematicians?

Chapter 8. Some Farther Considerations Concerning Our Simple Ideas

1. Positive ideas from privative causes. Concerning the simple ideas of sensation it is to be considered that whatsoever is so constituted in nature as to be able, by affecting our senses, to cause any perception in the mind, doth thereby produce in the understanding a simple idea; which, whatever be the external cause of it, when it comes to be taken notice of by our discerning faculty, it is by the mind looked on and considered there to be a real positive idea in the understanding, as much as any other whatsoever; though perhaps the cause of it be but a privation of the subject.

2. Ideas in the mind distinguished from that in things which gives rise to them. Thus the ideas of heat and cold, light and darkness, white and black, motion and rest, are equally clear and positive ideas in the mind; though perhaps some of the causes which produce them are barely privations in subjects, from whence our senses derive those ideas. These the understanding, in its view of them, considers all as distinct positive ideas, without taking notice of the causes that produce them: Which is an enquiry not belonging to the idea, as it is in the understanding, but to the nature of the things existing without us. These are two very different things, and carefully to be distinguished; it being one thing to perceive and know the idea of white or black, and quite another to examine what kind of particles they must be, and how ranged in the superficies, to make any object appear white or black.

3. We may have ideas when we are ignorant of their physical causes. A painter or dyer, who never enquired into their causes, hath the ideas of white and black, and other colors, as clearly, perfectly, and distinctly in his understanding, and perhaps more distinctly, than the philosopher, who hath busied himself in considering their natures, and thinks he knows how far either of them is in its cause positive or privative; and the idea of black is no less positive in his mind, than that of white, however the cause of that color in the external object may be only a privation.

4. Why a privative cause in nature may occasion a positive idea. If it were the design of my present undertaking to enquire into the natural causes and manner of perception, I should offer this as a reason why a privative cause might. in some cases at least, produce a positive idea, viz. that all sensation being produced in us only by different degrees and modes of motion in our animal spirits, variously agitated by external objects, the abatement of any former motion must as necessarily produce a new sensation, as the variation or increase of it; and so introduce a new idea, which depends only on a different motion of the animal spirits in that organ.

5. Negative names need not be meaningless. But whether this be so or no, I will not here determine, but appeal to every one's own experience, whether the shadow of a man, though it consists of nothing but the absence of light (and the more the absence of light is, the more discernible is the shadow) does not, when a man looks on it, cause as clear and positive idea in his mind, as a man himself, though covered over with clear sunshine? and the picture of a shadow is a positive thing. Indeed we have negative names, which stand not directly for positive ideas, but for their absence, such as insipid, silence, nihil, &c. which words denote positive ideas, v.g. taste, sound, being, with a signification of their absence.

6. Whether any ideas are due to causes really privative. And thus one may truly be said to see darkness. For supposing a hole perfectly dark, from whence no light is reflected, it is certain one may see the figure of it, or it may be painted: Or whether the ink I write with makes any other idea, is a question. The privative causes I have here assigned of positive ideas are according to the common opinion; but in truth it will be hard to determine, whether there be really any ideas from a privative cause, till it be determined, whether rest be any more a privation than motion.

7. Ideas in the mind, qualities of bodies. To discover the nature of our ideas the better, and to discourse of them intelligibly, it will be convenient to distinguish them as they are ideas or perceptions in our minds, and as they are modifications of matter in the bodies that cause such perceptions in us: That so we may not think (as perhaps usually is done) that they are exactly the images and resemblances of some thing inherent in the subject; most of those of sensation being in the mind no more the likeness of some thing existing without us, than the names that stand for them are the likeness of our ideas, which yet upon hearing they are apt to excite in us.

8. Our ideas and the qualities of bodies. Whatsoever the mind perceives in itself, or is the immediate object of perception, thought, or understanding, that I call idea; and the power to produce any idea in our mind I call a quality of the subject wherein that power is. Thus a snow-ball having the power to produce in us the ideas of white, cold, and round, the power to produce those ideas in us, as they are in the snow-ball, I call qualities; and as they are sensations or perceptions in our understandings, I call them ideas; which ideas, if I speak of sometimes, as in the things themselves, I would be understood to mean those qualities in the objects which produce them in us.

9. Primary qualities of bodies. Qualities thus considered in bodies are, first, such as are utterly inseparable from the body, in what state soever it be; such as in all the alterations and changes it suffers, all the force can be used upon it, it constantly keeps; and such as sense constantly finds in every particle of matter which has bulk enough to be perceived, and the mind finds inseparable from every particle of matter, though less than to make itself singly be perceived by our senses, v.g. Take a grain of wheat, divide it into two parts, each part has still solidity, extension, figure, and mobility; divide it again, and it retains still the same qualities; and so divide it on till the parts become insensible, they must retain still each of them all those qualities. For division (which is all that a mill, or pestle, or any other body does upon another, in reducing it to insensible parts) can never take away either solidity, extension, figure, or mobility from any body, but only makes two or more distinct separate masses of matter, of that which was but one before: All which distinct masses, reckoned as so many distinct bodies, after division make a certain number. These I call original or primary qualities of body, which I think we may observe to produce simple ideas in us, viz. solidity, extension, figure, motion or rest, and number.

10. Secondary qualities of bodies. Secondly, such qualities which in truth are nothing in the objects themselves, but powers to produce various sensations in us by their primary qualities, i.e. by the bulk, figure, texture, and motion of their insensible parts, as colors, sounds, tastes, &c. these I call secondary qualities. To these might be added a third sort, which are allowed to be barely powers, though they are as much real qualities in the subject, as those which I, to comply with the common way of speaking, call qualities, but for distinction, secondary qualities. For the power in fire to produce a new color, or consistency, in wax or clay, by its primary qualities, is as much a quality in fire, as the power it has to produce in me a new idea or sensation of warmth or burning, which I felt not before by the same primary qualities, viz. the bulk, texture, and motion of its insensible parts.

11. How primary qualities produce their ideas. The next thing to be considered is, how bodies produce ideas in us; and that is manifestly by impulse, the only way which we can conceive bodies to operate in.

12. By motions both external and in us. If then external objects be not united to our minds, when they produce ideas therein, and yet we perceive these original qualities in such of them as singly fall under our senses, it is evident that some motion must be thence continued by our nerves, or animal spirits, by some parts of our bodies, to the brains or the seat of sensation, there to produce in our minds the particular ideas we have of them. And since the extension, figure, number, and motion of bodies, of an observable bigness, may be perceived at a distance by the sight, it is evident some singly imperceptible bodies must come from them to the eyes, and thereby convey to the brain some motion, which produces these ideas which we have of them in us.

13. How secondary. After the same manner that the ideas of these original qualities are produced in us, we may conceive that the ideas of secondary qualities are also produced, viz. by the operation of insensible particles on our senses. For it being manifest that there are bodies and good store of bodies, each whereof are so small, that we cannot, by any of our senses, discover either their bulk, figure, or motion as is evident in the particles of the air and water, and others extremely smaller than those, perhaps as much smaller than the particles of air and water, as the particles of air and water are smaller than peas or hail-stones: Let us suppose at present, that the different motions and figures, bulk and number of such particles, affecting the several organs of our senses, produce in us those different sensations, which we have from the colors and smells of bodies; v.g. that a violet, by the impulse of such insensible particles of matter of peculiar figures and bulks, and in different degrees and modifications of their motions, causes the ideas of the blue color and sweet scent of that flower, to be produced in our minds; it being no more impossible to conceive that God should annex such ideas to such motions, with which they have no similitude, than that he should annex the idea of pain to the motion of a piece of steel dividing our flesh, with which that idea hath no resemblance.

14. They depend on the primary qualities. What I have said concerning colors and smells may be understood also of tastes and sounds, and other the like sensible qualities; which, whatever reality we by mistake attribute to them, are in truth nothing in the objects themselves, but powers to produce various sensations in us, and depend on those primary qualities, viz. bulk, figure, texture, and motion of parts; as I have said.

15. Ideas of primary qualities are resemblances; of secondary, not. From whence I think it easy to draw this observation, that the ideas of primary qualities of bodies are resemblances of them, and their patterns do really exist in the bodies themselves; but the ideas, produced in us by these secondary qualities, have no resemblance of them at all. There is nothing like our ideas existing in the bodies themselves. They are in the bodies, we denominate from them, only a power to produce those sensations in us: And what is sweet, blue, or warm in idea, is but the certain bulk, figure, and motion of the insensible parts in the bodies themselves, which we call so.

16. Examples. Flame is denominated hot and light; snow, white and cold; and manna, white and sweet, from the ideas they produce in us: Which qualities are commonly thought to be the same in those bodies that those ideas are in us, the one the perfect resemblance of the other, as they are in a mirror; and it would by most men be judged very extravagant, if one should say otherwise. And yet he that will consider that the same fire, that at one distance produces in us the sensation of warmth, does at a nearer approach produce in us the far different sensation of pain, ought to bethink himself what reason he has to say, that his idea of warmth, which was produced in him by the fire, is actually in the fire; and his idea of pain, which the same fire produced in him the same way, is not in the fire. Why are whiteness and coldness in snow, and pain not, when it produces the one and the other idea in us; and can do neither, but by the bulk, figure, number, and motion of its solid parts?

17. The idea of the primary alone really exist. The particular bulk, number, figure, and motion of the parts of fire or snow are really in them, whether any one's senses perceive them or no: And therefore they may be called real qualities, because they really exist in those bodies: But light, heat, whiteness or coldness, are no more really in them, than sickness or pain is in manna. Take away the sensation of them; let not the eyes see light, or colors, nor the ears hear sounds; let the palate not taste, nor the nose smell; and all colors, tastes, odors, and sounds, as they are such particular ideas, vanish and cease, and are reduced to their causes, i.e. bulk, figure, and motion of parts.

18. Secondary exist only as modes of the primary. A piece of manna of a sensible bulk is able to produce in us the idea of a round or square figure, and, by being removed from one place to another, the idea of motion. This idea of motion represents it as it really is in the manna moving: A circle or square are the same, whether in idea or existence, in the mind, or in the manna; and this both motion and figure are really in the manna, whether we take notice of them or no: This every body is ready to agree to. Besides, manna, by the bulk, figure, texture, and motion of its parts, has a power to produce the sensations of sickness, and sometimes of acute pains or gripings in us. That these ideas of sickness and pain are not in the manna, but effects of its operations on us, and are nowhere when we feel them not; this also every one readily agrees to. And yet men are hardly to be brought to think, that sweetness and whiteness are not really in manna; which are but the effects of the operations of manna by the motion, size, and figure of its particles on the eyes and palate; as the pain and sickness caused by manna are confessedly nothing but the effects of its operations on the stomach and guts, by the size, motion, and figure of its insensible parts (for by nothing else can a body operate, as has been proved): As if it could not operate on the eyes and palate, and thereby produce in the mind particular distinct ideas, which in itself it has not, as well as we allow it can operate on the guts and stomach, and thereby produce distinct ideas, which in itself it has not. These ideas, being all effects of the operations of manna, on several parts of our bodies, by the size, figure, number, and motion of its parts: Why those produced by the eyes and palate should rather be thought to be really in the manna, than those produced by the stomach and guts; or why the pain and sickness, ideas that are the effect of manna, should be thought to be no-where when they are not felt; and yet the sweetness and whiteness, effects of the same manna on other parts of the body, by ways equally as unknown, should be thought to exist in the manna, when they are not seen or tasted, would need some reason to explain.

19. Examples. Let us consider the red and white colors in porphyry: Hinder light from striking on it, and its colors vanish, it no longer produces any such ideas in us; upon the return of light, it produces these appearances on us again. Can any one think any real alterations are made in the porphyry, by the presence or absence of light; and that those ideas of whiteness and redness are really in porphyry in the light, when it is plain it has no color in the dark? It has, indeed, such a configuration of particles, both night and day, as are apt, by the rays of light rebounding from some parts of that hard stone, to produce in us the idea of redness, and from others the idea of whiteness; but whiteness or redness are not in it at any time, but such a texture, that hath the power to produce such a sensation in us. . . .

23. Three sorts of qualities in bodies. The qualities then that are in bodies rightly considered, are of three sorts.

First, the bulk, figure, number, situation, and motion, or rest of their solid parts; those are in them, whether we perceive them or no; and when they are of that size, that we can discover them, we have by these an idea of the thing as it is in itself, as is plain in artificial things. These I call primary qualities.

Secondly, The power that is in any body, by reason of its insensible primary qualities, to operate after a peculiar manner on any of our senses, and thereby produce in us the different ideas of several colors, sounds, smells, tastes, &c. These are usually called sensible qualities.

Thirdly, the power that is in any body, by reason of the particular constitution of its primary qualities, to make such a change in the bulk, figure, texture, and motion of another body, as to make it operate on our senses differently from what it did before. Thus the sun has a power to make wax white, and fire to make lead fluid. These are usually called powers.

The first of these, as has been said, I think, may be properly called real, original, or primary qualities, because they are in the things themselves, whether they are perceived or no: And upon their different modifications it is, that the secondary qualities depend.

The other two are only powers to act differently upon other things, which powers result from the different modifications of those primary qualities.

24. The first are resemblances; the second thought resemblances, but are not; the third neither are, nor are thought so. But though the two latter sorts of qualities are powers barely, and nothing but powers, relating to several other bodies, and resulting from the different modifications of the original qualities; yet they are generally otherwise thought of. For the second sort, viz. the powers to produce several ideas in us by our senses, are looked upon as real qualities, in the things thus affecting us: But the third sort are called and esteemed barely powers, v.g. the idea of heat, or light, which we receive by our eyes or touch from the sun, are commonly thought real qualities, existing in the sun, and some thing more than mere powers in it. But when we consider the sun, in reference to wax, which it melts or blanches, we look on the whiteness and softness produced in the wax, not as qualities in the sun, but effects produced by powers in it: Whereas, if rightly considered, these qualities of light and warmth, which are perceptions in me when I am warmed, or enlightened by the sun, are no otherwise in the sun, than the changes made in the wax, when it is blanched or melted, are in the sun. They are all of them equally powers in the sun, depending on its primary qualities; whereby it is able, in the one case, so to alter the bulk, figure, texture, or motion of some of the insensible parts of my eyes or hands, as thereby to produce in me the idea of light or heat; and in the other it is able so to alter the bulk, figure, texture, or motion of the insensible parts of the wax, as to make them fit to produce in me the distinct ideas of white and fluid.

25. Why the secondary are ordinarily taken for real qualities, and not for bare powers. The reason why the one are ordinarily taken for real qualities, and the other only for bare powers, seems to be, because the ideas we have of distinct colors, sounds, &c. containing nothing at all in them of bulk, figure, or motion, we are not apt to think them the effects of these primary qualities, which appear not, to our senses, to operate in their production; and with which they have not any apparent congruity, or conceivable connexion. Hence it is that we are so forward to imagine, that those ideas are the resemblances of some thing really existing in the objects themselves: Since sensation discovers nothing of bulk, figure, or motion of parts in their production; nor can reason shew how bodies, by their bulk, figure, and motion, should produce in the mind the ideas of blue or yellow, &c. But in the other case, in the operations of bodies changing the qualities one of another, we plainly discover, that the quality produced hath commonly no resemblance with any thing in the thing producing it; wherefore we look on it as a bare effect of power. For though receiving the idea of heat, or light, from the sun, we are apt to think it is a perception and resemblance of such a quality in the sun; yet when we see wax, or a fair face, receive change of color from the sun, we cannot imagine that to be the reception or resemblance of any thing in the sun, because we find not those different colors in the sun itself. For our senses being able to observe a likeness or unlikeness of sensible qualities in two different external objects, we forwardly enough conclude the production of any sensible quality, in any subject to be an effect of bare power, and not the communication of any quality, which was really in the efficient, when we find no such sensible quality in the thing that produced it. But our senses not being able to discover any unlikeness between the idea produced in us, and the quality of the object producing it; we are apt to imagine, that our ideas are resemblances of something, in the objects, and not the effects of certain powers placed in the modification of their primary qualities, with which primary qualities the ideas produced in us have no resemblance.

26. Secondary qualities two fold; first, immediately perceivable; secondly, mediately perceivable. To conclude, beside those before mentioned primary qualities in bodies, viz. bulk, figure, extension, number, and motion of their solid parts; all the rest whereby we take notice of bodies, and distinguish them one from another, are nothing else but several powers in them depending on those primary qualities; whereby they are fitted, either by immediately operating on our bodies to produce several different ideas, or else, by operating on other bodies, so to change their primary qualities, as to render them capable of producing ideas in us, different from what before they did. The former of these, I think, may be called secondary qualities, immediately perceivable: The latter, secondary qualities, mediately perceivable.

Chapter 9. Of Perception

1. It is the first simple idea of reflection. Perception, as it is the first faculty of the mind exercised about our ideas; so it is the first and simplest idea we have from reflection, and is by some called thinking in general. Though thinking, in the propriety of the English tongue, signifies that sort of operation in the mind about its ideas, wherein the mind is active; where it, with some degree of voluntary attention, considers any thing. For in bare naked perception, the mind is, for the most part, only passive: And what it perceives, it cannot avoid perceiving.

2. Perception is only when the mind receives the impression. What perception is, every one will know better by reflecting on what he does himself, when he sees, hears, feels, &c. or thinks, than by any discourse of mine. Whoever reflects on what passes in his own mind, cannot miss it: And if he does not reflect, all the words in the world cannot make him have any notion of it.

3. This is certain, that whatever alterations are made in the body, if they reach not the mind; whatever impressions are made on the outward parts, if they are not taken notice of within; there is no perception. Fire may burn our bodies, with no other effect, than it does a billet, unless the motion be continued to the brain, and there the sense of heat, or idea of pain, be produced in the mind, wherein consists actual perception.

4. How often may a man observe in himself, that whilst his mind is intently employed in the contemplation of some objects, and curiously surveying some ideas that are there, it takes no notice of impressions of sounding bodies made upon the organ of hearing, with the same alteration that uses to be for the producing the idea of sound? A sufficient impulse there may be on the organ; but it not reaching the observation of the mind, there follows no perception: And though the motion that uses to produce the idea of sound be made in the ear, yet no sound is heard. Want of sensation, in this case, is not through any defect in the organ, or that the man's ears are less affected than at other times when he does hear; but that which uses to produce the idea, though conveyed in by the usual organ, not being taken notice of in the understanding, and so imprinting no idea in the mind, there follows no sensation. So that wherever there is sense, or perception, there some idea is actually produced, and present in the understanding.

5. Children, though they have ideas in the womb, have none innate. Therefore I doubt not but children, by the exercise of their senses about objects that affect them in the womb, receive some few ideas before they are born; as the unavoidable effects, either of the bodies that environ them, or else of those wants or diseases they suffer: Amongst which (if one may conjecture concerning things not very capable of examination) I think the ideas of hunger and warmth are two; which probably are some of the first that children have, and which they scarce ever part with again.

6. But though it be reasonable to imagine that children receive some ideas before they come into the world, yet these simple ideas are far from those innate principles which some contend for, and we above have rejected. There here mentioned being the effects of sensation, are only from some affections of the body, which happen to them there, and so depend on some thing exterior to the mind: No otherwise differing in their manner of production from other ideas derived from sense, but only in the precedency of time; whereas those innate principles are supposed to be quite of another nature; not coming into the mind by any accidental alterations in, or operations on the body; but, as it were, original characters impressed upon it, in the very first moment of its being and constitution.

7. Which ideas first, is not evident. As there are some ideas which we may reasonably suppose may be introduced into the minds of children in the womb, subservient to the necessities of their life and being there; so after they are born, those ideas are the earliest imprinted which happen to be the sensible qualities which first occur to them: Amongst which, light is not the least considerable, nor of the weakest efficacy. And how covetous the mind is to be furnished with all such ideas as have no pain accompanying them, may be a little guessed, by what is observable in children new-born, who always turn their eyes to that part from whence the light comes, lay them how you please. But the ideas that are most familiar at first being various, according to the divers circumstances of children's first entertainment in the world; the order wherein the several ideas come at first into the mind is very various and uncertain also; neither is it much material to know it.

8. Ideas of sensation often changed by the judgment. We are further to consider concerning perception, that the ideas we receive by sensation are often in grown people altered by the judgment, without our taking notice of it. When we set before our eyes a round globe, of any uniform color, v.g. gold, alabaster, or jet; it is certain that the idea thereby imprinted in our mind, is of a flat circle variously shadowed, with several degrees of light and brightness coming to our eyes. But we having by use been accustomed to perceive what kind of appearance convex bodies are wont to make in us, what alterations are made in the reflections of light by the difference of the sensible figures of bodies; the judgment presently, by an habitual custom, alters the appearances into their causes; so that from that which is truly variety of shadow or color, collecting the figure, it makes it pass for a mark of figure, and frames to itself the perception of a convex figure and an uniform color; when the idea we receive from thence is only a plane variously colored, as is evident in painting. To which purpose I shall here insert a problem of that very ingenious and studious promoter of real knowledge, the learned and worthy Mr. Molineaux, which he was pleased to send me in a letter some months since; and it is this: Suppose a man born blind, and now adult, and taught by his touch to distinguish between a cube and a sphere of the same metal, and nighly of the same bigness, so as to tell, when he felt one and the other, which is the cube, which the sphere. Suppose then the cube and sphere placed on a table, and the blind man be made to see: Quaere, "whether by his sight, before he touched them, he could now distinguish and tell, which is the globe, which the cube?" to which the acute and judicious proposer answers: Not. For though he has obtained the experience of how a globe, how a cube affects his touch; yet he has not yet obtained the experience, that what affects his touch so or so, must affect his sight so or so: Or that a protuberant angle in the cube, that pressed his hand unequally, shall appear to his eye as it does in the cube. I agree with this thinking gentleman, whom I am proud to call my friend, in his answer to this problem; and am of opinion, that the blind man at first sight, would not be able with certainty to say which was the globe, which the cube, whilst he only saw them: Though he could unerringly name them by his touch, and certainly distinguish them by the difference of their figures felt. This I have set down, and leave with my reader, as an occasion for him to consider how much he may be beholden to experience, improvement, and acquired notions, where he thinks he had not the least use of, or help from them: And the rather, because this observing gentleman further adds, that having, upon the occasion of my book, proposed this to divers very ingenious men, he hardly ever met with one, that at first gave the answer to it which he thinks true, till by hearing his reasons they were convinced.

9. But this is not, I think, usual in any of our ideas, but those received by sight: Because sight, the most comprehensive of all our senses, conveying to our minds the ideas of light and colors, which are peculiar only to that sense; and also the far different ideas of space, figure, and motion, the several varieties whereof change the appearances of its proper object, viz. light and colors; we bring ourselves by use to judge of the one by the other. This, in many cases, by a settled habit, in things whereof we have frequent experience, is performed so constantly and so quick, that we take that for the perception of our sensation, which is an idea formed by our judgment; so that one, viz. that of sensation, serves only to excite the other, and is scarce taken notice of itself: As a man who reads or hears with attention and understanding, takes little notice of the characters, or sounds, but of the ideas that are excited in him by them.

10. Nor need we wonder that this is done with so little notice, if we consider how quick the actions of the mind are performed: For as itself is thought to take up no space, to have no extension; so its actions seem to require no time, but many of them seem to be crowded into an instant. I speak this in comparison to the actions of the body. Any one may easily observe this in his own thoughts, who will take the pains to reflect on them. How, as it were in an instant, do our minds with one glance see all the parts of a demonstration, which may very well be called a long one, if we consider the time it will require to put it into words, and step by step shew it another? Secondly, we shall not be so much surprised, that this is done in us with so little notice, if we consider how the facility which we get of doing things, by a custom of doing, makes them often pass in us without our notice. Habits, especially such as are begun very early, come at last to produce actions in us, which often escape our observation. How frequently do we, in a day, cover our eyes with our eye-lids, without perceiving that we are at all in the dark? Men that by custom have got the use of a by-word, do almost in every sentence pronounce sounds which, though taken notice of by others, they themselves neither hear nor observe. And therefore it is not so strange, that our mind should often change the idea of its sensation into that of its judgment, and make one serve only to excite the other without our taking notice of it.

11. Perception puts the difference between animals and inferior beings. This faculty of perception seems to me to be that, which puts the distinction betwixt the animal kingdom and the inferior parts of nature. For however vegetables have, many of them, some degrees of motion, and upon the different application of other bodies to them, do very briskly alter their figures and motions, and so have obtained the name of sensitive plants, from a motion which has some resemblance to that which in animals follows upon sensation: Yet, I suppose, it is all bare mechanism; and no otherwise produced, than the turning of a wild oat-beard, by the insinuation of the particles of moisture, or the shortening of a rope, by the affusion of water. All which is done without any sensation in the subject, or the having or receiving any ideas.

12. Perception, I believe, is in some degree in all sorts of animals; though in some, possibly, the avenues provided by nature for the reception of sensations are so few, and the perception they are received with so obscure and dull, that it comes extremely short of the quickness and variety of sensation which is in other animals; but yet it is sufficient for, and wisely adapted to, the state and condition of that sort of animals who are thus made. So that the wisdom and goodness of the Maker plainly appear in all the parts of this stupendous fabric, and all the several degrees and ranks of creatures in it.

13. We may, I think, from the make of an oyster, or cockle, reasonably conclude that it has not so many, nor so quick senses, as a man, or several other animals; nor if it had, would it, in that state and incapacity of transferring itself from one place to another, be bettered by them. What good would sight and hearing do to a creature, that cannot move itself to, or from the objects wherein at a distance it perceives good or evil? And would not quickness of sensation be an inconvenience to an animal that must lie still, where chance has once placed it; and there receive the afflux of colder or warmer, clear or foul water, as it happens to come to it?

14. But yet I cannot but think there is some small dull perception, whereby they are distinguished from perfect insensibility. And that this may be so, we have plain instances even in mankind itself. Take one, in whom decrepit old age has blotted out the memory of his past knowledge, and clearly wiped out the ideas his mind was formerly stored with; and has, by destroying his sight, hearing, and smell quite, and his taste to a great degree, stopped up almost all the passages for new ones to enter; or if there be some of the inlets yet half open, the impressions made are scarce perceived, or not at all retained. How far such an one (notwithstanding all that is boasted of innate principles) is in his knowledge, and intellectual faculties, above the condition of a cockle or an oyster, I leave to be considered. And if a man had passed sixty years in such a state, as it is possible he might, as well as three days; I wonder what difference there would have been, in any intellectual perfections, between him and the lowest degree of animals.

15. Perception the inlet of knowledge. Perception then being the first step and degree towards knowledge, and the inlet of all the materials of it; the fewer senses any man, as well as any other creature, hath, and the fewer and duller the impressions are that are made by them, and the duller the faculties are that are employed about them; the more remote are they from that knowledge, which is to be found in some men. But this being in great variety of degrees (as may be perceived amongst men) cannot certainly be discovered in the several species of animals, much less in their particular individuals. It suffices me only to have remarked here, that perception is the first operation of all our intellectual faculties, and the inlet of all knowledge in our minds. And I am apt too to imagine, that it is perception in the lowest degree of it, which puts the boundaries between animals and the inferior ranks of creatures. But this I mention only as my conjecture by the by; it being indifferent to the matter in hand, which way the learned shall determine of it.

Chapter 23. Of the Complex Ideas of Substance

14. Complex ideas of substance. But to return to the matter in hand, the ideas we have of substances, and the ways we come by them; I say, our specific ideas of substances are nothing else but a collection of a certain number of simple ideas, considered as united in one thing. These ideas of substances, though they are commonly simple apprehensions, and the names of them simple terms; yet in effect are complex and compounded. Thus the idea which an Englishman signifies by the name Swan, is white color, long neck, red beak, black legs, and whole feet, and all these of a certain size, with a power of swimming in the water, and making a certain kind of noise: And perhaps, to a man who has long observed this kind of bird, some other properties which all terminate in sensible simple ideas, all united in one common subject.

15. Idea of spiritual substances, as clear as of bodily substances. Besides the complex ideas we have of material sensible substances, of which I have last spoken, by the simple ideas we have taken from those operations of our own minds, which we experiment daily in ourselves, as thinking, understanding, willing, knowing, and power of beginning motion, &c. co-existing in some substance: We are able to frame the complex idea of an immaterial spirit. And thus by putting together the ideas of thinking, perceiving, liberty, and power of moving themselves, and other things, we have as clear a perception and notion of immaterial substances, as we have of material. For putting together the ideas of thinking and willing, or the power of moving or quieting corporeal motion, joined to substance of which we have no distinct idea, we have the idea of an immaterial spirit; and by putting together the ideas of coherent solid parts, and a power of being moved, joined with substance, of which likewise we have no positive idea, we have the idea of matter. The one is as clear and distinct an idea as the other: The idea of thinking, and moving a body, being as clear and distinct ideas, as the ideas of extension, solidity, and being moved. For our idea of substance is equally obscure, or none at all in both: It is but a supposed I know not what, to support those ideas we call accidents. It is for want of reflection that we are apt to think, that our senses shew us nothing but material things. Every act of sensation, when duly considered, gives us an equal view of both parts of nature, the corporeal and spiritual. For whilst I know, by seeing or hearing, &c. that there is some corporeal being without me, the object of that sensation; I do more certainly know, that there is some spiritual being within me, that sees and hears. This, I must be convinced, cannot be the action of bare insensible matter; nor ever could be, without an immaterial thinking being.

BOOK IV

Chapter 1. Of Knowledge in General

1. Our knowledge conversant about our ideas. Since the mind, in all its thoughts and reasonings, hath no other immediate object but its own ideas, which it alone does or can contemplate; it is evident, that our knowledge is only conversant about them.

2. Knowledge is the perception of the agreement or disagreement of two ideas. Knowledge then seems to me to be nothing but the perception of the connexion and agreement, or disagreement and repugnancy, of any of our ideas. In this alone it consists. Where this perception is, there is knowledge; and where it is not, there, though we may fancy, guess, or believe, yet we always come short of knowledge. For when we know that white is not black, what do we else but perceive that these two ideas do not agree? When we possess ourselves with the utmost security of the demonstration, that the three angles of a triangle are equal to two right ones, what do we more but perceive, that equality to two right ones does necessarily agree to, and is inseparable from the three angles of a triangle?

3. This agreement is fourfold. But to understand a little more distinctly wherein this agreement or disagreement consists, I think we may reduce it all to these four sorts: 1. Identity, or diversity; 2. Relation; 3. Co-existence, or necessary connexion; 4. Real existence.

4. First, Of Identity or Diversity. As to the first sort of agreement or disagreement, viz. identity or diversity. It is the first act of the mind, when it has any sentiments or ideas at all, to perceive its ideas; and so far as it perceives them, to know each what it is, and thereby also to perceive their difference, and that one is not another. This is so absolutely necessary, that without it there could be no knowledge, no reasoning, no imagination, no distinct thoughts, at all. By this the mind clearly and infallibly perceives each idea to agree with itself, and to be what it is; and all distinct ideas to disagree, i.e. the one not to be the other: And this it does without pains, labour, or deduction; but at first view, by its natural power of perception and distinction. And though men of art have reduced this into those general rules, "what is, is"; and "it is impossible for the same thing to be and not to be"; for ready application in all cases, wherein there may be occasion to reflect on it: Yet it is certain, that the first exercise of this faculty is about particular ideas. A man infallibly knows, as soon as ever he has them in his mind, that the ideas he calls white and round, are the very ideas they are, and that they are not other ideas which he calls red or square. Nor can any maxim or proposition in the world make him know it clearer or surer than he did before, and without any such general rule. This then is the first agreement or disagreement, which the mind perceives in its ideas; which it always perceives at first sight: And if there ever happen any doubt about it, it will always be found to be about the names, and not the ideas themselves, whose identity and diversity will always be perceived, as soon and clearly as the ideas themselves are; nor can it possibly be otherwise.

5. Secondly, Relative. The next sort of agreement or disagreement, the mind perceives in any of its ideas, may, I think, be called relative, and is nothing but the perception of the relation between any two ideas, of what kind soever, whether substances, modes, or any other. For since all distinct ideas must eternally be known not to be the same, and so be universally and constantly denied one of another, there could be no room for any positive knowledge at all, if we could not perceive any relation between our ideas, and find out the agreement or disagreement they have one with another, in several ways the mind takes of comparing them.

6. Thirdly, Of Coexistence. The third sort of agreement, or disagreement, to be found in our ideas, which the perception of the mind is employed about, is co-existence, or non-co-existence in the same subject; and this belongs particularly to substances. Thus when we pronounce concerning gold that it is fixed, our knowledge of this truth amounts to no more but this, that fixedness, or a power to remain in the fire unconsumed, is an idea that always accompanies, and is joined with that particular sort of yellowness, weight, fusibility, malleableness, and solubility in aqua regia (royal water), which make our complex idea, signified by the word gold.

7. Fourthly, Of Real Existence. The last sort is that of actual real existence agreeing to any idea. Within these four sorts of agreement or disagreement, is, I suppose, contained all the knowledge we have, or are capable of: For all the inquiries we can make concerning any of our ideas, all that we know or can affirm concerning any of them, is, that it is, or is not, the same with some other; that it does or does not, always co-exist with some other idea in the same subject; that it has this or that relation with some other idea; or that it has a real existence without the mind. Thus "blue is not yellow"; is of identity: "two triangles upon equal bases between two parallels are equal"; is of relation: "iron is susceptible of magnetical impressions"; is of co-existence: "God is"; is of real existence. Though identity and co-existence are truly nothing but relations, yet they are such peculiar ways of agreement or disagreement of our ideas, that they deserve well to be considered as distinct heads, and not under relation in general; since they are so different grounds of affirmation and negation, as will easily appear to any one, who will but reflect on what is said in several places of this essay. I should now proceed to examine the several degrees of our knowledge, but that it is necessary first to consider the different acceptations of the word knowledge.

8. Knowledge Actual or Habitual. There are several ways wherein the mind is possessed of truth, each of which is called knowledge.

1. There is actual knowledge which is the present view the mind has of the agreement or disagreement of any of its ideas, or of the relation they have one to another.

2. A man is said to know any proposition, which having been once laid before his thoughts, he evidently perceived the agreement or disagreement of the ideas whereof it consists; and so lodged it in his memory, that whenever that proposition comes again to be reflected on, he, without doubt or hesitation, embraces the right side, assents to, and is certain of the truth of it. This, I think, one may call habitual knowledge: And thus a man may be said to know all those truths which are lodged in his memory, by a foregoing, clear and full perception, whereof the mind is assured past doubt, as often as it has occasion to reflect on them. For our finite understandings being able to think clearly and distinctly but on one thing at once, if men had no knowledge of any more than what they actually thought on, they would all be very ignorant; and he that knew most, would know but one truth, that being all he was able to think on at one time.

9. Habitual knowledge twofold. Of habitual knowledge, there are also, vulgarly speaking, two degrees:

First, the one is of such truths laid up in the memory as, whenever they occur to the mind, it actually perceives the relation is between those ideas. And this is in all those truths whereof we have an intuitive knowledge; where the ideas themselves, by an immediate view, discover their agreement or disagreement one with another.

Secondly, The other is of such truths whereof the mind having been convinced, it retains the memory of the conviction, without the proofs. Thus a man that remembers certainly that he once perceived the demonstration, that the three angles of a triangle are equal to two right ones, is certain that he knows it, because he cannot doubt the truth of it. In his adherence to a truth, where the demonstration by which it was at first known is forgot, though a man may be thought rather to believe his memory than really to know, and this way of entertaining a truth seemed formerly to me like something between opinion and knowledge; a sort of assurance which exceeds bare belief, for that relies on the testimony of another: Yet upon a due examination I find it comes not short of perfect certainty, and is in effect true knowledge. That which is apt to mislead our first thoughts into a mistake in this matter, is, that the agreement or disagreement of the ideas in this case is not perceived, as it was at first, by an actual view of all the intermediate ideas, whereby the agreement or disagreement of those in the proposition was at first perceived; but by other intermediate ideas, that show the agreement or disagreement of the ideas contained in the proposition whose certainty we remember. For example, in this proposition, that "the three angles of a triangle are equal to two right ones," one who has seen and clearly perceived the demonstration of this truth, knows it to be true, when that demonstration is gone out of his mind; so that at present it is not actually in view, and possibly cannot be recollected: But he knows it in a different way from what he did before. The agreement of the two ideas joined in that proposition is perceived, but it is by the intervention of other ideas than those which at first produced that perception. He remembers, i.e. he knows (for remembrance is but the reviving of some past knowledge) that he was once certain of the truth of this proposition, that the three angles of a triangle are equal to two right ones. The immutability of the same relations between the same immutable things, is now the idea that shows him, that if the three angles of a triangle were once equal to two right ones, they will always be equal to two right ones. And hence he comes to be certain, that what was once true in the case, is always true; what ideas once agreed, will always agree; and consequently what he once knew to be true, he will always know to be true; as long as he can remember that he once knew it. Upon this ground it is, that particular demonstrations in mathematics afford general knowledge. If then the perception that the same ideas will eternally have the same habitudes and relations, but not a sufficient ground of knowledge, there could be no knowledge of general propositions in mathematics; for no mathematical demonstration would be any other than particular: And when a man had demonstrated any proposition concerning one triangle or circle, his knowledge would not reach beyond that particular diagram. If he would extend it farther, he must renew his demonstration in another instance, before he could know it to be true in another like triangle, and so on: By which means one could never come to the knowledge of any general propositions. Nobody, I think, can deny that Mr. Newton certainly knows any proposition, that he now at any time reads in his book, to be true; though he has not in actual view that admirable chain of intermediate ideas, whereby he at first discovered it to be true. Such a memory as that, able to retain such a train of particulars, may be well thought beyond the reach of human faculties; when the very discovery, perception, and laying together that wonderful connexion of ideas, is found to surpass most readers' comprehension. But yet it is evident, the author himself knows the proposition to be true, remembering he once saw the connexion of those ideas, as certainly as he knows such a man wounded another, remembering that he saw him run him through. But because the memory is not always so clear as actual perception, and does in all men more or less decay in length of time, this amongst other differences is one, which shows that demonstrative knowledge is much more imperfect than intuitive. . . .

Chapter 2. Of the Degrees of Our Knowledge

1. Intuitive. All our knowledge consisting, as I have said, in the view the mind has of its own ideas, which is the utmost light and greatest certainty we, with our faculties, and in our way of knowledge, are capable of; it may not be amiss to consider a little the degrees of its evidence. The different clearness of our knowledge seems to me to lie in the different way of perception the mind has of the agreement or disagreement of any of its ideas. For if we will reflect on our own ways of thinking, we shall find, that sometimes the mind perceives the agreement or disagreement of two ideas immediately by themselves, without the intervention of any other: And this, I think, we may call intuitive knowledge. For in this the mind is at no pains of proving or examining, but perceives the truth, as the eye doth light, only by being directed towards it. Thus the mind perceives, that white is not black, that a circle is not a triangle, that three are more than two, and equal to one and two. Such kinds of truths the mind perceives at the first sight of the ideas together, by bare intuition, without the intervention of any other idea; and this kind of knowledge is the clearest and most certain, that human frailty is capable of. This part of knowledge is irresistible, and like bright sunshine forces itself immediately to be perceived, as soon as ever the mind turns its view that way; and leaves no room for hesitation, doubt, or examination, but the mind is presently filled with the clear light of it. It is on this intuition that depends all the certainty and evidence of all our knowledge; which certainty every one finds to be so great, that he cannot imagine, and therefore not require a greater: For a man cannot conceive himself capable of a greater certainty, than to know that any idea in his mind is such as he perceives it to be; and that two ideas wherein he perceives a difference, are different and not precisely the same. He that demands a greater certainty than this, demands he knows not what, and shows only that he has a mind to be a skeptic, without being able to be so. Certainty depends so wholly on this intuition, that in the next degree of knowledge, which I call demonstrative, this intuition is necessary in all the connexions of the intermediate ideas, without which we cannot attain knowledge and certainty.

2. Demonstrative. The next degree of knowledge is, where the mind perceives the agreement or disagreement of any ideas, but not immediately. Though wherever the mind perceives the agreement or disagreement of any of its ideas, there be certain knowledge: Yet it does not always happen, that the mind sees that agreement or disagreement which there is between them, even where it is discoverable: And in that case remains in ignorance, and at most gets no farther than a probable conjecture. The reason why the mind cannot always perceive presently the agreement or disagreement of two ideas, is, because those ideas, concerning whose agreement or disagreement the inquiry is made, cannot by the mind be so put together as to show it. In this case then, when the mind cannot so bring its ideas together, as by their immediate comparison, and as it were juxta-position or application one to another, to perceive their agreement or disagreement, it is fain, by the intervention of other ideas (one or more, as it happens) to discover the agreement or disagreement which it searches; and this is that which we call reasoning. Thus the mind being willing to know the agreement or disagreement in bigness, between the three angles of a triangle and two right ones, cannot by an immediate view and comparing them do it: Because the three angles of a triangle cannot be brought at once, and be compared with any other one or two angles; and so of this the mind has no immediate, no intuitive knowledge. In this case the mind is fain to find out some other angles, to which the three angles of a triangle have an equality; and, finding those equal to two right ones, comes to know their equality to two right ones.

3. Depends on Proofs. Those intervening ideas which serve to show the agreement of any two others, are called proofs; and where the agreement and disagreement is by this means plainly and clearly perceived, it is called demonstration, it being shown to the understanding, and the mind made to see that it is so. A quickness in the mind to find out these intermediate ideas (that shall discover the agreement or disagreement of any other) and to apply them right, is, I suppose, that which is called sagacity.

4. But not so easy. This knowledge by intervening proofs, though it be certain, yet the evidence of it is not altogether so clear and bright, nor the assent so ready, as in intuitive knowledge. For though, in demonstration, the mind does at last perceive the agreement or disagreement of the ideas it considers; yet it is not without pains and attention: There must be more than one transient view to find it. A steady application and pursuit are required to this discovery: And there must be a progression by steps and degrees, before the mind can in this way arrive at certainty, and come to perceive the agreement or repugnancy between two ideas that need proofs and the use of reason to show it.

5. Not without precedent doubt. Another difference between intuitive and demonstrative knowledge is, that though in the latter all doubt be removed, when by the intervention of the intermediate ideas the agreement or disagreement is perceived; yet before the demonstration there was a doubt, which in intuitive knowledge cannot happen to the mind, that has its faculty of perception left to a degree capable of distinct ideas, no more than it can be a doubt to the eye (that can distinctly see white and black) whether this ink and this paper be all of a color. If there be sight in the eyes, it will at first glimpse, without hesitation, perceive the words printed on this paper different from the color of the paper: And so if the mind have the faculty of distinct perception, it will perceive the agreement or disagreement of those ideas that produce intuitive knowledge. If the eyes have lost the faculty of seeing, or the mind of perceiving, we in vain inquire after the quickness of sight in one, or clearness of perception in the other.

6. Not so clear. It is true the perception produced by demonstration is also very clear, yet it is often with a great abatement of that evident lustre and full assurance, that always accompany that which I call intuitive; like a face reflected by several mirrors one to another, where as long as it retains the similitude and agreement with the object, it produces a knowledge; but it is still in every successive reflection with a lessening of that perfect clearness and distinctness, which is in the first; till at last, after many removes, it has a great mixture of dimness, and is not at first sight so knowable, especially to weak eyes. Thus it is with knowledge made out by a long train of proof.

7. Each step must have intuitive evidence. Now, in every step reason makes in demonstrative knowledge, there is an intuitive knowledge of that agreement or disagreement it seeks with the next intermediate idea, which it uses as a proof; for if it were not so, that yet would need a proof; since without the perception of such agreement or disagreement, there is no knowledge produced. . . . This intuitive perception of the agreement or disagreement of the intermediate ideas, in each step and progression of the demonstration, must also be carried exactly in the mind, and a man must be sure that no part is left out: Which because in long deductions, and the use of many proofs, the memory does not always so readily and exactly retain; therefore it comes to pass, that this is more imperfect than intuitive knowledge, and men embrace often falsehood for demonstrations. . . .

9. Demonstration not limited to quantity. It has been generally taken for granted, that mathematics alone are capable of demonstrative certainty; but to have such an agreement or disagreement, as may intuitively be perceived, being, as I imagine, not the privilege of the ideas of number, extension, and figure alone, it may possibly be the want of due method and application in us, and not of sufficient evidence in things, that demonstration has been thought to have so little to do in other parts of knowledge, and been scarce so much as aimed at by any but mathematicians. For whatever ideas we have, wherein the mind can perceive the immediate agreement or disagreement that is between them, there the mind is capable of intuitive knowledge; and where it can perceive the agreement or disagreement of any two ides, by an intuitive perception of the agreement or disagreement they have with any intermediate ideas, there the mind is capable of demonstration, which is not limited to ideas of extension, figure, number, and their modes.

10. Why it has been so thought. The reason why it has been generally sought for, and supposed to be only in those, I imagine has been not only the general usefulness of those sciences; but because, in comparing their equality or excess, the modes of numbers have every the least difference very clear and perceivable; and though in extension, every the least excess is not so perceptible, yet the mind has found out ways to examine and discover demonstratively the just equality of two angles, or extensions, or figures: And both these, i.e. numbers and figures, can be set down by visible and lasting marks, wherein the ideas under consideration are perfectly determined; which for the most part they are not, where they are marked only by names and words.

11. Modes of quantity demonstrable, modes of qualities not. But in other simple ideas, whose modes and differences are made and counted by degrees, and not quantity, we have not so nice and accurate a distinction of their differences, as to perceive, or find ways to measure their just equality, or the least differences. For those other simple ideas, being appearances of sensations, produced in us by the size, figure, number, and motion of minute corpuscles singly insensible; their different degrees also depend upon the variation of some, or of all those causes: Which since it cannot be observed by us in particles of matter, whereof each is too subtile to be perceived, it is impossible for us to have any exact measures of the different degrees of these simple ideas. . . .

13. Secondary Qualities not discovered by demonstration. Not knowing therefore what number of particles, nor what motion of them is fit to produce any precise degree of whiteness, we cannot demonstrate the certain equality of any two degrees of whiteness; because we have no certain standard to measure them by, nor means to distinguish every the least real difference, the only help we have being from our senses, which in this point fail us. But where the difference is so great, as to produce in the mind clearly distinct ideas, whose differences can be perfectly retained, there these ideas or colors, as we see in different kinds, as blue and red, are as capable of demonstration, as ideas of number and extension. What I have here said of whiteness and colors, I think, holds true in all secondary qualities, and their modes.

14. Sensitive knowledge of particular existence. These two, viz. intuition and demonstration, are the degrees of our knowledge; whatever comes short of one of these, with what assurance soever embraced, is but faith, or opinion, but not knowledge, at least in all general truths. There is, indeed, another perception of the mind, employed about the particular existence of finite beings without us; which going beyond bare probability, and yet not reaching perfectly to either of the foregoing degrees of certainty, passes under the name of knowledge. There can be nothing more certain, than that the idea we receive from an external object is in our minds; this is intuitive knowledge. But whether there be any thing more than barely that idea in our minds; whether we can thence certainly infer the existence of any thing without us, which corresponds to that idea, is that, hereof some men think there may be a question made; because men may have such ideas in their minds, when no such thing exists, no such object affects their senses. But yet here, I think, we are provided with an evidence, that puts us past doubting: For I ask any one, whether he be not invincibly conscious to himself of a different perception, when he looks on the sun by day, and thinks on it by night; when he actually tastes wormwood, or smells a rose, or only thinks on that savor or odor? We as plainly find the difference there is between any idea revived in our minds by our own memory, and actually coming into our minds by our senses, as we do between any two distinct ideas. If any one say, a dream may do the same thing, and all these ideas may be produced in us without any external objects; he may please to dream that I make him this answer: 1. That it is no great matter, whether I remove his scruple or no: Where all is but dream, reasoning and arguments are of no use, truth and knowledge nothing. 2. That I believe he will allow a very manifest difference between dreaming of being in the fire, and being actually in it. But yet if he be resolved to appear so sceptical, as to maintain, that what I call being actually in the fire is nothing but a dream; and that we cannot thereby certainly know, that any such thing as fire actually exists without us: I answer, that we certainly finding that pleasure or pain follows upon the application of certain objects to us, whose existence we perceive, or dream that we perceive by our senses; this certainty is as great as our happiness or misery, beyond which we have no concernment to know or to be. So that, I think, we may add to the two former sorts of knowledge this also of the existence of particular external objects, by that perception and consciousness we have of the actual entrance of ideas from them, and allow these three degrees of knowledge, viz. intuitive, demonstrative, and sensitive: In each of which there are different degrees and ways of evidence and certainty.

Chapter 3. Of the Extent of Human Knowledge

1. Extent of our knowledge. Knowledge, as has been said, lying in the perception of the agreement or disagreement of any of our ideas, it follows from hence, That,

First, we can have knowledge no farther than we have ideas.

2. Not farther than we have ideas. Secondly, that we can have no knowledge farther than we can have perceptions of that agreement or disagreement. Which perception being, 1. Either by intuition, or the immediate comparing any two ideas; or, 2. By reason, examining the agreement or disagreement of two ideas, by the intervention of some others; or, 3.

By sensation, perceiving the existence of particular things: Hence it also follows,

3. Intuitive knowledge extends itself not to all the relations of all our ideas. Thirdly, that we cannot have an intuitive knowledge, that shall extend itself to all our ideas, and all that we would know about them; because we cannot examine and perceive all the relations they have one to another by juxta-position, or an immediate comparison one with another. Thus having the ideas of an obtuse and an acute angled triangle, both drawn from equal bases, and between parallels, I can, by intuitive knowledge, perceive the one not to be the other, but cannot that way know whether they be equal or no; because their agreement or disagreement in equality can never be perceived by an immediate comparing them: The difference of figure makes their parts incapable of an exact immediate application; and therefore there is need of some intervening quantities to measure them by, which is demonstration, or rational knowledge.

4. Nor demonstrative knowledge. Fourthly, it follows also, from what is above observed, that our rational knowledge cannot reach to the whole extent of our ideas: Because between two different ideas we would examine, we cannot always find such mediums, as we can connect one to another with an intuitive knowledge, in all the parts of the deduction; and wherever that fails, we come short of knowledge and demonstration.

5. Sensitive knowledge narrower than either. Fifthly, sensitive knowledge reaching no farther than the existence of things actually present to our senses, is yet much narrower than either of the former.

6. Our knowledge, therefore, narrower than either. From all which it is evident, that the extent of our knowledge comes not only short of the reality of things, but even of the extent of our own ideas. Though our knowledge be limited to our ideas, and cannot exceed them either in extent or perfection; and though these be very narrow bounds, in respect of the extent of all being, and far short of what we may justly imagine to be in some even created understandings, not tied down to the dull and narrow information, is to be received from some few, and not very acute ways of perception, such as are our senses; yet it would be well with us if our knowledge were but as large as our ideas, and there were not many doubts and inquiries concerning the ideas we have, whereof we are not, nor I believe ever shall be in this world resolved. Nevertheless I do not question but that human knowledge, under the present circumstances of our beings and constitutions, may be carried much farther than it has hitherto been, if men would sincerely, and with freedom of mind, employ all that industry and labour of thought, in improving the means of discovering truth, which they do for the coloring or support of falsehood, to maintain a system, interest, or party, they are once engaged in. But yet after all, I think I may, without injury to human perfection, be confident, that our knowledge would never reach to all we might desire to know concerning those ideas we have: Nor be able to surmount all the difficulties, and resolve all the questions that might arise concerning any of them. We have the ideas of a square, a circle, and equality; and yet, perhaps, shall never be able to find a circle equal to a square, and certainly know that it is so. We have the ideas of matter and thinking, but possibly shall never be able to know, whether any mere material being thinks, or no; it being impossible for us, by the contemplation of our own ideas, without revelation, to discover, whether omnipotency has not given to some systems of matter fitly disposed, a power to perceive and think, or else joined and fixed to matter so disposed a thinking immaterial substance: It being, in respect of our notions, not much more remote from our comprehension to conceive, that God can, if he pleases, superadd to matter a faculty of thinking, than that he should superadd to it another substance with a faculty of thinking; since we know not wherein thinking consists, nor to what sort of substances the Almighty has been pleased to give that power, which cannot be in any created being, but merely by the good pleasure and bounty of the Creator. For I see no contradiction in it, that the first eternal thinking Being or omnipotent Spirit should, if he pleased, give to certain systems of created senseless matter, put together as he thinks fit, some degrees of sense, perception, and thought: Though, as I think, I have proved, lib. iv. ch. 10, sec. 14, &c. it is no less than a contradiction to suppose matter (which is evidently in its own nature void of sense and thought) should be that eternal first-thinking being. What certainty of knowledge can any one have that some perceptions, such as, v.g. pleasure and pain, should not be in some bodies themselves, after a certain manner modified and moved, as well as that they should be in an immaterial substance, upon the motion of the parts of body? Body, as far as we can conceive, being able only to strike and affect body; and motion, according to the utmost reach of our ideas, being able to produce nothing but motion: So that when we allow it to produce pleasure or pain, or the idea of a color or sound, we are fain to quit our reason, go beyond our ideas, and attribute it wholly to the good pleasure of our Maker. For since we must allow he has annexed effects to motion, which we can no way conceive motion able to produce, what reason have we to conclude that he could not order them as well to be produced in a subject we cannot conceive capable of them, as well as in a subject we cannot conceive the motion of matter can any way operate upon? I say not this, that I would any way lessen the belief of the soul's immateriality: I am not here speaking of probability, but knowledge; and I think not only, that it becomes the modesty of philosophy not to pronounce magisterially, where we want that evidence that can produce knowledge; but also, that it is of use to us to discern how far our knowledge does reach; for the state we are at present in, not being that of vision, we must, in many things, content ourselves with faith and probability; and in the present question, about the immateriality of the soul, if our faculties cannot arrive at demonstrative certainty, we need not think it strange. All the great ends of morality and religion are well enough secured, without philosophical proofs of the soul's immateriality; since it is evident, that he who made us at the beginning to subsist here, sensible intelligent beings, and for several years continued us in such a state, can and will restore us to the like state of sensibility in another world, and make us capable there to receive the retribution he has designed to men, according to their doings in this life. And therefore it is not of such mighty necessity to determine one way or the other, as some, over-zealous for or against the immateriality of the soul, have been forward to make the world believe. Who, either on the one side, indulging too much their thoughts, immersed altogether in matter, can allow no existence to what is not material: Or who, on the other side, finding not cogitation within the natural powers of matter, examined over and over again by the utmost intention of mind, have the confidence to conclude, that omnipotency itself cannot give perception and thought to a substance which has the modification of solidity. He that considers how hardly sensation is, in our thoughts, reconcilable to extended matter; or existence to any thing that hath no extension at all; will confess that he is very far from certainly knowing what his soul is. It is a point which seems to me to be put out of the reach of our knowledge: And he who will give himself leave to consider freely, and look into the dark and intricate part of each hypothesis, will scarce find his reason able to determine him fixedly for or against the soul's materiality. Since on which side soever he views it, either as an unextended substance, or as a thinking extended matter; the difficulty to conceive either will, whilst either alone is in his thoughts, still drive him to the contrary side. An unfair way which some men take with themselves; who, because of the inconceivableness of something they find in one, throw themselves violently into the contrary hypothesis, though altogether as unintelligible to an unbiased understanding. This serves not only to shew the weakness and the scantiness of our knowledge, but the insignificant triumph of such sort of arguments, which, drawn from our own views, may satisfy us that we can find no certainty on one side of the question; but do not at all thereby help us to truth by running into the opposite opinion, which, on examination, will be found clogged with equal difficulties. For what safety, what advantage to any one is it, for the avoiding the seeming absurdities, and to him unsurmountable rubs he meets with in one opinion, to take refuge in the contrary, which is built on something altogether as inexplicable, and as far remote from his comprehension? It is past controversy, that we have in us something that thinks; our very doubts about what it is confirm the certainty of its being, though we must content ourselves in the ignorance of what kind of being it is: And it is in vain to go about to be sceptical in this, as it is unreasonable in most other cases to be positive against the being of any thing, because we cannot comprehend its nature. For I would fain know what substance exists, that has not something in it which manifestly baffles our understandings. Other spirits, who see and know the nature and inward constitution of things, how much must they exceed us in knowledge? To which if we add larger comprehension, which enables them at one glance to see the connexion and agreement of very many ideas, and readily supplies to them the intermediate proofs, which we by single and slow steps, and long poring in the dark, hardly at last find out, and are often ready to forget one before we have hunted out another: We may guess at some part of the happiness of superior ranks of spirits, who have a quicker and more penetrating sight, as well as a larger field of knowledge. But to return to the argument in hand; our knowledge, I say, is not only limited to the paucity and imperfections of the ideas we have, and which we employ it about, but even comes short of that too.

Chapter 11. Of Our Knowledge of the Existence of Other Things

1. Is to be had only by sensation. The knowledge of our own being we have by intuition. The existence of a God reason clearly makes known to us, as has been shown.

The knowledge of the existence of any other thing, we can have only by sensation: For there being no necessary connexion of real existence with any idea a man hath in his memory, nor of any other existence but that of God, with the existence of any particular man; no particular man can know the existence of any other being, but only when by actual operating upon him, it makes itself perceived by him. For the having the idea of any thing in our mind, no more proves the existence of that thing, than the picture of a man evidences his being in the world, or the visions of a dream make thereby a true history.

2. Instance, whiteness of this paper. It is therefore the actual receiving of ideas from without, that gives us notice of the existence of other things, and makes us know that something doth exist at that time without us, which causes that idea in us, though perhaps we neither know nor consider how it does it: For it takes not from the certainty of our senses, and the ideas we receive by them, that we know not the manner wherein they are produced: V.g. whilst I write this, I have, by the paper affecting my eyes, that idea produced in my mind, which whatever object causes, I call white; by which I know that that quality or accident (i.e. whose appearance before my eyes always causes that idea) doth really exist, and hath a being without me. And of this, the greatest assurance I can possibly have, and to which my faculties can attain, is the testimony of my eyes, which are the proper and sole judges of this thing, whose testimony I have reason to rely on as so certain, that I can no more doubt, whilst I write this, that I see white and black, and that something really exists, that causes that sensation in me, than that I write or move my hand; which is a certainty as great as human nature is capable of, concerning the existence of any thing, but a man's self alone, and of God.

3. This, though not so certain as demonstration, yet may be called knowledge, and proves the existence of things without us. The notice we have by our senses, of the existing of things without us, though it be not altogether so certain as our intuitive knowledge, or the deductions of our reason employed about the clear abstract ideas of our own minds; yet it is an assurance that deserves the name of knowledge. If we persuade ourselves, that our faculties act and inform us right, concerning the existence of those objects that affect them, it cannot pass for an ill-grounded confidence: For I think nobody can, in earnest, be so sceptical, as to be uncertain of the existence of those things which he sees and feels. At least, he that can doubt so far (whatever he may have with his own thoughts) will never have any controversy with me; since he can never be sure I say any thing contrary to his own opinion. As to myself, I think God has given me assurance enough of the existence of things without me; since by their different application I can produce in myself both pleasure and pain, which is one great concernment of my present state. This is certain; the confidence that our faculties do not herein deceive us is the greatest assurance we are capable of, concerning the existence of material beings. For we cannot act any thing but by our faculties; nor talk of knowledge itself, but by the help of those faculties, which are fitted to apprehend even what knowledge is. But besides the assurance we have from our senses themselves, that they do not err in the information they give us, of the existence of things without us, when they are affected by them, we are farther confirmed in this assurance by other concurrent reasons.

4. Because we cannot have them but by the inlets of the senses. First, it is plain those perceptions are produced in us by exterior causes affecting our senses; because those that want the organs of any sense, never can have the ideas belonging to that sense produced in their minds. This is too evident to be doubted: And therefore we cannot but be assured, that they come in by the organs of that sense, and no other way. The organs themselves, it is plain, do not produce them, for then the eyes of a man in the dark would produce colors, and his nose smell roses in the winter: But we see nobody gets the relish of a pine-apple, till he goes to the Indies, where it is, and tastes it.

5. Because an idea from actual sensation, and another from memory, are very distinct perceptions. Secondly, because sometimes I find, that I cannot avoid the having those ideas produced in my mind. For though when my eyes are shut, or windows fast, I can at pleasure recall to my mind the ideas of light, or the sun, which former sensations had lodged in my memory; so I can at pleasure lay by that idea, and take into my view that of the smell of a rose, or taste of sugar. But, if I turn my eyes at noon towards the sun, I cannot avoid the ideas, which the light, or sun, then produces in me. So that there is a manifest difference between the ideas laid up in my memory, (over which, if they were there only, I should have constantly the same power to dispose of them, and lay them by at pleasure) and those which force themselves upon me, and I cannot avoid having. And therefore it must needs be some exterior cause, and the brisk acting of some objects without me, whose efficacy I cannot resist, that produces those ideas in my mind, whether I will or no. Besides, there is nobody who doth not perceive the difference in himself between contemplating the sun, as he hath the idea of it in his memory, and actually looking upon it: Of which two, his perception is so distinct, that few of his ideas are more distinguishable one from another. And therefore he hath certain knowledge that they are not both memory, or the actions of his mind, and fancies only within him; but that actual seeing hath a cause without.

6. Pleasure and Pain, which accompanies actual sensation, accompanies not the returning of those ideas, without the external objects. Thirdly, add to this, that many of those ideas are produced in us with pain, which afterwards we remember without the least offence. Thus the pain of heat or cold, when the idea of it is revived in our minds, gives us no disturbance; which, when felt, was very troublesome, and is again, when actually repeated; which is occasioned by the disorder the external object causes in our bodies when applied to it. And we remember the pains of hunger, thirst, or the headache, without any pain at all; which would either never disturb us, or else constantly do it, as often as we thought of it, were there nothing more but ideas floating in our minds, and appearances entertaining our fancies, without the real existence of things affecting us from abroad. The same may be said of pleasure, accompanying several actual sensations: And though mathematical demonstration depends not upon sense, yet the examining them by diagrams gives great credit to the evidence of our sight, and seems to give it a certainty approaching to that of demonstration itself. For it would be very strange, that a man should allow it for an undeniable truth, that two angles of a figure, which he measures by lines and angles of a diagram, should be bigger one than the other; and yet doubt of the existence of those lines and angles, which by looking on he makes use of to measure that by.

7. Our senses assist one another's testimony of the existence of outward things. Fourthly, our senses in many cases bear witness to the truth of each other's report, concerning the existence of sensible things without us. He that sees a fire, may, if he doubt whether it be any thing more than a bare fancy, feel it too; and be convinced by putting his hand in it. Which certainly could never be put into such exquisite pain, by a bare idea or phantom, unless that the pain be a fancy too: Which yet he cannot, when the burn is well, by raising the idea of it, bring upon himself again.

Thus I see, whilst I write this, I can change the appearance of the paper: And by designing the letters tell before-hand what new idea it shall exhibit the very next moment, by barely drawing my pen over it: Which will neither appear (let me fancy as much as I will) if my hands stand still; or though I move my pen, if my eyes be shut: Nor when those characters are once made on the paper, can I choose afterwards but see them as they are; that is, have the ideas of such letters as I have made. Whence it is manifest, that they are not barely the sport and play of my own imagination, when I find that the characters, that were made at the pleasure of my own thoughts, do not obey them; nor yet cease to be, whenever I shall fancy it; but continue to affect my senses constantly and regularly, according to the figures I made them. To which if we will add, that the sight of those shall, from another man, draw such sounds, as I beforehand design they shall stand for; there will be little reason left to doubt, that those words I write do really exist without me, when they cause a long series of regular sounds to affect my ears, which could not be the effect of my imagination, nor could my memory retain them in that order.

8. This certainty is as great as our condition needs. But yet, if after all this any one will be so sceptical, as to distrust his senses, and to affirm that all we see and hear, feel and taste, think and do, during our whole being, is but the series and deluding appearances of a long dream, whereof there is no reality; and therefore will question the existence of all things, or our knowledge of any thing; I must desire him to consider, that if all be a dream, then he doth but dream, that he makes the question; and so it is not much matter, that a waking man should answer him. But yet, if he pleases, he may dream that I make him this answer, that the certainty of things existing in rerum natura, when we have the testimony of our senses for it, is not only as great as our frame can attain to, but as our condition needs. For our faculties being suited not to the full extent of being, nor to a perfect, clear, comprehensive knowledge of things free from all doubt and scruple; but to the preservation of us, in whom they are; and accommodated to the use of life; they serve to our purpose well enough, if they will but give us certain notice of those things, which are convenient or inconvenient to us. For he that sees a candle burning, and hath experimented the force of its flame, by putting his finger in it, will little doubt that this is something existing without him, which does him harm, and puts him to great pain: Which is assurance enough, when no man requires greater certainty to govern his actions by, than what is as certain as his actions themselves. And if our dreamer pleases to try, whether the glowing heat of a glass furnace be barely a wandering imagination in a drowsy man's fancy; by putting his hand into it, he may perhaps be wakened into a certainty greater than he could wish, that it is something more than bare imagination. So that this evidence is as great as we can desire, being as certain to us as our pleasure or pain, i.e. happiness or misery; beyond which we have no concernment, either of knowing or being. Such an assurance of the existence of things without us is sufficient to direct us in the attaining the good, and avoiding the evil, which is caused by them; which is the important concernment we have of being made acquainted with them.

9. But reaches no farther than actual sensation. In fine then, when our senses do actually convey into our understandings any idea, we cannot but be satisfied that there doth something at that time really exist without us, which doth affect our senses, and by them give notice of itself to our apprehensive faculties, and actually produce that idea which we then perceive: And we cannot so far distrust their testimony, as to doubt, that such collections of simple ideas, as we have observed by our senses to be united together, do really exist together. But this knowledge extends as far as the present testimony of our senses, employed about particular objects that do then affect them, and no farther. For if I saw such a collection of simple ideas, as is wont to be called man, existing together one minute since, and am now alone, I cannot be certain that the same man exists now, since there is no necessary connexion of his existence a minute since, with his existence now: By a thousand ways he may cease to be, since I had the testimony of my senses for his existence. And if I cannot be certain, that the man I saw last to-day is now in being, I can less be certain that he is so, who hath been longer removed from my senses, and I have not seen since yesterday, or since the last year; and much less can I be certain of the existence of men that I never saw. And therefore though it be highly probable, that millions of men do now exist, yet, whilst I am alone writing this, I have not that certainty of it which we strictly call knowledge; though the great likelihood of it puts me past doubt, and it be reasonable for me to do several things upon the confidence that there are men (and men also of my acquaintance, with whom I have to do) now in the world: But this is but probability, not knowledge.

10. Folly to expect demonstration in every thing. Whereby yet we may observe, how foolish and vain a thing it is, for a man of a narrow knowledge, who having reason given him to judge of the different evidence and probability of things, and to be swayed accordingly; how vain, I say, it is to expect demonstration and certainty in things not capable of it; and refuse assent to very rational propositions, and act contrary to very plain and clear truths, because they cannot be made out so evident, as to surmount every the least (I will not say reason, but) pretence of doubting. He that in the ordinary affairs of life would admit of nothing but direct plain demonstration, would be sure of nothing in this world, but of perishing quickly. The wholesomeness of his meat or drink would not give him reason to venture on it: And I would fain know, what it is he could do upon such grounds, as are capable of no doubt, no objection.

Chapter 21

George Berkeley

George Berkeley (1685–1753), an Irish philosopher and Anglican bishop, was educated at Trinity College, Dublin, where he subsequently taught. There he wrote *An Essay Towards a New Theory of Vision* (1709), *A Treatise Concerning the Principles of Human Knowledge* (1710), and *Three Dialogues Between Hylas and Philonous* (1713) from which the present selection is taken. At this time he became an Anglican priest and moved to London. In the 1720s he helped plan a college in Bermuda for sons of settlers and native Americans. In 1728 he married Anne Forster and sailed to Newport, Rhode Island, where he waited for promised government support for the college. It never came, and the college was never established. In 1731 he returned to London, where he wrote *The Theory of Vision* (1733). From 1734 to 1752 he served as Bishop of Cloyne, Ireland. A deeply committed Christian, he sought to reconcile science with his faith by proving that matter does not exist, and that the laws of physics, being God's laws, govern a universe made up of ideas.

Berkeley's fame rests on his development of a type of Idealism, better called "ideaism" or "Immaterialism," and for his incisive critique of Locke's Representationalism. It should be noted that Berkeley's Idealism is different from traditional idealism (e.g., Plato's), in that it is not rationalistic. It does not adhere to independently existing ideas, but rather it assumes an empirical foundation. It agrees with Locke that all ideas originate in sense experience, and proceeds to show that all we ever experience is ideas, our sensations or sense perceptions. The only reality there is to be known is perceivers and perceptions.

Concerning Locke's theory of knowledge, Berkeley argued, first, that the primary/secondary qualities distinction was exceedingly weak. The primary qualities are no more "in" the objects of perception than the secondary ones. Second, he argued that there were logical problems in the theory that our perceptions resembled physical objects ("an idea can be like nothing but an idea"). Third, he undermined the whole notion of substance which Locke needed to maintain his theory. What is the difference, Berkeley rhetorically asked, between a "something I know not what" (Locke's notion of substance) and nothing at all? Ultimately, Locke's Representationalism leads back to skepticism. Finally, Locke's theory was an explanatory failure. Locke asserted that ideas in the Mind were caused by mechanical actions upon our sense organs and brains. But Berkeley pointed out that this fails to explain mental events both in detail and principle: in *detail* because it was impossible to explain why a certain physical event should produce certain but quite different (in character) mental states (e.g., light waves producing the color red); in *principle* because the whole notion of dualistic interactionism was incoherent, misusing the notion of "cause." A cause makes something happen, but for this you need a notion of a WILL, agency—all causation is agent causation, but events in Nature do not make other events happen. One sees only two events in temporal succession—with regularity. But this only signals the reality of a cause; it is not the cause, for it is not an agent and exerts no will.

Berkeley held that there were only two realities: minds and mental events; ideas exist in the mind alone. All qualities are essentially secondary and have their reality by being perceived (*esse est percipi*—"To be is to be perceived."). There is no material world. Physical objects are simply mental events. "The table I write on exists, that is, I see and feel it; and if I were out of my study I should say it existed—meaning thereby that if I was in my study I might perceive it, or that some other spirit actually perceives it." All physical objects are mental phenomena that would cease to exist if they were not perceived. Why do physical objects continue to exist when no one is perceiving them? What happens to them when we are not looking at trees or mountains? Do they cease to be? No, someone is always perceiving them. God's eye keeps the world from dissolving.

There was a young man who said, "God
Must think it exceedingly odd
If he finds that this tree
Continues to be,
While there's no one about in the quad."

Dear Sir, your astonishment's odd
I'm always about in the quad,
And that's why the tree
Continues to be,
Since observed by,

Yours faithfully,

God

FOR FURTHER READING

Bennett, Jonathan. *Locke, Berkeley and Hume: Central Themes.* (Oxford University Press, 1971).
Luce, A. A. *The Dialectic of Immaterialism: An Account of the Making of Berkeley's Principles* (Hodder and Stoughton, 1963).
Martin, C. B. and D. M. Armstrong, eds. *Locke and Berkeley: A Collection of Critical Essays.* (Doubleday, 1968).
Muehlmann, Robert. *Berkeley's Ontology.* (Hackett Publishing Co., 1992).
Pitcher, George. *Berkeley.* (Routledge & Kegan Paul, 1977).
Turbayne, Colin, ed. *Berkeley: Critical and Interpretive Essays.* (University of Minnesota Press, 1987).
Urmson, J. O. *Berkeley.* (Oxford University Press, 1982).
Warnock, G. J. *Berkeley.* (Penguin Books, 1953).
Winkler, Kenneth. *Berkeley: The Philosophy of Immaterialism.* (Oxford University Press, 1989).

Three Dialogues Between Hylas and Philonous in Opposition to Sceptics and Atheists

THE FIRST DIALOGUE

PHILONOUS: Good morrow, Hylas: I did not expect to find you abroad so early.

HYLAS: It is indeed something unusual: but my thoughts were so taken up with a subject I was discoursing of last night, that finding I could not sleep, I resolved to rise and take a turn in the garden.

PHIL: It happened well, to let you see what innocent and agreeable pleasures you lose every morning. Can there be a pleasanter time of the day, or a more delightful season of the year? That purple sky, those wild but sweet notes of birds, the fragrant bloom upon the trees and flowers, the gentle influence of the rising sun, these and a thousand nameless beauties of nature inspire the soul with secret transports; its faculties too being at this time fresh and lively, are fit for these meditations, which the solitude of a garden and tranquillity of the morning naturally dispose us to. But I am afraid I interrupt your thoughts; for you seemed very intent on something.

HYL: It is true, I was, and shall be obliged to you if you will permit me to go on in the same vein; not that I would by any means deprive myself of your company, for my thoughts always flow more easily in conversation with a friend, than when I am alone: but my request is, that you would suffer me to impart my reflections to you.

PHIL: With all my heart, it is what I should have requested myself, if you had not prevented me.

HYL: I was considering the odd fate of those men who have in all ages, through an affectation of being distinguished from the vulgar, or some unaccountable turn of thought, pretended either to believe nothing at all, or to believe the most extravagant things in the world. This however might be borne, if their paradoxes and scepticism did not draw after them some consequences of general disadvantage to mankind. But the mischief lieth here; that when men of less leisure see them who are supposed to have spent their whole time in the pursuits of knowledge, professing an entire ignorance of all things, or advancing such notions as are repugnant to plain and commonly received principles, they will be tempted to entertain suspicions concerning the most important truths, which they had hitherto held sacred and unquestionable.

PHIL: I entirely agree with you, as to the ill tendency of the affected doubts of some philosophers, and fantastical conceits of others. I am even so far gone of late in this way of thinking, that I have quitted several of the sublime notions I had got in their schools for vulgar opinions. And I give it you on my word, since this revolt from metaphysical notions to the plain dictates of nature and common sense, I find my understanding strangely enlightened, so that I can now easily comprehend a great many things which before were all mystery and riddle.

HYL: I am glad to find there was nothing in the accounts I heard of you.

PHIL: Pray, what were those?

HYL: You were represented in last night's conversation, as one who maintained the most extravagant opinion that ever entered into the mind of man, to wit, that there is no such thing as material substance in the world.

PHIL: That there is no such thing as what philosophers call material substance, I am seriously persuaded: but if I were made to see any thing absurd or sceptical in this, I should then have the same reason to renounce this, that I imagine I have now to reject the contrary opinion.

HYL: What! can any thing be more fantastical, more repugnant to common sense, or a more manifest piece of scepticism, than to believe there is no such thing as matter?

PHIL: Softly, good Hylas. What if it should prove, that you who hold there is, are by virtue of that opinion a greater sceptic, and maintain more paradoxes and repugnancies to common sense, than I who believe no such thing?

HYL: You may as soon persuade me, the part is greater than the whole, as that, in order to avoid absurdity and scepticism, I should ever be obliged to give up my opinion in this point.

PHIL: Well then, are you content to admit that opinion for true, which upon examination shall appear most agreeable to common sense, and remote from scepticism?

HYL: With all my heart. Since you are for raising disputes about the plainest things in nature, I am content for once to hear what you have to say.

PHIL: Pray, Hylas, what do you mean by a sceptic?

HYL: I mean what all men mean, one that doubts of every thing.

PHIL: He then who entertains no doubt concerning some particular point, with regard to that point cannot be thought a sceptic.

HYL: I agree with you.

PHIL: Whether doth doubting consist in embracing the affirmative or negative side of a question?

HYL: In neither; for whoever understands English, cannot but know that doubting signifies a suspense between both.

PHIL: He then that denieth any point, can no more be said to doubt of it than he who affirmeth it with the same degree of assurance.

HYL: True.

PHIL: And consequently, for such his denial is no more to be esteemed a sceptic than the other.

HYL: I acknowledge it.

PHIL: How cometh it to pass then, Hylas, that you pronounce me a sceptic, because I deny what you affirm, to wit, the existence of matter? Since, for ought you can tell, I am as peremptory in my denial, as you in your affirmation.

HYL: Hold, Philonous, I have been a little out in my definition; but every false step a man makes in discourse is not to be insisted on. I said, indeed, that a sceptic was one who doubted of every thing; but I should have added, or who denies the reality and truth of things.

PHIL: What things? Do you mean the principles and theorems of sciences? but these you know are universal intellectual notions, and consequently independent of matter; the denial therefore of this doth not imply the denying them.

HYL: I grant it. But are there no other things? What think you of distrusting the senses, of denying the real existence of sensible things, or pretending to know nothing of them? Is not this sufficient to denominate a man a sceptic?

PHIL: Shall we therefore examine which of us it is that denies the reality of sensible things, or professes the greatest ignorance of them; since, if I take you rightly, he is to be esteemed the greatest sceptic?

HYL: That is what I desire.

PHIL: What mean you by sensible things?

HYL: Those things which are perceived by the senses. Can you imagine that I mean any thing else?

PHIL: Pardon me, Hylas, if I am desirous clearly to apprehend your notions, since this may much shorten our inquiry. Suffer me then to ask you this further question. Are those things only perceived by the senses which are perceived immediately? or may those things properly be said to be sensible, which are perceived mediately, or not without the intervention of others?

HYL: I do not sufficiently understand you.

PHIL: In reading a book, what I immediately perceive are the letters, but mediately, or by means of these, are suggested to my mind the notions of God, virtue, truth &c. Now that the letters are truly sensible things, or perceived by sense, there is no doubt: but I would know whether you take the things suggested by them to be so too.

HYL: No, certainly, it were absurd to think God or virtue sensible things, though they may be signified and suggested to the mind by sensible marks, with which they have an arbitrary connexion.

PHIL: It seems then, that by sensible things you mean those only which can be perceived immediately by sense.

HYL: Right.

PHIL: Doth it not follow from this, that though I see one part of the sky red, and another blue, and that my reason doth thence evidently conclude there must be some cause of that diversity of colours, yet that cause cannot be said to be a sensible thing, or perceived by the sense of seeing?

HYL: It doth.

PHIL: In like manner, though I hear variety of sounds, yet I cannot be said to hear the causes of those sounds.

HYL: You cannot.

PHIL: And when by my touch I perceive a thing to be hot and heavy, I cannot say with any truth or propriety, that I feel the cause of its heat or weight.

HYL: To prevent any more questions of this kind, I tell you once for all, that by sensible things I mean those only which are perceived by sense, and that in truth the senses perceive nothing which they do not perceive immediately: for they make no inferences. The deducing therefore of causes or occasions from effects and appearances, which alone are perceived by sense, entirely relates to reason.

PHIL: This point then is agreed between us, that

sensible things are those only which are immediately perceived by sense. You will further inform me, whether we immediately perceive by sight any thing beside light, and colours, and figures: or by hearing any thing but sounds: by the palate, any thing besides tastes: by the smell, besides odours: or by the touch, more than tangible qualities.

HYL: We do not.

PHIL: It seems therefore, that if you take away all sensible qualities, there remains nothing sensible.

HYL: I grant it.

PHIL: Sensible things therefore are nothing else but so many sensible qualities, or combinations of sensible qualities.

HYL: Nothing else.

PHIL: Heat then is a sensible thing.

HYL: Certainly.

PHIL: Doth the reality of sensible things consist in being perceived? or, is it something distinct from their being perceived, and that bears no relation to the mind?

HYL: To exist is one thing, and to be perceived is another.

PHIL: I speak with regard to sensible things only; and of these I ask, whether by their real existence you mean a subsistence exterior to the mind, and distinct from their being perceived?

HYL: I mean a real absolute being, distinct from, and without any relation to their being perceived.

PHIL: Heat therefore, if it be allowed a real being, must exist without the mind.

HYL: It must.

PHIL: Tell me, Hylas, is this real existence equally compatible to all degrees of heat, which we perceive: or is there any reason why we should attribute it to some, and deny it others? and if there be, pray let me know that reason.

HYL: Whatever degree of heat we perceive by sense, we may be sure the same exists in the object that occasions it.

PHIL: What, the greatest as well as the least?

HYL: I tell you, the reason is plainly the same in respect of both: they are both perceived by sense; nay, the greater degree of heat is more sensibly perceived; and consequently, if there is any difference, we are more certain of its real existence than we can be of the reality of a lesser degree.

PHIL: But is not the most vehement and intense degree of heat a very great pain?

HYL: No one can deny it.

PHIL: And is any unperceiving thing capable of pain or pleasure?

HYL: No certainly.

PHIL: Is your material substance a senseless being, or a being endowed with sense and perception?

HYL: It is senseless without doubt.

PHIL: It cannot therefore be the subject of pain.

HYL: By no means.

PHIL: Nor consequently of the greatest heat perceived by sense, since you acknowledge this to be no small pain.

HYL: I grant it.

PHIL: What shall we say then of your external object; is it a material substance, or no?

HYL: It is a material substance with the sensible qualities inhering in it.

PHIL: How then can a great heat exist in it, since you own it cannot in a material substance? I desire you would clear this point.

HYL: Hold, Philonous; I fear I was out in yielding intense heat to be a pain. It should seem rather, that pain is something distinct from heat, and the consequence or effect of it.

PHIL: Upon putting your hand near the fire, do you perceive one simple uniform sensation, or two distinct sensations?

HYL: But one simple sensation.

PHIL: Is not the heat immediately perceived?

HYL: It is.

PHIL: And the pain?

HYL: True.

PHIL: Seeing therefore they are both immediately perceived at the same time, and the fire affects you only with one simple, or uncompounded idea, it follows that this same simple idea is both the intense heat immediately perceived, and the pain; and consequently, that the intense heat immediately perceived, is nothing distinct from a particular sort of pain.

HYL: It seems so.

PHIL: Again, try in your thoughts, Hylas, if you can conceive a vehement sensation to be without pain, or pleasure.

HYL: I cannot.

PHIL: Or can you frame to yourself an idea of sensible pain or pleasure in general, abstracted from every particular idea of heat, cold, tastes, smells, &c.?

HYL: I do not find that I can.

PHIL: Doth it not therefore follow, that sensible

pain is nothing distinct from those sensations or ideas, in an intense degree?

HYL: It is undeniable; and to speak the truth, I begin to suspect a very great heat cannot exist but in a mind perceiving it.

PHIL: What! are you then in that sceptical state of suspense, between affirming and denying?

HYL: I think I may be positive in the point. A very violent and painful heat cannot exist without the mind.

PHIL: It hath not therefore, according to you, any real being.

HYL: I own it.

PHIL: Is it therefore certain, that there is no body in nature really hot?

HYL: I have not denied there is any real heat in bodies. I only say, there is no such thing as an intense real heat.

PHIL: But did you not say before, that all degrees of heat were equally real: or if there was any difference, that the greater were more undoubtedly real than the lesser?

HYL: True: but it was, because I did not then consider the ground there is for distinguishing between them, which I now plainly see. And it is this: because intense heat is nothing else but a particular kind of painful sensation; and pain cannot exist but in a perceiving being; it follows that no intense heat can really exist in an unperceiving corporeal substance. But this is no reason why we should deny heat in an inferior degree to exist in such a substance.

PHIL: But how shall we be able to discern those degrees of heat which exist only in the mind, from those which exist without it?

HYL: That is no difficult matter. You know, the least pain cannot exist unperceived; whatever therefore degree of heat is a pain, exists only in the mind. But as for all other degrees of heat, nothing obliges us to think the same of them.

PHIL: I think you granted before, that no unperceiving being was capable of pleasure, any more than of pain.

HYL: I did.

PHIL: And is not warmth, or a more gentle degree of heat than what causes uneasiness, a pleasure?

HYL: What then?

PHIL: Consequently it cannot exist without the mind in any unperceiving substance, or body.

HYL: So it seems.

PHIL: Since therefore, as well those degrees of heat that are not painful, as those that are, can exist only in a thinking substance; may we not conclude that external bodies are absolutely incapable of any degree of heat whatsoever?

HYL: On second thoughts, I do not think it so evident that warmth is a pleasure, as that a great degree of heat is a pain.

PHIL: I do not pretend that warmth is as great a pleasure as heat is a pain. But if you grant it to be even a small pleasure, it serves to make good my conclusion.

HYL: I could rather call it an indolence. It seems to be nothing more than a privation of both pain and pleasure. And that such a quality or state as this may agree to an unthinking substance, I hope you will not deny.

PHIL: If you are resolved to maintain that warmth, or a gentle degree of heat, is no pleasure, I know not how to convince you otherwise, than by appealing to your own sense. But what think you of cold?

HYL: The same that I do of heat. An intense degree of cold is a pain; for to feel a very great cold, is to perceive a great uneasiness: it cannot therefore exist without the mind; but a lesser degree of cold may, as well as a lesser degree of heat.

PHIL: Those bodies therefore, upon whose application to our own we perceive a moderate degree of heat, must be concluded to have a moderate degree of heat or warmth in them: and those, upon whose application we feel a like degree of cold, must be thought to have cold in them.

HYL: They must.

PHIL: Can any doctrine be true that necessarily leads a man into an absurdity?

HYL: Without doubt it cannot.

PHIL: Is it not an absurdity to think that the same thing should be at the same time both cold and warm?

HYL: It is.

PHIL: Suppose now one of your hands hot, and the other cold, and that they are both at once put into the same vessel of water, in an intermediate state; will not the water seem cold to one hand, and warm to the other?

HYL: It will.

PHIL: Ought we not therefore by your principles to conclude, it is really both cold and warm at the same time, that is, according to your own concession, to believe an absurdity?

HYL: I confess it seems so.

PHIL: Consequently, the principles themselves are false, since you have granted that no true principle leads to an absurdity.

HYL: But after all, can any thing be more absurd than to say, there is no heat in the fire?

PHIL: To make the point still clearer; tell me, whether in two cases exactly alike, we ought not to make the same judgment?

HYL: We ought.

PHIL: When a pin pricks your finger, doth it not rend and divide the fibres of your flesh?

HYL: It doth.

PHIL: And when a coal burns your finger, doth it any more?

HYL: It doth not.

PHIL: Since therefore you neither judge the sensation itself occasioned by the pin, nor any thing like it to be in the pin; you should not, conformably to what you have now granted, judge the sensation occasioned by the fire, or any thing like it, to be in the fire.

HYL: Well, since it must be so, I am content to yield this point, and acknowledge, that heat and cold are only sensations existing in our minds: but there still remain qualities enough to secure the reality of external things.

PHIL: But what will you say, Hylas, if it shall appear that the case is the same with regard to all other sensible qualities, and that they can no more be supposed to exist without the mind, than heat and cold?

HYL: Then indeed you will have done something to the purpose; but that is what I despair of seeing proved.

PHIL: Let us examine them in order. What think you of tastes, do they exist without the mind, or no?

HYL: Can any man in his senses doubt whether sugar is sweet, or wormwood bitter?

PHIL: Inform me, Hylas. Is a sweet taste a particular kind of pleasure or pleasant sensation, or is it not?

HYL: It is.

PHIL: And is not bitterness some kind of uneasiness or pain?

HYL: I grant it.

PHIL: If therefore sugar and wormwood are unthinking corporeal substances existing without the mind, how can sweetness and bitterness, that is, pleasure and pain, agree to them?

HYL: Hold, Philonous; I now see what it was deluded me all this time. You asked whether heat and cold, sweetness and bitterness, were not particular sorts of pleasure and pain; to which I answered simply, that they were. Whereas I should have thus distinguished: those qualities, as perceived by us, are pleasures or pains, but not as existing in the external objects. We must not therefore conclude absolutely, that there is no heat in the fire, or sweetness in the sugar, but only that heat or sweetness, as perceived by us, are not in the fire or sugar. What say you to this?

PHIL: I say it is nothing to the purpose. Our discourse proceeded altogether concerning sensible things, which you defined to be the things we immediately perceive by our senses. Whatever other qualities therefore you speak of, as distinct from these, I know nothing of them, neither do they at all belong to the point in dispute. You may indeed pretend to have discovered certain qualities which you do not perceive, and assert those insensible qualities exist in fire and sugar. But what use can be made of this to your present purpose, I am at a loss to conceive. Tell me then once more, do you acknowledge that heat and cold, sweetness and bitterness (meaning those qualities which are perceived by the senses), do not exist without the mind?

HYL: I see it is to no purpose to hold out, so I give up the cause as to those mentioned qualities. Though I profess it sounds oddly, to say that sugar is not sweet.

PHIL: But for your further satisfaction, take this along with you: that which at other times seems sweet, shall to a distempered palate appear bitter. And nothing can be plainer, than that divers persons perceive different tastes in the same food, since that which one man delights in, another abhors. And how could this be, if the taste was something really inherent in the food?

HYL: I acknowledge I know not how.

PHIL: In the next place, odours are to be considered. And with regard to these, I would fain know, whether what hath been said of tastes doth not exactly agree to them? Are they not so many pleasing or displeasing sensations?

HYL: They are.

PHIL: Can you then conceive it possible that they should exist in an unperceiving thing?

HYL: I cannot.

PHIL: Or can you imagine, that filth and ordure affect those brute animals that feed on them out of choice, with the same smells which we perceive in them?

HYL: By no means.

PHIL: May we not therefore conclude of smells, as of the other forementioned qualities, that they cannot exist in any but a perceiving substance or mind?

HYL: I think so.

PHIL: Then as to sounds, what must we think of them: are they accidents really inherent in external bodies, or not?

HYL: That they inhere not in the sonorous bodies, is plain from hence; because a bell struck in the exhausted receiver of an air-pump, sends forth no sound. The air therefore must be thought the subject of sound.

PHIL: What reason is there for that, Hylas?

HYL: Because when any motion is raised in the air, we perceive a sound greater or lesser, in proportion to the air's motion; but without some motion in the air, we never hear any sound at all.

PHIL: And granting that we never hear a sound but when some motion is produced in the air, yet I do not see how you can infer from thence, that the sound itself is in the air.

HYL: It is this very motion in the external air, that produces in the mind the sensation of sound. For striking on the drum of the ear, it causeth a vibration, which by the auditory nerves being communicated to the brain, the soul is thereupon affected with the sensation called sound.

PHIL: What! is sound then a sensation?

HYL: I tell you, as perceived by us, it is a particular sensation in the mind.

PHIL: And can any sensation exist without the mind?

HYL: No, certainly.

PHIL: How then can sound, being a sensation, exist in the air, if by the air you mean a senseless substance existing without the mind.

HYL: You must distinguish, Philonous, between sound, as it is perceived by us, and as it is in itself; or, (which is the same thing) between the sound we immediately perceive, and that which exists without us. The former indeed is a particular kind of sensation, but the latter is merely a vibrative or undulatory motion in the air.

PHIL: I thought I had already obviated that distinction by the answer I gave when you were applying it in a like case before. But to say no more of that; are you sure then that sound is really nothing but motion?

HYL: I am.

PHIL: Whatever therefore agrees to real sound, may with truth be attributed to motion.

HYL: It may.

PHIL: It is then good sense to speak of motion, as of a thing that is loud, sweet, acute, or grave.

HYL: I see you are resolved not to understand me. Is it not evident, those accidents or modes belong only to sensible sound, or sound in the common acceptation of the word, but not to sound in the real and philosophic sense, which, as I just now told you, is nothing but a certain motion of the air?

PHIL: It seems then there are two sorts of sound, the one vulgar, or that which is heard, the other philosophical and real.

HYL: Even so.

PHIL: And the latter consists in motion.

HYL: I told you so before.

PHIL: Tell me, Hylas, to which of the senses, think you, the idea of motion belongs: to the hearing?

HYL: No, certainly, but to the sight and touch.

PHIL: It should follow then, that according to you, real sounds may possibly be seen or felt, but never heard.

HYL: Look you, Philonous, you may if you please make a jest of my opinion, but that will not alter the truth of things. I own, indeed, the inferences you draw me into sound something oddly: but common language, you know, is framed by, and for the use of the vulgar: we must not therefore wonder, if expressions adapted to exact philosophic notions, seem uncouth and out of the way.

PHIL: Is it come to that? I assure you, I imagine myself to have gained no small point, since you make so light of departing from common phrases and opinions; it being a main part of our inquiry, to examine whose notions are widest of the common road, and most repugnant to the general sense of the world. But can you think it no more than a philosophical paradox, to say that real sounds are never heard, and that the idea of them is obtained by some other sense. And is there nothing in this contrary to nature and the truth of things?

HYL: To deal ingenuously, I do not like it. And after the concessions already made, I had as well grant that sounds too have no real being without the mind.

PHIL: And I hope you will make no difficulty to acknowledge the same of colours.

HYL: Pardon me; the case of colours is very different. Can any thing be plainer, than that we see them on the objects?

PHIL: The objects you speak of are, I suppose, corporeal substances existing without the mind.

HYL: They are.

PHIL: And have true and real colours inhering in them?

HYL: Each visible object hath that colour which we see in it.

PHIL: How! is there any thing visible but what we perceive by sight?

HYL: There is not.

PHIL: And do we perceive any thing by sense, which we do not perceive immediately?

HYL: How often must I be obliged to repeat the same thing? I tell you, we do not.

PHIL: Have patience, good Hylas; and tell me once more whether there is any thing immediately perceived by the senses, except sensible qualities. I know you asserted there was not: but I would now be informed, whether you still persist in the same opinion.

HYL: I do.

PHIL: Pray, is your corporeal substance either a sensible quality or made up of sensible qualities?

HYL: What a question that is! who ever thought it was?

PHIL: My reason for asking was, because in saying, each visible object hath that colour which we see in it, you make visible objects to be corporeal substances; which implies either that corporeal substances are sensible qualities, or else that there is something beside sensible qualities perceived by sight: but as this point was formerly agreed between us, and is still maintained by you, it is a clear consequence, that your corporeal substance is nothing distinct from sensible qualities.

HYL: You may draw as many absurd consequences as you please, and endeavour to perplex the plainest things; but you shall never persuade me out of my senses. I clearly understand my own meaning.

PHIL: I wish you would make me understand it too. But since you are unwilling to have your notion of corporeal substance examined, I shall urge that point no further. Only be pleased to let me know, whether the same colours which we see, exist in external bodies, or some other.

HYL: The very same.

PHIL: What! are then the beautiful red and purple we see on yonder clouds, really in them? Or do you imagine they have in themselves any other form than that of a dark mist or vapour?

HYL: I must own, Philonous, those colours are not really in the clouds as they seem to be at this distance. They are only apparent colours.

PHIL: Apparent call you them? how shall we distinguish these apparent colours from real?

HYL: Very easily. Those are to be thought apparent, which, appearing only at a distance, vanish upon a nearer approach.

PHIL: And those I suppose are to be thought real, which are discovered by the most near and exact survey.

HYL: Right.

PHIL: Is the nearest and exactest survey made by the help of a microscope, or by the naked eye?

HYL: By a microscope, doubtless.

PHIL: But a microscope often discovers colours in an object different from those perceived by the unassisted sight. And in case we had microscopes magnifying to any assigned degree; it is certain, that no object whatsoever viewed through them, would appear in the same colour which it exhibits to the naked eye.

HYL: And what will you conclude from all this? You cannot argue that there are really and naturally no colours on objects; because by artificial managements they may be altered, or made to vanish.

PHIL: I think it may evidently be concluded from your own concessions, that all the colours we see with our naked eyes, are only apparent as those on the clouds, since they vanish upon a more close and accurate inspection, which is afforded us by a microscope. Then as to what you say by way of prevention; I ask you, whether the real and natural state of an object is better discovered by a very sharp and piercing sight, or by one which is less sharp.

HYL: By the former without doubt.

PHIL: Is it not plain from dioptrics, that microscopes make the sight more penetrating, and represent objects as they would appear to the eye, in case it were naturally endowed with a most exquisite sharpness?

HYL: It is.

PHIL: Consequently the microscopical representation is to be thought that which best sets forth the real nature of the thing, or what it is in itself. The colours therefore by it perceived, are more genuine and real, than those perceived otherwise.

HYL: I confess there is something in what you say.

PHIL: Besides, it is not only possible but manifest, that there actually are animals, whose eyes are by nature framed to perceive those things, which by reason of their minuteness escape our sight. What think you of those inconceivably small animals perceived by glasses? must we suppose they are all stark blind? Or, in case they see, can it be imagined their sight hath not the same use in preserving their bodies from injuries, which appears in that of all other animals? And if it hath, is it not evident, they must see particles less than their own bodies, which will present them with a far different view in each object, from that which strikes our senses? Even our own eyes do not always represent objects to us after the same manner. In the jaundice, every one knows that all things seem yellow. Is it not therefore highly probable, those animals in whose eyes we discern a very different texture from that of ours, and whose bodies abound with different humours, do not see the same colours in every object that we do? From all of which, should it not seem to follow that all colours are equally apparent, and that none of those which we perceive are really inherent in any outward object?

HYL: It should.

PHIL: The point will be past all doubt, if you consider, that in case colours were real properties or affections inherent in external bodies, they could admit of no alteration, without some change wrought in the very bodies themselves: but is it not evident from what hath been said, that upon the use of microscopes, upon a change happening in the humours of the eye, or a variation of distance, without any manner of real alteration in the thing itself, the colours of any object are either changed, or totally disappear? Nay, all other circumstances remaining the same, change but the situation of some objects, and they shall present different colours to the eye. The same thing happens upon viewing an object in various degrees of light. And what is more known, than that the same bodies appear differently coloured by candle-light from what they do in the open day? Add to these the experiment of a prism, which, separating the heterogeneous rays of light, alters the colour of any object; and will cause the whitest to appear of a deep blue or red to the naked eye. And now tell me, whether you are still of opinion, that every body hath its true, real colour inhering in it; and if you think it hath, I would fain know further from you, what certain distance and position of the object, what peculiar texture and formation of the eye, what degree or kind of light is necessary for ascertaining that true colour, and distinguishing it from apparent ones.

HYL: I own myself entirely satisfied, that they are all equally apparent; and that there is no such thing as colour really inhering in external bodies, but that it is altogether in the light. And what confirms me in this opinion, is, that in proportion to the light, colours are still more or less vivid; and if there be no light, then are there no colours perceived. Besides, allowing there are colours on external objects, yet how is it possible for us to perceive them? For no external body affects the mind, unless it act first on our organs of sense. But the only action of bodies is motion; and motion cannot be communicated otherwise than by impulse. A distant object therefore cannot act on the eye, nor consequently make itself or its properties perceivable to the soul. Whence it plainly follows, that it is immediately some contiguous substance, which operating on the eye occasions a perception of colours: and such is light.

PHIL: How! is light then a substance?

HYL: I tell you, Philonous, external light is nothing but a thin fluid substance, whose minute particles being agitated with a brisk motion, and in various manners reflected from the different surfaces of outward objects to the eyes, communicate different motions to the optic nerves; which being propagated to the brain, cause therein various impressions: and these are attended with the sensations of red, blue, yellow, &c.

PHIL: It seems, then, the light doth no more than shake the optic nerves.

HYL: Nothing else.

PHIL: And consequent to each particular motion of the nerves the mind is affected with a sensation, which is some particular colour.

HYL: Right.

PHIL: And these sensations have no existence without the mind.

HYL: They have not.

PHIL: How then do you affirm that colours are in the light, since by light you understand a corporeal substance external to the mind?

HYL: Light and colours, as immediately perceived by us, I grant cannot exist without the mind. But in themselves they are only the motions and configurations of certain insensible particles of matter.

PHIL: Colours then, in the vulgar sense, or taken for the immediate objects of sight, cannot agree to any but a perceiving substance.

HYL: That is what I say.

PHIL: Well then, since you give up the point as to those sensible qualities, which are alone thought colours by all mankind beside, you may hold what you please with regard to those invisibles ones of the philosophers. It is not my business to dispute about them; only I would advise you to bethink yourself, whether, considering the inquiry we are upon, it be prudent for you to affirm the red and blue which we see are not real colours, but certain unknown motions and figures which no man ever did or can see, are truly so. Are not these shocking notions, and are not they subject to as many ridiculous inferences, as those you were obliged to renounce before in the case of sounds?

HYL: I frankly own, Philonous, that it is in vain to stand out any longer. Colours, sounds, tastes, in a word, all those termed secondary qualities, have certainly no existence without the mind. But by this acknowledgment I must not be supposed to derogate any thing from the reality of matter or external objects, seeing it is no more than several philosophers maintain, who nevertheless are the furthest imaginable from denying matter. For the clearer understanding of this, you must know sensible qualities are by philosophers divided into primary and secondary. The former are extension, figure, solidity, gravity, motion, and rest. And these they hold exist really in bodies. The latter are those above enumerated; or briefly, all sensible qualities beside the primary, which they assert are only so many sensations or ideas existing no where but in the mind. But all this, I doubt not, you are already apprised of. For my part, I have been a long time sensible there was such an opinion current among philosophers, but was never thoroughly convinced of its truth till now.

PHIL: You are still then of opinion, that extension and figures are inherent in external unthinking substances.

HYL: I am.

PHIL: But what if the same arguments which are brought against secondary qualities, will hold proof against these also?

HYL: Why then I shall be obliged to think, they too exist only in the mind.

PHIL: Is it your opinion, the very figure and extension which you perceive by sense, exist in the outward object or material substance?

HYL: It is.

PHIL: Have all other animals as good grounds to think the same of the figure and extension which they see and feel?

HYL: Without doubt, if they have any thought at all.

PHIL: Answer me, Hylas. Think you the senses were bestowed upon all animals for their preservation and well-being in life? or were they given to men alone for this end?

HYL: I make no question but they have the same use in all other animals.

PHIL: If so, is it not necessary they should be enabled by them to perceive their own limbs, and those bodies which are capable of harming them?

HYL: Certainly.

PHIL: A mite therefore must be supposed to see his own foot, and things equal or even less than it, as bodies of some considerable dimension; though at the same time they appear to you scarce discernible, or at best as so many visible points.

HYL: I cannot deny it.

PHIL: And to creatures less than the mite they will seem yet larger.

HYL: They will.

PHIL: Insomuch that what you can hardly discern, will to another extremely minute animal appear as some huge mountain.

HYL: All this I grant.

PHIL: Can one and the same thing be at the same time in itself of different dimensions?

HYL: That were absurd to imagine.

PHIL: But from what you have laid down it follows, that both the extension by you perceived, and that perceived by the mite itself, as likewise all those perceived by lesser animals, are each of them the true extension of the mite's foot, that is to say, by your own principles you are led into an absurdity.

HYL: There seems to be some difficulty in the point.

PHIL: Again, have you not acknowledged that no real inherent property of any object can be changed, without some change in the thing itself?

HYL: I have.

PHIL: But as we approach to or recede from an object, the visible extension varies, being at one distance ten or a hundred times greater than at another. Doth it not therefore follow from hence likewise, that it is not really inherent in the object?

HYL: I own I am at a loss what to think.

PHIL: Your judgment will soon be determined, if you will venture to think as freely concerning this quality, as you have done concerning the rest. Was it not admitted as a good argument, that neither heat nor cold was in the water, because it seemed warm to one hand, and cold to the other?

HYL: It was.

PHIL: Is it not the very same reasoning to conclude, there is no extension or figure in an object, because to one eye it shall seem little, smooth, and round, when at the same time it appears to the other, great, uneven, and angular?

HYL: The very same. But doth this latter fact ever happen?

PHIL: You may at any time make the experiment, by looking with one eye bare, and with the other through a microscope.

HYL: I know not how to maintain it, and yet I am loath to give up extension, I see so many odd consequences following upon such a concession.

PHIL: Odd, say you? After the concessions already made, I hope you will stick at nothing for its oddness. But on the other hand should it not seem very odd, if the general reasoning which includes all other sensible qualities did not also include extension? If it be allowed that no idea nor any thing like an idea can exist in an unperceiving substance, then surely it follows, that no figure or mode of extension, which we can either perceive or imagine, or have any idea of, can be really inherent in matter; not to mention the peculiar difficulty there must be, in conceiving a material substance, prior to and distinct from extension, to be the substratum of extension. Be the sensible quality what it will, figure, or sound, or colour; it seems alike impossible it should subsist in that which doth not perceive it.

HYL: I give up the point for the present, reserving still a right to retract my opinion, in case I shall hereafter discover any false step in my progress to it.

PHIL: That is a right you cannot be denied. Figures and extension being despatched, we proceed next to motion. Can a real motion in any external body be at the same time both very swift and very slow?

HYL: It cannot.

PHIL: Is not the motion of a body swift in a reciprocal proportion to the time it takes up in describing any given space? Thus a body that describes a mile in an hour, moves three times faster than it would in case it described only a mile in three hours.

HYL: I agree with you.

PHIL: And is not time measured by the succession of ideas in our minds?

HYL: It is.

PHIL: And is it not possible ideas should succeed one another twice as fast in your mind, as they do in mine, or in that of some spirit of another kind.

HYL: I own it.

PHIL: Consequently the same body may to another seem to perform its motion over any space in half the time that it doth to you. And the same reasoning will hold as to any other proportion: that is to say, according to your principles (since the motions perceived are both really in the object) it is possible one and the same body shall be really moved the same way at once, both very swift and very slow. How is this consistent either with common sense, or with what you just now granted?

HYL: I have nothing to say to it.

PHIL: Then as for solidity: either you do not mean any sensible quality by that word, and so it is beside our inquiry: or if you do, it must be either hardness or resistance. But both the one and the other are plainly relative to our senses: it being evident, that what seems hard to one animal, may appear soft to another, who hath greater force and firmness of limbs. Nor is it less plain, that the resistance I feel is not in the body.

HYL: I own the very sensation of resistance, which is all you immediately perceive, is not in the body, but the cause of that sensation is.

PHIL: But the causes of our sensations are not things immediately perceived, and therefore not sensible. This point I thought had been already determined.

HYL: I own it was; but you will pardon me if I seem a little embarrassed: I know not how to quit my old notions.

PHIL: To help you out, do but consider, that if extension be once acknowledged to have no existence without the mind, the same must necessarily be granted of motion, solidity, and gravity, since they all evidently suppose extension. It is therefore superfluous to inquire particularly concerning each of them. In denying extension, you have denied them all to have any real existence.

HYL: I wonder, Philonous, if what you say be true, why those philosophers who deny the secondary qualities any real existence, should yet attribute it to the primary. If there is no difference between them, how can this be accounted for?

PHIL: It is not my business to account for every opinion of the philosophers. But among other reasons which may be assigned for this, it seems probable, that pleasure and pain being rather annexed to the former than the latter, may be one. Heat and cold, tastes and smells, have something more vividly pleasing or disagreeable than the ideas of extension, figure, and motion, affect us with. And it being too visibly absurd to hold, that pain or pleasure can be in an unperceiving substance, men are more easily weaned from believing the external existence of the secondary, than the primary qualities. You will be satisfied there is something in this, if you recollect the difference you made between an intense and more moderate degree of heat, allowing the one a real existence, while you denied it to the other. But after all, there is no rational ground for that distinction; for surely an indifferent sensation is as truly a sensation, as one more pleasing or painful; and consequently should not any more than they be supposed to exist in an unthinking subject.

HYL: It is just come into my head, Philonous, that I have somewhere heard of a distinction between absolute and sensible extension. Now though it be acknowledged that great and small, consisting merely in the relation which other extended beings have to the parts of our own bodies, do not really inhere in the substances themselves; yet nothing obliges us to hold the same with regard to absolute extension, which is something abstracted from great and small, from this or that particular magnitude or figure. So likewise as to motion, swift and slow are altogether relative to the succession of ideas in our own minds. But it doth not follow, because those modifications of motion exist not without the mind, that therefore absolute motion abstracted from them doth not.

PHIL: Pray what is it that distinguishes one motion, or one part of extension from another? Is it not something sensible, as some degree of swiftness or slowness, some certain magnitude or figure peculiar to each?

HYL: I think so.

PHIL: These qualities therefore, stripped of all sensible properties, are without all specific and numerical differences, as the schools call them.

HYL: They are.

PHIL: That is to say, they are extension in general, and motion in general.

HYL: Let it be so.

PHIL: But it is a universally received maxim, that every thing which exists is particular. How then can motion in general, or extension in general, exist in any corporeal substance?

HYL: I will take time to solve your difficulty.

PHIL: But I think the point may be speedily decided. Without doubt you can tell, whether you are able to frame this or that idea. Now I am content to put our dispute on this issue. If you can frame in your thoughts a distinct abstract idea of motion or extension, divested of all those sensible modes, as swift and slow, great and small, round and square, and the like, which are acknowledged to exist only in the mind, I will then yield the point you contend for. But if you cannot, it will be unreasonable on your side to insist any longer upon what you have no notion of.

HYL: To confess ingenuously, I cannot.

PHIL: Can you even separate the ideas of extension and motion, from the ideas of all those qualities which they who make the distinction term secondary?

HYL: What! is it not an easy matter, to consider extension and motion by themselves, abstracted from all other sensible qualities? Pray how do the mathematicians treat of them?

PHIL: I acknowledge, Hylas, it is not difficult to form general propositions and reasonings about those qualities, without mentioning any other; and in this sense to consider or treat of them abstractedly. But how doth it follow that because I can pronounce the word motion by itself, I can form the idea of it in my mind exclusive of body? Or because theorems may be made of extension and figures, without any mention of great or small, or any other sensible mode or quality; that therefore it is possible such an abstract idea of extension, without any particular size or figure, or sensible quality, should be distinctly formed, and apprehended by the mind? Mathematicians treat of quantity, without regarding what other sensible qualities it is attended with, as being altogether indifferent to their demonstrations. But when laying aside the words, they contemplate the bare ideas, I believe you will find, they are not the pure abstracted ideas of extension.

HYL: But what say you to pure intellect? May not abstracted ideas be framed by that faculty?

PHIL: Since I cannot frame abstract ideas at all, it is plain, I cannot frame them by the help of pure intellect, whatsoever faculty you understand by those words. Besides, not to inquire into the nature of pure intellect and its spiritual objects, as virtue, reason, God, or the like, thus much seems manifest, that sensible things are only to be perceived by sense, or represented by the imagination. Figures therefore and extension, being originally perceived by sense, do not belong to pure intellect. But for your further satisfaction, try if you can frame the idea of any figure, abstracted from all particularities of size, or even from other sensible qualities.

HYL: Let me think a little—I do not find that I can.

PHIL: And can you think it possible, that should really exist in nature, which implies a repugnancy in its conception?

HYL: By no means.

PHIL: Since therefore it is impossible even for the mind to disunite the ideas of extension and motion from all other sensible qualities, doth it not follow, that where the one exist, there necessarily the other exist likewise?

HYL: It should seem so.

PHIL: Consequently the very same arguments which you admitted, as conclusive against the secondary qualities, are without any further application of force against the primary too. Besides, if you will trust your senses, is it not plain all sensible qualities co-exist, or to them appear as being in the same place? Do they ever represent a motion, or figure, as being divested of all other visible and tangible qualities?

HYL: You need say no more on this head. I am free to own, if there be no secret error or oversight in our proceedings hitherto, that all sensible qualities are alike to be denied existence without the mind. But my fear is, that I have been too liberal in my former concessions, or overlooked some fallacy or other. In short, I did not take time to think.

PHIL: For that matter, Hylas, you may take what time you please in reviewing the progress of our inquiry. You are at liberty to recover any slips you might have made, or offer whatever you have omitted, which makes for your first opinion.

HYL: One great oversight I take to be this: that I did not sufficiently distinguish the object from the sensation. Now though this latter may not exist without the mind, yet it will not thence follow that the former cannot.

PHIL: What object do you mean? The object of the senses?

HYL: The same.

PHIL: It is then immediately perceived?

HYL: Right.

PHIL: Make me to understand the difference between what is immediately perceived, and a sensation.

HYL: The sensation I take to be an act of the mind perceiving; beside which, there is something perceived; and this I call the object. For example, there is red and yellow on that tulip. But then the act of perceiving those colours is in me only, and not in the tulip.

PHIL: What tulip do you speak of? is it that which you see?

HYL: The same.

PHIL: And what do you see beside colour, figure, and extension?

HYL: Nothing.

PHIL: What you would say then is, that the red and yellow are co-existent with the extension; is it not?

HYL: That is not all: I would say, they have a real existence without the mind, in some unthinking substance.

PHIL: That the colours are really in the tulip which I see, is manifest. Neither can it be denied, that this tulip may exist independent of your mind or mine; but that any immediate object of the senses, that is, any idea, or combination of ideas, should exist in an unthinking substance, or exterior to all minds, is in itself an evident contradiction. Nor can I imagine how this follows from what you said just now, to wit that the red and yellow were on the tulip you saw, since you do not pretend to see that unthinking substance.

HYL: You have an artful way, Philonous, of diverting our inquiry from the subject.

PHIL: I see you have no mind to be pressed that way. To return then to your distinction between sensation and object; if I take you right, you distinguish in every perception two things, the one an action of the mind, the other not.

HYL: True.

PHIL: And this action cannot exist in, or belong to any unthinking thing; but whatever beside is implied in a perception, may.

HYL: That is my meaning.

PHIL: So that if there was a perception without any act of the mind, it were possible such a perception should exist in an unthinking substance.

HYL: I grant it. But it is impossible there should be such a perception.

PHIL: When is the mind said to be active?

HYL: When it produces, puts an end to, or changes any thing.

PHIL: Can the mind produce, discontinue, or change any thing but by an act of the will?

HYL: It cannot.

PHIL: The mind therefore is to be accounted active in its perceptions, so far forth as volition is included in them.

HYL: It is.

PHIL: In plucking this flower, I am active, because I do it by the motion of my hand, which was consequent upon my volition; so likewise in applying it to my nose. But is either of these smelling?

HYL: No.

PHIL: I act too in drawing the air through my nose; because my breathing so rather than otherwise, is the effect of my volition. But neither can this be called smelling: for if it were, I should smell every time I breathed in that manner.

HYL: True.

PHIL: Smelling then is somewhat consequent to all this.

HYL: It is.

PHIL: But I do not find my will concerned any further. Whatever more there is, as that I perceive such a particular smell or any smell at all, this is independent of my will, and therein I am altogether passive. Do you find it otherwise with you, Hylas?

HYL: No, the very same.

PHIL: Then as to seeing, is it not in your power to open your eyes, or keep them shut; to turn them this or that way?

HYL: Without doubt.

PHIL: But doth it in like manner depend on your will, that in looking on this flower, you perceive white rather than any other colour? Or directing your open eyes towards yonder part of the heaven, can you avoid seeing the sun? Or is light or darkness the effect of your volition?

HYL: No, certainly.

PHIL: You are then in these respects altogether passive.

HYL: I am.

PHIL: Tell me now, whether seeing consists in perceiving light and colours, or in opening and turning the eyes?

HYL: Without doubt, in the former.

PHIL: Since therefore you are in the very perception of light and colours altogether passive, what is become of that action you were speaking of, as an ingredient in every sensation? And doth it not follow from your own concessions, that the perception of light and colours, including no action in it, may exist in an unperceiving substance? And is not this a plain contradiction?

HYL: I know not what to think of it.

PHIL: Besides, since you distinguish the active and passive in every perception, you must do it in that of pain. But how is it possible that pain, be it as little active as you please, should exist in an unperceiving substance? In short, do but consider the point, and then confess ingenuously, whether light and colours, tastes, sounds, &c., are not all equally passions or sensations in the soul. You may indeed call them external objects, and give them in words what subsistence you please. But examine your own thoughts, and then tell me whether it be not as I say?

HYL: I acknowledge, Philonous, that upon a fair observation of what passes in my mind, I can discover nothing else, but that I am a thinking being, affected with variety of sensations; neither is it possible to conceive how a sensation should exist in an unperceiving substance. But then on the other hand, when I look on sensible things in a different view, considering them as so many modes and qualities, I find it necessary to suppose a material substratum, without which they cannot be conceived to exist.

PHIL: Material substratum call you it? Pray, by which of your senses came you acquainted with that being?

HYL: It is not itself sensible; its modes and qualities only being perceived by the senses.

PHIL: I presume then, it was by reflection and reason you obtained the idea of it.

HYL: I do not pretend to any proper positive idea of it. However I conclude it exists, because qualities cannot be conceived to exist without a support.

PHIL: It seems then you have only a relative notion of it, or that you conceive it not otherwise than by conceiving the relation it bears to sensible qualities.

HYL: Right.

PHIL: Be pleased therefore to let me know wherein that relation consists.

HYL: Is it not sufficiently expressed in the term substratum, or substance?

PHIL: If so, the word substratum should import, that it is spread under the sensible qualities or accidents.

HYL: True.

PHIL: And consequently under extension.

HYL: I own it.

PHIL: It is therefore somewhat in its own nature entirely distinct from extension.

HYL: I tell you, extension is only a mode, and matter is something that supports modes. And is it not evident the thing supported is different from the thing supporting?

PHIL: So that something distinct from, and exclusive of extension, is supposed to be the substratum of extension.

HYL: Just so.

PHIL: Answer me, Hylas. Can a thing be spread without extension? or is not the idea of extension necessarily included in spreading?

HYL: It is.

PHIL: Whatsoever therefore you suppose spread under any thing, must have in itself an extension distinct from the extension of that thing under which it is spread.

HYL: It must.

PHIL: Consequently every corporeal substance being the substratum of extension, must have in itself another extension by which it is qualified to be a substratum: and so on to infinity. And I ask whether this be not absurd in itself, and repugnant to what you granted just now, to wit, that the substratum was something distinct from, and exclusive of extension.

HYL: Aye but Philonous, you take me wrong. I do not mean that matter is spread in a gross literal sense under extension. The word substratum is used only to express in general the same thing with substance.

PHIL: Well then, let us examine the relation implied in the term substance. Is it not that it stands under accidents?

HYL: The very same.

PHIL: But that one thing may stand under or support another, must it not be extended?

HYL: It must.

PHIL: Is not therefore this supposition liable to the same absurdity with the former?

HYL: You still take things in a strict literal sense: that is not fair, Philonous.

PHIL: I am not for imposing any sense on your words: you are at liberty to explain them as you please. Only I beseech you, make me understand something by them. You tell me, matter supports or stands under accidents. How! is it as your legs support your body?

HYL: No; that is the literal sense.

PHIL: Pray let me know any sense, literal, or not literal, that you understand it in.—How long must I wait for an answer, Hylas?

HYL: I declare I know not what to say. I once thought I understood well enough what was meant by matter's supporting accidents. But now the more I think on it, the less can I comprehend it; in short, I find that I know nothing of it.

PHIL: It seems then you have no idea at all, neither relative nor positive, of matter; you know neither what it is in itself, nor what relation it bears to accidents.

HYL: I acknowledge it.

PHIL: And yet you asserted, that you could not conceive how qualities or accidents should really exist, without conceiving at the same time a material support of them.

HYL: I did.

PHIL: That is to say, when you conceive the real existence of qualities, you do withal conceive something which you cannot conceive.

HYL: It was wrong, I own. But still I fear there is some fallacy or other. Pray what think you of this? It is just come into my head, that the ground of all our mistakes lies in your treating of each quality by itself. Now, I grant that each quality cannot singly subsist without the mind. Colour cannot without extension, neither can figure without some other sensible quality. But as the several qualities united or blended together form entire sensible things, nothing hinders why such things may not be supposed to exist without the mind.

PHIL: Either, Hylas, you are jesting, or have a very bad memory. Though indeed we went through all the qualities by name one after another; yet my arguments, or rather your concessions no where tended to prove, that the secondary qualities did not subsist each alone by itself; but that they were not at all without the mind. Indeed in treating of figure and motion, we concluded they could not exist without the mind, because it was impossible even in thought to separate them from all secondary qualities, so as to conceive them existing by themselves. But then this was not the only argument made use of upon that occasion. But (to pass by all that hath been hitherto said, and reckon it for nothing, if you will have it so) I am content to put the whole upon this issue. If you can conceive it possible for any mixture or combination of qualities, or any sensible object whatever, to exist without the mind, then I will grant it actually to be so.

HYL: If it comes to that, the point will soon be decided. What more easy than to conceive a tree or house existing by itself, independent of, and unperceived by any mind whatsoever? I do at this present time conceive them existing after that manner.

PHIL: How say you, Hylas, can you see a thing which is at the same time unseen?

HYL: No, that were a contradiction.

PHIL: Is it not as great a contradiction to talk of conceiving a thing which is unconceived?

HYL: It is.

PHIL: The tree or house therefore which you think of, is conceived by you.

HYL: How should it be otherwise?

PHIL: And what is conceived is surely in the mind.

HYL: Without question, that which is conceived is in the mind.

PHIL: How then came you to say, you conceived a house or tree existing independent and out of all minds whatsoever?

HYL: That was, I own, an oversight; but stay, let me consider what led me into it. It is a pleasant mistake enough. As I was thinking of a tree in a solitary place, where no one was present to see it, methought that was to conceive a tree as existing unperceived or unthought of, not considering that I myself conceived it all the while. But now I plainly see, that all I can do is to frame ideas in my own mind. I may indeed conceive in my own thoughts the idea of a tree, or a house, or a mountain, but that is all. And this is far from proving, that I can conceive them existing out of the minds of all spirits.

PHIL: You acknowledge then that you cannot possibly conceive how any one corporeal sensible thing should exist otherwise than in a mind?

HYL: I do.

PHIL: And yet you will earnestly contend for the truth of that which you cannot so much as conceive?

HYL: I profess I know not what to think, but still there are some scruples remain with me. Is it not certain I see things at a distance? Do we not perceive the stars and moon, for example, to be a great way off? Is not this, I say, manifest to the senses?

PHIL: Do you not in a dream too perceive those or the like objects?

HYL: I do.

PHIL: And have they not then the same appearance of being distant?

HYL: They have.

PHIL: But you do not thence conclude the apparitions in a dream to be without the mind?

HYL: By no means.

PHIL: You ought not therefore to conclude that sensible objects are without the mind, from their appearance or manner wherein they are perceived.

HYL: I acknowledge it. But doth not my sense deceive me in those cases?

PHIL: By no means. The idea or thing which you immediately perceive, neither sense nor reason inform you that it actually exists without the mind. By sense you only know that you are affected with such certain sensations of light and colours, &c. And these you will not say are without the mind.

HYL: True: but beside all that, do you not think the sight suggests something of outness or distance?

PHIL: Upon approaching a distant object, do the visible size and figure change perpetually, or do they appear the same at all distances?

HYL: They are in a continual change.

PHIL: Sight therefore doth not suggest or any way inform you, that the visible object you immediately perceive, exists at a distance, or will be perceived when you advance further onward, there being a continued series of visible objects succeeding each other, during the whole time of your approach.

HYL: It doth not; but still I know, upon seeing an object, what object I shall perceive after having passed over a certain distance: no matter whether it be exactly the same or no: there is still something of distance suggested in the case.

PHIL: Good Hylas, do but reflect a little on the point, and then tell me whether there be any more in it than this. From the ideas you actually perceive by sight, you have by experience learned to collect what other ideas you will (according to the standing order of nature) be affected with, after such a certain succession of time and motion.

HYL: Upon the whole, I take it to be nothing else.

PHIL: Now is it not plain, that if we suppose a man born blind was on a sudden made to see, he could at first have no experience of what may be suggested by sight.

HYL: It is.

PHIL: He would not then, according to you, have any notion of distance annexed to the things he saw; but would take them for a new set of sensations existing only in his mind.

HYL: It is undeniable.

PHIL: But to make it still more plain: is not distance a line turned endwise to the eye?

HYL: It is.

PHIL: And can a line so situated be perceived by sight?

HYL: It cannot.

PHIL: Doth it not therefore follow that distance is not properly and immediately perceived by sight?

HYL: It should seem so.

PHIL: Again, is it your opinion that colours are at a distance?

HYL: It must be acknowledged, they are only in the mind.

PHIL: But do not colours appear to the eye as co-existing in the same place with extension and figures?

HYL: They do.

PHIL: How can you then conclude from sight, that figures exist without, when you acknowledge colours do not; the sensible appearance being the very same with regard to both?

HYL: I know not what to answer.

PHIL: But allowing that distance was truly and immediately perceived by the mind, yet it would not thence follow it existed out of the mind. For whatever is immediately perceived is an idea: and can any idea exist out of the mind?

HYL: To suppose that were absurd: but inform me, Philonous, can we perceive or know nothing beside our ideas?

PHIL: As for the rational deducing of causes from effects, that is beside our inquiry. And by the senses you can best tell, whether you perceive any thing which is not immediately perceived. And I ask you, whether the things immediately perceived, are other than your own sensations or ideas? You have indeed more than once, in the course of this conversation, declared yourself on those points; but you seem, by this last question, to have departed from what you then thought.

HYL: To speak the truth, Philonous, I think there are two kinds of objects, the one perceived immediately, which are likewise called ideas; the other are real things or external objects perceived by the mediation of ideas, which are their images and representations. Now I own, ideas do not exist without the mind; but the latter sort of objects do. I am sorry I did not think of this distinction sooner; it would probably have cut short your discourse.

PHIL: Are those external objects perceived by sense, or by some other faculty?

HYL: They are perceived by sense.

PHIL: How! is there any thing perceived by sense, which is not immediately perceived?

HYL: Yes, Philonous, in some sort there is. For example, when I look on a picture or statue of Julius Caesar, I may be said, after a manner, to perceive him (though not immediately) by my senses.

PHIL: It seems, then, you will have our ideas, which alone are immediately perceived, to be pictures of external things: and that these also are perceived by sense, inasmuch as they have a conformity or resemblance to our ideas.

HYL: That is my meaning.

PHIL: And in the same way that Julius Caesar, in himself invisible, is nevertheless perceived by sight; real things, in themselves imperceptible, are perceived by sense.

HYL: In the very same.

PHIL: Tell me, Hylas, when you behold the picture of Julius Caesar, do you see with your eyes any more than some colours and figures, with a certain symmetry and composition of the whole?

HYL: Nothing else.

PHIL: And would not a man, who had never known any thing of Julius Caesar, see as much?

HYL: He would.

PHIL: Consequently he hath his sight, and the use of it, in as perfect a degree as you.

HYL: I agree with you.

PHIL: Whence comes it then that your thoughts are directed to the Roman emperor and his are not? This cannot proceed from the sensations or ideas of sense by you then perceived; since you acknowledge you have no advantage over him in that respect. It should seem therefore to proceed from reason and memory: should it not?

HYL: It should.

PHIL: Consequently it will not follow from that instance, that any thing is perceived by sense which is not immediately perceived. Though I grant we may in one acceptation be said to perceive sensible things mediately by sense: that is, when from a frequently perceived connexion, the immediate perception of ideas by one sense suggests to the mind others perhaps belonging to another sense, which are wont to be connected with them. For instance, when I hear a coach drive along the streets, immediately I perceive only the sound; but from the experience I have had that such a sound is connected with a coach, I am said to hear the coach. It is nevertheless evident, that in truth and strictness, nothing can be heard but sound: and the coach is not then properly perceived by sense, but suggested from experience. So likewise when we are said to see a red-hot bar of iron; the solidity and heat of the iron are not the objects of sight, but suggested to the imagination by the colour and figure, which are properly perceived by that sense. In short, those things alone are actually and strictly perceived by any sense, which would have been perceived, in case that same sense had then been first conferred on us. As for other things, it is plain they are only suggested to the mind by experience grounded on former perceptions. But to return to your comparison of Caesar's picture, it is plain, if you keep to that, you must hold the real things or archetypes of our ideas are not perceived by sense, but by some internal faculty of the soul, as reason or memory. I would therefore fain know, what arguments you can draw from reason for the existence of what you call real things or material objects; or whether you remember to have seen them formerly as they are in themselves; or if you have heard or read of any one that did.

HYL: I see, Philonous, you are disposed to raillery; but that will never convince me.

PHIL: My aim is only to learn from you the way to come at the knowledge of material beings. Whatever we perceive, is perceived either immediately or mediately: by sense, or by reason and reflection. But as you have excluded sense, pray show me what reason you have to believe their existence; or what medium you can possibly make use of to prove it, either to mine or your own understanding.

HYL: To deal ingenuously, Philonous, now I consider the point, I do not find I can give you any good reason for it. But thus much seems pretty plain, that it is at least possible such things may really exist; and as long as there is no absurdity in supposing them, I am resolved to believe as I did, till you bring good reasons to the contrary.

PHIL: What! is it come to this, that you only believe the existence of material objects, and that your belief is founded barely on the possibility of its being true? Then you will have me bring reasons against it: though another would think it reasonable, the proof should lie on him who holds the affirmative. And after all, this very point which you are now resolved to maintain without any reason, is, in effect, what you have more than once, during this discourse, seen good reason to give up. But to pass over all this; if I understand you rightly, you say our ideas do not exist without the mind; but that they are copies, images, or representations of certain originals that do.

HYL: You take me right.

PHIL: They are then like external things.

HYL: They are.

PHIL: Have those things a stable and permanent nature independent of our senses; or are they in a perpetual change, upon our producing any motions in our bodies, suspending, exerting, or altering our faculties or organs of sense.

HYL: Real things, it is plain, have a fixed and real nature, which remains the same, notwithstanding any change in our senses, or in the posture and motion of our bodies; which, indeed, may affect the ideas in our minds, but it were absurd to think they had the same effect on things existing without the mind.

PHIL: How then is it possible, that things perpetually fleeting and variable as our ideas, should be copies or images of any thing fixed and constant? or in other words, since all sensible qualities, as size, figure, colour, &c., that is, our ideas, are continually changing upon every alteration in the distance, medium, or instruments of sensation; how can any determinate material objects be properly represented or painted forth by several distinct things, each of which is so different from and unlike the rest? Or if you say it resembles some one only of our ideas, how shall we be able to distinguish the true copy from all the false ones?

HYL: I profess, Philonous, I am at a loss. I know not what to say to this.

PHIL: But neither is this all. Which are material objects in themselves, perceptible or imperceptible?

HYL: Properly and immediately nothing can be perceived but ideas. All material things therefore are in themselves insensible, and to be perceived only by their ideas.

PHIL: Ideas then are sensible, and their archetypes or originals insensible.

HYL: Right.

PHIL: But how can that which is sensible be like that which is insensible? Can a real thing in itself invisible be like a colour; or a real thing which is not audible, be like a sound? In a word, can any thing be like a sensation or idea, but another sensation or idea?

HYL: I must own, I think not.

PHIL: Is it possible there should be any doubt in the point? Do you not perfectly know your own ideas?

HYL: I know them perfectly; since what I do not perceive or know, can be no part of my idea.

PHIL: Consider therefore, and examine them, and then tell me if there be any thing in them which can exist without the mind: or if you can conceive any thing like them existing without the mind.

HYL: Upon inquiry, I find it is impossible for me to conceive or understand how any thing but an idea can be like an idea. And it is most evident, that no idea can exist without the mind.

PHIL: You are therefore by your principles forced to deny the reality of sensible things, since you made it to consist in an absolute existence exterior to the mind. That is to say, you are a downright sceptic.

So I have gained my point, which was to show your principles led to scepticism.

HYL: For the present I am, if not entirely convinced, at least silenced.

PHIL: I would fain know what more you would require in order to a perfect conviction. Have you not had the liberty of explaining yourself all manner of ways? Were any little slips is discourse laid hold and insisted on? Or were you not allowed to retract or reinforce any thing you had offered, as best served your purpose? Hath not every thing you could say been heard and examined with all the fairness imaginable? In a word, have you not in every point been convinced out of your own mouth? And if you can at present discover any flaw in any of your former concessions, or think of any remaining subterfuge, any new distinction, colour, or comment whatsoever, why do you not produce it?

HYL: A little patience, Philonous. I am at present so amazed to see myself ensnared, and as it were imprisoned in the labyrinths you have drawn me into, that on the sudden it cannot be expected I should find my way out. You must give me time to look about me, and recollect myself. . . .

[Philonous and Hylas agree to meet on the morrow]

THE SECOND DIALOGUE

HYLAS: I beg your pardon, Philonous, for not meeting you sooner. All this morning my head was so filled with our late conversation, that I had not leisure to think of the time of the day, or indeed of any thing else.

PHILONOUS: I am glad you were so intent upon it, in hopes if there were any mistakes in your concessions, or fallacies in my reasonings from them, you will now discover them to me.

HYL: I assure you, I have done nothing ever since I saw you, but search after mistakes and fallacies, and with that view have minutely examined the whole series of yesterday's discourse: but all in vain, for the notions it led me into, upon review appear still more clear and evident; and the more I consider them, the more irresistibly do they force my assent.

PHIL: And is not this, think you, a sign that they are genuine, that they proceed from nature, and are comformable to right reason? Truth and beauty are in this alike, that the strictest survey sets them both off to advantage. While the false lustre of error and disguise cannot endure being reviewed, or too nearly inspected.

HYL: I own there is a great deal in what you say. Nor can any one be more entirely satisfied of the truth of those odd consequences, so long as I have in view the reasonings that lead to them. But when these are out of my thoughts, there seems on the other hand something so satisfactory, so natural and intelligible in the modern way of explaining things, that I profess I know now how to reject it.

PHIL: I know not what way you mean.

HYL: I mean the way of accounting for our sensations or ideas.

PHIL: How is that?

HYL: It is supposed the soul makes her residence in some part of the brain, from which the nerves take their rise, and are thence extended to all parts of the body: and that outward objects, by the different impressions they make on the organs of sense, communicate certain vibrative motions to the nerves; and these being filled with spirits, propagate them to the brain or seat of the soul, which according to the various impressions or traces thereby made in the brain, is variously affected with ideas.

PHIL: And call you this an explication of the manner whereby we are affected with ideas?

HYL: Why not, Philonous? have you any thing to object against it?

PHIL: I would first know whether I rightly understand your hypothesis. You make certain traces in the brain to be the causes or occasions of our ideas. Pray tell me, whether by the brain you mean any sensible thing?

HYL: What else think you I could mean?

PHIL: Sensible things are all immediately perceivable; and those things which are immediately perceivable, are ideas; and these exist only in the mind. Thus much you have, if I mistake not, long since agreed to.

HYL: I do not deny it.

PHIL: The brain therefore you speak of, being a sensible thing, exists only in the mind. Now, I would fain know whether you think it reasonable to suppose, that one idea or thing existing in the mind, occasions all other ideas. And if you think so, pray how do you account for the origin of that primary idea or brain itself?

HYL: I do not explain the origin of our ideas by that brain which is perceivable to sense, this being itself only a combination of sensible ideas, but by another which I imagine.

PHIL: But are not things imagined as truly in the mind as things perceived?

HYL: I must confess they are.

PHIL: It comes therefore to the same thing; and you have been all this while accounting for ideas, by certain motions or impressions in the brain, that is, by some alterations in an idea, whether sensible or imaginable, it matters not.

HYL: I begin to suspect my hypothesis.

PHIL: Beside spirits, all that we know or conceive are our own ideas. When therefore you say, all ideas are occasioned by impressions in the brain, do you conceive this brain or no? If you do, then you talk of ideas imprinted in an idea, causing that same idea, which is absurd. If you do not conceive it, you talk unintelligibly, instead of forming a reasonable hypothesis.

HYL: I now clearly see it was a mere dream. There is nothing in it.

PHIL: You need not be much concerned at it; for after all, this way of explaining things, as you called it, could never have satisfied any reasonable man. What connexion is there between a motion in the nerves, and the sensations of sound or colour in the mind? Or how is it possible these should be the effect of that?

HYL: But I could never think it had so little in it, as now it seems to have.

PHIL: Well then, are you at length satisfied that no sensible things have a real existence; and that you are in truth an arrant sceptic?

HYL: It is too plain to be denied.

PHIL: Look! are not the fields covered with a delightful verdure? Is there not something in the woods and groves, in the rivers and clear springs, that sooths, that delights, that transports the soul? At the prospect of the wide and deep ocean, or some huge mountain whose top is lost in the clouds, or of an old gloomy forest, are not our minds filled with a pleasing horror? Even in rocks and deserts, is there not an agreeable wildness? How sincere a pleasure is it to behold the natural beauties of the earth! to preserve and renew our relish for them, is not the veil of night alternately drawn over her face, and doth she not change her dress with the seasons? How aptly are the elements disposed! What variety and use in the meanest production of nature! What delicacy, what beauty, what contrivance in animal and vegetable bodies? How exquisitely are all things suited as well to their particular ends, as to constitute opposite parts of the whole! and while they mutually aid and support, do they not also set off and illustrate each other! Raise now your thoughts from this ball of earth, to all those glorious luminaries that adorn the high arch of heaven. The motion and situation of the planets, are they not admirable for use and order. Were those (miscalled erratic) globes ever known to stray, in their repeated journeys through the pathless void? Do they not measure areas round the sun ever proportioned to the times? So fixed, so immutable are the laws by which the unseen Author of nature actuates the universe. How vivid and radiant is the lustre of the fixed stars! how magnificent and rich that negligent profusion, with which they appear to be scattered throughout the whole azure vault! yet if you take the telescope, it brings into your sight a new host of stars that escape the naked eye. Here they seem contiguous and minute, but to a nearer view immense orbs of light at various distances, far sunk in the abyss of space. Now you must call imagination to your aid. The feeble narrow sense cannot descry innumerable worlds revolving round the central fires; and in those worlds the energy of an all-perfect mind displayed in endless forms. But neither sense nor imagination are big enough to comprehend the boundless extent with all its glittering furniture. Though the labouring mind exert and strain each power to its utmost reach, there still stands out ungrasped a surplusage immeasurable. Yet all the vast bodies that compose this mighty frame, how distant and remove soever, are by some secret mechanism, some divine art and force, linked in a mutual dependence and intercourse with each other, even with this earth, which was almost slipped from my thoughts, and lost in the crowd of worlds. Is not the whole system immense, beautiful, glorious beyond expression and beyond thought? What treatment then do those philosophers deserve, who would deprive these noble and delightful scenes of all reality? How should those principles be entertained, that lead us to think all the visible beauty of the creation a false imaginary glare? To be plain, can you expect this scepticism of yours will not be thought extravagantly absurd by all men of sense?

HYL: Other men may think as they please: but for your part you have nothing to reproach me with. My comfort is, you are as much a sceptic as I am.

PHIL: There, Hylas, I must beg leave to differ from you.

HYL: Wait! have you all along agreed to the premises, and do you now deny the conclusion, and leave me to maintain these paradoxes by myself which you led me into? This surely is not fair.

PHIL: I deny that I agreed with you in those notions that led to scepticism. You indeed said, the reality of sensible things consisted in an absolute existence out of the minds of spirits, or distinct from their being perceived. And pursuant to this notion of reality, you are obliged to deny sensible things any real existence: that is, according to your own definition, you profess yourself a sceptic. But I neither said nor thought the reality of sensible things was to be defined after that manner. To me it is evident, for the reasons you allow of, that sensible things cannot exist otherwise than in a mind or spirit. Whence I conclude, not that they have no real existence, but that seeing they depend not on my thought, and have an existence distinct from being perceived by me, there must be some other mind wherein they exist. As sure therefore as the sensible world really exists, so sure is there an infinite, omnipresent Spirit who contains and supports it.

HYL: What! this is no more than I and all Christians hold; nay, and all others too who believe there is a God, and that he knows and comprehends all things.

PHIL: Ay, but here lies the difference. Men commonly believe that all things are known or perceived by God, because they believe the being of a God, whereas I, on the other side, immediately and necessarily conclude the being of a God, because all sensible things must be perceived by him.

HYL: But so long as we all believe the same thing, what matter is it how we come by that belief?

PHIL: But neither do we agree in the same opinion. For philosophers, though they acknowledge all corporeal beings to be perceived by God, yet they attribute to them an absolute subsistence distinct from their being perceived by any mind whatever, which I do not. Besides, is there no difference between saying, there is a God, therefore he perceives all things: and saying, sensible things do really exist: and if they really exist, they are necessarily perceived by an infinite mind: therefore there is an infinite mind, or God. This furnishes you with a direct and immediate demonstration, from a most evident principle, of the being of a God. Divines and philosophers had proved beyond all controversy, from the beauty and usefulness of the several parts of the creation, that it was the workmanship of God. But that setting aside all help of astronomy and natural philosophy, all contemplation of the contrivance, order, and adjustment of things, an infinite mind should be necessarily inferred from the bare existence of the sensible world, is an advantage peculiar to them only who have made this easy reflection: that the sensible world is that which we perceive by our several senses; and that nothing is perceived by the senses beside ideas; and that no idea or archetype of an idea can exist otherwise than in a mind.

You may now, without any laborious search into the sciences, without any subtilty of reason, or tedious length of discourse, oppose and baffle the most strenuous advocate for atheism. Those miserable refuges, whether in an eternal succession of unthinking causes and effects, or in a fortuitous concourse of atoms; those wild imaginations of Vanini, Hobbes, and Spinoza; in a word, the whole system of atheism, is it not entirely overthrown by this single reflection on the repugnancy included in supposing the whole, or any part, even the most rude and shapeless of the visible world, to exist without a mind? Let any one of those abettors of impiety but look into his own thoughts, and there try if he can conceive how so much as a rock, a desert, a chaos, or confused jumble of atoms; how any thing at all, either sensible or imaginable, can exist independent of a mind, and he need go no further to be convinced of his folly. Can any thing be fairer than to put a dispute on such an issue, and leave it to a man himself to see if he can conceive, even in thought, what he holds to be true in fact, and from a notional to allow it a real existence?

HYL: It cannot be denied, there is something highly serviceable to religion in what you advance. But do you not think it looks very like a notion entertained by some eminent moderns, of seeing all things in God?

PHIL: I would gladly know that opinion; pray explain it to me.

HYL: They conceive that the soul being immaterial, is incapable of being united with material things, so as to perceive them in themselves, but that she perceives them by her union with the substance of God, which being spiritual is therefore purely intelligible, or capable of being the immediate object of a spirit's thought. Besides, the divine essence contains in it perfections correspondent to each created being; and which are, for that reason, proper to exhibit or represent them to the mind. . . .

PHIL: I do not pretend to be a setter-up of new notions. My endeavours tend only to unite and place in a clearer light that truth, which was before shared between the vulgar and the philosophers: the former being of opinion, that those things they immediately perceive are the real things: and the latter, that the things immediately perceived are ideas which exist only in the mind. Which two notions put together, do in effect constitute the substance of what I advance.

HYL: I have been a long time distrusting my senses; methought I saw things by a dim light, and through false glasses. Now the glasses are removed, and a new light breaks in upon my understanding. I am clearly convinced that I see things in their native forms; and am no longer in pain about their unknown natures or absolute existence. This is the state I find myself in at present: though indeed the course that brought me to it I do not yet thoroughly comprehend. You set out upon the same principles that Academics, Cartesians, and the like sects, usually do; and for a long time it looked as if you were advancing their philosophical scepticism; but in the end your conclusions are directly opposite to theirs.

PHIL: You see, Hylas, the water of yonder fountain, how it is forced upwards, in a round column, to a certain height; at which it breaks and falls back into the bason from whence it rose: its ascent, as well as descent, proceeding from the same uniform law or principle of gravitation. Just so, the same principles which at first view lead to scepticism, pursued to a certain point, bring men back to common sense.

Chapter 22

WILLIAM PALEY

William Paley (1743–1805), archdeacon of Carlisle, was a leading evangelical apologist. His most important work is *Natural Theology, or Evidences of the Existence and Attributes of the Deity Collected from the Appearances of Nature* (1802), the first chapter of which is reprinted here. Paley argues that just as we infer an intelligent designer to account for the purpose-revealing watch, so likewise we must infer an intelligent grand designer to account for the purpose-revealing world.

Natural Theology, or Evidences of the Existence and Attributes of the Deity Collected from the Appearances of Nature

STATEMENT OF THE ARGUMENT

In crossing a heath, suppose I pitched my foot against a *stone,* and were asked how the stone came to be there, I might possibly answer, that, for anything I knew to the contrary, it had lain there for ever; nor would it, perhaps, be very easy to show the absurdity of this answer. But suppose I found a *watch* upon the ground, and it should be inquired how the watch happened to be in that place, I should hardly think of the answer which I had given—that, for anything I knew, the watch might have always been there. Yet why should not this answer serve for the watch as well as for the stone? why is it not as admissible in the second case as in the first? For this reason, and for no other; viz., that, when we come to inspect the watch, we perceive (what we could not discover in the stone) that its several parts are framed and put together for a purpose, e.g. that they are so formed and adjusted as to produce motion, and that motion so regulated as to point out the hour of the day; that, if the different parts had been differently shaped from what they are, if a different size from what they are, or placed after any other manner, or in any other order than that in which they are placed, either no motion at all would have been carried on in the machine, or none which would have answered the use that is now served by it. To reckon up a few of the plainest of these parts, and of their offices, all tending to one result:—We see a cylindrical box containing a coiled elastic spring, which, by its endeavor to relax itself, turns round the box. We next observe a flexible chain (artificially wrought for the sake of flexure) communicating the action of the spring from the box to the fusee. We then find a series of wheels, the teeth of which catch in, and apply to, each other, conducting the motion from the fusee to the balance, and from the balance to the pointer, and, at the same time, by the size and shape of those wheels, so regulating that motion as to terminate in causing an index, by an equable and measured progression, to pass over a given space in a given time. We take notice that the wheels are made of brass, in order to keep them from rust; the springs of steel, no other metal being so elastic; that over the face of the watch there is placed a glass, a material employed in no other part of the work, but in the room of which, if there had been any other than a transparent substance, the hour could not be seen without opening the case. This mechanism being observed, (it requires indeed an examination of the instrument, and perhaps some previous knowledge of the subject, to perceive and understand it; but being once, as we have said, observed and understood,) the inference, we think, is inevitable, that the watch must have had a maker; that there must have existed, at some time, and at some place or other, an artificer or artificers who formed it for the purpose which we find it actually to answer; who comprehended its construction, and designed its use.

I. Nor would it, I apprehend, weaken the conclusion, that we have never seen a watch made; that we had never known an artist capable of making one; that we were altogether incapable of executing such a piece of workmanship ourselves, or of understanding in what manner it was performed; all this being no more than what is true of some exquisite remains of ancient art, of some lost arts, and, to the generality of mankind, of the more curious productions of modern manufacture. Does one man in a million know how oval frames are turned? Ignorance of this kind exalts our opinion of the unseen and unknown artist's skill, if he be unseen and unknown, but raises no doubt in our minds of the existence and agency of such an artist, at some former time, and in some place or other. Nor can I perceive that it varies at all the inference, whether the question arise concerning a human agent, or concerning an agent of a different species, or an agent possessing, in some respect, a different nature.

II. Neither, secondly, would it invalidate our conclusion, that the watch sometimes went wrong, or that it seldom went exactly right. The purpose of the machinery, the design, and the designer, might be evident, and, in the case supposed, would be evident, in whatever way we accounted for the irregularity of the movement, or whether we could account for it or not. It is not necessary that a machine be perfect, in order to show with what design it was made; still less necessary, where the only question is, whether it were made with any design at all.

III. Nor, thirdly, would it bring any uncertainty into the argument, if there were a few parts of the watch, concerning which we could not discover, or had not yet discovered, in what manner they conduced to the general effect; or even some parts, concerning which we could not ascertain whether they conduced to that effect in any manner whatever. For, as to the first branch of the case, if by the loss, or disorder, or decay of the parts in question, the movement of the watch were found in fact to be stopped, or disturbed, or retarded, no doubt would remain in our minds as to the utility or intention of these parts, although we should be unable to investigate the manner according to which, or the connection by which, the ultimate effect depended upon their action or assistance; and the more complex is the machine, the more likely is this obscurity to arise. Then, as to the second thing supposed, namely, that there were parts which might be spared without prejudice to the movement of the watch, and that he had proved this by experiment, these superfluous parts, even if we were completely assured that they were such, would not vacate the reasoning which we had instituted concerning other parts. The indication of contrivance remains, with respect to them, nearly as it was before.

IV. Nor, fourthly, would any man in his senses think the existence of the watch, with its various machinery, accounted for, by being told that it was one out of possible combinations of material forms; that whatever he had found in the place where he found the watch, must have contained some internal configuration or other; and that this configuration might be the structure now exhibited, viz., of the works of a watch, as well as a different structure.

V. Nor, fifthly, would it yield his inquiry more satisfaction, to be answered, that there existed in things a principle of order, which had disposed the parts of the watch into their present form and situation. He never knew a watch made by the principle of order; nor can he even form to himself an idea of what is meant by a principle of order, distinct from the intelligence of the watchmaker.

VI. Sixthly, he would be surprised to hear that the mechanism of the watch was no proof of contrivance, only a motive to induce the mind to think so:

VII. And not less surprised to be informed, that the watch in his hand was nothing more than the result of the laws of *metallic* nature. It is a perversion of language to assign any law as the efficient, operative cause of anything. A law presupposes an agent; for it is only the mode according to which an agent proceeds; it implies a power; for it is the order according to which that power acts. Without this agent, without this power, which are both distinct from itself, the *law* does nothing, is nothing. The expression, "the law of metallic nature," may sound strange and harsh to a philosophic ear; but it seems quite as justifiable as some others which are more familiar to him such as "the law of vegetable nature," "the law of animal nature," or, indeed, as "the law of nature" in general, when assigned as the cause of phenomena in exclusion of agency and power, or when it is substituted into the place of these.

VIII. Neither, lastly, would our observer be driven out of his conclusion, or from his confidence in its truth, by being told that he knew nothing at all about the matter. He knows enough for his argument: he knows the utility of the end: he knows the subserviency and adaptation of the means to the end. These points being known, his ignorance of other points, his doubts concerning other points, affect not the certainty of his reasoning. The consciousness of knowing little need not beget a distrust of that which he does know. . . .

APPLICATION OF THE ARGUMENT

Every indication of contrivance, every manifestation of design, which existed in the watch, exists in the works of nature; with the difference, on the side of nature, of being greater and more, and that in a degree which exceeds all computation. I mean that the contrivances of nature surpass the contrivances of art, in the complexity, subtlety, and curiosity of the mechanism; and still more, if possible, do they go beyond them in number and variety; yet in a multitude of cases, are not less evidently mechanical, not less evidently contrivances, not less evidently accommodated to their end, or suited to their office, than are the most perfect productions of human ingenuity. . . .

Chapter 23

DAVID HUME

David Hume was born in Edinburgh in 1711 into a strict Scottish Presbyterian family. He was taught at home until the age of twelve, when he entered the University of Edinburgh, where he was to pursue a legal career. Instead he fell in love with philosophy. He lost his religious faith and tended toward skepticism. Still in his early twenties he tried a career in business, but it was not suitable to his personality. He suffered exhaustion and in 1734 he traveled to France and eventually found lodging at La Fleche, Descartes' alma mater. There he argued with the Jesuits about miracles and completed his *Treatise on Human Nature*. The book was published in England in January 1739, but sold few copies and received very little attention. Hume noted in his autobiography that it "fell dead-born from the press." Today this work of the youthful Hume is considered one of the classics of philosophy. Encouraged by the success of his work *Essays Moral and Political* (1741), he decided to revise the *Treatise* and published it under the title *An Enquiry Concerning Human Understanding* (1748). The entire book is reprinted below. In 1752 Hume became the Librarian to the Faculty of Advocates in Edinburgh. While in this position he wrote his famous history of England. Hume never married. He was disappointed in love, having been rejected by the woman he proposed to marry—apparently she found him obese and clumsy. He was, nevertheless, a charming man with a good sense of humor, popular at social occasions, modest, mild, and moral, a generous friend. He died of cancer of the bowel on August 25, 1776, the year of the signing of the American Declaration of Independence. Hume's final masterpiece, *Dialogues Concerning Natural Religion*, had been written around 1751 but was left unpublished until after his death. Hume apparently thought its critique of religion too dangerous to publish. It appeared in print in 1779. It is reprinted below.

HUME'S THEORY OF KNOWLEDGE

Whereas Descartes was a Rationalist, who believed that reason could discover all truth, especially metaphysical truth, Hume, like Locke, is an Empiricist, who believes that we must start with our perceptions and reason from there. Descartes was a global skeptic, doubting even mathematical truth, whereas Hume is a *local* skeptic. He does not doubt truths of mathematics or logic as well as commonsense truth (e.g., memory reports and sensory impressions), but he doubts all metaphysical propositions: the existence of God, miracles, the idea of a self, material substance, free will, cause and effect, and induction.

Hume divides perceptions into two kinds: impressions and ideas. Impressions (both internal and external, the emotions, and sense experiences) are more forceful and lively when they strike the mind, whereas ideas are the faint copies of impressions we have when we remember past experiences or reason. All sensations, feelings, and passions are impressions. All thinking consists of ideas.

Hume's most original insight consists in his skepticism about causality and inductive reasoning. Before Hume philosophers thought that there was a *necessary connection* between cause and effect. Neither Locke nor Berkeley, nor anyone else before Hume, questioned the basic principle of causality. Hume asks, What is the origin of the idea of causality? Since ideas are copies of impressions, Hume asks what impressions give us the idea of causality. None can be discovered. Certainly, there is no impression of a necessary connection. Then how does the idea arise in the mind? Hume eventually concludes that it is brought on by a habit of association at seeing two types of events in constant conjunction.

Similarly, Hume challenges our notion of induction, the belief that the future will be like the past. Hume points out that, unlike truths of reason (logical and mathematical truths), it is never contradictory to deny a matter of fact. It is not logically necessary that the earth is now rotating or revolving around the sun, nor that it will do so tomorrow. These are mere contingent truths. "That the sun will not rise tomorrow is no less intelligible a proposition, and implies no more a contradiction than the affirmation that it will rise." And if the sun's not rising is possible, what reason do we have for thinking it won't actually happen?

What is our justification for the belief regarding matters of fact? Hume asks. He replies that we justify that belief by our belief in causal laws and relationships. We believe that a causal order rooted in nature's laws operates to produce all that is. But what is the foundation of all our reasoning concerning cause and effect? Experience, Hume replies, like a good Empiricist. All our experience corroborates such relations. But, Hume relentlessly continues, "What is the foundation of all conclusions from experience?" His reply, "In reality, all arguments from experience are founded on the similarity which we discover among natural objects, and by which we are induced to expect effects similar to those which we have found to follow from such objects." Only a fool or a lunatic would pretend to dispute this faith in causality based on experience.

But only experience shows us that certain objects and events regularly give rise to a number of uniform effects. From a body of like color and consistency with bread we "expect nourishment and support. But this surely is a step of the mind," which stands in need of explanation. Reasoning from the proposition "I have always found so and so to happen in the past" to the proposition "So and so will continue to happen in the future" is a great leap that stands in need of justification.

We must admit "that the inference is not intuitive; neither is it demonstrative. Of what nature is it then? To say it is experimental is begging the question. For all inferences from experience suppose, as their foundation, that the future will resemble the past. It is impossible, therefore, that any argument from experience can prove this resemblance of the past to the future; since all these arguments are founded on the supposition of that resemblance."

Hume shows that our belief that the future will be like the past is based on our belief in the uniformity of nature, which in turn is based on our past experience, which is an inadequate premise for arguing for the future. The argument "The uniformity of nature has been reliable in the past so it will likely be reliable in the future," is not a sound deductive argument, because the conclusion contains more information than the premises. Inductive generalizations are "ampliative," adding more data than the premises contain. Since Hume's time there have been many attempts to solve this problem of induction.

HUME'S PHILOSOPHY OF RELIGION

Our second selection consists of most of *Dialogues Concerning Natural Religion* (1779), in which Hume critiques the teleological and cosmological arguments for the existence of God and raises the problem of evil. Hume asserts that we cannot prove the existence of God via a priori reasoning (such as the ontological argument seeks to do) because the claim that God exists is a factual claim and it is never contradictory to deny a factual claim. So one must attempt to demonstrate God's existence via a posteriori arguments, those which begin with the observation that there is a world that needs to be accounted for and that there is order which suggests a designer (see Paley's Watch Argument, Chapter 22). But Hume argues that such a posteriori arguments are filled with insuperable problems. Hume's several criticisms have engaged philosophers for over two hundred years. I trust that they will stimulate you to work out your own answers to the problems they raise.

It may help you to know that Cleanthes, who opens the dialogue, is a natural theologian, similar to Paley in our previous section. Demea is an orthodox believer, and the skeptic Philo, who puts forth the arguments against the argument from design, seems to represent Hume's position.

FOR FURTHER READING

Ayer, A. J. *Hume.* (Oxford University Press, 1981).
Bennett, Jonathan. *Locke, Berkeley and Hume: Central Themes.* (Oxford University Press, 1971).
Chappell, V. C., ed. *Hume: A Collection of Critical Essays.* (University of Notre Dame Press, 1968).
Flew, Anthony. *Hume's Philosophy of Belief.* (Routledge & Kegan Paul, 1961).
Hendel, William. *Studies in the Philosophy of David Hume.* (Princeton University Press, 1925).
Kemp Smith, N. *The Philosophy of David Hume.* (Macmillan, 1941).
Mackie, J. L. *Hume's Moral Theory.* (Routledge & Kegan Paul, 1980).
Mossner, E. C. *The Life of David Hume.* (Clarendon Press, 1954, 1980).
Norton, David. *David Hume: Common Sense Moralist, Sceptical Metaphysician.* (Princeton University Press, 1982).
Skyrms, Brian. *Choice and Chance.* (Wadsworth Publishing Company, 1986).
Stove, D. C. *Probability and Hume's Induction.* (Clarendon Press, 1973).
Stroud, Barry. *Hume.* (Routledge & Kegan Paul, 1978).
Swinburne, Richard. *The Existence of God.* (Clarendon Press, 1979).

An Enquiry Concerning Human Understanding

SECTION I: OF THE DIFFERENT SPECIES OF PHILOSOPHY

Moral philosophy, or the science of human nature, may be treated after two different manners; each of which has its peculiar merit, and may contribute to the entertainment, instruction, and reformation of mankind. The one considers man chiefly as born for action; and as influenced in his measures by taste and sentiment; pursuing one object, and avoiding another, according to the value which these objects seem to possess, and according to the light in which they present themselves. As virtue, of all objects, is allowed to be the most valuable, this species of philosophers paint her in the most amiable colours; borrowing all helps from poetry and eloquence, and treating their subject in an easy and obvious manner, and such as is best fitted to please the imagination, and engage the affections. They select the most striking observations and instances from common life; place opposite characters in a proper contrast; and alluring us into the paths of virtue by the views of glory and happiness, direct our steps in these paths by the soundest precepts and most illustrious examples. They make us feel the difference between vice and virtue; they excite and regulate our sentiments; and so they can but bend our hearts to the love of probity and true honour, they think, that they have fully attained the end of all their labors.

The other species of philosophers consider man in the light of a reasonable rather than an active being, and endeavor to form his understanding more than cultivate his manners. They regard human nature as a subject of speculation; and with a narrow scrutiny examine it, in order to find those principles, which regulate our understanding, excite our sentiments, and make us approve or blame any particular object, action, or behavior. They think it a reproach to all literature, that philosophy should not yet have fixed, beyond controversy, the foundation of morals, reasoning, and criticism; and should for ever talk of truth and falsehood, vice and virtue, beauty and deformity, without being able to determine the source of these distinctions. While they attempt this arduous task, they are deterred by no difficulties; but proceeding from particular instances to general principles, they still push on their enquiries to principles more general, and rest not satisfied till they arrive at those original principles, by which, in every science, all human curiosity must be bounded. Though their speculations seem abstract, and even unintelligible to common readers, they aim at the approbation of the learned and the wise; and think themselves sufficiently compensated for the labour of their whole lives, if they can discover some hidden truths, which may contribute to the instruction of posterity.

It is certain that the easy and obvious philosophy will always, with the generality of mankind, have the preference above the accurate and abstruse; and by many will be recommended, not only as more agreeable, but more useful than the other. It enters more into common life; molds the heart and affections; and, by touching those principles which actuate men, reforms their conduct, and brings them nearer to that model of perfection which it describes. On the contrary, the abstruse philosophy, being founded on a turn of mind, which cannot enter into business and action, vanishes when the philosopher leaves the shade, and comes into open day; nor can its principles easily retain any influence over our conduct and behavior. The feelings of our heart, the agitation of our passions, the vehemence of our affections, dissipate all its conclusions, and reduce the profound philosopher to a mere plebeian.

This also must be confessed, that the most durable, as well as justest fame, has been acquired by the easy philosophy, and that abstract reasoners seem hitherto to have enjoyed only a momentary reputation, from the caprice or ignorance of their own age, but have not been able to support their renown with more equitable posterity. It is easy for a profound philosopher to commit a mistake in his subtile reasonings; and one mistake is the necessary parent of another, while he pushes on his consequences, and is not deterred from embracing any conclusion, by its unusual appearance, or its contradiction to popular opinion. But a philosopher, who purposes only to represent the common sense of mankind in more beautiful and more engaging colours, if by accident he falls into error, goes no farther; but renewing his appeal to common sense, and the natural sentiments of the mind, returns into the right path, and secures himself from any dangerous illusions. The fame of Cicero flourishes at present; but that of Aristotle is utterly decayed. La Bruyere passes the seas, and still maintains his reputation: But the glory of Malebranche is confined to his own nation, and to his own age. And Addison, perhaps, will be read with pleasure, when Locke shall be entirely forgotten.

The mere philosopher is a character, which is commonly but little acceptable in the world, as being supposed to contribute nothing either to the advantage or pleasure of society; while he lives remote from communication with mankind, and is wrapped up in principles and notions equally remote from their comprehension. On the other hand, the mere ignorant is still more despised; nor is any thing deemed a surer sign of an illiberal genius in an age and nation where the sciences flourish, than to be entirely destitute of all relish for those noble entertainments. The most perfect character is supposed to lie between those extremes; retaining an equal ability and taste for books, company, and business; preserving in conversation that discernment and delicacy which arise from polite letters; and in business, that probity and accuracy which are the natural result of a just philosophy. In order to diffuse and cultivate so accomplished a character, nothing can be more useful than compositions of the easy style and manner, which draw not too much from life, require no deep application or retreat to be comprehended, and send back the student among mankind full of noble sentiments and wise precepts, applicable to every exigence of human life. By means of such compositions, virtue becomes amiable, science agreeable, company instructive, and retirement entertaining.

Man is a reasonable being; and as such, receives from science his proper food and nourishment: But so narrow are the bounds of human understanding, that little satisfaction can be hoped for in this particular, either from the extent or security of his acquisitions. Man is a sociable, no less than a reasonable being: But neither can he always enjoy company agreeable and amusing, or preserve the proper relish for them. Man is also an active being; and from that disposition, as well as from the various necessities of human life, must submit to business and occupation: But the mind requires some relaxation, and cannot always support its bent to care and industry. It seems, then, that nature has pointed out a mixed kind of life as most suitable to human race, and secretly admonished them to allow none of these biases to draw too much, so as to incapacitate them for other occupations and entertainments. Indulge your passion for science, says she, but let your science be human, and such as may have a direct reference to action and society. Abstruse thought and profound researches I prohibit, and will severely punish, by the pensive melancholy which they introduce, by the endless uncertainty in which they involve you, and by the cold retention which your pretended discoveries shall meet with, when communicated. Be a philosopher; but, amidst all your philosophy, be still a man.

Were the generality of mankind contented to prefer the easy philosophy to the abstract and profound, without throwing any blame or contempt on the latter, it might not be improper, perhaps, to comply with this general opinion, and allow every man to enjoy, without opposition, his own taste and sentiment. But as the matter is often carried farther, even to the absolute rejecting of all profound reasonings, or what is commonly called metaphysics, we shall now proceed to consider what can reasonably be pleaded in their behalf.

We may begin with observing, that one considerable advantage, which results from the accurate and abstract philosophy, is, its subserviency to the easy and humane; which, without the former, can never attain a sufficient degree of exactness in its sentiments, precepts, or reasonings. All polite letters are nothing but pictures of human life in various attitudes and situations; and inspire us with different sentiments, of praise or blame, admiration or ridicule, according to the qualities of the object, which they set before us. An artist must be better qualified to succeed in this undertaking, who, besides a delicate taste and a quick apprehension, possesses an accurate knowledge of the internal fabric, the operations of the understanding, the workings of the passions, and the various species of sentiment which discriminate vice and virtue. How painful soever this inward search or enquiry may appear, it becomes, in some measure, requisite to those, who would describe with success the obvious and outward appearances of life and manners. The anatomist presents to the eye the most hideous and disagreeable objects; but his science is useful to the painter in delineating even a Venus or an Helen. While the latter employs all the richest colours of his art, and gives his figures the most graceful and engaging airs; he must still carry his attention to the inward structure of the human body, the position of the muscles, the fabric of the bones, and the use and figure of every part or organ. Accuracy is, in every case, advantageous to beauty, and just reasoning to delicate sentiment. In vain would we exalt the one by depreciating the other.

Besides, we may observe, in every art or profession, even those which most concern life or action, that a spirit of accuracy, however acquired, carries all of them nearer their perfection, and renders them more subservient to the interests of society. And though a philosopher may live remote from business, the genius of philosophy, if carefully cultivated by several, must gradually diffuse itself throughout the whole society, and bestow a similar correctness on every art and calling. The politician will acquire greater foresight and subtility, in the subdividing and balancing of power; the lawyer more method and finer principles in his reasonings; and the general more regularity in his discipline, and more caution in his plans and operations. The stability of modern governments above the ancient, and the accuracy of modern philosophy, have improved, and probably will still improve, by similar gradations.

Were there no advantage to be reaped from these studies, beyond the gratification of an innocent curiosity, yet ought not even this to be despised; as being one accession to those few safe and harmless pleasures, which are bestowed on human race. The sweetest and most inoffensive path of life leads through the avenues of science and learning; and whoever can either remove any obstructions in this way, or open up any new prospect, ought so far to be esteemed a benefactor to mankind. And though these researches may appear painful and fatiguing, it is with some minds as with some bodies, which being endowed with vigorous and florid health, require severe exercise, and reap a pleasure from what, to the generality of mankind, may seem burdensome and laborious. Obscurity, indeed, is painful to the mind as well as to the eye; but to bring light from obscurity, by whatever labour, must needs be delightful and rejoicing.

But this obscurity in the profound and abstract philosophy, is objected to, not only as painful and fatiguing, but as the inevitable source of uncertainty and error. Here indeed lies the justest and most plausible objection against a considerable part of metaphysics, that they are not properly a science; but arise either from the fruitless efforts of human vanity, which would penetrate into subjects utterly inaccessible to the understanding, or from the craft of popular superstitions, which, being unable to defend themselves on fair ground, raise these entangling brambles to cover and protect their weakness. Chased from the open country, these robbers fly into the forest, and lie in wait to break in upon every unguarded avenue of the mind, and overwhelm it with religious fears and prejudices. The stoutest antagonist, if he remit his watch a moment, is oppressed. And many, through cowardice and folly, open the gates to the enemies, and willingly receive them with reverence and submission, as their legal sovereigns.

But is this a sufficient reason, why philosophers should desist from such researches, and leave superstition still in possession of her retreat? Is it not proper to draw an opposite conclusion, and perceive the necessity of carrying the war into the most secret recesses of the enemy? In vain do we hope, that men, from frequent disappointment, will at last abandon such airy sciences, and discover the proper province of human reason. For, besides, that many persons find too sensible an interest in perpetually recalling such topics; besides this, I say, the motive of blind despair can never reasonably have place in the sciences; since, however unsuccessful former attempts may have proved, there is still room to hope, that the industry, good fortune, or improved sagacity of succeeding generations may reach discoveries unknown to former ages. Each adventurous genius will still leap at the arduous prize, and find himself stimulated, rather than discouraged, by the failures of his predecessors; while he hopes that the glory of achieving so hard an adventure is reserved for him alone. The only method of freeing learning, at once, from these abstruse questions, is to enquire seriously into the nature of human understanding, and shew, from an exact analysis of its powers and capacity, that it is by no means fitted for such remote and abstruse subjects. We must submit to this fatigue, in order to live at ease ever after: and must cultivate true metaphysics with some care, in order to destroy the false and adulterate. Indolence, which, to some persons, affords a safeguard against this deceitful philosophy, is, with others, overbalanced by curiosity; and despair, which, at some moments, prevails, may give place afterwards to sanguine hopes and expectations. Accurate and just reasoning is the only catholic remedy, fitted for all persons and all dispositions; and is alone able to subvert that abstruse philosophy and metaphysical jargon, which, being mixed up with popular superstition, renders it in a manner impenetrable to careless reasoners, and gives it the air of science and wisdom.

Besides this advantage of rejecting, after deliberate enquiry, the most uncertain and disagreeable part of learning, there are many positive advantages, which result from an accurate scrutiny into the powers and faculties of human nature. It is remarkable concerning the operations of the mind, that, though most intimately present to us, yet, whenever they become the object of reflection, they seem involved in obscurity; nor can the eye readily find those lines and boundaries, which discriminate and distinguish them. The objects are too fine to remain long in the same aspect or situation; and must be apprehended in an instant, by a superior penetration, derived from nature, and improved by habit and reflection. It becomes, therefore, no inconsiderable part of science barely to know the different operations of the mind, to separate them from each other, to class them under their proper heads, and to correct all that seeming disorder, in which they lie involved, when made the object of reflection and enquiry. This task of ordering and distinguishing, which has no merit, when performed with regard to external bodies, the objects of our senses, rises in its value, when directed towards the operations of the mind, in proportion to the difficulty and labour, which we meet with in performing it. And if we can go no farther than this mental geography, or delineation of the distinct parts and powers of the mind, it is at least a satisfaction to go so far; and the more obvious this science may appear (and it is by no means obvious) the more contemptible still must the ignorance of it be esteemed, in all pretenders to learning and philosophy.

Nor can there remain any suspicion, that this science is uncertain and chimerical; unless we should entertain such a scepticism as is entirely subversive of all speculation, and even action. It cannot be doubted, that the mind is endowed with several powers and faculties, that these powers are distinct from each other, that what is really distinct to the immediate perception may be distinguished by reflection; and consequently, that there is a truth and falsehood in all propositions on this subject, and a truth and falsehood, which lie not beyond the compass of human understanding. There are many obvious distinctions of this kind, such as those between the will and understanding, the imagination and passions, which fall within the comprehension of every human creature; and the finer and more philosophical distinctions are no less real and certain, though more difficult to be comprehended. Some instances, especially late ones, of success in these enquiries, may give us a juster notion of the certainty and solidity of this branch of learning. And shall we esteem it worthy the labour of a philosopher to give us a true system of the planets, and adjust the position and order of those remote bodies; while we affect to overlook those, who, with so much success, delineate the parts of the mind, in which we are so intimately concerned?

But may we not hope, that philosophy, if cultivated with care, and encouraged by the attention of the public, may carry its researches still farther, and discover, at least in some degree, the secret springs and principles, by which the human mind is actuated in its operations? Astronomers had long contented themselves with proving, from the phenomena, the true motions, order, and magnitude of the heavenly bodies: Till a philosopher, at last, arose, who seems, from the happiest reasoning, to have also determined the laws and forces, by which the revolutions of the planets are governed and directed. The like has been performed with regard to other parts of nature. And there is no reason to despair of equal success in our enquiries concerning the mental powers and economy, if prosecuted with equal capacity and caution. It is probable, that one operation and principle of the mind depends on another; which, again, may be resolved into one more general and universal: And how far these researches may possibly be carried, it will be difficult for us, before, or even after, a careful trial, exactly to determine. This is certain, that attempts of this kind are every day made even by those who philosophize the most negligently: And nothing can be more requisite than to enter upon the enterprise with thorough care and attention; that, if it lie within the compass of human understanding, it may at last be happily achieved; if not, it may, however, be rejected with some confidence and security. This last conclusion, surely, is not desirable; nor ought it to be embraced too rashly. For how much must we diminish from the beauty and value of this species of philosophy, upon such a supposition? Moralists have hitherto been accustomed, when they considered the vast multitude and diversity of those actions that excite our approbation or dislike, to search for some common principle, on which this variety of sentiments might depend. And though they have sometimes carried the matter too far, by their passion for some one general principle; it must, however, be confessed, that they are excusable in expecting to find some general principles, into which all the vices and virtues were justly to be resolved. The like has been the endeavor of critics, logicians, and even politicians; Nor have their attempts been wholly unsuccessful; though perhaps longer time, greater accuracy, and more ardent application may bring these sciences still nearer their perfection. To throw up at once all pretensions of this kind may justly be deemed more rash, precipitate, and dogmatical, than even the boldest and most affirmative philosophy, that has ever attempted to impose its crude dictates and principles on mankind.

What though these reasonings concerning human nature seem abstract, and of difficult comprehension? This affords no presumption of their falsehood. On the contrary, it seems impossible, that what has hitherto escaped so many wise and profound philosophers can be very obvious and easy. And whatever pains these researches may cost us, we may think ourselves sufficiently rewarded, not only in point of profit but of pleasure, if, by that means, we can make any addition to our stock of knowledge, in subjects of such unspeakable importance.

But as, after all, the abstractedness of these speculations is no recommendation, but rather a disadvantage to them, and as this difficulty may perhaps be surmounted by care and art, and the avoiding of all unnecessary detail, we have, in the following enquiry, attempted to throw some light upon subjects, from which uncertainty has hitherto deterred the wise, and obscurity the ignorant. Happy, if we can unite the boundaries of the different species of philosophy, by reconciling profound enquiry with clearness, and truth with novelty! And still more happy, if, reasoning in this easy manner, we can undermine the foundations of an abstruse philosophy, which seems to have hitherto served only as a shelter to superstition, and a cover to absurdity and error!

SECTION II: OF THE ORIGIN OF IDEAS

Every one will readily allow, that there is a considerable difference between the perceptions of the mind, when a man feels the pain of excessive heat, or the pleasure of moderate warmth, and when he afterwards recalls to his memory this sensation, or anticipates it by his imagination. These faculties may mimic or copy the perceptions of the senses; but they never can entirely reach the force and vivacity of the original sentiment. The utmost we say of them, even when they operate with greatest vigor, is, that they represent their object in so lively a manner, that we could almost say we feel or see it: But, except the mind be disordered by disease or madness, they never can arrive at such a pitch of vivacity, as to render these perceptions altogether undistinguishable. All the colours of poetry, however splendid, can never paint natural objects in such a manner as to make the description be taken for a real landscape. The most lively thought is still inferior to the dullest sensation.

We may observe a like distinction to run through all the other perceptions of the mind. A man in a fit of anger, is actuated in a very different manner from one who only thinks of that emotion. If you tell me, that any person is in love, I easily understand your meaning, and form a just conception of his situation; but never can mistake that conception for the real disorders and agitations of the passion. When we reflect on our past sentiments and affections, our thought is a faithful mirror, and copies its objects truly; but the colours which it employs are faint and dull, in comparison of those in which our original perceptions were clothed. It requires no nice discernment or metaphysical head to mark the distinction between them.

Here therefore we may divide all the perceptions of the mind into two classes or species, which are distinguished by their different degrees of force and vivacity. The less forcible and lively are commonly denominated Thoughts or Ideas. The other species want a name in our language, and in most others; I suppose, because it was not requisite for any, but philosophical purposes, to rank them under a general term or appellation. Let us, therefore, use a little freedom, and call them Impressions; employing that word in a sense somewhat different from the usual. By the term impression, then, I mean all our more lively perceptions, when we hear, or see, or feel, or love, or hate, or desire, or will. And impressions are distinguished from ideas, which are the less lively perceptions, of which we are conscious, when we reflect on any of those sensations or movements above mentioned.

Nothing, at first view, may seem more unbounded than the thought of man, which not only escapes all human power and authority, but is not even restrained within the limits of nature and reality. To form monsters, and join incongruous shapes and appearances, costs the imagination no more trouble than to conceive the most natural and familiar objects. And while the body is confined to one planet, along which it creeps with pain and difficulty; the thought can in an instant transport us into the most distant regions of the universe; or even beyond the universe, into the unbounded chaos, where nature is supposed to lie in total confusion. What never was seen, or heard of, may yet be conceived; nor is any thing beyond the power of thought, except what implies an absolute contradiction.

But though our thought seems to possess this unbounded liberty, we shall find, upon a nearer examination, that it is really confined within very narrow limits, and that all this creative power of the mind amounts to no more than the faculty of compounding, transposing, augmenting, or diminishing the materials afforded us by the senses and experience. When we think of a golden mountain, we only join two consistent ideas, gold, and mountain, with which we were formerly acquainted. A virtuous horse we can conceive; because, from our own feeling, we can conceive virtue; and this we may unite to the figure and shape of a horse, which is an animal familiar to us. In short, all the materials of thinking are derived either from our outward or inward sentiment: The mixture and composition of these belongs alone to the mind and will. Or, to express myself in philosophical language, all our ideas or more feeble perceptions are copies of our impressions or more lively ones.

To prove this, the two following arguments will, I hope, be sufficient. First, when we analyze our thoughts or ideas, however compounded or sublime, we always find, that they resolve themselves into such simple ideas as were copied from a precedent feeling or sentiment. Even those ideas, which, at first view, seem the most wide of this origin, are found, upon a nearer scrutiny, to be derived from it. The idea of God, as meaning an infinitely intelligent, wise, and good Being, arises from reflecting on the operations of our own mind, and augmenting, without limit, those qualities of goodness and wisdom. We may prosecute this enquiry to what length we please; where we shall always find, that every idea which we examine is copied from a similar impression. Those who would assert, that this position is not universally true nor without exception, have only one, and that an easy method of refuting it; by producing that idea, which, in their opinion, is not derived from this source. It will then be incumbent on us, if we would maintain our doctrine, to produce the impression or lively perception, which corresponds to it.

Secondly, If it happen, from a defect of the organ, that a man is not susceptible of any species of sensation, we always find, that he is as little susceptible of the correspondent ideas. A blind man can form no notion of colours; a deaf man of sounds. Restore either of them that sense, in which he is deficient; by opening this new inlet for his sensations, you also open an inlet for the ideas; and he finds no difficulty in conceiving these objects. The case is the same, if the object, proper for exciting any sensation, has never been applied to the organ. A Laplander or Negro, has no notion of the relish of wine. And though there are few or no instances of a like deficiency in the mind, where a person has never felt or is wholly incapable of a sentiment or passion that belongs to his species; yet we find the same observation to take place in a less degree. A man of mild manners can form no idea of inveterate revenge or cruelty; nor can a selfish heart easily conceive the heights of friendship and generosity. It is readily allowed, that other beings may possess many senses of which we can have no conception; because the ideas of them have never been introduced to us, in the only manner, by which an idea can have access to the mind, to wit, by the actual feeling and sensation.

There is, however, one contradictory phenomenon, which may prove, that it is not absolutely impossible for ideas to arise, independent of their correspondent impressions. I believe it will readily be allowed, that the several distinct ideas of colour, which enter by the eye, or those of sound, which are conveyed by the ear, are really different from each other; though, at the same time, resembling. Now if this be true of different colours, it must be no less so of the different shades of the same colour; and each shade produces a distinct idea, independent of the rest. For if this should be denied, it is possible, by the continual gradation of shades, to run a colour insensibly into what is most remote from it; and if you will not allow any of the means to be different, you cannot, without absurdity, deny the extremes to be the same. Suppose, therefore, a person to have enjoyed his sight for thirty years, and to have become perfectly acquainted with colours of all kinds, except one particular shade of blue, for instance, which it never has been his fortune to meet with. Let all the different shades of that colour, except that single one, be placed before him, descending gradually from the deepest to the lightest; it is plain, that he will perceive a blank, where that shade is wanting, and will be sensible, that there is a greater distance in that place between the contiguous colours than in any other. Now I ask, whether it be possible for him, from his own imagination, to supply this deficiency, and raise up to himself the idea of that particular shade, though it had never been conveyed to him by his senses? I believe there are few but will be of opinion that he can: And this may serve as a proof, that the simple ideas are not always, in every instance, derived from the correspondent impressions; though this instance is so singular, that it is scarcely worth our observing, and does not merit, that for it alone we should alter our general maxim.

Here, therefore, is a proposition, which not only seems, in itself, simple and intelligible; but, if a proper use were made of it, might render every dispute equally intelligible, and banish all that jargon, which has so long taken possession of metaphysical reasonings, and drawn disgrace upon them. All ideas, especially abstract ones, are naturally faint and obscure: The mind has but a slender hold of them: they are apt to be confounded with other resembling ideas; and when we have often employed any term, though without a distinct meaning, we are apt to imagine it has a determinate idea, annexed to it. On the contrary, all impressions, that is, all sensations, either outward or inward, are strong and vivid: The limits between them are more exactly determined: Nor is it easy to fall into any error or mistake with regard to them. When we entertain, therefore, any suspicion, that a philosophical term is employed without any meaning or idea (as is but too frequent), we need but enquire, from what impression is that supposed idea derived? And if it be impossible to assign any, this will serve to confirm our suspicion. By bringing ideas into so clear a light, we may reasonably hope to remove all dispute, which may arise, concerning their nature and reality.

SECTION III: OF THE ASSOCIATION OF IDEAS

It is evident, that there is a principle of connexion between the different thoughts or ideas of the mind, and that, in their appearance to the memory or imagination, they introduce each other with a certain degree of method and regularity. In our more serious thinking or discourse, this is so observable, that any particular thought, which breaks in upon the regular tract or chain of ideas, is immediately remarked and rejected. And even in our wildest and most wandering reveries, nay in our very dreams, we shall find, if we reflect, that the imagination ran not altogether at adventures, but that there was still a connexion upheld among the different ideas, which succeeded each other. Were the loosest and freest conversation to be transcribed, there would immediately be observed something, which connected it in all its transitions. Or where this is wanting, the person, who broke the thread of discourse, might still inform you, that there had secretly revolved in his mind a succession of thought, which had gradually led him from the subject of conversation. Among different languages, even where we cannot suspect the least connexion or communication, it is found, that the words, expressive of ideas, the most compounded, do yet nearly correspond to each other: A certain proof, that the simple ideas, comprehended in the compound ones, were bound together by some universal principle, which had an equal influence on all mankind.

Though it be too obvious to escape observation, that different ideas are connected together; I do not find, that any philosopher has attempted to enumerate or class all the principles of association; a subject, however, that seems worthy of curiosity. To me, there appear to be only three principles of connexion among ideas, namely, Resemblance, Contiguity in time or place, and Cause or Effect.

That these principles serve to connect ideas will not, I believe, be much doubted. A picture naturally leads our thoughts to the original: The mention of one apartment in a building naturally introduces an enquiry or discourse concerning the others: and if we think of a wound, we can scarcely forbear reflecting on the pain which follows it. But that this enumeration is complete, and that there are no other principles of association, except these, may be difficult to prove to the satisfaction of the reader, or even to a man's own satisfaction. All we can do, in such cases, is to run over several instances, and examine carefully the principle, which binds the different thoughts to each other, never stopping till we render the principle as general as possible. The more instances we examine, and the more care we employ, the more assurance shall we acquire, that the enumeration, which we form from the whole, is complete and entire.

SECTION IV: SCEPTICAL DOUBTS CONCERNING THE OPERATIONS OF THE UNDERSTANDING

Part I

All the objects of human reason or enquiry may naturally be divided into two kinds, to wit, Relations of Ideas, and Matters of Fact. Of the first kind are the sciences of Geometry, Algebra, and Arithmetic; and in short, every affirmation, which is either intuitively or demonstratively certain. That the square of the hypothenuse is equal to the squares of the two sides, is a proposition, which expresses a relation between these figures. That three times five is equal to the half of thirty, expresses a relation between these numbers. Propositions of this kind are discoverable by the mere operation of thought, without dependence on what is any where existent in the universe. Though there never were a circle or triangle in nature, the truths, demonstrated by Euclid, would for ever retain their certainty and evidence.

Matters of fact, which are the second objects of human reason, are not ascertained in the same manner; nor is our evidence of their truth, however great, of a like nature with the foregoing. The contrary of every matter of fact is still possible; because it can never imply a contradiction, and is conceived by the mind with the same facility and distinctness, as if ever so conformable to reality. That the sun will not rise to-morrow is no less intelligible a proposition, and implies no more contradiction, than the affirmation, that it will rise. We should in vain, therefore, attempt to demonstrate its falsehood. Were it demonstratively false, it would imply a contradiction, and could never be distinctly conceived by the mind.

It may, therefore, be a subject worthy of curiosity, to enquire what is the nature of that evidence, which assures us of any real existence and matter of fact, beyond the present testimony of our senses, or the records of our memory. This part of philosophy, it is observable, has been little cultivated, either by the ancients or moderns; and therefore our doubts and errors, in the prosecution of so important an enquiry, may be the more excusable; while we march through such difficult paths, without any guide or direction. They may even prove useful, by exciting curiosity, and destroying that implicit faith and security, which is the bane of all reasoning and free enquiry. The discovery of defects in the common philosophy, if any such there be, will not, I presume, be a discouragement, but rather an incitement, as is usual, to attempt something more full and satisfactory, than has yet been proposed to the public.

All reasonings concerning matter of fact seem to be founded on the relation of Cause and Effect. By means of that relation alone we can go beyond the evidence of our memory and senses. If you were to ask a man, why he believes any matter of fact, which is absent; for instance, that his friend is in the country, or in France; he would give you a reason; and this reason would be some other fact; as a letter received from him, or the knowledge of his former resolutions and promises. A man, finding a watch or any other machine in a desert island, would conclude, that there had once been men in that island. All our reasonings concerning fact are of the same nature. And here it is constantly supposed, that there is a connexion between the present fact and that which is inferred from it. Were there nothing to bind them together, the inference would be entirely precarious. The hearing of an articulate voice and rational discourse in the dark assures us of the presence of some person: Why? because these are the effects of the human make and fabric, and closely connected with it. If we anatomize all the other reasonings of this nature, we shall find, that they are founded on the relation of cause and effect, and that this relation is either near or remote, direct or collateral. Heat and light are collateral effects of fire, and the one effect may justly be inferred from the other.

If we would satisfy ourselves, therefore, concerning the nature of that evidence, which assures us of matters of fact, we must enquire how we arrive at the knowledge of cause and effect.

I shall venture to affirm, as a general proposition, which admits of no exception, that the knowledge of this relation is not, in any instance, attained by reasonings a priori; but arises entirely from experience, when we find, that any particular objects are constantly conjoined with each other. Let an object be presented to a man of ever so strong natural reason and abilities; if that object be entirely new to him, he will not be able, by the most accurate examination of its sensible qualities, to discover any of its causes or effects. Adam, though his rational faculties be supposed, at the very first, entirely perfect, could not have inferred from the fluidity, and transparency of water, that it would suffocate him, or from the light and warmth of fire, that it would consume him. No object ever discovers, by the qualities which appear to the senses, either the causes which produced it, or the effects which will arise from it; nor can our reason, unassisted by experience, ever draw any inference concerning real existence and matter of fact.

This proposition, that causes and effects are discoverable, not by reason but by experience, will readily be admitted with regard to such objects, as we remember to have once been altogether unknown to us; since we must be conscious of the utter inability, which we then lay under, of foretelling, what would arise from them. Present two smooth pieces of marble to a man, who has no tincture of natural philosophy; he will never discover, that they will adhere together, in such a manner as to require great force to separate them in a direct line, while they make so small a resistance to a lateral pressure. Such events, as bear little analogy to the common course of nature, are also readily confessed to be known only by experience; nor does any man imagine that the explosion of gunpowder, or the attraction of a loadstone, could ever be discovered by arguments a priori. In like manner, when an effect is supposed to depend upon an intricate machinery or secret structure of parts, we make no difficulty in attributing all our knowledge of it to experience. Who will assert, that he can give the ultimate reason, why milk or bread is proper nourishment for a man, not for a lion or a tiger?

But the same truth may not appear, at first sight, to have the same evidence with regard to events, which have become familiar to us from our first appearance in the world, which bear a close analogy to the whole course of nature, and which are supposed to depend on the simple qualities of objects, without any secret structure of parts. We are apt to imagine, that we could discover these effects by the mere operation of our reason, without experience. We fancy, that were we brought, on a sudden, into this world, we could at first have inferred, that one Billiard-ball would communicate motion to another upon impulse; and that we needed not to have waited for the event, in order to pronounce with certainty concerning it. Such is the influence of custom, that, where it is strongest, it not only covers our natural ignorance, but even conceals itself, and seems not to take place, merely because it is found in the highest degree.

But to convince us, that all the laws of nature, and all the operations of bodies without exception, are known only by experience, the following reflections may, perhaps, suffice. Were any object presented to us, and were we required to pronounce concerning the effect, which will result from it, without consulting past observation; after what manner, I beseech you, must the mind proceed in this operation? It must invent or imagine some event, which it ascribes to the object as its effect; and it is plain that this invention must be entirely arbitrary. The mind can never possibly find the effect in the supposed cause, by the most accurate scrutiny and examination. For the effect is totally different from the cause, and consequently can never be discovered in it. Motion in the second Billiard-ball is a quite distinct event from motion in the first; nor is there any thing in the one to suggest the smallest hint of the other. A stone or piece of metal raised into the air, and left without any support, immediately falls: But to consider the matter a priori, is there any thing we discover in this situation, which can beget the idea of a downward, rather than an upward, or any other motion, in the stone or metal?

And as the first imagination or invention of a particular effect, in all natural operations, is arbitrary, where we consult not experience; so must we also esteem the supposed tie or connexion between the cause and effect, which binds them together, and renders it impossible, that any other effect could result from the operation of that cause. When I see, for instance, a Billiard-ball moving in a straight line towards another; even suppose motion in the second ball should by accident be suggested to me, as the result of their contact or impulse; may I not conceive, that a hundred different events might as well follow from that cause? May not both these balls remain at absolute rest? May not the first ball return in a straight line, or leap off from the second in any line or direction? All these suppositions are consistent and conceivable. Why then should we give the preference to one, which is no more consistent or conceivable than the rest? All our reasonings a priori will never be able to shew us any foundation for this preference.

In a word, then, every effect is a distinct event from its cause. It could not, therefore, be discovered in the cause, and the first invention or conception of it, a priori, must be entirely arbitrary. And even after it is suggested, the conjunction of it with the cause must appear equally arbitrary; since there are always many other effects, which, to reason, must seem fully as consistent and natural. In vain, therefore, should we pretend to determine any single event, or infer any cause or effect, without the assistance of observation and experience.

Hence we may discover the reason, why no philosopher, who is rational and modest, has ever pretended to assign the ultimate cause of any natural operation, or to show distinctly the action of that power, which produces any single effect in the universe. It is confessed, that the utmost effort of human reason is to reduce the principles, productive of natural phenomena, to a greater simplicity, and to resolve the many particular effects into a few general causes, by means of reasonings from analogy, experience, and observation. But as to the causes of these general causes, we should in vain attempt their discovery; nor shall we ever be able to satisfy ourselves, by any particular explication of them. These ultimate springs and principles are totally shut up from human curiosity and enquiry. Elasticity, gravity, cohesion of parts, communication of motion by impulse; these are probably the ultimate causes and principles which we shall ever discover in nature; and we may esteem ourselves sufficiently happy, if, by accurate enquiry and reasoning, we can trace up the particular phenomena to, or near to, these general principles. The most perfect philosophy of the natural kind only staves off our ignorance a little longer: As perhaps the most perfect philosophy of the moral or metaphysical kind serves only to discover larger portions of it. Thus the observation of human blindness and weakness is the result of all philosophy, and meets us, at every turn, in spite of our endeavors to elude or avoid it.

Nor is geometry, when taken into the assistance of natural philosophy, ever able to remedy this defect, or lead us into the knowledge of ultimate causes, by all that accuracy of reasoning, for which it is so justly celebrated. Every part of mixed mathematics proceeds upon the supposition, that certain laws are established by nature in her operations; and abstract reasonings are employed, either to assist experience in the discovery of these laws, or to determine their influence in particular instances, where it depends upon any precise degree of distance and quantity. Thus, it is a law of motion, discovered by experience, that the moment or force of any body in motion is in the compound ratio or proportion of its solid contents and its velocity; and consequently, that a small force may remove the greatest obstacle or raise the greatest weight, if, by any contrivance or machinery, we can increase the velocity of that force, so as to make it an overmatch for its antagonist. Geometry assists us in the application of this law, by giving us the just dimensions of all the parts and figures, which can enter into any species of machine; but still the discovery of the law itself is owing merely to experience, and all the abstract reasonings in the world could never lead us one step towards the knowledge of it. When we reason a priori, and consider merely any object or cause, as it appears to the mind, independent of all observation, it never could suggest to us the notion of any distinct object, such as its effect; much less, shew us the inseparable and inviolable connexion between them. A man must be very sagacious, who could discover by reasoning that crystal is the effect of heat, and ice of cold, without being previously acquainted with the operation of these qualities.

Part II

But we have not, yet, attained any tolerable satisfaction with regard to the question first proposed. Each solution still gives rise to a new question as difficult as the foregoing, and leads us on to farther enquiries. When it is asked, What is the nature of all our reasonings concerning matter of fact? the proper answer seems to be, that they are founded on the relation of cause and effect. When again it is asked, What is the foundation of all our reasonings and conclusions concerning that relation? it may be replied in one word, Experience. But if we still carry on our sifting humor, and ask, What is the foundation of all conclusions from experience? this implies a new question, which may be of more difficult solution and explication. Philosophers, that give themselves airs of superior wisdom and sufficiency, have a hard task, when they encounter persons of inquisitive dispositions, who push them from every corner, to which they retreat, and who are sure at last to bring them to some dangerous dilemma. The best expedient to prevent this confusion, is to be modest in our pretensions; and even to discover the difficulty ourselves before it is objected to us. By this means, we may make a kind of merit of our very ignorance.

I shall content myself, in this section, with an easy task, and shall pretend only to give a negative answer to the question here proposed. I say then, that, even after we have experience of the operations of cause and effect, our conclusions from that experience are not founded on reasoning, or any process of the understanding. This answer we must endeavor, both to explain and to defend.

It must certainly be allowed, that nature has kept us at a great distance from all her secrets, and has afforded us only the knowledge of a few superficial qualities of objects; while she conceals from us those powers and principles, on which the influence of these objects entirely depends. Our senses inform us of the colour, weight, and consistence of bread; but neither sense nor reason can ever inform us of those qualities, which fit it for the nourishment and support of a human body. Sight or feeling conveys an idea of the actual motion of bodies; but as to that wonderful force or power, which would carry on a moving body for ever in a continued change of place, and which bodies never lose but by communicating it to others; of this we cannot form the most distant conception. But notwithstanding this ignorance of natural powers and principles, we always presume, when we see like sensible qualities, that they have like secret powers, and expect, that effects, similar to those which we have experienced, will follow from them. If a body of like colour and consistence with that bread, which we have formerly eaten, be presented to us, we make no scruple of repeating the experiment, and foresee, with certainty, like nourishment and support. Now this is a process of the mind or thought, of which I would willingly know the foundation. It is allowed on all hands, that there is no known connexion between the sensible qualities and the secret powers; and consequently, that the mind is not led to form such a conclusion concerning their constant and regular conjunction, by any thing which it knows of their nature. As to past Experience, it can be allowed to give direct and certain information of those precise objects only, and that precise period of time, which fell under its cognizance: But why this experience should be extended to future times, and to other objects, which for aught we know, may be only in appearance similar; this is the main question on which I would insist. The bread, which I formerly eat, nourished me; that is, a body of such sensible qualities, was, at that time, endued with such secret powers: But does it follow, that other bread must also nourish me at another time, and that like sensible qualities must always be attended with like secret powers? The consequence seems nowise necessary. At least, it must be acknowledged, that there is here a consequence drawn by the mind; that there is a certain step taken; a process of thought, and an inference, which wants to be explained. These two propositions are far from being the same, I have found that such an object has always been attended with such an effect, and I foresee, that other objects, which are, in appearance, similar, will be attended with similar effects. I shall allow, if you please, that the one proposition may justly be inferred from the other: I know in fact, that it always is inferred. But if you insist, that the inference is made by a chain of reasoning, I desire you to produce that reasoning. The connexion between these propositions is not intuitive. There is required a medium, which may enable the mind to draw such an inference, if indeed it be drawn by reasoning and argument. What that medium is, I must confess, passes my comprehension; and it is incumbent on those to produce it, who assert, that it really exists, and is the origin of all our conclusions concerning matter of fact.

This negative argument must certainly, in process of time, become altogether convincing, if many penetrating and able philosophers shall turn their enquiries this way; and no one be ever able to discover any connecting proposition or intermediate step, which supports the understanding in this conclusion. But as the question is yet new, every reader may not trust so far to his own penetration, as to conclude, because an argument escapes his enquiry, that therefore it does not really exist. For this reason it may be requisite to venture upon a more difficult task; and enumerating all the branches of human knowledge, endeavor to shew, that none of them can afford such an argument.

All reasonings may be divided into two kinds, namely demonstrative reasoning, or that concerning relations of ideas, and moral reasoning, or that concerning matter of fact and existence. That there are no demonstrative arguments in the case, seems evident; since it implies no contradiction, that the course of nature may change, and that an object, seemingly like those which we have experienced, may be attended with different or contrary effects. May I not clearly and distinctly conceive, that a body, falling from the clouds, and which, in all other respects, resembles snow, has yet the taste of salt or feeling of fire? Is there any more intelligible proposition than to affirm, that all the trees will flourish in December and January, and decay in May and June? Now whatever is intelligible, and can be distinctly conceived, implies no contradiction, and can never be proved false by any demonstrative argument or abstract reasoning a priori.

If we be, therefore, engaged by arguments to put trust in past experience, and make it the standard of our future judgment, these arguments must be probable only, or such as regard matter of fact and real existence, according to the division above mentioned. But that there is no argument of this kind, must appear, if our explication of that species of reasoning be admitted as solid and satisfactory. We have said, that all arguments concerning existence are founded on the relation of cause and effect; that our knowledge of that relation is derived entirely from experience; and that all our experimental conclusions proceed upon the supposition, that the future will be conformable to the past. To endeavor, therefore, the proof of this last supposition by probable arguments, or arguments regarding existence, must be evidently going in a circle, and taking that for granted, which is the very point in question.

In reality, all arguments from experience are founded on the similarity, which we discover among natural objects, and by which we are induced to expect effects similar to those, which we have found to follow from such objects. And though none but a fool or madman will ever pretend to dispute the authority of experience, or to reject that great guide of human life; it may surely be allowed a philosopher to have so much curiosity at least, as to examine the principle of human nature, which gives this mighty authority to experience, and makes us draw advantage from that similarity, which nature has placed among different objects. From causes, which appear similar, we expect similar effects. This is the sum of all our experimental conclusions. Now it seems evident, that, if this conclusion were formed by reason, it would be as perfect at first, and upon one instance, as after ever so long a course of experience. But the case is far otherwise. Nothing so like as eggs; yet no one, on account of this appearing similarity, expects the same taste and relish in all of them. It is only after a long course of uniform experiments in any kind, that we attain a firm reliance and security with regard to a particular event. Now where is that process of reasoning, which, from one instance, draws a conclusion, so different from that which it infers from a hundred instances, that are nowise different from that single one? This question I propose as much for the sake of information, as with an intention of raising difficulties. I cannot find, I cannot imagine any such reasoning. But I keep my mind still open to instruction, if any one will vouchsafe to bestow it on me.

Should it be said, that, from a number of uniform experiments, we infer a connexion between the sensible qualities and the secret powers; this, I must confess, seems the same difficulty, couched in different terms. The question still recurs, on what process of argument this inference is founded? Where is the medium, the interposing ideas, which join propositions so very wide of each other? It is confessed, that the colour, consistence, and other sensible qualities of bread appear not, of themselves, to have any connexion with the secret powers of nourishment and support. For otherwise we could infer these secret powers from the first appearance of these sensible qualities, without the aid of experience; contrary to the sentiment of all philosophers, and contrary to plain matter of fact. Here then is our natural state of ignorance with regard to the powers and influence of all objects. How is this remedied by experience? It only shows us a number of uniform effects, resulting from certain objects, and teaches us, that those particular objects, at that particular time, were endowed with such powers and forces. When a new object, endowed with similar sensible qualities, is produced, we expect similar powers and forces, and look for a like effect. From a body of like colour and consistence with bread, we expect like nourishment and support. But this surely is a step or progress of the mind, which wants to be explained. When a man says, I have found, in all past instances, such sensible qualities conjoined with such secret powers: And when he says, Similar sensible qualities will always be conjoined with similar secret powers; he is not guilty of a tautology, nor are these propositions in any respect the same. You say that the one proposition is an inference from the other. But you must confess that the inference is not intuitive; neither is it demonstrative: Of what nature is it then? To say it is experimental, is begging the question. For all inferences from experience suppose, as their foundation, that the future will resemble the past, and that similar powers will be conjoined with similar sensible qualities. If there be any suspicion, that the course of nature may change, and that the past may be no rule for the future, all experience becomes useless, and can give rise to no inference or conclusion. It is impossible, therefore, that any arguments from experience can prove this resemblance of the past to the future; since all these arguments are founded on the supposition of that resemblance. Let the course of things be allowed hitherto ever so regular; that alone, without some new argument or inference, proves not, that, for the future, it will continue so. In vain do you pretend to have learned the nature of bodies from your past experience. Their secret nature, and consequently, all their effects and influence, may change, without any change in their sensible qualities. This happens sometimes, and with regard to some objects: Why may it not happen always, and with regard to all objects? What logic, what process of argument secures you against this supposition? My practice, you say, refutes my doubts. But you mistake the purport of my question. As an agent, I am quite satisfied in the point; but as a philosopher, who has some share of curiosity, I will not say scepticism, I want to learn the foundation of this inference. No reading, no enquiry has yet been able to remove my difficulty, or give me satisfaction in a matter of such importance. Can I do better than propose the difficulty to the public, even though, perhaps, I have small hopes of obtaining a solution? We shall at least, by this means, be sensible of our ignorance, if we do not augment our knowledge.

I must confess, that a man is guilty of unpardonable arrogance, who concludes, because an argument has escaped his own investigation, that therefore it does not really exist. I must also confess, that, though all the learned, for several ages, should have employed themselves in fruitless search upon any subject, it may still, perhaps, be rash to conclude positively, that the subject must, therefore, pass all human comprehension. Even though we examine all the sources of our knowledge, and conclude them unfit for such a subject, there may still remain a suspicion, that the enumeration is not complete, or the examination not accurate. But with regard to the present subject, there are some considerations, which seem to remove all this accusation of arrogance or suspicion of mistake.

It is certain, that the most ignorant and stupid peasants, nay infants, nay even brute beasts, improve by experience, and learn the qualities of natural objects, by observing the effects, which result from them. When a child has felt the sensation of pain from touching the flame of a candle, he will be careful not to put his hand near any candle; but will expect a similar effect from a cause, which is similar in its sensible qualities and appearance. If you assert, therefore, that the understanding of the child is led into this conclusion by any process of argument or ratiocination, I may justly require you to produce that argument; nor have you any pretence to refuse so equitable a demand. You cannot say, that the argument is abstruse, and may possibly escape your enquiry; since you confess, that it is obvious to the capacity of a mere infant. If you hesitate, therefore, a moment, or if, after reflection, you produce any intricate or profound argument, you, in a manner, give up the question, and confess, that it is not reasoning which engages us to suppose the past resembling the future, and to expect similar effects from causes, which are, to appearance, similar. This is the proposition which I intended to enforce in the present section. If I be right, I pretend not to have made any mighty discovery. And if I be wrong, I must acknowledge myself to be indeed a very backward scholar; since I cannot now discover an argument, which, it seems, was perfectly familiar to me, long before I was out of my cradle.

SECTION V: SCEPTICAL SOLUTION OF THESE DOUBTS

Part I

The passion for philosophy, like that for religion, seems liable to this inconvenience, that, though it aims at the correction of our manners, and extirpation of our vices, it may only serve, by imprudent management, to foster a predominant inclination, and push the mind, with more determined resolution, towards that side, which already draws too much, by the bias and propensity of the natural temper. It is certain, that, while we aspire to the magnanimous firmness of the philosophic sage, and endeavor to confine our pleasures altogether within our own minds, we may, at last, render our philosophy like that of Epictetus, and other Stoics, only a more refined system of selfishness, and reason ourselves out of all virtue, as well as social enjoyment. While we study with attention the vanity of human life, and turn all our thoughts towards the empty and transitory nature of riches and honors, we are, perhaps, all the while, flattering our natural indolence, which, hating the bustle of the world, and drudgery of business, seeks a presence of reason to give itself a full and uncontrolled indulgence. There is, however, one species of philosophy, which seems little liable to this inconvenience, and that because it strikes in with no disorderly passion of the human mind, nor can mingle itself with any natural affection or propensity; and that is the Academic or Sceptical philosophy. The academics always talk of doubt and suspense of judgment, of danger in hasty determinations, of confining to very narrow bounds the enquiries of the understanding, and of renouncing all speculations which lie not within the limits of common life and practice. Nothing, therefore, can be more contrary than such a philosophy to the supine indolence of the mind, its rash arrogance, its lofty pretensions, and its superstitious credulity. Every passion is mortified by it, except the love of truth; and that passion never is, nor can be, carried to too high a degree. It is surprising, therefore, that this philosophy, which, in almost every instance, must be harmless and innocent, should be the subject of so much groundless reproach and obloquy. But, perhaps, the very circumstance, which renders it so innocent, is what chiefly exposes it to the public hatred and resentment. By flattering no irregular passion, it gains few partisans: By opposing so many vices and follies, it raises to itself abundance of enemies, who stigmatize it as libertine, profane, and irreligious.

Nor need we fear, that this philosophy, while it endeavors to limit our enquiries to common life, should ever undermine the reasonings of common life, and carry its doubts so far as to destroy all action, as well as speculation. Nature will always maintain her rights, and prevail in the end over any abstract reasoning whatsoever. Though we should conclude, for instance, as in the foregoing section, that, in all reasonings from experience, there is a step taken by the mind, which is not supported by any argument or process of the understanding, there is no danger, that these reasonings, on which almost all knowledge depends, will ever be affected by such a discovery. If the mind be not engaged by argument to make this step, it must be induced by some other principle of equal weight and authority; and that principle will preserve its influence as long as human nature remains the same. What that principle is, may well be worth the pains of enquiry.

Suppose a person, though endowed with the strongest faculties of reason and reflection, to be brought on a sudden into this world; he would, indeed, immediately observe a continual succession of objects, and one event following another; but he would not be able to discover any thing farther. He would not, at first, by any reasoning, be able to reach the idea of cause and effect; since the particular powers, by which all natural operations are performed, never appear to the senses; nor is it reasonable to conclude, merely because one event, in one instance, precedes another, that therefore the one is the cause, the other the effect. Their conjunction may be arbitrary and casual. There may be no reason to infer the existence of one from the appearance of the other. And in a word, such a person, without more experience, could never employ his conjecture or reasoning concerning any matter of fact, or be assured of any thing beyond what was immediately present to his memory and senses.

Suppose again, that he has acquired more experience, and has lived so long in the world as to have observed similar objects or events to be constantly conjoined together; what is the consequence of this experience? He immediately infers the existence of one object from the appearance of the other. Yet he has not, by all his experience, acquired any idea or knowledge of the secret power, by which the one object produces the other; nor is it, by any process of reasoning, he is engaged to draw this inference. But still he finds himself determined to draw it: And though he should be convinced, that his understanding has no part in the operation, he would nevertheless continue in the same course of thinking. There is some other principle, which determines him to form such a conclusion.

This principle is Custom or Habit. For wherever the repetition of any particular act or operation produces a propensity to renew the same act or operation, without being impelled by any reasoning or process of the understanding; we always say, that this propensity is the effect of Custom. By employing that word, we pretend not to have given the ultimate reason of such a propensity. We only point out a principle of human nature, which is universally acknowledged, and which is well known by its effects. Perhaps, we can push our enquiries no farther, or pretend to give the cause of this cause; but must rest contented with it as the ultimate principle, which we can assign, of all our conclusions from experience. It is sufficient satisfaction, that we can go so far; without repining at the narrowness of our faculties, because they will carry us no farther. And it is certain we here advance a very intelligible proposition at least, if not a true one, when we assert, that, after the constant conjunction of two objects, heat and flame, for instance, weight and solidity, we are determined by custom alone to expect the one from the appearance of the other. This hypothesis seems even the only one, which explains the difficulty, why we draw, from a thousand instances, an inference, which we are not able to draw from one instance, that is, in no respect, different from them. Reason is incapable of any such variation. The conclusions, which it draws from considering one circle, are the same which it would form upon surveying all the circles in the universe. But no man, having seen only one body move after being impelled by another, could infer, that every other body will move after a like impulse. All inferences from experience, therefore, are effects of custom, not of reasoning.

Custom, then, is the great guide of human life. It is that principle alone, which renders our experience useful to us, and makes us expect, for the future, a similar train of events with those which have appeared in the past. Without the influence of custom, we should be entirely ignorant of every matter of fact, beyond what is immediately present to the memory and senses. We should never know how to adjust means to ends, or to employ our natural powers in the production of any effect. There would be an end at once of all action, as well as of the chief part of speculation.

But here it may be proper to remark that though our conclusions from experience carry us beyond our memory and senses, and assure us of matters of fact, which happened in the most distant places and most remote ages; yet some fact must always be present to the senses or memory, from which we may first proceed in drawing these conclusions. A man, who should find in a desert country the remains of pompous buildings, would conclude, that the country had, in ancient times, been cultivated by civilized inhabitants; but did nothing of this nature occur to him, he could never form such an inference. We learn the events of former ages from history; but then we must peruse the volumes, in which this instruction is contained, and thence carry up our inferences from one testimony to another, till we arrive at the eye-witnesses and spectators of these distant events. In a word, if we proceed not upon some fact, present to the memory or senses, our reasonings would be merely hypothetical; and however the particular links might be connected with each other, the whole chain of inferences would have nothing to support it, nor could we ever, by its means, arrive at the knowledge of any real existence. If I ask why you believe any particular matter of fact, which you relate, you must tell me some reason; and this reason will be some other fact, connected with it. But as you cannot proceed after this manner, in infinitum, you must at last terminate in some fact, which is present to your memory or senses; or must allow that your belief is entirely without foundation.

What then is the conclusion of the whole matter? A simple one; though, it must be confessed, pretty remote from the common theories of philosophy. All belief of matter of fact or real existence is derived merely from some object, present to the memory or senses, and a customary conjunction between that and some other object. Or in other words; having found, in many instances, that any two kinds of objects, flame and heat, snow and cold, have always been conjoined together; if flame or snow be presented anew to the senses, the mind is carried by custom to expect heat or cold, and to believe, that such a quality does exist, and will discover itself upon a nearer approach. This belief is the necessary result of placing the mind in such circumstances. It is an operation of the soul, when we are so situated, as unavoidable as to feel the passion of love, when we receive benefits: or hatred, when we meet with injuries. All these operations are a species of natural instincts, which no reasoning or process of the thought and understanding is able, either to produce, or to prevent.

At this point, it would be very allowable for us to stop our philosophical researches. In most questions, we can never make a single step farther; and in all questions, we must terminate here at last, after our most restless and curious enquiries. But still our curiosity will be pardonable, perhaps commendable, if it carry us on to still farther researches, and make us examine more accurately the nature of this belief, and of the customary conjunction, whence it is derived. By this means we may meet with some explications and analogies, that will give satisfaction; at least to such as love the abstract sciences, and can be entertained with speculations, which, however accurate, may still retain a degree of doubt and uncertainty. As to readers of a different taste; the remaining part of this section is not calculated for them, and the following enquiries may well be understood, though it be neglected.

Part II

Nothing is more free than the imagination of man; and though it cannot exceed that original stock of ideas, furnished by the internal and external senses, it has unlimited power of mixing, compounding, separating, and dividing these ideas, in all the varieties of fiction and vision. It can feign a train of events, with all the appearance of reality, ascribe to them a particular time and place, conceive them as existent, and paint them out to itself with every circumstance, that belongs to any historical fact, which it believes with the greatest certainty. Wherein, therefore, consists the difference between such a fiction and belief? It lies not merely in any peculiar idea, which is annexed to such a conception as commands our assent, and which is wanting to every known fiction. For as the mind has authority over all its ideas, it could voluntarily annex this particular idea to any fiction, and consequently be able to believe whatever it pleases; contrary to what we find by daily experience. We can, in our conception, join the head of a man to the body of a horse; but it is not in our power to believe, that such an animal has ever really existed.

It follows, therefore, that the difference between fiction and belief lies in some sentiment or feeling, which is annexed to the latter, not to the former, and which depends not on the will, nor can be commanded at pleasure. It must be excited by nature, like all other sentiments; and must arise from the particular situation, in which the mind is placed at any particular juncture. Whenever any object is presented to the memory or senses, it immediately, by the force of custom, carries the imagination to conceive that object, which is usually conjoined to it; and this conception is attended with a feeling or sentiment, different from the loose reveries of the fancy. In this consists the whole nature of belief. For as there is no matter of fact which we believe so firmly, that we cannot conceive the contrary, there would be no difference between the conception assented to, and that which is rejected, were it not for some sentiment, which distinguishes the one from the other. If I see a billiard-ball moving towards another, on a smooth table, I can easily conceive it to stop upon contact. This conception implies no contradiction; but still it feels very differently from that conception, by which I represent to myself the impulse, and the communication of motion from one ball to another.

Were we to attempt a definition of this sentiment, we should, perhaps, find it a very difficult, if not an impossible task; in the same manner as if we should endeavor to define the feeling of cold or passion of anger, to a creature who never had any experience of these sentiments. Belief is the true and proper name of this feeling; and no one is ever at a loss to know the meaning of that term; because every man is every moment conscious of the sentiment represented by it. It may not, however, be improper to attempt a description of this sentiment; in hopes we may, by that means, arrive at some analogies, which may afford a more perfect explication of it. I say then, that belief is nothing but a more vivid, lively, forcible, firm, steady conception of an object, than what the imagination alone is ever able to attain. This variety of terms, which may seem so unphilosophical, is intended only to express that act of the mind, which renders realities, or what is taken for such, more present to us than fictions, causes them to weigh more in the thought, and gives them a superior influence on the passions and imagination. Provided we agree about the thing, it is needless to dispute about the terms. The imagination has the command over all its ideas, and can join and mix and vary them, in all the ways possible. It may conceive fictitious objects with all the circumstances of place and time. It may set them, in a manner, before our eyes, in their true colours, just as they might have existed. But as it is impossible, that this faculty of imagination can ever, of itself, reach belief, it is evident, that belief consists not in the peculiar nature or order of ideas, but in the manner of their conception, and in their feeling to the mind. I confess, that it is impossible perfectly to explain this feeling or manner of conception. We may make use of words, which express something near it. But its true and proper name, as we observed before, is belief; which is a term, that every one sufficiently understands in common life. And in philosophy, we can go no farther than assert, that belief is something felt by the mind, which distinguishes the ideas of the judgment from the fictions of the imagination. It gives them more weight and influence; makes them appear of greater importance; enforces them in the mind; and renders them the governing principle of our actions. I hear at present, for instance, a person's voice, with whom I am acquainted; and the sound comes as from the next room. This impression of my senses immediately conveys my thought to the person, together with all the surrounding objects. I paint them out to myself as existing at present, with the same qualities and relations, of which I formerly knew them possessed. These ideas take faster hold of my mind, than ideas of an enchanted castle. They are very different to the feeling, and have a much greater influence of every kind, either to give pleasure or pain, joy or sorrow.

Let us, then, take in the whole compass of this doctrine, and allow, that the sentiment of belief is nothing but a conception more intense and steady than what attends the mere fictions of the imagination, and that this manner of conception arises from a customary conjunction of the object with something present to the memory or senses: I believe that it will not be difficult, upon these suppositions, to find other operations of the mind analogous to it, and to trace up these phenomena to principles still more general.

We have already observed, that nature has established connexions among particular ideas, and that no sooner one idea occurs to our thoughts than it introduces its correlative, and carries our attention towards it, by a gentle and insensible movement. These principles of connexion or association we have reduced to three, namely, Resemblance, Contiguity, and Causation; which are the only bonds, that unite our thoughts together, and beget that regular train of reflection or discourse, which, in a greater or less degree, takes place among all mankind. Now here arises a question, on which the solution of the present difficulty will depend. Does it happen, in all these relations, that, when one of the objects is presented to the senses or memory, the mind is not only carried to the conception of the correlative, but reaches a steadier and stronger conception of it than what otherwise it would have been able to attain? This seems to be the case with that belief, which arises from the relation of cause and effect. And if the case be the same with the other relations or principles of association, this may be established as a general law, which takes place in all the operations of the mind.

We may, therefore, observe, as the first experiment to our present purpose, that, upon the appearance of the picture of an absent friend, our idea of him is evidently enlivened by the resemblance, and that every passion, which that idea occasions, whether of joy or sorrow, acquires new force and vigor. In producing this effect, there concur both a relation and a present impression. Where the picture bears him no resemblance, at least was not intended for him, it never so much as conveys our thought to him: And where it is absent, as well as the person; though the mind may pass from the thought of the one to that of the other; it feels its idea to be rather weakened than enlivened by that transition. We take a pleasure in viewing the picture of a friend, when it is set before us; but when it is removed, rather choose to consider him directly, than by reflection in an image, which is equally distant and obscure.

The ceremonies of the Roman Catholic religion may be considered as instances of the same nature. The devotees of that superstition usually plead in excuse for the mummeries, with which they are upbraided, that they feel the good effect of those external motions, and postures, and actions, in enlivening their devotion and quickening their fervor, which otherwise would decay, if directed entirely to distant and immaterial objects. We shadow out the objects of our faith, say they, in sensible types and images, and render them more present to us by the immediate presence of these types, than it is possible for us to do, merely by an intellectual view and contemplation. Sensible objects have always a greater influence on the fancy than any other; and this influence they readily convey to those ideas, to which they are related, and which they resemble. I shall only infer from these practices, and this reasoning, that the effect of resemblance in enlivening the ideas is very common; and as in every case a resemblance and a present impression must concur, we are abundantly supplied with experiments to prove the reality of the foregoing principle.

We may add force to these experiments by others of a different kind, in considering the effects of contiguity as well as of resemblance. It is certain, that distance diminishes the force of every idea, and that, upon our approach to any object; though it does not discover itself to our senses; it operates upon the mind with an influence, which imitates an immediate impression. The thinking on any object readily transports the mind to what is contiguous; but it is only the actual presence of an object, that transports it with a superior vivacity. When I am a few miles from home, whatever relates to it touches me more nearly than when I am two hundred leagues distant; though even at that distance the reflecting on any thing in the neighborhood of my friends or family naturally produces an idea of them. But as in this latter case, both the objects of the mind are ideas; notwithstanding there is an easy transition between them; that transition alone is not able to give a superior vivacity to any of the ideas, for want of some immediate impression.

No one can doubt but causation has the same influence as the other two relations of resemblance and contiguity. Superstitious people are fond of the relics of saints and holy men, for the same reason, that they seek after types or images, in order to enliven their devotion, and give them a more intimate and strong conception of those exemplary lives, which they desire to imitate. Now it is evident, that one of the best relics, which a devotee could procure, would be the handiwork of a saint; and if his clothes and furniture are ever to be considered in this light, it is because they were once at his disposal, and were moved and affected by him; in which respect they are to be considered as imperfect effects, and as connected with him by a shorter chain of consequences than any of those, by which we learn the reality of his existence.

Suppose, that the son of a friend, who had been long dead or absent, were presented to us; it is evident, that this object would instantly revive its correlative idea, and recall to our thoughts all past intimacies and familiarities, in more lively colours than they would otherwise have appeared to us. This is another phenomenon, which seems to prove the principle above-mentioned.

We may observe, that, in these phenomena, the belief of the correlative object is always presupposed; without which the relation could have no effect. The influence of the picture supposes, that we believe our friend to have once existed. Contiguity to home can never excite our ideas of home, unless we believe that it really exists. Now I assert, that this belief, where it reaches beyond the memory or senses, is of a similar nature, and arises from similar causes, with the transition of thought and vivacity of conception here explained. When I throw a piece of dry wood into a fire, my mind is immediately carried to conceive, that it augments, not extinguishes the flame. This transition of thought from the cause to the effect proceeds not from reason. It derives its origin altogether from custom and experience. And as it first begins from an object, present to the senses, it renders the idea or conception of flame more strong and lively than any loose, floating reverie of the imagination. That idea arises immediately. The thought moves instantly towards it, and conveys to it all that force of conception, which is derived from the impression present to the senses. When a sword is levelled at my breast, does not the idea of wound and pain strike me more strongly, than when a glass of wine is presented to me, even though by accident this idea should occur after the appearance of the latter object? But what is there in this whole matter to cause such a strong conception, except only a present object and a customary transition to the idea of another object, which we have been accustomed to conjoin with the former? This is the whole operation of the mind, in all our conclusions concerning matter of fact and existence; and it is a satisfaction to find some analogies, by which it may be explained. The transition from a present object does in all cases give strength and solidity to the related idea.

Here, then, is a kind of pre-established harmony between the course of nature and the succession of our ideas; and though the powers and forces, by which the former is governed, be wholly unknown to us; yet our thoughts and conceptions have still, we find, gone on in the same train with the other works of nature. Custom is that principle, by which this correspondence has been effected; so necessary to the subsistence of our species, and the regulation of our conduct, in every circumstance and occurrence of human life. Had not the presence of an object instantly excited the idea of those objects, commonly conjoined with it, all our knowledge must have been limited to the narrow sphere of our memory and senses; and we should never have been able to adjust means to ends, or employ our natural powers, either to the producing of good, or avoiding of evil. Those, who delight in the discovery and contemplation of final causes, have here ample subject to employ their wonder and admiration.

I shall add, for a further confirmation of the foregoing theory, that, as this operation of the mind, by which we infer like effects from like causes, and vice versa, is so essential to the subsistence of all human creatures, it is not probable, that it could be trusted to the fallacious deductions of our reason, which is slow in its operations; appears not, in any degree, during the first years of infancy; and at best is, in every age and period of human life, extremely liable to error and mistake. It is more conformable to the ordinary wisdom of nature to secure so necessary an act of the mind, by some instinct or mechanical tendency, which may be infallible in its operations, may discover itself at the first appearance of life and thought, and may be independent of all the labored deductions of the understanding. As nature has taught us the use of our limbs, without giving us the knowledge of the muscles and nerves, by which they are actuated; so has she implanted in us an instinct, which carries forward the thought in a correspondent course to that which she has established among external objects: though we are ignorant of those powers and forces, on which this regular course and succession of objects totally depends.

SECTION VI: OF PROBABILITY

Though there be no such thing as Chance in the world; our ignorance of the real cause of any event has the same influence on the understanding, and begets a like species of belief or opinion.

There is certainly a probability, which arises from a superiority of chances on any side; and according as this superiority increases, and surpasses the opposite chances, the probability receives a proportionable increase, and begets still a higher degree of belief or assent to that side, in which we discover the superiority. If a dye were marked with one figure or number of spots on four sides, and with another figure or number of spots on the two remaining sides, it would be more probable, that the former would turn up than the latter; though, if it had a thousand sides marked in the same manner, and only one side different, the probability would be much higher, and our belief or expectation of the event more steady and secure. This process of the thought or reasoning may seem trivial and obvious; but to those who consider it more narrowly, it may, perhaps, afford matter for curious speculation.

It seems evident, that, when the mind looks forward to discover the event, which may result from the throw of such a dye, it considers the turning up of each particular side as alike probable; and this is the very nature of chance, to render all the particular events, comprehended in it, entirely equal. But finding a greater number of sides concur in the one event than in the other, the mind is carried more frequently to that event, and meets it oftener, in revolving the various possibilities or chances, on which the ultimate result depends. This concurrence of several views in one particular event begets immediately, by an inexplicable contrivance of nature, the sentiment of belief, and gives that event the advantage over its antagonist, which is supported by a smaller number of views, and recurs less frequently to the mind. If we allow, that belief is nothing but a firmer and stronger conception of an object than what attends the mere fictions of the imagination, this operation may, perhaps, in some measure be accounted for. The concurrence of these several views or glimpses imprints the idea more strongly on the imagination; gives it superior force and vigor; renders its influence on the passions and affections more sensible; and in a word, begets that reliance or security, which constitutes the nature of belief and opinion.

The case is the same with the probability of causes, as with that of chance. There are some causes, which are entirely uniform and constant in producing a particular effect; and no instance has ever yet been found of any failure or irregularity in their operation. Fire has always burned, and water suffocated every human creature: The production of motion by impulse and gravity is an universal law, which has hitherto admitted of no exception. But there are other causes, which have been found more irregular and uncertain; nor has rhubarb always proved a purge, or opium a soporific to every one, who has taken these medicines. It is true, when any cause fails of producing its usual effect, philosophers ascribe not this to any irregularity in nature; but suppose, that some secret causes, in the particular structure of parts, have prevented the operation. Our reasonings, however, and conclusions concerning the event are the same as if this principle had no place. Being determined by custom to transfer the past to the future, in all our inferences; where the past has been entirely regular and uniform, we expect the event with the greatest assurance, and leave no room for any contrary supposition. But where different effects have been found to follow from causes, which are to appearance exactly similar, all these various effects must occur to the mind in transferring the past to the future, and enter into our consideration, when we determine the probability of the event. Though we give the preference to that which has been found most usual, and believe that this effect will exist, we must not overlook the other effects, but must assign to each of them a particular weight and authority, in proportion as we have found it to be more or less frequent. It is more probable, in almost every country of Europe, that there will be frost sometime in January, than that the weather will continue open throughout that whole month; though this probability varies according to the different climates, and approaches to a certainty in the more northern kingdoms. Here then it seems evident, that, when we transfer the past to the future, in order to determine the effect, which will result from any cause, we transfer all the different events, in the same proportion as they have appeared in the past, and conceive one to have existed a hundred times, for instance, another ten times, and another once. As a great number of views do here concur in one event, they fortify and confirm it to the imagination, beget that sentiment which we call belief, and give its object the preference above the contrary event, which is not supported by an equal number of experiments, and recurs not so frequently to the thought in transferring the past to the future. Let any one try to account for this operation of the mind upon any of the received systems of philosophy, and he will be sensible of the difficulty. For my part, I shall think it sufficient, if the present hints excite the curiosity of philosophers, and make them sensible how defective all common theories are in treating of such curious and such sublime subjects.

SECTION VII: OF THE IDEA OF NECESSARY CONNEXION

Part I

The great advantage of the mathematical sciences above the moral consists in this, that the ideas of the former, being sensible, are always clear and determinate, the smallest distinction between them is immediately perceptible, and the same terms are still expressive of the same ideas, without ambiguity or variation. An oval is never mistaken for a circle, nor an hyperbola for an ellipsis. The isosceles and scalenum are distinguished by boundaries more exact than vice and virtue, right and wrong. If any term be defined in geometry, the mind readily, of itself, substitutes, on all occasions, the definition for the term defined: Or even when no definition is employed, the object itself may be presented to the senses, and by that means be steadily and clearly apprehended. But the finer sentiments of the mind, the operations of the understanding, the various agitations of the passions, though really in themselves distinct, easily escape us, when surveyed by reflection; nor is it in our power to recall the original object, as often as we have occasion to contemplate it. Ambiguity, by this means, is gradually introduced into our reasonings: Similar objects are readily taken to be the same: And the conclusion becomes at last very wide of the premises.

One may safely, however, affirm, that, if we consider these sciences in a proper light, their advantages and disadvantages nearly compensate each other, and reduce both of them to a state of equality. If the mind, with greater facility, retains the ideas of geometry clear and determinate, it must carry on a much longer and more intricate chain of reasoning, and compare ideas much wider of each other, in order to reach the abstruser truths of that science. And if moral ideas are apt, without extreme care, to fall into obscurity and confusion, the inferences are always much shorter in these disquisitions, and the intermediate steps, which lead to the conclusion, much fewer than in the sciences which treat of quantity and number. In reality, there is scarcely a proposition in Euclid so simple, as not to consist of more parts, than are to be found in any moral reasoning which runs not into chimera and conceit. Where we trace the principles of the human mind through a few steps, we may be very well satisfied with our progress; considering how soon nature throws a bar to all our enquiries concerning causes, and reduces us to an acknowledgment of our ignorance. The chief obstacle, therefore, to our improvement in the moral or metaphysical sciences is the obscurity of the ideas, and ambiguity of the terms. The principal difficulty in the mathematics is the length of inferences and compass of thought, requisite to the forming of any conclusion. And, perhaps, our progress in natural philosophy is chiefly retarded by the want of proper experiments and phenomena, which are often discovered by chance, and cannot always be found, when requisite, even by the most diligent and prudent enquiry. As moral philosophy seems hitherto to have received less improvement than either geometry or physics, we may conclude, that, if there be any difference in this respect among these sciences, the difficulties, which obstruct the progress of the former, require superior care and capacity to be surmounted.

There are no ideas, which occur in metaphysics, more obscure and uncertain, than those of power, force, energy or necessary connexion, of which it is every moment necessary for us to treat in all our disquisitions. We shall, therefore, endeavor, in this section, to fix, if possible, the precise meaning of these terms, and thereby remove some part of that obscurity, which is so much complained of in this species of philosophy.

It seems a proposition, which will not admit of much dispute, that all our ideas are nothing but copies of our impressions, or, in other words, that it is impossible for us to think of any thing, which we have not antecedently felt, either by our external or internal senses. I have endeavored to explain and prove this proposition, and have expressed my hopes, that, by a proper application of it, men may reach a greater clearness and precision in philosophical reasonings, than what they have hitherto been able to attain. Complex ideas may, perhaps, be well known by definition, which is nothing but an enumeration of those parts or simple ideas, that compose them. But when we have pushed up definitions to the most simple ideas, and find still some ambiguity and obscurity; what resource are we then possessed of? By what invention can we throw light upon these ideas, and render them altogether precise and determinate to our intellectual view? Produce the impressions or original sentiments, from which the ideas are copied. These impressions are all strong and sensible. They admit not of ambiguity. They are not only placed in a full light themselves, but may throw light on their correspondent ideas, which lie in obscurity. And by this means, we may, perhaps, attain a new microscope or species of optics, by which, in the moral sciences, the most minute, and most simple ideas may be so enlarged as to fall readily under our apprehension, and be equally known with the grossest and most sensible ideas, that can be the object of our enquiry.

To be fully acquainted, therefore, with the idea of power or necessary connexion, let us examine its impression; and in order to find the impression with greater certainty, let us search for it in all the sources, from which it may possibly be derived.

When we look about us towards external objects, and consider the operation of causes, we are never able, in a single instance, to discover any power or necessary connexion; any quality, which binds the effect to the cause, and renders the one an infallible consequence of the other. We only find, that the one does actually, in fact, follow the other. The impulse of one billiard-ball is attended with motion in the second. This is the whole that appears to the outward senses. The mind feels no sentiment or inward impression from this succession of objects: Consequently, there is not, in any single, particular instance of cause and effect, any thing which can suggest the idea of power or necessary connexion.

From the first appearance of an object, we never can conjecture what effect will result from it. But were the power or energy of any cause discoverable by the mind, we could foresee the effect, even without experience; and might, at first, pronounce with certainty concerning it, by the mere dint of thought and reasoning.

In reality, there is no part of matter, that does ever, by its sensible qualities, discover any power or energy, or give us ground to imagine, that it could produce any thing, or be followed by any other object, which we could denominate its effect. Solidity, extension, motion; these qualities are all complete in themselves, and never point out any other event which may result from them. The scenes of the universe are continually shifting, and one object follows another in an uninterrupted succession; but the power or force, which actuates the whole machine, is entirely concealed from us, and never discovers itself in any of the sensible qualities of body. We know, that, in fact, heat is a constant attendant of flame; but what is the connexion between them, we have no room so much as to conjecture or imagine. It is impossible, therefore, that the idea of power can be derived from the contemplation of bodies, in single instances of their operation; because no bodies ever discover any power, which can be the original of this idea.

Since, therefore, external objects as they appear to the senses, give us no idea of power or necessary connexion, by their operation in particular instances, let us see, whether this idea be derived from reflection on the operations of our own minds, and be copied from any internal impression. It may be said, that we are every moment conscious of internal power; while we feel, that, by the simple command of our will, we can move the organs of our body, or direct the faculties of our mind. An act of volition produces motion in our limbs, or raises a new idea in our Imagination. This influence of the will we know by consciousness. Hence we acquire the idea of power or energy; and are certain, that we ourselves and all other intelligent beings are possessed of power. This idea, then, is an idea of reflection, since it arises from reflecting on the operations of our own mind, and on the command which is exercised by will, both over the organs of the body and faculties of the soul.

We shall proceed to examine this pretension; and first with regard to the influence of volition over the organs of the body. This influence, we may observe, is a fact, which, like all other natural events, can be known only by experience, and can never be foreseen from any apparent energy or power in the cause, which connects it with the effect, and renders the one an infallible consequence of the other. The motion of our body follows upon the command of our will. Of this we are every moment conscious. But the means, by which this is effected; the energy, by which the will performs so extraordinary an operation; of this we are so far from being immediately conscious, that it must for ever escape our most diligent enquiry.

For first; is there any principle in all nature more mysterious than the union of soul with body; by which a supposed spiritual substance acquires such an influence over a material one, that the most refined thought is able to actuate the grossest matter? Were we empowered, by a secret wish, to remove mountains, or control the planets in their orbit; this extensive authority would not be more extraordinary, nor more beyond our comprehension. But if by consciousness we perceived any power or energy in the will, we must know this power; we must know its connexion with the effect; we must know the secret union of soul and body, and the nature of both these substances; by which the one is able to operate, in so many instances, upon the other.

Secondly, We are not able to move all the organs of the body with a like authority; though we cannot assign any reason besides experience, for so remarkable a difference between one and the other. Why has the will an influence over the tongue and fingers, not over the heart or liver? This question would never embarrass us, were we conscious of a power in the former case, not in the latter. We should then perceive, independent of experience, why the authority of will over the organs of the body is circumscribed within such particular limits. Being in that case fully acquainted with the power or force, by which it operates, we should also know, why its influence reaches precisely to such boundaries, and no farther.

A man, suddenly struck with a palsy in the leg or arm, or who had newly lost those members, frequently endeavors, at first to move them, and employ them in their usual offices. Here he is as much conscious of power to command such limbs, as a man in perfect health is conscious of power to actuate any member which remains in its natural state and condition. But consciousness never deceives. Consequently, neither in the one case nor in the other, are we ever conscious of any power. We learn the influence of our will from experience alone. And experience only teaches us, how one event constantly follows another; without instructing us in the secret connexion, which binds them together, and renders them inseparable.

Thirdly, We learn from anatomy, that the immediate object of power in voluntary motion, is not the member itself which is moved, but certain muscles, and nerves, and animal spirits and, perhaps, something still more minute and more unknown, through which the motion is successively propagated, ere it reach the member itself whose motion is the immediate object of volition. Can there be a more certain proof that the power, by which this whole operation is performed, so far from being directly and fully known by an inward sentiment or consciousness, is, to the last degree, mysterious and unintelligible? Here the mind wills a certain event: Immediately another event, unknown to ourselves, and totally different from the one intended, is produced: This event produces another, equally unknown: Till at last, through a long succession, the desired event is produced. But if the original power were felt, it must be known: Were it known, its effect must also be known; since all power is relative to its effect. And vice versa, if the effect be not known, the power cannot be known nor felt. How indeed can we be conscious of a power to move our limbs, when we have no such power; but only that to move certain animal spirits, which, though they produce at last the motion of our limbs, yet operate in such a manner as is wholly beyond our comprehension?

We may, therefore, conclude from the whole, I hope, without any temerity, though with assurance; that our idea of power is not copied from any sentiment or consciousness of power within ourselves, when we give rise to animal motion, or apply our limbs, to their proper use and office. That their motion follows the command of the will is a matter of common experience, like other natural events: But the power or energy by which this is effected, like that in other natural events, is unknown and inconceivable.

Shall we then assert, that we are conscious of a power or energy in our own minds, when, by an act or command of our will, we raise up a new idea, fix the mind to the contemplation of it, turn it on all sides, and at last dismiss it for some other idea, when we think that we have surveyed it with sufficient accuracy? I believe the same arguments will prove, that even this command of the will gives us no real idea of force or energy.

First, It must be allowed, that, when we know a power, we know that very circumstance in the cause, by which it is enabled to produce the effect: For these are supposed to be synonymous. We must, therefore, know both the cause and effect, and the relation between them. But do we pretend to be acquainted with the nature of the human soul and the nature of an idea, or the aptitude of the one to produce the other? This is a real creation; a production of something out of nothing: Which implies a power so great, that it may seem, at first sight, beyond the reach of any being, less than infinite. At least it must be owned, that such a power is not felt, nor known, nor even conceivable by the mind. We only feel the event, namely, the existence of an idea, consequent to a command of the will: But the manner, in which this operation is performed, the power by which it is produced, is entirely beyond our comprehension.

Secondly, The command of the mind over itself is limited, as well as its command over the body; and these limits are not known by reason, or any acquaintance with the nature of cause and effect, but only by experience and observation, as in all other natural events and in the operation of external objects. Our authority over our sentiments and passions is much weaker than that over our ideas; and even the latter authority is circumscribed within very narrow boundaries. Will any one pretend to assign the ultimate reason of these boundaries, or shew why the power is deficient in one case, not in another?

Thirdly, This self-command is very different at different times. A man in health possesses more of it than one languishing with sickness. We are more master of our thoughts in the morning than in the evening: Fasting, than after a full meal. Can we give any reason for these variations, except experience? Where then is the power, of which we pretend to be conscious? Is there not here, either in a spiritual or material substance, or both, some secret mechanism or structure of parts, upon which the effect depends, and which, being entirely unknown to us, renders the power or energy of the will equally unknown and incomprehensible?

Volition is surely an act of the mind, with which we are sufficiently acquainted. Reflect upon it. Consider it on all sides. Do you find anything in it like this creative power, by which it raises from nothing a new idea, and with a kind of Fiat, imitates the omnipotence of its Maker, if I may be allowed so to speak, who called forth into existence all the various scenes of nature? So far from being conscious of this energy in the will, it requires as certain experience, as that of which we are possessed, to convince us, that such extraordinary effects do ever result from a simple act of volition.

The generality of mankind never find any difficulty in accounting for the more common and familiar operations of nature; such as the descent of heavy bodies, the growth of plants, the generation of animals, or the nourishment of bodies by food: But suppose, that, in all these cases, they perceive the very force or energy of the cause, by which it is connected with its effect, and is for ever infallible in its operation. They acquire, by long habit, such a turn of mind, that, upon the appearance of the cause, they immediately expect with assurance its usual attendant, and hardly conceive it possible, that any other event could result from it. It is only on the discovery of extraordinary phenomena, such as earthquakes, pestilence, and prodigies of any kind, that they find themselves at a loss to assign a proper cause, and to explain the manner, in which the effect is produced by it. It is usual for men, in such difficulties, to have recourse to some invisible intelligent principle, as the immediate cause of that event, which surprises them, and which, they think, cannot be accounted for from the common powers of nature. But philosophers, who carry their scrutiny a little farther, immediately perceive, that, even in the most familiar events, the energy of the cause is as unintelligible as in the most unusual, and that we only learn by experience the frequent Conjunction of objects, without being ever able to comprehend anything like Connexion between them. Here then, many philosophers think themselves obliged by reason to have recourse, on all occasions, to the same principle, which the vulgar never appeal to but in cases, that appear miraculous and supernatural. They acknowledge mind and intelligence to be, not only the ultimate and original cause of all things, but the immediate and sole cause of every event, which appears in nature. They pretend, that those objects, which are commonly denominated causes, are in reality nothing but occasions; and that the true and direct principle of every effect is not any power or force in nature, but a volition of the Supreme Being, who wills, that such particular objects should, for ever, be conjoined with each other. Instead of saying, that one billiard-ball moves another, by a force, which it has derived from the author of nature; it is the Deity himself, they say, who, by a particular volition, moves the second ball, being determined to this operation by the impulse of the first ball: in consequence of those general laws, which he has laid down to himself in the government of the universe. But philosophers advancing still in their enquiries, discover, that, as we are totally ignorant of the power, on which depends the mutual operation of bodies, we are no less ignorant of that power, on which depends the operation of mind on body, or of body on mind; nor are we able, either from our senses or consciousness, to assign the ultimate principle in one case, more than in the other. The same ignorance, therefore, reduces them to the same conclusion. They assert, that the Deity is the immediate cause of the union between soul and body; and that they are not the organs of sense, which, being agitated by external objects, produce sensations in the mind; but that it is a particular volition of our omnipotent Maker, which excites such a sensation, in consequence of such a motion in the organ. In like manner, it is not any energy in the will, that produces local motion in our members: It is God himself, who is pleased to second our will, in itself impotent, and to command that motion, which we erroneously attribute to our own power and efficacy. Nor do philosophers stop at this conclusion. They sometimes extend the same inference to the mind itself, in its internal operations. Our mental vision or conception of ideas is nothing but a revelation made to us by our Maker. When we voluntarily turn our thoughts to any object, and raise up its image in the fancy; it is not the will which creates that idea: It is the universal Creator, who discovers it to the mind, and renders it present to us.

Thus, according to these philosophers, every thing is full of God. Not content with the principle, that nothing exists but by his will, that nothing possesses any power but by his concession: They rob nature, and all created beings, of every power, in order to render their dependence on the Deity still more sensible and immediate. They consider not, that, by this theory, they diminish, instead of magnifying, the grandeur of those attributes, which they affect so much to celebrate. It argues surely more power in the Deity to delegate a certain degree of power to inferior creatures, than to produce every thing by his own immediate volition. It argues more wisdom to contrive at first the fabric of the world with such perfect foresight, that, of itself, and by its proper operation, it may serve all the purposes of providence, than if the great Creator were obliged every moment to adjust its parts, and animate by his breath all the wheels of that stupendous machine.

But if we would have a more philosophical confutation of this theory, perhaps the two following reflections may suffice.

First, It seems to me, that this theory of the universal energy and operation of the Supreme Being, is too bold ever to carry conviction with it to a man, sufficiently apprized of the weakness of human reason, and the narrow limits, to which it is confined in all its operations. Though the chain of arguments which conduct to it, were ever so logical, there must arise a strong suspicion, if not an absolute assurance, that it has carried us quite beyond the reach of our faculties, when it leads to conclusions so extraordinary, and so remote from common life and experience. We are got into fairy land, long ere we have reached the last steps of our theory; and there we have no reason to trust our common methods of argument, or to think that our usual analogies and probabilities have any authority. Our line is too short to fathom such immense abysses. And however we may flatter ourselves, that we are guided, in every step which we take, by a kind of verisimilitude and experience; we may be assured, that this fancied experience has no authority, when we thus apply it to subjects, that lie entirely out of the sphere of experience. But on this we shall have occasion to touch afterwards.

Secondly, I cannot perceive any force in the arguments, on which this theory is founded. We are ignorant, it is true, of the manner in which bodies operate on each other: Their force or energy is entirely incomprehensible: But are we not equally ignorant of the manner or force by which a mind, even the supreme mind, operates either on itself or on body? Whence, I beseech you, do we acquire any idea of it? We have no sentiment or consciousness of this power in ourselves. We have no idea of the Supreme Being but what we learn from reflection on our own faculties. Were our ignorance, therefore, a good reason for rejecting any thing, we should be led into that principle of denying all energy in the Supreme Being as much as in the grossest matter. We surely comprehend as little the operations of one as of the other. Is it more difficult to conceive, that motion may arise from impulse, than that it may arise from volition? All we know is our profound ignorance in both cases.

Part II

But to hasten to a conclusion of this argument, which is already drawn out to too great a length: We have sought in vain for an idea of power or necessary connexion, in all the sources from which we could suppose it to be derived. It appears, that, in single instances of the operation of bodies, we never can, by our utmost scrutiny, discover any thing but one event following another; without being able to comprehend any force or power, by which the cause operates, or any connexion between it and its supposed effect. The same difficulty occurs in contemplating the operations of mind on body; where we observe the motion of the latter to follow upon the volition of the former; but are not able to observe or conceive the tie which binds together the motion and volition, or the energy by which the mind produces this effect. The authority of the will over its own faculties and ideas is not a whit more comprehensible: So that, upon the whole, there appears not, throughout all nature, any one instance of connexion, which is conceivable by us. All events seem entirely loose and separate. One event follows another; but we never can observe any tie between them. They seem conjoined, but never connected. And as we can have no idea of any thing, which never appeared to our outward sense or inward sentiment, the necessary conclusion seems to be, that we have no idea of connexion or power at all, and that these words are absolutely without any meaning, when employed either in philosophical reasonings, or common life.

But there still remains one method of avoiding this conclusion, and one source which we have not yet examined. When any natural object or event is presented, it is impossible for us, by any sagacity or penetration, to discover, or even conjecture, without experience, what event will result from it, or to carry our foresight beyond that object, which is immediately present to the memory and senses. Even after one instance or experiment, where we have observed a particular event to follow upon another, we are not entitled to form a general rule, or foretell what will happen in like cases; it being justly esteemed an unpardonable temerity to judge of the whole course of nature from one single experiment, however accurate or certain. But when one particular species of event has always, in all instances, been conjoined with another, we make no longer any scruple of foretelling one upon the appearance of the other, and of employing that reasoning, which can alone assure us of any matter of fact or existence. We then call the one object, Cause; the other, Effect. We suppose, that there is some connexion between them; some power in the one, by which it infallibly produces the other, and operates with the greatest certainty and strongest necessity.

It appears, then, that this idea of a necessary connexion among events arises from a number of similar instances, which occur, of the constant conjunction of these events; nor can that idea ever be suggested by any one of these instances, surveyed in all possible lights and positions. But there is nothing in a number of instances, different from every single instance, which is supposed to be exactly similar; except only, that after a repetition of similar instances, the mind is carried by habit, upon the appearance of one event, to expect its usual attendant, and to believe, that it will exist. This connexion, therefore, which we feel in the mind, this customary transition of the imagination from one object to its usual attendant, is the sentiment or impression, from which we form the idea of power or necessary connexion. Nothing farther is in the case. Contemplate the subject on all sides; you will never find any other origin of that idea. This is the sole difference between one instance, from which we can never receive the idea of connexion, and a number of similar instances, by which it is suggested. The first time a man saw the communication of motion by impulse, as by the shock of two billiard-balls, he could not pronounce that the one event was connected: but only that it was conjoined with the other. After he has observed several instances of this nature, he then pronounces them to be connected. What alteration has happened to give rise to this new idea of connexion? Nothing but that he now feels these events to be connected in his imagination, and can readily foretell the existence of one from the appearance of the other. When we say, therefore, that one object is connected with another, we mean only, that they have acquired a connexion in our thought, and give rise to this inference, by which they become proofs of each other's existence: A conclusion, which is somewhat extraordinary; but which seems founded on sufficient evidence. Nor will its evidence be weakened by any general diffidence of the understanding, or sceptical suspicion concerning every conclusion, which is new and extraordinary. No conclusions can be more agreeable to scepticism than such as make discoveries concerning the weakness and narrow limits of human reason and capacity.

And what stronger instance can be produced of the surprising ignorance and weakness of the understanding, than the present? For surely, if there be any relation among objects, which it imports to us to know perfectly, it is that of cause and effect. On this are founded all our reasonings concerning matter of fact or existence. By means of it alone we attain any assurance concerning objects, which are removed from the present testimony of our memory and senses. The only immediate utility of all sciences, is to teach us, how to control and regulate future events by their causes. Our thoughts and enquiries are, therefore, every moment, employed about this relation: Yet so imperfect are the ideas which we form concerning it, that it is impossible to give any just definition of cause, except what is drawn from something extraneous and foreign to it. Similar objects are always conjoined with similar. Of this we have experience. Suitably to this experience, therefore, we may define a cause to be an object, followed by another, and where all the objects, similar to the first, are followed by objects similar to the second. Or, in other words, where, if the first object had not been, the second never had existed. The appearance of a cause always conveys the mind, by a customary transition, to the idea of the effect. Of this also we have experience. We may, therefore, suitably to this experience, form another definition of cause; and call it, an object followed by another, and whose appearance always conveys the thought to that other. But though both these definitions be drawn from circumstances foreign to the cause, we cannot remedy this inconvenience, or attain any more perfect definition, which may point out that circumstance in the cause, which gives it a connexion with its effect. We have no idea of this connexion; nor even any distinct notion what it is we desire to know, when we endeavor at a conception of it. We say, for instance, that the vibration of this string is the cause of this particular sound. But what do we mean by that affirmation? We either mean, that this vibration is followed by this sound, and that all similar vibrations have been followed by similar sounds: Or, that this vibration is followed by this sound, and that upon the appearance of one, the mind anticipates the senses, and forms immediately an idea of the other. We may consider the relation of cause and effect in either of these two lights; but beyond these, we have no idea of it.

To recapitulate, therefore, the reasonings of this section: Every idea is copied from some preceding impression or sentiment; and where we cannot find any impression, we may be certain that there is no idea. In all single instances of the operation of bodies or minds, there is nothing that produces any impression, nor consequently can suggest any idea of power or necessary connexion. But when many uniform instances appear, and the same object is always followed by the same event; we then begin to entertain the notion of cause and connexion. We then feel a new sentiment or impression, to wit, a customary connexion in the thought or imagination between one object and its usual attendant; and this sentiment is the original of that idea which we seek for. For as this idea arises from a number of similar instances, and not from any single instance, it must arise from that circumstance, in which the number of instances differ from every individual instance. But this customary connexion or transition of the imagination is the only circumstance in which they differ. In every other particular they are alike. The first instance which we saw of motion, communicated by the shock of two billiard-balls (to return to this obvious illustration) is exactly similar to any instance that may, at present, occur to us; except only, that we could not, at first, infer one event from the other; which we are enabled to do at present, after so long a course of uniform experience. I know not whether the reader will readily apprehend this reasoning. I am afraid, that, should I multiply words about it, or throw it into a greater variety of lights, it would only become more obscure and intricate. In all abstract reasonings, there is one point of view, which, if we can happily hit, we shall go farther towards illustrating the subject than by all the eloquence and copious expression in the world. This point of view we should endeavor to reach, and reserve the flowers of rhetoric for subjects which are more adapted to them.

SECTION VIII: OF LIBERTY AND NECESSITY

Part I

It might reasonably be expected, in questions, which have been canvassed and disputed with great eagerness, since the first origin of science and philosophy, that the meaning of all the terms, at least, should have been agreed upon among the disputants; and our enquiries, in the course of two thousand years, been able to pass from words to the true and real subject of the controversy. For how easy may it seem to give exact definitions of the terms employed in reasoning, and make these definitions, not the mere sound of words, the object of future scrutiny and examination? But if we consider the matter more narrowly, we shall be apt to draw a quite opposite conclusion. From this circumstance alone, that a controversy has been long kept on foot, and remains still undecided, we may presume, that there is some ambiguity in the expression, and that the disputants affix different ideas to the terms employed in the controversy. For as the faculties of the mind are supposed to be naturally alike in every individual; otherwise nothing could be more fruitless than to reason or dispute together; it were impossible, if men affix the same ideas to their terms, that they could so long form different opinions of the same subject; especially when they communicate their views, and each party turn themselves on all sides, in search of arguments, which may give them the victory over their antagonists. It is true; if men attempt the discussion of questions, which lie entirely beyond the reach of human capacity, such as those concerning the origin of worlds, or the economy of the intellectual system or region of spirits, they may long beat the air in their fruitless contests, and never arrive at any determinate conclusion. But if the question regard any subject of common life and experience; nothing, one would think, could preserve the dispute so long undecided, but some ambiguous expressions, which keep the antagonists still at a distance, and hinder them from grappling with each other.

This has been the case in the long disputed question concerning liberty and necessity; and to so remarkable a degree, that, if I be not much mistaken, we shall find, that all mankind, both learned and ignorant, have always been of the same opinion with regard to this subject, and that a few intelligible definitions would immediately have put an end to the whole controversy. I own, that this dispute has been so much canvassed on all hands, and has led philosophers into such a labyrinth of obscure sophistry, that it is no wonder, if a sensible reader indulge his ease so far as to turn a deaf ear to the proposal of such a question, from which he can expect neither instruction nor entertainment. But the state of the argument here proposed may, perhaps, serve to renew his attention; as it has more novelty, promises at least some decision of the controversy, and will not much disturb his ease by any intricate or obscure reasoning.

I hope, therefore, to make it appear, that all men have ever agreed in the doctrine both of necessity and of liberty, according to any reasonable sense, which can be put on these terms; and that the whole controversy has hitherto turned merely upon words. We shall begin with examining the doctrine of necessity.

It is universally allowed that matter, in all its operations, is actuated by a necessary force, and that every natural effect is so precisely determined by the energy of its cause, that no other effect, in such particular circumstances, could possibly have resulted from it. The degree and direction of every motion is, by the laws of nature, prescribed with such exactness, that a living creature may as soon arise from the shock of two bodies, as motion, in any other degree or direction than what is actually produced by it. Would we, therefore, form a just and precise idea of necessity, we must consider whence that idea arises, when we apply it to the operation of bodies.

It seems evident, that, if all the scenes of nature were continually shifted in such a manner, that no two events bore any resemblance to each other, but every object was entirely new, without any similitude to whatever had been seen before, we should never, in that case, have attained the least idea of necessity, or of a connexion among these objects. We might say, upon such a supposition, that one object or event has followed another; not that one was produced by the other. The relation of cause and effect must be utterly unknown to mankind. Inference and reasoning concerning the operations of nature would, from that moment, be at an end; and the memory and senses remain the only canals, by which the knowledge of any real existence could possibly have access to the mind. Our idea, therefore, of necessity and causation arises entirely from the uniformity, observable in the operations of nature; where similar objects are constantly conjoined together, and the mind is determined by custom to infer the one from the appearance of the other. These two circumstances form the whole of that necessity, which we ascribe to matter. Beyond the constant conjunction of similar objects, and the consequent inference from one to the other, we have no notion of any necessity, or connexion.

If it appear, therefore, that all mankind have ever allowed, without any doubt or hesitation, that these two circumstances take place in the voluntary actions of men, and in the operations of mind; it must follow, that all mankind have ever agreed in the doctrine of necessity, and that they have hitherto disputed, merely for not understanding each other.

As to the first circumstance, the constant and regular conjunction of similar events; we may possibly satisfy ourselves by the following considerations. It is universally acknowledged, that there is a great uniformity among the actions of men, in all nations and ages, and that human nature remains still the same, in its principles and operations. The same motives always produce the same actions: The same events follow from the same causes. Ambition, avarice, self-love, vanity, friendship, generosity, public spirit; these passions, mixed in various degrees, and distributed through society, have been, from the beginning of the world, and still are, the source of all the actions and enterprises, which have ever been observed among mankind. Would you know the sentiments, inclinations, and course of life of the Greeks and Romans? Study well the temper and actions of the French and English: You cannot be much mistaken in transferring to the former most of the observations, which you have made with regard to the latter. Mankind are so much the same, in all times and places, that history informs us of nothing new or strange in this particular. Its chief use is only to discover the constant and universal principles of human nature, by showing men in all varieties of circumstances and situations, and furnishing us with materials, from which we may form our observations, and become acquainted with the regular springs of human action and behavior. These records of wars, intrigues, factions, and revolutions, are so many collections of experiments, by which the politician or moral philosopher fixes the principles of his science; in the same manner as the physician or natural philosopher becomes acquainted with the nature of plants, minerals, and other external objects, by the experiments, which he forms concerning them. Nor are the earth, water, and other elements, examined by Aristotle, and Hippocrates, more like to those, which at present lie under our observation than the men, described by Polybius and Tacitus, are to those, who now govern the world.

Should a traveller, returning from a far country, bring us an account of men, wholly different from any, with whom we were ever acquainted; men, who were entirely divested of avarice, ambition, or revenge; who knew no pleasure but friendship, generosity, and public spirit; we should immediately, from these circumstances, detect the falsehood, and prove him a liar, with the same certainty as if he had stuffed his narration with stories of centaurs and dragons, miracles and prodigies. And if we would explode any forgery in history, we cannot make use of a more convincing argument, than to prove, that the actions, ascribed to any person, are directly contrary to the course of nature, and that no human motives, in such circumstances, could ever induce him to such a conduct. The veracity of Quintus Curtius is as much to be suspected, when he describes the supernatural courage of Alexander, by which he was hurried on singly to attack multitudes, as when he describes his supernatural force and activity, by which he was able to resist them. So readily and universally do we acknowledge a uniformity in human motives and actions as well as in the operations of body.

Hence likewise the benefit of that experience, acquired by long life and a variety of business and company, in order to instruct us in the principles of human nature, and regulate our future conduct, as well as speculation. By means of this guide, we mount up to the knowledge of men's inclinations and motives, from their actions, expressions, and even gestures; and again, descend to the interpretation of their actions from our knowledge of their motives and inclinations. The general observations, treasured up by a course of experience, give us the clue of human nature, and teach us to unravel all its intricacies. Pretexts and appearances no longer deceive us. Public declarations pass for the specious coloring of a cause. And though virtue and honour be allowed their proper weight and authority, that perfect disinterestedness, so often pretended to, is never expected in multitudes and parties; seldom in their leaders; and scarcely even in individuals of any rank or station. But were there no uniformity in human actions, and were every experiment, which we could form of this kind, irregular and anomalous, it were impossible to collect any general observations concerning mankind; and no experience, however accurately digested by reflection, would ever serve to any purpose. Why is the aged husbandman more skillful in his calling than the young beginner, but because there is a certain uniformity in the operation of the sun, rain, and earth towards the production of vegetables; and experience teaches the old practitioner the rules, by which this operation is governed and directed?

We must not, however, expect, that this uniformity of human actions should be carried to such a length, as that all men, in the same circumstances, will always act precisely in the same manner, without making any allowance for the diversity of characters, prejudices, and opinions. Such a uniformity in every particular, is found in no part of nature. On the contrary, from observing the variety of conduct in different men, we are enabled to form a greater variety of maxims, which still suppose a degree of uniformity and regularity.

Are the manners of men different in different ages and countries? We learn thence the great force of custom and education, which mould the human mind from its infancy, and form it into a fixed and established character. Is the behavior and conduct of the one sex very unlike that of the other? It is thence we become acquainted with the different characters, which nature has impressed upon the sexes, and which she preserves with constancy and regularity. Are the actions of the same person much diversified in the different periods of his life, from infancy to old age? This affords room for many general observations concerning the gradual change of our sentiments and inclinations, and the different maxims, which prevail in the different ages of human creatures. Even the characters, which are peculiar to each individual, have a uniformity in their influence; otherwise our acquaintance with the persons and our observation of their conduct, could never teach us their dispositions, or serve to direct our behavior with regard to them.

I grant it possible to find some actions, which seem to have no regular connexion with any known motives, and are exceptions to all the measures of conduct, which have ever been established for the government of men. But if we would willingly know, what judgment should be formed of such irregular and extraordinary actions; we may consider the sentiments, commonly entertained with regard to those irregular events, which appear in the course of nature, and the operations of external objects. All causes are not conjoined to their usual effects, with like uniformity. An artificer, who handles only dead matter, may be disappointed of his aim, as well as the politician, who directs the conduct of sensible and intelligent agents.

The vulgar, who take things according to their first appearance, attribute the uncertainty of events to such an uncertainty in the causes as makes the latter often fail of their usual influence; though they meet with no impediment in their operation. But philosophers, observing, that, almost in every part of nature, there is contained a vast variety of springs and principles, which are hid, by reason of their minuteness or remoteness, find, that it is at least possible the contrariety of events may not proceed from any contingency in the cause, but from the secret operation of contrary causes. This possibility is converted into certainty by farther observation; when they remark, that, upon an exact scrutiny, a contrariety of effects always betrays a contrariety of causes, and proceeds from their mutual opposition. A peasant can give no better reason for the stopping of any clock or watch than to say that it does not commonly go right: But an artist easily perceives that the same force in the spring or pendulum has always the same influence on the wheels; but fails of its usual effect, perhaps by reason of a grain of dust, which puts a stop to the whole movement. From the observation of several parallel instances, philosophers form a maxim, that the connexion between all causes and effects is equally necessary, and that its seeming uncertainty in some instances proceeds from the secret opposition of contrary causes.

Thus for instance, in the human body, when the usual symptoms of health or sickness disappoint our expectation; when medicines operate not with their wonted powers; when irregular events follow from any particular cause; the philosopher and physician are not surprised at the matter, nor are ever tempted to deny, in general, the necessity and uniformity of those principles, by which the animal economy is conducted. They know, that a human body is a mighty complicated machine: That many secret powers lurk in it, which are altogether beyond our comprehension: That to us it must often appear very uncertain in its operations: And that therefore the irregular events, which outwardly discover themselves, can be no proof, that the laws of nature are not observed with the greatest regularity in its internal operations and government.

The philosopher, if he be consistent, must apply the same reasoning to the actions and volitions of intelligent agents. The most irregular and unexpected resolutions of men may frequently be accounted for by those, who know every particular circumstance of their character and situation. A person of an obliging disposition gives a peevish answer: But he has the toothache, or has not dined. A stupid fellow discovers an uncommon alacrity in his carriage: But he has met with a sudden piece of good fortune. Or even when an action, as sometimes happens, cannot be particularly accounted for, either by the person himself or by others; we know, in general, that the characters of men are, to a certain degree, inconstant and irregular. This is, in a manner, the constant character of human nature; though it be applicable, in a more particular manner, to some persons, who have no fixed rule for their conduct, but proceed in a continued course of caprice and inconstancy. The internal principles and motives may operate in a uniform manner, notwithstanding these seeming irregularities; in the same manner as the winds, rain, clouds, and other variations of the weather are supposed to be governed by steady principles; though not easily discoverable by human sagacity and enquiry.

Thus it appears, not only that the conjunction between motives and voluntary actions is as regular and uniform, as that between the cause and effect in any part of nature; but also that this regular conjunction has been universally acknowledged among mankind, and has never been the subject of dispute, either in philosophy or common life. Now, as it is from past experience, that we draw all inferences concerning the future, and as we conclude, that objects will always be conjoined together, which we find to have always been conjoined; it may seem superfluous to prove, that this experienced uniformity in human actions is a source, whence we draw inferences concerning them. But in order to throw the argument into a greater variety of lights, we shall also insist, though briefly, on this latter topic.

The mutual dependence of men is so great, in all societies, that scarce any human action is entirely complete in itself, or is performed without some reference to the actions of others, which are requisite to make it answer fully the intention of the agent. The poorest artificer, who labors alone, expects at least the protection of the magistrate, to ensure him the enjoyment of the fruits of his labour. He also expects, that, when he carries his goods to market, and offers them at a reasonable price, he shall find purchasers; and shall be able, by the money he acquires, to engage others to supply him with those commodities, which are requisite for his subsistence. In proportion as men extend their dealings, and render their intercourse with others more complicated, they always comprehend, in their schemes of life, a greater variety of voluntary actions, which they expect, from the proper motives, to co-operate with their own. In all these conclusions, they take their measures from past experience, in the same manner as in their reasonings concerning external objects; and firmly believe, that men, as well as all the elements, are to continue, in their operations, the same, that they have ever found them. A manufacturer reckons upon the labour of his servants, for the execution of any work, as much as upon the tools, which he employs, and would be equally surprised, were his expectations disappointed. In short, this experimental inference and reasoning concerning the actions of others enters so much into human life, that no man, while awake, is ever a moment without employing it. Have we not reason, therefore, to affirm, that all mankind have always agreed in the doctrine of necessity, according to the foregoing definition and explication of it?

Nor have philosophers ever entertained a different opinion from the people in this particular. For not to mention, that almost every action of their life supposes that opinion; there are even few of the speculative parts of learning, to which it is not essential. What would become of history, had we not a dependence on the veracity of the historian, according to the experience, which we have had of mankind? How could politics be a science, if laws and forms of government had not a uniform influence upon society? Where would be the foundation of morals, if particular characters had no certain or determinate power to produce particular sentiments, and if these sentiments had no constant operation on actions? And with what presence could we employ our criticism upon any poet or polite author, if we could not pronounce the conduct and sentiments of his actors, either natural or unnatural, to such characters, and in such circumstances? It seems almost impossible, therefore, to engage, either in science or action of any kind, without acknowledging the doctrine of necessity, and this inference from motives to voluntary actions; from characters to conduct.

And indeed, when we consider how aptly natural and moral evidence link together, and form only one chain of argument, we shall make no scruple to allow, that they are of the same nature, and derived from the same principles. A prisoner, who has neither money nor interest, discovers the impossibility of his escape, as well when he considers the obstinacy of the jailer, as the walls and bars, with which he is surrounded; and, in all attempts for his freedom, chooses rather to work upon the stone and iron of the one, than upon the inflexible nature of the other. The same prisoner, when conducted to the scaffold, foresees his death as certainly from the constancy and fidelity of his guards, as from the operation of the ax or wheel. His mind runs along a certain train of ideas: The refusal of the soldiers to consent to his escape; the action of the executioner; the separation of the head and body; bleeding, convulsive motions, and death. Here is a connected chain of natural causes and voluntary actions; but the mind feels no difference between them, in passing from one link to another: Nor is less certain of the future event than if it were connected with the objects present to the memory or senses, by a train of causes, cemented together by what we are pleased to call a physical necessity. The same experienced union has the same effect on the mind, whether the united objects be motives, volition, and actions; or figure and motion. We may change the names of things; but their nature and their operation on the understanding never change.

Were a man, whom I know to be honest and opulent, and with whom I live in intimate friendship, to come into my house, where I am surrounded with my servants, I rest assured, that he is not to stab me before he leaves it, in order to rob me of my silver standish; and I no more suspect this event, than the falling of the house itself which is new, and solidly built and founded.—But he may have been seized with a sudden and unknown frenzy.—So may a sudden earthquake arise, and shake and tumble my house about my ears. I shall therefore change the suppositions. I shall say, that I know with certainty, that he is not to put his hand into the fire, and hold it there, till it be consumed: And this event, I think I can foretell with the same assurance, as that, if he throw himself out at the window, and meet with no obstruction, he will not remain a moment suspended in the air. No suspicion of an unknown frenzy can give the least possibility to the former event, which is so contrary to all the known principles of human nature. A man who at noon leaves his purse full of gold on the pavement at Charing-Cross, may as well expect that it will fly away like a feather, as that he will find it untouched an hour after. Above one half of human reasonings contain inferences of a similar nature, attended with more or less degrees of certainty, proportioned to our experience of the usual conduct of mankind in such particular situations.

I have frequently considered, what could possibly be the reason why all mankind, though they have ever, without hesitation, acknowledged the doctrine of necessity, in their whole practice and reasoning, have yet discovered such a reluctance to acknowledge it in words, and have rather strewn a propensity, in all ages, to profess the contrary opinion. The matter, I think, may be accounted for, after the following manner. If we examine the operations of body, and the production of effects from their causes, we shall find that all our faculties can never carry us farther in our knowledge of this relation, than barely to observe, that particular objects are constantly conjoined together, and that the mind is carried, by a customary transition, from the appearance of one to the belief of the other. But though this conclusion concerning human ignorance be the result of the strictest scrutiny of this subject, men still entertain a strong propensity to believe, that they penetrate farther into the powers of nature, and perceive something like a necessary connexion between the cause and the effect. When again they turn their reflections towards the operations of their own minds, and feel no such connexion of the motive and the action; they are thence apt to suppose, that there is a difference between the effects, which result from material force, and those which arise from thought and intelligence. But being once convinced, that we know nothing farther of causation of any kind, than merely the constant conjunction of objects, and the consequent inference of the mind from one to another and finding, that these two circumstances are universally allowed to have place in voluntary actions; we may be more easily led to own the same necessity common to all causes. And though this reasoning may contradict the systems of many philosophers, in ascribing necessity to the determinations of the will, we shall find, upon reflection, that they dissent from it in words only, not in their real sentiment. Necessity, according to the sense, in which it is here taken, has never yet been rejected, nor can ever, I think, be rejected by any philosopher. It may only, perhaps, be pretended, that the mind can perceive, in the operations of matter, some farther connexion between the cause and effect; and a connexion that has not place in the voluntary actions of intelligent beings. Now whether it be so or not, can only appear upon examination; and it is incumbent on these philosophers to make good their assertion, by defining or describing that necessity, and pointing it out to us in the operations of material causes.

It would seem, indeed, that men begin at the wrong end of this question concerning liberty and necessity, when they enter upon it by examining the faculties of the soul, the influence of the understanding, and the operations of the will. Let them first discuss a more simple question, namely, the operations of body and of brute unintelligent matter; and try whether they can there form any idea of causation and necessity, except that of a constant conjunction of objects, and subsequent inference of the mind from one to another. If these circumstances form, in reality, the whole of that necessity, which we conceive in matter, and if these circumstances be also universally acknowledged to take place in the operations of the mind, the dispute is at an end; at least, must be owned to be thenceforth merely verbal. But as long as we will rashly suppose, that we have some farther idea of necessity and causation in the operations of external objects; at the same time, that we can find nothing farther, in the voluntary actions of the mind; there is no possibility of bringing the question to any determinate issue, while we proceed upon so erroneous a supposition. The only method of undeceiving us, is, to mount up higher; to examine the narrow extent of science when applied to material causes; and to convince ourselves, that all we know of them, is, the constant conjunction and inference above mentioned. We may, perhaps, find, that it is with difficulty we are induced to fix such narrow limits to human understanding: But we can afterwards find no difficulty when we come to apply this doctrine to the actions of the will. For as it is evident, that these have a regular conjunction with motives and circumstances and characters, and as we always draw inferences from one to the other, we must be obliged to acknowledge in words, that necessity, which we have already avowed, in every deliberation of our lives, and in every step of our conduct and behavior.

But to proceed in this reconciling project with regard to the question of liberty and necessity; the most contentious question, of metaphysics, the most contentious science; it will not require many words to prove, that all mankind have ever agreed in the doctrine of liberty as well as in that of necessity, and that the whole dispute, in this respect also, has been hitherto merely verbal. For what is meant by liberty, when applied to voluntary actions? We cannot surely mean, that actions have so little connexion with motives, inclinations, and circumstances, that one does not follow with a certain degree of uniformity from the other, and that one affords no inference by which we can conclude the existence of the other. For these are plain and acknowledged matters of fact. By liberty, then, we can only mean a power of acting or not acting, according to the determinations of the will; that is, if we choose to remain at rest, we may; if we choose to move, we also may. Now this hypothetical liberty is universally allowed to belong to every one, who is not a prisoner and in chains. Here then is no subject of dispute.

Whatever definition we may give of liberty, we should be careful to observe two requisite circumstances; first, that it be consistent with plain matter of fact; secondly, that it be consistent with itself. If we observe these circumstances, and render our definition intelligible, I am persuaded that all mankind will be found of one opinion with regard to it.

It is universally allowed that nothing exists without a cause of its existence, and that chance, when strictly examined, is a mere negative word, and means not any real power, which has any where, a being in nature. But it is pretended, that some causes are necessary, some not necessary. Here then is the advantage of definitions. Let any one define a cause, without comprehending, as a part of the definition, a necessary connexion with its effect; and let him shew distinctly the origin of the idea, expressed by the definition; and I shall readily give up the whole controversy. But if the foregoing explication of the matter be received, this must be absolutely impracticable. Had not objects a regular conjunction with each other, we should never have entertained any notion of cause and effect; and this regular conjunction produces that inference of the understanding, which is the only connexion, that we can have any comprehension of. Whoever attempts a definition of cause, exclusive of these circumstances, will be obliged, either to employ unintelligible terms, or such as are synonymous to the term, which he endeavors to define. And if the definition above mentioned be admitted; liberty, when opposed to necessity, not to constraint, is the same thing with chance; which is universally allowed to have no existence.

Part II

There is no method of reasoning more common, and yet none more blameable, than, in philosophical disputes, to endeavor the refutation of any hypothesis, by a pretence of its dangerous consequences to religion and morality. When any opinion leads to absurdities, it is certainly false; but it is not certain that an opinion is false, because it is of dangerous consequence. Such topics, therefore, ought entirely to be forborne; as serving nothing to the discovery of truth, but only to make the person of an antagonist odious. This I observe in general, without pretending to draw any advantage from it. I frankly submit to an examination of this kind, and shall venture to affirm, that the doctrines, both of necessity and of liberty, as above explained, are not only consistent with morality, but are absolutely essential to its support.

Necessity may be defined two ways, conformably to the two definitions of cause, of which it makes an essential part. It consists either in the constant conjunction of like objects, or in the inference of the understanding from one object to another. Now necessity, in both these senses, (which, indeed, are, at bottom, the same) has universally, though tacitly, in the schools, in the pulpit, and in common life, been allowed to belong to the will of man; and no one has ever pretended to deny, that we can draw inferences concerning human actions, and that those inferences are founded on the experienced union of like actions, with like motives, inclinations, and circumstances. The only particular, in which any one can differ, is, that either, perhaps, he will refuse to give the name of necessity to this property of human actions: But as long as the meaning is understood, I hope the word can do no harm: Or that he will maintain it possible to discover something farther in the operations of matter. But this, it must be acknowledged, can be of no consequence to morality or religion, whatever it may be to natural philosophy or metaphysics. We may here be mistaken in asserting, that there is no idea of any other necessity or connexion in the actions of body: But surely we ascribe nothing to the actions of the mind, but what every one does, and must readily allow of. We change no circumstance in the received orthodox system with regard to the will, but only in that with regard to material objects and causes. Nothing therefore can be more innocent, at least, than this doctrine.

All laws being founded on rewards and punishments, it is supposed as a fundamental principle, that these motives have a regular and uniform influence on the mind, and both produce the good and prevent the evil actions. We may give to this influence what name we please; but, as it is usually conjoined with the action, it must be esteemed a cause, and be looked upon as an instance of that necessity, which we would here establish.

The only proper object of hatred or vengeance, is a person or creature, endowed with thought and consciousness; and when any criminal or injurious actions excite that passion, it is only by their relation to the person, or connexion with him. Actions are, by their very nature, temporary and perishing; and where they proceed not from some cause in the character and disposition of the person who performed them, they can neither redound to his honour, if good; nor infamy, if evil. The actions themselves may be blameable; they may be contrary to all the rules of morality and religion: But the person is not answerable for them; and as they proceeded from nothing in him, that is durable and constant, and leave nothing of that nature behind them, it is impossible he can, upon their account, become the object of punishment or vengeance. According to the principle, therefore, which denies necessity, and consequently causes, a man is as pure and untainted, after having committed the most horrid crime, as at the first moment of his birth, nor is his character any wise concerned in his actions; since they are not derived from it, and the wickedness of the one can never be used as a proof of the depravity of the other.

Men are not blamed for such actions, as they perform ignorantly and casually, whatever may be the consequences. Why? but because the principles of these actions are only momentary, and terminate in them alone. Men are less blamed for such actions as they perform hastily and unpremeditatedly, than for such as proceed from deliberation. For what reason? but because a hasty temper, though a constant cause or principle in the mind, operates only by intervals, and infects not the whole character. Again, repentance wipes off every crime, if attended with a reformation of life and manners. How is this to be accounted for? but by asserting, that actions render a person criminal, merely as they are proofs of criminal principles in the mind; and when, by an alteration of these principles, they cease to be just proofs, they likewise cease to be criminal. But, except upon the doctrine of necessity, they never were just proofs, and consequently never were criminal.

It will be equally easy to prove, and from the same arguments, that liberty, according to that definition above mentioned, in which all men agree, is also essential to morality, and that no human actions, where it is wanting, are susceptible of any moral qualities, or can be the objects either of approbation or dislike. For as actions are objects of our moral sentiment, so far only as they are indications of the internal character, passions, and affections; it is impossible that they can give rise either to praise or blame, where they proceed not from these principles, but are derived altogether from external violence.

I pretend not to have obviated or removed all objections to this theory, with regard to necessity and liberty. I can foresee other objections, derived from topics, which have not here been treated of. It may be said, for instance, that, if voluntary actions be subjected to the same laws of necessity with the operations of matter, there is a continued chain of necessary causes, pre-ordained and pre-determined, reaching from the original cause of all, to every single volition of every human creature. No contingency any where in the universe; no indifference; no liberty. While we act, we are, at the same time, acted upon. The ultimate Author of all our volitions is the Creator of the world, who first bestowed motion on this immense machine, and placed all beings in that particular position, whence every subsequent event, by an inevitable necessity, must result. Human actions, therefore, either can have no moral turpitude at all, as proceeding from so good a cause; or if they have any turpitude, they must involve our Creator in the same guilt, while he is acknowledged to be their ultimate cause and author. For as a man, who fired a mine, is answerable for all the consequences, whether the train he employed be long or short; so wherever a continued chain of necessary causes is fixed, that Being, either finite or infinite, who produces the first, is likewise the author of all the rest, and must both bear the blame and acquire the praise, which belong to them. Our clear and unalterable ideas of morality establish this rule, upon unquestionable reasons, when we examine the consequences of any human action; and these reasons must still have greater force, when applied to the volitions and intentions of a Being, infinitely wise and powerful. Ignorance or impotence may be pleaded for so limited a creature as man; but those imperfections have no place in our Creator. He foresaw, he ordained, he intended all those actions of men, which we so rashly pronounce criminal. And we must therefore conclude, either that they are not criminal, or that the Deity, not man, is accountable for them. But as either of these positions is absurd and impious, it follows, that the doctrine, from which they are deduced, cannot possibly be true, as being liable to all the same objections. An absurd consequence, if necessary, proves the original doctrine to be absurd; in the same manner as criminal actions render criminal the original cause, if the connexion between them be necessary and inevitable.

This objection consists of two parts, which we shall examine separately; First, that, if human actions can be traced up, by a necessary chain, to the Deity, they can never be criminal; on account of the infinite perfection of that Being, from whom they are derived, and who can intend nothing but what is altogether good and laudable. Or, Secondly, if they be criminal, we must retract the attribute of perfection, which we ascribe to the Deity, and must acknowledge him to be the ultimate author of guilt and moral turpitude in all his creatures.

The answer to the first objection seems obvious and convincing. There are many philosophers, who, after an exact scrutiny of all the phenomena of nature, conclude, that the WHOLE, considered as one system, is, in every period of its existence, ordered with perfect benevolence; and that the utmost possible happiness will, in the end, result to all created beings, without any mixture of positive or absolute ill and misery. Every physical ill, say they, makes an essential part of this benevolent system, and could not possibly be removed, even by the Deity himself, considered as a wise agent, without giving entrance to greater ill, or excluding greater good, which will result from it. From this theory, some philosophers, and the ancient Stoics among the rest, derived a topic of consolation under all afflictions, while they taught their pupils, that those ills, under which they labored, were, in reality, goods to the universe; and that to an enlarged view, which could comprehend the whole system of nature, every event became an object of joy and exultation. But though this topic be specious and sublime, it was soon found in practice weak and ineffectual. You would surely more irritate, than appease a man, lying under the racking pains of the gout, by preaching up to him the rectitude of those general laws, which produced the malignant humors in his body, and led them through the proper canals, to the sinews and nerves, where they now excite such acute torments. These enlarged views may, for a moment, please the imagination of a speculative man, who is placed in ease and security; but neither can they dwell with constancy on his mind, even though undisturbed by the emotions of pain or passion; much less can they maintain their ground, when attacked by such powerful antagonists. The affections take a narrower and more natural survey of their object; and by an economy, more suitable to the infirmity of human minds, regard alone the beings around us, and are actuated by such events as appear good or ill to the private system.

The case is the same with moral as with physical ill. It cannot reasonably be supposed, that those remote considerations, which are found of so little efficacy with regard to one, will have a more powerful influence with regard to the other. The mind of man is so formed by nature, that, upon the appearance of certain characters, dispositions, and actions, it immediately feels the sentiment of approbation or blame; nor are there any emotions more essential to its frame and constitution. The characters, which engage our approbation, are chiefly such as contribute to the peace and security of human society; as the characters, which excite blame, are chiefly such as tend to public detriment and disturbance: Whence it may reasonably be presumed, that the moral sentiments arise, either mediately or immediately, from a reflection of these opposite interests. What though philosophical meditations establish a different opinion or conjecture; that every thing is right with regard to the WHOLE, and that the qualities, which disturb society, are, in the main, as beneficial, and are as suitable to the primary intention of nature, as those which more directly promote its happiness and welfare? Are such remote and uncertain speculations able to counterbalance the sentiments, which arise from the natural and immediate view of the objects? A man who is robbed of a considerable sum; does he find his vexation for the loss any wise diminished by these sublime reflections? Why then should his moral resentment against the crime be supposed incompatible with them? Or why should not the acknowledgment of a real distinction between vice and virtue be reconcilable to all speculative systems of philosophy, as well as that of a real distinction between personal beauty and deformity? Both these distinctions are founded in the natural sentiments of the human mind: And these sentiments are not to be controlled or altered by any philosophical theory or speculation whatsoever.

The second objection admits not of so easy and satisfactory an answer; nor is it possible to explain distinctly, how the Deity can be the mediate cause of all the actions of men, without being the author of sin and moral turpitude. These are mysteries, which mere natural and unassisted reason is very unfit to handle; and whatever system she embraces, she must find herself involved in inextricable difficulties, and even contradictions, at every step which she takes with regard to such subjects. To reconcile the indifference and contingency of human actions with prescience; or to defend absolute decrees, and yet free the Deity from being the author of sin, has been found hitherto to exceed all the power of philosophy. Happy, if she be thence sensible of her temerity, when she pries into these sublime mysteries; and leaving a scene so full of obscurities and perplexities, return, with suitable modesty, to her true and proper province, the examination of common life; where she will find difficulties enough to employ her enquiries, without launching into so boundless an ocean of doubt, uncertainty, and contradiction!

SECTION IX: OF THE REASON OF ANIMALS

All our reasonings concerning matter of fact are founded on a species of Analogy, which leads us to expect from any cause the same events, which we have observed to result from similar causes. Where the causes are entirely similar, the analogy is perfect, and the inference, drawn from it, is regarded as certain and conclusive: Nor does any man ever entertain a doubt, where he sees a piece of iron, that it will have weight and cohesion of parts; as in all other instances, which have ever fallen under his observation. But where the objects have not so exact a similarity, the analogy is less perfect, and the inference is less conclusive; though still it has some force, in proportion to the degree of similarity and resemblance. The anatomical observations, formed upon one animal, are, by this species of reasoning, extended to all animals; and it is certain, that when the circulation of the blood, for instance, is clearly proved to have place in one creature, as a frog, or fish, it forms a strong presumption, that the same principle has place in all. These analogical observations may be carried farther, even to this science, of which we are now treating; and any theory, by which we explain the operations of the understanding, or the origin and connexion of the passions in man, will acquire additional authority, if we find, that the same theory is requisite to explain the same phenomena in all other animals. We shall make trial of this, with regard to the hypothesis, by which, we have, in the foregoing discourse, endeavored to account for all experimental reasonings; and it is hoped, that this new point of view will serve to confirm all our former observations.

First, It seems evident, that animals, as well as men, learn many things from experience, and infer, that the same events will always follow from the same causes. By this principle they become acquainted with the more obvious properties of external objects, and gradually, from their birth, treasure up a knowledge of the nature of fire, water, earth, stones, heights, depths, &c., and of the effects, which result from their operation. The ignorance and inexperience of the young are here plainly distinguishable from the cunning and sagacity of the old, who have learned, by long observation, to avoid what hurt them, and to pursue what gave ease or pleasure. A horse, that has been accustomed to the field, becomes acquainted with the proper height, which he can leap, and will never attempt what exceeds his force and ability. An old greyhound will trust the more fatiguing part of the chase to the younger, and will place himself so as to meet the hare in her doubles; nor are the conjectures, which he forms on this occasion, founded in any thing but his observation and experience.

This is still more evident from the effects of discipline and education on animals, who, by the proper application of rewards and punishments, may be taught any course of action, the most contrary to their natural instincts and propensities. Is it not experience, which renders a dog apprehensive of pain, when you menace him, or lift up the whip to beat him? Is it not even experience, which makes him answer to his name, and infer, from such an arbitrary sound, that you mean him rather than any of his fellows, and intend to call him, when you pronounce it in a certain manner, and with a certain tone and accent?

In all these cases, we may observe, that the animal infers some fact beyond what immediately strikes his senses; and that this inference is altogether founded on past experience, while the creature expects from the present object the same consequences, which it has always found in its observation to result from similar objects.

Secondly, It is impossible, that this inference of the animal can be founded on any process of argument or reasoning, by which he concludes, that like events must follow like objects, and that the course of nature will always be regular in its operations. For if there be in reality any arguments of this nature, they surely lie too abstruse for the observation of such imperfect understandings; since it may well employ the utmost care and attention of a philosophic genius to discover and observe them. Animals, therefore, are not guided in these inferences by reasoning: Neither are children: Neither are the generality of mankind, in their ordinary actions and conclusions: Neither are philosophers themselves, who, in all the active parts of life, are, in the main, the same with the vulgar, and are governed by the same maxims. Nature must have provided some other principle, of more ready, and more general use and application; nor can an operation of such immense consequence in life, as that of inferring effects from causes, be trusted to the uncertain process of reasoning and argumentation. Were this doubtful with regard to men, it seems to admit of no question with regard to the brute creation; and the conclusion being once firmly established in the one, we have a strong presumption, from all the rules of analogy, that it ought to be universally admitted, without any exception or reserve. It is custom alone, which engages animals, from every object, that strikes their senses, to infer its usual attendant, and carries their imagination, from the appearance of the one, to conceive the other, in that particular manner, which we denominate belief. No other explication can be given of this operation, in all the higher, as well as lower classes of sensitive beings, which fall under our notice and observation.

But though animals learn many parts of their knowledge from observation, there are also many parts of it, which they derive from the original hand of nature; which much exceed the share of capacity they possess on ordinary occasions; and in which they improve, little or nothing, by the longest practice and experience. These we denominate Instincts, and are so apt to admire as something very extraordinary, and inexplicable by all the disquisitions of human understanding. But our wonder will, perhaps, cease or diminish; when we consider, that the experimental reasoning itself, which we possess in common with beasts, and on which the whole conduct of life depends, is nothing but a species of instinct or mechanical power, that acts in us unknown to ourselves; and in its chief operations, is not directed by any such relations or comparisons of ideas, as are the proper objects of our intellectual faculties. Though the instinct be different, yet still it is an instinct, which teaches a man to avoid the fire; as much as that, which teaches a bird, with such exactness, the art of incubation, and the whole economy and order of its nursery.

SECTION X: OF MIRACLES

Part I

There is, in Dr. Tillotson's writings, an argument against the real presence, which is as concise, and elegant, and strong as any argument can possibly be supposed against a doctrine, so little worthy of a serious refutation. It is acknowledged on all hands, says that learned prelate, that the authority, either of the scripture or of tradition, is founded merely in the testimony of the apostles, who were eye-witnesses to those miracles of our Savior, by which he proved his divine mission. Our evidence, then, for the truth of the Christian religion is less than the evidence for the truth of our senses; because, even in the first authors of our religion, it was no greater; and it is evident it must diminish in passing from them to their disciples; nor can any one rest such confidence in their testimony, as in the immediate object of his senses. But a weaker evidence can never destroy a stronger; and therefore, were the doctrine of the real presence ever so clearly revealed in scripture, it were directly contrary to the rules of just reasoning to give our assent to it. It contradicts sense, though both the scripture and tradition, on which it is supposed to be built, carry not such evidence with them as sense; when they are considered merely as external evidences, and are not brought home to every one's breast, by the immediate operation of the Holy Spirit.

Nothing is so convenient as a decisive argument of this kind, which must at least silence the most arrogant bigotry and superstition, and free us from their impertinent solicitations. I flatter myself, that I have discovered an argument of a like nature, which, if just, will, with the wise and learned, be an everlasting check to all kinds of superstitious delusion, and consequently, will be useful as long as the world endures. For so long, I presume, will the accounts of miracles and prodigies be found in all history, sacred and profane.

Though experience be our only guide in reasoning concerning matters of fact; it must be acknowledged, that this guide is not altogether infallible, but in some cases is apt to lead us into errors. One, who in our climate, should expect better weather in any week of June than in one of December, would reason justly, and conformably to experience; but it is certain, that he may happen, in the event, to find himself mistaken. However, we may observe, that, in such a case, he would have no cause to complain of experience; because it commonly informs us beforehand of the uncertainty, by that contrariety of events, which we may learn from a diligent observation. All effects follow not with like certainty from their supposed causes. Some events are found, in all countries and all ages, to have been constantly conjoined together: Others are found to have been more variable, and sometimes to disappoint our expectations; so that, in our reasonings concerning matter of fact, there are all imaginable degrees of assurance, from the highest certainty to the lowest species of moral evidence.

A wise man, therefore, proportions his belief to the evidence. In such conclusions as are founded on an infallible experience, he expects the event with the last degree of assurance, and regards his past experience as a full proof of the future existence of that event. In other cases, he proceeds with more caution: He weighs the opposite experiments: He considers which side is supported by the greater number of experiments: To that side he inclines, with doubt and hesitation; and when at last he fixes his judgment, the evidence exceeds not what we properly call probability. All probability, then, supposes an opposition of experiments and observations, where the one side is found to overbalance the other, and to produce a degree of evidence, proportioned to the superiority. A hundred instances or experiments on one side, and fifty on another, afford a doubtful expectation of any event; though a hundred uniform experiments, with only one that is contradictory, reasonably beget a pretty strong degree of assurance. In all cases, we must balance the opposite experiments, where they are opposite, and deduct the smaller number from the greater, in order to know the exact force of the superior evidence.

To apply these principles to a particular instance; we may observe, that there is no species of reasoning more common, more useful, and even necessary to human life, than that which is derived from the testimony of men, and the reports of eye-witnesses and spectators. This species of reasoning, perhaps, one may deny to be founded on the relation of cause and effect. I shall not dispute about a word. It will be sufficient to observe, that our assurance in any argument of this kind is derived from no other principle than our observation of the veracity of human testimony, and of the usual conformity of facts to the reports of witnesses. It being a general maxim, that no objects have any discoverable connexion together, and that all the inferences, which we can draw from one to another, are founded merely on our experience of their constant and regular conjunction; it is evident, that we ought not to make an exception to this maxim in favour of human testimony, whose connexion with any event seems, in itself, as little necessary as any other. Were not the memory tenacious to a certain degree; had not men commonly an inclination to truth and a principle of probity; were they not sensible to shame, when detected in a falsehood: Were not these, I say, discovered by experience to be qualities, inherent in human nature, we should never repose the least confidence in human testimony. A man delirious, or noted for falsehood and villainy, has no manner of authority with us.

And as the evidence, derived from witnesses and human testimony, is founded on past experience, so it varies with the experience, and is regarded either as a proof or a probability, according as the conjunction between any particular kind of report and any kind of object has been found to be constant or variable. There are a number of circumstances to be taken into consideration in all judgments of this kind; and the ultimate standard, by which we determine all disputes, that may arise concerning them, is always derived from experience and observation. Where this experience is not entirely uniform on any side, it is attended with an unavoidable contrariety in our judgments, and with the same opposition and mutual destruction of argument as in every other kind of evidence. We frequently hesitate concerning the reports of others. We balance the opposite circumstances, which cause any doubt or uncertainty; and when we discover a superiority on any side, we incline to it; but still with a diminution of assurance, in proportion to the force of its antagonist.

This contrariety of evidence, in the present case, may be derived from several different causes; from the opposition of contrary testimony; from the character or number of the witnesses; from the manner of their delivering their testimony; or from the union of all these circumstances. We entertain a suspicion concerning any matter of fact, when the witnesses contradict each other; when they are but few, or of a doubtful character; when they have an interest in what they affirm; when they deliver their testimony with hesitation, or on the contrary, with too violent asseverations. There are many other particulars of the same kind, which may diminish or destroy the force of any argument, derived from human testimony.

Suppose, for instance, that the fact, which the testimony endeavors to establish, partakes of the extraordinary and the marvelous; in that case, the evidence, resulting from the testimony, admits of a diminution, greater or less, in proportion as the fact is more or less unusual. The reason, why we place any credit in witnesses and historians, is not derived from any connexion, which we perceive a priori, between testimony and reality, but because we are accustomed to find a conformity between them. But when the fact attested is such a one as has seldom fallen under our observation, here is a contest of two opposite experiences; of which the one destroys the other, as far as its force goes, and the superior can only operate on the mind by the force, which remains. The very same principle of experience, which gives us a certain degree of assurance in the testimony of witnesses, gives us also, in this case, another degree of assurance against the fact, which they endeavor to establish; from which contradiction there necessarily arises a counterpoise, and mutual destruction of belief and authority.

I should not believe such a story were it told me by Cato; was a proverbial saying in Rome, even during the lifetime of that philosophical patriot. The incredibility of a fact, it was allowed, might invalidate so great an authority.

The INDIAN prince, who refused to believe the first relations concerning the effects of frost, reasoned justly; and it naturally required very strong testimony to engage his assent to facts, that arose from a state of nature, with which he was unacquainted, and which bore so little analogy to those events, of which he had had constant and uniform experience. Though they were not contrary to his experience, they were not conformable to it.

But in order to increase the probability against the testimony of witnesses, let us suppose, that the fact, which they affirm, instead of being only marvelous, is really miraculous; and suppose also, that the testimony, considered apart and in itself, amounts to an entire proof; in that case, there is proof against proof, of which the strongest must prevail, but still with a diminution of its force, in proportion to that of its antagonist.

A miracle is a violation of the laws of nature; and as a firm and unalterable experience has established these laws, the proof against a miracle, from the very nature of the fact, is as entire as any argument from experience can possibly be imagined. Why is it more than probable, that all men must die; that lead cannot, of itself, remain suspended in the air; that fire consumes wood, and is extinguished by water; unless it be, that these events are found agreeable to the laws of nature, and there is required a violation of these laws, or in other words, a miracle to prevent them? Nothing is esteemed a miracle, if it ever happen in the common course of nature. It is no miracle that a man, seemingly in good health, should die on a sudden: because such a kind of death, though more unusual than any other, has yet been frequently observed to happen. But it is a miracle, that a dead man should come to life; because that has never been observed, in any age or country. There must, therefore, be an uniform experience against every miraculous event, otherwise the event would not merit that appellation. And as a uniform experience amounts to a proof, there is here a direct and full proof, from the nature of the fact, against the existence of any miracle; nor can such a proof be destroyed, or the miracle rendered credible, but by an opposite proof, which is superior.

The plain consequence is (and it is a general maxim worthy of our attention), 'That no testimony is sufficient to establish a miracle, unless the testimony be of such a kind, that its falsehood would be more miraculous, than the fact, which it endeavors to establish: And even in that case there is a mutual destruction of arguments, and the superior only gives us an assurance suitable to that degree of force, which remains, after deducting the inferior.' When any one tells me, that he saw a dead man restored to life, I immediately consider with myself, whether it be more probable, that this person should either deceive or be deceived, or that the fact, which he relates, should really have happened. I weigh the one miracle against the other; and according to the superiority, which I discover, I pronounce my decision, and always reject the greater miracle. If the falsehood of his testimony would be more miraculous, than the event which he relates; then, and not till then, can he pretend to command my belief or opinion.

Part II

In the foregoing reasoning we have supposed, that the testimony, upon which a miracle is founded, may possibly amount to an entire proof, and that the falsehood of that testimony would be a real prodigy: But it is easy to shew, that we have been a great deal too liberal in our concession, and that there never was a miraculous event established on so full an evidence.

For first, there is not to be found in all history, any miracle attested by a sufficient number of men, of such unquestioned good-sense, education, and learning, as to secure us against all delusion in themselves; of such undoubted integrity, as to place them beyond all suspicion of any design to deceive others; of such credit and reputation in the eyes of mankind, as to have a great deal to lose in case of their being detected in any falsehood; and at the same time, attesting facts performed in such a public manner, and in so celebrated a part of the world, as to render the detection unavoidable: All which circumstances are requisite to give us a full assurance in the testimony of men.

Secondly. We may observe in human nature a principle, which, if strictly examined, will be found to diminish extremely the assurance, which we might, from human testimony, have, in any kind of prodigy. The maxim, by which we commonly conduct ourselves in our reasonings, is, that the objects, of which we have no experience, resemble those, of which we have; that what we have found to be most usual is always most probable; and that where there is an opposition of arguments, we ought to give the preference to such as are founded on the greatest number of past observations. But though, in proceeding by this rule, we readily reject any fact which is unusual and incredible in an ordinary degree; yet in advancing farther, the mind observes not always the same rule; but when anything is affirmed utterly absurd and miraculous, it rather the more readily admits of such a fact, upon account of that very circumstance, which ought to destroy all its authority. The passion of surprise and wonder, arising from miracles, being an agreeable emotion, gives a sensible tendency towards the belief of those events, from which it is derived. And this goes so far, that even those who cannot enjoy this pleasure immediately, nor can believe those miraculous events, of which they are informed, yet love to partake of the satisfaction at second-hand or by rebound, and place a pride and delight in exciting the admiration of others.

With what greediness are the miraculous accounts of travellers received, their descriptions of sea and land monsters, their relations of wonderful adventures, strange men, and uncouth manners? But if the spirit of religion join itself to the love of wonder, there is an end of common sense; and human testimony, in these circumstances, loses all pretensions to authority. A religionist may be an enthusiast, and imagine he sees what has no reality: He may know his narrative to be false, and yet persevere in it, with the best intentions in the world, for the sake of promoting so holy a cause: Or even where this delusion has not place, vanity, excited by so strong a temptation, operates on him more powerfully than on the rest of mankind in any other circumstances; and self-interest with equal force. His auditors may not have, and commonly have not, sufficient judgment to canvass his evidence: What judgment they have, they renounce by principle, in these sublime and mysterious subjects: Or if they were ever so willing to employ it, passion and a heated imagination disturb the regularity of its operations. Their credulity increases his impudence: And his impudence overpowers their credulity.

Eloquence, when at its highest pitch, leaves little room for reason or reflection; but addressing itself entirely to the fancy or the affections, captivates the willing hearers, and subdues their understanding. Happily, this pitch it seldom attains. But what a Tully or a Demosthenes could scarcely effect over a Roman or Athenian audience, every Capuchin, every itinerant or stationary teacher can perform over the generality of mankind, and in a higher degree, by touching such gross and vulgar passions.

The many instances of forged miracles, and prophecies, and supernatural events, which, in all ages, have either been detected by contrary evidence, or which detect themselves by their absurdity, prove sufficiently the strong propensity of mankind to the extraordinary and the marvelous, and ought reasonably to beget a suspicion against all relations of this kind. This is our natural way of thinking, even with regard to the most common and most credible events. For instance: There is no kind of report, which rises so easily, and spreads so quickly, especially in country places and provincial towns, as those concerning marriages; insomuch that two young persons of equal condition never see each other twice, but the whole neighborhood immediately join them together. The pleasure of telling a piece of news so interesting, of propagating it, and of being the first reporters of it, spreads the intelligence. And this is so well known, that no man of sense gives attention to these reports, till he find them confirmed by some greater evidence. Do not the same passions, and others still stronger, incline the generality of mankind to believe and report, with the greatest vehemence and assurance, all religious miracles?

Thirdly. It forms a strong presumption against all supernatural and miraculous relations, that they are observed chiefly to abound among ignorant and barbarous nations; or if a civilized people has ever given admission to any of them, that people will be found to have received them from ignorant and barbarous ancestors, who transmitted them with that inviolable sanction and authority, which always attend received opinions. When we peruse the first histories of all nations, we are apt to imagine ourselves transported into some new world; where the whole frame of nature is disjointed, and every element performs its operations in a different manner, from what it does at present. Battles, revolutions, pestilence, famine, and death, are never the effect of those natural causes, which we experience. Prodigies, omens, oracles, judgments, quite obscure the few natural events, that are intermingled with them. But as the former grow thinner every page, in proportion as we advance nearer the enlightened ages, we soon learn, that there is nothing mysterious or supernatural in the case, but that all proceeds from the usual propensity of mankind towards the marvelous, and that, though this inclination may at intervals receive a check from sense and learning, it can never be thoroughly extirpated from human nature.

It is strange, a judicious reader is apt to say, upon the perusal of these wonderful historians, that such prodigious events never happen in our days. But it is nothing strange, I hope, that men should lie in all ages. You must surely have seen instances enough of that frailty. You have yourself heard many such marvelous relations started, which, being treated with scorn by all the wise and judicious, have at last been abandoned even by the vulgar. Be assured, that those renowned lies, which have spread and flourished to such a monstrous height, arose from like beginnings; but being sown in a more proper soil, shot up at last into prodigies almost equal to those which they relate.

It was a wise policy in that false prophet, Alexander, who, though now forgotten, was once so famous, to lay the first scene of his impostures in Paphlagonia, where, as Lucian tells us, the people were extremely ignorant and stupid, and ready to swallow even the grossest delusion. People at a distance, who are weak enough to think the matter at all worth enquiry, have no opportunity of receiving better information. The stories come magnified to them by a hundred circumstances. Fools are industrious in propagating the imposture; while the wise and learned are contented, in general, to deride its absurdity, without informing themselves of the particular facts, by which it may be distinctly refuted. And thus the impostor above-mentioned was enabled to proceed, from his ignorant Paphlagonians, to the enlisting of votaries, even among the Grecian philosophers, and men of the most eminent rank and distinction in Rome: Nay, could engage the attention of that sage emperor Marcus Aurelius; so far as to make him trust the success of a military expedition to his delusive prophecies.

The advantages are so great, of starting an imposture among an ignorant people, that, even though the delusion should be too gross to impose on the generality of them (which, though seldom, is sometimes the case) it has a much better chance for succeeding in remote countries, than if the first scene had been laid in a city renowned for arts and knowledge. The most ignorant and barbarous of these barbarians carry the report abroad. None of their countrymen have a large correspondence, or sufficient credit and authority to contradict and beat down the delusion. Men's inclination to the marvelous has full opportunity to display itself. And thus a story, which is universally exploded in the place where it was first started, shall pass for certain at a thousand miles distance. But had Alexander fixed his residence at Athens, the philosophers of that renowned mart of learning had immediately spread, throughout the whole Roman empire, their sense of the matter; which, being supported by so great authority, and displayed by all the force of reason and eloquence, had entirely opened the eyes of mankind. It is true; Lucian, passing by chance through Paphlagonia, had an opportunity of performing this good office. But, though much to be wished, it does not always happen, that every Alexander meets with a Lucian, ready to expose and detect his impostures.

I may add as a fourth reason, which diminishes the authority of prodigies, that there is no testimony for any, even those which have not been expressly detected, that is not opposed by an infinite number of witnesses; so that not only the miracle destroys the credit of testimony, but the testimony destroys itself. To make this the better understood, let us consider, that, in matters of religion, whatever is different is contrary; and that it is impossible the religions of ancient Rome, of Turkey, of Siam, and of China should, all of them, be established on any solid foundation. Every miracle, therefore, pretended to have been wrought in any of these religions (and all of them abound in miracles), as its direct scope is to establish the particular system to which it is attributed; so has it the same force, though more indirectly, to overthrow every other system. In destroying a rival system, it likewise destroys the credit of those miracles, on which that system was established; so that all the prodigies of different religions are to be regarded as contrary facts, and the evidences of these prodigies, whether weak or strong, as opposite to each other. According to this method of reasoning, when we believe any miracle of Mahomet or his successors, we have for our warrant the testimony of a few barbarous Arabians: And on the other hand, we are to regard the authority of Titus Livius, Plutarch, Tacitus, and, in short, of all the authors and witnesses, Grecian, Chinese, and Roman Catholic, who have related any miracle in their particular religion; I say, we are to regard their testimony in the same light as if they had mentioned that Mahometan miracle, and had in express terms contradicted it, with the same certainty as they have for the miracle they relate. This argument may appear over subtile and refined; but is not in reality different from the reasoning of a judge, who supposes, that the credit of two witnesses, maintaining a crime against any one, is destroyed by the testimony of two others, who affirm him to have been two hundred leagues distant, at the same instant when the crime is said to have been committed.

One of the best attested miracles in all profane history, is that which Tacitus reports of Vespasian, who cured a blind man in Alexandria, by means of his spittle, and a lame man by the mere touch of his foot; in obedience to a vision of the god Serapis, who had enjoined them to have recourse to the Emperor, for these miraculous cures. The story may be seen in that fine historian; where every circumstance seems to add weight to the testimony, and might be displayed at large with all the force of argument and eloquence, if any one were now concerned to enforce the evidence of that exploded and idolatrous superstition. The gravity, solidity, age, and probity of so great an emperor, who, through the whole course of his life, conversed in a familiar manner with his friends and courtiers, and never affected those extraordinary airs of divinity assumed by Alexander and Demetrius. The historian, a contemporary writer, noted for candor and veracity, and withal, the greatest and most penetrating genius, perhaps, of all antiquity; and so free from any tendency to credulity, that he even lies under the contrary imputation, of atheism and profaneness: The persons, from whose authority he related the miracle, of established character for judgment and veracity, as we may well presume; eye-witnesses of the fact, and confirming their testimony, after the Flavian family was despoiled of the empire, and could no longer give any reward, as the price of a lie. Those who were present recount both even now that a lie is no longer rewarded. To which if we add the public nature of the facts, as related, it will appear, that no evidence can well be supposed stronger for so gross and so palpable a falsehood.

There is also a memorable story related by Cardinal de Retz, which may well deserve our consideration. When that intriguing politician fled into Spain, to avoid the persecution of his enemies, he passed through Saragossa, the capital of Arragon, where he was shewn, in the cathedral, a man, who had served seven years as a door-keeper, and was well known to every body in town, that had ever paid his devotions at that church. He had been seen, for so long a time, wanting a leg; but recovered that limb by the rubbing of holy oil upon the stump; and the cardinal assures us that he saw him with two legs. This miracle was vouched by all the canons of the church; and the whole company in town were appealed to for a confirmation of the fact; whom the cardinal found, by their zealous devotion, to be thorough believers of the miracle. Here the relater was also contemporary to the supposed prodigy, of an incredulous and libertine character, as well as of great genius; the miracle of so singular a nature as could scarcely admit of a counterfeit, and the witnesses very numerous, and all of them, in a manner, spectators of the fact, to which they gave their testimony. And what adds mightily to the force of the evidence, and may double our surprise on this occasion, is, that the cardinal himself, who relates the story, seems not to give any credit to it, and consequently cannot be suspected of any concurrence in the holy fraud. He considered justly, that it was not requisite, in order to reject a fact of this nature, to be able accurately to disprove the testimony, and to trace its falsehood, through all the circumstances of knavery and credulity which produced it. He knew, that, as this was commonly altogether impossible at any small distance of time and place; so was it extremely difficult, even where one was immediately present, by reason of the bigotry, ignorance, cunning, and roguery of a great part of mankind. He therefore concluded, like a just reasoner, that such an evidence carried falsehood upon the very face of it, and that a miracle supported by any human testimony, was more properly a subject of derision than of argument.

There surely never was a greater number of miracles ascribed to one person, than those, which were lately said to have been wrought in France upon the tomb of Abbe Paris, the famous Jansenist, with whose sanctity the people were so long deluded. The curing of the sick, giving hearing to the deaf, and sight to the blind, were every where talked of as the usual effects of that holy sepulchre. But what is more extraordinary; many of the miracles were immediately proved upon the spot, before judges of unquestioned integrity, attested by witnesses of credit and distinction, in a learned age, and on the most eminent theater that is now in the world. Nor is this all: A relation of them was published and dispersed every where; nor were the Jesuits, though a learned body, supported by the civil magistrate, and determined enemies to those opinions, in whose favour the miracles were said to have been wrought, ever able distinctly to refute or detect them. Where shall we find such a number of circumstances, agreeing to the corroboration of one fact? And what have we to oppose to such a cloud of witnesses, but the absolute impossibility or miraculous nature of the events, which they relate? And this surely, in the eyes of all reasonable people, will alone be regarded as a sufficient refutation.

Is the consequence just, because some human testimony has the utmost force and authority in some cases, when it relates the battle of Philippi or Pharsalia for instance; that therefore all kinds of testimony must, in all cases, have equal force and authority? Suppose that the Caesarean and Pompeian factions had, each of them, claimed the victory in these battles, and that the historians of each party had uniformly ascribed the advantage to their own side: how could mankind, at this distance, have been able to determine between them? The contrariety is equally strong between the miracles related by Herodotus or Plutarch, and those delivered by Mariana, Bede, or any monkish historian.

The wise lend a very academic faith to every report which favors the passion of the reporter; whether it magnifies his country, his family, or himself, or in any other way strikes in with his natural inclinations and propensities. But what greater temptation than to appear a missionary, a prophet, an ambassador from heaven? Who would not encounter many dangers and difficulties, in order to attain so sublime a character? Or if, by the help of vanity and a heated imagination, a man has first made a convert of himself, and entered seriously into the delusion; who ever scruples to make use of pious frauds, in support of so holy and meritorious a cause?

The smallest spark may here kindle into the greatest flame; because the materials are always prepared for it. The crowd hungry for gossip, the gazing populace, receive greedily, without examination, whatever soothes superstition, and promotes wonder.

How many stories of this nature, have, in all ages, been detected and exploded in their infancy? How many more have been celebrated for a time, and have afterwards sunk into neglect and oblivion? Where such reports, therefore, fly about, the solution of the phenomenon is obvious; and we judge in conformity to regular experience and observation, when we account for it by the known and natural principles of credulity and delusion. And shall we, rather than have a recourse to so natural a solution, allow of a miraculous violation of the most established laws of nature?

I need not mention the difficulty of detecting a falsehood in any private or even public history, at the place, where it is said to happen; much more when the scene is removed to ever so small a distance. Even a court of judicature, with all the authority, accuracy, and judgment, which they can employ, find themselves often at a loss to distinguish between truth and falsehood in the most recent actions. But the matter never comes to any issue, if trusted to the common method of altercation and debate and flying rumors; especially when men's passions have taken part on either side.

In the infancy of new religions, the wise and learned commonly esteem the matter too inconsiderable to deserve their attention or regard. And when afterwards they would willingly detect the cheat, in order to undeceive the deluded multitude, the season is now past, and the records and witnesses, which might clear up the matter, have perished beyond recovery.

No means of detection remain, but those which must be drawn from the very testimony itself of the reporters: And these, though always sufficient with the judicious and knowing, are commonly too fine to fall under the comprehension of the vulgar.

Upon the whole, then, it appears, that no testimony for any kind of miracle has ever amounted to a probability, much less to a proof; and that, even supposing it amounted to a proof, it would be opposed by another proof; derived from the very nature of the fact, which it would endeavor to establish. It is experience only, which gives authority to human testimony; and it is the same experience, which assures us of the laws of nature. When, therefore, these two kinds of experience are contrary, we have nothing to do but subtract the one from the other, and embrace an opinion, either on one side or the other, with that assurance which arises from the remainder. But according to the principle here explained, this subtraction, with regard to all popular religions, amounts to an entire annihilation; and therefore we may establish it as a maxim, that no human testimony can have such force as to prove a miracle, and make it a just foundation for any such system of religion.

I beg the limitations here made may be remarked, when I say, that a miracle can never be proved, so as to be the foundation of a system of religion. For I own, that otherwise, there may possibly be miracles, or violations of the usual course of nature, of such a kind as to admit of proof from human testimony; though, perhaps, it will be impossible to find any such in all the records of history. Thus, suppose, all authors, in all languages, agree, that, from the first of January 1600, there was a total darkness over the whole earth for eight days: Suppose that the tradition of this extraordinary event is still strong and lively among the people: That all travellers, who return from foreign countries, bring us accounts of the same tradition, without the least variation or contradiction: It is evident, that our present philosophers, instead of doubting the fact, ought to receive it as certain, and ought to search for the causes whence it might be derived. The decay, corruption, and dissolution of nature, is an event rendered probable by so many analogies, that any phenomenon, which seems to have a tendency towards that catastrophe, comes within the reach of human testimony, if that testimony be very extensive and uniform.

But suppose, that all the historians who treat of England, should agree, that, on the first of January 1600, Queen Elizabeth died; that both before and after her death she was seen by her physicians and the whole court, as is usual with persons of her rank; that her successor was acknowledged and proclaimed by the parliament; and that, after being interred a month, she again appeared, resumed the throne, and governed England for three years: I must confess that I should be surprised at the concurrence of so many odd circumstances, but should not have the least inclination to believe so miraculous an event. I should not doubt of her pretended death, and of those other public circumstances that followed it: I should only assert it to have been pretended, and that it neither was, nor possibly could be real. You would in vain object to me the difficulty, and almost impossibility of deceiving the world in an affair of such consequence; the wisdom and solid judgment of that renowned queen; with the little or no advantage which she could reap from so poor an artifice: All this might astonish me; but I would still reply, that the knavery and folly of men are such common phenomena, that I should rather believe the most extraordinary events to arise from their concurrence, than admit of so signal a violation of the laws of nature.

But should this miracle be ascribed to any new system of religion; men, in all ages, have been so much imposed on by ridiculous stories of that kind, that this very circumstance would be a full proof of a cheat, and sufficient, with all men of sense, not only to make them reject the fact, but even reject it without farther examination. Though the Being to whom the miracle is ascribed, be, in this case, Almighty, it does not, upon that account, become a whit more probable; since it is impossible for us to know the attributes or actions of such a Being, otherwise than from the experience which we have of his productions, in the usual course of nature. This still reduces us to past observation, and obliges us to compare the instances of the violation of truth in the testimony of men, with those of the violation of the laws of nature by miracles, in order to judge which of them is most likely and probable. As the violations of truth are more common in the testimony concerning religious miracles, than in that concerning any other matter of fact; this must diminish very much the authority of the former testimony, and make us form a general resolution, never to lend any attention to it, with whatever specious presence it may be covered.

Lord Bacon seems to have embraced the same principles of reasoning. 'We ought,' says he, 'to make a collection or particular history of all monsters and prodigious births of productions, and in a word of every thing new, rare, and extraordinary in nature. But this must be done with the most severe scrutiny, lest we depart from truth. Above all, every relation must be considered as suspicious, which depends in any degree upon religion, as the prodigies of Livy: And no less so, every thing that is to be found in the writers of natural magic or alchemy, or such authors, who seem, all of them, to have an unconquerable appetite for falsehood and fable.'

I am the better pleased with the method of reasoning here delivered, as I think it may serve to confound those dangerous friends or disguised enemies to the Christian Religion, who have undertaken to defend it by the principles of human reason. Our most holy religion is founded on Faith, not on reason; and it is a sure method of exposing it to put it to such a trial as it is, by no means, fitted to endure. To make this more evident, let us examine those miracles, related in scripture; and not to lose ourselves in too wide a field, let us confine ourselves to such as we find in the Pentateuch, which we shall examine, according to the principles of these pretended Christians, not as the word or testimony of God himself, but as the production of a mere human writer and historian. Here then we are first to consider a book, presented to us by a barbarous and ignorant people, written in an age when they were still more barbarous, and in all probability long after the facts which it relates, corroborated by no concurring testimony, and resembling those fabulous accounts, which every nation gives of its origin. Upon reading this book, we find it full of prodigies and miracles. It gives an account of a state of the world and of human nature entirely different from the present: Of our fall from that state: Of the age of man, extended to near a thousand years: Of the destruction of the world by a deluge: Of the arbitrary choice of one people, as the favorites of heaven; and that people the countrymen of the author: Of their deliverance from bondage by prodigies the most astonishing imaginable: I desire any one to lay his hand upon his heart, and after a serious consideration declare, whether he thinks that the falsehood of such a book, supported by such a testimony, would be more extraordinary and miraculous than all the miracles it relates; which is, however, necessary to make it be received, according to the measures of probability above established.

What we have said of miracles may be applied, without any variation, to prophecies; and indeed, all prophecies are real miracles, and as such only, can be admitted as proofs of any revelation. If it did not exceed the capacity of human nature to foretell future events, it would be absurd to employ any prophecy as an argument for a divine mission or authority from heaven. So that, upon the whole, we may conclude, that the Christian Religion not only was at first attended with miracles, but even at this day cannot be believed by any reasonable person without one. Mere reason is insufficient to convince us of its veracity: And whoever is moved by Faith to assent to it, is conscious of a continued miracle in his own person, which subverts all the principles of his understanding, and gives him a determination to believe what is most contrary to custom and experience.

SECTION XI: OF A PARTICULAR PROVIDENCE AND OF A FUTURE STATE

I was lately engaged in conversation with a friend who loves sceptical paradoxes; where, though he advanced many principles, of which I can by no means approve, yet as they seem to be curious, and to bear some relation to the chain of reasoning carried on throughout this enquiry, I shall here copy them from my memory as accurately as I can, in order to submit them to the judgment of the reader.

Our conversation began with my admiring the singular good fortune of philosophy, which, as it requires entire liberty above all other privileges, and chiefly flourishes from the free opposition of sentiments and argumentation, received its first birth in an age and country of freedom and toleration, and was never cramped, even in its most extravagant principles, by any creeds, confessions, or penal statutes. For, except the banishment of Protagoras, and the death of Socrates, which last event proceeded partly from other motives, there are scarcely any instances to be met with, in ancient history, of this bigoted jealousy, with which the present age is so much infested. Epicurus lived at Athens to an advanced age, in peace and tranquillity: Epicureans were even admitted to receive the sacerdotal character, and to officiate at the altar, in the most sacred rites of the established religion: And the public encouragement of pensions and salaries was afforded equally, by the wisest of all the Roman emperors, to the professors of every sect of philosophy. How requisite such kind of treatment was to philosophy, in her early youth, will easily be conceived, if we reflect, that, even at present, when she may be supposed more hardy and robust, she bears with much difficulty the inclemency of the seasons, and those harsh winds of calumny and persecution, which blow upon her.

You admire, says my friend, as the singular good fortune of philosophy, what seems to result from the natural course of things, and to be unavoidable in every age and nation. This pertinacious bigotry, of which you complain, as so fatal to philosophy, is really her offspring, who, after allying with superstition, separates himself entirely from the interest of his parent, and becomes her most inveterate enemy and persecutor. Speculative dogmas of religion, the present occasions of such furious dispute, could not possibly be conceived or admitted in the early ages of the world; when mankind, being wholly illiterate, formed an idea of religion more suitable to their weak apprehension, and composed their sacred tenets of such tales chiefly as were the objects of traditional belief, more than of argument or disputation. After the first alarm, therefore, was over, which arose from the new paradoxes and principles of the philosophers; these teachers seem ever after, during the ages of antiquity, to have lived in great harmony with the established superstition, and to have made a fair partition of mankind between them; the former claiming all the learned and wise, the latter possessing all the vulgar and illiterate.

It seems then, say I, that you leave politics entirely out of the question, and never suppose, that a wise magistrate can justly be jealous of certain tenets of philosophy, such as those of Epicurus, which, denying a divine existence, and consequently a providence and a future state, seem to loosen, in a great measure, the ties of morality, and may be supposed, for that reason, pernicious to the peace of civil society.

I know, replied he, that in fact these persecutions never, in any age, proceeded from calm reason, or from experience of the pernicious consequences of philosophy; but arose entirely from passion and prejudice. But what if I should advance farther, and assert, that, if Epicurus had been accused before the people, by any of the sycophants or informers of those days, he could easily have defended his cause, and proved his principles of philosophy to be as salutary as those of his adversaries, who endeavored, with such zeal, to expose him to the public hatred and jealousy?

I wish, said I, you would try your eloquence upon so extraordinary a topic, and make a speech for Epicurus, which might satisfy, not the mob of Athens, if you will allow that ancient and polite city to have contained any mob, but the more philosophical part of his audience, such as might be supposed capable of comprehending his arguments.

The matter would not be difficult, upon such conditions, replied he: And if you please, I shall suppose myself Epicurus for a moment, and make you stand for the Athenian people, and shall deliver you such an harangue as will fill all the urn with white beans, and leave not a black one to gratify the malice of my adversaries.

Very well: Pray proceed upon these suppositions.

I come hither, O ye Athenians, to justify in your assembly what I maintained in my school, and I find myself impeached by furious antagonists, instead of reasoning with calm and dispassionate inquirers. Your deliberations, which of right should be directed to questions of public good, and the interest of the commonwealth, are diverted to the disquisitions of speculative philosophy; and these magnificent, but perhaps fruitless enquiries, take place of your more familiar but more useful occupations. But so far as in me lies, I will prevent this abuse. We shall not here dispute concerning the origin and government of worlds. We shall only enquire how far such questions concern the public interest. And if I can persuade you, that they are entirely indifferent to the peace of society and security of government, I hope that you will presently send us back to our schools, there to examine, at leisure, the question, the most sublime, but, at the same time, the most speculative of all philosophy.

The religious philosophers, not satisfied with the tradition of your forefathers, and doctrine of your priests (in which I willingly acquiesce), indulge a rash curiosity, in trying how far they can establish religion upon the principles of reason; and they thereby excite, instead of satisfying, the doubts, which naturally arise from a diligent and scrutinous enquiry. They paint, in the most magnificent colours, the order, beauty, and wise arrangement of the universe; and then ask, if such a glorious display of intelligence could proceed from the fortuitous concourse of atoms, or if chance could produce what the greatest genius can never sufficiently admire. I shall not examine the justness of this argument. I shall allow it to be as solid as my antagonists and accusers can desire. It is sufficient, if I can prove, from this very reasoning, that the question is entirely speculative, and that, when, in my philosophical disquisitions, I deny a providence and a future state, I undermine not the foundations of society, but advance principles, which they themselves, upon their own topics, if they argue consistently, must allow to be solid and satisfactory.

You then, who are my accusers, have acknowledged, that the chief or sole argument for a divine existence (which I never questioned) is derived from the order of nature; where there appear such marks of intelligence and design, that you think it extravagant to assign for its cause, either chance, or the blind and unguided force of matter. You allow, that this is an argument drawn from effects to causes. From the order of the work, you infer, that there must have been project and forethought in the workman. If you cannot make out this point, you allow, that your conclusion fails; and you pretend not to establish the conclusion in a greater latitude than the phenomena of nature will justify. These are your concessions. I desire you to mark the consequences.

When we infer any particular cause from an effect, we must proportion the one to the other, and can never be allowed to ascribe to the cause any qualities, but what are exactly sufficient to produce the effect. A body of ten ounces raised in any scale may serve as a proof, that the counterbalancing weight exceeds ten ounces; but can never afford a reason that it exceeds a hundred. If the cause, assigned for any effect, be not sufficient to produce it, we must either reject that cause, or add to it such qualities as will give it a just proportion to the effect. But if we ascribe to it farther qualities, or affirm it capable of producing other effects, we can only indulge the license of conjecture, and arbitrarily suppose the existence of qualities and energies, without reason or authority.

The same rule holds, whether the cause assigned be brute unconscious matter, or a rational intelligent being. If the cause be known only by the effect, we never ought to ascribe to it any qualities, beyond what are precisely requisite to produce the effect: Nor can we, by any rules of just reasoning, return back from the cause, and infer other effects from it, beyond those by which alone it is known to us. No one, merely from the sight of one of Zeuxis's pictures, could know, that he was also a statuary or architect, and was an artist no less skillful in stone and marble than in colours. The talents and taste, displayed in the particular work before us; these we may safely conclude the workman to be possessed of. The cause must be proportioned to the effect; and if we exactly and precisely proportion it, we shall never find in it any qualities, that point farther, or afford an inference concerning any other design or performance. Such qualities must be somewhat beyond what is merely requisite for producing the effect, which we examine.

Allowing, therefore, the gods to be the authors of the existence or order of the universe; it follows, that they possess that precise degree of power, intelligence, and benevolence, which appears in their workmanship; but nothing farther can ever be proved, except we call in the assistance of exaggeration and flattery to supply the defects of argument and reasoning. So far as the traces of any attributes, at present, appear, so far may we conclude these attributes to exist. The supposition of farther attributes is mere hypothesis; much more the supposition, that, in distant regions of space or periods of time, there has been, or will be, a more magnificent display of these attributes, and a scheme of administration more suitable to such imaginary virtues. We can never be allowed to mount up from the universe, the effect, to Jupiter, the cause; and then descend downwards, to infer any new effect from that cause; as if the present effects alone were not entirely worthy of the glorious attributes, which we ascribe to that deity. The knowledge of the cause being derived solely from the effect, they must be exactly adjusted to each other; and the one can never refer to any thing farther, or be the foundation of any new inference and conclusion.

You find certain phenomena in nature. You seek a cause or author. You imagine that you have found him. You afterwards become so enamored of this offspring of your brain, that you imagine it impossible, but he must produce something greater and more perfect than the present scene of things, which is so full of ill and disorder. You forget, that this superlative intelligence and benevolence are entirely imaginary, or, at least, without any foundation in reason; and that you have no ground to ascribe to him any qualities, but what you see he has actually exerted and displayed in his productions. Let your gods, therefore, O philosophers, be suited to the present appearances of nature: And presume not to alter these appearances by arbitrary suppositions, in order to suit them to the attributes, which you so fondly ascribe to your deities.

When priests and poets, supported by your authority, O Athenians, talk of a golden or silver age, which preceded the present state of vice and misery, I hear them with attention and with reverence. But when philosophers, who pretend to neglect authority, and to cultivate reason, hold the same discourse, I pay them not, I own, the same obsequious submission and pious deference. I ask; who carried them into the celestial regions, who admitted them into the councils of the gods, who opened to them the book of fate, that they thus rashly affirm, that their deities have executed, or will execute, any purpose beyond what has actually appeared? If they tell me, that they have mounted on the steps or by the gradual ascent of reason, and by drawing inferences from effects to causes, I still insist, that they have aided the ascent of reason by the wings of imagination; otherwise they could not thus change their manner of inference, and argue from causes to effects; presuming, that a more perfect production than the present world would be more suitable to such perfect beings as the gods, and forgetting that they have no reason to ascribe to these celestial beings any perfection or any attribute, but what can be found in the present world.

Hence all the fruitless industry to account for the ill appearances of nature, and save the honour of the gods; while we must acknowledge the reality of that evil and disorder, with which the world so much abounds. The obstinate and intractable qualities of matter, we are told, or the observance of general laws, or some such reason, is the sole cause, which controlled the power and benevolence of Jupiter, and obliged him to create mankind and every sensible creature so imperfect and so unhappy. These attributes, then, are, it seems, beforehand, taken for granted, in their greatest latitude. And upon that supposition, I own, that such conjectures may, perhaps, be admitted as plausible solutions of the ill phenomena. But still I ask; Why take these attributes for granted, or why ascribe to the cause any qualities but what actually appear in the effect? Why torture your brain to justify the course of nature upon suppositions, which, for aught you know, may be entirely imaginary, and of which there are to be found no traces in the course of nature?

The religious hypothesis, therefore, must be considered only as a particular method of accounting for the visible phenomena of the universe: But no just reasoner will ever presume to infer from it any single fact, and alter or add to the phenomena, in any single particular. If you think, that the appearances of things prove such causes, it is allowable for you to draw an inference concerning the existence of these causes. In such complicated and sublime subjects, every one should be indulged in the liberty of conjecture and argument. But here you ought to rest. If you come backward, and arguing from your inferred causes, conclude, that any other fact has existed, or will exist, in the course of nature, which may serve as a fuller display of particular attributes; I must admonish you, that you have departed from the method of reasoning, attached to the present subject, and have certainly added something to the attributes of the cause, beyond what appears in the effect; otherwise you could never, with tolerable sense or propriety, add any thing to the effect, in order to render it more worthy of the cause.

Where, then, is the odiousness of that doctrine, which I teach in my school, or rather, which I examine in my gardens? Or what do you find in this whole question, wherein the security of good morals, or the peace and order of society is in the least concerned?

I deny a providence, you say, and supreme governor of the world, who guides the course of events, and punishes the vicious with infamy and disappointment, and rewards the virtuous with honour and success, in all their undertakings. But surely, I deny not the course itself of events, which lies open to every one's enquiry and examination. I acknowledge, that, in the present order of things, virtue is attended with more peace of mind than vice, and meets with a more favorable reception from the world. I am sensible, that, according to the past experience of mankind, friendship is the chief joy of human life, and moderation the only source of tranquillity and happiness. I never balance between the virtuous and the vicious course of life; but am sensible, that, to a well disposed mind, every advantage is on the side of the former. And what can you say more, allowing all your suppositions and reasonings? You tell me, indeed, that this disposition of things proceeds from intelligence and design. But whatever it proceeds from, the disposition itself, on which depends our happiness or misery, and consequently our conduct and deportment in life, is still the same. It is still open for me, as well as you, to regulate my behavior, by my experience of past events. And if you affirm, that, while a divine providence is allowed, and a supreme distributive justice in the universe, I ought to expect some more particular reward of the good, and punishment of the bad, beyond the ordinary course of events; I here find the same fallacy, which I have before endeavored to detect. You persist in imagining, that, if we grant that divine existence, for which you so earnestly contend, you may safely infer consequences from it, and add something to the experienced order of nature, by arguing from the attributes which you ascribe to your gods. You seem not to remember, that all your reasonings on this subject can only be drawn from effects to causes; and that every argument, deduced from causes to effects, must of necessity be a gross sophism; since it is impossible for you to know any thing of the cause, but what you have antecedently, not inferred, but discovered to the full, in the effect.

But what must a philosopher think of those vain reasoners, who, instead of regarding the present scene of things as the sole object of their contemplation, so far reverse the whole course of nature, as to render this life merely a passage to something farther; a porch, which leads to a greater, and vastly different building; a prologue, which serves only to introduce the piece, and give it more grace and propriety? Whence, do you think, can such philosophers derive their idea of the gods? From their own conceit and imagination surely. For if they derived it from the present phenomena, it would never point to anything farther, but must be exactly adjusted to them. That the divinity may possibly be endowed with attributes, which we have never seen exerted; may be governed by principles of action, which we cannot discover to be satisfied: All this will freely be allowed. But still this is mere possibility and hypothesis. We never can have reason to infer any attributes, or any principles of action in him, but so far as we know them to have been exerted and satisfied.

Are there any marks of a distributive justice in the world? If you answer in the affirmative, I conclude, that, since justice here exerts itself, it is satisfied. If you reply in the negative, I conclude, that you have then no reason to ascribe justice, in our sense of it, to the gods. If you hold a medium between affirmation and negation, by saying, that the justice of the gods, at present, exerts itself in part, but not in its full extent; I answer, that you have no reason to give it any particular extent, but only so far as you see it, at present, exert itself.

Thus I bring the dispute, O Athenians, to a short issue with my antagonists. The course of nature lies open to my contemplation as well as to theirs. The experienced train of events is the great standard, by which we all regulate our conduct. Nothing else can be appealed to in the field, or in the senate. Nothing else ought ever to be heard of in the school, or in the closet. In vain would our limited understanding break through those boundaries, which are too narrow for our fond imagination. While we argue from the course of nature, and infer a particular intelligent cause, which first bestowed, and still preserves order in the universe, we embrace a principle, which is both uncertain and useless. It is uncertain; because the subject lies entirely beyond the reach of human experience. It is useless; because our knowledge of this cause being derived entirely from the course of nature, we can never, according to the rules of just reasoning, return back from the cause with any new inference, or making additions to the common and experienced course of nature, establish any new principles of conduct and behavior.

I observe (said I, finding he had finished his harangue) that you neglect not the artifice of the demagogues of old; and as you were pleased to make me stand for the people, you insinuate yourself into my favour by embracing those principles, to which, you know, I have always expressed a particular attachment. But allowing you to make experience (as indeed I think you ought) the only standard of our judgment concerning this, and all other questions of fact; I doubt not but, from the very same experience, to which you appeal, it may be possible to refute this reasoning, which you have put into the mouth of Epicurus. If you saw, for instance, a half-finished building, surrounded with heaps of brick and stone and mortar, and all the instruments of masonry; could you not infer from the effect, that it was a work of design and contrivance? And could you not return again, from this inferred cause, to infer new additions to the effect, and conclude, that the building would soon be finished, and receive all the further improvements, which art could bestow upon it? If you saw upon the sea-shore the print of one human foot, you would conclude, that a man had passed that way, and that he had also left the traces of the other foot, though effaced by the rolling of the sands or inundation of the waters. Why then do you refuse to admit the same method of reasoning with regard to the order of nature? Consider the world and the present life only as an imperfect building, from which you can infer a superior intelligence; and arguing from that superior intelligence, which can leave nothing imperfect; why may you not infer a more finished scheme or plan, which will receive its completion in some distant point of space or time? Are not these methods of reasoning exactly similar? And under what pretence can you embrace the one, while you reject the other?

The infinite difference of the subjects, replied he, is a sufficient foundation for this difference in my conclusions. In works of human art and contrivance, it is allowable to advance from the effect to the cause, and returning back from the cause, to form new inferences concerning the effect, and examine the alterations, which it has probably undergone, or may still undergo. But what is the foundation of this method of reasoning? Plainly this; that man is a being, whom we know by experience, whose motives and designs we are acquainted with, and whose projects and inclinations have a certain connexion and coherence, according to the laws which nature has established for the government of such a creature. When, therefore, we find, that any work has proceeded from the skill and industry of man; as we are otherwise acquainted with the nature of the animal, we can draw a hundred inferences concerning what may be expected from him; and these inferences will all be founded in experience and observation. But did we know man only from the single work or production which we examine, it were impossible for us to argue in this manner; because our knowledge of all the qualities, which we ascribe to him, being in that case derived from the production, it is impossible they could point to any thing farther, or be the foundation of any new inference. The print of a foot in the sand can only prove, when considered alone, that there was some figure adapted to it, by which it was produced: But the print of a human foot proves likewise, from our other experience, that there was probably another foot, which also left its impression, though effaced by time or other accidents. Here we mount from the effect to the cause; and descending again from the cause, infer alterations in the effect; but this is not a continuation of the same simple chain of reasoning. We comprehend in this case a hundred other experiences and observations, concerning the usual figure and members of that species of animal, without which this method of argument must be considered as fallacious and sophistical.

The case is not the same with our reasonings from the works of nature. The Deity is known to us only by his productions, and is a single being in the universe, not comprehended under any species or genus, from whose experienced attributes or qualities, we can, by analogy, infer any attribute or quality in him. As the universe shows wisdom and goodness, we infer wisdom and goodness. As it shows a particular degree of these perfections, we infer a particular degree of them, precisely adapted to the effect which we examine. But farther attributes or farther degrees of the same attributes, we can never be authorized to infer or suppose, by any rules of just reasoning. Now, without some such license of supposition, it is impossible for us to argue from the cause, or infer any alteration in the effect, beyond what has immediately fallen under our observation. Greater good produced by this Being must still prove a greater degree of goodness: A more impartial distribution of rewards and punishments must proceed from a greater regard to justice and equity. Every supposed addition to the works of nature makes an addition to the attributes of the Author of nature; and consequently, being entirely unsupported by any reason or argument, can never be admitted but as mere conjecture and hypothesis.

The great source of our mistake in this subject, and of the unbounded license of conjecture, which we indulge, is, that we tacitly consider ourselves, as in the place of the Supreme Being, and conclude, that he will, on every occasion, observe the same conduct, which we ourselves, in his situation, would have embraced as reasonable and eligible. But, besides that the ordinary course of nature may convince us, that almost everything is regulated by principles and maxims very different from ours; besides this, I say, it must evidently appear contrary to all rules of analogy to reason, from the intentions and projects of men, to those of a Being so different, and so much superior. In human nature, there is a certain experienced coherence of designs and inclinations; so that when, from any fact, we have discovered one intention of any man, it may often be reasonable, from experience, to infer another, and draw a long chain of conclusions concerning his past or future conduct. But this method of reasoning can never have place with regard to a Being, so remote and incomprehensible, who bears much less analogy to any other being in the universe than the sun to a waxen taper, and who discovers himself only by some faint traces or outlines, beyond which we have no authority to ascribe to him any attribute or perfection. What we imagine to be a superior perfection, may really be a defect. Or were it ever so much a perfection, the ascribing of it to the Supreme Being, where it appears not to have been really exerted, to the full, in his works, savors more of flattery and panegyric, than of just reasoning and sound philosophy. All the philosophy, therefore, in the world, and all the religion, which is nothing but a species of philosophy, will never be able to carry us beyond the usual course of experience, or give us measures of conduct and behavior different from those which are furnished by reflections on common life. No new fact can ever be inferred from the religious hypothesis; no event foreseen or foretold; no reward or punishment expected or dreaded, beyond what is already known by practice and observation. So that my apology for Epicurus will still appear solid and satisfactory; nor have the political interests of society any connexion with the philosophical disputes concerning metaphysics and religion.

There is still one circumstance, replied I, which you seem to have overlooked. Though I should allow your premises, I must deny your conclusion. You conclude, that religious doctrines and reasonings can have no influence on life, because they ought to have no influence; never considering, that men reason not in the same manner you do, but draw many consequences from the belief of a divine Existence, and suppose that the Deity will inflict punishments on vice, and bestow rewards on virtue, beyond what appear in the ordinary course of nature. Whether this reasoning of theirs be just or not, is no matter. Its influence on their life and conduct must still be the same. And, those, who attempt to disabuse them of such prejudices, may, for aught I know, be good reasoners, but I cannot allow them to be good citizens and politicians; since they free men from one restraint upon their passions, and make the infringement of the laws of society, in one respect, more easy and secure.

After all, I may, perhaps, agree to your general conclusion in favour of liberty, though upon different premises from those, on which you endeavor to found it. I think, that the state ought to tolerate every principle of philosophy; nor is there an instance, that any government has suffered in its political interests by such indulgence. There is no enthusiasm among philosophers; their doctrines are not very alluring to the people; and no restraint can be put upon their reasonings, but what must be of dangerous consequence to the sciences, and even to the state, by paving the way for persecution and oppression in points, where the generality of mankind are more deeply interested and concerned.

But there occurs to me (continued I) with regard to your main topic, a difficulty, which I shall just propose to you, without insisting on it; lest it lead into reasonings of too nice and delicate a nature. In a word, I much doubt whether it be possible for a cause to be known only by its effect (as you have all along supposed) or to be of so singular and particular a nature as to have no parallel and no similarity with any other cause or object, that has ever fallen under our observation. It is only when two species of objects are found to be constantly conjoined, that we can infer the one from the other; and were an effect presented, which was entirely singular, and could not be comprehended under any known species, I do not see, that we could form any conjecture or inference at all concerning its cause. If experience and observation and analogy be, indeed, the only guides which we can reasonably follow in inferences of this nature; both the effect and cause must bear a similarity and resemblance to other effects and causes, which we know, and which we have found, in many instances, to be conjoined with each other. I leave it to your own reflection to pursue the consequences of this principle. I shall just observe, that, as the antagonists of Epicurus always suppose the universe, an effect quite singular and unparalleled, to be the proof of a Deity, a cause no less singular and unparalleled; your reasonings, upon that supposition, seem, at least, to merit our attention. There is, I own, some difficulty, how we can ever return from the cause to the effect, and, reasoning from our ideas of the former, infer any alteration on the latter, or any addition to it.

SECTION XII: OF THE ACADEMICAL OR SCEPTICAL PHILOSOPHY

Part I

There is not a greater number of philosophical reasonings, displayed upon any subject, than those, which prove the existence of a Deity, and refute the fallacies of Atheists; and yet the most religious philosophers still dispute whether any man can be so blinded as to be a speculative atheist. How shall we reconcile these contradictions? The knights-errant, who wandered about to clear the world of dragons and giants, never entertained the least doubt with regard to the existence of these monsters.

The Sceptic is another enemy of religion, who naturally provokes the indignation of all divines and graver philosophers; though it is certain, that no man ever met with any such absurd creature, or conversed with a man, who had no opinion or principle concerning any subject, either of action or speculation. This begets a very natural question; What is meant by a sceptic? And how far it is possible to push these philosophical principles of doubt and uncertainty?

There is a species of scepticism, antecedent to all study and philosophy, which is much inculcated by Descartes and others, as a sovereign preservative against error and precipitate judgment. It recommends an universal doubt, not only of all our former opinions and principles, but also of our very faculties; of whose veracity, say they, we must assure ourselves, by a chain of reasoning, deduced from some original principle, which cannot possibly be fallacious or deceitful. But neither is there any such original principle, which has a prerogative above others, that are self-evident and convincing: Or if there were, could we advance a step beyond it, but by the use of those very faculties, of which we are supposed to be already diffident. The Cartesian doubt, therefore, were it ever possible to be attained by any human creature (as it plainly is not) would be entirely incurable; and no reasoning could ever bring us to a state of assurance and conviction upon any subject.

It must, however, be confessed, that this species of scepticism, when more moderate, may be understood in a very reasonable sense, and is a necessary preparative to the study of philosophy, by preserving a proper impartiality in our judgments, and weaning our mind from all those prejudices, which we may have imbibed from education or rash opinion. To begin with clear and self-evident principles, to advance by timorous and sure steps, to review frequently our conclusions, and examine accurately all their consequences; though by these means we shall make both a slow and a short progress in our systems; are the only methods, by which we can ever hope to reach truth, and attain a proper stability and certainty in our determinations.

There is another species of scepticism, consequent to science and enquiry, when men are supposed to have discovered, either the absolute fallaciousness of their mental faculties, or their unfitness to reach any fixed determination in all those curious subjects of speculation, about which they are commonly employed. Even our very senses are brought into dispute, by a certain species of philosophers; and the maxims of common life are subjected to the same doubt as the most profound principles or conclusions of metaphysics and theology. As these paradoxical tenets (if they may be called tenets) are to be met with in some philosophers, and the refutation of them in several, they naturally excite our curiosity, and make us enquire into the arguments, on which they may be founded.

I need not insist upon the more trite topics, employed by the sceptics in all ages, against the evidence of sense; such as those which are derived from the imperfection and fallaciousness of our organs, on numberless occasions; the crooked appearance of an oar in water; the various aspects of objects, according to their different distances; the double images which arise from the pressing one eye; with many other appearances of a like nature. These sceptical topics, indeed, are only sufficient to prove, that the senses alone are not implicitly to be depended on; but that we must correct their evidence by reason, and by considerations, derived from the nature of the medium, the distance of the object, and the disposition of the organ, in order to render them, within their sphere, the proper criteria of truth and falsehood. There are other more profound arguments against the senses, which admit not of so easy a solution.

It seems evident, that men are carried, by a natural instinct or prepossession, to repose faith in their senses; and that, without any reasoning, or even almost before the use of reason, we always suppose an external universe, which depends not on our perception, but would exist, though we and every sensible creature were absent or annihilated. Even the animal creation are governed by a like opinion, and preserve this belief of external objects, in all their thoughts, designs, and actions.

It seems also evident, that, when men follow this blind and powerful instinct of nature, they always suppose the very images, presented by the senses, to be the external objects, and never entertain any suspicion, that the one are nothing but representations of the other. This very table, which we see white, and which we feel hard, is believed to exist, independent of our perception, and to be something external to our mind, which perceives it. Our presence bestows not being on it: Our absence does not annihilate it. It preserves its existence uniform and entire, independent of the situation of intelligent beings, who perceive or contemplate it.

But this universal and primary opinion of all men is soon destroyed by the slightest philosophy, which teaches us, that nothing can ever be present to the mind but an image or perception, and that the senses are only the inlets, through which these images are conveyed, without being able to produce any immediate intercourse between the mind and the object. The table, which we see, seems to diminish, as we remove farther from it: But the real table, which exists independent of us, suffers no alteration: It was, therefore, nothing but its image, which was present to the mind. These are the obvious dictates of reason; and no man, who reflects, ever doubted, that the existences, which we consider, when we say, this house and that tree, are nothing but perceptions in the mind, and fleeting copies or representations of other existences, which remain uniform and independent.

So far, then, are we necessitated by reasoning to contradict or depart from the primary instincts of nature, and to embrace a new system with regard to the evidence of our senses. But here philosophy finds herself extremely embarrassed, when she would justify this new system, and obviate the cavils and objections of the sceptics. She can no longer plead the infallible and irresistible instinct of nature: For that led us to a quite different system, which is acknowledged fallible and even erroneous. And to justify this pretended philosophical system, by a chain of clear and convincing argument, or even any appearance of argument, exceeds the power of all human capacity.

By what argument can it be proved, that the perceptions of the mind must be caused by external objects, entirely different from them, though resembling them (if that be possible) and could not arise either from the energy of the mind itself, or from the suggestion of some invisible and unknown spirit, or from some other cause still more unknown to us? It is acknowledged, that, in fact, many of these perceptions arise not from any thing external, as in dreams, madness, and other diseases. And nothing can be more inexplicable than the manner, in which body should so operate upon mind as ever to convey an image of itself to a substance, supposed of so different, and even contrary a nature.

It is a question of fact, whether the perceptions of the senses be produced by external objects, resembling them: how shall this question be determined? By experience surely; as all other questions of a like nature. But here experience is, and must be entirely silent. The mind has never any thing present to it but the perceptions, and cannot possibly reach any experience of their connexion with objects. The supposition of such a connexion is, therefore, without any foundation in reasoning.

To have recourse to the veracity of the supreme Being, in order to prove the veracity of our senses, is surely making a very unexpected circuit. If his veracity were at all concerned in this matter, our senses would be entirely infallible; because it is not possible that he can ever deceive. Not to mention, that, if the external world be once called in question, we shall be at a loss to find arguments, by which we may prove the existence of that Being or any of his attributes.

This is a topic, therefore, in which the profounder and more philosophical sceptics will always triumph, when they endeavor to introduce an universal doubt into all subjects of human knowledge and enquiry. Do you follow the instincts and propensities of nature, may they say, in assenting to the veracity of sense? But these lead you to believe, that the very perception or sensible image is the external object. Do you disclaim this principle, in order to embrace a more rational opinion, that the perceptions are only representations of something external? You here depart from your natural propensities and more obvious sentiments; and yet are not able to satisfy your reason, which can never find any convincing argument from experience to prove, that the perceptions are connected with any external objects.

There is another sceptical topic of a like nature, derived from the most profound philosophy; which might merit our attention, were it requisite to dive so deep, in order to discover arguments and reasonings, which can so little serve to any serious purpose. It is universally allowed by modern inquirers, that all the sensible qualities of objects, such as hard, soft, hot, cold, white, black, &c. are merely secondary, and exist not in the objects themselves, but are perceptions of the mind, without any external archetype or model, which they represent. If this be allowed, with regard to secondary qualities, it must also follow, with regard to the supposed primary qualities of extension and solidity; nor can the latter be any more entitled to that denomination than the former. The idea of extension is entirely acquired from the senses of sight and feeling; and if all the qualities, perceived by the senses, be in the mind, not in the object, the same conclusion must reach the idea of extension, which is wholly dependent on the sensible ideas or the ideas of secondary qualities. Nothing can save us from this conclusion, but the asserting, that the ideas of those primary qualities are attained by Abstraction; an opinion, which, if we examine it accurately, we shall find to be unintelligible, and even absurd. An extension, that is neither tangible nor visible, cannot possibly be conceived: And a tangible or visible extension, which is neither hard nor soft, black nor white, is equally beyond the reach of human conception. Let any man try to conceive a triangle in general, which is neither Isosceles nor Scalenum, nor has any particular length or proportion of sides; and he will soon perceive the absurdity of all the scholastic notions with regard to abstraction and general ideas.

Thus the first philosophical objection to the evidence of sense or to the opinion of external existence consists in this, that such an opinion, if rested on natural instinct, is contrary to reason, and if referred to reason, is contrary to natural instinct, and at the same time carries no rational evidence with it, to convince an impartial enquirer. The second objection goes farther, and represents this opinion as contrary to reason: at least, if it be a principle of reason, that all sensible qualities are in the mind, not in the object. Bereave matter of all its intelligible qualities, both primary and secondary, you in a manner annihilate it, and leave only a certain unknown, inexplicable something, as the cause of our perceptions; a notion so imperfect, that no sceptic will think it worth while to contend against it.

Part II

It may seem a very extravagant attempt of the sceptics to destroy reason by argument and ratiocination; yet is this the grand scope of all their enquiries and disputes. They endeavor to find objections, both to our abstract reasonings, and to those which regard matter of fact and existence.

The chief objection against all abstract reasonings is derived from the ideas of space and time; ideas, which, in common life and to a careless view, are very clear and intelligible, but when they pass through the scrutiny of the profound sciences (and they are the chief object of these sciences) afford principles, which seem full of absurdity and contradiction. No priestly dogmas, invented on purpose to tame and subdue the rebellious reason of mankind, ever shocked common sense more than the doctrine of the infinite divisibility of extension, with its consequences; as they are pompously displayed by all geometricians and metaphysicians, with a kind of triumph and exultation. A real quantity, infinitely less than any finite quantity, containing quantities infinitely less than itself, and so on in infinitum; this is an edifice so bold and prodigious, that it is too weighty for any pretended demonstration to support, because it shocks the clearest and most natural principles of human reason. But what renders the matter more extraordinary, is, that these seemingly absurd opinions are supported by a chain of reasoning, the clearest and most natural; nor is it possible for us to allow the premises without admitting the consequences. Nothing can be more convincing and satisfactory than all the conclusions concerning the properties of circles and triangles; and yet, when these are once received, how can we deny, that the angle of contact between a circle and its tangent is infinitely less than any rectilinear angle, that as you may increase the diameter of the circle in infinitum, this angle of contact becomes still less, even in infinitum, and that the angle of contact between other curves and their tangents may be infinitely less than those between any circle and its tangent, and so on, in infinitum? The demonstration of these principles seems as unexceptionable as that which proves the three angles of a triangle to be equal to two right ones, though the latter opinion be natural and easy, and the former big with contradiction and absurdity. Reason here seems to be thrown into a kind of amazement and suspense, which, without the suggestions of any sceptic, gives her a diffidence of herself, and of the ground on which she treads. She sees a full light, which illuminates certain places; but that light borders upon the most profound darkness. And between these she is so dazzled and confounded, that she scarcely can pronounce with certainty and assurance concerning any one object.

The absurdity of these bold determinations of the abstract sciences seems to become, if possible, still more palpable with regard to time than extension. An infinite number of real parts of time, passing in succession, and exhausted one after another, appears so evident a contradiction, that no man, one should think, whose judgment is not corrupted, instead of being improved, by the sciences, would ever be able to admit of it.

Yet still reason must remain restless, and unquiet, even with regard to that scepticism, to which she is driven by these seeming absurdities and contradictions. How any clear, distinct idea can contain circumstances, contradictory to itself, or to any other clear, distinct idea, is absolutely incomprehensible; and is, perhaps, as absurd as any proposition, which can be formed. So that nothing can be more sceptical, or more full of doubt and hesitation, than this scepticism itself, which arises from some of the paradoxical conclusions of geometry or the science of quantity.

The sceptical objections to moral evidence, or to the reasonings concerning matter of fact, are either popular or philosophical. The popular objections are derived from the natural weakness of human understanding; the contradictory opinions, which have been entertained in different ages and nations; the variations of our judgment in sickness and health, youth and old age, prosperity and adversity; the perpetual contradiction of each particular man's opinions and sentiments; with many other topics of that kind. It is needless to insist farther on this head. These objections are but weak. For as, in common life, we reason every moment concerning fact and existence, and cannot possibly subsist, without continually employing this species of argument, any popular objections, derived from thence, must be insufficient to destroy that evidence. The great subverter of Pyrrhonism or the excessive principles of scepticism, is action, and employment, and the occupations of common life. These principles may flourish and triumph in the schools; where it is, indeed, difficult, if not impossible, to refute them. But as soon as they leave the shade, and by the presence of the real objects, which actuate our passions and sentiments, are put in opposition to the more powerful principles of our nature, they vanish like smoke, and leave the most determined sceptic in the same condition as other mortals.

The sceptic, therefore, had better keep within his proper sphere, and display those philosophical objections, which arise from more profound researches. Here he seems to have ample matter of triumph; while he justly insists, that all our evidence for any matter of fact, which lies beyond the testimony of sense or memory, is derived entirely from the relation of cause and effect; that we have no other idea of this relation than that of two objects, which have been frequently conjoined together; that we have no argument to convince us, that objects, which have, in our experience, been frequently conjoined, will likewise, in other instances, be conjoined in the same manner; and that nothing leads us to this inference but custom or a certain instinct of our nature; which it is indeed difficult to resist, but which, like other instincts, may be fallacious and deceitful. While the sceptic insists upon these topics, he shows his force, or rather, indeed, his own and our weakness; and seems, for the time at least, to destroy all assurance and conviction. These arguments might be displayed at greater length, if any durable good or benefit to society could ever be expected to result from them.

For here is the chief and most confounding objection to excessive scepticism, that no durable good can ever result from it; while it remains in its full force and vigor. We need only ask such a sceptic, What his meaning is? And what he proposes by all these curious researches? He is immediately at a loss, and knows not what to answer. A Copernican or Ptolemaic, who supports each his different system of astronomy, may hope to produce a conviction, which will remain constant and durable, with his audience. A Stoic or Epicurean displays principles, which may not only be durable, but which have an effect on conduct and behavior. But a Pyrrhonian cannot expect, that his philosophy will have any constant influence on the mind: or if it had, that its influence would be beneficial to society. On the contrary, he must acknowledge, if he will acknowledge any thing, that all human life must perish, were his principles universally and steadily to prevail. All discourse, all action would immediately cease; and men remain in a total lethargy, till the necessities of nature, unsatisfied, put an end to their miserable existence. It is true; so fatal an event is very little to be dreaded. Nature is always too strong for principle. And though a Pyrrhonian may throw himself or others into a momentary amazement and confusion by his profound reasonings; the first and most trivial event in life will put to flight all his doubts and scruples, and leave him the same, in every point of action and speculation, with the philosophers of every other sect, or with those who never concerned themselves in any philosophical researches. When he awakes from his dream, he will be the first to join in the laugh against himself, and to confess, that all his objections are mere amusement, and can have no other tendency than to shew the whimsical condition of mankind, who must act and reason and believe; though they are not able, by their most diligent enquiry, to satisfy themselves concerning the foundation of these operations, or to remove the objections, which may be raised against them.

Part III

There is, indeed, a more mitigated scepticism or academical philosophy, which may be both durable and useful, and which may, in part, be the result of this Pyrrhonism, or excessive scepticism, when its undistinguished doubts are, in some measure, corrected by common sense and reflection. The greater part of mankind are naturally apt to be affirmative and dogmatical in their opinions; and while they see objects only on one side, and have no idea of any counterpoising argument, they throw themselves precipitately into the principles, to which they are inclined; nor have they any indulgence for those who entertain opposite sentiments. To hesitate or balance perplexes their understanding, checks their passion, and suspends their action. They are, therefore, impatient till they escape from a state, which to them is so uneasy; and they think, that they can never remove themselves far enough from it, by the violence of their affirmations and obstinacy of their belief. But could such dogmatical reasoners become sensible of the strange infirmities of human understanding, even in its most perfect state, and when most accurate and cautious in its determinations; such a reflection would naturally inspire them with more modesty and reserve, and diminish their fond opinion of themselves, and their prejudice against antagonists. The illiterate may reflect on the disposition of the learned, who, amidst all the advantages of study and reflection, are commonly still diffident in their determinations: And if any of the learned be inclined, from their natural temper, to haughtiness and obstinacy, a small tincture of Pyrrhonism might abate their pride, by showing them, that the few advantages, which they may have attained over their fellows, are but inconsiderable, if compared with the universal perplexity and confusion, which is inherent in human nature. In general, there is a degree of doubt, and caution, and modesty, which, in all kinds of scrutiny and decision, ought for ever to accompany a just reasoner.

Another species of mitigated scepticism, which may be of advantage to mankind, and which may be the natural result of the Pyrrhonian doubts and scruples, is the limitation of our enquiries to such subjects as are best adapted to the narrow capacity of human understanding. The imagination of man is naturally sublime, delighted with whatever is remote and extraordinary, and running, without control, into the most distant parts of space and time in order to avoid the objects, which custom has rendered too familiar to it. A correct Judgment observes a contrary method, and avoiding all distant and high enquiries, confines itself to common life, and to such subjects as fall under daily practice and experience; leaving the more sublime topics to the embellishment of poets and orators, or to the arts of priests and politicians. To bring us to so salutary a determination, nothing can be more serviceable, than to be once thoroughly convinced of the force of the Pyrrhonian doubt, and of the impossibility, that any thing, but the strong power of natural instinct, could free us from it. Those who have a propensity to philosophy, will still continue their researches; because they reflect, that, besides the immediate pleasure, attending such an occupation, philosophical decisions are nothing but the reflections of common life, methodized and corrected. But they will never be tempted to go beyond common life, so long as they consider the imperfection of those faculties which they employ, their narrow reach, and their inaccurate operations. While we cannot give a satisfactory reason, why we believe, after a thousand experiments, that a stone will fall, or fire burn; can we ever satisfy ourselves concerning any determination, which we may form, with regard to the origin of worlds, and the situation of nature, from, and to eternity?

This narrow limitation, indeed, of our enquiries, is, in every respect, so reasonable, that it suffices to make the slightest examination into the natural powers of the human mind and to compare them with their objects, in order to recommend it to us. We shall then find what are the proper subjects of science and enquiry.

It seems to me, that the only objects of the abstract sciences or of demonstration are quantity and number, and that all attempts to extend this more perfect species of knowledge beyond these bounds are mere sophistry and illusion. As the component parts of quantity and number are entirely similar, their relations become intricate and involved; and nothing can be more curious, as well as useful, than to trace, by a variety of mediums, their equality or inequality, through their different appearances. But as all other ideas are clearly distinct and different from each other, we can never advance farther, by our utmost scrutiny, than to observe this diversity, and, by an obvious reflection, pronounce one thing not to be another. Or if there be any difficulty in these decisions, it proceeds entirely from the undeterminate meaning of words, which is corrected by juster definitions. That the square of the hypothenuse is equal to the squares of the other two sides, cannot be known, let the terms be ever so exactly defined, without a train of reasoning and enquiry. But to convince us of this proposition, that where there is no property, there can be no injustice, it is only necessary to define the terms, and explain injustice to be a violation of property. This proposition is, indeed, nothing but a more imperfect definition. It is the same case with all those pretended syllogistical reasonings, which may be found in every other branch of learning, except the sciences of quantity and number; and these may safely, I think, be pronounced the only proper objects of knowledge and demonstration.

All other enquiries of men regard only matter of fact and existence; and these are evidently incapable of demonstration. Whatever is may not be. No negation of a fact can involve a contradiction. The nonexistence of any being, without exception, is as clear and distinct an idea as its existence. The proposition, which affirms it not to be, however false, is no less conceivable and intelligible, than that which affirms it to be. The case is different with the sciences, properly so called. Every proposition, which is not true, is there confused and unintelligible. That the cube root of 64 is equal to the half of 10, is a false proposition, and can never be distinctly conceived. But that Caesar, or the angel Gabriel, or any being never existed, may be a false proposition, but still is perfectly conceivable, and implies no contradiction.

The existence, therefore, of any being can only be proved by arguments from its cause or its effect; and these arguments are founded entirely on experience. If we reason a priori, any thing may appear able to produce any thing. The falling of a pebble may, for aught we know, extinguish the sun; or the wish of a man control the planets in their orbits. It is only experience, which teaches us the nature and bounds of cause and effect, and enables us to infer the existence of one object from that of another. Such is the foundation of moral reasoning, which forms the greater part of human knowledge, and is the source of all human action and behavior.

Moral reasonings are either concerning particular or general facts. All deliberations in life regard the former; as also all disquisitions in history, chronology, geography, and astronomy.

The sciences, which treat of general facts, are politics, natural philosophy, physic, chemistry, &c. where the qualities, causes and effects of a whole species of objects are enquired into.

Divinity or Theology, as it proves the existence of a Deity, and the immortality of souls, is composed partly of reasonings concerning particular, partly concerning general facts. It has a foundation in reason, so far as it is supported by experience. But its best and most solid foundation is faith and divine revelation.

Morals and criticism are not so properly objects of the understanding as of taste and sentiment. Beauty, whether moral or natural, is felt, more properly than perceived. Or if we reason concerning it, and endeavor to fix its standard, we regard a new fact, to wit, the general taste of mankind, or some such fact, which may be the object of reasoning and enquiry.

When we run over libraries, persuaded of these principles, what havoc must we make? If we take in our hand any volume; of divinity or school metaphysics, for instance; let us ask, Does it contain any abstract reasoning concerning quantity or number? No. Does it contain any experimental reasoning concerning matter of fact and existence? No. Commit it then to the flames: For it can contain nothing but sophistry and illusion.

Dialogues Concerning Natural Religion

PAMPHILUS TO HERMIPPUS

It has been remarked, my Hermippus, that though the ancient philosophers conveyed most of their instruction in the form of dialogue, this method of composition has been little practiced in later ages, and has seldom succeeded in the hands of those who have attempted it. Accurate and regular argument, indeed, such as is now expected of philosophical enquirers, naturally throws a man into the methodical and didactic manner; where he can immediately, without preparation, explain the point at which he aims; and thence proceed, without interruption, to deduce the proofs on which it is established. To deliver a SYSTEM in conversation, scarcely appears natural; and while the dialogue-writer desires, by departing from the direct style of composition, to give a freer air to his performance, and avoid the appearance of Author and Reader, he is apt to run into a worse inconvenience, and convey the image of Pedagogue and Pupil. Or, if he carries on the dispute in the natural spirit of good company, by throwing in a variety of topics, and preserving a proper balance among the speakers, he often loses so much time in preparations and transitions, that the reader will scarcely think himself compensated, by all the graces of dialogue, for the order, brevity, and precision, which are sacrificed to them.

There are some subjects, however, to which dialogue-writing is peculiarly adapted, and where it is still preferable to the direct and simple method of composition.

Any point of doctrine, which is so obvious that it scarcely admits of dispute, but at the same time so important that it cannot be too often inculcated, seems to require some such method of handling it; where the novelty of the manner may compensate the triteness of the subject; where the vivacity of conversation may enforce the precept; and where the variety of lights, presented by various personages and characters, may appear neither tedious nor redundant.

Any question of philosophy, on the other hand, which is so obscure and uncertain, that human reason can reach no fixed determination with regard to it; if it should be treated at all, seems to lead us naturally into the style of dialogue and conversation. Reasonable men may be allowed to differ, where no one can reasonably be positive. Opposite sentiments, even without any decision, afford an agreeable amusement; and if the subject be curious and interesting, the book carries us, in a manner, into company; and unites the two greatest and purest pleasures of human life, study and society.

Happily, these circumstances are all to be found in the subject of NATURAL RELIGION. What truth so obvious, so certain, as the being of a God, which the most ignorant ages have acknowledged, for which the most refined geniuses have ambitiously striven to produce new proofs and arguments? What truth so important as this, which is the ground of all our hopes, the surest foundation of morality, the firmest support of society, and the only principle which ought never to be a moment absent from our thoughts and meditations? But, in treating of this obvious and important truth, what obscure questions occur concerning the nature of that Divine Being, his attributes, his decrees, his plan of providence? These have been always subjected to the disputations of men; concerning these human reason has not reached any certain determination. But these are topics so interesting, that we cannot restrain our restless enquiry with regard to them; though nothing but doubt, uncertainty, and contradiction, have as yet been the result of our most accurate researches.

This I had lately occasion to observe, while I passed, as usual, part of the summer season with Cleanthes, and was present at those conversations of his with Philo and Demea, of which I gave you lately some imperfect account. Your curiosity, you then told me, was so excited, that I must, of necessity, enter into a more exact detail of their reasonings, and display those various systems which they advanced with regard to so delicate a subject as that of natural religion. The remarkable contrast in their characters still further raised your expectations; while you opposed the accurate philosophical turn of Cleanthes to the careless scepticism of Philo, or compared either of their dispositions with the rigid inflexible orthodoxy of Demea. My youth rendered me a mere auditor of their disputes; and that curiosity, natural to the early season of life, has so deeply imprinted in my memory the whole chain and connexion of their arguments, that, I hope, I shall not omit or confound any considerable part of them in the recital.

Part I

After I joined the company, whom I found sitting in Cleanthes's library, Demea paid Cleanthes some compliments on the great care which he took of my education, and on his unwearied perseverance and constancy in all his friendships. The father of Pamphilus, said he, was your intimate friend: The son is your pupil; and may indeed be regarded as your adopted son, were we to judge by the pains which you bestow in conveying to him every useful branch of literature and science. You are no more wanting, I am persuaded, in prudence, than in industry. I shall, therefore, communicate to you a maxim, which I have observed with regard to my own children, that I may learn how far it agrees with your practice. The method I follow in their education is founded on the saying of an ancient, "That students of philosophy ought first to learn logics, then ethics, next physics, last of all the nature of the gods." This science of natural theology, according to him, being the most profound and abstruse of any, required the maturest judgment in its students; and none but a mind enriched with all the other sciences, can safely be intrusted with it.

Are you so late, says Philo, in teaching your children the principles of religion? Is there no danger of their neglecting, or rejecting altogether those opinions of which they have heard so little during the whole course of their education? It is only as a science, replied Demea, subjected to human reasoning and disputation, that I postpone the study of Natural Theology. To season their minds with early piety, is my chief care; and by continual precept and instruction, and I hope too by example, I imprint deeply on their tender minds an habitual reverence for all the principles of religion. While they pass through every other science, I still remark the uncertainty of each part; the eternal disputations of men; the obscurity of all philosophy; and the strange, ridiculous conclusions, which some of the greatest geniuses have derived from the principles of mere human reason. Having thus tamed their mind to a proper submission and self-diffidence, I have no longer any scruple of opening to them the greatest mysteries of religion; nor apprehend any danger from that assuming arrogance of philosophy, which may lead them to reject the most established doctrines and opinions.

Your precaution, says Philo, of seasoning your children's minds early with piety, is certainly very reasonable; and no more than is requisite in this profane and irreligious age. But what I chiefly admire in your plan of education, is your method of drawing advantage from the very principles of philosophy and learning, which, by inspiring pride and self-sufficiency, have commonly, in all ages, been found so destructive to the principles of religion. The vulgar, indeed, we may remark, who are unacquainted with science and profound enquiry, observing the endless disputes of the learned, have commonly a thorough contempt for philosophy; and rivet themselves the faster, by that means, in the great points of theology which have been taught them. Those who enter a little into study and enquiry, finding many appearances of evidence in doctrines the newest and most extraordinary, think nothing too difficult for human reason; and, presumptuously breaking through all fences, profane the inmost sanctuaries of the temple. But Cleanthes will, I hope, agree with me, that, after we have abandoned ignorance, the surest remedy, there is still one expedient left to prevent this profane liberty. Let Demea's principles be improved and cultivated: let us become thoroughly sensible of the weakness, blindness, and narrow limits of human reason: let us duly consider its uncertainty and endless contrarieties, even in subjects of common life and practice: let the errors and deceits of our very senses be set before us; the insuperable difficulties which attend first principles in all systems; the contradictions which adhere to the very ideas of matter, cause and effect, extension, space, time, motion; and in a word, quantity of all kinds, the object of the only science that can fairly pretend to any certainty or evidence. When these topics are displayed in their full light, as they are by some philosophers and almost all divines; who can retain such confidence in this frail faculty of reason as to pay any regard to its determinations in points so sublime, so abstruse, so remote from common life and experience? When the coherence of the parts of a stone, or even that composition of parts which renders it extended; when these familiar objects, I say, are so inexplicable, and contain circumstances so repugnant and contradictory; with what assurance can we decide concerning the origin of worlds, or trace their history from eternity to eternity?

While Philo pronounced these words, I could observe a smile in the countenance both of Demea and Cleanthes. That of Demea seemed to imply an unreserved satisfaction in the doctrines delivered: but, in Cleanthes's features, I could distinguish an air of finesse; as if he perceived some raillery or artificial malice in the reasonings of Philo.

You propose then, Philo, said Cleanthes, to erect religious faith on philosophical scepticism; and you think, that if certainty or evidence be expelled from every other subject of enquiry, it will all retire to these theological doctrines, and there acquire a superior force and authority. Whether your scepticism be as absolute and sincere as you pretend, we shall learn by and by, when the company breaks up: we shall then see, whether you go out at the door or the window; and whether you really doubt if your body has gravity, or can be injured by its fall; according to popular opinion, derived from our fallacious senses, and more fallacious experience. And this consideration, Demea, may, I think, fairly serve to abate our ill-will to this humourous sect of the sceptics. If they be thoroughly in earnest, they will not long trouble the world with their doubts, cavils, and disputes: if they be only in jest, they are, perhaps, bad railers; but can never be very dangerous, either to the state, to philosophy, or to religion.

In reality, Philo, continued he, it seems certain, that though a man, in a flush of humour, after intense reflection on the many contradictions and imperfections of human reason, may entirely renounce all belief and opinion, it is impossible for him to persevere in this total scepticism, or make it appear in his conduct for a few hours. External objects press in upon him; passions solicit him; his philosophical melancholy dissipates; and even the utmost violence upon his own temper will not be able, during any time, to preserve the poor appearance of scepticism. And for what reason impose on himself such a violence? This is a point in which it will be impossible for him ever to satisfy himself, consistently with his sceptical principles. So that, upon the whole, nothing could be more ridiculous than the principles of the ancient Pyrrhonians; if in reality they endeavoured, as is pretended, to extend, throughout, the same scepticism which they had learned from the declamations of their schools, and which they ought to have confined to them.

In this view, there appears a great resemblance between the sects of the Stoics and Pyrrhonians, though perpetual antagonists; and both of them seem founded on this erroneous maxim, That what a man can perform sometimes, and in some dispositions, he can perform always, and in every disposition. When the mind, by Stoical reflections, is elevated into a sublime enthusiasm of virtue, and strongly smit with any species of honour or public good, the utmost bodily pain and sufferings will not prevail over such a high sense of duty; and it is possible, perhaps, by its means, even to smile and exult in the midst of tortures. If this sometimes may be the case in fact and reality, much more may a philosopher, in his school, or even in his closet, work himself up to such an enthusiasm, and support in imagination the acutest pain or most calamitous event which he can possibly conceive. But how shall he support this enthusiasm itself? The bent of his mind relaxes, and cannot be recalled at pleasure; avocations lead him astray; misfortunes attack him unawares; and the philosopher sinks by degrees into the plebeian.

I allow of your comparison between the Stoics and Sceptics, replied Philo. But you may observe, at the same time, that though the mind cannot, in Stoicism, support the highest flights of philosophy, yet, even when it sinks lower, it still retains somewhat of its former disposition; and the effects of the Stoic's reasoning will appear in his conduct in common life, and through the whole tenor of his actions. The ancient schools, particularly that of Zeno, produced examples of virtue and constancy which seem astonishing to present times.

> Vain Wisdom all and false Philosophy.
> Yet with a pleasing sorcery could charm
> Pain, for a while, or anguish; and excite
> Fallacious Hope, or arm the obdurate breast
> With stubborn Patience, as with triple steel.

In like manner, if a man has accustomed himself to sceptical considerations on the uncertainty and narrow limits of reason, he will not entirely forget them when he turns his reflection on other subjects; but in all his philosophical principles and reasoning, I dare not say in his common conduct, he will be found different from those, who either never formed any opinions in the case, or have entertained sentiments more favourable to human reason.

To whatever length any one may push his speculative principles of scepticism, he must act, I own, and live, and converse, like other men; and for this conduct he is not obliged to give any other reason, than the absolute necessity he lies under of so doing. If he ever carries his speculations further than this necessity constrains him, and philosophizes either on natural or moral subjects, he is allured by a certain pleasure and satisfaction which he finds in employing himself after that manner. He considers besides, that every one, even in common life, is constrained to have more or less of this philosophy; that from our earliest infancy we make continual advances in forming more general principles of conduct and reasoning; that the larger experience we acquire, and the stronger reason we are endued with, we always render our principles the more general and comprehensive; and that what we call philosophy is nothing but a more regular and methodical operation of the same kind. To philosophize on such subjects, is nothing essentially different from reasoning on common life; and we may only expect greater stability, if not greater truth, from our philosophy, on account of its exacter and more scrupulous method of proceeding.

But when we look beyond human affairs and the properties of the surrounding bodies: when we carry our speculations into the two eternities, before and after the present state of things; into the creation and formation of the universe; the existence and properties of spirits; the powers and operations of one universal Spirit existing without beginning and without end; omnipotent, omniscient, immutable, infinite, and incomprehensible: we must be far removed from the smallest tendency to scepticism not to be apprehensive, that we have here got quite beyond the reach of our faculties. So long as we confine our speculations to trade, or morals, or politics, or criticism, we make appeals, every moment, to common sense and experience, which strengthen our philosophical conclusions, and remove, at least in part, the suspicion which we so justly entertain with regard to every reasoning that is very subtile and refined. But, in theological reasonings, we have not this advantage; while, at the same time, we are employed upon objects, which, we must be sensible, are too large for our grasp, and of all others, require most to be familiarized to our apprehension. We are like foreigners in a strange country, to whom every thing must seem suspicious, and who are in danger every moment of transgressing against the laws and customs of the people with whom they live and converse. We know not how far we ought to trust our vulgar methods of reasoning in such a subject; since, even in common life, and in that province which is peculiarly appropriated to them, we cannot account for them, and are entirely guided by a kind of instinct or necessity in employing them.

All sceptics pretend, that, if reason be considered in an abstract view, it furnishes invincible arguments against itself; and that we could never retain any conviction or assurance, on any subject, were not the sceptical reasonings so refined and subtile, that they are not able to counterpoise the more solid and more natural arguments derived from the senses and experience. But it is evident, whenever our arguments lose this advantage, and run wide of common life, that the most refined scepticism comes to be upon a footing with them, and is able to oppose and counterbalance them. The one has no more weight than the other. The mind must remain in suspense between them; and it is that very suspense or balance, which is the triumph of scepticism.

But I observe, says Cleanthes, with regard to you, Philo, and all speculative sceptics, that your doctrine and practice are as much at variance in the most abstruse points of theory as in the conduct of common life. Wherever evidence discovers itself, you adhere to it, notwithstanding your pretended scepticism; and I can observe, too, some of your sect to be as decisive as those who make greater professions of certainty and assurance. In reality, would not a man be ridiculous, who pretended to reject Newton's explication of the wonderful phenomenon of the rainbow, because that explication gives a minute anatomy of the rays of light; a subject, forsooth, too refined for human comprehension? And what would you say to one, who, having nothing particular to object to the arguments of Copernicus and Galileo for the motion of the earth, should withhold his assent, on that general principle, that these subjects were too magnificent and remote to be explained by the narrow and fallacious reason of mankind?

There is indeed a kind of brutish and ignorant scepticism, as you well observed, which gives the vulgar a general prejudice against what they do not easily understand, and makes them reject every principle which requires elaborate reasoning to prove and establish it. This species of scepticism is fatal to knowledge, not to religion; since we find, that those who make greatest profession of it, give often their assent, not only to the great truths of Theism and natural theology, but even to the most absurd tenets which a traditional superstition has recommended to them. They firmly believe in witches, though they will not believe nor attend to the most simple proposition of Euclid. But the refined and philosophical sceptics fall into an inconsistence of an opposite nature. They push their researches into the most abstruse corners of science; and their assent attends them in every step, proportioned to the evidence which they meet with. They are even obliged to acknowledge, that the most abstruse and remote objects are those which are best explained by philosophy. Light is in reality anatomized. The true system of the heavenly bodies is discovered and ascertained. But the nourishment of bodies by food is still an inexplicable mystery. The cohesion of the parts of matter is still incomprehensible. These sceptics, therefore, are obliged, in every question, to consider each particular evidence apart, and proportion their assent to the precise degree of evidence which occurs. This is their practice in all natural, mathematical, moral, and political science. And why not the same, I ask, in the theological and religious? Why must conclusions of this nature be alone rejected on the general presumption of the insufficiency of human reason, without any particular discussion of the evidence? Is not such an unequal conduct a plain proof of prejudice and passion?

Our senses, you say, are fallacious; our understanding erroneous; our ideas, even of the most familiar objects, extension, duration, motion, full of absurdities and contradictions. You defy me to solve the difficulties, or reconcile the repugnancies which you discover in them. I have not capacity for so great an undertaking: I have not leisure for it: I perceive it to be superfluous. Your own conduct, in every circumstance, refutes your principles, and shews the firmest reliance on all the received maxims of science, morals, prudence, and behaviour.

I shall never assent to so harsh an opinion as that of a celebrated writer, who says, that the Sceptics are not a sect of philosophers: they are only a sect of liars. I may, however, affirm (I hope without offence), that they are a sect of jesters or railers. But for my part, whenever I find myself disposed to mirth and amusement, I shall certainly choose my entertainment of a less perplexing and abstruse nature. A comedy, a novel, or at most a history, seems a more natural recreation than such metaphysical subtilties and abstractions.

In vain would the sceptic make a distinction between science and common life, or between one science and another. The arguments employed in all, if just, are of a similar nature, and contain the same force and evidence. Or if there be any difference among them, the advantage lies entirely on the side of theology and natural religion. Many principles of mechanics are founded on very abstruse reasoning; yet no man who has any pretensions to science, even no speculative sceptic, pretends to entertain the least doubt with regard to them. The Copernican system contains the most surprising paradox, and the most contrary to our natural conceptions, to appearances, and to our very senses: yet even monks and inquisitors are now constrained to withdraw their opposition to it. And shall Philo, a man of so liberal a genius and extensive knowledge, entertain any general undistinguished scruples with regard to the religious hypothesis, which is founded on the simplest and most obvious arguments, and, unless it meets with artificial obstacles, has such easy access and admission into the mind of man?

And here we may observe, continued he, turning himself towards Demea, a pretty curious circumstance in the history of the sciences. After the union of philosophy with the popular religion, upon the first establishment of Christianity, nothing was more usual, among all religious teachers, than declamations against reason, against the senses, against every principle derived merely from human research and enquiry. All the topics of the ancient Academics were adopted by the fathers; and thence propagated for several ages in every school and pulpit throughout Christendom. The Reformers embraced the same principles of reasoning, or rather declamation; and all panegyrics on the excellency of faith, were sure to be interlarded with some severe strokes of satire against natural reason. A celebrated prelate too, of the Romish communion, a man of the most extensive learning, who wrote a demonstration of Christianity, has also composed a treatise, which contains all the cavils of the boldest and most determined Pyrrhonism. Locke seems to have been the first Christian who ventured openly to assert, that faith was nothing but a species of reason; that religion was only a branch of philosophy; and that a chain of arguments, similar to that which established any truth in morals, politics, or physics, was always employed in discovering all the principles of theology, natural and revealed. The ill use which Bayle and other libertines made of the philosophical scepticism of the fathers and first reformers, still further propagated the judicious sentiment of Mr. Locke: and it is now in a manner avowed, by all pretenders to reasoning and philosophy, that Atheist and Sceptic are almost synonymous. And as it is certain that no man is in earnest when he professes the latter principle, I would fain hope that there are as few who seriously maintain the former.

Don't you remember, said Philo, the excellent saying of Lord Bacon on this head? That a little philosophy, replied Cleanthes, makes a man an Atheist: a great deal converts him to religion. That is a very judicious remark too, said Philo. But what I have in my eye is another passage, where, having mentioned David's fool, who said in his heart there is no God, this great philosopher observes, that the Atheists nowadays have a double share of folly; for they are not contented to say in their hearts there is no God, but they also utter that impiety with their lips, and are thereby guilty of multiplied indiscretion and imprudence. Such people, though they were ever so much in earnest, cannot, methinks, be very formidable.

But though you should rank me in this class of fools, I cannot forbear communicating a remark that occurs to me, from the history of the religious and irreligious scepticism with which you have entertained us. It appears to me, that there are strong symptoms of priestcraft in the whole progress of this affair. During ignorant ages, such as those which followed the dissolution of the ancient schools, the priests perceived, that Atheism, Deism, or heresy of any kind, could only proceed from the presumptuous questioning of received opinions, and from a belief that human reason was equal to every thing. Education had then a mighty influence over the minds of men, and was almost equal in force to those suggestions of the senses and common understanding, by which the most determined sceptic must allow himself to be governed. But at present, when the influence of education is much diminished, and men, from a more open commerce of the world, have learned to compare the popular principles of different nations and ages, our sagacious divines have changed their whole system of philosophy, and talk the language of Stoics, Platonists, and Peripatetics, not that of Pyrrhonians and Academics. If we distrust human reason, we have now no other principle to lead us into religion. Thus, sceptics in one age, dogmatists in another; whichever system best suits the purpose of these reverend gentlemen, in giving them an ascendant over mankind, they are sure to make it their favourite principle, and established tenet.

It is very natural, said Cleanthes, for men to embrace those principles, by which they find they can best defend their doctrines; nor need we have any recourse to priestcraft to account for so reasonable an expedient. And, surely nothing can afford a stronger presumption, that any set of principles are true, and ought to be embraced, than to observe that they tend to the confirmation of true religion, and serve to confound the cavils of Atheists, Libertines, and Freethinkers of all denominations.

Part II

I must own, Cleanthes, said Demea, that nothing can more surprise me, than the light in which you have all along put this argument. By the whole tenor of your discourse, one would imagine that you were maintaining the Being of a God, against the cavils of Atheists and Infidels; and were necessitated to become a champion for that fundamental principle of all religion. But this, I hope, is not by any means a question among us. No man, no man at least of common sense, I am persuaded, ever entertained a serious doubt with regard to a truth so certain and self-evident. The question is not concerning the BEING, but the NATURE of GOD. This, I affirm, from the infirmities of human understanding, to be altogether incomprehensible and unknown to us. The essence of that supreme Mind, his attributes, the manner of his existence, the very nature of his duration; these, and every particular which regards so divine a Being, are mysterious to men. Finite, weak, and blind creatures, we ought to humble ourselves in his august presence; and, conscious of our frailties, adore in silence his infinite perfections, which eye hath not seen, ear hath not heard, neither hath it entered into the heart of man to conceive. They are covered in a deep cloud from human curiosity. It is profaneness to attempt penetrating through these sacred obscurities. And, next to the impiety of denying his existence, is the temerity of prying into his nature and essence, decrees and attributes.

But lest you should think that my piety has here got the better of my philosophy, I shall support my opinion, if it needs any support, by a very great authority. I might cite all the divines, almost, from the foundation of Christianity, who have ever treated of this or any other theological subject: but I shall confine myself, at present, to one equally celebrated for piety and philosophy. It is Father Malebranche, who, I remember, thus expresses himself. "One ought not so much," says he, "to call God a spirit, in order to express positively what he is, as in order to signify that he is not matter. He is a Being infinitely perfect: of this we cannot doubt. But in the same manner as we ought not to imagine, even supposing him corporeal, that he is clothed with a human body, as the Anthropomorphites asserted, under colour that that figure was the most perfect of any; so, neither ought we to imagine that the spirit of God has human ideas, or bears any resemblance to our spirit, under colour that we know nothing more perfect than a human mind. We ought rather to believe, that as he comprehends the perfections of matter without being material . . . he comprehends also the perfections of created spirits without being spirit, in the manner we conceive spirit: that his true name is, He that is; or, in other words, Being without restriction, All Being, the Being infinite and universal."

After so great an authority, Demea, replied Philo, as that which you have produced, and a thousand more which you might produce, it would appear ridiculous in me to add my sentiment, or express my approbation of your doctrine. But surely, where reasonable men treat these subjects, the question can never be concerning the Being, but only the Nature, of the Deity. The former truth, as you well observe, is unquestionable and self-evident. Nothing exists without a cause; and the original cause of this universe (whatever it be) we call God; and piously ascribe to him every species of perfection. Whoever scruples this fundamental truth, deserves every punishment which can be inflicted among philosophers, to wit, the greatest ridicule, contempt, and disapprobation. But as all perfection is entirely relative, we ought never to imagine that we comprehend the attributes of this divine Being, or to suppose that his perfections have any analogy or likeness to the perfections of a human creature. Wisdom, Thought, Design, Knowledge; these we justly ascribe to him; because these words are honorable among men, and we have no other language or other conceptions by which we can express our adoration of him. But let us beware, lest we think that our ideas anywise correspond to his perfections, or that his attributes have any resemblance to these qualities among men. He is infinitely superior to our limited view and comprehension; and is more the object of worship in the temple, than of disputation in the schools.

In reality, Cleanthes, continued he, there is no need of having recourse to that affected scepticism so displeasing to you, in order to come at this determination. Our ideas reach no further than our experience. We have no experience of divine attributes and operations. I need not conclude my syllogism. You can draw the inference yourself. And it is a pleasure to me (and I hope to you too) that just reasoning and sound piety here concur in the same conclusion, and both of them establish the adorably mysterious and incomprehensible nature of the Supreme Being.

Not to lose any time in circumlocutions, said Cleanthes, addressing himself to Demea, much less in replying to the pious declamations of Philo; I shall briefly explain how I conceive this matter. Look round the world: contemplate the whole and every part of it: you will find it to be nothing but one great machine, subdivided into an infinite number of lesser machines, which again admit of subdivisions to a degree beyond what human senses and faculties can trace and explain. All these various machines, and even their most minute parts, are adjusted to each other with an accuracy which ravishes into admiration all men who have ever contemplated them. The curious adapting of means to ends, throughout all nature, resembles exactly, though it much exceeds, the productions of human contrivance; of human designs, thought, wisdom, and intelligence. Since, therefore, the effects resemble each other, we are led to infer, by all the rules of analogy, that the causes also resemble; and that the Author of Nature is somewhat similar to the mind of man, though possessed of much larger faculties, proportioned to the grandeur of the work which he has executed. By this argument a posteriori, and by this argument alone, do we prove at once the existence of a Deity, and his similarity to human mind and intelligence.

I shall be so free, Cleanthes, said Demea, as to tell you, that from the beginning, I could not approve of your conclusion concerning the similarity of the Deity to men; still less can I approve of the mediums by which you endeavor to establish it. What! No demonstration of the Being of God! No abstract arguments! No proofs a priori! Are these, which have hitherto been so much insisted on by philosophers, all fallacy, all sophism? Can we reach no further in this subject than experience and probability? I will not say that this is betraying the cause of a Deity: but surely, by this affected candor, you give advantages to Atheists, which they never could obtain by the mere dint of argument and reasoning.

What I chiefly scruple in this subject, said Philo, is not so much that all religious arguments are by Cleanthes reduced to experience, as that they appear not to be even the most certain and irrefragable of that inferior kind. That a stone will fall, that fire will burn, that the earth has solidity, we have observed a thousand and a thousand times; and when any new instance of this nature is presented, we draw without hesitation the accustomed inference. The exact similarity of the cases gives us a perfect assurance of a similar event; and a stronger evidence is never desired nor sought after. But wherever you depart, in the least, from the similarity of the cases, you diminish proportionately the evidence; and may at last bring it to a very weak analogy, which is confessedly liable to error and uncertainty. After having experienced the circulation of the blood in human creatures, we make no doubt that it takes place in Titius and Maevius. But from its circulation in frogs and fishes, it is only a presumption, though a strong one, from analogy, that it takes place in men and other animals. The analogical reasoning is much weaker, when we infer the circulation of the sap in vegetables from our experience that the blood circulates in animals; and those, who hastily followed that imperfect analogy, are found, by more accurate experiments, to have been mistaken.

If we see a house, Cleanthes, we conclude, with the greatest certainty, that it had an architect or builder; because this is precisely that species of effect which we have experienced to proceed from that species of cause. But surely you will not affirm, that the universe bears such a resemblance to a house that we can with the same certainty infer a similar cause, or that the analogy is here entire and perfect. The dissimilitude is so striking, that the utmost you can here pretend to is a guess, a conjecture, a presumption concerning a similar cause; and how that pretension will be received in the world, I leave you to consider.

It would surely be very ill received, replied Cleanthes; and I should be deservedly blamed and detested, did I allow, that the proofs of a Deity amounted to no more than a guess or conjecture. But is the whole adjustment of means to ends in a house and in the universe so slight a resemblance? The economy of final causes? The order, proportion, and arrangement of every part? Steps of a stair are plainly contrived, that human legs may use them in mounting; and this inference is certain and infallible. Human legs are also contrived for walking and mounting; and this inference, I allow, is not altogether so certain, because of the dissimilarity which you remark; but does it, therefore, deserve the name only of presumption or conjecture?

Good God! cried Demea, interrupting him, where are we? Zealous defenders of religion allow, that the proofs of a Deity fall short of perfect evidence! And you, Philo, on whose assistance I depended in proving the adorable mysteriousness of the Divine Nature, do you assent to all these extravagant opinions of Cleanthes? For what other name can I give them? or, why spare my censure, when such principles are advanced, supported by such an authority, before so young a man as Pamphilus?

You seem not to apprehend, replied Philo, that I argue with Cleanthes in his own way; and, by showing him the dangerous consequences of his tenets, hope at last to reduce him to our opinion. But what sticks most with you, I observe, is the representation which Cleanthes has made of the argument a posteriori; and finding that that argument is likely to escape your hold and vanish into air, you think it so disguised, that you can scarcely believe it to be set in its true light. Now, however much I may dissent, in other respects, from the dangerous principles of Cleanthes, I must allow that he has fairly represented that argument; and I shall endeavor so to state the matter to you, that you will entertain no further scruples with regard to it.

Were a man to abstract from every thing which he knows or has seen, he would be altogether incapable, merely from his own ideas, to determine what kind of scene the universe must be, or to give the preference to one state or situation of things above another. For as nothing which he clearly conceives could be esteemed impossible or implying a contradiction, every chimera of his fancy would be upon an equal footing; nor could he assign any just reason why he adheres to one idea or system, and rejects the others which are equally possible.

Again; after he opens his eyes, and contemplates the world as it really is, it would be impossible for him at first to assign the cause of any one event, much less of the whole of things, or of the universe. He might set his fancy a rambling; and she might bring him in an infinite variety of reports and representations. These would all be possible; but being all equally possible, he would never of himself give a satisfactory account for his preferring one of them to the rest. Experience alone can point out to him the true cause of any phenomenon.

Now, according to this method of reasoning, Demea, it follows, (and is, indeed, tacitly allowed by Cleanthes himself,) that order, arrangement, or the adjustment of final causes, is not of itself any proof of design; but only so far as it has been experienced to proceed from that principle. For ought we can know a priori, matter may contain the source or spring of order originally within itself as well as mind does; and there is no more difficulty in conceiving, that the several elements, from an internal unknown cause, may fall into the most exquisite arrangement, than to conceive that their ideas, in the great universal mind, from a like internal unknown cause, fall into that arrangement. The equal possibility of both these suppositions is allowed. But, by experience, we find, (according to Cleanthes,) that there is a difference between them. Throw several pieces of steel together, without shape or form; they will never arrange themselves so as to compose a watch. Stone, and mortar, and wood, without an architect, never erect a house. But the ideas in a human mind, we see, by an unknown, inexplicable economy, arrange themselves so as to form the plan of a watch or house. Experience, therefore, proves, that there is an original principle of order in mind, not in matter. From similar effects we infer similar causes. The adjustment of means to ends is alike in the universe, as in a machine of human contrivance. The causes, therefore, must be resembling.

I was from the beginning scandalized, I must own, with this resemblance, which is asserted, between the Deity and human creatures; and must conceive it to imply such a degradation of the Supreme Being as no sound Theist could endure. With your assistance, therefore, Demea, I shall endeavor to defend what you justly call the adorable mysteriousness of the Divine Nature, and shall refute this reasoning of Cleanthes, provided he allows that I have made a fair representation of it.

When Cleanthes had assented, Philo, after a short pause, proceeded in the following manner.

That all inferences, Cleanthes, concerning fact, are founded on experience; and that all experimental reasonings are founded on the supposition that similar causes prove similar effects, and similar effects similar causes; I shall not at present much dispute with you. But observe, I entreat you, with what extreme caution all just reasoners proceed in the transferring of experiments to similar cases. Unless the cases be exactly similar, they repose no perfect confidence in applying their past observation to any particular phenomenon. Every alteration of circumstances occasions a doubt concerning the event; and it requires new experiments to prove certainly, that the new circumstances are of no moment or importance. A change in bulk, situation, arrangement, age, disposition of the air, or surrounding bodies; any of these particulars may be attended with the most unexpected consequences: and unless the objects be quite familiar to us, it is the highest temerity to expect with assurance, after any of these changes, an event similar to that which before fell under our observation. The slow and deliberate steps of philosophers here, if any where, are distinguished from the precipitate march of the vulgar, who, hurried on by the smallest similitude, are incapable of all discernment or consideration.

But can you think, Cleanthes, that your usual phlegm and philosophy have been preserved in so wide a step as you have taken, when you compared to the universe houses, ships, furniture, machines, and, from their similarity in some circumstances, inferred a similarity in their causes? Thought, design, intelligence, such as we discover in men and other animals, is no more than one of the springs and principles of the universe, as well as heat or cold, attraction or repulsion, and a hundred others, which fall under daily observation. It is an active cause, by which some particular parts of nature, we find, produce alterations on other parts. But can a conclusion, with any propriety, be transferred from parts to the whole? Does not the great disproportion bar all comparison and inference? From observing the growth of a hair, can we learn any thing concerning the generation of a man? Would the manner of a leaf's blowing, even though perfectly known, afford us any instruction concerning the vegetation of a tree?

But, allowing that we were to take the operations of one part of nature upon another, for the foundation of our judgment concerning the origin of the whole, (which never can be admitted,) yet why select so minute, so weak, so bounded a principle, as the reason and design of animals is found to be upon this planet? What peculiar privilege has this little agitation of the brain which we call thought, that we must thus make it the model of the whole universe? Our partiality in our own favour does indeed present it on all occasions; but sound philosophy ought carefully to guard against so natural an illusion.

So far from admitting, continued Philo, that the operations of a part can afford us any just conclusion concerning the origin of the whole, I will not allow any one part to form a rule for another part, if the latter be very remote from the former. Is there any reasonable ground to conclude, that the inhabitants of other planets possess thought, intelligence, reason, or any thing similar to these faculties in men? When nature has so extremely diversified her manner of operation in this small globe, can we imagine that she incessantly copies herself throughout so immense a universe? And if thought, as we may well suppose, be confined merely to this narrow corner, and has even there so limited a sphere of action, with what propriety can we assign it for the original cause of all things? The narrow views of a peasant, who makes his domestic economy the rule for the government of kingdoms, is in comparison a pardonable sophism.

But were we ever so much assured, that a thought and reason, resembling the human, were to be found throughout the whole universe, and were its activity elsewhere vastly greater and more commanding than it appears in this globe; yet I cannot see, why the operations of a world constituted, arranged, adjusted, can with any propriety be extended to a world which is in its embryo state, and is advancing towards that constitution and arrangement. By observation, we know somewhat of the economy, action, and nourishment of a finished animal; but we must transfer with great caution that observation to the growth of a foetus in the womb, and still more in the formation of an animalcule in the loins of its male parent. Nature, we find, even from our limited experience, possesses an infinite number of springs and principles, which incessantly discover themselves on every change of her position and situation. And what new and unknown principles would actuate her in so new and unknown a situation as that of the formation of a universe, we cannot, without the utmost temerity, pretend to determine.

A very small part of this great system, during a very short time, is very imperfectly discovered to us; and do we then pronounce decisively concerning the origin of the whole?

Admirable conclusion! Stone, wood, brick, irons brass, have not, at this time, in this minute globe of earth, an order or arrangement without human art and contrivance; therefore the universe could not originally attain its order and arrangement, without something similar to human art. But is a part of nature a rule for another part very wide of the former? Is it a rule for the whole? Is a very small part a rule for the universe? Is nature in one situation, a certain rule for nature in another situation vastly different from the former?

And can you blame me, Cleanthes, if I here imitate the prudent reserve of Simonides, who, according to the noted story, being asked by Hiero, What God was? desired a day to think of it, and then two days more; and after that manner continually prolonged the term, without ever bringing in his definition or description? Could you even blame me, if I answered at first, that I did not know, and was sensible that this subject lay vastly beyond the reach of my faculties? You might cry out sceptic and rallier, as much as you pleased: but having found, in so many other subjects much more familiar, the imperfections and even contradictions of human reason, I never should expect any success from its feeble conjectures, in a subject so sublime, and so remote from the sphere of our observation. When two species of objects have always been observed to be conjoined together, I can infer, by custom, the existence of one wherever I see the existence of the other; and this I call an argument from experience. But how this argument can have place, where the objects, as in the present case, are single, individual, without parallel, or specific resemblance, may be difficult to explain. And will any man tell me with a serious countenance, that an orderly universe must arise from some thought and art like the human, because we have experience of it? To ascertain this reasoning, it were requisite that we had experience of the origin of worlds; and it is not sufficient, surely, that we have seen ships and cities arise from human art and contrivance.

Philo was proceeding in this vehement manner, somewhat between jest and earnest, as it appeared to me, when he observed some signs of impatience in Cleanthes, and then immediately stopped short. What I had to suggest, said Cleanthes, is only that you would not abuse terms, or make use of popular expressions to subvert philosophical reasonings. You know, that the vulgar often distinguish reason from experience, even where the question relates only to matter of fact and existence; though it is found, where that reason is properly analyzed, that it is nothing but a species of experience. To prove by experience the origin of the universe from mind, is not more contrary to common speech, than to prove the motion of the earth from the same principle. And a caviller might raise all the same objections to the Copernican system, which you have urged against my reasonings. Have you other earths, might he say, which you have seen to move? Have . . .

Yes! cried Philo, interrupting him, we have other earths. Is not the moon another earth, which we see to turn round its centre? Is not Venus another earth, where we observe the same phenomenon? Are not the revolutions of the sun also a confirmation, from analogy, of the same theory? All the planets, are they not earths, which revolve about the sun? Are not the satellites moons, which move round Jupiter and Saturn, and along with these primary planets round the sun? These analogies and resemblances, with others which I have not mentioned, are the sole proofs of the Copernican system; and to you it belongs to consider, whether you have any analogies of the same kind to support your theory.

In reality, Cleanthes, continued he, the modern system of astronomy is now so much received by all inquirers, and has become so essential a part even of our earliest education, that we are not commonly very scrupulous in examining the reasons upon which it is founded. It is now become a matter of mere curiosity to study the first writers on that subject, who had the full force of prejudice to encounter, and were obliged to turn their arguments on every side in order to render them popular and convincing. But if we peruse Galileo's famous Dialogues concerning the system of the world, we shall find, that that great genius, one of the sublimest that ever existed, first bent all his endeavors to prove, that there was no foundation for the distinction commonly made between elementary and celestial substances. The schools, proceeding from the illusions of sense, had carried this distinction very far; and had established the latter substances to be ingenerable, incorruptible, unalterable, impassible; and had assigned all the opposite qualities to the former. But Galileo, beginning with the moon, proved its similarity in every particular to the earth; its convex figure, its natural darkness when not illuminated, its density, its distinction into solid and liquid, the variations of its phases, the mutual illuminations of the earth and moon, their mutual eclipses, the inequalities of the lunar surface, etc. After many instances of this kind, with regard to all the planets, men plainly saw that these bodies became proper objects of experience; and that the similarity of their nature enabled us to extend the same arguments and phenomena from one to the other.

In this cautious proceeding of the astronomers, you may read your own condemnation, Cleanthes; or rather may see, that the subject in which you are engaged exceeds all human reason and enquiry. Can you pretend to shew any such similarity between the fabric of a house, and the generation of a universe? Have you ever seen nature in any such situation as resembles the first arrangement of the elements? Have worlds ever been formed under your eye; and have you had leisure to observe the whole progress of the phenomenon, from the first appearance of order to its final consummation? If you have, then cite your experience, and deliver your theory.

Part III

How the most absurd argument, replied Cleanthes, in the hands of a man of ingenuity and invention, may acquire an air of probability! Are you not aware, Philo, that it became necessary for Copernicus and his first disciples to prove the similarity of the terrestrial and celestial matter; because several philosophers, blinded by old systems, and supported by some sensible appearances, had denied that similarity? but that it is by no means necessary, that Theists should prove the similarity of the works of Nature to those of Art; because this similarity is self-evident and undeniable? The same matter, a like form; what more is requisite to shew an analogy between their causes, and to ascertain the origin of all things from a divine purpose and intention? Your objections, I must freely tell you, are no better than the abstruse cavils of those philosophers who denied motion; and ought to be refuted in the same manner, by illustrations, examples, and instances, rather than by serious argument and philosophy.

Suppose, therefore, that an articulate voice were heard in the clouds, much louder and more melodious than any which human art could ever reach: suppose, that this voice were extended in the same instant over all nations, and spoke to each nation in its own language and dialect: suppose, that the words delivered not only contain a just sense and meaning, but convey some instruction altogether worthy of a benevolent Being, superior to mankind: could you possibly hesitate a moment concerning the cause of this voice? and must you not instantly ascribe it to some design or purpose? Yet I cannot see but all the same objections (if they merit that appellation) which lie against the system of Theism, may also be produced against this inference.

Might you not say, that all conclusions concerning fact were founded on experience: that when we hear an articulate voice in the dark, and thence infer a man, it is only the resemblance of the effects which leads us to conclude that there is a like resemblance in the cause: but that this extraordinary voice, by its loudness, extent, and flexibility to all languages, bears so little analogy to any human voice, that we have no reason to suppose any analogy in their causes: and consequently, that a rational, wise, coherent speech proceeded, you know not whence, from some accidental whistling of the winds, not from any divine reason or intelligence? You see clearly your own objections in these cavils, and I hope too you see clearly, that they cannot possibly have more force in the one case than in the other.

But to bring the case still nearer the present one of the universe, I shall make two suppositions, which imply not any absurdity or impossibility. Suppose that there is a natural, universal, invariable language, common to every individual of human race; and that books are natural productions, which perpetuate themselves in the same manner with animals and vegetables, by descent and propagation. Several expressions of our passions contain a universal language: all brute animals have a natural speech, which, however limited, is very intelligible to their own species. And as there are infinitely fewer parts and less contrivance in the finest composition of eloquence, than in the coarsest organized body, the propagation of an Iliad or Aeneid is an easier supposition than that of any plant or animal.

Suppose, therefore, that you enter into your library, thus peopled by natural volumes, containing the most refined reason and most exquisite beauty; could you possibly open one of them, and doubt, that its original cause bore the strongest analogy to mind and intelligence? When it reasons and discourses; when it expostulates, argues, and enforces its views and topics; when it applies sometimes to the pure intellect, sometimes to the affections; when it collects, disposes, and adorns every consideration suited to the subject; could you persist in asserting, that all this, at the bottom, had really no meaning; and that the first formation of this volume in the loins of its original parent proceeded not from thought and design? Your obstinacy, I know, reaches not that degree of firmness: even your sceptical play and wantonness would be abashed at so glaring an absurdity.

But if there be any difference, Philo, between this supposed case and the real one of the universe, it is all to the advantage of the latter. The anatomy of an animal affords many stronger instances of design than the perusal of Livy or Tacitus; and any objection which you start in the former case, by carrying me back to so unusual and extraordinary a scene as the first formation of worlds, the same objection has place on the supposition of our vegetating library. Choose, then, your party, Philo, without ambiguity or evasion; assert either that a rational volume is no proof of a rational cause, or admit of a similar cause to all the works of nature.

Let me here observe too, continued Cleanthes, that this religious argument, instead of being weakened by that scepticism so much affected by you, rather acquires force from it, and becomes more firm and undisputed. To exclude all argument or reasoning of every kind, is either affectation or madness. The declared profession of every reasonable sceptic is only to reject abstruse, remote, and refined arguments; to adhere to common sense and the plain instincts of nature; and to assent, wherever any reasons strike him with so full a force that he cannot, without the greatest violence, prevent it. Now the arguments for Natural Religion are plainly of this kind; and nothing but the most perverse, obstinate metaphysics can reject them. Consider, anatomize the eye; survey its structure and contrivance; and tell me, from your own feeling, if the idea of a contriver does not immediately flow in upon you with a force like that of sensation. The most obvious conclusion, surely, is in favour of design; and it requires time, reflection, and study, to summon up those frivolous, though abstruse objections, which can support Infidelity. Who can behold the male and female of each species, the correspondence of their parts and instincts, their passions, and whole course of life before and after generation, but must be sensible, that the propagation of the species is intended by Nature? Millions and millions of such instances present themselves through every part of the universe; and no language can convey a more intelligible irresistible meaning, than the curious adjustment of final causes. To what degree, therefore, of blind dogmatism must one have attained, to reject such natural and such convincing arguments?

Some beauties in writing we may meet with, which seem contrary to rules, and which gain the affections, and animate the imagination, in opposition to all the precepts of criticism, and to the authority of the established masters of art. And if the argument for Theism be, as you pretend, contradictory to the principles of logic; its universal, its irresistible influence proves clearly, that there may be arguments of a like irregular nature. Whatever cavils may be urged, an orderly world, as well as a coherent, articulate speech, will still be received as an incontestable proof of design and intention.

It sometimes happens, I own, that the religious arguments have not their due influence on an ignorant savage and barbarian; not because they are obscure and difficult, but because he never asks himself any question with regard to them. Whence arises the curious structure of an animal? From the copulation of its parents. And these whence? From their parents? A few removes set the objects at such a distance, that to him they are lost in darkness and confusion; nor is he actuated by any curiosity to trace them further. But this is neither dogmatism nor scepticism, but stupidity: a state of mind very different from your sifting, inquisitive disposition, my ingenious friend. You can trace causes from effects: you can compare the most distant and remote objects: and your greatest errors proceed not from barrenness of thought and invention, but from too luxuriant a fertility, which suppresses your natural good sense, by a profusion of unnecessary scruples and objections.

Here I could observe, Hermippus, that Philo was a little embarrassed and confounded: but while he hesitated in delivering an answer, luckily for him, Demea broke in upon the discourse, and saved his countenance.

Your instance, Cleanthes, said he, drawn from books and language, being familiar, has, I confess, so much more force on that account: but is there not some danger too in this very circumstance; and may it not render us presumptuous, by making us imagine we comprehend the Deity, and have some adequate idea of his nature and attributes? When I read a volume, I enter into the mind and intention of the author: I become him, in a manner, for the instant; and have an immediate feeling and conception of those ideas which revolved in his imagination while employed in that composition. But so near an approach we never surely can make to the Deity. His ways are not our ways. His attributes are perfect, but incomprehensible. And this volume of nature contains a great and inexplicable riddle, more than any intelligible discourse or reasoning.

The ancient Platonists, you know, were the most religious and devout of all the Pagan philosophers; yet many of them, particularly Plotinus, expressly declare, that intellect or understanding is not to be ascribed to the Deity; and that our most perfect worship of him consists, not in acts of veneration, reverence, gratitude, or love; but in a certain mysterious self-annihilation, or total extinction of all our faculties. These ideas are, perhaps, too far stretched; but still it must be acknowledged, that, by representing the Deity as so intelligible and comprehensible, and so similar to a human mind, we are guilty of the grossest and most narrow partiality, and make ourselves the model of the whole universe.

All the sentiments of the human mind, gratitude, resentment, love, friendship, approbation, blame, pity, emulation, envy, have a plain reference to the state and situation of man, and are calculated for preserving the existence and promoting the activity of such a being in such circumstances. It seems, therefore, unreasonable to transfer such sentiments to a supreme existence, or to suppose him actuated by them; and the phenomena besides of the universe will not support us in such a theory. All our ideas derived from the senses are confusedly false and illusive; and cannot therefore be supposed to have place in a supreme intelligence: and as the ideas of internal sentiment, added to those of the external senses, compose the whole furniture of human understanding, we may conclude, that none of the materials of thought are in any respect similar in the human and in the divine intelligence. Now, as to the manner of thinking; how can we make any comparison between them, or suppose them anywise resembling? Our thought is fluctuating, uncertain, fleeting, successive, and compounded; and were we to remove these circumstances, we absolutely annihilate its essence, and it would in such a case be an abuse of terms to apply to it the name of thought or reason. At least if it appear more pious and respectful (as it really is) still to retain these terms, when we mention the Supreme Being, we ought to acknowledge, that their meaning, in that case, is totally incomprehensible; and that the infirmities of our nature do not permit us to reach any ideas which in the least correspond to the ineffable sublimity of the Divine attributes.

Part IV

It seems strange to me, said Cleanthes, that you, Demea, who are so sincere in the cause of religion, should still maintain the mysterious, incomprehensible nature of the Deity, and should insist so strenuously that he has no manner of likeness or resemblance to human creatures. The Deity, I can readily allow, possesses many powers and attributes of which we can have no comprehension: but if our ideas, so far as they go, be not just, and adequate, and correspondent to his real nature, I know not what there is in this subject worth insisting on. Is the name, without any meaning, of such mighty importance? Or how do you mystics, who maintain the absolute incomprehensibility of the Deity, differ from Sceptics or Atheists, who assert, that the first cause of all is unknown and unintelligible? Their temerity must be very great, if, after rejecting the production by a mind, I mean a mind resembling the human, (for I know of no other,) they pretend to assign, with certainty, any other specific intelligible cause: and their conscience must be very scrupulous indeed, if they refuse to call the universal unknown cause a God or Deity; and to bestow on him as many sublime eulogies and unmeaning epithets as you shall please to require of them.

Who could imagine, replied Demea, that Cleanthes, the calm philosophical Cleanthes, would attempt to refute his antagonists by affixing a nickname to them; and, like the common bigots and inquisitors of the age, have recourse to invective and declamation, instead of reasoning? Or does he not perceive, that these topics are easily retorted, and that Anthropomorphite is an appellation as invidious, and implies as dangerous consequences, as the epithet of Mystic, with which he has honored us? In reality, Cleanthes, consider what it is you assert when you represent the Deity as similar to a human mind and understanding. What is the soul of man? A composition of various faculties, passions, sentiments, ideas; united, indeed, into one self or person, but still distinct from each other. When it reasons, the ideas, which are the parts of its discourse, arrange themselves in a certain form or order; which is not preserved entire for a moment, but immediately gives place to another arrangement. New opinions, new passions, new affections, new feelings arise, which continually diversify the mental scene, and produce in it the greatest variety and most rapid succession imaginable. How is this compatible with that perfect immutability and simplicity which all true Theists ascribe to the Deity? By the same act, say they, he sees past, present, and future: his love and hatred, his mercy and justice, are one individual operation: he is entire in every point of space; and complete in every instant of duration. No succession, no change, no acquisition, no diminution. What he is implies not in it any shadow of distinction or diversity. And what he is this moment he ever has been, and ever will be, without any new judgment, sentiment, or operation. He stands fixed in one simple, perfect state: nor can you ever say, with any propriety, that this act of his is different from that other; or that this judgment or idea has been lately formed, and will give place, by succession, to any different judgment or idea.

I can readily allow, said Cleanthes, that those who maintain the perfect simplicity of the Supreme Being, to the extent in which you have explained it, are complete Mystics, and chargeable with all the consequences which I have drawn from their opinion. They are, in a word, Atheists, without knowing it. For though it be allowed, that the Deity possesses attributes of which we have no comprehension, yet ought we never to ascribe to him any attributes which are absolutely incompatible with that intelligent nature essential to him. A mind, whose acts and sentiments and ideas are not distinct and successive; one, that is wholly simple, and totally immutable, is a mind which has no thought, no reason, no will, no sentiment, no love, no hatred; or, in a word, is no mind at all. It is an abuse of terms to give it that appellation; and we may as well speak of limited extension without figure, or of number without composition.

Pray consider, said Philo, whom you are at present inveighing against. You are honoring with the appellation of Atheist all the sound, orthodox divines, almost, who have treated of this subject; and you will at last be, yourself, found, according to your reckoning, the only sound Theist in the world. But if idolaters be Atheists, as, I think, may justly be asserted, and Christian Theologians the same, what becomes of the argument, so much celebrated, derived from the universal consent of mankind?

But because I know you are not much swayed by names and authorities, I shall endeavor to shew you, a little more distinctly, the inconveniences of that Anthropomorphism, which you have embraced; and shall prove, that there is no ground to suppose a plan of the world to be formed in the Divine mind, consisting of distinct ideas, differently arranged, in the same manner as an architect forms in his head the plan of a house which he intends to execute.

It is not easy, I own, to see what is gained by this supposition, whether we judge of the matter by Reason or by Experience. We are still obliged to mount higher, in order to find the cause of this cause, which you had assigned as satisfactory and conclusive.

If Reason (I mean abstract reason, derived from enquiries a priori) be not alike mute with regard to all questions concerning cause and effect, this sentence at least it will venture to pronounce, That a mental world, or universe of ideas, requires a cause as much, as does a material world, or universe of objects; and, if similar in its arrangement, must require a similar cause. For what is there in this subject, which should occasion a different conclusion or inference? In an abstract view, they are entirely alike; and no difficulty attends the one supposition, which is not common to both of them.

Again, when we will needs force Experience to pronounce some sentence, even on these subjects which lie beyond her sphere, neither can she perceive any material difference in this particular, between these two kinds of worlds; but finds them to be governed by similar principles, and to depend upon an equal variety of causes in their operations. We have specimens in miniature of both of them. Our own mind resembles the one; a vegetable or animal body the other. Let experience, therefore, judge from these samples. Nothing seems more delicate, with regard to its causes, than thought; and as these causes never operate in two persons after the same manner, so we never find two persons who think exactly alike. Nor indeed does the same person think exactly alike at any two different periods of time. A difference of age, of the disposition of his body, of weather, of food, of company, of books, of passions; any of these particulars, or others more minute, are sufficient to alter the curious machinery of thought, and communicate to it very different movements and operations. As far as we can judge, vegetables and animal bodies are not more delicate in their motions, nor depend upon a greater variety or more curious adjustment of springs and principles.

How, therefore, shall we satisfy ourselves concerning the cause of that Being whom you suppose the Author of Nature, or, according to your system of Anthropomorphism, the ideal world, into which you trace the material? Have we not the same reason to trace that ideal world into another ideal world, or new intelligent principle? But if we stop, and go no further; why go so far? why not stop at the material world? How can we satisfy ourselves without going on in infinitum? And, after all, what satisfaction is there in that infinite progression? Let us remember the story of the Indian philosopher and his elephant. It was never more applicable than to the present subject. If the material world rests upon a similar ideal world, this ideal world must rest upon some other; and so on, without end. It were better, therefore, never to look beyond the present material world. By supposing it to contain the principle of its order within itself, we really assert it to be God; and the sooner we arrive at that Divine Being, so much the better. When you go one step beyond the mundane system, you only excite an inquisitive humor which it is impossible ever to satisfy.

To say, that the different ideas which compose the reason of the Supreme Being, fall into order of themselves, and by their own nature, is really to talk without any precise meaning. If it has a meaning, I would fain know, why it is not as good sense to say, that the parts of the material world fall into order of themselves and by their own nature. Can the one opinion be intelligible, while the other is not so?

We have, indeed, experience of ideas which fall into order of themselves, and without any known cause. But, I am sure, we have a much larger experience of matter which does the same; as, in all instances of generation and vegetation, where the accurate analysis of the cause exceeds all human comprehension. We have also experience of particular systems of thought and of matter which have no order; of the first in madness, of the second in corruption. Why, then, should we think, that order is more essential to one than the other? And if it requires a cause in both, what do we gain by your system, in tracing the universe of objects into a similar universe of ideas? The first step which we make leads us on for ever. It were, therefore, wise in us to limit all our enquiries to the present world, without looking further. No satisfaction can ever be attained by these speculations, which so far exceed the narrow bounds of human understanding.

It was usual with the Peripatetics, you know, Cleanthes, when the cause of any phenomenon was demanded, to have recourse to their faculties or occult qualities; and to say, for instance, that bread, nourished by its nutritive faculty, and senna purged by its purgative. But it has been discovered, that this subterfuge was nothing but the disguise of ignorance; and that these philosophers, though less ingenuous, really said the same thing with the sceptics or the vulgar, who fairly confessed that they knew not the cause of these phenomena. In like manner, when it is asked, what cause produces order in the ideas of the Supreme Being; can any other reason be assigned by you, Anthropomorphites, than that it is a rational faculty, and that such is the nature of the Deity? But why a similar answer will not be equally satisfactory in accounting for the order of the world, without having recourse to any such intelligent creator as you insist on, may be difficult to determine. It is only to say, that such is the nature of material objects, and that they are all originally possessed of a faculty of order and proportion. These are only more learned and elaborate ways of confessing our ignorance; nor has the one hypothesis any real advantage above the other, except in its greater conformity to vulgar prejudices.

You have displayed this argument with great emphasis, replied Cleanthes. You seem not sensible how easy it is to answer it. Even in common life, if I assign a cause for any event, is it any objection, Philo, that I cannot assign the cause of that cause, and answer every new question which may incessantly be started? And what philosophers could possibly submit to so rigid a rule? philosophers, who confess ultimate causes to be totally unknown; and are sensible, that the most refined principles into which they trace the phenomena, are still to them as inexplicable as these phenomena themselves are to the vulgar. The order and arrangement of nature, the curious adjustment of final causes, the plain use and intention of every part and organ; all these bespeak in the clearest language an intelligent cause or author. The heavens and the earth join in the same testimony: the whole chorus of Nature raises one hymn to the praises of its Creator. You alone, or almost alone, disturb this general harmony. You start abstruse doubts, cavils, and objections: you ask me, what is the cause of this cause? I know not; I care not; that concerns not me. I have found a Deity; and here I stop my enquiry. Let those go further, who are wiser or more enterprising.

I pretend to be neither, replied Philo: and for that very reason, I should never perhaps have attempted to go so far; especially when I am sensible, that I must at last be contented to sit down with the same answer, which, without further trouble, might have satisfied me from the beginning. If I am still to remain in utter ignorance of causes, and can absolutely give an explication of nothing, I shall never esteem it any advantage to shove off for a moment a difficulty, which, you acknowledge, must immediately, in its full force, recur upon me. Naturalists indeed very justly explain particular effects by more general causes, though these general causes themselves should remain in the end totally inexplicable; but they never surely thought it satisfactory to explain a particular effect by a particular cause, which was no more to be accounted for than the effect itself. An ideal system, arranged of itself, without a precedent design, is not a whit more explicable than a material one, which attains its order in a like manner; nor is there any more difficulty in the latter supposition than in the former.

Part V

But to shew you still more inconveniences, continued Philo, in your Anthropomorphism, please to take a new survey of your principles. Like effects prove like causes. This is the experimental argument; and this, you say too, is the sole theological argument. Now, it is certain, that the liker the effects are which are seen, and the liker the causes which are inferred, the stronger is the argument. Every departure on either side diminishes the probability, and renders the experiment less conclusive. You cannot doubt of the principle; neither ought you to reject its consequences.

All the new discoveries in astronomy, which prove the immense grandeur and magnificence of the works of Nature, are so many additional arguments for a Deity, according to the true system of Theism; but, according to your hypothesis of experimental Theism, they become so many objections, by removing the effect still further from all resemblance to the effects of human art and contrivance. For, if Lucretius, even following the old system of the world, could exclaim, Who is strong enough to rule the sum, who to hold in hand and control the mighty bridle of the unfathomable deep? Who to turn about all the heavens at one time, and warm the fruitful worlds with ethereal fires, or to be present in all places and at all times.

If Tully esteemed this reasoning so natural as to put it into the mouth of his Epicurean:

What power of mental vision enabled your master Plato to descry the vast and elaborate architectural process which, as he makes out, the deity adopted in building the structure of the universe? What method of engineering was employed? What tools and levers and derricks? What agents carried out so vast an understanding? And how were air, fire, water, and earth enabled to obey and execute the will of the architect?

If this argument, I say, had any force in former ages, how much greater must it have at present, when the bounds of Nature are so infinitely enlarged, and such a magnificent scene is opened to us? It is still more unreasonable to form our idea of so unlimited a cause from our experience of the narrow productions of human design and invention.

The discoveries by microscopes, as they open a new universe in miniature, are still objections, according to you, arguments, according to me. The further we push our researches of this kind, we are still led to infer the universal cause of all to be vastly different from mankind, or from any object of human experience and observation.

And what say you to the discoveries in anatomy, chemistry, botany? . . . These surely are no objections, replied Cleanthes; they only discover new instances of art and contrivance. It is still the image of mind reflected on us from innumerable objects. Add, a mind like the human, said Philo. I know of no other, replied Cleanthes. And the liker the better, insisted Philo. To be sure, said Cleanthes.

Now, Cleanthes, said Philo, with an air of alacrity and triumph, mark the consequences. First, By this method of reasoning, you renounce all claim to infinity in any of the attributes of the Deity. For, as the cause ought only to be proportioned to the effect, and the effect, so far as it falls under our cognizance, is not infinite; what pretensions have we, upon your suppositions, to ascribe that attribute to the Divine Being? You will still insist, that, by removing him so much from all similarity to human creatures, we give in to the most arbitrary hypothesis, and at the same time weaken all proofs of his existence.

Secondly, You have no reason, on your theory, for ascribing perfection to the Deity, even in his finite capacity, or for supposing him free from every error, mistake, or incoherence, in his undertakings. There are many inexplicable difficulties in the works of Nature, which, if we allow a perfect author to be proved a priori, are easily solved, and become only seeming difficulties, from the narrow capacity of man, who cannot trace infinite relations. But according to your method of reasoning, these difficulties become all real; and perhaps will be insisted on, as new instances of likeness to human art and contrivance. At least, you must acknowledge, that it is impossible for us to tell, from our limited views, whether this system contains any great faults, or deserves any considerable praise, if compared to other possible, and even real systems. Could a peasant, if the Aeneid were read to him, pronounce that poem to be absolutely faultless, or even assign to it its proper rank among the productions of human wit, he, who had never seen any other production?

But were this world ever so perfect a production, it must still remain uncertain, whether all the excellences of the work can justly be ascribed to the workman. If we survey a ship, what an exalted idea must we form of the ingenuity of the carpenter who framed so complicated, useful, and beautiful a machine? And what surprise must we feel, when we find him a stupid mechanic, who imitated others, and copied an art, which, through a long succession of ages, after multiplied trials, mistakes, corrections, deliberations, and controversies, had been gradually improving? Many worlds might have been botched and bungled, throughout an eternity, ere this system was struck out; much labour lost, many fruitless trials made; and a slow, but continued improvement carried on during infinite ages in the art of world-making. In such subjects, who can determine, where the truth; nay, who can conjecture where the probability lies, amidst a great number of hypotheses which may be proposed, and a still greater which may be imagined?

And what shadow of an argument, continued Philo, can you produce, from your hypothesis, to prove the unity of the Deity? A great number of men join in building a house or ship, in rearing a city, in framing a commonwealth; why may not several deities combine in contriving and framing a world? This is only so much greater similarity to human affairs. By sharing the work among several, we may so much further limit the attributes of each, and get rid of that extensive power and knowledge, which must be supposed in one deity, and which, according to you, can only serve to weaken the proof of his existence. And if such foolish, such vicious creatures as man, can yet often unite in framing and executing one plan, how much more those deities or demons, whom we may suppose several degrees more perfect!

To multiply causes without necessity, is indeed contrary to true philosophy: but this principle applies not to the present case. Were one deity antecedently proved by your theory, who were possessed of every attribute requisite to the production of the universe; it would be needless, I own, (though not absurd,) to suppose any other deity existent. But while it is still a question, Whether all these attri-butes are united in one subject, or dispersed among several independent beings, by what phenomena in nature can we pretend to decide the controversy? Where we see a body raised in a scale, we are sure that there is in the opposite scale, however concealed from sight, some counterpoising weight equal to it; but it is still allowed to doubt, whether that weight be an aggregate of several distinct bodies, or one uniform united mass. And if the weight requisite very much exceeds any thing which we have ever seen conjoined in any single body, the former supposition becomes still more probable and natural. An intelligent being of such vast power and capacity as is necessary to produce the universe, or, to speak in the language of ancient philosophy, so prodigious an animal exceeds all analogy, and even comprehension.

But further, Cleanthes: men are mortal, and renew their species by generation; and this is common to all living creatures. The two great sexes of male and female, says Milton, animate the world. Why must this circumstance, so universal, so essential be excluded from those numerous and limited deities? Behold, then, the theogony of ancient times brought back upon us.

And why not become a perfect Anthropomorphite? Why not assert the deity or deities to be corporeal, and to have eyes, a nose, mouth, ears, etc.? Epicurus maintained, that no man had ever seen reason but in a human figure; therefore the gods must have a human figure. And this argument, which is deservedly so much ridiculed by Cicero, becomes, according to you, solid and philosophical.

In a word, Cleanthes, a man who follows your hypothesis is able perhaps to assert, or conjecture, that the universe, sometime, arose from something like design: but beyond that position he cannot ascertain one single circumstance; and is left afterwards to fix every point of his theology by the utmost license of fancy and hypothesis. This world, for aught he knows, is very faulty and imperfect, compared to a superior standard; and was only the first rude essay of some infant deity, who afterwards abandoned it, ashamed of his lame performance: it is the work only of some dependent, inferior deity; and is the object of derision to his superiors: it is the production of old age and dotage in some superannuated deity; and ever since his death, has run on at adventures, from the first impulse and active force which it received from him. You justly give signs of horror, Demea, at these strange suppositions; but these, and a thousand more of the same kind, are Cleanthes's suppositions, not mine. From the moment the attributes of the Deity are supposed finite, all these have place. And I cannot, for my part, think that so wild and unsettled a system of theology is, in any respect, preferable to none at all.

These suppositions I absolutely disown, cried Cleanthes: they strike me, however, with no horror, especially when proposed in that rambling way in which they drop from you. On the contrary, they give me pleasure, when I see, that, by the utmost indulgence of your imagination, you never get rid of the hypothesis of design in the universe, but are obliged at every turn to have recourse to it. To this concession I adhere steadily; and this I regard as a sufficient foundation for religion.

Part VI

It must be a slight fabric, indeed, said Demea, which can be erected on so tottering a foundation. While we are uncertain whether there is one deity or many; whether the deity or deities, to whom we owe our existence, be perfect or imperfect, subordinate or supreme, dead or alive, what trust or confidence can we repose in them? What devotion or worship address to them? What veneration or obedience pay them? To all the purposes of life the theory of religion becomes altogether useless: and even with regard to speculative consequences, its uncertainty, according to you, must render it totally precarious and unsatisfactory.

To render it still more unsatisfactory, said Philo, there occurs to me another hypothesis, which must acquire an air of probability from the method of reasoning so much insisted on by Cleanthes. That like effects arise from like causes: this principle he supposes the foundation of all religion. But there is another principle of the same kind, no less certain, and derived from the same source of experience; that where several known circumstances are observed to be similar, the unknown will also be found similar. Thus, if we see the limbs of a human body, we conclude that it is also attended with a human head, though hid from us. Thus, if we see, through a chink in a wall, a small part of the sun, we conclude, that, were the wall removed, we should see the whole body. In short, this method of reasoning is so obvious and familiar, that no scruple can ever be made with regard to its solidity.

Now, if we survey the universe, so far as it falls under our knowledge, it bears a great resemblance to an animal or organized body, and seems actuated with a like principle of life and motion. A continual circulation of matter in it produces no disorder: a continual waste in every part is incessantly repaired: the closest sympathy is perceived throughout the entire system: and each part or member, in performing its proper offices, operates both to its own preservation and to that of the whole. The world, therefore, I infer, is an animal; and the Deity is the SOUL of the world, actuating it, and actuated by it.

You have too much learning, Cleanthes, to be at all surprised at this opinion, which, you know, was maintained by almost all the Theists of antiquity, and chiefly prevails in their discourses and reasonings. For though, sometimes, the ancient philosophers reason from final causes, as if they thought the world the workmanship of God; yet it appears rather their favorite notion to consider it as his body, whose organization renders it subservient to him. And it must be confessed, that, as the universe resembles more a human body than it does the works of human art and contrivance, if our limited analogy could ever, with any propriety, be extended to the whole of nature, the inference seems juster in favour of the ancient than the modern theory.

There are many other advantages, too, in the former theory, which recommended it to the ancient theologians. Nothing more repugnant to all their notions, because nothing more repugnant to common experience, than mind without body; a mere spiritual substance, which fell not under their senses nor comprehension, and of which they had not observed one single instance throughout all nature. Mind and body they knew, because they felt both: an order, arrangement, organization, or internal machinery, in both, they likewise knew, after the same manner: and it could not but seem reasonable to transfer this experience to the universe; and to suppose the divine mind and body to be also coeval, and to have, both of them, order and arrangement naturally inherent in them, and inseparable from them.

Here, therefore, is a new species of Anthropomorphism, Cleanthes, on which you may deliberate; and a theory which seems not liable to any considerable difficulties. You are too much superior, surely, to systematical prejudices, to find any more difficulty in supposing an animal body to be, originally, of itself, or from unknown causes, possessed of order and organization, than in supposing a similar order to belong to mind. But the vulgar prejudice, that body and mind ought always to accompany each other, ought not, one should think, to be entirely neglected; since it is founded on vulgar experience, the only guide which you profess to follow in all these theological enquiries. And if you assert, that our limited experience is an unequal standard, by which to judge of the unlimited extent of nature; you entirely abandon your own hypothesis, and must thenceforward adopt our Mysticism, as you call it, and admit of the absolute incomprehensibility of the Divine Nature.

This theory, I own, replied Cleanthes, has never before occurred to me, though a pretty natural one; and I cannot readily, upon so short an examination and reflection, deliver any opinion with regard to it. You are very scrupulous, indeed, said Philo: were I to examine any system of yours, I should not have acted with half that caution and reserve, in starting objections and difficulties to it. However, if any thing occur to you, you will oblige us by proposing it.

Why then, replied Cleanthes, it seems to me, that, though the world does, in many circumstances, resemble an animal body; yet is the analogy also defective in many circumstances the most material: no organs of sense; no seat of thought or reason; no one precise origin of motion and action. In short, it seems to bear a stronger resemblance to a vegetable than to an animal, and your inference would be so far inconclusive in favour of the soul of the world.

But, in the next place, your theory seems to imply the eternity of the world; and that is a principle, which, I think, can be refuted by the strongest reasons and probabilities. I shall suggest an argument to this purpose, which, I believe, has not been insisted on by any writer. Those, who reason from the late origin of arts and sciences, though their inference wants not force, may perhaps be refuted by considerations derived from the nature of human society, which is in continual revolution, between ignorance and knowledge, liberty and slavery, riches and poverty; so that it is impossible for us, from our limited experience, to foretell with assurance what events may or may not be expected. Ancient learning and history seem to have been in great danger of entirely perishing after the inundation of the barbarous nations; and had these convulsions continued a little longer, or been a little more violent, we should not probably have now known what passed in the world a few centuries before us. Nay, were it not for the superstition of the Popes, who preserved a little jargon of Latin, in order to support the appearance of an ancient and universal church, that tongue must have been utterly lost; in which case, the Western world, being totally barbarous, would not have been in a fit disposition for receiving the Greek language and learning, which was conveyed to them after the sacking of Constantinople. When learning and books had been extinguished, even the mechanical arts would have fallen considerably to decay; and it is easily imagined, that fable or tradition might ascribe to them a much later origin than the true one. This vulgar argument, therefore, against the eternity of the world, seems a little precarious.

But here appears to be the foundation of a better argument. Lucullus was the first that brought cherry-trees from Asia to Europe; though that tree thrives so well in many European climates, that it grows in the woods without any culture. Is it possible, that throughout a whole eternity, no European had ever passed into Asia, and thought of transplanting so delicious a fruit into his own country? Or if the tree was once transplanted and propagated, how could it ever afterwards perish? Empires may rise and fall, liberty and slavery succeed alternately, ignorance and knowledge give place to each other; but the cherry-tree will still remain in the woods of Greece, Spain, and Italy, and will never be affected by the revolutions of human society.

It is not two thousand years since vines were transplanted into France, though there is no climate in the world more favorable to them. It is not three centuries since horses, cows, sheep, swine, dogs, corn, were known in America. Is it possible, that during the revolutions of a whole eternity, there never arose a Columbus, who might open the communication between Europe and that continent? We may as well imagine, that all men would wear stockings for ten thousand years, and never have the sense to think of garters to tie them. All these seem convincing proofs of the youth, or rather infancy of the world; as being founded on the operation of principles more constant and steady than those by which human society is governed and directed. Nothing less than a total convulsion of the elements will ever destroy all the European animals and vegetables which are now to be found in the Western world.

And what argument have you against such convulsions? replied Philo. Strong and almost incontestable proofs may be traced over the whole earth, that every part of this globe has continued for many ages entirely covered with water. And though order were supposed inseparable from matter, and inherent in it; yet may matter be susceptible of many and great revolutions, through the endless periods of eternal duration. The incessant changes, to which every part of it is subject, seem to intimate some such general transformations; though, at the same time, it is observable, that all the changes and corruptions of which we have ever had experience, are but passages from one state of order to another; nor can matter ever rest in total deformity and confusion. What we see in the parts, we may infer in the whole; at least, that is the method of reasoning on which you rest your whole theory. And were I obliged to defend any particular system of this nature, which I never willingly should do, I esteem none more plausible than that which ascribes an eternal inherent principle of order to the world, though attended with great and continual revolutions and alterations. This at once solves all difficulties; and if the solution, by being so general, is not entirely complete and satisfactory, it is at least a theory that we must sooner or later have recourse to, whatever system we embrace. How could things have been as they are, were there not an original inherent principle of order somewhere, in thought or in matter? And it is very indifferent to which of these we give the preference. Chance has no place, on any hypothesis, sceptical or religious. Every thing is surely governed by steady, inviolable laws. And were the inmost essence of things laid open to us, we should then discover a scene, of which, at present, we can have no idea. Instead of admiring the order of natural beings, we should clearly see that it was absolutely impossible for them, in the smallest article, ever to admit of any other disposition.

Were any one inclined to revive the ancient Pagan Theology, which maintained, as we learn from Hesiod, that this globe was governed by thirty thousand deities, who arose from the unknown powers of nature: you would naturally object, Cleanthes, that nothing is gained by this hypothesis; and that it is as easy to suppose all men animals, beings more numerous, but less perfect, to have sprung immediately from a like origin. Push the same inference a step further, and you will find a numerous society of deities as explicable as one universal deity, who possesses within himself the powers and perfections of the whole society. All these systems, then, of Scepticism, Polytheism, and Theism, you must allow, on your principles, to be on a like footing, and that no one of them has any advantage over the others. You may thence learn the fallacy of your principles.

Part VII

But here, continued Philo, in examining the ancient system of the soul of the world, there strikes me, all on a sudden, a new idea, which, if just, must go near to subvert all your reasoning, and destroy even your first inferences, on which you repose such confidence. If the universe bears a greater likeness to animal bodies and to vegetables, than to the works of human art, it is more probable that its cause resembles the cause of the former than that of the latter, and its origin ought rather to be ascribed to generation or vegetation, than to reason or design. Your conclusion, even according to your own principles, is therefore lame and defective.

Pray open up this argument a little further, said Demea, for I do not rightly apprehend it in that concise manner in which you have expressed it.

Our friend Cleanthes, replied Philo, as you have heard, asserts, that since no question of fact can be proved otherwise than by experience, the existence of a Deity admits not of proof from any other medium. The world, says he, resembles the works of human contrivance; therefore its cause must also resemble that of the other. Here we may remark, that the operation of one very small part of nature, to wit man, upon another very small part, to wit that inanimate matter lying within his reach, is the rule by which Cleanthes judges of the origin of the whole; and he measures objects, so widely disproportioned, by the same individual standard. But to waive all objections drawn from this topic, I affirm, that there are other parts of the universe (besides the machines of human invention) which bear still a greater resemblance to the fabric of the world, and which, therefore, afford a better conjecture concerning the universal origin of this system. These parts are animals and vegetables. The world plainly resembles more an animal or a vegetable, than it does a watch or a knitting-loom. Its cause, therefore, it is more probable, resembles the cause of the former. The cause of the former is generation or vegetation. The cause, therefore, of the world, we may infer to be something similar or analogous to generation or vegetation.

But how is it conceivable, said Demea, that the world can arise from any thing similar to vegetation or generation?

Very easily, replied Philo. In like manner as a tree sheds its seeds into the neighbouring fields, and produces other trees; so the great vegetable, the world, or this planetary system, produces within itself certain seeds, which, being scattered into the surrounding chaos, vegetate into new worlds. A comet, for instance, is the seed of a world; and after it has been fully ripened, by passing from sun to sun, and star to star, it is at last tossed into the unformed elements which every where surround this universe, and immediately sprouts up into a new system.

Or if, for the sake of variety (for I see no other advantage), we should suppose this world to be an animal; a comet is the egg of this animal: and in like manner as an ostrich lays its egg in the sand, which, without any further care, hatches the egg, and produces a new animal; so . . . I understand you, says Demea: but what wild, arbitrary suppositions are these! What data have you for such extraordinary conclusions? And is the slight, imaginary resemblance of the world to a vegetable or an animal sufficient to establish the same inference with regard to both? Objects, which are in general so widely different, ought they to be a standard for each other?

Right, cries Philo: this is the topic on which I have all along insisted. I have still asserted, that we have no data to establish any system of cosmogony. Our experience, so imperfect in itself, and so limited both in extent and duration, can afford us no probable conjecture concerning the whole of things. But if we must needs fix on some hypothesis; by what rule, pray, ought we to determine our choice? Is there any other rule than the greater similarity of the objects compared? And does not a plant or an animal, which springs from vegetation or generation, bear a stronger resemblance to the world, than does any artificial machine, which arises from reason and design?

But what is this vegetation and generation of which you talk? said Demea. Can you explain their operations, and anatomize that fine internal structure on which they depend?

As much, at least, replied Philo, as Cleanthes can explain the operations of reason, or anatomize that internal structure on which it depends. But without any such elaborate disquisitions, when I see an animal, I infer, that it sprang from generation; and that with as great certainty as you conclude a house to have been reared by design. These words, generation, reason, mark only certain powers and energies in nature, whose effects are known, but whose essence is incomprehensible; and one of these principles, more than the other, has no privilege for being made a standard to the whole of nature.

In reality, Demea, it may reasonably be expected, that the larger the views are which we take of things, the better will they conduct us in our conclusions concerning such extraordinary and such magnificent subjects. In this little corner of the world alone, there are four principles, reason, instinct, generation, vegetation, which are similar to each other, and are the causes of similar effects. What a number of other principles may we naturally suppose in the immense extent and variety of the universe, could we travel from planet to planet, and from system to system, in order to examine each part of this mighty fabric? Any one of these four principles above mentioned, (and a hundred others which lie open to our conjecture,) may afford us a theory by which to judge of the origin of the world; and it is a palpable and egregious partiality to confine our view entirely to that principle by which our own minds operate. Were this principle more intelligible on that account, such a partiality might be somewhat excusable: but reason, in its internal fabric and structure, is really as little known to us as instinct or vegetation; and, perhaps, even that vague, undeterminate word, Nature, to which the vulgar refer every thing, is not at the bottom more inexplicable. The effects of these principles are all known to us from experience; but the principles themselves, and their manner of operation, are totally unknown; nor is it less intelligible, or less conformable to experience, to say, that the world arose by vegetation, from a seed shed by another world, than to say that it arose from a divine reason or contrivance, according to the sense in which Cleanthes understands it.

But methinks, said Demea, if the world had a vegetative quality, and could sow the seeds of new worlds into the infinite chaos, this power would be still an additional argument for design in its author. For whence could arise so wonderful a faculty but from design? Or how can order spring from any thing which perceives not that order which it bestows?

You need only look around you, replied Philo, to satisfy yourself with regard to this question. A tree bestows order and organization on that tree which springs from it, without knowing the order; an animal in the same manner on its offspring; a bird on its nest; and instances of this kind are even more frequent in the world than those of order, which arise from reason and contrivance. To say, that all this order in animals and vegetables proceeds ultimately from design, is begging the question; nor can that great point be ascertained otherwise than by proving, a priori, both that order is, from its nature, inseparably attached to thought; and that it can never of itself, or from original unknown principles, belong to matter.

But further, Demea; this objection which you urge can never be made use of by Cleanthes, without renouncing a defence which he has already made against one of my objections. When I enquired concerning the cause of that supreme reason and intelligence into which he resolves every thing; he told me, that the impossibility of satisfying such enquiries could never be admitted as an objection in any species of philosophy. We must stop somewhere, says he; nor is it ever within the reach of human capacity to explain ultimate causes, or shew the last connexions of any objects. It is sufficient, if any steps, so far as we go, are supported by experience and observation. Now, that vegetation and generation, as well as reason, are experienced to be principles of order in nature, is undeniable. If I rest my system of cosmogony on the former, preferably to the latter, it is at my choice. The matter seems entirely arbitrary. And when Cleanthes asks me what is the cause of my great vegetative or generative faculty, I am equally entitled to ask him the cause of his great reasoning principle. These questions we have agreed to forbear on both sides; and it is chiefly his interest on the present occasion to stick to this agreement. Judging by our limited and imperfect experience, generation has some privileges above reason: for we see every day the latter arise from the former, never the former from the latter.

Compare, I beseech you, the consequences on both sides. The world, say I, resembles an animal; therefore it is an animal, therefore it arose from generation. The steps, I confess, are wide; yet there is some small appearance of analogy in each step. The world, says Cleanthes, resembles a machine; therefore it is a machine, therefore it arose from design. The steps are here equally wide, and the analogy less striking. And if he pretends to carry on my hypothesis a step further, and to infer design or reason from the great principle of generation, on which I insist; I may, with better authority, use the same freedom to push further his hypothesis, and infer a divine generation or theogony from his principle of reason. I have at least some faint shadow of experience, which is the utmost that can ever be attained in the present subject. Reason, in innumerable instances, is observed to arise from the principle of generation, and never to arise from any other principle.

Hesiod, and all the ancient mythologists, were so struck with this analogy, that they universally explained the origin of nature from an animal birth, and copulation. Plato too, so far as he is intelligible, seems to have adopted some such notion in his Timaeus.

The Brahmins assert, that the world arose from an infinite spider, who spun this whole complicated mass from his bowels, and annihilates afterwards the whole or any part of it, by absorbing it again, and resolving it into his own essence. Here is a species of cosmogony, which appears to us ridiculous; because a spider is a little contemptible animal, whose operations we are never likely to take for a model of the whole universe. But still here is a new species of analogy, even in our globe. And were there a planet wholly inhabited by spiders, (which is very possible,) this inference would there appear as natural and irrefragable as that which in our planet ascribes the origin of all things to design and intelligence, as explained by Cleanthes. Why an orderly system may not be spun from the belly as well as from the brain, it will be difficult for him to give a satisfactory reason.

I must confess, Philo, replied Cleanthes, that of all men living, the task which you have undertaken, of raising doubts and objections, suits you best, and seems, in a manner, natural and unavoidable to you. So great is your fertility of invention, that I am not ashamed to acknowledge myself unable, on a sudden, to solve regularly such out-of-the-way difficulties as you incessantly start upon me: though I clearly see, in general, their fallacy and error. And I question not, but you are yourself, at present, in the same case, and have not the solution so ready as the objection: while you must be sensible, that common sense and reason are entirely against you; and that such whimsies as you have delivered, may puzzle, but never can convince us.

Part VIII

What you ascribe to the fertility of my invention, replied Philo, is entirely owing to the nature of the subject. In subjects adapted to the narrow compass of human reason, there is commonly but one determination, which carries probability or conviction with it; and to a man of sound judgment, all other suppositions, but that one, appear entirely absurd and chimerical. But in such questions as the present, a hundred contradictory views may preserve a kind of imperfect analogy; and invention has here full scope to exert itself. Without any great effort of thought, I believe that I could, in an instant, propose other systems of cosmogony, which would have some faint appearance of truth, though it is a thousand, a million to one, if either yours or any one of mine be the true system.

For instance, what if I should revive the old Epicurean hypothesis? This is commonly, and I believe justly esteemed the most absurd system that has yet been proposed; yet I know not whether, with a few alterations, it might not be brought to bear a faint appearance of probability. Instead of supposing matter infinite, as Epicurus did, let us suppose it finite. A finite number of particles is only susceptible of finite transpositions: and it must happen, in an eternal duration, that every possible order or position must be tried an infinite number of times. This world, therefore, with all its events, even the most minute, has before been produced and destroyed, and will again be produced and destroyed, without any bounds and limitations. No one, who has a conception of the powers of infinite, in comparison of finite, will ever scruple this determination.

But this supposes, said Demea, that matter can acquire motion, without any voluntary agent or first mover.

And where is the difficulty, replied Philo, of that supposition? Every event, before experience, is equally difficult and incomprehensible; and every event, after experience, is equally easy and intelligible. Motion, in many instances, from gravity, from elasticity, from electricity, begins in matter, without any known voluntary agent: and to suppose always, in these cases, an unknown voluntary agent, is mere hypothesis; and hypothesis attended with no advantages. The beginning of motion in matter itself is as conceivable a priori as its communication from mind and intelligence.

Besides, why may not motion have been propagated by impulse through all eternity, and the same stock of it, or nearly the same, be still upheld in the universe? As much is lost by the composition of motion, as much is gained by its resolution. And whatever the causes are, the fact is certain, that matter is, and always has been, in continual agitation, as far as human experience or tradition reaches. There is not probably, at present, in the whole universe, one particle of matter at absolute rest.

And this very consideration too, continued Philo, which we have stumbled on in the course of the argument, suggests a new hypothesis of cosmogony, that is not absolutely absurd and improbable. Is there a system, an order, an economy of things, by which matter can preserve that perpetual agitation which seems essential to it, and yet maintain a constancy in the forms which it produces? There certainly is such an economy; for this is actually the case with the present world. The continual motion of matter, therefore, in less than infinite transpositions, must produce this economy or order; and by its very nature, that order, when once established, supports itself, for many ages, if not to eternity. But wherever matter is so poised, arranged, and adjusted, as to continue in perpetual motion and yet preserve a constancy in the forms, its situation must, of necessity, have all the same appearance of art and contrivance which we observe at present. All the parts of each form must have a relation to each other, and to the whole; and the whole itself must have a relation to the other parts of the universe; to the element in which the form subsists; to the materials with which it repairs its waste and decay; and to every other form which is hostile or friendly. A defect in any of these particulars destroys the form; and the matter of which it is composed is again set loose, and is thrown into irregular motions and fermentations, till it unite itself to some other regular form. If no such form be prepared to receive it, and if there be a great quantity of this corrupted matter in the universe, the universe itself is entirely disordered; whether it be the feeble embryo of a world in its first beginnings that is thus destroyed, or the rotten carcass of one languishing in old age and infirmity. In either case, a chaos ensues; till finite, though innumerable revolutions produce at last some forms, whose parts and organs are so adjusted as to support the forms amidst a continued succession of matter.

Suppose (for we shall endeavor to vary the expression), that matter were thrown into any position, by a blind, unguided force; it is evident that this first position must, in all probability, be the most confused and most disorderly imaginable, without any resemblance to those works of human contrivance, which, along with a symmetry of parts, discover an adjustment of means to ends, and a tendency to self-preservation. If the actuating force cease after this operation, matter must remain for ever in disorder, and continue an immense chaos, without any proportion or activity. But suppose that the actuating force, whatever it be, still continues in matter, this first position will immediately give place to a second, which will likewise in all probability be as disorderly as the first, and so on through many successions of changes and revolutions. No particular order or position ever continues a moment unaltered. The original force, still remaining in activity, gives a perpetual restlessness to matter. Every possible situation is produced, and instantly destroyed. If a glimpse or dawn of order appears for a moment, it is instantly hurried away, and confounded, by that never-ceasing force which actuates every part of matter.

Thus the universe goes on for many ages in a continued succession of chaos and disorder. But is it not possible that it may settle at last, so as not to lose its motion and active force (for that we have supposed inherent in it), yet so as to preserve an uniformity of appearance, amidst the continual motion and fluctuation of its parts? This we find to be the case with the universe at present. Every individual is perpetually changing, and every part of every individual; and yet the whole remains, in appearance, the same. May we not hope for such a position, or rather be assured of it, from the eternal revolutions of unguided matter; and may not this account for all the appearing wisdom and contrivance which is in the universe? Let us contemplate the subject a little, and we shall find, that this adjustment, if attained by matter of a seeming stability in the forms, with a real and perpetual revolution or motion of parts, affords a plausible, if not a true solution of the difficulty.

It is in vain, therefore, to insist upon the uses of the parts in animals or vegetables, and their curious adjustment to each other. I would fain know, how an animal could subsist, unless its parts were so adjusted? Do we not find, that it immediately perishes whenever this adjustment ceases, and that its matter corrupting tries some new form? It happens indeed, that the parts of the world are so well adjusted, that some regular form immediately lays claim to this corrupted matter: and if it were not so, could the world subsist? Must it not dissolve as well as the animal, and pass through new positions and situations, till in great, but finite succession, it falls at last into the present or some such order?

It is well, replied Cleanthes, you told us, that this hypothesis was suggested on a sudden, in the course of the argument. Had you had leisure to examine it, you would soon have perceived the insuperable objections to which it is exposed. No form, you say, can subsist, unless it possess those powers and organs requisite for its subsistence: some new order or economy must be tried, and so on, without intermission; till at last some order, which can support and maintain itself, is fallen upon. But according to this hypothesis, whence arise the many conveniences and advantages which men and all animals possess? Two eyes, two ears, are not absolutely necessary for the subsistence of the species. Human race might have been propagated and preserved, without horses, dogs, cows, sheep, and those innumerable fruits and products which serve to our satisfaction and enjoyment. If no camels had been created for the use of man in the sandy deserts of Africa and Arabia, would the world have been dissolved? If no loadstone had been framed to give that wonderful and useful direction to the needle, would human society and the human kind have been immediately extinguished? Though the maxims of Nature be in general very frugal, yet instances of this kind are far from being rare; and any one of them is a sufficient proof of design, and of a benevolent design, which gave rise to the order and arrangement of the universe.

At least, you may safely infer, said Philo, that the foregoing hypothesis is so far incomplete and imperfect, which I shall not scruple to allow. But can we ever reasonably expect greater success in any attempts of this nature? Or can we ever hope to erect a system of cosmogony, that will be liable to no exceptions, and will contain no circumstance repugnant to our limited and imperfect experience of the analogy of Nature? Your theory itself cannot surely pretend to any such advantage, even though you have run into Anthropomorphism, the better to preserve a conformity to common experience. Let us once more put it to trial. In all instances which we have ever seen, ideas are copied from real objects, and are ectypal, not archetypal, to express myself in learned terms: you reverse this order, and give thought the precedence. In all instances which we have ever seen, thought has no influence upon matter, except where that matter is so conjoined with it as to have an equal reciprocal influence upon it. No animal can move immediately any thing but the members of its own body; and indeed, the equality of action and reaction seems to be an universal law of nature: but your theory implies a contradiction to this experience. These instances, with many more, which it were easy to collect, (particularly the supposition of a mind or system of thought that is eternal, or, in other words, an animal ingenerable and immortal); these instances, I say, may teach all of us sobriety in condemning each other, and let us see, that as no system of this kind ought ever to be received from a slight analogy, so neither ought any to be rejected on account of a small incongruity. For that is an inconvenience from which we can justly pronounce no one to be exempted.

All religious systems, it is confessed, are subject to great and insuperable difficulties. Each disputant triumphs in his turn; while he carries on an offensive war, and exposes the absurdities, barbarities, and pernicious tenets of his antagonist. But all of them, on the whole, prepare a complete triumph for the Sceptic; who tells them, that no system ought ever to be embraced with regard to such subjects: for this plain reason, that no absurdity ought ever to be assented to with regard to any subject. A total suspense of judgment is here our only reasonable resource. And if every attack, as is commonly observed, and no defence, among Theologians, is successful; how complete must be his victory, who remains always, with all mankind, on the offensive, and has himself no fixed station or abiding city, which he is ever, on any occasion, obliged to defend?

Part IX

But if so many difficulties attend the argument a posteriori, said Demea, had we not better adhere to that simple and sublime argument a priori, which, by offering to us infallible demonstration, cuts off at once all doubt and difficulty? By this argument, too, we may prove the INFINITY of the Divine attributes, which, I am afraid, can never be ascertained with certainty from any other topic. For how can an effect, which either is finite, or, for aught we know, may be so; how can such an effect, I say, prove an infinite cause? The unity too of the Divine Nature, it is very difficult, if not absolutely impossible, to deduce merely from contemplating the works of nature; nor will the uniformity alone of the plan, even were it allowed, give us any assurance of that attribute. Whereas the argument a priori. . .

You seem to reason, Demea, interposed Cleanthes, as if those advantages and conveniences in the abstract argument were full proofs of its solidity. But it is first proper, in my opinion, to determine what argument of this nature you choose to insist on; and we shall afterwards, from itself, better than from its useful consequences, endeavor to determine what value we ought to put upon it.

The argument, replied Demea, which I would insist on, is the common one. Whatever exists must have a cause or reason of its existence; it being absolutely impossible for any thing to produce itself, or be the cause of its own existence. In mounting up, therefore, from effects to causes, we must either go on in tracing an infinite succession, without any ultimate cause at all; or must at last have recourse to some ultimate cause, that is necessarily existent: now, that the first supposition is absurd, may be thus proved. In the infinite chain or succession of causes and effects, each single effect is determined to exist by the power and efficacy of that cause which immediately preceded; but the whole eternal chain or succession, taken together, is not determined or caused by any thing; and yet it is evident that it requires a cause or reason, as much as any particular object which begins to exist in time. The question is still reasonable, why this particular succession of causes existed from eternity, and not any other succession, or no succession at all. If there be no necessarily existent being, any supposition which can be formed is equally possible; nor is there any more absurdity in Nothing's having existed from eternity, than there is in that succession of causes which constitutes the universe. What was it, then, which determined Something to exist rather than Nothing, and bestowed being on a particular possibility, exclusive of the rest? External causes, there are supposed to be none. Chance is a word without a meaning. Was it Nothing? But that can never produce any thing. We must, therefore, have recourse to a necessarily existent Being, who carries the REASON of his existence in himself, and who cannot be supposed not to exist, without an express contradiction. There is, consequently, such a Being; that is, there is a Deity.

I shall not leave it to Philo, said Cleanthes, though I know that the starting objections is his chief delight, to point out the weakness of this metaphysical reasoning. It seems to me so obviously ill-grounded, and at the same time of so little consequence to the cause of true piety and religion, that I shall myself venture to shew the fallacy of it.

I shall begin with observing, that there is an evident absurdity in pretending to demonstrate a matter of fact, or to prove it by any arguments a priori. Nothing is demonstrable, unless the contrary implies a contradiction. Nothing, that is distinctly conceivable, implies a contradiction. Whatever we conceive as existent, we can also conceive as non-existent. There is no being, therefore, whose non-existence implies a contradiction. Consequently there is no being, whose existence is demonstrable. I propose this argument as entirely decisive, and am willing to rest the whole controversy upon it.

It is pretended that the Deity is a necessarily existent being; and this necessity of his existence is attempted to be explained by asserting, that if we knew his whole essence or nature, we should perceive it to be as impossible for him not to exist, as for twice two not to be four. But it is evident that this can never happen, while our faculties remain the same as at present. It will still be possible for us, at any time, to conceive the non-existence of what we formerly conceived to exist; nor can the mind ever lie under a necessity of supposing any object to remain always in being; in the same manner as we lie under a necessity of always conceiving twice two to be four. The words, therefore, necessary existence, have no meaning; or, which is the same thing, none that is consistent.

But further, why may not the material universe be the necessarily existent being, according to this pretended explication of necessity? We dare not affirm that we know all the qualities of matter; and for aught we can determine, it may contain some qualities, which, were they known, would make its non-existence appear as great a contradiction as that twice two is five. I find only one argument employed to prove, that the material world is not the necessarily existent Being: and this argument is derived from the contingency both of the matter and the form of the world. "Any particle of matter," it is said, "may be conceived to be annihilated; and any form may be conceived to be altered. Such an annihilation or alteration, therefore, is not impossible." But it seems a great partiality not to perceive, that the same argument extends equally to the Deity, so far as we have any conception of him; and that the mind can at least imagine him to be non-existent, or his attributes to be altered. It must be some unknown, inconceivable qualities, which can make his non-existence appear impossible, or his attributes unalterable: and no reason can be assigned, why these qualities may not belong to matter. As they are altogether unknown and inconceivable, they can never be proved incompatible with it.

Add to this, that in tracing an eternal succession of objects, it seems absurd to enquire for a general cause or first author. How can any thing, that exists from eternity, have a cause, since that relation implies a priority in time, and a beginning of existence?

In such a chain, too, or succession of objects, each part is caused by that which preceded it, and causes that which succeeds it. Where then is the difficulty? But the WHOLE, you say, wants a cause. I answer, that the uniting of these parts into a whole, like the uniting of several distinct countries into one kingdom, or several distinct members into one body, is performed merely by an arbitrary act of the mind, and has no influence on the nature of things. Did I shew you the particular causes of each individual in a collection of twenty particles of matter, I should think it very unreasonable, should you afterwards ask me, what was the cause of the whole twenty. This is sufficiently explained in explaining the cause of the parts.

Though the reasonings which you have urged, Cleanthes, may well excuse me, said Philo, from starting any further difficulties, yet I cannot forbear insisting still upon another topic. It is observed by arithmeticians, that the products of 9, compose always either 9, or some lesser product of 9, if you add together all the characters of which any of the former products is composed. Thus, of 18, 27, 36, which are products of 9, you make 9 by adding 1 to 8, 2 to 7, 3 to 6. Thus, 369 is a product also of 9; and if you add 3, 6, and 9, you make 18, a lesser product of 9. To a superficial observer, so wonderful a regularity may be admired as the effect either of chance or design: but a skillful algebraist immediately concludes it to be the work of necessity, and demonstrates, that it must forever result from the nature of these numbers. Is it not probable, I ask, that the whole economy of the universe is conducted by a like necessity, though no human algebra can furnish a key which solves the difficulty? And instead of admiring the order of natural beings, may it not happen, that, could we penetrate into the intimate nature of bodies, we should clearly see why it was absolutely impossible they could ever admit of any other disposition? So dangerous is it to introduce this idea of necessity into the present question! and so naturally does it afford an inference directly opposite to the religious hypothesis!

But dropping all these abstractions, continued Philo, and confining ourselves to more familiar topics, I shall venture to add an observation, that the argument a priori has seldom been found very convincing, except to people of a metaphysical head, who have accustomed themselves to abstract reasoning, and who, finding from mathematics, that the understanding frequently leads to truth through obscurity, and, contrary to first appearances, have transferred the same habit of thinking to subjects where it ought not to have place. Other people, even of good sense and the best inclined to religion, feel always some deficiency in such arguments, though they are not perhaps able to explain distinctly where it lies; a certain proof that men ever did, and ever will derive their religion from other sources than from this species of reasoning.

Part X

It is my opinion, I own, replied Demea, that each man feels, in a manner, the truth of religion within his own breast, and, from a consciousness of his imbecility and misery, rather than from any reasoning, is led to seek protection from that Being, on whom he and all nature is dependent. So anxious or so tedious are even the best scenes of life, that futurity is still the object of all our hopes and fears. We incessantly look forward, and endeavor, by prayers, adoration, and sacrifice, to appease those unknown powers, whom we find, by experience, so able to afflict and oppress us. Wretched creatures that we are! what resource for us amidst the innumerable ills of life, did not religion suggest some methods of atonement, and appease those terrors with which we are incessantly agitated and tormented?

I am indeed persuaded, said Philo, that the best, and indeed the only method of bringing every one to a due sense of religion, is by just representations of the misery and wickedness of men. And for that purpose a talent of eloquence and strong imagery is more requisite than that of reasoning and argument. For is it necessary to prove what every one feels within himself? It is only necessary to make us feel it, if possible, more intimately and sensibly.

The people, indeed, replied Demea, are sufficiently convinced of this great and melancholy truth. The miseries of life; the unhappiness of man; the general corruptions of our nature; the unsatisfactory enjoyment of pleasures, riches, honors; these phrases have become almost proverbial in all languages. And who can doubt of what all men declare from their own immediate feeling and experience?

In this point, said Philo, the learned are perfectly agreed with the vulgar; and in all letters, sacred and profane, the topic of human misery has been insisted on with the most pathetic eloquence that sorrow and melancholy could inspire. The poets, who speak from sentiment, without a system, and whose testimony has therefore the more authority, abound in images of this nature. From Homer down to Dr. Young, the whole inspired tribe have ever been sensible, that no other representation of things would suit the feeling and observation of each individual.

As to authorities, replied Demea, you need not seek them. Look round this library of Cleanthes. I shall venture to affirm, that, except authors of particular sciences, such as chemistry or botany, who have no occasion to treat of human life, there is scarce one of those innumerable writers, from whom the sense of human misery has not, in some passage or other, extorted a complaint and confession of it. At least, the chance is entirely on that side; and no one author has ever, so far as I can recollect, been so extravagant as to deny it.

There you must excuse me, said Philo: Leibnitz has denied it; and is perhaps the first who ventured upon so bold and paradoxical an opinion; at least, the first who made it essential to his philosophical system.

And by being the first, replied Demea, might he not have been sensible of his error? For is this a subject in which philosophers can propose to make discoveries especially in so late an age? And can any man hope by a simple denial (for the subject scarcely admits of reasoning), to bear down the united testimony of mankind, founded on sense and consciousness?

And why should man, added he, pretend to an exemption from the lot of all other animals? The whole earth, believe me, Philo, is cursed and polluted. A perpetual war is kindled amongst all living creatures. Necessity, hunger, want, stimulate the strong and courageous: fear, anxiety, terror, agitate the weak and infirm. The first entrance into life gives anguish to the new-born infant and to its wretched parent: weakness, impotence, distress, attend each stage of that life: and it is at last finished in agony and horror.

Observe too, says Philo, the curious artifices of Nature, in order to embitter the life of every living being. The stronger prey upon the weaker, and keep them in perpetual terror and anxiety. The weaker too, in their turn, often prey upon the stronger, and vex and molest them without relaxation. Consider that innumerable race of insects, which either are bred on the body of each animal, or, flying about, infix their stings in him. These insects have others still less than themselves, which torment them. And thus on each hand, before and behind, above and below, every animal is surrounded with enemies, which incessantly seek his misery and destruction.

Man alone, said Demea, seems to be, in part, an exception to this rule. For by combination in society, he can easily master lions, tigers, and bears, whose greater strength and agility naturally enable them to prey upon him.

On the contrary, it is here chiefly, cried Philo, that the uniform and equal maxims of Nature are most apparent. Man, it is true, can, by combination, surmount all his real enemies, and become master of the whole animal creation: but does he not immediately raise up to himself imaginary enemies, the demons of his fancy, who haunt him with superstitious terrors, and blast every enjoyment of life? His pleasure, as he imagines, becomes, in their eyes, a crime: his food and repose give them umbrage and offence: his very sleep and dreams furnish new materials to anxious fear: and even death, his refuge from every other ill, presents only the dread of endless and innumerable woes. Nor does the wolf molest more the timid flock, than superstition does the anxious breast of wretched mortals.

Besides, consider, Demea: this very society, by which we surmount those wild beasts, our natural enemies; what new enemies does it not raise to us? What woe and misery does it not occasion? Man is the greatest enemy of man. Oppression, injustice, contempt, contumely, violence, sedition, war, calumny, treachery, fraud; by these they mutually torment each other; and they would soon dissolve that society which they had formed, were it not for the dread of still greater ills, which must attend their separation.

But though these external insults, said Demea, from animals, from men, from all the elements, which assault us, form a frightful catalogue of woes, they are nothing in comparison of those which arise within ourselves, from the distempered condition of our mind and body. How many lie under the lingering torment of diseases? Hear the pathetic enumeration of the great poet.

> Intestine stone and ulcer, colic-pangs,
> Demoniac frenzy, moping melancholy,
> And moon-struck madness, pining atrophy,
> Marasmus, and wide-wasting pestilence.
> Dire was the tossing, deep the groans: DESPAIR
> Tended the sick, busiest from couch to couch.
> And over them triumphant DEATH his dart
> Shook: but delay'd to strike, though oft invok'd
> With vows, as their chief good and final hope.

The disorders of the mind, continued Demea, though more secret, are not perhaps less dismal and vexatious. Remorse, shame, anguish, rage, disappointment, anxiety, fear, dejection, despair; who has ever passed through life without cruel inroads from these tormentors? How many have scarcely ever felt any better sensations? Labour and poverty, so abhorred by every one, are the certain lot of the far greater number; and those few privileged persons, who enjoy ease and opulence, never reach contentment or true felicity. All the goods of life united would not make a very happy man; but all the ills united would make a wretch indeed; and any one of them almost (and who can be free from every one?) nay often the absence of one good (and who can possess all?) is sufficient to render life ineligible.

Were a stranger to drop on a sudden into this world, I would shew him, as a specimen of its ills, an hospital full of diseases, a prison crowded with malefactors and debtors, a field of battle strewed with carcass, a fleet foundering in the ocean, a nation languishing under tyranny, famine, or pestilence. To turn the gay side of life to him and give him a notion of its pleasures; whither should I conduct him? to a ball, to an opera, to court? He might justly think, that I was only showing him a diversity of distress and sorrow.

There is no evading such striking instances, said Philo, but by apologies, which still further aggravate the charge. Why have all men, I ask, in all ages, complained incessantly of the miseries of life? . . . They have no just reason, says one: these complaints proceed only from their discontented, repining, anxious disposition. . . . And can there possibly, I reply, be a more certain foundation of misery, than such a wretched temper?

But if they were really as unhappy as they pretend, says my antagonist, why do they remain in life? . . .

Not satisfied with life, afraid of death.

This is the secret chain, say I, that holds us. We are terrified, not bribed to the continuance of our existence.

It is only a false delicacy, he may insist, which a few refined spirits indulge, and which has spread these complaints among the whole race of mankind. . . . And what is this delicacy, I ask, which you blame? Is it any thing but a greater sensibility to all the pleasures and pains of life? and if the man of a delicate, refined temper, by being so much more alive than the rest of the world, is only so much more unhappy, what judgment must we form in general of human life?

Let men remain at rest, says our adversary, and they will be easy. They are willing artificers of their own misery. . . . No! reply I: an anxious languor follows their repose; disappointment, vexation, trouble, their activity and ambition.

I can observe something like what you mention in some others, replied Cleanthes: but I confess I feel little or nothing of it in myself, and hope that it is not so common as you represent it.

If you feel not human misery yourself, cried Demea, I congratulate you on so happy a singularity. Others, seemingly the most prosperous, have not been ashamed to vent their complaints in the most melancholy strains. Let us attend to the great, the fortunate emperor, Charles V., when, tired with human grandeur, he resigned all his extensive dominions into the hands of his son. In the last harangue which he made on that memorable occasion, he publicly avowed, that the greatest prosperities which he had ever enjoyed, had been mixed with so many adversities, that he might truly say he had never enjoyed any satisfaction or contentment. But did the retired life, in which he sought for shelter, afford him any greater happiness? If we may credit his son's account, his repentance commenced the very day of his resignation.

Cicero's fortune, from small beginnings, rose to the greatest lustre and renown; yet what pathetic complaints of the ills of life do his familiar letters, as well as philosophical discourses, contain? And suitably to his own experience, he introduces Cato, the great, the fortunate Cato, protesting in his old age, that had he a new life in his offer, he would reject the present.

Ask yourself, ask any of your acquaintance, whether they would live over again the last ten or twenty years of their lives. No! but the next twenty, they say, will be better:

> And from the dregs of life, hope to receive
> What the first sprightly running could not give.

Thus at last they find (such is the greatness of human misery, it reconciles even contradictions), that they complain at once of the shortness of life, and of its vanity and sorrow.

And is it possible, Cleanthes, said Philo, that after all these reflections, and infinitely more, which might be suggested, you can still persevere in your Anthropomorphism, and assert the moral attributes of the Deity, his justice, benevolence, mercy, and rectitude, to be of the same nature with these virtues in human creatures? His power we allow is infinite: whatever he wills is executed: but neither man nor any other animal is happy: therefore he does not will their happiness. His wisdom is infinite: he is never mistaken in choosing the means to any end: but the course of Nature tends not to human or animal felicity: therefore it is not established for that purpose. Through the whole compass of human knowledge, there are no inferences more certain and infallible than these. In what respect, then, do his benevolence and mercy resemble the benevolence and mercy of men?

Epicurus's old questions are yet unanswered.

Is he willing to prevent evil, but not able? then is he impotent. Is he able, but not willing? then is he malevolent. Is he both able and willing? whence then is evil?

You ascribe, Cleanthes (and I believe justly), a purpose and intention to Nature. But what, I beseech you, is the object of that curious artifice and machinery, which she has displayed in all animals? The preservation alone of individuals, and propagation of the species. It seems enough for her purpose, if such a rank be barely upheld in the universe, without any care or concern for the happiness of the members that compose it. No resource for this purpose: no machinery, in order merely to give pleasure or ease: no fund of pure joy and contentment: no indulgence, without some want or necessity accompanying it. At least, the few phenomena of this nature are overbalanced by opposite phenomena of still greater importance.

Our sense of music, harmony, and indeed beauty of all kinds, gives satisfaction, without being absolutely necessary to the preservation and propagation of the species. But what racking pains, on the other hand, arise from gouts, gravels, megrims, toothaches, rheumatisms, where the injury to the animal machinery is either small or incurable? Mirth, laughter, play, frolic, seems gratuitous satisfactions, which have no further tendency: spleen, melancholy, discontent, superstition, are pains of the same nature. How then does the Divine benevolence display itself, in the sense of you Anthropomorphites? None but we Mystics, as you were pleased to call us, can account for this strange mixture of phenomena, by deriving it from attributes, infinitely perfect, but incomprehensible.

And have you at last, said Cleanthes, smiling, betrayed your intentions, Philo? Your long agreement with Demea did indeed a little surprise me; but I find you were all the while erecting a concealed battery against me. And I must confess, that you have now fallen upon a subject worthy of your noble spirit of opposition and controversy. If you can make out the present point, and prove mankind to be unhappy or corrupted, there is an end at once of all religion. For to what purpose establish the natural attributes of the Deity, while the moral are still doubtful and uncertain?

You take umbrage very easily, replied Demea, at opinions the most innocent, and the most generally received, even amongst the religious and devout themselves: and nothing can be more surprising than to find a topic like this, concerning the wickedness and misery of man, charged with no less than Atheism and profaneness. Have not all pious divines and preachers, who have indulged their rhetoric on so fertile a subject; have they not easily, I say, given a solution of any difficulties which may attend it? This world is but a point in comparison of the universe; this life but a moment in comparison of eternity. The present evil phenomena, therefore, are rectified in other regions, and in some future period of existence. And the eyes of men, being then opened to larger views of things, see the whole connexion of general laws; and trace with adoration, the benevolence and rectitude of the Deity, through all the mazes and intricacies of his providence.

No! replied Cleanthes, No! These arbitrary suppositions can never be admitted, contrary to matter of fact, visible and uncontroverted. Whence can any cause be known but from its known effects? Whence can any hypothesis be proved but from the apparent phenomena? To establish one hypothesis upon another, is building entirely in the air; and the utmost we ever attain, by these conjectures and fictions, is to ascertain the bare possibility of our opinion; but never can we, upon such terms, establish its reality.

The only method of supporting Divine benevolence, and it is what I willingly embrace, is to deny absolutely the misery and wickedness of man. Your representations are exaggerated; your melancholy views mostly fictitious; your inferences contrary to fact and experience. Health is more common than sickness; pleasure than pain; happiness than misery. And for one vexation which we meet with, we attain, upon computation, a hundred enjoyments.

Admitting your position, replied Philo, which yet is extremely doubtful, you must at the same time allow, that if pain be less frequent than pleasure, it is infinitely more violent and durable. One hour of it is often able to outweigh a day, a week, a month of our common insipid enjoyments; and how many days, weeks, and months, are passed by several in the most acute torments? Pleasure, scarcely in one instance, is ever able to reach ecstasy and rapture; and in no one instance can it continue for any time at its highest pitch and altitude. The spirits evaporate, the nerves relax, the fabric is disordered, and the enjoyment quickly degenerates into fatigue and uneasiness. But pain often, good God, how often! rises to torture and agony; and the longer it continues, it becomes still more genuine agony and torture. Patience is exhausted, courage languishes, melancholy seizes us, and nothing terminates our misery but the removal of its cause, or another event, which is the sole cure of all evil, but which, from our natural folly, we regard with still greater horror and consternation.

But not to insist upon these topics, continued Philo, though most obvious, certain, and important; I must use the freedom to admonish you, Cleanthes, that you have put the controversy upon a most dangerous issue, and are unawares introducing a total scepticism into the most essential articles of natural and revealed theology. What! no method of fixing a just foundation for religion, unless we allow the happiness of human life, and maintain a continued existence even in this world, with all our present pains, infirmities, vexations, and follies, to be eligible and desirable! But this is contrary to every one's feeling and experience: it is contrary to an authority so established as nothing can subvert. No decisive proofs can ever be produced against this authority; nor is it possible for you to compute, estimate, and compare, all the pains and all the pleasures in the lives of all men and of all animals: and thus, by your resting the whole system of religion on a point, which, from its very nature, must for ever be uncertain, you tacitly confess, that system is equally uncertain.

But allowing you what never will be believed, at least what you never possibly can prove, that animal, or at least human happiness, in this life, exceeds its misery, you have yet done nothing: for this is not, by any means, what we expect from infinite power, infinite wisdom, and infinite goodness. Why is there any misery at all in the world? Not by chance surely. From some cause then. Is it from the intention of the Deity? But he is perfectly benevolent. Is it contrary to his intention? But he is almighty. Nothing can shake the solidity of this reasoning, so short, so clear, so decisive; except we assert, that these subjects exceed all human capacity, and that our common measures of truth and falsehood are not applicable to them; a topic which I have all along insisted on, but which you have, from the beginning, rejected with scorn and indignation.

But I will be contented to retire still from this entrenchment, for I deny that you can ever force me in it. I will allow, that pain or misery in man is compatible with infinite power and goodness in the Deity, even in your sense of these attributes: what are you advanced by all these concessions? A mere possible compatibility is not sufficient. You must prove these pure, unmixed, and uncontrollable attributes from the present mixed and confused phenomena, and from these alone. A hopeful undertaking! Were the phenomena ever so pure and unmixed, yet being finite, they would be insufficient for that purpose. How much more, where they are also so jarring and discordant!

Here, Cleanthes, I find myself at ease in my argument. Here I triumph. Formerly, when we argued concerning the natural attributes of intelligence and design, I needed all my sceptical and metaphysical subtilty to elude your grasp. In many views of the universe and of its parts, particularly the latter, the beauty and fitness of final causes strike us with such irresistible force, that all objections appear (what I believe they really are) mere cavils and sophisms; nor can we then imagine how it was ever possible for us to repose any weight on them. But there is no view of human life, or of the condition of mankind, from which, without the greatest violence, we can infer the moral attributes, or learn that infinite benevolence, conjoined with infinite power and infinite wisdom, which we must discover by the eyes of faith alone. It is your turn now to tug the laboring oar, and to support your philosophical subtilties against the dictates of plain reason and experience.

Part XI

I scruple not to allow, said Cleanthes, that I have been apt to suspect the frequent repetition of the word infinite, which we meet with in all theological writers, to savor more of panegyric than of philosophy; and that any purposes of reasoning, and even of religion, would be better served, were we to rest contented with more accurate and more moderate expressions. The terms, admirable, excellent, superlatively great, wise, and holy; these sufficiently fill the imaginations of men; and any thing beyond, besides that it leads into absurdities, has no influence on the affections or sentiments. Thus, in the present subject, if we abandon all human analogy, as seems your intention, Demea, I am afraid we abandon all religion, and retain no conception of the great object of our adoration. If we preserve human analogy, we must for ever find it impossible to reconcile any mixture of evil in the universe with infinite attributes; much less can we ever prove the latter from the former. But supposing the Author of Nature to be finitely perfect, though far exceeding mankind, a satisfactory account may then be given of natural and moral evil, and every untoward phenomenon be explained and adjusted. A less evil may then be chosen, in order to avoid a greater; inconveniences be submitted to, in order to reach a desirable end; and in a word, benevolence, regulated by wisdom, and limited by necessity, may produce just such a world as the present. You, Philo, who are so prompt at starting views, and reflections, and analogies, I would gladly hear, at length, without interruption, your opinion of this new theory; and if it deserve our attention, we may afterwards, at more leisure, reduce it into form.

My sentiments, replied Philo, are not worth being made a mystery of; and therefore, without any ceremony, I shall deliver what occurs to me with regard to the present subject. It must, I think, be allowed, that if a very limited intelligence, whom we shall suppose utterly unacquainted with the universe, were assured, that it were the production of a very good, wise, and powerful Being, however finite, he would, from his conjectures, form beforehand a different notion of it from what we find it to be by experience; nor would he ever imagine, merely from these attributes of the cause, of which he is informed, that the effect could be so full of vice and misery and disorder, as it appears in this life. Supposing now, that this person were brought into the world, still assured that it was the workmanship of such a sublime and benevolent Being; he might, perhaps, be surprised at the disappointment; but would never retract his former belief, if founded on any very solid argument; since such a limited intelligence must be sensible of his own blindness and ignorance, and must allow, that there may be many solutions of those phenomena, which will for ever escape his comprehension. But supposing, which is the real case with regard to man, that this creature is not antecedently convinced of a supreme intelligence, benevolent and powerful, but is left to gather such a belief from the appearances of things; this entirely alters the case, nor will he ever find any reason for such a conclusion. He may be fully convinced of the narrow limits of his understanding; but this will not help him in forming an inference concerning the goodness of superior powers, since he must form that inference from what he knows, not from what he is ignorant of. The more you exaggerate his weakness and ignorance, the more diffident you render him, and give him the greater suspicion that such subjects are beyond the reach of his faculties. You are obliged, therefore, to reason with him merely from the known phenomena, and to drop every arbitrary supposition or conjecture.

Did I shew you a house or palace, where there was not one apartment convenient or agreeable; where the windows, doors, fires, passages, stairs, and the whole economy of the building, were the source of noise, confusion, fatigue, darkness, and the extremes of heat and cold; you would certainly blame the contrivance, without any further examination. The architect would in vain display his subtilty, and prove to you, that if this door or that window were altered, greater ills would ensue. What he says may be strictly true: the alteration of one particular, while the other parts of the building remain, may only augment the inconveniences. But still you would assert in general, that, if the architect had skill and good intentions, he might have formed such a plan of the whole, and might have adjusted the parts in such a manner, as would have remedied all or most of these inconveniences. His ignorance, or even your own ignorance of such a plan, will never convince you of the impossibility of it. If you find any inconveniences and deformities in the building, you will always, without entering into any detail, condemn the architect.

In short, I repeat the question: Is the world, considered in general, and as it appears to us in this life, different from what a man, or such a limited being, would, beforehand, expect from a very powerful, wise, and benevolent Deity? It must be strange prejudice to assert the contrary. And from thence I conclude, that however consistent the world may be, allowing certain suppositions and conjectures, with the idea of such a Deity, it can never afford us an inference concerning his existence. The consistence is not absolutely denied, only the inference. Conjectures, especially where infinity is excluded from the Divine attributes, may perhaps be sufficient to prove a consistence, but can never be foundations for any inference.

There seems to be four circumstances, on which depend all, or the greatest part of the ills, that molest sensible creatures; and it is not impossible but all these circumstances may be necessary and unavoidable. We know so little beyond common life, or even of common life, that, with regard to the economy of a universe, there is no conjecture, however wild, which may not be just; nor any one, however plausible, which may not be erroneous. All that belongs to human understanding, in this deep ignorance and obscurity, is to be sceptical, or at least cautious, and not to admit of any hypothesis whatever, much less of any which is supported by no appearance of probability. Now, this I assert to be the case with regard to all the causes of evil, and the circumstances on which it depends. None of them appear to human reason in the least degree necessary or unavoidable; nor can we suppose them such, without the utmost license of imagination.

The first circumstance which introduces evil, is that contrivance or economy of the animal creation, by which pains, as well as pleasures, are employed to excite all creatures to action, and make them vigilant in the great work of self-preservation. Now pleasure alone, in its various degrees, seems to human understanding sufficient for this purpose. All animals might be constantly in a state of enjoyment: but when urged by any of the necessities of nature, such as thirst, hunger, weariness; instead of pain, they might feel a diminution of pleasure, by which they might be prompted to seek that object which is necessary to their subsistence. Men pursue pleasure as eagerly as they avoid pain; at least they might have been so constituted. It seems, therefore, plainly possible to carry on the business of life without any pain. Why then is any animal ever rendered susceptible of such a sensation? If animals can be free from it an hour, they might enjoy a perpetual exemption from it; and it required as particular a contrivance of their organs to produce that feeling, as to endow them with sight, hearing, or any of the senses. Shall we conjecture, that such a contrivance was necessary, without any appearance of reason? and shall we build on that conjecture as on the most certain truth?

But a capacity of pain would not alone produce pain, were it not for the second circumstance, viz. the conducting of the world by general laws; and this seems nowise necessary to a very perfect Being. It is true, if every thing were conducted by particular volitions, the course of nature would be perpetually broken, and no man could employ his reason in the conduct of life. But might not other particular volitions remedy this inconvenience? In short, might not the Deity exterminate all ill, wherever it were to be found; and produce all good, without any preparation, or long progress of causes and effects?

Besides, we must consider, that, according to the present economy of the world, the course of nature, though supposed exactly regular, yet to us appears not so, and many events are uncertain, and many disappoint our expectations. Health and sickness, calm and tempest, with an infinite number of other accidents, whose causes are unknown and variable, have a great influence both on the fortunes of particular persons and on the prosperity of public societies; and indeed all human life, in a manner, depends on such accidents. A being, therefore, who knows the secret springs of the universe, might easily, by particular volitions, turn all these accidents to the good of mankind, and render the whole world happy, without discovering himself in any operation. A fleet, whose purposes were salutary to society, might always meet with a fair wind. Good princes enjoy sound health and long life. Persons born to power and authority, be framed with good tempers and virtuous dispositions. A few such events as these, regularly and wisely conducted, would change the face of the world; and yet would no more seem to disturb the course of nature, or confound human conduct, than the present economy of things, where the causes are secret, and variable, and compounded. Some small touches given to Caligula's brain in his infancy, might have converted him into a Trajan. One wave, a little higher than the rest, by burying Caesar and his fortune in the bottom of the ocean, might have restored liberty to a considerable part of mankind. There may, for aught we know, be good reasons why Providence interposes not in this manner; but they are unknown to us; and though the mere supposition, that such reasons exist, may be sufficient to save the conclusion concerning the Divine attributes, yet surely it can never be sufficient to establish that conclusion.

If every thing in the universe be conducted by general laws, and if animals be rendered susceptible of pain, it scarcely seems possible but some ill must arise in the various shocks of matter, and the various concurrence and opposition of general laws; but this ill would be very rare, were it not for the third circumstance, which I proposed to mention, viz. the great frugality with which all powers and faculties are distributed to every particular being. So well adjusted are the organs and capacities of all animals, and so well fitted to their preservation, that, as far as history or tradition reaches, there appears not to be any single species which has yet been extinguished in the universe. Every animal has the requisite endowments; but these endowments are bestowed with so scrupulous an economy, that any considerable diminution must entirely destroy the creature. Wherever one power is increased, there is a proportional abatement in the others. Animals which excel in swiftness are commonly defective in force. Those which possess both are either imperfect in some of their senses, or are oppressed with the most craving wants. The human species, whose chief excellency is reason and sagacity, is of all others the most necessitous, and the most deficient in bodily advantages; without clothes, without arms, without food, without lodging, without any convenience of life, except what they owe to their own skill and industry. In short, nature seems to have formed an exact calculation of the necessities of her creatures; and, like a rigid master, has afforded them little more powers or endowments than what are strictly sufficient to supply those necessities. An indulgent parent would have bestowed a large stock, in order to guard against accidents, and secure the happiness and welfare of the creature in the most unfortunate concurrence of circumstances. Every course of life would not have been so surrounded with precipices, that the least departure from the true path, by mistake or necessity, must involve us in misery and ruin. Some reserve, some fund, would have been provided to insure happiness; nor would the powers and the necessities have been adjusted with so rigid an economy. The Author of Nature is inconceivably powerful: his force is supposed great, if not altogether inexhaustible: nor is there any reason, as far as we can judge, to make him observe this strict frugality in his dealings with his creatures. It would have been better, were his power extremely limited, to have created fewer animals, and to have endowed these with more faculties for their happiness and preservation. A builder is never esteemed prudent, who undertakes a plan beyond what his stock will enable him to finish.

In order to cure most of the ills of human life, I require not that man should have the wings of the eagle, the swiftness of the stag, the force of the ox, the arms of the lion, the scales of the crocodile or rhinoceros; much less do I demand the sagacity of an angel or cherubim. I am contented to take an increase in one single power or faculty of his soul. Let him be endowed with a greater propensity to industry and labour; a more vigorous spring and activity of mind; a more constant bent to business and application. Let the whole species possess naturally an equal diligence with that which many individuals are able to attain by habit and reflection; and the most beneficial consequences, without any alloy of ill, is the immediate and necessary result of this endowment. Almost all the moral, as well as natural evils of human life, arise from idleness; and were our species, by the original constitution of their frame, exempt from this vice or infirmity, the perfect cultivation of land, the improvement of arts and manufactures, the exact execution of every office and duty, immediately follow; and men at once may fully reach that state of society, which is so imperfectly attained by the best regulated government. But as industry is a power, and the most valuable of any, Nature seems determined, suitably to her usual maxims, to bestow it on men with a very sparing hand; and rather to punish him severely for his deficiency in it, than to reward him for his attainments. She has so contrived his frame, that nothing but the most violent necessity can oblige him to labour; and she employs all his other wants to overcome, at least in part, the want of diligence, and to endow him with some share of a faculty of which she has thought fit naturally to bereave him. Here our demands may be allowed very humble, and therefore the more reasonable. If we required the endowments of superior penetration and judgment, of a more delicate taste of beauty, of a nicer sensibility to benevolence and friendship; we might be told, that we impiously pretend to break the order of Nature; that we want to exalt ourselves into a higher rank of being; that the presents which we require, not being suitable to our state and condition, would only be pernicious to us. But it is hard; I dare to repeat it, it is hard, that being placed in a world so full of wants and necessities, where almost every being and element is either our foe or refuses its assistance; we should also have our own temper to struggle with, and should be deprived of that faculty which can alone fence against these multiplied evils.

The fourth circumstance, whence arises the misery and ill of the universe, is the inaccurate workmanship of all the springs and principles of the great machine of nature. It must be acknowledged, that there are few parts of the universe, which seem not to serve some purpose, and whose removal would not produce a visible defect and disorder in the whole. The parts hang all together; nor can one be touched without affecting the rest, in a greater or less degree. But at the same time, it must be observed, that none of these parts or principles, however useful, are so accurately adjusted, as to keep precisely within those bounds in which their utility consists; but they are, all of them, apt, on every occasion, to run into the one extreme or the other. One would imagine, that this grand production had not received the last hand of the maker; so little finished is every part, and so coarse are the strokes with which it is executed. Thus, the winds are requisite to convey the vapors along the surface of the globe, and to assist men in navigation: but how oft, rising up to tempests and hurricanes, do they become pernicious? Rains are necessary to nourish all the plants and animals of the earth: but how often are they defective? how often excessive? Heat is requisite to all life and vegetation; but is not always found in the due proportion. On the mixture and secretion of the humors and juices of the body depend the health and prosperity of the animal: but the parts perform not regularly their proper function. What more useful than all the passions of the mind, ambition, vanity, love, anger? But how oft do they break their bounds, and cause the greatest convulsions in society? There is nothing so advantageous in the universe, but what frequently becomes pernicious, by its excess or defect; nor has Nature guarded, with the requisite accuracy, against all disorder or confusion. The irregularity is never perhaps so great as to destroy any species; but is often sufficient to involve the individuals in ruin and misery.

On the concurrence, then, of these four circumstances, does all or the greatest part of natural evil depend. Were all living creatures incapable of pain, or were the world administered by particular volitions, evil never could have found access into the universe: and were animals endowed with a large stock of powers and faculties, beyond what strict necessity requires; or were the several springs and principles of the universe so accurately framed as to preserve always the just temperament and medium; there must have been very little ill in comparison of what we feel at present. What then shall we pronounce on this occasion? Shall we say that these circumstances are not necessary, and that they might easily have been altered in the contrivance of the universe? This decision seems too presumptuous for creatures so blind and ignorant. Let us be more modest in our conclusions. Let us allow, that, if the goodness of the Deity (I mean a goodness like the human) could be established on any tolerable reasons a priori, these phenomena, however untoward, would not be sufficient to subvert that principle; but might easily, in some unknown manner, be reconcilable to it. But let us still assert, that as this goodness is not antecedently established, but must be inferred from the phenomena, there can be no grounds for such an inference, while there are so many ills in the universe, and while these ills might so easily have been remedied, as far as human understanding can be allowed to judge on such a subject. I am Sceptic enough to allow, that the bad appearances, notwithstanding all my reasonings, may be compatible with such attributes as you suppose; but surely they can never prove these attributes. Such a conclusion cannot result from Scepticism, but must arise from the phenomena, and from our confidence in the reasonings which we deduce from these phenomena.

Look round this universe. What an immense profusion of beings, animated and organized, sensible and active! You admire this prodigious variety and fecundity. But inspect a little more narrowly these living existences, the only beings worth regarding. How hostile and destructive to each other! How insufficient all of them for their own happiness! How contemptible or odious to the spectator! The whole presents nothing but the idea of a blind Nature, impregnated by a great vivifying principle, and pouring forth from her lap, without discernment or parental care, her maimed and abortive children!

Here the Manichaean system occurs as a proper hypothesis to solve the difficulty: and no doubt, in some respects, it is very specious, and has more probability than the common hypothesis, by giving a plausible account of the strange mixture of good and ill which appears in life. But if we consider, on the other hand, the perfect uniformity and agreement of the parts of the universe, we shall not discover in it any marks of the combat of a malevolent with a benevolent being. There is indeed an opposition of pains and pleasures in the feelings of sensible creatures: but are not all the operations of Nature carried on by an opposition of principles, of hot and cold, moist and dry, light and heavy? The true conclusion is, that the original Source of all things is entirely indifferent to all these principles; and has no more regard to good above ill, than to heat above cold, or to drought above moisture, or to light above heavy.

There may four hypotheses be framed concerning the first causes of the universe: that they are endowed with perfect goodness; that they have perfect malice; that they are opposite, and have both goodness and malice; that they have neither goodness nor malice. Mixed phenomena can never prove the two former unmixed principles; and the uniformity and steadiness of general laws seem to oppose the third. The fourth, therefore, seems by far the most probable.

What I have said concerning natural evil will apply to moral, with little or no variation; and we have no more reason to infer, that the rectitude of the Supreme Being resembles human rectitude, than that his benevolence resembles the human. Nay, it will be thought, that we have still greater cause to exclude from him moral sentiments, such as we feel them; since moral evil, in the opinion of many, is much more predominant above moral good than natural evil above natural good.

But even though this should not be allowed, and though the virtue which is in mankind should be acknowledged much superior to the vice, yet so long as there is any vice at all in the universe, it will very much puzzle you Anthropomorphites, how to account for it. You must assign a cause for it, without having recourse to the first cause. But as every effect must have a cause, and that cause another, you must either carry on the progression in infinitum, or rest on that original principle, who is the ultimate cause of all things. . . .

Hold! hold! cried Demea: whither does your imagination hurry you? I joined in alliance with you, in order to prove the incomprehensible nature of the Divine Being, and refute the principles of Cleanthes, who would measure every thing by human rule and standard. But I now find you running into all the topics of the greatest libertines and infidels, and betraying that holy cause which you seemingly espoused. Are you secretly, then, a more dangerous enemy than Cleanthes himself?

And are you so late in perceiving it? replied Cleanthes. Believe me, Demea, your friend Philo, from the beginning, has been amusing himself at both our expense; and it must be confessed, that the injudicious reasoning of our vulgar theology has given him but too just a handle of ridicule. The total infirmity of human reason, the absolute incomprehensibility of the Divine Nature, the great and universal misery, and still greater wickedness of men; these are strange topics, surely, to be so fondly cherished by orthodox divines and doctors. In ages of stupidity and ignorance, indeed, these principles may safely be espoused; and perhaps no views of things are more proper to promote superstition, than such as encourage the blind amazement, the diffidence, and melancholy of mankind. But at present. . . . .

Blame not so much, interposed Philo, the ignorance of these reverend gentlemen. They know how to change their style with the times. Formerly it was a most popular theological topic to maintain, that human life was vanity and misery, and to exaggerate all the ills and pains which are incident to men. But of late years, divines, we find, begin to retract this position; and maintain, though still with some hesitation, that there are more goods than evils, more pleasures than pains, even in this life. When religion stood entirely upon temper and education, it was thought proper to encourage melancholy; as indeed mankind never have recourse to superior powers so readily as in that disposition. But as men have now learned to form principles, and to draw consequences, it is necessary to change the batteries, and to make use of such arguments as will endure at least some scrutiny and examination. This variation is the same (and from the same causes) with that which I formerly remarked with regard to Scepticism.

Thus Philo continued to the last his spirit of opposition, and his censure of established opinions. But I could observe that Demea did not at all relish the latter part of the discourse; and he took occasion soon after, on some presence or other, to leave the company.

Part XII

After Demea's departure, Cleanthes and Philo continued the conversation in the following manner. Our friend, I am afraid, said Cleanthes, will have little inclination to revive this topic of discourse, while you are in company; and to tell truth, Philo, I should rather wish to reason with either of you apart on a subject so sublime and interesting. Your spirit of controversy, joined to your abhorrence of vulgar superstition, carries you to strange lengths, when engaged in an argument; and there is nothing so sacred and venerable, even in your own eyes, which you spare on that occasion.

I must confess, replied Philo, that I am less cautious on the subject of Natural Religion than on any other; both because I know that I can never, on that head, corrupt the principles of any man of common sense; and because no one, I am confident, in whose eyes I appear a man of common sense, will ever mistake my intentions. You, in particular, Cleanthes, with whom I live in unreserved intimacy; you are sensible, that notwithstanding the freedom of my conversation, and my love of singular arguments, no one has a deeper sense of religion impressed on his mind, or pays more profound adoration to the Divine Being, as he discovers himself to reason, in the inexplicable contrivance and artifice of nature. A purpose, an intention, a design, strikes every where the most careless, the most stupid thinker; and no man can be so hardened in absurd systems, as at all times to reject it. That Nature does nothing in vain, is a maxim established in all the schools, merely from the contemplation of the works of Nature, without any religious purpose; and, from a firm conviction of its truth, an anatomist, who had observed a new organ or canal, would never be satisfied till he had also discovered its use and intention. One great foundation of the Copernican system is the maxim, That Nature acts by the simplest methods, and chooses the most proper means to any end; and astronomers often, without thinking of it, lay this strong foundation of piety and religion. The same thing is observable in other parts of philosophy: and thus all the sciences almost lead us insensibly to acknowledge a first intelligent Author; and their authority is often so much the greater, as they do not directly profess that intention.

It is with pleasure I hear Galen reason concerning the structure of the human body. The anatomy of a man, says he, discovers above six hundred different muscles; and whoever duly considers these, will find, that, in each of them, Nature must have adjusted at least ten different circumstances, in order to attain the end which she proposed; proper figure, just magnitude, right disposition of the several ends, upper and lower position of the whole, the due insertion of the several nerves, veins, and arteries: so that, in the muscles alone, above six thousand several views and intentions must have been formed and executed. The bones he calculates to be two hundred and eighty-four: the distinct purposes aimed at in the structure of each, above forty. What a prodigious display of artifice, even in these simple and homogeneous parts! But if we consider the skin, ligaments, vessels, glandules, humors, the several limbs and members of the body; how must our astonishment rise upon us, in proportion to the number and intricacy of the parts so artificially adjusted! The further we advance in these researches, we discover new scenes of art and wisdom: but descry still, at a distance, further scenes beyond our reach; in the fine internal structure of the parts, in the economy of the brain, in the fabric of the seminal vessels. All these artifices are repeated in every different species of animal, with wonderful variety, and with exact propriety, suited to the different intentions of Nature in framing each species. And if the infidelity of Galen, even when these natural sciences were still imperfect, could not withstand such striking appearances, to what pitch of pertinacious obstinacy must a philosopher in this age have attained, who can now doubt of a Supreme Intelligence!

Could I meet with one of this species (who, I thank God, are very rare), I would ask him: Supposing there were a God, who did not discover himself immediately to our senses, were it possible for him to give stronger proofs of his existence, than what appear on the whole face of Nature? What indeed could such a Divine Being do, but copy the present economy of things; render many of his artifices so plain, that no stupidity could mistake them; afford glimpses of still greater artifices, which demonstrate his prodigious superiority above our narrow apprehensions; and conceal altogether a great many from such imperfect creatures? Now, according to all rules of just reasoning, every fact must pass for undisputed, when it is supported by all the arguments which its nature admits of; even though these arguments be not in themselves, very numerous or forcible: how much more, in the present case, where no human imagination can compute their number, and no understanding estimate their cogency!

I shall further add, said Cleanthes, to what you have so well urged, that one great advantage of the principle of Theism, is, that it is the only system of cosmogony which can be rendered intelligible and complete, and yet can throughout preserve a strong analogy to what we every day see and experience in the world. The comparison of the universe to a machine of human contrivance, is so obvious and natural, and is justified by so many instances of order and design in Nature, that it must immediately strike all unprejudiced apprehensions, and procure universal approbation. Whoever attempts to weaken this theory, cannot pretend to succeed by establishing in its place any other that is precise and determinate: it is sufficient for him if he start doubts and difficulties; and by remote and abstract views of things, reach that suspense of judgment, which is here the utmost boundary of his wishes. But, besides that this state of mind is in itself unsatisfactory, it can never be steadily maintained against such striking appearances as continually engage us into the religious hypothesis. A false, absurd system, human nature, from the force of prejudice, is capable of adhering to with obstinacy and perseverance: but no system at all, in opposition to theory supported by strong and obvious reason, by natural propensity, and by early education, I think it absolutely impossible to maintain or defend.

So little, replied Philo, do I esteem this suspense of judgment in the present case to be possible, that I am apt to suspect there enters somewhat of a dispute of words into this controversy, more than is usually imagined. That the works of Nature bear a great analogy to the productions of art, is evident; and according to all the rules of good reasoning, we ought to infer, if we argue at all concerning them, that their causes have a proportional analogy. But as there are also considerable differences, we have reason to suppose a proportional difference in the causes; and in particular, ought to attribute a much higher degree of power and energy to the supreme cause, than any we have ever observed in mankind. Here then the existence of a DEITY is plainly ascertained by reason: and if we make it a question, whether, on account of these analogies, we can properly call him a mind or intelligence, notwithstanding the vast difference which may reasonably be supposed between him and human minds; what is this but a mere verbal controversy? No man can deny the analogies between the effects: to restrain ourselves from enquiring concerning the causes is scarcely possible. From this enquiry, the legitimate conclusion is, that the causes have also an analogy: and if we are not contented with calling the first and supreme cause a GOD or DEITY, but desire to vary the expression; what can we call him but MIND or THOUGHT, to which he is justly supposed to bear a considerable resemblance?

All men of sound reason are disgusted with verbal disputes, which abound so much in philosophical and theological enquiries; and it is found, that the only remedy for this abuse, must arise from clear definitions, from the precision of those ideas which enter into any argument, and from the strict and uniform use of those terms which are employed. But there is a species of controversy, which, from the very nature of language and of human ideas, is involved in perpetual ambiguity, and can never, by any precaution or any definitions, be able to reach a reasonable certainty or precision. These are the controversies concerning the degrees of any quality or circumstance. Men may argue to all eternity, whether Hannibal be a great, or a very great, or a superlatively great man, what degree of beauty Cleopatra possessed, what epithet of praise Livy or Thucydides is entitled to, without bringing the controversy to any determination. The disputants may here agree in their sense, and differ in the terms, or vice versa; yet never be able to define their terms, so as to enter into each other's meaning: because the degrees of these qualities are not, like quantity or number, susceptible of any exact mensuration, which may be the standard in the controversy. That the dispute concerning Theism is of this nature, and consequently is merely verbal, or perhaps, if possible, still more incurably ambiguous, will appear upon the slightest enquiry. I ask the Theist, if he does not allow, that there is a great and immeasurable, because incomprehensible difference between the human and the divine mind: the more pious he is, the more readily will he assent to the affirmative, and the more will he be disposed to magnify the difference: he will even assert, that the difference is of a nature which cannot be too much magnified. I next turn to the Atheist, who, I assert, is only nominally so, and can never possibly be in earnest; and I ask him, whether, from the coherence and apparent sympathy in all the parts of this world, there be not a certain degree of analogy among all the operations of Nature, in every situation and in every age; whether the rotting of a turnip, the generation of an animal, and the structure of human thought, be not energies that probably bear some remote analogy to each other: it is impossible he can deny it: he will readily acknowledge it. Having obtained this concession, I push him still further in his retreat; and I ask him, if it be not probable, that the principle which first arranged, and still maintains order in this universe, bears not also some remote inconceivable analogy to the other operations of nature, and, among the rest, to the economy of human mind and thought. However reluctant, he must give his assent. Where then, cry I to both these antagonists, is the subject of your dispute? The Theist allows, that the original intelligence is very different from human reason: the Atheist allows, that the original principle of order bears some remote analogy to it. Will you quarrel, gentlemen, about the degrees, and enter into a controversy, which admits not of any precise meaning, nor consequently of any determination? If you should be so obstinate, I should not be surprised to find you insensibly change sides; while the Theist, on the one hand, exaggerates the dissimilarity between the Supreme Being, and frail, imperfect, variable, fleeting, and mortal creatures; and the Atheist, on the other, magnifies the analogy among all the operations of Nature, in every period, every situation, and every position. Consider then, where the real point of controversy lies; and if you cannot lay aside your disputes, endeavor, at least, to cure yourselves of your animosity.

And here I must also acknowledge, Cleanthes, that as the works of Nature have a much greater analogy to the effects of our art and contrivance, than to those of our benevolence and justice, we have reason to infer, that the natural attributes of the Deity have a greater resemblance to those of men, than his moral have to human virtues. But what is the consequence? Nothing but this, that the moral qualities of man are more defective in their kind than his natural abilities. For, as the Supreme Being is allowed to be absolutely and entirely perfect, whatever differs most from him, departs the furthest from the supreme standard of rectitude and perfection.

These, Cleanthes, are my unfeigned sentiments on this subject; and these sentiments, you know, I have ever cherished and maintained. But in proportion to my veneration for true religion, is my abhorrence of vulgar superstitions; and I indulge a peculiar pleasure, I confess, in pushing such principles, sometimes into absurdity, sometimes into impiety. And you are sensible, that all bigots, notwithstanding their great aversion to the latter above the former, are commonly equally guilty of both.

My inclination, replied Cleanthes, lies, I own, a contrary way. Religion, however corrupted, is still better than no religion at all. The doctrine of a future state is so strong and necessary a security to morals, that we never ought to abandon or neglect it. For if finite and temporary rewards and punishments have so great an effect, as we daily find; how much greater must be expected from such as are infinite and eternal?

How happens it then, said Philo, if vulgar superstition be so salutary to society, that all history abounds so much with accounts of its pernicious consequences on public affairs? Factions, civil wars, persecutions, subversions of government, oppression, slavery; these are the dismal consequences which always attend its prevalency over the minds of men. If the religious spirit be ever mentioned in any historical narration, we are sure to meet afterwards with a detail of the miseries which attend it. And no period of time can be happier or more prosperous, than those in which it is never regarded or heard of.

The reason of this observation, replied Cleanthes, is obvious. The proper office of religion is to regulate the heart of men, humanize their conduct, infuse the spirit of temperance, order, and obedience; and as its operation is silent, and only enforces the motives of morality and justice, it is in danger of being overlooked, and confounded with these other motives. When it distinguishes itself, and acts as a separate principle over men, it has departed from its proper sphere, and has become only a cover to faction and ambition.

And so will all religion, said Philo, except the philosophical and rational kind. Your reasonings are more easily eluded than my facts. The inference is not just, because finite and temporary rewards and punishments have so great influence, that therefore such as are infinite and eternal must have so much greater. Consider, I beseech you, the attachment which we have to present things, and the little concern which we discover for objects so remote and uncertain. When divines are declaiming against the common behavior and conduct of the world, they always represent this principle as the strongest imaginable (which indeed it is); and describe almost all human kind as lying under the influence of it, and sunk into the deepest lethargy and unconcern about their religious interests. Yet these same divines, when they refute their speculative antagonists, suppose the motives of religion to be so powerful, that, without them, it were impossible for civil society to subsist; nor are they ashamed of so palpable a contradiction. It is certain, from experience, that the smallest grain of natural honesty and benevolence has more effect on men's conduct, than the most pompous views suggested by theological theories and systems. A man's natural inclination works incessantly upon him; it is for ever present to the mind, and mingles itself with every view and consideration: whereas religious motives, where they act at all, operate only by starts and bounds; and it is scarcely possible for them to become altogether habitual to the mind. The force of the greatest gravity, say the philosophers, is infinitely small, in comparison of that of the least impulse: yet it is certain, that the smallest gravity will, in the end, prevail above a great impulse; because no strokes or blows can be repeated with such constancy as attraction and gravitation.

Another advantage of inclination: it engages on its side all the wit and ingenuity of the mind; and when set in opposition to religious principles, seeks every method and art of eluding them: in which it is almost always successful. Who can explain the heart of man, or account for those strange salvos and excuses, with which people satisfy themselves, when they follow their inclinations in opposition to their religious duty? This is well understood in the world; and none but fools ever repose less trust in a man, because they hear, that from study and philosophy, he has entertained some speculative doubts with regard to theological subjects. And when we have to do with a man, who makes a great profession of religion and devotion, has this any other effect upon several, who pass for prudent, than to put them on their guard, lest they be cheated and deceived by him?

We must further consider, that philosophers, who cultivate reason and reflection, stand less in need of such motives to keep them under the restraint of morals; and that the vulgar, who alone may need them, are utterly incapable of so pure a religion as represents the Deity to be pleased with nothing but virtue in human behavior. The recommendations to the Divinity are generally supposed to be either frivolous observances, or rapturous ecstasies, or a bigoted credulity. We need not run back into antiquity, or wander into remote regions, to find instances of this degeneracy. Amongst ourselves, some have been guilty of that atrociousness, unknown to the Egyptian and Grecian superstitions, of declaiming in express terms, against morality; and representing it as a sure forfeiture of the Divine favour, if the least trust or reliance be laid upon it.

But even though superstition or enthusiasm should not put itself in direct opposition to morality; the very diverting of the attention, the raising up a new and frivolous species of merit, the preposterous distribution which it makes of praise and blame, must have the most pernicious consequences, and weaken extremely men's attachment to the natural motives of justice and humanity.

Such a principle of action likewise, not being any of the familiar motives of human conduct, acts only by intervals on the temper; and must be roused by continual efforts, in order to render the pious zealot satisfied with his own conduct, and make him fulfil his devotional task. Many religious exercises are entered into with seeming fervor, where the heart, at the time, feels cold and languid: a habit of dissimulation is by degrees contracted; and fraud and falsehood become the predominant principle. Hence the reason of that vulgar observation, that the highest zeal in religion and the deepest hypocrisy, so far from being inconsistent, are often or commonly united in the same individual character.

The bad effects of such habits, even in common life, are easily imagined; but where the interests of religion are concerned, no morality can be forcible enough to bind the enthusiastic zealot. The sacredness of the cause sanctifies every measure which can be made use of to promote it.

The steady attention alone to so important an interest as that of eternal salvation, is apt to extinguish the benevolent affections, and beget a narrow, contracted selfishness. And when such a temper is encouraged, it easily eludes all the general precepts of charity and benevolence.

Thus, the motives of vulgar superstition have no great influence on general conduct; nor is their operation favorable to morality, in the instances where they predominate.

Is there any maxim in politics more certain and infallible, than that both the number and authority of priests should be confined within very narrow limits; and that the civil magistrate ought, for ever, to keep his fasces and axes from such dangerous hands? But if the spirit of popular religion were so salutary to society, a contrary maxim ought to prevail. The greater number of priests, and their greater authority and riches, will always augment the religious spirit. And though the priests have the guidance of this spot, why may we not expect a superior sanctity of life, and greater benevolence and moderation, from persons who are set apart for religion, who are continually inculcating it upon others, and who must themselves imbibe a greater share of it? Whence comes it then, that, in fact, the utmost a wise magistrate can propose with regard to popular religions, is, as far as possible, to make a saving game of it, and to prevent their pernicious consequences with regard to society? Every expedient which he tries for so humble a purpose is surrounded with inconveniences. If he admits only one religion among his subjects, he must sacrifice, to an uncertain prospect of tranquillity, every consideration of public liberty, science, reason, industry, and even his own independency. If he gives indulgence to several sects, which is the wiser maxim, he must preserve a very philosophical indifference to all of them, and carefully restrain the pretensions of the prevailing sect; otherwise he can expect nothing but endless disputes, quarrels, factions, persecutions, and civil commotions.

True religion, I allow, has no such pernicious consequences: but we must treat of religion, as it has commonly been found in the world; nor have I any thing to do with that speculative tenet of Theism, which, as it is a species of philosophy, must partake of the beneficial influence of that principle, and at the same time must lie under a like inconvenience, of being always confined to very few persons.

Oaths are requisite in all courts of judicature; but it is a question whether their authority arises from any popular religion. It is the solemnity and importance of the occasion, the regard to reputation, and the reflecting on the general interests of society, which are the chief restraints upon mankind. Custom-house oaths and political oaths are but little regarded even by some who pretend to principles of honesty and religion; and a Quaker's asseveration is with us justly put upon the same footing with the oath of any other person. I know, that Polybius ascribes the infamy of Greek faith to the prevalency of the Epicurean philosophy: but I know also, that Punic faith had as bad a reputation in ancient times as Irish evidence has in modern; though we cannot account for these vulgar observations by the same reason. Not to mention that Greek faith was infamous before the rise of the Epicurean philosophy; and Euripides, in a passage which I shall point out to you, has glanced a remarkable stroke of satire against his nation, with regard to this circumstance.

Take care, Philo, replied Cleanthes, take care: push not matters too far: allow not your zeal against false religion to undermine your veneration for the true. Forfeit not this principle, the chief, the only great comfort in life; and our principal support amidst all the attacks of adverse fortune. The most agreeable reflection, which it is possible for human imagination to suggest, is that of genuine Theism, which represents us as the workmanship of a Being perfectly good, wise, and powerful; who created us for happiness; and who, having implanted in us immeasurable desires of good, will prolong our existence to all eternity, and will transfer us into an infinite variety of scenes, in order to satisfy those desires, and render our felicity complete and durable. Next to such a Being himself (if the comparison be allowed), the happiest lot which we can imagine, is that of being under his guardianship and protection.

These appearances, said Philo, are most engaging and alluring; and with regard to the true philosopher, they are more than appearances. But it happens here, as in the former case, that, with regard to the greater part of mankind, the appearances are deceitful, and that the terrors of religion commonly prevail above its comforts.

It is allowed, that men never have recourse to devotion so readily as when dejected with grief or depressed with sickness. Is not this a proof, that the religious spirit is not so nearly allied to joy as to sorrow?

But men, when afflicted, find consolation in religion, replied Cleanthes. Sometimes, said Philo: but it is natural to imagine, that they will form a notion of those unknown beings, suitably to the present gloom and melancholy of their temper, when they betake themselves to the contemplation of them. Accordingly, we find the tremendous images to predominate in all religions; and we ourselves, after having employed the most exalted expression in our descriptions of the Deity, fall into the flattest contradiction in affirming that the damned are infinitely superior in number to the elect.

I shall venture to affirm, that there never was a popular religion, which represented the state of departed souls in such a light, as would render it eligible for human kind that there should be such a state. These fine models of religion are the mere product of philosophy. For as death lies between the eye and the prospect of futurity, that event is so shocking to Nature, that it must throw a gloom on all the regions which lie beyond it; and suggest to the generality of mankind the idea of Cerberus and Furies; devils, and torrents of fire and brimstone.

It is true, both fear and hope enter into religion; because both these passions, at different times, agitate the human mind, and each of them forms a species of divinity suitable to itself. But when a man is in a cheerful disposition, he is fit for business, or company, or entertainment of any kind; and he naturally applies himself to these, and thinks not of religion. When melancholy and dejected, he has nothing to do but brood upon the terrors of the invisible world, and to plunge himself still deeper in affliction. It may indeed happen, that after he has, in this manner, engraved the religious opinions deep into his thought and imagination, there may arrive a change of health or circumstances, which may restore his good-humor, and raising cheerful prospects of futurity, make him run into the other extreme of joy and triumph. But still it must be acknowledged, that, as terror is the primary principle of religion, it is the passion which always predominates in it, and admits but of short intervals of pleasure.

Not to mention, that these fits of excessive, enthusiastic joy, by exhausting the spirits, always prepare the way for equal fits of superstitious terror and dejection; nor is there any state of mind so happy as the calm and equable. But this state it is impossible to support, where a man thinks that he lies in such profound darkness and uncertainty, between an eternity of happiness and an eternity of misery. No wonder that such an opinion disjoints the ordinary frame of the mind, and throws it into the utmost confusion. And though that opinion is seldom so steady in its operation as to influence all the actions; yet it is apt to make a considerable breach in the temper, and to produce that gloom and melancholy so remarkable in all devout people.

It is contrary to common sense to entertain apprehensions or terrors upon account of any opinion whatsoever, or to imagine that we run any risk hereafter, by the freest use of our reason. Such a sentiment implies both an absurdity and an inconsistency. It is an absurdity to believe that the Deity has human passions, and one of the lowest of human passions, a restless appetite for applause. It is an inconsistency to believe, that, since the Deity has this human passion, he has not others also; and, in particular, a disregard to the opinions of creatures so much inferior.

To know God, says Seneca, is to worship him. All other worship is indeed absurd, superstitious, and even impious. It degrades him to the low condition of mankind, who are delighted with entreaty, solicitation, presents, and flattery. Yet is this impiety the smallest of which superstition is guilty. Commonly, it depresses the Deity far below the condition of mankind; and represents him as a capricious demon, who exercises his power without reason and without humanity! And were that Divine Being disposed to be offended at the vices and follies of silly mortals, who are his own workmanship, ill would it surely fare with the votaries of most popular superstitions. Nor would any of human race merit his favour, but a very few, the philosophical Theists, who entertain, or rather indeed endeavor to entertain, suitable notions of his Divine perfections: as the only persons entitled to his compassion and indulgence would be the philosophical Sceptics, a sect almost equally rare, who, from a natural diffidence of their own capacity, suspend, or endeavor to suspend, all judgment with regard to such sublime and such extraordinary subjects.

If the whole of Natural Theology, as some people seem to maintain, resolves itself into one simple, though somewhat ambiguous, at least undefined proposition, *That the cause or causes of order in the universe probably bear some remote analogy to human intelligence*: if this proposition be not capable of extension, variation, or more particular explication: if it affords no inference that affects human life, or can be the source of any action or forbearance: and if the analogy, imperfect as it is, can be carried no further than to the human intelligence, and cannot be transferred, with any appearance of probability, to the qualities of the mind; if this really be the case, what can the most inquisitive, contemplative, and religious man do more than give a plain, philosophical assent to the proposition, as often as it occurs, and believe that the arguments on which it is established exceed the objections which lie against it? Some astonishment, indeed, will naturally arise from the greatness of the object; some melancholy from its obscurity; some contempt of human reason, that it can give no solution more satisfactory with regard to so extraordinary and magnificent a question. But believe me, Cleanthes, the most natural sentiment which a well-disposed mind will feel on this occasion, is a longing desire and expectation that Heaven would be pleased to dissipate, at least alleviate, this profound ignorance, by affording some particular revelation to mankind, and making discoveries of the nature, attributes, and operations of the Divine object of our faith. A person, seasoned with a just sense of the imperfections of natural reason, will fly to revealed truth with the greatest avidity: while the haughty Dogmatist, persuaded that he can erect a complete system of Theology by the mere help of philosophy, disdains any further aid, and rejects this adventitious instructor. To be a philosophical Sceptic is, in a man of letters, the first and most essential step towards being a sound, believing Christian; a proposition which I would willingly recommend to the attention of Pamphilus: and I hope Cleanthes will forgive me for interposing so far in the education and instruction of his pupil.

Cleanthes and Philo pursued not this conversation much further: and as nothing ever made greater impression on me, than all the reasonings of that day, so I confess, that, upon a serious review of the whole, I cannot but think, that Philo's principles are more probable than Demea's; but that those of Cleanthes approach still nearer to the truth.

Chapter 24

IMMANUEL KANT

Immanuel Kant (1724–1804), who was born in a deeply pietistic Lutheran family in Konigsberg, Germany, lived in that town his entire life. At sixteen he entered the University of Konigsberg, where he studied under the tutelage of Martin Knutzen, and read works of Leibniz and the Leibniz scholar Christian Wolff. After graduation he worked as a tutor, but in 1755 he was offered an unsalaried lectureship at his alma mater, receiving his fees directly from his students. He served in this capacity until 1770 when he was promoted to the Chair of Logic and Metaphysics at the University of Konigsberg. In his inaugural address he spoke of his goal of restructuring philosophy, resolving the debate between the rationalists (e.g., Descartes, Spinoza, Leibniz, and Wolff) and the empiricists (e.g., Newton, Bacon, Locke, and Hume). For the next ten years he worked on his magnus opus, *The Critique of Pure Reason* (1781), which accomplished that goal, a Copernican revolution of the theory of knowledge. In 1783 he wrote a shorter *Prolegomena to Any Future Metaphysics* "for the benefit of teachers," and in 1785 he wrote his first major work in ethics, *Foundation for the Metaphysic of Morals.* A successor to that work appeared in 1788, *Critique of Practical Reason,* and in 1793 he published his theory of rational religion, *Religion within the Limits of Reason Alone.*

Kant was an outstanding lecturer and excellent conversationalist, who was known for his generosity and friendliness. He lived a quiet, duty-bound, methodical life, so regular, that citizens were said to have set their clocks by his walks. He would leave his home at precisely 4:30 in the afternoon and walk up and down the street on which he lived exactly eight times.

In his own lifetime Kant was recognized as one of the premier philosophers in the Western tradition. Although he wrote on virtually every philosophical topic, he made his major contributions in epistemology and ethics, represented in the selections that follow. Let us briefly examine his thought in these areas.

KANT'S THEORY OF KNOWLEDGE

Building on a mathematical model, the rationalists from Plato through Descartes to Spinoza and Leibniz argued that reason alone is the ultimate source of knowledge, that we have innate or a priori knowledge of ultimate truth which can be accessed by introspection or pure reason. On the other hand, the British empiricists Locke and Hume set forth cogent criticisms against the rationalist projects and argued that experience is the only source of knowledge. The phenomenal success of Newton (1642–1727) in physics seemed to shift the balance of evidence to the empiricists. Empirical Science, not rationalist speculation, offered the best hope of attaining knowledge of the universe.

Kant began as a rationalist but on reading Hume was struck with the cogency of his argument. Hume "woke me from my dogmatic slumbers," Kant wrote, and henceforth accepted the idea that all of our knowledge begins with experience. But Kant thought that Hume had made an invalid inference in concluding that all our knowledge arises from experience. Kant sought to demonstrate that the rationalists had an invaluable insight, which had been lost in their flamboyant speculation, that there is something determinate in the mind that causes us to know what we know.

Kant argued that the mind is so structured and empowered that it imposes interpretive categories on our experience, so that we do not simply experience the world, as the empiricists alleged, but interpret it through the constitutive mechanisms of the mind. This is sometimes called Kant's Copernican Revolution.

> Until now we have assumed that all our knowledge must conform to objects. But every attempt to extend our knowledge of objects by establishing something in regard to them a priori, by means of concepts, have, on this assumption, ended in failure. Therefore, we must see whether we may have better success in our metaphysical task if we begin with the assumption that objects must conform to our knowledge. In this way we would have knowledge of objects a priori. We should then be proceeding in the same ways as Copernicus in his revolutionary hypothesis. After he failed to make progress in explaining the movements of the heavenly bodies on the supposition that they all revolved around the observer, he decided to reverse the relationship and made the observer revolve around the heavenly body, the sun, which was at rest. A similar experiment can be done in metaphysics with regard to the intuition of objects. If our intuition must conform to the constitution of the object, I do not see how we could know anything of the object a priori, but if the object of sense must conform to the constitution of our faculty of intuition, then a priori knowledge is possible (*Critique of Pure Reason* from the preface to the second edition, 1787, my translation).

A word is in order about a priori and a posteriori knowledge. *A priori* knowledge is that which we know *prior* to experience. It is opposed to *a posteriori* knowledge which is based on experience. You may recall that for Hume all knowledge of matters of fact was a posteriori and only analytic statements (e.g., mathematical truths or statements such as "All mothers are women") are known a priori. Kant rejects this formula. For him it is possible to have a priori matters of fact. "But though all our knowledge begins with experience, it does not follow that it all arises out of experience." Indeed, he thinks that mathematical truth is not analytic but synthetic (the predicate adds something to the subject) and that there is other synthetic a priori knowledge, such as our knowledge of time, space, causality, and the moral law.

KANT'S ETHICAL THEORY

In Kant's classic work, *The Foundations of the Metaphysic of Morals,* written in 1785 he outlines his ethical system. Kant is concerned to reject those ethical theories, such as the Theory of Moral Sentiments set forth by the Scottish moralists Francis Hutcheson (1694) and David Hume (1711–1776), in which morality is contingent and hypothetical. The Moral Sentiment view is contingent in that it is based on human nature and, in particular, on our feelings or sentiments. Had we been created differently, we would have a different nature and, hence, different moral duties. Morality, on this view, consists of hypothetical imperatives in that they depend on our desires for their realization. For example, we should obey the law because we want a peaceful, orderly society. We should seek peace because it is necessary for personal happiness. The naturalistic ethicists were typically utilitarians who sought to maximize human happiness.

Kant rejects this naturalistic, utilitarian account of ethics. Ethics is not *contingent* but *absolute,* and its duties or imperatives are not *hypothetical* but *categorical* (nonconditional). Ethics is based not on feeling but on reason. It is because we are rational beings that we are valuable and capable of discovering moral laws binding on all persons at all times. As such, our moral duties are not dependent on feelings but on reason. They are unconditional, universally valid, and necessary, regardless of the possible consequences or opposition to our inclinations.

Kant's first formulation of his *categorical imperative* is, "Act only on that maxim whereby thou canst at the same time will that it would become a universal law." This imperative is given as the criterion (or second order principle) by which to judge all other principles. If we could consistently will that everyone would do some type of action, then there is an application of the categorical imperative enjoining that type of action. If we cannot consistently will that everyone would do some type of action, then that type of action is morally wrong. Kant argues, for example, that we cannot consistently will that everyone make lying-promises, for the very institution of promising entails or depends on general adherence to keeping the promise or an intention to do so.

Kant offers a second formulation of the categorical imperative: "So act as to treat humanity, whether in your own person or in that of any other, in every case as an end and never as merely a means only." Each person by virtue of his or her reason has dignity and profound worth, which entails that he or she must never be exploited or manipulated or merely used as a means to our idea of what is for the general good. Kant thought that this formulation was substantively identical with the first, but the view is controversial.

FOR FURTHER READING

Acton, Harry. *Kant's Moral Philosophy.* (Macmillan, 1970).

Allison, Henry. *Kant's Transcendental Idealism.* (Yale University Press, 1983).

Beck, Lewis White. *A Commentary on Kant's Critique of Practical Reason.* (University of Chicago, 1960).

Beck, Lewis White, ed. *Studies in the Philosophy of Kant.* (Bobbs-Merrill, 1965).

Ewing, A. C. *A Short Commentary on Kant's Critique of Pure Reason.* (Methuen, 1950).

Hill, Thomas E. *Dignity and Practical Reason.* (Cornell University Press, 1992).

Kemp, John. *The Philosophy of Kant.* (Oxford University Press, 1968).

Kemp Smith, Norman. *A Commentary to Kant's "Critique of Pure Reason."* (Humanities Press, 1962).

Louden, Robert. *Morality and Moral Theory.* (Oxford University Press, 1991).

O'Neill, Onora. *Acting on Principle: An Essay on Kantian Ethics.* (Columbia University Press, 1975).

Ross, W. D. *Kant's Ethical Theory.* (Clarendon Press, 1954).

Strawson, P. F. *The Bounds of Sense: An Essay on Kant's Critique of Pure Reason.* (Methuen, 1966).

Sullivan, Roger. *An Introduction to Kant's Ethics.* (Cambridge University Press, 1994).

Sullivan, Roger. *Immanuel Kant's Moral Theory.* (Cambridge University Press, 1989).

Walker, Ralph C. S. *Kant: The Arguments of the Philosophers.* (Routledge & Kegan Paul, 1978).

Walker, Ralph C. S., ed. *Kant on Pure Reason.* (Oxford University Press, 1982).

Ward, Keith. *The Development of Kant's Views of Ethics.* (Blackwell's, 1972).

Werkmeister, W. H. *Kant.* (Open Court, 1980).

Wolff, Robert Paul, ed. *Kant.* (Doubleday, 1967).

Prolegomena To Any Future Metaphysics

INTRODUCTION

These *Prolegomena* are destined for the use, not of pupils, but of future teachers, and even the latter should not expect that they will be serviceable for the systematic exposition of a ready-made science, but merely for the discovery of the science itself.

There are scholarly men, to whom the history of philosophy (both ancient and modern) is philosophy itself; for these the present *Prolegomena* are not written. They must wait till those who endeavor to draw from the foundation of reason itself have completed their work; it will then be the historian's turn to inform the world of what has been done. Unfortunately, nothing can be said, which in their opinion has not been said before, and truly the same prophecy applies to all future time; for since the human reason has for many centuries speculated upon innumerable objects in various ways, it is hardly to be expected that we should not be able to discover analogies for every new idea among the old sayings of past ages.

My object is to persuade all those who think Metaphysics worth studying, that it is absolutely necessary to pause a moment, and, neglecting all that has been done, to propose first the preliminary question, "Whether such a thing as metaphysics be at all possible?"

If it be a science, how comes it that it cannot, like other sciences, obtain universal and permanent recognition? If not, how can it maintain its pretensions, and keep the human mind in suspense with hopes, never ceasing, yet never fulfilled? Whether then we demonstrate our knowledge or our ignorance in this field, we must come once for all to a definite conclusion respecting the nature of this so-called science, which cannot possibly remain on its present footing. It seems almost ridiculous, while every other science is continually advancing, that in this, which pretends to be Wisdom incarnate, for whose oracle every one inquires, we should constantly move round the same spot, without gaining a single step. And so its followers having melted away, we do not find men confident of their ability to shine in other sciences venturing their reputation here, where everybody, however ignorant in other matters, may deliver a final verdict, as in this domain there is as yet no standard weight and measure to distinguish sound knowledge from shallow talk.

After all it is nothing extraordinary in the elaboration of a science, when men begin to wonder how far it has advanced, that the question should at last occur, whether and how such a science is possible? Human reason so delights in constructions, that it has several times built up a tower, and then razed it to examine the nature of the foundation. It is never too late to become wise; but if the change comes late, there is always more difficulty in starting a reform.

The question whether a science be possible, presupposes a doubt as to its actuality. But such a doubt offends the men whose whole possessions consist of this supposed jewel; hence he who raises the doubt must expect opposition from all sides. Some, in the proud consciousness of their possessions, which are ancient, and therefore considered legitimate, will take their metaphysical compendia in their hands, and look down on him with contempt; others, who never see anything except it be identical with what they have seen before, will not understand him, and everything will remain for a time, as if nothing had happened to excite the concern, or the hope, for an impending change.

Nevertheless, I venture to predict that the independent reader of these *Prolegomena* will not only doubt his previous science, but ultimately be fully persuaded, that it cannot exist unless the demands here stated on which its possibility depends, be satisfied; and, as this has never been done, that there is, as yet, no such thing as Metaphysics. But as it can never cease to be in demand[1]—since the interests of common sense are intimately interwoven with it, he must confess that a radical reform, or rather a new birth of the science after an original plan, are unavoidable, however men may struggle against it for a while.

Translated by Paul Carus

1. Says Horace:
Rusticus expectat, dum defluat amnis, at ille
Labitur et labetur in omne volubilis aevum.
["A rustic fellow waiteth on the shore
For the river to flow away,
But the river flows, and flows on as before,
And it flows forever and aye."]

Since the *Essays* of Locke and Leibnitz, or rather since the origin of metaphysics so far as we know its history, nothing has ever happened which was more decisive to its fate than the attack made upon it by David Hume. He threw no light on this species of knowledge, but he certainly struck a spark from which light might have been obtained, had it caught some inflammable substance and had its smouldering fire been carefully nursed and developed.

Hume started from a single but important concept in Metaphysics, viz., that of Cause and Effect (including its derivatives force and action, etc.). He challenges reason, which pretends to have given birth to this idea from herself, to answer him by what right she thinks anything to be so constituted, that if that thing be posited, something else also must necessarily be posited; for this is the meaning of the concept of cause. He demonstrated irrefutably that it was perfectly impossible for reason to think *a priori* and by means of concepts a combination involving necessity. We cannot at all see why, in consequence of the existence of one thing, another must necessarily exist, or how the concept of such a combination can arise *a priori*. Hence he inferred, that reason was altogether deluded with reference to this concept, which she erroneously considered as one of her children, whereas in reality it was nothing but a bastard of imagination, impregnated by experience, which subsumed certain representations under the Law of Association, and mistook the subjective necessity of habit for an objective necessity arising from insight. Hence he inferred that reason had no power to think such combinations, even generally, because her concepts would then be purely fictitious, and all her pretended *a priori* cognitions nothing but common experiences marked with a false stamp. In plain language there is not, and cannot be, any such thing as metaphysics at all.[2]

However hasty and mistaken Hume's conclusion may appear, it was at least founded upon investigation, and this investigation deserved the concentrated attention of the brighter spirits of his day as well as determined efforts on their part to discover, if possible, a happier solution of the problem in the sense proposed by him, all of which would have speedily resulted in a complete reform of the science.

But Hume suffered the usual misfortune of metaphysicians, of not being understood. It is positively painful to see how utterly his opponents, Reid, Oswald, Beattie, and lastly Priestley, missed the point of the problem; for while they were ever taking for granted that which he doubted, and demonstrating with zeal and often with impudence that which he never thought of doubting, they so misconstrued his valuable suggestion that everything remained in its old condition, as if nothing had happened.

The question was not whether the concept of cause was right, useful, and even indispensable for our knowledge of nature, for this Hume had never doubted; but whether that concept could be thought by reason *a priori*, and consequently whether it possessed an inner truth, independent of all experience, implying a wider application than merely to the objects of experience. This was Hume's problem. It was a question concerning the *origin,* not concerning the *indispensable need* of the concept. Were the former decided, the conditions of the use and the sphere of its valid application would have been determined as a matter of course.

But to satisfy the conditions of the problem, the opponents of the great thinker should have penetrated very deeply into the nature of reason, so far as it is concerned with pure thinking—a task which did not suit them. They found a more convenient method of being defiant without any insight, viz., the appeal to *common sense*. It is indeed a great gift of God, to possess right, or (as they now call it) plain common sense. But this common sense must be shown practically, by well-considered and reasonable thoughts and words, not by appealing to it as an oracle, when no rational justification can be advanced. To appeal to common sense, when insight and science fail, and no sooner—this is one of the subtle discoveries of modern times, by means of which the most superficial ranter can safely enter the lists with the most thorough thinker, and hold his own. But as long as a particle of insight remains, no one would think of having recourse to this subterfuge. For what is it but an appeal to the opinion of the multitude, of whose applause the philosopher is ashamed, while the popular charlatan glories and confides in it? I should think that Hume might fairly

2. Nevertheless Hume called this very destructive science metaphysics and attached to it great value. Metaphysics and morals [he declares in the fourth part of his *Essays*] are the most important branches of science; mathematics and physics are not nearly so important. But the acute man merely regarded the negative use arising from the moderation of extravagant claims of speculative reason, and the complete settlement of the many endless and troublesome controversies that mislead mankind. He overlooked the positive injury which results, if reason be deprived of its most important prospects which can alone supply to the will the highest aim for all its endeavor.

have laid as much claim to common sense as Beattie, and in addition to a critical reason (such as the latter did not possess), which keeps common sense in check and prevents it from speculating, or, if speculations are under discussion, restrains the desire to decide because it cannot satisfy itself concerning its own arguments. By this means alone can common sense remain sound. Chisels and hammers may suffice to work a piece of wood, but for steel-engraving we require an engraver's needle. Thus common sense and speculative understanding are each serviceable in their own way, the former in judgments which apply immediately to experience, the latter when we judge universally from mere concepts, as in metaphysics, where sound common sense, so called in spite of the inapplicability of the word, has no right to judge at all.

I openly confess, the suggestion of David Hume was the very thing, which many years ago first interrupted my dogmatic slumber, and gave my investigations in the field of speculative philosophy quite a new direction. I was far from following him in the conclusions at which he arrived by regarding, not the whole of his problem, but a part, which by itself can give us no information. If we start from a well-founded, but undeveloped, thought, which another has bequeathed to us, we may well hope by continued reflection to advance farther than the acute man, to whom we owe the first spark of light.

I therefore first tried whether Hume's objection could not be put into a general form, and soon found that the concept of the connexion of cause and effect was by no means the only idea by which the understanding thinks the connexion of things *a priori,* but rather that metaphysics consists altogether of such connexions. I sought to ascertain their number, and when I had satisfactorily succeeded in this by starting from a single principle, I proceeded to the deduction of these concepts,which I was now certain were not deduced from experience, as Hume had apprehended, but sprang from the pure understanding. This deduction (which seemed impossible to my acute predecessor, which had never even occurred to any one else, though no one had hesitated to use the concepts without investigating the basis of their objective validity) was the most difficult task ever undertaken in the service of metaphysics; and the worst was that metaphysics, such as it then existed, could not assist me in the least, because this deduction alone can render metaphysics possible. But as soon as I had succeeded in solving Hume's problem not merely in a particular case, but with respect to the whole faculty of pure reason, I could proceed safely, though slowly, to determine the whole sphere of pure reason completely and from general principles, in its circumference as well as in its contents. This was required for metaphysics in order to construct its system according to a reliable method.

But I fear that the execution of Hume's problem in its widest extent (viz., my *Critique of Pure Reason*) will fare as the problem itself fared, when first proposed. It will be misjudged because it is misunderstood, and misunderstood because men choose to skim through the book, and not to think through it—a disagreeable task, because the work is dry, obscure, opposed to all ordinary notions, moreover long-winded. I confess, however, I did not expect to hear from philosophers complaints of want of popularity, entertainment, and facility, when the existence of a highly prized and indispensable cognition is at stake, which cannot be established otherwise, than by the strictest rules of methodic precision. Popularity may follow, but is inadmissible at the beginning. Yet as regards a certain obscurity, arising partly from the diffuseness of the plan, owing to which the principal points of the investigation are easily lost sight of, the complaint is just, and I intend to remove it by the present *Prolegomena.*

The first-mentioned work, which discusses the pure faculty of reason in its whole compass and bounds, will remain the foundation, to which the *Prolegomena,* as a preliminary exercise, refer; for our critique must first be established as a complete and perfected science, before we can think of letting Metaphysics appear on the scene, or even have the most distant hope of attaining it.

We have been long accustomed to seeing antiquated knowledge produced as new by taking it out of its former context, and reducing it to system in a new suit of any fancy pattern under new titles. Most readers will set out by expecting nothing else from the *Critique;* but these *Prolegomena* may persuade him that it is a perfectly new science, of which no one has ever even thought, the very idea of which was unknown, and for which nothing hitherto accomplished can be of the smallest use, except it be the suggestion of Hume's doubts. Yet even he did not suspect such a formal science, but ran his ship ashore, for safety's sake, landing on scepticism, there to let it lie and rot; whereas my object is rather to give it a pilot, who, by means of safe astronomical principles drawn from a knowledge of the globe, and provided with a complete chart and compass, may steer the ship safely, whither he listeth.

If in a new science, which is wholly isolated and unique in its kind, we started with the prejudice that we can judge of things by means of our previously acquired knowledge, which is precisely what has first to be called in question, we should only fancy we saw everywhere what we had already known, the expressions, having a similar sound, only that all would appear utterly metamorphosed, senseless and unintelligible, because we should have as a foundation our own notions, made by long habit a second nature, instead of the author's. But the longwindedness of the work, so far as it depends on the subject, and not the exposition, its consequent unavoidable dryness and its scholastic precision are qualities which can only benefit the science, though they may discredit the book.

Few writers are gifted with the subtlety, and at the same time with the grace, of David Hume, or with the depth, as well as the elegance, of Moses Mendelssohn. Yet I flatter myself I might have made my own exposition popular, had my object been merely to sketch out a plan and leave its completion to others, instead of having my heart in the welfare of the science, to which I had devoted myself so long; in truth, it required no little constancy, and even self-denial, to postpone the sweets of an immediate success to the prospect of a slower, but more lasting, reputation.

Making plans is often the occupation of an opulent and boastful mind, which thus obtains the reputation of a creative genius, by demanding what it cannot itself supply; by censuring, what it cannot improve; and by proposing, what it knows not where to find. And yet something more should belong to a sound plan of a general critique of pure reason than mere conjectures, if this plan is to be other than the usual declamations of pious aspirations. But pure reason is a sphere so separate and self-contained, that we cannot touch a part without affecting all the rest. We can therefore do nothing without first determining the position of each part, and its relation to the rest; for, as our judgment cannot be corrected by anything without, the validity and use of every part depends upon the relation in which it stands to all the rest within the domain of reason.

So in the structure of an organized body, the end of each member can only be deduced from the full conception of the whole. It may, then, be said of such a critique that it is never trustworthy except it be perfectly complete, down to the smallest elements of pure reason. In the sphere of this faculty you can determine either everything or nothing.

But although a mere sketch, preceding the *Critique of Pure Reason,* would be unintelligible, unreliable, and useless, it is all the more useful as a sequel. For so we are able to grasp the whole, to examine in detail the chief points of importance in the science, and to improve in many respects our exposition, as compared with the first execution of the work.

After the completion of the work I offer here such a plan which is sketched out after an analytical method, while the work itself had to be executed in the synthetical style, in order that the science may present all its articulations, as the structure of a peculiar cognitive faculty, in their natural combination. But should any reader find this plan, which I published as the *Prolegomena to any future Metaphysics,* still obscure, let him consider that not every one is bound to study Metaphysics, that many minds will succeed very well, in the exact and even in deep sciences, more closely allied to practical experience, while they cannot succeed in investigations dealing exclusively with abstract concepts. In such cases men should apply their talents to other subjects. But he who undertakes to judge, or still more, to construct, a system of Metaphysics, must satisfy the demands here made, either by adopting my solution, or by thoroughly refuting it, and substituting another. To evade it is impossible.

In conclusion, let it be remembered that this much-abused obscurity (frequently serving as a mere pretext under which people hide their own indolence or dullness) has its uses,since all who in other sciences observe a judicious silence, speak authoritatively in metaphysics and make bold decisions, because their ignorance is not here contrasted with the knowledge of others. Yet it does contrast with sound critical principles, which we may therefore commend in the words of Virgil:

Ignavum, fucos, pecus a praesepibus arcent.[3]

3. "Bees are defending their hives against drones, those indolent creatures."

PROLEGOMENA

Preamble on the Peculiarities of All Metaphysical Cognition

1. Of the Sources of Metaphysics

If it becomes desirable to formulate any cognition as science, it will be necessary first to determine accurately those peculiar features which no other science has in common with it, constituting its characteristics; otherwise the boundaries of all sciences become confused, and none of them can be treated thoroughly according to its nature.

The characteristics of a science may consist of a simple difference of object, or of the sources of cognition, or of the kind of cognition, or perhaps of all three conjointly. On this, therefore, depends the idea of a possible science and its territory.

First, as concerns the sources of metaphysical cognition, its very concept implies that they cannot be empirical. Its principles (including not only its maxims but its basic notions) must never be derived from experience. It must not be physical but metaphysical knowledge, viz., knowledge lying beyond experience. It can therefore have for its basis neither external experience, which is the source of physics proper, nor internal, which is the basis of empirical psychology. It is therefore *a priori* knowledge, coming from pure Understanding and pure Reason.

But so far Metaphysics would not be distinguishable from pure Mathematics; it must therefore be called pure philosophical cognition; and for the meaning of this term I refer to the *Critique of the Pure Reason* (II. "Method of Transcendentalism," Chap. I., Sec. i), where the distinction between these two employments of the reason is sufficiently explained. So far concerning the sources of metaphysical cognition.

2. Concerning the Kind of Cognition Which Can Alone Be Called Metaphysical

a) *Of the distinction between Analytical and Synthetical Judgments in general.*—The peculiarity of its sources demands that metaphysical cognition must consist of nothing but *a priori* judgments. But whatever be their origin, or their logical form, there is a distinction in judgments, as to their content, according to which they are either merely explicative, adding nothing to the content of the cognition, or expansive, increasing the given cognition: the former may be called analytical, the latter synthetical, judgments.

Analytical judgments express nothing in the predicate but what has been already actually thought in the concept of the subject, though not so distinctly or with the same (full) consciousness. When I say: All bodies are extended, I have not amplified in the least my concept of body, but have only analysed it, as extension was really thought to belong to that concept before the judgment was made, though it was not expressed. This judgment is therefore analytical. On the contrary, this judgment, All bodies have weight, contains in its predicate something not actually thought in the general concept of the body; it amplifies my knowledge by adding something to my concept, and must therefore be called synthetical.

b) *The Common Principles of all Analytical Judgments is the Law of Contradiction.*—All analytical judgments depend wholly on the law of Contradiction, and are in their nature *a priori* cognitions, whether the concepts that supply them with matter be empirical or not. For the predicate of an affirmative analytical judgment is already contained in the concept of the subject, of which it cannot be denied without contradiction. In the same way its opposite is necessarily denied of the subject in an analytical, but negative, judgment, by the same law of contradiction. Such is the nature of the judgments: all bodies are extended, and no bodies are unextended (i.e., simple).

For this very reason all analytical judgments are *a priori* even when the concepts are empirical, as, for example, Gold is a yellow metal; for to know this I require no experience beyond my concept of gold as a yellow metal: it is, in fact, the very concept, and I need only analyse it, without looking beyond it elsewhere.

c) *Synthetical Judgments require a different Principle from the Law of Contradiction.*—There are synthetical *a posteriori* judgments of empirical origin; but there are also others which are proved to be certain *a priori,* and which spring from pure Understanding and Reason. Yet they both agree in this, that they cannot possibly spring from the principle of analysis, viz., the law of contradiction, alone; they require a quite different principle, though, from whatever they may be deduced, they must be subject to the law of contradiction, which must never be violated, even though everything cannot be deduced from it. I shall first classify synthetical judgments.

1. *Empirical Judgments* are always synthetical. For it would be absurd to base an analytical judgment on experience, as our concept suffices for the purpose without requiring any testimony from experience. That body is extended, is a judgment established *a priori,* and not an empirical judgment. For before appealing to experience, we already have all the conditions of the judgment in the concept, from which we have but to elicit the predicate according to the law of contradiction, and thereby to become conscious of the necessity of the judgment, which experience could not even teach us.

2. *Mathematical Judgments* are all synthetical. This fact seems hitherto to have altogether escaped the observation of those who have analysed human reason; it even seems directly opposed to all their conjectures, though incontestably certain, and most important in its consequences. For as it was found that the conclusions of mathematicians all proceed according to the law of contradiction (as is demanded by all apodeictic certainty), men persuaded themselves that the fundamental principles were known from the same law. This was a great mistake, for a synthetical proposition can indeed be comprehended according to the law of contradiction, but only by presupposing another synthetical proposition from which it follows, but never in itself.

First of all, we must observe that all proper mathematical judgments are *a priori,* and not empirical, because they carry with them necessity, which cannot be obtained from experience. But if this be not conceded to me, very good; I shall confine my assertion to *pure Mathematics,* the very notion of which implies that it contains pure *a priori* and not empirical cognitions.

It might at first be thought that the proposition $7 + 5 = 12$ is a mere analytical judgment, following from the concept of the sum of seven and five, according to the law of contradiction. But on closer examination it appears that the concept of the sum of $7 + 5$ contains merely their union in a single number, without its being at all thought what the particular number is that unites them. The concept of twelve is by no means thought by merely thinking of the combination of seven and five; and analyse this possible sum as we may, we shall not discover twelve in the concept. We must go beyond these concepts, by calling to our aid some concrete image, i.e., either our five fingers, or five points (as Segner has it in his *Arithmetic*), and we must add successively the units of the five, given in some concrete image, to the concept of seven. Hence our concept is really amplified by the proposition $7 + 5 = 12$, and we add to the first a second, not thought in it. Arithmetical judgments are therefore synthetical, and the more plainly according as we take larger numbers; for in such cases it is clear that, however closely we analyse our concepts without calling visual images to our aid, we can never find the sum by such mere dissection.

All principles of geometry are no less analytical. That a straight line is the shortest path between two points, is a synthetical proposition. For my concept of straight contains nothing of quantity, but only a quality. The attribute of shortness is therefore altogether additional, and cannot be obtained by any analysis of the concept. Here, too, visualisation must come to aid us. It alone makes the synthesis possible.

Some other principles, assumed by geometers, are indeed actually analytical, and depend on the law of contradiction; but they only serve, as identical propositions, as a method of concatenation, and not as principles, e.g., $a = a$, the whole is equal to itself, or $a + b > a$, the whole is greater than its part. And yet even these, though they are recognised as valid from mere concepts, are only admitted in mathematics, because they can be represented in some visual form. What usually makes us believe that the predicate of such apodeictic[4] judgments is already contained in our concept, and that the judgment is therefore analytical, is the duplicity of the expression, requesting us to think a certain predicate as of necessity implied in the thought of a given concept, which necessity attaches to the concept. But the question is not what we are requested to join in thought *to* the given concept, but what we actually think together with and in it, though obscurely; and so it appears that the predicate belongs to these concepts necessarily indeed, yet not directly but indirectly by an added visualisation.

3. A Remark on the General Division of Judgments into Analytical and Synthetical

This division is indispensable, as concerns the critique of human understanding, and therefore deserves to be called classical, though otherwise it is of little use, but this is the reason why dogmatic philosophers, who always seek the sources of meta-

4. Kant borrows the term *apodeictic* from Aristotle who uses it in the sense of "certain beyond dispute."

physical judgments in Metaphysics itself, and not apart from it, in the pure laws of reason generally, altogether neglected this apparently obvious distinction. Thus the celebrated Wolf, and his acute follower Baumgarten, came to seek the proof of the principle of Sufficient Reason, which is clearly synthetical, in the principle of Contradiction. In Locke's Essay, however, I find an indication of my division. For in the fourth book (chap. iii. § 9, seq.), having discussed the various connexions of representations in judgments, and their sources, one of which he makes "identity and contradiction" (analytical judgments), and another the coexistence of representations in a subject, he confesses (§ 10) that our *a priori* knowledge of the latter is very narrow, and almost nothing. But in his remarks on this species of cognition, there is so little of what is definite, and reduced to rules, that we cannot wonder if no one, not even Hume, was led to make investigations concerning this sort of judgments. For such general and yet definite principles are not easily learned from other men, who have had them obscurely in their minds. We must hit on them first by our own reflexion, then we find them elsewhere, where we could not possibly have found them at first, because the authors themselves did not know that such an idea lay at the basis of their observations. Men who never think independently have nevertheless the acuteness to discover everything, after it has been once shown them, in what was said long since, though no one ever saw it there before.

4. The General Question of the Prolegomena.—Is Metaphysics at all Possible?

Were a metaphysics, which could maintain its place as a science, really in existence; could we say, here is metaphysics, learn it, and it will convince you irresistibly and irrevocably of its truth? This question would be useless, and there would only remain that other question (which would rather be a test of our acuteness, than a proof of the existence of the thing itself), "How is the science possible, and how does reason come to attain it?" But human reason has not been so fortunate in this case. There is no single book to which you can point as you do to Euclid, and say: This is Metaphysics; here you may find the noblest objects of this science, the knowledge of a highest Being, and of a future existence, proved from principles of pure reason. We can be shown indeed many judgments, demonstrably certain, and never questioned; but these are all analytical, and rather concern the materials and the scaffolding for Metaphysics, than the extension of knowledge, which is our proper object in studying it (§ 2). Even supposing you produce synthetical judgments (such as the law of Sufficient Reason, which you have never proved, as you ought to, from pure reason *a priori,* though we gladly concede its truth), you lapse when they come to be employed for your principal object, into such doubtful assertions, that in all ages one Metaphysics has contradicted another, either in its assertions, or their proofs, and thus has itself destroyed its own claim to lasting assent. Nay, the very attempts to set up such a science are the main cause of the early appearance of scepticism, a mental attitude in which reason treats itself with such violence that it could never have arisen save from complete despair of ever satisfying our most important aspirations. For long before men began to inquire into nature methodically, they consulted abstract reason, which had to some extent been exercised by means of ordinary experience; for reason is ever present, while laws of nature must usually be discovered with labor. So Metaphysics floated to the surface, like foam, which dissolved the moment it was scooped off. But immediately there appeared a new supply on the surface, to be ever eagerly gathered up by some, while others, instead of seeking in the depths the cause of the phenomenon, thought they showed their wisdom by ridiculing the idle labor of their neighbors.

The essential and distinguishing feature of pure mathematical cognition among all other *a priori* cognitions is, that it cannot at all proceed from concepts, but only by means of the construction of concepts (see *Critique* II., Method of Transcendentalism, chap. I., sect. I). As therefore in its judgments it must proceed beyond the concept to that which its corresponding visualisation contains, these judgments neither can, nor ought to, arise analytically, by dissecting the concept, but are all synthetical.

I cannot refrain from pointing out the disadvantage resulting to philosophy from the neglect of this easy and apparently insignificant observation. Hume being prompted (a task worthy of a philosopher) to cast his eye over the whole field of *a priori* cognitions in which human understanding claims such mighty possessions, heedlessly severed from it a whole, and indeed its most valuable, province, viz., pure mathematics; for he thought its nature, or, so to speak, the state-constitution of this empire, depended on totally different principles, namely, on the law of contradiction alone; and although he did not divide judgments in this manner formally and universally as I have done here, what he said was equivalent to this: that mathematics contains only analytical, but metaphysics synthetical, *a priori* judgments. In this, however, he was greatly mistaken, and the mistake had a decidedly injurious effect upon his whole conception. But for this, he would have extended his question concerning the origin of our synthetical judgments far beyond the metaphysical concept of Causality, and included in it the possibility of mathematics *a priori* also, for this latter he must have assumed to be equally synthetical. And then he could not have based his metaphysical judgments on mere experience without subjecting the axioms of mathematics equally to experience, a thing which he was far too acute to do. The good company into which metaphysics would thus have been brought, would have saved it from the danger of a contemptuous ill-treatment, for the thrust intended for it must have reached mathematics, which was not and could not have been Hume's intention. Thus that acute man would have been led into considerations which must needs be similar to those that now occupy us, but which would have gained inestimably by his inimitably elegant style.

Metaphysical judgments, properly so called, are all synthetical. We must distinguish judgments pertaining to metaphysics from metaphysical judgments properly so called. Many of the former are analytical, but they only afford the means for metaphysical judgments, which are the whole end of the science, and which are always synthetical. For if there be concepts pertaining to metaphysics (as, for example, that of substance), the judgments springing from simple analysis of them also pertain to metaphysics, as, for example, substance is that which only exists as subject; and by means of several such analytical judgments, we seek to approach the definition of the concept. But as the analysis of a pure concept of the understanding pertaining to metaphysics, does not proceed in any different manner from the dissection of any other, even empirical, concepts, not pertaining to metaphysics (such as: air is an elastic fluid, the elasticity of which is not destroyed by any known degree of cold), it follows that the concept indeed, but not the analytical judgment, is properly metaphysical. This science has something peculiar in the production of its *a priori* cognitions, which must therefore be distinguished from the features it has in common with other rational knowledge. Thus the judgment, that all the substance in things is permanent, is a synthetical and properly metaphysical judgment.

If the *a priori* principles, which constitute the materials of metaphysics, have first been collected according to fixed principles, then their analysis will be of great value; it might be taught as a particular part (as a *philosophia definitiva*), containing nothing but analytical judgments pertaining to metaphysics, and could be treated separately from the synthetical which constitute metaphysics proper. For indeed these analyses are not elsewhere of much value, except in metaphysics, i.e., as regards the synthetical judgments, which are to be generated by these previously analysed concepts.

The conclusion drawn in this section then is, that metaphysics is properly concerned with synthetical propositions *a priori*, and these alone constitute its end, for which it indeed requires various dissections of its concepts, viz., of its analytical judgments, but wherein the procedure is not different from that in every other kind of knowledge, in which we merely seek to render our concepts distinct by analysis. But the generation of *a priori* cognition by concrete images as well as by concepts, [together with] synthetical propositions *a priori* in philosophical cognition, constitutes the essential subject of Metaphysics.

Weary therefore as well of dogmatism, which teaches us nothing, as of scepticism, which does not even promise us anything, not even the quiet state of a contented ignorance; disquieted by the importance of knowledge so much needed; and lastly, rendered suspicious by long experience of all knowledge which we believe we possess, or which offers itself, under the title of pure reason: there remains but one critical question on the answer to which our future procedure depends, viz., *Is Metaphysics at all possible?* But this question must be answered not by sceptical objections to the asseverations of some actual system of metaphysics (for we do not as yet admit such a thing to exist), but from the conception, as yet only problematical, of a science of this sort.

In the *Critique of Pure Reason* I have treated this question synthetically, by making inquiries into pure reason itself, and endeavoring in this source to determine the elements as well as the laws of its pure use according to principles. The task is difficult, and requires a resolute reader to penetrate by degrees into a system, based on no data except reason itself, and which therefore seeks, without resting upon any fact, to unfold knowledge from its original germs. *Prolegomena,* however, are designed for preparatory exercises—they are intended rather to point out what we have to do in order if possible to actualise a science, than to propound it. They must therefore rest upon something already known as trustworthy, from which we can set out with confidence, and ascend to sources as yet unknown, the discovery of which will not only explain to us what we knew, but exhibit a sphere of many cognitions which all spring from the same sources. The method of *Prolegomena,* especially of those designed as a preparation for future metaphysics, is consequently analytical.

But it happens fortunately, that though we cannot assume metaphysics to be an actual science, we can say with confidence that certain pure *a priori* synthetical cognitions, pure Mathematics and pure Physics are actual and given; for both contain propositions, which are thoroughly recognised as apodeictically certain partly by mere reason, partly by general consent arising from experience, and yet as independent of experience. We have therefore some at least uncontested synthetical knowledge *a priori,* and need not ask *whether* it be possible, for it is actual, but how it is possible, in order that we may deduce from the principle which makes the given knowledge possible the possibility of all the rest.

5. The General Problem: How Is Knowledge from Pure Reason Possible?

We have above learned the significant distinction between analytical and synthetical judgments. The possibility of analytical propositions was easily comprehended, being entirely founded on the law of Contradiction. The possibility of synthetical *a posteriori* judgments, of those which are gathered from experience, also requires no particular explanation; for experience is nothing but a continual synthesis of perceptions. There remain therefore only synthetical propositions *a priori,* of which the possibility must be sought or investigated, because they must depend upon other principles than the law of contradiction.

But here we need not first establish the possibility of such propositions so as to ask whether they are possible. For there are enough of them which indeed are of undoubted certainty, and as our present method is analytical, we shall start from the fact, that such synthetical but purely rational cognition actually exists; but we must now inquire into the reason of this possibility, and ask, *how* such cognition is possible, in order that we may from the principles of its possibility be enabled to determine the conditions of its use, its sphere and its limits. The proper problem upon which all depends, when expressed with scholastic precision, is therefore:

How are Synthetical Propositions a priori *possible?*

For the sake of popularity I have above expressed this problem somewhat differently, as an inquiry into purely rational cognition, which I could do for once, without detriment to the desired comprehension, because, as we have only to do here with metaphysics and its sources, the reader will, I hope, after the foregoing remarks, keep in mind that when we speak of purely rational cognition, we do not mean analytical, but synthetical cognition.[5]

Metaphysics stands or falls with the solution of this problem: its very existence depends upon it. Let any one make metaphysical assertions with ever so much plausibility, let him overwhelm us with conclusions, if he has not previously proved able to answer this question satisfactorily, I have a right to say: this is all vain baseless philosophy and false wisdom. You speak through pure reason, and claim, as it were to create cognitions *a priori* by not only dissecting given concepts, but also by asserting connexions which do not rest upon the law of contradiction, and which you believe you conceive quite independently of all experience; how do you arrive at this, and how will you justify your pretensions? An appeal to the consent of the common sense of mankind cannot be allowed; for that is a witness whose authority depends merely upon rumor. Says Horace:

5. It is unavoidable that as knowledge advances, certain expressions which have become classical after having been used since the Infancy of science, will be found inadequate and unsuitable and a newer and more appropriate application of the terms will give rise to confusion. [This is the case with the term "analytical."] The analytical method, so far as it is opposed to the synthetical, is very different from that which constitutes the essence of analytical propositions: it signifies only that we start from what is sought, as if it were given, and ascend to the only conditions under which it is possible. In this method we often use nothing but synthetical propositions, as in mathematical analysis, and it were better to term it the regressive method, in contradistinction to the synthetic or progressive. A principal part of Logic too is distinguished by the name of Analytics, which here signifies the logic of truth in contrast to Dialectics without considering whether the cognitions belonging to it are analytical or synthetical.

Quodcunque ostendis mihi sic, incredulus odi[6]

The answer to this question, though indispensable, is difficult; and though the principal reason that it was not made long ago is, that the possibility of the question never occurred to anybody, there is yet another reason, which is this that a satisfactory answer to this one question requires a much more persistent, profound, and painstaking reflexion, than the most diffuse work on Metaphysics, which on its first appearance promised immortality to its author. And every intelligent reader, when he carefully reflects what this problem requires, must at first be struck with its difficulty, and would regard it as insoluble and even impossible, did there not actually exist pure synthetical cognitions *a priori*. This actually happened to David Hume, though he did not conceive the question in its entire universality as is done here, and as must be done, should the answer be decisive for all Metaphysics. For how is it possible, says that acute man, that when a concept is given me, I can go beyond it and connect with it another, which is not contained in it, in such a manner as if the latter necessarily belonged to the former? Nothing but experience can furnish us with such connexions (thus he concluded from the difficulty which he took to be an impossibility), and all that vaunted necessity, or, what is the same thing, all cognition assumed to be *a priori*, is nothing but a long habit of accepting something as true, and hence of mistaking subjective necessity for objective.

Should my reader complain of the difficulty and the trouble which I occasion him in the solution of this problem, he is at liberty to solve it himself in an easier way. Perhaps he will then feel under obligation to the person who has undertaken for him a labor of so profound research, and will rather be surprised at the facility with which, considering the nature of the subject, the solution has been attained. Yet it has cost years of work to solve the problem in its whole universality (using the term in the mathematical sense, viz., for that which is sufficient for all cases), and finally to exhibit it in the analytical form, as the reader finds it here.

All metaphysicians are therefore solemnly and legally suspended from their occupations till they shall have answered in a satisfactory manner the question, "How are synthetic cognitions *a priori* possible?" For the answer contains the only credentials which they must show when they have anything to offer in the name of pure reason. But if they do not possess these credentials, they can expect nothing else of reasonable people, who have been deceived so often, than to be dismissed without further ado.

If they on the other hand desire to carry on their business, not as a science, but as an art of wholesome oratory suited to the common sense of man, they cannot in justice be prevented. They will then speak the modest language of a rational belief, they will grant that they are not allowed even to conjecture, far less to know, anything which lies beyond the bounds of all possible experience, but only to assume (not for speculative use, which they must abandon, but for practical purposes only) the existence of something that is possible and even indispensable for the guidance of the understanding and of the will in life. In this manner alone can they be called useful and wise men, and the more so as they renounce the title of metaphysicians; for the latter profess to be speculative philosophers, and since, when judgments *a priori* are under discussion, poor probabilities cannot be admitted (for what is declared to be known *a priori* is thereby announced as necessary), such men cannot be permitted to play with conjectures, but their assertions must be either science, or are worth nothing at all.

It may be said, that the entire transcendental philosophy, which necessarily precedes all metaphysics, is nothing but the complete solution of the problem here propounded, in systematical order and completeness, and hitherto we have never had any transcendental philosophy; for what goes by its name is properly a part of metaphysics whereas the former science is intended first to constitute the possibility of the latter, and must therefore precede all metaphysics. And it is not surprising that when a whole science, deprived of all help from other sciences, and consequently in itself quite new, is required to answer a single question satisfactorily, we should find the answer troublesome and difficult, nay even shrouded in obscurity.

As we now proceed to this solution according to the analytical method, in which we assume that such cognitions from pure reasons actually exist, we can only appeal to two sciences of theoretical cognition (which alone is under consideration here), pure mathematics and pure natural science (physics). For these alone can exhibit to us objects in a definite and

6. "To all that which thou provest me thus I refuse to give credence and hate."

actualisable form, and consequently (if there should occur in them a cognition *a priori*) can show the truth or conformity of the cognition to the object *in concreto,* that is, its actuality, from which we could proceed to the reason of its possibility by the analytic method. This facilitates our work greatly for here universal considerations are not only applied to facts, but even start from them, while in a synthetic procedure they must strictly be derived *in abstracto* from concepts.

But, in order to rise from these actual and at the same time well-grounded pure cognitions *a priori* to such a possible cognition of the same as we are seeking, viz., to metaphysics as a science, we must comprehend that which occasions it, I mean the mere natural, though in spite of its truth still suspect, cognition *a priori* which lies at the bottom of that science, the elaboration of which without any critical investigation of its possibility is commonly called metaphysics. In a word, we must comprehend the natural conditions of such a science as a part of our inquiry, and thus the transcendental problem will be gradually answered by a division into four questions:

1. How is pure mathematics possible?

2. How is pure natural science possible?

3. How is metaphysics in general possible?

4. How is metaphysics as a science possible?

It may be seen that the solution of these problems, though chiefly designed to exhibit the essential matter of the *Critique,* has yet something peculiar, which for itself alone deserves attention. This is the search for the sources of given sciences in reason itself, so that its faculty of knowing something *a priori* may by its own deeds be investigated and measured. By this procedure these sciences gain, if not with regard to their contents, yet as to their proper use, and while they throw light on the higher question concerning their common origin, they give, at the same time, an occasion better to explain their own nature.

FIRST PART OF THE TRANSCENDENTAL PROBLEM

How Is Pure Mathematics Possible?

6. Here is a great and established branch of knowledge, encompassing even now a wonderfully large domain and promising an unlimited extension in the future. Yet it carries with it thoroughly apodeictical certainty, i.e., absolute necessity, which therefore rests upon no empirical grounds. Consequently it is a pure product of reason, and moreover is thoroughly synthetical. [Here the question arises:]

"How then is it possible for human reason to produce a cognition of this nature entirely *a priori*?"

Does not this faculty [which produces mathematics], as it neither is nor can be based upon experience, presuppose some ground of cognition *a priori,* which lies deeply hidden, but which might reveal itself by these its effects, if their first beginnings were but diligently ferreted out?

7. But we find that all mathematical cognition has this peculiarity: it must first exhibit its concept in a visual form and indeed *a priori,* therefore in a visual form which is not empirical, but pure. Without this mathematics cannot take a single step; hence its judgments are always visual, viz., "intuitive"; whereas philosophy must be satisfied with discursive judgments from mere concepts, and though it may illustrate its doctrines through a visual figure, can never derive them from it. This observation on the nature of mathematics gives us a clue to the first and highest condition of its possibility, which is, that some non-sensuous visualisation (called pure intuition) must form its basis, in which all its concepts can be exhibited or constructed, *in concreto* and yet *a priori.* If we can find out this pure intuition and its possibility, we may thence easily explain how synthetical propositions *a priori* are possible in pure mathematics, and consequently how this science itself is possible. Empirical intuition [viz., sense-perception] enables us without difficulty to enlarge the concept which we frame of an object of intuition [or sense-perception], by new predicates, which intuition [i.e., sense perception] itself presents synthetically in experience. Pure intuition [viz., the visualisation of forms in our imagination, from which every thing sensual, i.e., every thought of material qualities, is excluded] does so likewise, only with this difference, that in the latter case the synthetical judgment is *a priori* certain and apodeictical, in the former, only *a posteriori* and empirically certain; because this latter contains only that which occurs in contingent empirical intuition, but the former, that which must necessarily be discovered in pure intuition. Here intuition, being an intuition *a priori,* is *before all experience,* viz., before any perception of particular objects, inseparably conjoined with its concept.

8. But with this step our perplexity seems rather to increase than to lessen. for the question now is, "How is it possible to intuit [in a visual form] anything *a priori*?" An intuition [viz., a visual sense-perception] is such a representation as immediately depends upon the presence of the object. Hence it seems impossible to intuit from the outset *a priori*, because intuition would in that event take place without either a former or a present object to refer to, and by consequence could not be intuition. Concepts indeed are such, that we can easily form some of them *a priori*, viz., such as contain nothing but the thought of an object in general; and we need not find our selves in an immediate relation to the object. Take, for instance, the concepts of Quantity, of Cause, etc. But even these require, in order to make them understood, a certain concrete use—that is, an application to some sense-experience by which an object of them is given us. But how can the intuition of the object [its visualization] precede the object itself?

9. If our intuition [i.e., our sense-experience] were perforce of such a nature as to represent things as they are in themselves, there would not be any intuition *a priori*, but intuition would be always empirical. For I can only know what is contained in the object in itself when it is present and given to me. It is indeed even then incomprehensible how the visualising of a present thing should make me know this thing as it is in itself, as its properties cannot migrate into my faculty of representation. But even granting this possibility, a visualising of that sort would not take place *a priori*, that is, before the object were presented to me; for without this latter fact no reason of a relation between my representation and the object can be imagined, unless it depend upon a direct inspiration.

Therefore in one way only can my intuition anticipate the actuality of the object, and be a cognition *a priori*, viz.: if my intuition contains nothing but the form of sensibility, antedating in my subjectivity all the actual impressions through which I am affected by objects.

For that objects of sense can only be intuited according to this form of sensibility I can know *a priori*. Hence it follows: that propositions, which concern this form of sensuous intuition only, are possible and valid for objects of the senses; as also, conversely, that intuitions which are possible *a priori* can never concern any other things than objects of our senses.

10. Accordingly, it is only the form of sensuous intuition by which we can intuit things *a priori*, but by which we can know objects only as they appear to us (to our senses), not as they are in themselves; and this assumption is absolutely necessary if synthetical propositions *a priori* be granted as possible, or if, in case they actually occur, their possibility is to be comprehended and determined beforehand.

Now, the intuitions which pure mathematics lays at the foundation of all its cognitions and judgments which appear at once apodeictic and necessary are Space and Time. For mathematics must first have all its concepts in intuition, and pure mathematics in pure intuition, that is, it must construct them. If it proceeded in any other way, it would be impossible to make any headway, for mathematics proceeds, not analytically by dissection of concepts, but synthetically, and if pure intuition be wanting, there is nothing in which the matter for synthetical judgments *a priori* can be given. Geometry is based upon the pure intuition of space. Arithmetic accomplishes its concept of number by the successive addition of units in time; and pure mechanics especially cannot attain its concepts of motion without employing the representation of time. Both representations, however, are only intuitions; for if we omit from the empirical intuitions of bodies and their alterations (motion) everything empirical, or belonging to sensation, space and time still remain, which are therefore pure intuitions that lie *a priori* at the basis of the empirical. Hence they can never be omitted, but at the same time, by their being pure intuitions *a priori*, they prove that they are mere forms of our sensibility, which must precede all empirical intuition, or perception of actual objects, and conformably to which objects can be known *a priori*, but only as they appear to us.

11. The problem of the present section is therefore solved. Pure mathematics, as synthetical cognition *a priori*, is only possible by referring to no other objects than those of the senses. At the basis of their empirical intuition lies a pure intuition (of space and of time) which is *a priori*. This is possible, because the latter intuition is nothing but the mere form of sensibility, which precedes the actual appearance of the objects, in that it, in fact, makes them possible. Yet this faculty of intuiting *a priori* affects not the matter of the phenomenon (that is, the sense-element in it, for this constitutes that which is empirical), but its form, viz., space and time. Should any man venture to doubt that these are determinations adhering not to things in themselves, but to their relation to our sensibility, I should be glad to know how it can be possible to know the constitution of things *a priori*, viz., before we have any acquaintance with them and before they are presented to us. Such, however, is the case with space and time. But this is quite comprehensible as soon as both count for nothing more than formal conditions of our sensibility, while the objects count merely as phenomena; for then the form of the phenomenon, i.e., pure intuition, can by all means be represented as proceeding from ourselves, that is, *a priori*.

12. In order to add something by way of illustration and confirmation, we need only watch the ordinary and necessary procedure of geometers. All proofs of the complete congruence of two given figures (where the one can in every respect be substituted for the other) come ultimately to this that they may be made to coincide; which is evidently nothing else than a synthetical proposition resting upon immediate intuition, and this intuition must be pure, or given *a priori*, otherwise the proposition could not rank as apodeictically certain, but would have empirical certainty only. In that case, it could only be said that it is always found to be so, and holds good only as far as our perception reaches. That everywhere space (which [in its entirety] is itself no longer the boundary of another space) has three dimensions, and that space cannot in any way have more, is based on the proposition that not more than three lines can intersect at right angles in one point; but this proposition cannot by any means be shown from concepts, but rests immediately on intuition, and indeed on pure and *a priori* intuition, because it is apodeictically certain. That we can require a line to be drawn to infinity (*in indefinitum*), or that a series of changes (for example, space traversed by motion) shall be infinitely continued, presupposes a representation of space and time, which can only attach to intuition, namely, so far as it in itself is bounded by nothing, for from concepts it could never be inferred. Consequently, the basis of mathematics actually are pure intuitions, which make its synthetical and apodeictically valid propositions possible. Hence our transcendental deduction of the notions of space and of time explains at the same time the possibility of pure mathematics. Without some such deduction its truth may be granted, but its existence could by no means be understood, and we must assume "that everything which can be given to our senses (to the external senses in space, to the internal one in time) is intuited by us as it appears to us not as it is in itself."

13. Those who cannot yet rid themselves of the notion that space and time are actual qualities inhering in things in themselves, may exercise their acumen on the following paradox. When they have in vain attempted its solution, and are free from prejudices at least for a few moments, they will suspect that the degradation of space and of time to mere forms of our sensuous intuition may perhaps be well founded.

If two things are quite equal in all respects as much as can be ascertained by all means possible, quantitatively and qualitatively, it must follow, that the one can in all cases and under all circumstances replace the other, and this substitution would not occasion the least perceptible difference. This in fact is true of plane figures in geometry; but some spherical figures exhibit, notwithstanding a complete internal agreement, such a contrast in their external relation, that the one figure cannot possibly be put in the place of the other. For instance, two spherical triangles on opposite hemispheres, which have an arc of the equator as their common base, may be quite equal, both as regards sides and angles, so that nothing is to be found in either, if it be described for itself alone and completed, that would not equally be applicable to both; and yet the one cannot be put in the place of the other (being situated upon the opposite hemisphere). Here then is an internal difference between the two triangles, which difference our understanding cannot describe as internal, and which only manifests itself by external relations in space.

But I shall adduce examples, taken from common life, that are more obvious still.

What can be more similar in every respect and in every part more alike to my hand and to my ear, than their images in a mirror? And yet I cannot put such a hand as is seen in the glass in the place of its archetype; for if this is a right hand, that in the glass is a left one, and the image or reflexion of the right ear is a left one which never can serve as a substitute for the other. There are in this case no internal differences which our understanding could determine by thinking alone. Yet the differences are internal as the senses teach, for, notwithstanding their complete equality and similarity, the left hand cannot be enclosed in the same bounds as the right one (they are not congruent); the glove of one hand cannot be used for the other. What is the solution? These objects are not representations of things as they are in themselves, and as the pure understanding would cognise them, but sensuous intuitions that is, appearances, the possibility of which rests upon the relation of certain things unknown in themselves to something else, viz., to our sensibility. Space is the form of the external intuition of this sensibility, and the internal determination of every space is only possible by the determination of its external relation to the whole space, of which it is a part (in other words, by its relation to the external sense). That is to say, the part is only possible through the whole, which is never the case with things in themselves, as objects of the mere understanding, but with appearances only. Hence the difference between similar and equal things, which are yet not congruent (for instance, two symmetric helices), cannot be made intelligible by any concept, but only by the relation to the right and the left hands which immediately refers to intuition.

Remark I

Pure Mathematics, and especially pure geometry, can only have objective reality on condition that they refer to objects of sense. But in regard to the latter the principle holds good, that our sense representation is not a representation of things in themselves, but of the way in which they appear to us. Hence it follows, that the propositions of geometry are not the results of a mere creation of our poetic imagination, and that therefore they cannot be referred with assurance to actual objects; but rather that they are necessarily valid of space, and consequently of all that may be found in space, because space is nothing else than the form of all external appearances, and it is this form alone in which objects of sense can be given. Sensibility, the form of which is the basis of geometry, is that upon which the possibility of external appearance depends. Therefore these appearances can never contain anything but what geometry prescribes to them.

It would be quite otherwise if the senses were so constituted as to represent objects as they are in themselves. For then it would not by any means follow from the conception of space, which with all its properties serves to the geometer as an *a priori* foundation, together with what is thence inferred, must be so in nature. The space of the geometer would be considered a mere fiction, and it would not be credited with objective validity, because we cannot see how things must of necessity agree with an image of them, which we make spontaneously and previous to our acquaintance with them. But if this image, or rather this formal intuition, is the essential property of our sensibility, by means of which alone objects are given to us, and if this sensibility represents not things in themselves, but their appearances: we shall easily comprehend, and at the same time indisputably prove, that all external objects of our world of sense must necessarily coincide in the most rigorous way with the propositions of geometry; because sensibility by means of its form of external intuition, viz., by space, the same with which the geometer is occupied, makes those objects at all possible as mere appearances.

It will always remain a remarkable phenomenon in the history of philosophy, that there was a time, when even mathematicians, who at the same time were philosophers, began to doubt, not of the accuracy of their geometrical propositions so far as they concerned space, but of their objective validity and the applicability of this concept itself, and of all its corollaries, to nature. They showed much concern whether a line in nature might not consist of physical points, and consequently that true space in the object might not consist of physical points, and consequently that true space in the object might consist of simple [discrete] parts, while the space which the geometer has in his mind [being continuous] cannot be such. They did not recognise that this mental space renders possible the physical space, i.e., the extension of matter; that this pure space is not at all a quality of things in themselves, but a form of our sensuous faculty of representation; and that all objects in space are mere appearances, i.e., not things in themselves but representations of our sensuous intuition. But such is the case, for the space of the geometer is exactly the form of sensuous intuition which we find *a priori* in us, and contains the ground of the possibility of all external appearances (according to their form), and the latter must necessarily and most rigidly agree with the propositions of the geometer, which he draws not from any fictitious concept, but from the subjective basis of all external phenomena, which is sensibility itself. In this and no other way can geometry be made secure as to the undoubted objective reality of its propositions against all the intrigues of a shallow Metaphysics, which is surprised at them [the geometrical propositions], because it has not traced them to the sources of their concepts.

Remark II

Whatever is given us as object, must be given us in intuition. All our intuition however takes place by means of the senses only; the understanding intuits nothing, but only reflects. And as we have just shown that the senses never and in no manner enable us to know things in themselves, but only their appearances, which are mere representations of the sensibility, we conclude that "all bodies, together with the space in which they are, must be considered nothing but mere representations in us, and exist nowhere but in our thoughts." You will say: Is not this manifest idealism?

Idealism consists in the assertion, that there are none but thinking beings, all other things, which we think are perceived in intuition, being nothing but representations in the thinking beings, to which no object external to them corresponds in fact. Whereas I say, that things as objects of our senses existing outside us are given, but we know nothing of what they may be in themselves, knowing only their appearances, i.e., the representations which they cause in us by affecting our senses. Consequently I grant by all means that there are bodies without us, that is, things which, though quite unknown to us as to what they are in themselves, we yet know by the representations which their influence on our sensibility procures us, and which we call bodies, a term signifying merely the appearance of the thing which is unknown to us, but not therefore less actual. Can this be termed idealism? It is the very contrary.

Long before Locke's time, but assuredly since him, it has been generally assumed and granted without detriment to the actual existence of external things, that many of their predicates may be said to belong not to the things in themselves, but to their appearances, and to have no proper existence outside our representation. Heat, color, and taste, for instance, are of this kind. Now, if I go farther, and for weighty reasons rank as mere appearances the remaining qualities of bodies also, which are called primary, such as extension, place, and in general space, with all that which belongs to it (impenetrability or materiality, space, etc.)—no one in the least can adduce the reason of its being inadmissible. As little as the man who admits colors not to be properties of the object in itself, but only as modifications of the sense of sight, should on that account be called an idealist, so little can my system be named idealistic, merely because I find that more, nay,

All the properties which constitute the intuition of a body belong merely to its appearance.

The existence of the thing that appears is thereby not destroyed, as in genuine idealism, but it is only shown, that we cannot possibly know it by the senses as it is in itself.

I should be glad to know what my assertions must be in order to avoid all idealism. Undoubtedly, I should say, that the representation of space is not only perfectly conformable to the relation which our sensibility has to objects—that I have said—but that it is quite similar to the object,—an assertion in which I can find as little meaning as if I said that the sensation of red has a similarity to the property of vermilion, which in me excites this sensation.

Remark III

Hence we may at once dismiss an easily foreseen but futile objection, "that by admitting the ideality of space and of time the whole sensible world would be turned into mere sham." At first all philosophical insight into the nature of sensuous cognition was spoiled, by making the sensibility merely a confused mode of representation, according to which we still know things as they are, but without being able to reduce everything in this our representation to a clear consciousness; whereas proof is offered by us that sensibility consists, not in this logical distinction of clearness and obscurity, but in the genetical one of the origin of cognition itself. For sensuous perception represents things not at all as they are, but only the mode in which they affect our senses, and consequently by sensuous perception appearances only and not things themselves are given to the understanding for reflexion. After this necessary corrective, an objection rises from an unpardonable and almost intentional misconception, as if my doctrine turned all the things of the world of sense into mere illusion.

When an appearance is given us, we are still quite free as to how we should judge the matter. The appearance depends upon the senses, but the judgment upon the understanding, and the only question is, whether in the determination of the object there is truth or not. But the difference between truth and dreaming is not ascertained by the nature of the representations, which are referred to objects (for they are the same in both cases), but by their connexion according to those rules, which determine the coherence of the representations in the concept of an object, and by ascertaining whether they can subsist together in experience or not. And it is not the fault of the appearances if our cognition takes illusion for truth, i.e., if the intuition, by which an object is given us, is considered a concept of the thing or of its existence also, which the understanding can only think. The senses represent to us the paths of the planets as now progressive, now retrogressive, and herein is neither falsehood nor truth, because as long as we hold this path to be nothing but appearance, we do not judge of the objective nature of their motion. But as a false judgment may easily arise when the understanding is not on its guard against this subjective mode of representation being considered objective, we say they appear to move backward; it is not the senses however which must be charged with the illusion, but the understanding, whose province alone it is to give an objective judgment on appearances.

Thus, even if we did not at all reflect on the origin of our representations, whenever we connect our intuitions of sense (whatever they may contain), in space and in time, according to the rules of coherence of all cognition in experience, illusion or truth will arise according as we are negligent or careful. It is merely a question of the use of sensuous representations in the understanding, and not of their origin. In the same way, if I consider all the representations of the senses, together with their form, space and time, to be nothing but appearances, and space and time to be a mere form of the sensibility, which is not to be met with in objects out of it, and if I make use of these representations in reference to possible experience only, there is nothing in my regarding them as appearances that can lead astray or cause illusion. For all that they can correctly cohere according to rules of truth in experience. Thus all the propositions of geometry hold good of space as well as of all the objects of the senses, consequently of all possible experience, whether I consider space as a mere form of the sensibility, or as something cleaving to the things themselves. In the former case however I comprehend how I can know *a priori* these propositions concerning all the objects of external intuition. Otherwise everything else as regards all possible experience remains just as if I had not departed from the vulgar view.

But if I venture to go beyond all possible experience with my notions of space and time, which I cannot refrain from doing if I proclaim them qualities inherent in things in themselves (for what should prevent me from letting them hold good of the same things, even though my senses might be different, and unsuited to them?), then a grave error may arise due to illusion, for thus I would proclaim to be universally valid what is merely a subjective condition of the intuition of things and sure only for all objects of sense, viz., for all possible experience; I would refer this condition to things in themselves, and do not limit it to the conditions of experience.

My doctrine of the ideality of space and of time, therefore, far from reducing the whole sensible world to mere illusion, is the only means of securing the application of one of the most important cognitions (that which mathematics propounds *a priori*) to actual objects, and of preventing its being regarded as mere illusion. For without this observation it would be quite impossible to make out whether the intuitions of space and time, which we borrow from no experience, and which yet lie in our representation *a priori*, are not mere phantasms of our brain, to which objects do not correspond, at least not adequately, and consequently, whether we have been able to show its unquestionable validity with regard to all the objects of the sensible world just because they are mere appearances.

Secondly, though these my principles make appearances of the representations of the senses, they are so far from turning the truth of experience into mere illusion, that they are rather the only means of preventing the transcendental illusion, by which metaphysics has hitherto been deceived, leading to the childish endeavor of catching at bubbles, because appearances, which are mere representations, were taken for things in themselves. Here originated the remarkable event of the antimony of Reason which I shall mention by and by, and which is destroyed by the single observation, that appearance, as long as it is employed in experience, produces truth, but the moment it transgresses the bounds of experience, and consequently becomes transcendent, produces nothing but illusion.

Inasmuch, therefore, as I leave to things as we obtain them by the senses their actuality, and only limit our sensuous intuition of these things to this, that they represent in no respect, not even in the pure intuitions of space and of time, anything more than mere appearance of those things, but never their constitution in themselves, this is not a sweeping illusion invented for nature by me. My protestation too against all charges of idealism is so valid and clear as even to seem superfluous, were there not incompetent judges, who, while they would have an old name for every deviation from their perverse though common opinion, and never judge of the spirit of philosophic nomenclature, but cling to the letter only, are ready to put their own conceits in the place of well-defined notions, and thereby deform and distort them. I have myself given this my theory the name of transcendental idealism, but that cannot authorise any one to confound it either with the empirical idealism of Descartes, (indeed, his was only an insoluble problem, owing to which he thought every one at liberty to deny the existence of the corporeal world, because it could never be proved satisfactorily), or with the mystical and visionary idealism of Berkeley, against which and other similar phantasms our *Critique* contains the proper antidote. My idealism concerns not the existence of things (the doubting of which, however, constitutes idealism in the ordinary sense), since it never came into my head to doubt it, but it concerns the sensuous representation of things, to which space and time especially belong. Of these [viz., space and time], consequently of all appearances in general, I have only shown, that they are neither things (but mere modes of representation), nor determinations belonging to things in themselves. But the word "transcendental," which with me means a reference of our cognition, i.e., not to things, but only to the cognitive faculty, was meant to obviate this misconception. Yet rather than give further occasion to it by this word, I now retract it, and desire this idealism of mine to be called critical. But if it be really an objectionable idealism to convert actual things (not appearances) into mere representations by what name shall we call him who conversely changes mere representations to things? It may, I think, be called "dreaming idealism," in contradistinction to the former, which may be called "visionary," both of which are to be refuted by my transcendental, or, better, critical idealism.

SECOND PART OF THE TRANSCENDENTAL PROBLEM

How Is the Science of Nature Possible?

14. Nature is the existence of things, so far as it is determined according to universal laws. Should nature signify the existence of things in themselves, we could never cognise it either *a priori* or *a posteriori*. Not *a priori*, for how can we know what belongs to things in themselves, since this never can be done by the dissection of our concepts (in analytical judgments)? We do not want to know what is contained in our concept of a thing (for the [concept describes what] belongs to its logical being), but what is in the actuality of the thing superadded to our concept, and by what the thing itself is determined in its existence outside the concept. Our understanding, and the conditions on which alone it can connect the determinations of things in their existence, do not prescribe any rule to things themselves; these do not conform to our understanding, but it must conform itself to them; they must therefore be first given us in order to gather these determinations from them, wherefore they would not be cognised *a priori*.

A cognition of the nature of things in themselves *a posteriori* would be equally impossible. For, if experience is to teach us laws, to which the existence of things is subject, these laws, if they regard things in themselves, must belong to them of necessity even outside our experience. But experience teaches us what exists and how it exists, but never that it must necessarily exist so and not otherwise. Experience therefore can never teach us the nature of things in themselves.

15. We nevertheless actually possess a pure science of nature in which are propounded, *a priori* and with all the necessity requisite to apodeictical propositions, laws to which nature is subject. I need only call to witness that propaedeutic [introduction] of natural science which, under the title of the universal Science of Nature, precedes all Physics (which is founded upon empirical principles). In it we have Mathematics applied to appearance, and also merely discursive principles (or those derived from concepts), which constitute the philosophical part of the pure cognition of nature. But there are several things in it, which are not quite pure and independent of empirical sources: such as the concept of *motion*, that of *impenetrability* (upon which the empirical concept of matter rests), that of *inertia*, and many others, which prevent its being called a perfectly pure science of nature. Besides, it only refers to objects of the external sense, and therefore does not give an example of a universal science of nature, in the strict sense, for such a science must reduce nature in general, whether it regards the object of the external or that of the internal sense (the object of Physics as well as Psychology), to universal laws. But among the principles of this universal physics there are a few which actually have the required universality; for instance, the propositions that "substance is permanent," and that "every event is determined by a cause according to constant laws," etc. These are actually universal laws of nature, which subsist completely *a priori*. There is then in fact a pure science of nature, and the question arises, *How is it possible?*

16. The word "nature" assumes yet another meaning, which determines the object, whereas in the former sense it only denotes the conformity to law of the determinations of the existence of things generally. If we consider it *materialiter* (i.e., in the matter that forms its objects) "nature is the complex of all the objects of experience." And with this only are we now concerned, for besides, things which can never be objects of experience, if they must be cognised as to their nature, would oblige us to have recourse to concepts whose meaning could never be given *in concreto* (by any example of possible experience). Consequently we must form for ourselves a list of concepts of their nature, the reality whereof (i.e., whether they actually refer to objects, or are mere creations of thought) could never be determined. The cognition of what cannot be an object of experience would be hyperphysical, and with things hyperphysical we are here not concerned, but only with the cognition of nature, the actuality of which can be confirmed by experience, though it [the cognition of nature] is possible *a priori* and precedes all experience.

17. The former [aspect] of nature in this narrower sense is therefore the conformity to law of all the objects of experience, and so far as it is cognised *a priori*, their necessity conformity. But it has just been shown that the laws of nature can never be cognised *a priori* in objects so far as they are considered not in reference to possible experience, but as things in themselves. And our inquiry here extends not to things in themselves (the properties of which we pass by), but to things as objects of possible experience, and the complex of these is what we properly designate as nature. And now I ask, when the possibility of a cognition of nature *a priori* is in question, whether it is better to arrange the problem thus: How can we cognise *a priori* that things as objects of experience necessarily conform to law? or thus: How is it possible to cognise *a priori* the necessary conformity to law of experience itself as regards all its objects generally?

Closely considered, the solution of the problem, represented in either way, amounts, with regard to the pure cognition of nature (which is the point of the question at issue), entirely to the same thing. For the subjective laws, under which alone an empirical cognition of things is possible, hold good of these things, as objects of possible experience (not as things in themselves, which are not considered here). Either of the following statements means quite the same:

"A judgment of observation can never rank as experience without the law that whenever an event is observed, it is always referred to some antecedent, which it follows according to a universal rule."

"Everything, of which experience teaches that it happens, must have a cause."

It is, however, more commendable to choose the first formula. For we can *a priori* and previous to all given objects have a cognition of those conditions, on which alone experience is possible, but never of the laws to which things may in themselves be subject, without reference to possible experience. We cannot therefore study the nature of things *a priori* otherwise than by investigating the conditions and the universal (though subjective) laws, under which alone such a cognition as experience (as to mere form) is possible, and we determine accordingly the possibility of things, as objects of experience. For if I should choose the second formula, and seek the conditions *a priori*, on which nature as an object of experience is possible, I might easily fall into error, and fancy that I was speaking of nature as a thing in itself, and then move round in endless circles, in a vain search for laws concerning things of which nothing is given me.

Accordingly we shall here be concerned with experience only, and the universal conditions of its possibility which are given *a priori*. Thence we shall determine nature as the whole object of all possible experience. I think it will be understood that I here do not mean the rules of the observation of a nature that is already given, for these already presuppose experience. I do not mean how (through experience) we can study the laws of nature; for these would not then be laws *a priori*, and would yield us no pure science of nature; but [I mean to ask] how the conditions of the possibility of experience are at the same time the sources from which all the universal laws of nature must be derived.

18. In the first place we must state that, while all judgments of experience are empirical (i.e., have their ground in immediate sense-perception), vice versa, all empirical judgments are not judgments of experience, but, besides the empirical, and in general besides what is given to the sensuous intuition, particular, concepts must yet be superadded—concepts which have their origin quite *a priori* in the pure understanding, and under which every perception must be first of all subsumed and then by their means changed into experience.

Empirical judgments, so far as they have objective validity, are *judgments of experience;* but those which are only subjectively valid, I name mere *judgments of perception.* The latter require no pure concept of the understanding, but only the logical connexion of perception in a thinking subject. But the former always require, besides the representation of the sensuous intuition, particular *concepts originally begotten in the understanding,* which produce the objective validity of the judgment of experience.

All our judgments are at first merely judgments of perception; they hold good only for us (i.e., for our subject), and we do not till afterwards give them a new reference (to an object), and desire that they shall always hold good for us and in the same way for everybody else; for when a judgment agrees with an object, all judgments concerning the same object must likewise agree among themselves, and thus the objective validity of the judgment of experience signifies nothing else than its necessary universality of application. And conversely when we have reason to consider a judgment necessarily universal (which never depends upon perception, but upon the pure concept of the understanding, under which the perception is subsumed), we must consider it objective also, that is, that it expresses not merely a reference of our perception to a subject, but a quality of the object. For there would be no reason for the judgments of other men necessarily agreeing with mine, if it were not the unity of the object to which they all refer, and with which they accord; hence they must all agree with one another.

19. Therefore objective validity and necessary universality (for everybody) are equivalent terms, and though we do not know the object in itself, yet when we consider a judgment as universal, and also necessary, we understand it to have objective validity. By this judgment we cognise the object (though it remains unknown as it is in itself) by the universal and necessary connexion of the given perceptions. As this is the case with all objects of sense, judgments of experience take their objective validity not from the immediate cognition of the object (which is impossible), but from the condition of universal validity in empirical judgments, which, as already said, never rests upon empirical, or, in short, sensuous conditions, but upon a pure concept of the understanding. The object always remains unknown in itself; but when by the concept of the understanding the connexion of the representations of the object, which are given to our sensibility, is determined as universally valid, the object is determined by this relation, and it is the judgment that is objective.

To illustrate the matter: When we say, "the room is warm, sugar sweet, and wormwood bitter,"[7]—we have only subjectively valid judgments. I do not at all expect that I or any other person shall always find it as I now do; each of these sentences only expresses a relation of two sensations to the same subject, to myself, and that only in my present state of perception; consequently they are not valid of the object. Such are judgments of perception. Judgments of experience are of quite a different nature. What experience teaches me under certain circumstances, it must always teach me and everybody; and its validity is not limited to the subject nor to its state at a particular time. Hence I pronounce all such judgments as being objectively valid. For instance, when I say the air is elastic, this judgment is as yet a judgment of perception only—I do nothing but refer two of my sensations to one another. But, if I would have it called a judgment of experience, I require this connexion to stand under a condition, which makes it universally valid. I desire therefore that I and everybody else should always connect necessarily the same perceptions under the same circumstances.

20. We must consequently analyse experience in order to see what is contained in this product of the senses and of the understanding, and how the judgment of experience itself is possible. The foundation is the intuition of which I become conscious i.e., perception which pertains merely to the senses. But in the next place, there are acts of judging (which belong only to the understanding). But this judging

7. I freely grant that these examples do not represent such judgments of perception as ever could become judgments of experience, even though a concept of the understanding were superadded, because they refer merely to feeling, which everybody knows to be merely subjective, and which of course can never be attributed to the object, and consequently never become objective. I only wished to give here an example of a judgment that is merely subjectively valid, containing no ground for universal validity, and thereby for a relation to the object. An example of the judgments of perception, which become judgments of experience by superadded concepts of the understanding, will be given in the next note.

may be twofold—first, I may merely compare perceptions and connect them in a particular state of my consciousness; or, secondly, I may connect them in consciousness generally. The former judgment is merely a judgment of perception, and of subjective validity only: it is merely a connexion of perceptions in my mental state, without reference to the object. Hence it is not, as is commonly imagined, enough for experience to compare perceptions and to connect them in consciousness through judgment; there arises no universality and necessity, for which alone judgments can become objectively valid and be called experience.

Quite another judgment therefore is required before perception can become experience. The given intuition must be subsumed under a concept, which determines the form of judging in general relatively to the intuition, connects its empirical consciousness of intuition in consciousness generally, and thereby procures universal validity for empirical judgments. A concept of this nature is a pure *a priori* concept of the Understanding, which does nothing but determine for an intuition the general way in which it can be used for judgments. Let the concept be that of cause, then it determines the intuition which is subsumed under it, e.g., that of air, relative to judgments in general, viz., the concept of air serves with regard to its expansion in the relation of antecedent to consequent in a hypothetical judgment. The concept of cause accordingly is a pure concept of the understanding, which is totally disparate from all possible perception, and only serves to determine the representation subsumed under it, relatively to judgments in general, and so to make a universally valid judgment possible.

Before, therefore, a judgment of perception can become a judgment of experience, it is requisite that the perception should be subsumed under some such a concept of the understanding; for instance, air ranks under the concept of causes, which determines our judgment about it in regard to its expansion as hypothetical.[8] Thereby the expansion of the air is represented not as merely belonging to the perception of the air in my present state or in several states of mine, or in the state of perception of others, but as belonging to it necessarily. The judgment, "the air is elastic," becomes universally valid, and a judgment of experience, only by certain judgments preceding it, which subsume the intuition of air under the concept of cause and effect: and they thereby determine the perceptions not merely as regards one another in me, but relatively to the form of judging in general, which is here hypothetical, and in this way they render the empirical judgment universally valid.

If all our synthetical judgments are analysed so far as they are objectively valid, it will be found that they never consist of mere intuitions connected only (as is commonly believed) by comparison into a judgment; but that they would be impossible were not a pure concept of the understanding superadded to the concepts abstracted from intuition, under which concept these latter are subsumed, and in this manner only combined into an objectively valid judgment. Even the judgments of pure mathematics in their simplest axioms are not exempt from this condition. The principle, "a straight line is the shortest between two points," presupposes that the line is subsumed under the concept of quantity, which certainly is no mere intuition, but has its seat in the understanding alone, and serves to determine the intuition (of the line) with regard to the judgments which may be made about it, relatively to their quantity, that is, to plurality (as *judicia plurativa*).[9] For under them it is understood that in a given intuition there is contained a plurality of homogeneous parts.

21. To prove, then, the possibility of experience so far as it rests upon pure concepts of the understanding *a priori*, we must first represent what belongs to judgments in general and the various functions of the understanding, in a complete table. For the pure concepts of the understanding must run parallel to these functions, as such concepts are nothing more than concepts of intuitions in general, so

8. As an easier example, we may take the following: "When the sun shines on the stone, it grows warm." This judgment, however often I and others may have perceived it, is a mere judgment of perception, and contains no necessity; perceptions are only usually conjoined in this manner. But if I say, "The sun warms the stone," I add to the perception a concept of the understanding, viz., that of cause, which connects with the concept of sunshine that of heat as a necessary consequence, and the synthetical judgment becomes of necessity universally valid, viz., objective, and is converted from a perception into experience.

9. This name seems preferable to the term, *particularia,* which is used for these judgments in logic. For the latter implies the idea that they are not universal. But when I start from unity (in single judgments) and so proceed to universality, I must not [even indirectly and negatively] imply any reference to universality. I think plurality merely without universality, and not the exception from universality. This is necessary, if logical considerations shall form the basis of the pure concepts of the understanding. However, there is no need of making changes in logic.

far as these are determined by one or other of these functions of judging, in themselves, that is, necessarily and universally. Hereby also the *a priori* principles of the possibility of all experience, as of an objectively valid empirical cognition, will be precisely determined. For they are nothing but propositions by which all perception is (under certain universal conditions of intuition) subsumed under those pure concepts of the understanding.

Logical Table of Judgments.

1	2
As to Quantity.	*As to Quality.*
Universal.	Affirmative.
Particular.	Negative.
Singular.	Infinite.
3	4
As to Relation.	*As to Modality.*
Categorical.	Problematical.
Hypothetical.	Assertorial.
Disjunctive.	Apodeictical.

Transcendental Table of the Pure Concepts of the Understanding.

1	2
As to Quantity.	*As to Quality.*
Unity (the Measure).	Reality.
Plurality (the Quantity).	Negation.
Totality (the Whole).	Limitation.
3	4
As to Relation.	*As to Modality.*
Substance.	Possibility.
Cause.	Existence.
Community.	Necessity.

Pure Physiological Table of the Universal Principles of the Science of Nature.

1	2
Axioms of Intuition.	Anticipations of Perception.
3	4
Analogies of Experience	Postulates of Empirical Thinking generally

21*a*. In order to comprise the whole matter in one idea, it is first necessary to remind the reader that we are discussing not the origin of experience, but of that which lies in experience. The former pertains to empirical psychology, and would even then never be adequately explained without the latter, which belongs to the critique of cognition, and particularly of the understanding.

Experience consists of intuitions, which belongs to the sensibility, and of judgments, which are entirely a work of the understanding. But the judgments, which the understanding forms alone from sensuous intuitions, are far from being judgments of experience. For in the one case the judgment connects only the perceptions as they are given in the sensuous intuition, while in the other the judgments must express what experience in general, and not what the mere perception (which possesses only subjective validity) contains. The judgment of experience must therefore add to the sensuous intuition and its logical connexion in a judgment (after it has been rendered universal by comparison) something that determines the synthetical judgment as necessary and therefore as universally valid. This can be nothing else than that concept which represents the intuition as determined in itself with regard to one form of judgment rather than another, viz., a concept of that synthetical unity of intuitions which can only be represented by a given logical function of judgments.

22. The sum of the matter is this: the business of the senses is to intuit—that of the understanding is to think. But thinking is uniting representations in one consciousness. This union originates either merely relative to the subject, and is accidental and subjective, or is absolute, and is necessary or objective. The union of representations in one consciousness is judgment. Thinking therefore is the same as judging, or referring representations to judgments in general. Hence judgments are either merely subjective, when representations are referred to a consciousness in one subject only, and united in it, or objective, when they are united in a consciousness generally, that is, necessarily. The logical functions of all judgments are but various modes of uniting representations in consciousness. But if they serve for concepts, they are concepts of their necessary union in a consciousness, and so principles of objectively valid judgments. This union in a consciousness is either analytical, by identity, or synthetical, by the combination and addition of various representations one to another. Experience consists in the synthetical connexion of phenomena (perceptions) in consciousness, so far as this connexion is necessary. Hence the pure concepts of the understanding are those under which all perceptions must be subsumed before they can serve for judgments of experience, in which the synthetical unity of the perceptions is represented as necessary and universally valid.[10]

23. Judgments, when considered merely as the condition of the union of given representations in a consciousness, are rules. These rules, so far as they represent the union as necessary, are rules *a priori*, and so far as they cannot be deduced from higher rules, are fundamental principles. But in regard to the possibility of all experience, merely in relation to the form of thinking in it, no conditions of judgments of experience are higher than those which bring the phenomena, according to the various form of their intuition, under pure concepts of the understanding, and render the empirical judgment objectively valid. These concepts are therefore the *a priori* principles of possible experience.

The principles of possible experience are then at the same time universal laws of nature, which can be cognised *a priori*. And thus the problem in our second question, "How is the pure Science of Nature possible?" is solved. For the system which is required for the form of a science is to be met with in perfection here, because, beyond the above-mentioned formal conditions of all judgments in general offered in logic, no others are possible, and these constitute a logical system. The concepts grounded thereupon, which contain the *a priori* conditions of all synthetical and necessary judgments, accordingly constitute a transcendental system. Finally the principles, by means of which all phenomena are subsumed under these concepts, constitute a physical system, that is, a system of nature, which precedes all empirical cognition of nature, makes it even possible, and hence may in strictness be denominated the universal and pure science of nature.

10. But how does this proposition, "that judgments of experience contain necessity in the synthesis of perceptions," agree with my statement so often before inculcated that "experience as cognition *a posteriori* can afford contingent judgments only?" When I say that experience teaches me something I mean only the perception that lies in experience,—for example that heat always follows the shining of the sun on a stone; consequently the proposition of experience is always so far accidental. That this heat necessarily follows the shining of the sun is contained indeed in the judgment of experience (by means of the concept of cause), yet is a fact not learned by experience; for conversely experience is first of all generated by this addition of the concept of the understanding (of cause) to perception. How perception attains this addition may be seen by referring in the *Critique* itself to the section on the Transcendental faculty of Judgment.

24. The first one[11] of the physiological principles subsumes all phenomena, as intuitions in space and time, under the concept of Quantity, and is so far a principle of the application of Mathematics to experience. The second one subsumes the empirical element, viz., sensation, which denotes the real in intuitions, not indeed directly under the concept of quantity, because sensation is not an intuition that contains either space or time, though it places the respective object into both. But still there is between reality (sense-representation) and the zero, or total void of intuition in time, a difference which has a quantity. For between every given degree of light and of darkness, between every degree of heat and of absolute cold, between every degree of weight and of absolute lightness, between every degree of occupied space and of totally void space, diminishing degrees can be conceived, in the same manner as between consciousness and total unconsciousness (the darkness of a psychological blank) ever diminishing degrees obtain. Hence there is no perception that can prove an absolute absence of it; for instance, no psychological darkness that cannot be considered as a kind of consciousness, which is only outbalanced by a stronger consciousness. This occurs in all cases of sensation, and so the understanding can anticipate even sensations, which constitute the peculiar quality of empirical representations (appearances), by means of the principle: "that they all have (consequently that what is real in all phenomena has) a degree." Here is the second application of mathematics (*mathesis intensorum*) to the science of nature.

25. About the relation of appearances merely with a view to their existence, the determination is not mathematical but dynamical, and can never be objectively valid, consequently never fit for experience, if it does not come under *a priori* principles by which the cognition of experience relative to appearances becomes even possible. Hence appearances must be subsumed under the concept of Substance, which is the foundation of all determination of existence, as a concept of the thing itself; or secondly—so far as a succession is found among phenomena, that is, an event—under the concept of an

11. The three following paragraphs will hardly be understood unless reference be made to what the *Critique* itself says on the subject of the Principles; they will, however be of service in giving a general view of the Principles, and in fixing the attention on the main points.

Effect with reference to Cause; or lastly—so far as coexistence is to be known objectively, that is, by a judgment of experience—under the concept of Community (action and reaction). Thus *a priori* principles form the basis of objectively valid, through empirical judgments, that is, of the possibility of experience so far as it must connect objects as existing in nature. These principles are the proper laws of nature, which may be termed dynamical.

Finally the cognition of the agreement and connexion not only of appearances among themselves in experience, but of their relation to experience in general, belongs to the judgments of experience. This relation contains either their agreement with the formal conditions, which the understanding cognises, or their coherence with the materials of the senses and of perception, or combines both into one concept. Consequently it contains Possibility, Actuality, and Necessity according to universal laws of nature; and this constitutes the physical doctrine of method, or the distinction of truth and of hypotheses, and the bounds of the certainty of the latter.

26. The third table of Principles drawn from the nature of the understanding itself after the critical method, shows an inherent perfection, which raises it far above every other table which has hitherto though in vain been tried or may yet be tried by analysing the objects themselves dogmatically. It exhibits all synthetical *a priori* principles completely and according to one principle, viz., the faculty of judging in general, constituting the essence of experience as regards the understanding, so that we can be certain that there are no more such principles, which affords a satisfaction such as can never be attained by the dogmatical method. Yet is this not all: there is a still greater merit in it.

We must carefully bear in mind the proof which shows the possibility of this cognition *a priori*, and at the same time limits all such principles to a condition which must never be lost sight of, if we desire it not to be misunderstood, and extended in use beyond the original sense which the understanding attaches to it. This limit is that they contain nothing but the conditions of possible experience in general so far as it is subjected to laws *a priori*. Consequently I do not say, that things *in themselves* possess a quantity, that their actuality possesses a degree, their existence a connexion of accidents in a substance, etc. This nobody can prove, because such a synthetical connexion from mere concepts, without any reference to sensuous intuition on the one side, or connexion of it in a possible experience on the other, is absolutely impossible. The essential limitation of the concepts in these principles then is: That all things stand necessarily *a priori* under the aforementioned conditions, as objects of experience only.

Hence there follows secondly a specifically peculiar mode of proof of these principles: they are not directly referred to appearances and to their relations, but to the possibility of experience, of which appearances constitute the matter only, not the form. Thus they are referred to objectively and universally valid synthetical propositions, in which we distinguish judgments of experience from those of perception. This takes place because appearances, as mere intuitions, occupying a part of space and time, come under the concept of Quantity, which unites their multiplicity *a priori* according to rules synthetically. Again, so far as the perception contains, besides intuition, sensibility, and between the latter and nothing (i.e., the total disappearance of sensibility), there is an ever decreasing transition, it is apparent that that which is in appearances must have a degree, so far as it (viz., the perception) does not itself occupy any part of space or of time.[12] Still the transition to actuality from empty time or empty space is only possible in time; consequently though sensibility, as the quality of empirical intuition, can never be cognised *a priori*, by its specific difference from other sensibilities, yet it can, in a possible experience in general, as a quantity of perception be intensely distinguished from every other similar perception. Hence the application of mathematics to nature, as regards the sensuous intuition by which nature is given to us, becomes possible and is thus determined.

Above all, the reader must pay attention to the mode of proof of the principles which occur under the title of Analogies of experience. For these do not refer to the genesis of intuitions, as do the principles of applied mathematics, but to the connexion

12. Heat and light are in a small space just as large as to degree as in a large one; in like manner the internal representations, pain, consciousness in general, whether they last a short or a long time need not vary as to the degree. Hence the quantity is here in a point and in a moment just as great as in any space or time however great. Degrees are therefore capable of increase, but not of an intuition). Hence they can only be estimated quantitatively by the relation of 1 to 0, viz., by their capability of decreasing by infinite intermediate degrees to disappearance, or of increasing from naught through infinite gradations to a determinate sensation in a certain time. *Quantitas qualitas est gradus* [i.e., the degrees of quality is a quantity].

of their existence in experience; and this can be nothing but the determination of their existence in time according to necessary laws, under which alone the connexion is objectively valid, and thus becomes experience. The proof therefore does not turn on the synthetical unity in the connexion of things in themselves, but merely of perceptions, and of these not in regard to their matter, but to the determination of time and of the relation of their existence in it, according to universal laws. If the empirical determination in relative time is indeed objectively valid (i.e., experience), these universal laws contain the necessary determination of existence in time generally (viz., according to a rule of the understanding *a priori*).

In these *Prolegomena* I cannot further discuss the subject, but my reader (who has probably been long accustomed to consider experience a mere empirical synthesis of perceptions, and hence not considered that it goes much beyond them, as it imparts to empirical judgments universal validity, and for that purpose requires a pure and *a priori* unity of the understanding) is recommended to pay special attention to this distinction of experience from a mere aggregate of perceptions, and to judge the mode of proof from this point of view.

27. Now we are prepared to remove Hume's doubt. He justly maintains, that we cannot comprehend by reason the possibility of Causality, that is, of the reference of the existence of one thing to the existence of another, which is necessitated by the former. I add, that we comprehend just as little the concept of Subsistence, that is, the necessity that at the foundation of the existence of things there lies a subject which cannot itself be a predicate of any other thing; nay, we cannot even form a notion of the possibility of such a thing (though we can point out examples of its use in experience). The very same incomprehensibility affects the Community of things, as we cannot comprehend how from the state of one thing an inference to the state of quite another thing beyond it, and *vice versa,* can be drawn, and how substances which have each their own separate existence should depend upon one another necessarily. But I am very far from holding these concepts to be derived merely from experience, and the necessity represented in them, to be imaginary and a mere illusion produced in us by long habit. On the contrary, I have amply shown, that they and the theorems derived from them are firmly established *a priori*, or before all experience, and have their undoubted objective value, though only with regard to experience.

28. Though I have no notion of such a connexion of things in themselves, that they can either exist as substances, or act as causes, or stand in community with others (as parts of a real whole), and I can just as little conceive such properties in appearances as such (because those concepts contain nothing that lies in the appearances, but only what the understanding alone must think): we have yet a notion of such a connexion of representations in our understanding, and in judgments generally; consisting in this that representations appear in one sort of judgments as subject in relation to predicates, in another as reason in relation to consequences, and in a third as parts, which constitute together a total possible cognition. Besides we cognise *a priori* that without considering the representation of an object as determined in some of these respects, we can have no valid cognition of the object, and, if we should occupy ourselves about the object in itself, there is no possible attribute, by which I could know that it is determined under any of these aspects, that is, under the concept either of substance, or of cause, or (in relation to other substances) of community, for I have no notion of the possibility of such a connexion of existence. But the question is not how things in themselves, but how the empirical cognition of things is determined, as regards the above aspects of judgments in general, that is, how things, as objects of experience, can and shall be subsumed under these concepts of the understanding. And then it is clear, that I completely comprehend not only the possibility, but also the necessity of subsuming all phenomena under these concepts, that is, of using them for principles of the possibility of experience.

29. When making an experiment with Hume's problematical concept (his *crux metaphysicorum*), the concept of cause, we have, in the first place, given *a priori*, by means of logic, the form of a conditional judgment in general, i.e., we have one given cognition as antecedent and another as consequence. But it is possible, that in perception we may meet with a rule of relation, which runs thus: that a certain phenomenon is constantly followed by another (though not conversely), and this is a case for me to use the hypothetical judgment, and, for instance, to say, if the sun shines long enough upon a body, it grows warm. Here there is indeed as yet no necessity of connexion, or concept of cause. But I proceed and say, that if this proposition, which is merely a subjective connexion of perceptions, is to be a judgment of experience, it must be considered as necessary and universally valid. Such a proposition would be, "the sun is by its light the cause of heat." The empirical rule is now considered as a law, and as valid not merely of appearances but valid of them for the purposes of a possible experience which requires universal and therefore necessarily valid rules. I therefore easily comprehend the concept of cause, as a concept necessarily belonging to the mere form of experience, and its possibility as a synthetical union of perceptions in consciousness generally; but I do not at all comprehend the possibility of a thing generally as a cause, because the concept of cause denotes a condition not at all belonging to things, but to experience. It is nothing in fact but an objectively valid cognition of appearances and of their succession, so far as the antecedent can be conjoined with the consequent according to the rule of hypothetical judgments.

30. Hence if the pure concepts of the understanding do not refer to objects of experience but to things in themselves (noumena), they have no signification whatever. They serve, as it were, only to decipher appearances, that we may be able to read them as experience. The principles which arise from their reference to the sensible world, only serve our understanding for empirical use. Beyond this they are arbitrary combinations, without objective reality: and we can neither cognise their possibility *a priori*, nor verify their reference to objects, let alone make it intelligible by any example; because examples can only be borrowed from some possible experience, consequently the objects of these concepts can be found nowhere but in a possible experience.

This complete (though to its originator unexpected) solution of Hume's problem rescues for the pure concepts of the understanding their *a priori* origin, and for the universal laws of nature their validity, as laws of the understanding, yet in such a way as to limit their use to experience, because their possibility depends solely on the reference of the understanding to experience, but with a completely reversed mode of connexion which never occurred to Hume, not by deriving them from experience, but by deriving experience from them.

This is therefore the result of all our foregoing inquiries: "All synthetical principles *a priori* are nothing more than principles of possible experience, and can never be referred to things in themselves, but to appearances as objects of experience. And hence pure mathematics as well as a pure science of nature can never be referred to anything more than mere appearances, and can only represent either that which makes experience generally possible, or else that which, as it is derived from these principles, must always be capable of being represented in some possible experience."

31. And thus we have at last something definite, upon which to depend in all metaphysical enterprises, which have hitherto, boldly enough but always at random, attempted everything without discrimination. That the aim of their exertions should be so near, struck neither the dogmatical thinkers nor those who, confident in their supposed sound common sense, started with concepts and principles of pure reason (which were legitimate and natural, but destined for mere empirical use) in quest of fields of knowledge, to which they neither knew nor could know any determinate bound, because they had never reflected nor were able to reflect on the nature or even on the possibility of such a pure understanding.

Many a naturalist of pure reason (by which I mean the man who believes he can decide in matters of metaphysics without any science) may pretend, that he long ago by the prophetic spirit of his sound sense, not only suspected, but knew and comprehended, what is here propounded with so much ado, or, if he likes, with prolix and pedantic pomp: "that with all our reason we can never reach beyond the field of experience." But when he is questioned about his rational principles individually, he must grant, that there are many of them which he has not taken from experience, and which are therefore independent of it and valid *a priori*. How then and on what grounds will he restrain both himself and the dogmatist, who makes use of these concepts and principles beyond all possible experience, because they are recognised to be independent of it? And even he, this adept in sound sense, in spite of all his assumed and cheaply acquired wisdom, is not exempt from wandering inadvertently beyond objects of experience into the field of chimeras. He is often deeply enough involved in them, though in announcing everything as mere probability, rational conjecture, or analogy, he gives by his popular language a color to his groundless pretensions.

32. Since the oldest days of philosophy inquirers into pure reason have conceived, besides the things of sense, or appearances (*phenomena*), which make up the sensible world, certain creations of the understanding called noumena, which should constitute an intelligible world. And as appearance and illusion were by those men identified (a thing which we may well excuse in an undeveloped epoch), actuality was only conceded to the creations of thought.

And we indeed, rightly considering objects of sense as mere appearances, confess thereby that they are based upon a thing in itself, though we know not this thing in its internal constitution, but only know its appearances, viz., the way in which our senses are affected by this unknown something. The understanding therefore, by assuming appearances, grants the existence of things in themselves also, and so far we may say, that the representation of such things as form the basis of phenomena, consequently of mere creations of the understanding, is not only admissible, but unavoidable.

Our critical deduction by no means excludes things of that sort (noumena), but rather limits the principles of the Aesthetic (the science of the sensibility) to this, that they shall not extend to all things, as everything would then be turned into mere appearance, but that they shall only hold good of objects of possible experience. Hereby then objects of the understanding are granted, but with the inculcation of this rule which admits of no exception: "that we neither know nor can know anything at all definite of these pure objects of the understanding, because our pure concepts of the understanding as well as our pure intuitions extend to nothing but objects of possible experience, consequently to mere things of sense, and as soon as we leave this sphere these concepts retain no meaning whatever."

33. There is indeed something seductive in our pure concepts of the understanding, which tempts us to a transcendent use,—a use which transcends all possible experience. Not only are our concepts of substance, of power, of action, of reality, and others, quite independent of experience, containing nothing of sense appearance, and so apparently applicable to things in themselves (noumena), but, what strengthens this conjecture, they contain a necessity of determination in themselves, which experience never attains. The concept of cause implies a rule, according to which one state follows another necessarily; but experience can only show us, that one state of things often, or at most, commonly, follows another, and therefore affords neither strict universality, nor necessity.

Hence the Categories seem to have a deeper meaning and import than can be exhausted by their empirical use, and so the understanding inadvertently adds for itself to the house of experience a much more extensive wing, which it fills with nothing but creatures of thought, without ever observing that it has transgressed with its otherwise lawful concepts the bounds of their use.

34. Two important, and even indispensable, though very dry, investigations had therefore become indispensable in the *Critique of Pure Reason,*—viz., the two chapters "The Schematism of the Pure Concepts of the Understanding," and "The Ground of the Distinction of All Objects in general into Phenomena and Noumena." In the former it is shown, that the senses furnish not the pure concepts of the understanding *in concreto,* but only the schedule for their use, and that the object conformable to it occurs only in experience (as the product of the understanding from materials of the sensibility). In the latter it is shown, that, although our pure concepts of the understanding and our principles are independent of experience, and despite of the apparently greater sphere of their use, still nothing whatever can be thought by them beyond the field of experience, because they can do nothing but merely determine the logical form of the judgment relative to given intuitions. But as there is no intuition at all beyond the field of the sensibility, these pure concepts, as they cannot possibly be exhibited *in concreto,* are void of all meaning; consequently all these noumena, together with their complex, the intelligible world,[13] are nothing but representation of a problem, of which the object in itself is possible, but the solution, from the nature of our understanding, totally impossible. For our understanding is not a faculty of intuition, but of the connexion of given intuitions in experience. Experience must therefore contain all the objects for our concepts; but beyond it no concepts have any significance, as there is no intuition that might offer them a foundation.

35. The imagination may perhaps be forgiven for occasional vagaries, and for not keeping carefully

13. We speak of the "intelligible world" not (as the usual expression is) "intellectual world." For cognitions are intellectual through the understanding, and refer to our world of sense also; but objects so far as they can be represented merely by the understanding, and to which none of our sensible intuitions can refer, are termed "intelligible." But as some possible intuition must correspond to every object we would have to assume an understanding that intuits things immediately; but of such we have not the least notion, nor have we of the things of the understanding, to which it should be applied.

within the limits of experience, since it gains life and vigor by such flights, and since it is always easier to moderate its boldness, than to stimulate its languor. But the understanding which ought to *think* can never be forgiven for indulging in vagaries; for we depend upon it alone for assistance to set bounds, when necessary, to the vagaries of the imagination.

But the understanding begins its aberrations very innocently and modestly. It first elucidates the elementary cognitions, which inhere in it prior to all experience, but yet must always have their application in experience. It gradually drops these limits, and what is there to prevent it, as it has quite freely derived its principles from itself? And then it proceeds first to newly-imagined powers in nature, then to beings outside nature; in short to a world, for whose construction the materials cannot be wanting, because fertile fiction furnishes them abundantly, and though not confirmed, is never refuted, by experience. This is the reason that young thinkers are so partial to metaphysics of the truly dogmatical kind, and often sacrifice to it their time and their talents, which might be otherwise better employed.

But there is no use in trying to moderate these fruitless endeavors of pure reason by all manner of cautions as to the difficulties of solving questions so occult, by complaints of the limits of our reason, and by degrading our assertions into mere conjectures. For if their impossibility is not distinctly shown, and cognition of its own essence does not become a true science, in which the field of its right use is distinguished, so to say, with mathematical certainty from that of its worthless and idle use, these fruitless efforts will never be abandoned for good.

36. *How is Nature itself possible?* This question—the highest point that transcendental philosophy can ever reach, and to which, as its boundary and completion, it must proceed—properly contains two questions.

FIRST: How is nature at all possible in the material sense, by intuition, considered as the totality of appearances; how are space, time, and that which fills both—the object of sensation, in general possible? The answer is: By means of the constitution of our Sensibility, according to which it is specifically affected by objects, which are in themselves unknown to it, and totally distinct from those phenomena. This answer is given in the *Critique* itself in the transcendental Aesthetic, and in these *Prolegomena* by the solution of the first general problem.

SECONDLY: How is nature possible in the formal sense, as the totality of the rules, under which all phenomena must come, in order to be thought as connected in experience? The answer must be this: it is only possible by means of the constitution of our Understanding, according to which all the above representations of the sensibility are necessarily referred to a consciousness, and by which the peculiar way in which we think (viz., by rules), and hence experience also, are possible, but must be clearly distinguished from an insight into the objects in themselves. This answer is given in the *Critique* itself in the transcendental Logic, and in these *Prolegomena,* in the course of the solution of the second main problem.

But how this peculiar property of our sensibility itself is possible, or that of our understanding and of the apperception which is necessarily its basis and that of all thinking, cannot be further analysed or answered, because it is of them that we are in need for all our answers and for all our thinking about objects.

There are many laws of nature, which we can only know by means of experience; but conformity to law in the connexion of appearances, i.e., in nature in general, we cannot discover by any experience, because experience itself requires laws which are *a priori* at the basis of its possibility.

The possibility of experience in general is therefore at the same time the universal law of nature, and the principles of the experience are the very laws of nature. For we do not know nature but as the totality of appearances, i.e., of representations in us, and hence we can only derive the laws of its connexion from the principles of their connexion in us, that is, from the conditions of their necessary union in consciousness, which constitutes the possibility of experience.

Even the main proposition expounded throughout this section—that universal laws of nature can be distinctly cognised *a priori*—leads naturally to the proposition: that the highest legislation of nature must lie in ourselves, i.e., in our understanding, and that we must not seek the universal laws of nature in nature by means of experience, but conversely must seek nature, as to its universal conformity to law, in the conditions of the possibility of experience, which lie in our sensibility and in our understanding. For how were it otherwise possible to know *a priori* these laws, as they are not rules of analytical cognition, but truly synthetical extensions of it?

Such a necessary agreement of the principles of possible experience with the laws of the possibility of nature, can only proceed from one of two reasons: either these laws are drawn from nature by means of experience, or conversely nature is derived from the laws of the possibility of experience in general, and is quite the same as the mere universal conformity to law of the latter. The former is self-contradictory, for the universal laws of nature can and must be cognised *a priori* (that is, independent of all experience), and be the foundation of all empirical use of the understanding; the latter alternative therefore alone remains.[14]

But we must distinguish the empirical laws of nature, which always presuppose particular perceptions, from the pure or universal laws of nature, which, without being based on particular perceptions, contain merely the conditions of their necessary union in experience. In relation to the latter, nature and possible experience are quite the same, and as the conformity to law here depends upon the necessary connexion of appearances in experience (without which we cannot cognise any object whatever in the sensible world), consequently upon the original laws of the understanding, it seems at first strange, but is not the less certain, to say: *The understanding does not derive its laws (a priori) from, but prescribes them to, nature.*

37. We shall illustrate this seemingly bold proposition by an example, which will show, that laws, which we discover in objects of sensuous intuition (especially when these laws are cognised as necessary), are commonly held by us to be such as have been placed there by the understanding, in spite of their being similar in all points to the laws of nature, which we ascribed to experience.

38. If we consider the properties of the circle, by which this figure combines so many arbitrary determinations of space in itself, at once in a universal rule, we cannot avoid attributing a nature to this geometrical thing. Two right lines, for example, which intersect one another and the circle, howsoever they may be drawn, are always divided so that the rectangle constructed with the segments of the one is equal to that constructed with the segments of the other. The question now is: Does this law lie in the circle or in the understanding, that is, Does this figure, independently of the understanding, contain in itself the ground of the law, or does the understanding, having constructed according to its concepts (according to the quality of the radii) the figure itself, introduce into it this law of the chords cutting one another in geometrical proportion? When we follow the proofs of this law, we soon perceive, that it can only be derived from the condition on which the understanding founds the construction of this figure, and which is that of the equality of the radii. But, if we enlarge this concept, to pursue further the unity of various properties of geometrical figures under common laws, and consider the circle as a conic section, which of course is subject to the same fundamental conditions of construction as other conic sections, we shall find that all the chords which intersect within the ellipse, parabola, and hyperbola, always intersect so that the rectangles of their segments are not indeed equal, but always bear a constant ratio to one another. If we proceed still farther, to the fundamental laws of physical astronomy, we find a physical law of reciprocal attraction diffused over all material nature, the rule of which is: "that it decreases inversely as the square of the distance from each attracting point, i.e., as the spherical surfaces increase, over which this force spreads," which law seems to be necessarily inherent in the very nature of things, and hence is usually propounded as cognisable *a priori*. Simple as the sources of this law are, merely resting upon the relation of spherical surfaces of different radii, its consequences are so valuable with regard to the variety of their agreement and its regularity, that not only are all possible orbits of the celestial bodies conic sections, but such a relation of these orbits to each other results, that no other law of attraction, than that of the inverse square of the distance, can be imagined as fit for a cosmical system.

Here accordingly is a nature that rests upon laws which the understanding cognises *a priori* and chiefly from the universal principles of the determination of space. Now I ask:

Do the laws of nature lie in space, and does the understanding learn them by merely endeavoring to find out the enormous wealth of meaning that lies in space; or do they inhere in the understanding and in the way in which it determines space according

14. Crusius alone thought of a compromise that a Spirit, who can neither err nor deceive, implanted these laws in us originally. But since false principles often intrude themselves, as indeed the very system of this man shows in not a few examples, we are involved in difficulties as to the use of such a principle in the absence of sure criteria to distinguish the genuine origin from the spurious, as we never can know certainly what the Spirit of truth or the father of lies may have instilled into us.

to the conditions of the synthetical unity in which its concepts are all centered?

Space is something so uniform and as to all particular properties so indeterminate, that we should certainly not seek a store of laws of nature in it. Whereas that which determines space to assume the form of a circle or the figures of a cone and a sphere, is the understanding, so far as it contains the ground of the unity of their constructions.

The mere universal form of intuition, called space, must therefore be the substratum of all intuitions determinable to particular objects, and in it of course the condition of the possibility and of the variety of these intuitions lies. But the unity of the objects is entirely determined by the understanding,and on conditions which lie in its own nature; and thus the understanding is the origin of the universal order of nature, in that it comprehends all appearances under its own laws, and thereby first constructs, *a priori*, experience (as to its form), by means of which whatever is to be cognised only by experience, is necessarily subjected to its laws. For we are not now concerned with the nature of things in themselves, which is independent of the conditions both of our sensibility and our understanding, but with nature, as an object of possible experience, and in this case the understanding, whilst it makes experience possible, thereby insists that the sensuous world is either not an object of experience at all, or must be nature [viz., an existence of things, determined according to universal laws].

Appendix to the Pure Science of Nature

39. *Of the System of the Categories.* There can be nothing more desirable to a philosopher, than to be able to derive the scattered multiplicity of the concepts or the principles, which had occurred to him in concrete use, from a principle *a priori*, and to unite everything in this way in one cognition. He formerly only believed that those things, which remained after a certain abstraction, and seemed by comparison among one another to constitute a particular kind of cognitions, were completely collected; but this was only an Aggregate. Now he knows, that just so many, neither more nor less, can constitute the mode of cognition, and perceives the necessity of his division, which constitutes comprehension; and now only he has attained a *System*.

To search in our daily cognition for the concepts, which do not rest upon particular experience, and yet occur in all cognition of experience, where they as it were constitute the mere form of connexion, presupposes neither greater reflexion nor deeper insight, than to detect in a language the rules of the actual use of words generally, and thus to collect elements for a grammar. In fact both researches are very nearly related, even though we are not able to give a reason why each language has just this and no other formal constitution, and still less why an exact number of such formal determinations in general are found in it.

Aristotle collected ten pure elementary concepts under the name of Categories.[15] To these, which are also called predicaments, he found himself obliged afterwards to add five post-predicaments,[16] some of which however (*prius, simul,* and *motus*) are contained in the former; but this random collection must be considered (and commended) as a mere hint for future inquirers, not as a regularly developed idea, and hence it has, in the present more advanced state of philosophy, been rejected as quite useless.

After long reflexion on the pure elements of human knowledge (those which contain nothing empirical), I at last succeeded in distinguishing with certainty and in separating the pure elementary notions of the Sensibility (space and time) from those of the Understanding. Thus the 7th, 8th, and 9th Categories had to be excluded from the old list. And the others were of no service to me; because there was no principle [in them], on which the understanding could be investigated, measured in its completion, and all the functions, whence its pure concepts arise, determined exhaustively and with precision.

But in order to discover such a principle, I looked about for an act of the understanding which comprises all the rest, and is distinguished only by various modifications or phases, in reducing the multiplicity of representation to the unity of thinking in general: I found this act of the understanding to consist in judging. Here then the labors of the logicians were ready at hand, though not yet quite free from defects, and with this help I was enabled to exhibit a complete table of the pure functions of the understanding, which are however undetermined in regard to any object. I finally referred these functions of judging to objects in general, or rather to the condition of determining judgments as objectively valid,

15. 1. *Substantia*. 2. *Qualitas*. 3. *Quantitas*. 4. *Relatio*. 5. *Actio*. 6. *Passio*. 7. *Quando*. 8. *Ubi*. 9. *Situs*. 10. *Habitas*.

16. *Oppositum, Prius, Simul, Motus, Habere*.

and so there arose the pure concepts of the understanding, concerning which I could make certain, that these, and this exact number only, constitute our whole cognition of things from pure understanding. I was justified in calling them by their old name, *Categories,* while I reserved for myself the liberty of adding, under the title of *Predicables,* a complete list of all the concepts deducible from them, by combinations whether among themselves, or with the pure form of the appearance, i.e., space or time, or with its matter, so far as it is not yet empirically determined (viz., the object of sensation in general), as soon as a system of transcendental philosophy should be completed with the construction of which I am engaged in the *Critique of Pure Reason* itself.

Now the essential point in this system of Categories, which distinguishes it from the old rhapsodical collection without any principle, and for which alone it deserves to be considered as philosophy, consists in this: that by means of it the true significance of the pure concepts of the understanding and the condition of their use could be precisely determined. For here it became obvious that they are themselves nothing but logical functions, and as such do not produce the least concept of an object, but require some sensuous intuition as a basis. They therefore only serve to determine empirical judgments, which are otherwise undetermined and indifferent as regards all functions of judging, relatively to these functions, thereby procuring them universal validity, and by means of them making judgments of experience in general possible.

Such an insight into the nature of the categories, which limits them at the same time to the mere use of experience, never occurred either to their first author, or to any of his successors; but without this insight (which immediately depends upon their derivation or deduction), they are quite useless and only a miserable list of names, without explanation or rule for their use. Had the ancients conceived such an option, doubtless the whole study of the pure rational knowledge, which under the name of metaphysics has for centuries spoiled many a sound mind, would have reached us in quite another shape, and would have enlightened the human understanding, instead of actually exhausting it in obscure and vain speculations, thereby rendering it unfit for true science.

This system of categories makes all treatment of every object of pure reason itself systematic, and affords a direction or clue how and through what points of inquiry every metaphysical consideration must proceed, in order to be complete; for it exhausts all the possible movements of the understanding, among which every concept must be classed. In like manner the table of Principles has been formulated, the completeness of which we can only vouch for by the system of the categories. Even in the division of the concepts, which must go beyond the physical application of the understanding, it is always the very same clue, which, as it must always be determined *a priori* by the same fixed points of the human understanding, always forms a closed circle. There is no doubt that the object of a pure conception either of the understanding or of reason, so far as it is to be estimated philosophically and on *a priori* principles, can in this way be completely cognised. I could not therefore omit to make use of this clue with regard to one of the most abstract ontological divisions, viz., the various distinctions of "the notions of something and of nothing," and to construct accordingly (*Critique,* B 348) a regular and necessary table of their divisions.[17]

And this system, like every other true one founded on a universal principle, shows its inestimable value in this, that it excludes all foreign concepts, which might otherwise intrude among the pure concepts of the understanding, and determines the place of every cognition. Those concepts, which under the name of "concepts of reflexion" have been likewise arranged in a table according to the clue of the categories, intrude, without having any privilege or title to be among the pure concepts of the understanding in Ontology. They are concepts of connexion, and thereby of the objects themselves, whereas the former are only concepts of a mere comparison of concepts al-

17. On the table of the categories many neat observations may be made, for instance (1) that the third arises from the first and the second joined in one concept; (2) that in those of Quantity and of Quality there is merely a progress from unity to totality or from something to nothing (for this purpose the categories of Quality must stand thus: reality limitation total negation) without *correlata of opposita,* whereas those of Relation and of Modality have them; (3) that as in *Logic* categorical judgments are the basis of all others, so the category of Substance is the basis of all concepts of actual things; (4) that as Modality in the judgment is not a particular predicate, so by the modal concepts a determination is not superadded to things, etc., etc. Such observations are of great use. If we besides enumerate all the predicables which we can find pretty completely in any good ontology (for example, Baumgarten's), and arrange them in classes under the categories, in which operation we must not neglect to add as complete a dissection of all these concepts as possible, there will then arise a merely analytical part of metaphysics, which does not contain a single synthetical proposition, which might precede the second (the synthetical) and would by its precision and completeness be not only useful, but, in virtue of its system, be even to some extent elegant.

ready given, hence of quite another nature and use. By my systematic division[18] they are saved from this confusion. But the value of my special table of the categories will be still more obvious, when we separate the table of the transcendental concepts of Reason from the concepts of the understanding. The latter being of quite another nature and origin, they must have quite another form than the former. This so necessary separation has never yet been made in any system of metaphysics for, as a rule, these rational concepts are all mixed up with the categories, like children of one family, which confusion was unavoidable in the absence of a definite system of categories.

THIRD PART OF THE MAIN TRANSCENDENTAL PROBLEM

How is Metaphysics in General Possible?

40. Pure mathematics and pure science of nature had no occasion for such a deduction, as we have made of both, for their own safety and certainty. For the former rests upon its own evidence; and the latter (though sprung from pure sources of the understanding) upon experience and its thorough confirmation. Physics cannot altogether refuse and dispense with the testimony of the latter; because with all its certainty, it can never, as philosophy, rival mathematics. Both sciences therefore stood in need of this inquiry, not for themselves, but for the sake of another science, metaphysics.

Metaphysics has to do not only with concepts of nature, which always find their application in experience, but also with pure rational concepts, which never can be given in any possible experience. Consequently the objective reality of these concepts (viz., that they are not mere chimeras), and the truth or falsity of metaphysical assertions, cannot be discovered or confirmed by any experience. This part of metaphysics however is precisely what constitutes its essential end, to which the rest is only a means, and thus this science is in need of such a deduction for its own sake. The third question now proposed relates therefore as it were to the root and essential difference of metaphysics, i.e., the occupation of Reason with itself, and the supposed knowledge of objects arising immediately from this incubation of its own concepts, without requiring, or indeed being able to reach that knowledge through, experience.[19]

Without solving this problem reason never is justified. The empirical use to which reason limits the pure understanding, does not fully satisfy the proper destination of the latter. Every single experience is only a part of the whole sphere of its domain, but the absolute totality of all possible experience is itself not experience. Yet it is a necessary [concrete] problem for reason, the mere representation of which requires concepts quite different from the categories, whose use is only immanent, or refers to experience, so far as it can be given. Whereas the concepts of reason aim at the completeness, i.e., the collective unity of all possible experience, and thereby transcend every given experience. Thus they become *transcendent.*

As the understanding stands in need of categories for experience, reason contains in itself the source of ideas, by which I mean necessary concepts, whose object cannot be given in any experience. The latter are inherent in the nature of reason, as the former are in that of the understanding. While the former carry with them an illusion likely to mislead, the illusion of the latter is inevitable, though it certainly can be kept from misleading us.

Since all illusion consists in holding the subjective ground of our judgments to be objective, a self-knowledge of pure reason in its transcendent (exaggerated) use is the sole preservative from the aberrations into which reason falls when it mistakes its destination, and refers that to the object transcendently, which only regards its own subject and its guidance in all immanent use.

41. The distinction of ideas, that is, of pure concepts of reason, from categories, or pure concepts of the understanding, as cognitions of a quite distinct species, origin and use, is so important a point in founding a science which is to contain the system of all these *a priori* cognitions, that without this distinction metaphysics is absolutely impossible, or is at best a random, bungling attempt to build a castle in the air without a knowledge of the materials or of their fitness for any purpose. Had the *Critique of*

18. See *Critique of Pure Reason,* B 316.

19. If we can say, that a science is actual at least in the idea of all men, as soon as it appears that the problems which lead to it are proposed to everybody by the nature of human reason, and that therefore many (though faulty) endevours are unavoidably made in its behalf, then we are bound to say that metaphysics is subjectively (and indeed necessarily) actual, and therefore we justly ask, how is it (objectively) possible.

Pure Reason done nothing but first point out this distinction, it had thereby contributed more to clear up our conception of, and to guide to our inquiry in, the field of metaphysics, than all the vain efforts which have hitherto been made to satisfy the transcendent problems of pure reason, without ever surmising that we were in quite another field than that of the understanding, and hence classing concepts of the understanding and those of reason together, as if they were of the same kind.

42. All pure cognitions of the understanding have this feature, that their concepts present themselves in experience, and their principles can be confirmed by it; whereas the transcendent cognitions of reason cannot, either as ideas, appear in experience, or as propositions ever be confirmed or refuted by it. Hence whatever errors may slip in unawares, can only be discovered by pure reason itself—a discovery of much difficulty, because this very reason naturally becomes dialectical by means of its ideas, and this unavoidable illusion cannot be limited by any objective and dogmatical researches into things, but by a subjective investigation of reason itself as a source of ideas.

43. In the *Critique of Pure Reason* it was always my greatest care to endeavor not only carefully to distinguish the several species of cognition, but to derive concepts belonging to each one of them from their common source. I did this in order that by knowing whence they originated, I might determine their use with safety, and also have the unanticipated but invaluable advantage of knowing the completeness of my enumeration, classification and specification of concepts *a priori*, and therefore according to principles. Without this, metaphysics is mere rhapsody, in which no one knows whether he has enough, or whether and where something is still wanting. We can indeed have this advantage only in pure philosophy, but of this philosophy it constitutes the very essence.

As I had found the origin of the categories in the four logical functions of all the judgments of the understanding, it was quite natural to seek the origin of the ideas in the three functions of the syllogisms of reason. For as soon as these pure concepts of reason (the transcendental ideas) are given, they could hardly, except they be held innate, be found anywhere else, than in the same activity of reason, which, so far as it regards mere form, constitutes the logical element of the syllogisms of reason; but, so far as it represents judgments of the understanding with respect to the one or to the other form *a priori*, constitutes transcendental concepts of pure reason.

The formal distinction of syllogisms renders their division into categorical, hypothetical, and disjunctive necessary. The concepts of reason founded on them contained therefore, first, the idea of the complete subject (the substantial); secondly, the idea of the complete series of conditions; thirdly, the determination of all concepts in the idea of a complete complex of that which is possible.[20] The first idea is psychological, the second cosmological, the third theological, and, as all three give occasion to Dialectics, yet each in its own way, the division of the whole Dialectic of pure reason into its Paralogism, its Antinomy, and its Ideal, was arranged accordingly. Through this deduction we may feel assured that all the claims of pure reason are completely represented, and that none can be wanting; because the faculty of reason itself, whence they all take their origin, is thereby completely surveyed.

44. In these general considerations it is also remarkable that the ideas of reason are unlike the categories, of no service to the use of our understanding in experience, but quite dispensable, and become even an impediment to the maxims of a rational cognition of nature. Yet in another aspect still to be determined they are necessary. Whether the soul is or is not a simple substance, is of no consequence to us in the explanation of its phenomena. For we cannot render the notion of a simple being intelligible by any possible experience that is sensuous or concrete. The notion is therefore quite void as regards all hoped-for insight into the cause of phenomena, and cannot at all serve as a principle of the explanation of that which internal or external experience supplies. So the cosmological ideas of the beginning of the world or of its eternity (*a parte ante*) cannot be of any greater service to us for the explanation of any event in the world itself. And finally we must, according to a right maxim of the philosophy of na-

20. In disjunctive judgments we consider all possibility as divided in respect to a particular concept. By the ontological principle of the universal determination of a thing in general, I understand the principle that either the one or the other of all possible contradictory predicates must be assigned to any object. This is at the same time the principle of all disjunctive judgments, constituting the foundation of our conception of possibility, and in it the possibility of every object in general is considered as determined. This may serve as a slight explanation of the above proposition that the activity of reason in disjunctive syllogisms is formally the same as that by which it fashions the idea of a universal conception of all reality, containing in itself that which is positive in all contradictory predicates.

ture, refrain from all explanations of the design of nature, drawn from the will of a Supreme Being; because this would not be natural philosophy, but an acknowledgment that we have come to the end of it. The use of these ideas, therefore, is quite different from that of those categories by which (and by the principles built upon which) experience itself first becomes possible. But our laborious analytics of the understanding would be superfluous if we had nothing else in view than the mere cognition of nature as it can be given in experience; for reason does its work, both in mathematics and in the science of nature, quite safely and well without any of this subtle deduction. Therefore our critique of the understanding combines with the ideas of pure reason for a purpose which lies beyond the empirical use of the understanding; but this we have above declared to be in this aspect totally inadmissible, and without any object or meaning. Yet there must be a harmony between that of the nature of reason and that of the understanding, and the former must contribute to the perfection of the latter, and cannot possibly upset it.

The solution of this question is as follows: Pure reason does not in its ideas point to particular objects, which lie beyond the field of experience, but only requires completeness of the use of the understanding in the system of experience. But this completeness can be a completeness of principles only, not of intuitions and of objects. In order however to represent the ideas definitely, reason conceives them after the fashion of the cognition of an object. The cognition is as far as these rules are concerned completely determined, but the object is only an idea invented for the purpose of bringing the cognition of the understanding as near as possible to the completeness represented by that idea.

Prefatory Remark to the Dialectics of Pure Reason

45. We have above shown in 33 and 34 that the purity of the categories from all admixture of sensuous determinations may mislead reason into extending their use, quite beyond all experience, to things in themselves; though as these categories themselves find no intuition which can give them meaning or sense *in concreto,* they, as mere logical functions, can represent a thing in general, but not give by themselves alone a determinate concept of anything. Such hyperbolical objects are distinguished by the appellation of noumena, or pure beings of the understanding (or better, beings of thought), such as, for example, "substance," but conceived without permanence in time, or "cause," but not acting in time, etc. Here predicates, that only serve to make the conformity-to-law of experience possible, are applied to these concepts, and yet they are deprived of all the conditions of intuition, on which alone experience is possible, and so these concepts lose all significance.

There is no danger, however, of the understanding spontaneously making an excursion so very wantonly beyond its own bounds into the field of the mere creatures of thought, without being impelled by foreign laws. But when reason, which cannot be fully satisfied with any empirical use of the rules of the understanding, as being always conditioned, requires a completion of this chain of conditions, then the understanding is forced out of its sphere. And then it partly represents objects of experience in a series so extended that no experience can grasp, partly even (with a view to complete the series) it seeks entirely beyond it noumena, to which it can attach that chain, and so, having at last escaped from the conditions of experience, make its attitude as it were final. These are then the transcendental ideas, which, though according to the true but hidden ends of the natural determination of our reason, they may aim not at extravagant concepts, but at an unbounded extension of their empirical use, yet seduce the understanding by an unavoidable illusion to a transcendent use, which, though deceitful, cannot be restrained within the bounds of experience by any resolution, but only by scientific instruction and with much difficulty.

I. The Psychological Idea[21]

46. People have long since observed, that in all substances the proper subject, that which remains after all the accidents (as predicates) are abstracted, consequently that which forms the substance of things remains unknown, and various complaints have been made concerning these limits to our knowledge. But it will be well to consider that the human understanding is not to be blamed for its inability to know the substance of things, that is, to determine it by itself, but rather for requiring to cognise it which is a mere idea definitely as though it were a given object. Pure reason requires us to seek for every predicate of a thing its proper subject, and for this subject, which

21. See *Critique of Pure Reason,* "The Paralogisms of Pure Reason."

is itself necessarily nothing but a predicate, its subject, and so on indefinitely (or as far as we can reach). But hence it follows, that we must not hold anything, at which we can arrive, to be an ultimate subject, and that substance itself never can be thought by our understanding, however deep we may penetrate, even if all nature were unveiled to us. For the specific nature of our understanding consists in thinking everything discursively, that is, representing it by concepts, and so by mere predicates, to which therefore the absolute subject must always be wanting. Hence all the real properties, by which we cognise bodies, are mere accidents, not excepting impenetrability, which we can only represent to ourselves as the effect of a power of which the subject is unknown to us.

Now we appear to have this substance in the consciousness of ourselves (in the thinking subject), and indeed in an immediate intuition; for all the predicates of an internal sense refer to the *ego*, as a subject, and I cannot conceive myself as the predicate of any other subject. Hence completeness in the reference of the given concepts as predicates to a subject—not merely an idea, but an object—that is, the absolute subject itself, seems to be given in experience. But this expectation is disappointed. For the ego is not a concept,[22] but only the indication of the object of the internal sense, so far as we cognise it by no further predicate. Consequently it cannot be in itself a predicate of any other thing; but just as little can it be a determinate concept of an absolute subject, but is, as in all other cases, only the reference of the internal phenomena to their unknown subject. Yet this idea (which serves very well, as a regulative principle, totally to destroy all materialistic explanations of the internal phenomena of the soul) occasions by a very natural misunderstanding a very specious argument, which, from this supposed cognition of the substance of our thinking being, infers its nature, so far as the knowledge of its falls quite without the complex of experience.

47. But though we may call this thinking self (the soul) substance, as being the ultimate subject of thinking which cannot be further represented as the predicate of another thing; it remains quite empty and without significance, if permanence—the quality which renders the concept of substances in experience fruitful—cannot be proved of it.

But permanence can never be proved of the concept of a substance, as a thing in itself, but for the purposes of experience only. This is sufficiently shown by the first Analogy of Experience,[23] and whoever will not yield to this proof may try for himself whether he can succeed in proving, from the concept of a subject which does not exist itself as the predicate of another thing, that its existence is thoroughly permanent, and that it cannot either in itself or by any natural cause originate or be annihilated. These synthetical *a priori* propositions can never be proved in themselves, but only in reference to things as objects of possible experience.

48. If therefore from the concept of the soul as a substance, we would infer its permanence, this can hold good as regards possible experience only, not [of the soul] as a thing in itself and beyond all possible experience. But life is the subjective condition of all our possible experience, consequently we can only infer the permanence of the soul in life; for the death of man is the end of all experience which concerns the soul as an object of experience, except the contrary be proved, which is the very question in hand. The permanence of the soul can therefore only be proved (and no one cares for that) during the life of man, but not, as we desire to do, after death; and for this general reason, that the concept of substance, so far as it is to be considered necessarily combined with the concept of permanence, can be so combined only according to the principles of possible experience, and therefore for the purposes of experience only.[24]

22. Were the representation of the apperception (the Ego) a concept, by which anything could be thought, it could be used as a predicate of other things or contain predicates in itself. But it is nothing more than the feeling of an existence without the least definite conception and is only the representation of that to which all thinking stands in relation (*relatione accidentis*).

23. Cf. *Critique*, B224.

24. It is indeed very remarkable how carelessly metaphysicians have always passed over the principle of the permanence of substances without ever attempting a proof of it; doubtless because they found themselves abandoned by all proofs as soon as they began to deal with the concept of substance. Common sense, which felt distinctly that without this presupposition no union of perceptions in experience is possible, supplied the want by a postulate. From experience itself it never could derive such a principle, partly because substances cannot be so traced in all their alterations and dissolutions, that the matter can always be found undiminished, partly because the principle contains *necessity*, which is always the sign of an *a priori* principle. People then boldly applied this postulate to the concept of soul as a substance, and concluded a necessary continuance of the soul after the death of man (especially as the simplicity of this substance, which is inferred from the indivisibility of consciousness, secured it from destruction by dissolution). Had they found the genuine source of this principle—a discovery which requires deeper researches than they were ever inclined to make—they would have seen, that the law of the permanence of substances has place for the purposes of experience only, and hence can hold good of things so far as they are to be cognised and conjoined with others in experience, but never independently of all possible experience, and consequently cannot hold good of the soul after death.

49. That there is something real without us which not only corresponds, but must correspond, to our external perceptions, can likewise be proved to be not a connexion of things in themselves, but for the sake of experience. This means that there is something empirical, i.e., some phenomenon in space without us, that admits of a satisfactory proof, for we have nothing to do with other objects than those which belong to possible experience; because objects which cannot be given us in any experience, do not exist for us. Empirically without me is that which appears in space, and space, together with all the phenomena which it contains, belongs to the representations, whose connexion according to laws of experience proves their objective truth, just as the connexion of the phenomena of the internal sense provides the actuality of my soul (as an object of the internal sense). By means of external experience I am conscious of the actuality of bodies, as external phenomena in space, in the same manner as by means of the internal experience I am conscious of the existence of my soul in time, but this soul is only cognised as an object of the internal sense by phenomena that constitute an internal state, and of which the essence in itself, which forms the basis of these phenomena, is unknown. Cartesian idealism therefore does nothing but distinguish external experience from dreaming; and the conformity to law (as a criterion of its truth) of the former, from the irregularity and the false illusion of the latter. In both it presupposes space and time as conditions of the existence of objects, and it only inquires whether the objects of the external senses, which we when awake put in space, are as actually to be found in it, as the object of the internal sense, the soul, is in time; that is, whether experience carries with it sure criteria to distinguish it from imagination. This doubt, however, may easily be disposed of, and we always do so in common life by investigating the connexion of phenomena in both space and time according to universal laws of experience, and we cannot doubt, when the representation of external things throughout agrees therewith, that they constitute truthful experience. Material idealism, in which phenomena are considered as such only according to their connexion in experience, may accordingly be very easily refuted; and it is just as sure an experience, that bodies exist without us (in space), as that I myself exist according to the representation of the internal sense (in time): for the notion without us, only signifies existence in space. However as the Ego in the proposition, "I am," means not only the object of internal intuition (in space), but the thing-in-itself, which is the basis of this phenomenon; [as this is the case] the question, whether bodies (as phenomena of the external sense) exist as bodies apart from my thoughts, may without any hesitation be denied in nature. But the question, whether I myself as a phenomenon of the internal sense (the soul according to empirical psychology) exist apart from my faculty of representation in time, is an exactly similar inquiry, and must likewise be answered in the negative. And in this manner everything, when it is reduced to its true meaning, is decided and certain. The formal (which I have also called transcendental) actually abolishes the material, or Cartesian, idealism. For if space be nothing but a form of my sensibility, it is as a representation in me just as actual as I myself am, and nothing but the empirical truth of the representations in it remains for consideration. But, if this is not the case, if space and the phenomena in it are something existing without us, then all the criteria of experience beyond our perception can never prove the actuality of these objects without us.

II. The Cosmological Idea[25]

50. This product of pure reason in its transcendent use is its most remarkable curiosity. It serves as a very powerful agent to rouse philosophy from its dogmatic slumber, and to stimulate it to the arduous task of undertaking a critique of reason itself.

I term this idea cosmological, because it always takes its object only from the sensible world, and does not use any other than those whose object is given to sense, consequently it remains in this respect in its native home, it does not become transcendent, and is therefore so far not mere idea; whereas, to conceive the soul as a simple substance, already means to conceive such an object (the simple) as cannot be presented to the senses. Yet the cosmological idea extends the connexion of the conditioned with its condition (whether the connexion is mathematical or dynamical) so far, that experience never can keep up with it. It is therefore with regard to this point always an idea, whose object never can be adequately given in any experience.

51. In the first place, the use of a system of categories becomes here so obvious and unmistakable,

25. Cf. *Critique*, "The Antinomy of Pure Reason."

that even if there were not several other proofs of it, this alone would sufficiently prove it indispensable in the system of pure reason. There are only four such transcendent ideas, as there are so many classes of categories; in each of which, however, they refer only to the absolute completeness of the series of the conditions for a given conditioned. In analogy to these cosmological ideas there are only four kinds of dialectical assertions of pure reason, which, as they are dialectical, thereby prove, that to each of them, on equally specious principles of pure reason, a contradictory assertion stands opposed. As all the metaphysical art of the most subtle distinction cannot prevent this opposition, it compels the philosopher to recur to the first sources of pure reason itself. This Antinomy, not arbitrarily invented, but founded in the nature of human reason, and hence unavoidable and never ceasing, contains the following four theses together with their antitheses:

1

Thesis

The world has, as to time and space,
a beginning (limit).

Antithesis

The world is, as to time and space, infinite.

2

Thesis

Everything in the world consists of
[elements that are] simple.

Antithesis

There is nothing simple, but everything is composite.

3

Thesis

There are in the world causes through freedom.

Antithesis

There is no freedom, but all is nature.

4

Thesis

In the series of the world-causes there
is some necessary Being.

Antithesis

There is nothing necessary in the world,
but in this series all is contingent.

52*a*. Here is the most singular phenomenon of human reason, no other instance of which can be shown in any other use. If we, as is commonly done, represent to ourselves the appearances of the sensible world as things in themselves, if we assume the principles of their combination as principles universally valid of things in themselves and not merely of experience, as is usually, nay without our *Critique*, unavoidably done, there arises an unexpected conflict, which never can be removed in the common dogmatical way; because the thesis, as well as the antithesis, can be shown by equally clear, evident, and irresistible proofs—for I pledge myself as to the correctness of all these proofs—and reason therefore perceives that it is divided with itself, a state at which the sceptic rejoices, but which must make the critical philosopher pause and feel ill at ease.

52*b*. We may blunder in various ways in metaphysics without any fear of being detected in falsehood. For we never can be refuted by experience if we but avoid self-contradiction, which in synthetical, though purely fictitious propositions, may be done whenever the concepts, which we connect, are mere ideas, that cannot be given (in their whole content) in experience. For how can we make out by experience, whether the world is from eternity or had a beginning, whether matter is infinitely divisible or consists of simple parts? Such concepts cannot be given in any experience, be it ever so extensive, and consequently the falsehood either of the positive or the negative proposition cannot be discovered by this touch-stone.

The only possible way in which reason could have revealed unintentionally its secret Dialectics, falsely announced as Dogmatics, would be when it were made to ground an assertion upon a universally admitted principle and to deduce the exact contrary with the greatest accuracy of inference from another which is equally granted. This is actually here the case with regard to four natural ideas of reason, whence four assertions on the one side, and as many counter-assertions on the other arise, each consistently following from universally-acknowledged principles. Thus they reveal by the use of these principles the dialectical illusion of pure reason which would otherwise forever remain concealed.

This is therefore a decisive experiment, which must necessarily expose any error lying hidden in the assumptions of reason.[26] Contradictory proposi-

26. I therefore would be pleased to have the critical reader to devote to this antimony of pure reason his chief attention, because nature itself seems to have established it with a view to stagger reason in its daring pretensions, and to force it to self-examination. For every proof, which I have given, as well of the thesis as of the antithesis, I undertake to be responsible, and thereby to show the certainty of the inevitable antinomy of reason. When the reader is brought by this curious phenomenon to fall back upon the proof of the presumption upon which it rests, he will feel himself obliged to investigate the ultimate foundation of all the cognition of pure reason with me more thoroughly.

tions cannot both be false, except the concept, which is the subject of both, is self-contradictory; for example, the propositions, "a square circle is round, and a square circle is not round," are both false. For, as to the former it is false, that the circle is round, because it is quadrangular; and it is likewise false, that it is not round, that is, angular, because it is a circle. For the logical criterion of the impossibility of a concept consists in this, that if we presuppose it, two contradictory propositions both become false; consequently, as no middle between them is conceivable, nothing at all is thought by that concept.

52*c*. The first two antinomies, which I call mathematical, because they are concerned with the addition or division of the homogeneous, are founded on such a self-contradictory concept; and hence I explain how it happens, that both the Thesis and Antithesis of the two are false.

When I speak of objects in time and in space, it is not of things in themselves, of which I know nothing, but of things in appearance, that is, of experience, as the particular way of cognising objects which is afforded to man. I must not say of what I think in time or in space, that in itself, and independent of these my thoughts, it exists in space and in time; for in that case I contradict myself; because space and time, together with the appearances in them, are nothing existing in themselves and outside of my representations, but are themselves only modes of representation, and it is palpably contradictory to say, that a mere mode of representation exists without our representation. Objects of the senses therefore exist only in experience; whereas to give them a self-subsisting existence apart from experience or before it, is merely to represent to ourselves that experience actually exists apart from experience or before it.

Now if I inquire after the quantity of the world, as to space and time, it is equally impossible, as regards all my notions, to declare it infinite or to declare it finite. For neither assertion can be contained in experience, because experience either of an infinite space, or of an infinite time elapsed, or again, of the boundary of the world by a void space, or by an antecedent void time, is impossible; these are mere ideas. This quantity of the world, which is determined in either way, should therefore exist in the world itself apart from all experience. This contradicts the notion of a world of sense, which is merely a complex of the appearances whose existence and connexion occur only in our representations, that is, in experience, since this latter is not an object in itself, but a mere mode of representation. Hence it follows, that as the concept of an absolutely existing world of sense is self-contradictory, the solution of the problem concerning its quantity, whether attempted affirmatively or negatively, is always false.

The same holds good of the second antinomy, which relates to the division of phenomena. For these are mere representations, and the parts exist merely in their representation, consequently in the division, or in a possible experience where they are given, and the division reaches only as far as this latter reaches. To assume that an appearance, e.g., that of body, contains in itself before all experience all the parts, which any possible experience can ever reach, is to impute to a mere appearance, which can exist only in experience, an existence previous to experience. In other words, it would mean that mere representations exist before they can be found in our faculty of representation. Such an assertion is self-contradictory, as also every solution of our misunderstood problem, whether we maintain, that bodies in themselves consist of an infinite number of parts, or of a finite number of simple parts.

53. In the first (the mathematical) class of antinomies the falsehood of the assumption consists in representing in one concept something self-contradictory as if it were compatible (i.e., an appearance as an object in itself). But, as to the second (the dynamical) class of antinomies, the falsehood of the representation consists in representing as contradictory what is compatible; so that, as in the former case, the opposed assertions are both false, in this case, on the other hand, where they are opposed to one another by mere misunderstanding, they may both be true.

Any mathematical connexion necessarily presupposes homogeneity of what is connected (in the concept of magnitude), while the dynamical one by no means requires the same. When we have to deal with extended magnitudes, all the parts must be homogeneous with one another and with the whole: whereas in the connexion of cause and effect, homogeneity may indeed likewise be found, but is not necessary; for the concept of causality (by means of which something is posited through something else quite different from it), at all events, does not require it.

If the objects of the world of sense are taken for things in themselves, and the above laws of nature for the laws of things in themselves, the contradiction would be unavoidable. So also, if the subject of freedom were, like other objects, represented as mere appearance, the contradiction would be just as unavoidable, for the same predicate would at once be affirmed and denied of the same kind of object in the same sense. But if natural necessity is referred merely to appearances, and freedom merely to things in themselves, no contradiction arises, if we at once assume, or admit both kinds of causality, however difficult or impossible it may be to make the latter kind conceivable.

In appearance every effect is an event, or something that happens in time; it must, according to the universal law of nature, be preceded by a determination of the causality of its cause (a state), which follows according to a constant law. But this determination of the cause as causality must likewise be something that takes place or happens; the cause must have begun to act, otherwise no succession between it and the effect could be conceived. Otherwise the effect, as well as the causality of the cause, would have always existed. Therefore the determination of the cause to act must also have originated among appearances, and must consequently, as well as its effect, be an event, which must again have its cause, and so on; hence natural necessity must be the condition, on which effective causes are determined. Whereas if freedom is to be a property of certain causes of appearances, it must, as regards these, which are events, be a faculty of starting them spontaneously, that is, without the causality of the cause itself, and hence without requiring any other ground to determine its start. But then the cause, as to its causality, must not rank under time-determinations of its state, that is, it cannot be an appearance, and must be considered a thing in itself, while its effects would be only appearances.[27] If without contradiction we can think of the beings of understanding as exercising such an influence on appearances, then natural necessity will attach to all connexions of cause and effect in the sensuous world, though on the other hand, freedom can be granted to such cause, as is itself not an appearance (but the foundation of appearance). Nature therefore and freedom can without contradiction be attributed to the very same thing, but in different relations—on one side as a phenomenon, on the other as a thing in itself.

We have in us a faculty, which not only stands in connexion with its subjective determining grounds that are the natural causes of its actions, and is so far the faculty of a being that itself belongs to appearances, but is also referred to objective grounds, that are only ideas, so far as they can determine this faculty, a connexion which is expressed by the word *ought*. This faculty is called *reason*, and, so far as we consider a being (man) entirely according to this objectively determinable reason, he cannot be considered as a being of sense, but this property is that of a thing in itself, of which we cannot comprehend the possibility—I mean how the *ought* (which however has never yet taken place) should determine its activity, and can become the cause of actions, whose effect is an appearance in the sensible world. Yet the causality of reason would be freedom with regard to the effects in the sensuous world, so far as we can consider objective grounds, which are themselves ideas, as their determinants. For its action in that case would not depend upon subjective conditions, consequently not upon those of time, and of course not upon the law of nature, which serves to determine them, because grounds of reason give to actions the rule universally, according to principles, without the influence of the circumstances of either time or place.

What I adduce here is merely meant as an example to make the thing intelligible, and does not necessarily belong to our problem, which must be decided from mere concepts, independently of the properties which we meet in the actual world.

Now I may say without contradiction: that all the actions of rational beings, so far as they are appearances (occurring in any experience), are subject to the necessity of nature; but the same actions, as regards merely the rational subject and its faculty of acting according to mere reason, are free. For what is required for the necessity of nature? Nothing more than the determinability of every event in the world

27. The idea of freedom occurs only in the relation of the intellectual, as cause, to the appearance as effect. Hence we cannot attribute freedom to matter in regard to the incessant action by which it fills its space though this action takes place from an internal principle. We can likewise find no notion of freedom suitable to purely rational beings, for instance to God, so far as his action is immanent. For his action, though independent of external determining causes is determined in his eternal reason that is, in the divine *nature*. It is only if *something is to start* by an action, and so the effect occurs in the sequence of time, or in the world of sense (e.g., the beginning of the world), that we can put the question, whether the causality of the cause must in its turn have been started, or whether the cause can originate an effect without its causality itself beginning. In the former case the concept of this causality is a concept of natural necessity, in the latter that of freedom. From this the reader will see that as I explained freedom to be the faculty of starting an event spontaneously, I have exactly hit the notion which is the problem of metaphysics.

of sense according to constant laws, that is, a reference to cause in the appearance; in this process the thing in itself at its foundation and the causality remain unknown. But I say, that the law of nature remains, whether the rational being is the cause of the effects in the sensuous world from reason, that is, through freedom, or whether it does not determine them on grounds of reason. For, if the former is the case, the action is performed according to maxims, the effect of which as appearance is always conformable to constant laws; if the latter is the case, and the action not performed on principles of reason, it is subjected to the empirical laws of the sensibility, and in both cases the effects are connected according to constant laws; more than this we do not require or know concerning natural necessity. But in the former case reason is the cause of these laws of nature, and therefore free; in the latter the effects following according to mere natural laws of sensibility, because reason does not influence it; but reason itself is not determined on that account by the sensibility, and is therefore free in this case too. Freedom is therefore no hindrance to natural law in appearance, neither does this law abrogate the freedom of the practical use of reason, which is connected with things in themselves, as determining grounds.

Thus practical freedom, viz., the freedom in which reason possesses causality according to objectively determining grounds, is rescued and yet natural necessity is not in the least curtailed with regard to the very same effects, as appearances. The same remarks will serve to explain what we had to say concerning transcendental freedom and its compatibility with natural necessity (in the same subject, but not taken in the same reference). For, as to this, every beginning of the action of a being from objective causes regarded as determining grounds, is always a first start, though the same action is in the series of appearances only a subordinate start, which must be preceded by a state of the cause, which determines it, and is itself determined in the same manner by another immediately preceding. Thus we are able, in rational beings, or in beings generally, so far as their causality is determined in them as things in themselves, to imagine a faculty of beginning from itself a series of states, without falling into contradiction with the laws of nature. For the relation of the action to objective grounds of reason is not a time-relation; in this case that which determines the causality does not precede in time the action, because such determining grounds represent not a reference to objects of sense, e.g., to causes in the appearances, but to determining causes, as things in themselves, which do not rank under conditions of time. And in this way the action, with regard to the causality of reason, can be considered as a first start in respect to the series of appearances, and yet also as a merely subordinate beginning. We may therefore without contradiction consider it in the former aspect as free, but in the latter (in so far as it is merely appearance) as subject to natural necessity.

As to the fourth Antinomy, it is solved in the same way as the conflict of reason with itself in the third. For, provided the cause *in* the appearance is distinguished from the cause *of* the appearance (so far as it can be thought as a thing in itself), both propositions are perfectly reconcilable: the one, that there is nowhere in the sensuous world a cause (according to similar laws of causality), whose existence is absolutely necessary; the other, that this world is nevertheless connected with a Necessary Being as its cause (but of another kind and according to another law). The incompatibility of these propositions entirely rests upon the mistake of extending what is valid merely of appearances to things in themselves, and in general confusing both in one concept.

54. This then is the proposition and this the solution of the whole antinomy, in which reason finds itself involved in the application of its principles to the sensible world. The former alone (the mere proposition) would be a considerable service in the cause of our knowledge of human reason, even though the solution might fail to fully satisfy the reader, who has here to combat a natural illusion, which has been but recently exposed to him, and which he had hitherto always regarded as genuine. For one result at least is unavoidable. As it is quite impossible to prevent this conflict of reason with itself—so long as the objects of the sensible world are taken for things in themselves, and not for mere appearances, which they are in fact—the reader is thereby compelled to examine over again the deduction of all our *a priori* cognition and the proof which I have given of my deduction in order to come to a decision on the question. This is all I require at present; for when in this occupation he shall have thought himself deep enough into the nature of pure reason, those concepts by which alone the solution of the conflict of reason is possible, will become sufficiently familiar to him. Without this preparation I cannot expect an unreserved assent even from the most attentive reader.

III. The Theological Idea[28]

55. The third transcendental Idea, which affords matter for the most important, but, if pursued only speculatively, transcendent and thereby dialectical use of reason, is the ideal of pure reason. Reason in this case does not, as with the psychological and the cosmological Ideas, begin from experience, and err by exaggerating its grounds, in striving to attain, if possible, the absolute completeness of their series. It rather totally breaks with experience, and from mere concepts of what constitutes the absolute completeness of a thing in general, consequently by means of the idea of a most perfect primal Being, it proceeds to determine the possibility and therefore the actuality of all other things. And so the mere presupposition of a Being, who is conceived not in the series of experience, yet for the purposes of experience—for the sake of comprehending its connexion, order, and unity—i.e., the idea [the notion of it], is more easily distinguished from the concept of the understanding here, than in the former cases. Hence we can easily expose the dialectical illusion which arises from our making the subjective conditions of our thinking objective conditions of objects themselves, and an hypothesis necessary for the satisfaction of our reason, a dogma. As the observations of the *Critique* on the pretensions of transcendental theology are intelligible, clear, and decisive, I have nothing more to add on the subject.

General Remark on the Transcendental Ideas

56. The objects, which are given us by experience, are in many respects incomprehensible, and many questions, to which the law of nature leads us, when carried beyond a certain point (though quite conformably to the laws of nature), admit of no answer; as for example the question: why substances attract one another? But if we entirely quit nature, or in pursuing its combinations, exceed all possible experience, and so enter the realm of mere ideas, we cannot then say that the object is incomprehensible, and that the nature of things proposes to us insoluble problems. For we are not then concerned with nature or in general with given objects, but with concepts, which have their origin merely in our reason, and with mere creations of thought; and all the problems that arise from our notions of them must be solved, because of course reason can and must give a full account of its own procedure.[29] As the psychological, cosmological, and theological Ideas are nothing but pure concepts of reason, which cannot be given in any experience, the questions which reason asks us about them are put to us not by the objects, but by mere maxims of our reason for the sake of its own satisfaction. They must all be capable of satisfactory answers, which is done by showing that they are principles which bring our use of the understanding into thorough agreement, completeness, and synthetical unity, and that they so far hold good of experience only, but of experience as a whole.

Although an absolute whole of experience is impossible, the idea of a whole of cognition according to principles must impart to our knowledge a peculiar kind of unity, that of a system, without which it is nothing but piecework, and cannot be used for proving the existence of a highest purpose (which can only be the general system of all purposes), I do not here refer only to the practical, but also to the highest purpose of the speculative use of reason.

The transcendental Ideas therefore express the peculiar application of reason as a principle of systematic unity in the use of the understanding. Yet if we assume this unity of the mode of cognition to be attached to the object of cognition, if we regard that which is merely regulative to be constitutive, and if we persuade ourselves that we can by means of these Ideas enlarge our cognition transcendently, or far beyond all possible experience, while it only serves to render experience within itself as nearly complete as possible, i.e., to limit its progress by nothing that cannot belong to experience: we suffer from a mere misunderstanding in our estimate of the proper application of our reason and of its principles, and from a Dialectic, which both confuses the empirical use of reason, and also sets reason at variance with itself.

28. Cf. *Critique*, the chapter on "Transcendental Ideals."

29. Herr Platner in his *Aphorisms* acutely says (§§ 728, 729), "If reason be a criterion, no concept, which is incomprehensible to human reason, can be possible. Incomprehensibility has place in what is actual only. Here incomprehensibility arises from the insufficiency of the acquired ideas." It sounds paradoxical, but is otherwise not strange to say, that in nature there is much incomprehensible (e.g., the faculty of generation) but if we mount still higher, and even go beyond nature, everything again becomes comprehensible, for we then quit entirely the objects, which can be given us, and occupy ourselves merely about ideas, in which occupation we can easily comprehend the law that reason prescribes by them to the understanding for its use in experience, because the law is the reason's own production.

CONCLUSION

On the Determination of the Bounds of Pure Reason

57. Having adduced the clearest arguments, it would be absurd for us to hope that we can know more of any object, than belongs to the possible experience of it, or lay claim to the least atom of knowledge about anything not assumed to be an object of possible experience, which would determine it according to the constitution it has in itself. For how could we determine anything in this way, since time, space, and the categories, and still more all the concepts formed by empirical experience or perception in the sensible world, have and can have no other use, than to make experience possible. And if this condition is omitted from the pure concepts of the understanding, they do not determine any object, and have no meaning whatever.

But it would be on the other hand a still greater absurdity if we conceded no things in themselves, or set up our experience for the only possible mode of knowing things, our way of beholding them in space and in time for the only possible way, and our discursive understanding for the archetype of every possible understanding; in fact if we wished to have the principles of the possibility of experience considered universal conditions of things in themselves.

Our principles, which limit the use of reason to possible experience, might in this way become transcendent, and the limits of our reason be set up as limits of the possibility of things in themselves (as Hume's dialogues may illustrate), if a careful critique did not guard the bounds of our reason with respect to its empirical use, and set a limit to its pretensions. Scepticism originally arose from metaphysics and its licentious dialectics. At first it might, merely to favor the empirical use of reason, announce everything that transcends this use as worthless and deceitful; but by and by, when it was perceived that the very same principles that are used in experience, insensibly, and apparently with the same right, led still further than experience extends, then men began to doubt even the propositions of experience. But here there is no danger; for common sense will doubtless always assert its rights. A certain confusion, however, arose in science which cannot determine how far reason is to be trusted, and why only so far and no further, and this confusion can only be cleared up and all future relapses obviated by a formal determination, on principle, of the boundary of the use of our reason.

We cannot indeed, beyond all possible experience, form a definite notion of what things in themselves may be. Yet we are not at liberty to abstain entirely from inquiring into them; for experience never satisfies reason fully, but in answering questions, refers us further and further back, and leaves us dissatisfied with regard to their complete solution. This any one may gather from the Dialectics of pure reason, which therefore has its good subjective grounds. Having acquired, as regards the nature of our soul, a clear conception of the subject, and having come to the conviction, that its manifestations cannot be explained materialistically, who can refrain from asking what the soul really is, and, if no concept of experience suffices for the purpose, from accounting for it by a concept of reason (that of a simple immaterial being), though we cannot by any means prove its objective reality? Who can satisfy himself with mere empirical knowledge in all the cosmological questions of the duration and of the quantity of the world, of freedom or of natural necessity, since every answer given on principles of experience begets a fresh question, which likewise requires its answer and thereby clearly shows the insufficiency of all physical modes of explanation to satisfy reason? Finally, who does not see in the thorough-going contingency and dependence of all his thoughts and assumptions on mere principles of experience, the impossibility of stopping there? And who does not feel himself compelled, notwithstanding all interdictions against losing himself in transcendent ideas, to seek rest and contentment beyond all the concepts which he can vindicate by experience, in the concept of a Being, the possibility of which we cannot conceive, but at the same time cannot be refuted, because it relates to a mere being of the understanding, and without it reason must needs remain forever dissatisfied?

Bounds (in extended beings) always presuppose a space existing outside a certain definite place, and inclosing it; limits do not require this, but are mere negations, which affect a quantity, so far as it is not absolutely complete. But our reason, as it were, sees in its surroundings a space for the cognition of things in themselves, though we can never have definite notions of them, and are limited to appearances only.

As long as the cognition of reason is homogeneous, definite bounds to it are inconceivable. In mathematics and in natural philosophy human reason admits of limits, but not bounds, viz., that something indeed lies without it, at which it can never arrive, but not that it will at any point find completion in its internal progress. The enlarging of our views in mathematics, and the possibility of new discoveries, are infinite; and the same is the case with the discovery of new properties of nature, of new powers and laws, by continued experience and its rational combination. But limits cannot be mistaken here, for mathematics refers to appearances only, and what cannot be an object of sensuous contemplation, such as the concepts of metaphysics and of morals, lies entirely without its sphere, and it can never lead to them; neither does it require them. It is therefore not a continual progress and an approximation towards these sciences, and there is not, as it were, any point or line of contact. Natural science will never reveal to us the internal constitution of things, which though not appearance, yet can serve as the ultimate ground of explaining appearance. Nor does that science require this for its physical explanations. Nay even if such grounds should be offered from other sources (for instance, the influence of immaterial beings), they must be rejected and not used in the progress of its explanations. For these explanations must only be grounded upon that which as an object of sense can belong to experience, and be brought into connexion with our actual perceptions and empirical laws.

But metaphysics leads us towards bounds in the dialectical attempts of pure reason (not undertaken arbitrarily or wantonly, but stimulated hereto by the nature of reason itself). And the transcendental Ideas, as they do not admit of evasion, and are never capable of realisation, serve to point out to us actually not only the bounds of the pure use of reason, but also the way to determine them. Such is the end and the use of this natural predisposition of our reason, which has brought forth metaphysics as its favorite child, whose generation, like every other in the world, is not to be ascribed to blind chance, but to an original germ, wisely organised for great ends. For metaphysics, in its fundamental features, perhaps more than any other science, is placed in us by nature itself, and cannot be considered the production of an arbitrary choice or a casual enlargement in the progress of experience from which it is quite disparate.

Reason with all its concepts and laws of the understanding, which suffice for empirical use, i.e., within the sensible world, finds in itself no satisfaction because ever-recurring questions deprive us of all hope of their complete solution. The transcendental ideas, which have that completion in view, are such problems of reason. But it sees clearly, that the sensuous world cannot contain this completion, neither consequently can all the concepts, which serve merely for understanding the world of sense, such as space and time, and whatever we have adduced under the name of pure concepts of the understanding. The sensuous world is nothing but a chain of appearances connected according to universal laws; it has therefore no subsistence by itself; it is not the thing in itself, and consequently must point to that which contains the basis of this experience, to beings which cannot be cognised merely as phenomena, but as things in themselves. In the cognition of them alone reason can hope to satisfy its desire of completeness in proceeding from the conditioned to its conditions.

We have above (33, 34) indicated the limits of reason with regard to all cognition of mere creations of thought. Now, since the transcendental ideas have urged us to approach them, and thus have led us, as it were, to the spot where the occupied space (viz., experience) touches the void (that of which we can know nothing, viz., noumena), we can determine the bounds of pure reason. For in all bounds there is something positive (e.g., a surface is the boundary of corporeal space, and is therefore itself a space, a line is a space, which is the boundary of the surface, a point the boundary of the line,but yet always a place in space), whereas limits contain mere negations. The limits pointed out in those paragraphs are not enough after we have discovered that beyond them there still lies something (though we can never cognise what it is in itself). For the question now is, What is the attitude of our reason in this connexion of what we know with what we do not, and never shall, know? This is an actual connexion of a known thing with one quite unknown (and which will always remain so), and though what is unknown should not become the least more known—which we cannot even hope—yet the notion of this connexion must be definite, and capable of being rendered distinct.

We must therefore accept an immaterial being, a world of understanding, and a Supreme Being (all mere noumena), because in them only, as things in themselves, reason finds that completion and satisfaction, which it can never hope for in the derivation of appearances from their homogeneous grounds, and because these actually have reference to something distinct from them (and totally heterogeneous), as appearances always presuppose an object in itself, and therefore suggest its existence whether we can know more of it or not.

But as we can never cognise these beings of understanding as they are in themselves, that is, definitely, yet must assume them as regards the sensible world, and connect them with it by reason, we are at least able to think this connexion by means of such concepts as express their relation to the world of sense. Yet if we represent to ourselves a being of the understanding by nothing but pure concepts of the understanding, we then indeed represent nothing definite to ourselves, consequently our concept has no significance; but if we think it by properties borrowed from the sensuous world, it is no longer a being of understanding, but is conceived as an appearance, and belongs to the sensible world. Let us take an instance from the notion of the Supreme Being.

Our deistic conception is quite a pure concept of reason, but represents only a thing containing all realities, without being able to determine any one of them; because for that purpose an example must be taken from the world of sense, in which case we should have an object of sense only, not something quite heterogeneous, which can never be an object of sense. Suppose I attribute to the Supreme Being understanding, for instance; I have no concept of an understanding other than my own, one that must receive its perceptions by the senses, and which is occupied in bringing them under rules of the unity of consciousness. Then the elements of my concept would always lie in the appearance; I should however by the insufficiency of the appearance be necessitated to go beyond them to the concept of a being which neither depends upon appearance, nor is bound up with them as conditions of its determination. But if I separate understanding from sensibility to obtain a pure understanding, then nothing remains but the mere form of thinking without perception, by which form alone I can cognise nothing definite, and consequently no object. For that purpose I should conceive another understanding, such as would directly perceive its objects, but of which I have not the least notion; because the human understanding is discursive, and can not directly perceive, it can only cognise by means of general concepts. And the very same difficulties arise if we attribute a will to the Supreme Being; for we have this concept only by drawing it from our internal experience, and therefore from our dependence for satisfaction upon objects whose existence we require; and so the notion rests upon sensibility, which is absolutely incompatible with the pure concept of the Supreme Being.

Hume's objections to deism are weak, and affect only the proofs, and not the deistic assertion itself. But as regards theism, which depends on a stricter determination of the concept of the Supreme Being which in deism is merely transcendent, they are very strong, and as this concept is formed, in certain (in fact in all common) cases irrefutable. Hume always insists, that by the mere concept of an original being, to which we apply only ontological predicates (eternity, omnipresence, omnipotence), we think nothing definite, and that properties which can yield a concept *in concreto* must be superadded; that it is not enough to say, it is Cause, but we must explain the nature of its causality, for example, that of an understanding and of a will. He then begins his attacks on the essential point itself, i.e., theism, as he had previously directed his battery only against the proofs of deism, an attack which is not very dangerous to it in its consequences. All his dangerous arguments refer to anthropomorphism, which he holds to be inseparable from theism, and to make it absurd in itself; but if the former be abandoned, the latter must vanish with it, and nothing remain but deism, of which nothing can come, which is of no value, and which cannot serve as any foundation to religion or morals. If this anthropomorphism were really unavoidable, no proofs whatever of the existence of a Supreme Being, even were they all granted, could determine for us the concept of this Being without involving us in contradictions.

If we connect with the command to avoid all transcendent judgments of pure reason, the command (which apparently conflicts with it) to proceed to concepts that lie beyond the field of its immanent (empirical) use, we discover that both can subsist together, but only at the boundary of all lawful use of reason. For this boundary belongs as well to the field of experience, as to that of the creations of thought, and we are thereby taught, as well, how these so remarkable ideas serve merely for marking the bounds of human reason. On the one hand they give warning not boundlessly to extend cognition of experience, as if nothing but world remained for us to cognise, and yet, on the other hand, not to transgress the bounds of experience, and to think of judging about things beyond them, as things in themselves.

But we stop at this boundary if we limit our judgment merely to the relation which the world may have to a Being whose very concept lies beyond all the knowledge which we can attain within the world. For we then do not attribute to the Supreme Being any of the properties in themselves, by which we represent objects of experience, and thereby avoid dogmatic anthropomorphism; but we attribute them to his relation to the world, and allow ourselves a symbolical anthropomorphism, which in fact concerns language only, and not the object itself.

If I say that we are compelled to consider the world, as if it were the work of a Supreme Understanding and Will, I really say nothing more, than that a watch, a ship, a regiment, bears the same relation to the watchmaker, the shipbuilder, the commanding officer, as the world of sense (or whatever constitutes the substratum of this complex of appearances) does to the Unknown, which I do not hereby cognise as it is in itself, but as it is for me or in relation to the world, of which I am a part.

58. Such a cognition is one of analogy, and does not signify (as is commonly understood) an imperfect similarity of two things, but a perfect similarity of relations between two quite dissimilar things.[30] By means of this analogy, however, there remains a concept of the Supreme Being sufficiently determined *for us,* though we have left out everything that could determine it absolutely or in itself; for we determine it as regards the world and as regards ourselves, and more do we not require. The attacks which Hume makes upon those who would determine this concept absolutely, by taking the materials for so doing from themselves and the world, do not affect us; and he cannot object to us, that we have nothing left if we give up the objective anthropomorphism of the concept of the Supreme Being.

For let us assume at the outset (as Hume in his dialogues makes Philo grant Cleanthes), as a necessary hypothesis, the deistical concept of the First Being, in which this Being is thought by the mere ontological predicates of substance, of cause, etc. This must be done, because reason, actuated in the sensible world by mere conditions, which are themselves always conditional, cannot otherwise have any satisfaction, and it therefore can be done without falling into anthropomorphism (which transfers predicates from the world of sense to a Being quite distinct from the world), because those predicates are mere categories, which, though they do not give a determinate concept of God, yet give a concept not limited to any conditions of sensibility. Thus nothing can prevent our predicating of this Being a causality through reason with regard to the world, and thus passing to theism, without being obliged to attribute to God in himself this kind of reason, as a property inhering in him. For as to the former, the only possible way of prosecuting the use of reason (as regards all possible experience, in complete harmony with itself) in the world of sense to the highest point, is to assume a supreme reason as a cause of all the connexions in the world. Such a principle must be quite advantageous to reason and can hurt it nowhere in its application to nature. As to the latter, reason is thereby not transferred as a property to the First Being in himself, but only to his relation to the world of sense, and so anthropomorphism is entirely avoided. For nothing is considered here but the cause of the form of reason which is perceived everywhere in the world, and reason is attributed to the Supreme Being, so far as it contains the ground of this form of reason in the world, but according to analogy only, that is, so far as this expression shows merely the relation, which the Supreme Cause unknown to us has to the world, in order to determine everything in it conformably to reason in the highest degree. We are thereby kept from using reason as an attribute for the purpose of conceiving God, but instead of conceiving the world in such a manner as is necessary to have the greatest possible use of reason according to principle. We thereby acknowledge that the Supreme Being is quite inscrutable and even unthinkable in any definite way as to what he is in himself. We are thereby kept, on the one hand, from making a transcendent use of the concepts which we have of reason as an efficient cause (by means of the will), in order to determine the Divine Nature by properties, which are only bor-

30. There is, e.g., an analogy between the juridical relation of human actions and the mechanical relation of motive powers. I never can do anything to another man without giving him a right to do the same to me on the same conditions; just as no mass can act with its motive power on another mass without thereby occasioning the other to react equally against it. Here right and motive power are quite dissimilar things, but in their relation there is complete similarity. By means of such an analogy I can obtain a notion of the relation of things which absolutely are unknown to me. For instance as the promotion of the welfare of children (= a) is to the love of parents (= b), so the welfare of the human species (= c) is to that unknown [quantity which is] in God (= x), which we call love; not as if it had the least similarity to any human inclination, but because we can suppose its relation to the world to be similar to that which things of the world bear one another. But the concept of relation in this case is a mere category, vix., the concept of cause which has nothing to do with sensibility.

rowed from human nature, and from losing ourselves in gross and extravagant notions, and on the other hand from deluging the contemplation of the world with hyperphysical modes of explanation according to our notions of human reason, which we transfer to God, and so losing for this contemplation its proper application, according to which it should be a rational study of mere nature, and not a presumptuous derivation of its appearances from a Supreme Reason. The expression suited to our feeble notions is, that we conceive the world as if it came, as to its existence and internal plan, from a Supreme Reason, by which notion we both cognise the constitution, which belongs to the world itself, yet without pretending to determine the nature of its cause in itself, and on the other hand, we transfer the ground of this constitution (of the form of reason in the world) upon the relation of the Supreme Cause to the world, without finding the world sufficient by itself for that purpose.[31]

Thus the difficulties which seem to oppose theism disappear by combining with Hume's principle—"not to carry the use of reason dogmatically beyond the field of all possible experience"—this other principle, which he quite overlooked: "not to consider the field of experience as one which bounds itself in the eye of our reason." The *Critique of Pure Reason* here points out the true mean between dogmatism, which Hume combats, and skepticism, which he would substitute for it—a mean which is not like other means that we find advisable to determine for ourselves as it were mechanically (by adopting something from one side and something from the other), and by which nobody is taught a better way, but such a one as can be accurately determined on principles.

59. At the beginning of this annotation I made use of the metaphor of a boundary, in order to establish the limits of reason in regard to its suitable use. The world of sense contains merely appearances, which are not things in themselves, but the understanding must assume these latter ones, viz., noumena. In our reason both are comprised, and the question is, How does reason proceed to set boundaries to the understanding as regards both these fields? Experience, which contains all that belongs to the sensuous world, does not bound itself; it only proceeds in every case from the conditioned to some other equally conditioned object. Its boundary must lie quite without it, and this field is that of the pure beings of the understanding. But this field, so far as the determination of the nature of these beings is concerned, is an empty space for us, and if dogmatically-determined concepts alone are in question, we cannot pass out of the field of possible experience. But as a boundary itself is something positive, which belongs as well to that which lies within, as to the space that lies without the given complex, it is still an actual positive cognition, which reason only acquires by enlarging itself to this boundary, yet without attempting to pass it; because it there finds itself to this boundary, yet without attempting to pass it; because it there finds itself in the presence of an empty space, in which it can conceive forms of things, but not things themselves. But the setting of a boundary to the field of the understanding by something, which is otherwise unknown to it, is still a cognition which belongs to reason even at this standpoint, and by which it is neither confined within the sensible, nor straying without it, but only refers, as befits the knowledge of a boundary, to the relation between that which lies without it, and that which is contained within it.

Natural theology is such a concept at the boundary of human reason, being constrained to look beyond this boundary to the Idea of a Supreme Being (and, for practical purposes to that of an intelligible world also), not in order to determine anything relatively to this pure creation of the understanding, which lies beyond the world of sense, but in order to guide the use of reason within it according to principles of the greatest possible (theoretical as well as practical) unity. For this purpose we make use of the reference of the world of sense to an independent reason, as the cause of all its connexions. Thereby we do not purely invent a being, but, as beyond the sensible world there must be something that can only be thought by the pure understanding, we determine that something in this particular way, though only of course according to analogy.

And thus there remains our original proposition, which is the *résumé* of the whole *Critique*: "that reason by all its *a priori* principles never teaches us anything more than objects of possible experience, and even of these nothing more than can be cog-

31. I may say, that the causality of the Supreme Cause holds the same place with regard to the world that human reason does with regard to its works of art. Here the nature of the Supreme Cause itself remains unknown to me: I only compare its effects (the order of the world) which I know, and their conformity to reason, to the effects of human reason which I also know; and hence I term the former reason, without attributing to it on that account that I understand in man by this term, or attaching to it anything else known to me, as its property.

nised in experience." But this limitation does not prevent reason leading us to the objective boundary of experience, viz., to the reference to something which is not itself an object of experience, but is the ground of all experience. Reason does not however teach us anything concerning the thing in itself: it only instructs us as regards its own complete and highest use in the field of possible experience. But this is all that can be reasonably desired in the present case, and with which we have cause to be satisfied.

60. Thus we have fully exhibited metaphysics as it is actually given in the natural predisposition of human reason, and in that which constitutes the essential end of its pursuit, according to its subjective possibility. Though we have found, that this merely natural use of such a predisposition of our reason, if no discipline arising only from a scientific critique bridles and sets limits to it, involves us in transcendent, either apparently or really conflicting, dialectical syllogisms; and this fallacious metaphysics is not only unnecessary as regards the promotion of our knowledge of nature, but even disadvantageous to it: there yet remains a problem worthy of solution, which is to find out the natural ends intended by this disposition to transcendent concepts in our reason, because everything that lies in nature must be originally intended for some useful purpose.

Such an inquiry is of a doubtful nature; and I acknowledge, that what I can say about it is conjecture only, like every speculation about the first ends of nature. The question does not concern the objective validity of metaphysical judgments, but our natural predisposition to them, and therefore does not belong to the system of metaphysics but to anthropology.

When I compare all the transcendental Ideas, the totality of which constitutes the particular problem of natural pure reason, compelling it to quit the mere contemplation of nature, to transcend all possible experience, and in this endeavor to produce the thing (be it knowledge or fiction) called metaphysics, I think I perceive that the aim of this natural tendency is, to free our notions from the fetters of experience and from the limits of the mere contemplation of nature so far as at least to open to us a field containing mere objects for the pure understanding, which no sensibility can reach, not indeed for the purpose of speculatively occupying ourselves with them (for there we can find no ground to stand on), but because practical principles, which, without finding some such scope for their necessary expectation and hope, could not expand to the universality which reason unavoidably requires from a moral point of view.

So I find that the Psychological Idea (however little it may reveal to me the nature of the human soul, which is higher than all concepts of experience), shows the insufficiency of these concepts plainly enough, and thereby deters me from materialism, the psychological notion of which is unfit for any explanation of nature, and besides confines reason in practical respects. The Cosmological Ideas, by the obvious insufficiency of all possible cognition of nature to satisfy reason in its lawful inquiry, serve in the same manner to keep us from naturalism, which asserts nature to be sufficient for itself. Finally, all natural necessity in the sensible world is conditional, as it always presupposes the dependence of things upon others, and unconditional necessity must be sought only in the unity of a cause different from the world of sense. But as the causality of this cause, in its turn, were it merely nature, could never render the existence of the contingent (as its consequent) comprehensible, reason frees itself by means of the Theological Idea from fatalism, (both as a blind natural necessity in the coherence of nature itself, without a first principle, and as a blind causality of this principle itself), and leads to the concept of a cause possessing freedom, or of a Supreme Intelligence. Thus the transcendental Ideas serve, if not to instruct us positively, at least to destroy the rash assertions of Materialism, of Naturalism, and of Fatalism, and thus to afford scope for the moral Ideas beyond the field of speculation. These considerations, I should think, explain in some measure the natural predisposition of which I spoke.

The practical value, which a merely speculative science may have, lies without the bounds of this science, and can therefore be considered as a scholion merely, and like all scholia does not form part of the science itself. This application however surely lies within the bounds of philosophy, especially of philosophy drawn from the pure sources of reason, where its speculative use in metaphysics must necessarily be at unity with its practical use in morals. Hence the unavoidable dialectics of pure reason, considered in metaphysics, as a natural tendency, deserves to be explained not as an illusion merely, which is to be removed, but also, if possible, as a natural provision as regards its end, though this duty, a work of supererogation, cannot justly be assigned to metaphysics proper.

The solutions of these questions which are treated in the chapter on the Regulative Use of the Ideas of Pure Reason should be considered a second scholion which however has a greater affinity with the subject of metaphysics. For there certain rational principles are expounded which determine *a priori* the order of nature or rather of the understanding, which seeks nature's laws through experience. They seem to be constitutive and legislative with regard to experience, though they spring from pure reason, which cannot be considered, like the understanding, as a principle of possible experience. Now whether or not this harmony rests upon the fact, that just as nature does not inhere in appearances or in their source (the sensibility) itself, but only in so far as the latter is in relation to the understanding, as also a systematic unity in applying the understanding to bring about an entirety of all possible experience can only belong to the understanding when in relation to reason; and whether or not experience is in this way mediately subordinate to the legislation of reason: may be discussed by those who desire to trace the nature of reason even beyond its use in metaphysics, into the general principles of a history of nature; I have represented this task as important, but not attempted its solution, in the book itself.

And thus I conclude the analytical solution of the main question which I had proposed: "How is metaphysics in general possible?" by ascending from the data of its actual use in its consequences, to the grounds of its possibility.

Foundation for the Metaphysic of Morals

387|i

PREFACE

The Different Branches of Philosophy

Ancient Greek philosophy was divided into three sciences: *physics, ethics,* and *logic.* This division fits the nature of the subject perfectly, and there is no need to improve on it—except perhaps by adding the principle on which it is based. By so doing we may be able on the one hand to guarantee its completeness and on the other to determine correctly its necessary subdivisions.

All rational knowledge is either *material* and concerned with some object, or *formal* and concerned solely with the form of understanding and reason themselves—with the universal rules of thinking as such without regard to differences in its objects. Formal
ii mal philosophy is called *logic*; while material philosophy, which has to do with determinate objects and with the laws to which they are subject, is in turn divided into two, since the laws in question are laws either of *nature* or of *freedom.* The science of the first is called *physics,* that of the second *ethics.* The former is also called natural philosophy, the latter moral philosophy.

Logic can have no empirical part—that is, no part in which the universal and necessary laws of thinking are based on grounds taken from experience. Otherwise it would not be logic—that is, it would not be a canon for understanding and reason, valid for all thinking and capable of demonstration. As against this, both natural and moral philosophy can each have an empirical part, since the former has to formulate its laws for nature as an object of experience, and the latter for the will of man so far as affected by nature—the first set of laws being those in accordance with which everything happens, the second being those in accordance with which every- 388|iii
thing ought to happen, although they also take into account the conditions under which what ought to happen very often does not happen.

All philosophy so far as it rests on the basis of experience can be called *empirical* philosophy. If it sets forth its doctrines as depending entirely on *a priori* principles, it can be called *pure* philosophy.

Reprinted from Immanual Kant, *Groundwork of the Metaphysics of Morals* (London: Random House, 1948), translated by H. J. Paton.

The latter when wholly formal is called *logic*; but if it is confined to determinate objects of the understanding, it is then called *metaphysics*.

In this way there arises the Idea of a two-fold metaphysic—*a metaphysic of nature* and *a metaphysic of morals*. Thus physics will have its empirical part, but it will also have a rational one; and likewise ethics—although here the empirical part might be called specifically *practical anthropology*, while the rational part might properly be called *morals*.

The Need for Pure Ethics

All industries, arts, and crafts have gained by the di-
iv vision of labour—that is to say, one man no longer does everything, but each confines himself to a particular task, differing markedly from others in its technique, so that he may be able to perform it with the highest perfection and with greater ease. Where tasks are not so distinguished and divided, where every man is a jack of all trades, there industry is still sunk in utter barbarism. In itself it might well be a subject not unworthy of examination, if we asked whether pure philosophy in all its parts does not demand its own special craftsman. Would it not be better for the whole of this learned industry if those accustomed to purvey, in accordance with the public taste, a mixture of the empirical and the rational in various proportions unknown even to themselves—the self-styled 'creative thinkers' as opposed to the 'hair-splitters' who attend to the purely rational part—were to be warned against carrying on at once two jobs very different in their technique,
v each perhaps requiring a special talent and the combination of both in one person producing mere bunglers? Here, however, I confine myself to asking whether the nature of science does not always require that the empirical part should be scrupulously separated from the rational one, and that (empirical) physics proper should be prefaced by a metaphysic of nature, while practical anthropology should be prefaced by a metaphysic of morals—each metaphysic having to be scrupulously cleansed of everything empirical if we are to know how much pure reason can accomplish in both cases and from what
389 sources it can by itself draw its own *a priori* teaching. I leave it an open question whether the latter business is to be conducted by all moralists (whose name is legion) or only by those who feel a vocation for the subject.

Since my aim here is directed strictly to moral philosophy, I limit my proposed question to this point only—Do we not think it a matter of the utmost necessity to work out for once a pure moral philosophy completely cleansed of everything that can only be empirical and appropriate to anthropology? That there must be such a philosophy is already obvious from the common Idea of duty and from the laws of morality. Every one must admit that a law has to carry with it absolute necessity if it is to be valid morally—valid, that is, as a ground of obligation; that the command 'Thou shalt not lie' could not hold merely for men, other rational beings having no obligation to abide by it—and similarly with all other genuine moral laws; that here consequently the ground of obligation must be looked for, not in the nature of man nor in the circumstances of the world in which he is placed, but solely *a priori* in the concepts of pure reason; and that every other precept based on principles of mere experience—and even a precept that may in a certain sense be considered universal, so far as it rests in its slightest part, perhaps only in its motive, on empirical grounds—can indeed be called a practical rule, but never a moral law.

Thus in practical knowledge as a whole, not only are moral laws, together with their principles, essentially different from all the rest in which there is some empirical element, but the whole of moral philosophy is based entirely on the part of it that is pure. When applied to man it does not borrow in the slightest from acquaintance with him (in anthropology), but gives him laws *a priori* as a rational being. These laws admittedly require in addition a power of judgement sharpened by experience, partly in order to distinguish the cases to which they apply, partly to procure for them admittance to the will of man and influence over practice; for man, affected as he is by so many inclinations, is capable of the Idea of a pure practical reason, but he has not so easily the power to realize the Idea *in concreto* in his conduct of life.

A metaphysic of morals is thus indispensably necessary, not merely in order to investigate, from motives of speculation, the source of practical principles which are present *a priori* in our reason, but 390]viii
because morals themselves remain exposed to corruption of all sorts as long as this guiding thread is lacking, this ultimate norm for correct moral judgement. For if any action is to be morally good, it is not enough that it should *conform* to the moral law—

it must also be done *for the sake of the moral law*: where this is not so, the conformity is only too contingent and precarious, since the non-moral ground at work will now and then produce actions which accord with the law, but very often actions which transgress it. Now the moral law in its purity and genuineness (and in the field of action it is precisely this that matters most) is to be looked for nowhere else than in a pure philosophy. Hence pure philosophy (that is, metaphysics) must come first, and without it there can be no moral philosophy at all. Indeed a philosophy which mixes up these pure principles with empirical ones does not deserve the name of philosophy (since philosophy is distinguished from ordinary rational knowledge precisely because it sets forth in a separate science what the latter apprehends only as confused with other
ix things). Still less does it deserve the name of moral philosophy, since by this very confusion it undermines even the purity of morals themselves and acts against its own proper purpose.

The Philosophy of Willing As Such

It must not be imagined that in the propaedeutics prefixed to his moral philosophy by the celebrated *Wolff*—that is, in the '*Universal Practical Philosophy*', as he called it—we already have what is here demanded and consequently do not need to break entirely new ground. Precisely because it was supposed to be a universal practical philosophy, it has taken into consideration, not a special kind of will—not such a will as is completely determined by *a priori* principles apart from any empirical motives and so can be called a pure will—but willing as such, together with all activities and conditions belonging to it in this general sense. Because of this it differs from a metaphysic of morals in the same way as
x general logic differs from transcendental philosophy, the first of which sets forth the activities and rules of thinking *as such*, while the second expounds the special activities and rules of *pure* thinking—that is, of the thinking whereby objects are known completely *a priori*; for a metaphysic of morals has to investigate the idea and principles of a possible *pure* will, and not the activities and conditions of human willing as such, which are drawn for the most
391 part from psychology. The fact that in this 'universal practical philosophy' there is also talk (though quite unjustifiably) about moral laws and duty is no objection to what I say. For the authors of this science remain true to their Idea of it on this point as well: they do not distinguish motives which, as such, are conceived completely *a priori* by reason alone and are genuinely moral, from empirical motives which understanding raises to general concepts by the mere comparison of experiences. On the contrary, without taking into account differences in their origin they consider motives only as regards their xi
relative strength or weakness (looking upon all of them as homogeneous) and construct on this basis their concept of *obligation*. This concept is anything but moral; but its character is only such as is to be expected from a philosophy which never decides, as regards the *source* of all practical concepts, whether they arise only *a posteriori* or arise *a priori* as well.

The Aim of the Groundwork

Intending, as I do, to publish some day a metaphysic of morals, I issue this *Groundwork* in advance. For such a metaphysic there is strictly no other foundation than a critique of *pure practical reason*, just as for metaphysics there is no other foundation than the critique of pure speculative reason which I have already published. Yet, on the one hand, there is not the same extreme necessity for the former critique as for the latter, since human reason can, in matters of morality, be easily brought to a high degree of accuracy and precision even in the most ordinary intelligence, whereas in its theoretical, but pure, activity it is, on the contrary, out and out dialectical; xii
and, on the other hand, a critique of practical reason, if it is to be complete, requires, on my view, that we should be able at the same time to show the unity of practical and theoretical reason in a common principle, since in the end there can only be one and the same reason, which must be differentiated solely in its application. Here, however, I found myself as yet unable to bring my work to such completeness without introducing considerations of quite another sort and so confusing the reader. This is why, instead of calling it a '*Critique of Pure Practical Reason*', I have adopted the title '*Groundwork of the Metaphysic of Morals*'.

But, in the third place, since a metaphysic of morals, in spite of its horrifying title, can be in a high degree popular and suited to the ordinary intelligence, I think it useful to issue separately this preparatory work on its foundations so that later I need not insert the subtleties inevitable in these mat- 392|xiii
ters into doctrines more easy to understand.

The sole aim of the present Groundwork is to seek out and establish *the supreme principle of morality.* This by itself is a business which by its very purpose constitutes a whole and has to be separated off from every other enquiry. The application of the principle to the whole system would not doubt throw much light on my answers to this central question, so important and yet hitherto so far from being satisfactorily discussed; and the adequacy it manifests throughout would afford it strong confirmation. All the same, I had to forego this advantage, which in any case would be more flattering to myself than helpful to others, since the convenience of a principle in use and its seeming adequacy afford no completely safe proof of its correctness. They rather awaken a certain bias against examining and weighing it in all strictness for itself without any regard to its consequences.

The Method of the Groundwork

xiv

The method I have adopted in this book is, I believe, one which will work best if we proceed analytically from common knowledge to the formulation of its supreme principle and then back again synthetically from an examination of this principle and its origins to the common knowledge in which we find its application. Hence the division turns out to be as follows:—

1. *Chapter I*: Passage from ordinary rational knowledge of morality to philosophical.
2. *Chapter II*: Passage from popular moral philosophy to a metaphysic of morals.
3. *Chapter III*: Final step from a metaphysic of morals to a critique of pure practical reason.

CHAPTER I
PASSAGE FROM ORDINARY RATIONAL KNOWLEDGE OF MORALITY TO PHILOSOPHICAL

The Good Will

It is impossible to conceive anything at all in the world, or even out of it, which can be taken as good without qualification, except a *good will.* Intelligence, wit, judgement, and any other *talents* of the mind we may care to name, or courage, resolution, and constancy of purpose, as qualities of *temperament,* are without doubt good and desirable in many respects; but they can also be extremely bad and hurtful when the will is not good which has to make use of these gifts of nature, and which for this reason has the term '*character*' applied to its peculiar quality. It is exactly the same with *gifts of fortune.* Power, wealth, honour, even health and that complete well-being and contentment with one's state which goes 2
by the name of '*happiness*', produce boldness, and as a consequence often over-boldness as well, unless a good will is present by which their influence on the mind—and so too the whole principle of action—may be corrected and adjusted to universal ends; not to mention that a rational and impartial spectator can never feel approval in contemplating the uninterrupted prosperity of a being graced by no touch of a pure and good will, and that consequently a good will seems to constitute the indispensable condition of our very worthiness to be happy.

Some qualities are even helpful to this good will itself and can make its task very much easier. They have none the less no inner unconditioned worth, but rather presuppose a good will which sets a limit to 394
the esteem in which they are rightly held and does not permit us to regard them as absolutely good. Moderation in affections and passions, self-control, and sober reflexion are not only good in many respects: they may even seem to constitute part of the *inner* worth of a person. Yet they are far from being properly described as good without qualification (however unconditionally they have been commended by the ancients). For without the principles of a good will they may become exceedingly bad; 3
and the very coolness of a scoundrel makes him, not merely more dangerous, but also immediately more abominable in our eyes than we should have taken him to be without it.

The Good Will and Its Results

A good will is not good because of what it effects or accomplishes—because of its fitness for attaining some proposed end: it is good through its willing alone—that is, good in itself. Considered in itself it is to be esteemed beyond comparison as far higher than anything it could ever bring about merely in order to favour some inclination or, if you like, the sum total of inclinations. Even if, by some special disfavour of destiny or by the niggardly endowment of step-motherly nature, this will is entirely lacking in power to carry out its intentions; if by its utmost

effort it still accomplishes nothing, and only good will is left (not, admittedly, as a mere wish, but as the straining of every means so far as they are in our control); even then it would still shine like a jewel for its own sake as something which has its full value in itself. Its usefulness or fruitlessness can neither add to, nor subtract from, this value. Its usefulness would be merely, as it were, the setting which enables us to handle it better in our ordinary dealings or to attract the attention of those not yet sufficiently
4 expert, but not to commend it to experts or to determine its value.

The Function of Reason

Yet in this Idea of the absolute value of a mere will, all useful results being left out of account in its assessment, there is something so strange that, in spite of all the agreement it receives even from ordinary reason, there must arise the suspicion that perhaps its secret basis is merely some high-flown fantasticality, and that we may have misunderstood the purpose of nature in attaching reason to our will as its
395 governor. We will therefore submit our Idea to an examination from this point of view.

In the natural constitution of an organic being—that is, of one contrived for the purpose of life—let us take it as a principle that in it no organ is to be found for any end unless it is also the most appropriate to that end and the best fitted for it. Suppose now that for a being possesses of reason and a will the real purpose of nature were his *preservation,* his *welfare*, or in a word his *happiness.* In that case nature would have hit on a very bad arrangement by choosing reason in the creature to carry out this purpose. For all the actions he has to perform with this
5 end in view, and the whole rule of his behaviour, would have been mapped out for him far more accurately by instinct; and the end in question could have been maintained far more surely by instinct than it ever can be by reason. If reason should have been imparted to this favoured creature as well, it would have had to serve him only for contemplating the happy disposition of his nature, for admiring it, for enjoying it, and for being grateful to its beneficient Cause—not for subjecting his power of appetition to such feeble and defective guidance or for meddling incompetently with the purposes of nature. In a word, nature would have prevented reason from striking out into a *practical use* and from presuming, with its feeble vision, to think out for itself a plan for happiness and for the means to its attainment. Nature would herself have taken over the choice, not only of ends, but also of means, and would with wise precaution have entrusted both to instinct alone.

In actual fact too we find that the more a cultivated reason concerns itself with the aim of enjoying life and happiness, the farther does man get away from true contentment. This is why there arises in many, and that too in those who have made most trial of this use of reason, if they are only candid enough to admit it, a certain degree of *misology*— 6
that is, a hatred of reason; for when they balance all the advantage they draw, I will not say from thinking out all the arts of ordinary indulgence, but even from science (which in the last resort seems to them to be also an indulgence of the mind), they discover that they have in fact only brought more trouble on their heads than they have gained in the way of hap- 396
piness. On this account they come to envy, rather than to despise, the more common run of men, who are closer to the guidance of mere natural instinct, and who do not allow their reason to have much influence on their conduct. So far we must admit that the judgement of those who seek to moderate—and even to reduce below zero—the conceited glorification of such advantages as reason is supposed to provide in the way of happiness and contentment with life is in no way soured or ungrateful to the goodness with which the world is governed. These judgements rather have as their hidden ground the Idea of another and much more worthy purpose of existence, for which, and not for happiness, reason is quite properly designed, and to which, therefore, as a supreme condition the private purposes of man must for the most part be subordinated.

For since reason is not sufficiently serviceable for guiding the will safely as regards its objects and the 7
satisfaction of all our needs (which it in part even multiplies)—a purpose for which an implanted natural instinct would have led us much more surely; and since none the less reason has been imparted to us as a practical power—that is, as one which is to have influence on the *will*; its true function must be to produce a *will* which is *good*, not as a *means* to some further end, but *in itself*; and for this function reason was absolutely necessary in a world where nature, in distributing her aptitudes, has everywhere else gone to work in a purposive manner. Such a will need not on this account be the sole and complete good, but it must be the highest good and the

condition of all the rest, even of all our demands for happiness. In that case we can easily reconcile with the wisdom of nature our observation that the cultivation of reason which is required for the first and unconditioned purpose may in many ways, at least in this life, restrict the attainment of the second purpose—namely, happiness—which is always conditioned; and indeed that it can even reduce happiness to less than zero without nature proceeding contrary to its purpose; for reason, which recognizes as its highest practical function the establishment of a good will, in attaining this end is capable only of its own peculiar kind of contentment—contentment in
8 fulfilling a purpose which in turn is determined by reason alone, even if this fulfillment should often involve interference with the purposes of inclination.

The Good Will and Duty

397 We have now to elucidate the concept of a will estimable in itself and good apart from any further end. This concept, which is already present in a sound natural understanding and requires not so much to be taught as merely to be clarified, always holds the highest place in estimating the total worth of our actions and constitutes the condition of all the rest. We will therefore take up the concept of *duty*, which includes that of a good will, exposed, however, to certain subjective limitations and obstacles. These, so far from hiding a good will or disguising it, rather bring it out by contrast and make it shine forth more brightly.

The Motive of Duty

I will here pass over all actions already recognized as contrary to duty, however useful they may be with a view to this or that end; for about these the question does not even arise whether they could have been done *for the sake of duty* inasmuch as they are directly opposed to it. I will also set aside actions which in fact accord with duty, yet for which men have *no immediate inclination*, but perform them because impelled to do so by some other inclination.
9 For there it is easy to decide whether the action which accords with duty has been done *from duty* or from some purpose of self-interest. This distinction is far more difficult to perceive when the action accords with duty and the subject has in addition an *immediate* inclination to the action. For example, it certainly accords with duty that a grocer should not overcharge his inexperienced customer; and where there is much competition a sensible shopkeeper refrains from so doing and keeps to a fixed and general price for everybody so that a child can buy from him just as well as anyone else. Thus people are served *honestly*; but this is not nearly enough to justify us in believing that the shopkeeper has acted in this way from duty or from principles of fair dealing; his interests required him to do so. We cannot assume him to have in addition an immediate inclination towards his customers, leading him, as it were out of love, to give no man preference over another in the matter of price. Thus the action was done neither from duty nor from immediate inclination, but solely from purposes of self-interest.

On the other hand, to preserve one's life is a duty, and besides this every one has also an immediate inclination to do so. But on account of this the often anxious precautions taken by the greater part of mankind for this purpose have no inner worth, and the maxim of their action is without moral content. They do protect their lives *in conformity with duty,* 398
but not *from the motive of duty*. When on the con- 10
trary, disappointments and hopeless misery have quite taken away the taste for life; when a wretched man, strong in soul and more angered at his fate than faint-hearted or cast down, longs for death and still preserves his life without loving it—not from inclination or fear but from duty; then indeed his maxim has a moral content.

To help others where one can is a duty, and besides this there are many spirits of so sympathetic a temper that, without any further motive of vanity or self-interest, they find an inner pleasure in spreading happiness around them and can take delight in the contentment of others as their own work. Yet I maintain that in such a case an action of this kind, however right and however amiable it may be, has still no genuinely moral worth. It stands on the same footing as other inclinations—for example, the inclination for honour, which if fortunate enough to hit on something beneficial and right and consequently honourable, deserves praise and encouragement, but not esteem; for its maxim lacks moral content, namely, the performance of such actions, not from inclination, but *from duty*. Suppose then that the mind of this friend of man were overclouded by sorrows of his own which extinguished all sympa- 11
thy with the fate of others, but that he still had power to help those in distress, though no longer stirred by the need of others because sufficiently occupied with his own; and suppose that, when no longer moved

by any inclination, he tears himself out of this deadly insensibility and does the action without any inclination for the sake of duty alone; then for the first time his action has its genuine moral worth. Still further: if nature had implanted little sympathy in this or that man's heart; if (being in other respects an honest fellow) he were cold in temperament and indifferent to the sufferings of others—perhaps because, being endowed with the special gift of patience and robust endurance in his own sufferings, he assumed the like in others or even demanded it; if such a man (who would in truth not be the worst product of nature) were not exactly fashioned by her to be a philanthropist, would he not still find in himself a source from which he might draw a worth far higher than any that a good-natured temperament can have? Assuredly he would. It is precisely in this
399 that the worth of character begins to show—a moral worth and beyond all comparison the highest—namely, that he does good, not from inclination, but from duty.

To assure one's own happiness is a duty (at least indirectly); for discontent with one's state, in a press
12 of cares and amidst unsatisfied wants, might easily become a great *temptation to the transgression of duty.* But here also, apart from regard to duty, all men have already of themselves the strongest and deepest inclination towards happiness, because precisely in this Idea of happiness all inclinations are combined into a sum total. The prescription for happiness is, however, often so constituted as greatly to interfere with some inclinations, and yet men cannot form under the name of 'happiness' any determinate and assured conception of the satisfaction of all inclinations as a sum. Hence it is not to be wondered at that a single inclination which is determinate as to what it promises and as to the time of its satisfaction may outweigh a wavering Idea; and that a man, for example, a sufferer from gout, may choose to enjoy what he fancies and put up with what he can—on the ground that on balance he has here at least not killed the enjoyment of the present moment because of some possibly groundless expectations of the good fortune supposed to attach to soundness of health. But in this case also, when the universal inclination towards happiness has failed to determine his will, when good health, at least for him, has not entered into his calculations as so necessary, what remains over, here as in other cases, is
13 a law—the law of furthering his happiness, not from inclination, but from duty; and in this for the first time his conduct has a real moral worth.

It is doubtless in this sense that we should understand too the passages from Scripture in which we are commanded to love our neighbour and even our enemy. For love out of inclination cannot be commanded; but kindness done from duty—although no inclination impels us, and even although natural and unconquerable disinclination stands in our way—is *practical,* and not *pathological,* love, residing in the will and not in the propensions of feeling, in principles of action and not of melting compassion; and it is this practical love alone which can be an object of command.

The Formal Principle of Duty

Our second proposition is this: An action done from duty has its moral worth, *not in the purpose* to be attained by it, but in the maxim in accordance with
which it is decided upon; it depends therefore, not 400
on the realization of the object of the action, but solely on the *principle* of *volition* in accordance with which, irrespective of all objects of the faculty of desire, the action has been performed. That the purposes we may have in our actions, and also their effects considered as ends and motives of the will, can give to actions no unconditioned and moral worth is clear from what has gone before. Where then can this worth be found if we are not to find it in the will's relation to the effect hoped for from the action? It can be found nowhere but *in the principle* 14
of the will, irrespective of the ends which can be brought about by such an action; for between its *a priori* principle, which is formal, and its *a posteriori* motive, which is material, the will stands, so to speak, at a parting of the ways; and since it must be determined by some principle, it will have to be determined by the formal principle of volition when an action is done from duty, where, as we have seen, every material principle is taken away from it.

Reverence for the Law

Our third proposition, as an inference from the two preceding, I would express thus: *Duty is the necessity to act out of reverence for the law.* For an object as the effect of my proposed action I can have an *inclination,* but *never reverence,* precisely because it is merely the effect, and not the activity, of a will. Similarly for inclination as such, whether my own or that of another, I cannot have reverence: I can at most in the first case approve, and in the sec-

ond case sometimes even love—that is, regard it as favourable to my own advantage. Only something which is conjoined with my will solely as a ground and never as an effect—something which does not serve my inclination, but outweighs it or at least
15 leaves it entirely out of account in my choice—and therefore only bare law for its own sake, can be an object of reverence and therewith a command. Now an action done from duty has to set aside altogether the influence of inclination, and along with inclination every object of the will; so there is nothing left able to determine the will except objectively the *law* and subjectively *pure reverence* for this practical law, and therefore the maxim[1] of obeying this law
401 even to the detriment of all my inclinations.

Thus the moral worth of an action does not depend on the result expected from it, and so too does not depend on any principle of action that needs to borrow its motive from this expected result. For all these results (agreeable states and even the promotion of happiness in others) could have been brought about by other causes as well, and consequently their production did not require the will of a rational being, in which, however, the highest and unconditioned good can alone be found. Therefore nothing but the *idea of the law* in itself, *which admittedly is*
16 *present only in a rational being*—so far as it, and not an expected result, is the ground determining the will—can constitute that pre-eminent good which we call moral, a good which is already present in the person acting on this idea and has not to be awaited merely from the result.[2]

The Categorical Imperative

But what kind of law can this be the thought of 402|17
which, even without regard to the results expected from it, has to determine the will if this is to be called good absolutely and without qualification? Since I have robbed the will of every inducement that might arise for it as a consequence of obeying any particular law, nothing is left but the conformity of actions to universal law as such, and this alone must serve the will as its principle. That is to say, I ought never to act except in such a way *that I can also will that my maxim should become a universal law.* Here bare conformity to universal law as such (without having as its base any law prescribing particular actions) is what serves the will as its principle, and must so serve it if duty is not to be everywhere an empty delusion and a chimerical concept. The ordinary reason of mankind also agrees with this completely in its practical judgements and always has the aforesaid principle before its eyes.

Take this question, for example. May I not, when 18
I am hard pressed, make a promise with the intention of not keeping it? Here I readily distinguish the two senses which the question can have—Is it prudent, or is it right, to make a false promise? The first no doubt can often be the case. I do indeed see that it is not enough for me to extricate myself from present embarrassment by this subterfuge: I have to consider whether from this lie there may not subsequently accrue to me much greater inconvenience than that from which I now escape, and also—since, with all my supposed *astuteness,* to foresee the consequences is not so easy that I can be sure there is no chance, once confidence in me is lost, of this proving far more disadvantageous than all the ills I now think to avoid—whether it may not be a *more prudent* action to proceed here on a general maxim and make it my habit not to give a promise except with the intention of keeping it. Yet it becomes clear to me at once that such a maxim is always founded solely on fear of consequences. To tell the truth for the sake of duty is something entirely different from doing so out of concern for inconvenient results; for in the first case the

---

15 1. A *maxim* is the subjective principle of a volition: an objective principle (that is, one which would also serve subjectively as a practical principle for all rational beings if reason had full control over the faculty of desire) is a practical *law.*

16 2. It might be urged against me that I have merely tried, under cover of the world '*reverence*', to take refuge in an obscure feeling instead of giving a clearly articulated answer to the question by means of a concept of reason. Yet although reverence is a feeling, it is not a feeling *received* through outside influence, but one *self-produced* by a rational concept, and therefore specifically distinct from feelings of the first kind, all of which can be reduced to inclination or fear. What I recognize immediately as law for me, I recognize with reverence, which means merely consciousness of the *subordination* of my will to a law without the mediation of external influences on my senses. Immediate determination of the will by the law and consciousness of this determination is called '*reverence*', so that reverence is regarded as the *effect* of the law on the subject and not as the *cause* of the law. Reverence is properly awareness of a value which demolishes my self-love. Hence there is something which is regarded neither as an object of inclination nor as an object of fear, though it has at the same time some analogy with both. The *object* of reverence is the *law* alone—that law which we impose *on ourselves* but yet as necessary in itself. Considered as a law, we are subject to it without any consultation of self-love; considered as self-imposed it is a consequence of our will. In the first respect it is analogous to fear, in the second to inclination. All 17
reverence for a person is properly only reverence for the law (of honesty and so on) of which that person gives us an example. Because we regard the development of our talents as a duty, we see too in a man of talent a sort of *example of the law* (the law of becoming like him by practice), and this is what constitutes our reverence for him. All moral *interest,* so-called, consists solely in *reverence* for the law.

concept of the action already contains in itself a law for me, while in the second case I have first of all to look around elsewhere in order to see what effects
19 may be bound up with it for me. When I deviate from
403 the principle of duty, this is quite certainly bad; but if I desert my prudential maxim, this can often be greatly to my advantage, though it is admittedly safer to stick to it. Suppose I seek, however, to learn in the quickest way and yet unerringly how to solve the problem 'Does a lying promise accord with duty?' I have then to ask myself 'Should I really be content that my maxim (the maxim of getting out of a difficulty by a false promise) should hold as a universal law (one valid both for myself and others)? And could I really say to myself that every one may make a false promise if he finds himself in a difficulty from which he can extricate himself in no other way?' I then become aware at once that I can indeed will to lie, but I can by no means will a universal law of lying; for by such a law there could properly be no promises at all, since it would be futile to profess a will for future action to others who would not believe my profession or who, if they did so over-hastily, would pay me back in like coin; and consequently my maxim, as soon as it was made a universal law, would be bound to annul itself.

Thus I need no far-reaching ingenuity to find out what I have to do in order to possess a good will. In-
20 experienced in the course of world affairs and incapable of being prepared for all the chances that happen in it, I ask myself only 'Can you also will that your maxim should become a universal law?' Where you cannot, it is to be rejected, and that not because of a prospective loss to you or even to others, but because it cannot fit as a principle into a possible enactment of universal law. For such an enactment reason compels my immediate reverence, into whose grounds (which the philosopher may investigate) I have as yet no *insight*, although I do at least understand this much: reverence is the assessment of a worth which far outweighs all the worth of what is commended by inclination, and the necessity for me to act out of *pure* reverence for the practical law is what constitutes duty, to which every other motive must give way because it is the condition of a will good *in itself*, whose value is above all else.

Ordinary Practical Reason

In studying the moral knowledge of ordinary human reason we have now arrived at its first principle. This principle it admittedly does not conceive thus abstractly in its universal form; but it does always have it actually before its eyes and does use it as a norm of judgement. It would be easy to show here how hu-
man reason, with this compass in hand, is well able 404
to distinguish, in all cases that present themselves, 21
what is good or evil, right or wrong—provided that, without the least attempt to teach it anything new, we merely make reason attend, as Socrates did, to its own principle; and how in consequence there is no need of science or philosophy for knowing what man has to do in order to be honest and good, and indeed to be wise and virtuous. It might even be surmised in advance that acquaintance with what every man is obliged to do, and so also to know, will be the affair of every man, even the most ordinary. Yet we cannot observe without admiration the great advantage which the power of practical judgement has over that of theoretical in the minds of ordinary men. In theoretical judgements, when ordinary reason ventures to depart from the laws of experience and the perceptions of sense, it falls into sheer unintelligibility and self-contradiction, or at least into a chaos of uncertainty, obscurity, and vacillation. On the practical side, however, the power of judgement first begins to show what advantages it has in itself when the ordinary mind excludes all sensuous motives from its practical laws. Then ordinary intelligence becomes even
subtle—it may be in juggling with conscience or with 22
other claims as to what is to be called right, or in trying to determine honestly for its own instruction the value of various actions; and, what is most important, it can in the latter case have as good hope of hitting the mark as any that a philosopher can promise himself. Indeed it is almost surer in this than even a philosopher, because he can have no principle different from that of ordinary intelligence, but may easily confuse his judgement with a mass of alien and irrelevant considerations and cause it to swerve from the straight path. Might it not then be more advisable in moral questions to abide by the judgement of ordinary reason and, at the most, to bring in philosophy only in order to set forth the system of morals more fully and intelligibly and to present its rules in a form more convenient for use (though still more so for disputation)—but not in order to lead ordinary human intelligence away from its happy simplicity in respect of action and to set it by means of philosophy on a new path of enquiry and instruction?

The Need for Philosophy

Innocence is a splendid thing, only it has the misfortune not to keep very well and to be easily misled.

On this account even wisdom—which in itself consists more in doing and not doing than in knowing—does require science as well, not in order to learn from it, but in order to win acceptance and durability for 23 its own prescriptions. Man feels in himself a powerful counterweight to all the commands of duty presented to him by reason as so worthy of esteem—the counterweight of his needs and inclinations, whose total satisfaction he grasps under the name of 'happiness'. But reason, without promising anything to inclination, enjoins its commands relentlessly, and therefore, so to speak, with disregard and neglect of these turbulent and seemingly equitable claims (which refuse to be suppressed by any command). From this there arises a *natural dialectic*—that is, a disposition to quibble with these strict laws of duty, to throw doubt on their validity or at least on their purity and strictness, and to make them, where possible, more adapted to our wishes and inclinations; that is, to pervert their very foundations and destroy their whole dignity—a result which in the end even ordinary human reason is unable to approve.

In this way the *common reason of mankind* is impelled, not by any need for speculation (which never assails it so long as it is content to be mere sound reason), but on practical grounds themselves, to leave its own sphere and take a step into the field of *practical philosophy.* It there seeks to acquire in-
24 formation and precise instruction about the source of its own principle, and about the correct function of this principle in comparison with maxims based on need and inclination, in order that it may escape from the embarrassment of antagonistic claims and may avoid the risk of losing all genuine moral principles because of the ambiguity into which it easily falls. Thus ordinary reason, when cultivated in its practical use, gives rise insensibly to a *dialectic* which constrains it to seek help in philosophy, just as happens in its theoretical use; and consequently in the first case as little as in the second will it anywhere else than in a full critique of our reason be able to find peace.

406|25

CHAPTER II
PASSAGE FROM POPULAR MORAL PHILOSOPHY TO A METAPHYSIC OF MORALS

The Use of Examples

If so far we have drawn our concept of duty from the ordinary use of our practical reason, it must by no means be inferred that we have treated it as a concept of experience. On the contrary, when we pay attention to our experience of human conduct, we meet frequent and—as we ourselves admit—justified complaints that we can adduce no certain examples of the spirit which acts out of pure duty, and that, although much may be done *in accordance with* the commands of *duty*, it remains doubtful whether it really is done *for the sake of duty* and so has a moral value. Hence at all times there have been philosophers who have absolutely denied the presence of this spirit in human actions and have ascribed everything to a more or less refined self-love. Yet they have not cast doubt on the rightness of the concept of morality. They have spoken rather with deep regret of the frailty and impurity of human nature, which is on their view noble enough to take as its rule an Idea so worthy of reverence, but at the same time too weak to follow it: the reason which 26
should serve it for making laws it uses only to look after the interest of inclinations, whether singly or—at the best—in their greatest mutual compatibility.

In actual fact it is absolutely impossible for ex- 407
perience to establish with complete certainty a single case in which the maxim of an action in other respects right has rested solely on moral grounds and on the thought of one's duty. It is indeed at times the case that after the keenest self-examination we find nothing that without the moral motive of duty could have been strong enough to move us to this or that good action and to so great a sacrifice; but we cannot infer from this with certainty that it is not some secret impulse of self-love which has actually, under the mere show of the Idea of duty, been the cause genuinely determining our will. We are pleased to flatter ourselves with the false claim to a nobler motive, but in fact we can never, even by the most strenuous self-examination, get to the bottom of our secret impulsions; for when moral value is in question, we are concerned, not with the actions which we see, but with their inner principles, which we cannot see.

Furthermore, to those who deride all morality as the mere phantom of a human imagination which gets above itself out of vanity we can do no service more pleasing than to admit that the concepts of duty must be drawn solely from experience (just as out of slackness we willingly persuade ourselves that this is so in the case of all other concepts); for by so doing we prepare for them an assured triumph. Out of love for humanity I am willing to allow that most of our actions may accord with duty; but if we

look more closely at our scheming and striving, we everywhere come across the dear self, which is always turning up; and it is on this that the purpose of our actions is based—not on the strict command of duty, which would often require self-denial. One need not be exactly a foe to virtue, but merely a dispassionate observer declining to take the liveliest wish for goodness straight away as its realization, in order at certain moments (particularly with advancing years and with a power of judgement at once made shrewder by experience and also more keen in observation) to become doubtful whether any genuine virtue is actually to be encountered in the world. And then nothing can protect us against a complete falling away from our Ideas of duty, or can preserve in the soul a grounded reverence for its law, except the clear conviction that even if there never have been actions springing from such pure sources, the
408|28 question at issue here is not whether this or that has happened; that, on the contrary, reason by itself and independently of all appearances commands what ought to happen; that consequently actions of which the world has perhaps hitherto given no example—actions whose practicability might well be doubted by those who rest everything on experience—are nevertheless commanded unrelentingly by reason; and that, for instance, although up to now there may have existed no loyal friend, pure loyalty in friendship can be no less required from every man, inasmuch as this duty, prior to all experience, is contained as duty in general in the Idea of a reason which determines the will by *a priori* grounds.

It may be added that unless we wish to deny to the concept of morality all truth and all relation to a possible object, we cannot dispute that its law is of such widespread significance as to hold, not merely for men, but for all *rational beings as such*—not merely subject to contingent conditions and exceptions, but *with absolute necessity*. It is therefore clear that no experience can give us occasion to infer even the possibility of such apodeictic laws. For
29 by what right can we make what is perhaps valid only under the contingent conditions of humanity into an object of unlimited reverence as a universal precept for every rational nature? And how could laws for determining *our* will be taken as laws for determining the will of a rational being as such—and only because of this for determining ours—if these laws were merely empirical and did not have their source completely *a priori* in pure, but practical, reason?

What is more, we cannot do morality a worse service than by seeking to derive it from examples. Every example of it presented to me must first itself be judged by moral principles in order to decide if it is fit to serve as an original example—that is, as a model: it can in no way supply the prime source for the concept of morality. Even the Holy One of the gospel must first be compared with our ideal of moral perfection before we can recognize him to be such. He also says of himself: 'Why callest thou me (whom thou seest) good? There is none good (the archetype of the good) but one, that is, God (whom thou seest not)'. But where do we get the concept
of God as the highest good? Solely from the *Idea* of 409
moral perfection, which reason traces *a priori* and conjoins inseparably with the concept of a free will. Imitation has no place in morality, and examples
serve us only for encouragement—that is, they set 30
beyond doubt the practicability of what the law commands; they make perceptible what the practical law expresses more generally; but they can never entitle us to set aside their true original, which resides in reason, and to model ourselves upon examples.

Popular Philosophy

If there can be no genuine supreme principle of morality which is not grounded on pure reason alone independently of all experience, it should be unnecessary, I think, even to raise the question whether it is a good thing to set forth in general (*in abstracto*) these concepts which hold *a priori*, together with their corresponding principles, so far as our knowledge is to be distinguished from ordinary knowledge and described as philosophical. Yet in our days it may well be necessary to do so. For if we took a vote on which is to be preferred, pure rational knowledge detached from everything empirical—that is to say, a metaphysic of morals—or popular practical philosophy, we can guess at once on which side the preponderance would fall.

It is certainly most praiseworthy to come down to the level of popular thought when we have previously risen to the principles of pure reason and are
fully satisfied of our success. This could be de- 31
scribed as first *grounding* moral philosophy on metaphysics and subsequently winning *acceptance* for it by giving it a popular character after it has been established. But it is utterly senseless to aim at popularity in our first enquiry, upon which the whole correctness of our principles depends. It is not

merely that such a procedure can never lay claim to the extremely rare merit of a truly *philosophical popularity,* since we require no skill to make ourselves intelligible to the multitude once we renounce all profundity of thought: what it turns out is a disgusting hotchpotch of second-hand observations and semi-rational principles on which the empty-headed regale themselves, because this is something that can be used in the chit-chat of daily life. Men of insight, on the other hand, feel confused by it and avert their eyes with a dissatisfaction which, however, they are unable to cure. Yet philosophers, who can perfectly well see through this deception, get little hearing
410 when they summon us for a time from this would-be popularity in order that they may win the right to be genuinely popular only after definite insight has been attained.

We need only look at the attempts to deal with morality in this favoured style. What we shall encounter in an amazing medley is at one time the particular character of human nature (but along with this also the Idea of a rational nature as such), at an-
32 other perfection, at another happiness; here moral feeling and there the fear of God; something of this and also something of that. But it never occurs to these writers to ask whether the principles of morality are to be sought at all in our acquaintance with human nature (which we can get only from experience); nor does it occur to them that if this is not so—if these principles are to be found completely *a priori* and free from empirical elements in the concepts of pure reason and absolutely nowhere else even to the slightest extent—they had better adopt the plan of separating off this enquiry altogether as pure practical philosophy or (if one may use a name
33 so much decried) as a metaphysic[3] of morals; of bringing this to full completeness entirely by itself; and of bidding the public which demands popularity to await in hope the outcome of this undertaking.

Nevertheless such a completely isolated metaphysic of morals, mixed with no anthropology, no theology, no physics or hyperphysics, still less with occult qualities (which might be called hypophysical), is not only an indispensable substratum of all theoretical and precisely defined knowledge of duties, but is at the same time a desideratum of the utmost importance for the actual execution of moral precepts. Unmixed with the alien element of added empirical inducements, the pure thought of duty, and in general of the moral law, has by way of reason alone (which first learns from this that by itself it is able to be practical as well as theoretical) an influence on the human heart so much more powerful than all the further impulsions[4] capable of being
called up from the field of experience that in the 411
consciousness of its own dignity reason despises these impulsions and is able gradually to become their master. In place of this, a mixed moral philosophy, compounded of impulsions from feeling and inclination and at the same time of rational concepts, must make the mind waver between motives which
can be brought under no single principle and which 34
can guide us only by mere accident to the good, but very often also to the evil.

Review of Conclusions

From these considerations the following conclusions emerge. All moral concepts have their seat and origin in reason completely *a priori*, and indeed in the most ordinary human reason just as much as in the most highly speculative: they cannot be abstracted from any empirical, and therefore merely contingent, knowledge. In this purity of their origin is to be found their very worthiness to serve as supreme practical principles, and everything empirical added to them is just so much taken away from their genuine influence and from the absolute value of the corresponding actions. It is not only a requirement of the utmost necessity in respect of theory, where

3. We can, if we like, distinguish pure moral philosophy (metaphysics) from applied (applied, that is, to human nature)—just as pure mathematics is distinguished from applied mathematics and pure logic from applied logic. By this terminology we are at once reminded that moral principles are not grounded on the peculiarities of human nature, but must be established *a priori* by themselves; and yet that from such principles it must be possible to derive practical rules for human nature as well, just as it is for every kind of rational nature.

4. I have a letter from the late distinguished Professor *Sulzer*, in which he asks me what it is that makes moral instruction so ineffective, however convincing it may be in the eyes of reason. Because of my efforts to make it complete, my answer came too late. Yet it is just this: the teachers themselves do not make their concepts pure, but—since they try to do too well by hunting everywhere for inducements to be moral—they spoil their medicine altogether by their very attempt to make it really powerful. For the most ordinary observation shows that when a righteous act is represented as being done with a steadfast mind in complete disregard of any advantage in this or in another world, and even under the greatest temptations of affliction or allurement, it leaves far behind it any similar action affected even in the slightest degree by an alien impulsion and casts it into the shade: it uplifts the soul and rouses a wish that we too could act in this way. Even children of moderate age feel this impression, and duties should never be presented to them in any other way.

35 our concern is solely with speculation, but is also of the utmost practical importance, to draw these concepts and laws from pure reason, to set them forth pure and unmixed, and indeed to determine the extent of this whole practical, but pure, rational knowledge—that is, to determine the whole power of pure practical reason. We ought never—as speculative philosophy does allow and even at times finds necessary—to make principles depend on the special
412 nature of human reason. Since moral laws have to hold for every rational being as such, we ought rather to derive our principles from the general concept of a rational being as such, and on this basis to expound the whole of ethics—which requires anthropology for its *application* to man—at first independently as pure philosophy, that is, entirely as metaphysics (which we can very well do in this wholly abstract kind of knowledge). We know well that without possessing such a metaphysics it is a futile endeavour, I will not say to determine accurately for speculative judgement the moral element of duty in all that accords with duty—but that it is impossible, even in ordinary and practical usage, particularly in that of moral instruction, to base morals on their genuine principles and so to bring about pure moral dispositions and engraft them on men's minds for the highest good of the world.

In this task of ours we have to progress by nat-
36 ural stages, not merely from ordinary moral judgement (which is here worthy of great respect) to philosophical judgement, as we have already done, but from popular philosophy, which goes no further than it can get by fumbling about with the aid of examples, to metaphysics. (This no longer lets itself be held back by anything empirical, and indeed—since it must survey the complete totality of this kind of knowledge—goes right to Ideas, where examples themselves fail.) For this purpose we must follow—and must portray in detail—the power of practical reason from the general rules determining it right up to the point where there springs from it the concept of duty.

Imperatives in General

Everything in nature works in accordance with laws. Only a rational being has the power to act *in accordance with his idea* of laws—that is, in accordance with principles—and only so has he a *will*. Since *reason* is required in order to derive actions from laws, the will is nothing but practical reason. If reason infallibly determines the will, then in a being of this kind the actions which are recognized to be objectively necessary are also subjectively necessary—that is to say, the will is then a power to choose *only that* which reason independently of inclination recognizes to be practically necessary, that is, to be good. But if reason solely by itself is not sufficient to determine the will; if the will is exposed 37
also to subjective conditions (certain impulsions) which do not always harmonize with the objective ones; if, in a word, the will is not *in itself* completely in accord with reason (as actually happens in the 413
case of men); then actions which are recognized to be objectively necessary are subjectively contingent, and the determining of such a will in accordance with objective laws is *necessitation*. That is to say, the relation of objective laws to a will not good through and though is conceived as one in which the will of a rational being, although it is determined by principles of reason, does not necessarily follow these principles in virtue of its own nature.

The conception of an objective principle so far as this principle is necessitating for a will is called a command (of reason), and the formula of this command is called an *Imperative*.

All imperatives are expressed by an '*ought*' (*Sollen*). By this they mark the relation of an objective law of reason to a will which is not necessarily determined by this law in virtue of its subjective constitution (the relation of necessitation). They say that something would be good to do or to leave undone; only they say it to a will which does not always do a thing because it has been informed that this is a good thing to do. The practically *good* is that which 38
determines the will by concepts of reason, and therefore not by subjective causes, but objectively—that is, on grounds valid for every rational being as such. It is distinguished from the *pleasant* as that which influences the will, not as a principle of reason valid for every one, but solely through the medium of sensation by purely subjective causes valid only for the senses of this person or that.[5]

5. The dependence of the power of appetition on sensations is called an inclination, and thus an inclination always indicates a *need*. The dependence of a contingently determinable will on principles of reason is called an *interest*. Hence an interest is found only where there is a dependent will which in itself is not always in accord with reason: to a divine will we cannot ascribe any interest. But even the human will can *take an interest* in something without therefore *acting from interest*. The first expression signifies *practical* interest in the action; the second *pathological* interest in the object of the action. The first indicates only dependence of the will on principles of reason by itself; the

414|39 A perfectly good will would thus stand quite as much under objective laws (laws of the good), but it could not on this account be conceived as *necessitated* to act in conformity with law, since of itself, in accordance with its subjective constitution, it can be determined only by the concept of the good. Hence for the *divine* will, and in general for a *holy* will, there are no imperatives: '*I ought*' is here out of place, because '*I will*' is already of itself necessarily in harmony with the law. Imperatives are in consequence only formulae for expressing the relation of objective laws of willing to the subjective imperfection of the will of this or that rational being—for example, of the human will.

Classification of Imperatives

All *imperatives* command either *hypothetically* or *categorically*. Hypothetical imperatives declare a possible action to be practically necessary as a means to the attainment of something else that one wills (or that one may will). A categorical imperative would be one which represented an action as objectively necessary in itself apart from its relation to a further end.

Every practical law represents a possible action as good and therefore as necessary for a subject whose
40 actions are determined by reason. Hence all imperatives are formulae for determining an action which is necessary in accordance with the principle of a will in some sense good. If the action would be good solely as a means *to something else*, the imperative is *hypothetical*; if the action is represented as good *in itself* and therefore as necessary, in virtue of its principle, for a will which itself accords with reason, then the imperative is *categorical*.

An imperative therefore tells me which of my possible actions would be good; and it formulates a practical rule for a will that does not perform an action straight away because the action is good—whether because the subject does not always know that it is good or because, even if he did know this, he might still act on maxims contrary to the objective principles of practical reason.

A hypothetical imperative thus says only that an action is good for some purpose or other, either *possible* or *actual*. In the first case it is a *problematic*
practical principle; in the second case an *assertoric* ii415
practical principle. A categorical imperative, which declares an action to be objectively necessary in itself without reference to some purpose—that is, even without any further end—ranks as an *apodeictic* practical principle.

Everything that is possible only through the ef- 41
forts of some rational being can be conceived as a possible purpose of some will; and consequently there are in fact innumerable principles of action so far as action is thought necessary in order to achieve some possible purpose which can be effected by it. All sciences have a practical part consisting of problems which suppose that some end is possible for us and of imperatives which tell us how it is to be attained. Hence the latter can in general be called imperatives of *skill*. Here there is absolutely no question about the rationality or goodness of the end, but only about what must be done to attain it. A prescription required by a doctor in order to cure his man completely and one required by a poisoner in order to make sure of killing him are of equal value so far as each serves to effect its purpose perfectly. Since in early youth we do not know what ends may present themselves to us in the course of life, parents seek above all to make their children learn things *of many kinds*; they provide carefully for *skill* in the use of means to all sorts of *arbitrary* ends, of none of which can they be certain that it could not in the future become an actual purpose of their ward, while it is always *possible* that he might adopt it. Their care in this matter is so great that they commonly neglect on this account to form and correct the judgement of their children about the worth of the things which they
might possibly adopt as ends. 42

There is, however, *one* end that can be presupposed as actual in all rational beings (so far as they are dependent beings to whom imperatives apply); and thus there is one purpose which they not only *can* have, but which we can assume with certainty that they all *do* have by a natural necessity—the purpose, namely, of *happiness*. A hypothetical imperative which affirms the practical necessity of an action as a means to the furtherance of happiness is *assertoric*. We may represent it, not simply as necessary to an uncertain, merely possible purpose, but as necessary to a purpose which we can presuppose

second its dependence on principles of reason at the service of inclination—that is to say, where reason merely supplies a practical rule for meeting the need of inclination. In the first case what interests me is the action; in the second case what interests me is the object of the action (so far as this object is pleasant to me). We have seen in Chapter I that in an action done for the sake of duty we must have regard, not to interest in the object, but to interest in the action itself and in its rational principle (namely, the law).

a priori and with certainty to be present in every man because it belongs to his very being. Now skill in the choice of means to one's own greatest well-
416 being can be called *prudence*[6] in the narrowest sense. Thus an imperative concerned with the choice of means to one's own happiness—that is, a precept of prudence–still remains *hypothetical*: an action is
43 commanded, not absolutely, but only as a means to a further purpose.

Finally, there is an imperative which, without being based on, and conditioned by, any further purpose to be attained by a certain line of conduct, enjoins this conduct immediately. This imperative is *categorical*. It is concerned, not with the matter of the action and its presumed results, but with its form and with the principle from which it follows; and what is essentially good in the action consists in the mental disposition, let the consequences be what they may. This imperative may be called the imperative of *morality*.

Willing in accordance with these three kinds of principle is also sharply distinguished by a *dissimilarity* in the necessitation of the will. To make this dissimilarity obvious we should, I think, name these kinds of principle most appropriately in their order if we said they were either *rules* of skill or *counsels* of prudence or *commands* (*laws*) of morality. For only *law* carries with it the concept
44 of an *unconditioned*, and yet objective and so universally valid, *necessity*; and commands are laws which must be obeyed—that is, must be followed even against inclination. *Counsel* does indeed involve necessity, but necessity valid only under a subjective and contingent condition—namely, if this or that man counts this or that as belonging to his happiness. As against this, a categorical imperative is limited by no condition and can quite precisely be called a command, as being absolutely, although practically, necessary. We could also call imperatives of the first kind *technical*
417 (concerned with art); of the second kind *pragmatic*[7] (concerned with well-being); of the third kind *moral* (concerned with free conduct as such—that is, with morals).

How are Imperatives Possible?

The question now arises 'How are all these imperatives possible?' This question does not ask how we can conceive the execution of an action commanded by the imperative, but merely how we can conceive the necessitation of the will expressed by the imperative in setting us a task. How an imperative of skill is possible requires no special discussion. Who
wills the end, wills (so far as reason has decisive in- 45
fluence on his actions) also the means which are indispensably necessary and in his power. So far as willing is concerned, this proposition is analytic: for in my willing of an object as an effect there is already conceived the causality of myself as an acting cause—that is, the use of means; and from the concept of willing an end the imperative merely extracts the concept of actions necessary to this end. (Synthetic propositions are required in order to determine the means to a proposed end, but these are concerned, not with the reason for performing the act of will, but with the cause which produces the object.) That in order to divide a line into two equal parts on a sure principle I must from its ends describe two intersecting arcs—this is admittedly taught by mathematics only in synthetic propositions; but when I know that the aforesaid effect can be produced only by such an action, the proposition 'If I fully will the effect, I also will the action required for it' is analytic; for it is one and the same thing to conceive something as an effect possible in a certain way through me and to conceive myself as acting in the same way with respect to it.

If it were only as easy to find a determinate con-
cept of happiness, the imperatives of prudence 46
would agree entirely with those of skill and would be equally analytic. For here as there it could alike be said 'Who wills the end, wills also (necessarily, if he accords with reason) the sole means which are

6. The word 'prudence' (*Klugheit*) is used in a double sense: in one sense it can have the name of 'worldly wisdom' (*Weltklugheit*); in a second sense that of 'personal wisdom' (*Privatklugheit*). The first is the skull of a man in influencing others in order to use them for his own ends. The second is sagacity in combining all these ends to his own lasting advantage. The latter is properly that to which the value of the former can itself be traced; and of him who is prudent in the first sense, but not in the second, we might better say that he is clever and astute, but on the whole imprudent.

7. It seems to me that the proper meaning of the word '*pragmatic*' can be defined most accurately in this way. For those *Sanctions* are called Pragmatic which, properly speaking, do not spring as necessary laws from the Natural Right of States, but from *forethought* in regard to the general welfare. A *history* is written pragmatically when it teaches *prudence*—that is, when it instructs the world of to-day how to provide for its own advantage better than, or at least as well as, the world of other times.

418 in his power'. Unfortunately, however, the concept of happiness is so indeterminate a concept that although every man wants to attain happiness, he can never say definitely and in unison with himself what it really is that he wants and wills. The reason for this is that all the elements which belong to the concept of happiness are without exception empirical—that is, they must be borrowed from experience; but that none the less there is required for the idea of happiness an absolute whole, a maximum of well-being in my present, and in every future, state. Now it is impossible for the most intelligent, and at the same time most powerful, but nevertheless finite, being to form here a determinate concept of what he really wills. Is it riches that he wants? How much anxiety, envy, and pestering might he not bring in this way on his own head! Is it knowledge and insight? This might perhaps merely give him an eye so sharp that it would make evils at present hidden from him and yet unavoidable seem all the more frightful, or would add a load of still further needs to the desires which already give him trouble enough. Is it long life? Who will guarantee that it
47 would not be a long misery? Is it at least health? How often has infirmity of body kept a man from excesses into which perfect health would have let him fall!—and so on. In short, he has no principle by which he is able to decide with complete certainty what will make him truly happy, since for this he would require omniscience. Thus we cannot act on determinate principles in order to be happy, but only on empirical counsels, for example, of diet, frugality, politeness, reserve, and so on—things which experience shows contribute most to well-being on the average. From this it follows that imperatives of prudence, speaking strictly, do not command at all—that is, cannot exhibit actions objectively as practically *necessary*; that they are rather to be taken as recommendations (*consilia*), than as commands (*praecepta*), of reason; that the problem of determining certainly and universally what action will promote the happiness of a rational being is completely insoluble; and consequently that in regard to this there is no imperative possible which in the strictest sense could command us to do what will make us happy, since happiness is an Ideal, not of reason, but of imagination—an Ideal resting merely on empirical grounds, of which it is vain to expect that they should determine an action by which we
419 could attain the totality of a series of consequences
48 which is in fact infinite. Nevertheless, if we assume that the means to happiness could be discovered with certainty, this imperative of prudence would be an analytic practical proposition; for it differs from the imperative of skill only in this—that in the latter the end is merely possible, while in the former the end is given. In spite of this difference, since both command solely the means to something assumed to be willed as an end, the imperative which commands him who wills the end to will the means is in both cases analytic. Thus there is likewise no difficulty in regard to the possibility of an imperative of prudence.

Beyond all doubt, the question 'How is the imperative of *morality* possible?' is the only one in need of a solution; for it is in no way hypothetical, and consequently we cannot base the objective necessity which it affirms on any presupposition, as we can with hypothetical imperatives. Only we must never forget here that it is impossible to settle *by an example,* and so empirically, whether there is any imperative of this kind at all: we must rather suspect that all imperatives which seem to be categorical may none the less be covertly hypothetical. Take, for example, the saying 'Thou shalt make no false promises'. Let us assume that the necessity for this abstention is no mere advice for the avoidance of some further evil—as it might be said 'You ought not to make a lying promise lest, when this comes 49
to light, you destroy your credit'. Let us hold, on the contrary, that an action of this kind must be considered as bad in itself, and that the imperative of prohibition is therefore categorical. Even so, we cannot with any certainty show by an example that the will is determined here solely by the law without any further motive, although it may appear to be so; for it is always possible that fear of disgrace, perhaps also hidden dread of other risks, may unconsciously influence the will. Who can prove by experience that a cause is not present? Experience shows only that it is not perceived. In such a case, however, the so-called moral imperative, which as such appears to be categorical and unconditioned, would in fact be only a pragmatic prescription calling attention to our advantage and merely bidding us take this into account.

We shall thus have to investigate the possibility of a *categorical* imperative entirely *a priori*, since here we do not enjoy the advantage of having its re- 420
ality given in experience and so of being obliged merely to explain, and not to establish, its possibility. So much, however, can be seen provisionally—

that the categorical imperative alone purports to be
50 a practical *law*, while all the rest may be called *principles* of the will but not laws; for an action necessary merely in order to achieve an arbitrary purpose can be considered as in itself contingent, and we can always escape from the precept if we abandon the purpose; whereas an unconditioned command does not leave it open to the will to do the opposite at its discretion and therefore alone carries with it that necessity which we demand from a law.

In the second place, with this categorical imperative or law of morality the reason for our difficulty (in comprehending its possibility) is a very serious one. We have here a synthetic *a priori* practical proposition;[8] and since in theoretical knowledge there is so much difficulty in comprehending the possibility of propositions of this kind, it may readily be gathered that in practical knowledge the difficulty will be no less.

The Formula of Universal Law

51 In this task we wish first to enquire whether perhaps the mere concept of a categorical imperative may not also provide us with the formula containing the only proposition that can be a categorical imperative; for even when we know the purport of such an absolute command, the question of its possibility will still require a special and troublesome effort, which we postpone to the final chapter.

When I conceive a *hypothetical* imperative in general, I do not know beforehand what it will contain—until its condition is given. But if I conceive a *cate-*
421 *gorical* imperative, I know at once what it contains. For since besides the law this imperative contains only the necessity that our maxim[9] should conform to this law, while the law, as we have seen, contains no condition to limit it, there remains nothing over to which the maxim has to conform except the universality of a law as such; and it is this conformity alone 52
that the imperative properly asserts to be necessary.

There is therefore only a single categorical imperative and it is this: '*Act only on that maxim through which you can at the same time will that it should become a universal law*'.

Now if all imperatives of duty can be derived from this one imperative as their principle, then even although we leave it unsettled whether what we call duty may not be an empty concept, we shall still be able to show at least what we understand by it and what the concept means.

The Formula of the Law of Nature

Since the universality of the law governing the production of effects constitutes what is properly called *nature* in its most general sense (nature as regards its form)—that is, the existence of things so far as determined by universal laws—the universal imperative of duty may also run as follows: '*Act as if the maxim of your action were to become through your will a universal law of nature.*'

Illustrations

We will now enumerate a few duties, following their 53
customary division into duties towards self and duties towards others and into perfect and imperfect duties.[10]

1. A man feels sick of life as the result of a series of misfortunes that has mounted to the point of 422
despair, but he is still so far in possession of his reason as to ask himself whether taking his own life may not be contrary to his duty to himself. He now applies the test 'Can the maxim of my action really become a universal law of nature?' His maxim is 'From self-love I make it my principle to shorten my life if its continuance threatens more evil than it promises pleasure'. The only further question to ask is whether this principle of self-love can become a universal law of nature. It is then seen at once that

8. Without presupposing a condition taken from some inclination I connect an action with the will *a priori* and therefore necessarily (although only objectively so—that is, only subject to the Idea of a reason having full power over all subjective impulses to action). Here we have a practical proposition in which the willing of an action is not derived analytically from some other willing already presupposed (for we do not possess any such perfect will), but is on the contrary connected immediately with the concept of the will of a rational being as something which is not contained in this concept.

9. A *maxim* is a subjective principle of action and must be distinguished from an *objective principle*—namely, a practical law. The former contains a practical rule determined by reason in accordance with the conditions of the subject (often his ignorance or again his inclination): it is thus a principle on which the subject *acts*. A law, on the other hand, is an objective principle valid for every rational being; and it is a principle on which he *ought to act*—that is, an imperative.

10. It should be noted that I reserve my division of duties entirely for a future *Metaphysic of Morals* and that my present division is therefore put forward as arbitrary (merely for the purpose of arranging my examples). Further, I understand here by a perfect duty one which allows no exception in the interests of inclination, and so I recognize among *perfect duties*, not only outer ones, but also inner. This is contrary to the accepted usage of the schools, but I do not intend to justify it here, since for my purpose it is all one whether this point is conceded or not.

a system of nature by whose law the very same feel-
54 ing whose function (*Bestimmung*) is to stimulate the furtherance of life should actually destroy life would contradict itself and consequently could not subsist as a system of nature. Hence this maxim cannot possibly hold as a universal law of nature and is therefore entirely opposed to the supreme principle of all duty.

2. Another finds himself driven to borrowing money because of need. He well knows that he will not be able to pay it back; but he sees too that he will get no loan unless he gives a firm promise to pay it back within a fixed time. He is inclined to make such a promise; but he has still enough conscience to ask 'Is it not unlawful and contrary to duty to get out of difficulties in this way?' Supposing, however, he did resolve to do so, the maxim of his action would run thus: 'Whenever I believe myself short of money, I will borrow money and promise to pay it back, though I know that this will never be done'. Now this principle of self-love or personal advantage is perhaps quite compatible with my own entire future welfare; only there remains the question 'Is it right?' I therefore transform the demand of self-love into a universal law and frame my question thus: 'How would things stand if my maxim became a universal law?' I then see straight away that this maxim can never rank as a universal law
55 of nature and be self-consistent, but must necessarily contradict itself. For the universality of a law that every one believing himself to be in need can make any promise he pleases with the intention not to keep it would make promising, and the very purpose of promising, itself impossible, since no one would believe he was being promised anything, but would laugh at utterances of this kind as empty shams.

423 **3.** A third finds in himself a talent whose cultivation would make him a useful man for all sorts of purposes. But he sees himself in comfortable circumstances, and he prefers to give himself up to pleasure rather than to bother about increasing and improving his fortunate natural aptitudes. Yet he asks himself further 'Does my maxim of neglecting my natural gifts, besides agreeing in itself with my tendency to indulgence, agree also with what is called duty?' He then sees that a system of nature could indeed always subsist under such a universal law, although (like the South Sea Islanders) every man should let his talents rust and should be bent on devoting his life solely to idleness, indulgence, procreation, and, in a word, to enjoyment. Only he cannot possibly *will* that this should become a universal law of nature or should be implanted in us as such a law by a natural instinct. For as a rational be- 56
ing he necessarily wills that all his powers should be developed, since they serve him, and are given him, for all sorts of possible ends.

4. Yet a *fourth* is himself flourishing, but he sees others who have to struggle with great hardships (and whom he could easily help); and he thinks 'What does it matter to me? Let every one be as happy as Heaven wills or as he can make himself; I won't deprive him of anything; I won't even envy him; only I have no wish to contribute anything to his well-being or to his support in distress!' Now admittedly if such an attitude were a universal law of nature, mankind could get on perfectly well—better no doubt than if everybody prates about sympathy and goodwill, and even takes pains, on occasion, to practise them, but on the other hand cheats where he can, traffics in human rights, or violates them in other ways. But although it is possible that a universal law of nature could subsist in harmony with this maxim, yet it is impossible to *will* that such a principle should hold everywhere as a law of nature. For a will which decided in this way would be in conflict with itself, since many a situation might arise in which the man needed love and sympathy from others, and in which, by such a law of nature sprung from his own will, he would rob himself of 57
all hope of the help he wants for himself.

The Canon of Moral Judgement

These are some of the many actual duties—or at least of what we take to be such—whose derivation from the single principle cited above leaps to the eye. We must *be able to will* that a maxim of our 424
action should become a universal law—this is the general canon for all moral judgement of action. Some actions are so constituted that their maxim cannot even be *conceived* as a universal law of nature without contradiction, let alone be *willed* as what *ought* to become one. In the case of others we do not find this inner impossibility, but it is still impossible to *will* that their maxim should be raised to the universality of a law of nature, because such a will would contradict itself. It is easily seen that the first kind of action is opposed to strict or narrow (rigorous) duty, the second only to wider (meritorious) duty; and thus that by these examples all duties—so far as the type of obligation is concerned

(not the object of dutiful action)—are fully set out in their dependence on our single principle.

If we now attend to ourselves whenever we transgress a duty, we find that we in fact do not will that
58 our maxim should become a universal law—since this is impossible for us—but rather that its opposite should remain a law universally: we only take the liberty of making an *exception* to it for ourselves (or even just for this once) to the advantage of our inclination. Consequently if we weighed it all up from one and the same point of view—that of reason—we should find a contradiction in our own will, the contradiction that a certain principle should be objectively necessary as a universal law and yet subjectively should not hold universally but should admit of exceptions. Since, however, we first consider our action from the point of view of a will wholly in accord with reason, and then consider precisely the same action from the point of view of a will affected by inclination, there is here actually no contradiction, but rather an opposition of inclination to the precept of reason (*antagonismus),* whereby the universality of the principle (*universalitas*) is turned into a mere generality (*generalitas*) so that the practical principle of reason may meet our maxim half-way. this procedure, though in our own impartial judgement it cannot be justified, proves none the less that we in fact recognize the validity of the categorical imperative and (with all respect for it) merely permit ourselves a few exceptions which are, as we pretend, in-
59 considerable and apparently forced upon us.

425 We have thus at least shown this much—that if duty is a concept which is to have meaning and real legislative authority for our actions, this can be expressed only in categorical imperatives and by no means in hypothetical ones. At the same time—and this is already a great deal—we have set forth distinctly, and determinately for every type of application, the content of the categorical imperative, which must contain the principle of all duty (if there is to be such a thing at all). But we are still not so far advanced as to prove *a priori* that there actually is an imperative of this kind—that there is a practical law which by itself commands absolutely and without any further motives, and that the following of this law is duty.

The Need for Pure Ethics

For the purpose of achieving this proof it is of the utmost importance to take warning that we should not dream for a moment of trying to derive the reality of this principle from *the special characteristics of human nature.* For duty has to be a practical, unconditioned necessity of action; it must therefore hold for all rational beings (to whom alone an imperative can apply at all), and *only because of this* can it also be a law for all human wills. Whatever, on the other hand, is derived from the special predisposition of humanity, from certain feelings and 60
propensities, and even, if this were possible, from some special bent peculiar to human reason and not holding necessarily for the will of every rational being—all this can indeed supply a personal maxim, but not a law: it can give us a subjective principle—one on which we have a propensity and inclination to act—but not an objective one on which we should be *directed* to act although our every propensity, inclination, and natural bent were opposed to it; so much so that the sublimity and inner worth of the command is the more manifest in a duty, the fewer are the subjective causes for obeying it and the more those against—without, however, on this account weakening in the slightest the necessitation exercised by the law or detracting anything from its validity.

It is here that philosophy is seen in actual fact to be placed in a precarious position, which is supposed to be firm although neither in heaven nor on earth is there anything from which it depends or on which it is based. It is here that she has to show her purity as the authoress of her own laws—not as the mouthpiece of laws whispered to her by some implanted sense or by who knows what tutelary nature, all of which laws together, though they may always be better than nothing, can never furnish us with principles dictated by reason. These principles must have 426
an origin entirely and completely *a priori* and must at the same time derive from this their sovereign authority—that they expect nothing from the inclinations of men, but everything from the supremacy of the law and from the reverence due to it, or in default of this condemn man to self-contempt and in- 61
ward abhorrence.

Hence everything that is empirical is, as a contribution to the principle of morality, not only wholly unsuitable for the purpose, but is even highly injurious to the purity of morals; for in morals the proper worth of an absolutely good will, a worth elevated above all price, lies precisely in this—that the principle of action is free from all influence by contingent grounds, the only kind that experience can supply. Against the slack, or indeed ignoble, attitude which seeks for the moral principle among empirical motives and laws we cannot give a warning too strongly or too often; for human reason in its weariness is fain to rest upon this pillow and in a dream of sweet illusions (which lead it to embrace a cloud in mistake for Juno) to foist into the place of morality some misbegotten mongrel patched up from limbs of very varied ancestry and looking like anything you please, only not like virtue, to him who has once beheld her in her true shape.[11]

62 Our question therefore is this: 'Is it a necessary law *for all rational beings* always to judge their actions by reference to those maxims of which they can themselves will that they should serve as universal laws?' If there is such a law, it must already be connected (entirely *a priori*) with the concept of the will of a rational being as such. But in order to discover this connexion we must, however much we may bristle, take a step beyond it—that is, into metaphysics, although into a region of it different from that of speculative philosophy, namely, the metaphysic of morals. In practical philosophy we are not concerned
427 with accepting reasons for what *happens*, but with accepting laws of what *ought to happen,* even if it never does happen—that is, objective practical laws. And here we have no need to set up an enquiry as to the reasons why anything pleases or displeases; how the pleasure of mere sensation differs from taste, and whether the latter differs from a universal approval by reason; whereon feelings of pleasure and displeasure are based; how from these feelings there arise desires and inclinations; and how from these in turn, with the co-operation of reason, there arise maxims. All this belongs to empirical psychology, which would constitute the second part of the doctrine of nature, if we take this doctrine to be the *philosophy*
63 *of nature* so far as grounded on *empirical laws*. Here, however, we are discussing objective practical laws, and consequently the relation of a will to itself as determined solely by reason. Everything related to the empirical then falls away of itself; for if *reason entirely by itself* determines conduct (and it is the possibility of this which we now wish to investigate), it must necessarily do so *a priori*.

11. To behold virtue in her proper shape is nothing other than to show morality stripped of all admixture with the sensuous and of all the spurious adornments of reward or self-love. How much she then casts into the shade all else that appears attractive to the inclinations can be readily perceived by every man if he will exert his reason in the slightest—provided he has not entirely ruined it for all abstractions.

The Formula of the End in Itself

The will is conceived as a power of determining oneself to action *in accordance with the idea of certain laws*. And such a power can be found only in rational beings. Now what serves the will as a subjective ground of its self-determination is an *end*; and this, if it is given by reason alone, must be equally valid for all rational beings. What, on the other hand, contains merely the ground of the possibility of an action whose effect is an end is called a *means*. The subjective ground of a desire is an *impulsion* (*Triebfeder*); the objective ground of a volition is a *motive* (*Bewegungsgrund*). Hence the difference be- 64
tween subjective ends, which are based on impulsions, and objective ends, which depend on motives valid for every rational being. Practical principles are *formal* if they abstract from all subjective ends; they are *material*, on the other hand, if they are based on such ends and consequently on certain impulsions. Ends that a rational being adopts arbitrarily as *effects* of his action (material ends) are in every case only relative; for it is solely their relation to special characteristics in the subject's power of appetition which gives them their value. Hence this value can provide no universal principles, no principles valid and necessary for all rational beings and also for every volition—that is, no practical laws. Consequently all these relative ends can be the ground only of hypothetical imperatives. 428

Suppose, however, there were something *whose existence* has *in itself* an absolute value, something which as *an end in itself* could be a ground of determinate laws; then in it, and in it alone, would there be the ground of a possible categorical imperative—that is, of a practical law.

Now I say that man, and in general every rational being, *exists* as an end in himself, *not merely as a means* for arbitrary use by this or that will: he must in all his actions, whether they are directed to himself or to other rational beings, always be viewed *at the same time as an end*. All the objects of inclina- 65
tion have only a conditioned value; for if there were not these inclinations and the needs grounded on them, their object would be valueless. Inclinations themselves, as sources of needs are so far from having an absolute value to make them desirable for their own sake that it must rather be the universal wish of every rational being to be wholly free from them. Thus the value of all objects that can *be produced* by our action is always conditioned. Beings

whose existence depends, not on our will, but on nature, have none the less, if they are non-rational beings, only a relative value as means and are consequently called *things*. Rational beings, on the other hand, are called *persons* because their nature already marks them out as ends in themselves—that is, as something which ought not to be used merely as a means—and consequently imposes to that extent a limit on all arbitrary treatment of them (and is an object of reverence). Persons, therefore, are not merely subjective ends whose existence as an object of our actions has a value *for us*: they are *objective ends*—that is, things whose existence is in itself an end, and indeed an end such that in its place we can put no other end to which they should serve *simply* as means; for unless this is so, nothing at all of *absolute* value would be found anywhere. But if all
66 value were conditioned—that is, contingent—then no supreme principle could be found for reason at all.

If then there is to be a supreme practical principle and—so far as the human will is concerned—a categorical imperative, it must be such that from the idea of something which is necessarily an end for every one because it is an *end in itself* it forms an *objective* principle of the will and consequently can serve as a practical law. The ground of this princi-
429 ple is: *Rational nature exists as an end in itself.* This is the way in which a man necessarily conceives his own existence: it is therefore so far a *subjective* principle of human actions. But it is also the way in which every other rational being conceives his existence on the same rational ground which is valid also for me;[12] hence it is at the same time an *objective* principle, from which, as a supreme practical ground, it must be possible to derive all laws for the will. The practical imperative will therefore be as follows: *Act in such a way that you always treat humanity, whether in your own person or in the person of any other, never simply as a means, but al-*
67 *ways at the same time as an end.* We will now consider whether this can be carried out in practice.

Illustrations

Let us keep to our previous examples.

First, as regards the concept of necessary duty to oneself, the man who contemplates suicide will ask 'Can my action be compatible with the Idea of humanity *as an end in itself?*' If he does away with himself in order to escape from a painful situation, he is making use of a person merely as *a means* to maintain a tolerable state of affairs till the end of his life. But man is not a thing–not something to be used *merely* as a means: he must always in all his actions be regarded as an end in himself. Hence I cannot dispose of man in my person by maiming, spoiling, or killing. (A more precise determination of this principle in order to avoid all misunderstanding—for example, about having limbs amputated to save myself or about exposing my life to danger in order to preserve it, and so on—I must here forego: this question belongs to morals proper.)

Secondly, so far as necessary or strict duty to others is concerned, the man who has a mind to make a false promise to others will see at once that he is intending to make use of another man *merely as a* 68
means to an end he does not share. For the man whom I seek to use for my own purposes by such a promise cannot possibly agree with my way of behaving to him, and so cannot himself share the end of the action. This incompatibility with the principle of duty to others leaps to the eye more obviously when we bring in examples of attempts on the free- 430
dom and property of others. For then it is manifest that a violator of the rights of man intends to use the person of others merely as a means without taking into consideration that, as rational beings, they ought always at the same time to be rated as ends—that is, only as beings who must themselves be able to share in the end of the very same action.[13]

Thirdly, in regard to contingent (meritorious) duty to oneself, it is not enough that an action should re- 69
frain from conflicting with humanity in our own person as an end in itself: it must also *harmonize with this end.* Now there are in humanity capacities for greater perfection which form part of nature's purpose for humanity in our person. To neglect these can admittedly be compatible with the *maintenance* of humanity as an end in itself, but not with the *promotion* of this end.

66 12. This proposition I put forward here as a postulate. The grounds for it will be found in the final chapter.

13. Let no one think that here the trivial '*quod tibi non vis fieri, etc.*' 68
can serve as a standard or principle. For it is merely derivative from our principle, although subject to various qualifications: it cannot be a universal law since it contains the ground neither of duties to oneself nor of duties of kindness to others (for many a man would readily agree that others should not help him if only he could be dispensed from affording help to them), nor finally of strict duties towards others; for on this basis the criminal would be able to dispute with the judges who punish him, and so on.

Fourthly, as regards meritorious duties to others, the natural end which all men seek is their own happiness. Now humanity could no doubt subsist if everybody contributed nothing to the happiness of others but at the same time refrained from deliberately impairing their happiness. This is, however, merely to agree negatively and not positively with *humanity as an end in itself* unless every one endeavours also, so far as in him lies, to further the ends of others. For the ends of a subject who is an end in himself must, if this conception is to have its *full* effect in me, be also, as far as possible, *my* ends.

The Formula of Autonomy

This principle of humanity, and in general of every rational agent, *as an end in itself* (a principle which is the supreme limiting condition of every man's free-
431|70 dom of action) is not borrowed from experience; firstly, because it is universal, applying as it does to all rational beings as such, and no experience is adequate to determine universality; secondly, because in it humanity is conceived, not as an end of man (subjectively)—that is, an object which, as a matter of fact, happens to be made an end—but as an objective end—one which, be our ends what they may, must, as a law, constitute the supreme limiting condition of all subjective ends and so must spring from pure reason. That is to say, the ground for every enactment of practical law lies *objectively in the rule* and in the form of universality which (according to our first principle) makes the rule capable of being a law (and indeed a law of nature); *subjectively*, however, it lies in the *end*; but (according to our second principle) the subject of all ends is to be found in every rational being as an end in himself. From this there now follows our third practical principle for the will—as the supreme condition of the will's conformity with universal practical reason—namely, the Idea *of the will of every rational being as a will which makes universal law.*

By this principle all maxims are repudiated which cannot accord with the will's own enactment of universal law. The will is therefore not merely subject
71 to the law, but is so subject that it must be considered as also *making the law* for itself and precisely on this account as first of all subject to the law (of which it can regard itself as the author).

The Exclusion of Interest

Imperatives as formulated above—namely, the imperative enjoining conformity of actions to universal *supremacy* of rational beings in themselves *as ends*—did, by the mere fact that they were represented as categorical, exclude from their sovereign authority every admixture of interest as a motive. They were, however, merely *assumed* to be categorical because we were found to make this assumption if we wished to explain the concept of duty. That there were practical propositions which commanded categorically could not itself be proved, any more than it can be proved in this chapter generally; but one thing could have been done—namely, to show that in willing for the sake of duty renunciation of all interest, as the specific mark distinguishing a categorical from a hypothetical imperative, was expressed in the very imperative itself by means of some determination inherent in it. This is
what is done in the present third formulation of the 423
principle—namely, in the Idea of the will of every rational being as *a will which makes universal law.*

Once we conceive a will of this kind, it becomes 72
clear that while a will *which is subject to law* may be bound to this law by some interest, nevertheless a will which is itself a supreme lawgiver cannot possibly as such depend on any interest; for a will which is dependent in this way would itself require yet a further law in order to restrict the interest of self-love to the condition that this interest should itself be valid as a universal law.

Thus the *principle* that every human will is *a will which by all its maxims enacts universal law*[14]—provided only that it were right in other ways—would be *well suited* to be a categorical imperative in this respect: that precisely because of the Idea of making universal law it is *based on no interest* and consequently can alone among all possible imperatives be *unconditioned.* Or better still—to convert the proposition—if there is a categorical imperative (that is, a law for the will of every rational being), it can command us only to act always on the maxim of such a will in us as can at the same time look
upon itself as making universal law; for only then 73
is the practical principle and the imperative which we obey unconditioned, since it is wholly impossible for it to be based on any interest.

We need not now wonder, when we look back upon all the previous efforts that have been made to discover the principle of morality, why they have

14. I may be excused from bringing forward examples to illustrate this principle, since those which were first used as illustrations of the categorical imperative and its formula can all serve this purpose here.

one and all been bound to fail. Their authors saw man as tied to laws by his duty, but it never occurred to them that he is subject only to *laws which are made by himself* and yet are *universal*, and that he is bound only to act in conformity with a will which is his own but has as nature's purpose for it the function of making universal law. For when they thought of man merely as subject to a law (whatever it might
433 be), the law had to carry with it some interest in order to attract or compel, because it did not spring as a law from *his own* will: in order to conform with the law his will had to be necessitated by *something else* to act in a certain way. This absolutely inevitable conclusion meant that all the labour spent in trying to find a supreme principle of duty was lost beyond recall; for what they discovered was never duty, but only the necessity of acting from a certain interest. This interest might be one's own or another's; but on such a view the imperative was bound to be always a conditioned one and could not possibly serve as a moral law. I will therefore call my
74 principle the principle of the *Autonomy* of the will in contrast with all others, which I consequently class under *Heteronomy*.

The Formula of the Kingdom of Ends

The concept of every rational being as one who must regard himself as making universal law by all the maxims of his will, and must seek to judge himself and his actions from this point of view, leads to a closely connected and very fruitful concept—namely, that of *a kingdom of ends*.

I understand by a '*kingdom*' a systematic union of different rational beings under common laws. Now since laws determine ends as regards their universal validity, we shall be able—if we abstract from the personal differences between rational beings, and also from all the content of their private ends—to conceive a whole of all ends in systematic conjunction (a whole both of rational beings as ends in themselves and also of the personal ends which each may set before himself); that is, we shall be able to conceive a kingdom of ends which is possible in accordance with the above principles.

For rational beings all stand under the *law* that each of them should treat himself and all others,
75 *never merely as a means*, but always *at the same time as an end in himself*. But by so doing there arises a systematic union of rational beings under common objective laws—that is, a kingdom. Since these laws are directed precisely to the relation of such beings to one another as ends and means, this kingdom can be called a kingdom of ends (which is admittedly only an Ideal).

A rational being belongs to the kingdom of ends as a *member*, when, although he makes its universal laws, he is also himself subject to these laws. He belongs to it as its *head*, when as the maker of laws he is himself subject to the will of no other.

A rational being must always regard himself as 434
making laws in a kingdom of ends which is possible through freedom of the will—whether it be as member or as head. The position of the latter he can maintain, not in virtue of the maxim of his will alone, but only if he is a completely independent being, without needs and with an unlimited power adequate to his will.

Thus morality consists in the relation of all action to the making of laws whereby alone a kingdom of ends is possible. This making of laws must be found in every rational being himself and must be able to spring from his will. The principle of his will is therefore never to perform an action except on a 76
maxim such as can also be a universal law, and consequently such *that the will can regard itself as at the same time making universal law by means of its maxim*. Where maxims are not already by their very nature in harmony with this objective principle of rational beings as makers of universal law, the necessity of acting on this principle is practical necessitation—that is, *duty*. Duty does not apply to the head in a kingdom of ends, but it does apply to every member and to all members in equal measure.

The practical necessity of acting on this principle—that is, duty—is in no way based on feelings, impulses, and inclinations, but only on the relation of rational beings to one another, a relation in which the will of a rational being must always be regarded as *making universal law*, because otherwise he could not be conceived as *an end in himself*. Reason thus relates every maxim of the will, considered as making universal law, to every other will and also to every action towards oneself: it does so, not because of any further motive or future advantage, but from the Idea of the 77
dignity of a rational being who obeys no law other than that which he at the same time enacts himself.

The Dignity of Virtue

In the kingdom of ends everything has either a *price* or a *dignity*. If it has a price, something else can be put in its place as an *equivalent*; if it is exalted above all price and so admits of no equivalent, then it has a dignity.

What is relative to universal human inclinations and needs has a *market price*; what, even without
435 presupposing a need, accords with a certain taste—that is, with satisfaction in the mere purposeless play of our mental powers—has a *fancy price* (*Affektionspreis*); but that which constitutes the sole condition under which anything can be an end in itself has not merely a relative value—that is, a price—but has an intrinsic value—that is, *dignity*.

Now morality is the only condition under which a rational being can be an end in himself; for only through this is it possible to be a law-making member in a kingdom of ends. Therefore morality, and humanity so far as it is capable of morality, is the
78 only thing which has dignity. Skill and diligence in work have a market price; wit, lively imagination, and humour have a fancy price; but fidelity to promises and kindness based on principle (not on instinct) have an intrinsic worth. In default of these, nature and art alike contain nothing to put in their place; for their worth consists, not in the effects which result from them, not in the advantage or profit they produce, but in the attitudes of mind—that is, in the maxims of the will—which are ready in this way to manifest themselves in action even if they are not favoured by success. Such actions too need no recommendation from any subjective disposition or taste in order to meet with immediate favour and approval; they need no immediate propensity or feeling for themselves; they exhibit the will which performs them as an object of immediate reverence; nor is anything other than reason required to *impose* them upon the will, not to *coax* them from the will—which last would anyhow be a contradiction in the case of duties. This assessment reveals as dignity the value of such a mental attitude and puts it infinitely above all price, with which it cannot be brought into reckoning or comparison without, as it were, a profanation of its sanctity.

What is it then that entitles a morally good atti-
79 tude of mind—or virtue—to make claims so high? It is nothing less than the *share* which it affords to a rational being *in the making of universal law*, and which therefore fits him to be a member in a possible kingdom of ends. For this he was already marked out in virtue of his own proper nature as an end in himself and consequently as a maker of laws in the kingdom of ends—as free in respect of all laws of nature, obeying only those laws which he makes himself and in virtue of which his maxims can have their part in the making of universal law (to which he at the same time subjects himself). For nothing can have a value other than that determined for it by the law. But the law-making which determines all value must for this reason have a dignity—that is, 436
an unconditioned and incomparable worth—for the appreciation of which, as necessarily given by a rational being, the word '*reverence*' is the only becoming expression. *Autonomy* is therefore the ground of the dignity of human nature and of every rational nature.

Review of the Formulae

The aforesaid three ways of representing the principle of morality are at bottom merely so many formulations of precisely the same law, one of them by itself containing a combination of the other two. There is nevertheless a difference between them, which, however, is subjectively rather than objectively practical: that is to say, its purpose is to bring an Idea of reason nearer to intuition (in accordance with a certain analogy) and so nearer to feeling. All 80
maxims have, in short,

1. a *form*, which consists in their universality; and in this respect the formula of the moral imperative is expressed thus: 'Maxims must be chosen as if they had to hold as universal laws of nature';
2. a *matter*—that is, an end; and in this respect the formula says: 'A rational being, as by his very nature an end and consequently an end in himself, must serve for every maxim as a condition limiting all merely relative and arbitrary ends';
3. a *complete determination* of all maxims by the following formula, namely: 'All maxims as proceeding from our own making of law ought to harmonize with a possible kingdom of ends as a kingdom of nature'.[15] This progression may be said to take place through the categories of the *unity* of the form of will (its universality); of the *multiplicity* of its matter (its objects—that is, its

15. Teleology views nature as a kingdom of ends; ethics views a possible kingdom of ends as a kingdom of nature. In the first case the kingdom of ends is a theoretical Idea used to explain what exists. In the second case it is a practical Idea used to bring into existence what does not exist but can be made actual by our conduct—and indeed to bring it into existence in conformity with this Idea.

ends); and of the *totality* or completeness of its system of ends. It is, however, better if in moral
81 *judgement* we proceed always in accordance with the strict method and take as our basis the universal formula of the categorical imperative: '*Act on the maxim which can at the same time be made*
437 *a universal law*'. If, however, we wish also to secure acceptance for the moral law, it is very useful to bring one and the same action under the above-mentioned three concepts and so, as far as we can, to bring the universal formula nearer to intuition.

Review of the Whole Argument

We can now end at the point from which we started out at the beginning—namely, the concept of an unconditionally good will. The *will is absolutely good* if it cannot be evil—that is, if its maxim, when made into a universal law, can never be in conflict with itself. This principle is therefore also its supreme law: 'Act always on that maxim whose universality as a law you can at the same time will'. This is the one principle on which a will can never be in conflict with itself, and such an imperative is categorical. Because the validity of the will as a universal law for possible actions is analogous to the universal interconnexion of existent things in accordance with universal laws—which constitutes the formal aspect of nature as such—we can also express the categorical imperative as follows: '*Act on that maxim which can at the same time have for its object itself as a universal law of nature*'. In this way we provide the formula for an absolutely
82 good will.

Rational nature separates itself out from all other things by the fact that it sets itself an end. An end would thus be the matter of every good will. But in the Idea of a will which is absolutely good—good without any qualifying condition (namely, that it should attain this or that end)—there must be complete abstraction from every end that has to be *produced* (as something which would make every will only relatively good). Hence the end must here be conceived, not as an end to be produced, *but as a self-existent* end. It must therefore be conceived only negatively—that is, as an end against which we should never act, and consequently as one which in all our willing we must never rate *merely* as a means, but always at the same time as an end. Now this end can be nothing other than the subject of all possible ends himself, because this subject is also the subject of a will that may be absolutely good; for such a will cannot without contradiction be subordinated to any other object. The principle 'So act in relation to every rational being (both to yourself and to others) that he may at the same time count in your maxim as an end in himself' is thus at bottom the same as the principle 'Act on a maxim which at the same time contains in itself its own universal validity for every rational being'. For to say that in using means 438
to every end I ought to restrict my maxim by the condition that it should also be universally valid as a law for every subject is just the same as to say 83
this—that a subject of ends, namely, a rational being himself, must be made the ground for all maxims of action, never *merely* as a means, but as a supreme condition restricting the use of every means—that is, always also as an end.

Now from this it unquestionably follows that every rational being, as an end in himself, must be able to regard himself as also the maker of universal law in respect of any law whatever to which he may be subjected; for it is precisely the fitness of his maxims to make universal law that marks him out as an end in himself. It follows equally that this dignity (or prerogative) of his above all the mere things of nature carries with it the necessity of always choosing his maxims from the point of view of himself—and also of every other rational being—as a maker of law (and this is why they are called persons). It is in this way that a world of rational beings (*mundus intelligibilis*) is possible as a kingdom of ends—possible, that is, through the making of their own laws by all persons as its members. Accordingly every rational being must so act as if he were through his maxims always a law-making member in the universal kingdom of ends. The formal principle of such maxims is 'So act as 84
if your maxims had to serve at the same time as a universal law (for all rational beings)'. Thus a kingdom of ends is possible only on the analogy of a kingdom of nature; yet the kingdom of ends is possible only through maxims—that is, self-imposed rules—while nature is possible only through laws concerned with causes whose action is necessitated from without. In spite of this difference, we give to nature as a whole, even although it is regarded as a machine, the name of a 'kingdom of nature' so far as—and for the reason that—it stands in a relation to rational beings as its ends. Now a king-

dom of ends would actually come into existence through maxims which the categorical imperative prescribes as a rule for all rational beings, *if these maxims were universally followed.* Yet even if a rational being were himself to follow such a maxim strictly, he cannot count on everybody else being faithful to it on this ground, nor can he be confident that the kingdom of nature and its purposive order will work in harmony with him, as a fitting member, towards a kingdom of ends made possi-
439 ble by himself—or, in other words, that it will favour his expectation of happiness. But in spite of this the law 'Act on the maxims of a member who makes universal laws for a merely possible kingdom of ends' remains in full force, since its command is categorical. And precisely here we en-
85 counter the paradox that without any further end or advantage to be attained the mere dignity of humanity, that is, of rational nature in man—and consequently that reverence for a mere Idea—should function as an inflexible precept for the will; and that it is just this freedom from dependence on interested motives which constitutes the sublimity of a maxim and the worthiness of every rational subject to be a law-making member in the kingdom of ends; for otherwise he would have to be regarded as subject only to the law of nature—the law of his own needs. Even if it were thought that both the kingdom of nature and the kingdom of ends were united under one head and that thus the latter kingdom ceased to be a mere Idea and achieved genuine reality, the Idea would indeed gain by this the addition of a strong motive, but never any increase in its intrinsic worth; for, even if this were so, it would still be necessary to conceive the unique and absolute lawgiver himself as judging the worth of rational beings solely by the disinterested behaviour they prescribed to themselves in virtue of this Idea alone. The essence of things does not vary with their external relations; and where there is something which, without regard to such relations, constitutes by itself the absolute worth of man, it is by this that man must also be judged by everyone whatsoever—even by the Supreme Being. Thus *morality* lies in the relation of actions to the autonomy of the will—that is, to a possible making of universal law by means of its maxims. An
86 action which is compatible with the autonomy of the will is *permitted*; one which does not harmonize with it is *forbidden*. A will whose maxims necessarily accord with the laws of autonomy is a *holy*, or absolutely good, will. The dependence of a will not absolutely good on the principle of autonomy (that is, moral necessitation) is *obligation*. Obligation can thus have no reference to a holy being. The objective necessity to act from obligation is called *duty*.

From what was said a little time ago we can now easily explain how it comes about that, although in the concept of duty we think of subjection to the law, yet we also at the same time attribute to the person who fulfils all his duties a certain sublimity and
dignity. For it is not in so far as he is *subject* to the 440
law that he has sublimity, but rather in so far as, in regard to this very same law, he is at the same time its *author* and is subordinated to it only on this ground. We have also shown above how neither fear nor inclination, but solely reverence for the law, is the motive which can give an action moral worth. Our own will, provided it were to act only under the condition of being able to make universal law by means of its maxims—this ideal will which can be ours is the proper object of reverence; and the dig-
nity of man consists precisely in his capacity to make 87
universal law, although only on condition of being himself also subject to the law he makes.

Autonomy of the Will *as the Supreme Principle of Morality*

Autonomy of the will is the property the will has of being a law to itself (independently of every property belonging to the objects of volition). Hence the principle of autonomy is 'Never to choose except in such a way that in the same volition the maxims of your choice are also present as universal law'. That this practical rule is an imperative—that is, that the will of every rational being is necessarily bound to the rule as a condition—cannot be proved by mere analysis of the concepts contained in it, since it is a synthetic proposition. For proof we should have to go beyond knowledge of objects and pass to a critique of the subject—that is, of pure practical reason—since this synthetic proposition, as commanding apodeictically,
must be capable of being known entirely *a priori*. This 88
task does not belong to the present chapter. None the less by mere analysis of the concepts of morality we can quite well show that the above principle of autonomy is the sole principle of ethics. For analysis finds that the principle of morality must be a categorical imperative, and that this in turn commands nothing more nor less than precisely this autonomy.

441 **Heteronomy of the Will** ***as the Source of all Spurious Principles of Morality***

If the will seeks the law that is to determine it *anywhere else* than in the fitness of its maxims for its own making of universal law—if therefore in going beyond itself it seeks this law in the character of any of its objects—the result is always *heteronomy.* In that case the will does not give itself the law, but the object does so in virtue of its relation to the will. This relation, whether based on inclination or on rational ideas, can give rise only to hypothetical imperative: 'I ought to do something *because I will something else*'. As against this, the moral, and therefore categorical, imperative, says: 'I ought to will thus or thus, although I have not willed some-
89 thing else'. For example, the first says: 'I ought not to lie if I want to maintain my reputation'; while the second says: 'I ought not to lie even if so doing were to bring me not the slightest disgrace'. The second imperative must therefore abstract from all objects to this extent—they should be without any *influence* at all on the will so that practical reason (the will) may not merely administer an alien interest but may simply manifest its own sovereign authority as the supreme maker of law. Thus, for example, the reason why I ought to promote the happiness of others is not because the realization of their happiness is of consequence to myself (whether on account of immediate inclination or on account of some satisfaction gained indirectly through reason), but solely because a maxim which excludes this cannot also be present in one and the same volition as a universal law.

Classification ***of All Possible Principles of Morality Based on the Assumption of Heteronomy as Their Fundamental Concept.***

Here, as everywhere else, human reason in its pure use—so long as it lacks a critique—pursues every possible wrong way before it succeeds in finding the only right one.

All the principles that can be adopted from this
90 point of view are either *empirical* or *rational.* The *first* kind, drawn from the principle of *happiness,* are based either on natural, or on moral, feeling. The *second* kind, drawn from the principle of *perfection,*
442 are based either on the rational concept of perfection as a possible effect of our will or else on the concept of a self-existent perfection (God's will) as a determining cause of our will.

Empirical Principles of Heteronomy

Empirical principles are always unfitted to serve as a ground for moral laws. The universality with which these laws should hold for all rational beings without exception—the unconditioned practical necessity which they thus impose—falls away if their basis is taken from the *special constitution of human nature* or from the accidental circumstances in which it is placed. The principle of *personal happiness* is, however, the most objectionable, not merely because it is false and because its pretence that well-being always adjusts itself to well-being is contradicted by experience; nor merely because it contributes nothing whatever towards establishing morality, since making a man happy is quite different from making him good and making him prudent or astute in seeking his advantage quite different from making him virtuous; but because it bases morality on sensuous motives which rather undermine it and totally destroy its sublimity, inasmuch as the motives of virtue are put in the same class as those of vice and we are
instructed only to become better at calculation, the 91
specific difference between virtue and vice being completely wiped out. On the other hand, moral feeling, this alleged special sense[16] (however shallow be the appeal to it when men who are unable to *think* hope to help themselves out by *feeling,* even when the question is solely one of universal law, and however little feelings, differing as they naturally do from one another by an infinity of degrees, can supply a uniform measure of good and evil—let alone that one man by his feeling can make no valid judgements at all for others)—moral feeling still remains closer to morality and to its dignity in this respect: it does virtue the honour of
ascribing to her *immediately* the approval and es- 443
teem in which she is held, and does not, as it were, tell her to her face that we are attached to her, not for her beauty, but only for our own advantage.

16. I class the principle of moral feeling with that of happiness because every empirical principle promises a contribution to our well-being merely from the satisfaction afforded by something—whether this satisfaction is given immediately and without any consideration of advantage or is given in respect of such advantage. Similarly we must with *Hutcheson* class the principle of sympathy for the happiness of others along with the principle of moral sense as adopted by him.

Rational Principles of Heteronomy

Among the *rational* bases of morality—those 92 springing from reason—the ontological concept of *perfection* (however empty, however indefinite it is, and consequently unless for discovering in the boundless field of possible reality the maximum reality appropriate to us; and however much, in trying to distinguish specifically between the reality here in question and every other, it shows an inevitable tendency to go round in a circle and is unable to avoid covertly presupposing the morality it has to explain)—this concept none the less is better than the theological concept which derives morality from a divine and supremely perfect will; not merely because we cannot intuit God's perfection and can only derive it from our own concepts, among which that of morality is the most eminent; but because, if we do not do this (and to do so would be to give a crudely circular explanation), the concept of God's will still remaining to us—one drawn from such characteristics as lust for glory and domination and bound up with frightful ideas of power and vengefulness—would inevitably form the basis for a moral system which would be in direct opposition to morality.

Yet if I had to choose between the concept of moral sense and that of perfection in general (both of which at least do not undermine morality, though they are totally incompetent to support it as its foun- 93 dation), I should decide for the latter; for this, since it at least withdraws the settlement of this question from sensibility and brings it before the court of pure reason, even although it there gets no decision, does still preserve unfalsified for more precise determination the indeterminate Idea (of a will good in itself).

The Failure of Heteronomy

For the rest I believe I may be excused from a lengthy refutation of all these systems. This is so easy and is presumably so well understood even by those whose office requires them to declare themselves for one or other of these theories (since their audience will not lightly put up with a suspension of judgement) that to spend time on it would be merely superfluous labour. But what is of more interest to us here is to know that these principles never lay down anything but heteronomy as the first basis of morality and must in consequence necessarily fail in their object.

Wherever an object of the will has to be put down 444 as the basis for prescribing a rule to determine the will, there the rule is heteronomy; the imperative is conditioned, as follows; '*If*, or *because*, you will this object, you ought to act thus or thus'; consequently it can never give a moral—that is, a categorical—command. However the object determines the will—whether by means of inclination, as in the principle of personal happiness, or by means of reason directed to objects of our possible volitions generally, as in the principle of perfection—the will never de- 94 termines itself *immediately* by the thought of an action, but only by the impulsion which the anticipated effect of the action exercises on the will: '*I ought to do something because I will something else*'. And the basis for this must be yet a further law in me as a subject, whereby I necessarily will this 'something else'—which law in turn requires an imperative to impose limits on this maxim. The impulsion supposed to be exercised on the will of the subject, in accordance with his natural constitution, by the idea of a result to be attained by his own powers belongs to the nature of the subject—whether to his sensibility (his inclinations and taste) or to his understanding and reason, whose operation on an object is accompanied by satisfaction in virtue of the special equipment of their nature—and consequently, speaking strictly, it is nature which would make the law. This law, as a law of nature, not only must be known and proved by experience and therefore is in itself contingent and consequently unfitted to serve as an apodeictic rule of action such as a moral rule must be, but it is *always merely heteronomy of the will*: the will does not give itself the law, but an alien impulsion does so through the medium of the sub- 95 ject's own nature as tuned for its reception.

The Position of the Argument

An absolutely good will, whose principle must be a categorical imperative, will therefore, being undetermined in respect of all objects, contain only the *form* of *willing*, and that as autonomy. In other words, the fitness of the maxim of every good will to make itself a universal law is itself the sole law which the will of every rational being spontaneously imposes on itself without basing it on any impulsion or interest.

How such a synthetic a priori *proposition is possible* and why it is necessary—this is a problem whose solution lies no longer within the bounds of

445 a metaphysic of morals; nor have we here asserted the truth of this proposition, much less pretended to have a proof of it in our power. We have merely shown by developing the concept of morality generally in vogue that autonomy of the will is unavoidably bound up with it or rather is its very basis. Any one therefore who takes morality to be something, and not merely a chimerical Idea without truth, must at the same time admit the principle
96 we have put forward. This chapter, consequently, like the first, has been merely analytic. In order to prove that morality is no mere phantom of the brain—a conclusion which follows if the categorical imperative, and with it the autonomy of the will, is true and is absolutely necessary as an *a priori* principle—we require a *possible synthetic use of pure practical reason.* On such a use we cannot venture without prefacing it by a *critique* of this power of reason itself—a critique whose main features, so far as is sufficient for our purpose, we must outline in our final chapter.

446 CHAPTER III PASSAGE FROM A METAPHYSIC OF MORALS TO A CRITIQUE OF PURE PRACTICAL REASON

The Concept of Freedom is the Key to Explain Autonomy of the Will

Will is a kind of causality belonging to living beings so far as they are rational. *Freedom* would then be the property this causality has of being able to work independently of *determination* by alien causes; just as *natural necessity* is a property characterizing the causality of all non-rational beings—the property of being determined to activity by the influence of alien causes.

The above definition of freedom is *negative* and consequently unfruitful as a way of grasping its essence; but there springs from it a *positive* concept, which, as positive, is richer and more fruitful. The concept of causality carries with it that of *laws* (*Gesetze*) in accordance with which, because of
98 something we call a cause, something else—namely, its effect—must be posited (*gesetzt*). Hence freedom of will, although it is not the property of conforming to laws of nature, is not for this reason lawless: it must rather be a causality conforming to immutable laws, though of a special kind; for otherwise a free will would be self-contradictory. Natural necessity, as we have seen, is a heteronomy of efficient causes; for every effect is possible only in conformity with the law that something else determines the efficient cause to causal action. What else then 447
can freedom of will be but autonomy—that is, the property which will has of being a law to itself? The proposition 'Will is in all its actions a law to itself' expresses, however, only the principle of acting on no maxim other than one which can have for its object itself as at the same time a universal law. This is precisely the formula of the categorical imperative and the principle of morality. Thus a free will and a will under moral laws are one and the same.

Consequently if freedom of the will is presupposed, morality, together with its principle, follows by mere analysis of the concept of freedom. Nevertheless the principle of morality is still a synthetic proposition, namely: 'An absolutely good will is one 99
whose maxim can always have as its content itself considered as a universal law'; for we cannot discover this characteristic of its maxim by analysing the concept of an absolutely good will. Such synthetic propositions are possible only because two cognitions are bound to one another by their connexion with a third term in which both of them are to be found. The *positive* concept of freedom furnishes this third term, which cannot, as in the case of physical causes, be the nature of the sensible world (in the concept of which there come together the concepts of something as cause and of *something else* as effect in their relation to one another). What this third term is to which freedom directs us and of which we have an Idea *a priori*, we are not yet in a position to show here straight away, nor can we as yet make intelligible the deduction of the concept of freedom from pure practical reason and so the possibility of a categorical imperative: we require some further preparation.

Freedom must be Presupposed as a Property of the Will of all Rational Beings

It is not enough to ascribe freedom to our will, on whatever ground, unless we have sufficient reason for attributing the same freedom to all rational beings as well. For since morality is a law for us only 100
as *rational beings*, it must be equally valid for all rational beings; and since it must be derived solely from the property of freedom, we have got to prove that freedom too is a property of the will of all ra-

tional beings. It is not enough to demonstrate freedom from certain alleged experiences of human nature (though to do this is in any case absolutely impossible and freedom can be demonstrated only *a*
448 *priori*): we must prove that it belongs universally to the activity of rational beings endowed with a will. Now I assert that every being who cannot act except *under the Idea of freedom* is by this alone—from a practical point of view—really free; that is to say, for him all the laws inseparably bound up with freedom are valid just as much as if his will could be pronounced free in itself on grounds valid for theo-
101 retical philosophy.[1] And I maintain that to every rational being possessed of a will we must also lend the Idea of freedom as the only one under which he can act. For in such a being we conceive a reason which is practical—that is, which exercises causality in regard to its objects. But we cannot possibly conceive of a reason as being consciously directed from outside in regard to its judgements; for in that case the subject would attribute the determination of his power of judgement, not to his reason, but to an impulsion. Reason must look upon itself as the author of its own principles independently of alien influences. Therefore as practical reason, or as the will of a rational being, it must be regarded by itself as free; that is, the will of a rational being can be a will of his own only under the Idea of freedom, and such a will must therefore—from a practical point of view—be attributed to all rational beings.

The Interest Attached to the Ideas of Morality

Moral Interest and the Vicious Circle

We have at last traced the determinate concept of morality back to the Idea of freedom, but we have been quite unable to demonstrate freedom as something actual in ourselves and in human nature: we
449 saw merely that we must presuppose it if we wish to conceive a being as rational and as endowed with
102 consciousness of his causality in regard to actions—that is, as endowed with a will. Thus we find that on precisely the same ground we must attribute to every being endowed with reason and a will this property of determining himself to action under the Idea of his own freedom.

From the presupposition of this Idea there springs, as we further saw, consciousness of a law of action, the law that subjective principles of action—that is, maxims—must always be adopted in such a way that they can also hold as principles objectively—that is, universally—and can therefore serve for our own enactment of universal law. But why should I subject myself to this principle simply as a rational being and in so doing also subject to it every other being endowed with reason? I am willing to admit that no interest *impels* me to do so since this would not produce a categorical imperative; but all the same I must necessarily *take* an interest in it and understand how this happens; for this 'I ought' is properly an 'I will' which holds necessarily for every rational being—provided that reason in him is practical without any hindrance. For beings who, like us, are affected also by sensibility—that is, by motives of a different kind—and who do not always act as reason by itself would act, this necessity is expressed as an 'I 103
ought,' and the subjective necessity is distinct from the objective one.

It looks as if, in our Idea of freedom, we have in fact merely taken the moral law for granted—that is, the very principle of the autonomy of the will—and have been unable to give an independent proof of its reality and objective necessity. In that case we should still have made a quite considerable gain inasmuch as we should at least have formulated the genuine principle more precisely than has been done before. As regards its validity, however, and the practical necessity of subjecting ourselves to it we should have got no further. Why must the validity of our maxim as a universal law be a condition limiting our action? On what do we base the worth we attach to this way of acting—a worth supposed to be so great that there cannot be any interest which is higher? And how does it come about that in this 450
alone man believes himself to feel his own personal worth, in comparison with which that of a pleasurable or painful state is to count as nothing? To these questions we should have been unable to give any 104
sufficient answer.

We do indeed find ourselves able to take an interest in a personal characteristic which carries with it no interest in mere states, but only makes us fit to have a share in such states in the event of their be-

1. This method takes it as sufficient for our purpose if freedom is presupposed merely *as an Idea* by all rational beings in their actions; and I adopt it in order to avoid the obligation of having to prove freedom from a theoretical point of view as well. For even if this latter problem is left unsettled, the same laws as would bind a being who was really free are equally valid for a being who cannot act except under the Idea of his own freedom. In this way we can relieve ourselves of the burden which weighs upon theory.

ing distributed by reason. That is to say, the mere fact of deserving happiness can by itself interest us even without the motive of getting a share in this happiness. Such a judgement, however, is in fact merely the result of the importance we have already assumed to belong to moral laws (when we detach ourselves from every empirical interest by our Idea of freedom). But on this basis we can as yet have no insight into the principle that we ought to detach ourselves from such interest—that is, that we ought to regard ourselves as free in our actions and yet to hold ourselves bound by certain laws in order to find solely in our own person a worth which can compensate us for the loss of everything that makes our state valuable. We do not see how this is possible nor consequently *how the moral law can be binding*.

In this, we must frankly admit, there is shown a kind of circle, from which, as it seems, there is no way of escape. In the order of efficient causes we take ourselves to be free so that we may conceive ourselves to be under moral laws in the order of ends; and we then proceed to think of ourselves as subject to moral laws on the ground that we have described our will as free. Freedom and the will's enactment of its own laws are indeed both auton-
105 omy—and therefore are reciprocal concepts—but precisely for this reason one of them cannot be used to explain the other or to furnish its ground. It can at most be used for logical purposes in order to bring seemingly different ideas of the same object under a single concept (just as different fractions of equal value can be reduced to their simplest expression).

The Two Standpoints

One shift, however, still remains open to us. We can enquire whether we do not take one standpoint when by means of freedom we conceive ourselves as causes acting *a priori*, and another standpoint when we contemplate ourselves with reference to our actions as effects which we see before our eyes.

One observation is possible without any need for subtle reflexion and, we may assume, can be made by the most ordinary intelligence—no doubt in its
451 own fashion through some obscure discrimination of the power of judgement known to it as 'feeling.' The observation is this—that all ideas coming to us apart from our own volition (as do those of the senses) enable us to know objects only as they affect ourselves: what they may be in themselves remains unknown. Consequently, ideas of this kind, even with the greatest effort of attention and clarification brought to bear by understanding, serve only 106
for knowledge of *appearances,* never of *things in themselves*. Once this distinction is made (it may be merely by noting the difference between ideas given to us from without, we ourselves being passive, and those which we produce entirely from ourselves, and so manifest our own activity), it follows of itself that behind appearances we must admit and assume something else which is not appearance—namely, things in themselves—although, since we can never be acquainted with these, but only with the way in which they affect us, we must resign ourselves to the fact that we can never get any nearer to them and can never know what they are in themselves. This must yield us a distinction, however rough, between the *sensible world* and the *intelligible world*, the first of which can vary a great deal according to differences of sensibility in sundry observers, while the second, which is its ground, always remains the same. Even as regards himself—so far as man is acquainted with himself by inner sensation—he cannot claim to know what he is in himself. For since he does not, so to say, make himself, and since he acquires his concept of self not *a priori* but empirically, it is natural that even about himself he should get information through sense—that is, through inner sense—and consequently only through the mere appearance of his own nature and through the way 107
in which his consciousness is affected. Yet beyond this character of himself as a subject made up, as it is, of mere appearances he must suppose there to be something else which is its ground—namely, his Ego as this may be constituted in itself; and thus as regards mere perception and the capacity for receiving sensations he must count himself as belonging to the *sensible world*, but as regards whatever there may be in him of pure activity (whatever comes into consciousness, not through affection of the senses, but immediately) he must count himself as belonging to the *intellectual world*, of which, however, he knows nothing further.

A conclusion of this kind must be reached by a thinking man about everything that may be presented to him. It is presumably to be found even in 452
the most ordinary intelligence, which, as is well known, is always very much disposed to look behind the objects of the senses for something further that is invisible and is spontaneously active; but it goes on to spoil this by immediately sensifying this

invisible something in its turn—that is to say, it wants to make it an object of intuition, and so by this procedure it does not become in any degree wiser.

Now man actually finds in himself a power which distinguishes him from all other things—and even
108 from himself so far as he is affected by objects. This power is *reason.* As pure spontaneity reason is elevated even above *understanding* in the following respect. Understanding—although it too is spontaneous activity and is not, like sense, confined to ideas which arise only when we are affected by things (and therefore are passive)—understanding cannot produce by its own activity any concepts other than those whose sole service is *to bring sensuous ideas under rules* and so to unite them in one consciousness: without this employment of sensibility it would think nothing at all. Reason, on the other hand—in what are called 'Ideas'—shows a spontaneity so pure that it goes far beyond anything sensibility can offer: it manifests its highest function in distinguishing the sensible and intelligible worlds from one another and so in marking out limits for understanding itself.

Because of this a rational being must regard himself *qua intelligence* (and accordingly not on the side of his lower faculties) as belonging to the intelligible world, not to the sensible one. He has therefore two points of view from which he can regard himself and from which he can know laws governing the employment of his powers and consequently governing all his actions. He can consider himself *first*—so far as he belongs to the sensible world—
109 to be under laws of nature (heteronomy); and *secondly*—so far as he belongs to the intelligible world—to be under laws which, being independent of nature, are not empirical but have their ground in reason alone.

As a rational being, and consequently as belonging to the intelligible world, man can never conceive the causality of his own will except under the Idea of freedom; for to be independent of determination by causes in the sensible world (and this is what reason must
453 always attribute to itself) is to be free. To the Idea of freedom there is inseparably attached the concept of *autonomy*, and to this in turn the universal principle of morality—a principle which in Idea forms the ground for all the actions of *rational* beings, just as the law of nature does for all appearances.

The suspicion which we raised above is now removed—namely, that there might be a hidden circle in our inference from freedom to autonomy and from autonomy to the moral law; that in effect we had perhaps assumed the Idea of freedom only because of the moral law in order subsequently to infer the moral law in its turn from freedom; and that consequently we had been able to assign no ground at all for the moral law, but had merely assumed it by begging a principle which well-meaning souls will gladly concede us, but which we could never put forward as a demonstrable proposition. We see now that when we think of ourselves as free, we transfer ourselves into the intelligible world as mem- 110
bers and recognize the autonomy of the will together with its consequence—morality; whereas when we think of ourselves as under obligation, we look upon ourselves as belonging to the sensible world and yet to the intelligible world at the same time.

How is a Categorical Imperative Possible?

A rational being counts himself, *qua* intelligence, as belonging to the intelligible world, and solely *qua* efficient cause belonging to the intelligible world does he give to his causality the name of '*will*'. On the other side, however, he is conscious of himself as also a part of the sensible world, where his actions are encountered as mere appearances of this causality. Yet the possibility of these actions cannot be made intelligible by means of such causality, since with this we have no direct acquaintance; and instead these actions, as belonging to the sensible world, have to be understood as determined by other appearances—namely, by desires and inclinations. Hence, if I were solely a member of the intelligible world, all my actions would be in perfect conformity with the principle of the autonomy of a pure will; if I were solely a part of the sensible world, they would have to be taken as in complete conformity with the law of nature governing desires and inclinations—that is, with the heteronomy of nature.
(In the first case they would be grounded on the 111
supreme principle of morality; in the second case on that of happiness.) *But the intelligible world contains the ground of the sensible world and therefore also of its laws*; and so in respect of my will, for which (as belonging entirely to the intelligible world) it gives laws immediately, it must also be conceived as containing such a ground. Hence, in spite of regarding myself from one point of view as a being that belongs to the sensible world, I shall have to recognize that, *qua* intelligence, I am sub- 454

ject to the law of the intelligible world—that is, to the reason which contains this law in the Idea of freedom, and so to the autonomy of the will—and therefore I must look on the laws of the intelligible world as imperatives for me and on the actions which conform to this principle as duties.

And in this way categorical imperatives are possible because the Idea of freedom makes me a member of an intelligible world. This being so, if I were solely a member of the intelligible world, all my actions *would* invariably accord with the autonomy of the will; but because I intuit myself at the same time as a member of the sensible world, they *ought* so to accord. This *categorical* 'ought' presents us with a synthetic *a priori* proposition, since to my will as affected by sensuous desires there is added the Idea of the same will, viewed, however, as a pure will belonging to the intelligible world and active on its
112 own account—a will which contains the supreme condition of the former will, so far as reason is concerned. This is roughly like the way in which concepts of the understanding, which by themselves signify nothing but the form of law in general, are added to intuitions of the sensible world and so make synthetic *a priori* propositions possible on which all our knowledge of nature is based.

The practical use of ordinary human reason confirms the rightness of this deduction. There is no one, not even the most hardened scoundrel—provided only he is accustomed to use reason in other ways—who, when presented with examples of honesty in purpose, of faithfulness to good maxims, of sympathy, and of kindness towards all (even when these are bound up with great sacrifices of advantage and comfort), does not wish that he too might be a man of like spirit. He is unable to realize such an aim in his own person—though only on account of his desires and impulses; but yet at the same time he wishes to be free from these inclinations, which are a burden to himself. By such a wish he shows that having a will free from sensuous impulses he transfers himself in thought into an order of things quite different from that of his desires in the field of sensibility; for from the fulfilment of this wish he can expect no gratification of his sensuous desires and consequently no state which would satisfy any
113 of his actual or even conceivable inclinations (since by such an expectation the very Idea which elicited the wish would be deprived of its superiority); all he can expect is a greater inner worth of his own
455 person. This better person he believes himself to be when he transfers himself to the standpoint of a member of the intelligible world. He is involuntarily constrained to do so by the Idea of freedom—that is, of not being dependent on *determination* by causes in the sensible world; and from this standpoint he is conscious of possessing a good will which, on his own admission, constitutes the law for the bad will belonging to him as a member of the sensible world—a law of whose authority he is aware even in transgressing it. The moral 'I ought' is thus an 'I will' for man as a member of the intelligible world; and it is conceived by him as an 'I ought' only in so far as he considers himself at the same time to be a member of the sensible world.

The Extreme Limit of Practical Philosophy

The Antinomy of Freedom and Necessity

All men think of themselves as having a free will. From this arise all judgements that actions are such as *ought to have been done*, although they *have not been done*. This freedom is no concept of experience, nor can it be such, since it continues to hold although experience shows the opposite of those requirements which are regarded as necessary under the presupposition of freedom. On the other hand, it 114
is just as necessary that everything which takes place should be infallibly determined in accordance with the laws of nature; and this necessity of nature is likewise no concept of experience, precisely because it carries with it the concept of necessity and so of *a priori* knowledge. The concept of nature is, however, confirmed by experience and must inevitably be presupposed if experience—that is, coherent knowledge of sensible objects in accordance with universal laws—is to be possible. Hence, while freedom is only an *Idea* of reason whose objective reality is in itself questionable, nature is a *concept of the understanding*, which proves, and must necessarily prove, its reality in examples from experience.

From this there arises a dialectic of reason, since the freedom attributed to the will seems incompatible with the necessity of nature; and although at this parting of the ways reason finds the road of natural necessity much more beaten and serviceable than that of freedom for *purposes of speculation*, yet for *purposes of action* the footpath of freedom is the only one on which we can make use of reason in our conduct. Hence to argue freedom away is as im- 456
possible for the most abstruse philosophy as it is for the most ordinary human reason. Reason must there- 115

fore suppose that no genuine contradiction is to be found between the freedom and the natural necessity ascribed to the very same human actions; for it can abandon the concept of nature as little as it can abandon that of freedom.

All the same we must at least get rid of this seeming contradiction in a convincing fashion—although we shall never be able to comprehence how freedom is possible. For if the thought of freedom is self-contradictory or incompatible with nature—a concept which is equally necessary—freedom would have to be completely abandoned in favour of natural necessity.

The Two Standpoints

From this contradiction it would be impossible to escape if the subject who believes himself free were to conceive himself *in the same sense*, or *in precisely the same relationship*, when he calls himself free as when he holds himself subject to the law of nature in respect of the same action. Hence speculative philosophy has the unavoidable task of showing at least this—that its illusion about the contradiction rests on our conceiving man in one sense and relationship when we call him free and in another when we consider him, as a part of nature, to be sub-
116 ject to nature's laws; and that both characteristics not merely *can* get on perfectly well together, but must be conceived as *necessarily combined* in the same subject; for otherwise we could not explain why we should trouble reason with an Idea which—even if it can *without contradiction* be combined with a different and adequately verified concept—does yet involve us in a business which puts reason to sore straits in its theoretical use. This duty is incumbent on speculative philosophy solely in order that it may clear a path for practical philosophy. Thus it is not left to the discretion of philosophers whether they will remove the seeming contradiction or leave it untouched; for in the latter case the theory on this topic becomes *bonum vacans* [unoccupied property], of which the fatalist can justifiably take possession and can chase all morality out of its supposed property, which it has no title to hold.

Nevertheless at this point we cannot yet say that the boundary of practical philosophy begins. For practical philosophy has no part in the settlement of
457 this controversy: it merely requires speculative reason to bring to an end the dissension in which it is entangled on theoretical questions so that practical reason may have peace and security from external attacks capable of bringing into dispute the territory it seeks to cultivate.

The lawful title to freedom of will claimed even 117
by ordinary human reason is grounded on a consciousness—and an accepted presupposition—that reason is independent of purely subjective determination by causes which collectively make up all that belongs to sensation and comes under the general name of sensibility. In thus regarding himself as intelligence man puts himself into another order of things, and into relation with determining causes of quite another sort, when he conceives himself as intelligence endowed with a will and consequently with causality, than he does when he perceives himself as a phenomenon in the sensible world (which he actually is as well) and subjects his causality to external determination in accordance with laws of nature. He then becomes aware at once that both of these can, and indeed must, take place at the same time; for there is not the slightest contradiction in holding that a *thing as an appearance* (as belonging to the sensible world) is subject to certain laws of which it is independent *as a thing* or being *in itself*. That he must represent and conceive himself in this double way rests, as regards the first side, on consciousness of himself as an object affected through the senses; as concerns the second side, on consciousness of himself as intelligence—that is, as independent of sensuous impressions in his use of reason (and so as belonging to the intelligible world).

Hence it comes about that man claims for himself 118
a will which does not impute to itself anything appertaining merely to his desires and inclinations; and, on the other hand, that he conceives as possible through its agency, and indeed as necessary, actions which can be done only by disregarding all desires and incitements of sense. The causality of such actions lies in man as intelligence and in the laws of such effects and actions as accord with the principles of an intelligible world. Of that world he knows no more than this—that in it reason alone, and indeed pure reason independent of sensibility, is the source of law; and also that since he is there his proper self only as intelligence (while as a human being he is merely an appearance of himself), these laws apply to him immediately and categorically. It follows that incitements from desires and impulses (and therefore from the whole sensible world of nature) cannot impair the laws which gov-

ern his will as intelligence. Indeed he does not an-
458 swer for the former nor impute them to his proper self—that is, to his will; but he does impute to himself the indulgence which he would show them if he admitted their influence on his maxims to the detriment of the rational laws governing his will.

There Is No Knowledge of the Intelligible World

By *thinking* itself into the intelligible world practical reason does not overstep its limits in the least: it would do so only if it sought to *intuit or feel itself* into that world. The thought in question is a
119 merely negative one with respect to the sensible world: it gives reason no laws for determining the will and is positive only in this one point, that it combines freedom as a negative characteristic with a (positive) power as well—and indeed with a causality of reason called by us 'a will'—a power so to act that the principle of our actions may accord with the essential character of a rational cause, that is, with the condition that the maxim of these actions should have the validity of a universal laws. If practical reason were also to import an *object of the will*—that is, a motive of action—from the intelligible world, it would overstep its limits and pretend to an acquaintance with something of which it has no knowledge. The concept of the intelligible world is thus only *a point of view* which reason finds itself constrained to adopt outside appearances *in order to conceive itself as practical.* To conceive itself thus would not be possible if the influences of sensibility were able to determine man; but it is none the less necessary as far as we are not to deny him consciousness of himself as intelligence and consequently as a rational cause which is active by means of reason—that is, which is free in its operation. This thought admittedly carries with it the Idea of an order and a legislation different from that of the mechanism of nature appropriate to the world of sense. It makes necessary
120 the concept of an intelligible world (that is, of the totality of rational beings as things in themselves); but it makes not the slightest pretension to do more than conceive such a world with respect to its *formal* condition—to conceive it, that is, as conforming to the condition that the maxim of the will should have the universality of a law, and so as conforming to the autonomy of the will, which alone is compatible with freedom. In contrast with this all laws determined by reference to an object give us heteronomy, which can be found only in laws of nature and can apply only to the world of sense.

There is No Explanation of Freedom

Reason would overstep all its limits if it took upon itself to *explain how* pure reason can be practical.
This would be identical with the task of explaining 459
how freedom is possible.

We are unable to explain anything unless we can bring it under laws which can have an object given in some possible experience. Freedom, however, is a mere Idea: its objective validity can in no way be exhibited by reference to laws of nature and consequently cannot be exhibited in any possible experience. Thus the Idea of freedom can never admit of full comprehension, or indeed of insight, since it can never by any analogy have an example falling under it. It holds only as a necessary presupposition of reason in a being who believes himself to be conscious of a will—that is, of a power distinct from mere appetition (a power, namely, of determining himself to act as intelligence and consequently to act in accordance with laws of reason independently of natural instincts).
But where determination by laws of nature comes 121
to an end, all *explanation* comes to an end as well. Nothing is left but *defence*—that is, to repel the objections of those who profess to have seen more deeply into the essence of things and on this ground audaciously declare freedom to be impossible. We can only show them that their pretended discovery of a contradiction in it consists in nothing but this: in order to make the law of nature apply to human actions they have necessarily had to consider man as an appearance; and now that they are asked to conceive him, *qua* intelligence, as a thing in himself as well, they continue to look upon him as an appearance in this respect also. In that case, admittedly, to exempt man's causality (that is, his will) from all the natural laws of the sensible world would, in one and the same subject, give rise to a contradiction. The contradiction would fall away if they were willing to reflect and to admit, as is reasonable, that things in themselves (although hidden) must lie behind appearances as their ground, and that we cannot require the laws of their operations to be identical with those that govern their appearances.

There is No Explanation of Moral Interest

The subjective impossibility of *explaining* freedom
122 of will is the same as the impossibility of finding out and making comprehensible what *interest*[2] man can take in moral laws; and yet he does in fact take
460 such an interest. The basis of this in ourselves we call 'moral feeling'. Some people have mistakenly given out this feeling to be the gauge of our moral judgements: it should be regarded rather as the *subjective* effect exercises on our will by the law and having its objective ground in reason alone.

If we are to will actions for which reason by itself prescribes an 'ought' to a rational, yet sensuously affected, being, it is admittedly necessary that reason should have a power of *infusing* a *feeling of pleasure* or satisfaction in the fulfilment of duty, and consequently that it should possess a kind of causality by which it can determine sensibility in accor-
123 dance with rational principles. It is, however, wholly impossible to comprehend—that is, to make intelligible *a priori*—how a mere thought containing nothing sensible in itself can bring about a sensation of pleasure or displeasure; for there is here a special kind of causality, and—as with all causality—we are totally unable to determine its character *a priori*: on this we must consult experience alone. The latter cannot provide us with a relation of cause and effect except between two objects of experience—whereas here pure reason by means of mere Ideas (which furnish absolutely no objects for experience) has to be the cause of an effect admittedly found in experience. Hence for us men it is wholly impossible to explain how and why the *universality of a maxim as a law*—and therefore morality—should interest us. This much only is certain: the law is not valid for us *because it interests us* (for this is het-
461 eronomy and makes practical reason depend on sensibility—that is to say, on an underlying feeling—in which case practical reason could never give us moral law); the law interests us because it is valid for us as men in virtue of having sprung from our will as intelligence and so from our proper self; *but what belongs to mere appearance is necessarily subordinated by reason to the character of the thing in itself.*

General Review of the Argument

Thus the question 'How is a categorical imperative
possible?' can be answered so far as we can supply 124
the sole presupposition under which it is possible—namely, the Idea of freedom—and also so far as we can have insight into the necessity of this presupposition. This is sufficient for the *practical use* of reason—that is, for conviction of the *validity of this imperative,* and so too of the moral law. But how this presupposition itself is possible is never open to the insight of any human reason. Yet, on the presupposition that the will of an intelligence is free, there follows necessarily its *autonomy* as the formal condition under which alone it can be determined. It is not only perfectly *possible* (as speculative philosophy can show) to presuppose such freedom of the will (without contradicting the principle that natural necessity governs the connexion of appearances in the sensible world); it is also *necessary*, without any further condition, for a rational being conscious of exercising causality by means of reason and so of having a will (which is distinct from desires) to make such freedom in practice—that is, in Idea—underlie all his voluntary actions as their condition. But *how* pure reason can be practical in itself without further motives drawn from some other source; that is, how the bare *principle of the universal validity of all its maxims as laws* (which would admittedly be the form of a pure practical reason) can
by itself—without any matter (or object) of the will 125
in which we could take some antecedent interest—supply a motive and create an interest which could be called purely *moral*; or, in other words, *how pure reason can be practical*—all human reason is totally incapable of explaining this, and all the effort and labour to seek such an explanation is wasted.

It is precisely the same as if I sought to fathom how freedom itself is possible as the causality of a will. There I abandon a philosophical basis of ex-
planation, and I have no other. I could, no doubt, 462
proceed to flutter about in the intelligible world, which still remains left to me—the world of intelli-

2. An interest is that in virtue of which reason becomes practical—that is, becomes a cause determining the will. Hence only of a rational being do we say that he takes an interest in something: non-rational creatures merely feel sensuous impulses. Reason takes an immediate interest in an action only when the universal validity of the maxim of the action is a ground sufficient to determine the will. Such an interest alone is pure. When reason is able to determine the will only by means of some further object of desire or under the presupposition of some special feeling in the subject, then it takes only a mediate interest in the action; and since reason entirely by itself without the aid of experience can discover neither objects for the will nor a special feeling underlying the will, the latter interest would be merely empirical, and not a pure rational interest. The logical interest of reason (interest in promoting its own insight) is never immediate, but presupposes purposes for which reason can be employed.

gences; but although I have an *Idea* of it, which has its own good grounds, yet I have not the slightest *acquaintance* with such a world, nor can I ever attain such acquaintance by all the efforts of my natural power of reason. My Idea signifies only a 'something' that remains over when I have excluded from the grounds determining my will everything that belongs to the world of sense: its sole purpose is to restrict the principle that all motives come from the field of sensibility, by setting bounds to this field and by showing that it does not comprise all in all within itself, but that there is still more beyond it;
126 yet with this 'more' I have no further acquaintance. Of the pure reason which conceives this Ideal, after I have set aside all matter—that is, all knowledge of objects—there remains nothing over for me except its form—namely, the practical law that maxims should be universally valid—and the corresponding conception of reason, in its relation to a purely intelligible world, as a possible efficient cause, that is, a cause determining the will. Here all sensuous motives must entirely fail; this Idea of an intelligible world would itself have to be the motive or to be that wherein reason originally took an interest. To make this comprehensible is, however, precisely the problem that we are unable to solve.

The Extreme Limit of Moral Enquiry

Here then is the extreme limit of all moral enquiry. To determine this limit is, however, of great importance in this respect: by so doing reason may be kept, on the one hand, from searching around in the sensible world—greatly to the detriment of morality—for the supreme motive and for some interest, comprehensible indeed, but empirical; and it may be kept, on the other hand, from flapping its wings impotently, without leaving the spot, in a space that for it is empty—the space of transcendent concepts known as 'the intelligible world'—and so from getting lost among mere phantoms of the brain. For the rest, the Idea of a purely intelligible world, as a whole of all intelligences to which we ourselves belong as rational beings (although from another point
127 of view we are members of the sensible world as well), remains always a serviceable and permitted Idea for the purposes of a rational belief, though all knowledge ends at its boundary: it serves to produce in us a lively interest in the moral law by means of the splendid ideal of a universal kingdom of *ends in themselves* (rational beings), to which we can belong as members only if we are scrupulous to live
in accordance with maxims of freedom as if they 463
were laws of nature.

Concluding Note

The speculative use of reason *in regard to nature* leads to the absolute necessity of some supreme cause of the *world*; the practical use of reason *with respect to freedom* leads also to absolute necessity—but only to the absolute necessity *of the laws of action* for a rational being as such. Now it is an essential *principle* for every use of reason to push its knowledge to the point where we are conscious of its *necessity* (for without necessity it would not be knowledge characteristic of reason). It is an equally essential *limitation* of the same reason that it cannot have insight into the *necessity* either of what is or what happens, or of what ought to happen, except on the basis of a *condition* under which it is or happens or ought to happen. In this way, however, the
satisfaction of reason is merely postponed again and 128
again by continual enquiry after a condition. Hence reason unrestingly seeks the unconditionally necessary and sees itself compelled to assume this without any means of making it comprehensible—happy enough if only it can find a concept compatible with this presupposition. Thus it is no discredit to our deduction of the supreme principle of morality, but rather a reproach which must be brought against reason as such, that it cannot make comprehensible the absolute necessity of an unconditioned practical law (such as the categorical imperative must be). For its unwillingness to do this by means of a condition—namely, by basing this necessity on some underlying interest—reason cannot be blamed, since in that case there would be no moral law, that is, no supreme law of freedom. And thus, while we do not comprehend the practical unconditioned necessity of the moral imperative, we do comprehend its *incomprehensibility*. This is all that can fairly be asked of a philosophy which presses forward in its principles to the very limit of human reason.

Chapter 25

Georg Wilhelm Friedrich Hegel

Georg W. F. Hegel was born in Stuttgart, Germany, in 1770, and became the most prominent Continental philosopher in the nineteenth century. Taught Greek by his mother, he developed a love of Greek philosophy while still in high school. In 1788 he entered the University of Tubingen to study theology. As a student he became friends with the poet Holderlin and the philosopher Schelling. After graduating from the university in 1793, he became a family tutor in Bern and Frankfurt for six years. In 1799 he became an unsalaried lecturer at the University of Jena. While there he wrote his major work, *The Phenomenology of Mind,* a portion of which is reprinted below.The work was completed just as Napoleon launched the Battle of Jena, which closed the university. Hegel became the principal of a high school, married, and had two sons. In 1816 he joined the faculty of Heidelberg, where he continued to develop his ideas, publishing the *Science of Logic* (1816). In 1818 he was appointed to the prestigious Chair of Philosophy at the University of Berlin, where he published his *Philosophy of Right* (1821). He died of cholera in 1831.

Hegel is the pivotal philosopher between Kant and Marx. He was profoundly influenced by Kant, yet criticized him and then transformed his system into Absolute Idealism. He himself was then subjected to the same treatment by Karl Marx (see chapter 29), who criticized and transformed his dialectical idealism into dialectical materialism. Hegel thought that Kant had brought philosophy to a new crisis by denying knowledge of metaphysical truth. Hegel accepted Kant's criticisms of previous rationalist thought but thought Kant had not gone far enough. He rejected Kant's theory of knowledge, which claimed that we had no metaphysical knowledge, that we must be in ignorance regarding the thing-in-itself, ultimate reality. Following criticisms inaugurated by his friend Johann Fichte (1762–1814), Hegel pointed out that Kant's system contained an apparent contradiction: he says that we are both ignorant of the thing-in-itself, reality (the *noumenal world*), and that we know that it exists and *causes* our appearances. If we are ignorant of the noumenal world, how do we know that it exists at all? and how do we know that *it* causes our perceptions?

Hegel transformed Kant's categories of the mind into his system of Absolute Idealism, building a comprehensive and coherentist metaphysical system. Whereas Kant thought the categories were purely subjective, part of the structure of our minds, Hegel argued that they had objective reality.

The intricacies of Hegel's dialectical method, the overcoming internal contradictions inherent in the traidic process of "Being-Nothingness," in "Becoming" and the resolution of the dichotomy of "Idea-Nature" in "Spirit" have challenged some of the greatest minds in Western philosophy. Hegel defines "dialectics" this way:

> There are three aspects in every thought which is logically real or true: (1) the abstract or rational form, which says what something is; (2) the dialectical negation, which says what something is not; and (3) the speculative-concrete comprehension:

> A is also that which it is not, A is not-A. These three aspects do not constitute three parts of logic, but are moments of everything that is logically real or true. They belong to every philosophical concept. Every concept is rational, is abstractly opposed to another, and is united in comprehension together with its opposites. The is the definition of dialectic (*Encyclopedia of Philosophy,* p. 82).

Take Hegel's notion of being. This a pure category or concept that we must think, not the being of this or that, but pure being, such as we might arrive at by subtracting all other qualities from any existing object until we are left simply with its *existence*. Take this table (or pen or any object you like). Let us abstract its properties, in the case of the table, its shape, its size, its wood, its color, its hardness, and every other property it has, and leave only its bare existence. What do we have left? Mere "isness," "existence"—that which this table has in common with every other existent but which it doesn't have in common with possible but nonexistent tables, centaurs, unicorns, and so forth. Such being has in it no *determinations* or qualities whatsoever, for we have subtracted all of these determinations from it. It is therefore completely indeterminate, vacant, and empty. It has no content, whatsoever. It is simply nothing. Being, therefore, amounts to nothing. And the pure concept of being is thus seen to contain—dialectically—the idea of nothingness. So we have deduced the idea of nothingness from the idea of being.

Of course, this doesn't mean that existing things like tables and chairs are nothing, only that being itself is identical with nothing. Since being and nothing are identical, and we can deduce one from another, we can speak of a *passage* from being to nothing—and vice versa. Nothing is an emptiness, emptiness is pure being, hence nothing is pure being. So there is a two-way traffic between the concepts, and hence we arrived at the third category, *becoming,* the passage from being to nothing.

Hegel applies this method to history. Spirit or Mind demands an opposite, which Hegel shows to be Nature (or Matter in motion), its other. In overcoming this otherness, Spirit truly becomes itself. Nature is the other which is implicit in spirit but which is, in the first instance, opposed to it.

> Nature must be seen as a set of stages, leading up from inert mechanisms and mutual externality to organized life, which in its higher, animal forms is conscious and spiritual, and spirit must develop from a state in which it can understand and transform nature, and ultimately achieve the philosophico-religious understanding of itself as the immanent end of nature, thereby achieving absoluteness.

The Absolute Spirit is Hegel's interpretation of God, that which works through history, suffering and struggling to realize perfection, to find unity through plurality, to overcome alienation and bring forth the ultimate synthesis. "It is only in and through the Golgotha of the Absolute Spirit that its truth and kingdom are secured."

We will note the diverse reactions to this method and Hegel's vision in Kierkegaard and Marx.

In our selection from *The Phenomenology of Mind,* Hegel develops his dialectic of consciousness where the master finds himself in bondage to and dependent on the slave for his status and well-being. The solution is to reach a state of freedom, where there is neither oppressor or oppressed.

FOR FURTHER READING

Kaufmann, Walter. *Hegel: Reinterpretation, Text, and Commentary.* (Doubleday, 1965).

Inwood, Michael, ed. *Hegel.* (Oxford University Press, 1985).

MacIntyre, Alasdair, ed. *Hegel: A Collection of Critical Essays.* (University of Notre Dame Press, 1972).
Mure, G. R. *An Introduction to Hegel.* (Oxford University Press, 1940).
Norman, Richard. *Hegel's Phenomenology: A Philosophical Introduction.* (Brighton, 1976).
Singer, Peter. *Hegel.* (Oxford University Press, 1983).
Soll, Ivan. *An Introduction to Hegel's Metaphysics.* (University of Chicago, 1969).
Solomon, Robert. *From Hegel to Existentialism.* (Oxford University Press, 1987).
Stace, W. T. *The Philosophy of Hegel.* (Dover Reprint, 1924, 1955).
Taylor, Charles, *Hegel.* (Cambridge University Press, 1975).

Phenomenology of Spirit

LORDSHIP AND BONDAGE

Self-consciousness exists in itself and for itself, in that, and by the fact that it exists for another self-consciousness; that is to say, it *is* only by being acknowledged or "recognized." The conception of this its unity in its duplication, of infinitude realizing itself in self-consciousness, has many sides to it and encloses within it elements of varied significance. Thus its moments must on the one hand be strictly kept apart in detailed distinctiveness, and, on the other, in this distinction must, at the same time, also be taken as not distinguished, or must always be accepted and understood in their opposite sense. This double meaning of what is distinguished lies in the nature of self-consciousness:—of its being infinite, or directly the opposite of the determinateness in which it is fixed. The detailed exposition of the notion of this spiritual unity in its duplication will bring before us the process of Recognition.

Self-consciousness has before it another self-consciousness; it has come outside itself. This has a double significance. First it has lost its own self, since it finds itself as an *other* being; secondly, it has thereby sublated that other, for it does not regard the other as essentially real, but sees its own self in the other.

It must cancel this its other. To do so is the sublation of that first double meaning, and is therefore a second double meaning. First, it must set itself to sublate the other independent being, in order thereby to become certain of itself as true being, secondly, it thereupon proceeds to sublate its own self, for this other is itself.

This sublation in a double sense of its otherness in a double sense is at the same time a return in a double sense into its self. For, firstly, through sublation, it gets back itself, because it becomes one with itself again through the canceling of *its* otherness; but secondly, it likewise gives otherness back again to the other self-consciousness, for it was aware of being in the other, it cancels this its own being in the other and thus lets the other again go free.

This process of self-consciousness in relation to another self-consciousness has in this manner been represented as the action of one alone. But this action on the part of the one has itself the double significance of being at once its own action and the action of that other as well. For the other is likewise independent, shut up within itself, and there is nothing in it which is not there through itself. The first does not have the object before it only in the passive form characteristic primarily of the object of desire, but as an object existing independently for itself, over which therefore it has no power to do anything for its own behoof, if that object does not *per se* do what the first does too it. The process then is absolutely the double process of both self-consciousness. Each sees the other do the same as itself; each itself does what it demands on the part of the other, and for that reason does what it does only so far as the other does the same. Action from one

From *The Phenomenology of Mind*, trans. J.B. Baillie (1910). Reprinted with permission.

side only would be useless, because what is to happen can only be brought about by means of both.

The action has then a *double entente* not only in the sense that it is an act done to itself as well as to the other, but also in the sense that the act *simpliciter* is the act of the one as well as of the other regardless of their distinction.

In this movement we see the process repeated which came before us as the play of forces; in the present case, however, it is found in consciousness. What in the former had effect only for us [contemplating experience], holds here for the terms themselves. The middle term is self-consciousness which breaks itself up into the extremes; and each extreme is this interchange of its own determinateness, and complete transition into the opposite. While *qua* consciousness, it no doubt comes outside itself, still, in being outside itself, it is at the same time restrained within itself, it exists for itself, and its self-externalization is for consciousness. *Consciousness* finds that it immediately is and is not another consciousness, as also that this other is for itself only when it cancels itself as existing for itself, and has self-existence only in the self-existence of the other. Each is the mediating term to the other, through which each mediates and unites itself with itself; and each is to itself and to the other an immediate self-existing reality, which, at the same time, exists thus for itself only through this mediation. They recognize themselves as mutually recognizing one another.

This pure conception of recognition, of duplication of self-consciousness within its unity, we must now consider in the way its process appears for self-consciousness. It will, in the first place, present the aspect of the disparity of the two, or the break-up of the middle term into the extremes, which, *qua* extremes, are opposed to one another, and of which one is merely recognized, while the other only recognizes.

Self-consciousness is primarily simply existence for self, self-identity by exclusion of every other from itself. It takes its essential nature and absolute object to be Ego; and in this immediacy, in this bare fact of its self-existence, it is individual. That which for it is other stands as unessential object, as object with the impress and character of negation. But the other is also a self-consciousness; an individual makes its appearance in antithesis to an individual. Appearing thus in their immediacy, they are for each other in the manner of ordinary objects. They are independent individual forms, modes of consciousness that have not risen above the bare level of life (for the existent object here has been determined as life). They are, moreover, forms of consciousness which have not yet accomplished for one another the process of absolute abstraction, of uprooting all immediate existence, and of being merely the bare, negative fact of self-identical consciousness; or, in other words, have not yet revealed themselves to each other as existing purely for themselves, i.e., as self-consciousness. Each is indeed certain of its own self, but not of the other, and hence its own certainty of itself is still without truth. For its truth would be merely that its own individual existence for itself would be shown to it to be an independent object or, which is the same thing, that the object would be exhibited as this pure certainty of itself. By the notion of recognition, however, this is not possible, except in the form that as the other is for it, so it is for the other; each in its self through its own action and again through the action of the other achieves this pure abstraction of existence for self.

The presentation of itself, however, as pure abstraction of self-consciousness consists in showing itself as a pure negation of its objective form, or in showing that it is fettered to no determinate existence, that it is not bound at all by the particularity everywhere characteristic of existence as such, and is *not* tied up with life. The process of bringing all this out involves a twofold action—action on the part of the other and action on the part of itself. In so far as it is the other's action, each aims at the destruction and death of the other. But in this there is implicated also the second kind of action, self-activity; for the former implies that it risks its own life. The relation of both self-consciousnesses is in this way so constituted that they prove themselves and each other through a life-and-death struggle. They must enter into this struggle, for they must bring their certainty of themselves, the certainty of being for themselves, to the level of objective truth, and make this a fact both in the case of the other and in their own case as well. And it is solely by risking life that freedom is obtained; only thus is it tried and proved that the essential nature of self-consciousness is not bare existence, is not the merely immediate form in which it at first makes its appearance, is not its mere absorption in the expanse of life. Rather it is thereby guaranteed that there is nothing present but what might be taken as a vanishing moment—that self-consciousness is merely pure self-existence, being-for-self. The individual, who has not staked his life, may, no doubt, be recognized as a Person; but he has not attained the truth of this recognition as an independent self-consciousness. In the same way each must aim at the death of the other, as it risks its own life thereby; for that other is to it of no more worth than itself; the other's reality is presented to the former as an external other, as outside itself; it must cancel that externality. The other is a purely existent consciousness and entangled in manifold ways; it must view its otherness as pure existence for itself or as absolute negation.

This trial by death, however, cancels both the truth which was to result from it, and therewith the certainty of self altogether. For just as life is the natural "position" of consciousness, independence without absolute negativity, so death is the natural "negation" of consciousness, negation without independence, which thus remains without the requisite significance of actual recognition. Through death, doubtless, there has arisen the certainty that both did stake their life, and held it lightly both in their own case and in the case of the other; but that is not for those who underwent this struggle. They cancel their consciousness which had its place in this alien element of natural existence; in other words, they cancel themselves and are sublated as terms or extremes seeking to have existence on their own account. But along with this there vanishes from the play of change the essential moment, viz. that of breaking up into extremes with opposite characteristics; and the middle term collapses into a lifeless unity which is broken up into lifeless extremes, merely existent and not opposed. And the two do not mutually give and receive one another back from each other through consciousness; they let one another go quite indifferently, like things. Their act is abstract negation, not the negation characteristic of consciousness, which cancels in such a way that it preserves and maintains what is sublated, and thereby survives its being sublated.

In this experience self-consciousness becomes aware that *life* is as essential to it as pure self-consciousness. In immediate self-consciousness the simple ego is absolute object, which, however, is for us or in itself absolute mediation, and has as its essential moment substantial and solid independence. The dissolution of that simple unit is the result of the first experience; through this there is posited a pure self-consciousness, and a consciousness which is not purely for itself, but for another, i.e. as an existent consciousness, consciousness in the form and shape of thinghood. Both moments are essential, since, in the first instance, they are unlike and opposed, and their reflexion into unity has not yet come to light, they stand as two opposed forms or modes of consciousness. The one is independent, and its essential nature is to be for itself; the other is dependent, and its essence is life or existence for another. The former is the Master, or Lord, the latter the Bondsman.

The master is the consciousness that exists for *itself*; but no longer merely the general notion of existence for self. Rather, it is a consciousness existing on its own account which is mediated with itself through an other consciousness, i.e. through an other whose very nature implies that it is bound up with an independent being or with thinghood in general. The master brings himself into relation to both these moments, to a thing as such, the object of desire, and to the consciousness whose essential character is thinghood. And since the master, is (*a*) *qua* notion of self-consciousness, an immediate relation of self-existence, but (*b*) is now moreover at the same time mediation, or a being-for-self which is for itself only through an other—he [the master] stands in relation (*a*) immediately to both (*b*) mediately to each through the other. The master relates himself to the bondsman mediately through independent existence, for that is precisely what keeps the bondsman in thrall; it is his chain, from which he could not in the struggle get away, and for that reason he proved himself to be dependent, to have his independence in the shape of thinghood. The master, however, is the power controlling this state of existence, for he has shown in the struggle that he holds it to be merely something negative. Since he is the power dominating existence, while this existence again is the power controlling the other [the bondsman], the master holds, *par consequence,* the other in subordination. In the same way the master relates himself to the thing mediately through the bondsman. The bondsman being a self-consciousness in the broad sense, also takes up a negative attitude to things and cancels them; but the thing is, at the same time, independent for him, and, in consequence, he cannot, with all his negating, get so far as to annihilate it outright and be done with it; that is to say, he merely works on it. To the master, on the other hand, by means of this mediating process, belongs the immediate relation, in the sense of the pure negation of it, in other words he gets the enjoyment. What mere desire did not attain, he now succeeds in attaining, viz. to have done with the thing, and find satisfaction in enjoyment. Desire alone did not get the length of this, because of the independence of the thing. The master, however, who has interposed the bondsman between it and himself, thereby relates himself merely to the dependence of the thing, and enjoys it without qualification and without reserve. The aspect of its independence he leaves to the bondsman, who labours upon it.

In these two moments, the master gets his recognition through an other consciousness, for in them the latter affirms itself as unessential, both by working upon the thing, and, on the other hand, by the fact of being dependent on a determinate existence; in neither case can this other get the mastery over existence, and succeed in absolutely negating it. We have thus here this moment of recognition, viz. that the other consciousness cancels itself as self-existent, and, *ipso facto*, itself does what the first does to it. In the same way we have the other moment, that this action on the part of the second is the action proper of the first; for what is done by the bondsman is properly an action on the part of the master. The latter exists only for himself, that is his essential nature; he is the negative power without qualification, a power to which the thing is naught. And he is thus the absolutely essential act in this situation, while the bondsman is not so, he is an unessential activity. But for recognition proper there is needed the moment that what the master does to the other he should also do to himself, and what the bondsman does to himself, he should do to the other also. On that account a form of recognition has arisen that is one-sided and unequal.

In all this, the unessential consciousness is, for the master, the object which embodies the truth of his certainty of himself. But it is evident that this object does not correspond to its notion; for, just where the master has effectively achieved lordship, he really finds that something has come about quite different from an independent consciousness. It is not an independent, but rather a dependent consciousness that he has achieved. He is thus not assured of self-existence as his truth; he finds that his truth is rather the unessential consciousness, and the fortuitous unessential action of that consciousness.

The truth of the independent consciousness is accordingly the consciousness of the bondsman. This doubtless appears in the first instance outside itself, and not as the truth of self-consciousness. But just as lordship showed its essential nature to be the reverse of what it wants to be, so, too, bondage will, when completed, pass into the opposite of what it immediately is: being a consciousness repressed within itself, it will enter into itself, and change round into real and true independence.

We have seen what bondage is only in relation to lordship. But it is a self-consciousness, and we have now to consider what it is, in this regard, in and for itself. In the first instance, the master is taken to be the essential reality for the state of bondage; hence, for it, the truth is the independent consciousness existing for itself, although this truth is not taken yet as inherent in bondage itself. Still, it does in fact contain within itself this truth of pure negativity and self-existence, because it has experienced this reality within it. For this consciousness was not in peril and fear for this element or that, nor for this or that moment of time, it was afraid for its entire being; it felt the fear of death, the sovereign master. It has been in that experience melted to its inmost soul, has trembled throughout its every fibre, and all that was fixed and steadfast has quaked within it. This complete perturbation of its entire substance, this absolute dissolution of all its stability into fluent continuity, is, however, the simple, ultimate nature of self-consciousness, absolute negativity, pure self-referent existence, which consequently is involved in this type of consciousness. This moment of pure self-existence is moreover a fact for it; for in the master it finds this as its object. Further, this bondsman's consciousness is not only this total dissolution in a general way; in serving and toiling the bondsman actually carries this out. By serving he cancels in every particular aspect his dependence on and attachment to natural existence, and by his work removes this existence away.

The feeling of absolute power, however, realized both in general and in the particular form of service, is only dissolution implicitly; and albeit the fear of the lord is the beginning of wisdom, consciousness is not therein aware of being self-existent. Through work and labour, however, this consciousness of the bondsman comes to itself. In the moment which corresponds to desire in the case of the master's consciousness, the aspect of the non-essential relation to the thing seemed to fall to the lot of the servant, since the thing there retained its independence. Desire has reserved to itself the pure negating of the object and thereby unalloyed feeling of self. This satisfaction, however, just for that reason is itself only a state of evanescence, for it lacks objectivity or subsistence. Labour, on the other hand, is desire restrained and checked, evanescence delayed and postponed; in other words, labour shapes and fashions the thing. The negative relation to the object passes into the *form* of the object, into something that is permanent and remains; because it is just for the labourer that the object has independence. This negative mediating agency, this activity giving shape and form, is at the same time the individual existence, the pure self-existence of that consciousness, which now in the work it does is externalized and passes into the condition of permanence. The consciousness that toils and serves accordingly attains by this means the directs apprehension of that independent being as its self.

But again, shaping or forming the object has not only the positive significance that the bondsman becomes thereby aware of himself as factually and objectively self-existent; this type of consciousness has also a negative import, in contrast with its first moment, the element of fear. For in shaping the thing it only becomes aware of its own proper negativity, its existence on its own account, as an object, through the fact that it cancels the actual form confronting it. But this objective negative element is precisely the alien, external reality, before which it trembled. Now, however, it destroys this extraneous alien negative, affirms and sets itself up as a negative in the element of permanence, and thereby becomes for itself a self-existence being. In the master, the bondsman feels self-existence to be something external, an objective fact; in fear self-existence is present within himself; in fashioning the thing, self-existence comes to be felt explicitly as his own proper being, and he attains the consciousness that he himself exists in its own right and on it own account (*an und für sich*). By the fact that the form is objectified, it does not become something other than the consciousness moulding the thing through work; for just that form is his pure self-existence, which therein becomes truly realized. Thus precisely in labour where there seemed to be merely some outsider's mind and ideas involved, the bondsman becomes aware, through this re-discovery of himself by himself, of having by himself, of having and being a "mind of his own."

For this reflexion of self into self the two moments, fear and service in general, as also that of formative activity, are necessary: and at the same time both must exist in a universal manner. Without the discipline of service and obedience, fear remains formal and does not spread over the whole known reality of existence. Without the formative activity shaping the thing, fear remains inward and mute, and consciousness does not become objective for itself. Should consciousness shape and form the thing without the initial state of absolute fear, then it has a merely vain and futile "mind of its own"; for its form or negativity is not negativity *per se*, and hence its formative activity cannot furnish the consciousness of itself as essentially real. If it has endured not absolute fear, but merely some slight anxiety, the negative reality has remained external to it, its substance has not been through and through infected thereby. Since the entire content of its natural consciousness has not tottered and shaken, it is still inherently a determinate mode of being; having a "mind of its own" (*der eigene Sinn*) is simply stubbornness (*Eigensinn*), a type of freedom which does not get beyond the attitude of bondage. As little as the pure form can become its essential nature, so little is that form, considered as extending over particulars, a universal formative activity, an absolute notion; it is rather a piece of cleverness which has mastery within a certain range, but not over the universal power nor over the entire objective reality.

Chapter 26

ARTHUR SCHOPENHAUER

Arthur Schopenhauer (1788–1860) was born in Danzig, Germany. His father was a successful, cultured businessman, his mother a novelist. At the age of seventeen he went to work as a clerk in the office of a man named Jenisch. Shortly after he began work, his father apparently committed suicide. Distraught by the loss of his father and by the dullness of his job, Schopenhauer experienced a deep depression and begged his mother to release him from his employment. After two years of the worst years in his life, he was allowed to leave his work and attend high school and then, in 1809, Gottingen University. He started out in medicine but found philosophy more to this liking. His doctoral dissertation *On the Four-Fold Root of Sufficient Reason*, dealing with four basic types of explanation (causal, empirical, space-time, and motivational) won him a doctorate from the University of Jena in 1813. In 1818 he wrote his most famous work, *The World as Will and Representation*. In 1820 he decided to become a university lecturer at the University of Berlin. He chose to give his lectures at the very same hour as the famous Hegel, whom he regarded as a charlatan. When no one came to hear his lectures, he was given the option of giving up his lectures or changing his hour. He chose to give up his lectures. Schopenhauer was notorious for his stubborn doggedness.

Schopenhauer's philosophy is distinguished by three salient features: (1) his reinterpretation of Kant's distinction between the noumenal and phenomenal world, (2) his deep pessimism, and (3) his inclusion of Eastern philosophy, especially the Hindu Upanishads, into his system. Regarding (1) he thought he had developed Kant's distinction between the noumenal and phenomenal worlds to its highest point. He begins his *The World as Will and Representation* with the sentence "The world is my idea." In a manner reminiscent of Berkeley, Schopenhauer argues that all our thoughts about the world are creations of our mind, our appearances, phenomena. But what is the noumena? Our will: the subjective side of our lives, the desires and intentions. We know ourselves as will. He wrote, "My body and my will are one." The body is the phenomenal form of the will and the will the noumenal form of the body, the thing in itself.

Regarding (2) pessimism, Schopenhauer thought that life is intrinsically miserable. He referred to a pessimism as "a noble displeasure that arises only out of a better nature revolting against wickedness." The will, our deepest self, manifests itself as the will to live, the motive to stay alive, virtually, at all costs. The goal of life is not happiness but the lessening of suffering, and eventually extinction. Meanwhile, there are two ways open to us to ameliorate pessimism: (a) ethics and (b) aesthetics, the denial of the self through (a) compassion for others and (b) the contemplation of beauty.

Regarding (3) Hinduism, Schopenhauer read the *Upanishads* in 1814 and was influenced by its notion of *maya* or illusion—which is what all our appearances of the world are. He was also drawn to the idea of the oneness of the self with all things, signified in the phrase "Tat tvam asi" (this art thou). Similarly, Eastern ideas influenced him to develop a theory of reincarnation (metempsychosis or palingenesis), described in the last part of our first reading.

Our first reading is *On Death and Its Relation to the Indestructibility of Our Inner Nature,* which sets forth Schopenhauer's reflections of the fear of death in the light of his view of the self as will to life. Our second reading is *Essay on the Freedom of the Will,* which first won Schopenhauer acclaim and in which he sets forth a wholly deterministic account of human action.

FOR FURTHER READING

Atwell, John. *Schopenhauer: The Human Character.* (Temple University Press, 1990).
Copleston, F. C. *Arthur Schopenhauer: Philosopher of Pessimism.* (Barnes & Noble, 1975).
Fox, Michael. *Schopenhauer: His Philosophical Achievement.* (Barnes & Noble, 1980).
Jacquette, Dale, ed. *Schopenhauer, Philosophy and the Arts.* (Cambridge University Press, 1996).
Janaway, Christopher. *Schopenhauer.* (Oxford University Press, 1994).
Magee, Bryan. *The Philosophy of Schopenhauer.* (Oxford University Press, 1983).
Schopenhauer, Arthur. *The World as Will and Representation,* 2 vols. trans. E. F. J. Payne. (Dover, 1958).

The World as Will and Representation

ON DEATH AND ITS RELATION TO THE INDESTRUCTIBILITY OF OUR INNER NATURE

Death is the real inspiring genius or Musagetes of philosophy, and for this reason Socrates defined philosophy as "Preparation for death." Indeed, without death there would hardly have been any philosophizing. It will therefore be quite in order for a special consideration of this subject to have its place here at the beginning of the last, most serious, and most important of our books.

The animal lives without any real knowledge of death; therefore the individual animal immediately enjoys the absolute imperishableness and immortality of the species, since it is conscious of itself only as endless. With man the terrifying certainty of death necessarily appeared along with the faculty of reason. But just as everywhere in nature a remedy, or at any rate a compensation, is given for every evil, so the same reflection that introduced the knowledge of death also assists us in obtaining *metaphysical* points of view. Such views console us concerning death, and the animal is neither in need of nor capable of them. All religions and philosophical systems are directed principally to this end, and are thus primarily the antidote to the certainty of death which reflecting reason produces from its own resources. The degree in which they attain this end is, however, very different, and *one* religion or philosophy will certainly enable man, far more than the others will, to look death calmly in the face. Brahmanism and Buddhism, which teach man to regard himself as Brahman, as the original being himself, to whom all arising and passing away are essentially foreign, will achieve much more in this respect than will those religions that represent man as being made out of nothing and as actually beginning at his birth the existence he has received from another. In keeping with this we find in India a confidence and a contempt for death of which we in Europe have no conception. It is indeed a ticklish business to force on man through early impression weak and untenable notions in this important respect, and thus to render him for ever incapable of adopting more correct and stable views. For example, to teach him that he came but recently from nothing, that consequently he has been nothing throughout an eternity, and yet for the future is to be imperishable and immortal, is just like teaching him that, although he is through and through the work of another, he shall nevertheless be responsible to all eternity for his commissions and omissions. Thus if with a mature mind and with the appearance of reflection the untenable nature of such doctrines forces itself on him, he has nothing better to put in their place; in fact, he is no longer capable of understanding anything better, and in this way is deprived of the consolation that nature had provided for him as compensation for the certainty of death. In consequence of such a development, we now (1844) see in England the Socialists among the demoralized and corrupted factory workers, and in Germany the young Hegelians among the demoralized and corrupted students, sink to the absolutely physical viewpoint. This leads to the result: "Eat and drink, after death there is no more rejoicing" and to this extent can be described as bestiality.

According, however, to all that has been taught about death, it cannot be denied that, at any rate in Europe, the opinion of men, often in fact even of the same individual, very frequently vacillates afresh between the conception of death as absolute annihilation and the assumption that we are, so to speak with skin and hair, immortal. Both are equally false, but we have not so much to find a correct mean as rather to gain the higher standpoint from which such views disappear of themselves.

With these considerations, I wish to start first of all from the entirely empirical viewpoint. Here we have primarily before us the undeniable fact that, according to natural consciousness, man not only fears death for his own person more than anything else, but also weeps violently over the death of his friends and relations. It is evident, indeed, that he does this not egoistically over his own loss, but out of sympathy for the great misfortune that has befallen them. He therefore censures as hard-hearted and unfeeling those who in such a case do not weep and show no grief. Parallel with this is the fact that, in its highest degrees, the thirst for revenge seeks the death of the adversary as the greatest evil that can be inflicted on him. Opinions change according to time and place, but the voice of nature remains always and everywhere the same, and is therefore to be heeded before everything else. Now here it seems clearly to assert that death is a great evil. In the language of nature, *death* signifies annihilation; and that death is a serious matter could already be inferred from the fact that, as everyone knows, life is no joke. Indeed we must not deserve anything better than these two.

The fear of death is, in fact, independent of all knowledge, for the animal has it, although it does not know death. Everything that is born already brings this fear into the world. Such fear of death, however, is *a priori* only the reverse side of the will-to-live, which indeed we all are. Therefore in every animal the fear of its own destruction, like the care for its maintenance, is inborn. Thus it is this fear of death, and not the mere avoidance of pain, that shows itself in the anxious care and caution with which the animal seeks to protect itself, and still more its brood, from everyone who might become dangerous. Why does the animal flee, tremble, and try to conceal itself? Because it is simply the will-to-live, but as such it is forfeit to death and would like to gain time. By nature man is just the same. The greatest of evils, the worst thing that can threaten anywhere, is death; the greatest anxiety is the anxiety of death. Nothing excites us so irresistibly to the most lively interest as does danger to the lives of others; nothing is more dreadful than an execution. Now the boundless attachment to life which appears here cannot have sprung from knowledge and reflection. To these, on the contrary, it appears foolish, for the objective value of life is very uncertain, and it remains at least doubtful whether existence is to be preferred to non-existence; in fact, if experience and reflection have their say, non-existence must certainly win. If we knocked on the graves and asked the dead whether they would like to rise again, they would shake their heads. In Plato's *Apology* this is also the opinion of Socrates, and even the cheerful and amiable Voltaire cannot help saying: "We like life, but all the same nothingness also has its good points. . . . I do not know what eternal life is, but this present life is a bad joke." Moreover, in any case life must end soon, so that the few years which possibly we have still to exist vanish entirely before the endless time when we shall be no more. Accordingly, to reflection it appears even ludicrous for us to be so very anxious about this span of time, to tremble so much when our own life or another's is endangered, and to write tragedies whose terrible aspect has as its main theme merely the fear of death. Consequently, this powerful attachment to life is irrational and blind; it can be explained only from the fact that our whole being-in-itself is the will-to-live, to which life therefore must appear as the highest good, however embittered, of non-existence. To the hope of immortality of the soul there is always added that of a "better world"; an indication that the present world is not worth much. Notwithstanding all this, the question of our state after death has certainly been discussed verbally and in books ten thousand times more often than that of our state before birth. Theoretically, however, the one is a problem just as near at hand and just as legitimate as the other; moreover, he who answered the one would likewise be fully enlightened about the other. We have fine declamations about how shocking it would be to think that the mind of man, which embraces the world and has so many excellent ideas, should sink with him into the grave; but we hear nothing about this mind having allowed a whole infinity of time to elapse before it arose with these its qualities, and how for just as long a time the world had to manage without it. Yet to knowledge uncorrupted by the will no question presents itself more naturally than this, namely: An infinite time has run its course before my birth; what was I throughout all that time? Metaphysically, the answer might perhaps be: "I was always I; that is, all who throughout that time said I, were just I." But let us turn away from this to our present entirely empirical point of view, and assume that I did not exist at all. But I can then console myself for the infinite time after my death when I shall not exist, with the infinite time when I did not as yet exist, as a quite customary and really very comfortable state. For the infinity "after life" without me cannot be any more fearful than the infinity "before life" without me, since the two are not distinguished by anything except by the intervention of an ephemeral life-dream. All proofs of continued existence after death may also be applied just as well *in partem ante*, where they then demonstrate existence before life, in assuming which the Hindus and Buddhists therefore show themselves to be very consistent. Only Kant's ideality of time solves all these riddles; but we are not discussing this at the moment. But this much follows from what has been said, namely that to mourn for the time when we shall no longer exist is just as absurd as it would be to mourn for the time when we did not as yet exist; for it is all the same whether the time our existence does not fill is related to that which it does fill as future or as past.

But quite apart even from these considerations of time, it is in and by itself absurd to regard non-existence as an evil; for every evil, like every good, presupposes existence, indeed even consciousness. But this ceases with life, as well as in sleep and in a fainting fit; therefore the absence of consciousness is well known and familiar to us as a state containing no evil at all; in any case, its occurrence is a matter of a moment. Epicurus considered death from this point of view, and therefore said quite rightly: *ὁ θάνατος μηδὲν πρὸς ἡμᾶς* (Death does not concern us), with the explanation that when we are, death is not, and when death is, we are not (Diogenes Laërtius, x, 27). To have lost what cannot be missed is obviously no evil; therefore we ought to be just as little disturbed by the fact that we shall not exist as by the fact that we did not exist. Accordingly, from the standpoint of knowledge, there appears to be absolutely no ground for fearing death; but consciousness consists in knowing, and thus for consciousness death is no evil. Moreover, it is not really this *knowing* part of our *ego* that fears death, but *fuga mortis* comes simply and solely from the blind *will*, with which every living thing is filled. But, as already mentioned, this *fuga mortis* is essential to it, just because it is the will-to-live, whose whole inner nature consists in a craving for life and existence. Knowledge is not originally inherent in it, but appears only in consequence of the will's objectification in animal individuals. Now if by means of knowledge the will beholds death as the end of the phenomenon with which it has identified itself, and to which it therefore sees itself limited, its whole nature struggles against this with all its might. We shall investigate later on whether it really has anything to fear from death, and shall then remember the real source of the fear of death which is indicated here with a proper distinction between the willing and knowing part of our true nature.

According to this, what makes death so terrible for us is not so much the end of life—for this cannot seem to anyone specially worthy of regret—as the destruction of the organism, really because this organism is the will itself manifested as body. But actually, we feel this destruction only in the evils of illness or of old age; on the other hand, for the *subject*, death itself consists merely in the moment when consciousness vanishes, since the activity of the brain ceases. The extension of the stoppage to all the other parts of the organism which follows this is really already an event after death. Therefore, in a subjective respect, death concerns only consciousness. Now from going to sleep everyone can, to some extent, judge what the vanishing of consciousness may be; and whoever has had a real fainting fit knows it even better. The transition here is not so gradual, nor is it brought about by dreams; but first of all, while we are still fully conscious, the power of sight disappears, and then immediately supervenes the deepest unconsciousness. As far as the accompanying sensation goes, it is anything but unpleasant; and undoubtedly just as sleep is the brother of death, so is the fainting fit its twin-brother. Violent death also cannot be painful, for, as a rule, even severe wounds are not felt at all till some time afterwards, and are often noticed only from their external symptoms. If they are rapidly fatal, consciousness will vanish before this discovery; if they result in death later, it is the same as with other illnesses. All who have lost consciousness in water, through charcoal fumes, or through hanging, also state, as is well known, that it happened without pain. And finally, even death through natural causes proper, death through old age, euthanasia, is a gradual vanishing and passing out of existence in an imperceptible manner. In old age, passions and desires, together with the susceptibility to their objects, are gradually extinguished; the emotions no longer find any excitement, for the power to make representations or mental pictures becomes weaker and weaker, and its images feebler. The impressions no longer stick to us, but pass away without a trace; the days roll by faster and faster; events lose their significance; everything grows pale. The old man, stricken in years, totters about or rests in a corner, now only a shadow, a ghost, of his former self. What still remains there for death to destroy? One day a slumber is his last, and his dreams are ——. They are the dreams that Hamlet asks about in the famous monologue. I believe that we dream them just now.

I have still to observe that, although the maintenance of the life-process has a metaphysical basis, it does not take place without resistance, and hence without effort. It is this to which the organism yields every evening, for which reason it then suspends the brain-function, and diminishes certain secretions, respiration, pulse, and the development of heat. From this it may be concluded that the entire cessation of the life-process must be a wonderful relief for its driving force. Perhaps this is partly responsible for the expression of sweet contentment on the faces of most of the dead. In general, the moment of dying may be similar to that of waking from a heavy nightmare.

So far, the result for us is that death cannot really be an evil, however much it is feared, but that it often appears even as a good thing, as something desired, as a friend. All who have encountered insuperable obstacles to their existence or to their efforts, who suffer from incurable disease or from inconsolable grief, have the return into the womb of nature as the last resource that is often open to them as a matter of course. Like everything else, they emerged from this womb for a short time, enticed by the hope of more favourable conditions of existence than those that have fallen to their lot, and from this the same path always remains open to them. That return is the "Surrender of property" of the living. Yet even here it is entered into only after a physical or moral conflict, so hard does everyone struggle against returning to the place from which he came forth so readily and willingly to an existence that has so many sorrows and so few joys to offer. To Yama, the god of death, the Hindus give two faces, one very fearful and terrible, one very cheerful and benevolent. This is already explained in part from the observations we have just made.

From the empirical standpoint, at which we are still placed, the following consideration is one which presents itself automatically, and therefore merits being defined accurately by elucidation, and thus kept within its limits. The sight of a corpse shows me that sensibility, irritability, blood circulation, reproduction, and so on in it have ceased. From this I conclude with certainty that that which previously actuated them, which was nevertheless something always unknown to me, now actuates them no longer, and so has departed from them. But if I now wished to add that this must have been just what I have known only as consciousness, and consequently as intelligence (soul), this would be a conclusion not merely unjustified, but obviously false. For consciousness has always shown itself to me not as the cause, but as a product and result of organic life, since it rose and sank in consequence thereof at the different periods of life, in health and sickness, in sleep, in a faint, in awaking, and so on. Thus it always appeared as the effect, never as a cause, of organic life, always showed itself as something arising and passing away and again arising, so long as the conditions for this still exist, but not apart from them. Indeed, I may also have seen that the complete derangement of consciousness, madness, far from dragging down with it and depressing the other forces, or even endangering life, greatly enhances these, especially irritability or muscular force, and lengthens rather than shortens life, if there are no other competing causes. Then I knew individuality as a quality or attribute of everything organic, and when this was a self-conscious organism, of consciousness also. But there exists no occasion for concluding now that individuality is inherent in that vanished principle which imparts life and is wholly unknown to me; the less so, as everywhere in nature I see each particular phenomenon to be the work of a universal force active in thousands of similar phenomena. But on the other hand there is just as little occasion for concluding that, because organized life has here ceased, the force that actuated it hitherto has also become nothing; just as little as there is to infer from the stopping of the spinning-wheel the death of the spinner. If, by finding its centre of gravity again, a pendulum finally comes to rest, and thus its individual apparent life has ceased, no one will suppose that gravitation is annihilated, but everyone sees that now as always it is active in innumerable phenomena. Of course, it might be objected to this comparison that even in the pendulum gravitation has not ceased to be active, but has merely given up manifesting its activity visibly. He who insists on this may think, instead, of an electrical body in which, after its discharge, electricity has really ceased to be active. I wished only to show by this that we directly attribute an eternity and ubiquity even to the lowest forces of nature; and the transitoriness of their fleeting phenomenon does not for a moment confuse us with regard thereto. So much less, therefore, should it occur to us to regard the cessation of life as the annihilation of the living principle, and thus death as the entire destruction of man. Because the strong arm that three thousand years ago bent the bow of Ulysses no longer exists, no reflective and well-regulated understanding will look upon the force that acted so energetically in it as entirely annihilated. Therefore, on further reflection, it will not be assumed that the force that bends the bow today, first began to exist with that arm. Much nearer to us is the idea that the force that formerly actuated a life now vanished is the same force that is active in the life now flourishing; indeed this thought is almost inevitable. However, we certainly know that, as was explained in the second book, only that is perishable which is involved in the causal chain; but merely the states and forms are so involved. Untouched, however, by the change of these, which is produced by causes, there remain matter on the one hand, and the natural forces on the other; for both are the presupposition of all those changes. But the principle that gives us life must first be conceived at any rate as a force of nature, until a profounder investigation may perhaps let us know what it is in itself. Thus, taken already as a force of nature, vital force remains entirely untouched by the change of forms and states, which the bond of cause and effect introduces and carries off again, and which alone are subject to arising and passing away, just as these processes lie before us in experience. To this extent, therefore, the imperishableness of our true inner nature could already be certainly demonstrated. But this, of course, will not satisfy the claims usually made on proofs of our continued existence after death, nor will it afford the consolation expected from such proofs. Yet it is always something, and whoever fears death as his absolute annihilation cannot afford to disdain the perfect certainty that the innermost principle of his life remains untouched by it. In fact, we might advance the paradox that that second thing which, like the forces of nature, remains untouched by the continuous change of states under the guidance of causality, i.e., matter, also assures us through its absolute permanence of an indestructibility; and by virtue of this, he who might be incapable of grasping any other could yet be confident of a certain imperishability. But it will be asked: "How is the permanence of mere dust, of crude matter, to be regarded as a continuance of our true inner nature?" Oh! do you know this dust then? Do you know what it is and what it can do? Learn to know it before you despite it. This matter, now lying there as dust and ashes, will soon form into crystals when dissolved in water; it will shine as metal; it will then emit electric sparks. By means of its galvanic tension it will manifest a force which, decomposing the strongest and firmest combinations, reduces earths to metals. It will, indeed of its own accord, form itself into plant and animal; and from its mysterious womb it will develop that life, about the loss of which you in your narrowness of mind are so nervous and anxious. Is it, then, so absolutely and entirely nothing to continue to exist as such matter? Indeed, I seriously assert that even this permanence of matter affords evidence of the indestructibility of our true inner being, although only as in an image and simile, or rather only as in a shadowy outline. To see this, we need only recall the discussion on matter given in chapter 24, the conclusion of which was that mere formless matter—this basis of the world of experience, never perceived by itself alone, but assumed as always permanent—is the immediate reflection, the visibility in general, of the thing-in-itself, that is, of the will. Therefore, what absolutely pertains to the will in itself holds good of matter under the conditions of experience, and it reproduces the true eternity of the will under the image of temporal imperishability. Because, as we have already said, nature does not lie, no view which has sprung from a purely objective comprehension of her, and has been logically thought out, can be absolutely and entirely false; in the worst case it is only very one-sided and imperfect. But such a view is unquestionably consistent materialism, for instance that of Epicurus, just as is the absolute idealism opposed to it, like that of Berkeley, and generally every fundamental view of philosophy which has come from a correct *aperçu* and has been honestly worked out. Only they are all extremely one-sided interpretations, and therefore, in spite of their contrasts, are *simultaneously* true, each from a definite point of view. But as soon as we rise above this point, they appear to be true only relatively and conditionally. The highest standpoint alone, from which we survey them all and recognize them in their merely relative truth, and also beyond this in their falseness, can be that of absolute truth, in so far as such a truth is in general attainable. Accordingly, as was shown above, we see even in the really very crude, and therefore very old, fundamental view of materialism the indestructibility of our true inner being-in-itself still represented as by a mere shadow of it, namely through the imperishability of matter; just as in the already higher naturalism of an absolute physics we see it represented by the ubiquity and eternity of natural forces, among which vital force is at least to be reckoned. Hence even these crude fundamental views contain the assertion that the living being does not suffer any absolute annihilation through death, but continues to exist in and with the whole of nature.

The considerations which have brought us to this point, and with which the further discussions are connected, started from the remarkable fear of death which affects all living beings. But now we wish to alter the point of view, and to consider how, in contrast to individual beings, the *whole* of nature behaves with regard to death; yet here we still remain always on the ground and soil of the empirical.

We know, of course, of no higher gamble than that for life and death. We watch with the utmost attention, interest, and fear every decision concerning them; for in our view all in all is at stake. On the other hand, *nature*, which never lies, but is always frank and sincere, speaks quite differently on this theme, as Krishna does in the *Bhagavadgita*. Her statement is that the life or death of the individual is of absolutely no consequence. She expresses this by abandoning the life of every animal, and even of man, to the most insignificant accidents without coming to the rescue. Consider the insect on your path; a slight unconscious turning of your foot is decisive as to its life or death. Look at the wood-snail that has no means of flight, of defence, of practising deception, of concealment, a ready prey to all. Look at the fish carelessly playing in the still open net; at the frog prevented by its laziness from the flight that could save it; at the bird unaware of the falcon soaring above it; at the sheep eyed and examined from the thicket by the wolf. Endowed with little caution, all these go about guilelessly among the dangers which at every moment threaten their existence. Now, since nature abandons without reserve her organisms constructed with such inexpressible skill, not only to the predatory instinct of the stronger, but also to the blindest chance, the whim of every fool, and the mischievousness of every child, she expresses that the annihilation of these individuals is a matter of indifference to her, does her no harm, is of no significance at all, and that in these cases the effect is of no more consequence than is the cause. Nature states this very clearly, and she never lies; only she does not comment on her utterances, but rather expresses them in the laconic style of the oracle. Now if the universal mother carelessly sends forth her children without protection to a thousand threatening dangers, this can be only because she knows that, when they fall, they fall back into her womb, where they are safe and secure; therefore their fall is only a jest. With man she does not act otherwise than she does with the animals; hence her declaration extends also to him; the life or death of the individual is a matter of indifference to her. Consequently, they should be, in a certain sense, a matter of indifference to us; for in fact, we ourselves are nature. If only we saw deeply enough, we should certainly agree with nature, and regard life or death as indifferently as does she. Meanwhile, by means of reflection, we must attribute nature's careless and indifferent attitude concerning the life of individuals to the fact that the destruction of such a phenomenon does not in the least disturb its true and real inner being.

As we have just been considering, not only are life and death dependent on the most trifling accidents, but the existence of organic beings generally is also ephemeral; animal and plant arise today and tomorrow pass away; birth and death follow in quick succession, whereas to inorganic things, standing so very much lower, an incomparably longer duration is assured, but an infinitely long one only to absolutely formless matter, to which we attribute this even *a priori*. Now if we ponder over all this, I think the merely empirical, but objective and unprejudiced, comprehension of such an order of things must be followed as a matter of course by the thought that this order is only a superficial phenomenon, that such a constant arising and passing away cannot in any way touch the root of things, but can be only relative, indeed only apparent. The true inner being of everything, which, moreover, evades our glance everywhere and is thoroughly mysterious, is not affected by that arising and passing away, but rather continues to exist undisturbed thereby. Of course, we can neither perceive nor comprehend the way in which this happens, and must therefore think of it only generally as a kind of "Conjuring trick" that took place here. For whereas the most imperfect thing, the lowest, the inorganic, continues to exist unassailed, it is precisely the most perfect beings, namely living things with their infinitely complicated and inconceivably ingenious organizations, which were supposed always to arise afresh from the very bottom, and after a short span of time to become absolutely nothing, in order to make room once more for new ones like them coming into existence out of nothing. This is something so obviously absurd that it can never be the true order of things, but rather a mere veil concealing such an order, or more correctly a phenomenon conditioned by the constitution of our intellect. In fact, the entire existence and non-existence of these individual beings, in reference to which life and death are opposites, can be only relative. Hence the language of nature, in which it is given to us as something absolute, cannot be the true and ultimate expression of the quality and constitution of things and of the order of the world, but really only a "Provincial dialect," in other words, something merely relatively true, something self-styled, to be understood *cum grano salis*, or properly speaking, something conditioned by our intellect. I say that an immediate, intuitive conviction of the kind I have here tried to describe in words will force itself on everyone, of course only on everyone whose mind is not of the utterly common species. Such common minds are capable of knowing absolutely only the particular thing, simply and solely as such, and are strictly limited to knowledge of individuals, after the manner of the animal intellect. On the other hand, whoever, through an ability of an only somewhat higher power, even just begins to see in individual beings their universal, their Ideas, will also to a certain extent participate in that conviction, a conviction indeed that is immediate and therefore certain. Indeed, it is also only small, narrow minds that quite seriously fear death as their annihilation; those who are specially favoured with decided capacity are entirely remote from such terrors. Plato rightly founded the whole of philosophy on knowledge of the doctrine of Ideas, in other words, on the perception of the universal in the particular. But the conviction here described and arising directly out of the apprehension of nature must have been extremely lively in those sublime authors of the *Upanishads* of the *Vedas*, who can scarcely be conceived as mere human beings. For this conviction speaks to us so forcibly from an immense number of their utterances that we must ascribe this immediate illumination of their mind to the fact that, standing nearer to the origin of our race as regards time, these sages apprehended the inner essence of things more clearly and profoundly than the already enfeebled race, "As mortals now are," is capable of doing. But, of course, their comprehension was also assisted by the natural world of India, which is endowed with life in quite a different degree from that in which our northern world is. Thorough reflection, however, as carried through by Kant's great mind, also leads to just the same result by a different path; for it teaches us that our intellect, in which that rapidly changing phenomenal world exhibits itself, does not comprehend the true, ultimate essence of things, but merely its appearance or phenomenon; and indeed, as I add, because originally such an intellect is destined only to present motives to our will, in other words, to be serviceable to it in the pursuit of its paltry aims.

But let us continue still farther our objective and unprejudiced consideration of nature. If I kill an animal, be it a dog, a bird, a frog, or even only an insect, it is really inconceivable that this being, or rather the primary and original force by virtue of which such a marvellous phenomenon displayed itself only a moment before in its full energy and love of life, could through my wicked or thoughtless act have become nothing. Again, on the other hand, the millions of animals of every kind which come into existence at every moment in endless variety, full of force and drive, can never have been absolutely nothing before the act of their generation, and can never have arrived from nothing to an absolute beginning. If in this way I see one of these creatures withdraw from my sight without my ever knowing where it goes to, and another appear without my ever knowing where it comes from; moreover, if both still have the same form, the same inner nature, the same character, but not the same matter, which they nevertheless continue to throw off and renew during their existence; then of course the assumption that what vanishes and what appears in its place are one and the same thing, which has experienced only a slight change, a renewal of the form of its existence, and consequently that death is for the species what sleep is for the individual—this assumption, I say, is so close at hand, that it is impossible for it not to occur to us, unless our minds, perverted in early youth by the impression of false fundamental views, hurry it out of the way, even from afar, with superstitious fear. But the opposite assumption that an animal's birth is an arising out of nothing, and accordingly that its death is an absolute annihilation, and this with the further addition that man has also come into existence out of nothing, yet has an individual and endless future existence, and that indeed with consciousness, whereas the dog, the ape, and the elephant are annihilated by death—is really something against which the sound mind must revolt, and must declare to be absurd. If, as is often enough repeated, the comparison of a system's result with the utterances of common sense is supposed to be a touchstone of its truth, I wish that the adherents of that fundamental view, handed down by Descartes to the pre-Kantian eclectics, and indeed still prevalent even now among the great majority of cultured people in Europe, would once apply this touchstone here.

The genuine symbol of nature is universally and everywhere the circle, because it is the schema or form of recurrence; in fact, this is the most general form in nature. She carries it through in everything from the course of the constellations down to the death and birth of organic beings. In this way alone, in the restless stream of time and its content, a continued existence, i.e., a nature, becomes possible.

In autumn we observe the tiny world of insects, and see how one prepares its bed, in order to sleep the long, benumbing winter-sleep; another spins a cocoon, in order to hibernate as a chrysalis, and to awake in spring rejuvenated and perfected; finally, how most of them, intending to rest in the arms of death, carefully arrange a suitable place for depositing their eggs, in order one day to come forth from these renewed. This is nature's great doctrine of immortality, which tries to make it clear to us that there is no radical difference between sleep and death, but that the one endangers existence just as little as the other. The care with which the insect prepares a cell, or hole, or nest, deposits therein its egg, together with food for the larva that will emerge from it in the following spring, and then calmly dies, is just like the care with which a person in the evening lays out his clothes and his breakfast ready for the following morning, and then calmly goes to bed; and at bottom it could not take place at all, unless the insect that dies in autumn were in itself and according to its true essence just as identical with the insect hatched in spring as the person who lies down to sleep is with the one who gets up.

After these considerations, we now return to ourselves and our species; we then cast our glance forward far into the future, and try to picture to ourselves future generations with the millions of their individuals in the strange form of their customs and aspirations. But then we interpose with the question: Whence will all these come? Where are they now? Where is the abundant womb of that nothing which is pregnant with worlds, and which still conceals them, the coming generations? Would not the smiling and true answer to this be: Where else could they be but there where alone the real always was and will be, namely in the present and its content?—hence with you, the deluded questioner, who in this mistaking of his own true nature is like the leaf on the tree. Fading in the autumn and about to fall, this leaf grieves over its own extinction, and will not be consoled by looking forward to the fresh green which will clothe the tree in spring, but says as a lament: "I am not these! These are quite different leaves!" Oh, foolish leaf! Whither do you want to go? And whence are the others supposed to come? Where is the nothing, the abyss of which you fear? Know your own inner being, precisely that which is so filled with the thirst for existence; recognize it once more in the inner, mysterious, sprouting force of the tree. This force is always *one* and the same in all the generations of leaves, and it remains untouched by arising and passing away. And now

> "As the leaves on the tree, so are the generations of human beings." [*Iliad*, vi, 146.]

Whether the fly now buzzing round me goes to sleep in the evening and buzzes again the following morning, or whether it dies in the evening and in spring another fly buzzes which has emerged from its egg, this in itself is the same thing. But then the knowledge that presents these as two fundamentally different things is not unconditioned, but relative, a knowledge of the phenomenon, not of the thing-in-itself. In the morning the fly exists again; it also exists again in the spring. For the fly what distinguishes the winter from the night? In Burdach's *Physiologie,* Vol. I, § 275, we read: "Up till ten o'clock in the morning no *Cercaria ephemera* (one of the infusoria) is yet to be seen (in the infusion), and at twelve the whole water swarms with them. In the evening they die, and the next morning new ones come into existence again. It was thus observed for six days in succession by Nitzsch."

Thus everything lingers only for a moment, and hurries on to death. The plant and the insect die at the end of the summer, the animal and man after a few years; death reaps unweariedly. But despite all this, in fact as if this were not the case at all, everything is always there and in its place, just as if everything were imperishable. The plant always flourishes and blooms, the insect hums, animal and man are there in evergreen youth, and every summer we again have before us the cherries that have already been a thousand times enjoyed. Nations also exist as immortal individuals, though sometimes they change their names. Even their actions, what they do and suffer, are always the same, though history always pretends to relate something different; for it is like the kaleidoscope, that shows us a new configuration at every turn, whereas really we always have the same thing before our eyes. Therefore, what forces itself on us more irresistibly than the thought that that arising and passing away do not concern the real essence of things, but that this remains untouched by them, hence is imperishable, consequently that each and every thing that *wills* to exist actually does exist continuously and without end? Accordingly, at every given point of time all species of animals, from the gnat to the elephant, exist together complete. They have already renewed themselves many thousands of times, and withal have remained the same. They know nothing of others like them who have lived before them, or who will live after them; it is the species that always lives, and the individuals cheerfully exist in the consciousness of the imperishability of the species and their identity with it. The will-to-live manifests itself in an endless present, because this is the form of the life of the species, which therefore does not grow old, but remains always young. Death is for the species what sleep is for the individual, or winking for the eye; when the Indian gods appear in human form, they are recognized by their not winking. Just as at nightfall the world vanishes, yet does not for a moment cease to exist, so man and animal apparently pass away through death, yet their true inner being continues to exist just as undisturbed. Let us now picture to ourselves that alternation of birth and death in infinitely rapid vibrations, and we have before us the persistent and enduring objectification of the will, the permanent Ideas of beings, standing firm like the rainbow on the waterfall. This is temporal immortality. In consequence of this, in spite of thousands of years of death and decay, there is still nothing lost, no atom of matter, still less anything of the inner being exhibiting itself as nature. Accordingly we can at any moment cheerfully exclaim: "In spite of time, death, and decay, we are still all together!"

Perhaps an exception would have to be made of the man who should once have said from the bottom of his heart with regard to this game: "I no longer like it." But this is not yet the place to speak of that.

Attention, however, must indeed be drawn to the fact that the pangs of birth and the bitterness of death are the two constant conditions under which the will-to-live maintains itself in its objectification, in other words, our being-in-itself, untouched by the course of time and by the disappearance of generations, exists in an everlasting present, and enjoys the fruit of the affirmation of the will-to-live. This is analogous to our being able to remain awake during the day only on condition that we sleep every night; indeed, this is the commentary furnished by nature for an understanding of that difficult passage. For the suspension of the animal functions is sleep; that of the organic functions is death.

The substratum or filling out, the pleroma or material of the *present*, is really the same through all time. The impossibility of directly recognizing this identity is just *time*, a form and limitation of our intellect. The fact that by virtue of it, for example, the future event does not as yet exist, rests on a delusion of which we become aware when the event has come to pass. The essential form of our intellect produces such a delusion, and this is explained and justified from the fact that the intellect has come forth from the hands of nature by no means for the purpose of comprehending the inner being of things, but merely for the purpose of comprehending motives, and hence to serve an individual and temporal phenomenon of will. . . .

The very remarkable passage in Diderot's *Jacques le Fataliste,* which in its place is surprising, deserves to be mentioned: "An immense castle over the front entrance of which one read: 'I belong to no one, and I belong to all the world; you were in it before you entered it, and you will still be in it when you have gone out of it.' "

Of course in that sense in which he arises out of nothing when he is begotten, man becomes nothing through death. But really to become so thoroughly acquainted with this nothing would be very interesting, for it requires only moderate discernment to see that this empirical nothing is by no means an absolute nothing, in other words, such as would be nothing in every sense. We are already led to this insight by the observation that all the features and characteristics of the parents are found once again in their children, and have thus surmounted death.

There is on greater contrast than that between ceaseless, irresistible flight of time carrying its whole content away with it, and the rigid immobility of what is actually existing, which is at all times one and the same; and if, from this point of view, we fix our really objective glace on the immediate events of life, the Eternal Now becomes clear and visible to us in the center of the wheel of time. To the eye of a being who lived an incomparably longer life and took in at a single glance the human race in its whole duration, the constant alternation of birth and death would not occur to it at all to see in it a constantly new coming out of nothing and passing into nothing, but, just as to our glance the rapidly turning spark appears as a continuous circle, the rapidly vibrating spring as a permanent triangle, the vibrating cord as a spindle, so to its glance the species would appear as that which is and remains, birth and death as vibrations.

We shall have false notions about the indestructibility of our true nature through death, so long as we do not make up our minds to study it first of all in the animals, and claim for ourselves alone a class apart from them under the boastful name of immortality. But it is this presumption alone and the narrowness of view from which it proceeds, on account of which most people struggle so obstinately against recognizing the obvious truth that, essentially and in the main, we are the same as the animals; in fact that such people recoil at every hint of our relationship with these. Yet it is this denial of the truth which, more than anything else, bars to them the way to real knowledge of the indestructibility of our true nature. For if we seek anything on a wrong path, we have in so doing forsaken the right; and on the wrong path we shall never attain to anything in the end but belated disillusionment. Therefore, pursue truth straight away, not according to preconceived freaks and fancies, but guided by the hand of nature! First of all learn to recognize, when looking at every young animal, the never-aging existence of the species, which, as a reflection of its own eternal youth, bestows on every new individual a temporal youth, and lets it step forth as new, as fresh, as if the world were of today. Ask yourself honestly whether the swallow of this year's spring is an entirely different one from the swallow of the first spring, and whether actually between the two the miracle of creation out of nothing has been renewed a million times, in order to work just as often into the hands of absolute annihilation. I know quite well that anyone would regard me as mad if I seriously assured him that the cat, playing just now in the yard, is still the same one that did the same jumps and tricks there three hundred years ago; but I also know that it is much more absurd to believe that the cat of today is through and through and fundamentally an entirely different one from that cat of three hundred years ago. We need only become sincerely and seriously engrossed in the contemplation of one of these higher vertebrates, in order to become distinctly conscious that this unfathomable inner being, taken as a whole as it exists, cannot possibly become nothing, and yet, on the other hand, we know its transitoriness. This rests on the fact that in this animal the eternity of its Idea (species) is distinctly marked in the finiteness of the individual. For in a certain sense it is of course true that in the individual we always have before us a different being, namely in the sense resting on the principle of sufficient reason, under which are also included time and space; these constitute the *principium individuationis.* But in another it is not true, namely in the sense in which reality belongs only to the permanent forms of things, to the Ideas, and which was so clearly evident to Plato that it became his fundamental thought, the centre of his philosophy; the comprehension of it became his criterion for the ability to philosophize generally.

Just as the spraying drops of the roaring waterfall change with lightning rapidity, while the rainbow, of which they are the supporter, remains immovably at rest, quite untouched by that restless change, so every Idea, i.e., every *species* of living beings remains entirely untouched by the constant change of its individuals. But it is the *Idea* or the species in which the will-to-live is really rooted and manifests itself; therefore the will is really concerned only in the continuance of the species. For example, the lions that are born and that die are like the drops of the waterfall; but *leonitas*, the Idea or form or shape of the lion, is like the unshaken and unmoved rainbow on the waterfall. Plato therefore attributed real and true being only to the *Ideas*, i.e., to the species; but to the individuals he attributed only a restless arising and passing away. From the deepest consciousness of his imperishable nature there also spring the confidence and serenity with which every animal and even every human individual move along light-heartedly amid a host of chances and hazards that may annihilate them at any moment, and moreover move straight on to death. Out of his eyes, however, there glances the peace of the species, which is unaffected and untouched by that destruction and extinction. Not even to man could this peace and calm be vouchsafed by uncertain and changing dogmas. As I have said, however, the sight of every animal teaches us that death is no obstacle to the kernel of life, the will in its manifestation. Yet what an unfathomable mystery lies in every animal! Look at the nearest one; look at your dog, and see how cheerfully and calmly he stands there! Many thousands of dogs have had to die before it was this dog's turn to live; but the death and extinction of those thousands have not affected the *Idea* of the dog. This Idea has not in the least been disturbed by all that dying. Therefore the dog stands there as fresh and endowed with original force as if this day were his first and none could be his last, and out of his eyes there shines the indestructible principle in him, the archaeus. Now what has died throughout those thousands of years? Not the dog; he stands there before us intact and unscratched; merely his shadow, his image or copy in our manner of knowing, which is bound to time. Yet how can we ever believe that that passes away which exists for ever and ever, and fills all time? The matter is, of course, explainable empirically, namely according as death destroyed the individuals, generation brought forth new ones. This empirical explanation, however, is only an apparent explanation; it puts one riddle in place of the other. Although a metaphysical understanding of the matter is not to be had so cheaply, it is nevertheless the only true and satisfactory one.

In his subjective method, Kant brought to light the great though negative truth that time cannot belong to the thing-in-itself, because it lies preformed in our apprehension. Now death is the temporal end of the temporal phenomenon; but as soon as we take away time, there is no longer any end at all, and the word has lost all meaning. But here, on the objective path, I am now trying to show the positive aspect of the matter, namely that the thing-in-itself remains untouched by time and by that which is possible only through time, that is, by arising and passing away, and that the phenomena in time could not have even that restless, fleeting existence that stands next to nothingness, unless there were in them a kernel of eternity. It is true that *eternity* is a concept having no perception as its basis; for this reason, it is also of merely negative content, and thus implies a timeless existence. *Time*, however, is a mere image of eternity, "Time is a copy or image of eternity," as Plotinus has it; and in just the same way, our temporal existence is the mere image of our true inner being. This must lie in eternity, just because time is only the form of our knowing; but by virtue of this form alone we know our own existence and that of all things as transitory, finite, and subject to annihilation.

In the second book I have explained that the adequate objectivity of the will as thing-in-itself is the (Platonic) *Idea* at each of its grades. Similarly in the third book I have shown that the Ideas of beings have as their correlative the pure subject of knowing, consequently that the knowledge of them appears only by way of exception and temporarily under specially favourable conditions. For individual knowledge, on the other hand, and hence in time, the *Idea* exhibits itself under the form of the *species*, and this is the Idea drawn apart by entering into time. The *species* is therefore the most immediate objectification of the thing-in-itself, i.e., of the will-to-live. Accordingly, the innermost being of every animal and of man also lies in the *species*; thus the will-to-live, which is so powerfully active, has its root in the species, not really in the individual. On the other hand, immediate consciousness if to be found only in the individual; therefore it imagines itself to be different from the species, and thus fears death. The will-to-live manifests itself in reference to the individual as hunger and fear of death; in reference to the species, as sexual impulse and passionate care for the offspring. In agreement with this, we find nature, as being free from that delusion of the individual, just as careful for the maintenance of the species as she is indifferent to the destruction of the individuals; for her the latter are always only means, the former the end. Therefore, a glaring contrast appears between her niggardliness in the equipment of individuals and her lavishness when the species is at stake. From *one* individual often a hundred thousand seeds or more are obtained annually, for example, from trees, fish, crabs, termites, and many others. In the case of her niggardliness, on the other hand, only barely enough in the way of strength and organs is given to each to enable it with ceaseless exertion to maintain a bare living. If, therefore, an animal is crippled or weakened, it must, as a rule, die of starvation. And where an occasional economy was possible, through the circumstance that a part could be dispensed with in an emergency, it has been withheld, even out of order. Hence, for example, many caterpillars are without eyes; the poor animals grope about in the dark from leaf to leaf, and in the absence of antennae they do this by moving three quarters of their body to and fro in the air, till they come across an object. In this way they often miss their food that is to be found close at hand. But this happens in consequence of the *lex parsimoniae naturae,* to the expression of which, "Nature does nothing in vain and creates nothing superfluous; . . . and she gives away nothing." The same tendency of nature shows itself also in the fact that the fitter an individual is for propagation by virtue of his age, the more powerfully does "The healing power of nature" manifest itself in him. His wounds, therefore, heal easily, and he easily recovers from illnesses. This diminishes with the power of procreation, and sinks low after this power is extinguished; for in the eyes of nature the individual has now become worthless.

Now if we cast a glance at the scale of beings together with the gradation of consciousness that accompanies them, from the polyp to man, we see this wonderful pyramid kept in ceaseless oscillation certainly by the constant death of the individuals, yet enduring in the species throughout the endlessness of time by means of the bond of generation. Now, whereas, as was explained above, the *objective*, the species, manifests itself as indestructible, the *subjective*, consisting merely in the self-consciousness of these beings, seems to be of the shortest duration, and to be incessantly destroyed, in order just as often to come forth again out of nothing in an incomprehensible way. But a man must really be very short-sighted to allow himself to be deceived by this appearance, and not to understand that, although the form of temporal permanence belongs only to the objective, the subjective—i.e., the *will*, living and appearing in everything, and with it the subject of *knowing* in which this exhibits itself—must be no less indestructible. For the permanence of the objective, or the external, can indeed be only the phenomenal appearance of the indestructibility of the subjective, or the internal, since the former cannot possess anything that it had not received in fee from the latter; it cannot be essentially and originally something objective, a phenomenon, and then secondarily and accidentally something subjective, a thing-in-itself, something conscious of itself. For obviously, the former as phenomenon or appearance presupposes something that appears, just as being-for-another presupposes being-for-self, and object presupposes subject; but not conversely, since everywhere the root of things must lie in that which they are by themselves, hence in the subjective, not in the objective, not in that which they are only for others, not in the consciousness of another. Accordingly we found in the first book that the correct starting-point for philosophy is essentially and necessarily the subjective, i.e., the idealistic, just as the opposite starting-point, proceeding from the objective, leads to materialism. Fundamentally, however, we are far more at one with the world than we usually think; its inner nature is our will, and its phenomenal appearance our representation. The difference between the continuance of the external world after his death and his own continuance after death would vanish for anyone who could bring this unity or identity of being to distinct consciousness; the two would present themselves to him as one and the same thing; in fact, he would laugh at the delusion that could separate them. For an understanding of the indestructibility of our true nature coincides with that of the identity of macrocosm and microcosm. Meanwhile we can elucidate what has here been said by a peculiar experiment that is to be carried out by means of the imagination, and might be called metaphysical. Let a person attempt to present vividly to his mind the time, not in any case very distant, when he will be dead. He then thinks himself away, and allows the world to go on existing; but soon, to his own astonishment, he will discover that nevertheless he still exists. For he imagined he made a mental representation of the world without himself; but the I or ego is in consciousness that which is immediate, by which the world is first brought about, and for which alone the world exists. This centre of all existence, this kernel of all reality, is to be abolished, and yet the world is to be allowed to go on existing; it is an idea that may, of course, be conceived in the abstract, but not realized. The endeavour to achieve this, the attempt to think the secondary without the primary, the conditioned without the condition, the supported without the supporter, fails every time, much in the same way as the attempt fails to conceive an equilateral right-angled triangle, or an arising and passing away of matter, and similar impossibilities. Instead of what was intended, the feeling here forces itself on us that the world is no less in us than we are in it, and that the source of all reality lies within ourselves. The result is really that the time when I shall not be will come objectively; but subjectively it can never come. Indeed, it might therefore be asked how far anyone in his heart actually believes in a thing that he cannot really conceive at all; or whether, since the deep consciousness of the indestructibility of our real inner nature is associated with that merely intellectual experiment that has, however, already been carried out more or less distinctly by everyone, whether, I say, our own death is not perhaps for us at bottom the most incredible thing in the world.

The deep conviction of the impossibility of our extermination by death, which, as the inevitable qualms of conscience at the approach of death also testify, everyone carries at the bottom of his heart, depends entirely on the consciousness of our original and eternal nature; therefore Spinoza expresses it thus: "We feel and experience that we are *eternal*." For a reasonable person can think of himself as imperishable only in so far as he thinks of himself as beginningless, as eternal, in fact as timeless. On the other hand, he who regards himself as having come out of nothing must also think that he becomes nothing again; for it is a monstrous idea that an infinity of time elapsed before he was, but that a second infinity has begun throughout which he will never cease to be. Actually the most solid ground for our imperishable nature is the old aphorism: "Nothing comes out of nothing, and nothing can again become nothing." Therefore, Theophrastus Parcelsus says very pertinently: "The soul in me has come from something, therefore it does not come to nothing; for it comes out of something." He states the true reason. But he who regards man's birth as his absolute beginning must regard death as his absolute end. For both are what they are in the same sense; consequently everyone can think of himself as *immortal* only in so far as he also thinks of himself as *unborn*, and in the same sense. What birth is, that also is death, according to its true nature and significance; it is the same line drawn in two directions. If the former is an actual arising out of nothing, the latter is also an actual annihilation. In truth, however, it is only by means of the *eternity* of our real inner nature that am imperishableness of it is conceivable; consequently such an imperishableness is not temporal. The assumption that man is created out of nothing necessarily leads to the assumption that death is his absolute end. In this respect, therefore, the Old Testament is quite consistent; for no doctrine of immortality is appropriate to a creation out of nothing. New Testament Christianity has such a doctrine, because it is Indian in spirit, and therefore, more than probably, Indian in origin, although only indirectly, through Egypt. Such a doctrine, however, is as little suited to the Jewish stem on which that Indian wisdom had to be grafted in the Holy Land as the freedom of the will is to the will's being created, or as

> "If a painter wanted to join a human head to the neck of a horse." [Horace, *Ars poetica,* 1.]

It is always bad if we are not allowed to be thoroughly original and to carve out of the whole wood. Brahmanism and Buddhism, on the other hand, quite consistently with a continued existence after death, have an existence before birth, and the purpose of this life is to atone for the guilt of that previous existence. The following passage from Colebrooke's *History of Indian Philosophy* in the *Transactions of the Asiatic London Society,* Vol. I, p. 577, shows also how clearly conscious they are of the necessary consistency in this: "Against the system of the Bhagavatas, which is but partially heretical, the objection upon which the chief stress is laid by Vyasa is, that the soul would not be eternal, if it were a production, and consequently had a beginning." Further, in Upham's *Doctrine of Buddhism,* p. 110, it is said: "The lot in hell of impious persons call'd Deitty is the most severe: these are they who, discrediting the evidence of Buddha, adhere to the heretical doctrine, that all living beings had their beginning in the mother's womb, and will have their end in death."

He who conceives his existence as merely accidental, must certainly be afraid of losing it through death. On the other hand he who sees, even only in a general way, that his existence rests on some original necessity, will not believe that this necessity, which has produced so wonderful a thing, is limited to such a brief span of time, but that it is active at all times. But whoever reflects that up till now, when he exists, an infinite time, and thus an infinity of changes, has run its course, but yet notwithstanding this he exists, will recognize his existence as a necessary one. Therefore the entire possibility of all states and conditions has exhausted itself already without being able to eliminate his existence. *If ever he could not be, he would already not be now.* For the infinity of the time that has already elapsed, with the exhausted possibility of its events in it, guarantees that what *exists necessarily exists.* Consequently, everyone has to conceive himself as a necessary being, in other words, as a being whose existence would follow from its true and exhaustive definition, if only we had this. Actually in this train of thought is to be found the only immanent proof of the imperishableness of our real inner nature, that is to say, the only proof that keeps within the sphere of empirical data. Existence must be inherent in this inner nature, since it shows itself to be independent of all states or conditions that can possibly be brought about through the causal chain; for these states have already done what they could, and yet our existence has remained just as unshaken thereby, as the ray of light is by the hurricane that it cuts through. If from its own resources time could bring us to a happy state, we should already have been there long ago; for an infinite time lies behind us. But likewise, if time could lead us to destruction, we should already long ago have ceased to exist. It follows from the fact that we now exist, if the matter is well considered, that we are bound to exist at all times. For we ourselves are the inner nature that time has taken up into itself, in order to fill up its void; therefore this inner nature fills the *whole* of time, present, past, and future, in the same way; and it is just as impossible for us to fall out of existence as it is for us to fall out of space. If we carefully consider this, it is inconceivable that what once exists in all the force of reality could ever become nothing, and then not exist throughout an infinite time. From this have arisen the Christian doctrine of the restoration of all things, the Hindu doctrine of the constantly renewed creation of the world by Brahma, together with similar dogmas of the Greek philosophers. The great mystery of our existence and non-existence, to explain which these and all kindred dogmas were devised, ultimately rests on the fact that the same thing that objectively constitutes an infinite course of time is subjectively a point, an indivisible, ever-present present-moment; but who comprehends it? It has been most clearly expounded by Kant in his immortal doctrine of the ideality of time and of the sole reality of the thing-in-itself. For it follows from this that what is really essential in things, in man, in the world, lies permanently and enduringly in the *Nunc stans*, firm and immovable; and that the change of phenomena and of events is a mere consequence of our apprehension of it by means of our perception-form of time. Accordingly, instead of saying to men: "Ye have arisen through birth, but are immortal," one should say: "Ye are not nothing," and teach them to understand this in the sense of the saying attributed to Hermes Trismegistus: "For that which is must always be." Yet if this does not succeed, but the anxious heart breaks out into its old lament: "I see all beings arise out of nothing through birth, and again after a brief term return to nothing; even my existence, now in the present, will soon lie in the remote past, and I shall be nothing!" then the right answer is: "Do you not exist? Do you not possess the precious present, to which you children of time all aspire so eagerly, actually at this moment? And do you understand how you have attained to it? Do you know the paths which have led you to it, that you could see them barred to you by death? An existence of yourself after the destruction of your body is not possibly conceivable to you; but can it be more inconceivable to you than are your present existence and the way you have attained to it? Why should you doubt that the secret paths that stood open to you up to this present, will not also stand open to you to every future present?"

Therefore, if considerations of this kind are certainly calculated to awaken the conviction that there is something in us that death cannot destroy, this nevertheless happens only by our being raised to a point of view from which birth is not the beginning of our existence. It follows from this, however, that what is proved to be indestructible through death is not really the individual. Moreover, having arisen through generation and carrying within himself the qualities of the father and mother, this individual exhibits himself as a mere difference of the species, and as such can be only finite. Accordingly, just as the individual has no recollection of his existence before his birth, so can he have no recollection of his present existence after death. Everyone, however, places his I or ego in *consciousness*; therefore this seems to him to be tied to individuality. Moreover, with individuality there disappears all that which is peculiar to him, as to this, and which distinguishes him from others. Therefore his continued existence without individuality becomes for him indistinguishable from the continuance of all other beings, and he sees his I or ego become submerged. Now he who thus links his existence to the identity of *consciousness*, and therefore desires for this an endless existence after death, should bear in mind that in any case he can attain to this only at the price of just as endless a past before birth. For as he has no recollection of an existence before birth, and so his consciousness begins with birth, he must look upon his birth as an arising of his existence out of nothing. But then he purchases the endless time of his existence after death for just as long a time before birth; in this way the account is balanced without any profit to him. On the other hand, if the existence left untouched by death is different from that of individual consciousness, then it must be independent of birth just as it is of death. Accordingly, with reference to it, it must be equally true to say "I shall always be" and "I have always been," which then gives us two infinities for one. However, the greatest equivocation really lies in the word "I," as will be seen at once by anyone who calls to mind the contents of our second book and the separation there carried out of the willing part of our true inner nature from the knowing part. According as I understand this word, I can say: "Death is my entire end"; or else: "This my personal phenomenal appearance is just as infinitely small a part of my true inner nature as I am of the world." But the I or ego is the dark point in consciousness, just as on the retina the precise point of entry of the optic nerve is blind, the brain itself is wholly insensible, the body of the sun is dark, and the eye sees everything except itself. Our faculty of knowledge is directed entirely *outwards* in accordance with the fact that it is the product of a brain-function that has arisen for the purpose of mere self-maintenance, and hence for the search for nourishment and the seizing of prey. Therefore everyone knows of himself only as of this individual, just as it exhibits itself in external perception. If, on the other hand, he could bring to consciousness what he is besides and beyond this, he would willingly give up his individuality, smile at the tenacity of his attachment thereto, and say: "What does the loss of this individuality matter to me? for I carry within myself the possibility of innumerable individualities." He would see that, although there is not in store for him a continued existence of his individuality, it is nevertheless just as good as if he had such an existence, since he carries within himself a complete compensation for it. Besides this, however, it might also be taken into consideration that the individuality of most people is so wretched and worthless that they actually lose nothing in it, and that what in them may still have some value is the universal human element; but to this we can promise imperishableness. In fact, even the rigid unalterability and essential limitation of every individuality as such would, in the case of its endless duration, inevitably and necessarily produce ultimately such great weariness by its monotony, that we should prefer to become nothing, merely in order to be relieved of it. To desire immortality for the individual is really the same as wanting to perpetuate an error for ever; for at bottom every individuality is really only a special error, a false step, something that it would be better should not be, in fact something from which it is the real purpose of life to bring us back. This also finds confirmation in the fact that most, indeed really all, people are so constituted that they could not be happy, no matter in what world they might be placed. Insofar as such a world would exclude want and hardship, they would become a prey to boredom, and insofar as this was prevented, they would fall into misery, vexation, and suffering. Thus, for a blissful condition of man, it would not be by any means sufficient for him to be transferred to a "better world"; on the contrary, it would also be necessary for a fundamental change to occur in man himself, and hence for him to be no longer what he is, but rather to become what he is not. For this, however, he must first of all cease to be what he is; as a preliminary, this requirement is fulfilled by death, and the moral necessity of this can from this point of view already be seen. To be transferred to another world and to change one's entire nature are at bottom one and the same thing. On this also ultimately rests that dependence of the objective on the subjective which is explained by the idealism of our first book; accordingly, here is to be found the point of contact between transcendental philosophy and ethics. If we bear this in mind, we shall find that the awakening from the dream of life is possible only through the disappearance along with it of its whole fundamental fabric as well; but this is its organ itself, the intellect together with its forms. With this the dream would go on spinning itself for ever, so firmly is it incorporated with that organ. That which really dreamt the dream is, however, still different from it, and alone remains over. On the other hand, the fear that with death everything might be over and finished may be compared to the case of a person who in a dream should think that there were mere dreams without a dreamer. But would it even be desirable for an individual consciousness to be kindled again, after it had once been ended by death, in order that it might continue for ever? For the most part, often in fact entirely, its content is nothing but a stream of paltry, earthly, poor ideas, and endless worries and anxieties; let these then be finally silenced! Therefore with true instinct the ancients put on their tombstones: "To eternal security; . . . to good repose." But if even here, as has happened so often, we wanted continued existence of the individual consciousness, in order to connect with it a reward or punishment in the next world, then at bottom the aim would be merely the compatibility of virtue with egoism. But these two will never embrace; they are fundamentally opposed. On the other hand, the immediate conviction, which the sight of noble actions calls forth, is well founded, that the spirit of love enjoining one man to spare his enemies, and another, even at the risk of his life, to befriend a person never previously seen, can never pass away and become nothing.

The most complete answer to the question of the individual's continued existence after death is to be found in Kant's great doctrine of the *ideality of time*. Just here does this doctrine show itself to be specially fruitful and rich in important results, since it replaces dogmas, which lead to the absurd on the one path as on the other, by a wholly theoretical but well proved insight, and thus at once settles the most exciting of all metaphysical questions. To begin, to end, and to continue are concepts that derive their significance simply and solely from time; consequently they are valid only on the presupposition of time. But time has no absolute existence; it is not the mode and manner of the being-in-itself of things, but merely the form of our *knowledge* of the existence and inner being of ourselves and of all things; and for this reason such knowledge is very imperfect, and is limited to mere phenomena. Thus in reference to this knowledge alone do the concepts of ceasing and continuing find application, not in reference to that which manifests itself in them, namely the being-in-itself of things; applied to this, such concepts therefore no longer have any true meaning. For this is also seen in the fact that an answer to the question arising from those time-concepts becomes impossible, and every assertion of such an answer, whether on the one side or the other, is open to convincing objections. We might indeed assert that our being-in-itself continues after death, because it would be wrong to say that it was destroyed; but we might just as well assert that it is destroyed, because it would be wrong to say that it continues; at bottom, the one is just as true as the other. Accordingly, something like an antinomy could certainly be set up here, but it would rest on mere negations. In it one would deprive the subject of the judgement of two contradictorily opposite predicates, but only because the whole category of these predicates would not be applicable to that subject. But if one deprives it of those two predicates, not together but separately, it appears as if the contradictory opposite of the predicate, denied in each case, were thus proved of the subject of the judgement. This, however, is due to the fact that incommensurable quantities are here compared, inasmuch as the problem removes us to a scene that abolishes time, but yet asks about time-determinations. Consequently, it is equally false to attribute these to the subject and to deny them, which is equivalent to saying that the problem is transcendent. In this sense death remains a mystery.

On the other hand, adhering to that very distinction between phenomenon and thing-in-itself, we can make the assertion that man as phenomenon is certainly perishable, yet his true inner being is not affected by this. Hence this true inner being is indestructible, although, on account of the elimination of the time-concepts which is connected with this, we cannot attribute continuance to it. Accordingly, we should be led here to the concept of an indestructibility that was nevertheless not a continuance. Now this concept is one which, obtained on the path of abstraction, may possibly be thought in the abstract; yet it cannot be supported by any perception; consequently, it cannot really become distinct. On the other hand, we must here keep in mind that we have not, like Kant, absolutely given up the ability to know the thing-in-itself; on the contrary, we know that it is to be looked for in the will. It is true that we have never asserted an absolute and exhaustive knowledge of the thing-in-itself; indeed, we have seen quite well that is it impossible to know anything according to what it may be absolutely in and by itself. For as soon as I *know*, I have a representation, a mental picture; but just because this representation is mine, it cannot be identical with what is known; on the contrary, it reproduces in an entirely different form that which is known by making it a being-for-others out of a being-for-self; hence it is still always to be regarded as the *phenomenal appearance* of this. However, therefore, a *knowing* consciousness may be constituted, there can always be for it only phenomena. This is not entirely obviated even by the fact that my own inner being is that which is known; for, in so far as it falls within my *knowing* consciousness, it is already a reflex of my inner being, something different from this inner being itself, and so already in a certain degree phenomenon. Thus, in so far as I am that which knows, I have even in my own inner being really only a phenomenon; on the other hand, in so far as I am directly this inner being itself, I am not that which knows. For it is sufficiently proved in the second book that knowledge is only a secondary property of our inner being, and is brought about through the animal nature of this. Strictly speaking, therefore, we know even our own will always only as phenomenon, and not according to what it may be absolutely in and by itself. But in that second book, as well as in my work *On the Will in Nature,* it is fully discussed and demonstrated that if, in order to penetrate into the essence of things, we leave what is given only indirectly and from outside, and stick to the only phenomenon into whose inner nature an immediate insight is accessible to us from within, we quite definitely find in this the will as the ultimate thing and the kernel of reality. In the will, therefore, we recognize the thing-in-itself in so far as it no longer has space, but time for its form; consequently, we really know it only in its most immediate manifestation, and thus with the reservation that this knowledge of it is still not exhaustive and entirely adequate. In this sense, therefore, we here retain the concept of the will as that of the thing-in-itself.

The concept of ceasing to be is certainly applicable to man as phenomenon in time, and empirical knowledge plainly presents death as the end of this temporal existence. The end of the person is just as real as was its beginning, and in just that sense in which we did not exist before birth, shall we no longer exist after death. But no more can be abolished through death than was produced through birth; and so that cannot be abolished by which birth first of all became possible. In this sense "Born and unborn" is a fine expression. Now the whole of empirical knowledge affords us mere phenomena; thus only phenomena are affected by the temporal processes of arising and passing away, not that which appears, namely the being-in-itself. For this inner being the contrast, conditioned by the brain, between arising and passing away, does not exist at all; on the contrary, it has lost meaning and significance. This inner being, therefore, remains unaffected by the temporal end of a temporal phenomenon, and always retains that existence to which the concepts of beginning, end, and continuance are not applicable. But in so far as we can follow up this inner being, it is in every phenomenal being its will; so too in man. Consciousness, on the other hand, consists in knowledge; but this, as has been sufficiently demonstrated, belongs, as activity of the brain, and consequently as function of the organism, to the mere phenomenon, and therefore ends therewith. The will alone, of which the work or rather the copy was the body, is what is indestructible. The sharp distinction between will and knowledge, together with the former's primacy, a distinction that constitutes the fundamental characteristic of my philosophy, is therefore the only key to the contradiction that shows itself in many different ways, and always arises afresh in every consciousness, even the crudest. This contradiction is that death is our end, and yet we must be eternal and indestructible; hence it is the "We feel and experience that we are eternal" of Spinoza. All philosophers have made the mistake of placing that which is metaphysical, indestructible, and eternal in man in the *intellect.* It lies exclusively in the *will*, which is entirely different from the intellect, and alone is original. As was most thoroughly explained in the second book, the intellect is a secondary phenomenon, and is conditioned by the brain, and therefore begins and ends with this. The will alone is that which conditions, the kernel of the whole phenomenon; consequently, it is free from the forms of the phenomenon, one of which is time, and hence it is also indestructible. Accordingly, with death consciousness is certainly lost, but not what produced and maintained consciousness; life is extinguished, but with it not the principle of life which manifested itself in it. Therefore a sure and certain feeling says to everyone that there is in him something positively imperishable and indestructible. Even the freshness and vividness of recollections from earliest times, from early childhood, are evidence that something in us does not pass away with time, does not grow old, but endures unchanged. However, we were not able to see clearly what this imperishable element is. It is not consciousness any more than it is the body, on which consciousness obviously depends. On the contrary, it is that on which the body together with consciousness depends. It is, however, just that which, by entering into consciousness, exhibits itself as *will*. Of course, we cannot go beyond this most immediate phenomenal appearance of it, because we cannot go beyond consciousness. Therefore the question what that something may in so far as it does *not* enter into consciousness, in other words, what it is absolutely in itself, remains unanswerable.

In the phenomenon, and by means of its forms time and space, as *principium individuationis,* it is thus evident that the human individual perishes, whereas the human race remains and continues to live. But in the being-in-itself of things which is free from these forms, the whole difference between the individual and the race is also abolished, and the two are immediately one. The entire will-to-live is in the individual, as it is in the race, and thus the continuance of the species is merely the image of the individual's indestructibility.

Now, since the infinitely important understanding of the indestructibility of our true nature by death rests entirely on the difference between phenomenon and thing-in-itself, I wish to put this very difference in the clearest light by elucidating it in the opposite of death, hence in the origin of animal beings, i.e., in *generation*. For this process, that is just as mysterious as death, places most directly before our eyes the fundamental contrast between phenomenon and the being-in-itself of things, i.e., between the world as representation and the world as will, and also shows us the entire heterogeneity of the laws of these two. The act of procreation thus presents itself to us in a twofold manner: firstly for self-consciousness, whose sole object is, as I have often shown, the will with all its affections; and secondly for the consciousness of other things, i.e., of the world of the representation, or the empirical reality of things. Now from the side of the will, and thus inwardly, subjectively, for self-consciousness, that act manifests itself as the most immediate and complete satisfaction of the will, i.e., as sensual pleasure. On the other hand, from the side of the representation, and thus outwardly, objectively, for the consciousness of other things, this act is just the woof of the most ingenious of all fabrics, the foundation of the inexpressibly complicated animal organism which then needs only development in order to become visible to our astonished eyes. This organism, whose infinite complication and perfection are known only to the student of anatomy, is not to be conceived and thought of, from the side of the representation, as other than a system, devised with the most carefully planned combination and carried out with the most consummate skill and precision, the most arduous work of the profoundest deliberation. Now from the side of the will, we know through self-consciousness that the production of the organism is the result of an act the very opposite of all reflection and deliberation, of an impetuous, blind craving, an exceedingly voluptuous sensation. This contrast is exactly akin to the infinite contrast, shown above, between the absolute facility with which nature produces her works, together with the correspondingly boundless carelessness with which she abandons such works to destruction—and the incalculably ingenious and well-thought-out construction of these very works. To judge from these, it must have been infinitely difficult to make them, and therefore to provide for their maintenance with every conceivable care, whereas we have the very opposite before our eyes. Now if, by this naturally very unusual consideration, we have brought together in the sharpest manner the two heterogeneous sides of the world, and so to speak grasped them with one hand, we must now hold them firmly, in order to convince ourselves of the entire invalidity of the laws of the phenomenon, or of the world as representation, for that of the will, or of things-in-themselves. It will then become clearer to us that whereas, on the side of the representation, i.e., in the phenomenal world, there is exhibited to us first an arising out of nothing, then a complete annihilation of what has arisen, from that other side, or in itself, there lies before us an essence or entity, and when the concepts of arising and passing away are applied to it, they have absolutely no meaning. For by going back to the root, where, by means of self-consciousness, the phenomenon and the being-in-itself meet, we have just palpably apprehended, as it were, that the two are absolutely incommensurable. The whole mode of being of the one, together with all the fundamental laws of this being, signifies nothing, and less than nothing, in the other. I believe that this last consideration will be rightly understood only by a few, and that it will be unpleasant and even offensive to all who do not understand it. However, I shall never on this account omit anything that can serve to illustrate my fundamental idea.

At the beginning of this chapter I explained that the great attachment to life, or rather the fear of death, by no means springs from *knowledge,* for in that case it would be the result of the known value of life, but that that fear of death has its root directly in the *will*; it proceeds from the will's original and essential nature, in which that will is entirely without knowledge, and is therefore the blind will-to-live. Just as we are allured into life by the wholly illusory inclination for sensual pleasure, so are we firmly retained in life by the fear of death, certainly just as illusory. Both spring directly from the will that is in itself without knowledge. On the other hand, if man were a merely *knowing* being, death would necessarily be not only a matter of indifference, but even welcome to him. Now the consideration we have reached here teaches us that what is affected by death is merely the *knowing* consciousness; that the *will*, on the other hand, in so far as it is the thing-in-itself that lies at the root of every individual phenomenon, is free from everything that depends on determinations of time, and so is imperishable. Its striving for existence and manifestation, from which the world results, is always satisfied, for it is accompanied by this world just as the body is by the shadow, since the world is merely the visibility of the true inner nature of the will. Nevertheless, the will in us fears death, and this is because knowledge presents to this will its true nature merely in the individual phenomenon. From this there arises for the will the illusion that it perishes with this phenomenon, just as when the mirror is smashed my image in it seems to be destroyed at the same time. Therefore this fills the will with horror, because it is contrary to its original nature, which is a blind craving for existence. It follows from this that that in us which alone is capable of fearing death, and also alone fears it, namely the *will*, is not affected by it; and that, on the other hand, what is affected by it and actually perishes is that which, by its nature, is not capable of any fear, and generally of any desire or emotion, and is therefore indifferent to existence and nonexistence. I refer to the mere subject of knowledge, the intellect, the existence of which consists in its relation to the world of the representation, in other words the objective world; it is the correlative of this objective world, with whose existence its own existence is at bottom identical. Thus, although the individual consciousness does not survive death, that survives it which alone struggles against it, the will. From this is also explained the contradiction that, from the standpoint of knowledge, philosophers have at all times with cogent arguments shown death to be no evil; yet the fear of death remains impervious to them all, simply because it is rooted not in knowledge, but in the will alone. Just because the will alone, not the intellect, is the indestructible element, it follows that all religions and philosophies promise a reward in eternity only to the virtues of the will or heart, not to those of the intellect or head.

The following may also serve to illustrate this consideration. The will, which constitutes our being-in-itself, is of a simple nature; it merely wills and does not know. The subject of knowing, on the other hand, is a secondary phenomenon, arising out of the objectification of the will; it is the point of unity of the nervous system's sensibility, the focus, as it were, in which the rays of activity of all parts of the brain converge. Therefore with this brain the subject of knowing is bound to perish. In self-consciousness, as that which alone knows, the subject of knowing stands facing the will as a spectator, and although it has sprung from the will, it knows that will as something different from itself, something foreign to it, and thus only empirically, in time, piecemeal, in the successive agitations and acts of the will; only *a posteriori* and often very indirectly does it come to know the will's decisions. This is why our own inner being is a riddle to us, in other words, to our intellect, and why the individual regards himself as newly arisen and as perishable, although his inner being-in-itself is something timeless, and therefore eternal. Now just as the *will* does not *know*, so, conversely, the intellect, or the subject of knowledge, is simply and solely *knowing*, without ever willing. This can be proved even physically from the fact that, as already mentioned in the second book, the various emotions, according to Bichat, directly affect all parts of the organism and disturb their functions, with the exception of the brain as that which can be affected by them at most indirectly, in other words, in consequence of those very disturbances (*De la vie et de la mort,* art. 6, § 2). Yet it follows from this that the subject of knowing, by itself and as such, cannot take any part or interest in anything, but that the existence or non-existence of everything, in fact even of itself, is a matter of indifference to it. Now why should this indifferent being be immortal? It ends with the temporal phenomenon of the will, i.e., with the individual, just as it originated therewith. It is the lantern that after it has served its purpose is extinguished. The intellect, like the world of perception which exists in it alone, is mere phenomenon; but the finiteness of both does not affect that of which they are the phenomenal appearance. The intellect is the function of the cerebral nervous system; but this, like the rest of the body, is the objectivity of the *will*. The intellect, therefore, depends on the somatic life of the organism; but this organism itself depends on the will. Thus, in a certain sense, the organic body can be regarded as the link between the will and the intellect; although, properly speaking, the body is only the will itself spatially exhibiting itself in the perception of the intellect. Death and birth are the constant renewal and revival of the will's consciousness. In itself this will is endless and beginningless; it alone is, so to speak, the substance of existence (every such renewal, however, brings a new possibility of the denial of the will-to-live). Consciousness is the life of the subject of knowing, or of the brain, and death is its end. Therefore consciousness is finite, is always new, beginning each time at the beginning. The *will* alone is permanent; but permanence also concerns it alone, for it is the will-to-live. Nothing is of any consequence to the knowing subject by itself; yet the will and the knowing subject are united in the I or ego. In every animal being the will has achieved an intellect, and this is the light by which the will here pursues its ends. Incidentally, the fear of death may also be due partly to the fact that the individual will is so reluctant to separate itself from the intellect that has fallen to its lot through the course of nature, from its guide and guard, without which it knows that it is helpless and blind.

Finally, this explanation agrees also with that daily moral experience, teaching us that the will alone is real, while its objects, on the other hand, as conditioned by knowledge, are only phenomena, mere froth and vapour, like the wine provided by Mephistopheles in Auerbach's cellar; thus after every pleasure of the senses we say; "And yet it seemed as I were drinking wine" [Goethe's *Faust*].

The terrors of death rest for the most part on the false illusion that then the I or ego vanishes, and the world remains. But rather is the opposite true, namely that the world vanishes; on the other hand, the innermost kernel of the ego endures, the bearer and producer of that subject in whose representation alone the world had its existence. With the brain the intellect perishes, and with the intellect the objective world, this intellect's mere representation. The fact that in other brains a similar world lives and moves, now as before, is a matter of indifference with reference to the intellect that is perishing. If, therefore, reality proper did not lie in the *will*, and if the *moral* existence were not that which extended beyond death, then, as the intellect and with it its world are extinguished, the true essence of things generally would be nothing more than an endless succession of short and troubled dreams without connexion among themselves; for the permanence of nature-without-knowledge consists merely in the time-representation of nature that knows. Therefore a world-spirit, dreaming without aim or purpose dreams that are often heavy and troubled, would then be all in all.

When an individual experiences the dread of death, we really have the strange, and even ludicrous, spectacle of the lord of the worlds, who fills everything with his true nature, and through whom alone everything that is has its existence, in despair and afraid of perishing, of sinking into the abyss of eternal nothingness; whereas, in truth, everything is full of him, and there is no place where he would not be, no being in whom he would not live, for existence does not support him, but he [supports] existence. Yet it is he who despairs in the individual who suffers the dread of death, since he is exposed to the illusion, produced by the *principium, individuationis*, that his existence is limited to the being that is now dying. This illusion is part of the heavy dream into which he, as will-to-live, has fallen. However, we might say to the dying individual: "You are ceasing to be something which you would have done better never to become."

As long as no denial of that will has taken place, that of us which is left over by death is the seed and kernel of quite another existence, in which a new individual finds himself again so fresh and original, that he broods over himself in astonishment. Hence the enthusiastic, visionary, and dreamy disposition of noble youths at the time when this fresh consciousness has just been fully developed. What sleep is for the individual, death is for the will as thing-in-itself. It could not bear to continue throughout endless time the same actions and sufferings without true gain, if memory and individuality were left to it. It throws them off; this is Lethe; and through this sleep of death it reappears as a new being, refreshed and equipped with another intellect; "A new day beckons to a newer shore!"

As the self-affirming will-to-live, man has the root of his existence in the species. Accordingly, death is the losing of one individuality and the receiving of another, and consequently a changing of the individuality under the exclusive guidance of his own will. For in this alone lies the eternal force which was able to produce his existence with this ego, yet, on account of the nature of this ego, is unable to maintain it in existence. For death is the *démenti* that the essence (*essentia*) of everyone receives in its claim to existence (*existentia*), the appearance of a contradiction lying in every individual existence:

> for all things, from the Void
> Called forth, deserve to be destroyed.

Yet an infinite number of just such existences, each with its ego, stands within reach of the same force, that is, of the will, but these again will be just as perishable and transitory. Now as every ego has its separate consciousness, that infinite number of them, in respect of such an ego, is not different from a single one. From this point of view, it does not appear to me accidental that *aevum, αἰών*, signifies both the individual term of life and infinite time; thus it may be seen from this point, though indistinctly, that ultimately and in themselves both are the same. According to this it would really make no difference whether I existed only through my term of life or throughout an infinite time.

But of course we cannot obtain a notion of all that has been said above entirely without time-concepts; yet these should be excluded when we are dealing with the thing-in-itself. But it is one of the unalterable limitations of our intellect that it can never entirely cast off this first and most immediate form of all its representations, in order to operate without it. Therefore we naturally come here on a kind of metampsychosis, though with the important difference that this does not affect the whole *ψυχή*, and hence the *knowing* being, but the *will* alone, whereby so many absurdities that accompany the doctrine of metempsychosis disappear; and with the consciousness that the form of time here appears only as an unavoidable accommodation to the limitation of our intellect. If we now call in the assistance of the fact, to be discussed in chapter 43, that the character, i.e., the will, is inherited from the father, whereas the intellect comes from the mother, then this agrees very well with our view that the will of man, in itself individual, separates itself in death from the intellect that was obtained from the mother at procreation, and receives a new intellect in accordance with its now modified nature under the guidance of the absolutely necessary course of the world which harmonizes with this nature. With this new intellect, the will would become a new being that would have no recollection of a previous existence; for the intellect, alone having the faculty of recollection, is the mortal part or the form, whereas the will is the eternal part, the substance. Accordingly, the word palingenesis is more correct than metempsychosis for describing this doctrine. These constant rebirths then constitute the succession of the life-dreams of a will in itself indestructible, until, instructed and improved by so much and such varied and successive knowledge in a constantly new form, it would abolish itself.

The proper and, so to speak, esoteric doctrine of Buddhism, as we have come to know it through the most recent researches, also agrees with this view, since it teaches not metempsychosis, but a peculiar palingenesis resting on a moral basis, and it expounds and explains this with great depth of thought. . . .

Moreover, it must not be overlooked that even empirical grounds support a palingenesis of this kind. As a matter of fact, there does exist a connexion between the birth of the newly appearing beings and the death of those who are decrepit and worn out. It shows itself in the great fertility of the human race, arising as the result of devastating epidemics. When, in the fourteenth century, the Black Death had for the most part depopulated the Old World, a quite abnormal fertility appeared among the human race, and twin births were very frequent. Most remarkable also was the circumstance that none of the children born at this time acquired all their teeth; thus nature, exerting herself to the utmost, was niggardly in details. This is stated by F. Schnurrer in the *Chronik der Seuchen* (1825). Casper, *Die wahrscheinliche Lebensdauer des Menschen* (1835), also confirms the principle that, in a given population, the number of procreations has the most decided influence on the duration of life and on mortality, as it always keeps pace with the mortality; so that, everywhere and at all times, the births and deaths increase and decrease in equal ratio. This he places beyond doubt by accumulated evidence from many countries and their different provinces. And yet there cannot possibly be a *physical* causal connexion between my previous death and the fertility of a couple who are strangers to me, or *vice versa*. Here, then, the metaphysical appears undeniably and in an astonishing way as the immediate ground of explanation of the physical. Every new-born being comes fresh and blithe into the new existence, and enjoys it as a gift; but nothing is or can be freely given. Its fresh existence is paid for by the old age and death of a worn-out and decrepit existence which has perished, but which contained the indestructible seed. Out of this seed the new existence arose; the two existences are *one* being. To show the bridge between the two would, of course, be the solution to a great riddle.

The great truth here expressed has never been entirely overlooked, although it could not be reduced to its precise and correct meaning. This becomes possible only through the doctrine of the primary and metaphysical nature of the will and the secondary, merely organic, nature of the intellect. Thus we find the doctrine of metempsychosis, springing from the very earliest and noblest ages of the human race, always world-wide, as the belief of the great majority of mankind, in fact really as the doctrine of all religions, with the exception of Judaism and the two religions that have arisen from it. But, as already mentioned, we find this doctrine in its subtlest form, and coming nearest to the truth, in Buddhism. Accordingly, while Christians console themselves with the thought of meeting again in another world, in which they regain their complete personality and at once recognize one another, in those other religions the meeting is going on already, though incognito. Thus, in the round of births, and by virtue of metempsychosis or palingenesis, the persons who now stand in close connexion or contact with us will also be born simultaneously with us at the next birth, and will have the same, or analogous, relations and sentiments towards us as they now have, whether these are of a friendly or hostile nature. Of course, recognition is limited here to an obscure inkling, a reminiscence which is not to be brought to distinct consciousness, and which points to an infinite remoteness; with the exception, however, of the Buddha himself. He has the prerogative of distinctly knowing his own previous births and those of others; this is described in the *Jatakas*. But, in fact, if at favourable moments we look at the doings and dealings of men in real life in a purely objective way, the intuitive conviction is forced on us that they not only are and remain the same according to the (Platonic) Ideas, but also that the present generation, according to its real kernel, is precisely and substantially identical with every generation that previously existed. The question is only in what this kernel consists; the answer given to it by my teaching is well known. The above-mentioned intuitive conviction can be conceived as arising from the fact that the multiplying glasses, time and space, for a moment lose their effectiveness. With regard to the universal nature of the belief in metempsychosis, Obry rightly says in his excellent book *Du Nirvana indien*, p. 13: "This old belief has journeyed round the world, and was so widespread in ancient times that a learned follower of the Anglican Church judged it to be without father, without mother, without genealogy" (T. Burnet, in Beausobre, *Histoire du Manichéisme*, II, p. 391). Taught already in the *Vedas*, as in all the sacred books of India, metempsychosis is well known to be the kernel of Brahmanism and Buddhism. Accordingly it prevails even now in the whole of non-Mohammedan Asia, and thus among more than half of the human race, as the firmest of convictions, with an incredibly strong practical influence. It was also the belief of the Egyptians (Herodotus, ii, 123), from whom it was received with enthusiasm by Orpheus, Pythagoras, and Plato; the Pythagoreans in particular held firmly to it. That it was taught also in the mysteries of the Greeks follows undeniably from the ninth book of Plato's *Laws* (pp. 38 and 42, *ed. Bip.*). Nemesius even says (*De natura hominum,* c. 2): "Belief in a wandering from one body to another is common to all the Greeks, who declared that the soul was immortal." The *Edda*, particularly in the *Völuspá*, also teaches metempsychosis. No less was it the foundation of the religion of the Druids (Caesar, *De Bello Gallico,* vi. A. Pictet, *Le Mystère des Bardes de l'île de Bretagne,* 1856). Even a Mohammedan sect in India, the Bohrahs, of whom Colebrooke gives a detailed account in the *Asiatic Researches,* Vol. VII, pp. 336 *seqq*., believe in metempsychosis, and accordingly abstain from all animal food. Among American Indians and Negro tribes, indeed even among the natives of Australia, traces of this belief are found, as appears from an exact description, given in *The Times* of 29 January 1841, of the execution of two Australian savages for arson and murder. It says: "The younger of the 2 prisoners met his end with a dogged and determinate spirit, as it appear'd of revenge; the only intelligible expression he made use of conveyed an impression that he would rise up 'a white fellow,' which, it was considered, strengthened his resolution." In a book by Ungewitter, *Der Welttheil Australien* (1853), it is related also that the Papuans of New Holland regarded the whites as their own relations who had returned to the world. As the result of all this, belief in metempsychosis presents itself as the natural conviction of man whenever he reflects at all in an unprejudiced way. Accordingly, it would actually be that which Kant falsely asserts of his three pretended Ideas of reason, namely a philosopheme natural to human reason, and resulting from the forms of that faculty; and where this belief is not found, it would only be supplanted by positive religious doctrines coming from a different source. I have also noticed that it is at once obvious to everyone who hears of it for the first time. Just see how seriously even Lessing defends it in the last seven paragraphs of his *Erziehung des Menschengeschlechts*. Lichtenberg also says in his *Selbstcharakteristik*: "I cannot get rid of the idea that I had died before I was born." Even the exceedingly empirical Hume says in his sceptical essay on immortality, p. 23: "The metempsychosis is therefore the only system of this kind that philosophy can hearken to." What opposes this belief, which is spread over the whole human race and is evident to the wise as well as to the vulgar, is Judaism, together with the two religions that have sprung from it, inasmuch as they teach man's creation out of nothing. He then has the hard task of connecting this with the belief in an endless future existence *a parte post*. Of course, they have succeeded, with fire and sword, in driving that consoling, primitive belief of mankind out of Europe and of a part of Asia; for how long is still uncertain. The oldest Church history is evidence of precisely how difficult this was. Most of the heretics were attached to that primitive belief; for example, the Simonians, Basilidians, Valentinians, Marcionites, Gnostics, and Manichaeans. The Jews themselves have come to it to some extent, as is reported by Tertullian and Justin (in his dialogues). In the *Talmud* it is related that Abel's soul passed into the body of Seth, and then into that of Moses. Even the biblical passage, Matthew xvi, 13–15, takes on a rational meaning only when we understand it as spoken on the assumption of the dogma of metempsychosis. Luke, of course, who also has the passage (ix, 18–20), adds the words "That one of the old prophets is risen again" he thus attributes to the Jews the assumption that an ancient prophet can thus rise again with skin and hair; but, as they know that he has already been in the grave for six or seven hundred years, and consequently has long since turned to dust, such rising again would be a palpable absurdity. However, in Christianity the doctrine of original sin, in other words of atonement for the sin of another individual, has taken the place of the transmigration of souls and of the expiation by means thereof all the sins committed in a previous life. Thus both identify, and indeed with a moral tendency, the existing person with one who has existed previously; transmigration of souls does this directly, original sin indirectly.

Death is the great reprimand that the will-to-live, and more particularly the egoism essential thereto, receive through the course of nature; and it can be conceived as a punishment for our existence. Death is the painful untying of the knot that generation with sensual pleasure had tied; it is the violent destruction, bursting in from outside, of the fundamental error of our true nature, the great disillusionment. At bottom, we are something that ought not to be; therefore we cease to be. Egoism really consists in man's restricting all reality to his own person, in that he imagines he lives in this alone, and not in others. Death teaches him something better, since it abolishes this person, so that man's true nature, that is his will, will henceforth live only in other individuals. His intellect, however, which itself belonged only to the phenomenon, i.e., to the world as representation, and was merely the form of the external world, also continues to exist in the condition of being representation, in other words, in the *objective* being, *as such*, of things, hence also only in the existence of what was hitherto the external world. Therefore, from this time forward, his whole ego lives only in what he had hitherto regarded as non-ego; for the difference between external and internal ceases. Here we recall that the better person is the one who makes the least difference between himself and others, and does not regard them as absolutely non-ego; whereas to the bad person this difference is great, in fact absolute. I have discussed this at length in the essay *On the Basis of Morality*. The conclusion from the above remarks is that the degree in which death can be regarded as man's annihilation is in proportion to this difference. But if we start from the fact that the difference between outside me and inside me, as a spatial difference, is founded only in the phenomenon, not in the thing-in-itself, and so is not an absolutely real difference, then in the losing of our own individuality we shall see only the loss of a phenomenon, and thus only an apparent loss. However much reality that difference has in empirical consciousness, yet from the metaphysical standpoint the sentences "I perish, but the world endures," and "The world perishes, but I endure," are not really different at bottom.

But beyond all this, death is the great opportunity no longer to be I; to him, of course, who embraces it. During life, man's will is without freedom; on the basis of his unalterable character, his conduct takes place with necessity in the chain of motives. Now everyone carries in his memory very many things which he has done, about which he is not satisfied with himself. If he were to go on living, he would go on acting in the same way by virtue of the unalterability of his character. Accordingly, he must cease to be what he is, in order to be able to arise out of the germ of his true nature as a new and different being. Death, therefore, loosens those bonds; the will again becomes free, for freedom lies in the *esse,* not in the *operari.* "[Whoever beholds the highest and profoundest], has his heart's knot cut, all his doubts are resolved, and his works come to nought" is a very famous saying of the *Veda* often repeated by all Vedantists. Dying is the moment of that liberation from the one-sidedness of an individuality which does not constitute the innermost kernel of our true being, but is rather to be thought of as a kind of aberration thereof. The true original freedom again enters at this moment which in the sense stated can be regarded as a "Restoration to the former state." The peace and composure on the countenance of most dead people seem to have their origin in this. As a rule, the death of every good person is peaceful and gentle; but to die willingly, to die gladly, to die cheerfully, is the prerogative of the resigned, of him who gives up and denies the will-to-live. For he alone wishes to die *actually* and not merely *apparently,* and consequently needs and desires no continuance of his person. He willingly gives up the existence that we know; what comes to him instead of it is in our eyes *nothing,* because our existence in reference to that one is *nothing.* The Buddhist faith calls that existence *Nirvana,* that is to say, extinction.

Essay on the Freedom of the Will

1. DEFINITION OF CONCEPTS

1) What is freedom?

When carefully examined, this concept turns out to be negative. It signifies merely the absence of any hindrance and restraint. But this restraint, as it manifests power, must be positive. Corresponding to the possible nature of this restraint, the concept has three very different subspecies: physical, intellectual, and moral freedom.

a) *Physical freedom* is the absence of material hindrances of any sort. Thus we say: a clear sky, an open view, clear air, an open field, a vacant place free heat (which is not bound chemically), free electric charge, free flow of the stream where it is no longer checked by mountains or sluices, etc. Even such expressions as "free room and board," "free press," "post-free letter," signify the absence of those encumbering conditions which often attach themselves to such things and hinder their enjoyment. Most frequently, however, we conceive of freedom as an attribute of animate beings, whose distinctive feature is the ability to originate movements from their own will, that is, voluntarily. Thus such movements are called free when no material obstacles prevent them. Since these obstacles may be of very different kinds, but that with which they interfere is always the will, for the sake of simplicity one prefers to think of the concept of freedom in positive terms; the concept is used to cover everything that moves or acts only from its own will. This reversal of the concept changes nothing in essentials. Accordingly, in this physical meaning of the concept of freedom, animals and men are called free when their actions are not hindered by any physical or material obstacles—such as fetters, or prison,

Reprinted from Arthur Schopenhauer, *On Free Choice of the Will,* Bobbs-Merrill (1960), translated by Konstantine Kolenda.

or paralysis—but proceed in accordance with their will.

This physical meaning of the concept of freedom, especially when predicated on animate beings, is the original, immediate, and hence most frequent one. As such, the concept in this meaning is not subject to doubt or controversy, and its reality can always be authenticated empirically. For whenever an animate being acts only from its will, it is, in the physical sense, free. Here we do not take into account whatever may influence the will itself. For in its original, immediate, and therefore popular meaning, the concept of freedom refers only to the ability to act, that is, precisely to the absence of physical obstacles to its actions. Hence one says: free is the bird in the sky, the wild beast in the forest; man is by nature free; only the free are happy. We also call a nation free, meaning thereby that it is governed solely by laws, but that it has given itself these laws: for in that case it merely obeys its own will. Therefore, political freedom must be included under physical freedom.

However, as soon as we leave physical freedom . . . we are no longer dealing with the popular but with a philosophical sense of the concept. This, as is well known, leads to many difficulties. . . .

c) So I turn directly to . . . *moral freedom*. This is really the *liberum arbitrium* cited in the question of the Royal Society. This concept connects with that of physical freedom in a way which makes its necessarily much later origination understandable. Physical freedom, as noted above, has to do only with material obstacles; it is at once present when they are absent. But in some cases it has been observed that a man, without being hindered by material obstacles, was restrained by mere motives—such as threats, promises, dangers, and the like—from acting in a way which, if these motives were absent, would have certainly expressed his will. Consequently, the question was raised whether such a man was still free, or whether the actions which express his actual will could really be checked and prevented just as effectively by a strong countermotive as by a physical obstacle. A sound mind would find no difficulty in arriving at the answer: a motive can never act in the same ways as a physical obstacle. Undoubtedly the latter easily transcends human bodily powers unconditionally, while a motive can never be irresistible in itself and has no absolute power but can be always offset by a stronger countermotive, provided that such a countermotive is present and that the particular man can be determined by it. We often observe that even the strongest of all motives—to preserve one's life—is outweighed by other motives, for example, in suicide or in sacrificing one's life for others, for one's convictions, and for various causes. Conversely, all degrees of the most refined tortures on the rack have now and again been overcome by the mere thought that otherwise life would be lost. But even though it were evident from this that the motives bring with them no purely objective and absolute compulsion, still one could ascribe to them a subjective and relative compulsion, namely, relative to the person involved. In either case the result is the same. Hence the question remains: is the will itself free?

The concept of freedom, until now conceived only in respect to *ability*, was thus put in a relation to *willing*, and so the problem arose whether the willing itself is free. But on close inspection, the original, purely empirical, and hence popular concept of freedom shows itself incapable of becoming thus related to willing. For according to it "free" means "in accordance with one's own will." Consequently, to ask whether the will itself is free, is to ask whether the will is in accordance with itself. This, of course, is self-evident, but says also nothing at all. The empirical concept of freedom signifies: "I am free when I can *do what I will*." Here in the phrase "what I will" the freedom is already affirmed. But when we now inquire about the freedom of willing itself, the question would then take this form: "Can you also will your volitions?", as if a volition depended on another volition which lay behind it. Suppose that this question is answered in the affirmative, what them? Another question would arise: "Can you also will that which you will to will?" Thus we would be pushed back indefinitely, since we would think that a volition depended on a previous, deeper lying volition. In vain would we try to arrive in this way finally at a volition which we must think of and accept as dependent on nothing else. But if we were willing to accept such a volition, we could as well accept the first as the one we happened to make the last. Consequently, the question would be reduced to a simple: "Can you will?" But whether a mere affirmation of this question decides the problem of the freedom of the will, is what we wanted to know. So the problem remains unresolved.

We can see then that it is impossible to establish a direct connection between the concept of freedom—in its original, empirical meaning derived from action—and the concept of willing. In order nevertheless to be in a position to apply the concept of freedom to the will, one had to modify this concept by interpreting it more abstractly. This was accomplished by making the concept of freedom signify in general only the absence of any *necessity*. Thus interpreted, the concept retained its negative character, which I attributed to it from the very beginning. Accordingly, one must first investigate the concept of necessity, for this is the positive concept which gives meaning to the negative one.

So let us ask: What does one mean by "necessary"? The usual explanation: "necessary is that whose opposite is impossible, or which cannot be otherwise," is a mere word-definition, or paraphrase of the concept, which does not increase our understanding. As a real definition I propose the following: Something is necessary which follows from a given sufficient ground. This sentence, like any correct definition, can also be reversed. Depending on whether the ground in question is logical, or mathematical, or physical (i.e., called a cause), the necessity will be logical (e.g., of a conclusion, given the premises), or mathematical (e.g., equality of the sides of a triangle, given the equality of the angles), or physical, real (e.g., the occurrence of the effect, as soon as the cause is present). In all these cases, with equal strictness, the necessity is attached to the consequent when the ground is given. Only in so far as we comprehend something as the consequent of a given ground do we recognize it to be necessary. Conversely, as soon as we recognize something to be a consequent of a sufficient ground, we see that it is necessary. This is so because all grounds are compelling. This real definition is so adequate and exhaustive that the concept of necessity and the concept of consequent of a given sufficient ground are exchangeable concepts. In all cases, the one can be put in the place of the other.

According to this, the absence of necessity would be identical with the absence of a determining sufficient ground. Still, we think of the *accidental* as the opposite of the *necessary*. But there is no conflict between these two views; each accidental occurrence is only relatively so. For in the world of reality, where alone accidents can be encountered, every event is necessary in relation to its cause, while in relation to all other events which are contemporaneous and spatially contiguous with it, the event is accidental. But since the mark of freedom is absence of necessity, that which is free would have to be absolutely independent of any cause and would therefore have to be defined as absolutely accidental. This is a most problematic notion, and I don't guarantee that it is even conceivable. Nevertheless, it coincides in a singular fashion with the concept of freedom.

At any rate, that which is free remains that which is in no respect necessary, that is, not dependent on any ground. If this concept were applied to the will of man, this would mean that an individual will in its manifestations (volitions) would not be determined by causes or by sufficient grounds at all. Besides, since the consequent of a given ground (of whatever kind this may be) is always necessary, a man's acts would not be free but necessary. On this rests Kant's definition, according to which freedom is the capacity to initiate of oneself a series of changes. For in its true signification the expression "of oneself" means "without antecedent cause." This, however, is the same as "without necessity." So that, even though that definition gives to the concept of freedom the appearance of being positive, upon close scrutiny its negative nature emerges again.

A free will then would be the will which is not determined by grounds—and since everything that determines another must be a ground, in real things a real ground, that is, a cause—a free will would not be determined by anything at all. The particular manifestations of this will (volitions) would then proceed absolutely and quite originally from the will itself, without being brought about necessarily by antecedent conditions, and hence also without being determined by anything according to a rule. When we try to deal with this concept, clear thinking abandons us because, while the positing of a ground, in all of its meanings, is the essential form of our entire cognitive faculty, we are here asked to refrain from positing a ground. Still, there is no lack of a technical term also for this concept: this is *liberum arbitrium indifferentiae*. This is, by the way, the only clearly defined, firm, and positive concept of that which is called freedom of the will. One cannot therefore get away from it without involving oneself in vacillating, hazy explanations, behind which hides hesitant indecisions, as when one talks about grounds which do not necessarily bring about their consequents. Every consequent of a ground is necessary, and every necessity is the consequent of a ground. The positing of such a free will of indifference has an immediate consequence which characterizes this concept and must therefore be regarded as its peculiar feature. This is that for a human individual equipped with such a feature, under given external conditions which are thoroughly determined in every particular, two diametrically opposed actions are equally possible. . . .

2. THE WILL AND THE SELF-CONSCIOUSNESS

. . . As everyone may find out by introspection, that which the self-consciousness says about volitions, when freed of all foreign and inessential elements and reduced to its naked content, can be expressed by something like this: "I can will, and if I will an action, the movable members of my body will immediately perform it as soon as I will it, quite without fail." This means, in brief: "I can do what I will." Farther than this the assertion of the immediate self-consciousness does not go, no matter how one may try to turn it about and in what way one asks the question. What it asserts then always refers to the ability to act in accordance with the will. But this is the empirical, original, and popular concept of freedom which we set up at the very beginning, and according to which "free" means "in accordance with the will." The self-consciousness will absolutely affirm this freedom. But that is not the freedom we are asking about. The self-consciousness affirms the freedom of action—when the willing is presupposed. But what is being inquired into is precisely the freedom of *willing*.

We are searching for the relationship of the willing itself to the motive, and about this the assertion "I can do what I will" says nothing. The self-consciousness does indeed affirm the dependence of our behavior, that is, of our bodily actions, on our will. But this dependence is something quite different from an independence of external circumstances on the part of our volitions. Such an independence *would* constitute the freedom of the will, but the self-consciousness can assert nothing about it, because this independence lies outside of its sphere, as it concerns the causal relationship of the external world to our decisions (which is given to us as the consciousness of other things). The self-consciousness cannot judge of the relation of that which lies entirely outside its sphere to that which lies within it. For no cognitive faculty can establish a relationship one of whose terms is not given to it in any fashion. But obviously the objects of willing which determine a volition lie outside the boundary of the self-consciousness, namely in the consciousness of other things, while the volition itself is contained only in the self-consciousness. We, however, are inquiring into the causal relation of those other things to the self-consciousness. . . .

If we were to ask an unsophisticated person to describe that immediate consciousness which is so often regarded as that of an alleged freedom of the will, we would get something like the following answer: "I can do what I will: if I will to go to the left, I go to the left; if I will to go to the right, I go to the right. This depends entirely on my will; therefore, I am free." Of course this assertion is entirely true and correct, only the will is already presupposed in it, for it assumes that the will has already decided. Consequently, nothing can be established about its own freedom in this manner. The assertion does not at all speak about the dependence or independence of the *occurrence* of the act of volition itself, but only about the *effects* of this act as soon as it occurs, or, to be more precise, about its unfailing manifestation as bodily action. It is, however, nothing but the consciousness underlying this assertion that leads the layman, that is, the philosophically untrained person—who nevertheless in other areas can be very learned—to regard the freedom of the will as so immediately certain that he expresses it as indubitable truth and cannot really believe that philosophers seriously doubt it. Such a man believes in his heart that all this loose talk is a mere sparring exercise in academic dialectic and is at bottom a joke.

The certainty which is given to man through that consciousness and is indeed important is always very much at hand. Moreover, as primarily and essentially a practical, not a theoretical being, man is much more distinctly conscious of the active aspect of his volitions, that is, of their effectiveness, than of the passive aspect, that is, of their dependence. It is precisely for these reasons that it is difficult to make clear to a philosophically untrained person the real meaning of our problem and to make him understand that the question now is not about the *effects* but about the *grounds* of each act of willing. We grant that his *acting* depends entirely on his willing, but now we want to know on what his willing itself depends. Does it depend on nothing at all or on something? Of course, we say, he can do one thing when he wills it, and he can just as well do another thing when he wills it, but he should now consider whether he is able to will the one thing quite as well as the other. If, with this intention in mind, we ask a man a question like the following: "When two contrary wishes arise in you, can you really comply with the one just as well as with the other? For example, when you are to choose between two mutually exclusive objects of possession, can you prefer one as well as the other?" He will say: "Perhaps the choice will be difficult for me, but it will always depend completely on me whether I will choose one or the other and on no other power. I have complete freedom as to which of the two I shall will to choose, and in this I shall always follow my will alone." Now if one says: "But your willing itself, on what does *it* depend?", the man will fall back on the self-consciousness: "On nothing else but myself. I can will what I will: what I will, that I will." And he says this without intending it to be a tautology, or without even leaning in his innermost consciousness on the law of identity, by virtue of which alone this is true. But rather, being very hard put to it, he talks about a willing of his willing, which is the same as if he talked about the self of his self. One has pushed him back to the very heart of his self-consciousness, where he encounters his self and his will as indistinguishable, but where nothing remains to pass judgment on both of them.

The question is whether in that choice—assuming as given his person and the objects of his choice—his own willing of one thing and not the other could possibly have been somehow different from what it actually was, or whether, by virtue of the given data, his willing was as necessarily determined as is the fact that in a triangle the largest side lies opposite the largest angle. This question is so far removed from the natural self-consciousness that the latter even fails to comprehend the question, to say nothing of its containing the answer to it ready made, or even only as an undeveloped germ, which it would merely need to hand out naively. As already indicated, then, the ingenuous but philosophically untrained man will still try to escape the perplexity which the question, when really understood, must bring about, by hiding behind that immediate certainty "what I will, I can do, and I will what I will," as has been said above. This he will try again and again, countless times, so that it will be difficult to confront him with the real question, from which he all the time tries to escape. And one should not blame him for it, because the question is indeed most delicate. It penetrates searchingly into the very innermost being of man: it wants to know whether he also, like everything else in the world, is a being determined once for all by his own constitution which, like everything else in nature, has its definite, persisting properties, from which his reactions issue necessarily upon the occurrence of external stimuli. It wants to know whether, accordingly, these properties have an unalterable character in this respect, which leaves any possible modification in them fully at the mercy of determination by external stimuli, or whether man alone constitutes an exception to the whole of nature.

Should one finally succeed in confronting him with this delicate question and should one make clear to him that what is being searched for is the origin of his volitions themselves—whether they are subject to some rule or whether their emergence is completely lawless—one will discover that on this score no information is contained in the immediate self-consciousness. . . .

In the final analysis this is due to the fact that man's will is his authentic self, the true core of his being; hence it constitutes the ground of his consciousness as something which is simply given and present and beyond which he cannot go. For he himself is as he wills, and wills as he is. Therefore to ask him whether he could also will differently than he does is to ask whether he could also be other than himself; and that he does not know. For this very reason the philosopher, who differs from such a man only by virtue of his training, if he is to arrive at clarity in this difficult matter, must turn to his understanding, which provides knowledge a priori, to his reason, which reflects on such knowledge, and, as the final and the only competent court of appeal, to experience, which presents to him his acts and the acts of others, so that such apperceptions of the understanding can be interpreted and checked. The decision of this tribunal is, to be sure, not as easy, as immediate and simple as that of the self-consciousness, and yet in compensation it will be to the point and sufficient. It is the head that has posed the question, and the head must answer it. . . .

The answer which we received from the self-consciousness in response to our question I shall now restate in a shorter and easier wording. Everyone's self-consciousness asserts very clearly that he can do what he wills. But since we can conceive of him as willing quite opposite actions, it follows that if he so wills he can also *do* the opposite. Now the untutored understanding confuses this with the proposition that he, in a given case, can also *will* the opposite, and calls this the freedom of the will. But that in any given case he can will the opposite is absolutely not contained in the above proposition, but only this, namely, that of two contrary actions he can perform one action, if he wills it, or he can likewise perform the other one, if he wills that. But whether in a given case he can *will* the one as well as the other remains undetermined and calls for a deeper investigation than the one which mere self-consciousness could decide. . . .

Hence, that undeniable assertion of the self-consciousness, "I can do what I will," contains and decides nothing at all about the freedom of the will.

This freedom would consist in this, that the actual volition in each particular case and for a given particular character would not be determined necessarily by the external circumstances in which this man found himself, but could turn out now this way and now another way. But on this point the self-consciousness remains completely silent; for the matter lies entirely outside its realm, since it rests on the causal relation between the external world and the man. As a man who is of sound mind but who has no philosophical training in what the freedom of the will consists, which he so confidently maintained on the basis of the assertion of his self-consciousness, and he will answer: "It consists in this: I can do what I will provided I am not hindered physically." Hence it is always the relation of his acting to his willing that he speaks of. But this, as has been shown in the first section, is still merely *physical* freedom. If one asks him further whether in a given case he can will the one thing as well as he can its opposite, he will in his first zeal, to be sure, affirm this. But as soon as he starts to grasp the meaning of the question he will begin to have doubts, finally sink into uncertainty and confusion, and again prefer to take refuge behind his thesis "I can do what I will." There he will fortify himself against all grounds and all reasoning. But the corrected answer to his thesis, as I hope to free from all doubt in the next section, would be as follows: "You can do what you will, but in any given moment of your life you can *will* only one definite thing and absolutely nothing other than that one thing."

3. THE WILL AND THE CONSCIOUSNESS OF OTHER THINGS

. . . We are no longer dealing here with the will itself as accessible only to the inner space, but with those beings which will or are moved by the will, and which are the objects of the external senses. Even though in this procedure we suffer from the disadvantage of having to consider the actual object of our investigation only mediately and from a greater distance, this is outweighed by the advantage that we can now make use of a much more perfect instrument in our investigation than the dark, dull, one-sided, immediate self-consciousness, or the so-called inner sense. We can now use the understanding, equipped for objective apprehension with all external senses and all powers.

We find the most universal and fundamentally essential form of this understanding to be the law of causality. . . .

The law of causality is established a priori as the general rule to which all objects of the external world are subject without exception. This lack of exceptions is owing to its a priori character. The law refers essentially and exclusively to *changes* and means that wherever and whenever in the objective, real, material world *anything* changes to a lesser or greater extent, something else must necessarily have changed just before it, and that "something else" before that, and prior to that another one, and so on to infinity, without our ever seeing any starting point of this regressive series of changes which fill time as matter fills space. Such a starting point could not be thought possible, to say nothing of its being presupposed. For the question, which unremittingly renews itself, "What brought this change about?" never grants the understanding a final resting point, no matter how it may weary. For this reason a first cause is just as unthinkable as a beginning of time or a limit of space. The law of causality means no less definitely that when the earlier change—the cause—has occurred, then the later one which it brought about—the effect—must occur quite inevitably and therefore takes place necessarily. . . .

All changes taking place in the objects contained in the real external world are subject to the law of causality, and therefore, wherever and whenever they occur, they always occur necessarily and inevitably. To this there can be no exception, since the rule exists a priori for all the possibilities of experience. But as to its application to any given case one must only ask whether it concerns a change or a real object given in external experience. If it does, then its changes are subject to the application of the law of causality; that is, they must be brought about by a cause, but just for that reason *necessarily*. . . .

> "Cause" on the narrowest sense of the word is that whereby all mechanical, physical, and chemical changes in the objects of experience take place. It is always characterized by two features. First, to it applies Newton's third law, "action and reaction are equal to one another," that is, the antecedent state, called cause, experiences the same change as the following state, called effect. Second, according to Newton's second law, the degree of the effect always corresponds exactly to the degree of the cause. The strengthening of one therefore brings about an equal strengthening of the other, so that, when once the type of effect is known, the

degree of the effect can be immediately known, measured and calculated from the degree of the intensity of the cause, and vice versa. . . .

The second type of cause is the *stimulus*, that is, a cause which, first, does not itself experience a reaction caused by its action, and second, does not at all exhibit uniformity between its intensity and the intensity of its effect. Consequently, here the degree of the effect cannot be measured and determined beforehand from the degree of the cause. Rather, a small increase of the stimulus can cause a very great increase of the effect, or, quite the opposite, it may do away altogether with the antecedently produced effect, indeed it may bring about a contrary one. For example, as is well known, the growth of plants can be extraordinarily speeded up by means of heat or by adding calcium to the soil, since these causes stimulate their life force. If, however, the stimulus goes a little beyond the proper degree, instead of enhancing and accelerating the life of the plant, it will kill it. In the same fashion, by means of wine or opium we can intensify and considerably heighten our mental powers, but as soon as the right measure of stimulus is exceeded, the effect will be exactly the opposite.

This type of causes, namely stimuli, is the one which determines all changes of organisms as such. All changes and developments of plants, and all merely organic and vegetative changes or functions of animal bodies occur in response to stimuli. . . .

The third type of activating causes is that which is characteristic of animals. This is *motivation*, that is, causality which passes through cognition. In the hierarchy of natural organisms it enters at the point where, by virtue of having more complicated and hence manifold needs, the creature could no longer satisfy them in response to stimuli which must be waited for; it also had to be in a position to choose, to grasp, indeed to find the means of satisfaction. Therefore, in such organisms, in place of the mere receptivity to stimuli and the motion toward them, there enters a receptivity to motives, in other words, an imaginative faculty, an intellect in countless stages of perfection. Materially this manifests itself as nervous system and brain, and with these the consciousness enters the stage. It is well known that plant life which as such goes on only in response to stimuli serves as the basis of animal life. But all the movements which the animal performs as *animal* and which depend precisely on what physiology calls animal functions, take place as an effect of a cognized object, hence in response to motives. Accordingly an animal is any organism whose characteristic external movements and changes, appropriate to its nature, are always the result of motives, that is, of certain ideas which are present to the already presupposed consciousness. Even though the capacity for ideas, and hence consciousness, may have infinite gradations in the series of animals, every animal has enough to become aware of a motive and to be moved by it. In this process, the inner moving power whose particular manifestation is brought about by the motive makes itself known to the now present self-consciousness as that which we designate by the word "will". . . .

Animals, even the most clever ones, lack this ability [to form general concepts]; hence they have no ideas other than perceptual ones, and accordingly they know only that which is immediately present; they live only in the present. The motives by which their will is moved must, therefore, always be perceptual and actual. But the consequence of this is that they have extremely little choice. They can choose only among the things which spread themselves out perceptually before their limited field of vision and capacity to grasp, and so are present in time and space. That among them which is strongest as motive determines their will immediately, so that the causality of the motive is here very obvious. An apparent exception to this is made by training, which is fear operating through the medium of habit. A somewhat actual exception is instinct, insofar as by means of it in the total complex of its behavior the animal is set in motion not really by motives but through inner push and pull. However, in respect to particular actions and for every given moment, the proximate determination of this push and pull still proceeds from the motives, and thus reverts to the rule. . . .

On the other hand, by virtue of his capacity for non-perceptual ideas, by means of which he thinks and reflects, man has an infinitely larger field of vision, which includes the absent, the past, and the future. Because of this he can act from motives, and consequently exercise a choice, over a much greater range than the animal, which is limited to the narrow present. His action is not determined as a rule by that which lies before his sensuous perception and is present in space and time. Such determination proceeds rather from mere *thoughts* which he carries around everywhere in his head and which make him independent of the influence of the present. Whenever they fail to do that, one calls his actions irrational, and conversely, an action is praised as rational if it is performed strictly in accordance with well-considered thoughts and is therefore completely independent of the influence of the perceptual present. The very fact that man is activated by his own class of ideas (abstract concepts, thoughts), not possessed by the animal, is even externally visible. It impresses on all his actions, even the least significant ones, indeed on all his movements and steps, the character of the designed and intentional. Because of this, his activity is so visibly different from that of animals that one can positively see how his actions are guided, as it were, by fine, invisible threads (motives consisting of mere thoughts), whereas the actions of animals are pulled by rough, visible strings of what is perceptually present.

But the difference does not go further than that. The thought becomes a motive, as perception becomes a motive as soon as it can act on the particular will. All motives are causes, however, and all causality carries with it necessity. By means of his capacity to think, man can present to himself the motives whose influence on his will he feels in any order alternately and repeatedly, in order to hold them up to his will. This is called deliberation. Man is capable of deliberation, and thanks to his capacity he has a far greater choice than is possible for the animal. Because of this he is, of course, relatively free. He is free of the immediate compulsion of the perceptually present objects which act as motives on his will. To this the animal is subject absolutely. Man, on the other hand, determines himself independently of the present objects, namely by thoughts, which are *his* motives.

At bottom, it is probably this relative freedom that educated yet not deeply thinking people understand by the freedom of the will, clearly putting man ahead of the animals. This freedom, however, is only relative, namely, in relation to that which is present in perception, and only comparative, namely, in comparison with the animal. By its means only the type of motivation is altered, while the necessity of the effect of motives is not in the least obliterated, or even diminished. An abstract motive, consisting in a mere thought, is an external cause determining the will just as much as is a perceptual one, consisting in an actual and present object. Consequently, it is a cause like any other, and even consists always, like the others, in something real and material, insofar as it always rests ultimately on some impression, received sometime and somewhere from the outside. It only has the advantage of a longer conducting wire, by which expression I want to convey the idea that it is not, like mere perceptual motives, bound to a certain proximity in space and time, but can act across the greatest distance, the longest time, and through a mediation of concepts and thoughts in a long concatenation. This is the consequence of the constitution and the eminent sensitivity of the organ which first experiences the action of the motive and takes it in, namely, of the human brain, or of reason. This, however, does not in the last abolish its causality, nor the necessity which causality involves. Only a very superficial view, therefore, can regard that relative and comparative freedom as an absolute one, a *liberum arbitrium indifferentiae*.

The ability to deliberate, which arises from this relative freedom, yields in reality nothing but the very frequently distressing conflict of motives, which is dominated by indecision and has the whole soul and consciousness of man as its battlefield. This conflict makes the motives try out repeatedly, against one another, their effectiveness on the will. This puts the will in the same situation as that of the body on which different forces act in opposite directions, until finally the decidedly strongest motive drives the others from the field and determines the will. This outcome is called resolve, and it takes place with complete necessity as the result of the struggle. . . .

Let us imagine a man who, while standing on the street, would say to himself: "It is six o'clock in the evening, the working day is over. Now I can go for a walk, or I can go to the club; I can also climb up the tower to see the sun set; I can go to the theater; I can visit this friend or that one; indeed, I also can run out of the gate, into the wide world, and never return. All of this is strictly up to me, in this I have complete freedom. But still I shall do none of these things now, but with just as free a will I shall go home to my wife." This is exactly as if water spoke to itself: "I can make high waves (yes! in the sea during a storm), I can rush down hill (yes! in the river bed), I can plunge down foaming and gushing (yes! in the waterfall), I can rise freely as a stream of water into the air (yes! in the fountain), I can, finally, boil away and disappear (yes! at a certain temperature); but I am doing none of these things now, and am voluntarily remaining quiet and clear water in the reflecting pond."

As the water can do all those things only when the determining causes operate for the one or the other, so that man can do what he imagines himself able to do not otherwise than on the same condition. Until the causes begin to operate, this is impossible for him; but then, he *must*, as the water must, as soon as it is placed in the corresponding circumstances. His error and in general the delusion, which arises here from his falsely interpreted self-consciousness, that he can do all these things at this moment, rests, strictly speaking, on the fact that in his imagination only *one* picture at a time can be present and that for the moment it excludes everything else. When he imagines a motive for one of those actions which he proposes to himself as possible, he feels immediately its effect on his will, which is thereby solicited. This, in technical language, is called a *velleitas*. But then he thinks that he can raise this to the status of a *voluntas,* that is, that he can perform the proposed action. However, this is a delusion. For soon sober realization would set in and remind him of motives which pull in other directions or are contrary to the original one. And he would see that the action does not take place. In such successive imaginings of different, mutually exclusive motives, constantly accompanied by the inner "I can do what I will," the will turns, as it were, like a weather vane on a well-greased pivot and in a changeable wind, immediately toward any motive which imagination holds before it, and then in turn toward all of the motives which appear possible. In the case of each motive the man thinks that he can will it and so can fix the vane at this point, but this is sheer delusion. For his "I can will this" is in reality hypothetical and carries with it the additional clause, "if I did not prefer the other." But this addition annuls that ability to will.

Let us return to that man whom we had engaged in a deliberation at six o'clock. Suppose he noticed that I am standing behind him, philosophizing about him, and disputing his freedom to perform all those actions which are possible to him. It could easily happen that, in order to refute me, he would perform one of them. But then my denial and its effect on his contentious spirit would have been precisely the motive which forced him to do so. However, this motive would be able to move him only to one or the other of the easier of the above-mentioned actions, e.g., to go to the theater, but by no means to the last-mentioned, namely, to run out into the wide world; this motive would be far too weak for that. An equally erroneous supposition is made by a person who, holding a loaded pistol in his hand, thinks that he can shoot himself with it. For this the mechanical instrument is of the least importance; the main thing is an exceedingly strong and therefore rare motive which has the tremendous power required to outweigh the love of life, or, more correctly, the fear of death. Only after such a motive has entered in can he really shoot himself, and must do so; unless an even stronger countermotive, if such a one is at all possible, prevents the deed.

I can do what I will: I can, if I will, give everything I have to the poor and thus become poor myself—if I will! But I cannot will this, because the opposing motives have much too much power over me for me to be able to. On the other hand, if I had a different character, even to the extent that I were a saint, then I would be able to will it. But then I could not keep from willing it, and hence I would have to do so. . . .

It is definitely neither a metaphor nor a hyperbole but a quite dry and literal truth that, as little as a ball on a billiard table can move before receiving an impact, so little can a man get up from his chair before being drawn or driven by a motive. But then his getting up is as necessary and inevitable as the rolling of a ball after the impact. And to expect that anyone will do something to which absolutely no interest impels him is the same as to expect that a piece of wood shall move toward me without being pulled by a string. Should a man, maintaining this view in a gathering, encounter an obstinate opposition, he would get out of the affair in the shortest time if he had another man call out suddenly in a loud and solemn voice: "The roof is falling in." This would bring his opponents to the insight that a motive is just as capable of driving people out of the house as is the most robust mechanical cause.

For man, like all objects of experience, is a phenomenon in time and space, and since the law of causality holds for all such a priori and consequently without exception, he too must be subject to it. This is asserted a priori by the pure understanding, confirmed by the analogy found throughout the whole of nature, and attested by the experience of every moment, provided one does not succumb to the delusion arising from the consideration that, as natural beings become more complicated in the process of rising to a higher and higher level, and as their receptivity rises and becomes refined—from the merely mechanical to the chemical, electrical, irritable, sensible, intellectual, and, finally, rational—the nature of the activating causes must also proceed *pari passu* and correspond on each level to the beings which are to be activated. Consequently the causes must also present themselves as less and less palpable and material, so that in the end they are no longer visible to the eye but can indeed be reached by the understanding, which in each particular case presupposes them with unshakable confidence and discovers them too upon proper scrutiny. For here the acting causes are raised to the level of mere thoughts struggling with other thoughts, until the most powerful of them becomes decisive and sets the man in motion. All of this takes place with just such a strict causality as when purely mechanical causes work on one another in a complicated combination and the calculated effect occurs without fail. The appearance of causelessness due to the invisibility of the cause is found just as much among the electrified particles of cork which jump around in all directions in a glass as in the movements of man; but the eye is not entitled to judge, only the understanding.

If freedom of the will were presupposed, every human action would be an inexplicable miracle—an effect without a cause. And if one is bold enough to imagine such a *liberum arbitrium indifferentiae,* he will soon realize that in this effort the understanding is really at a standstill; it has no form with which to think such a thing. For the principle of sufficient reason, the principle of thoroughgoing determination and dependence of phenomena on one another, is the most universal form of our cognitive faculty, which, according to the difference of its objects, itself takes on different forms. But here we are supposed to think something which determines without being determined, which depends on nothing, but on which the other depends. This other, without any necessity, and consequently without any ground, produces A now, whereas it could just as well produce B, or C, or D. Furthermore, it could do this absolutely, under the same circumstances, that it is, without there being anything in A which would confer upon it a prerogative over B, C, or D (for this would be motivation, hence causality). Here we are led back to the concept of the absolutely accidental, posited in the very beginning. I repeat: in this case the understanding is really quite at a standstill, if only one can bring it to that.

However, let us now remind ourselves what a cause really is: an antecedent change which makes the following one necessary. No cause in the world ever brings about its effect all by itself, or produces it out of nothing. Rather there is something present every time on which it acts, and it produces a change merely at this particular time, in this place, and on this definite being. This change always corresponds to the nature of that being which, therefore, must already have the force to produce it. Thus every effect originates from two factors, an inner and an outer one, namely, from the original force of that which is being acted upon, and from the determining cause which forces the former to manifest itself in this case. . . .

Every action of a human being is the product of two factors: his character along with a motive.

The character of man is: 1) *individual*: in every one it is different. To be sure, the character of the species lies at the basis of all; therefore the main characteristics are repeated in every one. However, here there is such a significant difference of degree, such a difference of combination and mutual modification of characteristics, that one can assume the moral difference of characters to equal that of the intellectual capabilities; which is to say a great deal. It is also assumed that both are without comparison greater than the bodily difference between giant and dwarf, Apollo and Thersites. Therefore the effect of the same motive on different people is quite different; as the sunlight gives to wax white color and to chloric silver black, so the heat makes wax soft, but clay hard. Therefore from the knowledge of motives alone one cannot predict the act; in addition one must also have precise knowledge of the character in question.

2) The character of man is *empirical*: only through experience can one get to know it. This applies not only to others, but also to oneself. Therefore we are often disappointed with ourselves, as we are with others, when we discover that we do not have this or that quality, like justice, selflessness, or courage, in as high a degree as we most indulgently supposed. Hence too, in any difficult choice our own resolve, like that of another person, remains a mystery to us until the choice has been actually made. Now we believe that it will go in this direction and now in that, depending on whether the mind holds this or that motive more clearly before the will and the motive tries out its power, in which processes that "I can do what I will" produces the illusion of the will's freedom. Finally the stronger motive asserts its power over the will, and the choice often turns out quite differently than we initially supposed.

Therefore, finally, no one can know how another, and even how he himself, will act in a definite situation, until he has been in it. Only after the test has been passed is he sure of the other, and only then of himself too. But then he *is* sure: proved friends, tested servants are trustworthy. In general, we treat a person whom we know well like any other thing with whose properties we have already become familiar, and we know in advance what can be expected of him and what cannot. He who has done something once will do it again, good or bad, should the situation recur. For this reason the man who needs some great, extraordinary help will turn to the person who has proved himself generous; and he who wants to hire a murderer will look around among the people who have already had blood on their hands. . . .

Likewise, it is only out of experience and from opportunities to observe that our acquaintance with ourselves derives, on which self-trust or mistrust is based. Depending on whether in a given instance we have shown prudence, courage, honesty, discretion, astuteness, or whatever else the case might require, or whether the lack of such virtues has come to light, we are, as a result of the acquaintance made with ourselves, subsequently either satisfied or dissatisfied with ourselves. Only an exact knowledge of his own empirical character gives a man that which is called an acquired character. That man possesses it who knows accurately his own qualities, good as well as bad, and thus knows for certain with what he can trust himself, what he can expect of himself, and what he cannot. While till now, because of his empirical character, he played his role naturally, he now plays it artistically and methodically, with firmness and grace, without ever, as one says, being untrue to his character. Whenever a man is untrue to his character he shows that he was mistaken about his own self.

3) The character of man is *constant*: it remains the same, throughout the whole of life. Under the changeable shell of his years, his relationships, and even his store of knowledge and opinions, there hides, like a crab under its shell, the identical and real man, quite unchangeable and always the same. Only in respect to direction and content does his character undergo apparent modifications, which are the result of differences in one's age in life and its needs. Man never changes; as he has acted in one case, so he will always act again—given completely equal circumstances (which, however, includes also the correct knowledge of those circumstances). A confirmation of this truth can be gathered from everyday experience. But one encounters it in the most striking manner when after twenty or thirty years one meets an acquaintance again and soon catches him doing the same silly things as formerly.

It is true that many a man will deny this truth in words, but still such a man presupposes it in his actions. Finding a man dishonest once, he never trusts him again, but he readily relies on the one who has proved himself honest in the past. For on this truth rests the possibility of all knowledge of human beings, and of the firm trust in those that are tested, tried out, and confirmed. Even when such a trust has once disappointed us, we never say: "His character has changed," but "I was mistaken about him." This truth is also the basis of the fact that when we want to determine the moral worth of an action, we make a special effort to be sure about its motive, but then our praise or blame is not aimed at the motive but at the character which allowed itself to be determined by such a motive, the character being the second and the only factor in this act which inheres in the man himself. . . .

4) The individual character is *inborn*; it is not a work of art or of accidental circumstances, but the work of nature itself. It manifests itself already in the child and shows there on a small scale what it will be in the future on a large one. Hence two children who have exactly the same upbringing and surroundings will most clearly exhibit fundamentally different characters, characters which they will still have as old men. In its basic features character is even hereditary. . . .

The inborn character of a man determines in essentials even the goals toward which he unalterably strives: the means which he takes for this purpose are determined partly by the external circumstances and partly by his conception of them. The correctness of his conception depends in turn on his understanding and education. His particular actions take place as the end product of all of this, and so does the entire role which he plays in the world. The conclusion of the doctrine of the individual character, as presented here, finds an expression as accurate as it is poetic, in one of Goethe's most beautiful stanzas:

As on the day that gave you to the earth,
The sun greeted the planets in their course,
You, likewise, grew and throve, and from your
birth
Followed the law that was your primal source.
So must you be, your self you can't escape,
This said the sibyls, this the prophets hold;
And time and might are powerless to break
Predestined form, that living things unfold.[1]

Thus that assumption on which the necessity of the operations of *all* causes rests in the inner being of everything—be it merely a general natural force which manifests itself in it, or be it life force, or be it will. In every case the particular being, of whatever type, will react according to its special nature, whenever causes act upon it. This law, to which all things in the world are subject without exception, was expressed by the scholastics in the formula *operari sequitur esse.* According to it, the chemist tests substances by means of reagents, and a man tries out another man by means of tests which he applies to him. In all cases the external causes will necessarily call forth that which is hidden in a being; for this being cannot react otherwise than according to its nature.

Here one must be reminded that every existence presupposes an essence, that is, every thing-in-being must be *something*, must have a definite nature. It cannot exist and yet be nothing, it cannot be something like the *ens metaphysicum,* that is, a thing which simply *is* and no more than *is*, without any definitions and properties, and consequently, without a definite way of acting which flows from them. As little as an essence yields a reality without an existence . . . just as little can an existence do this without an essence. For every thing-in-being must have a nature which is essential and peculiar to it, in virtue of which it is what it is, which this being always maintains, and whose manifestations are called forth of necessity by causes; while on the other hand this nature itself is by no means the effect of those causes, nor can it be modified by them. But all this is just as true of man and his will as of all other beings in nature. He too has an essence in addition to existence, that is, fundamental properties which make up his character and require only an outside inducement in order to reveal themselves. Consequently, to expect that a man should act one time in one way, another time quite differently, in response to the same cause, would be no different than to expect that the same tree which bore cherries this summer should bear pears in the next. Freedom of the will, when carefully analyzed, means an existence without an essence, which means that something *is* and at the same time *is nothing,* which in turn means *is not*, and consequently is a self-contradiction.

The question of the freedom of the will is really a touchstone by which one can distinguish the deeply thinking minds from the superficial ones, or it is a milestone at which their ways part, all the former maintaining the necessary occurrence of an action when the character and the motive are given, and the latter, together with the great masses, clinging to the freedom of the will. There is also a type of middle-of-the-roader who, feeling embarrassed, tacks back and forth, shifts the target for himself and others, hides behind words and phrases, or turns and twists the question so long that one no longer knows what it amounted to . . . . But in order to make such vacillating talkers face the question, one must put it to them in the following way and insist that they answer it.

1) To a given man under given circumstances, are two actions possible, or only one?—The answer of all who think deeply: only one.

2) Let us consider that a man's character remains unchanged and also that the circumstances whose influence he had to experience were necessarily determined throughout and down to the least detail by external causes, which always take place with strict necessity and whose chain, entirely consisting of likewise necessary links, continues into infinity. Could the completed life course of such a man turn out in any respect, even the smallest, in any happening, any scene, differently from the way it did?—No! is the consistent and correct answer.

The conclusion from both propositions is: Everything that happens, from the largest to the smallest, happens necessarily. . . .

Anyone who is frightened by these propositions has still to learn some things and unlearn others. But then he will realize that they are the most abundant source of comfort and tranquility. Our acts are indeed not a first beginning; therefore nothing really new comes through them into being. But this is true: *through that which we do we only find out what we are. . . .*

Let me add just a few more considerations as

1. Johann Wolfgang von Goethe, "Orphisch," translated by Edith Fulton.

corollaries to the established doctrine of the necessity of all that happens.

What would become of this world if necessity did not permeate all things and hold them together, but especially govern the procreation of individuals? A monster, a rubbish heap, a caricature without sense and meaning—namely, the work of a true and real chaos.

To wish that some event had not taken place is a silly self-torture, for this means to wish something absolutely impossible, and is as irrational as is the wish that the sun should rise in the West. Precisely because everything that happens, great or small, happens with strict necessity, it is altogether useless to reflect on how insignificant and accidental were the causes which brought that event about, and how easily they could have been different. For this is illusory. All of them have happened with just as strict necessity and have done this work with just as full a power as that in virtue of which the sun rises in the East. We should rather consider the events, as they happen, with the same eye as we consider the printed word which we read, knowing full well that it was there before we read it.

Chapter 27

Soren Kierkegaard

The Danish philosopher Soren Aabye Kierkegaard (1813–1855) is widely recognized as the father of modern existentialism. He was born in Copenhagen, Denmark, into a deeply religious, but melancholy, Lutheran family with a brilliant self-taught father, Michael, who, though a successful businessman, was haunted by guilt. Soren suspected God had cursed him for his sins to suffer the penalty of outliving all members of his family, two wives and his seven children. Indeed, all but two children, including Soren, did precede Michael in death. Soren was the youngest child and received special nurturing from his father, playing games likely to expand the imagination.

In 1830 he entered the University of Copenhagen to study Theology, but spent most of his time reading literature and philosophy. He left the church, joined a fraternity, and lived a debauched life, spending his father's money. His father, brokenhearted by his son's immorality, reprimanded Kierkegaard, leading to a break between them.

In 1838, after spending eight years dallying at the University, Kierkegaard experienced a religious awakening, recommitted himself to the Christian faith, and was reunited with his father. He turned from his frivolous living, finished his degree within a year and earned the equivalent of a doctorate the next year, writing a long dissertation on Socratic Irony (1841).

While finishing his degree, in 1839, Kierkegaard fell in love with Regina Olsen, who was ten years younger than he, courted her, and the next year they became engaged. Almost immediately, he realized that the relationship would never work, that he was too melancholy for her, and that the relationship would destroy both of them. He sought to break the engagement and finally, a year later in 1841, succeeded, creating a citywide scandal.

Kierkegaard escaped from the public opprobrium by journeying to Berlin, where he wrote his first book *Either-Or*, contrasting the aesthetic (Epicurean) with the ethical (Stoic-Kantian) way of life. He published the two-volume work pseudonymously (under the name of "Victor Eremita"—the victorious hermit). It soon became a best seller, and all Copenhagen wondered who this brilliant author was. Other works followed, all written in different pseudonyms—Johannes de Silentio (Silent John), Vigilius Haufniensis (Watchman of the Harbor—Copenhagen is a harbor town), Johannes Climacus (John the Climber—to eternity), and so forth, some thirty books in all. He published all his work at his own expense. Only his first work made him a profit.

His life was filled with constant and intense suffering. He was frustrated in love, frustrated in his vocational aspirations—he was unable to get a teaching post, suffering a severe back ailment which may have led to his premature death. He was held in disrepute by most of his community. He opposed journalist corruption and suffered at the hands of the press. Yet he found solace in a deeply religious life. His last battle was with the organized state Lutheran Church, which he accused of betraying Christ. "As a religion, organized Christianity, as it is now practiced is just about as genuine as tea made from a bit of paper which once lay in a drawer beside another bit of paper which once had been used to wrap a few dried tea leaves from which tea had already been made three times."

Most of his works centered on the questions, "How shall I live my life? "What kind of life is worth living—the aesthetic, ethical or religious?" "What does it mean to have faith?" "What does it mean to love?" "What does it mean to accept one's suffering and how can one do this?" His discussion of these questions revealed philosophical acumen and literary brilliance.

In the first set of miscellaneous writings, we get a picture of Kierkegaard struggling to find meaning in his life. He rejects the abstract system-building philosophy of this day, especially Hegel's system, and opts for a philosophy that grows out of personal experience and for which one can live and die.

In the second reading from his most philosophical work, *Concluding Unscientific Postscript* (1844), Kierkegaard sets forth a radical version of fideism in which faith not only is said to be higher than reason but, in a sense, opposed to it. Faith, not reason, is the highest virtue a human can reach; faith is necessary for the deepest fulfillment. He argues that there is something misguided in trying to base one's religious faith on objective evidence or reason. It is both useless (it won't work) and a bad thing (it detracts one from the essential task of growing in faith). He then goes on to develop a theory of subjectivity wherein faith finds an authentic home. Even if we had direct proof for theism or Christianity, we would not want it, for such objective certainty would take the venture out of the religious pilgrimage, reducing it to a set of dull mathematical certainties.

FOR FURTHER READING

Bretall, Robert, ed. *A Kierkegaard Anthology.* (Modern Library, 1936).
Evans, C. Stephen. *Kierkegaard's "Fragments" and "Postscript."* (Humanities Press, 1983).
Gardiner, Patrick. *Kierkegaard.* (Oxford University Press, 1988).
Kaufmann, Walter, ed. *Existentialism from Dostoevski to Sartre.* (American Library, 1975).
Kierkegaard, Soren. *Fear and Trembling,* trans. Walter Lowrie. (Princeton University Press, 1954).
Kierkegaard, Soren. *Concluding Unscientific Postscript.* (Princeton University Press, 1946).
Krimse, Bruce. *Kierkegaard in Golden Age Denmark.* (University of Indiana Press, 1990).
Lowrie, Walter. *Kierkegaard.* (Oxford University Press, 1938).
Lowrie, Walter. *A Short Life of Kierkegaard.* (Princeton University Press, 1942).
Pojman, Louis. *The Logic of Subjectivity.* (University of Alabama Press, 1984).
Thomson, Josiah, ed. *Kierkegaard: A Collection of Critical Essays.* (Anchor Books, 1972).
Westphal, Merold. *Kierkegaard's Critique of Reason and Society.* (Mercer University Press, 1987).

Readings

AN ENTRY FROM THE JOURNAL OF THE YOUNG KIERKEGAARD

This entry was written by Soren Kierkegaard as a twenty-two-year-old university student on August 1, 1835, in Gilleleie on the northern coast of Denmark.

There is something missing in my life, and it has to do with my need to understand *what I must do,* not what I must know—except, of course, that a certain amount of knowledge is presupposed in every action. I need to understand my purpose in life, to see what God wants me to do, and this means that I must find a truth which is true for me, that I must find *that Idea for which I can live and die.*

For what would it profit me if I found the so-called 'objective truth', if I worked through all the systems

Translated by Louis P. Pojman

of philosophy and were able to analyze them and expose their inconsistencies; what would it profit me to develop a political theory and combine all the intricate details of politics into a complete whole, and so construct a world for the exhibition of others but in which I did not live; what would it profit me if I developed the correct interpretation of Christianity in which I resolved all the internal problems, if it had no deeper significance *for me and for my life;* what would it profit me if truth stood before me cold and naked, indifferent to whether I recognized her or not, creating in me paroxysms of anxiety rather than confident devotion?

I will not deny that I am presupposing an imperative of knowledge and that it can have an effect in our lives, but it *must be appropriated by me,* and this is what I now recognize as paramount. This is what my soul thirsts after as the African desert thirsts for water. This is what I lack, and why I am like a man who has just rented a house and completely furnished it but still has not found a lover with whom to share life's happiness and sorrows.

But in order to find this Idea, or better said, to find myself, it profits me nought to get involved in the world. And that is exactly the mistake I have been making! That is why I thought it would be good to plunge into the study of law, for I thought thereby to develop my mental acuity through analyzing the complications of life. Here was exactly that great mass of details wherein I would lose myself; here perhaps I could take the facts and construct a total view, an organism of theft, pursuing the darker side of the law (here a certain spirit of association is incredibly noteworthy!). Therefore I wished to become an attorney, so that by putting myself into another person's role, I could for all practical purposes find a substitute for my own life and find a certain distraction in outward events and circumstances.

The Idea was what I lacked in order *to live a complete human life* and not merely knowledge. So I could not base the development of my philosophy of life—yes, on something one calls 'objective'—on something not my own, but upon something which reaches to the deepest roots of my existence and wherein I am connected into the divine and held fast to it, even though the whole world falls apart. Yes, *this is what I lack and this is what I am striving for.*

THE SAYINGS OF KIERKEGAARD

Philosophy and Christianity will never allow themselves to be united, for if I hold to the most essential element in Christianity, namely, the redemption, so that if this element is to be something vital, it must be extended over the whole person. Or must I consider a person's moral ability as impaired while viewing his cognitive faculties as unimpaired? I certainly could consider the possibility of a philosophy according to Christianity, but it would be a Christian philosophy. The relation would not be philosophy's relation to Christianity, but Christianity's relation to Christian cognition [*Papers,* Oct. 17, 1835].

There is a major opposition between Augustine and Pelagius. The first will crush all in order to raise it. The second refers itself to man as he is. The first system views Christianity in three stages: creation; the fall through sin and with it a condition of death and impotence; and a new creation, whereby man becomes placed in a position where he can choose Christianity. The other system refers itself to man as he is (Christianity adapted to the world). The importance of the theory of inspiration is seen from the first system. Here one sees the relation between the synergistic and semi-pelagian conflict. It is the same question, only that the synergistic conflict has the Augustinian system's idea of new creation as its presupposition [*Papers* 1835].

Reasons are in general very curious things. If I lack passion, I look down on them with contempt. If I have passion, they grow up into something immense [*Papers* X].

All such scientific methods became particularly dangerous and pernicious when they encroach upon the spiritual field. Plants, animals, and stars may be handled in that way, but to handle the spirit of man in such a fashion is blasphemy which only weakens moral and religious passion. And so physiology spreads out over the kingdom of plants and animals, showing more and more analogies, which are not really analogies, since man is qualitatively different from plants and animals. Just as metaphysics has supplanted theology, physics will in the end supplant ethics. The whole modern statistical approach to morality is bent in this direction [*Papers* VII].

How ridiculous men are! They do not use the liberties they already possess, but they demand those they do not have. They have freedom of thought, but they demand freedom of speech [*Either/Or I*].

Do not check your soul's flight, do not grieve the better promptings within you, do not dull your spirit with half wishes and half thoughts. Ask yourself, and continue to ask until you find the answer. For one may have known a thing many times and acknowledged it, one may have willed a thing many times and attempted it; and yet it is only by the deep inward movements, only by the indescribable emotions of the hearts, that for the first time you are convinced that what you have known belongs to you, that no power can take it from you; for only the truth that edifies is truth for you [*Either/Or II*].

If there were no eternal consciousness in man, if at the foundation of all there lay only a wildly seething power which writhing with obscure passions produced everything that is great and everything that is insignificant, if a bottomless void never satiated lay hidden beneath all—what then would life be but despair? If such were the case, if there were no sacred bond which united mankind, if one generation arose after another like the leafage in the forest, if the human race passed through the desert, a thoughtless and fruitless activity, if an eternal oblivion were always lurking for its prey and there was no power strong enough to wrest it from its maw—how empty then and comfortless life would be! [*Fear and Trembling,* 1843].

If Hegel had written his whole logic and had written in the Preface that it was simply a thought experiment, he would have been the greatest thinker who has ever lived [*Papers,* VI].

Life can only be understood backwards, but it must be lived forward.

The only fundamental basis for understanding is that one understands only in proportion to becoming himself that which he understands [*Papers* V].

Both [proving and being convinced by an argument for the existence of God] are equally fantastic, for just as no one has ever proved the existence of God, so no one has ever been an atheist, although many have never willed to allow their knowledge of God's existence to get power over their mind. It is the same with immortality. . . . With regard to God's existence, immortality and all problems of immanence, recollection is valid; it is present in every man, only he is not aware of it; however, this in no way means that his concept is adequate [*Papers* V].

In making a choice it is not so much a question of choosing the right as of the energy, the earnest, the pathos with which one chooses. Thereby the personality is consolidated. Therefore, even if a man were to choose the wrong, he will nevertheless *discover, precisely by reason of the energy with which he chose, that he had chosen the wrong.* For the choice being made with the whole inwardness of his personality, his nature is purified and he himself brought into immediate relation with the eternal Power whose omnipotence interpenetrates the whole of existence [*Either/Or* II].

The absurd is a category, and the most developed thought is required to define the Christian absurd accurately and with conceptual correctness. The absurd is a category, the negative criterion, of the divine or of the relationship to the divine. *When the believer has faith, the absurd is not the absurd—* faith transforms it, but in every weak moment it is again more or less absurd to him. The passion of faith is the only thing which masters the absurd [*Papers,* X].

As a religion [organized Christianity] as it is now practiced is just about as genuine as tea made from a bit of paper which once lay in a drawer beside another bit of paper which once had been used to wrap up a few dried tea leaves from which tea had already been made three times [*Papers*].

Indeed, if the press were to hang a sign out like every other business, it would have to read as follows: Here people are demoralized in the shortest possible time on the largest possible scale for the smallest possible price. The lowest depths to which people can sink before God is defined by the word "Journalist." If I were a father and had a daughter who was seduced, I should not despair over her; I would hope for her salvation. But if I had a son who became a journalist, and continued to be one for five years, I would despair and give up on him [*Papers*].

Concluding Unscientific Postscript

The problem we are considering is not the truth of Christianity but the individual's relation to Christianity. Our discussion is not about the scholar's systematic zeal to arrange the truths of Christianity in nice tidy categories but about the individual's personal relationship to this doctrine, a relationship which is properly one of infinite interest to him. Simply stated, "I, Johannes Climacus, born in this city, now thirty years old, a decent fellow like most folk, suppose that there awaits me, as it awaits a maid and a professor, a highest good, which is called an eternal happiness. I have heard that Christianity is the way to that good, and so I ask, how may I establish a proper relationship to Christianity?"

I hear an intellectual's response to this, "What outrageous presumption! What egregious egoistic vanity in this theocentric and philosophically enlightened age, which is concerned with global history, to lay such inordinate weight on one's petty self."

I tremble at such a reproof and had I not already inured myself to these kinds of responses, I would slink away like a dog with his tail between his legs. But I have no guilt whatsoever about what I am doing, for it is not I who is presumptuous, but, rather, it is Christianity itself which compels me to ask the question in this way. For Christianity places enormous significance on my little self, and upon every other self however insignificant it may seem, in that it offers each self eternal happiness on the condition that a proper relationship between itself and the individual is established.

Although I am still an outsider to faith, I can see that the only unpardonable sin against the majesty of Christianity is for an individual to take his relationship to it for granted. However modest it may seem to relate oneself in this way, Christianity considers such a casual attitude to be imprudent. So I must respectfully decline all theocentric helpers and the helpers' helpers who would seek to help me through a detached relationship to this doctrine. I would rather remain where I am with my infinite concern about my spiritual existence, with the problem of how I may become a Christian. For while it is not impossible for one with an infinite concern for his eternal happiness to achieve salvation, it is entirely impossible for one who has lost all sensitivity to the relationship to achieve such a state.

The objective problem is: Is Christianity true? The subjective problem is: What is the individual's relationship to Christianity? Quite simply, how may I, Johannes Climacus, participate in the happiness promised by Christianity? The problem concerns myself alone; partly because, if it is properly set forth, it will concern everyone in exactly the same way; and partly because all the other points of view take faith for granted, as trivial.

In order to make my problem clear, I shall first describe the objective problem and show how it should be treated. In this way the historical aspect will be given its due. After this I shall describe the subjective problem.

The Objective Problem of the Truth of Christianity. From an objective point of view Christianity is a historical fact whose truth must be considered in a purely objective manner, for the modest scholar is far too objective not to leave himself outside—though as a matter of fact, he may count himself as a believer. 'Truth' in this objective sense may mean either (1) historical truth or (2) philosophical truth. As historical truth, the truth claims must be decided by a critical examination of the various sources in the same way we determine other historical claims. Considered philosophically, the doctrine that has been historically verified must be related to the eternal truth.

The inquiring, philosophical, and learned researcher raises the question of the truth, but not the subjective truth, that is, the truth as appropriated. The inquiring researcher is interested, but he is not infinitely, personally, and passionately interested in a way that relates his own eternal happiness to this truth. Far be it for the objective person to be so immodest, so presumptuous as that!

Such an inquirer must be in one of two states. Either he is already in faith convinced of the truth of Christianity—and in such a relationship he cannot be infinitely interested in the objective inquiry, since

Translated by Louis P. Pojman

faith itself consists in being infinitely concerned with Christianity and regards every competing interest as a temptation; or he is not in faith but objectively considering the subject matter, and as such not in a condition of being infinitely interested in the question.

I mention this in order to draw your attention to what will be developed in the second part of this work, namely, that the problem of the truth of Christianity is never appropriately set forth in this objective manner, that is, it does not arise at all, since Christianity lies in decision. Let the scholarly researcher work with indefatigable zeal even to the point of shortening his life in devoted service to scholarship. Let the speculative philosopher spare neither time nor effort. They are nevertheless not personally and passionately concerned. On the contrary, they wouldn't want to be but will want to develop an objective and disinterested stance. They are only concerned about objective truth, so that the question of personal appropriation is relatively unimportant, something that will follow their findings as a matter of course. In the last analysis what matters to the individual is of minor significance. Herein precisely lies the scholar's exalted equanimity as well as the comedy of his parrotlike pedantry.

The Historical Point of View. When Christianity is considered through its historical documents, it becomes vital to get a trustworthy account of what Christian doctrine really is. If the researcher is infinitely concerned with his relationship to this truth, he will immediately despair, because it is patently clear that in historical matters the greatest certainty is still only an approximation, and an approximation is too weak for one to build his eternal happiness upon, since its incommensurability with eternal happiness prevents it from obtaining. So the scholar, having only a historical interest in the truth of Christianity, begins his work with tremendous zeal and contributes important research until his seventieth year. Then just fourteen days before his death he comes upon a new document that casts fresh light over one whole side of his inquiry. Such an objective personality is the antithesis of the restless concern of the subject who is infinitely interested in eternal happiness and who surely deserves to have a decisive answer to the question concerning that happiness.

When one raises the historical question of the truth of Christianity or of what is and what is not Christian truth, we come directly to the Holy Scriptures as the central document. The historical investigation focuses first on the Bible.

The Holy Scriptures. It is very important that the scholar secure the highest possible reliability in his work. In this regard it is important for me not to pretend that I have learning or show that I have none, for my purpose here is more important. And that is to have it understood and remembered that even with the most impressive scholarly credentials and persistence, even if all the intelligence of all the critics met in one single head, still one would get no further than an approximation. We could never show more than that there is an incommensurability between the infinite personal concern for one's eternal happiness and the reliability of the documents.

When the Scriptures are considered as the ultimate arbiter, which determines what is and what is not Christian, it becomes imperative to secure their reliability through a critical historical investigation. So we must deal here with several issues: the canonicity of each book of the Bible, their authenticity, their integrity, the trustworthiness of the authors, and finally, we must assume a dogmatic guarantee: inspiration. When one thinks of the prodigious labors that the English are devoting to digging the tunnel under the Thames, the incredible expenditure of time and effort, and how a little accident can upset the whole project for a long time, one may be able to get some idea of what is involved in the undertaking that we are describing. How much time, what diligence, what glorious acumen, what remarkable scholarship from generation to generation have been requisitioned to accomplish this work of supreme wonder! And yet a single little dialectical doubt can suddenly touch the foundations and for a long time disturb the whole project, closing the underground way to Christianity, which one has tried to establish objectively and scientifically, instead of approaching the problem as it should be approached, above ground—subjectively.

But let us assume first that the critics have established everything that scholarly theologians in their happiest moments ever dreamed to prove about the Bible. These books and no others belong to the canon. They are authentic, complete, their authors are trustworthy—it is as though every letter were divinely inspired (one cannot say more than this, for inspiration is an object of faith and is qualitatively dialectical. It cannot be reached by a quantitative increment). Furthermore, there is not the slightest contradiction in these holy writings. For let us be careful in formulating our hypothesis. If there is even a word that is problematic, the parenthesis of uncertainty begins again, and the critical philological enterprise will lead one astray. In general, all that is needed to cause us to question our findings is a little circumspection, the renunciation of every learned middle-term, which could in a twinkle of the eye degenerate into a hundred-year parenthesis.

And so it comes to pass that everything we hoped for with respect to the Scriptures has been firmly established. What follows from this? Has anyone who didn't previously have faith come a single step closer to faith? Of course not, not a single step closer. For faith isn't produced through academic investigations. It doesn't come directly at all, but, on the contrary, it is precisely in objective analysis that one loses the infinite personal and passionate concern that is the requisite condition for faith, its ubiquitous ingredient, wherein faith comes into existence.

Has anyone who had faith gained anything in terms of faith's strength and power? No, not the least. Rather, his prodigious learning which lies like a dragon at faith's door, threatening to devour it, will become a handicap, forcing him to put forth an even greater prodigious effort in fear and trembling in order not to fall into temptation and confuse knowledge with faith. Whereas faith had uncertainty as a useful teacher, it now finds that certainty is its most dangerous enemy. Take passion away and faith disappears, for certainty and passion are incompatible. Let an analogy throw light on this point. He who believes that God exists and providentially rules the world finds it easier to preserve his faith (and not a fantasy) in an imperfect world where passion is kept awake, than in an absolutely perfect world; for in such an ideal world faith is unthinkable. This is the reason that we are taught that in eternity faith will be annulled.

Now let us assume the opposite, that the opponents have succeeded in proving what they desired to establish regarding the Bible and did so with a certainty that transcended their wildest hopes. What then? Has the enemy abolished Christianity? Now a whit. Has he harmed the believer? Not at all. Has he won the right of being free from the responsibility of becoming a believer? By no means. Simply because these books are not by these authors, are not authentic, lack integrity, do not seem to be inspired (though this cannot be demonstrated since it is a matter of faith), it in no way follows that these authors have not existed, and above all it does not follow that Christ never existed. In so far as faith perdures, the believer is at liberty to assume it, just as free (mark well!); for if he accepted the content of faith on the basis of evidence, he would now be on the verge of giving up faith. If things ever came this far, the believer is somewhat to blame, for he invited the procedure and began to play into the hands of unbelief by attempting to prove the content of faith.

Here is the heart of the matter, and I come back to learned theology. For whose sake is the proof sought? Faith does not need it. Yes, it must regard it as an enemy. But when faith begins to feel ashamed, when like a young woman for whom love ceases to suffice, who secretly feels ashamed of her lover and must therefore have it confirmed by others that he really is quite remarkable, so likewise when faith falters and begins to lose its passion, when it begins to cease to be faith, then proof becomes necessary in order to command respect from the side of unbelief.

So when the subject of faith is treated objectively, it becomes impossible for a person to relate himself to the decision of faith with passion, let alone with infinitely concerned passion. It is a self-contradiction and as such comical to be infinitely concerned about what at best can only be an approximation. If in spite of this, we still preserve passion, we obtain fanaticism. For the person with infinite passionate concern every relevant detail becomes something of infinite value. The error lies not in the infinite passion but in the fact that its object has become an approximation.

As soon as one takes subjectivity away—and with it subjectivity's passion—and with passion the infinite concern—it becomes impossible to make a decision—either with regard to this problem or any other; for every decision, every genuine decision, is a subjective action. A contemplator (i.e., an objective subject) experiences no infinite urge to make a decision and sees no need for a commitment anywhere. This is the falsity of objectivity and this is the problem with the Hegelian notion of mediation as the mode of transition in the continuous process, where nothing endures and where nothing is infinitely decided because the movement turns back on itself and again turns back; but the movement itself is a chimera and philosophy becomes wise afterwards. Objectively speaking, this method produces results in great supply, but it does not produce a single decisive result. This is as is expected, since decisiveness inheres in subjectivity, essentially in passion and maximally in the personal passion that is infinitely concerned about one's eternal happiness.

Christianity is spirit, spirit is inwardness, inwardness is subjectivity, subjectivity is essentially passion and at its maximum infinite personal and passionate concern about one's eternal happiness.

Becoming Subjective. Objectively we only consider the subject matter, subjectively we consider the subject and his subjectivity, and, behold, subjectivity is precisely our subject matter. It must constantly be kept in mind that the subjective problem is not about some other subject matter but simply about subjectivity itself. Since the problem is about a decision, and all decisions lie in subjectivity, it follows that not a trace of objectivity remains, for at the moment that subjectivity slinks away from the pain and crisis of decision, the problem becomes to a degree objective. If the Introduction still awaits another work before a judgment can be made on the subject matter, if the philosophical system still lacks a paragraph, if the speaker still has a final argument, the decision is postponed. We do not raise the question of the truth of Christianity in the sense that when it has been decided, subjectivity is ready and willing to accept it. No, the question is about the subject's acceptance of it, and it must be regarded as an infernal illusion or a deceitful evasion which seeks to avoid the decision by taking an objective treatment of the subject matter and assumes that a subjective commitment will follow from the objective deliberation as a matter of course. On the contrary, the decision lies in subjectivity and an objective acceptance is either a pagan concept or one devoid of all meaning.

Christianity will give the single individual eternal happiness, a good that cannot be divided into parts but can only be given to one person at a time. Although we presuppose that subjectivity is available to be appropriated, a possibility that involves accepting this good, it is not a subjectivity without qualification, without a genuine understanding of the meaning of this good. Subjectivity's development or transformation, its infinite concentration in itself with regard to an eternal happiness—this highest good of Infinity, an eternal happiness—this is subjectivity's developed possibility. As such, Christianity protests against all objectivity and will infinitely concern itself only with subjectivity. If there is any Christian truth, it first arises in subjectivity. Objectively it does not arise at all. If its truth is only in a single person, then Christianity exists in him alone, and there is greater joy in heaven over this one than over all world history and philosophical systems which, as objective forces, are incommensurable with the Christian idea.

Philosophy teaches that the way to truth is to become objective, but Christianity teaches that the way is to become subjective, that is, to become a subject in truth. Lest we seem to be trading on ambiguities, let it be said clearly that Christianity aims at intensifying passion to its highest pitch; but passion is subjectivity and does not exist objectively at all.

Subjective Truth, Inwardness; Truth is Subjectivity. For an objective reflection the truth becomes an object, something objective, and thought points away from the subject. For subjective reflection the truth becomes a matter of appropriation, of inwardness, of subjectivity, and thought must penetrate deeper and still deeper into the subject and his subjectivity. Just as in objective reflection, when objectivity had come into being, subjectivity disappeared, so here the subjectivity of the subject becomes the final stage, and objectivity disappears. It is not for an instant forgotten that the subject is an existing individual, and that existence is a process of becoming, and that therefore the idea of truth being an identity of thought and being is a chimera of abstraction; this is not because the truth is not such an identity but because the believer is an existing individual for whom the truth cannot be such an identity as long as he exists as a temporal being.

If an existing subject really could transcend himself, the truth would be something complete for him, but where is this point outside of himself? The I = I is a mathematical point that does not exist, and insofar as one would take this standpoint, he will not stand in another's way. It is only momentarily that the existential subject experiences the unity of the infinite and the finite, which transcends existence, and that moment is the moment of passion. While scribbling modern philosophy is contemptuous of passion, passion remains the highest point of existence for the individual who exists in time. In passion the existential subject is made infinite in imagination's eternity, and at the same time he is himself.

All essential knowledge concerns existence, or only that knowledge that relates to existence is essential knowledge. All knowledge that is not existential, that does not involve inward reflection, is really accidental knowledge, its degree and compass are essentially a matter of no importance. This essential knowledge that relates itself essentially to the existing individual is not to be equated with the above-mentioned abstract identity between thought and being. But it means that knowledge must relate itself to the knower, who is essentially an existing individual, and therefore all essential knowledge essentially relates itself to existence, to that which exists. But all ethical and all ethical-religious knowledge has this essential relationship to the existence of the knower.

In order to elucidate the difference between the objective way of reflection and the subjective way, I shall now show how subjective reflection makes its way back into inwardness. The highest point of inwardness in an existing person is passion, for passion corresponds to truth as a paradox, and the fact that the truth becomes a paradox is grounded in its relation to an existing individual. The one corresponds to the other. By forgetting that we are existing subjects, we lose passion and truth ceases to be a paradox, but the knowing subject begins to lose his humanity and becomes fantastic and the truth likewise becomes a fantastic object for this kind of knowledge.

When the question of truth is put forward in an objective manner, reflection is directed objectively to the truth as an object to which the knower is related. The reflection is not on the relationship but on whether he is related to the truth. If that which he is related to is the truth, the subject is in the truth. When the question of truth is put forward in a subjective manner, reflection is directed subjectively to the individual's relationship. If the relation's HOW is in truth, the individual is in truth, even if the WHAT to which he is related is not true.

We may illustrate this by examining the knowledge of God. Objectively the reflection is on whether the object is the true God; subjectively reflection is on whether the individual is related to a *what* in such a way that his relationship in truth is a God-relationship. On which side does the truth lie? Ah, let us not lean towards mediation and say, it is on neither side but in the mediation of both of them.

The existing individual who chooses the objective way enters upon the entire approximation process that is supposed to bring God into the picture. But this in all eternity cannot be done because God is Subject and therefore exists only for the subjective individual in inwardness. The existing individual who chooses the subjective way comprehends instantly the entire dialectical difficulty involved in having to use some time, perhaps a long time, in order to find God objectively. He comprehends this dialectical difficulty in all its pain because every moment without God is a moment lost—so important is the matter of being related to God. In this way God certainly becomes a postulate but not in the useless sense in which it is often taken. It becomes the only way in which an existing individual comes into a relation with God—when the dialectical contradiction brings passion to the point of despair and helps him embrace God with the category of despair (faith). Now the postulate is far from being arbitrary or optional. It becomes a life-saving necessity, so that it is no longer simply a postulate, but rather the individual's postulation of the existence of God is a necessity.

Now the problem is to calculate on which side there is the most truth: *either* the side of one who seeks the true God objectively and pursues the approximate truth of the God-idea *or* the side of one who is driven by infinite concern for his relationship to God. No one who has not been corrupted by science can have any doubt in the matter.

If one who lives in a Christian culture goes up to God's house, the house of the true God, with a true conception of God, with knowledge of God and prays—but prays in a false spirit; and one who lives in an idolatrous land prays with the total passion of the infinite, although his eyes rest on the image of an idol; where is there most truth? The one prays in truth to God, although he worships an idol. The other prays in untruth to the true God and therefore really worships an idol.

When a person objectively inquires about the problem of immortality and another person embraces it as an uncertainty with infinite passion, where is there most truth, and who really has the greater certainty? The one has entered into an inexhaustible approximation, for certainty of immortality lies precisely in the subjectivity of the individual. The other is immortal and fights against his uncertainty.

Let us consider Socrates. Today everyone is playing with some proof or other. Some have many, some fewer. But Socrates! He put the question objectively in a hypothetical manner: "*if* there is immortality." Compared to the modern philosopher with three proofs for immortality, should we consider Socrates a doubter? Not at all. On this little *if* he risks his entire life, he dares to face death, and he has directed his life with infinite passion so that the *if* is confirmed—*if* there is immortality. Is there any better proof for life after death? But those who have the three proofs do not at all pattern their lives in conformity with the idea. If there is an immortality, it must feel disgust over their lackadaisical manner of life. Can any better refutation be given of the three proofs? These crumbs of uncertainty helped Socrates because they hastened the process along, inciting the passions. The three proofs that that others have are of no help at all because they are dead to the spirit, and the fact that they need three proofs proves that they are spiritually dead. The Socratic ignorance that Socrates held fast with the entire passion of his inwardness was an expression of the idea that eternal truth is related to an existing individual, and that this will be in the form of a paradox as long as he exists; and yet it is just possible that there is more truth in Socratic ignorance than is contained in the "objective truth" of the philosophical systems, which flirts with the spirit of the times and cuddles up to associate professors.

The objective accent falls on *what* is said; the subjective accent falls on *how* it is said. This distinction is valid even for aesthetics and shows itself in the notion that what may be objectively true may in the mouth of certain people become false. This distinction is illustrated by the saying that the difference between the older days and our day is that in the old days only a few knew the truth while in ours all know it, except that the inwardness towards it is in inverse proportion to the scope of its possession. Aesthetically the contradiction that the truth becomes error in certain mouths is best understood comically. In the ethical-religious domain the accent is again on the *how*. But this is not to be understood as referring to decorum, modulation, delivery, and so on, but to the individual's relationship to the proposition, the way he relates himself to it. Objectively it is a question simply about the content of the proposition, but subjectively it is a question of inwardness. At its maximum this inward *how* is the passion of infinity and the passion of the infinite is itself the truth. But since the passion of the infinite is exactly subjectivity, subjectivity is the truth. Objectively there is no infinite decision or commitment, and so it is objectively correct to annul the difference between good and evil as well as the law of noncontradiction and the difference between truth and untruth. Only in subjectivity is there decision and commitment, so that to seek this in objectivity is to be in error. It is the passion of infinity that brings forth decisiveness, not its content, for its content is precisely itself. In this manner the subjective *how* and subjectivity are the truth.

But the *how* that is subjectively emphasized because the subject is an existing individual is also subject to a temporal dialectic. In passion's decisive moment, where the road swings off from the way to objective knowledge, it appears that the infinite decision is ready to be made. But in that moment the existing individual finds himself in time, and the subjective *how* becomes transformed into a striving, a striving that is motivated by and is repeatedly experienced in the decisive passion of the infinite. But this is still a striving.

When subjectivity is truth, subjectivity's definition must include an expression for an opposition to objectivity, a reminder of the fork in the road, and this expression must also convey the tension of inwardness. Here is such a definition of truth: *the objective uncertainty, held fast in an appropriation process of the most passionate inwardness is the truth,* the highest truth available for an existing person. There where the way swings off (and where that is cannot be discovered objectively but only subjectively), at that place objective knowledge is annulled. Objectively speaking he has only uncertainty, but precisely there the infinite passion of inwardness is intensified, and truth is precisely the adventure to choose objective uncertainty with the passion of inwardness.

When I consider nature in order to discover God, I do indeed see his omnipotence and wisdom, but I see much more that disturbs me. The result of all this is objective uncertainty, but precisely here is the place for inwardness because inwardness apprehends the objective uncertainty with the entire passion of infinity. In the case of mathematical statements objectivity is already given, but because of the nature of mathematics, this truth is existentially indifferent.

Now the above definition of truth is an equivalent description of faith. Without risk there is no faith. Faith is precisely the contradiction between the infinite passion of inwardness and objective uncertainty. If I can grasp God objectively, I do not believe, but because I cannot know God objectively, I must have faith, and if I will preserve myself in faith, I must constantly be determined to hold fast to the objective uncertainty, so as to remain out upon the ocean's deep, over seventy thousand fathoms of water, and still believe.

In the sentence 'subjectivity, inwardness is truth', we see the essence of Socratic wisdom, whose immortal service is exactly to have recognized the essential meaning of existence, that the knower is an *existing* subject, and for this reason in his ignorance Socrates enjoyed the highest relationship to truth within paganism. This is a truth that speculative philosophy unhappily again and again forgets: that the knower is an existing subject. It is difficult enough to recognize this fact in our objective age, long after the genius of Socrates.

When subjectivity, inwardness, is the truth, the truth becomes objectively determined as a paradox, and that it is paradoxical is made clear by the fact that subjectivity is truth, for it repels objectivity, and the expression for the objective repulsion is the intensity and measure of inwardness. The paradox is the objective uncertainty, which is the expression for the passion of inwardness, which is precisely the truth. This is the Socratic principle. The eternal, essential truth, that is, that which relates itself essentially to the individual because it concerns his existence (all other knowledge is, Socratically speaking, accidental, its degree and scope being indifferent), is a paradox. Nevertheless, the eternal truth is not essentially in itself paradoxical, but it becomes so by relating itself to an existing individual. Socratic ignorance is the expression of this objective uncertainty, the inwardness of the existential subject is the truth. To anticipate what I will develop later, Socratic ignorance is an analogy to the category of the absurd, only that there is still less objective certainty in the absurd, and therefore infinitely greater tension in its inwardness. The Socratic inwardness that involves existence is an analogy to faith, except that this inwardness is repulsed not by ignorance but by the absurd, which is infinitely deeper. Socratically the eternal, essential truth is by no means paradoxical in itself, but only by virtue of its relation to an existing individual.

Subjectivity, inwardness, is the truth. Is there a still more inward expression for this? Yes, there is. If subjectivity is seen as the truth, we may posit the opposite principle: that subjectivity is untruth, error. Socratically speaking, subjectivity is untruth if it fails to understand that subjectivity is truth and desires to understand itself objectively. But now we are presupposing that subjectivity in becoming the truth has a difficulty to overcome in as much as it is in untruth. So we must work backwards, back to inwardness. Socratically, the way back to the truth takes place through recollection, supposing that we have memories of that truth deep within us.

Let us call this untruth of the individual 'sin.' Seen from eternity the individual cannot be in sin, nor can he be eternally presupposed as having been in sin. So it must be that he becomes a sinner by coming into existence (for the beginning point is that subjectivity is untruth). He is not born as a sinner in the sense that he is sinful before he is born, but he is born in sin and as a sinner. We shall call this state *original sin.* But if existence has acquired such power over him, he is impotent to make his way back to eternity through the use of his memory (supposing that there is truth in the Platonic idea that we may discover truth through recollection). If it was already paradoxical that the eternal truth related itself to an existing individual, now it is absolutely paradoxical that it relates itself to such an individual. But the more difficult it is for him through memory to transcend existence, the more inwardness must increase in intense passion, and when it is made impossible for him, when he is held so fast in existence that the back door of recollection is forever closed to him through sin, then his inwardness will be the deepest possible.

Subjectivity is truth. Through this relationship between the eternal truth and the existing individual the paradox comes into existence. Let us now go further and suppose that the eternal truth is essentially a paradox. How does this paradox come into existence? By juxtaposing the eternal, essential truth with temporal existence. When we set them together within the truth itself, the truth becomes paradoxical. The eternal truth has come into time. This is the paradox. If the subject is hindered by sin from making his way back to eternity by looking inward through recollection, he need not trouble himself about this, for now the eternal essential truth is no longer behind him, but it is in front of him, through its being in existence or having existed, so that if the individual does not *existentially* get hold of the truth, he will never get hold of it.

It is impossible to accentuate existence more than this. When the eternal truth is related to an existing individual, truth becomes a paradox. The paradox repels the individual because of the objective uncertainty and ignorance towards inwardness. But since this paradox in itself is not paradoxical, it does not push the spirit far enough. For without risk there is no faith, and the greater the risk the greater the faith, and the more objective reliability, the less inwardness (for inwardness is precisely subjectivity). Indeed, the less objective reliability, the deeper becomes the possible inwardness. When the paradox is in itself paradoxical, it repels the individual by the power of the absurd, and the corresponding passion, which is produced in the process, is faith. But subjectivity, inwardness, is truth, for otherwise we have forgotten the Socratic contribution; but there is no more striking expression for inwardness than when the retreat from existence through recollection back to eternity is made impossible; and when the truth as paradox encounters the individual who is caught in the vice-grip of sin's anxiety and suffering, but who is also aware of the tremendous risk involved in faith—when he nevertheless makes the leap of faith—this is subjectivity at its height.

When Socrates believed in the existence of God, he held fast to an objective uncertainty in passionate inwardness, and in that contradiction, in that risk faith came into being. Now it is different. Instead of the objective uncertainty, there is objective certainty about the object—certainty that it is absurd, and it is, again, faith that holds fast to that object in passionate inwardness. Compared with the gravity of the absurd, Socratic ignorance is a joke, and compared with the strenuosity of faith in believing the paradox, Socratic existential inwardness is a Greek life of leisure.

What is the absurd? The absurd is that the eternal truth has entered time, that God has entered existence, has been born, has grown, and so on, has become precisely like any other human being, quite indistinguishable from other humans. The absurd is precisely by its objective repulsion the measure of the inwardness of faith. Suppose there is a man who desires to have faith. Let the comedy begin. He desires to obtain faith with the help of objective investigation and what the approximation process of evidential inquiry yields. What happens? With the help of the increment of evidence the absurd is transformed to something else; it becomes probable, it becomes more probable still, it becomes perhaps highly and overwhelmingly probable. Now that there is respectable evidence for the content of his faith, he is ready to believe it, and he prides himself that his faith is not like that of the shoemaker, the tailor, and the simple folk, but comes after a long investigation. Now he prepares himself to believe it. Any proposition that is almost probable, reasonably probable, highly and overwhelmingly probable, is something that is almost known and as good as known, highly and overwhelmingly known—but it is not believed, not through faith; for the absurd is precisely faith's object and the only positive attitude possible in relation to it is faith and not knowledge.

Christianity has declared itself to be the eternal that has entered time, that has proclaimed itself as the *paradox* and demands faith's inwardness in relation to that which is a scandal to the Jews and folly to the Greeks—and as absurd to the understanding. It is impossible to say this more strongly than by saying: subjectivity is truth, and objectivity is repelled by it—by virtue of the absurd.

Subjectivity culminates in passion. Christianity is the paradox; paradox and passion belong together as a perfect match, and the paradox is perfectly suited to one whose situation is to be in the extremity of existence. Indeed, there never has been found in all the world two lovers more suited to each other than passion and paradox, and the strife between them is a lover's quarrel, when they argue about which one first aroused the other's passion. And so it is here. The existing individual by means of the paradox has come to the extremity of existence. And what is more wonderful for lovers than to be granted a long time together with each other without anything disturbing their relationship except that which makes it more inwardly passionate? And this is what is granted to the unspeculative understanding between the passion and paradox, for they will dwell harmoniously together in time and be changed first in eternity.

But the speculative philosopher views things altogether differently. He believes but only to a certain degree. He puts his hand to the plow but quickly looks about for something to know. From a Christian perspective it is hard to see how he could reach the highest good in this manner.

Chapter 28

JOHN STUART MILL

John Stuart Mill (1806–1873), one of the most important British philosophers of the nineteenth century, was born in London and educated by his father, James Mill, a first-rate philosopher in his own right, learning Greek at the age of three and Latin at the age of eight. By the time he was fourteen he had received a thorough classic education at home. He began work as a clerk for the East India Company at the age of seventeen and eventually became a director of the company. Influenced by the work of Jeremy Bentham (1748–1832), he embraced utilitarianism and ardently worked for social reform. However, a crisis of meaning occurred in his twenty-second year. Mill describes it in his *Autobiography*. One day in 1826 he experienced a "dull state of nerves, such as everybody is occasionally liable to," when the following question occurred to him:

> Suppose that all your objects in life were realized; that all the changes in institutions and opinions which you are looking forward to, could be completely effected at this very instant: would this be a great joy and happiness to you? An irrepressible self-consciousness distinctly answered, "No!" At this my heart sank within me: the whole foundation on which my life was constructed fell down. All my happiness was to have been founded in the continual pursuit of this end. The end had ceased to charm, and how could there ever again be any interest in the means? I seemed to have nothing left to live for?

Mill went through a period of deep depression lasting several months. Eventually, he was restored to full emotional health and pursued his tasks with renewed vigor.

When he was twenty-five, Mill became close friends with Harriet Taylor, a married woman. Their mutual devotion and intimacy, though apparently Platonic, caused a scandal in a society where the only approved intimacy between the opposite sexes were familial, either as married couples or brother-sister. After Harriet's husband died, Mill married her (1851). Harriet's ideas changed Mill's and Mill regarded her as the most profound mind he had ever known. He claims that much of the credit for his work *On Liberty* (1859) goes to her. His arguments in *The Subjection of Women* (1861) show her influence.

Mill was a prolific writer. His *A System of Logic* (1848) is one of the most original works on inductive logic ever written. His *Utilitarianism* (1861) (see below) is the classic work on the topic. Mill was elected to Parliament in 1865. A man with an independent and penetrating mind, he fought for woman's suffrage, the rights of blacks in Jamaica, Irish land reform, the retention of capital punishment, and weighted votes for the better informed over the less educated ("It is not useful, but hurtful, that the constitution of the country should declare ignorance to be entitled to as much political power as knowledge").

Our first selection is his classic work *Utilitarianism.* Mill defends utilitarianism, a form of consequentialist ethics, against more rule-bound *deontological* systems, the sort of system we represented by Kant's categorical imperative in the *Foundation for the Metaphysic of Morals*. Traditionally, two major types of ethical systems have dominated the field, one in which the locus of value is the act or kind of act, the other in which the locus of value is the outcome or consequences of the act. The former type of theory is called *deontological* (from the Greek *deon* which means 'duty'), and the latter is called *teleological* (from the Greek *telos* which means 'end' or 'goal').

That is, the standard of right or wrong action for the teleologists is the comparative consequences of the available actions. That act is right which produces the best consequences. Whereas the deontologist is concerned only with the rightness of the act itself, the teleologist asserts that there is no such thing as an act having intrinsic worth. While there is something intrinsically bad about lying for the deontologist, the only thing wrong with lying for the teleologist is the bad consequences it produces. If you can reasonably calculate that lying will do even slightly more good than telling the truth, you have an obligation to lie.

Mill wrote *Utilitarianism* in response to criticisms about Jeremy Bentham's hedonistic version of utilitarianism, which failed to differentiate between kinds and quality of pleasure, and so received the name of "pig philosophy." Mill meets this charge by substituting a more complex theory of happiness for Bentham's undifferentiated pleasure.

In our second reading, *On Liberty,* Mill attempts to ground liberty in a utilitarian ethic. He argues for "utility in the largest sense, grounded on the permanent interests of man as a progressive being," from there defends the freedom of the individual to do whatever one likes so long as one is not interfering with the rights of others. He warns against the "tyranny of the majority" which can unjustifiably coerce liberty. The only grounds for interfering with another individual is to protect others from harm.

In our final essay, *The Subjection of Women,* he argues that powerful moral and prudential reasons exist for affording women equal education and, in general, equal opportunities with men.

FOR FURTHER READING

Britton, Karl. *John Stuart Mill.* (Dover, 1969).

Donner, Wendy. *The Liberal Self: John Stuart Mill's Moral and Political Philosophy.* (Cornell University Press, 1991).

Himmelfarb, Gertrude. *On Liberty and Liberalism: the Case of John Stuart Mill.* (Knopf, 1974).

McCloskey, H. J. *John Stuart Mill: A Critical Study.* (Macmillan, 1971).

Ryan, Alan. *J. S. Mill.* (Routledge & Kegan Paul, 1974).

Schneewind, J., ed. *Mill: A Collection of Critical Essays.* (Anchor Doubleday, 1968).

Sen, A. and B. Williams, eds. *Utilitarianism and Beyond.* (Cambridge University Press, 1982).

Smart, J. J. C. and Bernard Williams. *Utilitarianism: For and Against.* (Cambridge University Press, 1973).

Ten, C. L. *Mill on Liberty.* (Oxford University Press, 1980).

Utilitarianism

CHAPTER I GENERAL REMARKS

There are few circumstances among those which make up the present condition of human knowledge, more unlike what might have been expected, or more significant of the backward state in which speculation on the most important subjects still lingers, than the little progress which has been made in the decision of the controversy respecting the criterion of right and wrong. From the dawn of philosophy, the question concerning the summum bonum, or, what is the same thing, concerning the foundation of morality, has been accounted the main problem in speculative thought, has occupied the most gifted intellects, and divided them into sects and schools, carrying on a vigorous warfare against one another. And after more than two thousand years the same discussions continue, philosophers are still ranged under the same contending banners, and neither thinkers nor mankind at large seem nearer to being unanimous on the subject, than when the youth Socrates listened to the old Protagoras, and asserted (if Plato's dialogue be grounded on a real conversation) the theory of utilitarianism against the popular morality of the so-called sophist.

It is true that similar confusion and uncertainty, and in some cases similar discordance, exist respecting the first principles of all the sciences, not excepting that which is deemed the most certain of them, mathematics; without much impairing, generally indeed without impairing at all, the trustworthiness of the conclusions of those sciences. An apparent anomaly, the explanation of which is, that the detailed doctrines of a science are not usually deduced from, nor depend for their evidence upon, what are called its first principles. Were it not so, there would be no science more precarious, or whose conclusions were more insufficiently made out, than algebra; which derives none of its certainty from what are commonly taught to learners as its elements, since these, as laid down by some of its most eminent teachers, are as full of fictions as English law, and of mysteries as theology. The truths which are ultimately accepted as the first principles of a science, are really the last results of metaphysical analysis, practiced on the elementary notions with which the science is conversant; and their relation to the science is not that of foundations to an edifice, but of roots to a tree, which may perform their office equally well though they be never dug down to and exposed to light. But though in science the particular truths precede the general theory, the contrary might be expected to be the case with a practical art, such as morals or legislation. All action is for the sake of some end, and rules of action, it seems natural to suppose, must take their whole character and colour from the end to which they are subservient. When we engage in a pursuit, a clear and precise conception of what we are pursuing would seem to be the first thing we need, instead of the last we are to look forward to. A test of right and wrong must be the means, one would think, of ascertaining what is right or wrong, and not a consequence of having already ascertained it.

The difficulty is not avoided by having recourse to the popular theory of a natural faculty, a sense or instinct, informing us of right and wrong. For—besides that the existence of such a moral instinct is itself one of the matters in dispute—those believers in it who have any pretensions to philosophy, have been obliged to abandon the idea that it discerns what is right or wrong in the particular case in hand, as our other senses discern the sight or sound actually present. Our moral faculty, according to all those of its interpreters who are entitled to the name of thinkers, supplies us only with the general principles of moral judgments; it is a branch of our reason, not of our sensitive faculty; and must be looked to for the abstract doctrines of morality, not for perception of it in the concrete. The intuitive, no less than what may be termed the inductive, school of ethics, insists on the necessity of general laws. They both agree that the morality of an individual action is not a question of direct perception, but of the application of a law to an individual case. They recognize also, to a great extent, the same moral laws; but differ as to their evidence, and the source from which they derive their authority. According to the one opinion, the principles of morals are evident a priori, requiring nothing to command assent, except that the meaning of the terms be understood. According to the other doctrine, right and wrong, as well as truth and falsehood, are questions of observation and experience. But both hold equally that morality must be deduced from principles; and the intuitive school affirm as strongly as the inductive, that there is a science of morals. Yet they seldom attempt to make out a list of the a priori principles which are to serve as the premises of the science; still more rarely do they make any effort to reduce those various principles to one first principle, or common ground of obligation. They either assume the ordinary precepts of morals as of a priori authority, or they lay down as the common groundwork of those maxims, some generality much less obviously authoritative than the maxims themselves, and which has never succeeded in gaining popular acceptance. Yet to support their pretensions there ought either to be some one fundamental principle or law, at the root of all morality, or if there be several, there should be a determinate order of precedence among them; and the one principle, or the rule for deciding between the various principles when they conflict, ought to be self-evident.

To inquire how far the bad effects of this deficiency have been mitigated in practice, or to what extent the moral beliefs of mankind have been vitiated or made uncertain by the absence of any distinct recognition of an ultimate standard, would imply a complete survey and criticism of past and present ethical doctrine. It would, however, be easy to show that whatever steadiness or consistency these moral beliefs have attained, has been mainly due to the tacit influence of a standard not recognized. Although the non-existence of an acknowledged first principle has made ethics not so much a guide as a consecration of men's actual sentiments, still, as men's sentiments, both of favour and of aversion, are greatly influenced by what they suppose to be the effects of things upon their happiness, the principle of utility, or as Bentham latterly called it, the greatest happiness principle, has had a large share in forming the moral doctrines even of those who most scornfully reject its authority. Nor is there any school of thought which refuses to admit that the influence of actions on happiness is a most material and even predominant consideration in many of the details of morals, however unwilling to acknowledge it as the fundamental principle of morality, and the source of moral obligation. I might go much further, and say that to all those a priori moralists who deem it necessary to argue at all, utilitarian arguments are indispensable. It is not my present purpose to criticize these thinkers; but I cannot help referring, for illustration, to a systematic treatise by one of the most illustrious of them, the Metaphysics of Ethics, by Kant. This remarkable man, whose system of thought will long remain one of the landmarks in the history of philosophical speculation, does, in the treatise in question, lay down an universal first principle as the origin and ground of moral obligation; it is this:—'So act, that the rule on which thou actest would admit of being adopted as a law by all rational beings.' But when he begins to deduce from this precept any of the actual duties of morality, he fails, almost grotesquely, to show that there would be any contradiction, any logical (not to say physical) impossibility, in the adoption by all rational beings of the most outrageously immoral rules of conduct. All he shows is that the consequences of their universal adoption would be such as no one would choose to incur.

On the present occasion, I shall, without further discussion of the other theories, attempt to contribute something towards the understanding and appreciation of the Utilitarian or Happiness theory, and towards such proof as it is susceptible of. It is evident that this cannot be proof in the ordinary and popular meaning of the term. Questions of ultimate ends are not amenable to direct proof. Whatever can be proved to be good, must be so by being shown to be a means to something admitted to be good without proof. The medical art is proved to be good, by its conducing to health; but how is it possible to prove that health is good? The art of music is good, for the reason, among others, that it produces pleasure; but what proof is it possible to give that pleasure is good? If, then, it is asserted that there is a comprehensive formula, including all things which are in themselves good, and that whatever else is good, is not so as an end, but as a mean, the formula may be accepted or rejected, but is not a subject of what is commonly understood by proof. We are not, however, to infer that its acceptance or rejection must depend on blind impulse, or arbitrary choice. There is a larger meaning of the word proof, in which this question is as amenable to it as any other of the disputed questions of philosophy. The subject is within the cognizance of the rational faculty; and neither does that faculty deal with it solely in the way of intuition. Considerations may be presented capable of determining the intellect either to give or withhold its assent to the doctrine; and this is equivalent to proof.

We shall examine presently of what nature are these considerations; in what manner they apply to the case, and what rational grounds, therefore, can be given for accepting or rejecting the utilitarian formula. But it is a preliminary condition of rational acceptance or rejection, that the formula should be correctly understood. I believe that the very imperfect notion ordinarily formed of its meaning, is the chief obstacle which impedes its reception; and that could it be cleared, even from only the grosser misconceptions, the question would be greatly simplified, and a large proportion of its difficulties removed. Before, therefore, I attempt to enter into the philosophical grounds which can be given for assenting to the utilitarian standard, I shall offer some illustrations of the doctrine itself; with the view of showing more clearly what it is, distinguishing it from what it is not, and disposing of such of the practical objections to it as either originate in, or are closely connected with, mistaken interpretations of its meaning. Having thus prepared the ground, I shall afterwards endeavor to throw such light as I can upon the question, considered as one of philosophical theory.

CHAPTER II WHAT UTILITARIANISM IS

A passing remark is all that needs be given to the ignorant blunder of supposing that those who stand up for utility as the test of right and wrong, use the term in that restricted and merely colloquial sense in which utility is opposed to pleasure. An apology is due to the philosophical opponents of utilitarianism, for even the momentary appearance of confounding them with any one capable of so absurd a misconception; which is the more extraordinary, inasmuch as the contrary accusation, of referring everything to pleasure, and that too in its grossest form, is another of the common charges against utilitarianism: and, as has been pointedly remarked by an able writer, the same sort of persons, and often the very same persons, denounce the theory 'as impracticably dry when the word utility precedes the word pleasure, and as too practicably voluptuous when the word pleasure precedes the word utility.' Those who know anything about the matter are aware that every writer, from Epicurus to Bentham, who maintained the theory of utility, meant by it, not something to be contradistinguished from pleasure, but pleasure itself, together with exemption from pain; and instead of opposing the useful to the agreeable or the ornamental, have always declared that the useful means these, among other things. Yet the common herd, including the herd of writers, not only in newspapers and periodicals, but in books of weight and pretension, are perpetually falling into this shallow mistake. Having caught up the word utilitarian, while knowing nothing whatever about it but its sound, they habitually express by it the rejection, or the neglect, of pleasure in some of its forms; of beauty, of ornament, or of amusement. Nor is the term thus ignorantly misapplied solely in disparagement, but occasionally in compliment; as though it implied superiority to frivolity and the mere pleasures of the moment. And this perverted use is the only one in which the word is popularly known, and the one from which the new generation are acquiring their sole notion of its meaning. Those who introduced the word, but who had for many years discontinued it as a distinctive appellation, may well feel themselves called upon to resume it, if by doing so they can hope to contribute anything towards rescuing it from this utter degradation.

The creed which accepts as the foundation of morals, Utility, or the Greatest Happiness Principle, holds that actions are right in proportion as they tend to promote happiness, wrong as they tend to produce the reverse of happiness. By happiness is intended pleasure, and the absence of pain; by unhappiness, pain, and the privation of pleasure. To give a clear view of the moral standard set up by the theory, much more requires to be said; in particular, what things it includes in the ideas of pain and pleasure; and to what extent this is left an open question. But these supplementary explanations do not affect the theory of life on which this theory of morality is grounded namely, that pleasure, and freedom from pain, are the only things desirable as ends; and that all desirable things (which are as numerous in the utilitarian as in any other scheme) are desirable either for the pleasure inherent in themselves, or as means to the promotion of pleasure and the prevention of pain.

Now, such a theory of life excites in many minds, and among them in some of the most estimable in feeling and purpose, inveterate dislike. To suppose that life has (as they express it) no higher end than pleasure—no better and nobler object of desire and pursuit—they designate as utterly mean and grovelling; as a doctrine worthy only of swine, to whom the followers of Epicurus were, at a very early period, contemptuously likened; and modern holders of the doctrine are occasionally made the subject of equally polite comparisons by its German, French, and English assailants.

When thus attacked, the Epicureans have always answered, that it is not they, but their accusers, who represent human nature in a degrading light; since the accusation supposes human beings to be capable of no pleasures except those of which swine are capable. If this supposition were true, the charge could not be gainsaid, but would then be no longer an imputation; for if the sources of pleasure were precisely the same to human beings and to swine, the rule of life which is good enough for the one would be good enough for the other. The comparison of the Epicurean life to that of beasts is felt as degrading, precisely because a beast's pleasures do not satisfy a human being's conceptions of happiness. Human beings have faculties more elevated than the animal appetites, and when once made conscious of them, do not regard anything as happiness which does not include their gratification. I do not, indeed, consider the Epicureans to have been by any means faultless in drawing out their scheme of consequences from the utilitarian principle. To do this in any sufficient manner, many Stoic, as well as Christian elements require to be included. But there is no known Epicurean theory of life which does not assign to the pleasures of the intellect, of the feelings and imagination, and of the moral sentiments, a much higher value as pleasures than to those of mere sensation. It must be admitted, however, that utilitarian writers in general have placed the superiority of mental over bodily pleasures chiefly in the greater permanency, safety, uncostliness, &c., of the former—that is, in their circumstantial advantages rather than in their intrinsic nature. And on all these points utilitarians have fully proved their case; but they might have taken the other, and, as it may be called, higher ground, with entire consistency. It is quite compatible with the principle of utility to recognize the fact, that some kinds of pleasure are more desirable and more valuable than others. It would be absurd that while, in estimating all other things, quality is considered as well as quantity, the estimation of pleasures should be supposed to depend on quantity alone.

If I am asked, what I mean by difference of quality in pleasures, or what makes one pleasure more valuable than another, merely as a pleasure, except its being greater in amount, there is but one possible answer. Of two pleasures, if there be one to which all or almost all who have experience of both give a decided preference, irrespective of any feeling of moral obligation to prefer it, that is the more desirable pleasure. If one of the two is, by those who are competently acquainted with both, placed so far above the other that they prefer it, even though knowing it to be attended with a greater amount of discontent, and would not resign it for any quantity of the other pleasure which their nature is capable of, we are justified in ascribing to the preferred enjoyment a superiority in quality, so far outweighing quantity as to render it, in comparison, of small account.

Now it is an unquestionable fact that those who are equally acquainted with, and equally capable of appreciating and enjoying, both, do give a most marked preference to the manner of existence which employs their higher faculties. Few human creatures would consent to be changed into any of the lower animals, for a promise of the fullest allowance of a beast's pleasures; no intelligent human being would consent to be a fool, no instructed person would be an ignoramus, no person of feeling and conscience would be selfish and base, even though they should be persuaded that the fool, the dunce, or the rascal is better satisfied with his lot than they are with theirs. They would not resign what they possess more than he, for the most complete satisfaction of all the desires which they have in common with him. If they ever fancy they would, it is only in cases of unhappiness so extreme, that to escape from it they would exchange their lot for almost any other, however undesirable in their own eyes. A being of higher faculties requires more to make him happy, is capable probably of more acute suffering, and is certainly accessible to it at more points, than one of an inferior type; but in spite of these liabilities, he can never really wish to sink into what he feels to be a lower grade of existence. We may give what explanation we please of this unwillingness; we may attribute it to pride, a name which is given indiscriminately to some of the most and to some of the least estimable feelings of which mankind are capable; we may refer it to the love of liberty and personal independence, an appeal to which was with the Stoics one of the most effective means for the inculcation of it; to the love of power, or to the love of excitement, both of which do really enter into and contribute to it: but its most appropriate appellation is a sense of dignity, which all human beings possess in one form or other, and in some, though by no means in exact, proportion to their higher faculties, and which is so essential a part of the happiness of those in whom it is strong, that nothing which conflicts with it could be, otherwise than momentarily, an object of desire to them. Whoever supposes that this preference takes place at a sacrifice of happiness—that the superior being, in anything like equal circumstances, is not happier than the inferior—confounds the two very different ideas, of happiness, and content. It is indisputable that the being whose capacities of enjoyment are low, has the greatest chance of having them full satisfied; and a highly-endowed being will always feel that any happiness which he can look for, as the world is constituted, is imperfect. But he can learn to bear its imperfections, if they are at all bearable; and they will not make him envy the being who is indeed unconscious of the imperfections, but only because he feels not at all the good which those imperfections qualify. It is better to be a human being dissatisfied than a pig satisfied; better to be Socrates dissatisfied than a fool satisfied. And if the fool, or the pig, is of a different opinion, it is because they only know their own side of the question. The other party to the comparison knows both sides.

It may be objected, that many who are capable of the higher pleasures, occasionally, under the influence of temptation, postpone them to the lower. But this is quite compatible with a full appreciation of the intrinsic superiority of the higher. Men often, from infirmity of character, make their election for the nearer good, though they know it to be the less valuable; and this no less when the choice is between two bodily pleasures, than when it is between bodily and mental. They pursue sensual indulgences to the injury of health, though perfectly aware that health is the greater good. It may be further objected, that many who begin with youthful enthusiasm for everything noble, as they advance in years sink into indolence and selfishness. But I do not believe that those who undergo this very common change, voluntarily choose the lower description of pleasures in preference to the higher. I believe that before they devote themselves exclusively to the one, they have already become incapable of the other. Capacity for the nobler feelings is in most natures a very tender plant, easily killed, not only by hostile influences, but by mere want of sustenance; and in the majority of young persons it speedily dies away if the occupations to which their position in life has devoted them, and the society into which it has thrown them, are not favorable to keeping that higher capacity in exercise. Men lose their high aspirations as they lose their intellectual tastes, because they have not time or opportunity for indulging them; and they addict themselves to inferior pleasures, not because they deliberately prefer them, but because they are either the only ones to which they have access, or the only ones which they are any longer capable of enjoying. It may be questioned whether any one who has remained equally susceptible to both classes of pleasures, ever knowingly and calmly preferred the lower; though many, in all ages, have broken down in an ineffectual attempt to combine both.

From this verdict of the only competent judges, I apprehend there can be no appeal. On a question that is the best worth having of two pleasures, or which of two modes of existence is the most grateful to the feelings, apart from its moral attributes and from its consequences, the judgment of those who are qualified by knowledge of both, or, if they differ, that of the majority among them, must be admitted as final. And there needs be the less hesitation to accept this judgment respecting the quality of pleasures, since there is no other tribunal to be referred to even on the question of quantity. What means are there of determining which is the acutest of two pains, or the intensest of two pleasurable sensations, except the general suffrage of those who are familiar with both? Neither pains nor pleasures are homogeneous, and pain is always heterogeneous with pleasure. What is there to decide whether a particular pleasure is worth purchasing at the cost of a particular pain, except the feelings and judgment of the experienced? When, therefore, those feelings and judgment declare the pleasures derived from the higher faculties to be preferable in kind, apart from the question of intensity, to those of which the animal nature, disjoined from the higher faculties, is susceptible, they are entitled on this subject to the same regard.

I have dwelt on this point, as being a necessary part of a perfectly just conception of Utility or Happiness, considered as the directive rule of human conduct. But it is by no means an indispensable condition to the acceptance of the utilitarian standard; for that standard is not the agent's own greatest happiness, but the greatest amount of happiness altogether; and if it may possibly be doubted whether a noble character is always the happier for its nobleness, there can be no doubt that it makes other people happier, and that the world in general is immensely a gainer by it. Utilitarianism, therefore, could only attain its end by the general cultivation of nobleness of character, even if each individual were only benefited by the nobleness of others, and his own, so far as happiness is concerned, were a sheer deduction from the benefit. But the bare enunciation of such an absurdity as this last, renders refutation superfluous.

According to the Greatest Happiness Principle, as above explained, the ultimate end, with reference to and for the sake of which all other things are desirable (whether we are considering our own good or that of other people), is an existence exempt as far as possible from pain, and as rich as possible in enjoyments, both in point of quantity and quality; the test of quality, and the rule for measuring it against quantity, being the preference felt by those who in their opportunities of experience, to which must be added their habits of self-consciousness and self-observation, are best furnished with the means of comparison. This, being, according to the utilitarian opinion, the end of human action, is necessarily also the standard of morality; which may accordingly be defined, the rules and precepts for human conduct, by the observance of which an existence such as has been described might be, to the greatest extent possible, secured to all mankind; and not to them only, but, so far as the nature of things admits, to the whole sentient creation.

Against this doctrine, however, arises another class of objectors, who say that happiness, in any form, cannot be the rational purpose of human life and action; because, in the first place, it is unattainable: and they contemptuously ask, What right hast thou to be happy? a question which Mr. Carlyle clenches by the addition, What right, a short time ago, hadst thou even to be? Next, they say, that men can do without happiness; that all noble human beings have felt this, and could not have become noble but by learning the lesson of Entsagen, or renunciation; which lesson, thoroughly learnt and submitted to, they affirm to be the beginning and necessary condition of all virtue.

The first of these objections would go to the root of the matter were it well founded; for if no happiness is to be had at all by human beings, the attainment of it cannot be the end of morality, or of any rational conduct. Though, even in that case, something might still be said for the utilitarian theory; since utility includes not solely the pursuit of happiness, but the prevention or mitigation of unhappiness; and if the former aim be chimerical, there will be all the greater scope and more imperative need for the latter, so long at least as mankind think fit to live, and do not take refuge in the simultaneous act of suicide recommended under certain conditions by Novalis. When, however, it is thus positively asserted to be impossible that human life should be happy, the assertion, if not something like a verbal quibble, is at least an exaggeration. If by happiness be meant a continuity of highly pleasurable excitement, it is evident enough that this is impossible. A state of exalted pleasure lasts only moments, or in some cases, and with some intermissions, hours or days, and is the occasional brilliant flash of enjoyment, not its permanent and steady flame. Of this the philosophers who have taught that happiness is the end of life were as fully aware as those who taunt them. The happiness which they meant was not a life of rapture; but moments of such, in an existence made up of few and transitory pains, many and various pleasures, with a decided predominance of the active over the passive, and having as the foundation of the whole, not to expect more from life than it is capable of bestowing. A life thus composed, to those who have been fortunate enough to obtain it, has always appeared worthy of the name of happiness. And such an existence is even now the lot of many, during some considerable portion of their lives. The present wretched education, and wretched social arrangements, are the only real hindrance to its being attainable by almost all.

The objectors perhaps may doubt whether human beings, if taught to consider happiness as the end of life, would be satisfied with such a moderate share of it. But great numbers of mankind have been satisfied with much less. The main constituents of a satisfied life appear to be two, either of which by itself is often found sufficient for the purpose: tranquillity, and excitement. With much tranquillity, many find that they can be content with very little pleasure: with much excitement, many can reconcile themselves to a considerable quantity of pain. There is assuredly no inherent impossibility in enabling even the mass of mankind to unite both; since the two are so far from being incompatible that they are in natural alliance, the prolongation of either being a preparation for, and exciting a wish for, the other. It is only those in whom indolence amounts to a vice, that do not desire excitement after an interval of repose; it is only those in whom the need of excitement is a disease, that feel the tranquillity which follows excitement dull and insipid, instead of pleasurable in direct proportion to the excitement which preceded it. When people who are tolerably fortunate in their outward lot do not find in life sufficient enjoyment to make it valuable to them, the cause generally is, caring for nobody but themselves. To those who have neither public nor private affections, the excitements of life are much curtailed, and in any case dwindle in value as the time approaches when all selfish interests must be terminated by death: while those who leave after them objects of personal affection, and especially those who have also cultivated a fellow-feeling with the collective interests of mankind, retain as lively an interest in life on the eve of death as in the vigor of youth and health. Next to selfishness, the principal cause which makes life unsatisfactory is want of mental cultivation. A cultivated mind—I do not mean that of a philosopher, but any mind to which the fountains of knowledge have been opened, and which has been taught, in any tolerable degree, to exercise its faculties—finds sources of inexhaustible interest in all that surrounds it; in the objects of nature, the achievements of art, the imaginations of poetry, the incidents of history, the ways of mankind past and present, and their prospects in the future. It is possible, indeed, to become indifferent to all this, and that too without having exhausted a thousandth part of it; but only when one has had from the beginning no moral or human interest in these things, and has sought in them only the gratification of curiosity.

Now there is absolutely no reason in the nature of things why an amount of mental culture sufficient to give an intelligent interest in these objects of contemplation, should not be the inheritance of every one born in a civilized country. As little is there an inherent necessity that any human being should be a selfish egotist, devoid of every feeling or care but those which centre in his own miserable individuality. Something far superior to this is sufficiently common even now, to give ample earnest of what the human species may be made. Genuine private affections, and a sincere interest in the public good, are possible, though in unequal degrees, to every rightly brought up human being. In a world in which there is so much to interest, so much to enjoy, and so much also to correct and improve, every one who has this moderate amount of moral and intellectual requisites is capable of an existence which may be called enviable; and unless such a person, through bad laws, or subjection to the will of others, is denied the liberty to use the sources of happiness within his reach, he will not fail to find this enviable existence, if he escape the positive evils of life, the great sources of physical and mental suffering—such as indigence, disease, and the unkindness, worthlessness, or premature loss of objects of affection. The main stress of the problem lies, therefore, in the contest with these calamities, from which it is a rare good fortune entirely to escape; which, as things now are, cannot be obviated, and often cannot be in any material degree mitigated. Yet no one whose opinion deserves a moment's consideration can doubt that most of the great positive evils of the world are in themselves removable, and will, if human affairs continue to improve, be in the end reduced within narrow limits. Poverty, in any sense implying suffering, may be completely extinguished by the wisdom of society, combined with the good sense and providence of individuals. Even that most intractable of enemies, disease, may be indefinitely reduced in dimensions by good physical and moral education, and proper control of noxious influences; while the progress of science holds out a promise for the future of still more direct conquests over this detestable foe. And every advance in that direction relieves us from some, not only of the chances which cut short our own lives, but, what concerns us still more, which deprive us of those in whom our happiness is wrapped up. As for vicissitudes of fortune, and other disappointments connected with worldly circumstances, these are principally the effect either of gross imprudence, of ill-regulated desires, or of bad or imperfect social institutions. All the grand sources, in short, of human suffering are in a great degree, many of them almost entirely, conquerable by human care and effort; and though their removal is grievously slow—though a long succession of generations will perish in the breach before the conquest is completed, and this world becomes all that, if will and knowledge were not wanting, it might easily be made—yet every mind sufficiently intelligent and generous to bear a part, however small and inconspicuous, in the endeavor, will draw a noble enjoyment from the contest itself, which he would not for any bribe in the form of selfish indulgence consent to be without.

And this leads to the true estimation of what is said by the objectors concerning the possibility, and the obligation, of learning to do without happiness. Unquestionably it is possible to do without happiness; it is done involuntarily by nineteen-twentieths of mankind, even in those parts of our present world which are least deep in barbarism; and it often has to be done voluntarily by the hero or the martyr, for the sake of something which he prizes more than his individual happiness. But this something, what is it, unless the happiness of others, or some of the requisites of happiness? It is noble to be capable of resigning entirely one's own portion of happiness, or chances of it: but, after all, this self-sacrifice must be for some end; it is not its own end; and if we are told that its end is not happiness, but virtue, which is better than happiness, I ask, would the sacrifice be made if the hero or martyr did not believe that it would earn for others immunity from similar sacrifices? Would it be made if he thought that his renunciation of happiness for himself would produce no fruit for any of his fellow creatures, but to make their lot like his, and place them also in the condition of persons who have renounced happiness? All honour to those who can abnegate for themselves the personal enjoyment of life, when by such renunciation they contribute worthily to increase the amount of happiness in the world; but he who does it, or professes to do it, for any other purpose, is no more deserving of admiration than the ascetic mounted on his pillar. He may be an inspiriting proof of what men can do, but assuredly not an example of what they should.

Though it is only in a very imperfect state of the world's arrangements that any one can best serve the happiness of others by the absolute sacrifice of his own, yet so long as the world is in that imperfect state, I fully acknowledge that the readiness to make such a sacrifice is the highest virtue which can be found in man. I will add, that in this condition of the world, paradoxical as the assertion may be, the conscious ability to do without happiness gives the best prospect of realizing such happiness as is attainable. For nothing except that consciousness can raise a person above the chances of life, by making him feel that, let fate and fortune do their worst, they have not power to subdue him: which, once felt, frees him from excess of anxiety concerning the evils of life, and enables him, like many a Stoic in the worst times of the Roman Empire, to cultivate in tranquillity the sources of satisfaction accessible to him, without concerning himself about the uncertainty of their duration, any more than about their inevitable end.

Meanwhile, let utilitarians never cease to claim the morality of self-devotion as a possession which belongs by as good a right to them, as either to the Stoic or to the Transcendentalist. The utilitarian morality does recognize in human beings the power of sacrificing their own greatest good for the good of others. It only refuses to admit that the sacrifice is itself a good. A sacrifice which does not increase, or tend to increase, the sum total of happiness, it considers as wasted. The only self-renunciation which it applauds, is devotion to the happiness, or to some of the means of happiness, of others; either of mankind collectively, or of individuals within the limits imposed by the collective interests of mankind.

I must again repeat, what the assailants of utilitarianism seldom have the justice to acknowledge, that the happiness which forms the utilitarian standard of what is right in conduct, is not the agent's own happiness, but that of all concerned. As between his own happiness and that of others, utilitarianism requires him to be as strictly impartial as a disinterested and benevolent spectator. In the golden rule of Jesus of Nazareth, we read the complete spirit of the ethics of utility. To do as one would be done by, and to love one's neighbor as oneself, constitute the ideal perfection of utilitarian morality. As the means of making the nearest approach to this ideal, utility would enjoin, first, that laws and social arrangements should place the happiness, or (as speaking practically it may be called) the interest, of every individual, as nearly as possible in harmony with the interest of the whole; and secondly, that education and opinion, which have so vast a power over human character, should so use that power as to establish in the mind of every individual an indissoluble association between his own happiness and the good of the whole; especially between his own happiness and the practice of such modes of conduct, negative and positive, as regard for the universal happiness prescribes: so that not only he may be unable to conceive the possibility of happiness to himself, consistently with conduct opposed to the general good, but also that a direct impulse to promote the general good may be in every individual one of the habitual motives of action, and the sentiments connected therewith may fill a large and prominent place in every human being's sentient existence. If the impugners of the utilitarian morality represented it to their own minds in this its true character, I know not what recommendation possessed by any other morality they could possibly affirm to be wanting to it: what more beautiful or more exalted developments of human nature any other ethical system can be supposed to foster, or what springs of action, not accessible to the utilitarian, such systems rely on for giving effect to their mandates.

The objectors to utilitarianism cannot always be charged with representing it in a discreditable light. On the contrary, those among them who entertain anything like a just idea of its disinterested character, sometimes find fault with its standard as being too high for humanity. They say it is exacting too much to require that people shall always act from the inducement of promoting the general interests of society. But this is to mistake the very meaning of a standard of morals, and to confound the rule of action with the motive of it. It is the business of ethics to tell us what are our duties, or by what test we may know them; but no system of ethics requires that the sole motive of all we do shall be a feeling of duty; on the contrary, ninety-nine hundredths of all our actions are done from other motives, and rightly so done, if the rule of duty does not condemn them. It is the more unjust to utilitarianism that this particular misapprehension should be made a ground of objection to it, inasmuch as utilitarian moralists have gone beyond almost all others in affirming that the motive has nothing to do with the morality of the action, though much with the worth of the agent. He who saves a fellow creature from drowning does what is morally right, whether his motive be duty, or the hope of being paid for his trouble: he who betrays the friend that trusts him, is guilty of a crime, even if his object be to serve another friend to whom he is under greater obligations. But to speak only of actions done from the motive of duty, and in direct obedience to principle: it is a misapprehension of the utilitarian mode of thought, to conceive it as implying that people should fix their minds upon so wide a generality as the world, or society at large. The great majority of good actions are intended, not for the benefit of the world, but for that of individuals, of which the good of the world is made up; and the thoughts of the most virtuous man need not on these occasions travel beyond the particular persons concerned, except so far as is necessary to assure himself that in benefiting them he is not violating the rights—that is, the legitimate and authorized expectations—of any one else. The multiplication of happiness is, according to the utilitarian ethics, the object of virtue: the occasions on which any person (except one in a thousand) has it in his power to do this on an extended scale, in other words, to be a public benefactor, are but exceptional; and on these occasions alone is he called on to consider public utility; in every other case, private utility, the interest or happiness of some few persons, is all he has to attend to. Those alone the influence of whose actions extends to society in general, need concern themselves habitually about so large an object. In the case of abstinences indeed—of things which people forbear to do, from moral considerations, though the consequences in the particular case might be beneficial—it would be unworthy of an intelligent agent not to be consciously aware that the action is of a class which, if practiced generally, would be generally injurious, and that this is the ground of the obligation to abstain from it. The amount of regard for the public interest implied in this recognition, is no greater than is demanded by every system of morals; for they all enjoin to abstain from whatever is manifestly pernicious to society.

The same considerations dispose of another reproach against the doctrine of utility, founded on a still grosser misconception of the purpose of a standard of morality, and of the very meaning of the words right and wrong. It is often affirmed that utilitarianism renders men cold and unsympathizing; that it chills their moral feelings towards individuals; that it makes them regard only the dry and hard consideration of the consequences of actions, not taking into their moral estimate the qualities from which those actions emanate. If the assertion means that they do not allow their judgment respecting the rightness or wrongness of an action to be influenced by their opinion of the qualities of the person who does it, this is a complaint not against utilitarianism, but against having any standard of morality at all; for certainly no known ethical standard decides an action to be good or bad because it is done by a good or a bad man, still less because done by an amiable, a brave, or a benevolent man, or the contrary. These considerations are relevant, not to the estimation of actions, but of persons; and there is nothing in the utilitarian theory inconsistent with the fact that there are other things which interest us in persons besides the rightness and wrongness of their actions. The Stoics, indeed, with the paradoxical misuse of language which was part of their system, and by which they strove to raise themselves above all concern about anything but virtue, were fond of saying that he who has that has everything; that he, and only he, is rich, is beautiful, is a king. But no claim of this description is made for the virtuous man by the utilitarian doctrine. Utilitarians are quite aware that there are other desirable possessions and qualities besides virtue, and are perfectly willing to allow to all of them their full worth. They are also aware that a right action does not necessarily indicate a virtuous character, and that actions which are blameable often proceed from qualities entitled to praise. When this is apparent in any particular case, it modifies their estimation, not certainly of the act, but of the agent. I grant that they are, notwithstanding, of opinion, that in the long run the best proof of a good character is good actions; and resolutely refuse to consider any mental disposition as good, of which the predominant tendency is to produce bad conduct. This makes them unpopular with many people; but it is an unpopularity which they must share with every one who regards the distinction between right and wrong in a serious light; and the reproach is not one which a conscientious utilitarian need be anxious to repel.

If no more be meant by the objection than that many utilitarians look on the morality of actions, as measured by the utilitarian standard, with too exclusive a regard, and do not lay sufficient stress upon the other beauties of character which go towards making a human being loveable or admirable, this may be admitted. Utilitarians who have cultivated their moral feelings, but not their sympathies nor their artistic perceptions, do fall into this mistake; and so do all other moralists under the same conditions. What can be said in excuse for other moralists is equally available for them, namely, that if there is to be any error, it is better that it should be on that side. As a matter of fact, we may affirm that among utilitarians as among adherents of other systems, there is every imaginable degree of rigidity and of laxity in the application of their standard: some are even puritanically rigorous, while others are as indulgent as can possibly be desired by sinner or by sentimentalist. But on the whole, a doctrine which brings prominently forward the interest that mankind have in the repression and prevention of conduct which violates the moral law, is likely to be inferior to no other in turning the sanctions of opinion against such violations. It is true, the question, What does violate the moral law? is one on which those who recognize different standards of morality are likely now and then to differ. But difference of opinion on moral questions was not first introduced into the world by utilitarianism, while that doctrine does supply, if not always an easy, at all events a tangible and intelligible mode of deciding such differences.

It may not be superfluous to notice a few more of the common misapprehensions of utilitarian ethics, even those which are so obvious and gross that it might appear impossible for any person of candor and intelligence to fall into them: since persons, even of considerable mental endowments, often give themselves so little trouble to understand the bearings of any opinion against which they entertain a prejudice, and men are in general so little conscious of this voluntary ignorance as a defect, that the vulgarest misunderstandings of ethical doctrines are continually met with in the deliberate writings of persons of the greatest pretensions both to high principle and to philosophy. We not uncommonly hear the doctrine of utility inveighed against as a godless doctrine. If it be necessary to say anything at all against so mere an assumption, we may say that the question depends upon what idea we have formed of the moral character of the Deity. If it be a true belief that God desires, above all things, the happiness of his creatures, and that this was his purpose in their creation, utility is not only not a godless doctrine, but more profoundly religious than any other. If it be meant that utilitarianism does not recognize the revealed will of God as the supreme law of morals, I answer, that an utilitarian who believes in the perfect goodness and wisdom of God, necessarily believes that whatever God has thought fit to reveal on the subject of morals, must fulfil the requirements of utility in a supreme degree. But others besides utilitarians have been of opinion that the Christian revelation was intended, and is fitted, to inform the hearts and minds of mankind with a spirit which should enable them to find for themselves what is right, and incline them to do it when found, rather than to tell them, except in a very general way, what it is: and that we need a doctrine of ethics, carefully followed out, to interpret to us the will of God. Whether this opinion is correct or not, it is superfluous here to discuss; since whatever aid religion, either natural or revealed, can afford to ethical investigation, is as open to the utilitarian moralist as to any other. He can use it as the testimony of God to the usefulness or hurtfulness of an given course of action, by as good a right as others can use it for the indication of a transcendental law, having no connexion with usefulness or with happiness.

Again, Utility is often summarily stigmatized as an immoral doctrine by giving it the name of Expediency, and taking advantage of the popular use of that term to contrast it with Principle. But the Expedient, in the sense in which it is opposed to the Right, generally means that which is expedient for the particular interest of the agent himself; as when a minister sacrifices the interest of his country to keep himself in place. When it means anything better than this, it means that which is expedient for some immediate object, some temporary purpose, but which violates a rule whose observance is expedient in a much higher degree. The Expedient, in this sense, instead of being the same thing with the useful, is a branch of the hurtful. Thus, it would often be expedient, for the purpose of getting over some momentary embarrassment, or attaining some object immediately useful to ourselves or others, to tell a lie. But inasmuch as the cultivation in ourselves of a sensitive feeling on the subject of veracity, is one of the most useful, and the enfeeblement of that feeling one of the most hurtful, things to which our conduct can be instrumental; and inasmuch as any, even unintentional, deviation from truth, does that much towards weakening the trustworthiness of human assertion, which is not only the principal support of all present social well-being, but the insufficiency of which does more than any one thing that can be named to keep back civilization, virtue, everything on which human happiness on the largest scale depends; we feel that the violation, for a present advantage, of a rule of such transcendent expediency, is not expedient, and that he who, for the sake of a convenience to himself or to some other individual, does what depends on him to deprive mankind of the good, and inflict upon them the evil, involved in the greater or less reliance which they can place in each other's word, acts the part of one of their worst enemies. Yet that even this rule, sacred as it is, admits of possible exceptions, is acknowledged by all moralists; the chief of which is when the withholding of some fact (as of information from a malefactor, or of bad news from a person dangerously ill) would preserve some one (especially a person other than oneself) from great and unmerited evil, and when the withholding can only be effected by denial. But in order that the exception may not extend itself beyond the need, and may have the least possible effect in weakening reliance on veracity, it ought to be recognized, and, if possible, its limits defined; and if the principle of utility is good for anything, it must be good for weighing these conflicting utilities against one another, and marking out the region within which one or the other preponderates.

Again, defenders of utility often find themselves called upon to reply to such objections as this—that there is not time, previous to action, for calculating and weighing the effects of any line of conduct on the general happiness. This is exactly as if any one were to say that it is impossible to guide our conduct by Christianity, because there is not time, on every occasion on which anything has to be done, to read through the Old and New Testaments. The answer to the objection is, that there has been ample time, namely, the whole past duration of the human species. During all that time mankind have been learning by experience the tendencies of actions; on which experience all the prudence, as well as all the morality of life, is dependent. People talk as if the commencement of this course of experience had hitherto been put off, and as if, at the moment when some man feels tempted to meddle with the property or life of another, he had to begin considering for the first time whether murder and theft are injurious to human happiness. Even then I do not think that he would find the question very puzzling; but, at all events, the matter is now done to his hand. It is truly a whimsical supposition that if mankind were agreed in considering utility to be the test of morality, they would remain without any agreement as to what is useful, and would take no measures for having their notions on the subject taught to the young, and enforced by law and opinion. There is no difficulty in proving any ethical standard whatever to work ill, if we suppose universal idiocy to be conjoined with it; but on any hypothesis short of that, mankind must by this time have acquired positive beliefs as to the effects of some actions on their happiness; and the beliefs which have thus come down are the rules of morality for the multitude, and for the philosopher until he has succeeded in finding better. That philosophers might easily do this, even now, on many subjects; that the received code of ethics is by no means of divine right; and that mankind have still much to learn as to the effects of actions on the general happiness, I admit, or rather, earnestly maintain. The corollaries from the principle of utility, like the precepts of every practical art, admit of indefinite improvement, and, in a progressive state of the human mind, their improvement is perpetually going on. But to consider the rules of morality as improvable, is one thing; to pass over the intermediate generalizations entirely, and endeavor to test each individual action directly by the first principle, is another. It is a strange notion that the acknowledgment of a first principle is inconsistent with the admission of secondary ones. To inform a traveller respecting the place of his ultimate destination, is not to forbid the use of landmarks and direction-posts on the way. The proposition that happiness is the end and aim of morality, does not mean that no road ought to be laid down to that goal, or that persons going thither should not be advised to take one direction rather than another. Men really ought to leave off talking a kind of nonsense on this subject, which they would neither talk nor listen to on other matters of practical concernment. Nobody argues that the art of navigation is not founded on astronomy, because sailors cannot wait to calculate the Nautical Almanac. Being rational creatures, they go to sea with it ready calculated; and all rational creatures go out upon the sea of life with their minds made up on the common questions of right and wrong, as well as on many of the far more difficult questions of wise and foolish. And this, as long as foresight is a human quality, it is to be presumed they will continue to do. Whatever we adopt as the fundamental principle of morality, we require subordinate principles to apply it by: the impossibility of doing without them, being common to all systems, can afford no argument against any one in particular: but gravely to argue as if no such secondary principles could be had, and as if mankind had remained till now, and always must remain, without drawing any general conclusions from the experience of human life, is as high a pitch, I think, as absurdity has ever reached in philosophical controversy.

The remainder of the stock arguments against utilitarianism mostly consist in laying to its charge the common infirmities of human nature, and the general difficulties which embarrass conscientious persons in shaping their course through life. We are told that an utilitarian will be apt to make his own particular case an exception to moral rules, and, when under temptation, will see an utility in the breach of a rule, greater than he will see in its observance. But is utility the only creed which is able to furnish us with excuses for evil doing, and means of cheating our own conscience? They are afforded in abundance by all doctrines which recognize as a fact in morals the existence of conflicting considerations; which all doctrines do, that have been believed by sane persons. It is not the fault of any creed, but of the complicated nature of human affairs, that rules of conduct cannot be so framed as to require no exceptions, and that hardly any kind of action can safely be laid down as either always obligatory or always condemnable. There is no ethical creed which does not temper the rigidity of its laws, by giving a certain latitude, under the moral responsibility of the agent, for accommodation to peculiarities of circumstances; and under every creed, at the opening thus made, self-deception and dishonest casuistry get in. There exists no moral system under which there do not arise unequivocal cases of conflicting obligation. These are the real difficulties, the knotty points both in the theory of ethics, and in the conscientious guidance of personal conduct. They are overcome practically with greater or with less success according to the intellect and virtue of the individual; but it can hardly be pretended that any one will be the less qualified for dealing with them, from possessing an ultimate standard to which conflicting rights and duties can be referred. If utility is the ultimate source of moral obligations, utility may be invoked to decide between them when their demands are incompatible. Though the application of the standard may be difficult, it is better than none at all: while in other systems, the moral laws all claiming independent authority, there is no common umpire entitled to interfere between them; their claims to precedence one over another rest on little better than sophistry, and unless determined, as they generally are, by the unacknowledged influence of considerations of utility, afford a free scope for the action of personal desires and partialities. We must remember that only in these cases of conflict between secondary principles is it requisite that first principles should be appealed to. There is no case of moral obligation in which some secondary principle is not involved; and if only one, there can seldom be any real doubt which one it is, in the mind of any person by whom the principle itself is recognized.

CHAPTER III OF THE ULTIMATE SANCTION OF THE PRINCIPLE OF UTILITY

The question is often asked, and properly so, in regard to any supposed moral standard—What is its sanction? what are the motives to obey it? or more specifically, what is the source of its obligation? whence does it derive its binding force? It is a necessary part of moral philosophy to provide the answer to this question; which, though frequently assuming the shape of an objection to the utilitarian morality, as if it had some special applicability to that above others, really arises in regard to all standards. It arises, in fact, whenever a person is called on to adopt a standard, or refer morality to any basis on which he has not been accustomed to rest it. For the customary morality, that which education and opinion have consecrated, is the only one which presents itself to the mind with the feeling of being in itself obligatory; and when a person is asked to believe that this morality derives its obligation from some general principle round which custom has not thrown the same halo, the assertion is to him a paradox; the supposed corollaries seem to have a more binding force than the original theorem; the superstructure seems to stand better without, than with, what is represented as its foundation. He says to himself, I feel that I am bound not to rob or murder, betray or deceive; but why am I bound to promote the general happiness? If my own happiness lies in something else, why may I not give that the preference?

If the view adopted by the utilitarian philosophy of the nature of the moral sense be correct, this difficulty will always present itself, until the influences which form moral character have taken the same hold of the principle which they have taken of some of the consequences—until, by the improvement of education, the feeling of unity with our fellow creatures shall be (what it cannot be doubted that Christ intended it to be) as deeply rooted in our character, and to our own consciousness as completely a part of our nature, as the horror of crime is in an ordinarily well-brought up young person. In the mean time, however, the difficulty has no peculiar application to the doctrine of utility, but is inherent in every attempt to analyse morality and reduce it to principles; which, unless the principle is already in men's minds invested with as much sacredness as any of its applications, always seems to divest them of a part of their sanctity.

The principle of utility either has, or there is no reason why it might not have, all the sanctions which belong to any other system of morals. Those sanctions are either external or internal. Of the external sanctions it is not necessary to speak at any length. They are, the hope of favour and the fear of displeasure from our fellow creatures or from the Ruler of the Universe, along with whatever we may have of sympathy or affection for them, or of love and awe of Him, inclining us to do his will independently of selfish consequences. There is evidently no reason why all these motives for observance should not attach themselves to the utilitarian morality, as completely and as powerfully as to any other. Indeed, those of them which refer to our fellow creatures are sure to do so, in proportion to the amount of general intelligence; for whether there be any other ground of moral obligation than the general happiness or not, men do desire happiness; and however imperfect may be their own practice, they desire and commend all conduct in others towards themselves, by which they think their happiness is promoted. With regard to the religious motive, if men believe, as most profess to do, in the goodness of God, those who think that conduciveness to the general happiness is the essence, or even only the criterion, of good, must necessarily believe that it is also that which God approves. The whole force therefore of external reward and punishment, whether physical or moral, and whether proceeding from God or from our fellow men, together with all that the capacities of human nature admit, of disinterested devotion to either, become available to enforce the utilitarian morality, in proportion as that morality is recognized; and the more powerfully, the more the appliances of education and general cultivation are bent to the purpose.

So far as to external sanctions. The internal sanction of duty, whatever our standard of duty may be, is one and the same—a feeling in our own mind; a pain, more or less intense, attendant on violation of duty, which in properly-cultivated moral natures rises, in the more serious cases, into shrinking from it as an impossibility. This feeling, when disinterested, and connecting itself with the pure idea of duty, and not with some particular form of it, or with any of the merely accessory circumstances, is the essence of Conscience; though in that complex phenomenon as it actually exists, the simple fact is in general all encrusted over with collateral associations, derived from sympathy, from love, and still more from fear; from all the forms of religious feeling; from the recollections of childhood and of all our past life; from self-esteem, desire of the esteem of others, and occasionally even self-abasement. This extreme complication is, I apprehend, the origin of the sort of mystical character which, by a tendency of the human mind of which there are many other examples, is apt to be attributed to the idea of moral obligation, and which leads people to believe that the idea cannot possibly attach itself to any other objects than those which, by a supposed mysterious law, are found in our present experience to excite it. Its binding force, however, consists in the existence of a mass of feeling which must be broken through in order to do what violates our standard of right, and which, if we do nevertheless violate that standard, will probably have to be encountered afterwards in the form of remorse. Whatever theory we have of the nature or origin of conscience, this is what essentially constitutes it.

The ultimate sanction, therefore, of all morality (external motives apart) being a subjective feeling in our own minds, I see nothing embarrassing to those whose standard is utility, in the question, what is the sanction of that particular standard? We may answer, the same as of all other moral standards—the conscientious feelings of mankind. Undoubtedly this sanction has no binding efficacy on those who do not possess the feelings it appeals to; but neither will these persons be more obedient to any other moral principle than to the utilitarian one. On them morality of any kind has no hold but through the external sanctions. Meanwhile the feelings exist, a fact in human nature, the reality of which, and the great power with which they are capable of acting on those in whom they have been duly cultivated, are proved by experience. No reason has ever been shown why they may not be cultivated to as great intensity in connexion with the utilitarian, as with any other rule of morals.

There is, I am aware, a disposition to believe that a person who sees in moral obligation a transcendental fact, an objective reality belonging to the province of 'Things in themselves,' is likely to be more obedient to it than one who believes it to be entirely subjective, having its seat in human consciousness only. But whatever a person's opinion may be on this point of Ontology, the force he is really urged by is his own subjective feeling, and is exactly measured by its strength. No one's belief that Duty is an objective reality is stronger than the belief that God is so; yet the belief in God, apart from the expectation of actual reward and punishment, only operates on conduct through, and in proportion to, the subjective religious feeling. The sanction, so far as it is disinterested, is always in the mind itself; and the notion therefore of the transcendental moralists must be, that this sanction will not exist in the mind unless it is believed to have its root out of the mind; and that if a person is able to say to himself, This which is restraining me, and which is called my conscience, is only a feeling in my own mind, he may possibly draw the conclusion that when the feeling ceases the obligation ceases, and that if he find the feeling inconvenient, he may disregard it, and endeavor to get rid of it. But is this danger confined to the utilitarian morality? Does the belief that moral obligation has its seat outside the mind make the feeling of it too strong to be got rid of? The fact is so far otherwise, that all moralists admit and lament the ease with which, in the generality of minds, conscience can be silenced or stifled. The question, Need I obey my conscience? is quite as often put to themselves by persons who never heard of the principle of utility, as by its adherents. Those whose conscientious feelings are so weak as to allow of their asking this question, if they answer it affirmatively, will not do so because they believe in the transcendental theory, but because of the external sanctions.

It is not necessary, for the present purpose, to decide whether the feeling of duty is innate or implanted. Assuming it to be innate, it is an open question to what objects it naturally attaches itself; for the philosophic supporters of that theory are now agreed that the intuitive perception is of principles of morality, and not of the details. If there be anything innate in the matter, I see no reason why the feeling which is innate should not be that of regard to the pleasures and pains of others. If there is any principle of morals which is intuitively obligatory, I should say it must be that. If so, the intuitive ethics would coincide with the utilitarian, and there would be no further quarrel between them. Even as it is, the intuitive moralists, though they believe that there are other intuitive moral obligations, do already believe this to be one; for they unanimously hold that a large portion of morality turns upon the consideration due to the interests of our fellow creatures. Therefore, if the belief in the transcendental origin of moral obligation gives any additional efficacy to the internal sanction, it appears to me that the utilitarian principle has already the benefit of it.

On the other hand, if, as is my own belief, the moral feelings are not innate, but acquired, they are not for that reason the less natural. It is natural to man to speak, to reason, to build cities, to cultivate the ground, though these are acquired faculties. The moral feelings are not indeed a part of our nature, in the sense of being in any perceptible degree present in all of us; but this, unhappily, is a fact admitted by those who believe the most strenuously in their transcendental origin. Like the other acquired capacities above referred to, the moral faculty, if not a part of our nature, is a natural outgrowth from it; capable, like them, in a certain small degree, of springing up spontaneously; and susceptible of being brought by cultivation to a high degree of development. Unhappily it is also susceptible, by a sufficient use of the external sanctions and of the force of early impressions, of being cultivated in almost any direction: so that there is hardly anything so absurd or so mischievous that it may not, by means of these influences, be made to act on the human mind with all the authority of conscience. To doubt that the same potency might be given by the same means to the principle of utility, even if it had no foundation in human nature, would be flying in the face of all experience.

But moral associations which are wholly of artificial creation, when intellectual culture goes on, yield by degrees to the dissolving force of analysis: and if the feeling of duty, when associated with utility, would appear equally arbitrary; if there were no leading department of our nature, no powerful class of sentiments, with which that association would harmonize, which would make us feel it congenial, and incline us not only to foster it in others (for which we have abundant interested motives), but also to cherish it in ourselves; if there were not, in short, a natural basis of sentiment for utilitarian morality, it might well happen that his association also, even after it had been implanted by education, might be analysed away.

But there is this basis of powerful natural sentiment; and this it is which, when once the general happiness is recognized as the ethical standard, will constitute the strength of the utilitarian morality. This firm foundation is that of the social feelings of mankind; the desire to be in unity with our fellow creatures, which is already a powerful principle in human nature, and happily one of those which tend to become stronger, even without express inculcation, from the influences of advancing civilization. The social state is at once so natural, so necessary, and so habitual to man, that, except in some unusual circumstances or by an effort of voluntary abstraction, he never conceives himself otherwise than as a member of a body; and this association is riveted more and more, as mankind are further removed from the state of savage independence. Any condition, therefore, which is essential to a state of society, becomes more and more an inseparable part of every person's conception of the state of things which he is born into, and which is the destiny of a human being. Now, society between human beings, except in the relation of master and slave, is manifestly impossible on any other footing than that the interests of all are to be consulted. Society between equals can only exist on the understanding that the interests of all are to be regarded equally. And since in all states of civilization, every person, except an absolute monarch, has equals, ever one is obliged to live on these terms with somebody; and in every age some advance is made towards a state in which it will be impossible to live permanently on other terms with anybody. In this way people grow up unable to conceive as possible to them a state of total disregard of other people's interests. They are under a necessity of conceiving themselves as at least abstaining from all the grosser injuries, and (if only for their own protection) living in a state of constant protest against them. They are also familiar with the fact of co-operating with others, and proposing to themselves a collective, not an individual, interest, as the aim (at least for the time being) of their actions. So long as they are co-operating, their ends are identified with those of others; there is at least a temporary feeling that the interests of others are their own interests. Not only does all strengthening of social ties, and all healthy growth of society, give to each individual a stronger personal interest in practically consulting the welfare of others; it also leads him to identify his feelings more and more with their good, or at least with an ever greater degree of practical consideration for it. He comes, as though instinctively, to be conscious of himself as a being who of course pays regard to others. The good of others becomes to him a thing naturally and necessarily to be attended to, like any of the physical conditions of our existence. Now, whatever amount of this feeling a person has, he is urged by the strongest motives both of interest and of sympathy to demonstrate it, and to the utmost of his power encourage it in others; and even if he has none of it himself, he is as greatly interested as any one else that others should have it. Consequently the smallest germs of the feeling are laid hold of and nourished by the contagion of sympathy and the influences of education; and a complete web of corroborative association is woven round it, by the powerful agency of the external sanctions. This mode of conceiving ourselves and human life, as civilization goes on, is felt to be more and more natural. Every step in political improvement renders it more so, by removing the sources of opposition of interest, and levelling those inequalities of legal privilege between individuals or classes, owing to which there are large portions of mankind whose happiness it is still practicable to disregard. In an improving state of the human mind, the influences are constantly on the increase, which tend to generate in each individual a feeling of unity with all the rest; which feeling, if perfect, would make him never think of, or desire, any beneficial condition for himself, in the benefits of which they are not included. If we now suppose this feeling of unity to be taught as a religion, and the whole force of education, of institutions, and of opinion, directed, as it once was in the case of religion, to make every person grow up from infancy surrounded on all sides both by the profession and by the practice of it, I think that no one, who can realize this conception, will feel any misgiving about the sufficiency of the ultimate sanction for the Happiness morality. To any ethical student who finds the realization difficult, I recommend, as a means of facilitating it, the second of M. Comte's two principal works, the Systeme de Politique Positive. I entertain the strongest objections to the system of politics and morals set forth in that treatise; but I think it has superabundantly shown the possibility of giving to the service of humanity, even without the aid of belief in a Providence, both the psychical power and the social efficacy of a religion; making it take hold of human life, and colour all thought, feeling, and action, in a manner of which the greatest ascendancy ever exercised by any religion may be but a type and foretaste; and of which the danger is, not that it should be insufficient, but that it should be so excessive as to interfere unduly with human freedom and individuality.

Neither is it necessary to the feeling which constitutes the binding force of the utilitarian morality on those who recognize it, to wait for those social influences which would make its obligation felt by mankind at large. In the comparatively early state of human advancement in which we now live, a person cannot indeed feel that entireness of sympathy with all others, which would make any real discordance in the general direction of their conduct in life impossible; but already a person in whom the social feeling is at all developed, cannot bring himself to think of the rest of his fellow creatures as struggling rivals with him for the means of happiness, whom he must desire to see defeated in their object in order that he may succeed in his. The deeply-rooted conception which every individual even now has of himself as a social being, tends to make him feel it one of his natural wants that there should be harmony between his feelings and aims and those of his fellow creatures. If differences of opinion and of mental culture make it impossible for him to share many of their actual feelings—perhaps make him denounce and defy those feelings—he still needs to be conscious that his real aim and theirs do not conflict; that he is not opposing himself to what they really wish for, namely, their own good, but is, on the contrary, promoting it. This feeling in most individuals is much inferior in strength to their selfish feelings, and is often wanting altogether. But to those who have it, it possesses all the characters of a natural feeling. It does not present itself to their minds as a superstition of education, or a law despotically imposed by the power of society, but as an attribute which it would not be well for them to be without. This conviction is the ultimate sanction of the greatest happiness morality. This it is which makes any mind, of well-developed feelings, work with, and not against, the outward motives to care for others, afforded by what I have called the external sanctions; and when those sanctions are wanting, or act in an opposite direction, constitutes in itself a powerful internal binding force, in proportion to the sensitiveness and thoughtfulness of the character; since few but those whose mind is a moral blank, could bear to lay out their course of life on the plan of paying no regard to others except so far as their own private interest compels.

CHAPTER IV OF WHAT SORT OF PROOF THE PRINCIPLE OF UTILITY IS SUSCEPTIBLE

It has already been remarked, that questions of ultimate ends do not admit of proof, in the ordinary acceptation of the term. To be incapable of proof by reasoning is common to all first principles; to the first premises of our knowledge, as well as to those of our conduct. But the former, being matters of fact, may be the subject of a direct appeal to the faculties which judge of fact—namely, our senses, and our internal consciousness. Can an appeal be made to the same faculties on questions of practical ends? Or by what other faculty is cognizance taken of them?

Questions about ends are, in other words, questions what things are desirable. The utilitarian doctrine is, that happiness is desirable, and the only thing desirable, as an end; all other things being only desirable as means to that end. What ought to be required of this doctrine—what conditions is it requisite that the doctrine should fulfil—to make good its claim to be believed?

The only proof capable of being given that an object is visible, is that people actually see it. The only proof that a sound is audible, is that people hear it: and so of the other sources of our experience. In like manner, I apprehend, the sole evidence it is possible to produce that anything is desirable, is that people do actually desire it. If the end which the utilitarian doctrine proposes to itself were not, in theory and in practice, acknowledged to be an end, nothing could ever convince any person that it was so.

No reason can be given why the general happiness is desirable, except that each person, so far as he believes it to be attainable, desires his own happiness. This, however, being a fact, we have not only all the proof which the case admits of, but all which it is possible to require, that happiness is a good: that each person's happiness is a good to that person, and the general happiness, therefore, a good to the aggregate of all persons. Happiness has made out its title as one of the ends of conduct, and consequently one of the criteria of morality.

But it has not, by this alone, proved itself to be the sole criterion. To do that, it would seem, by the same rule, necessary to show, not only that people desire happiness, but that they never desire anything else. Now it is palpable that they do desire things which, in common language, are decidedly distinguished from happiness. They desire, for example, virtue, and the absence of vice, no less really than pleasure and the absence of pain. The desire of virtue is not as universal, but it is as authentic a fact, as the desire of happiness. And hence the opponents of the utilitarian standard deem that they have a right to infer that there are other ends of human action besides happiness, and that happiness is not the standard of approbation and disapprobation.

But does the utilitarian doctrine deny that people desire virtue, or maintain that virtue is not a thing to be desired? The very reverse. It maintains not only that virtue is to be desired, but that it is to be desired disinterestedly, for itself. Whatever may be the opinion of utilitarian moralists as to the original conditions by which virtue is made virtue; however they may believe (as they do) that actions and dispositions are only virtuous because they promote another end than virtue; yet this being granted, and it having been decided, from considerations of this description, what is virtuous, they not only place virtue at the very head of the things which are good as means to the ultimate end, but they also recognize as a psychological fact the possibility of its being, to the individual, a good in itself, without looking to any end beyond it; and hold, that the mind is not in a right state, not in a state conformable to Utility, not in the state most conducive to the general happiness, unless it does love virtue in this manner—as a thing desirable in itself, even although, in the individual instance, it should not produce those other desirable consequences which it tends to produce, and on account of which it is held to be virtue. This opinion is not, in the smallest degree, a departure from the Happiness principle. The ingredients of happiness are very various, and each of them is desirable in itself, and not merely when considered as swelling an aggregate. The principle of utility does not mean that any given pleasure, as music, for instance, or any given exemption from pain, as for example health, are to be looked upon as means to a collective something termed happiness, and to be desired on that account. They are desired and desirable in and for themselves; besides being means, they are a part of the end. Virtue, according to the utilitarian doctrine, is not naturally and originally part of the end, but it is capable of becoming so; and in those who love it disinterestedly it has become so, and is desired and cherished, not as a means to happiness, but as a part of their happiness.

To illustrate this farther, we may remember that virtue is not the only thing, originally a means, and which if it were not a means to anything else, would be and remain indifferent, but which by association with what it is a means to, comes to be desired for itself, and that too with the utmost intensity. What, for example, shall we say of the love of money? There is nothing originally more desirable about money than about any heap of glittering pebbles. Its worth is solely that of the things which it will buy; the desires for other things than itself, which it is a means of gratifying. Yet the love of money is not only one of the strongest moving forces of human life, but money is, in many cases, desired in and for itself; the desire to possess it is often stronger than the desire to use it, and goes on increasing when all the desires which point to ends beyond it, to be compassed by it, are falling off. It may be then said truly, that money is desired not for the sake of an end, but as part of the end. From being a means to happiness, it has come to be itself a principal ingredient of the individual's conception of happiness. The same may be said of the majority of the great objects of human life—power, for example, or fame; except that to each of these there is a certain amount of immediate pleasure annexed, which has at least the semblance of being naturally inherent in them; a thing which cannot be said of money. Still, however, the strongest natural attraction, both of power and of fame, is the immense aid they give to the attainment of our other wishes; and it is the strong association thus generated between them and all our objects of desire, which gives to the direct desire of them the intensity it often assumes, so as in some characters to surpass in strength all other desires. In these cases the means have become a part of the end, and a more important part of it than any of the things which they are means to. What was once desired as an instrument for the attainment of happiness, has come to be desired for its own sake. In being desired for its own sake it is, however, desired as part of happiness. The person is made, or thinks he would be made, happy by its mere possession; and is made unhappy by failure to obtain it. The desire of it is not a different thing from the desire of happiness, any more than the love of music, or the desire of health. They are included in happiness. They are some of the elements of which the desire of happiness is made up. Happiness is not an abstract idea, but a concrete whole; and these are some of its parts. And the utilitarian standard sanctions and approves their being so. Life would be a poor thing, very ill provided with sources of happiness, if there were not this provision of nature, by which things originally indifferent, but conducive to, or otherwise associated with, the satisfaction of our primitive desires, become in themselves sources of pleasure more valuable than the primitive pleasures, both in permanency, in the space of human existence that they are capable of covering, and even in intensity.

Virtue, according to the utilitarian conception, is a good of this description. There was no original desire of it, or motive to it, save its conduciveness to pleasure, and especially to protection from pain. But through the association thus formed, it may be felt a good in itself, and desired as such with as great intensity as any other good; and with this difference between it and the love of money, of power, or of fame, that all of these may, and often do, render the individual noxious to the other members of the society to which he belongs, whereas there is nothing which makes him so much a blessing to them as the cultivation of the disinterested love of virtue. And consequently, the utilitarian standard, while it tolerates and approves those other acquired desires, up to the point beyond which they would be more injurious to the general happiness than promotive of it, enjoins and requires the cultivation of the love of virtue up to the greatest strength possible, as being above all things important to the general happiness.

It results from the preceding considerations, that there is in reality nothing desired except happiness. Whatever is desired otherwise than as a means to some end beyond itself, and ultimately to happiness, is desired as itself a part of happiness, and is not desired for itself until it has become so. Those who desire virtue for its own sake, desire it either because the consciousness of it is a pleasure, or because the consciousness of being without it is a pain, or for both reasons united; as in truth the pleasure and pain seldom exist separately, but almost always together, the same person feeling pleasure in the degree of virtue attained, and pain in not having attained more. If one of these gave him to pleasure, and the other no pain, he would not love or desire virtue, or would desire it only for the other benefits which it might produce to himself or to persons whom he cared for.

We have now, then, an answer to the question, of what sort of proof the principle of utility is susceptible. If the opinion which I have now stated is psychologically true—if human nature is so constituted as to desire nothing which is not either a part of happiness or a means of happiness, we can have no other proof, and we require no other, that these are the only things desirable. If so, happiness is the sole end of human action, and the promotion of it the test by which to judge of all human conduct; from whence it necessarily follows that it must be the criterion of morality, since a part is included in the whole.

And now to decide whether this is really so; whether mankind do desire nothing for itself but that which is a pleasure to them, or of which the absence is a pain; we have evidently arrived at a question of fact and experience, dependent, like all similar questions, upon evidence. It can only be determined by practiced self-consciousness and self-observation, assisted by observation of others. I believe that these sources of evidence, impartially consulted, will declare that desiring a thing and finding it pleasant, aversion to it and thinking of it as painful, are phenomena entirely inseparable, or rather two parts of the same phenomenon; in strictness of language, two different modes of naming the same psychological fact: that to think of an object as desirable (unless for the sake of its consequences), and to think of it as pleasant, are one and the same thing; and that to desire anything, except in proportion as the idea of it is pleasant, is a physical and metaphysical impossibility.

So obvious does this appear to me, that I expect it will hardly be disputed: and the objection made will be, not that desire can possibly be directed to anything ultimately except pleasure and exemption from pain, but that the will is a different thing from desire; that a person of confirmed virtue, or any other person whose purposes are fixed, carries out his purposes without any thought of the pleasure he has in contemplating them, or expects to derive from their fulfilment; and persists in acting on them, even though these pleasures are much diminished, by changes in his character or decay of his passive sensibilities, or are outweighed by the pains which the pursuit of the purposes may bring upon him. All this I fully admit, and have stated it elsewhere, as positively and emphatically as any one. Will, the active phenomenon, is a different thing from desire, the state of passive sensibility, and though originally an offshoot from it, may in time take root and detach itself from the parent stock; so much so, that in the case of an habitual purpose, instead of willing the thing because we desire it, we often desire it only because we will it. This, however, is but an instance of that familiar fact, the power of habit, and is nowise confined to the case of virtuous actions. Many indifferent things, which men originally did from a motive of some sort, they continue to do from habit. Sometimes this is done unconsciously, the consciousness coming only after the action: at other times with conscious volition, but volition which has become habitual, and is put into operation by the force of habit, in opposition perhaps to the deliberate preference, as often happens with those who have contracted habits of vicious or hurtful indulgence. Third and last comes the case in which the habitual act of will in the individual instance is not in contradiction to the general intention prevailing at other times, but in fulfilment of it; as in the case of the person of confirmed virtue, and of all who pursue deliberately and consistently any determinate end. The distinction between will and desire thus understood, is an authentic and highly important psychological fact; but the fact consists solely in this—that will, like all other parts of our constitution, is amenable to habit, and that we may will from habit what we no longer desire for itself, or desire only because we will it. It is not the less true that will, in the beginning, is entirely produced by desire; including in that term the repelling influence of pain as well as the attractive one of pleasure. Let us take into consideration, no longer the person who has a confirmed will to do right, but him in whom that virtuous will is still feeble, conquerable by temptation, and not to be fully relied on; by what means can it be strengthened? How can the will to be virtuous, where it does not exist in sufficient force, be implanted or awakened? Only by making the person desire virtue—by making him think of it in a pleasurable light, or of its absence in a painful one. It is by associating the doing right with pleasure, or the doing wrong with pain, or by eliciting and impressing and bringing home to the person's experience the pleasure naturally involved in the one or the pain in the other, that it is possible to call forth that will to be virtuous, which, when confirmed, acts without any thought of either pleasure or pain. Will is the child of desire, and passes out of the dominion of its parent only to come under that of habit. That which is the result of habit affords no presumption of being intrinsically good; and there would be no reason for wishing that the purpose of virtue should become independent of pleasure and pain, were it not that the influence of the pleasurable and painful associations which prompt to virtue is not sufficiently to be depended on for unerring constancy of action until it has acquired the support of habit. Both in feeling and in conduct, habit is the only thing which imparts certainty; and it is because of the importance to others of being able to rely absolutely on one's feelings and conduct, and to oneself of being able to rely on one's own, that the will to do right ought to be cultivated into this habitual independence. In other words, this state of the will is a means to good, not intrinsically a good; and does not contradict the doctrine that nothing is a good to human beings but in so far as it is either itself pleasurable, or a means of attaining pleasure or averting pain.

But if this doctrine be true, the principle of utility is proved. Whether it is so or not, must now be left to the consideration of the thoughtful reader.

CHAPTER V ON THE CONNEXION BETWEEN JUSTICE AND UTILITY

In all ages of speculation, one of the strongest obstacles to the reception of the doctrine that Utility or Happiness is the criterion of right and wrong, has been drawn from the idea of Justice. The powerful sentiment, and apparently clear perception, which that word recalls with a rapidity and certainty resembling an instinct, have seemed to the majority of thinkers to point to an inherent quality in things; to show that the Just must have an existence in Nature as something absolute, generically distinct from every variety of the Expedient, and, in idea, opposed to it, though (as is commonly acknowledged) never, in the long run, disjoined from it in fact.

In the case of this, as of our other moral sentiments, there is no necessary connexion between the question of its origin, and that of its binding force. That a feeling is bestowed on us by Nature, does not necessarily legitimate all its promptings. The feeling of justice might be a peculiar instinct, and might yet require, like our other instincts, to be controlled and enlightened by a higher reason. If we have intellectual instincts, leading us to judge in a particular way, as well as animal instincts that prompt us to act in a particular way, there is no necessity that the former should be more infallible in their sphere than the latter in theirs: it may as well happen that wrong judgments are occasionally suggested by those, as wrong actions by these. But though it is one thing to believe that we have natural feelings of justice, and another to acknowledge them as an ultimate criterion of conduct, these two opinions are very closely connected in point of fact. Mankind are always predisposed to believe that any subjective feeling, not otherwise accounted for, is a revelation of some objective reality. Our present object is to determine whether the reality, to which the feeling of justice corresponds, is one which needs any such special revelation; whether the justice or injustice of an action is a thing intrinsically peculiar, and distinct from all its other qualities, or only a combination of certain of those qualities, presented under a peculiar aspect. For the purpose of this inquiry, it is practically important to consider whether the feeling itself, of justice and injustice, is sui generis like our sensations of colour and taste, or a derivative feeling, formed by a combination of others. And this it is the more essential to examine, as people are in general willing enough to allow, that objectively the dictates of justice coincide with a part of the field of General Expediency; but inasmuch as the subjective mental feeling of Justice is different from that which commonly attaches to simple expediency, and, except in extreme cases of the latter, is far more imperative in its demands, people find it difficult to see, in Justice, only a particular kind or branch of general utility, and think that its superior binding force requires a totally different origin.

To throw light upon this question, it is necessary to attempt to ascertain what is the distinguishing character of justice, or of injustice: what is the quality, or whether there is any quality, attributed in common to all modes of conduct designated as unjust (for justice, like many other moral attributes, is best defined by its opposite), and distinguishing them from such modes of conduct as are disapproved, but without having that particular epithet of disapprobation applied to them. If in everything which men are accustomed to characterize as just or unjust, some one common attribute or collection of attributes is always present, we may judge whether this particular attribute or combination of attributes would be capable of gathering round it a sentiment of that peculiar character and intensity by virtue of the general laws of our emotional constitution, or whether the sentiment is inexplicable, and requires to be regarded as a special provision of Nature. If we find the former to be the case, we shall, in resolving this question, have resolved also the main problem: if the latter, we shall have to seek for some other mode of investigating it.

To find the common attributes of a variety of objects, it is necessary to begin by surveying the objects themselves in the concrete. Let us therefore advert successively to the various modes of action, and arrangements of human affairs, which are classed, by universal or widely spread opinion, as Just or as Unjust. The things well known to excite the sentiments associated with those names, are of a very multifarious character. I shall pass them rapidly in review, without studying any particular arrangement.

In the first place, it is mostly considered unjust to deprive any one of his personal liberty, his property, or any other thing which belongs to him by law. Here, therefore, is one instance of the application of the terms just and unjust in a perfectly definite sense, namely, that it is just to respect, unjust to violate, the legal rights of any one. But this judgment admits of several exceptions, arising from the other forms in which the notions of justice and injustice present themselves. For example, the person who suffers the deprivation may (as the phrase is) have forfeited the rights which he is so deprived of: a case to which we shall return presently. But also,

Secondly; the legal rights of which he is deprived, may be rights which ought not to have belonged to him; in other words, the law which confers on him these rights, may be a bad law. When it is so, or when (which is the same thing for our purpose) it is supposed to be so, opinions will differ as to the justice or injustice of infringing it. Some maintain that no law, however bad, ought to be disobeyed by an individual citizen; that his opposition to it, if shown at all, should only be shown in endeavoring to get it altered by competent authority. This opinion (which condemns many of the most illustrious benefactors of mankind, and would often protect pernicious institutions against the only weapons which, in the state of things existing at the time, have any chance of succeeding against them) is defended, by those who hold it, on grounds of expediency; principally on that of the importance, to the common interest of mankind, of maintaining inviolate the sentiment of submission to law. Other persons, again, hold the directly contrary opinion, that any law, judged to be bad, may blamelessly be disobeyed, even though it be not judged to be unjust, but only inexpedient; while others would confine the license of disobedience to the case of unjust laws; but again, some say, that all laws which are inexpedient are unjust; since every law imposes some restriction on the natural liberty of mankind, which restriction is an injustice, unless legitimated by tending to their good. Among these diversities of opinion, it seems to be universally admitted that there may be unjust laws, and that law, consequently, is not the ultimate criterion of justice, but may give to one person a benefit, or impose on another an evil, which justice condemns. When, however, a law is thought to be unjust, it seems always to be regarded as being so in the same way in which a breach of law is unjust, namely, by infringing somebody's right; which, as it cannot in this case be a legal right, receives a different appellation, and is called a moral right. We may say, therefore, that a second case of injustice consists in taking or withholding from any person that to which he has a moral right.

Thirdly, it is universally considered just that each person should obtain that (whether good or evil) which he deserves; and unjust that he should obtain a good, or be made to undergo an evil, which he does not deserve. This is, perhaps, the clearest and most emphatic form in which the idea of justice is conceived by the general mind. As it involves the notion of desert, the question arises, what constitutes desert? Speaking in a general way, a person is understood to deserve good if he does right, evil if he does wrong; and in a more particular sense, to deserve good from those to whom he does or has done good, and evil from those to whom he does or has done evil. The precept of returning good for evil has never been regarded as a case of the fulfilment of justice, but as one in which the claims of justice are waved, in obedience to other considerations.

Fourthly, it is confessedly unjust to break faith with any one: to violate an engagement, either express or implied, or disappoint expectations raised by our own conduct, at least if we have raised those expectations knowingly and voluntarily. Like the other obligations of justice already spoken of, this one is not regarded as absolute, but as capable of being overruled by a stronger obligation of justice on the other side; or by such conduct on the part of the person concerned as is deemed to absolve us from our obligation to him, and to constitute a forfeiture of the benefit which he has been led to expect.

Fifthly, it is, by universal admission, inconsistent with justice to be partial; to show favour or preference to one person over another, in matters to which favour and preference do not properly apply. Impartiality, however, does not seem to be regarded as a duty in itself, but rather as instrumental to some other duty; for it is admitted that favour and preference are not always censurable, and indeed the cases in which they are condemned are rather the exception than the rule. A person would be more likely to be blamed than applauded for giving his family or friends no superiority in good offices over strangers, when he could do so without violating any other duty; and no one thinks it unjust to seek one person in preference to another as a friend, connexion, or companion. Impartiality where rights are concerned is of course obligatory, but this is involved in the more general obligation of giving to every one his right. A tribunal, for example, must be impartial, because it is bound to award, without regard to any other consideration, a disputed object to the one of two parties who has the right to it. There are other cases in which impartiality means, being solely influenced by desert; as with those who, in the capacity of judges, preceptors, or parents, administer reward and punishment as such. There are cases, again, in which it means, being solely influenced by consideration for the public interest; as in making a selection among candidates for a government employment. Impartiality, in short, as an obligation of justice, may be said to mean, being exclusively influenced by the considerations which it is supposed ought to influence the particular case in hand; and resisting the solicitation of any motives which prompt to conduct different from what those considerations would dictate.

Nearly allied to the idea of impartiality, is that of equality; which often enters as a component part both into the conception of justice and into the practice of it, and, in the eyes of many persons, constitutes its essence. But in this, still more than in any other case, the notion of justice varies in different persons, and always conforms in its variations to their notion of utility. Each person maintains that equality is the dictate of justice, except where he thinks that expediency requires inequality. The justice of giving equal protection to the rights of all, is maintained by those who support the most outrageous inequality in the rights themselves. Even in slave countries it is theoretically admitted that the rights of the slave, such as they are, ought to be as sacred as those of the master; and that a tribunal which fails to enforce them with equal strictness is wanting in justice; while, at the same time, institutions which leave to the slave scarcely any rights to enforce, are not deemed unjust, because they are not deemed inexpedient. Those who think that utility requires distinctions of rank, do not consider it unjust that riches and social privileges should be unequally dispensed; but those who think this inequality inexpedient, think it unjust also. Whoever thinks that government is necessary, sees no injustice in as much inequality as is constituted by giving to the magistrate powers not granted to other people. Even among those who hold levelling doctrines, there are as many questions of justice as there are differences of opinion about expediency. Some Communists consider it unjust that the produce of the labour of the community should be shared on any other principle than that of exact equality; others think it just that those should receive most whose needs are greatest; while others hold that those who work harder, or who produce more, or whose services are more valuable to the community, may justly claim a larger quota in the division of the produce. And the sense of natural justice may be plausibly appealed to in behalf of every one of these opinions.

Among so many diverse applications of the term Justice, which yet is not regarded as ambiguous, it is a matter of some difficulty to seize the mental link which holds them together, and on which the moral sentiment adhering to the term essentially depends. Perhaps, in this embarrassment, some help may be derived from the history of the word, as indicated by its etymology.

In most, if not in all, languages, the etymology of the word which corresponds to Just, points to an origin connected either with positive law, or with that which was in most cases the primitive form of law—authoritative custom. *Justum* is a form of *jussum,* that which has been ordered. *Jus* is of the same origin. [*Dikaion*] comes from [*dike*], of which the principal meaning, at least in the historical ages of Greece, was a suit at law. Originally, indeed, it meant only the mode or manner of doing things, but it early came to mean the prescribed manner; that which the recognized authorities, patriarchal, judicial, or political, would enforce. *Recht,* from which came right and righteous, is synonymous with law. The original meaning indeed of *recht* did not point to law, but to physical straightness; as wrong and its Latin equivalents meant twisted or tortuous; and from this it is argued that right did not originally mean law, but on the contrary law meant right. But however this may be, the fact that *recht* and *droit* became restricted in their meaning to positive law, although much which is not required by law is equally necessary to moral straightness or rectitude, is as significant of the original character of moral ideas as if the derivation had been the reverse way. The courts of justice, the administration of justice, are the courts and the administration of law. *La justice,* in French, is the established term for judicature. There can, I think, be no doubt that the *idee mere,* the primitive element, in the formation of the notion of justice, was conformity to law. It constituted the entire idea among the Hebrews, up to the birth of Christianity; as might be expected in the case of a people whose laws attempted to embrace all subjects on which precepts were required, and who believed those laws to be a direct emanation from the Supreme Being. But other nations, and in particular the Greeks and Romans, who knew that their laws had been made originally, and still continued to be made, by men, were not afraid to admit that those men might make bad laws; might do, by law, the same things, and from the same motives, which, if done by individuals without the sanction of law, would be called unjust. And hence the sentiment of injustice came to be attached, not to all violations of law, but only to violations of such laws as ought to exist, including such as ought to exist but do not; and to laws themselves, if supposed to be contrary to what ought to be law. In this manner the idea of law and of its injunctions was still predominant in the notion of justice, even when the laws actually in force ceased to be accepted as the standard of it.

It is true that mankind consider the idea of justice and its obligations as applicable to many things which neither are, nor is it desired that they should be, regulated by law. Nobody desires that laws should interfere with the whole detail of private life; yet every one allows that in all daily conduct a person may and does show himself to be either just or unjust. But even here, the idea of the breach of what ought to be law, still lingers in a modified shape. It would always give us pleasure, and chime in with our feelings of fitness, that acts which we deem unjust should be punished, though we do not always think it expedient that this should be done by the tribunals. We forego that gratification on account of incidental inconveniences. We should be glad to see just conduct enforced and injustice repressed, even in the minutest details, if we were not, with reason, afraid of trusting the magistrate with so unlimited an amount of power over individuals. When we think that a person is bound in justice to do a thing, it is an ordinary form of language to say, that he ought to be compelled to do it. We should be gratified to see the obligation enforced by anybody who had the power. If we see that its enforcement by law would be inexpedient, we lament the impossibility, we consider the impunity given to injustice as an evil, and strive to make amends for it by bringing a strong expression of our own and the public disapprobation to bear upon the offender. Thus the idea of legal constraint is still the generating idea of the notion of justice, though undergoing several transformations before that notion, as it exists in an advanced state of society, becomes complete.

The above is, I think, a true account, as far as it goes, of the origin and progressive growth of the idea of justice. But we must observe, that it contains, as yet, nothing to distinguish that obligation from moral obligation in general. For the truth is, that the idea of penal sanction, which is the essence of law, enters not only into the conception of injustice, but into that of any kind of wrong. We do not call anything wrong, unless we mean to imply that a person ought to be punished in some way or other for doing it; if not by law, by the opinion of his fellow creatures; if not by opinion, by the reproaches of his own conscience. This seems the real turning point of the distinction between morality and simple expediency. It is a part of the notion of Duty in every one of its forms, that a person may rightfully be compelled to fulfil it. Duty is a thing which may be exacted from a person, as one exacts a debt. Unless we think that it might be exacted from him, we do not call it his duty. Reasons of prudence, or the interest of other people, may militate against actually exacting it; but the person himself, it is clearly understood, would not be entitled to complain. There are other things, on the contrary, which we wish that people should do, which we like or admire them for doing, perhaps dislike or despise them for not doing, but yet admit that they are not bound to do; it is not a case of moral obligation; we do not blame them, that is, we do not think that they are proper objects of punishment. How we come by these ideas of deserving and not deserving punishment, will appear, perhaps, in the sequel; but I think there is no doubt that this distinction lies at the bottom of the notions of right and wrong; that we call any conduct wrong, or employ, instead, some other term of dislike or disparagement, according as we think that the person ought, or ought not, to be punished for it; and we say that it would be right to do so and so, or merely that it would be desirable or laudable, according as we would wish to see the person whom it concerns, compelled, or only persuaded and exhorted, to act in that manner.

This, therefore, being the characteristic difference which marks off, not justice, but morality in general, from the remaining provinces of Expediency and Worthiness; the character is still to be sought which distinguishes justice from other branches of morality. Now it is known that ethical writers divide moral duties into two classes, denoted by the ill-chosen expressions, duties of perfect and of imperfect obligation; the latter being those in which, though the act is obligatory, the particular occasions of performing it are left to our choice; as in the case of charity or beneficence, which we are indeed bound to practise, but not towards any definite person, nor at any prescribed time. In the more precise language of philosophic jurists, duties of perfect obligation are those duties in virtue of which a correlative right resides in some person or persons; duties of imperfect obligation are those moral obligations which do not give birth to any right. I think it will be found that this distinction exactly coincides with that which exists between justice and the other obligations of morality. In our survey of the various popular acceptations of justice, the term appeared generally to involve the idea of a personal right—a claim on the part of one or more individuals, like that which the law gives when it confers a proprietary or other legal right. Whether the injustice consists in depriving a person of a possession, or in breaking faith with him, or in treating him worse than he deserves, or worse than other people who have no greater claims, in each case the supposition implies two things—a wrong done, and some assignable person who is wronged. Injustice may also be done by treating a person better than others; but the wrong in this case is to his competitors, who are also assignable persons. It seems to me that this feature in the case—a right in some person, correlative to the moral obligation—constitutes the specific difference between justice, and generosity or beneficence. Justice implies something which it is not only right to do, and wrong not to do, but which some individual person can claim from us as his moral right. No one has a moral right to our generosity or beneficence, because we are not morally bound to practise those virtues towards an given individual. And it will be found with respect to this as with respect to every correct definition, that the instances which seem to conflict with it are those which most confirm it. For if a moralist attempts, as some have done, to make out that mankind generally, though not any given individual, have a right to all the good we can do them, he at once, by that thesis, includes generosity and beneficence within the category of justice. He is obliged to say, that our utmost exertions are due to our fellow creatures, thus assimilating them to a debt; or that nothing less can be a sufficient return for what society does for us, thus classing the case as one of gratitude; both of which are acknowledged cases of justice. Wherever there is a right, the case is one of justice, and not of the virtue of beneficence: and whoever does not place the distinction between justice and morality in general, where we have now placed it, will be found to make no distinction between them at all, but to merge all morality in justice.

Having thus endeavored to determine the distinctive elements which enter into the composition of the idea of justice, we are ready to enter on the inquiry, whether the feeling, which accompanies the idea, is attached to it by a special dispensation of nature, or whether it could have grown up, by any known laws, out of the idea itself; and in particular, whether it can have originated in considerations of general expediency.

I conceive that the sentiment itself does not arise from anything which would commonly, or correctly, be termed an idea of expediency; but that though the sentiment does not, whatever is moral in its does.

We have seen that the two essential ingredients in the sentiment of justice are, the desire to punish a person who has done harm, and the knowledge or belief that there is some definite individual or individuals to whom harm has been done.

Now it appears to me, that the desire to punish a person who has done harm to some individual, is a spontaneous outgrowth from two sentiments, both in the highest degree natural, and which either are or resemble instincts; the impulse of self-defence, and the feeling of sympathy.

It is natural to resent, and to repel or retaliate, any harm done or attempted against ourselves, or against those with whom we sympathize. The origin of this sentiment it is not necessary here to discuss. Whether it be an instinct or a result of intelligence, it is, we know, common to all animal nature; for every animal tries to hurt those who have hurt, or who it thinks are about to hurt, itself or its young. Human beings, on this point, only differ from other animals in two particulars. First, in being capable of sympathizing, not solely with their offspring, or, like some of the more noble animals, with some superior animal who is kind to them, but with all human, and even with all sentient, beings. Secondly, in having a more developed intelligence, which gives a wider range to the whole of their sentiments, whether self-regarding or sympathetic. By virtue of his superior intelligence, even apart from his superior range of sympathy, a human being is capable of apprehending a community of interest between himself and the human society of which he forms a part, such that any conduct which threatens the security of the society generally, is threatening to his own, and calls forth his instinct (if instinct it be) of self-defence. The same superiority of intelligence, joined to the power of sympathizing with human beings generally, enables him to attach himself to the collective idea of his tribe, his country, or mankind, in such a manner that any act hurtful to them rouses his instinct of sympathy, and urges him to resistance.

The sentiment of justice, in that one of its elements which consists of the desire to punish, is thus, I conceive, the natural feeling of retaliation or vengeance, rendered by intellect and sympathy applicable to those injuries, that is, to those hurts, which wound us through, or in common with, society at large. This sentiment, in itself, has nothing moral in it; what is moral is, the exclusive subordination of it to the social sympathies, so as to wait on and obey their call. For the natural feeling tends to make us resent indiscriminately whatever any one does that is disagreeable to us; but when moralized by the social feeling, it only acts in the directions conformable to the general good: just persons resenting a hurt to society, though not otherwise a hurt to themselves, and not resenting a hurt to themselves, however painful, unless it be of the kind which society has a common interest with them in the repression of.

It is no objection against this doctrine to say, that when we feel our sentiment of justice outraged, we are not thinking of society at large, or of any collective interest, but only of the individual case. It is common enough certainly, though the reverse of commendable, to feel resentment merely because we have suffered pain; but a person whose resentment is really a moral feeling, that is, who considers whether an act is blameable before he allows himself to resent it—such a person, though he may not say expressly to himself that he is standing up for the interest of society, certainly does feel that he is asserting a rule which is for the benefit of others as well as for his own. If he is not feeling this—if he is regarding the act solely as it affects him individually—he is not consciously just; he is not concerning himself about the justice of his actions. This is admitted even by anti-utilitarian moralists. When Kant (as before remarked) propounds as the fundamental principle of morals, 'So act, that thy rule of conduct might be adopted as a law by all rational beings,' he virtually acknowledges that the interest of mankind collectively, or at least of mankind indiscriminately, must be in the mind of the agent when conscientiously deciding on the morality of the act. Otherwise he uses words without a meaning: for, that a rule even of utter selfishness could not possibly be adopted by all rational beings—that there is an insuperable obstacle in the nature of things to its adoption—cannot be even plausibly maintained. To give any meaning to Kant's principle, the sense put upon it must be, that we ought to shape our conduct by a rule which all rational beings might adopt with benefit to their collective interest.

To recapitulate: the idea of justice supposes two things; a rule of conduct, and a sentiment which sanctions the rule. The first must be supposed common to all mankind, and intended for their good. The other (the sentiment) is a desire that punishment may be suffered by those who infringe the rule. There is involved, in addition, the conception of some definite person who suffers by the infringement; whose rights (to use the expression appropriated to the case) are violated by it. And the sentiment of justice appears to me to be, the animal desire to repel or retaliate a hurt or damage to oneself, or to those with whom one sympathizes, widened so as to include all persons, by the human capacity of enlarged sympathy, and the human conception of intelligent self-interest. From the latter elements, the feeling derives its morality; from the former, its peculiar impressiveness, and energy of self-assertion.

I have, throughout, treated the idea of a right residing in the injured person, and violated by the injury, not as a separate element in the composition of the idea and sentiment, but as one of the forms in which the other two elements clothe themselves. These elements are, a hurt to some assignable person or persons on the one hand, and a demand for punishment on the other. An examination of our own minds, I think, will show, that these two things include all that we mean when we speak of violation of a right. When we call anything a person's right, we mean that he has a valid claim on society to protect him in the possession of it, either by the force of law, or by that of education and opinion. If he has what we consider a sufficient claim, on whatever account, to have something guaranteed to him by society, we say that he has a right to it. If we desire to prove that anything does not belong to him by right, we think this done as soon as it is admitted that society ought not to take measures for securing it to him, but should leave it to chance, or to his own exertions. Thus, a person is said to have a right to what he can earn in fair professional competition; because society ought not to allow any other person to hinder him from endeavoring to earn in that manner as much as he can. But he has not a right to three hundred a-year, though he may happen to be earning it; because society is not called on to provide that he shall earn that sum. On the contrary, if he owns ten thousand pounds three per cent stock, he has a right to three hundred a-year; because society has come under an obligation to provide him with an income of that amount.

To have a right, then, is, I conceive, to have something which society ought to defend me in the possession of. If the objector goes on to ask why it ought, I can give him no other reason than general utility. If that expression does not seem to convey a sufficient feeling of the strength of the obligation, nor to account for the peculiar energy of the feeling, it is because there goes to the composition of the sentiment, not a rational only but also an animal element, the thirst for retaliation; and this thirst derives its intensity, as well as its moral justification, from the extraordinarily important and impressive kind of utility which is concerned. The interest involved is that of security, to every one's feelings the most vital of all interests. Nearly all other earthly benefits are needed by one person, not needed by another; and many of them can, if necessary, be cheerfully foregone, or replaced by something else; but security no human being can possibly do without; on it we depend for all our immunity from evil, and for the whole value of all and every good, beyond the passing moment; since nothing but the gratification of the instant could be of any worth to us, if we could be deprived of everything the next instant by whoever was momentarily stronger than ourselves. Now this most indispensable of all necessaries, after physical nutriment, cannot be had, unless the machinery for providing it is kept unintermittedly in active play. Our notion, therefore, of the claim we have on our fellow-creatures to join in making safe for us the very groundwork of our existence, gathers feelings round it so much more intense than those concerned in any of the more common cases of utility, that the difference in degree (as is often the case in psychology) becomes a real difference in kind. The claim assumes that character of absoluteness, that apparent infinity, and incommensurability with all other considerations, which constitute the distinction between the feeling of right and wrong and that of ordinary expediency and inexpediency. The feelings concerned are so powerful, and we count so positively on finding a responsive feeling in others (all being alike interested), that ought and should grow into must, and recognized indispensability becomes a moral necessity, analogous to physical, and often not inferior to it in binding force.

If the preceding analysis, or something resembling it, be not the correct account of the notion of justice; if justice be totally independent of utility, and be a standard per se, which the mind can recognize by simple introspection of itself; it is hard to understand why that internal oracle is so ambiguous, and why so many things appear either just or unjust, according to the light in which they are regarded.

We are continually informed that Utility is an uncertain standard, which every different person interprets differently, and that there is no safety but in the immutable, ineffaceable, and unmistakable dictates of Justice, which carry their evidence in themselves, and are independent of the fluctuations of opinion. One would suppose from this that on questions of justice there could be no controversy; that if we take that for our rule, its application to any given case could leave us in as little doubt as a mathematical demonstration. So far is this from being the fact, that there is as much difference of opinion, and as fierce discussion, about what is just, as about what is useful to society. Not only have different nations and individuals different notions of justice, but in the mind of one and the same individual, justice is not some one rule, principle, or maxim, but many, which do not always coincide in their dictates, and in choosing between which, he is guided either by some extraneous standard, or by his own personal predilections.

For instance, there are some who say, that it is unjust to punish any one for the sake of example to others; that punishment is just, only when intended for the good of the sufferer himself. Others maintain the extreme reverse, contending that to punish persons who have attained years of discretion, for their own benefit, is despotism and injustice, since if the matter at issue is solely their own good, no one has a right to control their own judgment of it; but that they may justly be punished to prevent evil to others, this being an exercise of the legitimate right of self-defence. Mr. Owen, again, affirms that it is unjust to punish at all; for the criminal did not make his own character; his education, and the circumstances which surround him, have made him a criminal, and for these he is not responsible. All these opinions are extremely plausible; and so long as the question is argued as one of justice simply, without going down to the principles which lie under justice and are the source of its authority, I am unable to see how any of these reasoners can be refuted. For in truth every one of the three builds upon rules of justice confessedly true. The first appeals to the acknowledged injustice of singling out an individual, and making him a sacrifice, without his consent, for other people's benefit. The second relies on the acknowledged justice of self-defence, and the admitted injustice of forcing one person to conform to another's notions of what constitutes his good. The Owenite invokes the admitted principle, that it is unjust to punish any one for what he cannot help. Each is triumphant so long as he is not compelled to take into consideration any other maxims of justice than the one he has selected; but as soon as their several maxims are brought face to face, each disputant seems to have exactly as much to say for himself as the others. No one of them can carry out his own notion of justice without trampling upon another equally binding. These are difficulties; they have always been felt to be such; and many devices have been invented to turn rather than to overcome them. As a refuge from the last of the three, men imagined what they called the freedom of the will; fancying that they could not justify punishing a man whose will is in a thoroughly hateful state, unless it be supposed to have come into that state through no influence of anterior circumstances. To escape from the other difficulties, a favorite contrivance has been the fiction of a contract, whereby at some unknown period all the members of society engaged to obey the laws, and consented to be punished for any disobedience to them; thereby giving to their legislators the right, which it is assumed they would not otherwise have had, of punishing them, either for their own good or for that of society. This happy thought was considered to get rid of the whole difficulty, and to legitimate the infliction of punishment, in virtue of another received maxim of justice, *Volenti non fit injuria;* that is not unjust which is done with the consent of the person who is supposed to be hurt by it. I need hardly remark, that even if the consent were not a mere fiction, this maxim is not superior in authority to the others which it is brought in to supersede. It is, on the contrary, an instructive specimen of the loose and irregular manner in which supposed principles of justice grow up. This particular one evidently came into use as a help to the coarse exigencies of courts of law, which are sometimes obliged to be content with very uncertain presumptions, on account of the greater evils which would often arise from any attempt on their part to cut finer. But even courts of law are not able to adhere consistently to the maxim, for they allow voluntary engagements to be set aside on the ground of fraud, and sometimes on that of mere mistake or misinformation.

Again, when the legitimacy of inflicting punishment is admitted, how many conflicting conceptions of justice come to light in discussing the proper apportionment of punishment to offences. No rule on this subject recommends itself so strongly to the primitive and spontaneous sentiment of justice, as the lex talionis, an eye for an eye and a tooth for a tooth. Though this principle of the Jewish and of the Mahomedan law has been generally abandoned in Europe as a practical maxim, there is, I suspect, in most minds, a secret hankering after it; and when retribution accidentally falls on an offender in that precise shape, the general feeling of satisfaction evinced, bears witness how natural is the sentiment to which this repayment in kind is acceptable. With many the test of justice in penal infliction is that the punishment should be proportioned to the offence; meaning that it should be exactly measured by the moral guilt of the culprit (whatever be their standard for measuring moral guilt): the consideration, what amount of punishment is necessary to deter from the offence, having nothing to do with the question of justice, in their estimation: while there are others to whom that consideration is all in all; who maintain that it is not just, at least for man, to inflict on a fellow-creature, whatever may be his offences, any amount of suffering beyond the least that will suffice to prevent him from repeating, and others from imitating, his misconduct.

To take another example from a subject already once referred to. In a co-operative industrial association, is it just or not that talent or skill should give a title to superior remuneration? On the negative side of the question it is argued, that whoever does the best he can, deserves equally well, and ought not in justice to be put in a position of inferiority for no fault of his own; that superior abilities have already advantages more than enough, in the admiration they excite, the personal influence they command, and the internal sources of satisfaction attending them, without adding to these a superior share of the world's goods; and that society is bound in justice rather to make compensation to the less favored, for this unmerited inequality of advantages, than to aggravate it. On the contrary side it is contended, that society receives more from the more efficient laborer; that his services being more useful, society owes him a larger return for them; that a greater share of the joint result is actually his work, and not to allow his claim to it is a kind of robbery; that if he is only to receive as much as others, he can only be justly required to produce as much, and to give a smaller amount of time and exertion, proportioned to his superior efficiency. Who shall decide between these appeals to conflicting principles of justice? Justice has in this case two sides to it, which it is impossible to bring into harmony, and the two disputants have chosen opposite sides; the one looks to what it is just that the individual should receive, the other to what it is just that the community should give. Each, from his own point of view, is unanswerable; and any choice between them, on grounds of justice, must be perfectly arbitrary. Social utility alone can decide the preference.

How many, again, and how irreconcilable, are the standards of justice to which reference is made in discussing the repartition of taxation. One opinion is, that payment to the State should be in numerical proportion to pecuniary means. Others think that justice dictates what they term graduated taxation; taking a higher percentage from those who have more to spare. In point of natural justice a strong case might be made for disregarding means altogether, and taking the same absolute sum (whenever it could be got) from every one: as the subscribers to a mess, or to a club, all pay the same sum for the same privileges, whether they can all equally afford it or not. Since the protection (it might be said) of law and government is afforded to, and is equally required by all, there is no injustice in making all buy it at the same price. It is reckoned justice, not injustice, that a dealer should charge to all customers the same price for the same article, not a price varying according to their means of payment. This doctrine, as applied to taxation, finds no advocates, because it conflicts strongly with men's feelings of humanity and perceptions of social expediency; but the principle of justice which it invokes is as true and as binding as those which can be appealed to against it. Accordingly, it exerts a tacit influence on the line of defence employed for other modes of assessing taxation. People feel obliged to argue that the State does more for the rich than for the poor, as a justification for its taking more from them: though this is in reality not true, for the rich would be far better able to protect themselves, in the absence of law or government, than the poor, and indeed would probably be successful in converting the poor into their slaves. Others, again, so far defer to the same conception of justice, as to maintain that all should pay an equal capitation tax for the protection of their persons (these being of equal value to all), and an unequal tax for the protection of their property, which is unequal. To this others reply, that the all of one man is as valuable to him as the all of another. From these confusions there is no other mode of extrication than the utilitarian.

Is, then, the difference between the Just and the Expedient a merely imaginary distinction? Have mankind been under a delusion in thinking that justice is a more sacred thing than policy, and that the latter ought only to be listened to after the former has been satisfied? By no means. The exposition we have given of the nature and origin of the sentiment, recognizes a real distinction; and no one of those who profess the most sublime contempt for the consequences of actions as an element in their morality, attaches more importance to the distinction than I do. While I dispute the pretensions of any theory which sets up an imaginary standard of justice not grounded on utility, I account the justice which is grounded on utility to be the chief part, and incomparably the most sacred and binding part, of all morality. Justice is a name for certain classes of moral rules, which concern the essentials of human well-being more nearly, and are therefore of more absolute obligation, than any other rules for the guidance of life; and the notion which we have found to be of the essence of the idea of justice, that of a right residing in an individual, implies and testifies to this more binding obligation.

The moral rules which forbid mankind to hurt one another (in which we must never forget to include wrongful interference with each other's freedom) are more vital to human well-being than any maxims, however important, which only point out the best mode of managing some department of human affairs. They have also the peculiarity, that they are the main element in determining the whole of the social feelings of mankind. It is their observance which alone preserves peace among human beings: if obedience to them were not the rule, and disobedience the exception, every one would see in every one else a probable enemy, against whom he must be perpetually guarding himself. What is hardly less important, these are the precepts which mankind have the strongest and the most direct inducements for impressing upon one another. By merely giving to each other prudential instruction or exhortation, they may gain, or think they gain, nothing: in inculcating on each other the duty of positive beneficence they have an unmistakable interest, but far less in degree: a person may possibly not need the benefits of others; but he always needs that they should not do him hurt. Thus the moralities which protect every individual from being harmed by others, either directly or by being hindered in his freedom of pursuing his own good, are at once those which he himself has most at heart, and those which he has the strongest interest in publishing and enforcing by word and deed. It is by a person's observance of these, that his fitness to exist as one of the fellowship of human beings, is tested and decided; for on that depends his being a nuisance or not to those with whom he is in contact. Now it is these moralities primarily, which compose the obligations of justice. The most marked cases of injustice, and those which give the tone to the feeling of repugnance which characterizes the sentiment, are acts of wrongful aggression, or wrongful exercise of power over some one; the next are those which consist in wrongfully withholding from him something which is his due; in both cases, inflicting on him a positive hurt, either in the form of direct suffering, or of the privation of some good which he had reasonable ground, either of a physical or of a social kind, for counting upon.

The same powerful motives which command the observance of these primary moralities, enjoin the punishment of those who violate them; and as the impulses of self-defence, of defence of others, and of vengeance, are all called forth against such persons, retribution, or evil for evil, becomes closely connected with the sentiment of justice, and is universally included in the idea. Good for good is also one of the dictates of justice; and this, though its social utility is evident, and though it carries with it a natural human feeling, has not at first sight that obvious connexion with hurt or injury, which, existing in the most elementary cases of just and unjust, is the source of the characteristic intensity of the sentiment. But the connexion, though less obvious, is not less real. He who accepts benefits, and denies a return of them when needed, inflicts a real hurt, by disappointing one of the most natural and reasonable of expectations, and one which he must at least tacitly have encouraged, otherwise the benefits would seldom have been conferred. The important rank, among human evils and wrongs, of the disappointment of expectation, is shown in the fact that it constitutes the principal criminality of two such highly immoral acts as a breach of friendship and a breach of promise. Few hurts which human beings can sustain are greater, and none wound more, than when that on which they habitually and with full assurance relied, fails them in the hour of need; and few wrongs are greater than this mere withholding of good; none excite more resentment, either in the person suffering, or in a sympathizing spectator. The principle, therefore, of giving to each what they deserve, that is, good for good as well as evil for evil, is not only included within the idea of Justice as we have defined it, but is a proper object of that intensity of sentiment, which places the Just, in human estimation, above the simply Expedient.

Most of the maxims of justice current in the world, and commonly appealed to in its transactions, are simply instrumental to carrying into effect the principles of justice which we have now spoken of. That a person is only responsible for what he has done voluntarily, or could voluntarily have avoided; that it is unjust to condemn any person unheard; that the punishment ought to be proportioned to the offence, and the like, are maxims intended to prevent the just principle of evil for evil from being perverted to the infliction of evil without that justification. The greater part of these common maxims have come into use from the practice of courts of justice, which have been naturally led to a more complete recognition and elaboration than was likely to suggest itself to others, of the rules necessary to enable them to fulfil their double function, of inflicting punishment when due, and of awarding to each person his right.

That first of judicial virtues, impartiality, is an obligation of justice, partly for the reason last mentioned; as being a necessary condition of the fulfilment of the other obligations of justice. But this is not the only source of the exalted rank, among human obligations, of those maxims of equality and impartiality, which, both in popular estimation and in that of the most enlightened, are included among the precepts of justice. In one point of view, they may be considered as corollaries from the principles already laid down. If it is a duty to do to each according to his deserts, returning good for good as well as repressing evil by evil, it necessarily follows that we should treat all equally well (when no higher duty forbids) who have deserved equally well of us, and that society should treat all equally well who have deserved equally well of it, that is, who have deserved equally well absolutely. This is the highest abstract standard of social and distributive justice; towards which all institutions, and the efforts of all virtuous citizens, should be made in the utmost possible degree to converge. But this great moral duty rests upon a still deeper foundation, being a direct emanation from the first principle of morals, and not a mere logical corollary from secondary or derivative doctrines. It is involved in the very meaning of Utility, or the Greatest-Happiness Principle. That principle is a mere form of words without rational signification, unless one person's happiness, supposed equal in degree (with the proper allowance made for kind), is counted for exactly as much as another's. Those conditions being supplied, Bentham's dictum, 'everybody to count for one, nobody for more than one,' might be written under the principle of utility as an explanatory commentary. The equal claim of everybody to happiness in the estimation of the moralist and the legislator, involves an equal claim to all the means of happiness, except in so far as the inevitable conditions of human life, and the general interest, in which that of every individual is included, set limits to the maxim; and those limits ought to be strictly construed. As every other maxim of justice, so this, is by no means applied or held applicable universally; on the contrary, as I have already remarked, it bends to every person's ideas of social expediency. But in whatever case it is deemed applicable at all, it is held to be the dictate of justice. All persons are deemed to have a right to equality of treatment, except when some recognized social expediency requires the reverse. And hence all social inequalities which have ceased to be considered expedient, assume the character not of simple inexpediency, but of injustice, and appear so tyrannical, that people are apt to wonder how they ever could have been tolerated; forgetful that they themselves perhaps tolerate other inequalities under an equally mistaken notion of expediency, the correction of which would make that which they approve seem quite as monstrous as what they have at last learnt to condemn. The entire history of social improvement has been a series of transitions, by which one custom or institution after another, from being a supposed primary necessity of social existence, has passed into the rank of an universally stigmatized injustice and tyranny. So it has been with the distinctions of slaves and freemen, nobles and serfs, patricians and plebeians; and so it will be, and in part already is, with the aristocracies of colour, race, and sex.

It appears from what has been said, that justice is a name for certain moral requirements, which, regarded collectively, stand higher in the scale of social utility, and are therefore of more paramount obligation, than any others; though particular cases may occur in which some other social duty is so important, as to overrule any one of the general maxims of justice. Thus, to save a life, it may not only be allowable, but a duty, to steal, or take by force, the necessary food or medicine, or to kidnap, and compel to officiate, the only qualified medical practitioner. In such cases, as we do not call anything justice which is not a virtue, we usually say, not that justice must give way to some other moral principle, but that what is just in ordinary cases is, by reason of that other principle, not just in the particular case. By this useful accommodation of language, the character of indefeasibility attributed to justice is kept up, and we are saved from the necessity of maintaining that there can be laudable injustice.

The considerations which have now been adduced resolve, I conceive, the only real difficulty in the utilitarian theory of morals. It has always been evident that all cases of justice are also cases of expediency: the difference is in the peculiar sentiment which attaches to the former, as contradistinguished from the latter. If this characteristic sentiment has been sufficiently accounted for; if there is no necessity to assume for it any peculiarity of origin; if it is simply the natural feeling of resentment, moralized by being made coextensive with the demands of social good; and if this feeling not only does but ought to exist in all the classes of cases to which the idea of justice corresponds; that idea no longer presents itself as a stumbling-block to the utilitarian ethics. Justice remains the appropriate name for certain social utilities which are vastly more important, and therefore more absolute and imperative, than any others are as a class (though not more so than others may be in particular cases); and which, therefore, ought to be, as well as naturally are, guarded by a sentiment not only different in degree, but also in kind; distinguished from the milder feeling which attaches to the mere idea of promoting human pleasure or convenience, at once by the more definite nature of its commands, and by the sterner character of its sanctions.

On Liberty

> The grand, leading principle, towards which every argument unfolded in these pages directly converges, is the absolute and essential importance of human development in its richest diversity.
>
> WILHELM VON HUMBOLDT: SPHERE AND DUTIES OF GOVERNMENT.

CHAPTER I. INTRODUCTORY

The subject of this Essay is not the so-called Liberty of the Will, so unfortunately opposed to the misnamed doctrine of Philosophical Necessity; but Civil, or Social Liberty: the nature and limits of the power which can be legitimately exercised by society over the individual. A question seldom stated, and hardly ever discussed, in general terms, but which profoundly influences the practical controversies of the age by its latent presence, and is likely soon to make itself recognized as the vital question of the future. It is so far from being new, that, in a certain sense, it has divided mankind, almost from the remotest ages; but in the stage of progress into which the more civilized portions of the species have now entered, it presents itself under new conditions, and requires a different and more fundamental treatment.

The struggle between Liberty and Authority is the most conspicuous feature in the portions of history with which we are earliest familiar, particularly in that of Greece, Rome, and England. But in old times this contest was between subjects, or some classes of subjects, and the Government. By liberty, was meant protection against the tyranny of the political rulers. The rulers were conceived (except in some of the popular governments of Greece) as in a necessarily antagonistic position to the people whom they ruled. They consisted of a governing One, or a governing tribe or caste, who derived their authority from inheritance or conquest, who, at all events, did not hold it at the pleasure of the governed, and whose supremacy men did not venture, perhaps did not desire, to contest, whatever precautions might be taken against its oppressive exercise. Their power was regarded as necessary, but also as highly dangerous; as a weapon which they would attempt to use against their subjects, no less than against external enemies. To prevent the weaker members of the community from being preyed upon by innumerable vultures, it was needful that there should be an animal of prey stronger than the rest, commissioned to keep them down. But as the king of the vultures would be no less bent upon preying on the flock than any of the minor harpies, it was indispensable to be in a perpetual attitude of defence against his beak and claws. The aim, therefore, of patriots was to set limits to the power which the ruler should be suffered to exercise over the community; and this limitation was what they meant by liberty. It was attempted in two ways. First, by obtaining a recognition of certain immunities, called political liberties or rights, which it was to be regarded as a breach of duty in the ruler to infringe, and which if he did infringe, specific resistance, or general rebellion, was held to be justifiable. A second, and generally a later expedient, was the establishment of constitutional checks, by which the consent of the community, or of a body of some sort, supposed to represent its interests, was made a necessary condition to some of the more important acts of the governing power. To the first of these modes of limitation, the ruling power, in most European countries, was compelled, more or less, to submit. It was not so with the second; and, to attain this, or when already in some degree possessed, to attain it more completely, became everywhere the principal object of the lovers of liberty. And so long as mankind were content to combat one enemy by another, and to be ruled by a master, on condition of being guaranteed more or less efficaciously against his tyranny, they did not carry their aspirations beyond this point.

A time, however, came, in the progress of human affairs, when men ceased to think it a necessity of nature that their governors should be an independent power, opposed in interest to themselves. It appeared to them much better that the various magistrates of the State should be their tenants or delegates, revocable at their pleasure. In that way alone, it seemed, could they have complete security that the powers of government would never be abused to their disadvantage. By degrees this new demand for elective and temporary rulers became the prominent object of the exertions of the popular party, wherever any such party existed; and superseded, to a considerable extent, the previous efforts to limit the power of rulers. As the struggle proceeded for making the ruling power emanate from the periodical choice of the ruled, some persons began to think that too much importance had been attached to the limitation of the power itself. That (it might seem) was a resource against rulers whose interests were habitually opposed to those of the people. What was now wanted was, that the rulers should be identified with the people; that their interest and will should be the interest and will of the nation. The nation did not need to be protected against its own will. There was no fear of its tyrannizing over itself. Let the rulers be effectually responsible to it, promptly removable by it, and it could afford to trust them with power of which it could itself dictate the use to be made. Their power was but the nation's own power, concentrated, and in a form convenient for exercise. This mode of thought, or rather perhaps of feeling, was common among the last generation of European liberalism, in the Continental section of which it still apparently predominates. Those who admit any limit to what a government may do, except in the case of such governments as they think ought not to exist, stand out as brilliant exceptions among the political thinkers of the Continent. A similar tone of sentiment might by this time have been prevalent in our own country, if the circumstances which for a time encouraged it, had continued unaltered.

But, in political and philosophical theories, as well as in persons, success discloses faults and infirmities which failure might have concealed from observation. The notion, that the people have no need to limit their power over themselves, might seem axiomatic, when popular government was a thing only dreamed about, or read of as having existed at some distant period of the past. Neither was that notion necessarily disturbed by such temporary aberrations as those of the French Revolution, the worst of which were the work of an usurping few, and which, in any case, belonged, not to the permanent working of popular institutions, but to a sudden and convulsive outbreak against monarchical and aristocratic despotism. In time, however, a democratic republic came to occupy a large portion of the earth's surface, and made itself felt as one of the most powerful members of the community of nations; and elective and responsible government became subject to the observations and criticisms which wait upon a great existing fact. It was now perceived that such phrases as 'self-government,' and 'the power of the people over themselves,' do not express the true state of the case. The 'people' who exercise the power are not always the same people with those over whom it is exercised; and the 'self-government' spoken of is not the government of each by himself, but of each by all the rest. The will of the people, moreover, practically means the will of the most numerous or the most active part of the people; the majority, or those who succeed in making themselves accepted as the majority; the people, consequently, may desire to oppress a part of their number; and precautions are as much needed against this as against any other abuse of power. The limitation, therefore, of the power of government over individuals loses none of its importance when the holders of power are regularly accountable to the community, that is, to the strongest party therein. This view of things, recommending itself equally to the intelligence of thinkers and to the inclination of those important classes in European society to whose real or supposed interests democracy is adverse, has had no difficulty in establishing itself; and in political speculations 'the tyranny of the majority' is now generally included among the evils against which society requires to be on its guard.

Like other tyrannies, the tyranny of the majority was at first, and is still vulgarly, held in dread, chiefly as operating through the acts of the public authorities. But reflecting persons perceived that when society is itself the tyrant—society collectively, over the separate individuals who compose it—its means of tyrannizing are not restricted to the acts which it may do by the hands of its political functionaries. Society can and does execute its own mandates: and if it issues wrong mandates instead of right, or any mandates at all in things with which it ought not to meddle, it practices a social tyranny more formidable than many kinds of political oppression, since, though not usually upheld by such extreme penalties, it leaves fewer means of escape, penetrating much more deeply into the details of life, and enslaving the soul itself. Protection, therefore, against the tyranny of the magistrate is not enough: there needs protection also against the tyranny of the prevailing opinion and feeling; against the tendency of society to impose, by other means than civil penalties, its own ideas and practices as rules of conduct on those who dissent from them; to fetter the development, and, if possible, prevent the formation, of any individuality not in harmony with its ways, and compel all characters to fashion themselves upon the model of its own. There is a limit to the legitimate interference of collective opinion with individual independence: and to find that limit, and maintain it against encroachment, is as indispensable to a good condition of human affairs, as protection against political despotism. . . .

The object of this Essay is to assert one very simple principle, as entitled to govern absolutely the dealings of society with the individual in the way of compulsion and control, whether the means used be physical force in the form of legal penalties, or the moral coercion of public opinion. That principle is, that the sole end for which mankind are warranted, individually or collectively, in interfering with the liberty of action of any of their number, is self-protection. That the only purpose for which power can be rightfully exercised over any member of a civilized community, against his will, is to prevent harm to others. His own good, either physical or moral, is not a sufficient warrant. He cannot rightfully be compelled to do or forbear because it will be better for him to do so, because it will make him happier, because, in the opinions of others, to do so would be wise, or even right. These are good reasons for remonstrating with him, or reasoning with him, or persuading him, or entreating him, but not for compelling him, or visiting him with any evil in case he do otherwise. To justify that, the conduct from which it is desired to deter him, must be calculated to produce evil to some one else. The only part of the conduct of any one, for which he is amenable to society, is that which concerns others. In the part which merely concerns himself, his independence is, of right, absolute. Over himself, over his own body and mind, the individual is sovereign.

It is, perhaps, hardly necessary to say that this doctrine is meant to apply only to human beings in the maturity of their faculties. We are not speaking of children, or of young persons below the age which the law may fix as that of manhood or womanhood. Those who are still in a state to require being taken care of by others, must be protected against their own actions as well as against external injury. For the same reason, we may leave out of consideration those backward states of society in which the race itself may be considered as in its nonage. The early difficulties in the way of spontaneous progress are so great, that there is seldom any choice of means for overcoming them; and a ruler full of the spirit of improvement is warranted in the use of any expedients that will attain an end, perhaps otherwise unattainable. Despotism is a legitimate mode of government in dealing with barbarians, provided the end be their improvement, and the means justified by actually effecting that end. Liberty, as a principle, has no application to any state of things anterior to the time when mankind have become capable of being improved by free and equal discussion. Until then, there is nothing for them but implicit obedience to an Akbar or a Charlemagne, if they are so fortunate as to find one. But as soon as mankind have attained the capacity of being guided to their own improvement by conviction or persuasion (a period long since reached in all nations with whom we need here concern ourselves), compulsion, either in the direct form or in that of pains and penalties for non-compliance, is no longer admissible as a means to their own good, and justifiable only for the security of others.

It is proper to state that I forgo any advantage which could be derived to my argument from the idea of abstract right, as a thing independent of utility. I regard utility as the ultimate appeal on all ethical questions; but it must be utility in the largest sense, grounded on the permanent interests of man as a progressive being. Those interests, I contend, authorize the subjection of individual spontaneity to external control, only in respect to those actions of each, which concern the interest of other people. If any one does an act hurtful to others, there is a prima facie case for punishing him, by law, or, where legal penalties are not safely applicable, by general disapprobation. There are also many positive acts for the benefit of others which he may rightfully be compelled to perform; such as, to give evidence in a court of justice; to bear his fair share in the common defence, or in any other joint work necessary to the interest of the society of which he enjoys the protection; and to perform certain acts of individual beneficence, such as saving a fellow-creature's life, or interposing to protect the defenceless against ill-usage, things which whenever it is obviously a man's duty to do, he may rightfully be made responsible to society for not doing. A person may cause evil to others not only by his actions but by his inaction, and in either case he is justly accountable to them for the injury. The latter case, it is true, requires a much more cautious exercise of compulsion than the former. To make any one answerable for doing evil to others, is the rule; to make him answerable for not preventing evil, is, comparatively speaking, the exception. Yet there are many cases clear enough and grave enough to justify that exception. In all things which regard the external relations of the individual, he is de jure amenable to those whose interests are concerned, and if need be, to society as their protector. There are often good reasons for not holding him to the responsibility; but these reasons must arise from the special expediencies of the case: either because it is a kind of case in which he is on the whole likely to act better, when left to his own discretion, than when controlled in any way in which society have it in their power to control him; or because the attempt to exercise control would produce other evils, greater than those which it would prevent. When such reasons as these preclude the enforcement of responsibility, the conscience of the agent himself should step into the vacant judgment seat, and protect those interests of others which have no external protection; judging himself all the more rigidly, because the case does not admit of his being made accountable to the judgment of his fellow-creatures.

But there is a sphere of action in which society, as distinguished from the individual, has, if any, only an indirect interest; comprehending all that portion of a person's life and conduct which affects only himself, or if it also affects others, only with their free, voluntary, and undeceived consent and participation. When I say only himself, I mean directly, and in the first instance: for whatever affects himself, may affect others through himself; and the objection which may be grounded on this contingency, will receive consideration in the sequel. This, then, is the appropriate region of human liberty. It comprises, first, the inward domain of consciousness; demanding liberty of conscience, in the most comprehensive sense; liberty of thought and feeling; absolute freedom of opinion and sentiment on all subjects, practical or speculative, scientific, moral, or theological. The liberty of expressing and publishing opinions may seem to fall under a different principle, since it belongs to that part of the conduct of an individual which concerns other people; but, being almost of as much importance as the liberty of thought itself, and resting in great part on the same reasons, is practically inseparable from it. Secondly, the principle requires liberty of tastes and pursuits; of framing the plan of our life to suit our own character; of doing as we like, subject to such consequences as may follow: without impediment from our fellow-creatures, so long as what we do does not harm them, even though they should think our conduct foolish, perverse, or wrong. Thirdly, from this liberty of each individual, follows the liberty, within the same limits, of combination among individuals; freedom to unite, for any purpose not involving harm to others: the persons combining being supposed to be of full age, and not forced or deceived.

No society in which these liberties are not, on the whole, respected, is free, whatever may be its form of government; and none is completely free in which they do not exist absolute and unqualified. The only freedom which deserves the name, is that of pursuing our own good in our own way, so long as we do not attempt to deprive others of theirs, or impede their efforts to obtain it. Each is the proper guardian of his own health, whether bodily, or mental and spiritual. Mankind are greater gainers by suffering each other to live as seems good to themselves, than by compelling each to live as seems good to the rest.

Though this doctrine is anything but new, and, to some persons, may have the air of a truism, there is no doctrine which stands more directly opposed to the general tendency of existing opinion and practice. Society has expended fully as much effort in the attempt (according to its lights) to compel people to conform to its notions of personal, as of social excellence. The ancient commonwealths thought themselves entitled to practise, and the ancient philosophers countenanced, the regulation of every part of private conduct by public authority, on the ground that the State had a deep interest in the whole bodily and mental discipline of every one of its citizens; a mode of thinking which may have been admissible in small republics surrounded by powerful enemies, in constant peril of being subverted by foreign attack or internal commotion, and to which even a short interval of relaxed energy and self-command might so easily be fatal, that they could not afford to wait for the salutary permanent effects of freedom. In the modern world, the greater size of political communities, and above all, the separation between spiritual and temporal authority (which placed the direction of men's consciences in other hands than those which controlled their worldly affairs), prevented so great an interference by law in the details of private life; but the engines of moral repression have been wielded more strenuously against divergence from the reigning opinion in self-regarding, then even in social matters; religion, the most powerful of the elements which have entered into the formation of moral feeling, having almost always been governed either by the ambition of a hierarchy, seeking control over every department of human conduct, or by the spirit of Puritanism. And some of those modern reformers who have placed themselves in strongest opposition to the religions of the past, have been noway behind either churches or sects in their assertion of the right of spiritual domination: M. Comte, in particular, whose social system, as unfolded in his Systeme de Politique Positive, aims at establishing (though by moral more than by legal appliances) a despotism of society over the individual, surpassing anything contemplated in the political ideal of the most rigid disciplinarian among the ancient philosophers.

Apart from the peculiar tenets of individual thinkers, there is also in the world at large an increasing inclination to stretch unduly the powers of society over the individual, both by the force of opinion and even by that of legislation: and as the tendency of all the changes taking place in the world is to strengthen society, and diminish the power of the individual, this encroachment is not one of the evils which tend spontaneously to disappear, but, on the contrary, to grow more and more formidable. The disposition of mankind, whether as rulers or as fellow-citizens, to impose their own opinions and inclinations as a rule of conduct on others, is so energetically supported by some of the best and by some of the worst feelings incident to human nature, that it is hardly ever kept under restraint by anything but want of power; and as the power is not declining, but growing, unless a strong barrier of moral conviction can be raised against the mischief, we must expect, in the present circumstances of the world, to see it increase.

It will be convenient for the argument, if, instead of at once entering upon the general thesis, we confine ourselves in the first instance to a single branch of it, on which the principle here stated is, if not fully, yet to a certain point, recognized by the current opinions. This one branch is the Liberty of Thought: from which it is impossible to separate the cognate liberty of speaking and of writing. Although these liberties, to some considerable amount, form part of the political morality of all countries which profess religious toleration and free institutions, the grounds, both philosophical and practical, on which they rest, are perhaps not so familiar to the general mind, nor so thoroughly appreciated by many even of the leaders of opinion, as might have been expected. Those grounds, when rightly understood, are of much wider application than to only one division of the subject, and a thorough consideration of this part of the question will be found the best introduction to the remainder. Those to whom nothing which I am about to say will be new, may therefore, I hope, excuse me, if on a subject which for now three centuries has been so often discussed, I venture on one discussion more.

CHAPTER II. OF THE LIBERTY OF THOUGHT AND DISCUSSION

The time, it is to be hoped, is gone by, when any defence would be necessary of the 'liberty of the press' as one of the securities against corrupt or tyrannical government. No argument, we may suppose, can now be needed, against permitting a legislature or an executive, not identified in interest with the people, to prescribe opinions to them, and determine what doctrines or what arguments they shall be allowed to hear. This aspect of the question, besides, has been so often and so triumphantly enforced by preceding writers, that it needs not be specially insisted on in this place. Though the law of England, on the subject of the press, is as servile to this day as it was in the time of the Tudors, there is little danger of its being actually put in force against political discussion, except during some temporary panic, when fear of insurrection drives ministers and judges from their propriety; and, speaking generally, it is not, in constitutional countries, to be apprehended, that the government, whether completely responsible to the people or not, will often attempt to control the expression of opinion, except when in doing so it makes itself the organ of the general intolerance of the public. Let us suppose, therefore, that the government is entirely at one with the people, and never thinks of exerting any power of coercion unless in agreement with what it conceives to be their voice. But I deny the right of the people to exercise such coercion, either by themselves or by their government. The power itself is illegitimate. The best government has no more title to it than the worst. It is as noxious, or more noxious, when exerted in accordance with public opinion, than when in opposition to it. If all mankind minus one, were of one opinion, and only one person were of the contrary opinion, mankind would be no more justified in silencing that one person, than he, if he had the power, would be justified in silencing mankind. Were an opinion a personal possession of no value except to the owner; if to be obstructed in the enjoyment of it were simply a private injury, it would make some difference whether the injury was inflicted only on a few persons or on many. But the peculiar evil of silencing the expression of an opinion is, that it is robbing the human race; posterity as well as the existing generation; those who dissent from the opinion, still more than those who hold it. If the opinion is right, they are deprived of the opportunity of exchanging error for truth: if wrong, they lose, what is almost as great a benefit, the clearer perception and livelier impression of truth, produced by its collision with error.

It is necessary to consider separately these two hypotheses, each of which has a distinct branch of the argument corresponding to it. We can never be sure that the opinion we are endeavoring to stifle is a false opinion; and if we were sure, stifling it would be an evil still.

First: the opinion which it is attempted to suppress by authority may possibly be true. Those who desire to suppress it, of course deny its truth; but they are not infallible. They have no authority to decide the question for all mankind, and exclude every other person from the means of judging. To refuse a hearing to an opinion, because they are sure that it is false, is to assume that their certainty is the same thing as absolute certainty. All silencing of discussion is an assumption of infallibility. Its condemnation may be allowed to rest on this common argument, not the worse for being common.

Unfortunately for the good sense of mankind, the fact of their fallibility is far from carrying the weight in their practical judgment, which is always allowed to it in theory; for while every one well knows himself to be fallible, few think it necessary to take any precautions against their own fallibility, or admit the supposition that any opinion, of which they feel very certain, may be one of the examples of the error to which they acknowledge themselves to be liable. Absolute princes, or others who are accustomed to unlimited deference, usually feel this complete confidence in their own opinions on nearly all subjects. People more happily situated, who sometimes hear their opinions disputed, and are not wholly unused to be set right when they are wrong, place the same unbounded reliance only on such of their opinions as are shared by all who surround them, or to whom they habitually defer: for in proportion to a man's want of confidence in his own solitary judgment, does he usually repose, with implicit trust, on the infallibility of 'the world' in general. And the world, to each individual, means the part of it with which he comes in contact; his party, his sect, his church, his class of society: the man may be called, by comparison, almost liberal and large-minded to whom it means anything so comprehensive as his own country or his own age. Nor is his faith in this collective authority at all shaken by his being aware that other ages, countries, sects, churches, classes, and parties have thought, and even now think, the exact reverse. He devolves upon his own world the responsibility of being in the right against the dissentient worlds of other people; and it never troubles him that mere accident has decided which of these numerous worlds is the object of his reliance, and that the same causes which make him a Churchman in London, would have made him a Buddhist or a Confucian in Pekin. Yet it is as evident in itself, as any amount of argument can make it, that ages are no more infallible than individuals; every age having held many opinions which subsequent ages have deemed not only false but absurd; and it is as certain that many opinions, now general, will be rejected by future ages, as it is that many, once general, are rejected by the present.

The objection likely to be made to this argument, would probably take some such form as the following. There is no greater assumption of infallibility in forbidding the propagation of error, than in any other thing which is done by public authority on its own judgment and responsibility. Judgment is given to men that they may use it. Because it may be used erroneously, are men to be told that they ought not to use it at all? To prohibit what they think pernicious, is not claiming exemption from error, but fulfilling the duty incumbent on them, although fallible, of acting on their conscientious conviction. If we were never to act on our opinions, because those opinions may be wrong, we should leave all our interests uncared for, and all our duties unperformed. An objection which applies to all conduct, can be no valid objection to any conduct in particular. It is the duty of governments, and of individuals, to form the truest opinions they can; to form them carefully, and never impose them upon others unless they are quite sure of being right. But when they are sure (such reasoners may say), it is not conscientiousness but cowardice to shrink from acting on their opinions, and allow doctrines which they honestly think dangerous to the welfare of mankind, either in this life or in another, to be scattered abroad without restraint, because other people, in less enlightened times, have persecuted opinions now believed to be true. Let us take care, it may be said, not to make the same mistake: but governments and nations have made mistakes in other things, which are not denied to be fit subjects for the exercise of authority: they have laid on bad taxes, made unjust wars. Ought we therefore to lay on no taxes, and, under whatever provocation, make no wars? Men, and governments, must act to the best of their ability. There is no such thing as absolute certainty, but there is assurance sufficient for the purposes of human life. We may, and must, assume our opinion to be true for the guidance of our own conduct: and it is assuming no more when we forbid bad men to pervert society by the propagation of opinions which we regard as false and pernicious.

I answer, that it is assuming very much more. There is the greatest difference between presuming an opinion to be true, because, with every opportunity for contesting it, it has not been refuted, and assuming its truth for the purpose of not permitting its refutation. Complete liberty of contradicting and disproving our opinion, is the very condition which justifies us in assuming its truth for purposes of action; and on no other terms can a being with human faculties have any rational assurance of being right.

When we consider either the history of opinion, or the ordinary conduct of human life, to what is it to be ascribed that the one and the other are no worse than they are? Not certainly to the inherent force of the human understanding; for, on any matter not self-evident, there a ninety-nine persons totally incapable of judging of it, for one who is capable; and the capacity of the hundredth person is only comparative; for the majority of the eminent men of every past generation held many opinions now known to be erroneous, and did or approved numerous things which no one will now justify. Why is it, then, that there is on the whole a preponderance among mankind of rational opinions and rational conduct? If there really is this preponderance—which there must be unless human affairs are, and have always been, in an almost desperate state—it is owning to a quality of the human mind, the source of everything respectable in man either as an intellectual or as a moral being, namely, that his errors are corrigible. He is capable of rectifying his mistakes, by discussion and experience. Not by experience alone. There must be discussion, to show how experience is to be interpreted. Wrong opinions and practices gradually yield to fact and argument: but facts and arguments, to produce any effect on the mind, must be brought before it. Very few facts are able to tell their own story, without comments to bring out their meaning. The whole strength and value, then, of human judgment, depending on the one property, that it can be set right when it is wrong, reliance can be placed on it only when the means of setting it right are kept constantly at hand. In the case of any person whose judgment is really deserving of confidence, how has it become so? Because he has kept his mind open to criticism of his opinions and conduct. Because it has been his practice to listen to all that could be said against him; to profit by as much of it as was just, and expound to himself, and upon occasion to others, the fallacy of what was fallacious. Because he has felt, that the only way in which a human being can make some approach to knowing the whole of a subject, is by hearing what can be said about it by persons of every variety of opinion, and studying all modes in which it can be looked at by every character of mind. No wise man ever acquired his wisdom in any mode but this; nor is it in the nature of human intellect to become wise in any other manner. The steady habit of correcting and completing his own opinion by collating it with those of others, so far from causing doubt and hesitation in carrying it into practice, is the only stable foundation for a just reliance on it: for, being cognizant of all that can, at least obviously, be said against him, and having taken up his position against all gainsayers—knowing that he has sought for objections and difficulties, instead of avoiding them, and has shut out no light which can be thrown upon the subject from any quarter—he has a right to think his judgment better than that of any person, or any multitude, who have not gone through a similar process. . . .

It is not too much to require that what the wisest of mankind, those who are best entitled to trust their own judgment, find necessary to warrant their relying on it, should be submitted to by that miscellaneous collection of a few wise and many foolish individuals, called the public. The most intolerant of churches, the Roman Catholic Church, even at the canonization of a saint, admits, and listens patiently to, a 'devil's advocate.' The holiest of men, it appears, cannot be admitted to posthumous honors, until all that the devil could say against him is known and weighed. If even the Newtonian philosophy were not permitted to be questioned, mankind could not feel as complete assurance of its truth as they now do. The beliefs which we have most warrant for, have no safeguard to rest on, but a standing invitation to the whole world to prove them unfounded. If the challenge is not accepted, or is accepted and the attempt fails, we are far enough from certainty still; but we have done the best that the existing state of human reason admits of; we have neglected nothing that could give the truth a chance of reaching us: if the lists are kept open, we may hope that if there be a better truth, it will be found when the human mind is capable of receiving it; and in the meantime we may rely on having attained such approach to truth, as is possible in our own day. This is the amount of certainty attainable by a fallible being, and this the sole way of attaining it.

Strange it is, that men should admit the validity of the arguments for free discussion, but object to their being 'pushed to an extreme;' not seeing that unless the reasons are good for an extreme case, they are not good for any case. Strange that they should imagine that they are not assuming infallibility, when they acknowledge that there should be free discussion on all subjects which can possibly be doubtful, but think that some particular principle or doctrine should be forbidden to be questioned because it is so certain, that is, because they are certain that it is certain. To call any proposition certain, while there is any one who would deny its certainty if permitted, but who is not permitted, is to assume that we ourselves, and those who agree with us, are the judges of certainty, and judges without hearing the other side.

In the present age—which has been described as 'destitute of faith, but terrified at scepticism'—in which people feel sure, not so much that their opinions are true, as that they should not know what to do without them—the claims of an opinion to be protected from public attack are rested not so much on its truth, as on its importance to society. There are, it is alleged, certain beliefs, so useful, not to say indispensable to well-being, that it is as much the duty of governments to uphold those beliefs, as to protect any other of the interests of society. In a case of such necessity, and so directly in the line of their duty, something less than infallibility may, it is maintained, warrant, and even bind, governments, to act on their own opinion, confirmed by the general opinion of mankind. It is also often argued, and still oftener thought, that none but bad men would desire to weaken these salutary beliefs; and there can be nothing wrong, it is thought, in restraining bad men, and prohibiting what only such men would wish to practise. This mode of thinking makes the justification of restraints on discussion not a question of the truth of doctrines, but of their usefulness; and flatters itself by that means to escape the responsibility of claiming to be an infallible judge of opinions. But those who thus satisfy themselves, do not perceive that the assumption of infallibility is merely shifted from one point to another. The usefulness of an opinion is itself matter of opinion; as disputable, as open to discussion, and requiring discussion as much, as the opinion itself. There is the same need of an infallible judge of opinions to decide an opinion to be noxious, as to decide it to be false, unless the opinion condemned has full opportunity of defending itself. And it will not do to say that the heretic may be allowed to maintain the utility or harmlessness of his opinion, though forbidden to maintain its truth. The truth of an opinion is part of its utility. If we would know whether or not it is desirable that a proposition should be believed, is it possible to exclude the consideration of whether or not it is true? In the opinion, not of bad men, but of the best men, no belief which is contrary to truth can be really useful: and can you prevent such men from urging that plea, when they are charged with culpability for denying some doctrine which they are told is useful, but which they believe to be false? Those who are on the side of received opinions, never fail to take all possible advantage of this plea; you do not find them handling the question of utility as if it could be completely abstracted from that of truth: on the contrary, it is, above all, because their doctrine is the 'truth,' that the knowledge or the belief of it is held to be so indispensable. There can be no fair discussion of the question of usefulness, when an argument so vital may be employed on one side, but not on the other. And in point of fact, when law or public feeling do not permit the truth of an opinion to be disputed, they are just as little tolerant of a denial of its usefulness. The utmost they allow is an extenuation of its absolute necessity, or of the positive guilt of rejecting it. . . .

Mankind can hardly be too often reminded, that there was once a man named Socrates, between whom and the legal authorities and public opinion of his time, there took place a memorable collision. Born in an age and country abounding in individual greatness, this man has been handed down to us by those who best knew both him and the age, as the most virtuous man in it; while we know him as the head and prototype of all subsequent teachers of virtue, the source equally of the lofty inspiration of Plato and the judicious utilitarianism of Aristotle, 'i maestri di color che sanno,' the two headsprings of ethical as of all other philosophy. This acknowledged master of all the eminent thinkers who have since lived—whose fame, still growing after more than two thousand years, all but outweighs the whole remainder of the names which make his native city illustrious—was put to death by his countrymen, after a judicial conviction, for impiety and immorality. Impiety, in denying the gods recognized by the State; indeed his accuser asserted (see the Apologia) that he believed in no gods at all. Immorality, in being, by his doctrines and instructions, a 'corruptor of youth.' Of these charges the tribunal, there is every ground for believing, honestly found him guilty, and condemned the man who probably of all then born had deserved best of mankind, to be put to death as a criminal.

To pass from this to the only other instance of judicial iniquity, the mention of which, after the condemnation of Socrates, would not be an anti-climax: the event which took place on Calvary rather more than eighteen hundred years ago. The man who left on the memory of those who witnessed his life and conversation, such an impression of his moral grandeur, that eighteen subsequent centuries have done homage to him as the Almighty in person, was ignominiously put to death, as what? As a blasphemer. Men did not merely mistake their benefactor; they mistook him for the exact contrary of what he was, and treated him as that prodigy of impiety, which they themselves are now held to be, for their treatment of him. The feelings with which mankind now regard these lamentable transactions, especially the later of the two, render them extremely unjust in their judgment of the unhappy actors. These were, to all appearance, not bad men—not worse than men commonly are, but rather the contrary; men who possessed in a full, or somewhat more than a full measure, the religious, moral, and patriotic feelings of their time and people: the very kind of men who, in all times, our own included, have every chance of passing through life blameless and respected. The high-priest who rent his garments when the words were pronounced, which, according to all the ideas of his country, constituted the blackest guilt, was in all probability quite as sincere in his horror and indignation, as the generality of respectable and pious men now are in the religious and moral sentiments they profess; and most of those who now shudder at his conduct, if they had lived in his time, and been born Jews, would have acted precisely as he did. Orthodox Christians who are tempted to think that those who stoned to death the first martyrs must have been worse men than they themselves are, ought to remember that one of those persecutors was Saint Paul. . . .

Aware of the impossibility of defending the use of punishment for restraining irreligious opinions . . . the enemies of religious freedom, when hard pressed, occasionally accept this consequence, and say, with Dr. Johnson, that the persecutors of Christianity were in the right; that persecution is an ordeal through which truth ought to pass, and always passes successfully, legal penalties being, in the end, powerless against truth, though sometimes beneficially effective against mischievous errors. This is a form of the argument for religious intolerance, sufficiently remarkable not to be passed without notice.

A theory which maintains that truth may justifiably be persecuted because persecution cannot possibly do it any harm, cannot be charged with being intentionally hostile to the reception of new truths; but we cannot commend the generosity of its dealing with the persons to whom mankind are indebted for them. To discover to the world something which deeply concerns it, and of which it was previously ignorant; to prove to it that it had been mistaken on some vital point of temporal or spiritual interest, is as important a service as a human being can render to his fellow-creatures, and in certain cases, as in those of the early Christians and of the Reformers, those who think with Dr. Johnson believe it to have been the most precious gift which could be bestowed on mankind. That the authors of such splendid benefits should be requited by martyrdom; that their reward should be to be dealt with as the vilest of criminals, is not, upon this theory, a deplorable error and misfortune, for which humanity should mourn in sackcloth and ashes, but the normal and justifiable state of things. The propounder of a new truth, according to this doctrine, should stand, as stood, in the legislation of the Locrians, the proposer of a new law, with a halter round his neck, to be instantly tightened if the public assembly did not, on hearing his reasons, then and there adopt his proposition. People who defend this mode of treating benefactors, cannot be supposed to set much value on the benefit; and I believe this view of the subject is mostly confined to the sort of persons who think that new truths may have been desirable once, but that we have had enough of them now.

But, indeed, the dictum that truth always triumphs over persecution, is one of those pleasant falsehoods which men repeat after one another till they pass into commonplaces, but which all experience refutes. History teems with instances of truth put down by persecution. If not suppressed for ever, it may be thrown back for centuries. To speak only of religious opinions: the Reformation broke out at least twenty times before Luther, and was put down. Arnold of Brescia was put down. Fra Dolcino was put down. Savonarola was put down. The Albigeois were put down. The Vaudois were put down. The Lollards were put down. The Hussites were put down. Even after the era of Luther, wherever persecution was persisted in, it was successful. In Spain, Italy, Flanders, the Austrian empire, Protestantism was rooted out; and, most likely, would have been so in England, had Queen Mary lived, or Queen Elizabeth died. Persecution has always succeeded, save where the heretics were too strong a party to be effectually persecuted. No reasonable person can doubt that Christianity might have been extirpated in the Roman Empire. It spread, and became predominant, because the persecutions were only occasional, lasting but a short time, and separated by long intervals of almost undisturbed propagandism. It is a piece of idle sentimentality that truth, merely as truth, has any inherent power denied to error, of prevailing against the dungeon and the stake. Men are not more zealous for truth than they often are for error, and a sufficient application of legal or even of social penalties will generally succeed in stopping the propagation of either. The real advantage which truth has, consists in this, that when an opinion is true, it may be extinguished once, twice, or many times, but in the course of ages there will generally be found persons to rediscover it, until some one of its reappearances falls on a time when from favorable circumstances it escapes persecution until it has made such head as to withstand all subsequent attempts to suppress it. . . .

Let us now pass to the second division of the argument, and dismissing the supposition that any of the received opinions may be false, let us assume them to be true, and examine into the worth of the manner in which they are likely to be held, when their truth is not freely and openly canvassed. However unwillingly a person who has a strong opinion may admit the possibility that his opinion may be false, he ought to be moved by the consideration that however true it may be, if it is not fully, frequently, and fearlessly discussed, it will be held as a dead dogma, not a living truth.

There is a class of persons (happily not quite so numerous as formerly) who think it enough if a person assents undoubtingly to what they think true, though he has no knowledge whatever of the grounds of the opinion, and could not make a tenable defence of it against the most superficial objections. Such persons, if they can once get their creed taught from authority, naturally think that no good, and some harm, comes of its being allowed to be questioned. Where their influence prevails, they make it nearly impossible for the received opinion to be rejected wisely and considerately, though it may still be rejected rashly and ignorantly; for to shut out discussion entirely is seldom possible, and when it once gets in, beliefs not grounded on conviction are apt to give way before the slightest semblance of an argument. Waving, however, this possibility—assuming that the true opinion abides in the mind, but abides as a prejudice, a belief independent of, and proof against, argument—this is not the way in which truth ought to be held by a rational being. This is not knowing the truth. Truth, thus held, is but one superstition the more, accidentally clinging to the words which enunciate a truth.

If the intellect and judgment of mankind ought to be cultivated, a thing which Protestants at least do not deny, on what can these faculties be more appropriately exercised by any one, than on the things which concern him so much that it is considered necessary for him to hold opinions on them? If the cultivation of the understanding consists in one thing more than in another, it is surely in learning the grounds of one's own opinions. Whatever people believe, on subjects on which it is of the first importance to believe rightly, they ought to be able to defend against at least the common objections. But, some one may say, 'Let them be taught the grounds of their opinions. It does not follow that opinions must be merely parroted because they are never heard controverted. Persons who learn geometry do not simply commit the theorems to memory, but understand and learn likewise the demonstrations; and it would be absurd to say that they remain ignorant of the grounds of geometrical truths, because they never hear any one deny, and attempt to disprove them.' Undoubtedly: and such teaching suffices on a subject like mathematics, where there is nothing at all to be said on the wrong side of the question. The peculiarity of the evidence of mathematical truths is, that all the argument is on one side. There are no objections, and no answers to objections. But on every subject on which difference of opinion is possible, the truth depends on a balance to be struck between two sets of conflicting reasons. Even in natural philosophy, there is always some other explanation possible of the same facts; some geocentric theory instead of heliocentric, some phlogiston instead of oxygen; and it has to be shown why that other theory cannot be the true one: and until this is shown, and until we know how it is shown, we do not understand the grounds of our opinion. But when we turn to subjects infinitely more complicated, to morals, religion, politics, social relations, and the business of life, three-fourths of the arguments for every disputed opinion consist in dispelling the appearances which favour some opinion different from it. The greatest orator, save one, of antiquity, has left it on record that he always studied his adversary's case with as great, if not with still greater, intensity than even his own. What Cicero practiced as the means of forensic success, requires to be imitated by all who study any subject in order to arrive at the truth. He who knows only his own side of the case, knows little of that. His reasons may be good, and no one may have been able to refute them. But if he is equally unable to refute the reasons on the opposite side; if he does not so much as know what they are, he has no ground for preferring either opinion. The rational position for him would be suspension of judgment, and unless he contents himself with that, he is either led by authority, or adopts, like the generality of the world, the side to which he feels most inclination. Nor is it enough that he should hear the arguments of adversaries from his own teachers, presented as they state them, and accompanied by what they offer as refutations. That is not the way to do justice to the arguments, or bring them into real contact with his own mind. He must be able to hear them from persons who actually believe them; who defend them in earnest, and do their very utmost for them. He must know them in their most plausible and persuasive form; he must feel the whole force of the difficulty which the true view of the subject has to encounter and dispose of; else he will never really possess himself of the portion of truth which meets and removes that difficulty. Ninety-nine in a hundred of what are called educated men are in this condition; even of those who can argue fluently for their opinions. Their conclusion may be true, but it might be false for anything they know: they have never thrown themselves into the mental position of those who think differently from them, and considered what such persons may have to say; and consequently they do not, in any proper sense of the word, know the doctrine which they themselves profess. They do not know those parts of it which explain and justify the remainder; the considerations which show that a fact which seemingly conflicts with another is reconcilable with it, or that, of two apparently strong reasons, one and not the other ought to be preferred. All that part of the truth which turns the scale, and decides the judgment of a completely informed mind, they are strangers to; nor is it ever really known, but to those who have attended equally and impartially to both sides, and endeavored to see the reasons of both in the strongest light. So essential is this discipline to a real understanding of moral and human subjects, that if opponents of all important truths do not exist, it is indispensable to imagine them, and supply them with the strongest arguments which the most skillful devil's advocate can conjure up.

To abate the force of these considerations, an enemy of free discussion may be supposed to say, that there is no necessity for mankind in general to know and understand all that can be said against or for their opinions by philosophers and theologians. That it is not needful for common men to be able to expose all the misstatements or fallacies of an ingenious opponent. That it is enough if there is always somebody capable of answering them, so that nothing likely to mislead uninstructed persons remains unrefuted. That simple minds, having been taught the obvious grounds of the truths inculcated on them, may trust to authority for the rest, and being aware that they have neither knowledge nor talent to resolve every difficulty which can be raised, may repose in the assurance that all those which have been raised have been or can be answered, by those who are specially trained to the task.

Conceding to this view of the subject the utmost that can be claimed for it by those most easily satisfied with the amount of understanding of truth which ought to accompany the belief of it; even so, the argument for free discussion is no way weakened. For even this doctrine acknowledges that mankind ought to have a rational assurance that all objections have been satisfactorily answered; and how are they to be answered if that which requires to be answered is not spoken? or how can the answer be known to be satisfactory, if the objectors have no opportunity of showing that it is unsatisfactory? If not the public, at least the philosophers and theologians who are to resolve the difficulties, must make themselves familiar with those difficulties in their most puzzling form; and this cannot be accomplished unless they are freely stated, and placed in the most advantageous light which they admit of. The Catholic Church has its own way of dealing with this embarrassing problem. It makes a broad separation between those who can be permitted to receive its doctrines on conviction, and those who must accept them on trust. Neither, indeed, are allowed any choice as to what they will accept; but the clergy, such at least as can be fully confided in, may admissibly and meritoriously make themselves acquainted with the arguments of opponents, in order to answer them, and may, therefore, read heretical books; the laity, not unless by special permission, hard to be obtained. This discipline recognizes a knowledge of the enemy's case as beneficial to the teachers, but finds means, consistent with this, of denying it to the rest of the world: thus giving to the elite more mental culture, though not more mental freedom, than it allows to the mass. By this device it succeeds in obtaining the kind of mental superiority which its purposes require; for though culture without freedom never made a large and liberal mind, it can make a clever nisi prius advocate of a cause. But in countries professing Protestantism, this resource is denied; since Protestants hold, at least in theory, that the responsibility for the choice of a religion must be borne by each for himself, and cannot be thrown off upon teachers. Besides, in the present state of the world, it is practically impossible that writings which are read by the instructed can be kept from the uninstructed. If the teachers of mankind are to be cognizant of all that they ought to know, everything must be free to be written and published without restraint.

If, however, the mischievous operation of the absence of free discussion, when the received opinions are true, were confined to leaving men ignorant of the grounds of those opinions, it might be thought that this, if an intellectual, is no moral evil, and does not affect the worth of the opinions, regarded in their influence on the character. The fact, however, is, that not only the grounds of the opinion are forgotten in the absence of discussion, but too often the meaning of the opinion itself. The words which convey it, cease to suggest ideas, or suggest only a small portion of those they were originally employed to communicate. Instead of a vivid conception and a living belief, there remain only a few phrases retained by rote; or, if any part, the shell and husk only of the meaning is retained, the finer essence being lost. The great chapter in human history which this fact occupies and fills, cannot be too earnestly studied and meditated on.

It is illustrated in the experience of almost all ethical doctrines and religious creeds. They are all full of meaning and vitality to those who originate them, and to the direct disciples of the originators. Their meaning continues to be felt in undiminished strength, and is perhaps brought out into even fuller consciousness, so long as the struggle lasts to give the doctrine or creed an ascendancy over other creeds. At last it either prevails, and becomes the general opinion, or its progress stops; it keeps possession of the ground it has gained, but ceases to spread further. When either of these results has become apparent, controversy on the subject flags, and gradually dies away. The doctrine has taken its place, if not as a received opinion, as one of the admitted sects or divisions of opinion: those who hold it have generally inherited, not adopted it; and conversion from one of these doctrines to another, being now an exceptional fact, occupies little place in the thoughts of their professors. Instead of being, as at first, constantly on the alert either to defend themselves against the world, or to bring the world over to them, they have subsided into acquiescence, and neither listen, when they can help it, to arguments against their creed, nor trouble dissentients (if there be such) with arguments in its favour. From this time may usually be dated the decline in the living power of the doctrine. We often hear the teachers of all creeds lamenting the difficulty of keeping up in the minds of believers a lively apprehension of the truth which they nominally recognize, so that it may penetrate the feelings, and acquire a real mastery over the conduct. No such difficulty is complained of while the creed is still fighting for its existence: even the weaker combatants then know and feel what they are fighting for, and the difference between it and other doctrines; and in that period of every creed's existence, not a few persons may be found, who have realized its fundamental principles in all the forms of thought, have weighed and considered them in all their important bearings, and have experienced the full effect on the character, which belief in that creed ought to produce in a mind thoroughly imbued with it. But when it has come to be an hereditary creed, and to be received passively, not actively—when the mind is no longer compelled, in the same degree as at first, to exercise its vital powers on the questions which its belief presents to it, there is a progressive tendency to forget all of the belief except the formularies, or to give it a dull and torpid assent, as if accepting it on trust dispensed with the necessity of realizing it in consciousness, or testing it by personal experience; until it almost ceases to connect itself at all with the inner life of the human being. Then are seen the cases, so frequent in this age of the world as almost to form the majority, in which the creed remains as it were outside the mind, incrusting and petrifying it against all other influences addressed to the higher parts of our nature; manifesting its power by not suffering any fresh and living conviction to get in, but itself doing nothing for the mind or heart, except standing sentinel over them to keep them vacant.

To what an extent doctrines intrinsically fitted to make the deepest impression upon the mind may remain in it as dead beliefs, without being ever realized in the imagination, the feelings, or the understanding, is exemplified by the manner in which the majority of believers hold the doctrines of Christianity. By Christianity I here mean what is accounted such by all churches and sects—the maxims and precepts contained in the New Testament. These are considered sacred, and accepted as laws, by all professing Christians. Yet it is scarcely too much to say that not one Christian in a thousand guides or tests his individual conduct by reference to those laws. The standard to which he does refer it, is the custom of his nation, his class, or his religious profession. He has thus, on the one hand, a collection of ethical maxims, which he believes to have been vouchsafed to him by infallible wisdom as rules for his government; and on the other, a set of every-day judgments and practices, which go a certain length with some of those maxims, not so great a length with others, stand in direct opposition to some, and are, on the whole, a compromise between the Christian creed and the interests and suggestions of worldly life. To the first of these standards he gives his homage; to the other his real allegiance. All Christians believe that the blessed are the poor and humble, and those who are ill-used by the world; that it is easier for a camel to pass through the eye of a needle than for a rich man to enter the kingdom of heaven; that they should judge not, lest they be judged; that they should swear not at all; that they should love their neighbor as themselves; that if one take their cloak, they should give him their coat also; that they should take no thought for the morrow; that if they would be perfect, they should sell all that they have and give it to the poor. They are not insincere when they say that they believe these things. They do believe them, as people believe what they have always heard lauded and never discussed. But in the sense of that living belief which regulates conduct, they believe these doctrines just up to the point to which it is usual to act upon them. The doctrines in their integrity are serviceable to pelt adversaries with; and it is understood that they are to be put forward (when possible) as the reasons for whatever people do that they think laudable. But any one who reminded them that the maxims require an infinity of things which they never even think of doing, would gain nothing but to be classed among those very unpopular characters who affect to be better than other people. The doctrines have no hold on ordinary believers—are not a power in their minds. They have an habitual respect for the sound of them, but no feeling which spreads from the words to things signified, and forces the mind to take them in, and make them conform to the formula. Whenever conduct is concerned, they look round for Mr. A and B to direct them how far to go in obeying Christ.

Now we may be well assured that the case was not thus, but far otherwise, with the early Christians. Had it been thus, Christianity never would have expanded from an obscure sect of the despised Hebrews into the religion of the Roman empire. When their enemies said, 'See how these Christians love one another' (a remark not likely to be made by anybody now), they assuredly had a much livelier feeling of the meaning of their creed than they have ever had since. And to this cause, probably, it is chiefly owing that Christianity now makes so little progress in extending its domain, and after eighteen centuries, is still nearly confined to Europeans and the descendants of Europeans. Even with the strictly religious, who are much in earnest about their doctrines, and attach a greater amount of meaning to many of them than people in general, it commonly happens that the part which is thus comparatively active in their minds is that which was made by Calvin, or Knox, or some such person much nearer in character to themselves. The sayings of Christ coexist passively in their minds, producing hardly any effect beyond what is caused by mere listening to words so amiable and bland. There are many reasons, doubtless, why doctrines which are the badge of a sect retain more of their vitality than those common to all recognized sects, and why more pains are taken by teachers to keep their meaning alive; but one reason certainly is, that the peculiar doctrines are more questioned, and have to be oftener defended against open gainsayers. Both teachers and learners go to sleep at their post, as soon as there is no enemy in the field.

The same thing holds true, generally speaking, of all traditional doctrines—those of prudence and knowledge of life, as well as of morals or religion. All languages and literatures are full of general observations on life, both as to what it is, and how to conduct oneself in it; observations which everybody knows, which everybody repeats, or hears with acquiescence, which are received as truisms, yet of which most people first truly learn the meaning, when experience, generally of a painful kind, has made it a reality to them. How often, when smarting under some unforeseen misfortune or disappointment, does a person call to mind some proverb or common saying, familiar to him all his life, the meaning of which, if he had ever before felt it as he does now, would have saved him from the calamity. There are indeed reasons for this, other than the absence of discussion: there are many truths of which the full meaning cannot be realized, until personal experience has brought it home. But much more of the meaning even of these would have been understood, and what was understood would have been far more deeply impressed on the mind, if the man had been accustomed to hear it argued pro and con by people who did understand it. The fatal tendency of mankind to leave off thinking about a thing when it is no longer doubtful, is the cause of half their errors. A contemporary author has well spoken of 'the deep slumber of a decided opinion.'

But what! (it may be asked) Is the absence of unanimity an indispensable condition of true knowledge? Is it necessary that some part of mankind should persist in error, to enable any to realize the truth? Does a belief cease to be real and vital as soon as it is generally received—and is a proposition never thoroughly understood and felt unless some doubt of it remains? As soon as mankind have unanimously accepted a truth, does the truth perish within them? The highest aim and best result of improved intelligence, it has hitherto been thought, is to unite mankind more and more in the acknowledgment of all important truths: and does the intelligence only last as long as it has not achieved its object? Do the fruits of conquest perish by the very completeness of the victory?

I affirm no such thing. As mankind improve, the number of doctrines which are no longer disputed or doubted will be constantly on the increase: and the well-being of mankind may almost be measured by the number and gravity of the truths which have reached the point of being uncontested. The cessation, on one question after another, of serious controversy, is one of the necessary incidents of the consolidation of opinion; a consolidation as salutary in the case of true opinions, as it is dangerous and noxious when the opinions are erroneous. But though this gradual narrowing of the bounds of diversity of opinion is necessary in both senses of the term, being at once inevitable and indispensable, we are not therefore obliged to conclude that all its consequences must be beneficial. The loss of so important an aid to the intelligent and living apprehension of a truth, as is afforded by the necessity of explaining it to, or defending it against, opponents, though not sufficient to outweigh, is no trifling drawback from, the benefit of its universal recognition. Where this advantage can no longer be had, I confess I should like to see the teachers of mankind endeavoring to provide a substitute for it; some contrivance for making the difficulties of the question as present to the learner's consciousness, as if they were pressed upon him by a dissentient champion, eager for his conversion.

But instead of seeking contrivances for this purpose, they have lost those they formerly had. The Socratic dialectics, so magnificently exemplified in the dialogues of Plato, were a contrivance of this description. They were essentially a negative discussion of the great questions of philosophy and life, directed with consummate skill to the purpose of convincing any one who had merely adopted the commonplaces of received opinion, that he did not understand the subject—that he as yet attached no definite meaning to the doctrines he professed; in order that, becoming aware of his ignorance, he might be put in the way to attain a stable belief, resting on a clear apprehension both of the meaning of doctrines and of their evidence. The school disputations of the middle ages had a somewhat similar object. They were intended to make sure that the pupil understood his own opinion, and (by necessary correlation) the opinion opposed to it, and could enforce the grounds of the one and confute those of the other. These last-mentioned contests had indeed the incurable defect, that the premises appealed to were taken from authority, not from reason; and, as a discipline in the mind, they were in every respect inferior to the powerful dialectics which formed the intellects of the 'Socratici viri:' but the modern mind owes far more to both than it is generally willing to admit, and the present modes of education contain nothing which in the smallest degree supplies the place either of the one or of the other. A person who derives all his instruction from teachers or books, even if he escape the besetting temptation of contenting himself with cram, is under no compulsion to hear both sides; accordingly it is far from a frequent accomplishment, even among thinkers, to know both sides; and the weakest part of what everybody says in defence of his opinion, is what he intends as a reply to antagonists. It is the fashion of the present time to disparage negative logic—that which points out weaknesses in theory or errors in practice, without establishing positive truths. Such negative criticism would indeed be poor enough as an ultimate result; but as a means to attaining any positive knowledge or conviction worthy the name, it cannot be valued too highly; and until people are again systematically trained to it, there will be few great thinkers, and a low general average of intellect, in any but the mathematical and physical departments of speculation. On any other subject no one's opinions deserve the name of knowledge, except so far as he has either had forced upon him by others, or gone through of himself, the same mental process which would have been required of him in carrying on an active controversy with opponents. That, therefore, which when absent, it is so indispensable, but so difficult, to create, how worse than absurd it is to forego, when spontaneously offering itself! If there are any persons who contest a received opinion, or who will do so if law or opinion will let them, let us thank them for it, open our minds to listen to them, and rejoice that there is some one to do for us what we otherwise ought, if we have any regard for either the certainty or the vitality of our convictions, to do with much greater labour for ourselves.

It still remains to speak of one of the principal causes which make diversity of opinion advantageous, and will continue to do so until mankind shall have entered a stage of intellectual advancement which at present seems at an incalculable distance. We have hitherto considered only two possibilities: that the received opinion may be false, and some other opinion, consequently, true; or that, the received opinion being true, a conflict with the opposite error is essential to a clear apprehension and deep feeling of its truth. But there is a commoner case then either of these; when the conflicting doctrines, instead of being one true and the other false, share the truth between them; and the nonconforming opinion is needed to supply the remainder of the truth, of which the received doctrine embodies only a part. Popular opinions, on subjects not palpable to sense, are often true, but seldom or never the whole truth. They are a part of the truth; sometimes a greater, sometimes a smaller part, but exaggerated, distorted, and disjoined from the truths by which they ought to be accompanied and limited. Heretical opinions, on the other hand, are generally some of these suppressed and neglected truths, bursting the bonds which kept them down, and either seeking reconciliation with the truth contained in the common opinion, or fronting it as enemies, and setting themselves up, with similar exclusiveness, as the whole truth. The latter case is hitherto the most frequent, as, in the human mind, one-sidedness has always been the rule, and many-sidedness the exception. Hence, even in revolutions of opinion, one part of the truth usually sets while another rises. Even progress, which ought to superadd, for the most part only substitutes, one partial and incomplete truth for another; improvement consisting chiefly in this, that the new fragment of truth is more wanted, more adapted to the needs of the time, than that which it displaces. Such being the partial character of prevailing opinions, even when resting on a true foundation, every opinion which embodies somewhat of the portion of truth which the common opinion omits, ought to be considered precious, with whatever amount of error and confusion that truth may be blended. No sober judge of human affairs will feel bound to be indignant because those who force on our notice truths which we should otherwise have overlooked, overlook some of those which we see. Rather, he will think that so long as popular truth is one-sided, it is more desirable than otherwise that unpopular truth should have one-sided asserters too; such being usually the most energetic, and the most likely to compel reluctant attention to the fragment of wisdom which they proclaim as if it were the whole.

Thus, in the eighteenth century, when nearly all the instructed, and all those of the uninstructed who were led by them, were lost in admiration of what is called civilization, and of the marvels of modern science, literature, and philosophy, and while greatly overrating the amount of unlikeness between the men of modern and those of ancient times, indulged the belief that the whole of the difference was in their own favour; with what a salutary shock did the paradoxes of Rousseau explode like bombshells in the midst, dislocating the compact mass of one-sided opinion, and forcing its elements to recombine in a better form and with additional ingredients. Not that the current opinions were on the whole farther from the truth than Rousseau's were; on the contrary, they were nearer to it; they contained more of positive truth, and very much less of error. Nevertheless there lay in Rousseau's doctrine, and has floated down the stream of opinion along with it, a considerable amount of exactly those truths which the popular opinion wanted; and these are the deposit which was left behind when the flood subsided. The superior worth of simplicity of life, the enervating and demoralizing effect of the trammels and hypocrisies of artificial society, are ideas which have never been entirely absent from cultivated minds since Rousseau wrote; and they will in time produce their due effect, though at present needing to be asserted as much as ever, and to be asserted by deeds, for words, on this subject, have nearly exhausted their power.

In politics, again, it is almost a commonplace, that a party of order or stability, and a party of progress or reform, are both necessary elements of a healthy state of political life; until the one or the other shall have so enlarged its mental grasp as to be a party equally of order and of progress, knowing and distinguishing what is fit to be preserved from what ought to be swept away. Each of these modes of thinking derives its utility from the deficiencies of the other; but it is in a great measure the opposition of the other that keeps each within the limits of reason and sanity. Unless opinions favorable to democracy and to aristocracy, to property and to equality, to co-operation and to competition, to luxury and to abstinence, to sociality and individuality, to liberty and discipline, and all the other standing antagonisms of practical life, are expressed with equal freedom, and enforced and defended with equal talent and energy, there is no chance of both elements obtaining their due; one scale is sure to go up, and the other down. Truth, in the great practical concerns of life, is so much a question of the reconciling and combining of opposites, that very few have minds sufficiently capacious and impartial to make the adjustment with an approach to correctness, and it has to be made by the rough process of a struggle between combatants fighting under hostile banners. On any of the great open questions just enumerated, if either of the two opinions has a better claim than the other, not merely to be tolerated, but to be encouraged and countenanced, it is the one which happens at the particular time and place to be in a minority. That is the opinion which, for the time being, represents the neglected interests, the side of human well-being which is in danger of obtaining less than its share. I am aware that there is not, in this country, any intolerance of differences of opinion on most of these topics. They are adduced to show, by admitted and multiplied examples, the universality of the fact, that only through diversity of opinion is there, in the existing state of human intellect, a chance of fair play to all sides of the truth. When there are persons to be found, who form an exception to the apparent unanimity of the world on any subject, even if the world is in the right, it is always probable that dissentients have something worth hearing to say for themselves, and that truth would lose something by their silence.

It may be objected, 'But some received principles, especially on the highest and most vital subjects, are more than half-truths. The Christian morality, for instance, is the whole truth on that subject, and if any one teaches a morality which varies from it, he is wholly in error.' As this is of all cases the most important in practice, none can be fitter to test the general maxim. But before pronouncing what Christian morality is or is not, it would be desirable to decide what is meant by Christian morality. If it means the morality of the New Testament, I wonder that any one who derives his knowledge of this from the book itself, can suppose that it was announced, or intended, as a complete doctrine of morals. The Gospel always refers to a pre-existing morality, and confines its precepts to the particulars in which that morality was to be corrected, or superseded by a wider and higher; expressing itself, moreover, in terms most general, often impossible to be interpreted literally, and possessing rather the impressiveness of poetry or eloquence than the precision of legislation. To extract from it a body of ethical doctrine, has never been possible without eking it out from the Old Testament, that is, from a system elaborate indeed, but in many respects barbarous, and intended only for a barbarous people. St. Paul, a declared enemy to this Judaical mode of interpreting the doctrine and filling up the scheme of his Master, equally assumes a pre-existing morality, namely that of the Greeks and Romans; and his advice to Christians is in a great measure a system of accommodation to that; even to the extent of giving an apparent sanction to slavery. What is called Christian, but should rather be termed theological, morality, was not the work of Christ or the Apostles, but is of much later origin, having been gradually built up by the Catholic church of the first five centuries, and though not implicitly adopted by moderns and Protestants, has been much less modified by them than might have been expected. For the most part, indeed, they have contented themselves with cutting off the additions which had been made to it in the middle ages, each sect supplying the place by fresh additions, adapted to its own character and tendencies. That mankind owe a great debt to this morality, and to its early teachers, I should be the last person to deny, but I do not scruple to say of it, that it is, in many important points, incomplete and one-sided, and that unless ideas and feelings, not sanctioned by it, had contributed to the formation of European life and character, human affairs would have been in a worse condition than they now are. Christian morality (so called) has all the characters of a reaction; it is, in great part, a protest against Paganism. Its ideal is negative rather than positive; passive rather than active; Innocence rather than Nobleness; Abstinence from Evil, rather than energetic Pursuit of Good: in its precepts (as has been well said) 'thou shalt not' predominates unduly over 'thou shalt.' In its horror of sensuality, it made an idol of asceticism, which has been gradually compromised away into one of legality. It holds out the hope of heaven and the threat of hell, as the appointed and appropriate motives to a virtuous life: in this falling far below the best of the ancients, and doing what lies in it to give to human morality an essentially selfish character, by disconnecting each man's feelings of duty from the interests of his fellow-creatures, except so far as a self-interested inducement is offered to him for consulting them. It is essentially a doctrine of passive obedience; it inculcates submission to all authorities found established; who indeed are not to be actively obeyed when they command what religion forbids, but who are not to be resisted, far less rebelled against, for any amount of wrong to ourselves. And while, in the morality of the best Pagan nations, duty to the State holds even a disproportionate place, infringing on the just liberty of the individual; in purely Christian ethics, that grand department of duty is scarcely noticed or acknowledged. It is in the Koran, not the New Testament, that we read the maxim—'A ruler who appoints any man to an office, when there is in his dominions another man better qualified for it, sins against God and against the State.' What little recognition the idea of obligation to the public obtains in modern morality, is derived from Greek and Roman sources, not from Christian; as, even in the morality of private life, whatever exists of magnanimity, highmindedness, personal dignity, even the sense of honour, is derived from the purely human, not the religious part of our education, and never could have grown out of a standard of ethics in which the only worth, professedly recognized, is that of obedience.

I am as far as any one from pretending that these defects are necessarily inherent in the Christian ethics, in every manner in which it can be conceived, or that the many requisites of a complete moral doctrine which it does not contain, do not admit of being reconciled with it. Far less would I insinuate this of the doctrines and precepts of Christ himself. I believe that the sayings of Christ are all, that I can see any evidence of their having been intended to be; that they are irreconcilable with nothing which a comprehensive morality requires; that everything which is excellent in ethics may be brought within them, with no greater violence to their language than has been done to it by all who have attempted to deduce from them any practical system of conduct whatever. But it is quite consistent with this, to believe that they contain, and were meant to contain, only a part of the truth; that many essential elements of the highest morality are among the things which are not provided for, nor intended to be provided for, in the recorded deliverances of the Founder of Christianity, and which have been entirely thrown aside in the system of ethics erected on the basis of those deliverances by the Christian Church. And this being so, I think it a great error to persist in attempting to find in the Christian doctrine that complete rule for our guidance, which its author intended it to sanction and enforce, but only partially to provide. I believe, too, that this narrow theory is becoming a grave practical evil, detracting greatly from the value of the moral training and instruction, which so many well-meaning persons are now at length exerting themselves to promote. I much fear that by attempting to form the mind and feelings on an exclusively religious type, and discarding those secular standards (as for want of a better name they may be called) which heretofore co-existed with and supplemented the Christian ethics, receiving some of its spirit, and infusing into it some of theirs, there will result, and is even now resulting, a low, abject, servile type of character, which, submit itself as it may to what it deems the Supreme Will, is incapable of rising to or sympathizing in the conception of Supreme Goodness. I believe that other ethics than any which can be evolved from exclusively Christian sources, must exist side by side with Christian ethics to produce the moral regeneration of mankind; and that the Christian system is no exception to the rule, that in an imperfect state of the human mind, the interests of truth require a diversity of opinions. It is not necessary that in ceasing to ignore the moral truths not contained in Christianity, men should ignore any of those which it does contain. Such prejudice, or oversight, when it occurs, is altogether an evil; but it is one from which we cannot hope to be always exempt, and must be regarded as the price paid for an inestimable good. The exclusive pretension made by a part of the truth to be the whole, must and ought to be protested against; and if a reactionary impulse should make the protestors unjust in their turn, this one-sidedness, like the other, may be lamented, but must be tolerated. If Christians would teach infidels to be just to Christianity, they should themselves be just to infidelity. It can do truth no service to blink the fact, known to all who have the most ordinary acquaintance with literary history, that a large portion of the noblest and most valuable moral teaching has been the work, not only of men who did not know, but of men who knew and rejected, the Christian faith.

I do not pretend that the most unlimited use of the freedom of enunciating all possible opinions would put an end to the evils of religious or philosophical sectarianism. Every truth which men of narrow capacity are in earnest about, is sure to be asserted, inculcated, and in many ways even acted on, as if no other truth existed in the world, or at all events none that could limit or qualify the first. I acknowledge that the tendency of all opinions to become sectarian is not cured by the freest discussion, but is often heightened and exacerbated thereby; the truth which ought to have been, but was not, seen, being rejected all the more violently because proclaimed by persons regarded as opponents. But it is not on the impassioned partisan, it is on the calmer and more disinterested bystander, that this collision of opinions works its salutary effect. Not the violent conflict between parts of the truth, but the quiet suppression of half of it, is the formidable evil; there is always hope when people are forced to listen to both sides; it is when they attend only to one that errors harden into prejudices, and truth itself ceases to have the effect of truth, by being exaggerated into falsehood. And since there are few mental attributes more rare than that judicial faculty which can sit in intelligent judgment between two sides of a question, of which only one is represented by an advocate before it, truth has no chance but in proportion as every side of it, every opinion which embodies any fraction of the truth, not only finds advocates, but is so advocated as to be listened to.

We have now recognized the necessity to the mental well-being of mankind (on which all their other well-being depends) of freedom of opinion, and freedom of the expression of opinion, on four distinct grounds; which we will now briefly recapitulate.

First, if any opinion is compelled to silence, that opinion may, for aught we can certainly know, be true. To deny this is to assume our own infallibility.

Secondly, though the silenced opinion be an error, it may, and very commonly does, contain a portion of truth; and since the general or prevailing opinion on any subject is rarely or never the whole truth, it is only by the collision of adverse opinions that the remainder of the truth has any chance of being supplied.

Thirdly, even if the received opinion be not only true, but the whole truth; unless it is suffered to be, and actually is, vigorously and earnestly contested, it will, by most of those who receive it, be held in the manner of a prejudice, with little comprehension or feeling of its rational grounds. And not only this, but, fourthly, the meaning of the doctrine itself will be in danger of being lost, or enfeebled, and deprived of its vital effect on the character and conduct: the dogma becoming a mere formal profession, inefficacious for good, but cumbering the ground, and preventing the growth of any real and heartfelt conviction, from reason or personal experience.

Before quitting the subject of freedom of opinion, it is fit to take some notice of those who say, that the free expression of all opinions should be permitted, on condition that the manner be temperate, and do not pass the bounds of fair discussion. Much might be said on the impossibility of fixing where these supposed bounds are to be placed; for if the test be offence to those whose opinion is attacked, I think experience testifies that this offence is given whenever the attack is telling and powerful, and that every opponent who pushes them hard, and whom they find it difficult to answer, appears to them, if he shows any strong feeling on the subject, an intemperate opponent. But this, though an important consideration in a practical point of view, merges in a more fundamental objection. Undoubtedly the manner of asserting an opinion, even though it be a true one, may be very objectionable, and may justly incur severe censure. But the principal offences of the kind are such as it is mostly impossible, unless by accidental self-betrayal, to bring home to conviction. The gravest of them is, to argue sophistically, to suppress facts or arguments, to misstate the elements of the case, or misrepresent the opposite opinion. But all this, even to the most aggravated degree, is so continually done in perfect good faith, by persons who are not considered, and in many other respects may not deserve to be considered, ignorant or incompetent, that it is rarely possible on adequate grounds conscientiously to stamp the misrepresentation as morally culpable; and still less could law presume to interfere with this kind of controversial misconduct. With regard to what is commonly meant by intemperate discussion, namely invective, sarcasm, personality, and the like, the denunciation of these weapons would deserve more sympathy if it were ever proposed to interdict them equally to both sides; but it is only desired to restrain the employment of them against the prevailing opinion: against the unprevailing they may not only be used without general disapproval, but will be likely to obtain for him who uses them the praise of honest zeal and righteous indignation. Yet whatever mischief arises from their use, is greatest when they are employed against the comparatively defenceless; and whatever unfair advantage can be derived by any opinion from this mode of asserting it, accrues almost exclusively to received opinions. The worst offence of this kind which can be committed by a polemic, is to stigmatize those who hold the contrary opinion as bad and immoral men. To calumny of this sort, those who hold any unpopular opinion are peculiarly exposed, because they are in general few and uninfluential, and nobody but themselves feels much interested in seeing justice done them; but this weapon is, from the nature of the case, denied to those who attack a prevailing opinion: they can neither use it with safety to themselves, nor, if they could, would it do anything but recoil on their own cause. In general, opinions contrary to those commonly received can only obtain a hearing by studied moderation of language, and the most cautious avoidance of unnecessary offence, from which they hardly ever deviate even in a slight degree without losing ground: while unmeasured vituperation employed on the side of the prevailing opinion, really does deter people from professing contrary opinions, and from listening to those who profess them. For the interest, therefore, of truth and justice, it is far more important to restrain this employment of vituperative language than the other; and, for example, if it were necessary to choose, there would be much more need to discourage offensive attacks on infidelity, than on religion. It is, however, obvious that law and authority have no business with restraining either, while opinion ought, in every instance, to determine its verdict by the circumstances of the individual case; condemning every one, on whichever side of the argument he places himself, in whose mode of advocacy either want of candor, or malignity, bigotry, or intolerance of feeling manifest themselves; but not inferring these vices from the side which a person takes, though it be the contrary side of the question to our own: and giving merited honour to every one, whatever opinion he may hold, who has calmness to see and honesty to state what his opponents and their opinions really are, exaggerating nothing to their discredit, keeping nothing back which tells, or can be supposed to tell, in their favour. This is the real morality of public discussion: and if often violated, I am happy to think that there are many controversialists who to a great extent observe it, and a still greater number who conscientiously strive towards it.

CHAPTER III. OF INDIVIDUALITY, AS ONE OF THE ELEMENTS OF WELL-BEING

Such being the reasons which make it imperative that human beings should be free to form opinions, and to express their opinions without reserve; and such the baneful consequences to the intellectual, and through that to the moral nature of man, unless this liberty is either conceded, or asserted in spite of prohibition; let us next examine whether the same reasons do not require that men should be free to act upon their opinions—to carry these out in their lives, without hindrance, either physical or moral, from their fellow-men, so long as it is at their own risk and peril. This last proviso is of course indispensable. No one pretends that actions should be as free as opinions. On the contrary, even opinions lose their immunity, when the circumstances in which they are expressed are such as to constitute their expression a positive instigation to some mischievous act. An opinion that corn-dealers are starvers of the poor, or that private property is robbery, ought to be unmolested when simply circulated through the press, but may justly incur punishment when delivered orally to an excited mob assembled before the house of a corn-dealer, or when handed about among the same mob in the form of a placard. Acts, of whatever kind, which, without justifiable cause, do harm to others, may be, and in the more important cases absolutely require to be, controlled by the unfavorable sentiments, and, when needful, by the active interference of mankind. The liberty of the individual must be thus far limited; he must not make himself a nuisance to other people. But if he refrains from molesting others in what concerns them, and merely acts according to his own inclination and judgment in things which concern himself, the same reasons which show that opinion should be free, prove also that he should be allowed, without molestation, to carry his opinions into practice at his own cost. That mankind are not infallible; that their truths, for the most part, are only half-truths; that unity of opinion, unless resulting from the fullest and freest comparison of opposite opinions, is not desirable, and diversity not an evil, but a good, until mankind are much more capable than at present of recognizing all sides of the truth, are principles applicable to men's modes of action, not less than to their opinions. As it is useful that while mankind are imperfect there should be different opinions, so is it that there should be different experiments of living; that free scope should be given to varieties of character, short of injury to others; and that the worth of different modes of life should be proved practically, when any one thinks fit to try them. It is desirable, in short, that in things which do not primarily concern others, individuality should assert itself. Where, not the person's own character, but the traditions or customs of other people are the rule of conduct, there is wanting one of the principal ingredients of human happiness, and quite the chief ingredient of individual and social progress.

In maintaining this principle, the greatest difficulty to be encountered does not lie in the appreciation of means towards an acknowledged end, but in the indifference of persons in general to the end itself. If it were felt that the free development of individuality is one of the leading essentials of well-being; that it is not only a co-ordinate element with all that is designated by the terms civilization, instruction, education, culture, but is itself a necessary part and condition of all those things; there would be no danger that liberty should be undervalued, and the adjustment of the boundaries between it and social control would present no extraordinary difficulty. But the evil is, that individual spontaneity is hardly recognized by the common modes of thinking, as having any intrinsic worth, or deserving any regard on its own account. The majority, being satisfied with the ways of mankind as they now are (for it is they who make them what they are), cannot comprehend why those ways should not be good enough for everybody; and what is more, spontaneity forms no part of the ideal of the majority of moral and social reformers, but is rather looked on with jealousy, as a troublesome and perhaps rebellious obstruction to the general acceptance of what these reformers, in their own judgment, think would be best for mankind. Few persons, out of Germany, even comprehend the meaning of the doctrine which Wilhelm Von Humboldt, so eminent both as a savant and as a politician, made the text of a treatise—that 'the end of man, or that which is prescribed by the eternal or immutable dictates of reason, and not suggested by vague and transient desires, is the highest and most harmonious development of his powers to a complete and consistent whole;' that, therefore, the objects 'towards which every human being must ceaselessly direct his efforts, and on which especially those who design to influence their fellow-men must ever keep their eyes, is the individuality of power and development;' that for this there are two requisites, 'freedom, and variety of situations;' and that from the union of these arise 'individual vigor and manifold diversity,' which combine themselves in 'originality.'

Little, however, as people are accustomed to a doctrine like that of Von Humboldt, and surprising as it may be to them to find so high a value attached to individuality, the question, one must nevertheless think, can only be one of degree. No one's idea of excellence in conduct is that people should do absolutely nothing but copy one another. No one would assert that people ought not to put into their mode of life, and into the conduct of their concerns, any impress whatever of their own judgment, or of their own individual character. On the other hand, it would be absurd to pretend that people ought to live as if nothing whatever had been known in the world before they came into it; as if experience has as yet done nothing towards showing that one mode of existence, or of conduct, is preferable to another. Nobody denies that people should be so taught and trained in youth, as to know and benefit by the ascertained results of human experience. But it is the privilege and proper condition of a human being, arrived at the maturity of his faculties, to use and interpret experience in his own way. It is for him to find out what part of recorded experience is properly applicable to his own circumstances and character. The traditions and customs of other people are, to a certain extent, evidence of what their experience has taught them; presumptive evidence, and as such, have a claim to his deference: but, in the first place, their experience may be too narrow; or they may not have interpreted it rightly. Secondly, their interpretation of experience may be correct, but unsuitable to him. Customs are made for customary circumstances, and customary characters; and his circumstances or his character may be uncustomary. Thirdly, though the customs be both good as customs, and suitable to him, yet to conform to custom, merely as custom, does not educate or develop in him any of the qualities which are the distinctive endowment of a human being. The human faculties of perception, judgment, discriminative feeling, mental activity, and even moral preference, are exercised only in making a choice. He who does anything because it is the custom, makes no choice. He gains no practice either in discerning or in desiring what is best. The mental and moral, like the muscular powers, are improved only by being used. The faculties are called into no exercise by doing a thing merely because others do it, no more than by believing a thing only because others believe it. If the grounds of an opinion are not conclusive to the person's own reason, his reason cannot be strengthened, but is likely to be weakened, by his adopting it: and if the inducements to an act are not such as are consentaneous to his own feelings and character (where affection, or the rights of others, are not concerned) it is so much done towards rendering his feelings and character inert and torpid, instead of active and energetic.

He who lets the world, or his own portion of it, choose his plan of life for him, has no need of any other faculty than the ape-like one of imitation. He who chooses his plan for himself, employs all his faculties. He must use observation to see, reasoning and judgment to foresee, activity to gather materials for decision, discrimination to decide, and when he has decided, firmness and self-control to hold to his deliberate decision. And these qualities he requires and exercises exactly in proportion as the part of his conduct which he determines according to his own judgment and feelings is a large one. It is possible that he might be guided in some good path, and kept out of harm's way, without any of these things. But what will be his comparative worth as a human being? It really is of importance, not only what men do, but also what manner of men they are that do it. Among the works of man, which human life is rightly employed in perfecting and beautifying, the first in importance surely is man himself. Supposing it were possible to get houses built, corn grown, battles fought, causes tried, and even churches erected and prayers said, by machinery—by automatons in human form—it would be a considerable loss to exchange for these automatons even the men and women who at present inhabit the more civilized parts of the world, and who assuredly are but starved specimens of what nature can and will produce. Human nature is not a machine to be built after a model, and set to do exactly the work prescribed for it, but a tree, which requires to grow and develop itself on all sides, according to the tendency of the inward forces which make it a living thing.

It will probably be conceded that it is desirable people should exercise their understandings, and that an intelligent following of custom, or even occasionally an intelligent deviation from custom, is better than a blind and simply mechanical adhesion to it. To a certain extent it is admitted, that our understanding should be our own: but there is not the same willingness to admit that our desires and impulses should be our own likewise; or that to possess impulses of our own, and of any strength, is anything but a peril and a snare. Yet desires and impulses are as much a part of a perfect human being, as beliefs and restraints: and strong impulses are only perilous when not properly balanced; when one set of aims and inclinations is developed into strength, while others, which ought to co-exist with them, remain weak and inactive. It is not because men's desires are strong that they act ill; it is because their consciences are weak. There is no natural connexion between strong impulses and a weak conscience. The natural connexion is the other way. To say that one person's desires and feelings are stronger and more various than those of another, is merely to say that he has more of the raw material of human nature, and is therefore capable, perhaps of more evil, but certainly of more good. Strong impulses are but another name for energy. Energy may be turned to bad uses; but more good may always be made of an energetic nature, than of an indolent and impassive one. Those who have most natural feeling, are always those whose cultivated feelings may be made the strongest. The same strong susceptibilities which make the personal impulses vivid and powerful, are also the source from whence are generated the most passionate love of virtue, and the sternest self-control. It is through the cultivation of these, that society both does its duty and protects its interests: not by rejecting the stuff of which heroes are made, because it knows not how to make them. A person whose desires and impulses are his own—are the expression of his own nature, as it has been developed and modified by his own culture—is said to have a character. One whose desires and impulses are not his own, has no character, no more than a steam-engine has a character. If, in addition to being his own, his impulses are strong, and are under the government of a strong will, he has an energetic character. Whoever thinks that individuality of desires and impulses should not be encouraged to unfold itself, must maintain that society has no need of strong natures—is not the better for containing many persons who have much character—and that a high general average of energy is not desirable.

In some early states of society, these forces might be, and were, too much ahead of the power which society then possessed of disciplining and controlling them. There has been a time when the element of spontaneity and individuality was in excess, and the social principle had a hard struggle with it. The difficulty then was, to induce men of strong bodies or minds to pay obedience to any rules which required them to control their impulses. To overcome this difficulty, law and discipline, like the Popes struggling against the Emperors, asserted a power over the whole man, claiming to control all his life in order to control his character—which society had not found any other sufficient means of binding. But society has now fairly got the better of individuality; and the danger which threatens human nature is not the excess, but the deficiency, of personal impulses and preferences. Things are vastly changed, since the passions of those who were strong by station or by personal endowment were in a state of habitual rebellion against laws and ordinances, and required to be rigorously chained up to enable the persons within their reach to enjoy any particle of security. In our times, from the highest class of society down to the lowest, every one lives as under the eye of a hostile and dreaded censorship. Not only in what concerns others, but in what concerns only themselves, the individual or the family do not ask themselves—what do I prefer? or, what would suit my character and disposition? or, what would allow the best and highest in me to have fair play, and enable it to grow and thrive? They ask themselves, what is suitable to my position? what is usually done by persons of my station and pecuniary circumstances? or (worse still) what is usually done by persons of a station and circumstances superior to mine? I do not mean that they choose what is customary, in preference to what suits their own inclination. It does not occur to them to have any inclination, except for what is customary. Thus the mind itself is bowed to the yoke: even in what people do for pleasure, conformity is the first thing thought of; they like in crowds; they exercise choice only among things commonly done: peculiarity of taste, eccentricity of conduct, are shunned equally with crimes: until by dint of not following their own nature, they have no nature to follow: their human capacities are withered and starved: they become incapable of any strong wishes or native pleasures, and are generally without either opinions or feelings of home growth, or properly their own. Now is this, or is it not, the desirable condition of human nature?

It is so, on the Calvinistic theory. According to that, the one great offence of man is self-will. All the good of which humanity is capable, is comprised in obedience. You have no choice; thus you must do, and no otherwise: 'whatever is not a duty, is a sin.' Human nature being radically corrupt, there is no redemption for any one until human nature is killed within him. To one holding this theory of life, crushing out any of the human faculties, capacities, and susceptibilities, is no evil: man needs no capacity, but that of surrendering himself to the will of God: and if he uses any of his faculties for any other purpose but to do that supposed will more effectually, he is better without them. This is the theory of Calvinism; and it is held, in a mitigated form, by many who do not consider themselves Calvinists; the mitigation consisting in giving a less ascetic interpretation to the alleged will of God; asserting it to be his will that mankind should gratify some of their inclinations; of course not in the manner they themselves prefer, but in the way of obedience, that is, in a way prescribed to them by authority; and, therefore, by the necessary conditions of the case, the same for all.

In some such insidious form there is at present a strong tendency to this narrow theory of life, and to the pinched and hidebound type of human character which it patronizes. Many persons, no doubt, sincerely think that human beings thus cramped and dwarfed, are as their Maker designed them to be; just as many have thought that trees are a much finer thing when clipped into pollards, or cut out into figures of animals, than as nature made them. But if it be any part of religion to believe that man was made by a good Being, it is more consistent with that faith to believe, that this Being gave all human faculties that they might be cultivated and unfolded, not rooted out and consumed, and that he takes delight in every nearer approach made by his creatures to the ideal conception embodied in them, every increase in any of their capabilities of comprehension, of action, or of enjoyment. There is a different type of human excellence from the Calvinistic; a conception of humanity as having its nature bestowed on it for other purposes than merely to be abnegated. 'Pagan self-assertion' is one of the elements of human worth, as well as 'Christian self-denial.' There is a Greek ideal of self-development, which the Platonic and Christian ideal of self-government blends with, but does not supersede. It may be better to be a John Knox than an Alcibiades, but it is better to be a Pericles than either; nor would a Pericles, if we had one in these days, be without anything good which belonged to John Knox.

It is not by wearing down into uniformity all that is individual in themselves, but by cultivating it and calling it forth, within the limits imposed by the rights and interests of others, that human beings become a noble and beautiful object of contemplation; and as the works partake the character of those who do them, by the same process human life also becomes rich, diversified, and animating, furnishing more abundant aliment to high thoughts and elevating feelings, and strengthening the tie which binds every individual to the race, by making the race infinitely better worth belonging to. In proportion to the development of his individuality, each person becomes more valuable to himself, and is therefore capable of being more valuable to others. There is a greater fullness of life about his own existence, and when there is more life in the units there is more in the mass which is composed of them. As much compression as is necessary to prevent the stronger specimens of human nature from encroaching on the rights of others, cannot be dispensed with; but for this there is ample compensation even in the point of view of human development. The means of development which the individual loses by being prevented from gratifying his inclinations to the injury of others, are chiefly obtained at the expense of the development of other people. And even to himself there is a full equivalent in the better development of the social part of his nature, rendered possible by the restraint put upon the selfish part. To be held to rigid rules of justice for the sake of others, develops the feelings and capacities which have the good of others for their object. But to be restrained in things not affecting their good, by their mere displeasure, develops nothing valuable, except such force of character as may unfold itself in resisting the restraint. If acquiesced in, it dulls and blunts the whole nature. To give any fair play to the nature of each, it is essential that different persons should be allowed to lead different lives. In proportion as this latitude has been exercised in any age, has that age been noteworthy to posterity. Even despotism does not produce its worst effects, so long as individuality exists under it; and whatever crushes individuality is despotism, by whatever name it may be called, and whether it professes to be enforcing the will of God or the injunctions of men.

Having said that Individuality is the same thing with development, and that it is only the cultivation of individuality which produces, or can produce, well-developed human beings, I might here close the argument: for what more or better can be said of any condition of human affairs, than that it brings human beings themselves nearer to the best thing they can be? or what worse can be said of any obstruction to good, than that it prevents this? Doubtless, however, these considerations will not suffice to convince those who most need convincing; and it is necessary further to show, that these developed human beings are of some use to the undeveloped—to point out to those who do not desire liberty, and would not avail themselves of it, that they may be in some intelligible manner rewarded for allowing other people to make use of it without hindrance.

In the first place, then, I would suggest that they might possibly learn something from them. It will not be denied by anybody, that originality is a valuable element in human affairs. There is always need of persons not only to discover new truths, and point out when what were once truths are true no longer, but also to commence new practices, and set the example of more enlightened conduct, and better taste and sense in human life. This cannot well be gainsaid by anybody who does not believe that the world has already attained perfection in all its ways and practices. It is true that this benefit is not capable of being rendered by everybody alike: there are but few persons, in comparison with the whole of mankind, whose experiments, if adopted by others, would be likely to be any improvement on established practice. But these few are the salt of the earth; without them, human life would become a stagnant pool. Not only is it they who introduce good things which did not before exist; it is they who keep the life in those which already existed. If there were nothing new to be done, would human intellect cease to be necessary? Would it be a reason why those who do the old things should forget why they are done, and do them like cattle, not like human beings? There is only too great a tendency in the best beliefs and practices to degenerate into the mechanical; and unless there were a succession of persons whose ever-recurring originality prevents the grounds of those beliefs and practices from becoming merely traditional, such dead matter would not resist the smallest shock from anything really alive, and there would be no reason why civilization should not die out, as in the Byzantine Empire. Persons of genius, it is true, are, and are always likely to be, a small minority; but in order to have them, it is necessary to preserve the soil in which they grow. Genius can only breathe freely in an atmosphere of freedom. Persons of genius are, ex vi termini, more individual than any other people—less capable, consequently, of fitting themselves, without hurtful compression, into any of the small number of molds which society provides in order to save its members the trouble of forming their own character. If from timidity they consent to be forced into one of these molds, and to let all that part of themselves which cannot expand under the pressure remain unexpanded, society will be little the better for their genius. If they are of a strong character, and break their fetters, they become a mark for the society which has not succeeded in reducing them to commonplace, to point at with solemn warning as 'wild,' 'erratic,' and the like; much as if one should complain of the Niagara river for not flowing smoothly between its banks like a Dutch canal.

I insist thus emphatically on the importance of genius, and the necessity of allowing it to unfold itself freely both in thought and in practice, being well aware that no one will deny the position in theory, but knowing also that almost every one, in reality, is totally indifferent to it. People think genius a fine thing if it enables a man to write an exciting poem, or paint a picture. But in its true sense, that of originality in thought and action, though no one says that it is not a thing to be admired, nearly all, at heart, think that they can do very well without it. Unhappily this is too natural to be wondered at. Originality is the one thing which unoriginal minds cannot feel the use of. They cannot see what it is to do for them: how should they? If they could see what it would do for them, it would not be originality. The first service which originality has to render them, is that of opening their eyes: which being once fully done, they would have a chance of being themselves original. Meanwhile, recollecting that nothing was ever yet done which some one was not the first to do, and that all good things which exist are the fruits of originality, let them be modest enough to believe that there is something still left for it to accomplish, and assure themselves that they are more in need of originality, the less they are conscious of the want.

In sober truth, whatever homage may be professed, or even paid, to real or supposed mental superiority, the general tendency of things throughout the world is to render mediocrity the ascendant power among mankind. In ancient history, in the middle ages, and in a diminishing degree through the long transition from feudality to the present time, the individual was a power in himself; and if he had either great talents or a high social position, he was a considerable power. At present individuals are lost in the crowd. In politics it is almost a triviality to say that public opinion now rules the world. The only power deserving the name is that of masses, and of governments while they make themselves the organ of the tendencies and instincts of masses. This is as true in the moral and social relations of private life as in public transactions. Those whose opinions go by the name of public opinion, are not always the same sort of public: in America they are the whole white population; in England, chiefly the middle class. But they are always a mass, that is to say, collective mediocrity. And what is a still greater novelty, the mass do not now take their opinions from dignitaries in Church or State, from ostensible leaders, or from books. Their thinking is done for them by men much like themselves, addressing them or speaking in their name, on the spur of the moment, through the newspapers. I am not complaining of all this. I do not assert that anything better is compatible, as a general rule, with the present low state of the human mind. But that does not hinder the government of mediocrity from being mediocre government. No government by a democracy or a numerous aristocracy, either in its political acts or in the opinions, qualities, and tone of mind which it fosters, ever did or could rise above mediocrity, except in so far as the sovereign. Many have let themselves be guided (which in their best times they always have done) by the counsels and influence of a more highly gifted and instructed One or Few. The initiation of all wise or noble things, comes and must come from individuals; generally at first from some one individual. The honour and glory of the average man is that he is capable of following that initiative; that he can respond internally to wise and noble things, and be led to them with his eyes open. I am not countenancing the sort of 'hero-worship' which applauds the strong man of genius for forcibly seizing on the government of the world and making it do his bidding in spite of itself. All he can claim is, freedom to point out the way. The power of compelling others into it, is not only inconsistent with the freedom and development of all the rest, but corrupting to the strong man himself. It does seem, however, that when the opinions of masses of merely average men are everywhere become or becoming the dominant power, the counterpoise and corrective to that tendency would be, the more and more pronounced individuality of those who stand on the higher eminences of thought. It is in these circumstances most especially, that exceptional individuals, instead of being deterred, should be encouraged in acting differently from the mass. In other times there was no advantage in their doing so, unless they acted not only differently, but better. In this age, the mere example of nonconformity, the mere refusal to bend the knee to custom, is itself a service. Precisely because the tyranny of opinion is such as to make eccentricity a reproach, it is desirable, in order to break through that tyranny, that people should be eccentric. Eccentricity has always abounded when and where strength of character has abounded; and the amount of eccentricity in a society has generally been proportional to the amount of genius, mental vigor, and moral courage which it contained. That so few now dare to be eccentric, marks the chief danger of the time.

I have said that it is important to give the freest scope possible to uncustomary things, in order that it may in time appear which of these are fit to be converted into customs. But independence of action, and disregard of custom, are not solely deserving of encouragement for the chance they afford that better modes of action, and customs more worthy of general adoption, may be struck out; nor is it only persons of decided mental superiority who have a just claim to carry on their lives in their own way. There is no reason that all human existence should be constructed on some one or some small number of patterns. If a person possesses any tolerable amount of common sense and experience, his own mode of laying out his existence is the best, not because it is the best in itself, but because it is his own mode. Human beings are not like sheep; and even sheep are not undistinguishably alike. A man cannot get a coat or a pair of boots to fit him, unless they are either made to his measure, or he has a whole warehouseful to choose from: and is it easier to fit him with a life than with a coat, or are human beings more like one another in their whole physical and spiritual conformation than in the shape of their feet? If it were only that people have diversities of taste, that is reason enough for not attempting to shape them all after one model. But different persons also require different conditions for their spiritual development; and can no more exist healthily in the same moral, than all the variety of plants can in the same physical, atmosphere and climate. The same things which are helps to one person towards the cultivation of his higher nature, are hindrances to another. The same mode of life is a healthy excitement to one, keeping all his faculties of action and enjoyment in their best order, while to another it is a distracting burden, which suspends or crushes all internal life. Such are the differences among human beings in their sources of pleasure, their susceptibilities of pain, and the operation on them of different physical and moral agencies, that unless there is a corresponding diversity in their modes of life, they neither obtain their fair share of happiness, nor grow up to the mental, moral, and aesthetic stature of which their nature is capable. Why then should tolerance, as far as the public sentiment is concerned, extend only to tastes and modes of life which extort acquiescence by the multitude of their adherents? Nowhere (except in some monastic institutions) is diversity of taste entirely unrecognized; a person may, without blame, either like or dislike rowing, or smoking, or music, or athletic exercises, or chess, or cards, or study, because both those who like each of these things, and those who dislike them, are too numerous to be put down. But the man, and still more the woman, who can be accused either of doing 'what nobody does,' or of not doing 'what everybody does,' is the subject of as much depreciatory remark as if he or she had committed some grave moral delinquency. Persons require to possess a title, or some other badge of rank, or of the consideration of people of rank, to be able to indulge somewhat in the luxury of doing as they like without detriment to their estimation. To indulge somewhat, I repeat: for whoever allow themselves much of that indulgence, incur the risk of something worse than disparaging speeches—they are in peril of a commission de lunatico, and of having their property taken from them and given to their relations.

There is one characteristic of the present direction of public opinion, peculiarly calculated to make it intolerant of any marked demonstration of individuality. The general average of mankind are not only moderate in intellect, but also moderate in inclinations: they have no tastes or wishes strong enough to incline them to do anything unusual, and they consequently do not understand those who have, and class all such with the wild and intemperate whom they are accustomed to look down upon. Now, in addition to this fact which is general, we have only to suppose that a strong movement has set in towards the improvement of morals, and it is evident what we have to expect. In these days such a movement has set in; much has actually been effected in the way of increased regularity of conduct, and discouragement of excesses; and there is a philanthropic spirit abroad, for the exercise of which there is no more inviting field than the moral and prudential improvement of our fellow-creatures. These tendencies of the times cause the public to be more disposed than at most former periods to prescribe general rules of conduct, and endeavor to make every one conform to the approved standard. And that standard, express or tacit, is to desire nothing strongly. Its ideal of character is to be without any marked character; to maim by compression, like a Chinese lady's foot, every part of human nature which stands out prominently, and tends to make the person markedly dissimilar in outline to commonplace humanity.

As is usually the case with ideals which exclude one-half of what is desirable, the present standard of approbation produces only an inferior imitation of the other half. Instead of great energies guided by vigorous reason, and strong feelings strongly controlled by a conscientious will, its result is weak feelings and weak energies, which therefore can be kept in outward conformity to rule without any strength either of will or of reason. Already energetic characters on any large scale are becoming merely traditional. There is now scarcely any outlet for energy in this country except business. The energy expended in this may still be regarded as considerable. What little is left from that employment, is expended on some hobby; which may be a useful, even a philanthropic hobby, but is always some one thing, and generally a thing of small dimensions. The greatness of England is now all collective: individually small, we only appear capable of anything great by our habit of combining; and with this our moral and religious philanthropists are perfectly contented. But it was men of another stamp than this that made England what it has been; and men of another stamp will be needed to prevent its decline.

The despotism of custom is everywhere the standing hindrance to human advancement, being in unceasing antagonism to that disposition to aim at something better than customary, which is called, according to circumstances, the spirit of liberty, or that of progress or improvement. The spirit of improvement is not always a spirit of liberty, for it may aim at forcing improvements on an unwilling people; and the spirit of liberty, in so far as it resists such attempts, may ally itself locally and temporarily with the opponents of improvement; but the only unfailing and permanent source of improvement is liberty, since by it there are as many possible independent centers of improvement as there are individuals. The progressive principle, however, in either shape, whether as the love of liberty or of improvement, is antagonistic to the sway of Custom, involving at least emancipation from that yoke; and the contest between the two constitutes the chief interest of the history of mankind. The greater part of the world has, properly speaking, no history, because the despotism of Custom is complete. This is the case over the whole East. Custom is there, in all things, the final appeal; justice and right mean conformity to custom; the argument of custom no one, unless some tyrant intoxicated with power, thinks of resisting. And we see the result. Those nations must once have had originality; they did not start out of the ground populous, lettered, and versed in many of the arts of life; they made themselves all this, and were then the greatest and most powerful nations of the world. What are they now? The subjects or dependents of tribes whose forefathers wandered in the forests when theirs had magnificent palaces and gorgeous temples, but over whom custom exercised only a divided rule with liberty and progress. A people, it appears, may be progressive for a certain length of time, and then stop: when does it stop? When it ceases to possess individuality. If a similar change should befall the nations of Europe, it will not be in exactly the same shape: the despotism of custom with which these nations are threatened is not precisely stationariness. It proscribes singularity, but it does not preclude change, provided all change together. We have discarded the fixed costumes of our forefathers; every one must still dress like other people, but the fashion may change once or twice a year. We thus take care that when there is change it shall be for change's sake, and not from any idea of beauty or convenience; for the same idea of beauty or convenience would not strike all the world at the same moment, and be simultaneously thrown aside by all at another moment. But we are progressive as well as changeable: we continually make new inventions in mechanical things, and keep them until they are again superseded by better; we are eager for improvement in politics, in education, even in morals, though in this last our idea of improvement chiefly consists in persuading or forcing other people to be as good as ourselves. It is not progress that we object to; on the contrary, we flatter ourselves that we are the most progressive people who ever lived. It is individuality that we war against: we should think we had done wonders if we had made ourselves all alike; forgetting that the unlikeness of one person to another is generally the first thing which draws the attention of either to the imperfection of his own type, and the superiority of another, or the possibility, by combining the advantages of both, of producing something better than either. We have a warning example in China—a nation of much talent, and, in some respects, even wisdom, owing to the rare good fortune of having been provided at an early period with a particularly good set of customs, the work, in some measure, of men to whom even the most enlightened European must accord, under certain limitations, the title of sages and philosophers. They are remarkable, too, in the excellence of their apparatus for impressing, as far as possible, the best wisdom they possess upon every mind in the community, and securing that those who have appropriated most of it shall occupy the posts of honour and power. Surely the people who did this have discovered the secret of human progressiveness, and must have kept themselves steadily at the head of the movement of the world. On the contrary, they have become stationary—have remained so for thousands of years; and if they are ever to be farther improved, it must be by foreigners. They have succeeded beyond all hope in what English philanthropists are so industriously working at—in making a people all alike, all governing their thoughts and conduct by the same maxims and rules; and these are the fruits. The modern regime of public opinion is, in an unorganized form, what the Chinese educational and political systems are in an organized; and unless individuality shall be able successfully to assert itself against this yoke, Europe, notwithstanding its noble antecedents and its professed Christianity, will tend to become another China.

What is it that has hitherto preserved Europe from this lot? What has made the European family of nations an improving, instead of a stationary portion of mankind? Not any superior excellence in them, which, when it exists, exists as the effect, not as the cause; but their remarkable diversity of character and culture. Individuals, classes, nations, have been extremely unlike one another: they have struck out a great variety of paths, each leading to something valuable; and although at every period those who travelled in different paths have been intolerant of one another, and each would have thought it an excellent thing if all the rest could have been compelled to travel his road, their attempts to thwart each other's development have rarely had any permanent success, and each has in time endured to receive the good which the others have offered. Europe is, in my judgment, wholly indebted to this plurality of paths for its progressive and many-sided development. But it already begins to possess this benefit in a considerably less degree. It is decidedly advancing towards the Chinese ideal of making all people alike. M. de Tocqueville, in his last important work, remarks how much more the Frenchmen of the present day resemble one another, than did those even of the last generation. The same remark might be made of Englishmen in a far greater degree. In a passage already quoted from Wilhelm von Humboldt, he points out two things as necessary conditions of human development, because necessary to render people unlike one another; namely, freedom, and variety of situations. The second of these two conditions is in this country every day diminishing. The circumstances which surround different classes and individuals, and shape their characters, are daily becoming more assimilated. Formerly, different ranks, different neighborhoods, different trades and professions, lived in what might be called different worlds; at present, to a great degree in the same. Comparatively speaking, they now read the same things, listen to the same things, see the same things, go to the same places, have their hopes and fears directed to the same objects, have the same rights and liberties, and the same means of asserting them. Great as are the differences of position which remain, they are nothing to those which have ceased. And the assimilation is still proceeding. All the political changes of the age promote it, since they all tend to raise the low and to lower the high. Every extension of education promotes it, because education brings people under common influences, and gives them access to the general stock of facts and sentiments. Improvements in the means of communication promote it, by bringing the inhabitants of distant places into personal contact, and keeping up a rapid flow of changes of residence between one place and another. The increase of commerce and manufactures promotes it, by diffusing more widely the advantages of easy circumstances, and opening all objects of ambition, even the highest, to general competition, whereby the desire of rising becomes no longer the character of a particular class, but of all classes. A more powerful agency than even all these, in bringing about a general similarity among mankind, is the complete establishment, in this and other free countries, of the ascendancy of public opinion in the State. As the various social eminences which enabled persons entrenched on them to disregard the opinion of the multitude, gradually become levelled; as the very idea of resisting the will of the public, when it is positively known that they have a will, disappears more and more from the minds of practical politicians; there ceases to be any social support for nonconformity—any substantive power in society, which, itself opposed to the ascendancy of numbers, is interested in taking under its protection opinions and tendencies at variance with those of the public.

The combination of all these causes forms so great a mass of influences hostile to Individuality, that it is not easy to see how it can stand its ground. It will do so with increasing difficulty, unless the intelligent part of the public can be made to feel its value—to see that it is good there should be differences, even though not for the better, even though, as it may appear to them, some should be for the worse. If the claims of Individuality are ever to be asserted, the time is now, while much is still wanting to complete the enforced assimilation. It is only in the earlier stages that any stand can be successfully made against the encroachment. The demand that all other people shall resemble ourselves, grows by what it feeds on. If resistance waits till life is reduced nearly to one uniform type, all deviations from that type will come to be considered impious, immoral, even monstrous and contrary to nature. Mankind speedily become unable to conceive diversity, when they have been for some time unaccustomed to see it.

CHAPTER IV. OF THE LIMITS TO THE AUTHORITY OF SOCIETY OVER THE INDIVIDUAL

What, then, is the rightful limit to the sovereignty of the individual over himself? Where does the authority of society begin? How much of human life should be assigned to individuality, and how much to society?

Each will receive its proper share, if each has that which more particularly concerns it. To individuality should belong the part of life in which it is chiefly the individual that is interested; to society, the part which chiefly interests society.

Though society is not founded on a contract, and though no good purpose is answered by inventing a contract in order to deduce social obligations from it, every one who receives the protection of society owes a return for the benefit, and the fact of living in society renders it indispensable that each should be bound to observe a certain line of conduct towards the rest. This conduct consists first, in not injuring the interests of one another; or rather certain interests, which, either by express legal provision or by tacit understanding, ought to be considered as rights; and secondly, in each person's bearing his share (to be fixed on some equitable principle) of the labors and sacrifices incurred for defending the society or its members from injury and molestation. These conditions society is justified in enforcing at all costs to those who endeavor to withhold fulfillment. Nor is this all that society may do. The acts of an individual may be hurtful to others, or wanting in due consideration for their welfare, without going the length of violating any of their constituted rights. The offender may then be justly punished by opinion, though not by law. As soon as any part of a person's conduct affects prejudicially the interests of others, society has jurisdiction over it, and the question whether the general welfare will or will not be promoted by interfering with it, becomes open to discussion. But there is no room for entertaining any such question when a person's conduct affects the interests of no persons besides himself, or needs not affect them unless they like (all the persons concerned being of full age, and the ordinary amount of understanding). In all such cases there should be perfect freedom, legal and social, to do the action and stand the consequences. . . .

The distinction here pointed out between the part of a person's life which concerns only himself, and that which concerns others, many persons will refuse to admit. How (it may be asked) can any part of the conduct of a member of society be a matter of indifference to the other members? No person is an entirely isolated being; it is impossible for a person to do anything seriously or permanently hurtful to himself, without mischief reaching at least to his near connexions, and often far beyond them. If he injures his property, he does harm to those who directly or indirectly derived support from it, and usually diminishes, by a greater or less amount, the general resources of the community. If he deteriorates his bodily or mental faculties, he not only brings evil upon all who depended on him for any portion of their happiness, but disqualifies himself for rendering the services which he owes to his fellow creatures generally; perhaps becomes a burden on their affection or benevolence; and if such conduct were very frequent, hardly any offence that is committed would detract more from the general sum of good. Finally, if by his vices or follies a person does no direct harm to others, he is nevertheless (it may be said) injurious by his example; and ought to be compelled to control himself, for the sake of those whom the sight or knowledge of his conduct might corrupt or mislead.

And even (it will be added) if the consequences of misconduct could be confined to the vicious or thoughtless individual, ought society to abandon to their own guidance those who are manifestly unfit for it? If protection against themselves is confessedly due to children and persons under age, is not society equally bound to afford it to persons of mature years who are equally incapable of self-government? If gambling, or drunkenness, or incontinence, or idleness, or uncleanliness, are as injurious to happiness, and as great a hindrance to improvement, as many or most of the acts prohibited by law, why (it may be asked) should not law, so far as is consistent with practicability and social convenience, endeavor to repress these also? And as a supplement to the unavoidable imperfections of law, ought not opinion at least to organize a powerful police against these vices, and visit rigidly with social penalties those who are known to practise them? There is no question here (it may be said) about restricting individuality, or impeding the trial of new and original experiments in living. The only things it is sought to prevent are things which have been tried and condemned from the beginning of the world until now; things which experience has shown not to be useful or suitable to any person's individuality. There must be some length of time and amount of experience, after which a moral or prudential truth may be regarded as established: and it is merely desired to prevent generation after generation from falling over the same precipice which has been fatal to their predecessors.

I fully admit that the mischief which a person does to himself may seriously affect, both through their sympathies and their interests, those nearly connected with him, and in a minor degree, society at large. When, by conduct of this sort, a person is led to violate a distinct and assignable obligation to any other person or persons, the case is taken out of the self-regarding class, and becomes amenable to moral disapprobation in the proper sense of the term. If, for example, a man, through intemperance or extravagance, becomes unable to pay his debts, or, having undertaken the moral responsibility of a family, becomes from the same cause incapable of supporting or educating them, he is deservedly reprobated, and might be justly punished; but it is for the breach of duty to his family or creditors, not for the extravagance. If the resources which ought to have been devoted to them, had been diverted from them for the most prudent investment, the moral culpability would have been the same. George Barnwell murdered his uncle to get money for his mistress, but if he had done it to set himself up in business, he would equally have been hanged. Again, in the frequent case of a man who causes grief to his family by addiction to bad habits, he deserves reproach for his unkindness or ingratitude; but so he may be cultivating habits not in themselves vicious, if they are painful to those with whom he passes his life, or who from personal ties are dependent on him for their comfort. Whoever fails in the consideration generally due to the interests and feelings of others, not being compelled by some more imperative duty, or justified by allowable self-preference, is a subject of moral disapprobation for that failure, but not for the cause of it, nor for the errors, merely personal to himself, which may have remotely led to it. In like manner, when a person disables himself, by conduct purely self-regarding, from the performance of some definite duty incumbent on him to the public, he is guilty of a social offence. No person ought to be punished simply for being drunk; but a soldier or a policeman should be punished for being drunk on duty. Whenever, in short, there is a definite damage, or a definite risk of damage, either to an individual or to the public, the case is taken out of the province of liberty, and placed in that of morality or law.

But with regard to the merely contingent, or, as it may be called, constructive injury which a person causes to society, by conduct which neither violates any specific duty to the public, nor occasions perceptible hurt to any assignable individual except himself; the inconvenience is one which society can afford to bear, for the sake of the greater good of human freedom. If grown persons are to be punished for not taking proper care of themselves, I would rather it were for their own sake, than under pretence of preventing them from impairing their capacity of rendering to society benefits which society does not pretend it has a right to exact. But I cannot consent to argue the point as if society had no means of bringing its weaker members up to its ordinary standard of rational conduct, except waiting till they do something irrational, and then punishing them, legally or morally, for it. Society has had absolute power over them during all the early portion of their existence: it has had the whole period of childhood and nonage in which to try whether it could make them capable of rational conduct in life. The existing generation is master both of the training and the entire circumstances of the generation to come; it cannot indeed make them perfectly wise and good, because it is itself so lamentably deficient in goodness and wisdom; and its best efforts are not always, in individual cases, its most successful ones; but it is perfectly well able to make the rising generation, as a whole, as good as, and a little better than, itself. If society lets any considerable number of its members grow up mere children, incapable of being acted on by rational consideration of distant motives, society has itself to blame for the consequences. Armed not only with all the powers of education, but with the ascendancy which the authority of a received opinion always exercises over the minds who are least fitted to judge for themselves; and aided by the natural penalties which cannot be prevented from falling on those who incur the distaste or the contempt of those who know them; let not society pretend that it needs, besides all this, the power to issue commands and enforce obedience in the personal concerns of individuals, in which, on all principles of justice and policy, the decision ought to rest with those who are to abide the consequences. Nor is there anything which tends more to discredit and frustrate the better means of influencing conduct, than a resort to the worse. If there be among those whom it is attempted to coerce into prudence or temperance, any of the material of which vigorous and independent characters are made, they will infallibly rebel against the yoke. No such person will ever feel that others have a right to control him in his concerns, such as they have to prevent him from injuring them in theirs; and it easily comes to be considered a mark of spirit and courage to fly in the face of such usurped authority, and do with ostentation the exact opposite of what it enjoins; as in the fashion of grossness which succeeded, in the time of Charles II, to the fanatical moral intolerance of the Puritans. With respect to what is said of the necessity of protecting society from the bad example set to others by the vicious or the self-indulgent; it is true that bad example may have a pernicious effect, especially the example of doing wrong to others with impunity to the wrongdoer. But we are now speaking of conduct which, while it does no wrong to others, is supposed to do great harm to the agent himself: and I do not see how those who believe this, can think otherwise than that the example, on the whole, must be more salutary than hurtful, since, if it displays the misconduct, it displays also the painful or degrading consequences which, if the conduct is justly censured, must be supposed to be in all or most cases attendant on it.

But the strongest of all the arguments against the interference of the public with purely personal conduct, is that when it does interfere, the odds are that it interferes wrongly, and in the wrong place. On questions of social morality, of duty to others, the opinion of the public, that is, of an overruling majority, though often wrong, is likely to be still oftener right; because on such questions they are only required to judge of their own interests; of the manner in which some mode of conduct, if allowed to be practiced, would affect themselves. But the opinion of a similar majority, imposed as a law on the minority, on questions of self-regarding conduct, is quite as likely to be wrong as right; for in these cases public opinion means, at the best, some people's opinion of what is good or bad for other people; while very often it does not even mean that; the public, with the most perfect indifference, passing over the pleasure or convenience of those whose conduct they censure, and considering only their own preference. There are many who consider as an injury to themselves any conduct which they have a distaste for, and resent it as an outrage to their feelings; as a religious bigot, when charged with disregarding the religious feelings of others, has been known to retort that they disregard his feelings, by persisting in their abominable worship or creed. But there is no parity between the feeling of a person for his own opinion, and the feeling of another who is offended at his holding it; no more than between the desire of a thief to take a purse, and the desire of the right owner to keep it. And a person's taste is as much his own peculiar concern as his opinion or his purse. It is easy for any one to imagine an ideal public, which leaves the freedom and choice of individuals in all uncertain matters undisturbed, and only requires them to abstain from modes of conduct which universal experience has condemned. But where has there been seen a public which set any such limit to its censorship? or when does the public trouble itself about universal experience? In its interferences with personal conduct it is seldom thinking of anything but the enormity of acting or feeling differently from itself; and this standard of judgment, thinly disguised, is held up to mankind as the dictate of religion and philosophy, by nine-tenths of all moralists and speculative writers. These teach that things are right because they are right; because we feel them to be so. They tell us to search in our own minds and hearts for laws of conduct binding on ourselves and on all others. What can the poor public do but apply these instructions, and make their own personal feelings of good and evil, if they are tolerably unanimous in them, obligatory on all the world?

The evil here pointed out is not one which exists only in theory; and it may perhaps be expected that I should specify the instances in which the public of this age and country improperly invests its own preferences with the character of moral laws. I am not writing an essay on the aberrations of existing moral feeling. That is too weighty a subject to be discussed parenthetically, and by way of illustration. Yet examples are necessary, to show that the principle I maintain is of serious and practical moment, and that I am not endeavoring to erect a barrier against imaginary evils. And it is not difficult to show, by abundant instances, that to extend the bounds of what may be called moral police, until it encroaches on the most unquestionably legitimate liberty of the individual, is one of the most universal of all human propensities.

CHAPTER V. APPLICATIONS

The principles asserted in these pages must be more generally admitted as the basis for discussion of details, before a consistent application of them to all the various departments of government and morals can be attempted with any prospect of advantage. The few observations I propose to make on questions of detail, are designed to illustrate the principles, rather than to follow them out to their consequences. I offer, not so much applications, as specimens of application; which may serve to bring into greater clearness the meaning and limits of the two maxims which together form the entire doctrine of this Essay, and to assist the judgment in holding the balance between them, in the cases where it appears doubtful which of them is applicable to the case.

The maxims are, first, that the individual is not accountable to society for his actions, in so far as these concern the interests of no person but himself.

Advice, instruction, persuasion, and avoidance by other people if thought necessary by them for their own good, are the only measures by which society can justifiably express its dislike or disapprobation of his conduct. Secondly, that for such actions as are prejudicial to the interests of others, the individual is accountable, and may be subjected either to social or to legal punishment, if society is of opinion that the one or the other is requisite for its protection.

In the first place, it must by no means be supposed, because damage, or probability of damage, to the interests of others, can alone justify the interference of society, that therefore it always does justify such interference. In many cases, an individual, in pursuing a legitimate object, necessarily and therefore legitimately causes pain or loss to others, or intercepts a good which they had a reasonable hope of obtaining. Such oppositions of interest between individuals often arise from bad social institutions, but are unavoidable while those institutions last; and some would be unavoidable under any institutions. Whoever succeeds in an overcrowded profession, or in a competitive examination; whoever is preferred to another in any contest for an object which both desire, reaps benefit from the loss of others, from their wasted exertion and their disappointment. But it is, by common admission, better for the general interest of mankind, that persons should pursue their objects undeterred by this sort of consequences. In other words, society admits no right, either legal or moral, in the disappointed competitors, to immunity from this kind of suffering; and feels called on to interfere, only when means of success have been employed which it is contrary to the general interest to permit—namely, fraud or treachery, and force.

Again, trade is a social act. Whoever undertakes to sell any description of goods to the public, does what affects the interest of other persons, and of society in general; and thus his conduct, in principle, comes within the jurisdiction of society: accordingly, it was once held to be the duty of governments, in all cases which were considered of importance, to fix prices, and regulate the processes of manufacture. But it is now recognized, though not till after a long struggle, that both the cheapness and the good quality of commodities are most effectually provided for by leaving the producers and sellers perfectly free, under the sole check of equal freedom to the buyers for supplying themselves elsewhere. This is the so-called doctrine of Free Trade, which rests on grounds different from, though equally solid with, the principle of individual liberty asserted in this Essay. Restrictions on trade, or on production for purposes of trade, are indeed restraints; and all restraint, qua restraint, is an evil: but the restraints in question affect only that part of conduct which society is competent to restrain, and are wrong solely because they do not really produce the results which it is desired to produce by them. As the principle of individual liberty is not involved in the doctrine of Free Trade, so neither is it in most of the questions which arise respecting the limits of that doctrine; as for example, what amount of public control is admissible for the prevention of fraud by adulteration; how far sanitary precautions, or arrangements to protect workpeople employed in dangerous occupations, should be enforced on employers. Such questions involve considerations of liberty, only in so far as leaving people to themselves is always better, caeteris paribus, than controlling them: but that they may be legitimately controlled for these ends, is in principle undeniable. On the other hand, there are questions relating to interference with trade, which are essentially questions of liberty; such as the Maine Law, already touched upon; the prohibition of the importation of opium into China; the restriction of the sale of poisons; all cases, in short, where the object of the interference is to make it impossible or difficult to obtain a particular commodity. These interferences are objectionable, not as infringements on the liberty of the producer or seller, but on that of the buyer.

One of these examples, that of the sale of poisons, opens a new question; the proper limits of what may be called the functions of police, how far liberty may legitimately be invaded for the prevention of crime, or of accident. It is one of the undisputed functions of government to take precautions against crime before it has been committed, as well as to detect and punish it afterwards. The preventive function of government, however, is far more liable to be abused, to the prejudice of liberty, then the punitory function; for there is hardly any part of the legitimate freedom of action of a human being which would not admit of being represented, and fairly too, as increasing the facilities for some form or other of delinquency. Nevertheless, if a public authority, or even a private person, sees any one evidently preparing to commit a crime, they are not bound to look on inactive until the crime is committed, but may interfere to prevent it. If poisons were never bought or used for any purpose except the commission of murder, it would be right to prohibit their manufacture and sale. They may, however, be wanted not only for innocent but for useful purposes, and restrictions cannot be imposed in the one case without operating in the other. Again, it is a proper office of public authority to guard against accidents. If either a public officer or any one else saw a person attempting to cross a bridge which had been ascertained to be unsafe, and there were no time to warn him of his danger, they might seize him and turn him back, without any real infringement of his liberty; for liberty consists in doing what one desires, and he does not desire to fall into the river. Nevertheless, when there is not a certainty, but only a danger of mischief, no one but the person himself can judge of the sufficiency of the motive which may prompt him to incur the risk: in this case, therefore (unless he is a child, or delirious, or in some state of excitement or absorption incompatible with the full use of the reflecting faculty), he ought, I conceive, to be only warned of the danger; not forcibly prevented from exposing himself to it. Similar considerations, applied to such a question as the sale of poisons, may enable us to decide which among the possible modes of regulation are or are not contrary to principle. Such a precaution, for example, as that of labelling the drug with some word expressive of its dangerous character, may be enforced without violation of liberty: the buyer cannot wish not to know that the thing he possesses has poisonous qualities. But to require in all cases the certificate of a medical practitioner, would make it sometimes impossible, always expensive, to obtain the article for legitimate uses. The only mode apparent to me, in which difficulties may be thrown in the way of crime committed through this means, without any infringement, worth taking into account, upon the liberty of those who desire the poisonous substance for other purposes, consists in providing what, in the apt language of Bentham, is called 'preappointed evidence.' This provision is familiar to every one in the case of contracts. It is usual and right that the law, when a contract is entered into, should require as the condition of its enforcing performance, that certain formalities should be observed, such as signatures, attestation of witnesses, and the like, in order that in case of subsequent dispute, there may be evidence to prove that the contract was really entered into, and that there was nothing in the circumstances to render it legally invalid: the effect being, to throw great obstacles in the way of fictitious contracts, or contracts made in circumstances which, if known, would destroy their validity. Precautions of a similar nature might be enforced in the sale of articles adapted to be instruments of crime. The seller, for example, might be required to enter in a register the exact time of the transaction, the name and address of the buyer, the precise quality and quantity sold; to ask the purpose for which it was wanted, and record the answer he received. When there was no medical prescription, the presence of some third person might be required, to bring home the fact to the purchaser, in case there should afterwards be reason to believe that the article had been applied to criminal purposes. Such regulations would in general be no material impediment to obtaining the article, but a very considerable one to making an improper use of it without detection.

The right inherent in society, to ward off crimes against itself by antecedent precautions, suggests the obvious limitations to the maxim, that purely self-regarding misconduct cannot properly be meddled with in the way of prevention or punishment. Drunkenness, for example, in ordinary cases, is not a fit subject for legislative interference; but I should deem it perfectly legitimate that a person, who had once been convicted of any act of violence to others under the influence of drink, should be placed under a special legal restriction, personal to himself; that if he were afterwards found drunk, he should be liable to a penalty, and that if when in that state he committed another offence, the punishment to which he would be liable for that other offence should be increased in severity. The making himself drunk, in a person whom drunkenness excites to do harm to others, is a crime against others. So, again, idleness, except in a person receiving support from the public, or except when it constitutes a breach of contract, cannot without tyranny be made a subject of legal punishment; but if, either from idleness or from any other avoidable cause, a man fails to perform his legal duties to others, as for instance to support his children, it is no tyranny to force him to fulfil that obligation, by compulsory labour, if no other means are available.

Again, there are many acts which, being directly injurious only to the agents themselves, ought not to be legally interdicted, but which, if done publicly, are a violation of good manners, and coming thus within the category of offences against others, may rightfully be prohibited. Of this kind are offences against decency; on which it is unnecessary to dwell, the rather as they are only connected indirectly with our subject, the objection to publicity being equally strong in the case of many actions not in themselves condemnable, nor supposed to be so.

There is another question to which an answer must be found, consistent with the principles which have been laid down. In cases of personal conduct supposed to be blameable, but which respect for liberty precludes society from preventing or punishing, because the evil directly resulting falls wholly on the agent; what the agent is free to do, ought other persons to be equally free to counsel or instigate? This question is not free from difficulty. The case of a person who solicits another to do an act, is not strictly a case of self-regarding conduct. To give advice or offer inducements to any one, is a social act, and may, therefore, like actions in general which affect others, be supposed amenable to social control. But a little reflection corrects the first impression, by showing that if the case is not strictly within the definition of individual liberty, yet the reasons on which the principle of individual liberty is grounded, are applicable to it. If people must be allowed, in whatever concerns only themselves, to act as seems best to themselves at their own peril, they must equally be free to consult with one another about what is fit to be so done; to exchange opinions, and give and receive suggestions. Whatever it is permitted to do, it must be permitted to advise to do. The question is doubtful, only when the instigator derives a personal benefit from his advice; when he makes it his occupation, for subsistence or pecuniary gain, to promote what society and the State consider to be an evil. Then, indeed, a new element of complication is introduced; namely, the existence of classes of persons with an interest opposed to what is considered as the public weal, and whose mode of living is grounded on the counteraction of it. Ought this to be interfered with, or not? Fornication, for example, must be tolerated, and so must gambling; but should a person be free to be a pimp, or to keep a gambling-house? The case is one of those which lie on the exact boundary line between two principles, and it is not at once apparent to which of the two it properly belongs. There are arguments on both sides. On the side of toleration it may be said, that the fact of following anything as an occupation, and living or profiting by the practice of it, cannot make that criminal which would otherwise be admissible; that the act should either be consistently permitted or consistently prohibited; that if the principles which we have hitherto defended are true, society has no business, as society, to decide anything to be wrong which concerns only the individual; that it cannot go beyond dissuasion, and that one person should be as free to persuade, as another to dissuade. In opposition to this it may be contended, that although the public, or the State, are not warranted in authoritatively deciding, for purposes of repression or punishment, that such or such conduct affecting only the interests of the individual is good or bad, they are fully justified in assuming, if they regard it as bad, that its being so or not is at least a disputable question: That, this being supposed, they cannot be acting wrongly in endeavoring to exclude the influence of solicitations which are not disinterested, of instigators who cannot possibly be impartial—who have a direct personal interest on one side, and that side the one which the State believes to be wrong, and who confessedly promote it for personal objects only. There can surely, it may be urged, be nothing lost, no sacrifice of good, by so ordering matters that persons shall make their election, either wisely or foolishly, on their own prompting, as free as possible from the arts of persons who stimulate their inclinations for interested purposes of their own. Thus (it may be said) though the statutes respecting unlawful games are utterly indefensible—though all persons should be free to gamble in their own or each other's houses, or in any place of meeting established by their own subscriptions, and open only to the members and their visitors—yet public gambling-houses should not be permitted. It is true that the prohibition is never effectual, and that, whatever amount of tyrannical power may be given to the police, gambling-houses can always be maintained under other pretenses; but they may be compelled to conduct their operations with a certain degree of secrecy and mystery, so that nobody knows anything about them but those who seek them; and more than this, society ought not to aim at. There is considerable force in these arguments. I will not venture to decide whether they are sufficient to justify the moral anomaly of punishing the accessory, when the principal is (and must be) allowed to go free; of fining or imprisoning the procurer, but not the fornicator, the gambling-house keeper, but not the gambler. Still less ought the common operations of buying and selling to be interfered with on analogous grounds. Almost every article which is bought and sold may be used in excess, and the sellers have a pecuniary interest in encouraging that excess; but no argument can be founded on this, in favour, for instance, of the Maine Law; because the class of dealers in strong drinks, though interested in their abuse, are indispensably required for the sake of their legitimate use. The interest, however, of these dealers in promoting intemperance is a real evil, and justifies the State in imposing restrictions and requiring guarantees which, but for that justification, would be infringements of legitimate liberty.

A further question is, whether the State, while it permits, should nevertheless indirectly discourage conduct which it deems contrary to the best interests of the agent; whether, for example, it should take measures to render the means of drunkenness more costly, or add to the difficulty of procuring them by limiting the number of the places of sale. On this as on most other practical questions, many distinctions require to be made. To tax stimulants for the sole purpose of making them more difficult to be obtained, is a measure differing only in degree from their entire prohibition; and would be justifiable only if that were justifiable. Every increase of cost is a prohibition, to those whose means do not come up to the augmented price; and to those who do, it is a penalty laid on them for gratifying a particular taste. Their choice of pleasures, and their mode of expending their income, after satisfying their legal and moral obligations to the State and to individuals, are their own concern, and must rest with their own judgment. These considerations may seem at first sight to condemn the selection of stimulants as special subjects of taxation for purposes of revenue. But it must be remembered that taxation for fiscal purposes is absolutely inevitable; that in most countries it is necessary that a considerable part of that taxation should be indirect; that the State, therefore, cannot help imposing penalties, which to some persons may be prohibitory, on the use of some articles of consumption. It is hence the duty of the State to consider, in the imposition of taxes, what commodities the consumers can best spare; and a fortiori, to select in preference those of which it deems the use, beyond a very moderate quantity, to be positively injurious. Taxation, therefore, of stimulants, up to the point which produces the largest amount of revenue (supposing that the State needs all the revenue which it yields) is not only admissible, but to be approved of.

The question of making the sale of these commodities a more or less exclusive privilege, must be answered differently, according to the purposes to which the restriction is intended to be subservient. All places of public resort require the restraint of a police, and places of this kind peculiarly, because offences against society are especially apt to originate there. It is, therefore, fit to confine the power of selling these commodities (at least for consumption on the spot) to persons of known or vouched-for respectability of conduct; to make such regulations respecting hours of opening and closing as may be requisite for public surveillance, and to withdraw the license if breaches of the peace repeatedly take place through the connivance or incapacity of the keeper of the house, or if it becomes a rendezvous for concocting and preparing offences against the law. Any further restriction I do not conceive to be, in principle, justifiable. The limitation in number, for instance, of beer and spirit houses, for the express purpose of rendering them more difficult of access, and diminishing the occasions of temptation, not only exposes all to an inconvenience because there are some by whom the facility would be abused, but is suited only to a state of society in which the laboring classes are avowedly treated as children or savages, and placed under an education of restraint, to fit them for future admission to the privileges of freedom. This is not the principle on which the laboring classes are professedly governed in any free country; and no person who sets due value on freedom will give his adhesion to their being so governed, unless after all efforts have been exhausted to educate them for freedom and govern them as freemen, and it has been definitively proved that they can only be governed as children. The bare statement of the alternative shows the absurdity of supposing that such efforts have been made in any case which needs be considered here. It is only because the institutions of this country are a mass of inconsistencies, that things find admittance into our practice which belong to the system of despotic, or what is called paternal, government, while the general freedom of our institutions precludes the exercise of the amount of control necessary to render the restraint of any real efficacy as a moral education.

It was pointed out in an early part of this Essay, that the liberty of the individual, in things wherein the individual is alone concerned, implies a corresponding liberty in any number of individuals to regulate by mutual agreement such things as regard them jointly, and regard no persons but themselves. This question presents no difficulty, so long as the will of all the persons implicated remains unaltered; but since that will may change, it is often necessary, even in things in which they alone are concerned, that they should enter into engagements with one another; and when they do, it is fit, as a general rule, that those engagements should be kept. Yet, in the laws, probably, of every country, this general rule has some exceptions. Not only persons are not held to engagements which violate the rights of third parties, but it is sometimes considered a sufficient reason for releasing them from an engagement, that it is injurious to themselves. In this and most other civilized countries, for example, an engagement by which a person should sell himself, or allow himself to be sold, as a slave, would be null and void; neither enforced by law nor by opinion. The ground for thus limiting his power of voluntarily disposing of his own lot in life, is apparent, and is very clearly seen in this extreme case. The reason for not interfering, unless for the sake of others, with a person's voluntary acts, is consideration for his liberty. His voluntary choice is evidence that what he so chooses is desirable, or at the least endurable, to him, and his good is on the whole best provided for by allowing him to take his own means of pursuing it. But by selling himself for a slave, he abdicates his liberty; he foregoes any future use of it beyond that single act. He therefore defeats, in his own case, the very purpose which is the justification of allowing him to dispose of himself. He is no longer free; but is thenceforth in a position which has no longer the presumption in its favour, that would be afforded by his voluntarily remaining in it. The principle of freedom cannot require that he should be free not to be free. It is not freedom, to be allowed to alienate his freedom. . . .

A person should be free to do as he likes in his own concerns, but he ought not to be free to do as he likes in acting for another, under the pretext that the affairs of the other are his own affairs. The State, while it respects the liberty of each in what specially regards himself, is bound to maintain a vigilant control over his exercise of any power which it allows him to possess over others. The obligation is almost entirely disregarded in the case of the family relations—a case, in its direct influence on human happiness, more important than all others taken together. The almost despotic power of husbands over wives needs not be enlarged upon here, because nothing more is needed for the complete removal of the evil than that wives should have the same rights and should receive the protection of law in the same manner as all other persons; and because, on this subject, the defenders of established injustice do not avail themselves of the plea of liberty but stand forth openly as the champions of power. It is in the case of children that misapplied notions of liberty are a real obstacle to the fulfillment by the State of its duties. One would almost think that a man's children were supposed to be literally, and not metaphorically, a part of himself, so jealous is opinion of the smallest interference of law with his absolute and exclusive control over them, more jealous than of almost any interference with his own freedom of action: so much less do the generality of mankind value liberty than power. Consider, for example, the case of education. Is it not almost a self-evident axiom that the State should require and compel the education, up to certain standard, of every human being who is born its citizen? Yet who is there that is not afraid to recognize and assert this truth? Hardly anyone, indeed, will deny that it is one of the most sacred duties of the parents, after summoning a human being into the world, to give to that being an education fitting him to perform his part well in life toward others and towards himself. But while this is unanimously declared to be the father's duty, scarcely anybody, in this country, will bear to hear of obliging him to perform it. Instead of his being required to make an exertion or sacrifice for securing education to his child, it is left to his choice to accept it or not when it is provided gratis! It still remains unrecognized that to bring a child into existence without a fair prospect of being able, not only to provide food for its body, but instruction and training for its mind is a moral crime, both against the unfortunate offspring and against society; and that if the parent does not fulfill this obligation, the State ought to see it fulfilled at the charge, as far as possible, of the parent. . . .

The worth of a State, in the long run, is the worth of the individuals composing it; and a State which postpones the interests of *their* mental expansion and elevation to a little more of administrative skill, or of that semblance of it which practice gives in the details of business; a State which dwarfs its men, in order that they may be more docile instruments in its hands even for the beneficial purposes—will find that with small men no great thing can really be accomplished; and that the perfection of machinery to which it has sacrificed everything will in the end avail it nothing, for want of the vital power which, in order that the machine might work more smoothly, it has preferred to banish.

The Subjection of Women

CHAPTER I

The object of this Essay is to explain as clearly as I am able, the grounds of an opinion which I have held from the very earliest period when I had formed any opinions at all on social or political matters, and which, instead of being weakened or modified, has been constantly growing stronger by the progress of reflection and the experience of life: That the principle which regulates the existing social relations between the two sexes—the legal subordination of one sex to the other—is wrong in itself, and now one of the chief hindrances to human improvement; and that it ought to be replaced by a principle of perfect equality, admitting no power or privilege on the one side, nor disability on the other. . . .

The generality of a practice is in some cases a strong presumption that it is, or at all events once was, conducive to laudable ends. This is the case, when the practice was first adopted, or afterwards kept up, as a means to such ends, and was grounded on experience of the mode in which they could be most effectually attained. If the authority of men over women, when first established, had been the result of a conscientious comparison between different modes of constituting the government of society; if, after trying various other modes of social organization—the government of women over men, equality between the two, and such mixed and divided modes of government as might be invented—it had been decided, on the testimony of experience, that the mode in which women are wholly under the rule of men, having no share at all in public concerns, and each in private being under the legal obligation of obedience to the man with whom she has associated her destiny, was the arrangement most conducive to the happiness and well being of both; its general adoption might then be fairly thought to be some evidence that, at the time when it was adopted, it was the best: though even then the considerations which recommended it may, like so many other primeval social facts of the greatest importance, have subsequently, in the course of ages, ceased to exist. But the state of the case is in every respect the reverse of this. In the first place, the opinion in favour of the present system, which entirely subordinates the weaker sex to the stronger, rests upon theory only; for there never has been trial made of any other: so that experience, in the sense in which it is vulgarly opposed to theory, cannot be pretended to have pronounced any verdict.

And in the second place, the adoption of this system of inequality never was the result of deliberation, or forethought, or any social ideas, or any notion whatever of what conduced to the benefit of humanity or the good order of society. It arose simply from the fact that from the very earliest twilight of human society, every woman (owing to the value attached to her by men, combined with her inferiority in muscular strength) was found in a state of bondage to some man. Laws and systems of polity always begin by recognising the relations they find already existing between individuals. They convert what was a mere physical fact into a legal right, give it the sanction of society, and principally aim at the substitution of public and organized means of asserting and protecting these rights, instead of the irregular and lawless conflict of physical strength. Those who had already been compelled to obedience became in this manner legally bound to it. Slavery, from being a mere affair of force between the master and the slave, became regularized and a matter of compact among the masters, who, binding themselves to one another for common protection, guaranteed by their collective strength the private possessions of each, including his slaves. In early times, the great majority of the male sex were slaves, as well as the whole of the female. And many ages elapsed, some of them ages of high cultivation, before any thinker was bold enough to question the rightfulness, and the absolute social necessity, either of the one slavery or of the other. By degrees such thinkers did arise: and (the general progress of society assisting) the slavery of the male sex has, in all the countries of Christian Europe at least (though, in one of them, only within the last few years) been at length abolished, and that of the female sex has been gradually changed into a milder form of dependence. But this dependence, as it exists at present, is not an original institution, taking a fresh start from considerations of justice and social expediency—it is the primitive state of slavery lasting on, through successive mitigations and modifications occasioned by the same causes which have softened the general manners, and brought all human relations more under the control of justice and the influence of humanity. It has not lost the taint of its brutal origin. No presumption in its favour, therefore, can be drawn from the fact of its existence. The only such presumption which it could be supposed to have, must be grounded on its having lasted till now, when so many other things which came down from the same odious source have been done away with. And this, indeed, is what makes it strange to ordinary ears, to hear it asserted that the inequality of rights between men and women has no other source than the law of the strongest. . . .

Some will object, that a comparison cannot fairly be made between the government of the male sex and the forms of unjust power which I have adduced in illustration of it, since these are arbitrary, and the effect of mere usurpation, while it on the contrary is natural. But was there ever any domination which did not appear natural to those who possessed it? There was a time when the division of mankind into two classes, a small one of masters and numerous one of slaves, appeared, even to the most cultivated minds, to be a natural, and the only natural, condition of the human race. No less an intellect, and one which contributed no less to the progress of human thought, than Aristotle, held this opinion without doubt or misgiving; and rested it on the same premises on which the same assertion in regard to the dominion of men over women is usually based, namely that there are different natures among mankind, free natures, and slave natures; that the Greeks were of a free nature, the barbarian races of Thracians and Asiatics of a slave nature. But why need I go back to Aristotle? Did not the slaveowners of the Southern United States maintain the same doctrine, with all the fanaticism with which men cling to the theories that justify their passions and legitimate their personal interests? Did they not call heaven and earth to witness that the dominion of the white man over the black is natural, that the black race is by nature incapable of freedom, and marked out for slavery? some even going so far as to say that the freedom of manual labourers is an unnatural order of things anywhere. Again, the theorists of absolute monarchy have always affirmed it to be the only natural form of government; issuing from the patriarchal, which was the primitive and spontaneous form of society, framed on the model of the paternal, which is anterior to society itself, and, as they contend, the most natural authority of all. Nay, for that matter, the law of force itself, to those who could not plead any other, has always seemed the most natural of all grounds for the exercise of authority.

Conquering races hold it to be Nature's own dictate that the conquered should obey the conquerors, or, as they euphoniously paraphrase it, that the feebler and more unwarlike races should submit to the braver and manlier. The smallest acquaintance with human life in the middle ages, shows how supremely natural the dominion of the feudal nobility over men of low condition appeared to the nobility themselves, and how unnatural the conception seemed, of a person of the inferior class claiming equality with them, or exercising authority over them. It hardly seemed less so to the class held in subjection. The emancipated serfs and burgesses, even in their most vigorous struggles, never made any pretension to a share of authority; they only demanded more or less of limitation to the power of tyrannizing over them. So true is it that unnatural generally means only uncustomary, and that everything which is usual appears natural. The subjection of women to men being a universal custom, any departure from it quite naturally appears unnatural. But how entirely, even in this case, the feeling is dependent on custom, appears by ample experience. Nothing so much astonishes the people of distant parts of the world, when they first learn anything about England, as to be told that it is under a queen: the thing seems to them so unnatural as to be almost incredible. To Englishmen this does not seem in the least degree unnatural, because they are used to it; but they do feel in unnatural that women should be soldiers or members of Parliament. In the feudal ages, on the contrary, war and politics were not thought unnatural to women, because not unusual; it seemed natural that women of the privileged classes should be of manly character, inferior in nothing but bodily strength to their husbands and fathers. The independence of women seemed rather less unnatural to the Greeks than to other ancients, on account of the fabulous Amazons (whom they believed to be historical), and the partial example afforded by the Spartan women; who, though no less subordinate by law than in other Greek states, were more free in fact, and being trained to bodily exercises in the same manner with men, gave ample proof that they were not naturally disqualified for them. There can be little doubt that Spartan experience suggested to Plato, among many other of his doctrines, that of the social and political equality of the two sexes.

But, it will be said, the rule of men over women differs from all these others in not being a rule of force: it is accepted voluntarily; women make no complaint, and are consenting parties to it. In the first place, a great number of women do not accept it. Every since there have been women able to make their sentiments known by their writings (the only mode of publicity which society permits to them), an increasing number of them have recorded protests against their present social condition: and recently many thousands of them, headed by the most eminent women known to the public, have petitioned Parliament for their admission to the Parliamentary Suffrage.

The claim of women to be educated as solidly, and in the same branches of knowledge, as men, is urged with growing intensity, and with a great prospect of success; while the demand for their admission into professions and occupations hitherto closed against them, becomes every year more urgent. . . .

It must be remembered, also, that no enslaved class ever asked for complete liberty at once. When Simon de Montfort called the deputies of the commons to sit for the first time in Parliament, did any of them dream of demanding that an assembly, elected by their constituents, should make and destroy ministries, and dictate to the king in affairs of state? No such thought entered into the imagination of the most ambitious of them. The nobility had already these pretensions; the commons pretended to nothing but to be exempt from arbitrary taxation, and from the gross individual oppression of the king's officers. It is a political law of nature that those who are under any power of ancient origin, never begin by complaining of the power itself, but only of its oppressive exercise. There is never any want of women who complain of ill usage by their husbands. There would be infinitely more, if complaint were not the greatest of all provocatives to a repetition and increase of the ill usage. It is this which frustrates all attempts to maintain the power but protect the woman against its abuses. In no other case (except that of a child) is the person who has been proved judicially to have suffered an injury, replaced under the physical power of the culprit who inflicted it. Accordingly wives, even in the most extreme and protracted cases of bodily ill usage, hardly every dare avail themselves of the laws made for their protection: and if, in a moment of irrepressible indignation, or by the interference of neighbours, they are induced to do so, their whole effort afterwards is to disclose as little as they can, and to beg off their tyrant from his merited chastisement.

All causes, social and natural, combine to make it unlikely that women should be collectively rebellious to the power of men. They are so far in a position different from all other subject classes, that their masters require something more from them than actual service. Men do not want solely the obedience of women, they want their sentiments. All men, except the most brutish, desire to have, in the woman most nearly connected with them, not a forced slave but a willing one, not a slave merely, but a favourite. They have therefore put everything in practice to enslave their minds. The masters of all other slaves rely, for maintaining obedience, on fear; either fear of themselves, or religious fears. The masters of women wanted more than simple obedience, and they turned the whole force of education to effect their purpose. All women are brought up from the very earliest years in the belief that their ideal of character is the very opposite to that of men; not self-will, and government by self-control, but submission, and yielding to the control of others. All the moralities tell them that it is the duty of women, and all the current sentimentalities that it is their nature, to live for others; to make complete abnegation of themselves, and to have no life but in their affections. And by their affections are meant the only ones they are allowed to have—those to the men with whom they are connected, or to the children who constitute an additional and indefeasible tie between them and a man.

When we put together three things—first, the natural attraction between opposite sexes; secondly, the wife's entire dependence on the husband, every privilege or pleasure she has being either his gift, or depending entirely on his will; and lastly, that the principal object of human pursuit, consideration, and all objects of social ambition, can in general be sought or obtained by her only through him, it would be a miracle if the object of being attractive to men had not become the polar star of feminine education and formation of character. And, this great means of influence over the minds of women having been acquired, an instinct of selfishness made men avail themselves of it to the utmost as a means of holding women in subjection, by representing to them meekness, submissiveness, and resignation of all individual will into the hands of a man, as an essential part of sexual attractiveness. Can it be doubted that any of the other yokes which mankind have succeeded in breaking, would have subsisted till now if the same means had existed, and had been as sedulously used, to bow down their minds to it? If it had been made the object of the life of every young plebeian to find personal favour in the eyes of some patrician, of every young serf with some seigneur; if domestication with him, and a share of his personal affections, had been held out as the prize which they all should look out for, the most gifted and aspiring being able to reckon on the most desirable prizes; and if, when this prize had been obtained, they had been shut out by a wall of brass from all interests not centering in him, all feelings and desires but those which he shared or inculcated; would not serfs and seigneurs, plebeians and patricians, have been as broadly distinguished at this day as men and women are? and would not all but a thinker here and there, have believed the distinction to be a fundamental and unalterable fact in human nature? . . .

The least that can be demanded is, that the question should not be considered as prejudged by existing fact and existing opinion, but open to discussion on its merits, as a question of justice and expediency: the decision on this, as on any of the other social arrangements of mankind, depending on what an enlightened estimate of tendencies and consequences may show to be most advantageous to humanity in general, without distinction of sex. And the discussion must be a real discussion, descending to foundations, and not resting satisfied with vague and general assertions. It will not do, for instance, to assert in general terms, that the experience of mankind has pronounced in favour of the existing system. Experience cannot possibly have decided between two courses, so long as there has only been experience of one. If it be said that the doctrine of the equality of the sexes rests only on theory, it must be remembered that the contrary doctrine also has only theory to rest upon. All that is proved in its favour by direct experience, is that mankind have been able to exist under it, and to attain the degree of improvement and prosperity which we now see; but whether that prosperity has been attained sooner, or is now greater, than it would have been under the other system, experience does not say. . . .

Neither does it avail anything to say that the nature of the two sexes adapts them to their present functions and position, and renders these appropriate to them. Standing on the ground of common sense and the constitution of the human mind, I deny that any one knows, or can know, the nature of the two sexes, as long as they have only been seen in their present relation to one another. If men had ever been found in society without women, or women without men, or if there had been a society of men and women in which the women were not under the control of the men, something might have been positively known about the mental and moral differences which may be inherent in the nature of each. What is now called the nature of women is an eminently artificial thing—the result of forced repression in some directions, unnatural stimulation in others. It may be asserted without scruple, that no other class of dependents have had their character so entirely distorted from its natural proportions by their relation with their masters; for, if conquered and slave races have been, in some respects, more forcibly repressed, whatever in them has not been crushed down by an iron heel has generally been let alone, and if left with any liberty of development, it has developed itself according to its own laws; but in the case of women, a hot-house and stove cultivation has always been carried on of some of the capabilities of their nature, for the benefit and pleasure of their masters. . . .

Of all difficulties which impede the progress of thought, and the formation of well-grounded opinions on life and social arrangements, the greatest is now the unspeakable ignorance and inattention of mankind in respect to the influences which form human character. Whatever any portion of the human species now are, or seem to be, such, it is supposed, they have a natural tendency to be: even when the most elementary knowledge of the circumstances in which they have been placed, clearly points out the causes that made them what they are. Because a cottier deeply in arrears to his landlord is not industrious, there are people who think that the Irish are naturally idle. Because constitutions can be overthrown when the authorities appointed to execute them turn their arms against them, there are people who think the French incapable of free government. Because the Greeks cheated the Turks, and the Turks only plundered the Greeks, there are persons who think that the Turks are naturally more sincere: and because women, as is often said, care nothing about politics except their personalities, it is supposed that the general good is naturally less interesting to women than to men. History, which is now so much better understood than formerly, teaches another lesson: if only by showing the extraordinary susceptibility of human nature to external influences, and the extreme variableness of those of its manifestations which are supposed to be most universal and uniform. But in history, as in travelling, men usually see only what they already had in their own minds; and few learn much from history, who do not bring much with them to its study.

Hence, in regard to that most difficult question, what are the natural differences between the two sexes—a subject on which it is impossible in the present state of society to obtain complete and correct knowledge—while almost everybody dogmatizes upon it, almost all neglect and make light of the only means by which any partial insight can be obtained into it. This is, an analytic study of the most important department of psychology, the laws of the influence of circumstances on character. For, however great and apparently ineradicable the moral and intellectual differences between men and women might be, the evidence of their being natural differences could only be negative. Those only could be inferred to be natural which could not possibly be artificial—the residuum, after deducting every characteristic of either sex which can admit of being explained from education or external circumstances. The profoundest knowledge of the laws of the formation of character is indispensable to entitle any one to affirm even that there is any difference, much more what the difference is, between the two sexes considered as moral and rational beings; and since no one, as yet, has that knowledge, (for there is hardly any subject which, in proportion to its importance, has been so little studied), no one is thus far entitled to any positive opinion on the subject. Conjectures are all that can at present be made; conjectures more or less probable, according as more or less authorized by such knowledge as we yet have of the laws of psychology, as applied to the formation of character.

Even the preliminary knowledge, what the differences between the sexes now are, apart from all question as to how they are made what they are, is still in the crudest and most incomplete state. Medical practitioners and physiologists have ascertained, to some extent, the differences in bodily constitution; and this is an important element to the psychologist: but hardly any medical practitioner is a psychologist. Respecting the mental characteristics of women; their observations are of no more worth than those of common men. It is a subject on which nothing final can be known, so long as those who alone can really know it, women themselves, have given but little testimony, and that little, mostly suborned. It is easy to know stupid women. Stupidity is much the same all the world over. A stupid person's notions and feelings may confidently be inferred from those which prevail in the circle by which the person is surrounded. Not so with those whose opinions and feelings are an emanation from their own nature and faculties. It is only a man here and there who has any tolerable knowledge of the character even of the women of his own family. I do not mean, of their capabilities; these nobody knows, not even themselves, because most of them have never been called out. I mean their actually existing thoughts and feelings. Many a man thinks he perfectly understands women, because he has had amatory relations with several, perhaps with many of them. If he is a good observer, and his experience extends to quality as well as quantity, he may have learnt something of one narrow department of their nature—an important department, no doubt. But of all the rest of it, few persons are generally more ignorant, because there are few from whom it is so carefully hidden. The most favourable case which a man can generally have for studying the character of a woman, is that of his own wife: for the opportunities are greater, and the cases of complete sympathy not so unspeakably rare. And in fact, this is the source from which any knowledge worth having on the subject has, I believe, generally come. But most men have not had the opportunity of studying in this way more than a single case: accordingly one can, to an almost laughable degree, infer what a man's wife is like, from his opinions about women in general. To make even this one case yield any result, the woman must be worth knowing, and the man not only a competent judge, but of a character so sympathetic in itself, and so well adapted to hers, that he can either read her mind by sympathetic intuition, or has nothing in himself which makes her shy of disclosing it.

Hardly anything, I believe, can be more rare than this conjunction. It often happens that there is the most complete unity of feeling and community of interests as to all external things, yet the one has as little admission into the internal life of the other as if they were common acquaintance. Even with true affection, authority on the one side and subordination on the other prevent perfect confidence. Though nothing may be intentionally withheld, much is not shown. In the analogous relation of parent and child, the corresponding phenomenon must have been in the observation of every one. As between father and son, how many are the cases in which the father, in spite of real affection on both sides, obviously to all the world does not know, nor suspect, parts of the son's character familiar to his companions and equals. The truth is, that the position of looking up to another is extremely unpropitious to complete sincerity and openness with him. The fear of losing ground in his opinion or in his feelings is so strong, that even in an upright character, there is an unconscious tendency to show only the best side, or the side which, though not the best, is that which he most likes to see: and it may be confidently said that thorough knowledge of one another hardly ever exists, but between persons who, besides being intimates, are equals. How much more true, then, must all this be, when the one is not only under the authority of the others, but has it inculcated on her as a duty to reckon everything else subordinate to his comfort and pleasure, and to let him neither see nor feel anything coming from her, except what is agreeable to him. All these difficulties stand in the way of a man's obtaining any thorough knowledge even of the one woman whom alone, in general, he has sufficient opportunity of studying. When we further consider that to understand one woman is not necessarily to understand any other woman; that even if he could study many women of one rank, or of one country, he would not thereby understand women of other ranks or countries; and even if he did, they are still only the women of a single period of history; we may safely assert that the knowledge which men can acquire of women, even as they have been and are, without reference to what they might be, is wretchedly imperfect and superficial, and always will be so, until women themselves have told all that they have to tell.

And this time has not come; nor will it come otherwise than gradually. It is but of yesterday that women have either been qualified by literary accomplishments, or permitted by society, to tell anything to the general public. As yet very few of them dare tell anything, which men, on whom their literary success depends, are unwilling to hear. Let us remember in what manner, up to a very recent time, the expression, even by a male author, of uncustomary opinions, or what are deemed eccentric feelings, usually was, and in some degree still is, received; and we may form some faint conception under what impediments a woman, who is brought up to think custom and opinion her sovereign rule, attempts to express in books anything drawn from the depths of her own nature. . . . The greater part of what women write about women is mere sycophancy to men. In the case of unmarried women, much of it seems only intended to increase their chance of a husband. Many, both married and unmarried, overstep the mark, and inculcate a servility beyond what is desired or relished by any man, except the very vulgarest. But this is not so often the case as, even at a quite late period, it still was. Literary women are becoming more freespoken, and more willing to express their real sentiments. Unfortunately, in this country especially, they are themselves such artificial products, that their sentiments are compounded of a small element of individual observation and consciousness, and a very large one of acquired associations. This will be less and less the case, but it will remain true to a great extent, as long as social institutions do not admit the same free development of originality in women which is possible to men. When that time comes, and not before, we shall see, and not merely hear, as much as it is necessary to know of the nature of women, and the adaptation of other things to it. . . .

One thing we may be certain of—that what is contrary to women's nature to do, they never will be made to do by simply giving their nature free play. The anxiety of mankind to interfere in behalf of nature, for fear lest nature should not succeed in effecting its purpose, is an altogether unnecessary solicitude. What women by nature cannot do, it is quite superfluous to forbid them from doing. What they can do, but not so well as the men who are their competitors, competition suffices to exclude them from; since nobody asks for protective duties and bounties in favour of women; it is only asked that the present bounties and protective duties in favour of men should be recalled. If women have a greater natural inclination for some things than for others, there is no need of laws or social inculcation to make the majority of them do the former in preference to the latter. Whatever women's services are most wanted for, the free play of competition will hold out the strongest inducements to them to undertake. And, as the words imply, they are most wanted for the things for which they are most fit; by the apportionment of which to them, the collective faculties of the two sexes can be applied on the whole with the greatest sum of valuable result.

The general opinion of men is supposed to be, that the natural vocation of a woman is that of a wife and mother. I say, is supposed to be, because, judging from acts—from the whole of the present constitution of society—one might infer that their opinion was the direct contrary. They might be supposed to think that the alleged natural vocation of women was of all things the most repugnant to their nature; insomuch that if they are free to do anything else—if any other means of living, or occupation of their time and faculties, is open, which has any chance of appearing desirable to them—there will not be enough of them who will be willing to accept the condition said to be natural to them. If this is the real opinion of men in general, it would be well that it should be spoken out. I should like to hear somebody openly enunciating the doctrine (it is already implied in much that is written on the subject)—"It is necessary to society that women should marry and produce children. They will not do so unless they are compelled. Therefore it is necessary to compel them." The merits of the case would then be clearly defined. It would be exactly that of the slaveholders of South Carolina and Louisiana. "It is necessary that cotton and sugar should be grown. White men cannot produce them. Negroes will not, for any wages which we choose to give. Ergo they must be compelled." An illustration still closer to the point is that of impressment. Sailors must absolutely be had to defend the country. It often happens that they will not voluntarily enlist. Therefore there must be the power of forcing them. How often has this logic been used! and, but for one flaw in it, without doubt it would have been successful up to this day. But it is open to the retort—First pay the sailors the honest value of their labour. When you have made it as well worth their while to serve you, as to work for other employers, you will have no more difficulty than others have in obtaining their services. To this there is no logical answer except "I will not:" and as people are now not only ashamed, but are not desirous, to rob the labourer of his hire, impressment is no longer advocated. Those who attempt to force women into marriage by closing all other doors against them, lay themselves open to a similar retort. If they mean what they say, their opinion must evidently be, that men do not render the married condition so desirable to women, as to induce them to accept it for its own recommendations. It is not a sign of one's thinking the boon one offers very attractive, when one allows only Hobson's choice, "that or none." . . . .

CHAPTER III

On the other point which is involved in the just equality of women, their admissibility to all the functions and occupations hitherto retained as the monopoly of the stronger sex. . . . I believe that their disabilities elsewhere are only clung to in order to maintain their subordination in domestic life; because the generality of the male sex cannot yet tolerate the idea of living with an equal. Were it not for that, I think that almost every one, in the existing state of opinion in politics and political economy, would admit the injustice of excluding half the human race from the greater number of lucrative occupations, and from almost all high social functions; ordaining from their birth either that they are not, and cannot by any possibility become, fit for employments which are legally open to the stupidest and basest of the other sex, or else that however fit they may be, those employments shall be interdicted to them, in order to be preserved for the exclusive benefit of males. In the last two centuries, when (which was seldom the case) any reason beyond the mere existence of the fact was thought to be required to justify the disabilities of women, people seldom assigned as a reason their inferior mental capacity; which, in times when there was a real trial of personal faculties (from which all women were not excluded) in the struggles of public life, no one really believed in. The reason given in those days was not women's unfitness, but the interest of society, by which was meant the interest of men: just as the raison d'etat, meaning the convenience of the government, and the support of existing authority, was deemed a sufficient explanation and excuse for the most flagitious crimes. In the present day, power holds a smoother language, and whomsoever it oppresses, always pretends to do so for their own good: accordingly, when anything is forbidden to women, it is thought necessary to say, and desirable to believe, that they are incapable of doing it, and that they depart from their real path of success and happiness when they aspire to it. But to make this reason plausible (I do not say valid), those by whom it is urged must be prepared to carry it to a much greater length than any one ventures to do in the face of present experience.

It is not sufficient to maintain that women on the average are less gifted than men on the average, with certain of the higher mental faculties, or that a smaller number of women than of men are fit for occupations and functions of the highest intellectual character. It is necessary to maintain that no women at all are fit for them, and that the most eminent women are inferior in mental faculties to the most mediocre of the men on whom those functions at present devolve. For if the performance of the function is decided either by competition, or by any mode of choice which secures regard to the public interest, there needs be no apprehension that any important employments will fall into the hands of women inferior to average men, or to the average of their male competitors. The only result would be that there would be fewer women than men in such employments; a result certain to happen in any case, if only from the preference always likely to be felt by the majority of women for the one vocation in which there is nobody to compete with them. Now, the most determined depreciator of women will not venture to deny, that when we add the experience of recent times to that of ages past, women, and not a few merely, but many women, have proved themselves capable of everything, perhaps without a single exception, which is done by men, and of doing it successfully and creditably. The utmost that can be said is, that there are many things which none of them have succeeded in doing as well as they have been done by some men—many in which they have not reached the very highest rank. But there are extremely few, dependent only on mental faculties, in which they have not attained the rank next to the highest. Is not this enough, and much more than enough, to make it a tyranny to them, and a detriment to society, that they should not be allowed to compete with men for the exercise of these functions? Is it not a mere truism to say, that such functions are often filled by men far less fit for them than numbers of women, and who would be beaten by women in any fair field of competition? What difference does it make that there may be men somewhere, fully employed about other things, who may be still better qualified for the things in question than these women? Does not this take place in all competitions? Is there so great a superfluity of men fit for high duties, that society can afford to reject the service of any competent person? Are we so certain of always finding a man made to our hands for any duty or function of social importance which falls vacant, that we lose nothing by putting a ban upon one-half of mankind, and refusing beforehand to make their faculties available, however distinguished they may be? And even if we could do without them, would it be consistent with justice to refuse to them their fair share of honour and distinction, or to deny to them the equal moral right of all human beings to choose their occupation (short of injury to others) according to their own preferences, at their own risk? Nor is the injustice confined to them: it is shared by those who are in a position to benefit by their services. To ordain that any kind of persons shall not be physicians, or shall not be advocates, or shall not be members of parliament, is to injure not them only, but all who employ physicians or advocates or elect members of parliament, and who are deprived of the stimulating effect of greater competition on the exertions of the competitors, as well as restricted to a narrower range of individual choice.

It will perhaps be sufficient if I confine myself, in the details of my argument, to functions of a public nature: since, if I am successful as to those, it probably will be readily granted that women should be admissible to all other occupations to which it is at all material whether they are admitted or not. . . .

With regard to the fitness of women, not only to participate in elections, but themselves to hold offices or practise professions involving important public responsibilities; I have already observed that this consideration is not essential to the practical question in dispute: since any woman, who succeeds in an open profession, proves by that very fact that she is qualified for it. And in the case of public offices, if the political system of the country is such as to exclude unfit men, it will equally exclude unfit women: while if it is not, there is no additional evil in the fact that the unfit persons whom it admits may be either women or men. As long therefore as it is acknowledged that even a few women may be fit for these duties, the laws which shut the door on those exceptions cannot be justified by any opinion which can be held respecting the capacities of women in general. But, though this last consideration is not essential, it is far from being irrelevant. An unprejudiced view of it gives additional strength to the arguments against the disabilities of women, and reinforces them by high considerations of practical utility.

Let us at first make entire abstraction to all psychological considerations tending to show, that any of the mental differences supposed to exist between women and men are but the natural effect of the differences in their education and circumstances, and indicate no radical difference, far less radical inferiority, of nature. Let us consider women only as they already are, or as they are known to have been; and the capacities which they have already practically shown. What they have done, that at least, if nothing else, it is proved that they can do. When we consider how sedulously they are all trained away from, instead of being trained towards, any of the occupations or objects reserved for men, it is evident that I am taking a very humble ground for them, when I rest their case on what they have actually achieved. For, in this case, negative evidence is worth little, while any positive evidence is conclusive. It cannot be inferred to be impossible that a woman should be a Homer, or an Aristotle, or a Michael Angelo, or a Beethoven, because no woman has yet actually produced works comparable to theirs in any of those lines of excellence. This negative fact at most leaves the question uncertain, and open to psychological discussion. But it is quite certain that a woman can be a Queen Elizabeth, or a Deborah, or a Joan of Arc, since this is not inference, but fact. Now it is a curious consideration, that the only things which the existing law excludes women from doing, are the things which they have proved that they are able to do. There is no law to prevent a woman from having written all the plays of Shakspeare, or composed all the operas of Mozart. But Queen Elizabeth or Queen Victoria, had they not inherited the throne, could not have been intrusted with the smallest of the political duties, of which the former showed herself equal to the greatest.

If anything conclusive could be inferred from experience, without psychological analysis, it would be that the things which women are not allowed to do are the very ones for which they are peculiarly qualified; since their vocation for government has made its way, and become conspicuous, through the very few opportunities which have been given; while in the lines of distinction which apparently were freely open to them, they have by no means so eminently distinguished themselves. We know how small a number of reigning queens history presents, in comparison with that of kings. Of this smaller number a far larger proportion have shown talents for rule; though many of them have occupied the throne in difficult periods. It is remarkable, too, that they have, in a great number of instances, been distinguished by merits the most opposite to the imaginary and conventional character of women: they have been as much remarked for the firmness and vigour of their rule, as for its intelligence. When, to queens and empresses, we add regents, and viceroys of provinces, the list of women who have been eminent rulers of mankind swells to a great length. This fact is so undeniable, that some one, long ago, tried to retort the argument, and turned the admitted truth into an additional insult, by saying that queens are better than kings, because under kings women govern, but under queens, men.

It may seem a waste of reasoning to argue against a bad joke; but such things do affect people's minds; and I have heard men quote this saying, with an air as if they thought that there was something in it. At any rate, it will serve as well as anything else for a starting point in discussion. I say, then, that it is not true that under kings, women govern. Such cases are entirely exceptional: and weak kings have quite as often governed ill through the influence of male favourites, as of female. When a king is governed by a woman merely through his amatory propensities, good government is not probable, though even then there are exceptions. But French history counts two kings who have voluntarily given the direction of affairs during many years, the one to his mother, the other to his sister: one of them, Charles VIII., was a mere boy, but in doing so he followed the intentions of his father Louis XI., the ablest monarch of his age. The other, Saint Louis, was the best, and one of the most vigorous rulers, since the time of Charlemagne. Both these princesses ruled in a manner hardly equalled by any prince among their contemporaries. The emperor Charles V., the most politic prince of his time, who had as great a number of able men in his service as a ruler ever had, and was one of the least likely of all sovereigns to sacrifice his interest to personal feelings, made two princesses of his family successively Governors of the Netherlands, and kept one or other of them in that post during his whole life, (they were afterwards succeeded by a third). Both ruled very successfully, and one of them, Margaret of Austria, was one of the ablest politicians of the age. So much for one side of the question. Now as to the other. When it is said that under queens men govern, is the same meaning to be understood as when kings are said to be governed by women? Is it meant that queens choose as their instruments of government, the associates of their personal pleasures? The case is rare even with those who are as unscrupulous on the latter point as Catherine II.: and it is not in these cases that the good government, alleged to arise from male influence, is to be found. If it be true, then, that the administration is in the hands of better men under a queen than under an average king, it must be that queens have a superior capacity for choosing them; and women must be better qualified than men both for the position of sovereign, and for that of chief minister; for the principal business of a prime minister is not to govern in person, but to find the fittest persons to conduct every department of public affairs. The more rapid insight into character, which is one of the admitted points of superiority in women over men, must certainly make them, with anything like parity of qualifications in other respects, more apt than men in that choice of instruments, which is nearly the most important business of every one who has to do with governing mankind. Even the unprincipled Catherine de' Medici could feel the value of a Chancellor de l'Hopital. But it is also true that most great queens have been great by their own talents for government, and have been well served precisely for that reason. They retained the supreme direction of affairs in their own hands: and if they listened to good advisers, they gave by that fact the strongest proof that their judgment fitted them for dealing with the great questions of government.

Is it reasonable to think that those who are fit for the greater functions of politics, are incapable of qualifying themselves for the less? Is there any reason in the nature of things, that the wives and sisters of princes should, whenever called on, be found as competent as the princes themselves to their business, but that the wives and sisters of statesmen, and administrators, and directors of companies, and managers of public institutions, should be unable to do what is done by their brothers and husbands? The real reason is plain enough; it is that princesses, being more raised above the generality of men by their rank than placed below them by their sex, have never been taught that it was improper for them to concern themselves with politics; but have been allowed to feel the liberal interest natural to any cultivated human being, in the great transactions which took place around them, and in which they might be called on to take a part. The ladies of reigning families are the only women who are allowed the same range of interests and freedom of development as men; and it is precisely in their case that there is not found to be any inferiority. Exactly where and in proportion as women's capacities for government have been tried, in that proportion have they been found adequate.

This fact is in accordance with the best general conclusions which the world's imperfect experience seems as yet to suggest, concerning the peculiar tendencies and aptitudes characteristic of women, as women have hitherto been. I do not say, as they will continue to be; for, as I have already said more than once, I consider it presumption in any one to pretend to decide what women are or are not, can or cannot be, by natural constitution. They have always hitherto been kept, as far as regards spontaneous development, in so unnatural a state, that their nature cannot but have been greatly distorted and disguised; and no one can safely pronounce that if women's nature were left to choose its direction as freely as men's, and if no artificial bent were attempted to be given to it except that required by the conditions of human society, and given to both sexes alike, there would be any material difference, or perhaps any difference at all, in the character and capacities which would unfold themselves. I shall presently show, that even the least contestable of the differences which now exist, are such as may very well have been produced merely by circumstances, without any difference of natural capacity. But, looking at women as they are known in experience, it may be said of them, with more truth than belongs to most other generalizations on the subject, that the general bent of their talents is towards the practical. This statement is conformable to all the public history of women, in the present and the past. It is no less borne out by common and daily experience. Let us consider the special nature of the mental capacities most characteristic of a woman of talent. They are all of a kind which fits them for practice, and makes them tend towards it. What is meant by a woman's capacity of intuitive perception? It means, a rapid and correct insight into present fact. It has nothing to do with general principles. Nobody ever perceived a scientific law of nature by intuition, nor arrived at a general rule of duty or prudence by it. These are results of slow and careful collection and comparison of experience; and neither the men nor the women of intuition usually shine in this department, unless, indeed, the experience necessary is such as they can acquire by themselves. For what is called their intuitive sagacity makes them peculiarly apt in gathering such general truths as can be collected from their individual means of observation. When, consequently, they chance to be as well provided as men are with the results of other people's experience, by reading and education (I use the word chance advisedly, for, in respect to the knowledge that tends to fit them for the greater concerns of life, the only educated women are the self-educated), they are better furnished than men in general with the essential requisites of skillful and successful practice. Men who have been much taught, are apt to be deficient in the sense of present fact; they do not see, in the facts which they are called upon to deal with, what is really there, but what they have been taught to expect. This is seldom the case with women of any ability. Their capacity of "intuition" preserves them from it. With equality of experience and of general faculties, a woman usually sees much more than a man of what is immediately before her. Now this sensibility to the present, is the main quality on which the capacity for practice, as distinguished from theory, depends. To discover general principles, belongs to the speculative faculty: to discern and discriminate the particular cases in which they are and are not applicable, constitutes practical talent: and for this, women as they now are have a peculiar aptitude. I admit that there can be no good practice without principles, and that the predominant place which quickness of observation holds among a woman's faculties, makes her particularly apt to build over-hasty generalizations upon her own observation; though at the same time no less ready in rectifying those generalizations, as her observation takes a wider range. But the corrective to this defect, is access to the experience of the human race; general knowledge—exactly the thing which education can best supply. A woman's mistakes are specifically those of a clever self-educated man, who often sees what men trained in routine do not see, but falls into errors for want of knowing things which have long been known. Of course he has acquired much of the pre-existing knowledge, or he could not have got on at all; but what he knows of it he has picked up in fragments and at random, as women do.

But this gravitation of women's minds to the present, to the real, to actual fact, while in its exclusiveness it is a source of errors, is also a most useful counteractive of the contrary error. The principal and most characteristic aberration of speculative minds as such, consists precisely in the deficiency of this lively perception and ever-present sense of objective fact. For want of this, they often not only overlook the contradiction which outward facts oppose to their theories, but lose sight of the legitimate purpose of speculation altogether, and let their speculative faculties go astray into regions not peopled with real beings, animate or inanimate, even idealized, but with personified shadows created by the illusions of metaphysics or by the mere entanglement of words, and think these shadows the proper objects of the highest, the most transcendent, philosophy. Hardly anything can be of greater value to a man of theory and speculation who employs himself not in collecting materials of knowledge by observation, but in working them up by processes of thought into comprehensive truths of science and laws of conduct, than to carry on his speculations in the companionship, and under the criticism, of a really superior woman. There is nothing comparable to it for keeping his thoughts within the limits of real things, and the actual facts of nature. A woman seldom runs wild after an abstraction. The habitual direction of her mind to dealing with things as individuals rather than in groups, and (what is closely connected with it) her more lively interest in the present feelings of persons, which makes her consider first of all, in anything which claims to be applied to practice, in what manner persons will be affected by it—these two things make her extremely unlikely to put faith in any speculation which loses sight of individuals, and deals with things as if they existed for the benefit of some imaginary entity, some mere creation of the mind, not resolvable into the feelings of living beings. Women's thoughts are thus as useful in giving reality to those of thinking men, as men's thoughts in giving width and largeness to those of women. In depth, as distinguished from breadth, I greatly doubt if even now, women, compared with men, are at any disadvantage. . . .

CHAPTER IV

He who would rightly appreciate the worth of personal independence as an element of happiness, should consider the value he himself puts upon it as an ingredient of his own. There is no subject on which there is a greater habitual difference of judgment between a man judging for himself, and the same man judging for other people. When he hears others complaining that they are not allowed freedom of action—that their own will has not sufficient influence in the regulation of their affairs—his inclination is, to ask, what are their grievances? what positive damage they sustain? and in what respect they consider their affairs to be mismanaged? and if they fail to make out, in answer to these questions, what appears to him a sufficient case, he turns a deaf ear, and regards their complaint as the fanciful querulousness of people whom nothing reasonable will satisfy. But he has a quite different standard of judgment when he is deciding for himself. Then, the most unexceptionable administration of his interests by a tutor set over him, does not satisfy his feelings: his personal exclusion from the deciding authority appears itself the greatest grievance of all, rendering it superfluous even to enter into the question of mismanagement. It is the same with nations. What citizen of a free country would listen to any offers of good and skillful administration, in return for the abdication of freedom? Even if he could believe that good and skillful administration can exist among a people ruled by a will not their own, would not the consciousness of working out their own destiny under their own moral responsibility be a compensation to his feelings for great rudeness and imperfection in the details of public affairs? Let him rest assured that whatever he feels on this point, women feel in a fully equal degree. Whatever has been said or written, from the time of Herodotus to the present, of the ennobling influence of free government—the nerve and spring which it gives to all the faculties, the larger and higher objects which it presents to the intellect and feelings, the more unselfish public spirit, and calmer and broader views of duty, that it engenders, and the generally loftier platform on which it elevates the individual as a moral, spiritual, and social being—is every particle as true of women as of men. Are these things no important part of individual happiness? Let any man call to mind what he himself felt on emerging from boyhood—from the tutelage and control of even loved and affectionate elders—and entering upon the responsibilities of manhood. Was it not like the physical effect of taking off a heavy weight, or releasing him from obstructive, even if not otherwise painful, bonds? Did he not feel twice as much alive, twice as much a human being, as before? And does he imagine that women have none of these feelings? But it is a striking fact, that the satisfactions and mortifications of personal pride, though all in all to most men when the case is their own, have less allowance made for them in the case of other people, and are less listened to as a ground or a justification of conduct, than any other natural human feelings; perhaps because men compliment them in their own case with the names of so many other qualities, that they are seldom conscious how mighty an influence these feelings exercise in their own lives. No less large and powerful is their part, we may assure ourselves, in the lives and feelings of women. Women are schooled into suppressing them in their most natural and most healthy direction, but the internal principle remains, in a different outward form. An active and energetic mind, if denied liberty, will seek for power: refused the command of itself, it will assert its personality by attempting to control others. To allow to any human beings no existence of their own but what depends on others, is giving far too high a premium on bending others to their purposes. Where liberty cannot be hoped for, and power can, power becomes the grand object of human desire; those to whom others will not leave the undisturbed management of their own affairs, will compensate themselves, if they can, by meddling for their own purposes with the affairs of others. Hence also women's passion for personal beauty, and dress and display; and all the evils that flow from it, in the way of mischievous luxury and social immorality. The love of power and the love of liberty are in eternal antagonism. Where there is least liberty, the passion for power is the most ardent and unscrupulous. The desire of power over others can only cease to be a depraving agency among mankind, when each of them individually is able to do without it: which can only be where respect for liberty in the personal concerns of each is an established principle.

But it is not only through the sentiment of personal dignity, that the free direction and disposal of their own faculties is a source of individual happiness, and to be fettered and restricted in it, a source of unhappiness, to human beings, and not least to women. There is nothing, after disease, indigence, and guilt, so fatal to the pleasurable enjoyment of life as the want of a worthy outlet for the active faculties. Women who have the cares of a family, and while they have the cares of a family, have this outlet, and it generally suffices for them: but what of the greatly increasing number of women, who have had no opportunity of exercising the vocation which they are mocked by telling them is their proper one? What of the women whose children have been lost to them by death or distance, or have grown up, married, and formed homes of their own? There are abundant examples of men who, after a life engrossed by business, retire with a competency to the enjoyment, as they hope, of rest, but to whom, as they are unable to acquire new interests and excitements that can replace the old, the change to a life of inactivity brings ennui, melancholy, and premature death. Yet no one thinks of the parallel case of so many worthy and devoted women, who, having paid that they are told is their debt to society—having brought up a family blamelessly to manhood and womanhood—having kept a house as long as they had a house needing to be kept—are deserted by the sole occupation for which they have fitted themselves; and remain with undiminished activity but with no employment for it, unless perhaps a daughter or daughter-in-law is willing to abdicate in their favour the discharge of the same functions in her younger household. Surely a hard lot for the old age of those who have worthily discharged, as long as it was given to them to discharge, what the world accounts their only social duty. Of such women, and of those others to whom this duty has not been committed at all—many of whom pine through life with the consciousness of thwarted vocations, and activities which are not suffered to expand—the only resources, speaking generally, are religion and charity. But their religion, though it may be one of feeling, and of ceremonial observance, cannot be a religion of action, unless in the form of charity. For charity many of them are by nature admirably fitted; but to practise it usefully, or even without doing mischief, requires the education, the manifold preparation, the knowledge and the thinking powers, of a skillful administrator. There are few of the administrative functions of government for which a person would not be fit, who is fit to bestow charity usefully. In this as in other cases (pre-eminently in that of the education of children), the duties permitted to women cannot be performed properly, without their being trained for duties which, to the great loss of society, are not permitted to them. And here let me notice the singular way in which the question of women's disabilities is frequently presented to view, by those who find it easier to draw a ludicrous picture of what they do not like, than to answer the arguments for it. When it is suggested that women's executive capacities and prudent counsels might sometimes be found valuable in affairs of state, these lovers of fun hold up to the ridicule of the world, as sitting in parliament or in the cabinet, girls in their teens, or young wives of two or three and twenty, transported bodily, exactly as they are, from the drawing-room to the House of Commons. They forget that males are not usually selected at this early age for a seat in Parliament, or for responsible political functions. Common sense would tell them that if such trusts were confided to women, it would be to such as having no special vocation for married life, or preferring another employment of their faculties (as many women even now prefer to marriage some of the few honorable occupations within their reach), have spent the best years of their youth in attempting to qualify themselves for the pursuits in which they desire to engage; or still more frequently perhaps, widows or wives of forty or fifty, by whom the knowledge of life and faculty of government which they have acquired in their families, could by the aid of appropriate studies be made available on a less contracted scale. There is no country of Europe in which the ablest men have not frequently experienced, and keenly appreciated, the value of the advice and help of clever and experienced women of the world, in the attainment both of private and of public objects; and there are important matters of public administration to which few men are equally competent with such women; among others, the detailed control of expenditure. But what we are now discussing is not the need which society has of the services of women in public business, but the full and hopeless life to which it so often condemns them, by forbidding then to exercise the practical abilities which many of them are conscious of, in any wider field than one which to some of them never was, and to others is no longer, open. If there is anything vitally important to the happiness of human beings, it is that they should relish their habitual pursuit. This requisite of an enjoyable life is very imperfectly granted, or altogether denied, to a large part of mankind; and by its absence many a life is a failure, which is provided, in appearance, with every requisite of success. But if circumstances which society is not yet skillful enough to overcome, render such failures often for the present inevitable, society need not itself inflict them. The injudiciousness of parents, a youth's own inexperience, or the absence of external opportunities for the congenial vocation, and their presence for an uncongenial, condemn numbers of men to pass their lives in doing one thing reluctantly and ill, when there are other things which they could have done well and happily. But on women this sentence is imposed by actual law, and by customs equivalent to law. What, in unenlightened societies, colour, race, religion, or in the case of a conquered country, nationality, are to some men, sex is to all women; a peremptory exclusion from almost all honorable occupations, but either such as cannot be fulfilled by others, or such as those others do not think worthy of their acceptance. Sufferings arising from causes of this nature usually meet with so little sympathy, that few persons are aware of the great amount of unhappiness even now produced by the feeling of a wasted life. The case will be even more frequent, as increased cultivation creates a greater and greater disproportion between the ideas and faculties of women, and the scope which society allows to their activity.

When we consider the positive evil caused to the disqualified half of the human race by their disqualification—first in the loss of the most inspiriting and elevating kind of personal enjoyment, and next in the weariness, disappointment, and profound dissatisfaction with life, which are so often the substitute for it; one feels that among all the lessons which men require for carrying on the struggle against the inevitable imperfections of their lot on earth, there is no lesson which they more need, than not to add to the evils which nature inflicts, by their jealous and prejudiced restrictions on one another. Their vain fears only substitute other and worse evils for those which they are idly apprehensive of: while every restraint on the freedom of conduct of any of their human fellow creatures (otherwise than by making them responsible for any evil actually caused by it), dries up pro tanto the principal fountain of human happiness, and leaves the species less rich, to an inappreciable degree, in all that makes life valuable to the individual human being.

Chapter 29

KARL MARX

Karl Marx (1818–1883) was born in Trier, Germany, and, although a Lutheran, was educated in Catholic schools and at the University of Berlin, where he received his doctorate at the age of twenty-three. At the university he fell under the influence of Hegel's thought and became a Hegelian. He accepted Hegel's triadic or dialectical method, seeing history as a process of overcoming opposition and, at the same time, being reconciled to it, incorporating it within its being. Soon, however, we became dissatisfied with Hegel's spiritualism and opted for a more materialist and economic interpretation of history, but the same dialectical method, the same determinism, the same inevitability would characterize his historical materialism that characterized Hegel's system.

Marx began his career in 1842 as a journalist for the liberal *Rheinische Zeitung*. He soon distinguished himself as a brilliant and radical thinker. He was described as follows: "He combines the deepest philosophical seriousness with the most biting wit. Imagine Rousseau, Voltaire, Holbach, Lessing, Heine, and Hegel fused into one person—I say fused, not juxtaposed—and you have Dr. Marx."[1] The next year he married Jenny von Westphalen. He soon began to be involved in radical politics, and was forced to emigrate to London. In England he was supported by his lifelong friend Friedrich Engels (1820–1895). Marx worked as a journalist but otherwise spent his time studying in the British Museum. He became a leader of the Communist International Working Men's Association. He played the dominant role in founding the Marxist movement. His principal works are *Economic and Philosophical Manuscripts of 1844, The Communist Manifesto* (with Friedrich Engels, 1848), and *Capital,* 3 vols., 1867, 1885, 1895. He died in 1883.

Marx wrote as a young man, "Hitherto, the various philosophies have only interpreted the world in various ways; the point is to change it." The message of our selections embodies that thesis. It combines socioeconomic analysis of the class struggle with a plan of action for overthrowing the existing oppressive conditions. Under capitalism the worker (proletariat) is a wage-slave, exploited by the capitalist, for the worker creates value for the capitalist who robs him of part of his labor. For example, suppose a chair takes an average of ten hours to make. Because the capitalist owns the shop and tools, the proletariat must sell his labor to him. So the proletariat gets paid for only half his labor (for five hours work on the chair) and the capitalist gets the rest, three hours worth to pay for the equipment and two hours in sheer profit. Without the profit motive, the driving force of capitalism, the capitalist would not invest in the chair-making business. Getting only half his value, the proletariat is robbed, and because he has no other option in an industrial society, he in effect becomes a wage-slave. He becomes alienated from his work.

Marx argues that the struggle between classes is the essential catalyst of historical change, but whereas in earlier times the structure of society was a complicated arrangement of hierarchical classes, in the present period of the bourgeoisie the social structure is developing toward a

1. (David McClellan's *Karl Marx* quoted in Viking Press, 1975, p. 3).

simple division of two classes: the bourgeoisie, owners of the means of production and the ruling class, and the proletariat, the worker-slaves. The proletariat are fast becoming self-conscious of their exploited state, and an international drama is unfolding in which they will create a violent revolution, throwing off their chains and, as new dictators, instantiating a new era of justice. "The Communists disdain to conceal their views and aims. They openly declare that their ends can be attained only by the forcible overthrow of all existing social conditions. Let the ruling classes tremble at a Communistic revolution. The proletariat have nothing to lose but their chains. They have a world to win. Working men of all countries, Unite!"

The result of the revolution will be a classless society in which everyone freely and equally participates, where the formula will be "from each according to his ability, to each according to his need," and "in which the free development of each is the condition for the free development of all."

The selections are from *Towards a Critique of Hegel's Philosophy of Right* (1843), the *Economic and Philosophical Manuscripts* (1843), and *The German Ideology* (1844).

FOR FURTHER READING

Acton, H. B. *The Illusion of the Epoch.* (Routledge & Kegan Paul, 1955).
Berlin, Isaiah. *Karl Marx: His Life and Environment.* (Oxford University Press, 1963).
Bottomore, Tom, ed. *Karl Marx: Early Writings.* (C. A. Watts, 1963).
Lichtheim, George. *Marxism: An Historical and Critical Study.* (Routledge & Kegan Paul, 1961).
Kolakowski, L. *Marxism and Beyond.* (London, 1968).
McLellan, David. *Karl Marx: His Life and Thought.* (Harper & Row, 1973).
Singer, Peter. *Marx.* (Oxford University Press, 1980).
Tucker, Robert, ed. *The Marx-Engels Reader.* (Norton, 1978).
Tucker, Robert. *Philosophy and Myth in Karl Marx.* (Cambridge University Press, 1967).
Wood, Alan. *Karl Marx.* (Routledge & Kegan Paul, 1981).

Towards a Critique of Hegel's Philosophy of Right

THE CRITIQUE OF RELIGION

As far as Germany is concerned, the criticism of religion is essentially complete, and the criticism of religion is the presupposition of all criticism.

The profane existence of error is compromised as soon as its heavenly *oratio pro aris et focis* [prayer for hearth and home] is refuted. Man has found in the imaginary reality of heaven where he looked for a superman only the reflection of his own self. He will therefore no longer be inclined to find only the appearance of himself, the non-man, where he seeks and must seek his true reality.

The foundation of irreligious criticism is this: man makes religion, religion does not make man. Religion is indeed the self-consciousness and self-awareness of man who either has not yet attained to himself or has already lost himself again. But man is no abstract being squatting outside the world. Man is the world of man, the state, society. This state, this society, produces religion's inverted attitude to the world, because they are an inverted world them-

Reprinted from *Karl Marx: Selected Writings*, edited by David McLellan (1977) by permission of Oxford University Press.

selves. Religion is the general theory of this world, its encyclopaedic compendium, its logic in popular form, its spiritual *point d'honneur,* its enthusiasm, its moral sanction, its solemn complement, its universal basis for consolation and justification. It is the imaginary realization of the human essence, because the human essence possesses no true reality. Thus, the struggle against religion is indirectly the struggle against the world whose spiritual aroma is religion.

Religious suffering is at the same time an expression of real suffering and a protest against real suffering. Religion is the sigh of the oppressed creature, the feeling of a heartless world, and the soul of soulless circumstances. It is the opium of the people.

The abolition of religion as the illusory happiness of the people is the demand for their real happiness. The demand to give up the illusions about their condition is a demand to give up a condition that requires illusion. The criticism of religion is therefore the germ of the criticism of the valley of tears whose halo is religion.

Criticism has plucked the imaginary flowers from the chains not so that man may bear chains without any imagination or comfort, but so that he may throw away the chains and pluck living flowers. The criticism of religion disillusions man so that he may think, act, and fashion his own reality as a disillusioned man come to his senses; so that he may revolve around himself as his real sun. Religion is only the illusory sun which revolves around man as long as he does not revolve around himself.

It is therefore the task of history, now the truth is no longer in the beyond, to establish the truth of the here and now. The first task of philosophy, which is in the service of history, once the holy form of human self-alienation has been discovered, is to discover self-alienation in its unholy forms. The criticism of heaven is thus transformed into the criticism of earth, the criticism of religion into the criticism of law, and the criticism of theology into the criticism of politics.

Economic and Philosophical Manuscripts

ALIENATED LABOUR

We started from the presuppositions of political economy. We accepted its vocabulary and its laws. We presupposed private property, the separation of labour, capital, and land, and likewise of wages, profit, and ground rent; also division of labour; competition; the concept of exchange value, etc. Using the very words of political economy we have demonstrated that the worker is degraded to the most miserable sort of commodity; that the misery of the worker is in inverse proportion to the power and size of his production; that the necessary result of competition is the accumulation of capital in a few hands, and thus a more terrible restoration of monopoly; and that finally the distinction between capitalist and landlord, and that between peasant and industrial worker disappears and the whole of society must fall apart into the two classes of the property owners and the propertyless workers.

Political economy starts with the fact of private property, it does not explain it to us. It conceives of the material process that private property goes through in reality in general abstract formulas which then have for it a value of laws. It does not understand these law, i.e. it does not demonstrate how they arise from the nature of private property. Political economy does not afford us any explanation of the reason for the separation of labour and capital, of capital and land. When, for example, political economy defines the relationship of wages to profit from capital, the interest of the capitalist is the ultimate court of appeal, that is, it presupposes what should be its result. In the same way competition enters the argument everywhere. It is explained by exterior circumstances. But political economy tells us nothing about how far these exterior, apparently fortuitous

Reprinted from *Karl Marx: Selected Writings,* edited by David McLellan (1977) by permission of Oxford University Press.

circumstances are merely the expression of a necessary development. We have seen how it regards exchange itself as something fortuitous. The only wheels that political economy sets in motion are greed and war among the greedy, competition.

It is just because political economy has not grasped the connections in the movement that new contradictions have arisen in its doctrines, for example, between that of monopoly and that of competition, freedom of craft and corporations, division of landed property and large estates. For competition, free trade, and the division of landed property were only seen as fortuitous circumstances created by will and force, not developed and comprehended as necessary, inevitable, and natural results of monopoly, corporations, and feudal property.

So what we have to understand now is the essential connection of private property, selfishness, the separation of labour, capital, and landed property, of exchange and competition, of the value and degradation of man, of monopoly and competition, etc.—the connection of all this alienation with the money system.

Let us not be like the political economist who, when he wishes to explain something, puts himself in an imaginary original state of affairs. Such an original stage of affairs explains nothing. He simply pushes the question back into a grey and nebulous distance. He presupposes as a fact and an event what he ought to be deducing, namely the necessary connection between the two things, for example, between the division of labour and exchange. Similarly, the theologian explains the origin of evil through the fall, i.e. he presupposes as an historical fact what he should be explaining.

We start with a contemporary fact of political economy:

The worker becomes poorer the richer is his production, the more it increases in power and scope. The worker becomes a commodity that is all the cheaper the more commodities he creates. The depreciation of the human world progresses in direct proportion to the increase in value of the world of things. Labour does not only produce commodities; it produces itself and the labourer as a commodity and that to the extent to which it produces commodities in general.

What this fact expresses is merely this: the object that labour produces, its product, confronts it as an alien being, as a power independent of the producer. The product of labour is labour that has solidified itself into an object, made itself into a thing, the objectification of labour. The realization of labour is its objectification. In political economy this realization of labour appears as a loss of reality for the worker, objectification as a loss of the object or slavery to it, and appropriation as alienation, as externalization.

The realization of labour appears as a loss of reality to an extent that the worker loses his reality by dying of starvation. Objectification appears as a loss of the object to such an extent that the worker is robbed not only of the objects necessary for his life but also of the objects of his work. Indeed, labour itself becomes an object he can only have in his power with the greatest of efforts and at irregular intervals. The appropriation of the object appears as alienation to such an extent that the more objects the worker produces, the less he can possess and the more he falls under the domination of his product, capital.

All these consequences follow from the fact that the worker relates to the product of his labour as to an alien object. For it is evident from this presupposition that the more the worker externalizes himself in his work, the more powerful becomes the alien, objective world that he creates opposite himself, the poorer he becomes himself in his inner life and the less he can call his own. It is just the same in religion. The more man puts into God, the less he retains in himself. The worker puts his life into the object and this means that it no longer belongs to him but to the object. So the greater this activity, the more the worker is without an object. What the product of his labour is, that he is not. So the greater this product the less he is himself. The externalization of the worker in his product implies not only that his labour becomes an object, an exterior existence but also that it exists outside him, independent and alien, and becomes a self-sufficient power opposite him, that the life that he has lent to the object affronts him, hostile and alien.

Let us now deal in more detail with objectification, the production of the worker, and the alienation, the loss of the object, his product, which is involved in it.

The worker can create nothing without nature, the sensuous exterior world. It is the matter in which his labour realizes itself, in which it is active, out of which and through which it produces.

But as nature affords the means of life for labour in the sense that labour cannot live without objects on which it exercises itself, so it affords a means of life in the narrower sense, namely the means for the physical subsistence of the worker himself.

Thus the more the worker appropriates the exterior world of sensuous nature by his labour, the more he doubly deprives himself of the means of subsistence, firstly since the exterior sensuous world increasingly ceases to be an object belonging to his work, a means of subsistence for his labour; secondly, since it increasingly ceases to be a means of subsistence in the direct sense, a means for the physical subsistence of the worker.

Thus in these two ways the worker becomes a slave to his object: firstly he receives an object of labour, that is he receives labour, and secondly, he receives the means of subsistence. Thus it is his object that permits him to exist first as a worker and secondly as a physical subject. The climax of this slavery is that only as a worker can he maintain himself as a physical subject and it is only as a physical subject that he is a worker.

(According to the laws of political economy the alienation of the worker in his object is expressed as follows: the more the worker produces the less he has to consume, the more values he creates the more valueless and worthless he becomes, the more formed the product the more deformed the worker, the more civilized the product, the more barbaric the worker, the more powerful the work the more powerless becomes the worker, the more cultured the work the more philistine the worker becomes and more of a slave to nature.)

Political economy hides the alienation in the essence of labour by not considering the immediate relationship between the worker (labour) and production. Labour produces works of wonder for the rich, but nakedness for the worker. It produces palaces, but only hovels for the worker; it produces beauty, but cripples the worker; it replaces labour by machines but throws a part of the workers back to a barbaric labour and turns the other part into machines. It produces culture, but also imbecility and cretinism for the worker.

The immediate relationship of labour to its products is the relationship of the worker to the objects of his production. The relationship of the man of means to the objects of production and to production itself is only a consequence of this first relationship. And it confirms it. We shall examine this other aspect later.

So when we ask the question: what relationship is essential to labour, we are asking about the relationship of the worker to production.

Up to now we have considered only one aspect of the alienation or externalization of the worker, his relationship to the products of his labour. But alienation shows itself not only in the result, but also in the act of production, inside productive activity itself. How would the worker be able to affront the product of his work as an alien being if he did not alienate himself in the act of production itself? For the product is merely the summary of the activity of production. So if the product of labour is externalization, production itself must be active externalization, the externalization of activity, the activity of externalization. The alienation of the object of labour is only the résumé of the alienation, the externalization in the activity of labour itself.

What does the externalization of labour consist of then?

Firstly, that labour is exterior to the worker, that is, it does not belong to his essence. Therefore he does not confirm himself in his work, he denies himself, feels miserable instead of happy, deploys no free physical and intellectual energy, but mortifies his body and ruins his mind. Thus the worker only feels a stranger. He is at home when he is not working and when he works he is not at home. His labour is therefore not voluntary but compulsory, forced labour. It is therefore not the satisfaction of a need but only a means to satisfy needs outside itself. How alien it really is is very evident from the fact that when there is no physical or other compulsion, labour is avoided like the plague. External labour, labour in which man externalizes himself, is a labour of self-sacrifice and mortification. Finally, the external character of labour for the worker shows itself in the fact that it is not his own but someone else's, that it does not belong to him, that he does not belong to himself in his labour but to someone else. As in religion the human imagination's own activity, the activity of man's head and his heart, reacts independently on the individual as an alien activity of gods or devils, so the activity of the worker is not his own spontaneous activity. It belongs to another and is the loss of himself.

The result we arrive at then is that man (the worker) only feels himself freely active in his animal functions of eating, drinking, and procreating, at most also in his dwelling and dress, and feels himself an animal in his human functions.

Eating, drinking, procreating, etc. are indeed truly

human functions. But in the abstraction that separates them from the other round of human activity and makes them into final and exclusive ends they become animal.

We have treated the act of alienation of practical human activity, labour, from two aspects. (1) The relationship of the worker to the product of his labour as an alien object that has power over him. This relationship is at the same time the relationship to the sensuous exterior world and to natural objects as to an alien and hostile world opposed to him. (2) The relationship of labour to the act of production inside labour. This relationship is the relationship of the worker to his own activity as something that is alien and does not belong to him; it is activity that is passivity, power that is weakness, procreation that is castration, the worker's own physical and intellectual energy, his personal life (for what is life except activity?) as an activity directed against himself, independent of him and not belonging to him. It is self-alienation, as above it was the alienation of the object.

We now have to draw a third characteristic of alienated labour from the two previous ones.

Man is a species-being not only in that practically and theoretically he makes both his own and other species into his objects, but also, and this is only another way of putting the same thing, he relates to himself as to the present, living species, in that he relates to himself as to a universal and therefore free being.

Both with man and with animals the species-life consists physically in the fact that man (like animals) lives from inorganic nature, and the more universal man is than animals the more more universal is the area of inorganic nature from which he lives. From the theoretical point of view, plants, animals, stones, air, light, etc. form part of human consciousness, partly as objects of natural science, partly as objects of art; they are his intellectual inorganic nature, his intellectual means of subsistence, which he must first prepare before he can enjoy and assimilate them. From the practical point of view, too, they form a part of human life and activity. Physically man lives solely from these products of nature, whether they appear as food, heating, clothing, habitation, etc. The universality of man appears in practice precisely in the universality that makes the whole of nature into his inorganic body in that it is both (i) his immediate means of subsistence and also (ii) the material object and tool of his vital activity. Nature is the inorganic body of a man, that is, in so far as it is not itself a human body. That man lives from nature means that nature is his body with which he must maintain a constant interchange so as not to die. That man's physical and intellectual life depends on nature merely means that nature depends on itself, for man is a part of nature.

While alienated labour alienates (1) nature from man, and (2) man from himself, his own active function, his vital activity, it also alienates the species from man; it turns his species-life into a means towards his individual life. Firstly it alienates species-life and individual life, and secondly in its abstraction it makes the latter into the aim of the former which is also conceived of in its abstract and alien form. For firstly, work, vital activity, and productive life itself appear to man only as a means to the satisfaction of a need, the need to preserve his physical existence. But productive life is species-life. It is life producing life. The whole character of a species, its generic character, is contained in its manner of vital activity, and free conscious activity is the species-characteristic of man. Life itself appears merely as a means to life.

The animal is immediately one with its vital activity. It is not distinct from it. They are identical. Man makes his vital activity itself into an object of his will and consciousness. He has a conscious vital activity. He is not immediately identical to any of his characterizations. Conscious vital activity differentiates man immediately from animal vital activity. It is this and this alone that makes man a species-being. He is only a conscious being, that is, his own life is an object to him, precisely because he is a species-being. This is the only reason for his activity being free activity. Alienated labour reverses the relationship so that, just because he is a conscious being, man makes his vital activity and essence a mere means to his existence.

The practical creation of an objective world, the working-over of inorganic nature, is the confirmation of man as a conscious species-being, that is, as a being that relates to the species as to himself and to himself as to the species. It is true that the animal, too, produces. It builds itself a nest, a dwelling, like the bee, the beaver, the ant, etc. But it only produces what it needs immediately for itself or its offspring; it produces one-sidedly whereas man produces universally; it produces only under the pressure of immediate physical need, whereas man produces freely from physical need and only truly produces when he is thus free; it produces only itself whereas man reproduces the whole of nature. Its product belongs immediately to its physical body whereas man can freely separate himself from his product. The animal only fashions things according to the standards and needs of the species it belongs to, whereas man knows how to produce according to the measure of every species and knows everywhere how to apply its inherent standard to the object; thus man also fashions things according to the laws of beauty.

Thus it is in the working over of the objective world that man first really affirms himself as a species-being. This production is his active species-life. Through it nature appears as his work and his reality. The object of work is therefore the objectification of the species-life of man; for he duplicates himself not only intellectually, in his mind, but also actively in reality and thus can look at his image in a world he has created. Therefore when alienated labour tears from man the object of his production, it also tears from him his species-life, the real objectivity of his species and turns the advantage he has over animals into a disadvantage in that his inorganic body, nature, is torn from him.

Similarly, in that alienated labour degrades man's own free activity to a means, it turns the species-life of man into a means for his physical existence.

Thus consciousness, which man derives from his species, changes itself through alienation so that species-life becomes a means for him.

Therefore alienated labour:

(3) makes the species-being of man, both nature and the intellectual faculties of his species, into a being that is alien to him, into a means for his individual existence. It alienates from man his own body, nature exterior to him, and his intellectual being, his human essence.

(4) An immediate consequence of man's alienation from the product of his work, his vital activity and his species-being, is the alienation of man from man. When man is opposed to himself, it is another man that is opposed to him. What is valid for the relationship of a man to his work, of the product of his work and himself, is also valid for the relationship of man to other men and of their labour and the objects of their labour.

In general, the statement that man is alienated from his species-being, means that one man is alienated from another as each of them is alienated from the human essence.

The alienation of man and in general of every relationship in which man stands to himself is first realized and expressed in the relationship with which man stands to other men.

Thus in the situation of alienated labour each man measures his relationship to other men by the relationship in which he finds himself placed as a worker.

We began with a fact of political economy, the alienation of the worker and his production. We have expressed this fact in conceptual terms: alienated, externalized labour. We have analysed this concept and thus analysed a purely economic fact.

Let us now see further how the concept of alienated, externalized labour must express and represent itself in reality.

If the product of work is alien to me, opposes me as an alien power, whom does it belong to then?

If my own activity does not belong to me and is an alien, forced activity to whom does it belong then?

To another being than myself.

Who is this being?

The gods? Of course in the beginning of history the chief production, as for example, the building of temples etc. in Egypt, India, and Mexico was both in the service of the gods and also belonged to them. But the gods alone were never the masters of the work. And nature just as little. And what a paradox it would be if, the more man mastered nature through his work and the more the miracles of the gods were rendered superfluous by the miracles of industry, the more man had to give up his pleasure in producing and the enjoyment in his product for the sake of these powers.

The alien being to whom the labour and the product of the labour belongs, whom the labour serves and who enjoys its product, can only be man himself. If the product of labour does not belong to the worker but stands over against him as an alien power, this is only possible in that it belongs to another man apart from the worker.

If his activity torments him it must be a joy and a pleasure to someone else. This alien power above man can be neither the gods nor nature, only man himself.

Consider further the above sentence that the relationship of man to himself first becomes objective and real to him through his relationship to other men. So if he relates to the product of his labour, his objectified labour, as to an object that is alien, hostile, powerful, and independent of him, this relationship implies that another man is the alien, hostile, powerful, and independent master of this object. If he relates to his own activity as to something unfree, it is a relationship to an activity that is under the domination, oppression, and yoke of another man.

Every self-alienation of man from himself and nature appears in the relationship in which he places himself and nature to other men distinct from himself. Therefore religious self-alienation necessarily appears in the relationship of layman to priest, or, because here we are dealing with a spiritual world, to a mediator, etc. In the practical, real world, the self-alienation can only appear through the practical, real relationship to other men. The means through which alienation makes progress are themselves practical. Through alienated labour, then, man creates not only his relationship to the object and act of production as to alien and hostile men; he creates too the relationship in which other men stand to his production and his product and the relationship in which he stand to these other men. Just as he turns his production into his own loss of reality and punishment and his own product into a loss, a product that does not belong to him, so he creates the domination of the man who does not produce over the production and the product. As he alienates his activity from himself, so he hands over to an alien person an activity that does not belong to him.

Up till now we have considered the relationship only from the side of the worker and we will later consider it from the side of the non-worker.

Thus through alienated, externalized labour the worker creates the relationship to this labour of a man who is alien to it and remains exterior to it. The relationship of the worker to his labour creates the relationship to it of the capitalist, or whatever else one wishes to call the master of the labour. Private property is thus the product, result, and necessary consequence of externalized labour, of the exterior relationship of the worker to nature and to himself.

Thus private property is the result of the analysis of the concept of externalized labour, i.e. externalized man, alienated work, alienated life, alienated man.

We have, of course, obtained the concept of externalized labour (externalized life) from political economy as the result of the movement of private property. But it is evident from the analysis of this concept that, although private property appears to be the ground and reason for externalized labour, it is rather a consequence of it, just as the gods are originally not the cause but the effect of the aberration of the human mind, although later this relationship reverses itself.

It is only in the final culmination of the development of private property that these hidden characteristics come once more to the fore, in that firstly it is the product of externalized labour and secondly it is the means through which labour externalizes itself, the realization of this externalization.

This development sheds light at the same time on several previously unresolved contradictions.

1. Political economy starts from labour as the veritable soul of production, and yet it attributes nothing to labour and everything to private property. Proudhon has drawn a conclusion from this contradiction that is favourable to labour and against private property. But we can see that this apparent contradiction is the contradiction of alienated labour with itself and that political economy has only expressed the laws of alienated labour.

We can therefore also see that wages and private property are identical: for wages, in which the product, the object of the labour, remunerates the labour itself, are just a necessary consequence of the alienation of labour. In the wage system the labour does not appear as the final aim but only as the servant of the wages. We will develop this later and for the moment only draw a few consequences.

An enforced raising of wages (quite apart from other difficulties, apart from the fact that, being an anomaly, it could only be maintained by force) would only mean a better payment of slaves and would not give this human meaning and worth either to the worker or to his labour.

Indeed, even the equality of wages that Proudhon demands only changes the relationship of the contemporary worker to his labour into that of all men to labour. Society is then conceived of as an abstract capitalist.

Wages are an immediate consequence of alienated labour and alienated labour is the immediate cause of private property. Thus the disappearance of one entails also the disappearance of the other.

2. It is a further consequence of the relationship of alienated labour to private property that the emancipation of society from private property, etc., from slavery, is expressed in its political form by the emancipation of the workers. This is not because only their emancipation is at stake but because general human emancipation is contained in their eman-

cipation. It is contained within it because the whole of human slavery is involved in the relationship of the worker to his product and all slave relationships are only modifications and consequences of this relationship.

Just as we have discovered the concept of private property through an analysis of the concept of alienated, externalized labour, so all categories of political economy can be deduced with the help of these two factors. We shall recognize in each category of market, competition, capital, money, only a particular and developed expression of these first two fundamental elements.

However, before we consider this structure let us try to solve two problems:

1. To determine the general essence of private property as it appears as a result of alienated labour in its relationship to truly human and social property.

2. We have taken the alienation and externalization of labour as a fact and analysed this fact. We now ask, how does man come to externalize, to alienate his labour? How is this alienation grounded in human development? We have already obtained much material for the solution of this problem, in that we have turned the question of the origin of private property into the question of the relationship of externalized labour to the development of human history. For when we speak of private property we think we are dealing with something that is exterior to man. When we speak of labour, then we are dealing directly with man. This new formulation of the problem already implies its solution.

To take point 1, the general nature of private property and its relationship to truly human property.

Externalized labour has been broken down into two component parts that determine each other or are only different expressions of one and the same relationship. Appropriation appears as alienation, as externalization, and externalization as appropriation, and alienation as true enfranchisement. We have dealt with one aspect, alienated labour as regards the worker himself, that is, the relationship of externalized labour to itself. As a product and necessary result of this relationship we have discovered the property relationship of the non-worker to the worker and his labour.

As the material and summary expression of alienated labour, private property embraces both relationships, both that of the worker to his labour, the product of his labour and the non-worker, and that of the non-worker to the worker and the product of his labour.

We have already seen that for the worker who appropriates nature through his work, this appropriation appears as alienation, his own activity as activity for and of someone else, his vitality as sacrifice of his life, production of objects as their loss to an alien power, an alien man: let us now consider the relationship that this man, who is alien to labour and the worker, has to the worker, to labour and its object.

The first remark to make is that everything that appears in the case of the worker to be an activity of externalization, of alienation, appears in the case of the non-worker to be a state of externalization, of alienation.

Secondly, the real, practical behaviour of the worker in production and towards his product (as a state of mind) appears in the case of the non-worker opposed to him as theoretical behaviour. Thirdly, the non-worker does everything against the worker that the worker does against himself but he does not do against himself what he does against the worker.

Let us consider these three relationships in more detail. . . . [The manuscript breaks off unfinished here.]

PRIVATE PROPERTY AND COMMUNISM

The overcoming of self-alienation follows the same course as self-alienation itself. At first, private property is considered only from its objective aspect, but still with labour as its essence. The form of its existence is therefore capital, that is to be abolished 'as such' (Proudhon). Or else the source of the harmfulness of private property, its alienation from human existence, is thought of as consisting in the particular type of labour, labour which is levelled down, fragmented, and therefore unfree. This is the view of Fourier, who like the physiocrats also considered agriculture as labour *par excellence*. Saint-Simon on the other hand declares industrial labour to be the essential type, and demands as well exclusive rule by industrialists and the improvement of the condition of the workers. Finally, communism is the positive expression of the overcoming of private property, appearing first of all as generalized private property. In making this relationship universal communism is:

1. In its original form only a generalization and completion of private property. As such it appears in a dual form: firstly, it is faced with such a great domination of material property that it wishes to destroy everything that cannot be possessed by everybody as private property; it wishes to abstract forcibly from talent, etc. It considers immediate physical ownership as the sole aim of life and being. The category of worker is not abolished but extended to all men. The relationship of the community to the world of things remains that of private property. Finally, this process of opposing general private property to private property is expressed in the animal form of opposing to marriage (which is of course a form of exclusive private property) the community of women where the woman becomes the common property of the community. One might say that the idea of the community of women reveals the open secret of this completely crude and unthinking type of communism. Just as women pass from marriage to universal prostitution, so the whole world of wealth, that is the objective essence of man, passes from the relationship of exclusive marriage to the private property owner to the relationship of universal prostitution with the community. By systematically denying the personality of man this communism is merely the consistent expression of private property which is just this negation. Universal envy setting itself up as a power is the concealed form of greed which merely asserts itself and satisfies itself in another way. The thoughts of every private property owner as such are at least turned against those richer than they as an envious desire to level down. This envious desire is precisely the essence of competition. Crude communism is only the completion of this envy and levelling down to a preconceived minimum. It has a particular and limited standard. How little this abolition of private property constitutes a real appropriation is proved by the abstract negation of the whole world of culture and civilization, a regression to the unnatural simplicity of the poor man without any needs who has not even arrived at the stage of private property, let alone got beyond it.

In this theory the community merely means a community of work and equality of the wages that the communal capital, the community as general capitalist, pays out. Both sides of the relationship are raised to a sham universality, labour being the defining characteristic applied to each man, while capital is the universality and power of society.

The infinite degradation in which man exists for himself is expressed in his relationship to woman as prey and servant of communal lust; for the secret of this relationship finds an unambiguous, decisive, open, and unveiled expression in the relationship of man to woman and the conception of the immediate and natural relationship of the sexes. The immediate, natural, and necessary relationship of human being to human being is the relationship of man to woman. In this natural relationship of the sexes man's relationship to nature is immediately his relationship to man, and his relationship to man is immediately his relationship to nature, his own natural function. Thus, in this relationship is sensuously revealed and reduced to an observable fact how far for man his essence has become nature or nature has become man's human essence. Thus, from this relationship the whole cultural level of man can be judged. From the character of this relationship we can conclude how far man has become a species-being, a human being, and conceives of himself as such; the relationship of man to woman is the most natural relationship of human being to human being. Thus it shows how far the natural behaviour of man has become human or how far the human essence has become his natural essence, how far his human nature has become nature for him. This relationship also shows how far the need of man has become a human need, how far his fellow men as men have become a need, how far in his most individual existence he is at the same time a communal being.

The first positive abolition of private property, crude communism, is thus only the form in which appears the ignominy of private property that wishes to establish itself as the positive essence of the community.

2. The second form of communism is: (*a*) still political in nature, whether democratic or despotic; (*b*) with the abolition of the state, but still incomplete and still under the influence of private property, i.e. the alienation of man. In both forms communism knows itself already to be the reintegration or return of man into himself, the abolition of man's self-alienation. But since it has not yet grasped the positive essence of private property or the human nature of needs, it is still imprisoned and contaminated by private property. It has understood its concept, but not yet its essence.

3. Thirdly, there is communism as the positive abolition of private property and thus of human self-alienation and therefore the real reappropriation of

the human essence by and for man. This is communism as the complete and conscious return of man conserving all the riches of previous development for man himself as a social, i.e. human being. Communism as completed naturalism is humanism and as completed humanism is naturalism. It is the genuine solution of the antagonism between man and nature and between man and man. It is the true solution of the struggle between existence and essence, between objectification and self-affirmation, between freedom and necessity, between individual and species. It is the solution to the riddle of history and knows itself to be this solution.

The whole movement of history, therefore, both as regards the real engendering of this communism, the birth of its empirical existence, and also as regards its consciousness and thought, is the consciously comprehended process of its becoming. On the other hand, the communism that is still incomplete seeks an historical proof for itself in what already exists by selecting isolated historical formations opposed to private property. It tears isolated phases out of the movement (Cabet, Villegardelle, etc. in particular ride this hobby horse) and asserts them as proofs of its historical pedigree. But all it succeeds in showing is that the disproportionately larger part of this movement contradicts its assertions and that if it has ever existed, it is precisely its past being that refutes its pretension to essential being.

We can easily see how necessary it is that the whole revolutionary movement should find not so much its empirical as its theoretical basis in the development of private property and particularly the economic system.

This material, immediately sensuous, private property, is the material, sensuous expression of man's alienated life. Its movement of production and consumption is the sensuous revelation of the movement of all previous production, i.e. the realization or reality of man. Religion, family, state, law, morality, science, and art are only particular forms of production and fall under its general law. The positive abolition of private property and the appropriation of human life is therefore the positive abolition of all alienation, thus the return of man out of religion, family, state, etc. into his human, i.e. social being. Religious alienation as such occurs only in man's interior consciousness, but economic alienation is that of real life, and its abolition therefore covers both aspects. It is obvious that the movement begins differently with different peoples according to whether the actual conscious life of the people is lived in their minds or in the outer world, is an ideal or a real life. Communism begins immediately with atheism (Owen) and atheism is at first still very far from being communism, for this atheism is still rather an abstraction.[1] The philanthropy of atheism is therefore at first only an abstract philosophical philanthropy whereas that of communism is immediately real and directly orientated towards action.

We have seen how, presupposing the positive supercession of private property, man produces man, himself and other men; how also the object, which is the direct result of his personal activity, is at the same time his own existence for other men and their existence for him. In the same way, both the materials of his labour and man its author are the result and at the same time the origin of the movement. (And private property is historically necessary precisely because there must be this origin.) So the general character of the whole movement is a social one; as society produces man as man, so it is produced by man. Activity and enjoyment are social both in their content and in their mode of existence; they are social activity and social enjoyment. The human significance of nature is only available to social man; for only to social man is nature available as a bond with other men, as the basis of his own existence for others and theirs for him, and as the vital element in human reality; only to social man is nature the foundation of his own human existence. Only as such has his natural existence become a human existence and nature itself become human. Thus society completes the essential unity of man and nature, it is the genuine resurrection of nature, the accomplished naturalism of man and the accomplished humanism of nature.

Social activity and social enjoyment by no means exist only in the form of a directly communal activity and directly communal enjoyment. But communal activity and enjoyment, i.e. activity and enjoyment that is expressed and confirmed in the real society of other men, will occur everywhere where this direct expression of sociability arises from the content of the activity or enjoyment and corresponds to its nature.

1. Prostitution is only a particular expression of the general prostitution of the worker, and because prostitution is a relationship which includes both the person prostituted and the person prostituting—whose baseness is even greater—thus the capitalist, too, etc. is included within this category. (Footnote by Marx.)

But even if my activity is a scientific one, etc., an activity that I can seldom perform directly in company with other men, I am still acting socially since I am acting as a man. Not only the material of my activity—like language itself for the thinker—is given to me as a social product, my own existence is social activity; therefore what I individually produce, I produce individually for society, conscious of myself as a social being.

My universal consciousness is only the theoretical form whose living form is the real community, society, whereas at the present time universal consciousness is an abstraction from real life and as such turns into its enemy. Thus the activity of my universal consciousness is as such my theoretical existence as a social being.

It is above all necessary to avoid restoring society as a fixed abstraction opposed to the individual. The individual is the social being. Therefore, even when the manifestation of his life does not take the form of a communal manifestation performed in the company of other men, it is still a manifestation and confirmation of social life. The individual and the species-life of man are not different, although, necessarily, the mode of existence of individual life is a more particular or a more general mode of species-life or the species-life is a more particular or more general individual life.

Man confirms his real social life in his species-consciousness and in his thought he merely repeats his real existence just as conversely his species-being is confirmed in his species-consciousness and exists for itself in its universality as a thinking being.

However much he is a particular individual (and it is precisely his particularity that makes him an individual and a truly individual communal being) man is just as much the totality, the ideal totality, the subjective existence of society as something thought and felt. Man exists also in reality both as the contemplation and true enjoyment of social existence and as the totality of human manifestations of life.

Thus thought and being are indeed distinct, but at the same time they together form a unity.

Death appears as the harsh victory of the species over the particular individual and seems to contradict their unity; but the particular individual is only a determinate species-being and thus mortal.

4. Private property is only the sensuous expression of the fact that man is both objective to himself and, even more, becomes a hostile and inhuman object to himself, that the expression of his life entails its externalization, its realization becomes the loss of its reality, an alien reality. Similarly the positive supersession of private property, that is, the sensuous appropriation by and for man of human essence and human life, of objective man and his works, should not be conceived of only as direct and exclusive enjoyment, as possession and having. Man appropriates his universal being in a universal manner, as a whole man. Each of his human relationships to the world—seeing, hearing, smell, tasting, feeling, thinking, contemplating, feeling, willing, acting, loving—in short all the organs of his individuality, just as the organs whose form is a directly communal one, are in their objective action, or their relation to the object, the appropriation of this object. The appropriation of human reality, their relationship to the object, is the confirmation of human reality. It is therefore as manifold as the determinations and activities of human nature. It is human effectiveness and suffering, for suffering, understood in the human sense, is an enjoyment of the self for man.

Private property has made us so stupid and narrow-minded that an object is only ours when we have it, when it exists as capital for us or when we directly possess, eat, drink, wear, inhabit it, etc. in short, when we use it. Yet private property itself in its turn conceives of all these direct realizations of property merely as means of life, and the life which they serve is that of private property, labour, and capitalization.

Thus all physical and intellectual senses have been replaced by the simple alienation of all these senses, the sense of having. Man's essence had to be reduced to this absolute poverty, so it might bring forth out of itself its own inner riches.

The supersession of private property is therefore the complete emancipation of all human senses and qualities, but it is this emancipation precisely in that these senses and qualities have become human, both subjectively and objectively. The eye has become a human eye when its object has become a social, human object produced by man and destined for him. Thus in practice the senses have become direct theoreticians. They relate to the thing for its own sake but the thing itself is an objective human relationship to itself and to man and vice versa. (I can in practice only relate myself humanly to an object if the object relates itself humanly to man.) Need and enjoyment have thus lost their egoistic nature and nature has lost its mere utility in that its utility has become human utility.

In the same way I can appropriate the senses and enjoyment of other men. Apart, then, from these immediate organs, social organs are constituted in the form of society: thus, for example, direct social activity with others is an organ of the manifestation of life and a manner in which to appropriate human life.

It is evident that the human eye enjoys things differently from the crude, inhuman eye, the human ear differently from the crude ear, etc.

We have seen that man does not lose himself in his object provided that it is a human object or objective humanity. This is only possible if it becomes a social object for him and he himself becomes a social being, while society becomes a being for him in this object.

Therefore in so far as generally in society reality becomes the reality of man's faculties, human reality, and thus the reality of his own faculties, all objects become for him the objectification of himself. They are objects that confirm and realize his individuality, his own objects, i.e. he becomes an object himself. How they become his own depends on the nature of the object and the faculty that corresponds to it. For it is just the distinctness of this relationship that constitutes the specific real mode of affirmation. The eye perceives an object differently from the ear and the object of the eye is different from that of the ear. What makes each faculty distinct is just its particular essence and thus also the particular mode of its objectification, of its objectively real, living being. Thus man is affirmed in the objective world not only in thought but through all his senses.

Just as society that is being born finds all the material for its cultural formation through the development of private property with its material and intellectual wealth and poverty, so society when formed produces man in the whole wealth of its being, man rich in profound and manifold sensitivity as its constant reality.

It can be seen how subjectivism and objectivism, spiritualism and materialism, activity and passivity lose their opposition and thus their existence as opposites only in a social situation; it can be seen how the solution of theoretical opposition is only possible in a practical way, only through the practical energy of man, and their solution is thus by no means an exercise in epistemology but a real problem of life that philosophy could not solve just because it conceived of it as a purely theoretical task.

It can be seen how the history of industry and its previous objective existence is an open book of man's faculties and his psychology available to view. It was previously not conceived of in its connection with man's essence but only under the exterior aspect of utility, because man, moving inside the sphere of alienation, could only apprehend religion as the generalized existence of man, or history in its abstract and universal form of politics, art, literature, etc., as the reality of human faculties and the human species-act. In everyday material industry (which one can just as well consider as a part of that general development, or the general development can be considered as a particular part of industry, because all human activity has hitherto been labour, i.e. industry, self-alienated activity) we have the objectified faculties of man before us in the form of sensuous, alien, utilitarian objects, in the form of alienation. A psychology for which this book, and therewith the most tangible and accessible part of history, remains closed cannot become a genuine science with a real content. What should one think of a science whose preconceptions disregarded this large field of man's labour and which is not conscious of its incompleteness even though so broad a wealth of man's labour means nothing to it apart, perhaps, from what can be expressed in a single word 'need', and 'common need'?

The natural sciences have developed an enormous activity and appropriated an ever-increasing amount of material. However, philosophy has remained as alien to them as they to philosophy. The momentary union was only an imaginary illusion. The wish was there, but the ability lacking. Historians themselves only afford natural science a passing glance, as making for enlightenment, utility, and isolated great discoveries. But natural science by means of industry has penetrated human life all the more effectively, changed its form and prepared for human emancipation, even though in the first place it lead to complete dehumanization. Industry is the real historical relationship of nature, and therefore of natural science, to man. If then it is conceived of as the open revelation of human faculties, then the human essence of nature or the natural essence of man will also be understood. Natural science will then lose its one-sidedly materialist, or rather idealistic, orientation and become the basis of human science as it has already, though in an alienated form, become the basis of actual human life. And to have one basis for life and another for science would be in itself a falsehood. Nature as it is formed in human history—the birth process of human society—is the real nature of man and thus nature as fashioned by industry is true anthropological nature, though in an alienated form.

Sense-experience (see Feuerbach) must be the basis of all science. Science is only real science when it starts from sense-experience in the dual form of sense perception and sensuous need, in other words when it starts from nature. The whole of history is a preparation for 'man' to become the object of sense perception and for needs to be the needs of 'man as man'. History itself is the real part of natural history, of nature's becoming man. Natural science will later comprise the science of man just as much as the science of man will embrace natural science; they will be one single science.

Man is the direct object of natural science; for directly sensuous nature for man is man's sense-experience (the expressions are identical) in the shape of other men presented to him in a sensuous way. For it is only through his fellow man that his sense-experience becomes human for him. But nature is the direct object of the science of man. Man's first object—man himself—is nature, sense-experience; and particular human sensuous faculties are only objectively realized in natural objects and can only attain to self-knowledge in the science of nature in general. The elements of thought itself, the element of the vital manifestation of thought, language, is sensuous in character. The social reality of nature and human natural science or the natural science of man are identical expressions.

It can be seen how the wealthy man and the plenitude of human need take the place of economic wealth and poverty. The wealthy man is the man who needs a complete manifestation of human life and a man in whom his own realization exists as an inner necessity, as a need. Not only the wealth of man but also his poverty contain equally, under socialism, a human and therefore social meaning. Poverty is the passive bond that lets man feel his greatest wealth, his fellow man, as a need. The domination of the objective essence within me, the sensuous eruption of my essential activity is the passion that here becomes the activity of my essence.

5. A being only counts itself as independent when it stands on its own feet and it stands on its own feet as long as it owes its existence to itself. A man who lives by grace of another considers himself a dependent being. But I live completely by the grace of another when I owe him not only the maintenance of my life but when he has also created my life, when he is the source of my life. And my life necessarily has such a ground outside itself if it is not my own creation. The idea of creation is thus one that it is very difficult to drive out of the minds of people. They find it impossible to conceive of nature and man existing through themselves since it contradicts all the evidences of practical life.

The idea of the creation of the world received a severe blow from the science of geogeny, the science which describes the formation and coming into being of the earth as a process of self-generation. Spontaneous generation is the only practical refutation of the theory of creation.

Now it is easy to say to the single individual what Aristotle already said: you are engendered by your father and your mother and so in your case it is the mating of two human beings, a human species-act, that has produced the human being. You see, too, that physically also man owes his existence to man. So you must not only bear in mind the aspect of the infinite regression and ask further: who engendered my father and his grandfather, etc., you must also grasp the circular movement observable in that progression whereby man renews himself by procreation and thus always remains the subject. But you will answer: I grant you this circular movement but then grant me the progression that pushes me ever further backwards until I ask, who created the first man and the world as a whole? I can only answer you: your question itself is a product of abstraction. Ask yourself how you come to ask such a question; ask yourself whether your question is not put from a standpoint that I cannot accept because it is an inverted one. Ask yourself whether that progress exists as such for rational thought. When you inquire about the creation of the world and man, then you abstract from man and the world. You suppose them non-existent and yet require me to prove to you that they exist. I say to you: give up your abstraction and you will give up your question, or if you wish to stick to your abstraction then be consistent, and if you think of man and the world as non-existent then think of yourself as non-existent, also, for you too are a part of the world and man. Do not think, do not ask me questions, for immediately you think and ask, your abstraction from the being of nature and man has no meaning. Or are you such an egoist that you suppose everything to be nothing and yet wish to exist yourself?

You can reply to me: I do not wish to suppose the nothingness of the world and so on; I am only asking you about their origins, as I ask an anatomist about the formation of bones, etc.

But since for socialist man what is called world history is nothing but the creation of man by human labour and the development of nature for man, he has the observable and irrefutable proof of his self-creation and the process of his origin. Once the essential reality of man in nature, man as the existence of nature for man, and nature for man as the existence of man, has become evident in practical life and sense experience, then the question of an alien being, of a being above nature and man—a question that implies an admission of the unreality of nature and man—has become impossible in practice. Atheism, as a denial of this unreality, has no longer any meaning, for atheism is a denial of God and tries to assert through this negation the existence of man; but socialism as such no longer needs this mediation; it starts from the theoretical and practical sense-perception of man and nature as the true reality. It is the positive self-consciousness of man no longer mediated through the negation of religion, just as real life is the positive reality of man no longer mediated through communism as the negation of private property. Communism represents the positive in the form of the negation of the negation and thus a phase in human emancipation and rehabilitation, both real and necessary at this juncture of human development. Communism is the necessary form and dynamic principle of the immediate future, but communism is not as such the goal of human development, the form of human society. . . .

Let us summarize our results:

The only liberation of Germany that is practically possible is the liberation from the theoretical standpoint that declares man to be the highest being for man. In Germany emancipation from the Middle Ages is only possible as an emancipation from the partial overcoming of the Middle Ages. In Germany no form of slavery can be broken without every form of slavery being broken. Germany is thorough and cannot make a revolution without its being a thorough one. The head of this emancipation is philosophy, its heart is the proletariat. Philosophy cannot realize itself without transcending the proletariat, the proletariat cannot transcend itself without realizing philosophy.

ON MONEY

What I have thanks to money, what I pay for, i.e. what money can buy, that is what I, the possessor of the money, am myself. My power is as great as the power of money. The properties of money are my—(its owner's)—properties and faculties. Thus what I am and what I am capable of is by no means determined by my individuality. I am ugly, but I can buy myself the most beautiful women. Consequently I am not ugly, for the effect of ugliness, its power of repulsion, is annulled by money. As an individual, I am lame, but money can create twenty-four feet for me; so I am not lame; I am a wicked, dishonest man without conscience or intellect, but money is honoured and so also is its possessor. Money is the highest good and so its possessor is good. Money relieves me of the trouble of being dishonest; so I am presumed to be honest. I may have no intellect, but money is the true mind of all things and so how should its possessor have no intellect? Moreover he can buy himself intellectuals and is not the man who has power over intellectuals not more intellectual than they? I who can get with money everything that the human heart longs for, do I not possess all human capacities? Does not my money thus change all my incapacities into their opposite?

If money is the bond that binds me to human life, that binds society to me and me to nature and men, is not money the bond of all bonds? Can it not tie and untie all bonds? Is it not, therefore, also the universal means of separation? It is the true agent both of separation and of union, the galvanochemical power of society.

Shakespeare brings out two particular properties of money:

1. It is the visible god-head, the transformation of all human and natural qualities into their opposites, the general confusion and inversion of things; it makes impossibilities fraternize.

2. It is the universal whore, the universal pander between men and peoples.

The inversion and confusion of all human and natural qualities, the fraternization of impossibilities, this divine power of money lies in its being the externalized and self-externalizing species-being of man. It is the externalized capacities of humanity.

What I cannot do as a man, thus what my individual faculties cannot do, this I can do through money. Thus money turns each of these faculties into something that it is not, i.e. into its opposite.

If I long for a meal, or wish to take the mail coach because I am not strong enough to make the journey on foot, then money procures the meal and the mail coach for me. This means that it changes my wishes from being imaginary, and translates them from their being in thought, imagination, and will into a sensuous, real being, from imagination to life, from imaginary being to real being. The truly creative force in this mediation is money.

Demand also exists for the man who has no money but his demand is simply an imaginary entity that has no effective existence for me, for a third party or for other men and thus remains unreal and without an object. The difference between a demand that is based on money and effective and one that is based on my needs, passions, wishes, etc. and is ineffective is the difference between being and thought, between a representation that merely exists within me and one that is outside me as a real object.

If I have no money for travelling, then I have no need, no real and self-realizing need, to travel. If I have a vocation to study, but have no money for it, then I have no vocation to study, no effective, genuine vocation. If, on the contrary, I do not really have a vocation to study, but have the will and the money, then I have an effective vocation thereto. Money is the universal means and power, exterior to man, not issuing from man as man or from human society as society, to turn imagination into reality and reality into mere imagination. Similarly it turns real human and natural faculties into mere abstract representations and thus imperfections and painful imaginings, while on the other hand it turns the real imperfections and imaginings, the really powerless faculties that exist only in the imagination of the individual, into real faculties and powers. This description alone suffices to make money the universal inversion of individualities that turns them into their opposites and gives them qualities at variance with their own. As this perverting power, money then appears as the enemy of man and social bonds that pretend to self-subsistence. It changes fidelity into infidelity, love into hate, hate into love, virtue into vice, vice into virtue, slave into master, mater into slave, stupidity into intelligence and intelligence into stupidity.

Since money is the existing and self-affirming concept of value and confounds and exchanges all things, it is the universal confusion and exchange of all things, the inverted world, the confusion and exchange of all natural and human qualities.

He who can buy courage is courageous though he be a coward. Because money can be exchanged not for a particular quality, for a particular thing or human faculty, but for the whole human and actual objective world, from the point of view of its possessor it can exchange any quality for any other, even contradictory qualities and objects; it is the fraternization of incompatibles and forces contraries to embrace.

If you suppose man to be man and his relationship to the world to be a human one, then you can only exchange love for love, trust for trust, etc. If you wish to appreciate art, then you must be a man with some artistic education; if you wish to exercise an influence on other men, you must be a man who has a really stimulating and encouraging effect on other men. Each of your relationships to man—and to nature—must be a definite expression of your real individual life that corresponds to the object of your will. If you love without arousing a reciprocal love, that is, if your loves does not as such produce love in return, if through the manifestation of yourself as a loving person you do not succeed in making yourself a beloved person, then your love is impotent and a misfortune. . . .

The German Ideology

THE NEED FOR REVOLUTION

Our investigation hitherto started from the instruments of production, and it has already shown that private property was a necessity for certain industrial stages. In *industrie extractive* [raw materials industry] private property still coincides with labour; in small industry and all agriculture up till now property is the necessary consequence of the existing instruments of production; in big industry the contradiction between the instrument of production and private property appears for the first time and is the product of big industry; moreover, big industry must be highly developed to produce this contradiction. And thus only with big industry does the abolition of private property become possible.

In big industry and competition the whole mass of conditions of existence, limitations, biases of individuals, are fused together into the two simplest forms: private property and labour. With money every form of intercourse, and intercourse itself, is considered fortuitous for the individuals. Thus money implies that all previous intercourse was only intercourse of individuals under particular conditions, not of individuals as individuals. These conditions are reduced to two: accumulated labour or private property, and actual labour. If both or one of these ceases, then intercourse comes to a standstill. The modern economists themselves, e.g. Sismondi, Cherbuliez, etc., oppose 'association of individuals' to 'association of capital'. On the other hand, the individuals themselves are entirely subordinated to the division of labour and hence are brought into the most complete dependence on one another. Private property, in so far as within labour itself it is opposed to labour, evolves out of the necessity of accumulation, and has still, to begin with, rather the form of the communality; but in its further development it approaches more and more the modern form of private property. The division of labour implies from the outset the division of the conditions of labour, of tools and materials, and thus the splitting-up of accumulated capital among different owners, and thus, also, the division between capital and labour, and the different forms of property itself. The more the division of labour develops and accumulation grows, the sharper are the forms that this process of differentiation assumes. Labour itself can only exist on the premiss of this fragmentation.

Thus two facts are here revealed. First the productive forces appear as a world for themselves, quite independent of and divorced from the individuals, alongside the individuals: the reason for this is that the individuals, whose forces they are, exist split up and in opposition to one another, while, on the other hand, these forces are only real forces in the intercourse and association of these individuals. Thus, on the one hand, we have a totality of productive forces, which have, as it were, taken on a material form and are for the individuals no longer the forces of the individuals but of private property, and hence of the individuals only in so far as they are owners of private property themselves. Never, in any earlier period, have the productive forces taken on a form so indifferent to the intercourse of individuals as individuals, because their intercourse itself was formerly a restricted one. On the other hand, standing over against these productive forces, we have the majority of the individuals from whom these forces have been wrested away, and who, robbed thus of all real life-content, have become abstract individuals, but who are, however, only by this fact put into a position to enter into relation with one another as individuals.

The only connection which still links them with the productive forces and with their own existence—labour—has lost all semblance of self-activity and only sustains their life by stunting it. While in the earlier periods self-activity and the production of material life were separated, in that they devolved on different persons, and while, on account of the narrowness of the individuals themselves, the production of material life was considered as a subordinate mode of self-activity, they now diverge to such an extent that altogether material life appears as the end, and what produces this material life,

Reprinted from *Karl Marx: Selected Writings,* edited by David McLellan (1977) by permission of Oxford University Press.

labour (which is now the only possible but, as we see, negative form of self-activity), as the means.

Thus things have now come to such a pass that the individuals must appropriate the existing totality of productive forces, not only to achieve self-activity, but also merely to safeguard their very existence. This appropriation is first determined by the object to be appropriated, the productive forces, which have been developed to a totality and which only exist within a universal intercourse. From this aspect alone, therefore, this appropriation must have a universal character corresponding to the productive forces and the intercourse.

The appropriation of these forces is itself nothing more than the development of the individual capacities corresponding to the material instruments of production. The appropriation of a totality of instruments of production is, for this very reason, the development of a totality of capacities in the individuals themselves.

This appropriation is further determined by the persons appropriating. Only the proletarians of the present day, who are completely shut off from all self-activity, are in a position to achieve a complete and no longer restricted self-activity, which consists in the appropriation of a totality of productive forces and in the thus postulated development of a totality of capacities. All earlier revolutionary appropriations were restricted; individuals, whose self-activity was restricted by a crude instrument of production and a limited intercourse, appropriated this crude instrument of production, and hence merely achieved a new state of limitation. Their instrument of production became their property, but they themselves remained subordinate to the division of labour and their own instrument of production. In all expropriations up to now, a mass of individuals remained subservient to a single instrument of production; in the appropriation by the proletarians, a mass of instruments of production must be made subject to each individual, and property to all. Modern universal intercourse can be controlled by individuals, therefore, only when controlled by all.

This appropriation is further determined by the manner in which it must be effected. It can only be effected through a union, which by the character of the proletariat itself can again only be a universal one, and through a revolution, in which, on the one hand, the power of the earlier mode of production and intercourse and social organization is overthrown, and, on the other hand, there develops the universal character and the energy of the proletariat, without which the revolution cannot be accomplished; and in which, further, the proletariat rids itself of everything that still clings to it from its previous position in society.

Only at this stage does self-activity coincide with material life, which corresponds to the development of individuals into complete individuals and the casting-off of all natural limitations. The transformation of labour into self-activity corresponds to the transformation of the earlier limited intercourse into the intercourse of individuals as such. With the appropriation of the total productive forces through united individuals, private property comes to an end. While previously in history a particular condition always appeared as accidental, now the isolation of individuals and the particular private gain of each man have themselves become accidental. . . .

Finally, from the conception of history we have sketched we obtain these further conclusions: (1) In the development of productive forces there comes a stage when productive forces and means of intercourse are brought into being, which, under the existing relationships, only cause mischief, and are no longer productive but destructive forces (machinery and money); and connected with this a class is called forth, which has to bear all the burdens of society without enjoying its advantages, which, ousted from society, is forced into the most decided antagonism to all other classes; a class which forms the majority of all members of society, and from which emanates the consciousness of the necessity of a fundamental revolution, the communist consciousness, which may, of course, arise among the other classes too through the contemplation of the situation of this class. (2) The conditions under which definite productive forces can be applied are the conditions of the rule of a definite class of society, whose social power, deriving from its property, has its practical-idealistic expression in each case in the form of the State; and, therefore, every revolutionary struggle is directed against a class, which till then has been in power. (3) In all revolutions up till now the mode of activity always remained unscathed and it was only a question of a different distribution of this activity, a new distribution of labour to other persons, while the communist revolution is directed against the preceding mode of activity, does away with labour, and abolishes the rule of all classes with the classes themselves, because it is carried through by the class which no longer counts as a class in society, is not recognized as a class, and is in itself the expression of the dissolution of all classes, nationalities, etc. within present society; and (4) Both for the production on a mass scale of this communist consciousness, and for the success of the cause itself, the alternation of men on a mass scale is necessary, an alteration which can only take place in a practical movement, a revolution; this revolution is necessary, therefore, not only because the ruling class cannot be overthrown in any other way, but also because the class overthrowing it can only in a revolution succeed in ridding itself of all the muck of ages and become fitted to found society anew. . . .

Chapter 30

Friedrich Nietzsche

Friedrich Nietzsche (1844–1900) was a German philosopher who has played a major role in contemporary intellectual development. Descended through both of his parents from Christian ministers, Nietzsche was brought up in a pious German Lutheran home and was known as "the little Jesus" by his schoolmates. He studied theology at the University of Bonn and philology at Leipzig, becoming an atheist in the process. At the age of twenty-four he was appointed professor of classical philology at the University of Basel in Switzerland, where he taught for ten years until forced by ill health to retire. Eventually he became mentally ill. He died on August 25, 1900.

Nietzsche believes that the fundamental creative force that motivates all creation is the will to power. We all seek to affirm ourselves, to flourish and dominate. Since we are essentially unequal in ability, it follows that the fittest will survive and be victorious in the contest with the weaker and the baser. There is great aesthetic beauty in the noble spirit coming to fruition, but this process is hampered by Judeo-Christian morality, which Nietzsche labels "slave morality." Slave morality, which is the invention of jealous priests, envious and resentful of the power of the noble, prescribes that we give up the will to power and excellence and become meek and mild, that we believe the lie of all humans having equal worth. In our reading, Nietzsche also refers to this as the ethics of resentment.

Nietzsche's ideas of inegalitarian ethics are based on his notion of the death of God. God plays no vital role in our culture—except as a protector of the slave morality, including the idea of equal worth of all persons. If we recognize that there is no rational basis for believing in God, we will see that the whole edifice of slave morality must crumble and with it the notion of equal worth. In its place will arise the morality of the noble person based on the virtues of the high courage, discipline, and intelligence, in the pursuit of self-affirmation and excellence.

We begin with some aphorisms, then his famous description of the madman who announces the death of God (from *Joyful Wisdom*), and then to longer passages from *Beyond Good and Evil, The Twilight of the Idols,* and *The Anti-Christ.*

FOR FURTHER READING

Copleston, F. C. *Friedrich Nietzsche, A Philosopher of Culture.* (Barnes & Noble, 1975).

Danto, Arthur. *Nietzsche As Philosopher.* (Macmillan, 1965).

Hollingdale, R. J. *Nietzsche.* (Routledge & Kegan Paul, 1973).

Kaufmann, W. *Nietzsche, Philosopher, Psychologist, Anti-Christ.* (Princeton University Press, 1968).

Nietzsche, Friedrich. *The Complete Works of Nietzsche,* ed. Oscar Levy. (Foulis, 1910).

Nietzsche, Friedrich. *The Portable Nietzsche,* ed. Walter Kaufmann. (Viking Press, 1954).

Richardson, John. *Nietzsche's System.* (Oxford University Press, 1996).

Solomon, Robert C. and Kathleen M. Higgins, eds. *Reading Nietzsche.* (Oxford University Press, 1988).

Stern, J. P. *A Study of Nietzsche.* (Cambridge University Press, 1977).

Aphorisms

THOUGHTS ON THE MEANING OF LIFE

"Man would sooner have the Void for his purpose than be void of Purpose."

"Hegel says, 'That at the bottom of history, and particularly of world history, there is a final aim, and that this has actually been realized in it and is being realized—the plan of Providence—that there is reason in history: that is to be shown philosophically and this as altogether necessary.' [This is balderdash] My life has no aim and this is evident even from the accidental nature of its origin. That I can posit an aim for myself is another matter. But a state has no aim; we alone give it an aim."

"Whatever does not kill me makes me stronger."

TRUTH AND UNTRUTH

"A belief, however necessary it may be for the preservation of a species, has nothing to do with truth."

"The falseness of a judgment is not for us necessarily an objection to a judgment. The question is to what extent it is life-promoting, life-preserving, species preserving, perhaps even species cultivating. To recognize untruth as a condition of life—that certainly means resisting accustomed value feelings in a dangerous way; and a philosophy that risks this would by that token alone place itself beyond good and evil." (Beyond Good and Evil, 4).

BEYOND GOOD AND EVIL

"To speak of right and wrong per se makes no sense at all. No act of violence, rape, exploitation, destruction, is intrinsically *unjust,* since life itself is violent, rapacious, exploitative, and destructive and cannot be conceived otherwise." (Genealogy of Morals 208)

WILL TO POWER

What is good? All that enhances the feeling of power, the Will to Power, and the power itself in man. What is bad?—All that proceeds from weakness. What is happiness?—The feeling that power is increasing—that resistance has been overcome.

Not contentment, but more power; not peace at any price but war; not virtue, but competence (virtue in the Renaissance sense, *virtu,* free from moralistic acid). The first principle of our humanism: The weak and the failures shall perish. They ought even to be helped to perish.

What is more harmful than any vice?—Practical sympathy and pity for all the failures and all the weak: Christianity.

STYLE AND CHARACTER

One thing is needful.—To give style to one's character—a great and rare art! It is practiced by those who survey all the strengths and weaknesses of their nature and then fit them into an artist plan until every one of them appears as art and reason and even weaknesses delight the eye. Here a large mass of second nature has been added; there a piece of original nature has been removed—both times through long practice and daily work at it. Here the ugly that could not be removed is concealed; there it has been reinterpreted and made sublime. Much that is vague and resisted shaping has been saved and exploited for distant views. . . . In the end, when the work is finished, it becomes evident how the constraint of a single taste governed and formed everything large and small. Whether this taste was good or bad is less important than one might suppose, if only it was a single taste!

THE ÜBERMENSCH (SUPERMAN)

We immoralists make it a point of honor to be affirmers. More and more our eyes have opened to that economy which needs and knows how to utilize all that the holy witlessness of the priest, of the diseased reason of the priest, rejects—that economy in the law of life which finds an advantage even in the disgusting species of the prigs, the priests, the virtuous. What advantage? Be we ourselves, we immoralists, are the answer."

ON INTERPRETATION

Everything is Interpretation: Against positivism, which halts at phenomena—Against those who say

"There are only facts," I say, "No, facts are precisely what there is not, only interpretations." We cannot establish any fact *in itself*. Perhaps it is folly to want to do such a thing.

"Everything is subjective," you say; but even here we have interpretation. The "subject" is not something given. It is something given; it is something added and invented and projected behind what there is. Finally, is it necessary to posit an interpreter behind the interpretation? Even this is invention, hypothesis.

Insofar as the word "knowledge" has any meaning, the world is knowable; but it is *interpretable* otherwise. It has no meaning behind it, but countless meanings.

PERSPECTIVISM

It is our needs that interpret the world; our drives and their For and Against. Every drive is a kind of lust to rule; each one has its perspective that it would like to compel all other drives to accept as a norm.

Joyful Wisdom

THE MADMAN AND THE DEATH OF GOD

Have you ever heard of the madman who on a bright morning lighted a lantern and ran to the market-place calling out unceasingly: "I seek God! I seek God!"—As there were many people standing about who did not believe in God, he caused a great deal of amusement. Why! is he lost? said one. Has he strayed away like a child? said another. Or does he keep himself hidden? Is he afraid of us? Has he taken a sea-voyage? Has he emigrated?—the people cried out laughingly, all in a hubbub. The insane man jumped into their midst and transfixed them with his glances. "Where is God gone?" he called out. "I mean to tell you! *We have killed him,*—you and I! We are all his murderers! But how have we done it? How were we able to drink up the sea? Who gave us the sponge to wipe away the whole horizon? What did we do when we loosened this earth from its sun? Whither does it now move? Whither do we move? Away from all suns? Do we not dash on unceasingly? Backwards, sideways, forewards, in all directions? Is there still an above and below? Do we not stray, as through infinite nothingness? Does not empty space breathe upon us? Has it not become colder? Does not night come on continually, darker and darker? Shall we not have to light lanterns in the morning? Do we not hear the noise of the gravediggers who are burying God? Do we not smell the divine putrefaction?—for even Gods putrefy! God is dead! God remains dead! And we have killed him! How shall we console ourselves, the most murderous of all murderers? The holiest and the mightiest that the world has hitherto possessed, has bled to death under our knife,—who will wipe the blood from us? With what water could we cleanse ourselves? What lustrums, what sacred games shall we have to devise? Is not the magnitude of this deed too great for us? Shall we not ourselves have to become Gods, merely to seem worthy of it? There never was a greater event,—and on account of it, all who are born after us belong to a higher history than any history hitherto!"—Here the madman was silent and looked again at his hearers; they also were silent and looked at him in surprise. At last he threw his lantern on the ground, so that it broke in pieces and was extinguished. "I come too early," he then said, "I am not yet at the right time. This prodigious event is still on its way, and is traveling,—it has not yet reached men's ears. Lightning and thunder need time, the light of the stars needs time, deeds need time, even after they are done, to be seen and heard. This deed is as yet further from them than the furthest star,—*and yet they have done it!*"—It is further stated that the madman made his way into different churches on the same day, and there intoned his *Requiem aeternam deo*. When led out and called to account, he always gave the reply: "What are these churches now, if they are not the tombs and monuments of God?"— . . .

Beyond Good and Evil

WHAT IS NOBLE?

Every elevation of the type "man," has hitherto been the work of an aristocratic society and so it will always be—a society believing in a long scale of gradations of rank and differences of worth among human beings, and requiring slavery in some form or other. Without the *pathos of distance,* such as grows out of the incarnated difference of classes, out of the constant outlooking and downlooking of the ruling caste on subordinates and instruments, and out of their equally constant practice of obeying and commanding, of keeping down and keeping at a distance—that other more mysterious pathos could never have arisen, the longing for an ever new widening of distance within the soul itself, the formation of ever higher, rarer, further, more extended, more comprehensive states, in short, just the elevation of the type "man," the continued "self-surmounting of man," to use a moral formula in a supermoral sense. To be sure, one must not resign oneself to any humanitarian illusions about the history of the origin of an aristocratic society (that is to say, of the preliminary condition for the elevation of the type "man"): the truth is hard. Let us acknowledge unprejudicedly how ever higher civilisation hitherto has *originated!* Men with a still natural nature, barbarians in every terrible sense of the word, men of prey, still in possession of unbroken strength of will and desire for power, threw themselves upon weaker, more moral, more peaceful races (perhaps trading or cattle-rearing communities), or upon old mellow civilisations in which the final vital force was flickering out in brilliant fireworks of wit and depravity. At the commencement, the noble caste was always the barbarian caste: their superiority did not consist first of all in their physical, but in their psychical power—they were more *complete* men (which at every point also implies the same as "more complete beasts").

Corruption—as the indication that anarchy threatens to break out among the instincts, and that the foundation of the emotions, called "life," is convulsed—is something radically different according to the organisation in which it manifests itself. When, for instance, an aristocracy like that of France at the beginning of the Revolution, flung away its privileges with sublime disgust and sacrificed itself to an excess of its moral sentiments, it was corruption:—it was really only the closing act of the corruption which had existed for centuries, by virtue of which that aristocracy had abdicated step by step its lordly prerogatives and lowered itself to a *function* of royalty (in the end even to its decoration and parade-dress). The essential thing, however, in a good and healthy aristocracy is that it should *not* regard itself as a function either of the kingship or the commonwealth, but as the *significance* and highest justification thereof—that it should therefore accept with a good conscience the sacrifice of a legion of individuals, who, *for its sake,* must be suppressed and reduced to imperfect men, to slaves and instruments. Its fundamental belief must be precisely that society is *not* allowed to exist for its own sake, but only as a foundation and scaffolding, by means of which a select class of beings may be able to elevate themselves to their higher duties, and in general to a higher *existence:* like those sun-seeking climbing plants in Java—they are called *Sipo Matador,*—which encircle an oak so long and so often with their arms, until at last, high above it, but supported by it, they can unfold their tops in the open light, and exhibit their happiness.

To refrain mutually from injury, from violence, from exploitation, and put one's will on a par with that of others: this may result in a certain rough sense in good conduct among individuals when the necessary conditions are given (namely, the actual similarity of the individuals in amount of force and degree of worth, and their co-relation within one organisation). As soon, however, as one wished to take this principle more generally, and if possible even as *the fundamental principle of society,* it would immediately disclose what it really is—namely, a Will to the *denial* of life, a principle of dissolution and decay. Here one must think profoundly to the very basis and resist all sentimental weakness: life itself is *essentially* appropriation, injury, conquest of the strange and weak, suppression, severity, obtrusion of peculiar forms, incorporation, and at the least, putting it mildest, exploitation;—but why should one for ever use precisely these words on which for ages a disparaging purpose has been stamped? Even the organisation within which, as was previously supposed, the individuals treat each other as equal—it takes place in every healthy aristocracy—must itself, if it be a living and not a dying organisation, do all that towards other bodies, which the individuals within it refrain from doing to each other: it will have to be the incarnated Will to Power, it will endeavour to grow, to gain ground, attract to itself and acquire ascendency—not owing to any morality or immorality, but because it *lives,* and because life *is* precisely Will to Power. On no point, however, is the ordinary consciousness of Europeans more unwilling to be corrected than on this matter; people now rave everywhere, even under the guise of science, about coming conditions of society in which "the exploiting character" is to be absent:—that sounds to my ears as if they promised to invent a mode of life which should refrain from all organic functions. "Exploitation" does not belong to a depraved, or imperfect and primitive society: it belongs to the *nature* of the living being as a primary organic function; it is a consequence of the intrinsic Will to Power, which is precisely the Will to Life.—Granting that as a theory this is a novelty—as a reality it is the *fundamental fact* of all history: let us be so far honest towards ourselves!

MASTER AND SLAVE MORALITY

In a tour through the many finer and coarser moralities which have hitherto prevailed or still prevail on the earth, I found certain traits recurring regularly together, and connected with one another, until finally two primary types revealed themselves to me, and a radical distinction was brought to light. There is *master-morality* and *slave-morality;*—I would at once add, however, that in all higher and mixed civilisations, there are also attempts at the reconciliation of the two moralities; but one finds still oftener the confusion and mutual misunderstanding of them, indeed, sometimes their close juxtaposition—even in the same man, within one soul. The distinctions of moral values have either originated in a ruling caste, pleasantly conscious of being different from the ruled—or among the ruled class, the slaves and dependents of all sorts. In the first case, when it is the rulers who determine the conception "good," it is the exalted, proud disposition which is regarded as the distinguishing feature, and that which determines the order of rank. The noble type of man separates from himself the beings in whom the opposite of this exalted, proud disposition displays itself: he despises them. Let it at once be noted that in this first kind of morality the antithesis "good" and "bad" means practically the same as "noble" and "despicable";—the antithesis "good" and "*evil*" is of a different origin. The cowardly, the timid, the insignificant, and those thinking merely of narrow utility are despised; moreover, also, the distrustful, with their constrained glances, the self-abasing, the dog-like kind of men who let themselves be abused, the mendicant flatterers, and above all the liars:—it is a fundamental belief of all aristocrats that the common people are untruthful. "We truthful ones"—the nobility in ancient Greece called themselves. It is obvious that everywhere the designations of moral value were at first applied to *men,* and were only derivatively and at a later period applied to *actions;* it is a gross mistake, therefore, when historians of morals start with questions like, "Why have sympathetic actions been praised?" The noble type of man regards *himself* as a determiner of values; he does not require to be approved of; he passes the judgment: "What is injurious to me is injurious in itself"; he knows that it is he himself only who confers honour on things; he is a *creator of values.* He honours whatever he recognises in himself: such morality is self-glorification. In the foreground there is the feeling of plenitude, of power, which seeks to overflow, the happiness of high tension, the consciousness of a wealth which would fain give and bestow:—the noble man also helps the unfortunate, but not—or scarcely—out of pity, but rather from an impulse generated by the superabundance of power. The noble man honours in himself the powerful one, him also who has power over himself, who knows how to speak and how to keep silence, who takes pleasure in subjecting himself to severity and hardness, and has reverence for all that is severe and hard. "Wotan placed a hard heart in my breast," says an old Scandinavian Saga: it is thus rightly expressed from the soul of a proud Viking. Such a type of man is even proud of *not* being made for sympathy; the hero of the Saga therefore adds warningly: "He who has not a hard heart when young, will never have one." The noble and brave who think thus are the furthest removed from the morality which sees precisely in sympathy, or in acting for the good of others, or in *désintéressement,* the characteristic of the moral; faith in oneself, pride in oneself, a radical enmity and irony towards "selflessness," belong as definitely to noble morality, as do a careless scorn and precaution in presence of sympathy and the "warm heart."—It is the powerful who *know* how to honour, it is their art, their domain for invention. The profound reverence for age and for tradition—all law rests on this double reverence,—the belief and prejudice in favour of ancestors and unfavourable to newcomers, is typical in the morality of the powerful; and if, reversely, men of "modern ideas" believe almost instinctively in "progress" and the "future," and are more and more lacking in respect for old age, the ignoble origin of these "ideas" has complacently betrayed itself thereby. A morality of the ruling class, however, is more especially foreign and irritating to present-day taste in the sternness of its principle that one has duties only to one's equals; that one may act towards beings of a lower rank, towards all that is foreign, just as seems good to one, or "as the heart desires," and in any case "beyond good and evil": it is here that sympathy and similar sentiments can have a place. The ability and obligation to exercise prolonged gratitude and prolonged revenge—both only within the circle of equals,—artfulness in retaliation, *raffinement* of the idea in friendship, a certain necessity to have enemies (as outlets for the emotions of envy, quarrelsomeness, arrogance—in fact, in order to be a good *friend*): all these are typical characteristics of the noble morality, which, as has been pointed out, is not the morality of "modern ideas," and is therefore at present difficult to realise and also to unearth and disclose.—It is otherwise with the second type of morality, *slave-morality.* Supposing that the abused, the oppressed, the suffering, the unemancipated, the weary, and those uncertain of themselves, should moralise, what will be the common element in their moral estimates? Probably a pessimistic suspicion with regard to the entire situation of man will find expression, perhaps a condemnation of man, together with his situation. The slave has an unfavourable eye for the virtues of the powerful; he has a scepticism and distrust, a *refinement* of distrust of everything "good" that is there honoured—he would fain persuade himself that the very happiness there is not genuine. On the other hand, *those* qualities which serve to alleviate the existence of sufferers are brought into prominence and flooded with light; it is here that sympathy, the kind, helping hand, the warm heart, patience, diligence, humility, and friendliness attain to honour; for here these are the most useful qualities, and almost the only means of supporting the burden of existence. Slave-morality is essentially the morality of utility. Here is the seat of the origin of the famous antithesis "good" and "evil":—power and dangerousness are assumed to reside in the evil, a certain dreadfulness, subtlety, and strength, which do not admit of being despised. According to slave-morality, therefore, the "evil" man arouses fear; according to master-morality, it is precisely the "good" man who arouses fear and seeks to arouse it, while the bad man is regarded as the despicable being. The contrast attains its maximum when, in accordance with the logical consequences of slave-morality, a shade of depreciation—it may be slight and well-intentioned—at last attaches itself to the "good" man of this morality; because, according to the servile mode of thought, the good man must in any case be the *safe* man: he is good-natured, easily deceived, perhaps a little stupid, *un bonhomme.* Everywhere that slave-morality gains the ascendency, language shows a tendency to approximate the significations of the words "good" and "stupid."—A last fundamental difference: the desire for *freedom,* the instinct for happiness and the refinements of the feeling of liberty belong as necessarily to slave-morals and morality, as artifice and enthusiasm in reverence and devotion are the regular symptoms of an aristocratic mode of thinking and estimating.—Hence we can understand without further detail why love *as a passion*—it is our European specialty—must absolutely be of noble origin; as is well known, its invention is due to the Provençal poet-cavaliers, those brilliant, ingenious men of the "*gai saber,*" to whom Europe owes so much, and almost owes itself. . . .

There is an *instinct for rank,* which more than anything else is already the sign of a *high* rank; there is a *delight* in the *nuances* of reverence which leads one to infer noble origin and habits. The refinement, goodness, and loftiness of a soul are put to a perilous test when something passes by that is of the highest rank, but is not yet protected by the awe of authority from obtrusive touches and incivilities: something that goes its way like a living touchstone, undistinguished, undiscovered, and tentative, perhaps voluntarily veiled and disguised. He whose task and practice it is to investigate souls, will avail himself of many varieties of this very art to determine the ultimate value of a soul, the unalterable, innate order of rank to which it belongs: he will test it by its *instinct for reverence. Différence engendre haine* [Difference engenders hate.—ED.]: the vulgarity of many a nature spurts up suddenly like dirty water, when any holy vessel, any jewel from closed shrines, any book bearing the marks of great destiny, is brought before it; while on the other hand, there is an involuntary silence, a hesitation of the eye, a cessation of all gestures, by which it is indicated that a soul *feels* the nearness of what is worthiest of respect. . . .

The revolt of the slaves in morals begins in the very principle of *resentment* becoming creative and giving birth to values—a resentment experienced by creatures who, deprived as they are of the proper outlet of action, are forced to find their compensation in an imaginary revenge. While every aristocratic morality springs from a triumphant affirmation of its own demands, the slave morality says "no" from the very outset to what is "outside itself," "different from itself," and "not itself": and this "no" is its creative deed. This reversal of the valuing standpoint—this *inevitable* gravitation to the objective instead of back to the subjective—is typical of "resentment": the slave-morality requires as the condition of its existence an external and objective world, to employ physiological terminology, it requires objective stimuli to be capable of action at all—its action is fundamentally a reaction. The contrary is the case when we come to the aristocrat's system of values: it acts and grows spontaneously, it merely seeks its antithesis in order to pronounce a more grateful and exultant "yes" to its own self;—its negative conception, "low," "vulgar," "bad," is merely a pale late-born foil in comparison with its positive and fundamental conception (saturated as it is with life and passion), of "we aristocrats, we good ones, we beautiful ones, we happy ones."

When the aristocratic morality goes astray and commits sacrilege on reality, this is limited to that particular sphere with which it is *not* sufficiently acquainted—a sphere, in fact, from the real knowledge of which it disdainfully defends itself. It misjudges, in some cases, the sphere which it despises, the sphere of the common vulgar man and the low people: on the other hand, due weight should be given to the consideration that in any case the mood of contempt, of disdain, of superciliousness, even on the supposition that it *falsely* portrays the object of its contempt, will always be far removed from that degree of falsity which will always characterise the attacks—in effigy, of course—of the vindictive hatred and revengefulness of the weak in onslaughts on their enemies. In point of fact, there is in contempt too strong an admixture of nonchalance, of casualness, of boredom, of impatience, even of personal exultation, for it to be capable of distorting its victim into a real caricature or a real monstrosity. Attention again should be paid to the almost benevolent *nuances* which, for instance, the Greek nobility imports into all the words by which it distinguishes the common people from itself; note how continuously a kind of pity, care, and consideration imparts its honeyed *flavour*, until at last almost all the words which are applied to the vulgar man survive finally as expressions for "unhappy," "worthy of pity". . .—and how, conversely, "bad," "low," "unhappy" have never ceased to ring in the Greek ear with a tone in which "unhappy" is the predominant note: this is a heritage of the old noble aristocratic morality, which remains true to itself even in contempt. . . . The "well-born" simply *felt* themselves the "happy"; they did not have to manufacture their happiness artificially through looking at their enemies, or in cases to talk and lie themselves into happiness (as is the custom with all resentful men); and similarly, complete men as they were, exuberant with strength, and consequently *necessarily* energetic, they were too wise to dissociate happiness from action—activity becomes in their minds necessarily counted as happiness (that is the etymology of *εὖ πράττειν*)—all in sharp contrast to the "happiness" of the weak and the oppressed, with their festering venom and malignity, among whom happiness appears essentially as a narcotic, a deadening, a quietude, a peace, a "Sabbath," an enervation of the mind and relaxation of the limbs,—in short, a purely *passive* phenomenon. While the aristocratic man lived in confidence and openness with himself (*γεν-ναῖος*, "noble-born," emphasises the nuance "sincere," and perhaps also "naïf"), the resentful man, on the other hand, is neither sincere nor naïf, nor honest and candid with himself. His soul *squints*; his mind loves hidden crannies, tortuous paths and backdoors, everything secret appeals to him as *his* world, *his* safety, *his* balm; he is past master in silence, in not forgetting, in waiting, in provisional self-depreciation and self-abasement. A race of such *resentful* men will of necessity eventually prove more *prudent* than any aristocratic race, it will honour prudence on quite a distinct scale, as, in fact, a paramount condition of existence, while prudence among aristocratic men is apt to be tinged with a delicate flavour of luxury and refinement; so among them it plays nothing like so integral a part as that complete certainty of function of the governing *unconscious* instincts, or as indeed a certain lack of prudence, such as a vehement and valiant charge, whether against danger or the enemy, or as those ecstatic bursts of rage, love, reverence, gratitude, by which at all times noble souls have recognised each other. When the resentment of the aristocratic man manifests itself, it fulfils and exhausts itself in an immediate reaction, and consequently instills no *venom:* on the other hand, it never manifests itself at all in countless instances, when in the case of the feeble and weak it would be inevitable. An inability to take seriously for any length of time their enemies, their disasters, their *misdeeds*—that is the sign of the full strong natures who possess a superfluity of moulding plastic force, that heals completely and produces forgetfulness: a good example of this in the modern world is Mirabeau, who had no memory for any insults and meannesses which were practised on him, and who was only incapable of forgiving because he forgot. Such a man indeed shakes off with a shrug many a worm which would have buried itself in another; it is only in characters like these that we see the possibility (supposing, of course, that there is such a possibility in the world) of the real "*love* of one's enemies." What respect for his enemies is found, forsooth, in an aristocratic man—and such a reverence is already a bridge to love! He insists on having his enemy to himself as his distinction. He tolerates no other enemy but a man in whose character there is nothing to despise and *much* to honour! On the other hand, imagine the "enemy" as the resentful man conceives him—and it is here exactly that we see his work, his creativeness; he has conceived "the evil enemy," the "evil one," and indeed that is the root idea from which he now evolves as a contrasting and corresponding figure a "good one," himself—his very self!

The method of this man is quite contrary to that of the aristocratic man, who conceives the root idea "good" spontaneously and straight away, that is to say, out of himself, and from that material then creates for himself a concept of "bad"! This "bad" of aristocratic origin and that "evil" out of the cauldron of unsatisfied hatred—the former an imitation, an "extra," an additional nuance; the latter, on the other hand, the original, the beginning, the essential act in the conception of a slave-morality—these two words "bad" and "evil," how great a difference do they make, in spite of the fact that they have an identical contrary in the idea "good." But the idea "good" is *not* the same: much rather let the question be asked, "Who is really evil according to the meaning of the morality of resentment?" In all sternness let it be answered thus:—*just* the good man of the other morality, just the aristocrat, the powerful one, the one who rules, but who is distorted by the venomous eye of resentfulness, into a new colour, a new signification, a new appearance. This particular point we would be the last to deny: the man who learnt to know those "good" ones only as enemies, learnt at the same time not to know them only as "*evil enemies,*" and the same men who . . . were kept so rigorously in bounds through convention, respect, custom, and gratitude, though much more through mutual vigilance and jealousy, . . . these men who in their relations with each other find so many new ways of manifesting consideration, self-control, delicacy, loyalty, pride, and friendship, these men are in reference to what is outside their circle (where the foreign element, a *foreign* country, begins), not much better than beasts of prey, which have been let loose. They enjoy their freedom from all social control, they feel that in the wilderness they can give vent with impunity to that tension which is produced by enclosure and imprisonment in the peace of society, they *revert* to the innocence of the beast-of-prey conscience, like jubilant monsters, who perhaps come from a ghostly bout of murder, arson, rape, and torture, with bravado and a moral equanimity, as though merely some wild student's prank had been played, perfectly convinced that the poets have now an ample theme to sing and celebrate. It is impossible not to recognise at the core of all these aristocratic races the beast of prey; the magnificent *blonde brute,* avidly rampant for spoil and victory; this hidden core needed an outlet from time to time, the beast must get loose again, must return into the wilderness—the Roman, Arabic, German, and Japanese nobility, the Homeric heroes, the Scandinavian Vikings, are all alike in this need. It is the aristocratic races who have left the idea "Barbarian" on all the tracks in which they have marched; nay, a consciousness of this very barbarianism, and even a pride in it, manifests itself even in their highest civilisation (for example, when Pericles says to his Athenians in that celebrated funeral oration, "Our audacity has forced a way over every land and sea, rearing everywhere imperishable memorials of itself for *good* and for *evil*"). This audacity of aristocratic races, mad, absurd, and spasmodic as may be its expression; the incalculable and fantastic nature of their enterprises, . . . their nonchalance and contempt for safety, body, life, and comfort, their awful joy and intense delight in all destruction, in all the ecstasies of victory and cruelty,—all these features become cystallised, for those who suffered thereby in the picture of the "barbarian," of the "evil enemy," perhaps of the "Goth" and of the "Vandal." The profound, icy mistrust which the German provokes, as soon as he arrives at power,—even at the present time,—is always still an aftermath of that inextinguishable horror with which for whole centuries Europe has regarded the wrath of the blonde Teuton beast. . . .

. . . One may be perfectly justified in being always afraid of the blonde beast that lies at the core of all aristocratic races, and in being on one's guard: but who would not a hundred times prefer to be afraid, when one at the same time admires, than to be immune from fear, at the cost of being perpetually obsessed with the loathsome spectacle of the distorted, the dwarfed, the stunted, the envenomed? And is that not our fate? What produces to-day our repulsion towards "man"?—for we *suffer* from "man," there is no doubt about it. It is not fear; it is rather that we have nothing more to fear from men; it is that the worm "man" is in the foreground and pullulates; it is that the "tame man," the wretched mediocre and unedifying creature, has learnt to consider himself a goal and a pinnacle, an inner meaning, an historic principle, a "higher man"; yes, it is that he has a certain right so to consider himself, in so far as he feels that in contrast to that excess of deformity, disease, exhaustion, and effeteness whose odour is beginning to pollute present-day Europe, he at any rate has achieved a relative success, he at any rate still says "yes" to life.

GOODNESS AND THE WILL TO POWER

What is good?—All that enhances the feeling of power, the Will to Power, and the power itself in man. What is bad?—All that proceeds from weakness. What is happiness?—The feeling that power is increasing—that resistance has been overcome.

Not contentment, but more power; not peace at any price but war; not virtue, but competence (virtue in the Renaissance sense, *virtu,* free from all moralistic acid). The first principle of our humanism: The weak and the failures shall perish. They ought even to be helped to perish.

What is more harmful than any vice?—Practical sympathy and pity for all the failures and all the weak: Christianity.

Christianity is the religion of pity. Pity opposes the noble passions which heighten our vitality. It has a depressing effect, depriving us of strength. As we multiply the instances of pity we gradually lose our strength of nobility. Pity makes suffering contagious and under certain conditions it may cause a total loss of life and vitality out of all proportion to the magnitude of the cause. . . . Pity is the practice of nihilism.

Twilight of the Idols

MAXIMS AND MISSILES

1. Idleness is the parent of all psychology. What? Is psychology then a—vice?

2. Even the pluckiest among us has but seldom the courage of what he really knows.

3. Aristotle says that in order to live alone, a man must be either an animal or a god. The third alternative is lacking: a man must be both—a *philosopher.*

4. "All truth is simple."—Is not this a double lie?

5. Once for all I wish to be blind to many things—Wisdom sets bounds even to knowledge.

6. A man recovers best from his exceptional nature—his intellectuality—by giving his animal instincts a chance.

7. Which is it? Is man only a blunder of God? Or is God only a blunder of man?

8. *From the military school of life.*—That which does not kill me, makes me stronger.

9. Help thyself, then everyone will help thee. A principle of neighbour-love.

10. A man should not play the coward to his deeds. He should not repudiate them once he has performed them. Pangs of conscience are indecent.

11. Can a donkey be tragic?—To perish beneath a load that one can neither bear nor throw off? This is the case of the Philosopher.

12. If a man knows the wherefore of his existence, then the manner of it can take care of itself. Man does not aspire to happiness; only the Englishman does that.

13. Man created women—out of what? Out of a rib of his god,—of his "ideal."

14. What? Art thou looking for something? Thou wouldst fain multiply thyself tenfold, a hundredfold? Thou seekest followers? Seek ciphers!

15. Posthumous men, like myself, are not so well understood as men who reflect their age, but they are heard with more respect. In plain English: we are never understood—hence our authority.

16. *Among women.*—"Truth? Oh, you do not know truth! Is it not an outrage on all our *pudeurs?*"—

17. There is an artist after my own heart, modest in his needs: he really wants only two things, his bread and his art—*panem et Circen.*

18. He who knows not how to plant his will in things at least endows them with some meaning: that is to say, he believes that a will is already present in them. (A principle of faith.)

19. What? Ye chose virtue and the heaving breast, and at the same time ye squint covetously at the advantages of the unscrupulous.—But with virtue ye renounce all "advantages" . . . (to be nailed to an Antisemite's door).

20. The perfect woman perpetrates literature as if it were a petty vice: as an experiment, *en passant,* and looking about her all the while to see whether anybody is noticing her, hoping that somebody *is* noticing her.

21. One should adopt only those situations in which one is in no need of sham virtues, but rather, like the tight-rope dancer on his tight rope, in which one must either fall or stand—or escape.

22. "Evil men have no songs."[1]—How is it that the Russians have songs?

23. "German intellect"; for eighteen years this has been a *contradictio in adjecto.*

24. By seeking the beginnings of things, a man becomes a crab. The historian looks backwards: in the end he also *believes* backwards.

25. Contentment preserves one even from catching cold. Has a woman who knew that she was well-dressed ever caught cold?—No, not even when she had scarcely a rag to her back.

26. I distrust all systematisers, and avoid them. The will to a system, shows a lack of honesty.

27. Man thinks woman profound—why? Because he can never fathom her depths. Woman is not even shallow.

28. When woman possesses masculine virtues, she is enough to make you run away. When she possesses no masculine virtues, she herself runs away.

29. "How often conscience had to bite in times gone by! What good teeth it must have had! And today, what is amiss?"—A dentist's question.

30. Errors of haste are seldom committed singly. The first time a man always does too much. And precisely on that account he commits a second error, and then he does too little.

31. The trodden worm curls up. This testifies to its caution. It thus reduces its chances of being trodden upon again. In the language of morality: Humility.—

32. There is such a thing as a hatred of lies and dissimulation, which is the outcome of a delicate sense of humour; there is also the selfsame hatred but as the result of cowardice, in so far as falsehood is forbidden by Divine law. Too cowardly to lie. . . .

33. What trifles constitute happiness! The sound of a bagpipe. Without music life would be a mistake. The German imagines even God as a songster.

34. *On ne peut penser et écrire qu'assis* (G. Flaubert). Here I have got you, you nihilist! A sedentary life is the real sin against the Holy Spirit. Only those thoughts that come by walking have any value.

35. There are times when we psychologists are like horses, and grow fretful. We see our own shadow rise and fall before us. The psychologist must look away from himself if he wishes to see anything at all.

1. This is a reference to Seume's poem "*Die Gesänge,*" the first verse of which is:—

> *"Wo man singet, lass dich ruhig nieder,*
> *Ohne Furcht, was man im Lande glaubt;*
> *Wo man singet, wird kein Mensch beraubt:*
> *Bösewichter haben keine Lieder."*

(Wherever people sing thou canst safely settle down without a qualm as to what the general faith of the land may be. Wherever people sing, no man is ever robbed; *rascals* have no songs.) Popular tradition, however, renders the lines thus:—

> *"Wo man singt, da lass dich ruhig nieder;*
> *Böse Menschen* [evil men] *haben keine Lieder."*

—Tr.

36. Do we immoralists injure virtue in any way? Just as little as the anarchists injure royalty. Only since they have been shot at do princes sit firmly on their thrones once more. Moral: *morality must be shot at.*

37. Thou runnest *ahead?*—Dost thou do so as a shepherd or as an exception? A third alternative would be the fugitive. . . . First question of conscience.

38. Art thou genuine or art thou only an actor? Art thou a representative or the thing represented, itself? Finally, art thou perhaps simply a copy of an actor? . . . Second question of conscience.

39. *The disappointed man speaks:*—I sought for great men, but all I found were the apes of their ideal.

40. Art thou one who looks on, or one who puts his own shoulder to the wheel?—Or art thou one who looks away, or who turns aside? . . . Third question of conscience.

41. Wilt thou go in company, or lead, or go by thyself? . . . A man should know what he desires, and that he desires something.—Fourth question of conscience.

42. They were but rungs in my ladder, on them I made my ascent:—to that end I had to go beyond them. But they imagined that I wanted to lay myself to rest upon them.

43. What matters it whether I am acknowledged to be right! I am much too right. And he who laughs best to-day, will also laugh last.

44. The formula of my happiness: a Yea, a Nay, a straight line, a *goal.* . . .

THE PROBLEM OF SOCRATES

1. In all ages the wisest have always agreed in their judgment of life: *it is no good.* At all times and places the same words have been on their lips,—words full of doubt, full of melancholy, full of weariness of life, full of hostility to life. Even Socrates' dying words were:—"To live—means to be ill a long while: I owe a cock to the God Æsculapius." Even Socrates had had enough of it. What does that prove? What does it point to? Formerly people would have said (—oh, it has been said, and loudly enough too; by our Pessimists loudest of all!): "In any case there must be some truth in this! The *consensus sapientium* is a proof of truth."—Shall we say the same to-day? *May* we do so? "In any case there must be some sickness here," we make reply. These great sages of all periods should first be examined more closely! Is it possible that they were, everyone of them, a little shaky on their legs, effete, rocky, decadent? Does wisdom perhaps appear on earth after the manner of a crow attracted by a slight smell of carrion?

2. This irreverent belief that the great sages were decadent types, first occurred to me precisely in regard to that case concerning which both learned and vulgar prejudice was most opposed to my view. I recognised Socrates and Plato as symptoms of decline, as instruments in the disintegration of Hellas, as pseudo-Greek, as anti-Greek ("The Birth of Tragedy," 1872). That *consensus sapientium,* as I perceived ever more and more clearly, did not in the least prove that they were right in the matter on which they agreed. It proved rather that these sages themselves must have been alike in some physiological particular, in order to assume the same negative attitude towards life—in order to be bound to assume that attitude. After all, judgments and valuations of life, whether for or against, cannot be true: their only value lies in the fact that they are symptoms; they can be considered only as symptoms,—*per se* such judgments are nonsense. You must therefore endeavour by all means to reach out and try to grasp this astonishingly subtle axiom, *that the value of life cannot be estimated.* A living man cannot do so, because he is a contending party, or rather the very object in the dispute, and not a judge; nor can a dead man estimate it—for other reasons. For a philosopher to see a problem in the value of life, is almost an objection against him, a note of interrogation set against his wisdom—a lack of wisdom. What? Is it possible that all these great sages were not only decadents, but that they were not even wise? Let me however return to the problem of Socrates.

3. To judge from his origin, Socrates belonged to the lowest of the low: Socrates was mob. You know, and you can still see it for yourself, how ugly he was. But ugliness, which in itself is an objection, was almost a refutation among the Greeks. Was Socrates really a Greek? Ugliness is not infrequently the expression of thwarted development, or of development arrested by crossing. In other cases it appears as a decadent development. The anthropologists among the criminal specialists declare that the typical criminal is ugly: *monstrum in fronte, mon-*

strum in animo. But the criminal is a decadent.[1] Was Socrates a typical criminal?—At all events this would not clash with that famous physiognomist's judgment which was so repugnant to Socrates friends. While on his way through Athens a certain foreigner who was no fool at judging by looks, told Socrates to his face that he was a monster, that his body harboured all the worst vices and passions. And Socrates replied simply: "You know me sir!"—

4. Not only are the acknowledged wildness and anarchy of Socrates' instincts indicative of decadence, but also that preponderance of the logical faculties and that malignity of the mis-shapen which was his special characteristic. Neither should we forget those aural delusions which were religiously interpreted as "the demon of Socrates." Everything in his is exaggerated, *buffo*, caricature, his nature is also full of concealment, of ulterior motives, and of underground currents. I try to understand the idiosyncrasy from which the Socratic equation:—Reason = Virtue = Happiness, could have arisen: the weirdest equation ever seen, and one which was essentially opposed to all the instincts of the older Hellenes.

5. With Socrates Greek taste veers round in favour of dialectics: what actually occurs? In the first place a noble taste is vanquished: with dialectics the mob comes to the top. Before Socrates' time, dialectical manners were avoided in good society: they were regarded as bad manners, they were compromising. Young men were cautioned against them. All such proffering of one's reasons was looked upon with suspicion. Honest things like honest men do not carry their reasons on their sleeve in such fashion. It is not good form to make a show of everything. That which needs to be proved cannot be worth much. Wherever authority still belongs to good usage, wherever men do not prove but command, the dialectician is regarded as a sort of clown. People laugh at him, they do not take him seriously. Socrates was a clown who succeeded in making men take him seriously: what then was the matter?

6. A man resorts to dialectics only when he has no other means to hand. People know that they excite suspicion with it and that it is not very convincing. Nothing is more easily dispelled than a dialectical effect: this is proved by the experience of every gathering in which discussions are held. It can be only the last defence of those who have no other weapons. One must require to extort one's right, otherwise one makes no use of it. That is why the Jews were dialecticians. Reynard the Fox was a dialectician: what?—and was Socrates one as well?

7. Is the Socratic irony an expression of revolt, of mob resentment? Does Socrates, as a creature suffering under oppression, enjoy his innate ferocity in the knife-thrusts of the syllogism? Does he wreak his revenge on the noblemen he fascinates?—As a dialectician a man has a merciless instrument to wield; he can play the tyrant with it: he compromises when he conquers with it. The dialectician leaves it to his opponent to prove that he is no idiot: he infuriates, he likewise paralyses. The dialectician cripples the intellect of his opponent. Can it be that dialectics was only a form of revenge in Socrates?

8. I have given you to understand in what way Socrates was able to repel: now it is all the more necessary to explain how he fascinated.—One reason is that he discovered a new kind of *Agon*, and that he was the first fencing-master in the best circles in Athens. He fascinated by appealing to the combative instinct of the Greeks,—he introduced a variation into the contests between men and youths. Socrates was also a great erotic.

9. But Socrates divined still more. He saw right through his noble Athenians; he perceived that his case, his peculiar case, was no exception even in his time. The same kind of degeneracy was silently preparing itself everywhere: ancient Athens was dying out. And Socrates understood that the whole world needed him,—his means, his remedy, his special artifice for self-preservation. Everywhere the instincts were in a state of anarchy; everywhere people were within an ace of excess: the *monstrum in animo* was the general danger. "The instincts would play the tyrant; we must discover a counter-tyrant who is stronger than they." On the occasion when that physiognomist had unmasked Socrates, and had told him what he was—a crater full of evil desires, the great Master of Irony let fall one or two words more, which provide the key to his nature. "This is true," he said, "but I overcame them all." How did Socrates succeed in mastering himself? His case was at bottom only the extreme and most apparent example of a state of distress which was beginning to be general: that state in which no one was able to master himself and in which the instincts turned one

1. It should be borne in mind that Nietzsche recognised two types of criminals,—the criminal from strength, and the criminal from weakness. This passage alludes to the latter, Aphorism 45, p. 103, alludes to the former.—Tr.

against the other. As the extreme example of this state, he fascinated—his terrifying ugliness made him conspicuous to every eye: it is quite obvious that he fascinated still more as a reply, as a solution, as an apparent cure of this case.

10. When a man finds it necessary, as Socrates did, to create a tyrant out of reason, there is no small danger that something else wishes to play the tyrant. Reason was then discovered as a saviour; neither Socrates nor his "patients" were at liberty to be rational or not, as they pleased; at that time it was *de rigueur,* it had become a last shift. The fanaticism with which the whole of Greek thought plunges into reason, betrays a critical condition of things: men were in danger; there were only two alternatives: either perish or else be absurdly rational. The moral bias of Greek philosophy from Plato onward, is the outcome of a pathological condition, as is also its appreciation of dialectics. Reason = Virtue= Happiness, simply means: we must imitate Socrates, and confront the dark passions permanently with the light of day—the light of reason. We must at all costs be clever, precise, clear: all yielding to the instincts, to the unconscious, leads downwards.

11. I have now explained how Socrates fascinated: he seemed to be a doctor, a Saviour. Is it necessary to expose the errors which lay in his faith in "reason at any price"?—It is a piece of self-deception on the part of philosophers and moralists to suppose that they can extricate themselves from degeneration by merely waging war upon it. They cannot thus extricate themselves: that which they choose as a means, as the road to salvation, is in itself again only an expression of degeneration—they only modify its mode of manifesting itself: they do not abolish it. Socrates was a misunderstanding. *The whole of the morality of amelioration—that of Christianity as well—was a misunderstanding.* The most blinding light of day: reason at any price; life made clear, cold, cautious, conscious, without instincts, opposed to the instincts, was in itself only a disease, another kind of disease—and by no means a return to "virtue," to "health," and to happiness. To be obliged to fight the instincts—this is the formula of degeneration: as long as life is in the ascending line, happiness is the same as instinct.

12. —Did he understand this himself, this most intelligent of self-deceivers? Did he confess this to himself in the end, in the wisdom of his courage before death. Socrates wished to die. Not Athens, but his own hand gave him the draught of hemlock; he drove Athens to the poisoned cup. "Socrates is not a doctor," he whispered to himself, "death alone can be a doctor here. . . . Socrates himself has only been ill a long while."

"REASON" IN PHILOSOPHY

1. You ask me what all idiosyncrasy is in philosophers? . . . For instance their lack of the historical sense, their hatred even of the idea of Becoming, their Egyptianism. They imagine that they do honour to a thing by divorcing it from history *sub specie æterni,*—when they make a mummy of it. All the ideas that philosophers have treated for thousands of years, have been mummied concepts; nothing real has ever come out of their hands alive. These idolaters of concepts merely kill and stuff things when they worship,—they threaten the life of everything they adore. Death, change, age, as well as procreation and growth, are in their opinion objections,—even refutations. That which is cannot evolve; that which evolves *is* not. Now all of them believe, and even with desperation, in Being. But, as they cannot lay hold of it, they try to discover reasons why this privilege is withheld from them. "Some merely apparent quality, some deception must be the cause of our not being able to ascertain the nature of Being: where is the deceiver?" "We have him," they cry rejoicing, "it is sensuality!" These senses, *which in other things are so immoral,* cheat us concerning the true world. Moral: we must get rid of the deception of the senses, of Becoming, of history, of falsehood.—History is nothing more than the belief in the senses, the belief in falsehood. Moral: we must say "no" to everything in which the senses believe: to all the rest of mankind: all that belongs to the "people." Let us be philosophers, mummies, monotono-theists, grave-diggers!—And above all, away with the *body,* this wretched *idée fixe* of the senses, infected with all the faults of logic that exist, refuted, even impossible, although it be impudent enough to pose as if it were real!

2. With a feeling of great reverence I except the name of *Heraclitus.* If the rest of the philosophic gang rejected the evidences of the senses, because the latter revealed a state of multifariousness and change, he rejected the same evidence because it revealed things as if they possessed permanence and unity. Even Heraclitus did an injustice to the senses. The latter lie neither as the Eleatics believed them to lie, nor as he believed them to lie,—they do not lie at all. The interpretations we give to their evidence is what first introduces falsehood into it; for instance the lie of unity, the lie of matter, of substance and of permanence. Reason is the cause of our falsifying the evidence of the senses. In so far as the senses show us a state of Becoming, of transiency, and of change, they do not lie. But in declaring that Being was an empty illusion, Heraclitus will remain eternally right. The "apparent" world is the only world: the "true world" is no more than a false adjunct thereto.

3. And what delicate instruments of observation we have in our senses! This human nose, for instance, of which no philosopher has yet spoken with reverence and gratitude, is, for the present, the most finely adjusted instrument at our disposal: it is able to register even such slight changes of movement as the spectroscope would be unable to record. Our scientific triumphs at the present day extend precisely so far as we have accepted the evidence of our senses,—as we have sharpened and armed them, and learned to follow them up to the end. What remains is abortive and not yet science—that is to say, metaphysics, theology, psychology, epistemology, or formal science, or a doctrine of symbols, like logic and its applied form mathematics. In all these things reality does not come into consideration at all, even as a problem; just as little as does the question concerning the general value of such a convention of symbols as logic.

4. The other idiosyncrasy of philosophers is no less dangerous; it consists in confusing the last and the first things. They place that which makes its appearance last—unfortunately! for it ought not to appear at all!—the "highest concept," that is to say, the most general, the emptiest, the last cloudy streak of evaporating reality, at the beginning as the beginning. This again is only their manner of expressing their veneration: the highest thing must not have grown out of the lowest, it must not have grown at all. . . . Moral: everything of the first rank must be *causa sui*. To have been derived from something else, is as good as an objection, it sets the value of a thing in question. All superior values are of the first rank, all the highest concepts—that of Being, of the Absolute, of Goodness, of Truth, and of Perfection; all these things cannot have been evolved, they must therefore be *causa sui*. All these things cannot however be unlike one another, they cannot be opposed to one another. Thus they attain to their stupendous concept "God." The last, most attenuated and emptiest thing is postulated as the first thing, as the absolute cause, as *ens realissimum*. Fancy humanity having to take the brain diseases of morbid cobweb-spinners seriously!—And it has paid dearly for having done so.

5. —Against this let us set the different manner in which we (—you observe that I am courteous enough to say "we") conceive the problem of the error and deceptiveness of things. Formerly people regarded change and evolution in general as the proof of appearance, as a sign of the fact that something must be there that leads us astray. To-day, on the other hand, we realise that precisely as far as the rational bias forces us to postulate unity, identity, permanence, substance, cause, materiality and being, we are in a measure involved in error, driven necessarily to error; however certain we may feel, as the result of a strict examination of the matter, that the error lies here. It is just the same here as with the motion of the sun: In its case it was our eyes that were wrong; in the matter of the concepts above mentioned it is our language itself that pleads most constantly in their favour. In its origin language belongs to an age of the most rudimentary forms of psychology: if we try to conceive of the first conditions of the metaphysics of language, *i.e.,* in plain English, of reason, we immediately find ourselves in the midst of a system of fetichism. For here, the doer and his deed are seen in all circumstances, will is believed in as a cause in general; the ego is taken for granted, the ego as Being, and as substance, and the faith in the ego as substance is projected into all things—in this way, alone, the concept "thing" is created. Being is thought into and insinuated into everything as cause; from the concept "ego," alone, can the concept "Being" proceed. At the beginning stands the tremendously fatal error of supposing the will to be something that actuates,—a faculty. Now we know that it is only a word.[1] Very much later, in a world a thousand times more enlightened, the assurance, the subjective certitude, in the handling of the categories of reason came into the minds of philosophers as a surprise. They concluded that these

1. Nietzsche here refers to the concept "free will" of the Christians; this does not mean that there is no such thing as will—that is to say a powerful determining force from within.—Tr.

categories could not be derived from experience,—on the contrary, the whole of experience rather contradicts them. *Whence do they come therefore?* In India, as in Greece, the same mistake was made: "we must already once have lived in a higher world (—instead of in a much lower one, which would have been the truth!), we must have been divine, for we possess reason!" . . . Nothing indeed has exercised a more simple power of persuasion hitherto than the error of Being, as it was formulated by the Eleatics for instance: in its favour are every word and every sentence that we utter!—Even the opponents of the Eleatics succumbed to the seductive powers of their concept of Being. Among others there was Democritus in his discovery of the atom. "Reason" in language!—oh what a deceptive old witch it has been! I fear we shall never be rid of God, so long as we still believe in grammar.

6. People will feel grateful to me if I condense a point of view, which is at once so important and so new, into four theses: by this means I shall facilitate comprehension, and shall likewise challenge contradiction.

Proposition One. The reasons upon which the apparent nature of "this" world have been based, rather tend to prove its reality,—any other kind of reality defies demonstration.

Proposition Two. The characteristics with which man has endowed the "true Being" of things, are the characteristics of non-Being, of *nonentity*. The "true world" has been erected upon a contradiction of the real world; and it is indeed an apparent world, seeing that it is merely a *moralo-optical* delusion.

Proposition Three. There is no sense in spinning yarns about another world, provided, of course, that we do not possess a mighty instinct which urges us to slander, belittle, and cast suspicion upon this life: in this case we should be avenging ourselves on this life with the phantasmagoria of "another," of a "better" life.

Proposition Four. To divide the world into a "true" and an "apparent" world, whether after the manner of Christianity or of Kant (after all a Christian in disguise), is only a sign of decadence,—a symptom of *degenerating* life. The fact that the artist esteems the appearance of a thing higher than reality, is no objection to this statement. For "appearance" signifies once more reality here, but in a selected, strengthened and corrected form. The tragic artist is no pessimist,—he says *Yea* to everything questionable and terrible, he is Dionysian.

HOW THE "TRUE WORLD" ULTIMATELY BECAME A FABLE

The History of an Error

1. The true world, attainable to the sage, the pious man and the man of virtue,—he lives in it, *he is it.*

(The most ancient form of the idea was relatively clever, simple, convincing. It was a paraphrase of the proposition "I, Plato, am the truth.")

2. The true world which is unattainable for the moment, is promised to the sage, to the pious man and to the man of virtue ("to the sinner who repents").

(Progress of the idea: it becomes more subtle, more insidious, more evasive,—*it becomes a woman,* it becomes Christian.)

3. The true world is unattainable, it cannot be proved, it cannot promise anything; but even as a thought, alone, it is a comfort, an obligation, a command.

(At bottom this is still the old sun; but seen through mist and scepticism: the idea has become sublime, pale, northern, Königsbergian.[2])

4. The true world—is it unattainable? At all events it is unattained. And as unattained it is also *unknown.* Consequently it no longer comforts, nor saves, nor constrains: what could something unknown constrain us to?

(The grey of dawn. Reason stretches itself and yawns for the first time. The cock-crow of positivism.)

5. The "true world"—an idea that no longer serves any purpose, that no longer constrains one to anything,—a useless idea that has become quite superfluous, consequently an exploded idea: let us abolish it!

(Bright daylight; breakfast; the return of common sense and of cheerfulness; Plato blushes for shame and all free-spirits kick up a shindy.)

6. We have suppressed the true world: what world survives? the apparent world perhaps? . . . Certainly not! *In abolishing the true world we have also abolished the world of appearance!*

2. Kant was a native of Königsberg and lived there all his life. Did Nietzsche know that Kant was simply a Scotch Puritan, whose family had settled in Germany?

(Noon; the moment of the shortest shadows; the end of the longest error; mankind's zenith; *Incipit Zarathustra.*)

MORALITY AS THE ENEMY OF NATURE

1. There is a time when all passions are simply fatal in their action, when they wreck their victims with the weight of their folly,—and there is a later period, a very much later period, when they marry with the spirit, when they "spiritualise" themselves. Formerly, owing to the stupidity inherent in passion, men waged war against passion itself: men pledged themselves to annihilate it,—all ancient moral-mongers were unanimous on this point, "*il faut tuer les passions.*" The most famous formula for this stands in the New Testament, in that Sermon on the Mount, where, let it be said incidentally, things are by no means regarded *from a height.* It is said there, for instance, with an application to sexuality: "if they eye offend thee, pluck it out": fortunately no Christian acts in obedience to this precept. To annihilate the passions and desires, simply on account of their stupidity, and to obviate the unpleasant consequences of their stupidity, seems to us to-day merely an aggravated form of stupidity. We no longer admire those dentists who extract teeth simply in order that they may not ache again. On the other hand, it will be admitted with some reason, that on the soil from which Christianity grew, the idea of the "spiritualisation of passion" could not possibly have been conceived. The early Church, as everyone knows, certainly did wage war against the "intelligent," in favour of the "poor in spirit." In these circumstances how could the passions be combated intelligently? The Church combats passion by means of excision of all kinds: its practice, its "remedy," is *castration.* It never inquires "how can a desire be spiritualised, beautified, deified?"—In all ages it has laid the weight of discipline in the process of extirpation (the extirpation of sensuality, pride, lust of dominion, lust of property, and revenge).—But to attack the passions at their roots, means attacking life itself at its source: the method of the Church is hostile to life.

2. The same means, castration and extirpation, are instinctively chosen for waging war against a passion, by those who are too weak of will, too degenerate, to impose some sort of moderation upon it; by those natures who, to speak in metaphor (—and without metaphor), need *la Trappe,* or some kind of ultimatum of war, a *gulf* set between themselves and a passion. Only degenerates find radical methods indispensable: weakness of will, or more strictly speaking, the inability not to react to a stimulus, is in itself simply another form of degeneracy. Radical and mortal hostility to sensuality, remains a suspicious symptom: it justifies one in being suspicious of the general state of one who goes to such extremes. Moreover, that hostility and hatred reach their height only when such natures no longer possess enough strength of character to adopt the radical remedy, to renounce their inner "Satan." Look at the whole history of the priests, the philosophers, and the artists as well: the most poisonous diatribes against the senses have not been said by the impotent, nor by the ascetics; but by those impossible ascetics, by those who found it necessary to be ascetics.

3. The spiritualisation of sensuality is called *love:* it is a great triumph over Christianity. Another triumph is our spiritualisation of hostility. It consists in the fact that we are beginning to realise very profoundly the value of having enemies: in short that with them we are forced to do and to conclude precisely the reverse of what we previously did and concluded. In all ages the Church wished to annihilate its enemies: we, the immoralists and Anti-christs, see our advantage in the survival of the Church. Even in political life, hostility has now become more spiritual,—much more cautious, much more thoughtful, and much more moderate. Almost every party sees its self-preservative interests in preventing the Opposition from going to pieces; and the same applies to politics on a grand scale. A new creation, more particularly, like the new Empire, has more need of enemies than friends: only as a contrast does it begin to feel necessary, only as a contrast does it *become* necessary. And we behave in precisely the same way to the "inner enemy": in this quarter too we have spiritualised enmity, in this quarter too we have understood its value. A man is productive only in so far as he is rich in contrasted instincts; he can remain young only on condition that his soul does not begin to take things easy and to yearn for peace. Nothing has grown more alien to us than that old desire—the "peace of the soul," which is the aim of Christianity. Nothing could make us less envious than the moral cow and the plump happiness of a clean conscience. The man who has renounced war has renounced a grand life. In many cases, of course, "peace of the soul" is merely a misunderstanding,—it is something *very different* which has failed to find a more honest name for itself. Without either circumlocution or prejudice I will suggest a few cases. "Peace of the soul" may for instance be the sweet effulgence of rich animality in the realm of morality (or religion). Or the first presage of weariness, the first shadow that evening, every kind of evening, is wont to cast. Or a sign that the air is moist, and that winds are blowing up from the south. Or unconscious gratitude for a good digestion (sometimes called "brotherly love"). Or the serenity of the convalescent, on whose lips all things have a new taste, and who bides his time. Or the condition which follows upon a thorough gratification of our strongest passion, the well-being of unaccustomed satiety. Or the senility of our will, of our desires, and of our vices. Or laziness, coaxed by vanity into togging itself out in a moral garb. Or the ending of a state of long suspense and of agonising uncertainty, by a state of certainty, of even terrible certainty. Or the expression of ripeness and mastery in the midst of a task, of a creative work, of a production, of a thing willed, the calm breathing that denotes that "freedom of will" has been attained. Who knows?—maybe *The Twilight of the Idols* is only a sort of "peace of the soul."

4. I will formulate a principle. All naturalism in morality—that is to say, every sound morality is ruled by a life instinct,—any one of the laws of life is fulfilled by the definite canon "thou shalt," "thou shalt not," and any sort of obstacle or hostile element in the road of life is thus cleared away. Conversely, the morality which is antagonistic to nature—that is to say, almost every morality that has been taught, honoured and preached hitherto, is directed precisely against the life-instincts,—it is a condemnation, now secret, now blatant and impudent, of these very instincts. Inasmuch as it says "God sees into the heart of man," it says Nay to the profoundest and most superior desires of life and takes God as the enemy of life. The saint in whom God is well pleased, is the ideal eunuch. Life terminates where the "Kingdom of God" begins.

5. Admitting that you have understood the villainy of such a mutiny against life as that which has become almost sacrosanct in Christian morality, you have fortunately understood something besides; and that is the futility, the fictitiousness, the absurdity and the falseness of such a mutiny. For the condemnation of life by a living creature is after all but the symptom of a definite kind of life: the question as to whether the condemnation is justified or the reverse is not even raised. In order even to approach the problem of the value of life, a man would need to be placed outside life, and moreover know it as well as one, as many, as all in fact, who have lived it. These are reasons enough to prove to us that this problem is an inaccessible one to us. When we speak of values, we speak under the inspiration, and through the optics of life: life itself urges us to determine values: life itself values through us when we determine values. From which it follows that even that morality which is antagonistic to life, and which conceives God as the opposite and the condemnation of life, is only a valuation of life—of what life? of what kind of life? But I have already answered this question: it is the valuation of declining, of enfeebled, of exhausted and of condemned life. Morality, as it has been understood hitherto—as it was finally formulated by Schopenhauer in the words "The Denial of the Will to Life," is the instinct of degeneration itself, which converts itself into an imperative: it says: "Perish!" It is the death sentence of men who are already doomed.

6. Let us at last consider how exceedingly simple it is on our part to say: "Man should be thus and thus!" Reality shows us a marvellous wealth of types, and a luxuriant variety of forms and changes: and yet the first wretch of a moral loafer that comes along cries "No! Man should be different!" He even knows what man should be like, does this sanctimonious prig: he draws his own face on the wall and declares: "*ecce homo!*" But even when the moralist addresses himself only to the individual and says "thus and thus shouldst thou be!" he still makes an ass of himself. The individual in his past and future is a piece of fate, one law the more, one necessity the more for all that is to come and is to be. To say to him "change thyself," is tantamount to saying that everything should change, even backwards as well. Truly these have been consistent moralists, they wished man to be different, *i.e.,* virtuous; they wished him to be after their own image,—that is to say sanctimonious humbugs. And to this end they denied the world! No slight form of insanity! No modest form of immodesty! Morality, in so far it condemns *per se,* and *not* out of any aim, consideration or motive of life, is a specific error, for which no one should feel any mercy, a degenerate idiosyncrasy, that has done an unutterable amount of harm. We others, we immoralists, on the contrary, have opened our hearts wide to all kinds of comprehension, understanding and approbation.[3] We do not deny readily, we glory in saying yea to things. Our eyes have opened ever wider and wider to that economy which still employs and knows how to use to its own advantage all that which the sacred craziness of priests and the morbid reason in priests, rejects; to that economy in the law of life which draws its own advantage even out of the repulsive race of bigots, the priests and the virtuous,—what advantage?—But we ourselves, we immoralists, are the reply to this question.

THE FOUR GREAT ERRORS

1. The error of the confusion of cause and effect.—There is no more dangerous error than to confound the effect with the cause: I call this error the intrinsic perversion of reason. Nevertheless this error is one of the most ancient and most recent habits of mankind. In one part of the world it has even been canonised; and it bears the name of "Religion" and "Morality." Every postulate formulated by religion and morality contains it. Priests and the promulgators of moral laws are the promoters of this perversion of reason.—Let me give you an example. Everybody knows the book of the famous Cornaro, in which he recommends his slender diet as the recipe for a long, happy and also virtuous life. Few books have been so widely read, and to this day many thousand copies of it are still printed annually in England. It do not doubt that there is scarcely a single book (the Bible of course excepted) that has worked more mischief, shortened more lives, than this well-meant curiosity. The reason of this is the confusion of effect and cause. This worthy Italian saw the cause of his long life in his diet: whereas the prerequisites of long life, which are exceptional slowness of molecular change, and a low rate of expenditure in energy, were the cause of his meagre diet. He was not at liberty to eat a small or a great amount. His frugality was not the result of free choice, he would have been ill had he eaten more. He who does not happen to be a carp, however, is not only wise to eat well, but is also compelled to do so. A scholar of the present day, with his rapid consumption of nervous energy, would soon go to the dogs on Cornaro's diet. *Crede experto.*—

2. The most general principle lying at the root of every religion and morality, is this: "Do this and that and avoid this and that—and thou wilt be happy. Otherwise—." Every morality and every religion is this Imperative—I call it the great original sin of reason,—*immortal unreason.* In my mouth this principle is converted into its opposite—first example of my "Transvaluation of all Values": a well-constituted man, a man who is one of "Nature's lucky strokes," *must* perform certain actions and instinctively fear other actions; he introduces the element of order, of which he is the physiological manifestation, into his relations with men and things. In a formula: his virtue is the consequence of his good constitution. Longevity and plentiful offspring are not the reward of virtue, virtue itself is on the contrary that retardation of the metabolic process which, among other things, results in a long life and in plentiful offspring, in short in *Cornarism.* The Church and morality say: "A race, a people perish through vice and luxury." My reinstated reason says: when a people are going to the dogs, when they are degenerating physiologically, vice and luxury (that is to say, the need of ever stronger and more frequent stimuli such as all exhausted natures are acquainted with) are bound to result. Such and such a young man grows pale and withered prematurely. His friends say this or that illness is the cause of it. I say: the fact that he became ill, the fact that he did not resist illness, was in itself already the outcome of impoverished life, of hereditary exhaustion. The newspaper reader says: such and such a party by committing such an error will meet its death. My superior politics say: a party that can make such mistakes, is in its last agony—it no longer possesses any certainty of instinct. Every mistake is in every sense the sequel to degeneration of the instincts, to disintegration of the will. This is almost the definition of evil, Everything valuable is instinct—and consequently easy, necessary, free. Exertion is an objection, the god is characteristically different from the hero (in my language: light feet are the first attribute of divinity).

3. The error of false causality. In all ages men have believed that they knew what a cause was: but whence did we derive this knowledge, or more accurately, this faith in the fact that we know? Out of the realm of the famous "inner facts of consciousness," not one of which has yet proved itself to be

3. *Cf.* Spinoza, who says in the *Tractatus politicus* (1677), Chap. I, § 4: "*Sedulo curavi, humanas actiones non ridere, non lugere, neque detestari, sed intelligere*" ("I have carefully endeavoured not to deride, or deplore, or detest human actions, but to understand them.").—Tr.

a fact. We believed ourselves to be causes even in the action of the will; we thought that in this matter at least we caught causality red-handed. No one doubted that all the *antecedentia* of an action were to be sought in consciousness, and could be discovered there—as "motive"—if only they were sought. Otherwise we should not be free to perform them, we should not have been responsible for them. Finally who would have questioned that a thought is caused? that the ego causes the thought? Of these three "facts of inner consciousness" by means of which causality seemed to be guaranteed, the first and most convincing is that of the will as cause; the conception of consciousness ("spirit") as a cause, and subsequently that of the ego (the "subject") as a cause, were merely born afterwards, once the causality of the will stood established as "given," as a fact of experience. Meanwhile we have come to our senses. To-day we no longer believe a word of all this. The "inner world" is full of phantoms and will-o'-the-wisps: the will is one of these. The will no longer actuates, consequently it no longer explains anything—all it does is to accompany processes; it may even be absent. The so-called "motive" is another error. It is merely a ripple on the surface of consciousness, a side issue of the action, which is much more likely to conceal than to reveal the *antecedentia* of the latter. And as for the ego! It has become legendary, fictional, a play upon words: it has ceased utterly and completely from thinking, feeling, and willing! What is the result of it all? There are no such things as spiritual causes. The whole of popular experience on this subject went to the devil! That is the result of it all. For we had blissfully abused that experience, we had built the world upon it as a world of causes, as a world of will, as a world of spirit. The most antiquated and most traditional psychology has been at work here, it has done nothing else: all phenomena were deeds in the light of this psychology, and all deeds were the result of will; according to it the world was a complex mechanism of agents, an agent (a "subject") lay at the root of all things. Man projected his three "inner facts of consciousness," the will, the spirit, and the ego in which he believed most firmly, outside himself. He first deduced the concept Being out of the concept Ego, he supposed "things" to exist as he did himself, according to his notion of the ego as cause. Was it to be wondered at that later on he always found in things only that which he had laid in them?—The thing itself, I repeat, the concept thing was merely a reflex of the belief in the ego as cause. And even your atom, my dear good Mechanists and Physicists, what an amount of error, of rudimentary psychology still adheres to it!—Not to speak of the "thing-in-itself," of the *horrendum pudendum* of the metaphysicians! The error of spirit regarded as a cause, confounded with reality! And made the measure of reality! And called *God!*

4. The Error of imaginary Causes. Starting out from dreamland, we find that to any definite sensation, like that produced by a distant cannon shot for instance, we are wont to ascribe a cause after the fact (very often quite a little romance in which the dreamer himself is, of course, the hero). Meanwhile the sensation becomes protracted like a sort of continuous echo, until, as it were, the instinct of causality allows it to come to the front rank, no longer however as a chance occurrence, but as a thing which has some meaning. The cannon shot presents itself in a *causal* manner, by means of an apparent reversal in the order of time. That which occurs last, the motivation, is experienced first, often with a hundred details which flash past like lightning, and the shot is the *result.* What has happened? The ideas suggested by a particular state of our senses, are misinterpreted as the cause of that state. As a matter of fact we proceed in precisely the same manner when we are awake. The greater number of our general sensations—every kind of obstacle, pressure, tension, explosion in the interplay of the organs, and more particularly the condition of the *nervus sympathicus*—stimulate our instinct of causality: we will have a reason which will account for our feeling thus or thus,—for feeling ill or well. We are never satisfied by merely ascertaining the fact that we feel thus or thus: we admit this fact—we become conscious of it—only when we have attributed it to some kind of motivation. Memory, which, in such circumstances unconsciously becomes active, adduces former conditions of a like kind, together with the causal interpretations with which they are associated,—but not their real cause. The belief that the ideas, the accompanying processes of consciousness, have been the causes, is certainly produced by the agency of memory. And in this way we become *accustomed* to a particular interpretation of causes which, truth to tell, actually hinders and even utterly prevents the investigation of the proper cause.

5. The Psychological Explanation of the above Fact. To trace something unfamiliar back to something familiar, is at once a relief, a comfort and a satisfaction, while it also produces a feeling of power. The unfamiliar involves danger, anxiety and care,—the fundamental instinct is to get rid of these painful circumstances. First principle: any explanation is better than none at all. Since, at bottom, it is only a question of shaking one's self free from certain oppressive ideas, the means employed to this end are not selected with overmuch punctiliousness: the first idea by means of which the unfamiliar is revealed as familiar, produces a feeling of such comfort that it is "held to be true." The proof of happiness ("of power") as the criterion of truth. The instinct of causality is therefore conditioned and stimulated by the feeling of fear. Whenever possible, the question "why?" should not only educe the cause as cause, but rather a certain kind of cause—a comforting, liberating and reassuring cause. The first result of this need is that something known or already experienced, and recorded in the memory, is posited as the cause. The new factor, that which has not been experienced and which is unfamiliar, is excluded from the sphere of causes. Not only do we try to find a certain kind of explanation as the cause, but those kinds of explanations are selected and preferred which dissipate most rapidly the sensation of strangeness, novelty and unfamiliarity,—in fact the most ordinary explanations. And the result is that a certain manner of postulating causes tends to predominate ever more and more, becomes concentrated into a system, and finally reigns supreme, to the complete exclusion of all other causes and explanations. The banker thinks immediately of business, the Christian of "sin," and the girl of her love affair.

6. The whole Domain of Morality and Religion may be classified under the Rubric "Imaginary Causes." The "explanation" of general unpleasant sensations. These sensations are dependent upon certain creatures who are hostile to us (evil spirits: the most famous example of this—the mistaking of hysterical women for witches). These sensations are dependent upon actions which are reprehensible (the feeling of "sin," "sinfulness" is a manner of accounting for a certain physiological disorder—people always find reasons for being dissatisfied with themselves). These sensations depend upon punishment, upon compensation for something which we ought not to have done, which we ought not to have been (this idea was generalised in a more impudent form by Schopenhauer, into that principle in which morality appears in its real colours,—that is to say, as a veritable poisoner and slanderer of life: "all great suffering, whether mental or physical, reveals what we deserve: for it could not visit us if we did not deserve it,"—"The World as Will and Idea," vol. 2, p. 666). These sensations are the outcome of ill-considered actions, having evil consequences, (—the passions, the senses, postulated as causes, as guilty. By means of other calamities distressing physiological conditions are interpreted as "merited").—The "explanation" of pleasant sensations. These sensations are dependent upon a trust in God. They may depend upon our consciousness of having done one or two good actions (a so-called "good conscience" is a physiological condition, which may be the outcome of good digestion). They may depend upon the happy issue of certain undertakings (—an ingenuous mistake: the happy issue of an undertaking certainly does not give a hypochondriac or a Pascal any general sensation of pleasure). They may depend upon faith, love and hope,—the Christian virtues. As a matter of fact all these pretended explanations are but the results of certain states, and as it were translations of feelings of pleasure and pain into a false dialect: a man is in a condition of hopefulness because the dominant physiological sensation of his being is again one of strength and wealth; he trusts in God because the feeling of abundance and power gives him a peaceful state of mind. Morality and religion are completely and utterly parts of the psychology of error: in every particular case cause and effect are confounded; as truth is confounded with the effect of that which is believed to be true; or a certain state of consciousness is confounded with the chain of causes which brought it about.

7. The Error of Free-Will. At present we no longer have any mercy upon the concept "free-will": we know only too well what it is—the most egregious theological trick that has ever existed for the purpose of making mankind "responsible" in a theological manner,—that is to say, to make mankind dependent upon theologians. I will now explain to you only the psychology of the whole process of inculcating the sense of responsibility. Wherever men try to trace responsibility home to anyone, it is the instinct of punishment and of the desire to judge which is active. Becoming is robbed of its innocence when any particular condition of things is traced to a will, to intentions and to responsible actions. The doctrine of the will was invented principally for the purpose of punishment,—that is to say, with the intention of tracing guilt. The whole of ancient psychology, or the psychology of the will, is the outcome of the fact that its originators, who were the priests at the head of ancient communities, wanted to create for themselves a right to administer punishments—or the right for God to do so. Men were thought of as "free" in order that they might be judged and punished—in order that they might be held guilty: consequently every action had to be regarded as voluntary, and the origin of every action had to be imagined as lying in consciousness (—in this way the most fundamentally fraudulent character of psychology was established as the very principle of psychology itself). Now that we have entered upon the opposite movement, now that we immoralists are trying with all our power to eliminate the concepts of guilt and punishment from the world once more, and to cleanse psychology, history, nature and all social institutions and customs of all signs of those two concepts, we recognise no more radical opponents than the theologians, who with their notion of "a moral order of things," still continue to pollute the innocence of Becoming with punishment and guilt. Christianity is the metaphysics of the hangman.

8. What then, alone, can our teaching be?—That no one gives man his qualities, neither God, society, his parents, his ancestors, nor himself (—this nonsensical idea which is at last refuted here, was taught as "intelligible freedom" by Kant, and perhaps even as early as Plato himself). No one is responsible for the fact that he exists at all, that he is constituted as he is, and that he happens to be in certain circumstances and in a particular environment. The fatality of his being cannot be divorced from the fatality of all that which has been and will be. This is not the result of an individual intention, of a will, of an aim, there is no attempt at attaining to any "ideal man," or "ideal happiness" or "ideal morality" with him,—it is absurd to wish him to be careering towards some sort of purpose. *We* invented the concept "purpose"; in reality purpose is altogether lacking. One is necessary, one is a piece of fate, one belongs to the whole, one is in the whole,—there is nothing that could judge, measure, compare, and condemn our existence, for that would mean judging, measuring, comparing and condemning the whole. *But there is nothing outside the whole!* The fact that no one shall any longer be made responsible, that the nature of existence may not be traced to a *causa prima,* that the world is an entity neither as a sensorium nor as a spirit—*this alone is the great deliverance,*—thus alone is the innocence of Becoming restored. . . . The concept "God" has been the greatest objection to existence hitherto. . . . We deny God, we deny responsibility in God: thus alone do we save the world.—

The Anti-Christ

1. Let us look each other in the face. We are hyperboreans,—we know well enough how far outside the crowd we stand. "Thou wilt find the way to the Hyperboreans neither by land nor by water": Pindar already knew this much about us. Beyond the north, the ice, and death—*our life, our happiness.* . . . We discovered happiness; we know the way; we found the way out of thousands of years of labyrinth. Who *else* would have found it?—Not the modern man, surely?—"I do not know where I am or what I am to do; I am everything that knows not where it is or what to do,"—sighs the modern man. We were made quite ill by *this* modernity,—with its indolent peace, its cowardly compromise, and the whole of the virtuous filth of its Yea and Nay. This tolerance and *largeur de cœur* which "forgives" everything because it "understands" everything, is a Sirocco for us. We prefer to live amid ice than to be breathed upon by modern virtues and other southerly winds! . . . We were brave enough; we spared neither ourselves nor others: but we were very far from knowing whither to direct our bravery. We were becoming gloomy; people called us fatalists. *Our* fate—it was the abundance, the tension and the storing up of power. We thirsted for thunderbolts and great deeds; we kept at the most respectful distance from the joy of the weakling, from "resignation." . . . Thunder was in our air, that part of nature which we are, became overcast—*for we had no direction.* The formula of our happiness: a Yea, a Nay, a straight line, a goal.

2. What is good? All that enhances the feeling of power, the Will to Power, and power itself in man. What is bad?—All that proceeds from weakness. What is happiness?—The feeling that power is *increasing,*—that resistance has been overcome.

Not contentment, but more power; not peace at any price, but war; not virtue, but efficiency[1] (virtue in the Renaissance sense, *virtù,* free from all moralic acid). The weak and the botched shall perish: first principle of our humanity. And they ought even to be helped to perish.

What is more harmful than any vice?—Practical sympathy with all the botched and the weak—Christianity.

3. The problem I set in this work is not what will replace mankind in the order of living beings (—Man is an *end*—); but, what type of man must be *reared,* must be *willed,* as having the highest value, as being the most worthy of life and the surest guarantee of the future.

This more valuable type has appeared often enough already: but as a happy accident, as an exception, never as *willed.* He has rather been precisely the most feared; hitherto he has been almost the terrible in itself;—and from out the very fear he provoked there arose the will to rear the type which has now been reared, *attained:* the domestic animal, the gregarious animal, the sick animal man,—the Christian.

4. Mankind does *not* represent a development towards a better, stronger or higher type, in the sense in which this is supposed to occur to-day. "Progress" is merely a modern idea—that is to say, a false idea.[2] The modern European is still far below the European of the Renaissance in value. The process of evolution does not by any means imply elevation, enhancement and increasing strength.

On the other hand isolated and individual cases are continually succeeding in different places on earth, as the outcome of the most different cultures, and in these a *higher type* certainly manifests itself: something which by the side of mankind in general, represents a kind of superman. Such lucky strokes of great success have always been possible and will perhaps always be possible. And even whole races, tribes and nations may in certain circumstances represent such *lucky strokes.*

5. We must not deck out and adorn Christianity: it has waged a deadly war upon this *higher* type of man, it has set a ban upon all the fundamental instincts of this type, and has distilled evil and the devil himself out of these instincts:—the strong man as the typical pariah, the villain. Christianity has sided with everything weak, low, and botched; it has made an ideal out of *antagonism* towards all the self-preservative instincts of strong life: it has corrupted even the reason of the strongest intellects, by teaching that the highest values of intellectuality are sinful, misleading and full of temptations. The most lamentable example of this was the corruption of Pascal, who believed in the perversion of his reason through original sin, whereas it had only been perverted by his Christianity.

6. A painful and ghastly spectacle has just risen before my eyes. I tore down the curtain which concealed mankind's *corruption.* This word in my mouth is at least secure from the suspicion that it contains a moral charge against mankind. It is—I would fain emphasise this again—free from moralic acid: to such an extent is this so, that I am most thoroughly conscious of the corruption in question precisely in those quarters in which hitherto people have aspired with most determination to "virtue" and to "godliness." As you have already surmised, I understand corruption in the sense of *decadence.* What I maintain is this, that all the values upon which mankind builds its highest hopes and desires are *decadent* values.

I call an animal, a species, an individual corrupt, when it loses its instincts, when it selects and *prefers* that which is detrimental to it. A history of the "higher feelings," of "human ideals"—and it is not impossible that I shall have to write it—would almost explain why man is so corrupt. Life itself, to my mind, is nothing more nor less than the instinct of growth, of permanence, of accumulating forces, of power: where the will to power is lacking, degeneration sets in. My contention is that all the highest values of mankind *lack* this will,—that the values of decline and of *nihilism* are exercising the

1. The German "*Tüchtigkeit*" has a nobler ring than our word "efficiency."—Tr.

2. *Cf.* Disraeli: "But enlightened Europe is not happy. Its existence is a fever which it calls progress. Progress to what?" ("Tancred," Book III., Chap. vii.).—Tr.

sovereign power under the cover of the holiest names.

7. Christianity is called the religion of *pity.*—Pity is opposed to the tonic passions which enhance the energy of the feeling of life: its action is depressing. A man loses power when he pities. By means of pity the drain on strength which suffering itself already introduces into the world is multiplied a thousand-fold. Through pity, suffering itself becomes infectious; in certain circumstances it may lead to a total loss of life and vital energy, which is absurdly out of proportion to the magnitude of the cause (—the case of the death of the Nazarene). This is the first standpoint; but there is a still more important one. Supposing one measures pity according to the value of the reactions it usually stimulates, its danger to life appears in a much more telling light. On the whole, pity thwarts the law of development which is the law of selection. It preserves that which is ripe for death, it fights in favour of the disinherited and the condemned of life; thanks to the multitude of abortions of all kinds which it maintains in life, it lends life itself a sombre and questionable aspect. People have dared to call pity a virtue (—in every *noble* culture it is considered as a weakness—); people went still further, they exalted it to *the* virtue, the root and origin of all virtues,—but, of course, what must never be forgotten is the fact that this was done from the standpoint of a philosophy which was nihilistic, and on whose shield the device *The Denial of Life* was inscribed. Schopenhauer was right in this respect: by means of pity, life is denied and made *more worthy of denial,*—pity is the *praxis* of Nihilism. I repeat, this depressing and infectious instinct thwarts those instincts which aim at the preservation and enhancement of the valuelife: by *multiplying* misery quite as much as by preserving all that is miserable, it is the principal agent in promoting decadence,—pity exhorts people to nothing, to *nonentity!* But they do not say "*nonentity,*" they say "Beyond," or "God," or "the true life"; or Nirvana, or Salvation, or Blessedness, instead. This innocent rhetoric, which belongs to the realm of the religio-moral idiosyncrasy, immediately appears to be *very much less innocent* if one realises what the tendency is which here tries to drape itself in the mantle of sublime expressions—the tendency of hostility to life. Schopenhauer was hostile to life: that is why he elevated pity to a virtue. . . . Aristotle, as you know, recognised in pity a morbid and dangerous state, of which it was wise to rid one's self from time to time by a purgative: he regarded tragedy as a purgative. For the sake of the instinct of life, it would certainly seem necessary to find some means of lancing any such morbid and dangerous accumulation of pity, as that which possessed Schopenhauer (and unfortunately the whole of our literary and artistic decadence as well, from St Petersburg to Paris, from Tolstoi to Wagner), if only to make it *burst.* . . . Nothing is more unhealthy in the midst of our unhealthy modernity, than Christian pity. To be doctors *here,* to be inexorable *here,* to wield the knife effectively *here,*—all this is our business, all this is *our* kind of love to our fellows, this is what makes *us* philosophers, us hyperboreans!— —

8. It is necessary to state whom we regard as our antithesis:—the theologians, and all those who have the blood of theologians in their veins—the whole of our philosophy. . . . A man must have had his very nose upon this fatality, or better still he must have experienced it in his own soul; he must almost have perished through it, in order to be unable to treat this matter lightly (—the free-spiritedness of our friends the naturalists and physiologists is, in my opinion, a *joke,*—what they lack in these questions is passion, what they lack is having suffered from these questions—). This poisoning extends much further than people think: I unearthed the "arrogant" instinct of the theologian, wherever nowadays people feel themselves idealists,—wherever, thanks to superior antecedents, they claim the right to rise above reality and to regard it with suspicion. . . . Like the priest the idealist has every grandiloquent concept in his hand (—and not only in his hand!), he wields them all with kindly contempt against the "understanding," the "senses," "honours," "decent living," "science"; he regards such things as *beneath* him, as detrimental and seductive forces, upon the face of which, "the Spirit" moves in pure absoluteness:—as if humility, chastity, poverty, in a word *holiness,* had not done incalculably more harm to life hitherto, than any sort of horror and vice. . . . Pure spirit is pure falsehood. . . . As long as the priest, the *professional* denier, calumniator and poisoner of life, is considered as the *highest* kind of man, there can be no answer to the question, what *is* truth? Truth has already been turned topsy-turvy, when the conscious advocate of nonentity and of denial passes as the representative of "truth."

9. It is upon this theological instinct that I wage

war. I find traces of it everywhere. Whoever has the blood of theologians in his veins, stands from the start in a false and dishonest position to all things. The pathos which grows out of this state, is called *Faith:* that is to say, to shut one's eyes once and for all, in order not to suffer at the sight of incurable falsity. People convert this faulty view of all things into a moral, a virtue, a thing of holiness. They endow their distorted vision with a good conscience,—they claim that no *other* point of view is any longer of value, once theirs has been made sacrosanct with the names "God," "Salvation," "Eternity." I unearthed the instinct of the theologian everywhere: it is the most universal, and actually the most subterranean form of falsity on earth. That which a theologian considers true, *must* of necessity be false: this furnishes almost the criterion of truth. It is his most profound self-preservative instinct which forbids reality ever to attain to honour in any way, or even to raise its voice. Whithersoever the influence of the theologian extends, *valuations* are topsy-turvy, and the concepts "true" and "false" have necessarily changed places: that which is most deleterious to life, is here called "true," that which enhances it, elevates it, says Yea to it, justifies it and renders it triumphant, is called "false." . . . If it should happen that theologians, *via* the "conscience" either of princes or of the people, stretch out their hand for power, let us not be in any doubt as to what results there from each time, namely:—the will to the end, the *nihilistic* will to power. . . .

10. Among Germans I am immediately understood when I say, that philosophy is ruined by the blood of theologians. The Protestant minister is the grandfather of German philosophy, Protestantism itself is the latter's *peccatum originale.* Definition of Protestantism: the partial paralysis of Christianity—and of reason. . . . One needs only to pronounce the word "Tübingen Seminary," in order to understand what German philosophy really is at bottom, *i.e.:*—theology *in disguise.* . . . The Swabians are the best liars in Germany, they lie innocently. . . . Whence came all the rejoicing with which the appearance of Kant was greeted by the scholastic world of Germany, three-quarters of which consist of clergymen's and schoolmasters' sons? Whence came the German conviction, which finds an echo even now, that Kant inaugurated a change for the *better?* The theologian's instinct in the German scholar divined what had once again been made possible. . . . A back-staircase leading into the old ideal was discovered, the concept "true world," the concept morality as the *essence* of the world (—those two most vicious errors that have ever existed!), were, thanks to a subtle and wily scepticism, once again, if not demonstrable, at least no longer *refutable.* . . . Reason, the *prerogative* of reason, does not extend so far. . . . Out of reality they had made "appearance"; and an absolutely false world—that of being—had been declared to be reality. Kant's success is merely a theologian's success. Like Luther, and like Leibniz, Kant was one brake the more upon the already squeaky wheel of German uprightness.

11. One word more against Kant as a *moralist.* A virtue *must* be *our* invention, our most personal defence and need: in every other sense it is merely a danger. That which does not constitute a condition of our life, is merely harmful to it: to possess a virtue merely because one happens to respect the concept "virtue," as Kant would have us do, is pernicious. "Virtue," "Duty," "Goodness in itself," goodness stamped with the character of impersonality and universal validity—these things are mere mental hallucinations, in which decline the final devitalisation of life and Kœnigsbergian Chinadom find expression. The most fundamental laws of preservation and growth, demand precisely the reverse, namely:—that each should discover *his* own virtue, his own Categorical Imperative. A nation goes to the dogs when it confounds its concept of duty with the general concept of duty. Nothing is more profoundly, more thoroughly pernicious, than every impersonal feeling of duty, than every sacrifice to the Moloch of abstraction.—Fancy no one's having thought Kant's Categorical Imperative *dangerous to life!* . . . The instinct of the theologist alone took it under its wing!—An action stimulated by the instinct of life, is proved to be a proper action by the happiness that accompanies it: and that nihilist with the bowels of a Christian dogmatist regarded happiness as an *objection.* . . . What is there that destroys a man more speedily than to work, think, feel, as an automaton of "duty," without internal promptings, without a profound personal predilection, without joy? This is the recipe *par excellence* of decadence and even of idiocy. . . . Kant became an idiot.—And he was the contemporary of Goethe! This fatal spider was regarded as *the* German philosopher,—is still regarded as such! . . . I refrain from saying what I think of the Germans. . . . Did Kant not see in the French Revolution the transition of the State from the inorganic to the *organic* form? Did he not ask himself whether there was a single event on record which could be explained otherwise than as a moral faculty of mankind; so that by means of it, "mankind's tendency towards good," might be *proved* once and for all? Kant's reply: "that is the Revolution." Instinct at fault in anything and everything, hostility to nature as an instinct, German decadence made into philosophy—*that is Kant!*

12. Except for a few sceptics, the respectable type in the history of philosophy, the rest do not know the very first pre-requisite of intellectual uprightness. They all behave like females, do these great enthusiasts and animal prodigies,—they regard "beautiful feelings" themselves as arguments, the "heaving breast" as the bellows of divinity, and conviction as the *criterion* of truth. In the end, even Kant, with "Teutonic" innocence, tried to dress this lack of intellectual conscience up in a scientific garb by means of the concept "practical reason." He deliberately invented a kind of reason which at times would allow one to dispense with reason, that is to say when "morality," when the sublime command "thou shalt," makes itself heard. When one remembers that in almost all nations the philosopher is only a further development of the priestly type, this heirloom of priesthood, this *fraud towards one's self,* no longer surprises one. When a man has a holy life-task, as for instance to improve, save, or deliver mankind, when a man bears God in his breast, and is the mouthpiece of imperatives from another world,—with such a mission he stands beyond the pale of all merely reasonable valuations. He is even sanctified by such a taste, and is already the type of a higher order! What does a priest care about science! He stands too high for that!—And until now the priest has *ruled!*—He it was who determined the concept "true and false."

13. Do not let us undervalue the fact that we *ourselves,* we free spirits, are already a "transvaluation of all values," an incarnate declaration of war against all the old concepts "true" and "untrue" and of a triumph over them. The most valuable standpoints are always the last to be found: but the most valuable standpoints are the methods. All the methods and the first principles of our modern scientific procedure, had for years to encounter the profoundest contempt: association with them meant exclusion from the society of decent people—one was regarded as an "enemy of God," as a scoffer at truth and as "one possessed." With one's scientific nature, one belonged to the Chandala. We have had the whole feeling of mankind against us; hitherto their notion of that which ought to be truth, of that which ought to serve the purpose of truth: every "thou shalt," has been directed against us. . . . Our objects, our practices, our calm, cautious distrustful manner—everything about us seemed to them absolutely despicable and beneath contempt. After all, it might be asked with some justice, whether the thing which kept mankind blindfold so long, was not an aesthetic taste: what they demanded of truth was a *picturesque* effect, and from the man of science what they expected was that he should make a forcible appeal to their senses. It was our *modesty* which ran counter to their taste so long . . . And oh! how well they guessed this, did these divine turkey-cocks!—

14. We have altered our standpoint. In every respect we have become more modest. We no longer derive man from the "spirit," and from the "godhead"; we have thrust him back among the beasts. We regard him as the strongest animal, because he is the craftiest: one of the results thereof is his intellectuality. On the other hand we guard against the vain pretension, which even here would fain assert itself: that man is the great *arrière pensée* of organic evolution! He is by no means the crown of creation, beside him, every other creature stands at the same stage of perfection. . . . And even in asserting this we go a little too far; for, relatively speaking, man is the most botched and diseased of animals, and he has wandered furthest from his instincts. Be all this as it may, he is certainly the most *interesting!* As regards animals, Descartes was the first, with really admirable daring, to venture the thought that the beast was *machina,* and the whole of our physiology is endeavouring to prove this proposition. Moreover, logically we do not set man apart, as Descartes did: the extent to which man is understood to-day goes only so far as he has been understood mechanistically. Formerly man was given "free will," as his dowry from a higher sphere; nowadays we have robbed him even of will, in view of the fact that no such faculty is any longer known. The only purpose served by the old word "will," is to designate a result, a sort of individual reaction which necessarily follows upon a host of partly discordant and partly harmonious stimuli:—the will no longer "effects" or "moves" anything. . . . Formerly people thought that man's consciousness, his "spirit," was a proof of his lofty origin, of his divinity. With the idea of perfecting man, he was conjured to draw his senses inside himself, after the manner of the tortoise, to cut off all relations with terrestrial things, and to divest himself of his mortal shell. Then the most important thing about him, the "pure spirit," would remain over. Even concerning these things we have improved our standpoint. Consciousness, "spirit," now seems to us rather a symptom of relative imperfection in the organism, as an experiment, a groping, a misapprehension, an affliction which absorbs an unnecessary quantity of nervous energy. We deny that anything can be done perfectly so long as it is done consciously. "Pure spirit" is a piece of "pure stupidity": if we discount the nervous system, the senses and the "mortal shell," we have miscalculated—that it is all! . . .

15. In Christianity, neither morality nor religion comes in touch at all with reality. Nothing but imaginary *causes* (God, the soul, the ego, spirit, free will—or even non-free will); nothing but imaginary *effects* (sin, salvation, grace, punishment, forgiveness of sins). Imaginary beings are supposed to have intercourse (God, spirits, souls); imaginary Natural History (anthropocentric: total lack of the notion "natural causes"); an imaginary *psychology* (nothing but misunderstandings of self, interpretations of pleasant or unpleasant general feelings; for instance of the states of the *nervus sympathicus,* with the help of the sign language of a religio-moral idiosyncrasy,—repentance, pangs of conscience, the temptation of the devil, the presence of God); an imaginary teleology (the Kingdom of God, the Last Judgment, Everlasting Life).—This purely fictitious world distinguishes itself very unfavourably from the world of dreams: the latter *reflects* reality, whereas the former falsifies, depreciates and denies it. Once the concept "nature" was taken to mean the opposite of the concept God, the word "natural" had to acquire the meaning of abominable,—the whole of that fictitious world takes its root in the hatred of nature (—reality!—), it is the expression of profound discomfiture in the presence of reality. . . . *But this explains everything.* What is the only kind of man who has reasons for wriggling out of reality by lies? The man who suffers from reality. But in order to suffer from reality one must be a bungled portion of it. The preponderance of pain over pleasure is the *cause* of that fictitious morality and religion: but any such preponderance furnishes the formula for decadence.

16. A criticism of the Christian concept of God inevitably leads to the same conclusion.—A nation that still believes in itself, also has its own God. In him it honours the conditions which enable it to remain uppermost,—that is to say, its virtues. It projects its joy over itself, its feeling of power, into a being, to whom it can be thankful for such things. He who is rich, will give of his riches: a proud people requires a God, unto whom it can *sacrifice* things. . . . Religion, when restricted to these principles, is a form of gratitude. A man is grateful for his own existence; for this he must have a God.—Such a God must be able to benefit and to injure him, he must be able to act the friend and the foe. He must be esteemed for his good as well as for his evil qualities. The monstrous castration of a God by making him a God only of goodness, would lie beyond the pale of the desires of such a community. The evil God is just as urgently needed as the good God: for a people in such a form of society certainly does not owe its existence to toleration and humaneness. . . . What would be the good of a God who knew nothing of anger, revenge, envy, scorn, craft, and violence?—who had perhaps never experienced the rapturous *ardeurs* of victory and of annihilation? No one would understand such a God: why should one possess him?—Of course, when a people is on the road to ruin; when it feels its belief in a future, its hope of freedom vanishing for ever; when it becomes conscious of submission as the most useful quality, and of the virtues of the submissive as self-preservative measures, then its God must also modify himself. He then becomes a tremulous and unassuming sneak; he counsels "peace of the soul," the cessation of all hatred, leniency and "love" even towards friend and foe. He is for ever moralising, he crawls into the heart of every private virtue, becomes a God for everybody, he retires from active service and becomes a Cosmopolitan. . . . Formerly he represented a people, the strength of a people, everything aggressive and desirous of power lying concealed in the heart of a nation: now he is merely the good God. . . . In very truth Gods have no other alternative, they are *either* the Will to Power—in which case they are always the Gods of whole nations,—or, on the other hand, the incapacity for power—in which case they necessarily become good.

17. Wherever the Will to Power, no matter in what form, begins to decline, a physiological retrogression, decadence, always supervenes. The godhead of *decadence,* shorn of its masculine virtues and passions is perforce converted into the God of the physiologically degraded, of the weak. Of course they do not call themselves the weak, they call themselves "the good." . . . No hint will be necessary to help you to understand at what moment in history the dualistic fiction of a good and an evil God first became possible. With the same instinct by which the subjugated reduce their God to "Goodness in itself," they also cancel the good qualities from their conquerer's God; they avenge themselves on their masters by diabolising the latter's God.—The *good God* and the devil as well:—both the abortions of decadence.—How is it possible that we are still so indulgent towards the simplicity of Christian theologians to-day, as to declare with them that the evolution of the concept God, from the "God of Israel," the God of a people, to the Christian God, the quintessence of all goodness, marks a *step forward?*—But even Renan does this. As if Renan had a right to simplicity! Why the very contrary stares one in the face. When the pre-requisites of *ascending* life, when everything strong, plucky, masterful and proud has been eliminated from the concept of God, and step by step he has sunk down to the symbol of a staff for the weary, of a last straw for all those who are drowning; when he becomes the pauper's God, the sinner's God, the sick man's God *par excellence,* and the attribute "Saviour," "Redeemer," remains *over* as the one essential attribute of divinity: what does such a metamorphosis, such an abasement of the godhead imply?—Undoubtedly, "the kingdom of God" has thus become larger. Formerly all he had was his people, his "chosen" people. Since then he has gone travelling over foreign lands, just as his people have done; since then he has never rested anywhere: until one day he felt at home everywhere, the Great Cosmopolitan,—until he got the "greatest number," and half the world on his side. But the God of the "greatest number," the democrat among gods, did not become a proud heathen god notwithstanding: he remained a Jew, he remained the God of the back streets, the God of all dark corners and hovels, of all the unwholesome quarters of the world! . . . His universal empire is now as ever a netherworld empire, an infirmary, a subterranean empire, a ghetto-empire. . . . And he himself is so pale, so weak, so decadent. . . . Even the palest of the pale were able to master him—our friends the metaphysicians, those albinos of thought. They spun their webs around him so long that ultimately he was hypnotised by their movements and himself became a spider, a metaphysician. Thenceforward he once more began spinning the world out of his inner being—*sub specie Spinozæ,*—thenceforward he transfigured himself into something ever thinner and ever more anæmic, became "ideal," became "pure spirit," became "*absolutum,*" and "thing-in-itself." . . . *The decline and fall of a god:* God became the "thing-in-itself."

18. The Christian concept of God—God as the deity of the sick, God as a spider, God as spirit—is one of the most corrupt concepts of God that has ever been attained on earth. Maybe it represents the low-water mark in the evolutionary ebb of the godlike type. God degenerated into the *contradiction of life,* instead of being its transfiguration and eternal Yea! With God war is declared on life, nature, and the will to life! God is the formula for every calumny of this world and for every lie concerning a beyond! In God, nonentity is deified, and the will to nonentity is declared holy!

19. The fact that the strong races of Northern Europe did not repudiate the Christian God, certainly does not do any credit to their religious power, not to speak of their taste. They ought to have been able successfully to cope with such a morbid and decrepit offshoot of decadence. And a curse lies on their heads; because they were unable to cope with him: they made illness, decrepitude and contradiction a part of all their instincts,—since then they have not *created* any other God! Two thousand years have passed and not a single new God! But still there exists, and as if by right,—like an *ultimum* and *maximum* of god-creating power,—the *creator spiritus* in man, this miserable God of Christian monotono-theism! This hybrid creature of decay, nonentity, concept and contradiction, in which all the instincts of decadence, all the cowardices and languors of the soul find their sanction!— —

20. With my condemnation of Christianity I should not like to have done an injustice to a religion which is related to it and the number of whose followers is even greater; I refer to Buddhism. As nihilistic religions, they are akin,—they are religions of decadence,—while each is separated from the other in the most extraordinary fashion. For being able to compare them at all, the critic of Christianity is profoundly grateful to Indian scholars.—Buddhism is a hundred times more realistic than Christianity,—it is part of its constitutional heritage to be able to face problems objectively and coolly, it is the outcome of centuries of lasting philosophical activity. The concept "God" was already exploded when it appeared. Buddhism is the only really *positive* religion to be found in history, even in its epistemology (which is strict phenomenalism)—it no longer speaks of the "struggle with *sin,*" but fully recognising the true nature of reality it speaks of the "struggle with *pain.*" It already has—and this distinguishes it fundamentally from Christianity,—the self-deception of moral concepts beneath it,—to use my own phraseology, it stands *Beyond Good and Evil.* The two physiological facts upon which it rests and upon which it bestows its attention are: in the first place excessive irritability of feeling, which manifests itself as a refined susceptibility to pain, *and also* as super-spiritualisation, an all-too-lengthy sojourn amid concepts and logical procedures, under the influence of which the personal instinct has suffered in favour of the "impersonal." (—Both of these states will be known to a few of my readers, the objective ones, who, like myself, will know them from experience.) Thanks to these physiological conditions, a state of depression set in, which Buddha sought to combat by means of hygiene. Against it, he prescribes life in the open, a life of travel; moderation and careful choice in food; caution in regard to all intoxicating liquor, as also in regard to all the passions which tend to create bile and to heat the blood; and he deprecates care either on one's own or on other people's account. He recommends ideas that bring one either peace or good cheer,—he invents means whereby the habit of contrary ideas may be lost. He understands goodness—being good—as promoting health. *Prayer* is out of the question, as is also *asceticism*; there is neither a Categorical Imperative nor any discipline whatsoever, even within the walls of a monastery (—it is always possible to leave it if one wants to). All these things would have been only a means of accentuating the excessive irritability already referred to. Precisely on this account he does not exhort his followers to wage war upon those who do not share their views; nothing is more abhorred in his doctrine than the feeling of revenge, of aversion, and of resentment (—"not through hostility doth hostility end": the touching refrain of the whole of Buddhism . . .). And in this he was right; for it is precisely these passions which are thoroughly unhealthy in view of the principal dietetic object. The mental fatigue which he finds already existent and which expresses itself in excessive "objectivity" (*i.e.,* the enfeeblement of the individual's interest—loss of ballast and of "egoism"), he combats by leading the spiritual interests as well imperatively back to the individual. In Buddha's doctrine egoism is a duty: the thing which is above all necessary, *i.e.,* "how canst thou be rid of suffering" regulates and defines the whole of the spiritual diet (—let anyone but think of that Athenian who also declared war upon pure "scientificality," Socrates, who made a morality out of personal egoism even in the realm of problems).

21. The pre-requisites for Buddhism are a very mild climate, great gentleness and liberality in the customs of a people and *no* militarism. The movement must also originate among the higher and even learned classes. Cheerfulness, peace and absence of desire, are the highest of inspirations, and they are *realised.* Buddhism is not a religion in which perfection is merely aspired to: perfection is the normal case. In Christianity all the instincts of the subjugated and oppressed come to the fore: it is the lowest classes who seek their salvation in this religion. Here the pastime, the manner of killing time is to practise the casuistry of sin, self-criticism, and conscience inquisition. Here the ecstasy in the presence of a *powerful being,* called "god," is constantly maintained by means of prayer; while the highest thing is regarded as unattainable, as a gift, as an act of "grace." Here plain dealing is also entirely lacking: concealment and the darkened room are Christian. Here the body is despised, hygiene is repudiated as sensual; the church repudiates even cleanliness (—the first Christian measure after the banishment of the Moors was the closing of the public baths, of which Cordova alone possessed 270). A certain spirit of cruelty towards one's self and others is also Christian: hatred of all those who do not share one's views; the will to persecute. Sombre and exciting ideas are in the foreground; the most coveted states and those which are endowed with the finest names, are really epileptic in their nature; diet is selected in such a way as to favour morbid symptoms and to over-excite the nerves. Christian, too, is the mortal hatred of the earth's rulers—the "noble,"—and at the same time a sort of concealed and secret competition with them (the subjugated leave the "body" to their master—all they want is the "soul"). Christian is the hatred of the intellect, of pride, of courage, freedom, intellectual *libertinage;* Christian is the hatred of the *senses,* of the joys of the senses, of joy in general.

22. When Christianity departed from its native soil, which consisted of the lowest classes, the *submerged masses* of the ancient world, and set forth in quest of power among barbaric nations, it no longer met with exhausted men but inwardly savage and self-lacerating men—the strong but bungled men. Here, dissatisfaction with one's self, suffering through one's self, is not as in the case of Buddhism, excessive irritability and susceptibility to pain, but rather, conversely, it is an inordinate desire for inflicting pain, for a discharge of the inner tension in hostile deeds and ideas. Christianity was in need of *barbaric* ideas and values, in order to be able to master barbarians: such are for instance, the sacrifice of the first-born, the drinking of blood at communion, the contempt of the intellect and of culture; torture in all its forms, sensual and non-sensual; the great pomp of the cult. Buddhism is a religion for *senile* men, for races which have become kind, gentle, and over-spiritual, and which feel pain too easily (—Europe is not nearly ripe for it yet—); it calls them back to peace and cheerfulness, to a regimen for the intellect, to a certain hardening of the body. Christianity aims at mastering *beasts of prey;* its expedient is to make them *ill,*—to render feeble is the Christian recipe for taming, for "civilisation." Buddhism is a religion for the close and exhaustion of civilisation; Christianity does not even find civilisation at hand when it appears, in certain circumstances it lays the foundation of civilisation.

23. Buddhism, I repeat, is a hundred times colder, more truthful, more objective. It no longer requires to justify pain and its susceptibility to suffering by the interpretation of sin,—it simply says what it thinks, "I suffer." To the barbarian, on the other hand, suffering in itself is not a respectable thing: in order to acknowledge to himself that he suffers, what he requires, in the first place, is an explanation (his instinct directs him more readily to deny his suffering, or to endure it in silence). In his case, the word "devil" was a blessing: man had an almighty and terrible enemy—he had no reason to be ashamed of suffering at the hands of such an enemy.—

At bottom there are in Christianity one or two subtleties which belong to the Orient. In the first place it knows that it is a matter of indifference whether a thing be true or not; but that it is of the highest importance that it should be believed to be true. Truth and the belief that something is true: two totally separate worlds of interest, almost *opposite worlds,* the road to the one and the road to the other lie absolutely apart. To be initiated into this fact almost constitutes one a sage in the Orient: the Brahmins understood it thus, so did Plato, and so does every disciple of esoteric wisdom. If for example it give anyone pleasure to believe himself delivered from sin, it is *not* a necessary prerequisite thereto that he should be sinful, but only that he should *feel* sinful. If, however, *faith* is above all necessary, then reason, knowledge, and scientific research must be brought into evil repute: the road to truth becomes the *forbidden* road.—Strong *hope* is a much greater stimulant of life than any single realised joy could be. Sufferers must be sustained by a hope which no actuality can contradict,—and which cannot ever be realised: the hope of another world. (Precisely on account of this power that hope has of making the unhappy linger on, the Greeks regarded it as the evil of evils, as the most *mischievous* evil: it remained behind in Pandora's box.) In order that *love* may be possible, God must be a person. In order that the lowest instincts may also make their voices heard God must be young. For the ardour of the women a beautiful saint, and for the ardour of the men a Virgin Mary has to be pressed into the foreground. All this on condition that Christianity wishes to rule over a certain soil, on which Aphrodisiac or Adonis cults had already determined the *notion* of a cult. To insist upon *chastity* only intensifies the vehemence and profundity of the religious instinct—it makes the cult warmer, more enthusiastic, more soulful.—Love is the state in which man sees things most widely different from what they are. The force of illusion reaches its zenith here, as likewise the sweetening and transfiguring power. When a man is in love he endures more than at other times; he submits to everything. The thing was to discover a religion in which it was possible to love: by this means the worst in life is overcome—it is no longer even seen.—So much for three Christian virtues Faith, Hope, and Charity: I call them the three Christian *precautionary measures.*—Buddhism is too full of aged wisdom, too positivistic to be shrewd in this way.

24. Here I only touch upon the problem of the origin of Christianity. The first principle of its solution reads: Christianity can be understood only in relation to the soil out of which it grew,—it is not a counter-movement against the Jewish instinct, it is the rational outcome of the latter, one step further in its appalling logic. In the formula of the Saviour: "for Salvation is of the Jews."—The second principle is: the psychological type of the Galilean is still recognisable, but it was only in a state of utter degeneration (which is at once a distortion and an overloading with foreign features) that he was able to serve the purpose for which he has been used,—namely, as the type of a Redeemer of mankind.

The Jews are the most remarkable people in the history of the world, because when they were confronted with the question of Being or non-Being, with simply uncanny deliberateness, they preferred Being *at any price:* this price was the fundamental *falsification* of all Nature, all the naturalness and all the reality, of the inner quite as much as of the outer world. They hedged themselves in behind all those conditions under which hitherto a people has been able to live, has been allowed to live; of themselves they created an idea which was the reverse of *natural* conditions,—each in turn, they twisted first religion, then the cult, then morality, history and psychology, about in a manner so perfectly hopeless that they were made *to contradict their natural value.* We meet with the same phenomena again, and exaggerated to an incalculable degree, although only as a copy:—the Christian Church as compared with the "chosen people," lacks all claim to originality. Precisely on this account the Jews are the most *fatal* people in the history of the world: their ultimate influence has falsified mankind to such an extent, that even to this day the Christian can be anti-Semitic in spirit, without comprehending that he himself is the *final consequence of Judaism.*

It was in my "Genealogy of Morals" that I first gave a psychological exposition of the idea of the antithesis noble- and *resentment*-morality, the latter having arisen out of an attitude of negation to the former: but this is Judæo-Christian morality heart and soul. In order to be able to say Nay to everything that represents the ascending movement of life, prosperity, power, beauty, and self-affirmation on earth, the instinct of resentment, become genius, had to invent *another* world, from the standpoint of which that *Yea-saying* to life appeared as *the* most evil and most abominable thing. From the psychological standpoint the Jewish people are possessed of the toughest vitality. Transplanted amid impossible conditions, with profound self-preservative intelligence, it voluntarily took the side of all the instincts of decadence,—*not* as though dominated by them, but because it detected a power in them by means of which it could assert itself *against* "the world." The Jews are the opposite of all *decadents:* they have been forced to represent them to the point of illusion, and with a *non plus ultra* of histrionic genius, they have known how to set themselves at the head of all decadent movements (St. Paul and Christianity for instance), in order to create something from them which is stronger than every party *saying Yea to life.* For the category of men which aspires to power in Judaism and Christianity,—that is to say, for the sacerdotal class, decadence is but a *means:* this category of men has a vital interest in making men sick, and in turning the notions "good" and "bad," "true" and "false," upside down in a manner which is not only dangerous to life, but also slanders it.

25. The history of Israel is invaluable as the typical history of every *denaturalisation* of natural values: let me point to five facts which relate thereto. Originally, and above all in the period of the kings, even Israel's attitude to all things was the *right* one—that is to say, the natural one. Its Jehovah was the expression of its consciousness of power, of its joy over itself, of its hope for itself: victory and salvation were expected from him, through him it was confident that Nature would give what a people requires—above all rain. Jehovah is the God of Israel, and *consequently* the God of justice: this is the reasoning of every people which is in the position of power, and which has a good conscience in that position. In the solemn cult both sides of this self-affirmation of a people find expression: it is grateful for the great strokes of fate by means of which it became uppermost; it is grateful for the regularity in the succession of the seasons and for all good fortune in the rearing of cattle and in the tilling of the soil.—This state of affairs remained the ideal for some considerable time, even after it had been swept away in a deplorable manner by anarchy from within and the Assyrians from without. But the people still retained, as their highest desideratum, that vision of a king who was a good soldier and a severe judge; and he who retained it most of all was that typical prophet (—that is to say, critic and satirist of the age), Isaiah.—But all hopes remained unrealised. The old God was no longer able to do what he had done formerly. He ought to have been dropped. What happened? The idea of him was changed,—the idea of him was denaturalised: this was the price they paid for retaining him.—Jehovah, the God of "Justice,"—is no longer one with Israel, no longer the expression of a people's sense of dignity: he is only a god on certain conditions. . . . The idea of him becomes a weapon in the hands of priestly agitators who henceforth interpret all happiness as a reward, all unhappiness as a punishment for disobedience to

God, for "sin": that most fraudulent method of interpretation which arrives at a so-called "moral order of the Universe," by means of which the concept "cause" and "effect" is turned upside down. Once natural causation has been swept out of the world by reward and punishment, a causation *hostile to nature* becomes necessary; whereupon all the forms of unnaturalness follow. A God who *demands,*—in the place of a God who helps, who advises, who is at bottom only a name for every happy inspiration of courage and of self-reliance. . . . Morality is no longer the expression of the conditions of life and growth, no longer the most fundamental instinct of life, but it has become abstract, it has become the opposite of life,—Morality as the fundamental perversion of the imagination, as the "evil eye" for all things. What is Jewish morality, what is Christian morality? Chance robbed of its innocence; unhappiness polluted with the idea of "sin"; well-being interpreted as a danger, as a "temptation"; physiological indisposition poisoned by means of the canker-worm of conscience. . . .

PART IV

THE CONTEMPORARY PERIOD

Chapter 31

W. K. CLIFFORD

William Kingdon Clifford (1845–1879), British mathematician and philosopher, was educated at Trinity College, Cambridge, and King's College, London, where he became Professor of Applied Mathematics. His promising career was cut short when he died of tuberculosis at the age of thirty-four. His best known work, *The Ethics of Belief,* deals with the relationship between evidence and belief. He attacks the kind of pragmatic justification for religious belief set forth by Pascal in his Wager Argument (see chapter 17). Clifford argues that there is an ethics of belief that makes immoral all believing without sufficient evidence. Pragmatic justifications are not justifications at all but counterfeits of genuine justifications, which must always be based on evidence.

Clifford illustrates his thesis with the example of a shipowner who sends an emigrant ship to sea. He knows that the ship is old and not well built, but he fails to have the ship inspected. Dismissing from his mind all doubts and suspicions that the vessel is not seaworthy, he trusts in Providence to care for his ship. He acquires a sincere and comfortable conviction in this way and collects his insurance money without a tinge of guilt after the ship sinks and all the passengers drown. Clifford argues that although the shipowner sincerely believed that all was well with the ship, his sincerity in no way exculpates him, because "he had no right to believe on such evidence as was before him." One has an obligation to get oneself in a position in which one will believe propositions only on sufficient evidence. His general conclusion is that it is "always wrong for anyone to believe anything on insufficient evidence."

FOR FURTHER READING

James, William. *The Will to Believe.* (Dover, 1956).

Mackie, J. L. *The Miracle of Theism: Arguments for and Against the Existence of God.* (Oxford University Press, 1982).

Meiland, Jack. "What Ought We to Believe? or the Ethics of Belief Revisited." (*American Philosophical Quarterly,* vol 17, 1980).

Pojman, Louis. *Religious Belief and the Will.* (Routledge & Kegan Paul, 1986).

Price, H. H. *Belief.* (Unwin & Allen, 1967).

Wainwright, William. *Reasons of the Heart.* (Cornell University Press, 1995).

Williams, Bernard. "Deciding to Believe" in *Problems of the Self.* (Cambridge University Press, 1972).

The Ethics of Belief

I. THE DUTY OF INQUIRY

A shipowner was about to send to sea an emigrant-ship. He knew that she was old, and not over-well built at the first; that she had seen many seas and climes, and often had needed repairs. Doubts had been suggested to him that possibly she was not seaworthy. These doubts preyed upon his mind, and made him unhappy; he thought that perhaps he ought to have her thoroughly overhauled and refitted, even though this should put him to great expense. Before the ship sailed, however, he succeeded in overcoming these melancholy reflections. He said to himself that she had gone safely through so many voyages and weathered so many storms that it was idle to suppose she would not come safely home from this trip also. He would put his trust in Providence, which could hardly fail to protect all these unhappy families that were leaving their fatherland to seek for better times elsewhere. He would dismiss from his mind all ungenerous suspicions about the honesty of builders and contractors. In such ways he acquired a sincere and comfortable conviction that his vessel was thoroughly safe and seaworthy; he watched her departure with a light heart, and benevolent wishes for the success of the exiles in their strange new home that was to be; and he got his insurance-money when she went down in mid-ocean and told no tales.

What shall we say of him? Surely this, that he was verily guilty of the death of those men. It is admitted that he did sincerely believe in the soundness of his ship; but the sincerity of his conviction can in no wise help him, because *he had no right to believe on such evidence as was before him.* He had acquired his belief not by honestly earning it in patient investigation, but by stifling his doubts. And although in the end he may have felt so sure about it that he could not think otherwise, yet inasmuch as he had knowingly and willingly worked himself into that frame of mind, he must be held responsible for it.

Let us alter the case a little, and suppose that the ship was not unsound after all; that she made her voyage safely, and many others after it. Will that diminish the guilt of her owner? Not one jot. When an action is once done, it is right or wrong for ever; no accidental failure of its good or evil fruits can possibly alter that. The man would not have been innocent, he would only have been not found out. The question of right or wrong has to do with the origin of his belief, not the matter of it; not what it was, but how he got it; not whether it turned out to be true or false, but whether he had a right to believe on such evidence as was before him.

There was once an island in which some of the inhabitants professed a religion teaching neither the doctrine of original sin nor that of eternal punishment. A suspicion got abroad that the professors of this religion had made use of unfair means to get their doctrines taught to children. They were accused of wresting the laws of their country in such a way as to remove children from the care of their natural and legal guardians; and even of stealing them away and keeping them concealed from their friends and relations. A certain number of men formed themselves into a society for the purpose of agitating the public about this matter. They published grave accusations against individual citizens of the highest position and character, and did all in their power to injure these citizens in the exercise of their professions. So great was the noise they made, that a Commission was appointed to investigate the facts; but after the Commission had carefully inquired into all the evidence that could be got, it appeared that the accused were innocent. Not only had they been accused on insufficient evidence, but the evidence of their innocence was such as the agitators might easily have obtained, if they had attempted a fair inquiry. After these disclosures the inhabitants of that country looked upon the members of the agitating society, not only as persons whose judgment was to be distrusted, but also as no longer to be counted honourable men. For although they had sincerely and conscientiously believed in the charges they had made, yet *they had no right to believe on such evidence as was before them.* Their sincere convictions, instead of being honestly earned by patient inquiring, were stolen by listening to the voice of prejudice and passion.

Let us vary this case also, and suppose, other things remaining as before, that a still more accurate investigation proved the accused to have been really guilty. Would this make any difference in the guilt of the accusers? Clearly not; the question is not whether their belief was true or false, but whether they entertained it on wrong grounds. They would no doubt say, "Now you see that we were right after all; next time perhaps you will believe us." And they might be believed, but they would not thereby become honourable men. They would not be innocent, they would only be not found out. Every one of them, if he chose to examine himself *in foro conscientiae,* would know that he had acquired and nourished a belief, when he had no right to believe on such evidence as was before him; and therein he would know that he had done a wrong thing.

It may be said, however, that in both of these supposed cases it is not the belief which is judged to be wrong, but the action following upon it. The shipowner might say, "I am perfectly certain that my ship is sound, but still I feel it my duty to have her examined, before trusting the lives of so many people to her." And it might be said to the agitator, "However convinced you were of the justice of your cause and the truth of your convictions, you ought not to have made a public attack upon any man's character until you had examined the evidence on both sides with the utmost patience and care."

In the first place, let us admit that, so far as it goes, this view of the case is right and necessary; right, because even when a man's belief is so fixed that he cannot think otherwise, he still has a choice in regard to the action suggested by it, and so cannot escape the duty of investigating on the ground of the strength of his convictions; and necessary, because those who are not yet capable of controlling their feelings and thoughts must have a plain rule dealing with overt acts.

But this being premised as necessary, it becomes clear that it is not sufficient, and that our previous judgment is required to supplement it. For it is not possible so to sever the belief from the action it suggests as to condemn the one without condemning the other. No man holding a strong belief on one side of a question, or even wishing to hold a belief on one side, can investigate it with such fairness and completeness as if he were really in doubt and unbiased; so that the existence of a belief not founded on fair inquiry unfits a man for the performance of this necessary duty.

Nor is that truly a belief at all which has not some influence upon the actions of him who holds it. He who truly believes that which prompts him to an action has looked upon the action to lust after it, he has committed it already in his heart. If a belief is not realized immediately in open deeds, it is stored up for the guidance of the future. It goes to make a part of that aggregate of beliefs which is the link between sensation and action at every moment of all our lives, and which is so organized and compacted together that no part of it can be isolated from the rest, but every new addition modifies the structure of the whole. No real belief, however trifling and fragmentary it may seem, is ever truly insignificant; it prepares us to receive more of its like, confirms those which resembled it before, and weakens others; and so gradually it lays a stealthy train in our inmost thoughts, which may some day explode into overt action, and leave its stamp upon our character for ever.

And no one man's belief is in any case a private matter which concerns himself alone. Our lives are guided by that general conception of the course of things which has been created by society for social purposes. Our words, our phrases, our forms and processes and modes of thought, are common property, fashioned and perfected from age to age; an heirloom which every succeeding generation inherits as a precious deposit and sacred trust to be handed on to the next one, not unchanged but enlarged and purified, with some clear marks of its proper handiwork. Into this, for good or ill, is woven every belief of every man who has speech of his fellows. An awful privilege, and an awful responsibility, that we should help to create the world in which posterity will live.

In the two supposed cases which have been considered, it has been judged wrong to believe on insufficient evidence, or to nourish belief by suppressing doubt and avoiding investigation. The reason of this judgment is not far to seek; it is that in both these cases the belief held by one man was of great importance to other men. But forasmuch as no belief held by one man, however seemingly trivial the belief, and however obscure the believer, is ever actually insignificant or without its effect on the fate of mankind, we have no choice but to extend our judgment to all cases of belief whatever. Belief, that sacred faculty which prompts the decisions of our will, and knits into harmonious working all the compacted energies of our being, is ours not for ourselves, but for humanity. It is rightly used on truths which have been established by long experience and waiting toil, and which have stood in the fierce light of free and fearless questioning. Then it helps to bind men together, and to strengthen and direct their common action. It is desecrated when given to unproved and unquestioned statements, for the solace and private pleasure of the believer; to add a tinsel splendour to the plain straight road of our life and display a bright mirage beyond it; or even to drown the common sorrows of our kind by a self-deception which allows them not only to cast down, but also to degrade us. Whoso would deserve well of his fellows in this matter will guard the purity of his belief with a very fanaticism of jealous care, lest at any time it should rest on an unworthy object, and catch a stain which can never be wiped away.

It is not only the leader of men, statesman, philosopher, or poet, that owes this bounden duty to mankind. Every rustic who delivers in the village alehouse his slow, infrequent sentences, may help to kill or keep alive the fatal superstitions which clog his race. Every hard-worked wife of an artisan may transmit to her children beliefs which shall knit society together, or rend it in pieces. No simplicity of mind, no obscurity of station, can escape the universal duty of questioning all that we believe.

It is true that this duty is a hard one, and the doubt which comes out of it is often a very bitter thing. It leaves us bare and powerless where we thought that we were safe and strong. To know all about anything is to know how to deal with it under all circumstances. We feel much happier and more secure when we think we know precisely what to do, no matter what happens, than when we have lost our way and do not know where to turn. And if we have supposed ourselves to know all about anything, and to be capable of doing what is fit in regard to it, we naturally do not like to find that we are really ignorant and powerless, that we have to begin again at the beginning, and try to learn what the thing is and how it is to be dealt with—if indeed anything can be learnt about it. It is the sense of power attached to a sense of knowledge that makes men desirous of believing, and afraid of doubting.

This sense of power is the highest and best of pleasures when the belief on which it is founded is a true belief, and has been fairly earned by investigation. For then we may justly feel that it is common property, and hold good for others as well as for ourselves. Then we may be glad, not that *I* have learned secrets by which I am safer and stronger, but that *we men* have got mastery over more of the world; and we shall be strong, not for ourselves, but in the name of Man and in his strength. But if the belief has been accepted on insufficient evidence, the pleasure is a stolen one. Not only does it deceive ourselves by giving us a sense of power which we do not really possess, but it is sinful, because it is stolen in defiance of our duty to mankind. That duty is to guard ourselves from such beliefs as from a pestilence, which may shortly master our own body and then spread to the rest of the town. What would be thought of one who, for the sake of a sweet fruit, should deliberately run the risk of bringing a plague upon his family and his neighbours?

And, as in other such cases, it is not the risk only which has to be considered; for a bad action is always bad at the time when it is done, no matter what happens afterwards. Every time we let ourselves believe for unworthy reasons, we weaken our powers of self-control, of doubting, of judicially and fairly weighing evidence. We all suffer severely enough from the maintenance and support of false beliefs and the fatally wrong actions which they lead to, and the evil born when one such belief is entertained is great and wide. But a greater and wider evil arises when the credulous character is maintained and supported, when a habit of believing for unworthy reasons is fostered and made permanent. If I steal money from any person, there may be no harm done by the mere transfer of possession; he may not feel the loss, or it may prevent him from using the money badly. But I cannot help doing this great wrong towards Man, that I make myself dishonest. What hurts society is not that it should lose its property, but that it should become a den of thieves; for then it must cease to be society. This is why we ought not to do evil that good may come; for at any rate this great evil has come, that we have done evil and are made wicked thereby. In like manner, if I let myself believe anything on insufficient evidence, there may be no great harm done by the mere belief; it may be true after all, or I may never have occasion to exhibit it in outward acts. But I cannot help doing this great wrong towards Man, that I make myself credulous. The danger to society is not merely that it should believe wrong things, though that is great enough; but that it should become credulous, and lose the habit of testing things and inquiring into them; for then it must sink back into savagery.

The harm which is done by credulity in a man is not confined to the fostering of a credulous character in others, and consequent support of false beliefs. Habitual want of care about what I believe leads to habitual want of care in others about the truth of what is told to me. Men speak the truth to one another when each reveres the truth in his own mind and in the other's mind; but how shall my friend revere the truth in my mind when I myself am careless about it, when I believe things because I want to believe them, and because they are comforting and pleasant? Will he not learn to cry, "Peace," to me, when there is no peace? By such a course I shall surround myself with a thick atmosphere of falsehood and fraud, and in that I must live. It may matter little to me, in my cloud-castle of sweet illusions and darling lies; but it matters much to Man that I have made my neighbours ready to deceive. The credulous man is father to the liar and the cheat; he lives in the bosom of this his family, and it is no marvel if he should become even as they are. So closely are our duties knit together, that whoso shall keep the whole law, and yet offend in one point, he is guilty of all.

To sum up: it is wrong always, everywhere, and for anyone, to believe anything upon insufficient evidence.

If a man, holding a belief which he was taught in childhood or persuaded of afterwards, keeps down and pushes away any doubts which arise about it in his mind, purposely avoids the reading of books and the company of men that call in question or discuss it, and regards as impious those questions which cannot easily be asked without disturbing it—the life of that man is one long sin against mankind.

If this judgment seems harsh when applied to those simple souls who have never known better, who have been brought up from the cradle with a horror of doubt, and taught that their eternal welfare depends on *what* they believe, then it leads to the very serious question, *Who hath made Israel to sin?*

It may be permitted me to fortify this judgment with the sentence of Milton—

"A man may be a heretic in the truth; and if he believe things only because his pastor says so, or the assembly so determine, without knowing other reason, though his belief be true, yet the very truth he holds becomes his heresy."

And with this famous aphorism of Coleridge—

"He who begins by loving Christianity better than Truth, will proceed by loving his own sect or Church better than Christianity, and end in loving himself better than all."

Inquiry into the evidence of a doctrine is not to be made once for all, and then taken as finally settled. It is never lawful to stifle a doubt; for either it can be honestly answered by means of the inquiry already made, or else it proves that the inquiry was not complete.

"But," says one, "I am a busy man; I have no time for the long course of study which would be necessary to make me in any degree a competent judge of certain questions, or even able to understand the nature of the arguments." Then he should have no time to believe.

Chapter 32

Charles Sanders Peirce

Charles Sanders Peirce (1839–1914), born in Cambridge, the son of a Harvard University mathematician, was a scientist and philosopher. He received his M. A. in mathematics and chemistry, and worked for three years at the Harvard astronomical observatory. From 1861 to 1891 he was associated with the U. S. Coastal and Geodetic Survey. He also lectured at Johns Hopkins University, but was never a permanent member of the faculty. Although he deplored the popularization of his thought by William James, James was a loyal friend who introduced Peirce's theories to the intellectual public. Peirce is primarily known for having identified a third type of reasoning in addition to the two standard forms, deduction and induction, which he named "abduction," and which has subsequently been known as reasoning to the best explanation. He is also the father of *pragmatism* (from the Greek word *pragma,* meaning act or deed), which emphasizes the practical nature of philosophy.

In the 1870s Peirce published a series in *Popular Science Monthly,* one of which was "The Fixation of Belief," which is reprinted below. The essay argues that the function of coming to believe something is to relieve the disturbance of uncertainty and doubt. He distinguishes four ways of coming to a settled belief about some issue or subject matter: the methods of tenacity, authority, natural preferences, and science, the method which Peirce prefers.

FOR FURTHER READING

Ayer, A. J. *Origins of Pragmatism: Studies in the Philosophy of Charles Sanders Peirce and William James.* (Macmillan, 1968).

Kuklick, Bruce. *The Rise of American Philosophy.* (Yale University Press, 1977).

Murphy, John. *Pragmatism: From Peirce to Davidson.* (Westview Press, 1990).

Peirce, C. S. *Essays in the Philosophy of Science.* (Liberal Arts Library, 1957).

Quine, W. V. and Joseph Ullian. *The Web of Belief,* 2nd ed. (Random House, 1978).

Scheffler, Israel. *Four Pragmatists.* (Humanities Press, 1974).

Smith, John. *The Spirit of American Philosophy.* (Oxford University Press, 1963).

The Fixation of Belief

1. SCIENCE AND LOGIC

358. Few persons care to study logic, because everybody conceives himself to be proficient enough in the art of reasoning already. But I observe that this satisfaction is limited to one's own ratiocination, and does not extend to that of other men.

359. We come to the full possession of our power of drawing inferences, the last of all our faculties; for it is not so much a natural gift as a long and difficult art. The history of its practice would make a grand subject for a book. The medieval schoolman, following the Romans, made logic the earliest of a boy's studies after grammar, as being very easy. So it was as they understood it. Its fundamental principle, according to them, was, that all knowledge rests either on authority or reason; but that whatever is deduced by reason depends ultimately on a premiss derived from authority. Accordingly, as soon as a boy was perfect in the syllogistic procedure, his intellectual kit of tools was held to be complete.

360. To Roger Bacon, that remarkable mind who in the middle of the thirteenth century was almost a scientific man, the schoolmen's conception of reasoning appeared only an obstacle to truth. He saw that experience alone teaches anything—a proposition which to us seems easy to understand, because a distinct conception of experience has been handed down to us from former generations; which to him likewise seemed perfectly clear, because its difficulties had not yet unfolded themselves. Of all kinds of experience, the best, he thought, was interior illumination, which teaches many things about Nature which the external senses could never discover, such as the transubstantiation of bread.

361. Four centuries later, the more celebrated Bacon, in the first book of his *Novum Organum,* gave his clear account of experience as something which must be open to verification and reëxamination. But, superior as Lord Bacon's conception is to earlier notions, a modern reader who is not in awe of his grandiloquence is chiefly struck by the inadequacy of his view of scientific procedure. That we have only to make some crude experiments, to draw up briefs of the results in certain blank forms, to go through these by rule, checking off everything disproved and setting down the alternatives, and that thus in a few years physical science would be finished up—what an idea! "He wrote on science like a Lord Chancellor," indeed, as Harvey, a genuine man of science said.

362. The early scientists, Copernicus, Tycho Brahe, Kepler, Galileo, Harvey, and Gilbert, had methods more like those of their modern brethren. Kepler undertook to draw a curve through the places of Mars, and to state the times occupied by the planet in describing the different parts of that curve; but perhaps his greatest service to science was in impressing on men's minds that this was the thing to be done if they wished to improve astronomy; that they were not to content themselves with inquiring whether one system of epicycles was better than another but that they were to sit down to the figures and find out what the curve, in truth, was. He accomplished this by his incomparable energy and courage, blundering along in the most inconceivable way (to us), from one irrational hypothesis to another, until, after trying twenty-two of these, he fell, by the mere exhaustion of his invention, upon the orbit which a mind well furnished with the weapons of modern logic would have tried almost at the outset.

363. In the same way, every work of science great enough to be well remembered for a few generations affords some exemplification of the defective state of the art of reasoning of the time when it was written; and each chief step in science has been a lesson in logic. It was so when Lavoisier and his contemporaries took up the study of Chemistry. The old chemist's maxim had been, "Lege, lege, lege, labora, ore, et relege." Lavoisier's method was not to read and pray, but to dream that some long and complicated chemical process would have a certain effect, to put it into practice with dull patience, after its inevitable failure, to dream that with some modification it would have another result, and to end by publishing the last dream as a fact: his way was to carry his mind into his laboratory, and literally to make of his alembics and cucurbits instruments of thought, giving a new conception of reasoning as something which was to be done with one's eyes open, in manipulating real things instead of words and fancies.

364. The Darwinian controversy is, in large part,

a question of logic. Mr. Darwin proposed to apply the statistical method to biology. The same thing has been done in a widely different branch of science, the theory of gases. Though unable to say what the movements of any particular molecule of gas would be on a certain hypothesis regarding the constitution of this class of bodies, Clausius and Maxwell were yet able, eight years before the publication of Darwin's immortal work, by the application of the doctrine of probabilities, to predict that in the long run such and such a proportion of the molecules would, under given circumstances, acquire such and such velocities; that there would take place, every second, such and such a relative number of collisions, etc.; and from these propositions were able to deduce certain properties of gases, especially in regard to their heat-relations. In like manner, Darwin, while unable to say what the operation of variation and natural selection in any individual case will be, demonstrates that in the long run they will, or would, adapt animals to their circumstances. Whether or not existing animal forms are due to such action, or what position the theory ought to take, forms the subject of a discussion in which questions of fact and questions of logic are curiously interlaced.

2. GUIDING PRINCIPLES

365. The object of reasoning is to find out, from the consideration of what we already know, something else which we do not know. Consequently, reasoning is good if it be such as to give a true conclusion from true premisses, and not otherwise. Thus, the question of validity is purely one of fact and not of thinking. A being the facts stated in the premisses and B being that concluded, the question is, whether these facts are really so related that if A were B would generally be. If so, the inference is valid; if not, not. It is not in the least the question whether, when the premisses are accepted by the mind, we feel an impulse to accept the conclusion also. It is true that we do generally reason correctly by nature. But that is an accident; the true conclusion would remain true if we had no impulse to accept it; and the false one would remain false, though we could not resist the tendency to believe in it.

366. We are, doubtless, in the main logical animals, but we are not perfectly so. Most of us, for example, are naturally more sanguine and hopeful than logic would justify. We seem to be so constituted that in the absence of any facts to go upon we are happy and selfsatisfied; so that the effect of experience is continually to contract our hopes and aspirations. Yet a lifetime of the application of this corrective does not usually eradicate our sanguine disposition. Where hope is unchecked by any experience, it is likely that our optimism is extravagant. Logicality in regard to practical matters (if this be understood, not in the old sense, but as consisting in a wise union of security with fruitfulness of reasoning) is the most useful quality an animal can possess, and might, therefore, result from the action of natural selection; but outside of these it is probably of more advantage to the animal to have his mind filled with pleasing and encouraging visions, independently of their truth; and thus, upon unpractical subjects, natural selection might occasion a fallacious tendency of thought.

367. That which determines us, from given premisses, to draw one inference rather than another, is some habit of mind, whether it be constitutional or acquired. The habit is good or otherwise, according as it produces true conclusions from true premisses or not; and an inference is regarded as valid or not, without reference to the truth or falsity of its conclusion specially, but according as the habit which determines it is such as to produce true conclusions in general or not. The particular habit of mind which governs this or that inference may be formulated in a proposition whose truth depends on the validity of the inferences which the habit determines; and such a formula is called a *guiding principle* of inference. Suppose, for example, that we observe that a rotating disk of copper quickly comes to rest when placed between the poles of a magnet, and we infer that this will happen with every disk of copper. The guiding principle is, that what is true of one piece of copper is true of another. Such a guiding principle with regard to copper would be much safer than with regard to many other substances—brass, for example.

368. A book might be written to signalize all the most important of these guiding principles of reasoning. It would probably be, we must confess, of no service to a person whose thought is directed wholly to practical subjects, and whose activity moves along thoroughly-beaten paths. The problems that present themselves to such a mind are matters of routine which he has learned once for all to handle in learning his business. But let a man venture into an unfamiliar field, or where his results are not continually checked by experience, and all history shows that the most masculine intellect will ofttimes lose his orientation and waste his efforts in directions which bring him no nearer to his goal, or even carry him entirely astray. He is like a ship in the open sea, with no one on board who understands the rules of navigation. And in such a case some general study of the guiding principles of reasoning would be sure to be found useful.

369. The subject could hardly be treated, however, without being first limited; since almost any fact may serve as a guiding principle. But it so happens that there exists a division among facts, such that in one class are all those which are absolutely essential as guiding principles, while in the others are all which have any other interest as objects of research. This division is between those which are necessarily taken for granted in asking why a certain conclusion is thought to follow from certain premisses, and those which are not implied in such a question. A moment's thought will show that a variety of facts are already assumed when the logical question is first asked. It is implied, for instance, that there are such states of mind as doubt and belief—that a passage from one to the other is possible, the object of thought remaining the same, and that this transition is subject to some rules by which all minds are alike bound. As these are facts which we must already know before we can have any clear conception of reasoning at all, it cannot be supposed to be any longer of much interest to inquire into their truth or falsity. On the other hand, it is easy to believe that those rules of reasoning which are deduced from the very idea of the process are the ones which are the most essential; and, indeed, that so long as it conforms to these it will, at least, not lead to false conclusions from true premisses. In point of fact, the importance of what may be deduced from the assumptions involved in the logical question turns out to be greater than might be supposed, and this for reasons which it is difficult to exhibit at the outset. The only one which I shall here mention is, that conceptions which are really products of logical reflection, without being readily seen to be so, mingle with our ordinary thoughts, and are frequently the causes of great confusion. This is the case, for example, with the conception of quality. A quality, as such, is never an object of observation. We can see that a thing is blue or green, but the quality of being blue and the quality of being green are not things which we see; they are products of logical reflections. The truth is, that common-sense, or thought as it first emerges above the level of the narrowly practical, is deeply imbued with that bad logical quality to which the epithet *metaphysical* is commonly applied; and nothing can clear it up but a severe course of logic.

3. DOUBT AND BELIEF

370. We generally know when we wish to ask a question and when we wish to pronounce a judgment, for there is a dissimilarity between the sensation of doubting and that of believing.

371. But this is not all which distinguishes doubt from belief. There is a practical difference. Our beliefs guide our desires and shape our actions. The Assassins, or followers of the Old Man of the Mountain, used to rush into death at his least command, because they believed that obedience to him would insure everlasting felicity. Had they doubted this, they would not have acted as they did. So it is with every belief, according to its degree. The feeling of believing is a more or less sure indication of there being established in our nature some habit which will determine our actions. Doubt never has such an effect.

372. Nor must we overlook a third point of difference. Doubt is an uneasy and dissatisfied state from which we struggle to free ourselves and pass into the state of belief; while the latter is a calm and satisfactory state which we do not wish to avoid, or to change to a belief in anything else. On the contrary, we cling tenaciously, not merely to believing, but to believing just what we do believe.

373. Thus, both doubt and belief have positive effects upon us, though very different ones. Belief does not make us act at once, but puts us into such a condition that we shall behave in some certain way, when the occasion arises. Doubt has not the least such active effect, but stimulates us to inquiry until it is destroyed. This reminds us of the irritation of a nerve and the reflex action produced thereby; while for the analogue of belief, in the nervous system, we must look to what are called nervous associations—for example, to that habit of the nerves in consequence of which the smell of a peach will make the mouth water.

THE END OF INQUIRY

374. The irritation of doubt causes a struggle to attain a state of belief. I shall term this struggle *Inquiry,* though it must be admitted that this is sometimes not a very apt designation.

375. The irritation of doubt is the only immediate motive for the struggle to attain belief. It is certainly best for us that our beliefs should be such as may truly guide our actions so as to satisfy our desires; and this reflection will make us reject every belief which does not seem to have been so formed as to insure this result. But it will only do so by creating a doubt in the place of that belief. With the doubt, therefore, the struggle begins, and with the cessation of doubt it ends. Hence, the sole object of inquiry is the settlement of opinion. We may fancy that this is not enough for us, and that we seek, not merely an opinion, but a true opinion. But put this fancy to the test, and it proves groundless; for as soon as a firm belief is reached we are entirely satisfied, whether the belief be true or false. And it is clear that nothing out of the sphere of our knowledge can be our object, for nothing which does not affect the mind can be the motive for mental effort. The most that can be maintained is, that we seek for a belief that we shall *think* to be true. But we think each one of our beliefs to be true, and, indeed, it is mere tautology to say so.

That the settlement of opinion is the sole end of inquiry is a very important proposition. It sweeps away, at once, various vague and erroneous conceptions of proof. A few of these may be noticed here.

376.

1. Some philosophers have imagined that to start an inquiry it was only necessary to utter a question whether orally or by setting it down on paper, and have even recommended us to begin our studies with questioning everything! But the mere putting of a proposition into the interrogative form does not stimulate the mind to any struggle after belief. There must be a real and living doubt, and without this all discussion is idle.
2. It is a very common idea that a demonstration must rest on some ultimate and absolutely indubitable propositions. These, according to one school, are first principles of a general nature; according to another, are first sensations. But, in point of fact, an inquiry, to have that completely satisfactory result called demonstration, has only to start with propositions perfectly free from all actual doubt. If the premisses are not in fact doubted at all, they cannot be more satisfactory than they are.
3. Some people seem to love to argue a point after all the world is fully convinced of it. But no further advance can be made. When doubt ceases, mental action on the subject comes to an end; and, if it did go on, it would be without a purpose.

5. METHODS OF FIXING BELIEF

377. If the settlement of opinion is the sole object of inquiry, and if belief is of the nature of a habit, why should we not attain the desired end, by taking as answer to a question any we may fancy, and constantly reiterating it to ourselves, dwelling on all which may conduce to that belief, and learning to turn with contempt and hatred from anything that might disturb it? This simple and direct method is really pursued by many men. I remember once being entreated not to read a certain newspaper lest it might change my opinion upon free-trade. "Lest I might be entrapped by its fallacies and misstatements," was the form of expression. "You are not," my friend said, "a special student of political economy. You might, therefore, easily be deceived by fallacious arguments upon the subject. You might, then, if you read this paper, be led to believe in protection. But you admit that free-trade is the true doctrine; and you do not wish to believe what is not true." I have often known this system to be deliberately adopted. Still oftener, the instinctive dislike of an undecided state of mind, exaggerated into a vague dread of doubt, makes men cling spasmodically to the views they already take. The man feels that, if he only holds to his belief without wavering, it will be entirely satisfactory. Nor can it be denied that a steady and immovable faith yields great peace of mind. It may, indeed, give rise to inconveniences, as if a man should resolutely continue to believe that fire would not burn him, or that he would be eternally damned if he received his *ingesta* otherwise than through a stomach-pump. But then the man who adopts this method will not allow that its inconveniences are greater than its advantages. He will say, "I hold steadfastly to the truth, and the truth is always wholesome." And in many cases it may very well be that the pleasure he derives from his calm faith overbalances any inconveniences resulting from its deceptive character. Thus, if it be true that death is annihilation, then the man who believes that he will certainly go straight to heaven when he dies, provided he have fulfilled certain simple observances in this life, has a cheap pleasure which will not be followed by the least disappointment. A similar consideration seems to have weight with many persons in religious topics, for we frequently hear it said, "Oh, I could not believe so-and-so, because I should be wretched if I did." When an ostrich buries its head in the sand as danger approaches, it very likely takes the happiest course. It hides the danger, and then calmly says there is no danger, and, if it feels perfectly sure there is none, why should it raise its head to see? A man may go through life, systematically keeping out of view all that might cause a change in his opinions, and if he only succeeds—basing his method, as he does, on two fundamental psychological laws—I do not see what can be said against his doing so. It would be an egotistical impertinence to object that his procedure is irrational, for that only amounts to saying that his method of settling belief is not ours. He does not propose to himself to be rational, and, indeed, will often talk with scorn of man's weak and illusive reason. So let him think as he pleases.

378. But this method of fixing belief, which may be called the method of tenacity, "will be unable to hold its ground in practice." The social impulse is against it. The man who adopts it will find that other men think differently from him, and it will be apt to occur to him, in some saner moment, that their opinions are quite as good as his own, and this will shake his confidence in his belief. This conception, that another man's thought or sentiment may be equivalent to one's own, is a distinctly new step, and a highly important one. It arises from an impulse too strong in man to be suppressed, without danger of destroying the human species. Unless we make ourselves hermits, we shall necessarily influence each other's opinions; so that the problem becomes how to fix belief, not in the individual merely, but in the community.

379. Let the will of the state act, then, instead of that of the individual. Let an institution be created which shall have for its object to keep correct doctrines before the attention of the people, to reiterate them perpetually, and to teach them to the young; having at the same time power to prevent contrary doctrines from being taught, advocated, or expressed. Let all possible causes of a change of mind be removed from men's apprehensions. Let them be kept ignorant, lest they should learn of some reason to think otherwise than they do. Let their passions be enlisted, so that they may regard private and unusual opinions with hatred and horror. Then, let all men who reject the established belief be terrified into silence. Let the people turn out and tar-and-feather such men, or let inquisitions be made into the manner of thinking of suspected persons, and when they are found guilty of forbidden beliefs, let them be subjected to some signal punishment. When complete agreement could not otherwise be reached, a general massacre of all who have not thought in a certain way has proved a very effective means of settling opinion in a country. If the power to do this be wanting, let a list of opinions be drawn up, to which no man of the least independence of thought can assent, and let the faithful be required to accept all these propositions, in order to segregate them as radically as possible from the influence of the rest of the world.

This method has, from the earliest times, been one of the chief means of upholding correct theological and political doctrines, and of preserving their universal or catholic character. In Rome, especially, it has been practiced from the days of Numa Pompilius to those of Pius Nonus. This is the most perfect example in history; but wherever there is a priesthood—and no religion has been without one—this method has been more or less made use of. Wherever there is an aristocracy, or a guild, or any association of a class of men whose interests depend, or are supposed to depend, on certain propositions, there will be inevitably found some traces of this natural product of social feeling. Cruelties always accompany this system; and when it is consistently carried out, they become atrocities of the most horrible kind in the eyes of any rational man. Nor should this occasion surprise, for the officer of a society does not feel justified in surrendering the interests of that society for the sake of mercy, as he might his own private interests. It is natural, therefore, that sympathy and fellowship should thus produce a most ruthless power.

380. In judging this method of fixing belief, which may be called the method of authority, we must, in the first place, allow its immeasurable mental and moral superiority to the method of tenacity. Its success is proportionately greater; and, in fact, it has over and over again worked the most majestic results. The mere structures of stone which it has caused to be put together—in Siam, for example, in Egypt, and in Europe—have many of them a sublimity hardly more than rivaled by the greatest works of Nature. And, except the geological epochs, there are no periods of time so vast as those which are measured by some of these organized faiths. If we scrutinize the matter closely, we shall find that there has not been one of their creeds which has remained always the same; yet the change is so slow as to be imperceptible during one person's life, so that individual belief remains sensibly fixed. For the mass of mankind, then, there is perhaps no better method than this. If it is their highest impulse to be intellectual slaves, then slaves they ought to remain.

381. But no institution can undertake to regulate opinions upon every subject. Only the most important ones can be attended to, and on the rest men's minds must be left to the action of natural causes. This imperfection will be no source of weakness so long as men are in such a state of culture that one opinion does not influence another—that is, so long as they cannot put two and two together. But in the most priest-ridden states some individuals will be found who are raised above that condition. These men possess a wider sort of social feeling; they see that men in other countries and in other ages have held to very different doctrines from those which they themselves have been brought up to believe; and they cannot help seeing that it is the mere accident of their having been taught as they have, and of their having been surrounded with the manners and associations they have, that has caused them to believe as they do and not far differently. Nor can their candour resist the reflection that there is no reason to rate their own views at a higher value than those of other nations and other centuries; thus giving rise to doubts in their minds.

382. They will further perceive that such doubts as these must exist in their minds with reference to every belief which seems to be determined by the caprice either of themselves or of those who originated the popular opinions. The willful adherence to a belief, and the arbitrary forcing of it upon others, must, therefore, both be given up. A different new method of settling opinions must be adopted, that shall not only produce an impulse to believe, but shall also decide what proposition it is which is to be believed. Let the action of natural preferences be unimpeded, then, and under their influence let men, conversing together and regarding matters in different lights, gradually develop beliefs in harmony with natural causes. This method resembles that by which conceptions of art have been brought to maturity. The most perfect example of it is to be found in the history of metaphysical philosophy. Systems of this sort have not usually rested upon any observed facts, at least not in any great degree. They have been chiefly adopted because their fundamental propositions seemed "agreeable to reason." This is an apt expression; it does not mean that which agrees with experience, but that which we find ourselves inclined to believe. Plato, for example, finds it agreeable to reason that the distances of the celestial spheres from one another should be proportional to the different lengths of strings which produce harmonious chords. Many philosophers have been led to their main conclusions by considerations like this; but this is the lowest and least developed form which the method takes, for it is clear that another man might find Kepler's theory, that the celestial spheres are proportional to the inscribed and circumscribed spheres of the different regular solids, more agreeable to *his* reason. But the shock of opinions will soon lead men to rest on preferences of a far more universal nature. Take, for example, the doctrine that man only acts selfishly—that is, from the consideration that acting in one way will afford him more pleasure than acting in another. This rests on no fact in the world, but it has had a wide acceptance as being the only reasonable theory.

383. This method is far more intellectual and respectable from the point of view of reason than either of the others which we have noticed. Indeed, as long as no better method can be applied, it ought to be followed, since it is then the expression of instinct which must be the ultimate cause of belief in all cases. But its failure has been the most manifest. It makes of inquiry something similar to the development of taste; but taste, unfortunately, is always more or less a matter of fashion, and accordingly metaphysicians have never come to any fixed agreement, but the pendulum has swung backward and forward between a more material and a more spiritual philosophy, from the earliest times to the latest. And so from this, which has been called the *a priori* method, we are driven, in Lord Bacon's phrase, to a true induction. We have examined into this *a priori* method as something which promised to deliver our opinions from their accidental and capricious element. But development, while it's a process which eliminates the effect of some casual circumstances, only magnifies that of others. This method, therefore, does not differ in a very essential way from that of authority. The government may not have lifted its finger to influence my convictions; I may have been left outwardly quite free to choose, we will say, between monogamy and polygamy, and, appealing to my conscience only, I may have concluded that the latter practice is in itself licentious. But when I come to see that the chief obstacle to the spread of Christianity among a people of as high culture as the Hindoos has been a conviction of the immorality of our way of treating women, I cannot help seeing that, though governments do not interfere, sentiments in their development will be very greatly determined by accidental causes. Now, there are some people, among whom I must suppose that my reader is to be found, who, when they see that any belief of theirs is determined by any circumstance extraneous to the facts, will from that moment not merely admit in words that that belief is doubtful, but will experience a real doubt of it, so that it ceases in some degree at least to be a belief.

384. To satisfy our doubts, therefore, it is necessary that a method should be found by which our beliefs may be determined by nothing human, but by some external permanency—by something upon which our thinking has no effect. Some mystics imagine that they have such a method in a private inspiration from on high. But that is only a form of the method of tenacity, in which the conception of truth as something public is not yet developed. Our external permanency would not be external, in our sense, if it was restricted in its influence to one individual. It must be something which affects, or might affect, every man. And, though these affections are necessarily as various as are individual conditions, yet the method must be such that the ultimate conclusion of every man shall be the same. Such is the method of science. Its fundamental hypothesis, restated in more familiar language, is this: There are Real things, whose characters are entirely independent of our opinions about them; those Reals affect our senses according to regular laws, and, though our sensations are as different as are our relations to the objects, yet, by taking advantage of the laws of perception, we can ascertain by reasoning how things really and truly are; and any man, if he have sufficient experience and he reason enough about it, will be led to the one True conclusion. The new conception here involved is that of Reality. It may be asked how I know that there are any Reals. If this hypothesis is the sole support of my method of inquiry, my method of inquiry must not be used to support my hypothesis. The reply is this: 1. If investigation cannot be regarded as proving that there are Real things, it at least does not lead to a contrary conclusion; but the method and the conception on which it is based remain ever in harmony. No doubts of the method, therefore, necessarily arise from its practice, as is the case with all the others. 2. The feeling which gives rise to any method of fixing belief is a dissatisfaction at two repugnant propositions. But here already is a vague concession that there is some *one* thing which a proposition should represent. Nobody, therefore, can really doubt that there are Reals, for, if he did, doubt would not be a source of dissatisfaction. The hypothesis, therefore, is one which every mind admits. So that the social impulse does not cause men to doubt it. 3. Everybody uses the scientific method about a great many things, and only ceases to use it when he does not know how to apply it. 4. Experience of the method has not led us to doubt it, but, on the contrary, scientific investigation has had the most wonderful triumphs in the way of settling opinion. These afford the explanation of my not doubting the method or the hypothesis which it supposes; and not having any doubt, nor believing that anybody else whom I could influence has, it would be the merest babble for me to say more about it. If there be anybody with a living doubt upon the subject, let him consider it.

385. To describe the method of scientific investigation is the object of this series of papers. At present I have only room to notice some points of contrast between it and other methods of fixing belief.

This is the only one of the four methods which presents any distinction of a right and a wrong way. If I adopt the method of tenacity, and shut myself out from all influences, whatever I think necessary to doing this, is necessary according to that method. So with the method of authority: the state may try to put down heresy by means which, from a scientific point of view, seem very ill—calculated to accomplish its purposes; but the only test *on that method* is what the state thinks; so that it cannot pursue the method wrongly. So with the *a priori* method. The very essence of it is to think as one is inclined to think. All metaphysicians will be sure to do that, however they may be inclined to judge each other to be perversely wrong. The Hegelian system recognizes every natural tendency of thought as logical, although it be certain to be abolished by counter-tendencies. Hegel thinks there is a regular system in the succession of these tendencies, in consequence of which, after drifting one way and the other for a long time, opinion will at last go right. And it is true that metaphysicians do get the right ideas at last; Hegel's system of Nature represents tolerably the science of his day; and one may be sure that whatever scientific investigation shall have put out of doubt will presently receive *a priori* demonstration on the part of the metaphysicians. But with the scientific method the case is different. I may start with known and observed facts to proceed to the unknown; and yet the rules which I follow in doing so may not be such as investigation would approve. The test of whether I am truly following the method is not an immediate appeal to my feelings and purposes, but, on the contrary, itself involves the application of the method. Hence it is that bad reasoning as well as good reasoning is possible; and this fact is the foundation of the practical side of logic.

386. It is not to be supposed that the first three methods of settling opinion present no advantage whatever over the scientific method. On the contrary, each has some peculiar convenience of its own. The *a priori* method is distinguished for its comfortable conclusions. It is the nature of the process to adopt whatever belief we are inclined to, and there are certain flatteries to the vanity of man which we all believe by nature, until we are awakened from our pleasing dream by rough facts. The method of authority will always govern the mass of mankind; and those who wield the various forms of organized force in the state will never be convinced that dangerous reasoning ought not to be suppressed in some way. If liberty of speech is to be untrammeled from the grosser forms of constraint, then uniformity of opinion will be secured by a moral terrorism to which the respectability of society will give its thorough approval. Following the method of authority is the path of peace. Certain non-conformities are permitted; certain others (considered unsafe) are forbidden. These are different in different countries and in different ages; but, wherever you are, let it be known that you seriously hold a tabooed belief, and you may be perfectly sure of being treated with a cruelty less brutal but more refined than hunting you like a wolf. Thus, the greatest intellectual benefactors of mankind have never dared, and dare not now, to utter the whole of their thought; and thus a shade of *prima facie* doubt is cast upon every proposition which is considered essential to the security of society. Singularly enough, the persecution does not all come from without; but a man torments himself and is oftentimes most distressed at finding himself believing propositions which he has been brought up to regard with aversion. The peaceful and sympathetic man will, therefore, find it hard to resist the temptation to submit his opinions to authority. But most of all I admire the method of tenacity for its strength, simplicity, and directness. Men who pursue it are distinguished for their decision of character, which becomes very easy with such a mental rule. They do not waste time in trying to make up their minds what they want, but, fastening like lightning upon whatever alternative comes first, they hold to it to the end, whatever happens, without an instant's irresolution. This is one of the splendid qualities which generally accompany brilliant, unlasting success. It is impossible not to envy the man who can dismiss reason, although we know how it must turn out at last

387. Such are the advantages which the other methods of settling opinion have over scientific investigation. A man should consider well of them; and then he should consider that, after all, he wishes his opinions to coincide with the fact, and that there is no reason why the results of those three first methods should do so. To bring about this effect is the prerogative of the method of science. Upon such considerations he has to make his choice—a choice which is far more than the adoption of any intellectual opinion, which is one of the ruling decisions of his life, to which, when once made, he is bound to adhere. The force of habit will sometimes cause a man to hold on to old beliefs, after he is in a condition to see that they have no sound basis. But reflection upon the state of the case will overcome these habits, and he ought to allow reflection its full weight. People sometimes shrink from doing this, having an idea that beliefs are wholesome which they cannot help feeling rest on nothing. But let such persons suppose an analogous though different case from their own. Let them ask themselves what they would say to a reformed Mussulman who should hesitate to give up his old notions in regard to the relations of the sexes; or to a reformed Catholic who should still shrink from reading the Bible. Would they not say that these persons ought to consider the matter fully, and clearly understand the new doctrine, and then ought to embrace it, in its entirety? But, above all, let it be considered that what is more wholesome than any particular belief is integrity of belief, and that to avoid looking into the support of any belief from a fear that it may turn out rotten is quite as immoral as it is disadvantageous. The person who confesses that there is such a thing as truth, which is distinguished from falsehood simply by this, that if acted on it should, on full consideration, carry us to the point we aim at and not astray, and then, though convinced of this, dares not know the truth and seeks to avoid it, is in a sorry state of mind indeed.

Yes, the other methods do have their merits: a clear logical conscience does cost something—just as any virtue, just as all that we cherish, costs us dear. But we should not desire it to be otherwise. The genius of a man's logical method should be loved and reverenced as his bride, whom he has chosen from all the world. He need not contemn the others; on the contrary, he may honor them deeply, and in doing so he only honors her the more. But she is the one that he has chosen, and he knows that he was right in making that choice. And having made it, he will work and fight for her, and will not complain that there are blows to take, hoping that there may be as many and as hard to give, and will strive to be the worthy knight and champion of her from the blaze of whose splendors he draws his inspiration and his courage.

Chapter 33

WILLIAM JAMES

William James (1842–1910), was an American philosopher and psychologist, born in New York City and educated at Harvard, the brother of Henry James, the novelist. James struggled through much of his life with ill heath. He studied science, medicine, and philosophy in France and Germany, earning a medical degree from Harvard in 1869, where he taught as a psychology instructor. In 1890 he published *Principles of Psychology,* a compendious textbook in experimental psychology. But his interests were more philosophical than scientific, so eventually he moved into the philosophy department at Harvard, where he taught for many years. Throughout his early years he was assailed by doubts over freedom of the will and the existence of God, and developed the philosophy of pragmatism, in part as a response to these difficulties. Pragmatism originated with James's friend Charles Peirce (Chapter 32), but underwent crucial changes and popularization in the hands of James. He wrote: "The whole function of philosophy ought to be to find out what definite difference it will make to you and me, at definite instants of our life, if this world-formula or that world-formula be the true one."

His principal works are *The Will to Believe* (1897), reprinted below; *The Varieties of Religious Experience* (1902); *Pragmatism, A New Name for Some Old Ways of Thinking* (1907), from which a selection is taken; and *Essays in Radical Empiricism* (1912).

In our first reading, *The Will to Believe,* James argues that life would be greatly impoverished if we confined our beliefs to such a Scrooge-like epistemology, as W. K. Clifford proposes: "It is wrong always, everywhere, and for anyone, to believe anything upon insufficient evidence." In everyday life, where the evidence for important propositions is often unclear, we must live by faith or cease to act at all. While we may not make leaps of faith just anywhere, sometimes practical considerations force us to make a decision regarding propositions which do not have their truth value written on their faces. "Belief" is defined as a live, momentous, optional hypothesis, on which we cannot avoid a decision, for not to choose is, in effect, to choose against the hypothesis. James claims that religion may be such an optional hypothesis for many people, and where it is, the individual has the right to believe the better story rather than the worse. To do so, one must will to believe what the evidence alone is inadequate to support.

The second reading is from *Pragmatism.* After a brief introduction to Pragmatism by way of a fascinating example of resolving a dispute about the correct characterization of a squirrel's behavior, James sets forth his view of truth. He holds that truth is dynamic rather that static and is to be defined in terms of beliefs that are useful or satisfying. Unlike the "intellectualists" (James's characterization of the traditional static approaches to the question of truth, viz., the correspondence theorists) truth is in process, still becoming, and changing. Yesterday's truth is today's falsehood, and today's truth is tomorrow's half-truth. What really matters is what you can *do* with an idea, what difference it makes to your life, its cash-value. His famous definition of truth is this: " 'The true' . . . is only the expedient in the way of our thinking, just as 'the right' is only the expedient in the way of our behaving" (by 'expedient' James means prudent or suitable to achieve success). Philosophers have debated the significance of this statement, especially what James meant by the phrase that truth is expedient "in the long run and on the whole." Bertrand Russell will present a radically different view (see chapter 34).

FOR FURTHER READING

Ayer, A. J. *Origins of Pragmatism: Studies in the Philosophy of Charles Sanders Peirce and William James.* (Macmillan, 1968).
James, William. *Pragmatism.* (Longmans, Green & Co., 1907).
Kuklick, Bruce. *The Rise of American Philosophy.* (Yale University Press, 1977).
McDermott, John, ed. *The Writings of William James.* (Random House, 1967).
Murphy, John. *Pragmatism: From Peirce to Davidson.* (Westview Press, 1990).
Myers, G. E. *William James: His Life and Thought.* (Yale University Press, 1986).
Perry, R. B. *The Thought and Character of William James,* 2 vols. (Harper, 1935).
Quine, W. V. and Joseph Ullian. *The Web of Belief,* 2nd ed. (Random House, 1978).
Scheffler, Israel. *Four Pragmatists.* (Humanities Press, 1974).
Smith, John. *The Spirit of American Philosophy.* (Oxford University Press, 1963).
Wild, John. *The Radical Empiricism of William James.* (Greenwood Press, 1980).

The Will to Believe

I

Let us give the name of hypothesis to anything that may be proposed to our belief; and just as the electricians speak of live and dead wires, let us speak of any hypothesis as either *live* or *dead.* A live hypothesis is one which appeals as a real possibility to him to whom it is proposed. If I ask you to believe in the Mahdi, the notion makes no electric connection with your nature—it refuses to scintillate with any credibility at all. As an hypothesis it is completely dead. To an Arab, however (even if he be not one of the Madhi's followers), the hypothesis is among the mind's possibilities: It is alive. This shows that deadness and liveness in an hypothesis are not intrinsic properties, but relations to the individual thinker. They are measured by his willingness to act. The maximum of liveness in an hypothesis means willingness to act irrevocably. Practically, that means belief; but there is some believing tendency wherever there is willingness to act at all.

Next, let us call the decision between two hypotheses an *option.* Options may be of several kinds. They may be first, *living* or *dead;* secondly, *forced* or *avoidable;* thirdly, *momentous* or *trivial;* and for our purposes we may call an option a *genuine* option when it is of the forced, living, and momentous kind.

1. A living option is one in which both hypotheses are live ones. If I say to you: "Be a theosophist or be a Mohammedan," it is probably a dead option, because for you neither hypothesis is likely to be alive. But if I say: "Be an agnostic or be a Christian," it is otherwise: trained as you are, each hypothesis makes some appeal, however small, to your belief.

2. Next, if I say to you: "Choose between going out with your umbrella or without it," I do not offer you a genuine option, for it is not forced. You can easily avoid it by not going out at all. Similarly, if I say, "Either love me or hate me," "Either call my theory true or call it false," your option is avoidable. You may remain indifferent to me, neither loving nor hating, and you may decline to offer any judgment as to my theory. But if I say, "Either accept this truth or go without it," I put on you a forced option, for there is no standing place outside of the alternative. Every dilemma based on a complete logical disjunction, with no possibility of not choosing, is an option of this forced kind.

3. Finally, if I were Dr. Nansen and proposed to you to join my North Pole expedition, your option would be momentous; for this would probably be your similar opportunity, and your choice now would either exclude you from the North Pole sort of immortality altogether or put at least the chance of it into your hands. He who refuses to embrace a unique opportunity loses the prize as surely as if he tried and failed. *Per contra,* the option is trivial when the opportunity is not unique, when the stake is insignificant, or when the decision is reversible if it later prove unwise. Such trivial options abound in the scientific life. A chemist finds an hypothesis live enough to spend a year in its verification: he believes in it to that extent. But if his experiments prove inconclusive either way, he is quit for his loss of time, no vital harm being done.

It will facilitate our discussion if we keep all these distinctions well in mind.

II

The next matter to consider is the actual psychology of human opinion. When we look at certain facts, it seems as if our passional and volitional nature lay at the root of all our convictions. When we look at others, it seems as if they could do nothing when the intellect had once said its say. Let us take the latter facts up first.

Does it not seem preposterous on the very face of it to talk of our opinions being modifiable at will? Can our will either help or hinder our intellect in its perceptions of truth? Can we, by just willing it, believe that Abraham Lincoln's existence is a myth, and that the portraits of him in *McClure's Magazine* are all of some one else? Can we, by any effort of our will, or by any strength of wish that it were true, believe ourselves well and about when we are roaring with rheumatism in bed, or feel certain that the sum of the two one-dollar bills in our pocket must be a hundred dollars? We can *say* any of these things, but we are absolutely impotent to believe them; and of just such things is the whole fabric of the truths that we do believe in made up—matters of fact, immediate or remote, as Hume said, and relations between ideas, which are either there or not there for us if we see them so, and which if not there cannot be put there by any action of our own.

In Pascal's *Thoughts* there is a celebrated passage known in literature as Pascal's wager. In it he tries to force us into Christianity by reasoning as if our concern with truth resembled our concern with the stakes in a game of chance. Translated freely his words are these: You must either believe or not believe that God is—which will you do? Your human reason cannot say. A game is going on between you and the nature of things which at the day of judgment will bring out either heads or tails. Weigh what your gains and your losses would be if you should stake all you have on heads, or God's existence: if you win in such case, you gain eternal beatitude; if you lose, you lose nothing at all. If there were an infinity of chances, and only one for God in this wager, still you ought to stake your all on God; for though you surely risk a finite loss by this procedure, any finite loss is reasonable, even a certain one is reasonable, if there is but the possibility of infinite gain. Go, then, and take holy water, and have masses said; belief will come and stupefy your scruples. . . . Why should you not? At bottom, what have you to lose?

You probably feel that when religious faith expresses itself thus, in the language of the gamingtable, it is put to its last trumps. Surely Pascal's own personal belief in masses and holy water had far other springs; and this celebrated page of his is but an argument for others, a last desperate snatch at a weapon against the hardness of the unbelieving heart. We feel that a faith in masses and holy water adopted wilfully after such a mechanical calculation would lack the inner soul of faith's reality; and if we were ourselves in the place of the Deity, we should probably take particular pleasure in cutting off believers of this pattern from their infinite reward. It is evident that unless there be some preexisting tendency to believe in masses and holy water, the option offered to the will by Pascal is not a living option. Certainly no Turk ever took to masses and holy water on its account; and even to us Protestants these means of salvation seem such foregone impossibilities that Pascal's logic, invoked for them specifically, leaves us unmoved. As well might the Mahdi write to us, saying, "I am the Expected One whom God has created in his effulgence. You shall be infinitely happy if you confess me; otherwise you shall be cut off from the light of the sun. Weigh, then, your infinite gain if I am genuine against your finite sacrifice if I am not!" His logic would be that of Pascal; but he would vainly use it on us, for the hypothesis he offers us is dead. No tendency to act on it exists in us to any degree.

The talk of believing by our volition seems, then, from one point of view, simply silly. From another point of view it is worse than silly, it is vile. When one turns to the magnificent edifice of the physical sciences, and sees how it was reared; what thousands of disinterested moral lives of men lie buried in its mere foundations; what patience and postponement, what choking down of preference, what submission to the icy laws of outer fact are wrought into its very stones and mortar; how absolutely impersonal it stands in its vast augustness—then how besotted and contemptible seems every little sentimentalist who comes blowing his voluntary smoke-wreaths, and pretending to decide things from out of his private dream! Can we wonder if those bred in the rugged and manly school of science should feel like spewing such subjectivism out of their mouths? The whole system of loyalties which grow up in the schools of science go dead against its toleration; so that it is only natural that those who have caught the scientific fever should pass over to the opposite extreme, and write sometimes as if the incorruptibly truthful intellect ought positively to prefer bitterness and unacceptableness to the heart in its cup.

> It fortifies my soul to know
> That though I perish, Truth is so

sings Clough, while Huxley exclaims: "My only consolation lies in the reflection that, however bad our posterity may become, so far as they hold by the plain rule of not pretending to believe what they have no reason to believe, because it may be to their advantage so to pretend [the word 'pretend' is surely here redundant], they will not have reached the lowest depth of immorality." And that delicious *enfant terrible* Clifford writes: "Belief is desecrated when given to unproved and unquestioned statements for the solace and private pleasure of the believer. . . . Whoso would deserve well of his fellows in this matter will guard the purity of his belief with a very fanaticism of jealous care, lest at any time it should rest on an unworthy object, and catch a stain which can never be wiped away. . . . If [a] belief has been accepted on insufficient evidence [even though the belief be true, as Clifford on the same page explains] the pleasure is a stolen one. . . . It is sinful because it is stolen in defiance of our duty to mankind. That duty is to guard ourselves from such beliefs as from a pestilence which may shortly master our own body and then spread to the rest of the town. . . . It is wrong always, everywhere, and for every one, to believe anything upon insufficient evidence."

III

All this strikes one as healthy, even when expressed, as by Clifford, with somewhat too much of robustious pathos in the voice. Free will and simple wishing do seem, in the matter of our credences, to be only fifth wheels to the coach. Yet if any one should thereupon assume that intellectual insight is what remains after wish and will and sentimental preference have taken wing, or that pure reason is what then settles our opinions, he would fly quite as directly in the teeth of the facts.

It is only our already dead hypotheses that our willing nature is unable to bring to life again. But what has made them dead for us is for the most part a previous action of our willing nature of an antagonistic kind. When I say "willing nature," I do not mean only such deliberate volitions as may have set up habits of belief that we cannot now escape from—I mean all such factors of belief as fear and hope, prejudice and passion, imitation and partisanship, the circumpressure of our caste and set. As a matter of fact we find ourselves believing, we hardly know how or why. Mr. Balfour gives the name of "authority" to all those influences, born of the intellectual climate, that make hypotheses possible or impossible for us, alive or dead. Here in this room, we all of us believe in molecules and the conservation of energy, in democracy and necessary progress, in Protestant Christianity and the duty of fighting for "the doctrine of the immortal Monroe," all for no reasons worthy of the name. We see into these matters with no more inner clearness, and probably with much less, than any disbeliever in them might possess. His unconventionality would probably have some grounds to show for its conclusions; but for us, not insight, but the *prestige* of the opinions, is what makes the spark shoot from them and light up our sleeping magazines of faith. Our reason is quite satisfied, in nine hundred and ninety-nine cases out of every thousand of us, if it can find a few arguments that will do to recite in case our credulity is criticized by some one else. Our faith is faith in some one else's faith, and in the greatest matters this is the most the case. . . .

Evidently, then, our non-intellectual nature does influence our convictions. There are passional tendencies and volitions which run before and others which come after belief, and it is only the latter that are too late for the fair; and they are not too late when the previous passional work has been already in their own direction. Pascal's argument, instead of being powerless, then seems a regular clincher, and is the last stroke needed to make our faith in masses and holy water complete. The state of things is evidently far from simple; and pure insight and logic, whatever they might do ideally, are not the only things that really do produce our creeds.

IV

Our next duty, having recognized this mixedup state of affairs, is to ask whether it be simply reprehensible and pathological, or whether, on the contrary, we must treat it as a normal element in making up our minds. The thesis I defend is, briefly stated, this: *Our passional nature not only lawfully may, but must, decide an option between propositions, whenever it is a genuine option that cannot by its nature be decided on intellectual grounds; for to say, under such circumstances, "Do not decide, but leave the question open," is itself a passional decision—just like deciding yes or no—and is attended with the same risk of losing the truth. . . .*

VII

One more point, small but important, and our preliminaries are done. There are two ways of looking at our duty in the matter of opinion—ways entirely different, and yet ways about whose difference the theory of knowledge seems hitherto to have shown very little concern. *We must know the truth; and we must avoid error*—these are our first and great commandments as would-be knowers; but they are not two ways of stating an identical commandment, they are two separable laws. Although it may indeed happen that when we believe the truth A, we escape as an incidental consequence from believing the falsehood B, it hardly ever happens that by merely disbelieving B we necessarily believe A. We may in escaping B fall into believing other falsehoods, C or D, just as bad as B; or we may escape B by not believing anything at all, not even A.

Believe truth! Shun error!—these, we see, are two materially different laws; and by choosing between them we may end by coloring differently our whole intellectual life. We may regard the chase for truth as paramount, and the avoidance of error as secondary; or we may, on the other hand, treat the avoidance of error as more imperative, and let truth take its chance. Clifford, in the instructive passage which I have quoted, exhorts us to the latter course. Believe nothing, he tells us, keep your mind in suspense forever, rather than by closing it on insufficient evidence incur the awful risk of believing lies. You, on the other hand, may think that the risk of being in error is a very small matter when compared with the blessings of real knowledge, and be ready to be duped many times in your investigation rather than postpone indefinitely the chance of guessing true. I myself find it impossible to go with Clifford. We must remember that these feelings of our duty about either truth or error are in any case only expressions of our passional life. Biologically considered, our minds are as ready to grind out falsehood as veracity, and he who says, "Better go without belief forever than believe a lie!" merely shows his own preponderant private horror of becoming a dupe. He may be critical of many of his desires and fears, but this fear he slavishly obeys. He cannot imagine any one questioning its binding force. For my own part, I have also a horror of being duped; but I can believe that worse things than being duped may happen to a man in this world: so Clifford's exhortation has to my ears a thoroughly fantastic sound. It is like a general informing his soldiers that it is better to keep out of battle forever than to risk a single wound. Not so are victories either over enemies or over nature gained. Our errors are surely not such awfully solemn things. In a world where we are so certain to incur them in spite of all our caution, a certain lightness of heart seems healthier than this excessive nervousness on their behalf. At any rate, it seems the fittest thing for the empiricist philosopher.

VIII

And now, after all this introduction, let us go straight at our question. I have said, and now repeat it, that not only as a matter of fact do we find our passional nature influencing us in our opinions, but that there are some options between opinions in which this influence must be regarded both as an inevitable and as a lawful determinant of our choice.

I fear here that some of you my hearers will begin to scent danger, and lend an inhospitable ear. Two first steps of passion you have indeed had to admit as necessary—we must think so as to avoid dupery, and we must think so as to gain truth; but the surest path to those ideal consummations, you will probably consider, is from now onwards to take no further passional step.

Well, of course, I agree as far as the facts will allow. Wherever the option between losing truth and gaining it is not momentous, we can throw the chance of *gaining truth* away, and at any rate save ourselves from any chance of *believing falsehood,* by not making up our minds at all till objective evidence has come. In scientific questions, this is almost always the case; and even in human affairs in general, the need of acting is seldom so urgent that a false belief to act on is better than no belief at all. Law courts, indeed, have to decide on the best evidence attainable for the moment, because a judge's duty is to make law as well as to ascertain it, and (as a learned judge once said to me) few cases are worth spending much time over: the great thing is to have them decided on *any* acceptable principle, and got out of the way. But in our dealings with objective nature we obviously are recorders, not makers, of the truth; and decisions for the mere sake of deciding promptly and getting on to the next business would be wholly out of place. Throughout the breadth of physical nature facts are what they are quite independently of us, and seldom is there any such hurry about them that the risks of being duped by believing a premature theory need be faced. The questions here are always trivial options, the hypotheses are hardly living (at any rate not living for us spectators), the choice between believing truth or falsehood is seldom forced. The attitude of sceptical balance is therefore the absolutely wise one if we would escape mistakes. What difference, indeed, does it make to most of us whether we have or have not a theory of the Röntgen rays, whether we believe or not in mind-stuff, or have a conviction about the causality of conscious states? It makes no difference. Such options are not forced on us. On every account it is better not to make them, but still keep weighing reasons *pro et contra* with an indifferent hand.

I speak, of course, here of the purely judging mind. For purposes of discovery such indifference is to be less highly recommended, and science would be far less advanced than she is if the passionate desires of individuals to get their own faiths confirmed had been kept out of the game. See for example the sagacity which Spencer and Weismann now display. On the other hand, if you want an absolute duffer in an investigation, you must, after all, take the man who has no interest whatever in its results: he is the warranted incapable, the positive fool. The most useful investigator, because the most sensitive observer, is always he whose eager interest in one side of the question is balanced by an equally keen nervousness lest he become deceived. Science has organized this nervousness into a regular *technique,* her so-called method of verification; and she has fallen so deeply in love with the method that one may even say she has ceased to care for truth by itself at all. It is only truth as technically verified that interests her. The truth of truths might come in merely affirmative form, and she would decline to touch it. Such truth as that, she might repeat with Clifford, would be stolen in defiance of her duty to mankind. Human passions, however, are stronger than technical rules. "*Le coeur a ses raisons,*" as Pascal says, "*que la raison ne connait pas*", and however indifferent to all but the bare rules of the game the umpire, the abstract intellect, may be, the concrete players who furnish him the materials to judge of are usually, each one of them, in love with some pet "live hypothesis" of his own. Let us agree, however, that wherever there is no forced option, the dispassionately judicial intellect with no pet hypothesis, saving us, as it does, from dupery at any rate, ought to be our ideal.

The question next arises: Are there not somewhere forced options in our speculative questions, and can we (as men who may be interested at least as much in positively gaining truth as in merely escaping dupery) always wait with impunity till the coercive evidence shall have arrived? It seems *a priori* improbable that the truth should be so nicely adjusted to our needs and powers as that. In the great boardinghouse of nature, the cakes and the butter and the syrup seldom come out so even and leave the plates so clean. Indeed, we should view them with scientific suspicion if they did.

IX

Moral questions immediately present themselves as questions whose solution cannot wait for sensible proof. A moral question is a question not of what sensibly exists, but of what is good, or would be good if it did exist. Science can tell us what exists; but to compare the *worths,* both of what exists and of what does not exist, we must consult not science, but what Pascal calls our heart. . . .

Turn now from these wide questions of good to a certain class of questions of fact, questions concerning personal relations, states of mind between one man and another. *Do you like me or not?*—for example. Whether you do or not depends, in countless instances, on whether I meet you halfway, am willing to assume that you must like me, and show you trust and expectation. The previous faith on my part in your liking's existence is in such cases what makes your liking come. But if I stand aloof, and refuse to budge an inch until I have objective evidence, until you shall have done something apt, as the absolutists say, *ad extorquendum assensum meum,* ten to one your liking never comes. How many women's hearts are vanquished by the mere sanguine insistence of some man that they *must* love him! He will not consent to the hypothesis that they cannot. The desire for a certain kind of truth here brings about that special truth's existence; and so it is in innumerable cases of other sorts. . . . *And where faith in a fact can help create the fact,* that would be an insane logic which should say that faith running ahead of scientific evidence is the "lowest kind of immorality" into which a thinking being can fall. Yet such is the logic by which our scientific absolutists pretend to regulate our lives!

X

In truths dependent on our personal action, then, faith based on desire is certainly a lawful and possibly an indispensable thing.

But now, it will be said, these are all childish human cases, and have nothing to do with great cosmical matters, like the question of religious faith. Let us then pass on to that. Religions differ so much in their accidents that in discussing the religious question we must make it very generic and broad. What then do we now mean by the religious hypothesis? Science says things are; morality says some things are better than other things; and religion says essentially two things.

First, she says that the best things are the more eternal things, the overlapping things, the things in the universe that throw the last stone, so to speak, and say the final word. "Perfection is eternal"—this phrase of Charles Secrétan seems a good way of putting this first affirmation of religion, an affirmation which obviously cannot yet be verified scientifically at all.

The second affirmation of religion is that we are better off even now if we believe her first affirmation to be true.

Now, let us consider what the logical elements of this situation are *in case the religious hypothesis in both its branches be really true.* (Of course, we must admit that possibility at the outset. If we are to discuss the question at all, it must involve a living option. If for any of you religion be a hypothesis that cannot, by any living possibility, be true, then you need go no farther. I speak to the "saving remnant" alone.) So proceeding, we see, first, that religion offers itself as a *momentous* option. We are supposed to gain, even now, by our belief, and to lose by our non-belief, a certain vital good. Secondly, religion is a *forced* option, so far as that good goes. We cannot escape the issue by remaining sceptical and waiting for more light, because, although we do avoid error in that way *if religion be untrue*, we lose the good, *if it be true*, just as certainly as if we positively chose to disbelieve. It is as if a man should hesitate indefinitely to ask a certain woman to marry him because he was not perfectly sure that she would prove an angel after he brought her home. Would he not cut himself off from that particular angel-possibility as decisively as if he went and married some one else? Scepticism, then, is not avoidance of option; it is option of a certain particular kind of risk. *Better risk loss of truth than chance of error*—that is your faithvetoer's exact position. He is actively playing his stake as much as the believer is; he is backing the field against the religious hypothesis, just as the believer is backing the religious hypothesis against the field. To preach scepticism to us as a duty until "sufficient evidence" for religion be found, is tantamount therefore to telling us, when in presence of the religious hypothesis, that to yield to our fear of its being error is wiser and better than to yield to our hope that it may be true. It is not intellect against all passions, then; it is only intellect with one passion laying down its law. And by what, forsooth, is the supreme wisdom of this passion warranted? Dupery for dupery, what proof is there that dupery through hope is so much worse than dupery through fear? I, for one, can see no proof; and I simply refuse obedience to the scientist's command to imitate his kind of option, in a case where my own stake is important enough to give me the right to choose my own form of risk. If religion be true and the evidence for it be still insufficient, I do not wish, by putting your extinguisher upon my nature (which feels to me as if it had after all some business in this matter), to forfeit my sole chance in life of getting upon the winning side—that chance depending, of course, on my willingness to run the risk of acting as if my passional need of taking the world religiously might he prophetic and right.

All this is on the supposition that it really may be prophetic and right, and that, even to us who are discussing the matter, religion is a live hypothesis which may be true. Now, to most of us religion comes in a still further way that makes a veto on our active faith even more illogical. The more perfect and more eternal aspect of the universe is represented in our religions as having personal form. The universe is no longer a mere *It* to us, but a *Thou,* if we are religious; and any relation that may be possible from person to person might be possible here. For instance, although in one sense we are passive portions of the universe, in another we show a curious autonomy, as if we were small active centers on our own account. We feel, too, as if the appeal of religion to us were made to our own active good-will, as if evidence might be forever withheld from us unless we met the hypothesis halfway. To take a trivial illustration: just as a man who in a company of gentlemen made no advances, asked a warrant for every concession, and believed no one's word without proof, would cut himself off by such churlishness from all the social rewards that a more trusting spirit would earn—so here, one who should shut himself up in snarling logicality and try to make the gods extort his recognition willy-nilly, or not get it at all, might cut himself off forever from his only opportunity of making the gods' acquaintance. This feeling, forced on us we know not whence that by obstinately believing that there are gods (although not to do so would be so easy both for our logic and our life) we are doing the universe the deepest service we can, seems part of the living essence of the religious hypothesis. If the hypothesis *were* true in all its parts, including this one, then pure intellectualism, with its veto on our making willing advances, would be an absurdity; and some participation of our sympathetic nature would be logically required. I therefore, for one, cannot see my way to accepting the agnostic rules for truth-seeking, or wilfully agree to keep my willing nature out of the game. I cannot do so for this plain reason, that *a rule of thinking which would absolutely prevent me from acknowledging certain kinds of truth if those kinds of truth were really there, would be an irrational rule.* That for me is the long and short of the formal logic of the situation, no matter what the kinds of truth might materially be.

I confess I do not see how this logic can be escaped. But sad experience makes me fear that some of you may still shrink from radically saying with me, *in abstracto,* that we have the right to believe at our own risk any hypothesis that is live enough to tempt our will. I suspect, however, that if this is so, it is because you have got away from the abstract logical point of view altogether, and are thinking (perhaps without realizing it) of some particular religious hypothesis which for you is dead. The freedom to "believe what we will" you apply to the case of some patent superstition; and the faith you think of is the faith defined by the schoolboy when he said, "Faith is when you believe something that you know ain't true." I can only repeat that this is misapprehension. *In concreto,* the freedom to believe can only cover living options which the intellect of the individual cannot by itself resolve; and living options never seem absurdities to him who has them to consider. When I look at the religious question as it really puts itself to concrete men, and when I think of all the possibilities which both practically and theoretically it involves, then this command that we shall put a stopper on our heart, instincts, and courage, and *wait*—acting of course meanwhile more or less as if religion were not true—till doomsday, or till such time as our intellect and senses working together may have raked in evidence enough—this command, I say, seems to me the queerest idol ever manufactured in the philosophic cave. Were we scholastic absolutists, there might be more excuse. If we had an infallible intellect with its objective certitudes, we might feel ourselves disloyal to such a perfect organ of knowledge in not trusting to it exclusively, in not waiting for its releasing word. But if we are empiricists, if we believe that no bell in us tolls to let us know for certain when truth is in our grasp, then it seems a piece of idle fantasticality to preach so solemnly our duty of waiting for the bell. Indeed we *may* wait if we will—I hope you do not think that I am denying that—but if we do so, we do so at our peril as much as if we believed. In either case we *act,* taking our life in our hands. No one of us ought to issue vetoes to the other, nor should we bandy words of abuse. We ought, on the contrary, delicately and profoundly to respect one another's mental freedom: then only shall we bring about the intellectual republic; then only shall we have that spirit of inner tolerance without which all our outer tolerance is soulless, and which is empiricism's glory; then only shall we live and let live, in speculative as well as in practical things.

I began by a reference to Fitz-James Stephen; let me end by a quotation from him. "What do you think of yourself? What do you think of the world? . . . These are questions with which all must deal as it seems good to them. They are riddles of the Sphinx, and in some way or other we must deal with them. . . . In all important transactions of life we have to take a leap in the dark. . . . If we decide to leave the riddles unanswered, that is a choice; if we waver in our answer, that, too, is a choice: but whatever choice we make, we make it at our peril. If a man chooses to turn his back altogether on God and the future, no one can prevent him; no one can show beyond reasonable doubt that he is mistaken. If a man thinks otherwise and acts as he thinks, I do not see that any one can prove that he is mistaken. Each must act as he thinks best; and if he is wrong, so much the worse for him. We stand on a mountain pass in the midst of whirling snow and blinding mist, through which we get glimpses now and then of paths which may be deceptive. If we stand still we shall be frozen to death. If we take the wrong road we shall be dashed to pieces. We do not certainly know whether there is any right one. What must we do? 'Be strong and of a good courage.' Act for the best, hope for the best, and take what comes. . . . If death ends all, we cannot meet death better."

Pragmatism

WHAT PRAGMATISM MEANS

Some years ago, being with a camping party in the mountains, I returned from a solitary ramble to find every one engaged in a ferocious metaphysical dispute. The *corpus* of the dispute was a squirrel—a live squirrel supposed to be clinging to one side of a treetrunk; while over against the tree's opposite side a human being was imagined to stand. This human witness tries to get sight of the squirrel by moving rapidly round the tree, but no matter how fast he goes, the squirrel moves as fast in the opposite direction, and always keeps the tree between himself and the man, so that never a glimpse of him is caught. The resultant metaphysical problem now is this: *Does the man go round the squirrel or not?* He goes round the tree, sure enough, and the squirrel is on the tree; but does he go round the squirrel? In the unlimited leisure of the wilderness, discussion had been worn threadbare. Everyone had taken sides, and was obstinate; and the numbers on both sides were even. Each side, when I appeared therefore appealed to me to make it a majority. Mindful of the scholastic adage that whenever you meet a contradiction you must make a distinction, I immediately sought and found one, as follows: "Which party is right," I said, "depends on what you *practically mean* by 'going round' the squirrel. If you mean passing from the north of him to the east, then to the south, then to the west, and then to the north of him again, obviously the man does go round him, for he occupies these successive positions. But if on the contrary you mean being first in front of him, then on the right of him, then behind him, then on his left, and finally in front again, it is quite as obvious that the man fails to go round him, for by the compensating movements the squirrel makes, he keeps his belly turned towards the man all the time, and his back turned away. Make the distinction, and there is no occasion for any farther dispute. You are both right and both wrong according as you conceive the verb 'to go round' in one practical fashion or the other."

Although one or two of the hotter disputants called my speech a shuffling evasion, saying they wanted no quibbling or scholastic hairsplitting, but meant just plain honest English 'round,' the majority seemed to think that the distinction had assuaged the dispute.

I tell this trivial anecdote because it is a peculiarly simple example of what I wish now to speak of as *the pragmatic method*. The pragmatic method is primarily a method of settling metaphysical disputes that otherwise might be interminable. Is the world one or many?—fated or free?—material or spiritual?—here are notions either of which may or may not hold good of the world; and disputes over such notions are unending. The pragmatic method in such cases is to try to interpret each notion by tracing its respective practical consequences. What difference would it practically make to any one if this notion rather than that notion were true? If no practical difference whatever can be traced, then the alternatives mean practically the same thing, and all dispute is idle. Whenever a dispute is serious, we ought to be able to show some practical difference that must follow from one side or the other's being right.

A glance at the history of the idea will show you still better what pragmatism means. The term is derived from the same Greek word πραγμα, meaning action, from which our words 'practice' and 'practical' come. It was first introduced into philosophy by Mr. Charles Peirce in 1878. In an article entitled 'How to Make Our Ideas Clear,' in the 'Popular Science Monthly' for January of that year[1] Mr. Peirce, after pointing out that our beliefs are really rules for action, said that, to develop a thought's meaning, we need only determine what conduct it is fitted to produce: that conduct is for us its sole significance. And the tangible fact at the root of all our thought-distinctions, however subtle, is that there is no one of them so fine as to consist in anything but a possible difference of practice. To attain perfect clearness in our thoughts of an object, then, we need only consider what conceivable effects of a practical kind the object may involve—what sensations we are to expect from it, and what reactions we must prepare. Our conception of these effects, whether immediate or remote, is then for us the whole of our conception of the object, so far as that conception has positive significance at all.

This is the principle of Peirce, the principle of pragmatism. It lay entirely unnoticed by any one for twenty years, until I, in an address before Professor Howison's philosophical union at the university of California, brought it forward again and made a special application of it to religion. By that date (1898) the times seemed ripe for its reception. The word 'pragmatism' spread, and at present it fairly spots the pages of the philosophic journals. On all hands we find the 'pragmatic movement' spoken of, sometimes with respect, sometimes with contumely, seldom with clear understanding. It is evident that the term applies itself conveniently to a number of tendencies that hitherto have lacked a collective name, and that it has 'come to stay.'

To take in the importance of Peirce's principle, one must get accustomed to applying it to concrete cases. I found a few years ago that Ostwald, the illustrious Leipzig chemist, had been making perfectly distinct use of the principle of pragmatism in his lectures on the philosophy of science, though he had not called it by that name.

"All realities influence our practice," he wrote me, "and that influence is their meaning for us. I am accustomed to put questions to my classes in this way: In what respects would the world be different if this alternative or that were true? If I can find nothing that would become different, then the alternative has no sense."

That is, the rival views mean practically the same thing, and meaning, other than practical, there is for us none. Ostwald in a published lecture gives this example of what he means. Chemists have long wrangled over the inner constitution of certain bodies called 'tautomerous.' Their properties seemed equally consistent with the notion that an instable hydrogen atom oscillates inside of them, or that they are instable mixtures of two bodies. Controversy raged, but never was decided. "It would never have begun," says Ostwald, "if the combatants had asked themselves what particular experimental fact could have been made different by one or the other view being correct. For it would then have appeared that no difference of fact could possibly ensue; and the quarrel was as unreal as if, theorizing in primitive times about the raising of dough by yeast, one party should have invoked a 'brownie,' while another insisted on an 'elf' as the true cause of the phenomenon."[2]

It is astonishing to see how many philosophical disputes collapse into insignificance the moment you subject them to this simple test of tracing a concrete consequence. There can *be* no difference anywhere

1. Translated in the *Revue Philosophique* for January, 1879 (vol. vii).

2. 'Theorie und Praxis,' *Zeitsch. des Oesterreichischen Ingenieur u. Architecten-Vereines*, 1905, Nr. 4 u. 6. I find a still more radical pragmatism than Ostwald's in an address by Professor W. S. Franklin: "I think that the sickliest notion of physics, even if a student gets it, is that it is 'the science of masses, molecules, and the ether.' And I think that the healthiest notion, even if a student does not wholly get it, is that physics is the science of the ways of taking hold of bodies and pushing them!" (*Science*, January 2, 1903.)

that doesn't *make* a difference elsewhere—no difference in abstract truth that doesn't express itself in a difference in concrete fact and in conduct consequent upon that fact, imposed on somebody, somehow, somewhere, and somewhen. The whole function of philosophy ought to be to find out what definite difference it will make to you and me, at definite instants of our life, if this world-formula or that world-formula be the true one.

There is absolutely nothing new in the pragmatic method. Socrates was an adept at it. Aristotle used it methodically. Locke, Berkeley, and Hume made momentous contributions to truth by its means. Shadworth Hodgson keeps insisting that realities are only what they are 'known as.' But these forerunners of pragmatism used it in fragments: they were preluders only. Not until in our time has it generalized itself, become conscious of a universal mission, pretended to a conquering destiny. I believe in that destiny, and I hope I may end by inspiring you with my belief.

Pragmatism represents a perfectly familiar attitude in philosophy, the empiricist attitude, but it represents it, as it seems to me, both in a more radical and in a less objectionable form than it has ever yet assumed. A pragmatist turns his back resolutely and once for all upon a lot of inveterate habits dear to professional philosophers. He turns away from abstraction and insufficiency, from verbal solutions, from bad *a priori* reasons, from fixed principles, closed systems, and pretended absolutes and origins. He turns towards concreteness and adequacy, towards facts, towards action and towards power. That means the empiricist temper regnant and the rationalist temper sincerely given up. It means the open air and possibilities of nature, as against dogma, artificiality, and the pretence of finality in truth.

At the same time it does not stand for any special results. It is a method only. But the general triumph of that method would mean an enormous change in what I called in my last lecture the 'temperament' of philosophy. Teachers of the ultra-rationalistic type would be frozen out, much as the courtier type is frozen out in republics, as the ultramontane type of priest is frozen out in protestant lands. Science and metaphysics would come much nearer together, would in fact work absolutely hand in hand.

Metaphysics has usually followed a very primitive kind of quest. You know how men have always hankered after unlawful magic, and you know what a great part in magic *words* have always played. If you have his name, or the formula of incantation that binds him, you can control the spirit, genie, afrite, or whatever the power may be. Solomon knew the names of all the spirits, and having their names, he held them subject to his will. So the universe has always appeared to the natural mind as a kind of enigma, of which the key must be sought in the shape of some illuminating or power-bringing word or name. That word names the universe's *principle,* and to possess it is after a fashion to possess the universe itself. 'God,' 'Matter,' 'Reason,' 'the Absolute,' 'Energy,' are so many solving names. You can rest when you have them. You are at the end of your metaphysical quest.

But if you follow the pragmatic method, you cannot look on any such word as closing your quest. You must bring out of each word its practical cash-value, set it at work within the stream of your experience. It appears less as a solution, then, than as a program for more work, and more particularly as an indication of the ways in which existing realities may be *changed.*

Theories thus become instruments, not answers to enigmas, in which we can rest. We don't lie back upon them, we move forward, and, on occasion, make nature over again by their aid. Pragmatism unstiffens all our theories, limbers them up and sets each one at work. Being nothing essentially new, it harmonizes with many ancient philosophic tendencies. It agrees with nominalism for instance, in always appealing to particulars; with utilitarianism in emphasizing practical aspects; with positivism in its disdain for verbal solutions, useless questions and metaphysical abstractions.

All these, you see, are *anti-intellectualist* tendencies. Against rationalism as a pretension and a method pragmatism is fully armed and militant. But, at the outset, at least, it stands for no particular results. It has no dogmas, and no doctrines save its method. As the young Italian pragmatist Papini has well said, it lies in the midst of our theories, like a corridor in a hotel. Innumerable chambers open out of it. In one you may find a man writing an atheistic volume; in the next some one on his knees praying for faith and strength; in a third a chemist investigating a body's properties. In a fourth a system of idealistic metaphysics is being excogitated; in a fifth the impossibility of metaphysics is being shown. But they all own the corridor, and all must pass through it if they want a practicable way of getting into or out of their respective rooms.

No particular results then, so far, but only an attitude of orientation, is what the pragmatic method means. *The attitude of looking away from first things, principles, 'categories,' supposed necessities; and of looking towards last things, fruits, consequences, facts.*

So much for the pragmatic method! You may say that I have been praising it rather than explaining it to you, but I shall presently explain it abundantly enough by showing how it works on some familiar problems. Meanwhile the word pragmatism has come to be used in a still wider sense, as meaning also a certain *theory of truth.* I mean to give a whole lecture to the statement of that theory, after first paving the way, so I can be very brief now. But brevity is hard to follow, so I ask for your redoubled attention for a quarter of an hour. If much remains obscure, I hope to make it clearer in the later lectures.

One of the most successfully cultivated branches of philosophy in our time is what is called inductive logic, the study of the conditions under which our sciences have evolved. Writers on this subject have begun to show a singular unanimity as to what the laws of nature and element of fact mean, when formulated by mathematicians, physicist and chemists. When the first mathematical, logical, and natural uniformities, the first *laws,* were discovered, men were so carried away by the clearness, beauty and simplification that resulted, that they believed themselves to have deciphered authentically the eternal thoughts of the Almighty. His mind also thundered and reverberated in syllogisms. He also thought in conic sections, squares and roots and ratios, and geometrized like Euclid. He made Kepler's laws for the planets to follow; he made velocity increase proportionally to the time in falling bodies; he made the law of the sines for light to obey when refracted; he established the classes, orders, families and genera of plants and animals, and fixed the distances between them. He thought the archetypes of all things, and devised their variations; and when we rediscover any one of these his wondrous institutions, we seize his mind in its very literal intention.

But as the sciences have developed farther, the notion has gained ground that most, perhaps all, of our laws are only approximations. The laws themselves, moreover, have grown so numerous that there is no counting them; and so many rival formulations are proposed in all the branches of science that investigators have become accustomed to the notion that no theory is absolutely a transcript of reality, but that any one of them may from some point of view be useful. Their great use is to summarize old facts and to lead to new ones. They are only a man-made language, a conceptual shorthand, as some one calls them, in which we write our reports of nature; and languages, as is well known, tolerate much choice of expression and many dialects.

Thus human arbitrariness has driven divine necessity from scientific logic. If I mention the names of Sigwart, Mach, Ostwald, Pearson, Milhaud, Poincaré, Duhem, Ruyssen, those of you who are students will easily identify the tendency I speak of, and will think of additional names.

Riding now on the front of this wave of scientific logic Messrs. Schiller and Dewey appear with their pragmatistic account of what truth everywhere signifies. Everywhere, these teachers say, 'truth' in our ideas and beliefs means the same thing that it means in science. It means, they say, nothing but this, *that ideas (which themselves are but parts of our experience) become true just in so far as they help us to get into satisfactory relation with other parts of our experience,* to summarize them and get about among them by conceptual short-cuts instead of following the interminable succession of particular phenomena. Any idea upon which we can ride, so to speak; any idea that will carry us prosperously from any one part of our experience to any other part, linking things satisfactorily, working securely, simplifying, saving labor; is true for just so much, true in so far forth, true *instrumentally.* This is the 'instrumental' view of truth taught so successfully at Chicago, the view that truth in our ideas means their power to 'work,' promulgated so brilliantly at Oxford.

Messrs. Dewey, Schiller and their allies, in reaching this general conception of all truth, have only followed the example of geologists, biologists and philologists. In the establishment of these other sciences, the successful stroke was always to take some simple process actually observable in operation—as denudation by weather, say, or variation from parental type, or change of dialect by incorporation of new words and pronunciations—and then to generalize it, making it apply to all times, and produce great results by summating its effects through the ages.

The observable process which Schiller and Dewey particularly singled out for generalization is the familiar one by which any individual settles into *new opinions.* The process here is always the same. The individual has a stock of old opinions already, but he meets a new experience that puts them to a strain. Somebody contradicts them; or in a reflective moment he discovers that they contradict each other; or he hears of facts with which they are incompatible; or desires arise in him which they cease to satisfy. The result is an inward trouble to which his mind till then had been a stranger, and from which he seeks to escape by modifying his previous mass of opinions. He saves as much of it as he can, for in this matter of belief we are all extreme conservatives. So he tries to change first this opinion, and then that (for they resist change very variously), until at last some new idea comes up which he can graft upon the ancient stock with a minimum of disturbance of the latter, some idea that mediates between the stock and the new experience and runs them into one another most felicitously and expediently.

This new idea is then adopted as the true one. It preserves the older stock of truths with a minimum of modification, stretching them just enough to make them admit the novelty, but conceiving that in ways as familiar as the case leaves possible. An *outrée* explanation, violating all our preconceptions, would never pass for a true account of a novelty. We should scratch round industriously till we found something less excentric. The most violent revolutions in an individual's beliefs leave most of his old order standing. Time and space, cause and effect, nature and history, and one's biography remain untouched. New truth is always a go-between, a smoother-over of transitions. It marries old opinion to new fact so as ever to show a minimum of jolt, a maximum of continuity. We hold a theory true just in proporation to its success in solving this 'problem of maxima and minima.' But success in solving this problem is eminently a matter of approximation. We say this theory solves it on the whole more satisfactorily than that theory; but that means more satisfactorily to ourselves, and individuals will emphasize their points of satisfaction differently. To a certain degree, therefore, everything here is plastic.

The point I now urge you to observe particularly is the part played by the older truths. Failure to take account of it is the source of much of the unjust criticism levelled against pragmatism. Their influence is absolutely controlling. Loyalty to them is the first principle—in most cases it is the only principle; for by far the most usual way of handling phenomena so novel that they would make for a serious rearrangement of our preconception is to ignore them altogether, or to abuse those who bear witness for them.

You doubtless wish examples of this process of truth's growth, and the only trouble is their superabundance. The simplest case of new truth is of course the mere numerical addition of new kinds of facts, or of new single facts of old kinds, to our experience—an addition that involves no alteration in the old beliefs. Day follows day, and its contents are simply added. The new contents themselves are not true, they simply *come* and *are*. Truth is *what we say about* them, and when we say that they have come, truth is satisfied by the plain additive formula.

But often the day's contents oblige a rearrangement. If I should now utter piercing shrieks and act like a maniac on this platform, it would make many of you revise your ideas as to the probable worth of my philosophy. 'Radium' came the other day as part of the day's content, and seemed for a moment to contradict our ideas of the whole order of nature, that order having come to be identified with what is called the conservation of energy. The mere sight of radium paying heat away indefinitely out of its own pocket seemed to violate that conservation. What to think? If the radiations from it were nothing but an escape of unsuspected 'potential' energy, pre-existent inside of the atoms, the principle of conservation would be saved. The discovery of 'helium' as the radiation's outcome, opened a way to this belief. So Ramsay's view is generally held to be true, because, although it extends our old ideas of energy, it causes a minimum of alteration in their nature.

I need not multiply instances. A new opinion counts as 'true' just in proportion as it gratifies the individual's desire to assimilate the novel in his experience to his beliefs in stock. It must both lean on old truth and grasp new fact; and its success (as I said a moment ago) in doing this, is a matter for the individual's appreciation. When old truth grows, then, by new truth's addition, it is for subjective reasons. We are in the process and obey the reasons. That new idea is truest which performs most felicitously its function of satisfying our double urgency. It makes itself true, gets itself classed as true, by the way it works; grafting itself then upon the ancient body of truth, which thus grows much as a tree grows by the activity of a new layer of cambium.

Now Dewey and Schiller proceed to generalize this observation and to apply it to the most ancient parts of truth. They also once were plastic. They also were called true for human reasons. They also mediated between still earlier truths and what in those days were novel observations. Purely objective truth, truth in whose establishment the function of giving human satisfaction in marrying previous parts of experience with newer parts played no rôle whatever, is nowhere to be found. The reasons why we call things true is the reason why they *are* true, for 'to be true' *means* only to perform this marriage-function.

The trail of the human serpent is thus over everything. Truth independent; truth that we *find* merely; truth no longer malleable to human need; truth incorrigible, in a word; such truth exists indeed superabundantly—or is supposed to exist by rationalistically minded thinkers; but then it means only the dead heart of the living tree, and its being there means only that truth also has its paleontology, and its 'prescription,' and may grow stiff with years of veteran service and petrified in men's regard by sheer antiquity. But how plastic even the oldest truths nevertheless really are has been vividly shown in our day by the transformation of logical and mathematical ideas, a transformation which seems even to be invading physics. The ancient formulas are reinterpreted as special expressions of much wider principles, principles that our ancestors never got a glimpse of in their present shape and formulation.

Mr. Schiller still gives to all this view of truth the name of 'Humanism,' but, for this doctrine too, the name of pragmatism seems fairly to be in the ascendant, so I will treat it under the name of pragmatism in these lectures.

Such then would be the scope of pragmatism—first, a method; and second, a genetic theory of what is meant by truth. And these two things must be our future topics.

What I have said of the theory of truth will, I am sure, have appeared obscure and unsatisfactory to most of you by reason of its brevity. I shall make amends for that hereafter. In a lecture on 'common sense' I shall try to show what I mean by truths grown petrified by antiquity. In another lecture I shall expatiate on the idea that our thoughts become true in proportion as they successfully exert their go-between function. In a third I shall show how hard it is to discriminate subjective from objective factors in Truth's development. You may not follow me wholly in these lectures; and if you do, you may not wholly agree with me. But you will, I know, regard me at least as serious, and treat my effort with respectful consideration.

You will probably be surprised to learn, then, that Messrs. Schiller's and Dewey's theories have suffered a hailstorm of contempt and ridicule. All rationalism has risen against them. In influential quarters Mr. Schiller, in particular, has been treated like an impudent schoolboy who deserves a spanking. I should not mention this, but for the fact that it throws so much sidelight upon that rationalistic temper to which I have opposed the temper of pragmatism. Pragmatism is uncomfortable away from facts. Rationalism is comfortable only in the presence of abstractions. This pragmatist talk about truths in the plural, about their utility and satisfactoriness, about the success with which they 'work,' etc., suggests to the typical intellectualist mind a sort of coarse lame second-rate makeshift article of truth. Such truths are not real truth. Such tests are merely subjective. As against this, objective truth must be something non-utilitarian, haughty, refined, remote, august, exalted. It must be an absolute correspondence of our thoughts with an equally absolute reality. It must be what we *ought* to think unconditionally. The conditioned ways in which we *do* think are so much irrelevance and matter for psychology. Down with psychology, up with logic, in all this question!

See the exquisite contrast of the types of mind! The pragmatist clings to facts and concreteness, observes truth at its work in particular cases, and generalizes. Truth, for him, becomes a class-name for all sorts of definite working-values in experience. For the rationalist it remains a pure abstraction, to the bare name of which we must defer. When the pragmatist undertakes to show in detail just *why* we must defer, the rationalist is unable to recognize the concretes from which his own abstraction is taken. He accuses us of *denying* truth; whereas we have only sought to trace exactly why people follow it and always ought to follow it. Your typical ultra-abstractionist fairly shudders at concreteness: other things equal, he positively prefers the pale and spectral. If the two universes were offered, he would always choose the skinny outline rather than the rich thicket of reality. It is so much purer, clearer, nobler.

I hope that as these lectures go on, the concreteness and closeness to facts of the pragmatism which they advocate may be what approves itself to you as its most satisfactory peculiarity. It only follows here the example of the sister-sciences, interpreting the unobserved by the observed. It brings old and new harmoniously together. It converts the absolutely empty notion of a static relation of 'correspondence' (what that may mean we must ask later) between our minds and reality, into that of a rich and active commerce (that any one may follow in detail and understand) between particular thoughts of ours, and the great universe of other experiences in which they play their parts and have their uses.

But enough of this at present? The justification of what I say must be postponed. I wish now to add a word in further explanation of the claim I made at our last meeting, that pragmatism may be a happy harmonizer of empiricist ways of thinking with the more religious demands of human beings.

Men who are strongly of the fact-loving temperament, you may remember me to have said, are liable to be kept at a distance by the small sympathy with facts which that philosophy from the present-day fashion of idealism offers them. It is far too intellectualistic. Old fashioned theism was bad enough, with its notion of God as an exalted monarch, made up of a lot of unintelligible or preposterous 'attributes'; but, so long as it held strongly by the argument from design, it kept some touch with concrete realities. Since, however, Darwinism has once for all displaced design from the minds of the 'scientific,' theism has lost that foothold; and some kind of an immanent or pantheistic deity working *in* things rather than above them is, if any, the kind recommended to our contemporary imagination. Aspirants to a philosophic religion turn, as a rule, more hopefully nowadays towards idealistic pantheism than towards the older dualistic theism, in spite of the fact that the latter still counts able defenders.

But, as I said in my first lecture, the brand of pantheism offered is hard for them to assimilate if they are lovers of facts, or empirically minded. It is the absolutistic brand, spurning the dust and reared upon pure logic. It keeps no connexion whatever with concreteness. Affirming the Absolute Mind, which is its substitute for God, to be the rational presupposition of all particulars of fact, whatever they may be, it remains supremely indifferent to what the particular facts in our world actually are. Be they what they may, the Absolute will father them. Like the sick lion in Esop's fable, all footprints lead into his den, but *nulla vestigia retrorsum.* You cannot redescend into the world of particulars by the Absolute's aid, or deduce any necessary consequences of detail important for your life from your idea of his nature. He gives you indeed the assurance that all is well with *Him,* and for his eternal way of thinking; but thereupon he leaves you to be finitely saved by your own temporal devices.

Far be it from me to deny the majesty of this conception, or its capacity to yield religious comfort to a most respectable class of minds. But from the human point of view, no one can pretend that it doesn't suffer from the faults of remoteness and abstractness. It is eminently a product of what I have ventured to call the rationalistic temper. It disdains empiricism's needs. It substitutes a pallid outline for the real world's richness. It is dapper, it is noble in the bad sense, in the sense in which to be noble is to be inapt for humble service. In this real world of sweat and dirt, it seems to me that when a view of things is 'noble,' that ought to count as a presumption against its truth, and as a philosophic disqualification. The prince of darkness may be a gentleman, as we are told he is, but whatever the God of earth and heaven is, he can surely be no gentleman. His menial services are needed in the dust of our human trials, even more than his dignity is needed in the empyrean.

Now pragmatism, devoted though she be to facts, has no such materialistic bias as ordinary empiricism labors under. Moreover, she has no objection whatever to the realizing of abstractions, so long as you get about among particulars with their aid and they actually carry you somewhere. Interested in no conclusions but those which our minds and our experiences work out together, she has no *a priori* prejudices against theology. *If theological ideas prove to have a value for concrete life, they will be true, for pragmatism, in the sense of being good for so much. For how much more they are true, will depend entirely on their relations to the other truths that also have to be acknowledged.*

What I said just now about the Absolute, of transcendental idealism, is a case in point. First, I called it majestic and said it yielded religious comfort to a class of minds, and then I accused it of remoteness and sterility. But so far as it affords such comfort, it surely is not sterile; it has that amount of value; it performs a concrete function. As a good pragmatist, I myself ought to call the Absolute true 'in so far forth,' then; and I unhesitatingly now do so.

But what does *true in so far forth* mean in this case? To answer, we need only apply the pragmatic method. What do believers in the Absolute mean by saying that their belief affords them comfort? They mean that since, in the Absolute finite evil is 'overruled' already, we may, therefore, whenever we wish, treat the temporal as if it were potentially the eternal, be sure that we can trust its outcome, and, without sin, dismiss our fear and drop the worry of our finite responsibility. In short, they mean that we have a right ever and anon to take a moral holiday, to let the world wag in its own way, feeling that its issues are in better hands than ours and are none of our business.

The universe is a system of which the individual members may relax their anxieties occasionally, in which the don't-care mood is also right for men, and moral holidays in order,—that, if I mistake not, is part, at least, of what the Absolute is 'known-as,' that is the great difference in our particular experiences which his being true makes, for us, that is his cash-value when he is pragmatically interpreted. Farther than that the ordinary lay-reader in philosophy who thinks favorably of absolute idealism does not venture to sharpen his conceptions. He can use the Absolute for so much, and so much is very precious. He is pained at hearing you speak incredulously of the Absolute, therefore, and disregards your criticisms because they deal with aspects of the conception that he fails to follow.

If the Absolute means this, and means no more than this, who can possibly deny the truth of it? To deny it would be to insist that men should never relax, and that holidays are never in order.

I am well aware how odd it must seem to some of you to hear me say that an idea is 'true' so long as to believe it is profitable to our lives. That it is *good,* for as much as it profits, you will gladly admit. If what we do by its aid is good, you will allow the idea itself to be good in so far forth, for we are the better for possessing it. But is it not a strange misuse of the word 'truth,' you will say, to call ideas also 'true' for this reason?

To answer this difficulty fully is impossible at this stage of my account. You touch here upon the very central point of Messrs. Schiller's, Dewey's, and my own doctrine of truth, which I can not discuss with detail until my sixth lecture. Let me now say only this, that truth is *one species of good,* and not, as is usually supposed, a category distinct from good, and co-ordinate with it. *The true is the name of whatever proves itself to be good in the way of belief, and good, too, for definite, assignable reasons.* Surely you must admit this, that if there were *no* good for life in true ideas, or if the knowledge of them were positively disadvantageous and false ideas the only useful ones, then the current notion that truth is divine and precious, and its pursuit a duty, could never have grown up or become a dogma. In a world like that, our duty would be to *shun* truth, rather. But in this world, just as certain foods are not only agreeable to our taste, but good for our teeth, our stomach, and our tissues; so certain ideas are not only agreeable to think about, or agreeable as supporting other ideas that we are fond of, but they are also helpful in life's practical struggles. If there be any life that it is really better we should lead, and if there be any idea which, if believed in, would help us to lead that life, then it would be really *better for us* to believe in that idea, *unless, indeed, belief in it incidentally clashed with other greater vital benefits.*

'What would be better for us to believe'! This sounds very like a definition of truth. It comes very near to saying 'what we *ought* to believe': and in *that* definition none of you would find any oddity. Ought we ever not to believe what it is *better for us* to believe? And can we then keep the notion of what is better for us, and what is true for us, permanently apart?

Pragmatism says no, and I fully agree with her. Probably you also agree, so far as the abstract statement goes, but with a suspicion that if we practically did believe everything that made for good in our own personal lives, we should be found indulging all kinds of fancies about this world's affairs, and all kinds of sentimental superstitions about a world hereafter. Your suspicion here is undoubtedly well founded, and it is evident that something happens when you pass from the abstract to the concrete that complicates the situation.

I said just now that what is better for us to believe is true *unless the belief incidentally clashes with some other vital benefit.* Now in real life what vital benefits is any particular belief of ours most liable to clash with? What indeed except the vital benefits yielded by *other beliefs* when these prove incompatible with the first ones? In other words, the greatest enemy of any one of our truths may be the rest of our truths. Truths have once for all this desperate instinct of self-preservation and of desire to extinguish whatever contradicts them. My belief in the Absolute, based on the good it does me, must run the gauntlet of all my other beliefs. Grant that it may be true in giving me a moral holiday. Nevertheless, as I conceive it,—and let me speak now confidentially, as it were, and merely in my own private person,—it clashes with other truths of mine whose benefits I hate to give up on its account. It happens to be associated with a kind of logic of which I am the enemy, I find that it entangles me in metaphysical paradoxes that are inacceptable, etc., etc. But as I have enough trouble in life already without adding the trouble of carrying these intellectual inconsistencies, I personally just give up the Absolute. I just *take* my moral holidays; or else as a professional philosopher, I try to justify them by some other principle.

If I could restrict my notion of the Absolute to its bare holiday-giving value, it wouldn't clash with my other truths. But we can not easily thus restrict our hypotheses. They carry supernumerary features, and these it is that clash so. My disbelief in the Absolute means then disbelief in those other supernumerary features, for I fully believe in the legitimacy of taking moral holidays.

You see by this what I meant when I called pragmatism a mediator and reconciler and said, borrowing the word from Papini, that she 'unstiffens' our theories. She has in fact no prejudices whatever, no obstructive dogmas, no rigid canons of what shall count as proof. She is completely genial. She will entertain any hypothesis, she will consider any evidence. It follows that in the religious field she is at a great advantage both over positivistic empiricism, with its anti-theological bias, and over religious rationalism, with its exclusive interest in the remote, the noble, the simple, and the abstract in the way of conception.

In short, she widens the field of search for God. Rationalism sticks to logic and the empyrean. Empiricism sticks to the external senses. Pragmatism is willing to take anything, to follow either logic or the senses and to count the humblest and most personal experiences. She will count mystical experiences if they have practical consequences. She will take a God who lives in the very dirt of private fact—if that should seem a likely place to find him.

Her only test of probable truth is what works best in the way of leading us, what fits every part of life best and combines with the collectivity of experience's demands, nothing being omitted. If theological ideas should do this, if the notion of God, in particular, should prove to do it, how could pragmatism possibly deny God's existence? She could see no meaning in treating as 'not true' a notion that was pragmatically so successful. What other kind of truth could there be, for her, than all this agreement with concrete reality?

PRAGMATISM'S CONCEPTION OF TRUTH

I fully expect to see the pragmatist view of truth run through the classic stages of a theory's career. First, you know, a new theory is attacked as absurd; then it is admitted to be true, but obvious and insignificant; finally it is seen to be so important that its adversaries claim that they themselves discovered it. Our doctrine of truth is at present in the first of these three stages, with symptoms of the second stage having begun in certain quarters. I wish that this lecture might help it beyond the first stage in the eyes of many of you.

Truth, as any dictionary will tell you, is a property of certain of our ideas. It means their "agreement," as falsity means their "disagreement," with "reality." Pragmatists and intellectualists both accept this definition as a matter of course. They begin to quarrel only after the question is raised as to what may precisely be meant by the term "agreement," and what by the term "reality," when reality is taken as something for our ideas to agree with.

In answering these questions the pragmatists are more analytic and painstaking, the intellectualists more offhand and irreflective. The popular notion is that a true idea must copy its reality. Like other popular views, this one follows the analogy of the most usual experience. Our true ideas of sensible things do indeed copy them. Shut your eyes and think of yonder clock on the wall, and you get just such a true picture or copy of its dial. But your idea of its "works" (unless you are a clockmaker) is much less of a copy, yet it passes muster, for it in no way clashes with the reality. Even though it should shrink to the mere word "works," that word still serves you truly; and when you speak of the "time-keeping function" of the clock, or of its spring's "elasticity," it is hard to see exactly what your ideas can copy.

You perceive that there is a problem here. Where our ideas cannot copy definitely their object, what does agreement with that object mean? Some idealists seem to say that they are true whenever they are what God means that we ought to think about that subject. Others hold the copy-view all through, and speak as if our ideas possessed truth just in proportion as they approach to being copies of the Absolute's eternal way of thinking.

These views, you see, invite pragmatistic discussion. But the great assumption of the intellectualists is that truth means essentially an inert static relation. When you've got your true idea of anything, there's an end of the matter. You're in possession; you *know*; you have fulfilled your thinking destiny. You are where you ought to be mentally; you have obeyed your categorical imperative; and nothing more need follow on that climax of your rational destiny. Epistemologically you are in stable equilibrium.

Pragmatism, on the other hand, asks its usual question. "Grant an idea or belief to be true," it says, "what concrete difference will its being true make in any one's actual life? How will the truth be realized? What experiences will be different from those which would obtain if the belief were false? What, in short, is the truth's cash-value in experiential terms?"

The moment pragmatism asks this question, it sees the answer: *True ideas are those that we can assimilate, validate, corroborate and verify. False ideas are those that we cannot.* That is the practical difference it makes to us to have true ideas, that, therefore, is the meaning of truth, for it is all that truth is known-as.

This thesis is what I have to defend. The truth of an idea is not a stagnant property inherent in it. Truth *happens* to an idea. It *becomes* true, is *made* true by events. Its verity *is* in fact an event, a process: the process namely of its verifying itself, its veri-*fication*. Its validity is the process of its valid-*ation*.

But what do the words verification and validation themselves pragmatically mean? They again signify certain practical consequences of the verified and validated idea. It is hard to find any one phrase that characterizes these consequences better than the ordinary agreement-formula—just such consequences being what we have in mind whenever we say that our ideas "agree" with reality. They lead us, namely, through the acts and other ideas which they instigate, into or up to, or towards, other parts of experience with which we feel all the while—such feeling being among our potentialities—that the original ideas remain in agreement. The connexions and transitions come to us from point to point as being progressive, harmonious, satisfactory. This function of agreeable leading is what we mean by an idea's verification. . . .

. . . The possession of true thoughts means everywhere the possession of invaluable instruments of action; and that our duty to gain truth, so far from being a blank command from out of the blue, or a "stunt" self-imposed by our intellect, can account for itself by excellent practical reasons.

The importance to human life of having true beliefs about matters of fact is a thing too notorious. We live in a world of realities that can be infinitely useful or infinitely harmful. Ideas that tell us which of them to expect count as the true ideas in all this primary sphere of verification, and the pursuit of such ideas is a primary human duty. The possession of truth, so far from being here an end in itself, is only a preliminary means towards other vital satisfactions. If I am lost in the woods and starved, and find what looks like a cow-path, it is of the utmost importance that I should think of a human habitation at the end of it, for if I do so and follow it, I save myself. The true thought is useful here because the house which is its object is useful. The practical value of true ideas is thus primarily derived from the practical importance of their objects to us. Their objects are, indeed, not important at all times. I may on another occasion have no use for the house; and then my idea of it, however verifiable, will be practically irrelevant, and had better remain latent. Yet since almost any object may some day become temporarily important, the advantage of having a general stock of *extra* truths, of ideas that shall be true of merely possible situations, is obvious. We store such extra truths away in our memories, and with the overflow we fill our books of reference. Whenever such an extra truth becomes practically relevant to one of our emergencies, it passes from cold-storage to do work in the world and our belief in it grows active. You can say of it then either that "it is useful because it is true" or that "it is true because it is useful." Both these phrases mean exactly the same thing, namely that here is an idea that gets fulfilled and can be verified. True is the name for whatever idea starts the verification-process, useful is the name for its completed function in experience. True ideas would never have been singled out as such, would never have acquired a class-name, least of all a name suggesting value, unless they had been useful from the outset in this way.

From this simple cue pragmatism gets her general notion of truth as something essentially bound up with the way in which one moment in our experience may lead us towards other moments which it will be worth while to have been led to. Primarily, and on the common-sense level, the truth of a state of mind means this function of *a leading that is worth while*. When a moment in our experience, of any kind whatever, inspires us with a thought that is true, that means that sooner or later we dip by that thought's guidance into the particulars of experience again and make advantageous connexion with them. This is a vague enough statement, but I beg you to retain it, for it is essential.

Our experience meanwhile is all shot through with regularities. One bit of it can warn us to get ready for another bit, can "intend" or be "significant of" that remoter object. The object's advent is the significance's verification. Truth, in these cases, meaning nothing but eventual verification, is manifestly incompatible with waywardness on our part. Woe to him whose beliefs play fast and loose with the order which realities follow in his experience; they will lead him nowhere or else make false connexions.

By "realities" or "objects" here, we mean either things of common sense, sensibly present, or else common-sense relations, such as dates, places, distances, kinds, activities. Following our mental image of a house along the cow-path, we actually come to see the house; we get the image's full verification. *Such simply and fully verified leadings are certainly the originals and prototypes of the truth-process.* Experience offers indeed other forms of truth-process, but they are all conceivable as being primary verifications arrested, multiplied or substituted one for another.

Take, for instance, yonder object on the wall. You and I consider it to be a "clock," altho no one of us has seen the hidden works that make it one. We let our notion pass for true without attempting to verify. If truths mean verification-process essentially, ought we then to call such unverified truths as this abortive? No, for they form the overwhelmingly large number of the truths we live by. Indirect as well as direct verifications pass muster. Where circumstantial evidence is sufficient, we can go without eye-witnessing. Just as we here assume Japan to exist without ever having been there, because it *works* to do so, everything we know conspiring with the belief, and nothing interfering, so we assume that thing to be a clock. We *use* it as a clock, regulating the length of our lecture by it. The verification of the assumption here means its leading to no frustration or contradiction. Verifi*ability* of wheels and weights and pendulum is as good as verification. For one truth-process completed there are a million in our lives that function in this state of nascency. They turn us *towards* direct verification; lead us into the *surroundings* of the objects they envisage; and then, if everything runs on harmoniously, we are so sure that verification is possible that we omit it, and are usually justified by all that happens.

Truth lives, in fact, for the most part on a credit system. Our thoughts and beliefs "pass," so long as nothing challenges them, just as banknotes pass so long as nobody refuses them. But this all points to direct face-to-face verifications somewhere, without which the fabric of truth collapses like a financial system with no cashbasis whatever. You accept my verification of one thing, I yours of another. We trade on each other's truth. But beliefs verified concretely by *somebody* are the posts of the whole superstructure.

Another great reason—beside economy of time—for waiving complete verification in the usual business of life is that all things exist in kinds and not singly. Our world is found once for all to have that peculiarity. So that when we have once directly verified our ideas about one specimen of a kind, we consider ourselves free to apply them to other specimens without verification. A mind that habitually discerns the kind of thing before it, and acts by the law of the kind immediately, without pausing to verify, will be a "true" mind in ninety-nine out of a hundred emergencies, proved so by its conduct fitting everything it meets, and getting no refutation.

Indirectly or only potentially verifying processes may thus he true as well as full verification-processes. They work as true processes would work, give us the same advantages, and claim our recognition for the same reasons. . . .

[James returns to the notion that truth is an agreement with reality.]

Here it is that pragmatism and intellectualism begin to part company. Primarily, no doubt, to agree means to copy, but we saw that the mere word "clock" would do instead of a mental picture of its works, and that of many realities our ideas can only be symbols and not copies. "Past time," "power," "spontaneity"—how can our mind copy such realities?

To "agree" in the widest sense with a reality *can only mean to be guided either straight up to it or into its surroundings, or to be put into such working touch with it as to handle either it or something connected with it better than if we disagreed.* Better either intellectually or practically! And often agreement will only mean the negative fact that nothing contradictory from the quarter of that reality comes to interfere with the way in which our ideas guide us elsewhere. To copy a reality is, indeed, one very important way of agreeing with it, but it is far from being essential. The essential thing is the process of being guided. Any idea that helps us to *deal,* whether practically or intellectually, with either the reality or its belongings, that doesn't entangle our progress in frustrations, that *fits,* in fact, and adapts our life to the reality's whole setting, will agree sufficiently to meet the requirement. It will hold true of that reality.

Thus, *names* are just as "true" or "false" as definite mental pictures are. They set up similar verification-processes, and lead to fully equivalent practical results.

All human thinking gets discursified; we exchange ideas; we lend and borrow verifications, get them from one another by means of social intercourse. All truth thus gets verbally built out, stored up, and made available for every one. Hence, we must *talk* consistently just as we must *think* consistently: for both in talk and thought we deal with kinds. Names are arbitrary, but once understood they must be kept to. We mustn't now call Abel "Cain" or Cain "Abel." If we do, we ungear ourselves from the whole book of Genesis, and from all its connexions with the universe of speech and fact down to the present time. We throw ourselves out of whatever truth that entire system of speech and fact may embody.

The overwhelming majority of our true ideas admit of no direct or face-to-face verification—those of past history, for example, as of Cain and Abel. The stream of time can be remounted only verbally, or verified directly by the present prolongations or effects of what the past harbored. Yet if they agree with these verbalities and effects, we can know that our ideas of the past are true. *As true as past time itself was,* so true was Julius Caesar, so true were antediluvian monsters all in their proper dates and settings. That past time itself was, is guaranteed by its coherence with everything that's present. True as the present *is,* the past *was* also.

Agreement thus turns out to be essentially an affair of leading—leading that is useful because it is into quarters that contain objects that are important. True ideas lead us into useful verbal and conceptual quarters as well as directly up to useful sensible termini. They lead to consistency, stability and flowing human intercourse. They lead away from excentricity and isolation, from foiled and barren thinking. The untrammelled flowing of the leading-process, its general freedom from clash and contradiction, passes for its indirect verification; but all roads lead to Rome, and in the end and eventually, all true processes must lead to the face of directly verifying sensible experiences *somewhere,* which somebody's ideas have copied.

Such is the large loose way in which the pragmatist interprets the word agreement. He treats it altogether practically. He lets it cover any process of conduction from a present idea to a future terminus, provided only it run prosperously. It is only thus that "scientific" ideas, flying as they do beyond common sense, can be said to agree with their realities. It is, as I have already said, *as if* reality were made of ether, atoms or electrons, but we mustn't think so literally. The term "energy" doesn't even pretend to stand for anything "objective." It is only a way of measuring the surface of phenomena so as to string their changes on a simple formula.

Yet in the choice of these man-made formulas we cannot be capricious with impunity any more than we can be capricious on the common-sense practical level. We must find a theory that will *work;* and that means something extremely difficult; for our theory must mediate between all previous truths and certain new experiences. It must derange common sense and previous belief as little as possible, and it must lead to some sensible terminus or other that can be verified exactly. To "work" means both these things; and the squeeze is so tight that there is little loose play for any hypothesis. Our theories are wedged and controlled as nothing else is. Yet sometimes alternative theoretic formulas are equally compatible with all the truths we know, and then we choose between them for subjective reasons. We choose the kind of theory to which we are already partial; we follow "elegance" or "economy." Clerk-Maxwell somewhere says it would be "poor scientific taste" to choose the more complicated of two equally well-evidenced conceptions; and you will all agree with him. Truth in science is what gives us the maximum possible sum of satisfactions, taste included, but consistency both with previous truth and with novel fact is always the most imperious claimant. . . .

Our account of truth is an account of truths in the plural, of processes of leading, realized *in rebus,*[3]

3. [in things]

and having only this quality in common, that they *pay*. They pay by guiding us into or towards some part of a system that dips at numerous points into sense-percepts, which we may copy mentally or not, but with which at any rate we are now in the kind of commerce vaguely designated as verification. Truth for us is simply a collective name for verification-processes, just as health, wealth, strength, etc., are names for other processes connected with life, and also pursued because it pays to pursue them. Truth is *made*, just as health, wealth and strength are made, in the course of experience.

Here rationalism is instantaneously up in arms against us. I can imagine a rationalist to talk as follows:

"Truth is not made," he will say; "it absolutely obtains, being a unique relation that does not wait upon any process, but shoots straight over the head of experience, and hits its reality every time. Our belief that yon thing on the wall is a clock is true already, altho no one in the whole history of the world should verify it. The bare quality of standing in that transcendent relation is what makes any thought true that possesses it, whether or not there be verification. You pragmatists put the cart before the horse in making truth's being reside in verification-processes. These are merely signs of its being, merely our lame ways of ascertaining after the fact, which of our ideas already has possessed the wondrous quality. The quality itself is timeless, like all essences and natures. Thoughts partake of it directly, as they partake of falsity or of irrelevancy. It can't be analyzed away into pragmatic consequences."

The whole plausibility of this rationalist tirade is due to the fact to which we have already paid so much attention. In our world, namely, abounding as it does in things of similar kinds and similarly associated, one verification serves for others of its kind, and one great use of knowing things is to be led not so much to them as to their associates, especially to human talk about them. The quality of truth, obtaining *ante rem,*[4] pragmatically means, then, the fact that in such a world innumerable ideas work better by their indirect or possible than by their direct and actual verification. Truth *ante rem* means only verifiability, then; or else it is a case of the stock rationalist trick of treating the *name* of a concrete phenomenal reality as an independent prior entity, and placing it behind the reality as its explanation. . . .

4. [before the thing]

In the case of "wealth" we all see the fallacy. We know that wealth is but a name for concrete processes that certain men's lives play a part in, and not a natural excellence found in Messrs. Rockefeller and Carnegie, but not in the rest of us.

Like wealth, "health" also lives *in rebus*. It is a name for processes, as digestion, circulation, sleep, etc., that go on happily, tho in this instance we are more inclined to think of it as a principle and to say the man digests and sleeps so well *because* he is so healthy.

With "strength" we are, I think, more rationalistic still, and decidedly inclined to treat it as an excellence pre-existing in the man and explanatory of the herculean performances of his muscles.

With "truth" most people go over the border entirely, and treat the rationalistic account as self-evident. But really all these words in *th* are exactly similar. Truth exists *ante rem* just as much and as little as the other things do.

The scholastics, following Aristotle, made much of the distinction between habit and act. Health *in actu* means, among other things, good sleeping and digesting. But a healthy man need not always be sleeping, or always digesting, any more than a wealthy man need be always handling money, or a strong man always lifting weights. All such qualities sink to the status of "habits" between their times of exercise; and similarly truth becomes a habit of certain of our ideas and beliefs in their intervals of rest from their verifying activities. But those activities are the root of the whole matter, and the condition of there being any habit to exist in the intervals.

"The true," to put it very briefly, is only the expedient in the way of our thinking, just as "the right" is only the expedient in the way of our behaving. Expedient in almost any fashion; and expedient in the long run and on the whole of course; for what meets expediently all the experience in sight won't necessarily meet all further experiences equally satisfactorily. Experience, as we know, has ways of *boiling over,* and making us correct our present formulas.

The "absolutely" true, meaning what no further experience will ever alter, is that ideal vanishing-point towards which we imagine that all our temporary truths will some day converge. It runs on all fours with the perfectly wise man, and with the absolutely complete experience; and, if these ideals are ever realized, they will all be realized together. Meanwhile we have to live today by what truth we can get today, and be ready tomorrow to call it falsehood. Ptolemaic astronomy, Euclidean space, Aristotelian logic, Scholastic metaphysics, were expedient for centuries, but human experience has boiled over those limits, and we now call these things only relatively true, or true within those borders of experience. "Absolutely" they are false; for we know that those limits were casual, and might have been transcended by past theorists just as they are by present thinkers.

When new experiences lead to retrospective judgments, using the past tense, what these judgments utter *was* true, even tho no past thinker had been led there. We live forwards, a Danish thinker [Kierkegaard] has said, but we understand backwards. The present sheds a backward light on the world's previous processes. They may have been truth-processes for the actors in them. They are not so for one who knows the latter revelations of the story.

This regulative notion of a potential better truth to be established later, possibly to be established some day absolutely, and having powers of retroactive legislation, turns its face, like all pragmatist notions, towards concreteness of fact, and towards the future. Like the half-truths, the absolute truth will have to be *made,* made as a relation incidental to the growth of a mass of verification-experience, to which the half-true ideas are all along contributing their quota.

I have already insisted on the fact that truth is made largely out of previous truths. Men's beliefs at any time are so much experience *funded.* But the beliefs are themselves parts of the sum total of the world's experience, and become matter, therefore, for the next day's funding operations. So far as reality means experienceable reality, both it and the truths men gain about it are everlastingly in process of mutation—mutation towards a definite goal, it may be—but still mutation.

Mathematicians can solve problems with two variables. On the Newtonian theory, for instance, acceleration varies with distance, but distance also varies with acceleration. In the realm of truth-processes facts come independently and determine our beliefs provisionally. But these beliefs make us act, and as fast as they do so, they bring into sight or into existence new facts which re-determine the beliefs accordingly. So the whole coil and ball of truth, as it rolls up, is the product of a double influence. Truths emerge from facts; but they dip forward into facts again and add to them; which facts again create or reveal new truth (the word is indifferent) and so on indefinitely. The "facts" themselves meanwhile are not *true.* They simply *are.* Truth is the function of the beliefs that start and terminate among them. . . .

The case is like a snowball's growth, due as it is to the distribution of the snow on the one hand, and to the successive pushes of the boys on the other, with these factors co-determining each other incessantly. . . .

I am well aware how odd it must seem to some of you to hear me say that an idea is "true" so long as to believe it is profitable to our lives. That it is *good,* for as much as it profits, you will gladly admit. If what we do by its aid is good, you will allow the idea itself to be good in so far forth, for we are the better for possessing it. But is it not a strange misuse of the word "truth," you will say, to call ideas also "true" for this reason? . . .

. . . Let me now say only this, that truth is *one species of good,* and not, as is usually supposed, a category distinct from good, and co-ordinate with it. *The true is the name of whatever proves itself to be good in the way of belief and good, too, for definite, assignable reasons.* Surely you must admit this, that if there were *no* good for life in true ideas, or if the knowledge of them were positively disadvantageous and false ideas the only useful ones, then the current notion that truth is divine and precious, and its pursuit a duty, could never have grown up or become a dogma. In a world like that, our duty would be to *shun* truth, rather. But in this world, just as certain foods are not only agreeable to our taste, but good for our teeth, our stomach, and our tissues; so certain ideas are not only agreeable to think about, or agreeable as supporting other ideas that we are fond of, but they are also helpful in life's practical struggles. If there be any life that it is really better we should lead, and if there be any idea which, if believed in, would help us to lead that life, then it would be really *better for us* to believe in that idea, *unless, indeed, belief in it incidentally clashed with other greater vital benefits.*

"What would be better for us to believe!" This sounds very like a definition of truth. It comes very near to saying "what we *ought* to believe"; and in *that* definition none of you would find any oddity. Ought we ever not to believe what it is *better for us* to believe? And can we then keep the notion of what is better for us, and what is true for us, permanently apart?

Pragmatism says no, and I fully agree with her. Probably you also agree, so far as the abstract statement goes, but with a suspicion that if we practically did believe everything that made for good in our own personal lives, we should be found indulging all kinds of fancies about this world's affairs, and all kinds of sentimental superstitions about a world hereafter. Your suspicion here is undoubtedly well founded, and it is evident that something happens when you pass from the abstract to the concrete that complicates the situation.

I said just now that what is better for us to believe is true *unless the belief incidentally clashes with some other vital benefit*. Now in real life what vital benefits is any particular belief of ours most liable to clash with? What indeed except the vital benefits yielded by *other beliefs* when these prove incompatible with the first ones? In other words, the greatest enemy of any one of our truths may be the rest of our truths. Truths have once for all this desperate instinct of self-preservation and of desire to extinguish whatever contradicts them.

Chapter 34

BERTRAND RUSSELL

Bertrand Russell was born in England in 1872, the godson of John Stuart Mill. His parents died when he was three and he was brought up by his deeply religious grandmother. He studied mathematics and philosophy, and later taught at Cambridge University. He traveled widely, to China and Russia, as well as to the United States, where he taught for a brief period. His work covers virtually all areas of philosophical inquiry, from logic through philosophy of religion and philosophy of mind to ethics. He made major contributions to logic, especially with his *Principia Matematica* (written with Alfred North Whitehead), philosophy of language, and epistemology.

Russell received the Nobel Prize for Literature in 1950.

Though he never was a doctrinaire pacifist, Russell's opposition to World War I and the Vietnam War, which he regarded as senseless slaughters, led to loss of his Cambridge fellowship and two imprisonments—on the last occasion at the age of ninety-four. An agnostic, he debated the Jesuit philosopher, Father F. C. Copleston on the existence of God. He was asked what he would say to God, when, after death, he was asked by God why he didn't believe in Him. Russell replied, "God, why did you make the evidence for your existence so insufficient?" He died in 1970 at the age of ninety-seven.

Our first reading, *The Problems of Philosophy,* is one of the most succinct, insightful outlines of the central notions of epistemology. Russell wrote in his preface, "In the following pages I have confined myself in the main to those problems of philosophy in regard to which I thought it possible to say something positive and constructive, since merely negative criticism seemed out of place. For this reason, theory of knowledge occupies a larger space than metaphysics in the present volume, and some topics much discussed by philosophers are treated very briefly, if at all." In the first few chapters Russell defends a Lockean (see John Locke, Chapter 20) or representationalist view of sense perception, holding that there is a real world but that we never know it directly. Of special importance is his defense of the Correspondence theory of truth (chapter XII), which may be contrasted with William James's Pragmatic theory of truth (see James, Chapter 33).

In our last selection, "A Free Man's Worship," Russell attempts to find meaning and morality in a life or world without God or a transcendental being. The world, Russell laments, is an absurd, godless tragedy, in which nature, omnipotent but blind, has brought forth rational, purposeful children who are superior to their mother, and as such can discover moral ideals with which to sustain themselves in this ultimately meaningless existence. Morality doesn't need religion for legitimation.

FOR FURTHER READING

Ayer, A. J. *Bertrand Russell.* (University of Chicago Press, 1988).
Clark, R. *The Life of Bertrand Russell.* (De Capo Press, 1990).

Russell, Bertrand. *The Autobiography of Bertrand Russell.* (Allen & Unwin, 1961).
Russell, Bertrand. *Human Knowledge.* (Simon & Schuster, 1962).
Bertrand Russell. *A History of Western Philosophy.* (Random House, 1945).
Sainsbury, M. *Russell.* (Routledge & Kegan Paul, 1979).
Schilpp, P. A., ed. *The Philosophy of Bertrand Russell.* (Harper & Row, 1963).

The Problems of Philosophy

CHAPTER I APPEARANCE AND REALITY

Is there any knowledge in the world which is so certain that no reasonable man could doubt it? This question, which at first sight might not seem difficult, is really one of the most difficult that can be asked. When we have realized the obstacles in the way of a straightforward and confident answer, we shall be well launched on the study of philosophy—for philosophy is merely the attempt to answer such ultimate questions, not carelessly and dogmatically, as we do in ordinary life and even in the sciences, but critically after exploring all that makes such questions puzzling, and after realizing all the vagueness and confusion that underlie our ordinary ideas.

In daily life, we assume as certain many things which, on a closer scrutiny, are found to be so full of apparent contradictions that only a great amount of thought enables us to know what it is that we really may believe. In the search for certainty, it is natural to begin with our present experiences, and in some sense, no doubt, knowledge is to be derived from them. But any statement as to what it is that our immediate experiences make us know is very likely to be wrong. It seems to me that I am now sitting in a chair, at a table of a certain shape, on which I see sheets of paper with writing or print. By turning my head I see out of the window buildings and clouds and the sun. I believe that the sun is about ninety-three million miles from the earth; that it is a hot globe many times bigger than the earth; that, owing to the earth's rotation, it rises every morning, and will continue to do so for an indefinite time in the future. I believe that, if any other normal person comes into my room, he will see the same chairs and tables and books and papers as I see, and that the table which I see is the same as the table which I feel pressing against my arm. All this seems to be so evident as to be hardly worth stating, except in answer to a man who doubts whether I know anything. Yet all this may be reasonably doubted, and all of it requires much careful discussion before we can be sure that we have stated it in a form that is wholly true.

To make our difficulties plain, let us concentrate attention on the table. To the eye it is oblong, brown and shiny, to the touch it is smooth and cool and hard; when I tap it, it gives out a wooden sound. Any one else who sees and feels and hears the table will agree with this description, so that it might seem as if no difficulty would arise; but as soon as we try to be more precise our troubles begin. Although I believe that the table is 'really' of the same colour all over, the parts that reflect the light look much brighter than the other parts, and some parts look white because of reflected light. I know that, if I move, the parts that reflect the light will be different, so that the apparent distribution of colours on the table will change. It follows that if several people are looking at the table at the same moment, no two of them will see exactly the same distribution of colours, because no two can see it from exactly the same point of view, and any change in the point of view makes some change in the way the light is reflected.

For most practical purposes these differences are unimportant, but to the painter they are all-important: the painter has to unlearn the habit of thinking that things seem to have the colour which common sense says they 'really' have, and to learn the habit of seeing things as they appear. Here we have already the beginning of one of the distinctions that cause most trouble in philosophy—the distinction between 'appearance' and 'reality', between what things seem to be and what they are. The painter wants to know what things seem to be, the practical man and the philosopher want to know what they are; but the philosopher's wish to know this is stronger than the practical man's, and is more troubled by knowledge as to the difficulties of answering the question.

To return to the table. It is evident from what we have found, that there is no colour which preeminently appears to be the colour of the table, or even of any one particular part of the table—it appears to be of different colours from different points of view, and there is no reason for regarding some of these as more really its colour than others. And we know that even from a given point of view the colour will seem different by artificial light, or to a colour-blind man, or to a man wearing blue spectacles, while in the dark there will be no colour at all, though to touch and hearing the table will be unchanged. This colour is not something which is inherent in the table, but something depending upon the table and the spectator and the way the light falls on the table. When, in ordinary life, we speak of the colour of the table, we only mean the sort of colour which it will seem to have to a normal spectator from an ordinary point of view under usual conditions of light. But the other colours which appear under other conditions have just as good a right to be considered real; and therefore, to avoid favouritism, we are compelled to deny that, in itself, the table has any one particular colour.

The same thing applies to the texture. With the naked eye one can see the grain, but otherwise the table looks smooth and even. If we looked at it through a microscope, we should see roughnesses and hills and valleys, and all sorts of differences that are imperceptible to the naked eye. Which of these is the 'real' table? We are naturally tempted to say that what we see through the microscope is more real, but that in turn would be changed by a still more powerful microscope. If, then, we cannot trust what we see with the naked eye, why should we trust what we see through a microscope? Thus, again, the confidence in our senses with which we began deserts us.

The shape of the table is no better. We are all in the habit of judging as to the 'real' shapes of things, and we do this so unreflectingly that we come to think we actually see the real shapes. But, in fact, as we all have to learn if we try to draw, a given thing looks different in shape from every different point of view. If our table is 'really' rectangular, it will look, from almost all points of view, as if it had two acute angles and two obtuse angles. If opposite sides are parallel, they will look as if they converged to a point away from the spectator; if they are of equal length, they will look as if the nearer side were longer. All these things are not commonly noticed in looking at a table, because experience has taught us to construct the 'real' shape from the apparant shape, and the 'real' shape is what interests us as practical men. But the 'real' shape is not what we see; it is something inferred from what we see. And what we see is constantly changing in shape as we move about the room; so that here again the senses seem not to give us the truth about the table itself, but only about the appearance of the table.

Similar difficulties arise when we consider the sense of touch. It is true that the table always gives us a sensation of hardness, and we feel that it resists pressure. But the sensation we obtain depends upon how hard we press the table and also upon what part of the body we press with; thus the various sensations due to various pressures or various parts of the body cannot be supposed to reveal directly any definite property of the table, but at most to be signs of some property which perhaps causes all the sensations, but is not actually apparent in any of them. And the same applies still more obviously to the sounds which can be elicited by rapping the table.

Thus it becomes evident that the real table, if there is one, is not the same as what we immediately experience by sight or touch or hearing. The real table, if there is one, is not immediately known to us at all, but must be an inference from what is immediately known. Hence, two very difficult questions at once arise; namely, (1) Is there a real table at all? (2) If so, what sort of object can it be?

It will help us in considering these questions to have a few simple terms of which the meaning is definite and clear. Let us give the name of 'sense-data' to the things that are immediately known in sensation: such things as colours, sounds, smells, hardnesses, roughnesses, and so on. We shall give the name 'sensation' to the experience of being immediately aware of these things. Thus, whenever we see a colour, we have a sensation of the colour, but the colour itself is a sense-datum, not a sensation. The colour is that of which we are immediately aware, and the awareness itself is the sensation. It is plain that if we are to know anything about the table, it must be by means of the sense-data—brown colour, oblong shape, smoothness, etc.—which we associate with the table; but, for the reasons which have been given, we cannot say that the table is the sense-data, or even that the sense-data are directly properties of the table. Thus a problem arise as to the relation of the sense-data to the real table, supposing there is such a thing.

The real table, if it exists, we will call a 'physical object'. Thus we have to consider the relation of sense-data to physical objects. The collection of all physical objects is called 'matter'. Thus our two questions may be re-stated as follows: (1) Is there any such thing as matter? (2) If so, what is its nature?

The philosopher who first brought prominently forward the reasons for regarding the immediate objects of our senses as not existing independently of us was Bishop Berkeley (1685–1753). His *Three Dialogues between Hylas and Philonous, in Opposition to Sceptics and Atheists*, undertake to prove that there is no such thing as matter at all, and that the world consists of nothing but minds and their ideas. Hylas has hitherto believed in matter, but he is no match for Philonous, who mercilessly drives him into contradictions and paradoxes, and makes his own denial of matter seem, in the end, as if it were almost common sense. The arguments employed are of very different value: some are important and sound, others are confused or quibbling. But Berkeley retains the merit of having shown that the existence of matter is capable of being denied without absurdity, and that if there are any things that exist independently of us they cannot be the immediate objects of our sensations.

There are two different questions involved when we ask whether matter exists, and it is important to keep them clear. We commonly mean by 'matter' something which is opposed to 'mind', something which we think of as occupying space and as radically incapable of any sort of thought or consciousness. It is chiefly in this sense that Berkeley denies matter; that is to say, he does not deny that the sense-data which we commonly take as signs of the existence of the table are really signs of the existence of something independent of us, but he does deny that this something is nonmental, that it is neither mind nor ideas entertained by some mind. He admits that there must be something which continues to exist when we go out of the room or shut our eyes, and that what we call seeing the table does really give us reason for believing in something which persists even when we are not seeing it. But he thinks that this something cannot be radically different in nature from what we see, and cannot be independent of seeing altogether, though it must be independent of our seeing. He is thus led to regard the 'real' table as an idea in the mind of God. Such an idea has the required permanence and independence of ourselves, without being—as matter would otherwise be—something quite unknowable, in the sense that we can only infer it, and can never be directly and immediately aware of it.

Other philosophers since Berkeley have also held that, although the table does not depend for its existence upon being seen by me, it does depend upon being seen (or otherwise apprehended in sensation) by some mind—not necessarily the mind of God, but more often the whole collective mind of the universe. This they hold, as Berkeley does, chiefly because they think there can be nothing real—or at any rate nothing known to be real except minds and their thoughts and feelings. We might state the argument by which they support their view in some such way as this: 'Whatever can be thought of is an idea in the mind of the person thinking of it; therefore nothing can be thought of except ideas in minds; therefore anything else is inconceivable, and what is inconceivable cannot exist.'

Such an argument, in my opinion, is fallacious; and of course those who advance it do not put it so shortly or so crudely. But whether valid or not, the argument has been very widely advanced in one form or another; and very many philosophers, perhaps a majority, have held that there is nothing real except minds and their ideas. Such philosophers are called 'idealists'. When they come to explaining matter, they either say, like Berkeley, that matter is really nothing but a collection of ideas, or they say, like Leibniz (1646–1716), that what happens as matter is really a collection of more or less rudimentary minds.

But these philosophers, though they deny matter as opposed to mind, nevertheless, in another sense, admit matter. It will be remembered that we asked two questions; namely, (1) Is there a real table at all? (2) If so, what sort of object can it be? Now both Berkeley and Leibniz admit that there is a real table, but Berkeley says it is certain ideas in the mind of God, and Leibniz says it is a colony of souls. Thus both of them answer our first question in the affirmative and only diverge from the views of ordinary mortals in their answer to our second question. In fact, almost all philosophers seem to be agreed that there is a real table. They almost all agree that, however much our sense-data—colour, shape, smoothness, etc.—may depend upon us, yet their occurrence is a sign of something existing independently of us, something differing, perhaps, completely from our sense-data whenever we are in a suitable relation to the real table.

Now obviously this point in which the philosophers are agreed—the view that there is a real table, whatever its nature may be is vitally important, and it will be worth while to consider what reasons there are for accepting this view before we go on to the further question as to the nature of the real table. Our next chapter, therefore, will be concerned with the reasons for supposing that there is a real table at all.

Before we go farther it will be well to consider for a moment what it is that we have discovered so far. It has appeared that, if we take any common object of the sort that is supposed to be known by the senses, what the senses immediately tell us is not the truth about the object as it is apart from us, but only the truth about certain sense-data which, so far as we can see, depend upon the relations between us and the object. Thus what we directly see and feel is merely 'appearance', which we believe to be a sign of some 'reality' behind. But if the reality is not what appears, have we any means of knowing whether there is any reality at all? And if so, have we any means of finding out what it is like?

Such questions are bewildering, and it is difficult to know that even the strangest hypotheses may not be true. Thus our familiar table, which has roused but the slightest thoughts in us hitherto, has become a problem full of surprising possibilities. The one thing we know about it is that it is not what it seems. Beyond this modest result, so far, we have the most complete liberty of conjecture. Leibniz tells us it is a community of souls: Berkeley tells us it is an idea in the mind of God; sober science, scarcely less wonderful, tells us it is a vast collection of electric charges in violent motion.

Among these surprising possibilities, doubt suggests that perhaps there is no table at all. Philosophy, if it cannot answer so many questions as we could wish, has at least the power of asking questions which increase the interest of the world, and show the strangeness and wonder lying just below the surface even in the commonest things of daily life.

CHAPTER II THE EXISTENCE OF MATTER

In this chapter we have to ask ourselves whether, in any sense at all, there is such a thing as matter. Is there a table which has a certain intrinsic nature, and continues to exist when I am not looking, or is the table merely a product of my imagination, a dream-table in a very prolonged dream? This question is of the greatest importance. For if we cannot be sure of the independent existence of objects, we cannot be sure of the independent existence of other people's bodies, and therefore still less of other people's minds, since we have no grounds for believing in their minds except such as are derived from observing their bodies. Thus if we cannot be sure of the independent existence of objects, we shall be left alone in a desert—it may be that the whole outer world is nothing but a dream, and that we alone exist. This is an uncomfortable possibility; but although it cannot be strictly proved to be false, there is not the slightest reason to suppose that it is true. In this chapter we have to see why this is the case.

Before we embark upon doubtful matters, let us try to find some more or less fixed point from which to start. Although we are doubting the physical existence of the table, we are not doubting the existence of the sense-data which made us think there was a table; we are not doubting that, while we look, a certain colour and shape appear to us, and while we press, a certain sensation of hardness is experienced by us. All this, which is psychological, we are not calling in question. In fact, whatever else may be doubtful, some at least of our immediate experiences seem absolutely certain.

Descartes (1596–1650), the founder of modern philosophy, invented a method which may still be used with profit—the method of systematic doubt. He determined that he would believe nothing which he did not see quite clearly and distinctly to be true. Whatever he could bring himself to doubt, he would doubt, until he saw reason for not doubting it. By applying this method he gradually became convinced that the only existence of which he could be quite certain was his own. He imagined a deceitful demon, who presented unreal things to his senses in a perpetual phantasmagoria; it might be very improbable that such a demon existed, but still it was possible, and therefore doubt concerning things perceived by the senses was possible.

But doubt concerning his own existence was not

possible, for if he did not exist, no demon could deceive him. If he doubted, he must exist; if he had any experiences whatever, he must exist. Thus his own existence was an absolute certainty to him. 'I think, therefore I am,' he said (Cogito, ergo sum); and on the basis of this certainty he set to work to build up again the world of knowledge which his doubt had laid in ruins. By inventing the method of doubt, and by showing that subjective things are the most certain, Descartes performed a great service to philosophy, and one which makes him still useful to all students of the subject.

But some care is needed in using Descartes' argument. 'I think, therefore I am' says rather more than is strictly certain. It might seem as though we were quite sure of being the same person to-day as we were yesterday, and this is no doubt true in some sense. But the real Self is as hard to arrive at as the real table and does not seem to have the absolute, convincing certainty that belongs to particular experiences. When I look at my table and see a certain brown colour, what is quite certain at once is not 'I am seeing a brown colour', but rather, 'a brown colour is being seen'. This of course involves something (or somebody) which (or who) sees the brown colour; but it does not of itself involve that more or less permanent person whom we call 'I'. So far as immediate certainty goes, it might be that the something which sees the brown colour is quite momentary, and not the same as the something which has some different experience the next moment.

Thus it is our particular thoughts and feelings that have primitive certainty. And this applies to dreams and hallucinations as well as to normal perceptions: when we dream or see a ghost, we certainly do have the sensations we think we have, but for various reasons it is held that no physical object corresponds to these sensations. Thus the certainty of our knowledge of our own experiences does not have to be limited in any way to allow for exceptional cases. Here, therefore, we have, for what it is worth, a solid basis from which to begin our pursuit of knowledge.

The problem we have to consider is this: Granted that we are certain of our own sense-data, have we any reason for regarding them as signs of the existence of something else, which we can call the physical object? When we have enumerated all the sense-data which we should naturally regard as connected with the table have we said all there is to say about the table, or is there still something else—something not a sense-datum, something which persists when we go out of the room? Common sense unhesitatingly answers that there is. What can be bought and sold and pushed about and have a cloth laid on it, and so on, cannot be a mere collection of sense-data. If the cloth completely hides the table, we shall derive no sense-data from the table, and therefore, if the table were merely sense-data, it would have ceased to exist, and the cloth would be suspended in empty air, resting, by a miracle, in the place where the table formerly was. This seems plainly absurd; but whoever wishes to become a philosopher must learn not to be frightened by absurdities.

One great reason why it is felt that we must secure a physical object in addition to the sense-data, is that we want the same object for different people. When ten people are sitting round a dinner-table, it seems preposterous to maintain that they are not seeing the same tablecloth, the same knives and forks and spoons and glasses. But the sense-data are private to each separate person; what is immediately present to the sight of one is not immediately present to the sight of another: they all see things from slightly different points of view, and therefore see them slightly differently. Thus, if there are to be public neutral objects, which can be in some sense known to many different people, there must be something over and above the private and particular sense-data which appear to various people. What reason, then, have we for believing that there are such public neutral objects?

The first answer that naturally occurs to one is that, although different people may see the table slightly differently, still they all see more or less similar things when they look at the table, and the variations in what they see follow the laws of perspective and reflection of light, so that it is easy to arrive at a permanent object underlying all the different people's sense-data. I bought my table from the former occupant of my room; I could not buy his sense-data, which died when he went away, but I could and did buy the confident expectation of more or less similar sense-data. Thus it is the fact that different people have similar sense-data, and that one person in a given place at different times has similar sense-data, which makes us suppose that over and above the sense-data there is a permanent public object which underlies or causes the sense-data of various people at various times.

Now in so far as the above considerations depend upon supposing that there are other people besides ourselves, they beg the very question at issue. Other people are represented to me by certain sense-data, such as the sight of them or the sound of their voices, and if I had no reason to believe that there were physical objects independent of my sense-data, I should have no reason to believe that other people exist except as part of my dream. Thus, when we are trying to show that there must be objects independent of our own sense-data, we cannot appeal to the testimony of other people, since this testimony itself consists of sense-data, and does not reveal other people's experiences unless our own sense-data are signs of things existing independently of us. We must therefore, if possible, find, in our own purely private experiences, characteristics which show, or tend to show, that there are in the world things other than ourselves and our private experiences.

In one sense it must be admitted that we can never prove the existence of things other than ourselves and our experiences. No logical absurdity results from the hypothesis that the world consists of myself and my thoughts and feelings and sensations, and that everything else is mere fancy. In dreams a very complicated world may seem to be present, and yet on waking we find it was a delusion; that is to say, we find that the sense-data in the dream do not appear to have corresponded with such physical objects as we should naturally infer from our sense-data. (It is true that, when the physical world is assumed, it is possible to find physical causes for the sense-data in dreams: a door banging, for instance, may cause us to dream of a naval engagement. But although, in this case, there is a physical cause for the sense-data, there is not a physical object corresponding to the sense-data in the way in which an actual naval battle would correspond.) There is no logical impossibility in the supposition that the whole of life is a dream, in which we ourselves create all the objects that come before us. But although this is not logically impossible, there is no reason whatever to suppose that it is true; and it is, in fact, a less simple hypothesis, viewed as a means of accounting for the facts of our own life, than the common-sense hypothesis that there really are objects independent of us, whose action on us causes our sensations.

The way in which simplicity comes in from supposing that there really are physical objects is easily seen. If the cat appears at one moment in one part of the room, and at another in another part, it is natural to suppose that it has moved from the one to the other, passing over a series of intermediate positions. But if it is merely a set of sense-data, it cannot have ever been in any place where I did not see it; thus we shall have to suppose that it did not exist at all while I was not looking, but suddenly sprang into being in a new place. If the cat exists whether I see it or not, we can understand from our own experience how it gets hungry between one meal and the next; but if it does not exist when I am not seeing it, it seems odd that appetite should grow during non-existence as fast as during existence. And if the cat consists only of sense-data, it cannot be hungry, since no hunger but my own can be a sense-datum to me. Thus the behaviour of the sense-data which represent the cat to me, though it seems quite natural when regarded as an expression of hunger, becomes utterly inexplicable when regarded as mere movements and changes of patches of colour, which are as incapable of hunger as triangle is of playing football.

But the difficulty in the case of the cat is nothing compared to the difficulty in the case of human beings. When human beings speak—that is, when we hear certain noises which we associate with ideas, and simultaneously see certain motions of lips and expressions of face—it is very difficult to suppose that what we hear is not the expression of a thought, as we know it would be if we emitted the same sounds. Of course similar things happen in dreams, where we are mistaken as to the existence of other people. But dreams are more or less suggested by what we call waking life, and are capable of being more or less accounted for on scientific principles if we assume that there really is a physical world. Thus every principle of simplicity urges us to adopt the natural view, that there really are objects other than ourselves and our sense-data which have an existence not dependent upon our perceiving them.

Of course it is not by argument that we originally come by our belief in an independent external world. We find this belief ready in ourselves as soon as we begin to reflect: it is what may be called an instinctive belief. We should never have been led to question this belief but for the fact that, at any rate in the case of sight, it seems as if the sense-datum itself was instinctively believed to be the independent object, whereas argument shows that the object cannot be identical with the sense-datum. This discovery, however—which is not at all paradoxical in the case of taste and smell and sound, and only slightly so in the case of touch—leaves undiminished our instinctive belief that there are objects corresponding to our sense-data. Since this belief does not lead to any difficulties, but on the contrary tends to simplify and systematize our account of our experiences, there seems no good reason for rejecting it. We may therefore admit—though with a slight doubt derived from dreams—that the external world does really exist, and is not wholly dependent for its existence upon our continuing to perceive it.

The argument which has led us to this conclusion is doubtless less strong than we could wish, but it is typical of many philosophical arguments, and it is therefore worth while to consider briefly its general character and validity. All knowledge, we find, must be built up upon our instinctive beliefs, and if these are rejected, nothing is left. But among our instinctive beliefs some are much stronger than others, while many have, by habit and association, become entangled with other beliefs, not really instinctive, but falsely supposed to be part of what is believed instinctively.

Philosophy should show us the hierarchy of our instinctive beliefs, beginning with those we hold most strongly, and presenting each as much isolated and as free from irrelevant additions as possible. It should take care to show that, in the form in which they are finally set forth, our instinctive beliefs do not clash, but form a harmonious system. There can never be any reason for rejecting one instinctive belief except that it clashes with others; thus, if they are found to harmonize, the whole system becomes worthy of acceptance.

It is of course possible that all or any of our beliefs may be mistaken, and therefore all ought to be held with at least some slight element of doubt. But we cannot have reason to reject a belief except on the ground of some other belief. Hence, by organizing our instinctive beliefs and their consequences, by considering which among them is most possible, if necessary, to modify or abandon, we can arrive, on the basis of accepting as our sole data what we instinctively believe, at an orderly systematic organization of our knowledge, in which, though the possibility of error remains, its likelihood is diminished by the interrelation of the parts and by the critical scrutiny which has preceded acquiescence.

This function, at least, philosophy can perform. Most philosophers, rightly or wrongly, believe that philosophy can do much more than this—that it can give us knowledge, not otherwise attainable, concerning the universe as a whole, and concerning the nature of ultimate reality. Whether this be the case or not, the more modest function we have spoken of can certainly be performed by philosophy, and certainly suffices, for those who have once begun to doubt the adequacy of common sense, to justify the arduous and difficult labours that philosophical problems involve.

CHAPTER III THE NATURE OF MATTER

In the preceding chapter we agreed, though without being able to find demonstrative reasons, that it is rational to believe that our sense-data—for example, those which we regard as associated with my table—are really signs of the existence of something independent of us and our perceptions. That is to say, over and above the sensations of colour, hardness, noise, and so on, which make up the appearance of the table to me, I assume that there is something else, of which these things are appearances. The colour ceases to exist if I shut my eyes, the sensation of hardness ceases to exist if I remove my arm from contact with the table, the sound ceases to exist if I cease to rap the table with my knuckles. But I do not believe that when all these things cease the table ceases. On the contrary, I believe that it is because the table exists continuously that all these sense-data will reappear when I open my eyes, replace my arm, and begin again to rap with my knuckles. The question we have to consider in this chapter is: What is the nature of this real table, which persists independently of my perception of it?

To this question physical science gives an answer, somewhat incomplete it is true, and in part still very hypothetical, but yet deserving of respect so far as it goes. Physical science, more or less unconsciously, has drifted into the view that all natural phenomena ought to be reduced to motions. Light and heat and sound are all due to wave-motions, which travel from the body emitting them to the person who sees light or feels heat or hears sound. That which has the wave-motion is either ether or 'gross matter', but in either case is what the philosopher would call matter. The only properties which science assigns to it are position in space, and the power of motion according to the laws of motion. Science does not deny that it may have other properties; but if so, such other properties are not useful to the man of science, and in no way assist him in explaining the phenomena.

It is sometimes said that 'light is a form of wave-motion', but this is misleading, for the light which we immediately see, which we know directly by means of our senses, is not a form of wave-motion, but something quite different—something which we all know if we are not blind, though we cannot describe it so as to convey our knowledge to a man who is blind. A wave-motion, on the contrary, could quite well be described to a blind man, since he can acquire a knowledge of space by the sense of touch; and he can experience a wave-motion by a sea voyage almost as well as we can. But this, which a blind man can understand, is not what we mean by light: we mean by light just that which a blind man can never understand, and which we can never describe to him.

Now this something, which all of us who are not blind know, is not, according to science, really to be found in the outer world: it is something caused by the action of certain waves upon the eyes and nerves and brain of the person who sees the light. When it is said that light is waves, what is really meant is that waves are the physical cause of our sensations of light. But light itself, the thing which seeing people experience and blind people do not, is not supposed by science to form any part of the world that is independent of us and our senses. And very similar remarks would apply to other kinds of sensations.

It is not only colours and sounds and so on that are absent from the scientific world of matter, but also space as we get it through sight or touch. It is essential to science that its matter should be in a space, but the space in which it is cannot be exactly the space we see or feel. To begin with, space as we see it is not the same as space as we get it by the sense of touch; it is only by experience in infancy that we learn how to touch things we see, or how to get a sight of things which we feel touching us. But the space of science is neutral as between touch and sight; thus it cannot be either the space of touch or the space of sight.

Again, different people see the same object as of different shapes, according to their point of view. A circular coin, for example, though we should always judge it to be circular, will look oval unless we are straight in front of it. When we judge that it is circular, we are judging that it has a real shape which is not its apparent shape, but belongs to it intrinsically apart from its appearance. But this real shape, which is what concerns science, must be in a real space, not the same as anybody's apparent space. The real space is public, the apparent space is private to the percipient. In different people's private spaces the same object seems to have different shapes; thus the real space, in which it has its real shape, must be different from the private spaces. The space of science, therefore, though connected with the spaces we see and feel, is not identical with them, and the manner of its connexion requires investigation.

We agreed provisionally that physical objects cannot be quite like our sense-data, but may be regarded as causing our sensations. These physical objects are in the space of science, which we may call 'physical' space. It is important to notice that, if our sensations are to be caused by physical objects, there must be a physical space containing these objects and our sense-organs and nerves and brain. We get a sensation of touch from an object when we are in contact with it; that is to say, when some part of our body occupies a place in physical space quite close to the space occupied by the object. We see an object (roughly speaking) when no opaque body is between the object and our eyes in physical space. Similarly, we only hear or smell or taste an object when we are sufficiently near to it, or when it touches the tongue, or has some suitable position in physical space relatively to our body. We cannot begin to state what different sensations we shall derive from a given object under different circumstances unless we regard the object and our body as both in one physical space, for it is mainly the relative positions of the object and our body that determine what sensations we shall derive from the object.

Now our sense-data are situated in our private spaces, either the space of sight or the space of touch or such vaguer spaces as other senses may give us. If, as science and common sense assume, there is one public all-embracing physical space in which physical objects are, the relative positions of physical objects in physical space must more or less correspond to the relative positions of sense-data in our private spaces. There is no difficulty in supposing this to be the case. If we see on a road one house nearer to us than another, our other senses will bear out the view that it is nearer; for example, it will be reached sooner if we walk along the road. Other people will agree that the house which looks nearer to us is nearer; the ordnance map will take the same view; and thus everything points to a spatial relation between the houses corresponding to the relation between the sense-data which we see when we look at the houses. Thus we may assume that there is a physical space in which physical objects have spatial relations corresponding to those which the corresponding sense-data have in our private spaces. It is this physical space which is dealt with in geometry and assumed in physics and astronomy.

Assuming that there is physical space, and that it does thus correspond to private spaces, what can we know about it? We can know only what is required in order to secure the correspondence. That is to say, we can know nothing of what it is like in itself, but we can know the sort of arrangement of physical objects which results from their spatial relations. We can know, for example, that the earth and moon and sun are in one straight line during an eclipse, though we cannot know what a physical straight line is in itself, as we know the look of a straight line in our visual space. Thus we come to know much more about the relations of distances in physical space than about the distances themselves; we may know that one distance is greater than another, or that it is along the same straight line as the other, but we cannot have that immediate acquaintance with physical distances that we have with distances in our private spaces, or with colours or sounds or other sense-data. We can know all those things about physical space which a man born blind might know through other people about the space of sight; but the kind of things which a man born blind could never know about the space of sight we also cannot know about physical space. We can know the properties of the relations required to preserve the correspondence with sense-data, but we cannot know the nature of the terms between which the relations hold.

With regard to time, our feeling of duration or of the lapse of time is notoriously an unsafe guide as to the time that has elapsed by the clock. Times when we are bored or suffering pain pass slowly, times when we are agreeably occupied pass quickly, and times when we are sleeping pass almost as if they did not exist. Thus, in so far as time is constituted by duration, there is the same necessity for distinguishing a public and a private time as there was in the case of space. But in so far as time consists in an order of before and after, there is no need to make such a distinction; the time-order which events seem to have is, so far as we can see, the same as the time-order which they do have. At any rate no reason can be given for supposing that the two orders are not the same. The same is usually true of space: if a regiment of men are marching along a road, the shape of the regiment will look different from different points of view, but the men will appear arranged in the same order from all points of view. Hence we regard the order as true also in physical space, whereas the shape is only supposed to correspond to the physical space so far as is required for the preservation of the order.

In saying that the time-order which events seem to have is the same as the time-order which they really have, it is necessary to guard against a possible misunderstanding. It must not be supposed that the various states of different physical objects have the same time-order as the sense-data which constitute the perceptions of those objects. Considered as physical objects, the thunder and lightning are simultaneous; that is to say, the lightning is simultaneous with the disturbance of the air in the place where the disturbance begins, namely, where the lightning is. But the sense-datum which we call hearing the thunder does not take place until the disturbance of the air has travelled as far as to where we are. Similarly, it takes about eight minutes for the sun's light to reach us; thus, when we see the sun we are seeing the sun of eight minutes ago. So far as our sense-data afford evidence as to the physical sun they afford evidence as to the physical sun of eight minutes ago; if the physical sun had ceased to exist within the last eight minutes, that would make no difference to the sense-data which we call 'seeing the sun'. This affords a fresh illustration of the necessity of distinguishing between sense-data and physical objects.

What we have found as regards space is much the same as what we find in relation to the correspondence of the sense-data with their physical counterparts. If one object looks blue and another red, we may reasonably presume that there is some corresponding difference between the physical objects; if two objects both look blue, we may presume a corresponding similarity. But we cannot hope to be acquainted directly with the quality in the physical object which makes it look blue or red. Science tells us that this quality is a certain sort of wave-motion, and this sounds familiar, because we think of wave-motions in the space we see. But the wave-motions must really be in physical space, with which we have no direct acquaintance; thus the real wave-motions have not that familiarity which we might have supposed them to have. And what holds for colours is closely similar to what holds for other sense-data.

Thus we find that, although the relations of physical objects have all sorts of knowable properties, derived from their correspondence with the relations of sense-data, the physical objects themselves remain unknown in their intrinsic nature, so far at least as can be discovered by means of the senses. The question remains whether there is any other method of discovering the intrinsic nature of physical objects.

The most natural, though not ultimately the most defensible, hypothesis to adopt in the first instance, at any rate as regards visual sense-data, would be that, though physical objects cannot, for the reasons we have been considering, be exactly like sense-data, yet they may be more or less like. According to this view, physical objects will, for example, really have colours, and we might, by good luck, see an object as of the colour it really is. The colour which an object seems to have at any given moment will in general be very similar, though not quite the same, from many different points of view; we might thus suppose the 'real' colour to be a sort of medium colour, intermediate between the various shades which appear from the different points of view.

Such a theory is perhaps not capable of being definitely refuted, but it can be shown to be groundless. To begin with, it is plain that the colour we see depends only upon the nature of the light-waves that strike the eye, and is therefore modified by the medium intervening between us and the object, as well as by the manner in which light is reflected from the object in the direction of the eye. The intervening air alters colours unless it is perfectly clear, and any strong reflection will alter them completely. Thus the colour we see is a result of the ray as it reaches the eye, and not simply a property of the object from which the ray comes. Hence, also, provided certain waves reach the eye, we shall see a certain colour, whether the object from which the waves start has any colour or not. Thus it is quite gratuitous to suppose that physical objects have colours, and therefore there is no justification for making such a supposition. Exactly similar arguments will apply to other sense-data.

It remains to ask whether there are any general philosophical arguments enabling us to say that, if matter is real, it must be of such and such a nature. As explained above, very many philosophers, perhaps most, have held that whatever is real must be in some sense mental, or at any rate that whatever we can know anything about must be in some sense mental. Such philosophers are called 'idealists'. Idealists tell us that what appears as matter is really something mental; namely, either (as Leibniz held) more or less rudimentary minds, or (as Berkeley contended) ideas in the minds which, as we should commonly say, 'perceive' the matter. Thus idealists deny the existence of matter as something intrinsically different from mind, though they do not deny that our sense-data are signs of something which exists independently of our private sensations. In the following chapter we shall consider briefly the reasons—in my opinion fallacious—which idealists advance in favour of their theory.

CHAPTER IV IDEALISM

The word 'idealism' is used by different philosophers in somewhat different senses. We shall understand by it the doctrine that whatever exists, or at any rate whatever can be known to exist, must be in some sense mental. This doctrine, which is very widely held among philosophers, has several forms, and is advocated on several different grounds. The doctrine is so widely held, and so interesting in itself, that even the briefest survey of philosophy must give some account of it.

Those who are unaccustomed to philosophical speculation may be inclined to dismiss such a doctrine as obviously absurd. There is no doubt that common sense regards tables and chairs and the sun and moon and material objects generally as something radically different from minds and the contents of minds, and as having an existence which might continue if minds ceased. We think of matter as having existed long before there were any minds, and it is hard to think of it as a mere product of mental activity. But whether true or false, idealism is not to be dismissed as obviously absurd.

We have seen that, even if physical objects do have an independent existence, they must differ very widely from sense-data, and can only have a correspondence with sense-data, in the same sort of way in which a catalogue has a correspondence with the things catalogued. Hence common sense leaves us completely in the dark as to the true intrinsic nature of physical objects, and if there were good reason to regard them as mental, we could not legitimately reject this opinion merely because it strikes us as strange. The truth about physical objects must be strange. It may be unattainable, but if any philosopher believes that he has attained it, the fact that what he offers as the truth is strange ought not to be made a ground of objection to his opinion.

The grounds on which idealism is advocated are generally grounds derived from the theory of knowledge, that is to say, from a discussion of the conditions which things must satisfy in order that we may be able to know them. The first serious attempt to establish idealism on such grounds was that of Bishop Berkeley. He proved first, by arguments which were largely valid, that our sense-data cannot be supposed to have an existence independent of us, but must be, in part at least, 'in' the mind, in the sense that their existence would not continue if there were no seeing or hearing or touching or smelling or tasting. So far, his contention was almost certainly valid, even if some of his arguments were not so. But he went on to argue that sense-data were the only things of whose existence our perceptions could assure us, and that to be known is to be 'in' a mind, and therefore to be mental. Hence he concluded that nothing can ever be known except what is in some mind, and that whatever is known without being in my mind must be in some other mind.

In order to understand his argument, it is necessary to understand his use of the word 'idea'. He gives the name 'idea' to anything which is immediately known, as, for example, sense-data are known. Thus a particular colour which we see is an idea; so is a voice which we hear, and so on. But the term is not wholly confined to sense-data. There will also be things remembered or imagined, for with such things also we have immediate acquaintance at the moment of remembering or imagining. All such immediate data he calls 'ideas'.

He then proceeds to consider common objects, such as a tree, for instance. He shows that all we know immediately when we 'perceive' the tree consists of ideas in his sense of the word, and he argues that there is not the slightest ground for supposing that there is anything real about the tree except what is perceived. Its being, he says, consists in being perceived: in the Latin of the schoolmen its 'esse' is 'percipi'. He fully admits that the tree must continue to exist even when we shut our eyes or when no human being is near it. But this continued existence, he says, is due to the fact that God continues to perceive it; the 'real' tree, which corresponds to what we called the physical object, consists of ideas in the mind of God, ideas more or less like those we have when we see the tree, but differing in the fact that they are permanent in God's mind so long as the tree continues to exist. All our perceptions, according to him, consist in a partial participation in God's perceptions, and it is because of this participation that different people see more or less the same tree. Thus apart from minds and their ideas there is nothing in the world, nor is it possible that anything else should ever be known, since whatever is known is necessarily an idea.

There are in this argument a good many fallacies which have been important in the history of philosophy, and which it will be as well to bring to light. In the first place, there is a confusion engendered by the use of the word 'idea'. We think of an idea as essentially something in somebody's mind, and thus when we are told that a tree consists entirely of ideas, it is natural to suppose that, if so, the tree must be entirely in minds. But the notion of being 'in' the mind is ambiguous. We speak of bearing a person in mind, not meaning that the person is in our minds, but that a thought of him is in our minds. When a man says that some business he had to arrange went clean out of his mind, he does not mean to imply that the business itself was ever in his mind, but only that a thought of the business was formerly in his mind, but afterwards ceased to be in his mind. And so when Berkeley says that the tree must be in our minds if we can know it, all that he really has a right to say is that a thought of the tree must be in our minds. To argue that the tree itself must be in our minds is like arguing that a person whom we bear in mind is himself in our minds. This confusion may seem too gross to have been really committed by any competent philosopher, but various attendant circumstances rendered it possible. In order to see how it was possible, we must go more deeply into the question as to the nature of ideas.

Before taking up the general question of the nature of ideas, we must disentangle two entirely separate questions which arise concerning sense-data and physical objects. We saw that, for various reasons of detail, Berkeley was right in treating the sense-data which constitute our perception of the tree as more or less subjective, in the sense that they depend upon us as much as upon the tree, and would not exist if the tree were not being perceived. But this is an entirely different point from the one by which Berkeley seeks to prove that whatever can be immediately known must be in a mind. For this purpose argument of detail as to the dependence of sense-data upon us are useless. It is necessary to prove, generally, that by being known, things are shown to be mental. This is what Berkeley believes himself to have done. It is this question, and not our previous question as to the difference between sense-data and the physical object, that must now concern us.

Taking the word 'idea' in Berkeley's sense, there are two quite distinct things to be considered whenever an idea is before the mind. There is on the one hand the thing of which we are aware—say the colour of my table—and on the other hand the actual awareness itself, the mental act of apprehending the thing. The mental act is undoubtedly mental, but is there any reason to suppose that the thing apprehended is in any sense mental? Our previous arguments concerning the colour did not prove it to be mental; they only proved that its existence depends upon the relation of our sense organs to the physical object—in our case, the table. That is to say, they proved that a certain colour will exist, in a certain light, if a normal eye is placed at a certain point relatively to the table. They did not prove that the colour is in the mind of the percipient.

Berkeley's view, that obviously the colour must be in the mind, seems to depend for its plausibility upon confusing the thing apprehended with the act of apprehension. Either of these might be called an 'idea'; probably either would have been called an idea by Berkeley. The act is undoubtedly in the mind; hence, when we are thinking of the act, we readily assent to the view that ideas must be in the mind. Then, forgetting that this was only true when ideas were taken as acts of apprehension, we transfer the proposition that 'ideas are in the mind' to ideas in the other sense, i.e. to the things apprehended by our acts of apprehension. Thus, by an unconscious equivocation, we arrive at the conclusion that whatever we can apprehend must be in our minds. This seems to be the true analysis of Berkeley's argument, and the ultimate fallacy upon which it rests.

This question of the distinction between act and object in our apprehending of things is vitally important, since our whole power of acquiring knowledge is bound up with it. The faculty of being acquainted with things other than itself is the main characteristic of a mind. Acquaintance with objects essentially consists in a relation between the mind and something other than the mind; it is this that constitutes the mind's power of knowing things. If we say that the things known must be in the mind, we are either unduly limiting the mind's power of knowing, or we are uttering a mere tautology. We are uttering a mere tautology if we mean by 'in the mind' the same as by 'before the mind', i.e. if we mean merely being apprehended by the mind. But if we mean this, we shall have to admit that what, in this sense, is in the mind, may nevertheless be not mental. Thus when we realize the nature of knowledge, Berkeley's argument is seen to be wrong in substance as well as in form, and his grounds for supposing that 'ideas'—i.e. the objects apprehended—must be mental, are found to have no validity whatever. Hence his grounds in favour of idealism may be dismissed. It remains to see whether there are any other grounds.

It is often said, as though it were a self-evident truism, that we cannot know that anything exists which we do not know. It is inferred that whatever can in any way be relevant to our experience must be at least capable of being known by us; whence it follows that if matter were essentially something with which we could not become acquainted, matter would be something which we could not know to exist, and which could have for us no importance whatever. It is generally also implied, for reasons which remain obscure, that what can have no importance for us cannot be real, and that therefore matter, if it is not composed of minds or of mental ideas, is impossible and a mere chimaera.

To go into this argument fully at our present stage would be impossible, since it raises points requiring a considerable preliminary discussion; but certain reasons for rejecting the argument may be noticed at once. To begin at the end: there is no reason why what cannot have any practical importance for us should not be real. It is true that, if theoretical importance is included, everything real is of some importance to us, since, as persons desirous of knowing the truth about the universe, we have some interest in everything that the universe contains. But if this sort of interest is included, it is not the case that matter has no importance for us, provided it exists even if we cannot know that it exists. We can, obviously, suspect that it may exist, and wonder whether it does; hence it is connected with our desire for knowledge, and has the importance of either satisfying or thwarting this desire.

Again, it is by no means a truism, and is in fact false, that we cannot know that anything exists which we do not know. The word 'know' is here used in two different senses. (1) In its first use it is applicable to the sort of knowledge which is opposed to error, the sense in which what we know is true, the sense which applies to our beliefs and convictions, i.e. to what are called judgements. In this sense of the word we know that something is the case. This sort of knowledge may be described as knowledge of truths. (2) In the second use of the word 'know' above, the word applies to our knowledge of things, which we may call acquaintance. This is the sense in which we know sense-data. (The distinction involved is roughly that between savoir and connaitre in French, or between wissen and kennen in German.)

Thus the statement which seemed like a truism becomes, when re-stated, the following: 'We can never truly judge that something with which we are not acquainted exists.' This is by no means a truism, but on the contrary a palpable falsehood. I have not the honour to be acquainted with the Emperor of China, but I truly judge that he exists. It may be said, of course, that I judge this because of other people's acquaintance with him. This, however, would be an irrelevant retort, since, if the principle were true, I could not know that any one else is acquainted with him. But further: there is no reason why I should not know of the existence of something with which nobody is acquainted. This point is important, and demands elucidation.

If I am acquainted with a thing which exists, my acquaintance gives me the knowledge that it exists. But it is not true that, conversely, whenever I can know that a thing of a certain sort exists, I or some one else must be acquainted with the thing. What happens, in cases where I have true judgement without acquaintance, is that the thing is known to me by description, and that, in virtue of some general principle, the existence of a thing answering to this description can be inferred from the existence of something with which I am acquainted. In order to understand this point fully, it will be well first to deal with the difference between knowledge by acquaintance and knowledge by description, and then to consider what knowledge of general principles, if any, has the same kind of certainty as our knowledge of the existence of our own experiences. These subjects will be dealt with in the following chapters.

CHAPTER V KNOWLEDGE BY ACQUAINTANCE AND KNOWLEDGE BY DESCRIPTION

In the preceding chapter we saw that there are two sorts of knowledge: knowledge of things, and knowledge of truths. In this chapter we shall be concerned exclusively with knowledge of things, of which in turn we shall have to distinguish two kinds. Knowledge of things, when it is of the kind we call knowledge by acquaintance, is essentially simpler than any knowledge of truths, and logically independent of knowledge of truths, though it would be rash to assume that human beings ever, in fact, have acquaintance with things without at the same time knowing some truth about them. Knowledge of things by description, on the contrary, always involves, as we shall find in the course of the present chapter, some knowledge of truths as its source and ground. But first of all we must make dear what we mean by 'acquaintance' and what we mean by 'description'.

We shall say that we have acquaintance with anything of which we are directly aware, without the intermediary of any process of inference or any knowledge of truths. Thus in the presence of my table I am acquainted with the sense-data that make up the appearance of my table—its colour, shape, hardness, smoothness, etc.; all these are things of which I am immediately conscious when I am seeing and touching my table. The particular shade of colour that I am seeing may have many things said about it—I may say that it is brown, that it is rather dark, and so on. But such statements, though they make me know truths about the colour, do not make me know the colour itself any better than I did before: so far a concerns knowledge of the colour itself, as opposed to knowledge of truths about it, I know the colour perfectly and completely when I see it, and no further knowledge of it itself is even theoretically possible. Thus the sense-data which make up the appearance of my table are things with which I have acquaintance, things immediately known to me just as they are.

My knowledge of the table as a physical object, on the contrary, is not direct knowledge. Such as it is, it is obtained through acquaintance with the sense-data that make up the appearance of the table. We have seen that it is possible, without absurdity, to doubt that there is a table at all, whereas it is not possible to doubt the sense-data. My knowledge of the table is of the kind which we shall call 'knowledge by description'. The table is 'the physical object which causes such-and-such sense-data'. This describes the table by means of the sense-data. In order to know anything at all about the table, we must know truths connecting it with things with which we have acquaintance: we must know that 'such-and-such sense-data are caused by a physical object'. There is no state of mind in which we are directly aware of the table; all our knowledge of the table is really knowledge of truths, and the actual thing which is the table is not, strictly speaking, known to us at all. We know a description and we know that there is just one object to which this description applies, though the object itself is not directly known to us. In such a case, we say that our knowledge of the object is knowledge by description.

All our knowledge, both knowledge of things and knowledge of truths, rests upon acquaintance as its foundation. It is therefore important to consider what kinds of things there are with which we have acquaintance.

Sense-data, as we have already seen, are among the things with which we are acquainted; in fact, they supply the most obvious and striking example of knowledge by acquaintance. But if they were the sole example, our knowledge would be very much more restricted than it is. We should only know what is now present to our senses: we could not know anything about the past—not even that there was a past—nor could we know any truths about our sense-data, for all knowledge of truths, as we shall show, demands acquaintance with things which are of an essentially different character from sense-data, the things which are sometimes called 'abstract ideas', but which we shall call 'universals'. We have therefore to consider acquaintance with other things besides sense-data if we are to obtain any tolerably adequate analysis of our knowledge.

The first extension beyond sense-data to be considered is acquaintance by memory. It is obvious that we often remember what we have seen or heard or had otherwise presented to our senses, and that in such cases we are still immediately aware of what we remember, in spite of the fact that it appears as past and not as present. This immediate knowledge by memory is the source of all our knowledge concerning the past: without it, there could be no knowledge of the past by inference, we should never know that there was anything past to be inferred.

The next extension to be considered is acquaintance by introspection. We are not only aware of things, but we are often aware of being aware of them. When I see the sun, I am often aware of my seeing the sun; thus 'my seeing the sun' is an object with which I have acquaintance. When I desire food, I may be aware of my desire for food; thus 'my desiring food' is an object with which I am acquainted. Similarly we may be aware of our feeling pleasure or pain, and generally of the events which happen in our minds. This kind of acquaintance, which may be called self-consciousness, is the source of all our knowledge of mental things. It is obvious that it is only what goes on in our own minds that can be thus known immediately. What goes on in the minds of others is known to us through our perception of their bodies, that is, the sense-data in us which are associated with their bodies. But for our acquaintance with the contents of our own minds, we should be unable to imagine the minds of others, and therefore we could never arrive at the knowledge that they have minds. It seems natural to suppose that self-consciousness is one of the things that distinguish men from animals: animals, we may suppose, though they have acquaintance with sense-data, never become aware of this acquaintance. I do not mean that they doubt whether they exist, but that they have never become conscious of the fact that they have sensations and feelings, nor therefore of the fact that they, the subjects of their sensations and feelings, exist.

We have spoken of acquaintance with the contents of our minds as self-consciousness, but it is not, of course, consciousness of our self: it is consciousness of particular thoughts and feelings. The question whether we are also acquainted with our bare selves, as opposed to particular thoughts and feelings, is a very difficult one, upon which it would be rash to speak positively. When we try to look into ourselves we always seem to come upon some particular thought or feeling, and not upon the 'I' which has the thought or feeling. Nevertheless there are some reasons for thinking that we are acquainted with the 'I', though the acquaintance is hard to disentangle from other things. To make clear what sort of reason there is, let us consider for a moment what our acquaintance with particular thoughts really involves.

When I am acquainted with 'my seeing the sun', it seems plain that I am acquainted with two different things in relation to each other. On the one hand there is the sense-datum which represents the sun to me, on the other hand there is that which sees this sense-datum. All acquaintance, such as my acquaintance with the sense-datum which represents the sun, seems obviously a relation between the person acquainted and the object with which the person is acquainted. When a case of acquaintance is one with which I can be acquainted (as I am acquainted with my acquaintance with the sense-datum representing the sun), it is plain that the person acquainted is myself. Thus, when I am acquainted with my seeing the sun, the whole fact with which I am acquainted is 'Self-acquainted-with-sense-datum'.

Further, we know the truth 'I am acquainted with this sense-datum'. It is hard to see how we could know this truth, or even understand what is meant by it, unless we were acquainted with something which we call 'I'. It does not seem necessary to suppose that we are acquainted with a more or less permanent person, the same to-day as yesterday, but it does seem as though we must be acquainted with that thing, whatever its nature, which sees the sun and has acquaintance with sense-data. Thus, in some sense it would seem we must be acquainted with our Selves as opposed to our particular experiences. But the question is difficult, and complicated arguments can be adduced on either side. Hence, although acquaintance with ourselves seems probably to occur, it is not wise to assert that it undoubtedly does occur.

We may therefore sum up as follows what has been said concerning acquaintance with things that exist. We have acquaintance in sensation with the data of the outer senses, and in introspection with the data of what may be called the inner sense—thoughts, feelings, desires, etc.; we have acquaintance in memory with things which have been data either of the outer senses or of the inner sense. Further, it is probable, though not certain, that we have acquaintance with Self, as that which is aware of things or has desires towards things.

In addition to our acquaintance with particular existing things, we also have acquaintance with what we shall call universals, that is to say, general ideas such as whiteness, diversity, brotherhood, and so on. Every complete sentence must contain at least one word which stands for a universal, since all verbs have a meaning which is universal. We shall return to universals later on, in Chapter IX; for the present, it is only necessary to guard against the supposition that whatever we can be acquainted with must be something particular and existent. Awareness of universals is called conceiving, and a universal of which we are aware is called a concept.

It will be seen that among the objects with which we are acquainted are not included physical objects (as opposed to sense-data), nor other people's minds. These things are known to us by what I call 'knowledge by description', which we must now consider.

By a 'description' I mean any phrase of the form 'a so-and-so' or 'the so-and-so'. A phrase of the form 'a so-and-so' I shall call an 'ambiguous' description; a phrase of the form 'the so-and-so' (in the singular) I shall call a 'definite' description. Thus 'a man' is an ambiguous description, and 'the man with the iron mask' is a definite description. There are various problems connected with ambiguous descriptions, but I pass them by, since they do not directly concern the matter we are discussing, which is the nature of our knowledge concerning objects in cases where we know that there is an object answering to a definite description, though we are not acquainted with any such object. This is a matter which is concerned exclusively with definite descriptions. I shall therefore, in the sequel, speak simply of 'descriptions' when I mean 'definite descriptions'. Thus a description will mean any phrase of the form 'the so-and-so' in the singular.

We say that an object is 'known by description' when we know that it is 'the so-and-so', i.e. when we know that there is one object, and no more, having a certain property; and it will generally be implied that we do not have knowledge of the same object by acquaintance. We know that the man with the iron mask existed, and many propositions are known about him; but we do not know who he was. We know that the candidate who gets the most votes will be elected, and in this case we are very likely also acquainted (in the only sense in which one can be acquainted with some one else) with the man who is, in fact, the candidate who will get most votes; but we do not know which of the candidates he is, i.e. we do not know any proposition of the form 'A is the candidate who will get most votes' where A is one of the candidates by name. We shall say that we have 'merely descriptive knowledge' of the so-and-so when, although we know that the so-and-so exists, and although we may possibly be acquainted with the object which is, in fact, the so-and-so, yet we do not know any proposition 'A is the so-and-so', where A is something with which we are acquainted.

When we say 'the so-and-so exists', we mean that there is just one object which is the so-and-so. The proposition 'A is the so-and-so' means that A has the property so-and-so, and nothing else has. 'Mr. A. is the Unionist candidate for this constituency' means 'Mr. A. is a Unionist candidate for this constituency, and no one else is'. 'The Unionist candidate for this constituency exists' means 'some one is a Unionist candidate for this constituency, and no one else is'. Thus, when we are acquainted with an object which is the so-and-so, we know that the so-and-so exists; but we may know that the so-and-so exists when we are not acquainted with any object which we know to be the so-and-so, and even when we are not acquainted with any object which, in fact, is the so-and-so.

Common words, even proper names, are usually really descriptions. That is to say, the thought in the mind of a person using a proper name correctly can generally only be expressed explicitly if we replace the proper name by a description. Moreover, the description required to express the thought will vary for different people, or for the same person at different times. The only thing constant (so long as the name is rightly used) is the object to which the name applies. But so long as this remains constant, the particular description involved usually makes no difference to the truth or falsehood of the proposition in which the name appears.

Let us take some illustrations. Suppose some statement made about Bismarck. Assuming that there is such a thing as direct acquaintance with oneself, Bismarck himself might have used his name directly to designate the particular person with whom he was acquainted. In this case, if he made a judgement about himself, he himself might be a constituent of the judgement. Here the proper name has the direct use which it always wishes to have, as simply standing for a certain object, and not for a description of the object. But if a person who knew Bismarck made a judgement about him, the case is different. What this person was acquainted with were certain sense-data which he connected (rightly, we will suppose) with Bismarck's body. His body, as a physical object, and still more his mind, were only known as the body and the mind connected with these sense-data. That is, they were known by description. It is, of course, very much a matter of chance which characteristics of a man's appearance will come into a friend's mind when he thinks of him; thus the description actually in the friend's mind is accidental. The essential point is that he knows that the various descriptions all apply to the same entity, in spite of not being acquainted with the entity in question.

When we, who did not know Bismarck, make judgement about him, the description in our minds will probably be some more or less vague mass of historical knowledge—far more, in most cases, than is required to identify him. But, for the sake of illustration, let us assume that we think of him as 'the first Chancellor of the German Empire'. Here all the words are abstract except 'German'. The word 'German' will, again, have different meanings for different people. To some it will recall travels in Germany, to some the look of Germany on the map, and so on. But if we are to obtain a description which we know to be applicable, we shall be compelled, at some point, to bring in a reference to a particular with which we are acquainted. Such reference is involved in any mention of past, present, and future (as opposed to definite dates), or of here and there, or of what others have told us. Thus it would seem that, in some way or other, a description known to be applicable to a particular must involve some reference to a particular with which we are acquainted, if our knowledge about the thing described is not to be merely what follows logically from the description. or example, 'the most long-lived of men' is a description involving only universals, which must apply to some man, but we can make no judgements concerning this man which involve knowledge about him beyond what the description gives. If, however, we say, 'The first Chancellor of the German Empire was an astute diplomatist', we can only be assured of the truth of our judgement in virtue of something with which we are acquainted—usually a testimony heard or read. Apart from the information we convey to others, apart from the fact about the actual Bismarck, which gives importance to our judgement, the thought we really have contains the one or more particulars involved, and otherwise consists wholly of concepts.

All names of places—London, England, Europe, the Earth, the Solar System—similarly involve, when used, descriptions which start from some one or more particulars with which we are acquainted. I suspect that even the Universe, as considered by metaphysics, involves such a connexion with particulars. In logic on the contrary, where we are concerned not merely with what does exist, but with whatever might or could exist or be, no reference to actual particulars is involved.

It would seem that, when we make a statement about something only known by description, we often intend to make our statement, not in the form involving the description, but about the actual thing described. That is to say, when we say anything about Bismarck, we should like, if we could, to make the judgement which Bismarck alone can make, namely, the judgement of which he himself is a constituent. In this we are necessarily defeated, since the actual Bismarck is unknown to us. But we know that there is an object B, called Bismarck, and that B was an astute diplomatist. We can thus describe the proposition we should like to affirm, namely, 'B was an astute diplomat', where B is the object which was Bismarck. If we are describing Bismarck as 'the first Chancellor of the German Empire', the proposition we should like to affirm may be described as 'the proposition asserting, concerning the actual object which was the first Chancellor of the German Empire, that this object an astute diplomatist'. What enables us to communicate in spite of the varying descriptions we employ is that we know there is a true proposition concerning the actual Bismarck, and that however we may vary the description (so long as the description is correct) the proposition described is still the same. This proposition, which is described and is known to be true, is what interests us; but we are not acquainted with the proposition itself, and do not know it, though we know it is true.

It will be seen that there are various stages in the removal from acquaintance with particulars: there is Bismarck to people who knew him; Bismarck to those who only know of him through history; the man with the iron mask; the longest-lived of men. These are progressively further removed from acquaintance with particulars; the first comes as near to acquaintance as is possible in regard to another person; in the second, we shall still be said to know 'who Bismarck was'; in the third, we do not know who was the man with the iron mask, though we can know many propositions about him which are not logically deducible from the fact that he wore an iron mask; in the fourth, finally, we know nothing beyond what is logically deducible from the definition of the man. There is a similar hierarchy in the region of universals. Many universals like many particulars, are only known to us by description. But here, as in the case of particulars, knowledge concerning what is known by description is ultimately reducible to knowledge concerning what is known by acquaintance.

The fundamental principle in the analysis of propositions containing descriptions is this: Every proposition which we can understand must be composed wholly of constituents with which we are acquainted.

We shall not at this stage attempt to answer all the objections which may be urged against this fundamental principle. For the present, we shall merely point out that, in some way or other, it must be possible to meet these objections, for it is scarcely conceivable that we can make a judgement or entertain a supposition without knowing what it is that we are judging or supposing about. We must attach some meaning to the words we use, if we are to speak significantly and not utter mere noise; and the meaning we attach to our words must be something with which we are acquainted. Thus when, for example, we make a statement about Julius Caesar, it is plain that Julius Caesar himself is not before our minds, since we are not acquainted with him. We have in mind some description of Julius Caesar: 'the man who was assassinated on the Ides of March', 'the founder of the Roman Empire', or, merely 'the man whose name was Julius Caesar'. (In this last description, Julius Caesar is a noise or shape with which we are acquainted.) Thus our statement does not mean quite what it seems to mean, but means something involving, instead of Julius Caesar, some description of him which is composed wholly of particulars and universals with which we are acquainted.

The chief importance of knowledge by description is that it enables us to pass beyond the limits of our experience. In spite of the fact that we can only know truths which are wholly composed of terms which we have experienced in acquaintance, we can yet have knowledge by description of things which we have never experienced. In view of the very narrow range of our immediate experience, this result is vital, and until it is understood, much of our knowledge must remain mysterious and therefore doubtful.

CHAPTER VI ON INDUCTION

In almost all our previous discussions we have been concerned in the attempt to get clear as to our data in the way of knowledge of existence. What things are there in the universe whose existence is known to us owing to our being acquainted with them? So far, our answer has been that we are acquainted with our sense-data, and, probably, with ourselves. These we know to exist. And past sense-data which are remembered are known to have existed in the past. This knowledge supplies our data.

But if we are to be able to draw inferences from these data—if we are to know of the existence of matter, of other people, of the past before our individual memory begins, or of the future, we must know general principles of some kind by means of which such inferences can be drawn. It must be known to us that the existence of some one sort of thing, A, is a sign of the existence of some other sort of thing, B, either at the same time as A or at some earlier or later time, as, for example, thunder is a sign of the earlier existence of lightning. If this were not known to us, we could never extend our knowledge beyond the sphere of our private experience; and this sphere, as we have seen, is exceedingly limited. The question we have now to consider is whether such an extension is possible, and if so, how it is effected.

Let us take as an illustration a matter about which none of us, in fact, feel the slightest doubt. We are all convinced that the sun will rise to-morrow. Why? Is this belief a mere blind outcome of past experience, or can it be justified as a reasonable belief? It is not easy to find a test by which to judge whether a belief of this kind is reasonable or not, but we can at least ascertain what sort of general beliefs would suffice, if true, to justify the judgement that the sun will rise to-morrow, and the many other similar judgements upon which our actions are based.

It is obvious that if we are asked why we believe the sun will rise to-morrow, we shall naturally answer, 'Because it always has risen every day'. We have a firm belief that it will rise in the future, because it has risen in the past. If we are challenged as to why we believe that it will continue to rise as heretofore, we may appeal to the laws of motion: the earth, we shall say, is a freely rotating body, and such bodies do not cease to rotate unless something interferes from outside, and there is nothing outside to interfere with the earth between now and to-morrow. Of course it might be doubted whether we are quite certain that there is nothing outside to interfere, but this is not the interesting doubt. The interesting doubt is as to whether the laws of motion will remain in operation until to-morrow. If this doubt is raised, we find ourselves in the same position as when the doubt about the sunrise was first raised.

The only reason for believing that the laws of motion remain in operation is that they have operated hitherto, so far as our knowledge of the past enables us to judge. It is true that we have a greater body of evidence from the past in favour of the laws of motion than we have in favour of the sunrise, because the sunrise is merely a particular case of fulfillment of the laws of motion, and there are countless other particular cases. But the real question is: Do any number of cases of a law being fulfilled in the past afford evidence that it will be fulfilled in the future? If not, it becomes plain that we have no ground whatever for expecting the sun to rise to-morrow, or for expecting the bread we shall eat at our next meal not to poison us, or for any of the other scarcely conscious expectations that control our daily lives. It is to be observed that all such expectations are only probable; thus we have not to seek for a proof that they must be fulfilled, but only for some reason in favour of the view that they are likely to be fulfilled.

Now in dealing with this question we must, to begin with, make an important distinction, without which we should soon become involved in hopeless confusions. Experience has shown us that, hitherto, the frequent repetition of some uniform succession or coexistence has been a cause of our expecting the same succession or coexistence on the next occasion. Food that has a certain appearance generally has a certain taste, and it is a severe shock to our expectations when the familiar appearance is found to be associated with an unusual taste. Things which we see become associated, by habit, with certain tactile sensations which we expect if we touch them; one of the horrors of a ghost (in many ghost-stories) is that it fails to give us any sensations of touch. Uneducated people who go abroad for the first time are so surprised as to be incredulous when they find their native language not understood.

And this kind of association is not confined to men; in animals also it is very strong. A horse which has been often driven along a certain road resists the attempt to drive him in a different direction. Domestic animals expect food when they see the person who feeds them. We know that all these rather crude expectations of uniformity are liable to be misleading. The man who has fed the chicken every day throughout its life at last wrings its neck instead, showing that more refined views as to the uniformity of nature would have been useful to the chicken.

But in spite of the misleadingness of such expectations, they nevertheless exist. The mere fact that something has happened a certain number of times causes animals and men to expect that it will happen again. Thus our instincts certainly cause us to believe the sun will rise to-morrow, but we may be in no better a position than the chicken which unexpectedly has its neck wrung. We have therefore to distinguish the fact that past uniformities cause expectations as to the future, from the question whether there is any reasonable ground for giving weight to such expectations after the question of their validity has been raised.

The problem we have to discuss is whether there is any reason for believing in what is called 'the uniformity of nature'. The belief in the uniformity of nature is the belief that everything that has happened or will happen is an instance of some general law to which there are no exceptions. The crude expectations which we have been considering are all subject to exceptions, and therefore liable to disappoint those who entertain them. But science habitually assumes, at least as a working hypothesis, that general rules which have exceptions can be replaced by general rules which have no exceptions. 'Unsupported bodies in air fall' is a general rule to which balloons and aeroplanes are exceptions. But the laws of motion and the law of gravitation, which account for the fact that most bodies fall, also account for the fact that balloons and aeroplanes can rise; thus the laws of motion and the law of gravitation are not subject to these exceptions.

The belief that the sun will rise to-morrow might be falsified if the earth came suddenly into contact with a large body which destroyed its rotation; but the laws of motion and the law of gravitation would not be infringed by such an event. The business of science is to find uniformities, such as the laws of motion and the law of gravitation, to which, so far as our experience extends, there are no exceptions. In this search science has been remarkably successful, and it may be conceded that such uniformities have held hitherto. This brings us back to the question: Have we any reason, assuming that they have always held in the past, to suppose that they will hold in the future?

It has been argued that we have reason to know that the future will resemble the past, because what was the future has constantly become the past, and has always been found to resemble the past, so that we really have experience of the future, namely of times which were formerly future, which we may call past futures. But such an argument really begs the very question at issue. We have experience of past futures, but not of future futures, and the question is: Will future futures resemble past futures? This question is not to be answered by an argument which starts from past futures alone. We have therefore still to seek for some principle which shall enable us to know that the future will follow the same laws as the past.

The reference to the future in this question is not essential. The same question arises when we apply the laws that work in our experience to past things of which we have no experience—as, for example, in geology, or in theories as to the origin of the Solar system. The question we really have to ask is: 'When two things have been found to be often associated, and no instance is known of the one occurring without the other, does the occurrence of one of the two, in a fresh instance, give any good ground for expecting the other?' On our answer to this question must depend the validity of the whole of our expectations as to the future, the whole of the results obtained by induction, and in fact practically all the beliefs upon which our daily life is based.

It must be conceded, to begin with, that the fact that two things have been found often together and never apart does not, by itself, suffice to prove demonstratively that they will be found together in the next case we examine. The most we can hope is that the oftener things are found together, the more probable becomes that they will be found together another time, and that, if they have been found together often enough, the probability will amount almost to certainty. It can never quite reach certainty, because we know that in spite of frequent repetitions there sometimes is a failure at the last, as in the case of the chicken whose neck is wrung. Thus probability is all we ought to seek.

It might be urged, as against the view we are advocating, that we know all natural phenomena to be subject to the reign of law, and that sometimes, on the basis of observation, we can see that only one law can possibly fit the facts of the case. Now to this view there are two answers. The first is that, even if some law which has no exceptions applies to our case, we can never, in practice, be sure that we have discovered that law and not one to which there are exceptions. The second is that the reign of law would seem to be itself only probable, and that our belief that it will hold in the future, or in unexamined cases in the past, is itself based upon the very principle we are examining.

The principle we are examining may be called the principle of induction, and its two parts may be stated as follows:

(a) When a thing of a certain sort A has been found to be associated with a thing of a certain other sort B, and has never been found dissociated from a thing of the sort B, the greater the number of cases in which A and B have been associated, the greater is the probability that they will be associated in a fresh case in which one of them is known to be present;

(b) Under the same circumstances, a sufficient number of cases of association will make the probability of a fresh association nearly a certainty, and will make it approach certainty without limit.

As just stated, the principle applies only to the verification of our expectation in a single fresh instance. But we want also to know that there is a probability in favour of the general law that things of the sort A are always associated with things of the sort B, provided a sufficient number of cases of association are known, and no cases of failure of association are known. The probability of the general law is obviously less than the probability of the particular case, since if the general law is true, the particular case must also be true, whereas the particular case may be true without the general law being true. Nevertheless the probability of the general law is increased by repetitions, just as the probability of the particular case is. We may therefore repeat the two parts of our principle as regards the general law, thus:

(a)The greater the number of cases in which a thing the sort A has been found associated with a thing the sort B, the more probable it is (if no cases of failure of association are known) that A is always associated with B;

(b) Under the same circumstances, a sufficient number of cases of the association of A with B will make it nearly certain that A is always associated with B, and will make this general law approach certainty without limit.

It should be noted that probability is always relative to certain data. In our case, the data are merely the known cases of coexistence of A and B. There may be other data, which might be taken into account, which would gravely alter the probability. For example, a man who had seen a great many white swans might argue by our principle, that on the data it was probable that all swans were white, and this might be a perfectly sound argument. The argument is not disproved by the fact that some swans are black, because a thing may very well happen in spite of the fact that some data render it improbable. In the case of the swans, a man might know that colour is a very variable characteristic in many species of animals, and that, therefore, an induction as to colour is peculiarly liable to error. But this knowledge would be a fresh datum, by no means proving that the probability relatively to our previous data had been wrongly estimated. The fact, therefore, that things often fail to fulfill our expectations is no evidence that our expectations will not probably be fulfilled in a given case or a given class of cases. Thus our inductive principle is at any rate not capable of being disproved by an appeal to experience.

The inductive principle, however, is equally incapable of being proved by an appeal to experience. Experience might conceivably confirm the inductive principle as regards the cases that have been already examined; but as regards unexamined cases, it is the inductive principle alone that can justify any inference from what has been examined to what has not been examined. All arguments which, on the basis of experience, argue as to the future or the unexperienced parts of the past or present, assume the inductive principle; hence we can never use experience to prove the inductive principle without begging the question. Thus we must either accept the inductive principle on the ground of its intrinsic evidence, or forgo all justification of our expectations about the future. If the principle is unsound, we have no reason to expect the sun to rise to-morrow, to expect bread to be more nourishing than a stone, or to expect that if we throw ourselves off the roof we shall fall. When we see what looks like our best friend approaching us, we shall have no reason to suppose that his body is not inhabited by the mind of our worst enemy or of some total stranger. All our conduct is based upon associations which have worked in the past, and which we therefore regard as likely to work in the future; and this likelihood is dependent for its validity upon the inductive principle.

The general principles of science, such as the belief in the reign of law, and the belief that every event must have a cause, are as completely dependent upon the inductive principle as are the beliefs of daily life. All such general principles are believed because mankind have found innumerable instances of their truth and no instances of their falsehood. But this affords no evidence for their truth in the future, unless the inductive principle is assumed.

Thus all knowledge which, on a basis of experience tells us something about what is not experienced, is based upon a belief which experience can neither confirm nor confute, yet which, at least in its more concrete applications, appears to be as firmly rooted in us as many of the facts of experience. The existence and justification of such beliefs—for the inductive principle, as we shall see, is not the only example—raises some of the most difficult and most debated problems of philosophy. We will, in the next chapter, consider briefly what may be said to account for such knowledge, and what is its scope and its degree of certainty.

CHAPTER VII ON OUR KNOWLEDGE OF GENERAL PRINCIPLES

We saw in the preceding chapter that the principle of Induction, while necessary to the validity of all arguments based on experience, is itself not capable of being proved by experience, and yet is unhesitatingly believed by every one, at least in all its concrete applications. In these characteristics the principle of induction does not stand alone. There are a number of other principles which cannot be proved or disproved by experience, but are used in arguments which start from what is experienced.

Some of these principles have even greater evidence than the principle of induction, and the knowledge of them has the same degree of certainty as the knowledge of the existence of sense-data. They constitute the means of drawing inferences from what is given in sensation; and if what we infer is to be true, it is just as necessary that our principles of inference should be true as it is that our data should be true. The principles of inference are apt to be overlooked because of their very obviousness—the assumption involved is assented to without our realizing that it is an assumption. But it is very important to realize the use of principles of inference, if a correct theory of knowledge is to be obtained; for our knowledge of them raises interesting and difficult questions.

In all our knowledge of general principles, what actually happens is that first of all we realize some particular application of the principle, and then we realize the particularity is irrelevant, and that there is a generality which may equally truly be affirmed. This is of course familiar in such matters as teaching arithmetic: 'two and two are four' is first learnt in the case of some particular pair of couples, and then in some other particular case, and so on, until at last it becomes possible to see that it is true of any pair of couples. The same thing happens with logical principles. Suppose two men are discussing what day of the month it is. One of them says, 'At least you will admit that if yesterday was the 15th to-day must the 16th.' 'Yes', says the other, 'I admit that.' 'And you know', the first continues, 'that yesterday was the 15th, because you dined with Jones, and your diary will tell you that was on the 15th.' 'Yes', says the second; 'therefore to-day is the 16th.'

Now such an argument is not hard to follow; and if it is granted that its premisses are true in fact, no one deny that the conclusion must also be true. But it depends for its truth upon an instance of a general logical principle. The logical principle is as follows: 'Suppose it known that if this is true, then that is true. Suppose it also known that this is true, then it follows that that is true.' When it is the case that if this is true, that is true, we shall say that this 'implies' that, that that 'follows from' this. Thus our principle states that if this implies that, and this is true, then that is true. In other words, 'anything implied by a proposition is true', or 'whatever follows from a true proposition is true'.

This principle is really involved—at least, concrete instances of it are involved—in all demonstrations. Whenever one thing which we believe is used to prove something else, which we consequently believe, this principle is relevant. If any one asks: 'Why should I accept the results of valid arguments based on true premisses?' we can only answer by appealing to our principle. In fact, the truth of the principle is impossible to doubt, and its obviousness is so great that at first sight it seems almost trivial. Such principles, however, are not trivial to the philosopher, for they show that we may have indubitable knowledge which is in no way derived from objects of sense.

The above principle is merely one of a certain number of self-evident logical principles. Some at least of these principles must be granted before any argument or proof becomes possible. When some of them have been granted, others can be proved, though these others, so long as they are simple, are just as obvious as the principles taken for granted. For no very good reason, three of these principles have been singled out by tradition under the name of 'Laws of Thought'.

They are as follows:

1. The law of identity: 'Whatever is, is.'
2. The law of contradiction: 'Nothing can both be and not be.'
3. The law of excluded middle: 'Everything must either be or not be.'

These three laws are samples of self-evident logical principles, but are not really more fundamental or more self-evident than various other similar principles: for instance, the one we considered just now, which states that what follows from a true premise is true. The name 'laws of thought' is also misleading, for what is important is not the fact that we think in accordance with these laws, but the fact that things behave in accordance with them; in other words, the fact that when we think in accordance with them we think truly. But this is a large question, to which we return at a later stage.

In addition to the logical principles which enable us to prove from a given premiss that something is *certainly* true, there are other logical principles which enable us to prove, from a given premiss, that there is a greater or less probability that something is true. An example of such principles—perhaps the most important example—is the inductive principle, which we considered in the preceding chapter.

One of the great historic controversies in philosophy is the controversy between the two schools called respectively 'empiricists' and 'rationalists'. The empiricists—who are best represented by the British philosophers, Locke, Berkeley, and Hume—maintained that all our knowledge is derived from experience; the rationalists—who are represented by the continental philosophers of the seventeenth century, especially Descartes and Leibniz—maintained that, in addition to what we know by experience, there are certain 'innate ideas' and 'innate principles', which we know independently of experience. It has now become possible to decide with some confidence as to the truth or falsehood of these opposing schools. It must be admitted, for the reasons already stated, that logical principles are known to us, and cannot be themselves proved by experience, since all proof presupposes them. In this, therefore, which was the most important point of the controversy, the rationalists were in the right.

On the other hand, even that part of our knowledge which is logically independent of experience (in the sense that experience cannot prove it) is yet elicited and caused by experience. It is on occasion of particular experiences that we become aware of the general laws which their connexions exemplify. It would certainly be absurd to suppose that there are innate principles in the sense that babies are born with a knowledge of everything which men know and which cannot be deduced from what is experienced. For this reason, the word 'innate' would not now be employed to describe our knowledge of logical principles. The phrase 'a priori' is less objectionable, and is more usual in modern writers. Thus, while admitting that all knowledge is elicited and caused by experience, we shall nevertheless hold that some knowledge is a priori, in the sense that the experience which makes us think of it does not suffice to prove it, but merely so directs our attention that we see its truth without requiring any proof from experience.

There is another point of great importance, in which the empiricists were in the right as against the rationalists. Nothing can be known to exist except by the help of experience. That is to say, if we wish to prove that something of which we have no direct experience exists, we must have among our premisses the existence of one or more things of which we have direct experience. Our belief that the Emperor of China exists, for example, rests upon testimony, and testimony consists, in the last analysis, of sense-data seen or heard in reading or being spoken to. Rationalists believed that, from general consideration as to what must be, they could deduce the existence of this or that in the actual world. In this belief they seem to have been mistaken. All the knowledge that we can acquire a priori concerning existence seems to be hypothetical: it tells us that if one thing exists, another must exist, or, more generally, that if one proposition is true another must be true. This is exemplified by principles we have already dealt with, such as 'if this is true, and this implies that, then that is true', of 'if this and that have been repeatedly found connected, they will probably be connected in the next instance in which one of them is found.' Thus the scope and power of a priori principles is strictly limited. All knowledge that something exists must be in part dependent on experience. When anything is known immediately, its existence is known by experience alone; when anything is proved to exist, without being known immediately, both experience and a priori principles must be required in the proof. Knowledge is called empirical when it rests wholly or partly upon experience. Thus all knowledge which asserts existence is empirical, and the only a priori knowledge concerning existence is hypothetical, giving connexions among things that exist or may exist, but not giving actual existence.

A priori knowledge is not all of the logical kind we have been hitherto considering. Perhaps the most important example of non-logical a priori knowledge is knowledge as to ethical value. I am not speaking of judgements as to what is useful or as to what is virtuous, for such judgements do require empirical premisses; I am speaking of judgements as to the intrinsic desirability of things. If something is useful, it must be useful because it secures some end, the end must, if we have gone far enough, be valuable on its own account, and not merely because it is useful for some further end. Thus all judgements as to what is useful depend upon judgements as to what has value on its own account.

We judge, for example, that happiness is more desirable than misery, knowledge than ignorance, goodwill than hatred, and so on. Such judgements must, in part at least, be immediate and a priori. Like our previous a priori judgements, they may be elicited by experience, and indeed they must be; for it seems not possible to judge whether anything is intrinsically valuable unless we have experienced something of the same kind. But it is fairly obvious that they cannot be proved by experience; for the fact that a thing exists or does not exist cannot prove either that it is good that it should exist or that it is bad. The pursuit of this subject belongs to ethics, where the impossibility of deducing what ought to be from what is has to established. In the present connexion, it is only important to realize that knowledge as to what is intrinsically of value is a priori in the same sense in which logic is a priori, namely in the sense that the truth of such knowledge can be neither proved nor disproved by experience.

All pure mathematics is a priori, like logic. This is strenuously denied by the empirical philosophers, who maintained that experience was as much the source of our knowledge of arithmetic as of our knowledge of geography. They maintained that by the repeated experience of seeing two things and two other things, and finding that altogether they made four things, we were led by induction to the conclusion that two things and two other things would always make four things altogether. If, however, this were the source of our knowledge that two and two are four we should proceed differently, in persuading ourselves of its truth, from the way in which we do actually proceed. In fact, a certain number of instances are needed to make us think of two abstractly, rather than of two coins or two books or two people, or two of any other specified kind. But as soon as we are able to divest our thoughts of irrelevant particularity, we become able to see the general principle that two and two are four; any one instance is seen to be typical and the examination of other instances becomes unnecessary.

The same thing is exemplified in geometry. If we want to prove some property of all triangles, we draw some one triangle and reason about it; but we can avoid making use of any property which it does not share with all other triangles, and thus, from our particular case, we obtain a general result. We do not, in fact, feel our certainty that two and two are four increased by fresh instances, because, as soon as we have seen the truth of this proposition, our certainty becomes so great as to be incapable of growing greater. Moreover, we feel some quality of necessity about the proposition 'two and two are four', which is absent from even the best attested empirical generalizations. Such generalizations always remain mere facts: we feel that there might be a world in which they were false, though in the actual world they happen to be true. In any possible world, on the contrary, we feel that two and two would be four: this is not a mere fact, but a necessity to which everything actual and possible must conform.

The case may be made clearer by considering a genuinely empirical generalization, such as 'All men are mortal.' It is plain that we believe this proposition, in the first place, because there is no known instance of men living beyond a certain age, and in the second place because there seem to be physiological grounds for thinking that an organism such as a man's body must sooner or later wear out. Neglecting the second ground, and considering merely our experience of men's mortality, it is plain that we should not be content with one quite clearly understood instance of a man dying, whereas, in the case of 'two and two are four', one instance does suffice, when carefully considered, to persuade us that the same must happen in any other instance. Also we can be forced to admit, on reflection, that there may be some doubt, however slight, as to whether all men are mortal. This may be made plain by the attempt to imagine two different worlds, in one of which there are men who are not mortal, while in the other two and two make five. When Swift invites us to consider the race of Struldbugs who never die, we are able to acquiesce in imagination. But a world where two and two make five seems quite on a different level. We feel that such a world, if there were one, would upset the whole fabric of our knowledge and reduce us to utter doubt.

The fact is that, in simple mathematical judgements such as 'two and two are four', and also in many judgements of logic, we can know the general proposition without inferring it from instances, although some instance is usually necessary to make clear to us what the general proposition means. This is why there is real utility in the process of deduction, which goes from the general to the general, or from the general to the particular, as well as in the process of induction, which goes from the particular to the particular, or from the particular to the general. It is an old debate among philosophers whether deduction ever gives new knowledge. We can now see that in certain cases, at least, it does do so. If we already know that two and two always make four, and we know that Brown and Jones are two, and so are Robinson and Smith, we can deduce that Brown and Jones and Robinson and Smith are four. This is new knowledge, not contained in our premisses, because the general proposition, 'two and two are four', never told us there were such people as Brown and Jones and Robinson and Smith, and the particular premisses do not tell us that there were four of them, whereas the particular proposition deduced does tell us both these things.

But the newness of the knowledge is much less certain if we take the stock instance of deduction that is always given in books on logic, namely, 'All men are mortal; Socrates is a man, therefore Socrates is mortal.' In this case, what we really know beyond reasonable doubt is that certain men, A, B, C, were mortal, since, in fact, they have died. If Socrates is one of these men, it is foolish to go the roundabout way through 'all men are mortal' to arrive at the conclusion that probably Socrates is mortal. If Socrates is not one of the men on whom our induction is based, we shall still do better to argue straight from our A, B, C, to Socrates, than to go round by the general proposition, 'all men are mortal'. For the probability that Socrates is mortal is greater, on our data, than the probability that all men are mortal. (This is obvious, because if all men are mortal, so is Socrates; but if Socrates is mortal, it does not follow that all men are mortal.) Hence we shall reach the conclusion that Socrates is mortal with a greater approach to certainty if we make our argument purely inductive than if we go by way of 'all men are mortal' and then use deduction.

This illustrates the difference between general propositions known a priori, such as 'two and two are four', and empirical generalizations such as 'all men are mortal'. In regard to the former, deduction is the right mode of argument, whereas in regard to the latter, induction is always theoretically preferable, and warrants a greater confidence in the truth of our conclusion, because all empirical generalizations are more uncertain than the instances of them.

We have now seen that there are propositions known a priori , and that among them are the propositions of logic and pure mathematics, as well as the fundamental propositions of ethics. The question which must next occupy us is this: How is it possible that there should be such knowledge? And more particularly, how can there be knowledge of general propositions in cases where we have not examined all the instances, and indeed never can examine them all, because their number is infinite? These questions, which were first brought prominently forward by the German philosopher Kant (1724–1804), are very difficult, and historically very important.

CHAPTER VIII HOW A PRIORI KNOWLEDGE IS POSSIBLE

Immanuel Kant is generally regarded as the greatest of the modern philosophers. Though he lived through the Seven Years War and the French Revolution, he never interrupted his teaching of philosophy at Konigsberg in East Prussia. His most distinctive contribution was the invention of what he called the 'critical' philosophy, which, assuming as a datum that there is knowledge of various kinds, inquired how such knowledge comes to be possible, and deduced, from the answer to this inquiry, many metaphysical results as to the nature of the world. Whether these results were valid may well be doubted. But Kant undoubtedly deserves credit for two things: first, for having perceived that we have a priori knowledge which is not purely 'analytic', i.e. such that the opposite would be self-contradictory; and secondly, for having made evident the philosophical importance of the theory of knowledge.

Before the time of Kant, it was generally held that whatever knowledge was a priori must be 'analytic'. What this word means will be best illustrated by examples. If I say, 'A bald man is a man', 'A plane figure is a figure', 'A bad poet is a poet', I make a purely analytic judgement: the subject spoken about is given as having at least two properties, of which one is singled out to be asserted of it. Such propositions as the above are trivial, and would never be enunciated in real life except by an orator preparing the way for a piece of sophistry. They are called 'analytic' because the predicate is obtained by merely analysing the subject. Before the time of Kant it was thought that all judgements of which we could be certain a priori were of this kind: that in all of them there was a predicate which was only part of the subject of which it was asserted. If this were so, we should be involved in a definite contradiction if we attempted to deny thinking that could be known a priori. 'A bald man is not bald' would assert and deny baldness of the same man, and would therefore contradict itself. Thus according to the philosophers before Kant, the law of contradiction, which asserts that nothing can at the same time have and not have a certain property, sufficed to establish the truth of all a priori knowledge.

Hume (1711–1776), who preceded Kant, accepting the usual view as to what makes knowledge a priori, discovered that, in many cases which had previously been supposed analytic, and notably in the case of cause and effect, the connexion was really synthetic. Before Hume, rationalists at least had supposed that the effect could be logically deduced from the cause, if only we had sufficient knowledge. Hume argued—correctly, as would now be generally admitted—that this could not be done. Hence he inferred the far more doubtful proposition that nothing could be known a priori about the connexion of cause and effect. Kant, who had been educated in the rationalist tradition, was much perturbed by Hume's skepticism, and endeavoured to find an answer to it. He perceived that not only the connexion of cause and effect, but all the propositions of arithmetic and geometry, are 'synthetic' i.e. not analytic: in all these propositions, no analysis of the subject will reveal the predicate. His stock instance was the proposition $7 + 5 = 12$. He pointed out, quite truly, that 7 and 5 have to be put together to give 12: the idea of 12 is not contained in them, nor even in the idea of adding them together. Thus he was led to the conclusion that all pure mathematics, though a priori, is synthetic; and this conclusion raised a new problem of which he endeavoured to find the solution.

The question which Kant put at the beginning of his philosophy, namely 'How is pure mathematics possible?' is an interesting and difficult one, to which every philosophy which is not purely sceptical must find some answer. The answer of the pure empiricists, that our mathematical knowledge is derived by induction from particular instances, we have already seen to be inadequate, for two reasons: first, that the validity of the inductive principle itself cannot be proved by induction; secondly, that the general propositions of mathematics, such as 'two and two always make four', can obviously be known with certainty by consideration of a single instance, and gain nothing by enumeration of other cases in which they have been found to be true. Thus our knowledge of the general propositions of mathematics (and the same applies to logic) must be accounted for otherwise than our (merely probable) knowledge of empirical generalizations such as 'all men are mortal'.

The problem arises through the fact that such knowledge is general, whereas all experience is particular. It seems strange that we should apparently be able to know some truths in advance about particular things of which we have as yet no experience; but it cannot easily be doubted that logic and arithmetic will apply to such things. We do not know who will be the inhabitants of London a hundred years hence; but we know that any two of them and any other two of them will make four of them. This apparent power of anticipating facts about things of which we have no experience is certainly surprising. Kant's solution of the problem, though not valid in my opinion, is interesting. It is, however, very difficult, and is differently understood by different philosophers. We can, therefore, only give the merest outline of it, and even that will be thought misleading by many exponents of Kant's system.

What Kant maintained was that in all our experience there are two elements to be distinguished, the one due to the object (i.e. to what we have called the 'physical object'), the other due to our own nature. We saw, in discussing matter and sense-data, that the physical object is different from the associated sense-data, and that the sense-data are to be regarded as resulting from an interaction between the physical object and ourselves. So far, we are in agreement with Kant. But what is distinctive of Kant is the way in which he apportions the shares of ourselves and the physical object respectively. He considers that the crude material given in sensation—the colour, hardness etc.—is due to the object, and that what we supply is the arrangement in space and time, and all the relations between sense-data which result from comparison or from considering one as the cause of the other or in any other way. His chief reason in favour of this view is that we seem to have a priori knowledge as to space and time and causality and comparison, but not as to the actual crude material of sensation. We can be sure, he says, that anything we shall ever experience must show the characteristics affirmed of it in our a priori knowledge, because these characteristics are due to our own nature, and therefore nothing can ever come into our experience without acquiring these characteristics.

The physical object, which he calls the 'thing in itself',[1] he regards as essentially unknowable; what can be known is the object as we have it in experience, which he calls the 'phenomenon'. The phenomenon, being a joint product of us and the thing in itself, is sure to have those characteristics which are due to us, and is therefore sure to conform to our a priori knowledge. Hence this knowledge, though true of all actual and possible experience, must not be supposed to apply outside experience. Thus in spite of the existence of a priori knowledge, we cannot know anything about the thing in itself or about what is not an actual or possible object of experience. In this way he tries to reconcile and harmonize the contentions of the rationalists with the arguments of the empiricists.

Apart from minor grounds on which Kant's philosophy may be criticized, there is one main objection which seems fatal to any attempt to deal with the problem of a priori knowledge by his method. The thing to be accounted for is our certainty that the facts must always conform to logic and arithmetic. To say that logic and arithmetic are contributed by us does not account for this. Our nature is as much a fact of the existing world as anything, and there can be no certainty that it will remain constant. It might happen, if Kant is right, that to-morrow our nature would so change as to make two and two become five. This possibility seems never to have occurred to him, yet it is one which utterly destroys the certainty and universality which he is anxious to vindicate for arithmetical propositions. It is true that this possibility, formally, is inconsistent with the Kantian view that time itself is a form imposed by the subject upon phenomena, so that our real Self is not in time and has no to-morrow. But he will still have to suppose that the time-order of phenomena is determined by characteristics of what is behind phenomena, and this suffices for the substance of our argument.

Reflection, moreover, seems to make it clear that, if there is any truth in our arithmetical beliefs, they must apply to things equally whether we think of them or not. Two physical objects and two other physical objects must make four physical objects, even if physical objects cannot be experienced. To assert this is certainly within the scope of what we mean when we state that two and two are four. Its truth is just as indubitable as the truth of the assertion that two phenomena and two other phenomena make four phenomena. Thus Kant's solution unduly limits the scope of a priori propositions, in addition to failing in the attempt at explaining their certainty.

Apart from the special doctrines advocated by Kant, it is very common among philosophers to regard what is a priori as in some sense mental, as concerned rather with the way we must think than with any fact of the outer world. We noted in the preceding chapter the three principles commonly called 'laws of thought'. The view which led to their being so named is a natural one, but there are strong reasons for thinking that it is erroneous. Let us take as an illustration the law of contradiction. This is commonly stated in the form 'Nothing can both be and not be', which is intended to express the fact that nothing can at once have and not have a given quality. Thus, for example, if a tree is a beech it cannot also be not a beech; if my table is rectangular it cannot also be not rectangular, and so on.

Now what makes it natural to call this principle a law of thought is that it is by thought rather than by outward observation that we persuade ourselves of its necessary truth. When we have seen that a tree is a beech, we do not need to look again in order to ascertain whether it is also not a beech; thought alone makes us know that this is impossible. But the conclusion that the law of contradiction is a law of thought is nevertheless erroneous. What we believe, when we believe the law of contradiction, is not that the mind is so made that it must believe the law of contradiction. This belief is a subsequent result of psychological reflection, which presupposes the belief in the law of contradiction. The belief in the law of contradiction is a belief about things, not only about thoughts. It is not, e.g., the belief that if we think a certain tree is a beech, we cannot at the same time think that it is not a beech; it is the belief that if a tree is a beech, it cannot at the same time be not a beech. Thus the law of contradiction is about

[1]Kant's 'thing in itself' is identical in definition with the physical object, namely, it is the cause of sensations. In the properties deduced from the definition it is not identical, since Kant held (in spite of some inconsistency as regards cause) that we can know that none of the categories are applicable to the 'thing in itself'.

things, and not merely about thoughts; and although belief in the law of contradiction is a thought, the law of contradiction itself is not a thought, but a fact concerning the things in the world. If this, which we believe when we believe the law of contradiction, were not true of the things in the world, the fact that we were compelled to think it true would not save the law of contradiction from being false; and this shows that the law is not a law of thought.

A similar argument applies to any other a priori judgement. When we judge that two and two are four, we are not making a judgement about our thoughts, but about all actual or possible couples. The fact that our minds are so constituted as to believe that two and two are four, though it is true, is emphatically not what we assert when we assert that two and two are four. And no fact about the constitution of our minds could make it true that two and two are four. Thus our a priori knowledge, if it is not erroneous, is not merely knowledge about the constitution of our minds, but is applicable to whatever the world may contain, both what is mental and what is non-mental.

The fact seems to be that all our a priori knowledge is concerned with entities which do not, properly speaking exist, either in the mental or in the physical world. These entities are such as can be named by parts of speech which are not substantives; they are such entities as qualities and relations. Suppose, for instance, that I am in my room. I exist, and my room exists; but does 'in' exist? Yet obviously the word 'in' has a meaning; it denotes a relation which holds between me and my room. This relation is something, although we cannot say that it exists in the same sense in which I and my room exist. The relation 'in' is something which we can think about and understand, for, if we could not understand it, we could not understand the sentence 'I am in my room'. Many philosophers, following Kant, have maintained that relations are the work of the mind, that things in themselves have no relations, but that the mind brings them together in one act of thought and thus produces the relations which it judges them to have.

This view, however, seems open to objections similar to those which we urged before against Kant. It seems plain that it is not thought which produces the truth of the proposition 'I am in my room'. It may be true that an earwig is in my room, even if neither I nor the earwig nor any one else is aware of this truth; for this truth concerns only the earwig and the room, and does not depend upon anything else. Thus relations, as we shall see more fully in the next chapter, must be placed in a world which is neither mental nor physical. This world is of great importance to philosophy, and in particular to the problems of a priori knowledge. In the next chapter we shall proceed to develop its nature and its bearing upon the questions with which we have been dealing.

CHAPTER IX THE WORLD OF UNIVERSALS

At the end of the preceding chapter we saw that such entities as relations appear to have a being which is in some way different from that of physical objects, and also different from that of minds and from that of sense-data. In the present chapter we have to consider what is the nature of this kind of being, and also what objects there are that have this kind of being. We will begin with the latter question.

The problem with which we are now concerned is a very old one, since it was brought into philosophy by Plato. Plato's 'theory of ideas' is an attempt to solve this very problem, and in my opinion it is one of the most successful attempts hitherto made. The theory to be advocated in what follows is largely Plato's, with merely such modifications as time has shown to be necessary.

The way the problem arose for Plato was more or less as follows. Let us consider, say, such a notion as justice. If we ask ourselves what justice is, it is natural to proceed by considering this, that, and the other just act, with a view to discovering what they have in common. They must all, in some sense, partake of a common nature, which will be found in whatever is just and in nothing else. This common nature, in virtue of which they are all just, will be justice itself, the pure essence the admixture of which with facts of ordinary life produces the multiplicity of just acts. Similarly with any other word which may be applicable to common facts, such as 'whiteness' for example. The word will be applicable to a number of particular things because they all participate in a common nature or essence. This pure essence is what Plato calls an 'idea' or 'form'. (It must not be supposed that 'ideas', in his sense, exist in minds, though they may be apprehended by minds.) The 'idea' justice is not identical with anything that is just: it is something other than particular things, which particular things partake of. Not being particular, it cannot itself exist in the world of sense. Moreover it is not fleeting or changeable like the things of sense: it is eternally itself, immutable and indestructible.

Thus Plato is led to a supra-sensible world, more real than the common world of sense, the unchangeable world of ideas, which alone gives to the world of sense whatever pale reflection of reality may belong to it. The truly real world, for Plato, is the world of ideas; for whatever we may attempt to say about things in the world of sense, we can only succeed in saying that they participate in such and such ideas, which, therefore, constitute all their character. Hence it is easy to pass on into a mysticism. We may hope, in a mystic illumination, to see the ideas as we see objects of sense; and we may imagine that the ideas exist in heaven. These mystical developments are very natural, but the basis of the theory is in logic, and it is as based in logic that we have to consider it.

The word 'idea' has acquired, in the course of time, many associations which are quite misleading when applied to Plato's 'ideas'. We shall therefore use the word 'universal' instead of the word 'idea', to describe what Plato meant. The essence of the sort of entity that Plato meant is that it is opposed to the particular things that are given in sensation. We speak of whatever is given in sensation, or is of the same nature as things given in sensation, as a particular; by opposition to this, a universal will be anything which may be shared by many particulars, and has those characteristics which, as we saw, distinguish justice and whiteness from just acts and white things.

When we examine common words, we find that, broadly speaking, proper names stand for particulars, while other substantives, adjectives, prepositions, and verbs stand for universals. Pronouns stand for particulars, but are ambiguous: it is only by the context or the circumstances that we know what particulars they stand for. The word 'now' stands for a particular, namely the present moment; but like pronouns, it stands for an ambiguous particular, because the present is always changing.

It will be seen that no sentence can be made up without at least one word which denotes a universal. The nearest approach would be some such statement as 'I like this'. But even here the word 'like' denotes a universal, for I may like other things, and other people may like things. Thus all truths involve universals, and all knowledge of truths involves acquaintance with universals.

Seeing that nearly all the words to be found in the dictionary stand for universals, it is strange that hardly anybody except students of philosophy ever realizes that there are such entities as universals. We do not naturally dwell upon those words in a sentence which do not stand for particulars; and if we are forced to dwell upon a word which stands for a universal, we naturally think of it as standing for some one of the particulars that come under the universal. When, for example, we hear the sentence, 'Charles I's head was cut off', we may naturally enough think of Charles I, of Charles I's head, and of the operation of cutting off his head, which are all particulars; but we do not naturally dwell upon what is meant by the word 'head' or the word 'cut', which is a universal. We feel such words to be incomplete and insubstantial; they seem to demand a context before anything can be done with them. Hence we succeed in avoiding all notice of universals as such, until the study of philosophy forces them upon our attention.

Even among philosophers, we may say, broadly, that only those universals which are named by adjectives or substantives have been much or often recognized, while those named by verbs and prepositions have been usually overlooked. This omission has had a very great effect upon philosophy; it is hardly too much to say that most metaphysics, since Spinoza, has been largely determined by it. The way this has occurred is, in outline, as follows: Speaking generally, adjectives and common nouns express qualities or properties of single things, whereas prepositions and verbs tend to express relations between two or more things. Thus the neglect of prepositions and verbs led to the belief that every proposition can be regarded as attributing a property to a single thing, rather than as expressing a relation between two or more things. Hence it was supposed that, ultimately, there can be no such entities as relations between things. Hence either there can be only one thing in the universe, or, if there are many things, they cannot possibly interact in any way, since any interaction would be a relation, and relations are impossible.

The first of these views, advocated by Spinoza and held in our own day by Bradley and many other philosophers, is called *monism*; the second, advocated by Leibniz but not very common nowadays, is called *monadism*, because each of the isolated things is called a *monad*. Both these opposing philosophies, interesting as they are, result, in my opinion, from an undue attention to one sort of universals, namely the sort represented by adjectives and substantives rather than by verbs and prepositions.

As a matter of fact, if any one were anxious to deny altogether that there are such things as universals, we should find that we cannot strictly prove that there are such entities as qualities, i.e. the universals represented by adjectives and substantives, whereas we can prove that there must be relations, i.e. the sort of universals generally represented by verbs and prepositions. Let us take in illustration the universal whiteness. If we believe that there is such a universal, we shall say that things are white because they have the quality of whiteness. This view, however, was strenuously denied by Berkeley and Hume, who have been followed in this by later empiricists. The form which their denial took was to deny that there are such things as 'abstract ideas'. When we want to think of whiteness, they said, we form an image of some particular white thing, and reason concerning this particular, taking care not to deduce anything concerning it which we cannot see to be equally true of any other white thing. As an account of our actual mental processes, this is no doubt largely true. In geometry, for example, when we wish to prove something about all triangles, we draw a particular triangle and reason about it, taking care not to use any characteristic which it does not share with other triangles. The beginner, in order to avoid error, often finds it useful to draw several triangles, as unlike each other as possible, in order to make sure that his reasoning is equally applicable to all of them. But a difficulty emerges as soon as we ask ourselves how we know that a thing is white or a triangle. If we wish to avoid the universals whiteness and triangularity, we shall choose some particular patch of white or some particular triangle, and say that anything is white or a triangle if it has the right sort of resemblance to our chosen particular. But then the resemblance required will have to be a universal. Since there are many white things, the resemblance must hold between many pairs of particular white things; and this is the characteristic of a universal. It will be useless to say that there is a different resemblance for each pair, for then we shall have to say that these resemblances resemble each other, and thus at last we shall be forced to admit resemblance as a universal. The relation of resemblance, therefore, must be a true universal. And having been forced to admit this universal, we find that it is no longer worth while to invent difficult and unplausible theories to avoid the admission of such universals as whiteness and triangularity.

Berkeley and Hume failed to perceive this refutation of their rejection of 'abstract ideas', because, like their adversaries, they only thought of qualities, and altogether ignored relations as universals. We have therefore here another respect in which the rationalists appear to have been in the right as against the empiricists, although, owing to the neglect or denial of relations, the deductions made by rationalists were, if anything, more apt to be mistaken than those made by empiricists.

Having now seen that there must be such entities as universals, the next point to be proved is that their being is not merely mental. By this is meant that whatever being belongs to them is independent of their being thought of or in any way apprehended by minds. We have already touched on this subject at the end of the preceding chapter, but we must now consider more fully what sort of being it is that belongs to universals.

Consider such a proposition as 'Edinburgh is north of London'. Here we have a relation between two places, and it seems plain that the relation subsists independently of our knowledge of it. When we come to know that Edinburgh is north of London, we come to know something which has to do only with Edinburgh and London: we do not cause the truth of the proposition by coming to know it, on the contrary we merely apprehend a fact which was there before we knew it. The part of the earth's surface where Edinburgh stands would be north of the part where London stands, even if there were no human being to know about north and south, and even if there were no minds at all in the universe. This is, of course, denied by many philosophers, either for Berkeley's reasons or for Kant's. But we have already considered these reasons, and decided that they are inadequate. We may therefore now assume it to be true that nothing mental is presupposed in the fact that Edinburgh is north of London. But this fact involves the relation 'north of', which is a universal; and it would be impossible for the whole fact to involve nothing mental if the relation 'north of', which is a constituent part of the fact, did involve anything mental. Hence we must admit that the relation, like the terms it relates, is not dependent upon thought, but belongs to the independent world which thought apprehends but does not create.

This conclusion, however, is met by the difficulty that the relation 'north of' does not seem to exist in the same sense in which Edinburgh and London exist. If we ask 'Where and when does this relation exist?' the answer must be 'Nowhere and nowhen'. There is no place or time where we can find the relation 'north of'. It does not exist in Edinburgh any more than in London, for it relates the two and is neutral as between them. Nor can we say that it exists at any particular time. Now everything that can be apprehended by the senses or by introspection exists at some particular time. Hence the relation 'north of' is radically different from such things. It is neither in space nor in time, neither material nor mental; yet it is something.

It is largely the very peculiar kind of being that belongs to universals which has led many people to suppose that they are really mental. We can think of a universal, and our thinking then exists in a perfectly ordinary sense, like any other mental act. Suppose, for example, that we are thinking of whiteness. Then in one sense it may be said that whiteness is 'in our mind'. We have here the same ambiguity as we noted in discussing Berkeley in Chapter IV. In the strict sense, it is not whiteness that is in our mind, but the act of thinking of whiteness. The connected ambiguity in the word 'idea', which we noted at the same time, also causes confusion here. In one sense of this word, namely the sense in which it denotes the object of an act of thought, whiteness is an 'idea'. Hence, if the ambiguity is not guarded against, we may come to think that whiteness is an 'idea' in the other sense, i.e. an act of thought; and thus we come to think that whiteness is mental. But in so thinking, we rob it of its essential quality of universality. One man's act of thought is necessarily a different thing from another man's; one man's act of thought at one time is necessarily a different thing from the same man's act of thought at another time. Hence, if whiteness were the thought as opposed to its object, no two different men could think of it, and no one man could think of it twice. That which many different thoughts of whiteness have in common is their object, and this object is different from all of them. Thus universals are not thoughts, though when known they are the objects of thoughts.

We shall find it convenient only to speak of things existing when they are in time, that is to say, when we can point to some time at which they exist (not excluding the possibility of their existing at all times). Thus thoughts and feelings, minds and physical objects exist. But universals do not exist in this sense; we shall say that they subsist or have being, where 'being' is opposed to 'existence' as being timeless. The world of universals, therefore, may also be described as the world of being. The world of being is unchangeable, rigid, exact, delightful to the mathematician, the logician, the builder of metaphysical systems, and all who love perfection more than life. The world of existence is fleeting, vague, without sharp boundaries, without any clear plan or arrangement, but it contains all thoughts and feelings, all the data of sense, and all physical objects, everything that can do either good or harm, everything that makes any difference to the value of life and the world. According to our temperaments, we shall prefer the contemplation of the one or of the other. The one we do not prefer will probably seem to us a pale shadow of the one we prefer, and hardly worthy to be regarded as in any sense real. But the truth is that both have the same claim on our impartial attention, both are real, and both are important to the metaphysician. Indeed no sooner have we distinguished the two worlds than it becomes necessary to consider their relations.

But first of all we must examine our knowledge of universals. This consideration will occupy us in the following chapter, where we shall find that it solves the problem of a priori knowledge, from which we were first led to consider universals.

CHAPTER X ON OUR KNOWLEDGE OF UNIVERSALS

In regard to one man's knowledge at a given time, universals, like particulars, may be divided into those known by acquaintance, those known only by description, and those not known either by acquaintance or by description.

Let us consider first the knowledge of universals by acquaintance. It is obvious, to begin with, that we are acquainted with such universals as white, red, black, sweet, sour, loud, hard, etc., i.e. with qualities which are exemplified in sense-data. When we see a white patch, we are acquainted, in the first instance, with the particular patch; but by seeing many white patches, we easily learn to abstract the whiteness which they all have in common, and in learning to do this we are learning to be acquainted with whiteness. A similar process will make us acquainted with any other universal of the same sort. Universals of this sort may be called 'sensible qualities'. They can be apprehended with less effort of abstraction than any others, and they seem less removed from particulars than other universals are.

We come next to relations. The easiest relations to apprehend are those which hold between the different parts of a single complex sense-datum. For example, I can see at a glance the whole of the page on which I am writing; thus the whole page is included in one sense-datum. But I perceive that some parts of the page are to the left of other parts, and some parts are above other parts. The process of abstraction in this case seems to proceed somewhat as follows: I see successively a number of sense-data in which one part is to the left of another; I perceive, as in the case of different white patches, that all these sense-data have something in common, and by abstraction I find that what they have in common is a certain relation between their parts, namely the relation which I call 'being to the left of'. In this way I become acquainted with the universal relation.

In like manner I become aware of the relation of before and after in time. Suppose I hear a chime of bells: when the last bell of the chime sounds, I can retain the whole chime before my mind, and I can perceive that the earlier bells came before the later ones. Also in memory I perceive that what I am remembering came before the present time. From either of these sources I can abstract the universal relation of before and after, just as I abstracted the universal relation 'being to the left of'. Thus time-relations, like space-relations, are among those with which we are acquainted.

Another relation with which we become acquainted in much the same way is resemblance. If I see simultaneously two shades of green, I can see that they resemble each other; if I also see a shade of red at the same time, I can see that the two greens have more resemblance to each other than either has to the red. In this way I become acquainted with the universal resemblance or similarity.

Between universals, as between particulars, there are relations of which we may be immediately aware. We have just seen that we can perceive that the resemblance between two shades of green is greater than the resemblance between a shade of red and a shade of green. Here we are dealing with a relation, namely 'greater than', between two relations. Our knowledge of such relations, though it requires more power of abstraction than is required for perceiving the qualities of sense-data, appears to be equally immediate, and (at least in some cases) equally indubitable. Thus there is immediate knowledge concerning universals well as concerning sense-data.

Returning now to the problem of a priori knowledge, which we left unsolved when we began the consideration of universals, we find ourselves in a position to deal with it in a much more satisfactory manner than was possible before. Let us revert to the proposition 'two and two are four'. It is fairly obvious, in view of what has been said, that this proposition states a relation between the universal 'two' and the universal 'four'. This suggests a proposition which we shall now endeavour to establish: namely, All a priori knowledge deals exclusively with the relations of universals. This proposition is of great importance, and goes a long way towards solving our previous difficulties concerning a priori knowledge.

The only case in which it might seem, at first sight, as if our proposition were untrue, is the case in which an a priori proposition states that all of one class of particulars belong to some other class, or (what comes the same thing) that all particulars having some one property also have some other. In this case it might seem as though we were dealing with the particulars that have the property rather than with the property. The proposition 'two and two are four' is really a case in point, for this may be stated in the form 'any two and any other two are four', or 'any collection formed of two twos is a collection of four'. If we can show that such statements as this really deal only with universals, our proposition may be regarded as proved.

One way of discovering what a proposition deals with is to ask ourselves what words we must understand—in other words, what objects we must be acquainted with—in order to see what the proposition means. As soon as we see what the proposition means, even if we do not yet know whether it is true or false, it is evident that we must have acquaintance with whatever is really dealt with by the proposition. By applying this test, it appears that many propositions which might seem to be concerned with particulars are really concerned only with universals. In the special case of 'two and two are four', even when we interpret it as meaning 'any collection formed of two twos is a collection of four', it is plain that we can understand the proposition, i.e.

we can see what it is that it asserts, as soon as we know what is meant by 'collection' and 'two' and 'four'. It is quite unnecessary to know all the couples in the world: if it were necessary, obviously we could never understand the proposition, since the couples are infinitely numerous and therefore cannot all be known to us. Thus although our general statement implies statements about particular couples, as soon as we know that there are such particular couples, yet it does not itself assert or imply that there are such particular couples, and thus fails to make any statement whatever about an actual particular couple. The statement made is about 'couple', the universal, and not about this or that couple.

Thus the statement 'two and two are four' deals exclusively with universals, and therefore may be known by anybody who is acquainted with the universals concerned and can perceive the relation between them which the statement asserts. It must be taken as a fact, discovered by reflecting upon our knowledge, that we have the power of sometimes perceiving such relations between universals, and therefore of sometimes knowing general a priori propositions such as those of arithmetic and logic. The thing that seemed mysterious, when we formerly considered such knowledge, was that it seemed to anticipate and control experience. This, however, we can now see to have been an error. No fact concerning anything capable of being experienced can be known independently of experience. We know a priori that two things and two other things together make four things, but we do not know a priori that if Brown and Jones are two, and Robinson and Smith are two, then Brown and Jones and Robinson and Smith are four. The reason is that this proposition cannot be understood at all unless we know that there are such people as Brown and Jones and Robinson and Smith, and this we can only know by experience. Hence, although our general proposition is a priori, all its applications to actual particulars involve experience and therefore contain an empirical element. In this way what seemed mysterious in our a priori knowledge is seen to have been based upon an error.

It will serve to make the point clearer if we contrast our genuine a priori judgement with an empirical generalization, such as 'all men are mortals'. Here as before, we can understand what the proposition means as soon as we understand the universals involved, namely man and mortal. It is obviously unnecessary to have an individual acquaintance with the whole human race in order to understand what our proposition means. Thus the difference between an a priori general proposition and an empirical generalization does not come in the meaning of the proposition; it comes in the nature of the evidence for it. In the empirical case, the evidence consists in the particular instances. We believe that all men are mortal because we know that there are innumerable instances of men dying, and no instances of their living beyond a certain age. We do not believe it because we see a connexion between the universal man and the universal mortal. It is true that if physiology can prove, assuming the general laws that govern living bodies, that no living organism can last for ever, that gives a connexion between man and mortality which would enable us to assert our proposition without appealing to the special evidence of men dying. But that only means that our generalization has been subsumed under a wider generalization, for which the evidence is still of the same kind, though more extensive. The progress of science is constantly producing such subsumptions, and therefore giving a constantly wider inductive basis for scientific generalizations. But although this gives a greater degree of certainty, it does not give a different kind: the ultimate ground remains inductive, i.e. derived from instances, and not an a priori connexion of universals such as we have in logic and arithmetic.

Two opposite points are to be observed concerning a priori general propositions. The first is that, if many particular instances are known, our general proposition may be arrived at in the first instance by induction, and the connexion of universals may be only subsequently perceived. For example, it is known that if we draw perpendiculars to the sides of a triangle from the opposite angles, all three perpendiculars meet in a point. It would be quite possible to be first led to this proposition by actually drawing perpendiculars in many cases, and finding that they always met in a point; this experience might lead us to look for the general proof and find it. Such cases are common in the experience of every mathematician.

The other point is more interesting, and of more philosophical importance. It is, that we may sometimes know a general proposition in cases where we do not know a single instance of it. Take such a case as the following: We know that any two numbers can be multiplied together, and will give a third called their product. We know that all pairs of integers the product of which is less than 100 have been actually multiplied together, and the value of the product recorded in the multiplication table. But we also know that the number of integers is infinite, and that only a finite number of pairs of integers ever have been or ever will be thought of by human beings. Hence it follows that there are pairs of integers which never have been and never will be thought of by human beings, and that all of them deal with integers the product of which is over 100. Hence we arrive at the proposition: 'All products of two integers, which never have been and never will be thought of by any human being, are over 100.' Here is a general proposition of which the truth is undeniable, and yet, from the very nature of the case, we can never give an instance; because any two numbers we may think of are excluded by the terms of the proposition.

This possibility, of knowledge of general propositions of which no instance can be given, is often denied, because it is not perceived that the knowledge of such propositions only requires a knowledge of the relations of universals, and does not require any knowledge of instances of the universals in question. Yet the knowledge of such general propositions is quite vital to a great deal of what is generally admitted to be known. For example, we saw, in our early chapters, that knowledge of physical objects, as opposed to sense-data, is only obtained by an inference, and that they are not things with which we are acquainted. Hence we can never know any proposition of the form 'this is a physical object', where 'this' is something immediately known. It follows that all our knowledge concerning physical objects is such that no actual instance can be given. We can give instances of the associated sense-data, but we cannot give instances of the actual physical objects. Hence our knowledge as to physical objects depends throughout upon this possibility of general knowledge where no instance can be given. And the same applies to our knowledge of other people's minds, or of any other class of things of which no instance is known to us by acquaintance.

We may now take a survey of the sources of our knowledge, as they have appeared in the course of our analysis. We have first to distinguish knowledge of things and knowledge of truths. In each there are two kinds, one immediate and one derivative. Our immediate knowledge of things, which we called acquaintance, consists of two sorts, according as the things known are particulars or universals. Among particulars, we have acquaintance with sense-data and (probably) with ourselves. Among universals, there seems to be no principle by which we can decide which can be known by acquaintance, but it is clear that among those that can be so known are sensible qualities, relations of space and time, similarity, and certain abstract logical universals. Our derivative knowledge of things, which we call knowledge by description, always involves both acquaintance with something and knowledge of truths. Our immediate knowledge of truths may be called intuitive knowledge, and the truths so known may be called self-evident truths. Among such truths are included those which merely state what is given in sense, and also certain abstract logical and arithmetical principles, and (though with less certainty) some ethical propositions. Our derivative knowledge of truths consists of everything that we can deduce from self-evident truths by the use of self-evident principles of deduction.

If the above account is correct, all our knowledge of truths depends upon our intuitive knowledge. It therefore becomes important to consider the nature and scope of intuitive knowledge, in much the same way as, at an earlier stage, we considered the nature and scope of knowledge by acquaintance. But knowledge of truths raises a further problem, which does not arise in regard to knowledge of things, namely the problem of error. Some of our beliefs turn out to be erroneous, and therefore it becomes necessary to consider how, if at all, we can distinguish knowledge from error. This problem does not arise with regard to knowledge by acquaintance, for, whatever may be the object of acquaintance, even in dreams and hallucinations, there is no error involved so long as we do not go beyond the immediate object: error can only arise when we regard the immediate object, i.e. the sense-datum, as the mark of some physical object. Thus the problems connected with knowledge of truths are more difficult than those connected with knowledge of things. As the first of the problems connected with knowledge of truths, let us examine the nature and scope of our intuitive judgements.

CHAPTER XI ON INTUITIVE KNOWLEDGE

There is a common impression that everything that we believe ought to be capable of proof, or at least of being shown to be highly probable. It is felt by many that a belief for which no reason can be given is an unreasonable belief. In the main, this view is just. Almost all our common beliefs are either inferred, or capable of being inferred, from other beliefs which may be regarded as giving the reason for them. As a rule, the reason has been forgotten, or has even never been consciously present to our minds. Few of us ever ask ourselves, for example, what reason there is to suppose the food we are just going to eat will not turn out to be poison. Yet we feel, when challenged, that a perfectly good reason could be found, even if we are not ready with it at the moment. And in this belief we are usually justified.

But let us imagine some insistent Socrates, who, whatever reason we give him, continues to demand a reason for the reason. We must sooner or later, and probably before very long, be driven to a point where we cannot find any further reason, and where it becomes almost certain that no further reason is even theoretically discoverable. Starting with the common beliefs of daily life, we can be driven back from point to point, until we come to some general principle, or some instance of a general principle, which seems luminously evident, and is not itself capable of being deduced from anything more evident. In most questions of daily life, such as whether our food is likely to be nourishing and not poisonous, we shall be driven back to the inductive principle, which we discussed in Chapter VI. But beyond that, there seems to be no further regress. The principle itself is constantly used in our reasoning, sometimes consciously, sometimes unconsciously; but there is no reasoning which, starting from some simpler self-evident principle, leads us to the principle of induction as its conclusion. And the same holds for other logical principles. Their truth is evident to us, and we employ them in constructing demonstrations; but they themselves, or at least some of them, are incapable of demonstration.

Self-evidence, however, is not confined to those among general principles which are incapable of proof. When a certain number of logical principles have been admitted, the rest can be deduced from them; but the propositions deduced are often just as self-evident as those that were assumed without proof. All arithmetic, moreover, can be deduced from the general principles of logic, yet the simple propositions of arithmetic, such as 'two and two are four', are just as self-evident as the principles of logic.

It would seem, also, though this is more disputable, that there are some self-evident ethical principles, such as 'we ought to pursue what is good'.

It should be observed that, in all cases of general principles, particular instances, dealing with familiar things, are more evident than the general principle. For example, the law of contradiction states that nothing can both have a certain property and not have it. This is evident as soon as it is understood, but it is not so evident as that a particular rose which we see cannot be both red and not red. (It is of course possible that parts of the rose may be red and parts not red, or that the rose may be of a shade of pink which we hardly know whether to call red or not; but in the former case it is plain that the rose as a whole is not red, while in the latter case the answer is theoretically definite as soon as we have decided on a precise definition of 'red'.) It is usually through particular instances that we come to be able to see the general principle. Only those who are practiced in dealing with abstractions can readily grasp a general principle without the help of instances.

In addition to general principles, the other kind of self-evident truths are those immediately derived from sensation. We will call such truths 'truths of perception', and the judgements expressing them we will call 'judgements of perception'. But here a certain amount of care is required in getting at the precise nature of the truths that are self-evident. The actual sense-data are neither true nor false. A particular patch of colour which I see, for example, simply exists: it is not the sort of thing that is true or false. It is true that there is such a patch, true that it has a certain shape and degree of brightness, true that it is surrounded by certain other colours. But the patch itself, like everything else in the world of sense, is of a radically different kind from the things that are true or false, and therefore cannot properly be said to be true. Thus whatever self-evident truths may be obtained from our senses must be different from the sense-data from which they are obtained.

It would seem that there are two kinds of self-evident truths of perception, though perhaps in the last analysis the two kinds may coalesce. First, there is the kind which simply asserts the existence of the sense-datum, without in any way analysing it. We see a patch of red, and we judge 'there is such-and-such a patch of red', or more strictly 'there is that'; this is one kind of intuitive judgement of perception. The other kind arises when the object of sense is complex, and we subject it to some degree of analysis. If, for instance, we see a round patch of red, we may judge 'that patch of red is round'. This is again a judgement of perception, but it differs from our previous kind. In our present kind we have a single sense-datum which has both colour and shape: the colour is red and the shape is round. Our judgement analyses the datum into colour and shape, and then recombines them by stating that the red colour is round in shape. Another example of this kind of judgement is 'this is to the right of that', where 'this' and 'that' are seen simultaneously. In this kind of judgement the sense-datum contains constituents which have some relation to each other, and the judgement asserts that these constituents have this relation.

Another class of intuitive judgements, analogous to those of sense and yet quite distinct from them, are judgements of memory. There is some danger of confusion as to the nature of memory, owing to the fact that memory of an object is apt to be accompanied by an image of the object, and yet the image cannot be what constitutes memory. This is easily seen by merely noticing that the image is in the present, whereas what is remembered is known to be in the past. Moreover, we are certainly able to some extent to compare our image with the object remembered, so that we often know, within somewhat wide limits, how far our image is accurate; but this would be impossible, unless the object, as opposed to the image, were in some way before the mind. Thus the essence of memory is not constituted by the image, but by having immediately before the mind an object which is recognized as past. But for the fact of memory in this sense, we should not know that there ever was a past at all, nor should we be able to understand the word 'past', any more than a man born blind can understand the word 'light'. Thus there must be intuitive judgements of memory, and it is upon them, ultimately, that all our knowledge of the past depends.

The case of memory, however, raises a difficulty, for it is notoriously fallacious, and thus throws doubt on the trustworthiness of intuitive judgements in general. This difficulty is no light one. But let us first narrow its scope as far as possible. Broadly speaking, memory is trustworthy in proportion to the vividness of the experience and to its nearness in time. If the house next door was struck by lightning half a minute ago, my memory of what I saw and heard will be so reliable that it would be preposterous to doubt whether there had been a flash at all. And the same applies to less vivid experiences, so long as they are recent. I am absolutely certain that half a minute ago I was sitting in the same chair in which I am sitting now. Going backward over the day, I find things of which I am quite certain, other things of which I am almost certain, other things of which I can become certain by thought and by calling up attendant circumstances, and some things of which I am by no means certain. I am quite certain that I ate my breakfast this morning, but if I were as indifferent to my breakfast as a philosopher should be, I should be doubtful. As to the conversation at breakfast, I can recall some of it easily, some with an effort, some only with a large element of doubt, and some not at all. Thus there is a continual gradation in the degree of self-evidence of what I remember, and a corresponding gradation in the trustworthiness of my memory.

Thus the first answer to the difficulty of fallacious memory is to say that memory has degrees of self-evidence, and that these correspond to the degrees of its trustworthiness, reaching a limit of perfect self-evidence and perfect trustworthiness in our memory of events which are recent and vivid.

It would seem, however, that there are cases of very firm belief in a memory which is wholly false. It is probable that, in these cases, what is really remembered, in the sense of being immediately before the mind, is something other than what is falsely believed in, though something generally associated with it. George IV is said to have at last believed that he was at the battle of Waterloo, because he had so often said that he was. In this case, what was immediately remembered was his repeated assertion; the belief in what he was asserting (if it existed) would be produced by association with the remembered assertion, and would therefore not be a genuine case of memory. It would seem that cases of fallacious memory can probably all be dealt with in this way, i.e. they can be shown to be not cases of memory in the strict sense at all.

One important point about self-evidence is made clear by the case of memory, and that is, that self-evidence has degrees: it is not a quality which is simply present or absent, but a quality which may be more or less present, in gradations ranging from absolute certainty down to an almost imperceptible faintness. Truths of perception and some of the principles of logic have the very highest degree of self-evidence; truths of immediate memory have an almost equally high degree. The inductive principle has less self-evidence than some of the other principles of logic, such as 'what follows from a true premiss must be true'. Memories have a diminishing self-evidence as they become remoter and fainter; the truths of logic and mathematics have (broadly speaking) less self-evidence as they become more complicated. Judgements of intrinsic ethical or aesthetic value are apt to have some self-evidence, but not much.

Degrees of self-evidence are important in the theory of knowledge, since, if propositions may (as seems likely) have some degree of self-evidence without being true, it will not be necessary to abandon all connexion between self-evidence and truth, but merely to say that, where there is a conflict, the more self-evident proposition is to be retained and the less self-evident rejected.

It seems, however, highly probable that two different notions are combined in 'self-evidence' as above explained; that one of them, which corresponds to the highest degree of self-evidence, is really an infallible guarantee of truth, while the other, which corresponds to all the other degrees, does not give an infallible guarantee, but only a greater or less presumption. This, however, is only a suggestion, which we cannot as yet develop further. After we have dealt with the nature of truth, we shall return to the subject of self-evidence, in connexion with the distinction between knowledge and error.

CHAPTER XII TRUTH AND FALSEHOOD

Our knowledge of truths, unlike our knowledge of things, has an opposite, namely error. So far as things are concerned, we may know them or not know them, but there is no positive state of mind which can be described as erroneous knowledge of things, so long, at any rate, as we confine ourselves to knowledge by acquaintance. Whatever we are acquainted with must be something; we may draw wrong inferences from our acquaintance, but the acquaintance itself cannot be deceptive. Thus there is no dualism as regards acquaintance. But as regards knowledge of truths, there is a dualism. We may believe what is false as well as what is true. We know that on very many subjects different people hold different and incompatible opinions: hence some beliefs must be erroneous. Since erroneous beliefs are often held just as strongly as true beliefs, it becomes a difficult question how they are to be distinguished from true beliefs. How are we to know, in a given case, that our belief is not erroneous? This is a question of the very greatest difficulty, to which no completely satisfactory answer is possible. There is, however, a preliminary question which is rather less difficult, and that is: What do we mean by truth and falsehood? It is this preliminary question which is to be considered in this chapter.

In this chapter we are not asking how we can know whether a belief is true or false: we are asking what is meant by the question whether a belief is true or false. It is to be hoped that a clear answer to this question may help us to obtain an answer to the question what beliefs are true, but for the present we ask only 'What is truth?' and 'What is falsehood?' not 'What beliefs are true?' and 'What beliefs are false?' It is very important to keep these different questions entirely separate, since any confusion between them is sure to produce an answer which is not really applicable to either.

There are three points to observe in the attempt to discover the nature of truth, three requisites which any theory must fulfill.

1. Our theory of truth must be such as to admit of its opposite, falsehood. A good many philosophers have failed adequately to satisfy this condition: they have constructed theories according to which all our thinking ought to have been true, and have then had the greatest difficulty in finding a place for falsehood. In this respect our theory of belief must differ from our theory of acquaintance, since in the case of acquaintance it was not necessary to take account of any opposite.

2. It seems fairly evident that if there were no beliefs there could be no falsehood, and no truth either, in the sense in which truth is correlative to falsehood. If we imagine a world of mere matter, there would be no room for falsehood in such a world, and although it would contain what may be called 'facts', it would not contain any truths, in the sense in which truths are things of the same kind as falsehoods. In fact, truth and falsehood are properties of beliefs and statements: hence a world of mere matter, since it would contain no beliefs or statements, would also contain no truth or falsehood.

3. But, as against what we have just said, it is to be observed that the truth or falsehood of a belief always depends upon something which lies outside the belief itself. If I believe that Charles I died on the scaffold, I believe truly, not because of any intrinsic quality of my belief, which could be discovered by merely examining the belief, but because of an historical event which happened two and a half centuries ago. If I believe that Charles I died in his bed, I believe falsely: no degree of vividness in my belief, or of care in arriving at it, prevents it from being false, again because of what happened long ago, and not because of any intrinsic property of my belief. Hence, although truth and falsehood are properties of beliefs, they are properties dependent upon the relations of the beliefs to other things, not upon any internal quality of the beliefs.

The third of the above requisites leads us to adopt the view—which has on the whole been commonest among philosophers—that truth consists in some form of correspondence between belief and fact. It is, however, by no means an easy matter to discover a form of correspondence to which there are no irrefutable objections. By this partly—and partly by the feeling that, if truth consists in a correspondence of thought with something outside thought, thought can never know when truth has been attained—many philosophers have been led to try to find some definition of truth which shall not consist in relation to something wholly outside belief. The most important attempt at a definition of this sort is the theory that truth consists in coherence. It is said that the mark of falsehood is failure to cohere in the body of our beliefs, and that it is the essence of a truth to form part of the completely rounded system which is The Truth.

There is, however, a great difficulty in this view, or rather two great difficulties. The first is that there is no reason to suppose that only one coherent body of beliefs is possible. It may be that, with sufficient imagination, a novelist might invent a past for the world that would perfectly fit on to what we know, and yet be quite different from the real past. In more scientific matters, it is certain that there are often two or more hypotheses which account for all the known facts on some subject, and although, in such cases, men of science endeavour to find facts which will rule out all the hypotheses except one, there is no reason why they should always succeed.

In philosophy, again, it seems not uncommon for two rival hypotheses to be both able to account for all the facts. Thus, for example, it is possible that life is one long dream, and that the outer world has only that degree of reality that the objects of dreams have; but although such a view does not seem inconsistent with known facts, there is no reason to prefer it to the common-sense view, according to which other people and things do really exist. Thus coherence as the definition of truth fails because there is no proof that there can be only one coherent system.

The other objection to this definition of truth is that it assumes the meaning of 'coherence' known, whereas, in fact, 'coherence' presupposes the truth of the laws of logic. Two propositions are coherent when both may be true, and are incoherent when one at least must be false. Now in order to know whether two propositions can both be true, we must know such truths as the law of contradiction. For example, the two propositions, 'this tree is a beech' and 'this tree is not a beech', are not coherent, because of the law of contradiction. But if the law of contradiction itself were subjected to the test of coherence, we should find that, if we choose to suppose it false, nothing will any longer be incoherent with anything else. Thus the laws of logic supply the skeleton or framework within which the test of coherence applies, and they themselves cannot be established by this test.

For the above two reasons, coherence cannot be accepted as giving the meaning of truth, though it is often a most important test of truth after a certain amount of truth has become known.

Hence we are driven back to correspondence with fact as constituting the nature of truth. It remains to define precisely what we mean by 'fact', and what is the nature of the correspondence which must subsist between belief and fact, in order that belief may be true.

In accordance with our three requisites, we have to seek a theory of truth which (1) allows truth to have an opposite, namely falsehood, (2) makes truth a property of beliefs, but (3) makes it a property wholly dependent upon the relation of the beliefs to outside things.

The necessity of allowing for falsehood makes it impossible to regard belief as a relation of the mind to a single object, which could be said to be what is believed. If belief were so regarded, we should find that, like acquaintance, it would not admit of the opposition of truth and falsehood, but would have to be always true. This may be made clear by examples. Othello believes falsely that Desdemona loves Cassio. We cannot say that this belief consists in a relation to a single object, 'Desdemona's love for Cassio', for if there were such an object, the belief would be true. There is in fact no such object, and therefore Othello cannot have any relation to such an object. Hence his belief cannot possibly consist in a relation to this object.

It might be said that his belief is a relation to a different object, namely 'that Desdemona loves Cassio'; but it is almost as difficult to suppose that there is such an object as this, when Desdemona does not love Cassio, as it was to suppose that there is 'Desdemona's love for Cassio'. Hence it will be better to seek for a theory of belief which does not make it consist in a relation of the mind to a single object.

It is common to think of relations as though they always held between two terms, but in fact this is not always the case. Some relations demand three terms, some four, and so on. Take, for instance, the relation 'between'. So long as only two terms come in, the relation 'between' is impossible: three terms are the smallest number that render it possible. York is between London and Edinburgh; but if London and Edinburgh were the only places in the world, there could be nothing which was between one place and another. Similarly jealousy requires three people: there can be no such relation that does not involve three at least. Such a proposition as 'A wishes B to promote C's marriage with D' involves a relation of four terms; that is to say, A and B and C and D all come in, and the relation involved cannot be expressed otherwise than in a form involving all four. Instances might be multiplied indefinitely, but enough has been said to show that there are relations which require more than two terms before they can occur.

The relation involved in judging or believing must, if falsehood is to be duly allowed for, be taken to be a relation between several terms, not between two. When Othello believes that Desdemona loves Cassio, he must not have before his mind a single object, 'Desdemona's love for Cassio', or 'that Desdemona loves Cassio', for that would require that there should be objective falsehoods, which subsist independently of any minds; and this, though not logically refutable, is a theory to be avoided if possible. Thus it is easier to account for falsehood if we take judgement to be a relation in which the mind and the various objects concerned all occur severally; that is to say, Desdemona and loving and Cassio must all be terms in the relation which subsists when Othello believes that Desdemona loves Cassio. This relation, therefore, is a relation of four terms, since Othello also is one of the terms of the relation. When we say that it is a relation of four terms, we do not mean that Othello has a certain relation to Desdemona, and has the same relation to loving and also to Cassio. This may be true of some other relation than believing; but believing, plainly, is not a relation which Othello has to each of the three terms concerned, but to all of them together: there is only one example of the relation of believing involved, but this one example knits together four terms. Thus the actual occurrence, at the moment when Othello is entertaining his belief, is that the relation called 'believing' is knitting together into one complex whole the four terms Othello, Desdemona, loving, and Cassio. What is called belief or judgement is nothing but this relation of believing or judging, which relates a mind to several things other than itself. An act of belief or of judgement is the occurrence between certain terms at some particular time, of the relation of believing or judging.

We are now in a position to understand what it is that distinguishes a true judgement from a false one. For this purpose we will adopt certain definitions. In every act of judgement there is a mind which judges, and there are terms concerning which it judges. We will call the mind the subject in the judgement, and the remaining terms the objects. Thus, when Othello judges that Desdemona loves Cassio, Othello is the subject, while the objects are Desdemona and loving and Cassio. The subject and the objects together are called the constituents of the judgement. It will be observed that the elation of judging has what is called a 'sense' or 'direction'. We may say, metaphorically, that it puts its objects in a certain order, which we may indicate by means of the order of the words in the sentence. (In an inflected language, the same thing will be indicated by inflections, e.g., by the difference between nominative and accusative.) Othello's judgement that Cassio loves Desdemona differs from his judgement that Desdemona loves Cassio, in spite of the fact that it consists of the same constituents, because the relation of judging places the constituents in a different order in the two cases. Similarly, if Cassio judges that Desdemona loves Othello, the constituents of the judgement are still the same, but their order is different. This property of having a 'sense' or 'direction' is one which the relation of judging shares with all other relations. The 'sense' of relations is the ultimate source of order and series and a host of mathematical concepts; but we need not concern ourselves further with this aspect.

We spoke of the relation called 'judging' or 'believing' as knitting together into one complex whole the subject and the objects. In this respect, judging is exactly like every other relation. Whenever a relation holds between two or more terms, it unites the terms into a complex whole. If Othello loves Desdemona, there is such a complex whole as 'Othello's love for Desdemona'. The terms united by the relation may be themselves complex, or may be simple, but the whole which results from their being united must be complex. Wherever there is a relation which relates certain terms, there is a complex object formed of the union of those terms; and conversely, wherever there is a complex object, there is a relation which relates its constituents. When an act of believing occurs, there is a complex, in which 'believing' is the uniting relation, and subject and objects are arranged in a certain order by the 'sense' of the relation of believing. Among the objects, as we saw in considering 'Othello believes that Desdemona loves Cassio', one must be a relation—in this instance, the relation 'loving'. But this relation, as it occurs in the act of believing, is not the relation which creates the unity of the complex whole consisting of the subject and the objects. The relation 'loving', as it occurs in the act of believing, is one of the objects—it is a brick in the structure, not the cement. The cement is the relation 'believing'. When the belief is true, there is another complex unity, in which the relation which was one of the objects of the belief relates the other objects. Thus, e.g., if Othello believes truly that Desdemona loves Cassio, then there is a complex unity, 'Desdemona's love for Cassio', which is composed exclusively of the objects of the belief, in the same order as they had in the belief, with the relation which was one of the objects occurring now as the cement that binds together the other objects of the belief. On the other hand, when a belief is false, there is no such complex unity composed only of the objects of the belief. If Othello believes falsely that Desdemona loves Cassio, then there is no such complex unity as 'Desdemona's love for Cassio'.

Thus a belief is *true* when it *corresponds* to a certain associated complex, and *false* when it does not. Assuming, for the sake of definiteness, that the objects of the belief are two terms and a relation, the terms being put in a certain order by the 'sense' of the believing, then if the two terms in that order are united by the relation into a complex, the belief is true; if not, it is false. This constitutes the definition of truth and falsehood that we were in search of. Judging or believing is a certain complex unity of which a mind is a constituent; if the remaining constituents, taken in the order which they have in the belief, form a complex unity, then the belief is true; if not, it is false.

Thus although truth and falsehood are properties of beliefs, yet they are in a sense extrinsic properties, for the condition of the truth of a belief is something not involving beliefs, or (in general) any mind at all, but only the objects of the belief. A mind, which believes, believes truly when there is a corresponding complex not involving the mind, but only its objects. This correspondence ensures truth, and its absence entails falsehood. Hence we account simultaneously for the two facts that beliefs (a) depend on minds for their *existence*, and (b) do not depend on minds for their *truth*.

We may restate our theory as follows: If we take such a belief as 'Othello believes that Desdemona loves Cassio', we will call Desdemona and Cassio the object-terms, and loving the object-relation. If there is a complex unity 'Desdemona's love for Cassio', consisting of the object-terms related by the object-relation in the same order as they have in the belief, then this complex unity is called the fact corresponding to the belief. Thus a belief is true when there is a corresponding fact, and is false when there is no corresponding fact.

It will be seen that minds do not create truth or falsehood. They create beliefs, but when once the beliefs are created, the mind cannot make them true or false, except in the special case where they concern future things which are within the power of the person believing, such as catching trains. What makes a belief true is a fact, and this fact does not (except in exceptional cases) in any way involve the mind of the person who has the belief.

Having now decided what we mean by truth and falsehood, we have next to consider what ways there are of knowing whether this or that belief is true or false. This consideration will occupy the next chapter.

CHAPTER XIII KNOWLEDGE, ERROR, AND PROBABLE OPINION

The question as to what we mean by truth and falsehood, which we considered in the preceding chapter, is of much less interest than the question as to how we can know what is true and what is false. This question will occupy us in the present chapter. There can be no doubt that some of our beliefs are erroneous; thus we are led to inquire what certainty we can ever have that such and such a belief is not erroneous. In other words, can we ever know anything at all, or do we merely sometimes by good luck believe what is true? Before we can attack this question, we must, however, first decide what we mean by 'knowing', and this question is not so easy as might be supposed.

At first sight we might imagine that knowledge could be defined as 'true belief'. When what we believe is true, it might be supposed that we had achieved a knowledge of what we believe. But this would not accord with the way in which the word is commonly used. To take a very trivial instance: If a man believes that the late Prime Minister's last name began with a B, he believes what is true, since the late Prime Minister was Sir Henry Campbell Bannerman. But if he believes that Mr. Balfour was the late Prime Minister, he will still believe that the late Prime Minister's last name began with a B, yet this belief, though true, would not be thought to constitute knowledge. If a newspaper, by an intelligent anticipation, announces the result of a battle before any telegram giving the result has been received, it may by good fortune announce what afterwards turns out to be the right result, and it may produce belief in some of its less experienced readers. But in spite of the truth of their belief, they cannot be said to have knowledge. Thus it is clear that a true belief is not knowledge when it is deduced from a false belief.

In like manner, a true belief cannot be called knowledge when it is deduced by a fallacious process of reasoning, even if the premisses from which it is deduced are true. If I know that all Greeks are men and that Socrates was a man, and I infer that Socrates was a Greek, I cannot be said to know that Socrates was a Greek, because, although my premisses and my conclusion are true, the conclusion does not follow from the premisses.

But are we to say that nothing is knowledge except what is validly deduced from true premisses? Obviously we cannot say this. Such a definition is at once too wide and too narrow. In the first place, it is too wide, because it is not enough that our premisses should be true, they must also be known. The man who believes that Mr. Balfour was the late Prime Minister may proceed to draw valid deductions from the true premiss that the late Prime Minister's name began with a B, but he cannot be said to know the conclusions reached by these deductions. Thus we shall have to amend our definition by saying that knowledge is what is validly deduced from known premisses. This, however, is a circular definition: it assumes that we already know what is meant by 'known premisses'. It can, therefore, at best define one sort of knowledge, the sort we call derivative, as opposed to intuitive knowledge. We may say: 'Derivative knowledge is what is validly deduced from premisses known intuitively'. In this statement there is no formal defect, but it leaves the definition of intuitive knowledge still to seek.

Leaving on one side, for the moment, the question of intuitive knowledge, let us consider the above suggested definition of derivative knowledge. The chief objection to it is that it unduly limits knowledge. It constantly happens that people entertain a true belief, which has grown up in them because of some piece of intuitive knowledge from which it is capable of being validly inferred, but from which it has not, as a matter of fact, been inferred by any logical process.

Take, for example, the beliefs produced by reading. If the newspapers announce the death of the King, we are fairly well justified in believing that the King is dead, since this is the sort of announcement which would not be made if it were false. And we are quite amply justified in believing that the newspaper asserts that the King is dead. But here the intuitive knowledge upon which our belief is based is knowledge of the existence of sense-data derived from looking at the print which gives the news. This knowledge scarcely rises into consciousness, except in a person who cannot read easily. A child may be aware of the shapes of the letters, and pass gradually and painfully to a realization of their meaning. But anybody accustomed to reading passes at once to what the letters mean, and is not aware, except on reflection, that he has derived this knowledge from the sense-data called seeing the printed letters. Thus although a valid inference from the letters to their meaning is possible, and could be performed by the reader, it is not in fact performed, since he does not in fact perform any operation which can be called logical inference. Yet it would be absurd to say that the reader does not know that the newspaper announces the King's death.

We must, therefore, admit as derivative knowledge whatever is the result of intuitive knowledge even if by mere association, provided there is a valid logical connexion, and the person in question could become aware of this connexion by reflection. There are in fact many ways, besides logical inference, by which we pass from one belief to another: the passage from the print to its meaning illustrates these ways. These ways may be called 'psychological inference'. We shall, then, admit such psychological inference as a means of obtaining derivative knowledge, provided there is a discoverable logical inference which runs parallel to the psychological inference. This renders our definition of derivative knowledge less precise than we could wish, since the word 'discoverable' is vague: it does not tell us how much reflection may be needed in order to make the discovery. But in fact 'knowledge' is not a precise conception: it merges into 'probable opinion', as we shall see more fully in the course of the present chapter. A very precise definition, therefore, should not be sought, since any such definition must be more or less misleading.

The chief difficulty in regard to knowledge, however, does not arise over derivative knowledge, but over intuitive knowledge. So long as we are dealing with derivative knowledge, we have the test of intuitive knowledge to fall back upon. But in regard to intuitive beliefs, it is by no means easy to discover any criterion by which to distinguish some as true and others as erroneous. In this question it is scarcely possible to reach any very precise result: all our knowledge of truths is infected with some degree of doubt, and a theory which ignored this fact would be plainly wrong. Something may be done, however, to mitigate the difficulties of the question.

Our theory of truth, to begin with, supplies the possibility of distinguishing certain truths as self-evident in a sense which ensures infallibility. When a belief is true, we said, there is a corresponding fact, in which the several objects of the belief form a single complex. The belief is said to constitute knowledge of this fact, provided it fulfills those further somewhat vague conditions which we have been considering in the present chapter. But in regard to any fact, besides the knowledge constituted by belief, we may also have the kind of knowledge constituted by perception (taking this word in its widest possible sense). For example, if you know the hour of the sunset, you can at that hour know the fact that the sun is setting: this is knowledge of the fact by way of knowledge of truths; but you can also, if the weather is fine, look to the west and actually see the setting sun: you then know the same fact by the way of knowledge of things.

Thus in regard to any complex fact, there are, theoretically, two ways in which it may be known: (1) by means of a judgement, in which its several parts are judged to be related as they are in fact related; (2) by means of acquaintance with the complex fact itself, which may (in a large sense) be called perception, though it is by no means confined to objects of the senses. Now it will be observed that the second way of knowing a complex fact, the way of acquaintance, is only possible when there really is such a fact, while the first way, like all judgement, is liable to error. The second way gives us the complex whole, and is therefore only possible when its parts do actually have that relation which makes them combine to form such a complex. The first way, on the contrary, gives us the parts and the relation severally, and demands only the reality of the parts and the relation: the relation may not relate those parts in that way, and yet the judgement may occur.

It will be remembered that at the end of Chapter XI we suggested that there might be two kinds of self-evidence, one giving an absolute guarantee of truth, the other only a partial guarantee. These two kinds can now be distinguished.

We may say that a truth is self-evident, in the first and most absolute sense, when we have acquaintance with the fact which corresponds to the truth. When Othello believes that Desdemona loves Cassio, the corresponding fact, if his belief were true, would be 'Desdemona's love for Cassio'. This would be a fact with which no one could have acquaintance except Desdemona; hence in the sense of self-evidence that we are considering, the truth that Desdemona loves Cassio (if it were a truth) could only be self-evident to Desdemona. All mental facts, and all facts concerning sense-data, have this same privacy: there is only one person to whom they can be self-evident in our present sense, since there is only one person who can be acquainted with the mental things or the sense-data concerned. Thus no fact about any particular existing thing can be self-evident to more than one person. On the other hand, facts about universals do not have this privacy. Many minds may be acquainted with the same universals; hence a relation between universals may be known by acquaintance to many different people. In all cases where we know by acquaintance a complex fact consisting of certain terms in a certain relation, we say that the truth that these terms are so related has the first or absolute kind of self-evidence, and in these cases the judgement that the terms are so related must be true. Thus this sort of self-evidence is an absolute guarantee of truth.

But although this sort of self-evidence is an absolute guarantee of truth, it does not enable us to be absolutely certain, in the case of any given judgement, that the judgement in question is true. Suppose we first perceive the sun shining, which is a complex fact, and thence proceed to make the judgement 'the sun is shining'. In passing from the perception to the judgement, it is necessary to analyse the given complex fact: we have to separate out 'the sun' and 'shining' as constituents of the fact. In this process it is possible to commit an error; hence even where a fact has the first or absolute kind of self-evidence, a judgement believed to correspond to the fact is not absolutely infallible, because it may not really correspond to the fact. But if it does correspond (in the sense explained in the preceding chapter), then it must be true.

The second sort of self-evidence will be that which belongs to judgements in the first instance, and is not derived from direct perception of a fact as a single complex whole. This second kind of self-evidence will have degrees, from the very highest degree down to a bare inclination in favour of the belief. Take, for example, the case of a horse trotting away from us along a hard road. At first our certainty that we hear the hoofs is complete; gradually, if we listen intently, there comes a moment when we think perhaps it was imagination or the blind upstairs or our own heartbeats; at last we become doubtful whether there was any noise at all; then we think we no longer hear anything, and at last we know we no longer hear anything. In this process, there is a continual gradation of self-evidence, from the highest degree to the least, not in the sense-data themselves, but in the judgements based on them.

Or again: Suppose we are comparing two shades of colour, one blue and one green. We can be quite sure they are different shades of colour; but if the green colour is gradually altered to be more and more like the blue, becoming first a blue-green, then a greeny-blue, then blue, there will come a moment when we are doubtful whether we can see any difference, and then a moment when we know that we cannot see any difference. The same thing happens in tuning a musical instrument, or in any other case where there is a continuous gradation. Thus self-evidence of this sort is a matter of degree; and it seems plain that the higher degrees are more to be trusted than the lower degrees.

In derivative knowledge our ultimate premisses must have some degree of self-evidence, and so must their connexion with the conclusions deduced from them. Take for example a piece of reasoning in geometry. It is not enough that the axioms from which we start should be self-evident: it is necessary also that, at each step in the reasoning, the connexion of premiss and conclusion should be self-evident. In difficult reasoning, this connexion has often only a very small degree of self-evidence; hence errors of reasoning are not improbable where the difficulty is great.

From what has been said it is evident that, both as regards intuitive knowledge and as regards derivative knowledge, if we assume that intuitive knowledge is trustworthy in proportion to the degree of its self-evidence, there will be a gradation in trustworthiness, from the existence of noteworthy sense-data and the simpler truths of logic and arithmetic, which may be taken as quite certain, down to judgements which seem only just more probable than their opposites. What we firmly believe, if it is true, is called knowledge, provided it is either intuitive or inferred (logically or psychologically) from intuitive knowledge from which it follows logically. What we firmly believe, if it is not true, is called error. What we firmly believe, if it is neither knowledge nor error, and also what we believe hesitatingly, because it is, or is derived from, something which has not the highest degree of self-evidence, may be called probable opinion. Thus the greater part of what would commonly pass as knowledge is more or less probable opinion.

In regard to probable opinion, we can derive great assistance from coherence, which we rejected as the definition of truth, but may often use as a criterion. A body of individually probable opinions, if they are mutually coherent, become more probable than any one of them would be individually. It is in this way that many scientific hypotheses acquire their probability. They fit into a coherent system of probable opinions, and thus become more probable than they would be in isolation. The same thing applies to general philosophical hypotheses. Often in a single case such hypotheses may seem highly doubtful, while yet, when we consider the order and coherence which they introduce into a mass of probable opinion, they become pretty nearly certain. This applies, in particular, to such matters as the distinction between dreams and waking life. If our dreams, night after night, were as coherent one with another as our days, we should hardly know whether to believe the dreams or the waking life. As it is, the test of coherence condemns the dreams and confirms the waking life. But this test, though it increases probability where it is successful, never gives absolute certainty, unless there is certainty already at some point in the coherent system. Thus the mere organization of probable opinion will never, by itself, transform it into indubitable knowledge.

CHAPTER XIV THE LIMITS OF PHILOSOPHICAL KNOWLEDGE

In all that we have said hitherto concerning philosophy, we have scarcely touched on many matters that occupy a great space in the writings of most philosophers. Most philosophers—or, at any rate, very many—profess to be able to prove, by a priori metaphysical reasoning, such things as the fundamental dogmas of religion, the essential rationality of the universe, the illusoriness of matter, the unreality of all evil, and so on. There can be no doubt that the hope of finding reason to believe such theses as these has been the chief inspiration of many life-long students of philosophy. This hope, I believe, is vain. It would seem that knowledge concerning the universe as a whole is not to be obtained by metaphysics, and that the proposed proofs that, in virtue of the laws of logic such and such things must exist and such and such others cannot, are not capable of surviving a critical scrutiny. In this chapter we shall briefly consider the kind of way in which such reasoning is attempted, with a view to discovering whether we can hope that it may be valid.

The great representative, in modern times, of the kind of view which we wish to examine, was Hegel (1770–1831). Hegel's philosophy is very difficult, and commentators differ as to the true interpretation of it. According to the interpretation I shall adopt, which is that of many, if not most, of the commentators and has the merit of giving an interesting and important type of philosophy, his main thesis is that everything short of the Whole is obviously fragmentary, and obviously incapable of existing without the complement supplied by the rest of the world. Just as a comparative anatomist, from a single bone, sees what kind of animal the whole must have been, so the metaphysician, according to Hegel, sees, from any one piece of reality, what the whole of reality must be—at least in its large outlines. Every apparently separate piece of reality has, as it were, hooks which grapple it to the next piece; the next piece, in turn, has fresh hooks, and so on, until the whole universe is reconstructed. This essential incompleteness appears, according to Hegel, equally in the world of thought and in the world of things. In the world of thought, if we take any idea which is abstract or incomplete, we find, on examination, that if we forget its incompleteness, we become involved in contradictions; these contradictions turn the idea in question into its opposite, or antithesis; and in order to escape, we have to find a new, less incomplete idea, which is the synthesis of our original idea and its antithesis. This new idea, though less incomplete than the idea we started with, will be found, nevertheless, to be still not wholly complete, but to pass into its antithesis, with which it must be combined in a new synthesis. In this way Hegel advances until he reaches the 'Absolute Idea', which, according to him, has no incompleteness, no opposite, and no need of further development. The Absolute Idea, therefore, is adequate to describe Absolute Reality; but all lower ideas only describe reality as it appears to a partial view, not as it is to one who simultaneously surveys the Whole. Thus Hegel reaches the conclusion that Absolute Reality forms one single harmonious system, not in space or time, not in any degree evil, wholly rational, and wholly spiritual. Any appearance to the contrary, in the world we know, can be proved logically—so he believes—to be entirely due to our fragmentary piecemeal view of the universe. If we saw the universe whole, as we may suppose God sees it, space and time and matter and evil and all striving and struggling would disappear, and we should see instead an eternal perfect unchanging spiritual unity.

In this conception, there is undeniably something sublime, something to which we could wish to yield assent. Nevertheless, when the arguments in support of it are carefully examined, they appear to involve much confusion and many unwarrantable assumptions. The fundamental tenet upon which the system is built up is that what is incomplete must be not self-subsistent, but must need the support of other things before it can exist. It is held that whatever has relations to things outside itself must contain some reference to those outside things in its own nature, and could not, therefore, be what it is if those outside things did not exist. A man's nature, for example, is constituted by his memories and the rest of his knowledge, by his loves and hatreds, and so on; thus, but for the objects which he knows or loves or hates, he could not be what he is. He is essentially and obviously a fragment: taken as the sum-total of reality he would be self-contradictory.

This whole point of view, however, turns upon the notion of the 'nature' of a thing, which seems to mean 'all the truths about the thing'. It is of course the case that a truth which connects one thing with another thing could not subsist if the other thing did not subsist. But a truth about a thing is not part of the thing itself, although it must, according to the above usage, be part of the 'nature' of the thing. If we mean by a thing's 'nature' all the truths about the thing, then plainly we cannot know a thing's 'nature' unless we know all the thing's relations to all the other things in the universe. But if the word 'nature' is used in this sense, we shall have to hold that the thing may be known when its 'nature' is not known, or at any rate is not known completely. There is a confusion, when this use of the word 'nature' is employed, between knowledge of things and knowledge of truths. We may have knowledge of a thing by acquaintance even if we know very few propositions about it—theoretically we need not know any propositions about it. Thus, acquaintance with a thing does not involve knowledge of its 'nature' in the above sense. And although acquaintance with a thing is involved in our knowing any one proposition about a thing, knowledge of its 'nature', in the above sense, is not involved. Hence, (1) acquaintance with a thing does not logically involve a knowledge of its relations, and (2) a knowledge of some of its relations does not involve a knowledge of all of its relations nor a knowledge of its 'nature' in the above sense. I may be acquainted, for example, with my toothache, and this knowledge may be as complete as knowledge by acquaintance ever can be, without knowing all that the dentist (who is not acquainted with it) can tell me about its cause, and without therefore knowing its 'nature' in the above sense. Thus the fact that a thing has relations does not prove that its relations are logically necessary. That is to say, from the mere fact that it is the thing it is we cannot deduce that it must have the various relations which in fact it has. This only seems to follow because we know it already.

It follows that we cannot prove that the universe as a whole forms a single harmonious system such as Hegel believes that it forms. And if we cannot prove this, we also cannot prove the unreality of space and time and matter and evil, for this is deduced by Hegel from the fragmentary and relational character of these things. Thus we are left to the piecemeal investigation of the world, and are unable to know the characters of those parts of the universe that are remote from our experience. This result, disappointing as it is to those whose hopes have been raised by the systems of philosophers, is in harmony with the inductive and scientific temper of our age, and is borne out by the whole examination of human knowledge which has occupied our previous chapters.

Most of the great ambitious attempts of metaphysicians have proceeded by the attempt to prove that such and such apparent features of the actual world were self-contradictory, and therefore could not be real. The whole tendency of modern thought, however, is more and more in the direction of showing that the supposed contradictions were illusory, and that very little can be proved a priori from considerations of what must be. A good illustration of this is afforded by space and time. Space and time appear to be infinite in extent, and infinitely divisible. If we travel along a straight line in either direction, it is difficult to believe that we shall finally reach a last point, beyond which there is nothing, not even empty space. Similarly, if in imagination we travel backwards or forwards in time, it is difficult to believe that we shall reach a first or last time, with not even empty time beyond it. Thus space and time appear to be infinite in extent.

Again, if we take any two points on a line, it seems evident that there must be other points between them, however small the distance between them may be: every distance can be halved, and the halves can be halved again, and so on ad infinitum. In time, similarly, however little time may elapse between two moments, it seems evident that there will be other moments between them. Thus space and time appear to be infinitely divisible. But as against these apparent facts—infinite extent and infinite divisibility—philosophers have advanced arguments tending to show that there could be no infinite collections of things, and that therefore the number of points in space, or of instants in time, must be finite. Thus a contradiction emerged between the apparent nature of space and time and the supposed impossibility of infinite collections.

Kant, who first emphasized this contradiction, deduced the impossibility of space and time, which he declared to be merely subjective; and since his time very many philosophers have believed that space and time are mere appearance, not characteristic of the world as it really is. Now, however, owing to the labours of the mathematicians, notably Georg Cantor, it has appeared that the impossibility of infinite collections was a mistake. They are not in fact self-contradictory, but only contradictory of certain rather obstinate mental prejudices. Hence the reasons for regarding space and time as unreal have become inoperative, and one of the great sources of metaphysical constructions is dried up.

The mathematicians, however, have not been content with showing that space as it is commonly supposed to be is possible; they have shown also that many other forms of space are equally possible, so far as logic can show. Some of Euclid's axioms, which appear to common sense to be necessary, and were formerly supposed to be necessary by philosophers, are now known to derive their appearance of necessity from our mere familiarity with actual space, and not from any a priori logical foundation. By imagining worlds in which these axioms are false, the mathematicians have used logic to loosen the prejudices of common sense, and to show the possibility of spaces differing—some more, some less—from that in which we live. And some of these spaces differ so little from Euclidean space, where distances such as we can measure are concerned, that it is impossible to discover by observation whether our actual space is strictly Euclidean or of one of these other kinds. Thus the position is completely reversed. Formerly it appeared that experience left only one kind of space to logic, and logic showed this one kind to be impossible. Now logic presents many kinds of space as possible apart from experience, and experience only partially decides between them. Thus, while our knowledge of what is has become less than it was formerly supposed to be, our knowledge of what may be is enormously increased. Instead of being shut in within narrow walls, of which every nook and cranny could be explored, we find ourselves in an open world of free possibilities, where much remains unknown because there is so much to know.

What has happened in the case of space and time has happened, to some extent, in other directions as well. The attempt to prescribe to the universe by means of a priori principles has broken down; logic instead of being, as formerly, the bar to possibilities, has become the great liberator of the imagination, presenting innumerable alternatives which are closed to unreflective common sense, and leaving to experience the task of deciding, where decision is possible, between the many worlds which logic offers for our choice. Thus knowledge as to what exists becomes limited to what we can learn from experience—not to what we can actually experience, for, as we have seen, there is much knowledge by description concerning things of which we have no direct experience. But in all cases of knowledge by description, we need some connexion of universals, enabling us, from such and such a datum, to infer an object of a certain sort as implied by our datum. Thus in regard to physical objects, for example, the principle that sense-data are signs of physical objects is itself a connexion of universals; and it is only in virtue of this principle that experience enables us to acquire knowledge concerning physical objects. The same applies to the law of causality, or, to descend to what is less general, to such principles as the law of gravitation.

Principles such as the law of gravitation are proved, or rather are rendered highly probable, by a combination of experience with some wholly a priori principle, such as the principle of induction. Thus our intuitive knowledge, which is the source of all our other knowledge of truths, is of two sorts: pure empirical knowledge, which tells us of the existence and some of the properties of particular things with which we are acquainted, and pure a priori knowledge, which gives us connexions between universals, and enables us to draw inferences from the particular facts given in empirical knowledge. Our derivative knowledge always depends upon some pure a priori knowledge and usually also depends upon some pure empirical knowledge.

Philosophical knowledge, if what has been said above is true, does not differ essentially from scientific knowledge; there is no special source of wisdom which is open to philosophy but not to science, and the results obtained by philosophy are not radically different from those obtained from science. The essential characteristic of philosophy which makes it a study distinct from science, is criticism. It examines critically the principles employed in science and in daily life; it searches out any inconsistencies there may be in these principles, and it only accepts them when, as the result of a critical inquiry, no reason for rejecting them has appeared. If, as many philosophers have believed, the principles underlying the sciences were capable, when disengaged from irrelevant detail, of giving us knowledge concerning the universe as a whole, such knowledge would have the same claim on our belief as scientific knowledge has; but our inquiry has not revealed any such knowledge, and therefore, as regards the special doctrines of the bolder metaphysicians, has had a mainly negative result. But as regards what would be commonly accepted as knowledge, our result is in the main positive: we have seldom found reason to reject such knowledge as the result of our criticism, and we have seen no reason to suppose man incapable of the kind of knowledge which he is generally believed to possess.

When, however, we speak of philosophy as a criticism of knowledge, it is necessary to impose a certain limitation. If we adopt the attitude of the complete sceptic, placing ourselves wholly outside all knowledge, and asking, from this outside position, to be compelled to return within the circle of knowledge, we are demanding what is impossible, and our scepticism can never be refuted. For all refutation must begin with some piece of knowledge which the disputants share; from blank doubt, no argument can begin. Hence the criticism of knowledge which philosophy employs must not be of this destructive kind, if any result is to be achieved. Against this absolute scepticism, no logical argument can be advanced. But it is not difficult to see that scepticism of this kind is unreasonable. Descartes' 'methodical doubt', with which modern philosophy began, is not of this kind, but is rather the kind of criticism which we are asserting to be the essence of philosophy. His 'methodical doubt' consisted in doubting whatever seemed doubtful; in pausing, with each apparent piece of knowledge, to ask himself whether, on reflection, he could feel certain that he really knew it. This is the kind of criticism which constitutes philosophy. Some knowledge, such as knowledge of the existence of our sense-data, appears quite indubitable, however calmly and thoroughly we reflect upon it. In regard to such knowledge, philosophical criticism does not require that we should abstain from belief. But there are beliefs—such, for example, as the belief that physical objects exactly resemble our sense-data—which are entertained until we begin to reflect, but are found to melt away when subjected to a close inquiry. Such beliefs philosophy will bid us reject, unless some new line of argument is found to support them. But to reject the beliefs which do not appear open to any objections, however closely we examine them, is not reasonable, and is not what philosophy advocates.

The criticism aimed at, in a word, is not that which, without reason, determines to reject, but that which considers each piece of apparent knowledge on its merits, and retains whatever still appears to be knowledge when this consideration is completed. That some risk of error remains must be admitted, since human beings are fallible. Philosophy may claim justly that it diminishes the risk of error, and that in some cases it renders the risk so small as to be practically negligible. To do more than this is not possible in a world where mistakes must occur; and more than this no prudent advocate of philosophy would claim to have performed.

CHAPTER XV THE VALUE OF PHILOSOPHY

Having now come to the end of our brief and very incomplete review of the problems of philosophy, it will be well to consider, in conclusion, what is the value of philosophy and why it ought to be studied. It is the more necessary to consider this question, in view of the fact that many men, under the influence of science or of practical affairs, are inclined to doubt whether philosophy is anything better than innocent but useless trifling, hair-splitting distinctions, and controversies on matters concerning which knowledge is impossible.

This view of philosophy appears to result, partly from a wrong conception of the ends of life, partly from a wrong conception of the kind of goods which philosophy strives to achieve. Physical science, through the medium of inventions, is useful to innumerable people who are wholly ignorant of it; thus the study of physical science is to be recommended, not only, or primarily, because of the effect on the student, but rather because of the effect on mankind in general. Thus utility does not belong to philosophy. If the study of philosophy has any value at all for others than students of philosophy, it must be only indirectly, through its effects upon the lives of those who study it. It is in these effects, therefore, if anywhere, that the value of philosophy must be primarily sought.

But further, if we are not to fail in our endeavour to determine the value of philosophy, we must first free our minds from the prejudices of what are wrongly called 'practical' men. The 'practical' man, as this word is often used, is one who recognizes only material needs, who realizes that men must have food for the body, but is oblivious of the necessity of providing food for the mind. If all men were well off, if poverty and disease had been reduced to their lowest possible point, there would still remain much to be done to produce a valuable society; and even in the existing world the goods of the mind are at least as important as the goods of the body. It is exclusively among the goods of the mind that the value of philosophy is to be found; and only those who are not indifferent to these goods can be persuaded that the study of philosophy is not a waste of time.

Philosophy, like all other studies, aims primarily at knowledge. The knowledge it aims at is the kind of knowledge which gives unity and system to the body of the sciences, and the kind which results from a critical examination of the grounds of our convictions, prejudices, and beliefs. But it cannot be maintained that philosophy has had any very great measure of success in its attempts to provide definite answers to its questions. If you ask a mathematician, a mineralogist, a historian, or any other man of learning, what definite body of truths has been ascertained by his science, his answer will last as long as you are willing to listen. But if you put the same question to a philosopher, he will, if he is candid, have to confess that his study has not achieved positive results such as have been achieved by other sciences. It is true that this is partly accounted for by the fact that, as soon as definite knowledge concerning any subject becomes possible, this subject ceases to be called philosophy, and becomes a separate science. The whole study of the heavens, which now belongs to astronomy, was once included in philosophy; Newton's great work was called 'the mathematical principles of natural philosophy'. Similarly, the study of the human mind, which was a part of philosophy, has now been separated from philosophy and has become the science of psychology. Thus, to a great extent, the uncertainty of philosophy is more apparent than real: those questions which are already capable of definite answers are placed in the sciences, while those only to which, at present, no definite answer can be given, remain to form the residue which is called philosophy.

This is, however, only a part of the truth concerning the uncertainty of philosophy. There are many questions—and among them those that are of the profoundest interest to our spiritual life—which, so far as we can see, must remain insoluble to the human intellect unless its powers become of quite a different order from what they are now. Has the universe any unity of plan or purpose, or is it a fortuitous concourse of atoms? Is consciousness a permanent part of the universe, giving hope of indefinite growth in wisdom, or is it a transitory accident on a small planet on which life must ultimately become impossible? Are good and evil of importance to the universe or only to man? Such questions are asked by philosophy, and variously answered by various philosophers. But it would seem that, whether answers be otherwise discoverable or not, the answers suggested by philosophy are none of them demonstrably true. Yet, however slight may be the hope of discovering an answer, it is part of the business of philosophy to continue the consideration of such questions, to make us aware of their importance, to examine all the approaches to them, and to keep alive that speculative interest in the universe which is apt to be killed by confining ourselves to definitely ascertainable knowledge.

Many philosophers, it is true, have held that philosophy could establish the truth of certain answers to such fundamental questions. They have supposed that what is of most importance in religious beliefs could be proved by strict demonstration to be true. In order to judge of such attempts, it is necessary to take a survey of human knowledge, and to form an opinion as to its methods and its limitations. On such a subject it would be unwise to pronounce dogmatically; but if the investigations of our previous chapters have not led us astray, we shall be compelled to renounce the hope of finding philosophical proofs of religious beliefs. We cannot, therefore, include as part of the value of philosophy any definite set of answers to such questions. Hence, once more, the value of philosophy must not depend upon any supposed body of definitely ascertainable knowledge to be acquired by those who study it.

The value of philosophy is, in fact, to be sought largely in its very uncertainty. The man who has no tincture of philosophy goes through life imprisoned in the prejudices derived from common sense, from the habitual beliefs of his age or his nation, and from convictions which have grown up in his mind without the co-operation or consent of his deliberate reason. To such a man the world tends to become definite, finite, obvious; common objects rouse no questions, and unfamiliar possibilities are contemptuously rejected. As soon as we begin to philosophize, on the contrary, we find, as we saw in our opening chapters, that even the most everyday things lead to problems to which only very incomplete answers can be given. Philosophy, though unable to tell us with certainty what is the true answer to the doubts which it raises, is able to suggest many possibilities which enlarge our thoughts and free them from the tyranny of custom. Thus, while diminishing our feeling of certainty as to what things are, it greatly increases our knowledge as to what they may be; it removes the somewhat arrogant dogmatism of those who have never travelled into the region of liberating doubt, and it keeps alive our sense of wonder by showing familiar things in an unfamiliar aspect.

Apart from its utility in showing unsuspected possibilities, philosophy has a value—perhaps its chief value—through the greatness of the objects which it contemplates, and the freedom from narrow and personal aims resulting from this contemplation. The life of the instinctive man is shut up within the circle of his private interests: family and friends may be included, but the outer world is not regarded except as it may help or hinder what comes within the circle of instinctive wishes. In such a life there is something feverish and confined, in comparison with which the philosophic life is calm and free. The private world of instinctive interests is a small one, set in the midst of a great and powerful world which must, sooner or later, lay our private world in ruins. Unless we can so enlarge our interests as to include the whole outer world, we remain like a garrison in a beleaguered fortress, knowing that the enemy prevents escape and that ultimate surrender is inevitable. In such a life there is no peace, but a constant strife between the insistence of desire and the powerlessness of will. In one way or another, if our life is to be great and free, we must escape this prison and this strife.

One way of escape is by philosophic contemplation. Philosophic contemplation does not, in its widest survey, divide the universe into two hostile camps—friends and foes, helpful and hostile, good and bad—it views the whole impartially. Philosophic contemplation, when it is unalloyed, does not aim at proving that the rest of the universe is akin to man. All acquisition of knowledge is an enlargement of the Self, but this enlargement is best attained when it is not directly sought. It is obtained when the desire for knowledge is alone operative, by a study which does not wish in advance that its objects should have this or that character, but adapts the Self to the characters which it finds in its objects. This enlargement of Self is not obtained when, taking the Self as it is, we try to show that the world is so similar to this Self that knowledge of it is possible without any admission of what seems alien. The desire to prove this is a form of self-assertion and, like all self-assertion, it is an obstacle to the growth of Self which it desires, and of which the Self knows that it is capable. Self-assertion, in philosophic speculation as elsewhere, views the world as a means to its own ends; thus it makes the world of less account than Self, and the Self sets bounds to the greatness of its goods. In contemplation, on the contrary, we start from the not-Self, and through its greatness the boundaries of Self are enlarged; through the infinity of the universe the mind which contemplates it achieves some share in infinity.

For this reason greatness of soul is not fostered by those philosophies which assimilate the universe to Man. Knowledge is a form of union of Self and not-Self; like all union, it is impaired by dominion, and therefore by any attempt to force the universe into conformity with what we find in ourselves. There is a widespread philosophical tendency towards the view which tells us that Man is the measure of all things, that truth is man-made, that space and time and the world of universals are properties of the mind, and that, if there be anything not created by the mind, it is unknowable and of no account for us. This view, if our previous discussions were correct, is untrue; but in addition to being untrue, it has the effect of robbing philosophic contemplation of all that gives it value, since it fetters contemplation to Self. What it calls knowledge is not a union with the not-Self, but a set of prejudices, habits, and desires, making an impenetrable veil between us and the world beyond. The man who finds pleasure in such a theory of knowledge is like the man who never leaves the domestic circle for fear his word might not be law.

The true philosophic contemplation, on the contrary, finds its satisfaction in every enlargement of the not-Self, in everything that magnifies the objects contemplated, and thereby the subject contemplating. Everything, in contemplation, that is personal or private, everything that depends upon habit, self-interest, or desire, distorts the object, and hence impairs the union which the intellect seeks. By thus making a barrier between subject and object, such personal and private things become a prison to the intellect.

The free intellect will see as God might see, without a here and now, without hopes and fears, without the trammels of customary beliefs and traditional prejudices, calmly, dispassionately, in the sole and exclusive desire of knowledge—knowledge as impersonal, as purely contemplative, as it is possible for man to attain. Hence also the free intellect will value more the abstract and universal knowledge into which the accidents of private history do not enter, than the knowledge brought by the senses, and dependent, as such knowledge must be, upon an exclusive and personal point of view and a body whose sense-organs distort as much as they reveal.

The mind which has become accustomed to the freedom and impartiality of philosophic contemplation will preserve something of the same freedom and impartiality in the world of action and emotion. It will view its purposes and desires as parts of the whole, with the absence of insistence that results from seeing them as infinitesimal fragments in a world of which all the rest is unaffected by any one man's deeds. The impartiality which, in contemplation, is the unalloyed desire for truth, is the very same quality of mind which, in action, is justice, and in emotion is that universal love which can be given to all, and not only to those who are judged useful or admirable. Thus contemplation enlarges not only the objects of our thoughts, but also the objects of our actions and our affections: it makes us citizens of the universe, not only of one walled city at war with all the rest. In this citizenship of the universe consists man's true freedom, and his liberation from the thraldom of narrow hopes and fears.

Thus, to sum up our discussion of the value of philosophy; Philosophy is to be studied, not for the sake of any definite answers to its questions since no definite answers can, as a rule, be known to be true, but rather for the sake of the questions themselves; because these questions enlarge our conception of what is possible, enrich our intellectual imagination and diminish the dogmatic assurance which closes the mind against speculation; but above all because, through the greatness of the universe which philosophy contemplates, the mind also is rendered great, and becomes capable of that union with the universe which constitutes its highest good.

A Free Man's Worship

This essay was written in 1903 during one of Russell's deepest personal crises. It shows his attempt to find meaning and morality in life, and is a classic essay on humanistic perspective.

The world, says Russell, is an absurd, godless tragedy in which nature, omnipotent but blind, has brought forth rational children who are superior to their mother, and as such can discover moral ideals with which to sustain themselves in this ultimately meaningless existence. Morality doesn't need religion for legitimation.

To Dr. Faustus in his study Mephistopheles told the history of the Creation, saying,

The endless praises of the choirs of angels had begun to grow wearisome; for, after all, did he not deserve their praise? Had he not given them endless joy? Would it not be more amusing to obtain undeserved praise, to be worshiped by beings whom he tortured? He smiled inwardly, and resolved that the great drama should be performed.

For countless ages the hot nebula whirled aimlessly through space. At length it began to take shape, the central mass threw off planets, the planets cooled, boiling seas and burning mountains heaved and tossed, from black masses of cloud hot sheets of rain deluged the barely solid crust. And now the first germ of life grew in the depths of the ocean and developed rapidly in the fructifying warmth into vast forest trees, huge ferns springing from the damp mold, sea monsters breeding, fighting, devouring, and passing away. And from the monsters, as the play unfolded itself, Man was born, with the power of thought, the knowledge of good and evil, and the cruel thirst for worship. And Man saw that all is passing in this mad, monstrous world, that all is struggling to snatch, at any cost, a few brief moments of life before Death's inexorable decree. And Man said, "There is a hidden purpose, could we but fathom it, and the purpose is good; for we must reverence something, and in the visible world there is nothing worthy of reverence." And Man stood aside from the struggle, resolving that

God intended harmony to come out of chaos by human efforts. And when he followed the instincts which God had transmitted to him from his ancestry of beasts of prey, he called it Sin, and asked God to forgive him. But he doubted whether he could be justly forgiven, until he invented a divine Plan by which God's wrath was to have been appeased. And seeing the present was bad, he made it yet worse, that thereby the future might be better. And he gave God thanks for the strength that enabled him to forgo even the joys that were possible. And God smiled; and when he saw that Man had become perfect in renunciation and worship, he sent another sun through the sky, which crashed into Man's sun; and all returned again to nebula.

> "Yes," he murmured, "it was a good play; I will have it performed again."

Such, in outline, but even more purposeless, more void of meaning, is the world which science presents for our belief. Amid such a world, if anywhere, our ideals henceforward must find a home. That man is the product of causes which had no prevision of the end they were achieving; that his origin, his growth, his hopes and fears, his loves and his beliefs, are but the outcome of accidental collocations of atoms; that no fire, no heroism, no intensity of thought and feeling, can preserve an individual life beyond the grave; that all the labors of the ages, all the devotion, all the inspiration, all the noonday brightness of human genius, are destined to extinction in the vast death of the solar system, and that the whole temple of man's achievement must inevitably be buried beneath the debris of a universe in ruins—all these things, if not quite beyond dispute, are yet so nearly certain that no philosophy which rejects them can hope to stand. Only within the scaffolding of these truths, only on the firm foundation of unyielding despair, can the soul's habitation henceforth be safely built.

How, in such an alien and inhuman world, can so powerless a creature as man preserve his aspirations untarnished? A strange mystery it is that nature, omnipotent but blind, in the revolutions of her secular hurryings through the abysses of space, has brought forth at last a child, subject still to her power, but gifted with sight, with knowledge of good and evil, with the capacity of judging all the works of his unthinking mother. In spite of death, the mark and seal of the parental control, man is yet free, during his brief years, to examine, to criticize, to know, and in imagination to create. To him alone, in the world with which he is acquainted, this freedom belongs; and in this lies his superiority to the resistless forces that control his outward life.

The savage, like ourselves, feels the oppression of his impotence before the powers of nature; but having in himself nothing that he respects more than power, he is willing to prostrate himself before his gods, without inquiring whether they are worthy of his worship. Pathetic and very terrible is the long history of cruelty and torture, of degradation and human sacrifice, endured in the hope of placating the jealous gods: surely, the trembling believer thinks, when what is most precious has been freely given, their lust for blood must be appeased, and more will not be required. The religion of Moloch—as such creeds may be generally called—is in essence the cringing submission of the slave, who dare not, even in his heart, allow the thought that his master deserves no adulation. Since the independence of ideals is not yet acknowledged, power may be freely worshiped and receive an unlimited respect, despite its wanton infliction of pain.

But gradually, as morality grows bolder, the claim of the ideal world begins to be felt; and worship, if it is not to cease, must be given to gods of another kind than those created by the savage. Some, though they feel the demands of the ideal, will still consciously reject them, still urging that naked power is worthy of worship. Such is the attitude inculcated in God's answer to Job out of the whirlwind: the divine power and knowledge are paraded, but of the divine goodness there is no hint. Such also is the attitude of those who, in our own day, base their morality upon the struggle for survival, maintaining that the survivors are necessarily the fittest. But others, not content with an answer so repugnant to the moral sense, will adopt the position which we have become accustomed to regard as specially religious, maintaining that, in some hidden manner, the world of fact is really harmonious with the world of ideals. Thus man created God, all-powerful and all-good, the mystic unity of what is and what should be.

But the world of fact, after all, is not good; and, in submitting our judgment to it, there is an element of slavishness from which our thoughts must be purged. For in all things it is well to exalt the dignity of man, by freeing him as far as possible from the tyranny of nonhuman power. When we have realized that power is largely bad, that man, with his knowledge of good and evil, is but a helpless atom in a world which has no such knowledge, the choice is again presented to us: Shall we worship force, or shall we worship goodness? Shall our God exist and be evil, or shall he be recognized as the creation of our own conscience?

The answer to this question is very momentous and affects profoundly our whole morality. The worship of force, to which Carlyle and Nietzsche and the creed of militarism have accustomed us, is the result of failure to maintain our own ideals against a hostile universe: it is itself a prostrate submission to evil, a sacrifice of our best to Moloch. If strength indeed is to be respected, let us respect rather the strength of those who refuse that false "recognition of facts" which fails to recognize that facts are often bad. Let us admit that, in the world we know, there are many things that would be better otherwise, and that the ideals to which we do and must adhere are not realized in the realm of matter. Let us preserve our respect for truth, for beauty, for the ideal of perfection which life does not permit us to attain, though none of these things meet with the approval of the unconscious universe. If power is bad, as it seems to be, let us reject it from our hearts. In this lies man's true freedom: in determination to worship only the God created by our own love of the good, to respect only the heaven which inspires the insight of our best moments. In action, in desire, we must submit perpetually to the tyranny of outside forces; but in thought, in aspiration, we are free, free from our fellow men, free from the petty planet on which our bodies impotently crawl, free even, while we live, from the tyranny of death. Let us learn, then, that energy of faith which enables us to live constantly in the vision of the good; and let us descend, in action, into the world of fact, with that vision always before us.

When first the opposition of fact and ideal grows fully visible, a spirit of fiery revolt, of fierce hatred of the gods, seems necessary to the assertion of freedom. To defy with Promethean constancy a hostile universe, to keep its evil always in view, always actively hated, to refuse no pain that the malice of power can invent, appears to be the duty of all who will not bow before the inevitable. But indignation is still a bondage, for it compels our thoughts to be occupied with an evil world; and in the fierceness of desire from which rebellion springs there is a kind of self-assertion which it is necessary for the wise to overcome. Indignation is a submission of our thoughts but not of our desires; the Stoic freedom in which wisdom consists is found in the submission of our desires but not of our thoughts. From the submission of our desires springs the virtue of resignation; from the freedom of our thoughts springs the whole world of art and philosophy, and the vision of beauty by which, at last, we half reconquer the reluctant world. But the vision of beauty is possible only to unfettered contemplation, to thoughts not weighted by the load of eager wishes; and thus freedom comes only to those who no longer ask of life that it shall yield them any of those personal goods that are subject to the mutations of time.

Although the necessity of renunciation is evidence of the existence of evil, yet Christianity, in preaching it, has shown a wisdom exceeding that of the Promethean philosophy of rebellion. It must be admitted that, of the things we desire, some, though they prove impossible, are yet real goods; others, however, as ardently longed for, do not form part of a fully purified ideal. The belief that what must be renounced is bad, though sometimes false, is far less often false than untamed passion supposes; and the creed of religion, by providing a reason for proving that it is never false, has been the means of purifying our hopes by the discovery of many austere truths.

But there is in resignation a further good element: even real goods, when they are unattainable, ought not to be fretfully desired. To every man comes, sooner or later, the great renunciation. For the young, there is nothing unattainable; a good thing desired with the whole force of a passionate will, and yet impossible, is to them not credible. Yet, by death, by illness, by poverty, or by the voice of duty, we must learn, each one of us, that the world was not made for us, and that, however beautiful may be the things we crave, Fate may nevertheless forbid them. It is the part of courage, when misfortune comes, to bear without repining the ruin of our hopes, to turn away our thoughts from vain regrets. This degree of submission to power is not only just and right: it is the very gate of wisdom.

But passive renunciation is not the whole of wisdom; for not by renunciation alone can we build a temple for the worship of our own ideals. Haunting foreshadowings of the temple appear in the realm of imagination, in music, in architecture, in the untroubled kingdom of reason, and in the golden sunset magic of lyrics, where beauty shines and glows, remote from the touch of sorrow, remote from the fear of change, remote from the failures and disenchantments of the world of fact. In the contemplation of these things the vision of heaven will shape itself in our hearts, giving at once a touchstone to judge the world about us and an inspiration by which to fashion to our needs whatever is not incapable of serving as a stone in the sacred temple.

Except for those rare spirits that are born without sin, there is a cavern of darkness to be traversed before that temple can be entered. The gate of the cavern is despair, and its floor is paved with the gravestones of abandoned hopes. There self must die; there the eagerness, the greed of untamed desire, must be slain, for only so can the soul be freed from the empire of Fate. But out of the cavern, the Gate of Renunciation leads again to the daylight of wisdom, by whose radiance a new insight, a new joy, a new tenderness, shine forth to gladden the pilgrim's heart.

When, without the bitterness of impotent rebellion, we have learned both to resign ourselves to the outward rule of Fate and to recognize that the non-human world is unworthy of our worship, it becomes possible at last so to transform and refashion the unconscious universe, so to transmute it in the crucible of imagination, that a new image of shining gold replaces the old idol of clay. In all the multiform facts of the world—in the visual shapes of trees and mountains and clouds, in the events of the life of man, even in the very omnipotence of death—the insight of creative idealism can find the reflection of a beauty which its own thoughts first made. In this way mind asserts its subtle mastery over the thoughtless forces of nature. The more evil the material with which it deals, the more thwarting to untrained desire, the greater is its achievement in inducing the reluctant rock to yield up its hidden treasures, the prouder its victory in compelling the opposing forces to swell the pageant of its triumph. Of all the arts, tragedy is the proudest, the most triumphant; for it builds its shining citadel in the very center of the enemy's country, on the very summit of his highest mountain; from its impregnable watchtowers, his camps and arsenals, his columns and forts, are all revealed; within its walls the free life continues, while the legions of death and pain and despair, and all the servile captains of tyrant Fate, afford the burghers of that dauntless city new spectacles of beauty. Happy those sacred ramparts, thrice happy the dwellers on that all-seeing eminence. Honor to those brave warriors who, through countless ages of warfare, have preserved for us the priceless heritage of liberty and have kept undefiled by sacrilegious invaders the home of the unsubdued.

But the beauty of tragedy does but make visible a quality which, in more or less obvious shapes, is present always and everywhere in life. In the spectacle of death, in the endurance of intolerable pain, and in the irrevocableness of a vanished past, there is a sacredness, an overpowering awe, a feeling of the vastness, the depth, the inexhaustible mystery of existence, in which, as by some strange marriage of pain, the sufferer is bound to the world by bonds of sorrow. In these moments of insight, we lose all eagerness of temporary desire, all struggling and striving for petty ends, all care for the little trivial things that, to a superficial view, make up the common life of day by day; we see, surrounding the narrow raft illumined by the flickering light of human comradeship, the dark ocean on whose rolling waves we toss for a brief hour; from the great night without, a chill blast breaks in upon our refuge; all the loneliness of humanity amid hostile forces is concentrated upon the individual soul, which must struggle alone, with what of courage it can command, against the whole weight of a universe that cares nothing for its hopes and fears. Victory, in this struggle with the powers of darkness, is the true baptism into the glorious company of heroes, the true initiation into the overmastering beauty of human existence. From that awful encounter of the soul with the outer world, renunciation, wisdom, and charity are born; and with their birth a new life begins. To take into the inmost shrine of the soul the irresistible forces whose puppets we seem to be—death and change, the irrevocableness of the past, and the powerlessness of man before the blind hurry of the universe from vanity to vanity—to feel these things and know them is to conquer them.

This is the reason why the past has such magical power. The beauty of its motionless and silent pictures is like the enchanted purity of late autumn, when the leaves, though one breath would make them fall, still glow against the sky in golden glory. The past does not change or strive; like Duncan, after life's fitful fever it sleeps well; what was eager and grasping, what was petty and transitory, has faded away; the things that were beautiful and eternal shine out of it like stars in the night. Its beauty, to a soul not worthy of it, is unendurable; but to a soul which has conquered Fate it is the key of religion.

The life of man, viewed outwardly, is but a small

thing in comparison with the forces of nature. The slave is doomed to worship Time and Fate and Death, because they are greater than anything he finds in himself, and because all his thoughts are of things which they devour. But, great as they are, to think of them greatly, to feel their passionless splendor, is greater still. And such thought makes us free men; we no longer bow before the inevitable in Oriental subjection, but we absorb it and make it a part of ourselves. To abandon the struggle for private happiness, to expel all eagerness of temporary desire, to burn with passion for eternal things—this is emancipation, and this is the free man's worship. And this liberation is effected by contemplation of Fate; for Fate itself is subdued by the mind which leaves nothing to be purged by the purifying fire of time.

United with his fellow men by the strongest of all ties, the tie of a common doom, the free man finds that a new vision is with him always, shedding over every daily task the light of love. The life of man is a long march through the night, surrounded by invisible foes, tortured by weariness and pain, toward a goal that few can hope to reach, and where none may tarry long. One by one, as they march, our comrades vanish from our sight, seized by the silent orders of omnipotent death. Very brief is the time in which we can help them, in which their happiness or misery is decided. Be it ours to shed sunshine on their path, to lighten their sorrows by the balm of sympathy, to give them the pure joy of a never-tiring affection, to strengthen failing courage, to instill faith in hours of despair. Let us not weigh in grudging scales their merits and demerits, but let us think only of their need—of the sorrows, the difficulties, perhaps the blindnesses, that make the misery of their lives; let us remember that they are fellow sufferers in the same darkness, actors in the same tragedy with ourselves. And so, when their day is over, when their good and their evil have become eternal by the immortality of the past, be it ours to feel that, where they suffered, where they failed, no deed of ours was the cause; but wherever a spark of the divine fire kindled in their hearts, we were ready with encouragement, with sympathy, with brave words in which high courage glowed.

Brief and powerless is man's life; on him and all his race the slow, sure doom falls pitiless and dark. Blind to good and evil, reckless of destruction, omnipotent matter rolls on its relentless way; for man, condemned today to lose his dearest, tomorrow himself to pass through the gate of darkness, it remains only to cherish, ere yet the blow fall, the lofty thoughts that ennoble his little day; disdaining the coward terrors of the slave of Fate, to worship at the shrine that his own hands have built; undismayed by the empire of chance, to preserve a mind free from the wanton tyranny that rules his outward life; proudly defiant of the irresistible forces that tolerate, for a moment, his knowledge and his condemnation, to sustain alone, a weary but unyielding Atlas, the world that his own ideals have fashioned despite the trampling march of unconscious power.

Chapter 35

G. E. MOORE

G. E. Moore (1873–1958) was Professor of Philosophy at Cambridge University and one of the leading philosophers of the first half of the twentieth century. As a student at Cambridge University, he was a close acquaintance, though more a rival than a friend, of Bertrand Russell. He was also the leader of the Bloomsbury group of writers and artists which included such illustrious intellectuals as John Maynard Keynes, Leonard and Virginia Woolf, and Lytton Strachey. He was editor of the British philosophy journal *Mind* from 1921 to 1947 and was appointed to the Order of Merit in 1951. Perhaps his most influential work is *Principia Ethica* (1903) where he argues for the indefinability of "good."

Moore was a defender of common sense against skeptics and others who derided our ordinary beliefs. He argued that there is a vast amount of shared knowledge about the world, expressible in ordinary language and about which we can be quite certain. In this essay-which is a combination of two of his articles, "A Defence of Common Sense" and "Proof of the External World"—Moore argues that skepticism is decisively refuted by common sense. The essence of the argument is as follows:

1. If skepticism is true, we do not have knowledge of the external world.

2. But we do have knowledge of the external world (Moore gives many examples).

Therefore

3. Skepticism is false.

FOR FURTHER READING

Baldwin, Thomas. *G.E. Moore* (London, 1990).
Copleston, F. C. *Contemporary Philosophy*. (Newman Press, 1963).
Moore, G. E. *Philosophical Papers*. (George Allen & Unwin, 1959).
Moore, G. E. *Some Main Problems of Philosophy*. (Collier Books, 1962).
Passmore, John. *A Hundred Years of Philosophy*. (Macmillan, 1957).
Schilpp, P.A. (ed.) *The Philosophy of G.E. Moore* (open Court, 1942).

Philosophical Papers

A DEFENSE OF COMMON SENSE

In what follows I have merely tried to state, one by one, some of the most important points in which my philosophical position differs from positions which have been taken up by *some* other philosophers. It may be that the points which I have had room to mention are not really the most important, and possibly some of them may be points as to which no philosopher has ever really differed from me. But, to the best of my belief, each is a point as to which many have really differed; although (in most cases, at all events) each is also a point as to which many have agreed with me.

I

The first point is a point which embraces a great many other points. And it is one which I cannot state as clearly as I wish to state it, except at some length. The method I am going to use for stating it is this. I am going to begin by enunciating, under the heading (1), a whole long list of propositions, which may seem, at first sight, such obvious truisms as not to be worth stating: they are, in fact, a set of propositions, every one of which (in my own opinion) I *know*, with certainty, to be true. I shall, next, under the heading (2), state a single proposition which makes an assertion about a whole set of *classes* of propositions—each class being defined, as the class consisting of all propositions which resemble *one* of the propositions in (1) in a certain respect. (2), therefore, is a proposition which could not be stated, until the list of propositions in (1), or some similar list, had already been given. (2) is itself a proposition which may seem such an obvious truism as not to be worth stating: and it is also a proposition which (in my own opinion) I know, with certainty, to be true. But, nevertheless, it is, to the best of my belief, a proposition with regard to which many philosophers have, for different reasons, differed from me; even if they have not directly denied (2) itself, they have held views incompatible with it. My first point, then, may be said to be that (2), together with all its implications, some of which I shall expressly mention, is true.

(1) I begin, then, with my list of truisms, every one of which (in my own opinion) I *know*, with certainty, to be true. The propositions to be included in this list are the following:

There exists at present a living human body, which is *my* body. This body was born at a certain time in the past, and has existed continuously ever since, though not without undergoing changes; it was, for instance, much smaller when it was born, and for some time afterwards, than it is now. Ever since it was born, it has been either in contact with or not far from the surface of the earth; and, at every moment since it was born, there have also existed many other things, having shape and size in three dimensions (in the same familiar sense in which it has), from which it has been *at various distances* (in the familiar sense in which it is now at a distance both from that mantelpiece and from that bookcase, and at a greater distance from the bookcase than it is from the mantelpiece); also there have (very often, at all events) existed some other things of this kind with which it was *in contact* (in the familiar sense in which it is now in contact with the pen I am holding in my right hand and with some of the clothes I am wearing). Among the things which have, in this sense, formed part of its environment (i.e. have been either in contact with it, or at *some* distance from it, however *great*) there have, at every moment since its birth, been large numbers of other living human bodies, each of which has, like it, (*a*) at some time been born, (*b*) continued to exist from some time after birth, (*c*) been, at every moment of its life after birth, either in contact with or not far from the surface of the earth; and many of these bodies have already died and ceased to exist. But the earth had existed also for many years before my body was born; and for many of these years, also, large numbers of human bodies had, at every moment, been alive upon it; and many of these bodies had died and ceased to exist before it was born. Fi-

Reprinted from G.E. Moore, *Philosophical Papers* (London: George Allen & Unwin, 1959) by permission of Timothy Moore.

nally (to come to a different class of propositions), I am a human being, and I have, at different times since my body was born, had many different experiences, of each of many different kinds: e.g. I have often perceived both my own body and other things which formed part of its environment, including other human bodies; I have not only perceived things of this kind, but have also observed facts about them, such as, for instance, the fact which I am now observing, that that mantel-piece is at present nearer to my body than that bookcase; I have been aware of other facts, which I was not at the time observing, such as, for instance, the fact, of which I am now aware, that my body existed yesterday and was then also for some time nearer to that mantelpiece than to that bookcase; I have had expectations with regard to the future, and many beliefs of other kinds, both true and false; I have thought of imaginary things and persons and incidents, in the reality of which I did not believe; I have had dreams; and I have had feelings of many different kinds. And, just as my body has been the body of a human being, namely myself, who has, during his lifetime, had many experiences of each of these (and other) different kinds; so, in the case of very many of the other human bodies which have lived upon the earth, each has been the body of a different human being, who has, during the lifetime of that body, had many different experiences of each of these (and other) different kinds.

(2) I now come to the single truism which, as will be seen, could not be stated except by reference to the whole list of truisms, just given in (1). This truism also (in my own opinion) I *know*, which certainty, to be true; and it is as follows:

In the case of *very many* (I do not say *all*) of the human beings belonging to the class (which includes myself) defined in the following way, i.e. as human beings who have had human bodies, that were born and lived for some time upon the earth, and who have, during the lifetime of those bodies, had many different experiences of each of the kinds mentioned in (1), it is true that each has frequently, during the life of his body, known, with regard to *him*self or *his* body, and with regard to some time earlier than any of the times at which I wrote down the propositions in (1), a proposition *corresponding* to each of the propositions in (1), in the sense that it asserts with regard to *himself* or *his* body and the earlier time in question (namely, in each case, the time at which he knew it), just what the corresponding proposition in (1) asserts with regard to *me* or *my* body and the time at which I wrote that proposition down.

In other words what (2) asserts is only (what seems an obvious enough truism) that each of *us* (meaning by 'us', very many human beings of the class defined) has frequently *known*, with regard to *him*self or *his* body and the time at which he knew it, everything which, in writing down my list of propositions in (1), I was claiming to know about *my*self or *my* body and the time at which I wrote that proposition down, i.e. just as *I* knew (when I wrote it down) 'There exists at present a living human body which is my body', so each of us has frequently known with regard to himself and some other time the different but corresponding proposition, which *he* could *then* have properly expressed by, 'There exists *at present* a human body which is *my* body'; just as *I* know 'Many human bodies other than mine have before now lived on the earth', so each of us has frequently known the different but corresponding proposition 'Many human bodies other than *mine* have before *now* lived on the earth'; just as *I* know 'Many human beings other than myself have before now perceived, and dreamed, and felt', so each of *us* has frequently known the different but corresponding proposition 'Many human beings other than *myself* have before *now* perceived, and dreamed, and felt'; and so on, in the case of *each* of the propositions enumerated in (1). . . .

PROOF OF AN EXTERNAL WORLD

In the preface to the second edition of Kant's *Critique of Pure Reason* some words occur, which, in Professor Kemp Smith's translations, are rendered as follows:

> It still remains a scandal to philosophy . . . that the existence of things outside of us . . . must be accepted merely on *faith*, and that, if anyone thinks good to doubt their existence, we are unable to counter his doubts by any satisfactory proof.[1]

It seems clear from these words that Kant thought it a matter of some importance to give a proof of 'the existence of things outside of us' or perhaps

[1]B xxxix, note: Kemp Smith, p. 34. The German words are 'so bleibt es immer ein Skandal de Philosophie . . ., das Dasein der Dinge ausser uns . . . bloss auf *Glauben* annehmen zu müssen, und wenn es jemand einfällt es zu bezweifeln, ihm keinin genugtuenden Beweis entgegenstellen zu können'.

rather (for it seems to me possible that the force of the German words is better rendered in this way) of 'the existence of *the* things outside of us'; for had he not thought it important that a proof should be given, he would scarcely have called it a 'scandal' that no proof had been given. And it seems clear also that he thought that the giving of such a proof was a task which fell properly within the province of philosophy; for, it if did not, the fact that no proof had been given could not possibly be a scandal to *philosophy*.

Now, even if Kant was mistaken in both of these two opinions, there seems to me to be no doubt whatever that it is a matter of some importance and also a matter which falls properly within the province of philosophy, to discuss the question what sort of proof, if any, can be given of 'the existence of things outside of us'. And to discuss this question was my object when I began to write the present lecture. But I may say at once that, as you will find, I have only, at most, succeeded in saying a very small part of what ought to be said about it.

The words 'it . . . remains a scandal to philosophy . . . that we are unable . . .' would, taken strictly, imply that, at the moment at which he wrote them, Kant himself was unable to produce a satisfactory proof of the point in question. But I think it is unquestionable that Kant himself did not think that he personally was at the time unable to produce such a proof. On the contrary, in the immediately preceding sentence, he has declared that he has, in the second edition of his *Critique*, to which he is now writing the Preface, given a 'rigorous proof' of this very thing; and has added that he believes this proof of his to be 'the only possible proof'. It is true that in this preceding sentence he does not describe the proof which he has given as a proof of 'the existence of things outside of us' or of 'the existence of the things outside of us', but describes it instead as a proof of 'the objective reality of outer intuition'. But the context leaves no doubt that he is using these two phrases, 'the objective reality of outer intuition' and 'the existence of things (*or* 'the things') outside of us', in such a way that whatever is a proof of the first is also necessarily a proof of the second. We must, therefore, suppose that when he speaks as if *we* are unable to give a satisfactory proof, he does not mean to say that he himself, as well as others, is *at the moment* unable; but rather that, until he discovered the proof which he has given, both he himself and everybody else *were* unable. Of course, if he is right in thinking that he has given a satisfactory proof, the state of things which he describes came to an end as soon as his proof was published. As soon as that happened, anyone who read it was able to give a satisfactory proof by simply repeating that which Kant had given, and the 'scandal' to philosophy had been removed once for all.

If, therefore, it were certain that the proof of the point in question given by Kant in the second edition is a satisfactory proof, it would be certain that at least one satisfactory proof can be given; and all that would remain of the question which I said I proposed to discuss would be, firstly, the question as to what *sort* of a proof this of Kant's is, and secondly the question whether (contrary to Kant's own opinion) there may not perhaps be other proofs, of the same or of a different sort, which are also satisfactory. But I think it is by no means certain that Kant's proof is satisfactory. I think it is by no means certain that he did succeed in removing once for all the state of affairs which he considered to be a scandal to philosophy. And I think, therefore, that the question whether it is possible to give *any* satisfactory proof of the point in question still deserves discussion.

But what is the point in question? I think it must be owned that the expression 'things outside of us' is rather an odd expression, and an expression the meaning of which is certainly not perfectly clear. It would have sounded less odd if, instead of 'things outside of us' I had said 'external things', and perhaps also the meaning of this expression would have seemed to be clearer; and I think we make the meaning of 'external things' clearer still if we explain that this phrase has been regularly used by philosophers as short for 'things external to *our minds*'. The fact is that there has been a long philosophical tradition, in accordance with which the three expressions 'external things', 'things external to *us*', and 'things external to *our minds*' have been used as equivalent to one another, and have, each of them, been used as if they needed no explanation. The origin of this usage I do not know. It occurs already in Descartes; and since he uses the expressions as if they needed no explanation, they had presumably been used with the same meaning before. Of the three, it seems to me that the expression 'external to *our minds*' is the clearest, since it at least makes clear that what is meant is not 'external to *our bodies*'; whereas both the other expressions might be taken to mean this: and indeed there has been a good deal of confusion, even among philosophers, as to the relation of the two conceptions 'external things' and 'things external to *our bodies*'. But even the expression 'things external to our minds' seems to me to be far from perfectly clear; and if I am to make really clear what I mean by 'proof of the existence of things outside of us', I cannot do it by merely saying that by 'outside of us' I mean 'external to our minds'. . . .

But now, if to say of anything, e.g. my body, that it is external to *my* mind, means merely that from a proposition to the effect that it existed at a specified time, there in no case follows the further proposition that *I* was having an experience at the time in question, then to say of anything that it is external to *our* minds, will mean similarly that from a proposition to the effect that it existed at a specified time, it in no case follows that any of *us* were having experiences at the time in question. And if by *our* minds be meant, as is, I think, usually meant, the minds of human beings living on the earth, then it will follow that any pains which animals may feel, any after-images they may see, any experiences they may have, though not external to *their* minds, yet are external to *ours*. And this at once makes plain how different is the conception 'external to our minds' from the conception 'to be met with in space'; for, of course, pains which animals feel or after-images which they see are no more to be met with in space than are pains which *we* feel or after-images which *we* see. From the proposition that there are external objects—objects that are not in any of *our* minds, it does *not* follow that there are things to be met with in space; and hence 'external to our minds' is not a mere synonym for 'to be met with in space': that is to say, 'external to our minds' and 'to be met with in space' are two different conceptions. And the true relation between these conceptions seems to me to be this. We have already seen that there are ever so many kinds of 'things', such that, in the case of each of these kinds, from the proposition that there is at least one thing of that kind there *follows* the proposition that there is at least one thing to be met with in space: e.g. this follows from 'There is at least one star', from 'There is at least one human body', from 'There is at least one shadow', etc. And I think we can say that of every kind of thing of which this is true, it is also true that from the proposition that there is at least one 'thing' of that kind there *follows* the proposition that there is at least one thing external to our minds: e.g. from 'There is at least one star' there follows not only 'There is at least one thing to be met with in space' but also 'There is at least one external thing', and similarly in all other cases. My reason for saying this is as follows. Consider any kind of thing, such that anything of that kind, if there is anything of it, must be 'to be met with in space': e.g. consider the kind 'soap-bubble'. If I say of anything which I am perceiving, 'That is a soap-bubble', I am, it seems to me, certainly implying that there would be no contradiction in asserting that it existed before I perceived it and that it will continue to exist, even if I cease to perceive it. This seems to me to be part of what is meant by saying that it is a real soap-bubble, as distinguished, for instance, from an hallucination of a soap-bubble. Of course, it by no means follows, that if it really is a soap-bubble, it did in fact exist before I perceived it or will continue to exist after I cease to perceive it: soap-bubbles are an example of a kind of 'physical object' and 'thing to be met with in space', in the case of which it is notorious that particular specimens of the kind often do exist only so long as they are perceived by a particular person. But a thing which I perceive would not be a soap-bubble unless its existence at any given time were *logically independent* of my perception of it at that time; unless that is to say, from the proposition, with regard to a particular time, that it existed at that time, it *never* follows that I perceived it at that time. But, if it is true that it would not be a soap-bubble, unless it *could* have existed at any given time without being perceived by me at that time, it is certainly also true that it would not be a soap-bubble, unless it *could* have existed at any given time, without its being true that I was having any experience of any kind at the time in question: it would not be a soap-bubble, unless, whatever time you take, from the proposition that it existed at that time it does *not* follow that I was having any experience at that time. That is to say, from the proposition with regard to anything which I am perceiving that it is a soap-bubble, there *follows* the proposition that it is external to *my* mind. But if, when I say that anything which I perceive is a soap-bubble, I am implying that it is external to *my* mind, I am, I think, certainly also implying that it is also external to all other minds: I am implying that it is not a thing of a sort such that things of that sort *can* only exist at a time when somebody is having an experience. I think, therefore, that from any proposition of the form 'There's a soap-bubble!' there does really *follow* the proposition 'There's an external object!' 'There's an object external to *all* our minds!' And, if this is true of the kind 'soap-bubble', it is certainly also true of any other kind (including the kind 'unicorn') which is such that, if there are any things of that kind, it follows that there are *some* things to be met with in space.

I think, therefore, that in the case of all kinds of 'things', which are such that if there is a pair of things, both of which are of one of these kinds, or a pair of things one of which is of one of them and one of them of another, then it will follow at once that there are some things to be met with in space, it is true also that if I can prove that there are a pair of things, one of which is of one of these kinds and another of another, or a pair both of which are of one of them, then I shall have proved *ipso facto* that there are at least two 'things outside of us'. That is to say, if I can prove that there exist now both a sheet of paper and a human hand, I shall have proved that there are now 'things outside of us'; if I can prove that there exist now both a shoe and sock, I shall have proved that there are not 'things outside of us'; etc.; and similarly I shall have proved it, if I can prove that there exist now two sheets of paper, or two human hands, or two shoes, or two socks, etc. Obviously, then, there are thousands of different things such that, if, at any time, I can prove any one of them, I shall have proved the existence of things outside of us. Cannot I prove any of these things?

It seems to me that, so far from its being true, as Kant declares to be his opinion, that there is only one possible proof of the existence of things outside of us, namely the one which he has given, I can now give a large number of different proofs, each of which is a perfectly rigorous proof; and that at many other times I have been in a position to give many others. I can prove now, for instance, that two human hands exist. How? By holding up my two hands, and saying, as I make a certain gesture with the right hand, 'Here is one hand', and adding, as I make a certain gesture with the left, 'and here is another'. And if, by doing this, I have proved *ipso facto* the existence of external things, you will all see that I can also do it now in numbers of other ways: there is no need to multiply examples.

But did I prove just now that two human hands were then in existence? I do want to insist that I did; that the proof which I gave was a perfectly rigorous one; and that it is perhaps impossible to give a better or more rigorous proof of anything whatever. Of course, it would not have been a proof unless three conditions were satisfied; namely (1) unless the premiss which I adduced as proof of the conclusion was different from the conclusion I adduced it to prove; (2) unless the premiss which I adduced was something which I *knew* to be the case, and not merely something which I believed but which was by no means certain, or something which, though in fact true, I did not know to be so; and (3) unless the conclusion did really follow from the premiss. But all these three conditions were in fact satisfied by my proof. (1) The premiss which I adduced in proof was quite certainly different from the conclusion, for the conclusion was merely 'Two human hands exist at this moment'; but the premiss was something far more specific than this—something which I expressed by showing you my hands, making certain gestures, and saying the words 'Here is one hand, and here is another'. It is quite obvious that the two were different, because it is quite obvious that the conclusion might have been true, even if the premiss had been false. In asserting the premiss I was asserting much more than I was asserting in asserting the conclusion. (2) I certainly did at the moment *know* that which I expressed by the combination of certain gestures with saying the words 'There is one hand and here is another'. I *knew* that there was one hand in the place indicated by combining a certain gesture with my first utterance of 'here' and that there was another in the different place indicated by combining a certain gesture with my second utterance of 'here'. How absurd it would be to suggest that I did not know it, but only believed it, and that perhaps it was not the case! You might as well suggest that I do not know that I am now standing up and talking—that perhaps after all I'm not, and that it's not quite certain that I am! And finally (3) it is quite certain that the conclusion did follow from the premiss. This is as certain as it is that if there is one hand here and another here *now*, then it follows that there are two hands in existence *now*.

My proof, then, of the existence of things outside of us did satisfy three of the conditions necessary for a rigorous proof. Are there any other conditions necessary for a rigorous proof, such that perhaps it did not satisfy one of them? Perhaps there may be; I do not know; but I do want to emphasize that, so far as I can see, we all of us do constantly take proofs of this sort as absolutely conclusive proofs of certain conclusions—as finally settling certain questions, as to which we were previously in doubt. Suppose, for instance, it were a question whether there were as many as three misprints on a certain page in a certain book. A says there are, B is inclined to doubt it. How could A prove that he is right? Surely he *could* prove it by taking the book, turning to the page, and pointing to three separate places on it, saying 'There's one misprint here, another here, and another here': surely that is a method by which it *might* be proved! Of course, A would not have proved, by doing this that there were at least three misprints on the page in question, unless it was certain that there was a misprint in each of the places to which he pointed. But to say that he *might* prove it in this way, is to say that it *might* be certain that there was. And if such a thing as that could ever be certain, then assuredly it was certain just now that there was one hand in one of the two places I indicated and another in the other.

I did, then, just now, give a proof that there were *then* external objects; and obviously, if I did, I could *then* have given many other proofs of the same sort that there were external objects *then*, and could now give many proofs of the same sort that there are external objects *now*.

But, if what I am asked to do is to prove that external objects have existed *in the past*, then I can give many different proofs of this also, but proofs which are in important respects of a different *sort* from those just given. And I want to emphasize that, when Kant says it is a scandal not to be able to give a proof of the existence of external objects, a proof of their existence in the past would certainly *help* to remove the scandal of which he is speaking. He says that, if it occurs to anyone to question their existence, we ought to be able to confront him with a satisfactory proof. But by a person who questions their existence, he certainly means not merely a person who questions whether any exist at the moment of speaking, but a person who questions whether any have *ever* existed; and a proof that some have existed in the past would certainly therefore be relevant to *part* of what such a person is questioning. How then can I prove that there have been external objects in the past? Here is one proof. I can say: 'I held up two hands above this desk not very long ago; therefore two hands existed not very long ago; therefore at least two external objects have existed at some time in the past, Q.E.D.' This is a perfectly good proof, provided I *know* what is asserted in the premiss. But I *do* know that I held up two hands above this desk not very long ago. As a matter of fact, in this case you all know it too. There's no doubt whatever that I did. Therefore I have given a perfectly conclusive proof that external objects have existed in the past; and you will all see at once that, if this is a conclusive proof, I could have given many others of the same sort, and could now give many others. But it is also quite obvious that this sort of proof differs in important respects from the sort of proof I gave just now that there were two hands existing *then*.

I have, then, given two conclusive proofs of the existence of external objects. The first was a proof that two human hands existed at the time when I gave the proof; the second was a proof that two human hands had existed at a time previous to that at which I gave the proof. These proofs were of a different sort in important respects. And I pointed out that I could have given, then, many other conclusive proofs of both sorts. It is also obvious that I could give many others of both sorts now. So that, if these are the sort of proof that is wanted, nothing is easier than to prove the existence of external objects.

But now I am perfectly well aware that, in spite of all that I have said, many philosophers will still feel that I have not given any satisfactory proof of the point in question. And I want briefly, in conclusion, to say something as to why this dissatisfaction with my proofs should be felt.

One reason why, is, I think, this. Some people understand 'proof of an external world' as including a proof of things which I haven't attempted to prove and haven't proved. It is not quite easy to say *what* it is that they want proved—*what* it is that is such that unless they got a proof of it, they would not say that they had a proof of the existence of external things; but I can make an approach to explaining what they want by saying that if I had proved the propositions which I used as *premises* in my two proofs, then they would perhaps admit that I had proved the existence of external things, but, in the absence of such a proof (which, of course, I have neither given nor attempted to give), they will say that I have not given what they mean by a proof of the existence of external things. In other words, they want a proof of what I assert *now* when I hold up my hands and say 'Here's one hand and here's another'; and, in the other case, they want a proof of what I assert *now* when I say 'I did hold up two hands above this desk just now'. Of course, what they really want is not merely a proof of these two propositions, but something like a general statement as to how *any* propositions of this sort may be proved. This, of course, I haven't given; and I do not believe it can be given: if this is what is meant by proof of the existence of external things, I do not believe that any proof of the existence of external things is possible. Of course, in some cases what might be called a proof of propositions which seem like these can be got. If one of you suspected that one of my hands was artificial he might be said to get a proof of my proposition 'Here's one hand, and here's another', by coming up and examining the suspected hand clsoe up, perhaps touching and pressing it, and so establishing that it really was a human hand. But I do not believe that any proof is possible in nearly all cases. How am I to prove now that 'Here's one hand, and here's another? I do not believe I can do it. In order to do it, I should need to prove for one thing, as Descartes pointed out, that I am not now dreaming. But how can I prove that I am not? I have, no doubt, conclusive reasons for asserting that I am not now dreaming; I have conclusive evidence that I am awake: but that is a very different thing from being able to prove it. I could not tell you what all my evidence is; and I should require to do this at least, in order to give you a proof.

But another reason why some people would feel dissatisfied with my proofs is, I think, not merely that they want a proof of something which I haven't proved, but that they think that, if I cannot give such extra proofs, then the proofs that I have given are not conclusive proofs at all. And this, I think, is a definite mistake. They would say: 'If you cannot prove your premiss that here is one hand and here is another, then you do not know it. But you yourself have admitted that, if you did not know it, then your proof was not conclusive. Therefore your proof was not, as you say it was, a conclusive proof.' This view that, if I cannot prove such things as these, I do not know them, is, I think, the view that Kant was expressing in the sentence which I quoted at the beginning of this lecture, when he implies that so long as we have no proof of the existence of external things, their existence must be accepted merely on *faith*. He means to say, I think, that if I cannot prove that there is a hand here, I must accept it merely as a matter of faith—I cannot know it. Such a view, though it has been very common among philosophers, can, I think, be shown to be wrong—though shown only by the use of premisses which are not known to be true, unless we do know of the existence of external things. I can know things, which I cannot prove; and among things which I certainly did know, even if (as I think) I could not prove them, were the premisses of my two proofs. I should say, therefore, that those, if any, who are dissatisfied with these proofs merely on the ground that I did not know their premisses, have no good reason for their dissatisfaction.

36

Ludwig Wittgenstein

Ludwig Wittgenstein (1889–1951) was born in Vienna into a wealthy, highly cultured family. His father was a Jew who had converted to Protestantism, his mother a Roman Catholic, in which religion Wittgenstein was brought up. Wittgenstein went to study engineering at the University of Manchester. Having read the work of Bertrand Russell, in 1912 he transferred to Cambridge University, where Russell was teaching, to study under him. Russell soon realized that his student was a genius and also an extremely eccentric and intense young man. Russell relates the following story about his pupil.

> At the end of his first term at Cambridge he came to me and said, "Will you please tell me whether I am a complete idiot or not?" I replied, "My dear fellow, I don't know. Why are you asking me?" He said, "Because, if I am a complete idiot, I shall become an aeronaut; but if not, I shall become a philosopher." I told him to write something during the vacation on some philosophical subject and I would then tell him whether he was a complete idiot or not. At the beginning of the following term he brought me the fulfillment of this suggestion. After reading only one sentence, I said to him, "No, you must not become an aeronaut."[1]

Wittgenstein returned to Austria to serve in the Austrian army during the First World War. He was captured by the Italians and spent time in a prisoner-of-war camp, where he finished writing his first work, *Tractatus Logico-Philosophicus* (1919). The work was to show the logical relationship between language and the world, to show what could and could not be said. He writes in the preface:

> The book deals with the problems of philosophy, and shows, I believe, that the reason why these problems are posed is that the logic of our language is misunderstood. The whole sense of the book might be summed up in the following words: what can be said at all can be said clearly, and what we cannot talk about we must pass over in silence.

A selection from this work is reprinted below.

After the war, he worked as a schoolmaster and gardener in a monastery before returning to Cambridge in 1929. There he submitted the *Tractatus* as his PhD dissertation. Russell and G. E. Moore were his examiners. He was appointed a lecturer at Cambridge and continued in that capacity until his death in 1951. His second book, *Philosophical Investigations*, was published posthumously in 1953.

1. Bertrand Russell, *Portraits from Memory* (George Allen & Unwin, 1956), 26–27.

Wittgenstein came to reject the reasoning of the *Tractatus*, believing his solution of giving logical structure to language solved the problem of how language related to the world. In this second work, Wittgenstein denies his earlier views that words have essences and that propositions have pictorial form which reflects the world. Instead he claimed that languages were various games that occurred within different cultures or forms of life. Philosophy cannot provide foundations for knowledge in general but only shows us that our practices are justified within forms of life. "Philosophy may in no way interfere with the actual use of language; it can in the end only describe it. For it cannot give it any foundation either. It leaves everything as it is."

FOR FURTHER READING

Ayer, A. J. *Wittgenstein.* (University of Chicago, 1986).
Grayling, A. C. *Wittgenstein.* (Oxford University Press, 1988).
Hacker, P. M. S. *Wittgenstein's Position in Twentieth Century Analytic Philosophy.* (Oxford University Press, 1996).
Kenny, Anthony. *Wittgenstein.* (Harvard University Press, 1974).
Malcolm, Norman. *Ludwig Wittgenstein: A Memoir.* (Oxford University Press, 1958).
Monk, Ray. *Ludwig Wittgenstein: The Duty of Genius.* (Free Press, 1990).
Rundle, Bede. *Wittgenstein on Language: Meaning, Use and Truth.* (Blackwell, 1990).
Wittgenstein, Ludwig. *Tractatus Logico-Philosophicus*, trans. D. Pears and B. McGuiness. (Routledge & Kegan Paul, 1961).

Tractatus Logico-Philosophicus

PREFACE

Perhaps this book will be understood only by someone who has himself already had the thoughts that are expressed in it—or at least similar thoughts.—So it is not a textbook.—Its purpose would be achieved if it gave pleasure to one person who read and understood it.

The book deals with the problems of philosophy, and shows, I believe, that the reason why these problems are posed is that the logic of our language is misunderstood. The whole sense of the book might be summed up in the following words: what can be said at all can be said clearly, and what we cannot talk about we must pass over in silence.

Thus the aim of the book is to draw a limit to thought, or rather—not to thought, but to the expressing of thoughts: for in order to be able to draw a limit to thought, we should have to find both sides of the limit thinkable (i.e. we should have to be able to think what cannot be thought).

It will therefore only be in language that the limit can be drawn, and what lies on the other side of the limit will simply be nonsense.

I do not wish to judge how far my efforts coincide with those of other philosophers. Indeed, what I have written here makes no claim to novelty in detail, and the reason why I give no sources is that it is a matter of indifference to me whether the thoughts that I have had have been anticipated by someone else.

I will only mention that I am indebted to Frege's great works and to the writings of my friend Mr. Bertrand Russell for much of the stimulation of my thoughts.

Reprinted from Ludwig Wittgenstein's *Tractatus Logico-Philosophicus*, translated by D. F. Pears and B. F. McGuiness (Routledge & Keegan Paul) by permission of Routledge.

If this work has any value, it consists in two things: the first is that thoughts are expressed in it, and on this score the better the thoughts are expressed—the more the nail has been hit on the head—the greater will be its value.—Here I am conscious of having fallen a long way short of what is possible. Simply because my powers are too slight for the accomplishment of the task.—May others come and do it better.

On the other hand the *truth* of the thoughts that are here communicated seems to me unassailable and definitive. I therefore believe myself to have found, on all essential points, the final solution of the problems. And if I am not mistaken in this belief, then the second thing in which the value of this work consists is that it shows how little is achieved when these problems are solved.

LANGUAGE AS PICTURE

1[1] The world is all that is the case.

1.1 The world is the totality of facts, not of things.

1.11 The world is determined by the facts, and by their being *all* the facts.

1.12 Totality of facts determines what is the case, and also whatever is not the case.

1.13 The facts in logical space are the world.

1.2 The world divides into facts.

1.21 Each item can be the case or not the case while everything else remains the same.

2 What is the case—a fact—is existence of states of affairs.

2.01 A state of affairs (a state of things) is a combination of objects (things).

2.011 It is essential to things that they should be possible constituents of states of affairs.

2.012 In logic nothing is accidental: if a thing can occur in a state of affairs, the possibility of the state of affairs must be written into the thing itself.

2.0121 It would seem to be a sort of accident, if it turned out that a situation would fit a thing that could already exist entirely on its own.

If things can occur in states of affairs, this possibility must be in them from the beginning.

(Nothing in the province of logic can be merely possible. Logic deals with every possibility and all possibilities are its facts.)

Just as we are quite unable to imagine spatial objects outside space or temporal objects outside time, so too there is no object that we can imagine excluded from the possibility of combining with others.

If I can imagine objects combined in states of affairs, I cannot imagine them excluded from the *possibility* of such combinations.

2.0122 Things are dependent in so far as they can occur in all *possible* situations, but this form of independence is a form of connexion with states of affairs, a form of dependence. (It is impossible for words to appear in two different roles: by themselves, and in propositions.)

2.0123 If I know an object I also know its possible occurrences in states of affairs.

(Every one of these possibilities must be part of the nature of the object.)

A new possibility cannot be discovered later.

2.01231 If I am to know an object, though I need not know its external properties, I must know all its internal properties.

2.0124 If all objects are given, then at the same time all *possible* states of affairs are also given.

2.013 Each thing is, as it were, in a space of possible states of affairs. This space I can imagine empty, but I cannot imagine the thing without the space.

2.0131 A spatial object must be situated in infinite space. (A spatial point is an argument-place.)

A speck in the visual field, though it need not be red, must have some colour: it is, so to speak, surrounded by colour-space. Notes must have *some* pitch, objects of the

1. The decimal numbers assigned to the individual propositions indicate the logical importance of the propositions, the stress laid on them in my exposition. The propositions *n*.1, *n*.2, *n*.3, etc. are comments of proposition no.*n*; the propositions *n.m*1, *n.m*2, etc. are comments on proposition no. *n.m*; and so on.Text of Footnote.

sense of touch *some* degree of hardness, and so on.

2.014 Objects contain the possibility of all situations.

2.0141 The possibility of its occurring in states of affairs is the form of an object.

2.02 Objects are simple.

2.0201 Every statement about complexes can be resolved into a statement about their constituents and into the propositions that describe the complexes completely.

2.021 Objects make up the substance of the world. That is why they cannot be composite.

2.0211 If the world had no substance, then whether a proposition had sense would depend on whether another proposition was true.

2.0212 In that case we could not sketch any picture of the world (true or false).

2.022 It is obvious that an imagined world, however different it may be from the real one, must have *something*—a form—in common with it.

2.023 Objects are just what constitute this unalterable form.

2.0231 The substance of the world *can* only determine a form, and not any material properties. For it is only by means of propositions that material properties are represented—only by the configuration of objects that they are produced.

2.0232 In a manner of speaking, objects are colourless.

2.0233 If two objects have the same logical form, the only distinction between them, apart from their external properties, is that they are different.

2.02331 Either a thing has properties that nothing else has, in which case we can immediately use a description to distinguish it from the others and refer to it; or, on the other hand, there are several things that have the whole set of their properties in common, in which case it is quite impossible to indicate one of them.

For if there is nothing to distinguish a thing, I cannot distinguish it, since otherwise it would be distinguished after all.

2.024 Substance is what subsists independently of what is the case.

2.025 It is form and content.

2.0251 Space, time, and colour (being coloured) are forms of objects.

2.026 There must be objects, if the world is to have an unalterable form.

2.027 Objects, the unalterable, and the subsistent are one and the same.

2.0271 Objects are what is unalterable and subsistent; their configuration is what is changing and unstable.

2.0272 The configuration of objects produces states of affairs.

2.03 In a state of affairs objects fit into one another like the links of a chain.

2.031 In a state of affairs objects stand in a determinate relation to one another.

2.032 The determinate way in which objects are connected in a state of affairs is the structure of the state of affairs.

2.033 Form is the possibility of structure.

2.034 The structure of a fact consists of the structures of states of affairs.

2.04 The totality of existing states of affairs is the world.

2.05 The totality of existing states of affairs also determines which states of affairs do not exist.

2.06 The existence and non-existence of states of affairs is reality. (We also call the existence of states of affairs a positive fact, and their non-existence a negative fact.)

2.061 States of affairs are independent of one another.

2.062 From the existence or non-existence of one state of affairs it is impossible to infer the existence or non-existence of another.

2.063 The sum-total of reality is the world.

2.1 We picture facts to ourselves.

2.11 A picture presents a situation in logical space, the existence and non-existence of states of affairs.

2.12 A picture is a model of reality.

2.13 In a picture objects have the elements of the picture corresponding to them.

2.131 In a picture the elements of the picture are the representatives of objects.

2.14 What constitutes a picture is that its elements are related to one another in a determinate way.

2.141 A picture is a fact.

2.15 The fact that the elements of a picture are related to one another in a determinate way represents that things are related to one another in the same way.

Let us call this connexion of its elements the structure of the picture, and let us call the possibility of this structure the pictorial form of the picture.

2.151 Pictorial form is the possibility that things are related to one another in the same way as the elements of a picture.

2.1511 *That* is how a picture is attached to reality; it reaches right out to it.

2.1512 It is laid against reality like a measure.

2.15121 Only the end-points of the graduating lines actually *touch* the object that is to be measured.

2.1513 So a picture, conceived in this way, also includes the pictorial relationship, which makes it into a picture.

2.1514 The pictorial relationship consists of the correlations of the picture's elements with things.

2.1515 These correlations are, as it were, the feelers of the picture's elemens, with which the picture touches reality.

2.16 If a fact is to be a picture, it must have something in common with what it depicts.

2.161 There must be something identical in a picture and what it depicts, to enable the one to be a picture of the other at all.

2.17 What a picture must have in common with reality, in order to be able to depict it—correctly or incorrectly—in the way it does, is its pictorial form.

2.171 A picture can depict any reality whose form it has.

A spatial picture can depict anything spatial, a coloured one anything coloured, etc.

2.172 A picture cannot, however, depict its pictorial form: it displays it.

2.173 A picture represents its subject from a position outside it. (Its standpoint is its representational form.) That is why a picture represents its subject correctly or incorrectly.

2.174 A picture cannot, however, place itself outside its representational form.

2.18 What any picture, of whatever form, must have in common with reality, in order to be able to depict it—correctly or incorrectly—in any way at all, is logical form, i.e. the form of reality.

2.181 A picture whose pictorial form is logical form is called logical picture.

2.182 Every picture is *at the same time* a logical one. (On the other hand, not every picture is, for example, a spatial one.)

2.19 Logical pictures can depict the world.

2.2 A picture has logico-pictorial form in common with what it depicts.

2.201 A picture depicts reality by representing a possibility of existence and non-existence of states of affairs.

2.202 A picture represents a possible situation in logical space.

2.203 A picture contains the possibility of the situation that it represents.

2.21 A picture agrees with reality or fails to agree; it is correct or incorrect, true or false.

2.22 What a picture represents it represents independently of its truth or falsity, by means of its pictorial form.

2.221 What a picture represents is its sense.

2.222 The agreement or disagreement of its sense with reality constitutes its truth or falsity.

2.223 In order to tell whether a picture is true or false we must compare it with reality.

2.224 It is impossible to tell from the picture alone whether it is true or false.

2.225 There are no pictures that are true a priori.

3 A logical picture of facts is a thought.

3.001 'A state of affairs is thinkable': what this means is that we can picture it to ourselves.

3.01 The totality of true thoughts is a picture of the world.

3.02 A thought contains the possibility of the situation of which it is the thought. What is thinkable is possible too.

3.03 Thought can never be of anything illogical, since, if it were, we should have to think illogically.

3.031 It used to be said that God could create anything except what would be contrary to the laws of logic.—The truth is that we could not *say* what an 'illogical' world would look like.

3.032 It is as impossible to represent in language anything that 'contradicts logic' as it is in geometry to represent by its co-ordinates a figure that contradicts the laws of space, or to give the co-ordinates of a point that does not exist.

3.0321 Though a state of affairs that would contravene the laws of physics can be represented by us spatially, one that would contravene the laws of geometry cannot.

3.04 If a thought were correct a priori, it would be a thought whose possibility ensured its truth.

3.05 A priori knowledge that a thought was true would be possible only if its truth were recognizable from the thought itself (without anything to compare it with).

3.1 In a proposition a thought finds an expression that can be perceived by the senses.

3.11 We use the perceptible sign of a proposition (spoken or written, etc.) as a projection of a possible situation.

The method of projection is to think of the sense of the proposition.

3.12 I call the sign with which we express a thought a propositional sign.—And a proposition is a propositional sign in its projective relation to the world.

3.13 A proposition includes all that the projection includes, but not what is projected.

Therefore, though what is projected is not itself included, its possibility is.

A proposition, therefore, does not actually contain its sense, but does contain the possibility of expressing it.

('The content of a proposition' means the content of a proposition that has sense.)

A proposition contains the form, but not the content, of its sense.

3.14 What constitutes a propositional sign is that in it its elements (the words) stand in a determinate relation to one another.

A propositional sign is a fact.

3.141 A proposition is not a blend of words.—(Just as a theme in music is not a blend of notes.)

A propositional is articulate.

3.142 Only facts can express a sense, a set of names cannot.

3.143 Although a propositional sign is a fact, this is obscured by the usual frm of expression in writing or print.

For in a printed proposition, for example, no essential difference is apparent between a propositional sign and a word.

(That is what made it possible for Frege to call a proposition a composite name.)

3.1431 The essence of a propositional sign is very clearly seen if we imagine one composed of spatial objects (such as tables, chairs, and books) instead of written signs.

3.1432 Instead of, 'The complex sign "*a*R*b*" says that *a* stands to *b* in the relation *R*', we ought to put, '*That* "*a*" stands to "*b*" in a certain relation says *that* *a*R*b*.'

3.144 Situations can be described but not *given names*.

(Names are like points; propositions like arrows—they have sense.)

3.2 In a proposition a thought can be expressed in such a way that elements of the propositional sign correspond to the objects of the thought.

3.201 I call such elements 'simple signs', and such a proposition 'completely analysed'.

3.202 The simple signs employed in propositions are called names.

3.203 A name means an object. The object is its meaning. ('*A*' is the same sign as '*A*'.)

3.21 The configuration of objects in a situation corresponds to the configuration of simple signs in the propositional sign.

3.22 In a proposition a name is the representative of an object.

3.221 Objects can only be *named*. Signs are their representatives. I can only speak *about* them: I cannot *put them into words*. Propositions can only say *how* things are, not *what* they are.

3.23 The requirement that simple signs be possible is the requirement that sense be determinate.

3.24 A proposition about a complex stands in an internal relation to a proposition about a constituent of the complex.

A complex can be given only by its description, which will be right or wrong. A proposition that mentions a complex will not be nonsensical, if the complex does not exist, but simply false.

When a propositional element signifies a complex, this can be seen from an indeterminateness in the propositions in which it occurs. In such cases we *know* that the proposition leaves something undetermined. (In fact the generality-sign *contains* a prototype.)

The contraction of a symbol for a complex into a simple symbol can be expressed in a definition.

3.25 A proposition has one and only one complete analysis.

3.251 What a proposition expresses it expresses in a determinate manner, which can be set out clearly: a proposition is articulated.

3.26 A name cannot be dissected any further by means of a definition: it is a primitive sign.

3.261 Every sign that has a definition signifies *via* the signs that serve to define it; and the definitions point the way.

Two signs cannot signify in the same manner if one is primitive and the other is defined by means of primitive signs. Names *cannot* be anatomized by means of definitions. (This cannot be done to any sign that has a meaning independently and on its own.)

3.262 What signs fail to express, their application shows. What signs slur over, their application says clearly.

3.263 The meanings of primitive signs can be explained by means of elucidations. Elucidations are propositions that contain the primitive signs. So they can only be understood if the meanings of those signs are already know.

3.3 Only propositions have sense; only in the nexus of a proposition does a name have meaning.

3.31 I call any part of a proposition that characterizes its sense an expression (or a symbol).

(A proposition is itself an expression.)

Everything essential to their sense that propositions can have in common with one another is an expression.

An expression is the mark of a form and a content.

3.311 An expression presupposes the forms of all the propositions in which it can occur. It is the common characteristic mark of a class of propositions.

3.312 It is therefore presented by means of the general form of the propositions that it characterizes.

In fact, in this form the expression will be *constant* and everything else *variable*.

3.313 Thus an expression is presented by means of a variable whose values are the propositions that contain the expression.

(In the limiting case the variable becomes a constant, the expression becomes a proposition.)

I call such a variable a 'propositional variable'.

3.314 An expression has meaning only in a proposition. All variables can be construed as propositional variables.

(Even variable names.)

3.315 If we turn a constituent of a proposition into a variable, there is a class of propositions all of which are values of the resulting variable proposition. In general, this class too will be dependent on the meaning that our arbitrary conventions have given to parts of the original proposition. But if all the signs in it that have arbitrarily determined meanings are turned into variables, we shall still get a class of this kind. This one, however, is not dependent on any convention, but solely on the nature of the proposition. It corresponds to a logical form—a logical prototype.

3.316 What values a propositional variable may take is something that is stipulated.

The stipulation of values *is* the variable.

3.317 To stipulate values for a propositional variable is *to give the propositions* whose common characteristic the variable is.

The stipulation is a description of those propositions.

The stipulation will therefore be concerned only with symbols, not with their meaning.

And the *only* thing essential to the stipulation is *that it is merely a description of symbols and states nothing about what is signified.*

How the description of the propositions is produced is not essential.

3.318 Like Frege and Russell I construe a proposition as a function of the expressions contained in it.

6.362 What can be described can also happen: and what the law of causality is meant to exclude cannot even be described.

6.363 The procedure of induction consists in accepting as true the *simplest* law that can be reconciled with our experiences.

6.3631 This procedure, however, has no logical justification but only a psychological one. It is clear that there are no grounds for believing that the simplest eventuality will in fact be realized.

6.36311 It is an hypothesis that the sun will rise tomorrow: and this means that we do not *know* whether it will rise.

6.37 There is no compulsion making one thing happen because another has happened. The only necessity that exists is *logical* necessity.

6.371 The whole modern conception of the world is founded on the illusion that the so-called laws of nature are the explanations of natural phenomena.

6.372 Thus people today stop at the laws of nature, treating them as something inviolable, just as God and Fate were treated in past ages.

And in fact both are right and both wrong: though the view of the ancients is clearer in so far as they have a clear and acknowledged terminus, while the modern system tries to make it look as if *everything* were explained.

6.373 The world is independent of my will.

6.374 Even if all that we wish for were to happen, still this would only be a favour granted by fate, so to speak: for there is no *logical* connexion between the will and the world, which would guarantee it, and the supposed physical connexion itself is surely not something that we could will.

6.375 Just as the only necessity that exists is *logical* necessity, so too the only impossibility that exists is *logical* impossibility.

6.3751 For example, the simultaneous presence of two colours at the same place in the visual field is impossible, in fact logically impossible, since it is ruled out by the logical structure of colour.

Let us think how this contradiction appears in physics: more or less as follows—a particle cannot have two velocities at the same time; that is to say, it cannot be in two places at the same time; that is to say, particles that are in different places at the same time cannot be identical.

(It is clear that the logical product of two elementary propositions can neither be a tautology nor a contradiction. The statement that a point in the visual field has two different colours at the same time is a contradiction.)

6.4 All propositions are of equal value.

6.41 The sense of the world must lie outside the world. In the world everything is as it is, and everything happens as it does happen: *in* it no value exists—and if it did exist, it would have no value.

If there is any value that does have values, it must lie outside the whole sphere of what happens and is the case. For all that happens and is the case is accidental.

What makes it non-accidental cannot lie *within* the world, since if it did it would itself be accidental.

It must lie outside the world.

6.42 So too it is impossible for there to be propositions of ethics.

Propositions can express nothing that is higher.

6.421 It is clear that ethics cannot be put into words.

Ethics is transcendental.

(Ethics and aesthetics are one and the same.)

6.422 When an ethical law of the form, 'Thou shalt . . .', is laid down, one's first thought is, 'And what if I do not do it?' It is clear, however, that ethics has nothing to do with punishment and reward in the usual sense of the terms. So our question about the *consequences* of an action must be unimportant.—At least those consequences should not be events. For there must be something right about the question we posed. There must indeed be some kind of ethical reward and ethical punishment, but they must reside in the action itself.

(And it is also clear that the reward must be something pleasant and the punishment something unpleasant.)

6.423 It is impossible to speak about the will in so far as it is the subject of ethical attributes.

And the will as a phenomenon is of interest only to psychology.

6.43 If the good or bad exercise of the will does alter the world, it can alter only the limits of the world, not the facts—not what can be expressed by means of language.

In short the effect must be that it becomes an altogether different world. It must, so to speak, wax and wane as a whole.

The world of the happy man is a different one from that of the unhappy man.

6.431 So too at death the world does not alter, but comes to an end.

6.4311 Death is not an event in life: we do not live to experience death.

If we take eternity to mean not infinite temporal duration but timelessness, then eternal life belongs to those who live in the present.

Our life has no end in just the way in which our visual field has no limits.

6.4312 Not only is there no guarantee of the temporal immortality of the human soul, that is to say of its eternal survival after death; but, in any case, this assumption completely fails to accomplish the purpose for which it has always been intended. Or is some riddle solved by my surviving for ever? Is not this eternal life itself as much of a riddle as our present life? The solution of the riddle of life in space and time lies *outside* space and time.

(It is certainly not the solution of any problems of natural science that is required.)

6.432 *How* things are in the world is a matter of complete indifference for what is higher. God does not reveal himself *in* the world.

6.4321 The facts all contribute only to settling the problem, not to its solution.

6.44 It is not *how* things are in the world that is mystical, but *that* it exists.

6.45 To view the world sub specie aeterni is to view it as a whole—a limited whole.

Feeling the world as a limited whole—it is this that is mystical.

6.5 When the answer cannot be put into words, neither can the question be put into words.

The riddle does not exist.

If a question can be framed at all, it is also *possible* to answer it.

6.51 Scepticism is *not* irrefutable, but obviously nonsensical when it tries to raise doubts where no questions can be asked.

For doubt can exist only where a question exists, a question only where an answer exists, and an answer only where something *can be said.*

6.52 We feel that even when all *possible* scientific questions have been answered, the problems of life remain completely untouched. Of course there are then no questions left, and this itself is the answer.

6.521 The solution of the problem of life is seen in the vanishing of the problem.

(Is not this the reason why those who have found after a long period of doubt that the sense of life became clear to them have then been unable to say what constituted sense?)

6.522 There are, indeed, things that cannot be put into words. They *make themselves manifest*. They are what is mystical.

6.53 The correct method in philosophy would really be the following: to say nothing except what can be said, i.e. propositions of natural science—i.e. something that has nothing to do with philosophy—and then, whenever someone else wanted to say something metaphysical, to demonstrate to him that he had failed to give a meaning to certain signs in his propositions. Although it would not be satisfying to the other person—he would not have the feeling that we were teaching him philosophy—*this* method would be the only strictly correct one.

6.54 My propositions serve as elucidations in the following way: anyone who understands me eventually recognizes them as nonsensical, when he has used them—as steps—to climb up beyond them. (He must, so to speak, throw away the ladder after he has climbed up it.)

He must transcend these propositions, and then he will see the world aright.

7 What we cannot speak about we must pass over in silence.

Philosophical Investigations

1. "When they (my elders) named some object, and accordingly moved towards something, I saw this and I grasped that the thing was called by the sound they uttered when they meant to point it out. Their intention was shewn by their bodily movements, as it were the natural language of all peoples: the expression of the face, the play of the eyes, the movement of other parts of the body, and the tone of voice which expresses our state of mind in seeking, having, rejecting, or avoiding something. Thus, as I heard words repeatedly used in their proper places in various sentences, I gradually learnt to understand what objects they signified; and after I had trained my mouth to form these signs, I used them to express my own desires." [Augustine, *Confessions*, I.8]

These words, it seems to me, give us a particular picture of the essense of human language. It is this: the individual words in language name objects—sentences are combinations of such names.—In this picture of language we find the roots of the following idea: Every word has a meaning. This meaning is correlated with the word. It is the object for which the word stands.

Augustine does not speak of there being any difference between kinds of word. If you describe the learning of language in this way you are, I believe, thinking primarily of nouns like "table", "chair", "bread", and of people's names, and only secondarily of the names of certain actions and properties; and of the remaining kinds of word as something that will take care of itself.

Now think of the following use of language: I send someone shopping. I give him a slip marked "five red apples". He takes the slip to the shopkeeper, who opens the drawer marked "apples"; then he looks up the word "red" in a table and finds a colour sample opposite it; then he says the series of cardinal numbers—I assume that he knows them by heart—up to the word "five" and for each number he takes an apple of the same colour as the sample out of the drawer.——It is in this and similar ways that one operates with words.——"But how does he know where and how he is to look up the word 'red' and what he is to do with the word 'five'?"——Well, I assume that he *acts* as I have described. Explanations come to an end somewhere.—But what is the meaning of the word "five"?—No such thing was in question here, only how the word "five" is used.

2. That philosophical concept of meaning has its place in a primitive idea of the way language functions. But one can also say that it is the idea of a language more primitive than ours.

Let us imagine a language for which the description given by Augustine is right. The language is meant to serve for communication between a builder A and an assistant B. A is building with building-stones: there are blocks, pillars, slabs and beams. B has to pass the stones, and that in the order in which A needs them. For this purpose they use a language consisting of the words "block", "pillar", "slab", "beam". A calls them out;—B brings the stone which he has learnt to bring at such-and-such a call.——Conceive this as a complete primitive language.

3. Augustine, we might say, does describe a system of communication; only not everything that we call language is this system. And one has to say this in many cases where the question arises "Is this an appropriate description or not?" The answer is: "Yes, it is appropriate, but only for this narrowly circumscribed region, not for the whole of what you were claiming to describe."

It is as if someone were to say: "A game consists in moving objects about on a surface according to certain rules . . ."—and we replied: You seem to be thinking of board games, but there are others. You can make your definition correct by expressly restricting it to those games.

4. Imagine a script in which the letters were used to stand for sounds, and also as signs of emphasis and punctuation. (A script can be conceived as a language for describing sound-patterns.) Now imagine someone interpreting that script as if there were simply a correspondence of letters to sounds and as if the letters had not also completely different functions. Augustine's conception of language is like such an over-simple conception of the script.

5. If we look at the example in §1, we may perhaps get an inkling how much this general notion of the meaning of a word surrounds the working of language with a haze which makes clear vision impossible. It disperses the fog to study the phenomena of language in primitive kinds of application in which one can command a clear view of the aim and functioning of the words.

A child uses such primitive forms of language when it learns to talk. Here the teaching of language is not explanation, but training.

6. We could imagine that the language of §2 was the *whole* language of A and B; even the whole language of a tribe. The children are brought up to perform *these* actions, to use *these* words as they do so, and to react in *this* way to the words of others.

An important part of the training will consist in the teacher's pointing to the objects, directing the child's attention to them, and at the same time uttering a word; for instance, the word "slab" as he points to that shape. (I do not want to call this "ostensive definition", because the child cannot as yet *ask* what the name is. I will call it "ostensive teaching of words".——I say that it will form an important part of the training, because it is so with human beings; not because it could not be imagined otherwise.) This ostensive teaching of words can be said to establish an association between the word and the thing. But what does this mean? Well, it may mean various things; but one very likely thinks first of all that a picture of the object comes before the child's mind when it hears the word. But now, if this does happen—is it the purpose of the word?—Yes, it *may* be the purpose.—I can imagine such a use of words (of series of sounds). (Uttering a word is like striking a note on the keyboard of the imagination.) But in the language of §2 it is *not* the purpose of the words to evoke images. (It may, of course, be discovered that that helps to attain the actual purpose.)

But if the ostensive teaching has this effect,—am I to say that it effects an understanding of the word? Don't you understand the call "Slab!" if you act upon it in such-and-such a way?—Doubtless the ostensive teaching helped to bring this about; but only together with a particular training. With different training the same ostensive teaching of these words would have effected a quite different understanding.

"I set the brake up by connecting up rod and lever."—Yes, given the whole of the rest of the mechanism. Only in conjunction with that is it a brake-lever, and separated from its support it is not even a lever; it may be anything, or nothing.

7. In the practice of the use of language (2) one party calls out the words, the other acts on them. In instruction in the language the following process will occur: the learner *names* the objects; that is, he utters the word when the teacher points to the stone.—And there will be this still simpler exercise: the pupil repeats the words after the teacher—both of these being processes resembling language.

We can also think of the whole process of using words in (2) as one of those games by means of which children learn their native language. I will call these games "language-games" and will sometimes speak of a primitive language as a language-game.

And the processes of naming the stones and of repeating words after someone might also be called language-games. Think of much of the use of words in games like ring-a-ring-a-roses.

I shall also call the whole, consisting of language and the actions into which it is woven, the "language-game".

8. Let us now look at an expansion of language (2). Besides the four words "block", "pillar", etc., let it contain a series of words used as the shopkeeper in (1) used the numerals (it can be the series of letters of the alphabet); further, let there be two words, which may as well be "there" and "this" (because this roughly indicates their purpose), that are used in connexion with a pointing gesture; and finally a number of colour samples. A gives an order like: "d—slab—there". At the same time he shews the assistant a colour sample, and when he says "there" he points to a place on the building site. From the stock of slabs B takes one for each letter of the alphabet up to "d", of the same colour as the sample, and brings them to the place indicated by A.—On other occasions A gives the order "this—there". At "this" he points to a building stone. And so on.

9. When a child learns this language, it has to learn the series of 'numerals' a, b, c, . . . by heart. And it has to learn their use.—Will this training include ostensive teaching of the words?—Well, people will, for example, point to slabs and count: "a, b, c slabs".—Something more like the ostensive teaching of the words "block", "pillar", etc. would be the ostensive teaching of numerals that serve not to count but to refer to groups of objects that can be taken in at a glance. Children do learn the use of the first five or six cardinal numerals in this way.

Are "there" and "this" also taught ostensively?—Imagine how one might perhaps teach their use. One will point to places and things—but in this case the pointing occurs in the *use* of the words too and not merely in learning the use.—

10. Now what do the words of this language *signify*?—What is supposed to shew what they signify, if not the kind of use they have? And we have already described that. So we are asking for the expression "This word signifies *this*" to be made a part of the description. In other words the description ought to take the form: "The word . . . . signifies . . . .".

Of course, one can reduce the description of the use of the word "slab" to the statement that this word signifies this object. This will be done when, for example, it is merely a matter of removing the mistaken idea that the word "slab" refers to the shape of building-stone that we in fact call a "block"—but the kind of '*referring*' this is, that is to say the use of these words for the rest, is already known.

Equally one can say that the signs "a", "b", etc. signify numbers; when for example this removes the mistaken idea that "a", "b", "c", play the part actually played in language by "block", "slab", "pillar". And one can also say that "c" means this number and not that one; when for example this serves to explain that the letters are to be used in the order a, b, c, d, etc. and not in the order a, b, d, c.

But assimilating the descriptions of the uses of words in this way cannot make the uses themselves any more like one another. For, as we see, they are absolutely unlike.

11. Think of the tools in a tool-box: there is a hammer, pliers, a saw, a screw-driver, a rule, a glue-pot, glue, nails and screws.—The functions of words are as diverse as the functions of these objects. (And in both cases there are similarities.)

Of course, what confuses us is the uniform appearance of words when we hear them spoken or meet them in script and print. For their *application* is not presented to us so clearly. Especially when we are doing philosophy!

12. It is like looking into the cabin of a locomotive. We see handles all looking more or less alike. (Naturally, since they are all supposed to be handled.) But one is the handle of a crank which can be moved continuously (it regulates the opening of a valve); another is the handle of a switch, which has only two effective positions, it is either off or on; a third is the handle of a brake-lever, the harder one pulls on it, the harder it brakes; a fourth, the handle of a pump: it has an effect only so long as it is moved to and fro.

13. When we say: "Every word in language signifies something" we have so far said *nothing whatever*; unless we have explained exactly *what* distinction we wish to make. (It might be, of course, that we wanted to distinguish the words of language (8) from words 'without meaning' such as occur in Lewis Carroll's poems, or words like "Lilliburlero" in songs.)

14. Imagine someone's saying: "*All* tools serve to modify something. Thus the hammer modifies the position of the nail, the saw the shape of the board, and so on."—And what is modified by the rule, the glue-pot, the nails?—"Our knowledge of a thing's length, the temperature of the glue, and the solidity of the box."——Would anything be gained by this assimilation of expressions?—

15. The word "to signify" is perhaps used in the most straightforward way when the object signified is marked with the sign. Suppose that the tools A uses in building bear certain marks. When A shews his assistant such a mark, he brings the tool that has that mark on it.

It is in this and more or less similar ways that a name means and is given to a thing.—It will often prove useful in philosophy to say to ourselves: naming something is like attaching a label to a thing.

16. What about the colour samples that A shews to B: are they part of the *language*? Well, it is as you please. They do not belong among the words; yet when I say to someone: "Pronounce the word 'the'", you will count the second "the" as part of the sentence. Yet it has a role just like that of a colour-sample in language-game (8); that is, it is a sample of what the other is meant to say.

It is most natural, and causes least confusion, to reckon the samples among the instruments of the language.

((Remark on the reflexive pronoun "*this* sentence".))

17. It will be possible to say: In language (8) we have different *kinds of word*. For the functions of the word "slab" and the word "block" are more alike than those of "slab" and "d". But how we group words into kinds will depend on the aim of the classification,—and on our own inclination.

Think of the different points of view from which one can classify tools or chess-men.

18. Do not be troubled by the fact that languages (2) and (8) consist only of orders. If you want to say that this shews them to be incomplete, ask yourself whether our language is complete;—whether it was so before the symbolism of chemistry and the notation of the infinitesimal calculus were incorporated in it; for these are, so to speak, suburbs of our language. (And how many houses or streets does it take before a town begins to be a town?) Our language can be seen as an ancient city: a maze of little streets and squares, of old and new houses, and of houses with additions from vaious periods; and this surrounded by a multitude of new boroughs with straight regular streets and uniform houses.

19. It is easy to imagine a language consisting only of orders and reports in battle.—Or a language consisting only of questions and expressions for answering yes and no. And innumerable others.——And to imagine a language means to imagine a form of life.

But what about this: is the call "Slab!" in example (2) a sentence or a word?—If a word, surely it has not the same meaning as the like-sounding word of our ordinary language, for in §2 it is a call. But if a sentence, it is surely not the elliptical sentence: "Slab!" of our language.——As far as the first question goes you can call "Slab!" a word and also a sentence; perhaps it could be appropriately called a 'degenerate sentence' (as one speaks of a degenerate hyperbola); in fact it *is* our 'elliptical' sentence.—But that is surely only a shortened form of the sentence "Bring me a slab", and there is no such sentence in example (2).—But why should I not on the contrary have called the sentence "Bring me a slab" a *lengthening* of the sentence "Slab!"?—Because if you shout "Slab!" you really mean: "Bring me a slab".—But how do you do this: how do you *mean that* while you *say* "Slab!"? Do you say the unshortened sentence to yourself? And why should I translate the call "Slab!" into a different expression in order to say what someone means by it? And if they mean the same thing—why should I not say: "When he says 'Slab!' he means 'Slab!' "? Again, if you can mean "Bring me the slab", why should you not be able to mean "Slab!"?——But when I call "Slab!", then what I want is, *that he should bring me a slab*!——Certainly, but does 'wanting this' consist in thinking in some form or other a different sentence from the one you utter?—

20. But now it looks as if when someone says "Bring me a slab" he could mean this expression as *one* long word corresponding to the single word "Slab!"——Then can one mean it sometimes as one word and sometimes as four? And how does one usually mean it?——I think we shall be inclined to say: we mean the sentence as *four* words when we use it in contrast with other sentences such as "*Hand* me a slab", "Bring *him* a slab", "Bring *two* slabs", etc.; that is, in contrast with sentences containing the separate words of our command in other combinations.——But what does using one sentence in contrast with others consist in? Do the others, perhaps, hover before one's mind? *All* of them? And *while* one is saying the one sentence, or before, or afterwards?—No. Even if such an explanation rather tempts us, we need only think for a moment of what actually happens in order to see that we are going astray here. We say that we use the command in contrast with other sentences because *our language* contains the possibility of those other sentences. Someone who did not understand our language, a foreigner, who had fairly often heard someone giving the order: "Bring me a slab!", might believe that this whole series of sounds was one word corresponding perhaps to the word for "building-stone" in his language. If he himself had then given this order perhaps he would have pronounced it differently, and we should say: he pronounces it so oddly because he takes it for a *single* word.——But then, is there not also something different going on in him when he pronounces it,—something corresponding to the fact that he conceives the sentence as a *single* word?——Either the same thing may go on in him, or something different. For what goes on in you when you give such an order? Are you conscious of its consisting of four words *while* you are uttering it? Of course you have a *mastery* of this language—which contains those other sentences as well—but is this having a mastery something that *happens* while you are uttering the sentence?—And I have admitted that the foreigner will probably pronounce a sentence differently if he conceives it differently; but what we call his wrong conception *need* not lie in anything that accompanies the utterance of the command.

The sentence is 'elliptical', not because it leaves out something that we think when we utter it, but because it is shortened—in comparison with a particular paradigm of our grammar.—Of course one might object here: "You grant that the shortened and the unshortened sentence have the same sense.—What is this sense, then? Isn't there a verbal expression for this sense?"——But doesn't the fact that sentences have the same sense consist in their having the same *use*?—(In Russian one says "stone red" instead of "the stone is red"; do they feel the copula to be missing in the sense, or attach it in *thought*?)

21. Imagine a language-game in which A asks and B reports the number of slabs or blocks in a pile, or the colours and shapes of the building-stones that are stacked in such-and-such a place.—Such a report might run: "Five slabs". Now what is the difference between the report or statement "Five slabs" and the order "Five slabs!"?—Well, it is the part which uttering these words plays in language-game. No doubt the tone of voice and the look with which they are uttered, and much else besides, will also be different. But we could also imagine the tone's being the same—for an order and a report can be spoken in a *variety* of tones of voice and with various expressions of face—the difference being only in the application. (Of course, we might use the words "statement" and "command" to stand for grammatical forms of sentence and intonations; we do in fact call "Isn't the weather glorious to-day?" a question, although it is used as a statement.) We could imagine a language in which *all* statements had the form and tone of rhetorical questions; or every command the form of the question "Would you like to . . .?". Perhaps it will then be said: "What he says has the form of a question but is really a command",—that is, has the function of a command in the technique of using the language. (Similarly one says "You will do this" not as a prophecy but as a command. What makes it the one or the other?)

22. Frege's idea that every assertion contains an assumption, which is the thing that is asserted, really rests on the possibility found in our language of writing every statement in the form: "It is asserted that such-and-such is the case."—But "that such-and-such is the case" is *not* a sentence in our language—so far it is not a *move* in the language-game. And if I write, not "It is asserted that . . . .", but "It is asserted: such-and-such is the case", the words "It is asserted" simply become superfluous.

We might very well also write every statement in the form of a question followed by a "Yes"; for instances: "Is it raining? Yes!: Would this shew that every statement contained a question?

Of course we have the right to use an assertion sign in contrast with a question-mark, for example, or if we want to distinguish an assertion from a fiction or a supposition. It is only a mistake if one thinks that the assertion consists of two actions, entertaining and asserting (assigning the truth-value, or something of the kind), and that in performing these actions we follow the propositional sign roughly as we sing from the musical score. Reading the written sentence loud or soft is indeed comparable with singing from a musical score, but '*meaning*' (thinking) the sentence that is read is not.

Frege's assertion sign marks the *beginning of the sentence*. Thus its function is like that of the full-stop. It distinguishes the whole period from a clause *within* the period. If I hear someone say "it's raining" but do not know whether I have heard the beginning and end of the period, so far this sentence does not serve to tell me anything.

23. But how many kinds of sentence are there? Say assertion, question, and command?—There are *countless* kinds: countless different kinds of use of what we call "symbols", "words", "sentences". And this multiplicity is not something fixed, given once for all; but new types of language, new language-games, as we may say, come into existence, and others become obsolete and get forgotten. (We can get a *rough picture* of this from the changes in mathematics.)

Here the term "language-*game*" is meant to bring into prominence the fact that the *speaking* of language is part of an activity, or of a form of life.

Review the multiplicity of language-games in the following examples, and in others:

Giving orders, and obeying them—

Describing the appearance of an object, or giving its measurements—

Constructing an object from a description (a drawing)—

Reporting an event—

Speculating about an event—

Forming and testing a hypothesis—

Presenting the results of an experiment in tables and diagrams—

Making up a story; and reading it—

Play-acting—

Singing catches—

Guessing riddles—

Making a joke; telling it—

Solving a problem in practical arithmetic—

Translating from one language into another—

Asking, thanking, cursing, greeting, praying.

—It is interesting to compare the multiplicity of the tools in language and of the ways they are used, the multiplicity of kinds of word and sentence, with what logicians have said about the structure of language. (Including the author of the *Tractatus Logico-Philosophicus*.)

24. If you do not keep the multiplicity of language-games in view you will perhaps be inclined to ask questions like: "What is a question?"—Is it the statement that I do not know such-and-such, or the statement that I wish the other person would tell me . . . .? Or is it the description of my mental state of uncertainty?—And is the cry "Help!" such a description?

Think how many different kinds of thing are called "description": description of a body's position bymeans of its co-ordinates; description of a facial expression; description of a sensation of touch; of a mood.

Of course it is possible to substitute the form of statement or description for the usual form of question: "I want to know whether . . . ." or "I am in doubt whether . . . ."—but this does not bring the different language-games any closer together.

The significance of such possibilities of transformation, for example of turning all statements into sentences beginning "I think" or "I believe" (and thus, as it were, into descriptions of *my* inner life) will become clearer in another place. (Solipsism.)

25. It is sometimes said that animals do not talk because they lack the mental capacity. And this means: "they do not think, and that is why they do not talk." But—they simply do not talk. Or to put it better: they do not use language—if we except the most primitive forms of language.—Commanding, questioning, recounting, chatting, are as much a part of our natural history as walking, eating, drinking, playing.

LANGUAGE AS LANGUAGE-GAMES

65. Here we come up against the great question that lies behind all these considerations.—For someone might object against me: "You take the easy way out! You talk about all sorts of language-games, but have nowhere said that the essence of a language-game, and hence of language, is: what is common to all these activities, and what makes them into language or parts of language. So you let yourself off the very part of the investigation that once gave you yourself most headache, the part about the *general form of propositions and of language*."

And this is true.—Instead of producing something common to all that we call language, I am saying that these phenomena have no one thing in common which makes us use the same word for all,—but that they are *related* to one another in many different ways. And it is because of this relationship, or these relationships, that we call them all "language." I will try to explain this.

66. Consider for example the proceedings that we call "games". I mean board-games, card-games, ball-games, Olympic games, and so on. What is common to them all?—Don't say: "There *must* be something common, or they would not be called 'games'—but *look and see* whether there is anything common to all.—For if you look at them you will not see something that is common to *all*, but similarities, relationships, and a whole series of them at that. To repeat: don't think, but look!—Look for example at board-games, with their multifarious relationships. Now pass to card-games; here you find many correspondences with the first group, but many common features drop out, and others appear. When we pass next to ball-games, much that is common is retained, but much is lost.—Are they all 'amusing'? Compare chess with noughts and crosses. Or is there always winning and losing, or competition between players? Think of patience. In ball games there is winning and losing; but when a child throws his ball at the wall and catches it again, this feature has disappeared. Look at the parts played by skill and luck; and at the difference between skill in chess and skill in tennis. Think now of games like ring-a-ring-a-roses; here is the element of amusement, but how many other characteristic features have disappeared! And we can go through the many, many other groups of games in the same way; can see how similarities crop up and disappear.

And the result of this examination is: we see a complicated network of similarities overlapping and criss-crossing: sometimes overall similarities, sometimes similarities of detail.

67. I can think of no better expression to characterize these similarities than "family resemblances"; for the various resemblances between members of a family: build, features, colour of eyes, gait, temperament, etc. etc. overlap and criss-cross in the same way.—And I shall say: 'games' form a family.

And for instance the kinds of number form a family in the same way. Why do we call something a "number"? Well, perhaps because it has a—direct—relationship with several things that have hitherto been called number; and this can be said to give it an indirect relationship to other things we call the same name. And we extend our concept of number as in spinning a thread we twist fibre on fibre. And the strength of the thread does not reside in the fact that some one fibre runs through its whole length, but in the overlapping of many fibres.

But if someone wished to say: "There is something common to all these constructions—namely the disjunction of all their common properties"—I should reply: Now you are only playing with words. One might as well say: "Something runs through the whole thread—namely the continuous overlapping of those fibres".

68. "All right: the concept of number is defined for you as the logical sum of these individual interrelated concepts: cardinal numbers, rational numbers, real numbers, etc.; and in the same way the concept of a game as the logical sum of a corresponding set of sub-concepts."—It need not be so. For I *can* give the concept 'number' rigid limits in this way, that is, use the word "number" for a rigidly limited concept, but I can also use it so that the extension of the concept is *not* closed by a frontier. And this is how we do use the word "game". For how is the concept of a game bounded? What still counts as a game and what no longer does? Can you give the boundary? No. You can *draw* one; for none has so far been drawn. (But that never troubled you before when you used the word "game".)

"But when the use of the word is unregulated, the 'game' we play with it is unregulated."—It is not everywhere circumscribed by rules; but no more are there any rules for how high one throws the ball in tennis, or how hard; yet tennis is a game for all that and has rules too.

69. How should we explain to someone what a game is? I imagine that we should describe *games* to him, and we might add: "This *and similar things* are called 'games'." And do we know any more about it ourselves? Is it only other people whom we cannot tell exactly what a game is?—But this is not ignorance. We do not know the boundaries because none have been drawn. To repeat, we can draw a boundary—for a special purpose. Does it take that to make the concept usable? Not at all! (Except for that special purpose.) No more than it took the definition: 1 pace = 75 cm. to make the measure of length 'one pace' usable. And if you want to say "But still, before that it wasn't an exact measure", then I reply: very well, it was an inexact one.—Though you still owe me a definition of exactness.

70. "But if the concept 'game' is uncircumscribed like that, you don't really know what you mean by a 'game'."—When I give the description: "The ground was quite covered with plants"—do you want to say I don't know what I am talking about until I can give a definition of a plant?

My meaning would be explained by, say, a drawing and the words "The ground looked roughly like this." Perhaps I even say "it looked *exactly* like this."—Then were just *this* grass and *these* leaves there, arranged just like this? No, that is not what it means. And I should not accept any picture as exact in *this* sense.

Someone says to me: "Shew the children a game." I teach them gaming with dice, and the other says

"I didn't mean that sort of game." Must the exclusion of the game with dice have come before his mind when he gave me the order? (Note added by Wittgenstein.)

71. One might say that the concept 'game' is a concept with blurred edges.—"But is a blurred concept a concept at all?—Is an indistinct photograph a picture of a person at all? Is it even always an advantage to replace an indistinct picture by a sharp one? Isn't the indistinct one often exactly what we need?

Frege compares a concept to an area and says that an area with vague boundaries cannot be called an area at all. This presumably means that we cannot do anything with it.—But is it senseless to say: "Stand roughly there"? Suppose that I were standing with someone in a city square and said that. As I say it I do not draw any kind of boundary, but perhaps point with my hand—as if I were indicating a particular *spot*. And this is just how one might explain to someone what a game is. One gives examples and intends them to be taken in a particular way.—I do not, however, mean by this that he is supposed to see in those examples that common thing which I—for some reason—was unable to express; but that he is now to *employ* those examples in a particular way. Here giving examples is not an *indirect* means of explaining—in default of a better. For any general definition can be misunderstood too. The point is that *this* is how we play the game. (I mean the language-game with the word "game".)

72. *Seeing what is common.* Suppose I shew someone various multicoloured pictures, and say: "The colour you see in all these is called 'yellow ochre'."—This is a definition, and the other will get to understand it by looking for and seeing what is common to the pictures. Then he can look *at*, can point *to*, the common thing.

Compare with this a case in which I shew him figures of different shapes all painted the same colour, and say: "What these have in common is called 'yellow ochre'."

And compare this case: I shew him samples of different shades of blue and say: "The colour that is common to all these is what I call 'blue'."

73. When someone defines the names of colours for me by pointing to samples and saying "This colour is called 'blue', this 'green' . . ." this case can be compared in many respects to putting a table in my hands, with the words written under the colour-samples.—Though this comparison may mislead in many ways.—One is now inclined to extend the comparison: to have understood the definition means to have in one's mind an idea of the thing defned, and that is a sample or picture. So if I am shewn various different leaves and told "This is called a 'leaf'," I get an idea of the shape of a leaf, a picture of it in my mind.—But what does the picture of a leaf look like when it does not shew us any particular shape, but 'what is common to all shapes of leaf'? Which shade is the 'sample in my mind' of the colour green—the sample of what is common to all shades of green.

"But might there not be such 'general' samples? Say a schematic leaf, or a sample of *pure* green?"—Certainly there might. But for such a schema to be understood as a *schema*, and not as the shape of a particular leaf, and for the slip of pure green to be understood as a sample of all that is greenish and not as a sample of pure green—this in turn resides in the way the samples are used.

Ask yourself: what *shape* must the sample of the colour green be? Should it be rectangular? Or would it then be the sample of a green rectangle?—So should it be 'irregular' in shape? And what is to prevent us then from regarding it—that is, from using it—only as a sample of irregularity of shape?

74. Here also belongs the idea that if you see this leaf as a samp of the 'leaf shape in general' you *see* it differently from someone who regards it as, say, a sample of this particular shape. Now this might well be so—though it is not so—for it would only be to say that, as a matter of experience, if you *see* the leaf in a particular way, you use it in such-and-such a way or according to such-and-such rules. Of course, there is such a thing as seeing in *this* way or *that*; and there are also cases where whoever sees a sample like *this* will in general use it in *this* way, and whoever sees it otherwise in another way. For example, if you see the schematic drawing of a cube as a plane figure consisting of a square and two rhombi you will, perhaps, carry out the order "Bring me something like this" differently from someone who sees the picture three-dimensionally.

75. What does it mean to know what a game is? What does it mean, to know it and not be able to say it? Is this knowledge somehow equivalent to an unformulated definition? So that if it were formulated I should be able to recognize it as the expression of my knowledge? Isn't my knowledge, my concept of a game, completely expressed in the explanations that I could give? That is, in my describing examples of various kinds of game; shewing how all sorts of other games can be constructed on the analogy of these; saying that I should scarcely include this or this among games; and so on.

76. If someone were to draw a sharp boundary I could not acknowledge it as the one that I too always wanted to draw, or had drawn in my mind. For I did not want to draw one at all. His concept can then be said to be not the same as mine, but akin to it. The kinship is that of two pictures, one of which consists of colour patches with vague contours, and the other of patches similarly shaped and distributed, but with clear contours. The kinship is just as undeniable as the difference.

77. And if we carry this comparison still further it is clear that the degree to which the sharp picture *can* resemble the blurred one depends on the latter's degree of vagueness. For imagine having to sketch a sharply defined picture 'corresponding' to a blurred one. In the latter there is a blurred red rectangle: for it you put down a sharply defined one. Of course—several such sharply defined rectangles can be drawn to correspond to the indefinite one.—But if the colours in the original merge without a hint of any outline won't it become a hopeless task to draw a sharp picture corresponding to the blurred one? Won't you then have to say: "Here I might just as well draw a circle or heart as a rectangle, for all the colours merge. Anything—and nothing—is right."—And this is the position you are in if you look for definitions corresponding to our concepts in aesthetics or ethics.

In such a difficulty always ask yourself: How did we *learn* the meaning of this word ("good" for instance)? From what sort of examples? in what language-games? Then it will be easier for you to see that the word must have a family of meanings.

Chapter 37

EDMUND HUSSERL

Edmund Husserl (1859–1938) was born in Moravia (now the Czech Republic). After attending the University of Leipzig where he studied mathematics and science, he went to Vienna to study under Franz Brentano, who awakened his thought in philosophical psychology. Brentano held that a basic form of consciousness was *intentionality*. All thought and desire is *about* something. One never just thinks or desires but thinks or desires something, even though the object may be vague and amorphous. Husserl developed Brentano's ideas, centering his studies on the nature or *phenomenology* of consciousness. He is considered the father of phenomenology, the basic ideas of which are outlined in the selection that follows.

In 1916 he became a professor at the University of Freiburg, Germany, where he remained until his retirement in 1929. During the last five years of his life he was barred from public activities because of his Jewish ancestry.

In our selection from *Ideas: General Introduction to Pure Phenomenology* (1913) Husserl focuses on his notion of phenomenological (or *eidetic*) reduction: all acts must be reduced to an essence of *eidos* (essential idea). The perceiver must perform an *epoche*, that is, suspend judgment on the existence of the objects of consciousness. For example, I should not focus on whether the computer before me really exists but on the essential features of the experience itself. He describes this as "bracketing" the experience. For Husserl I am neither a thinking substance (as Descartes thought), nor a bundle of perceptions (as Hume thought), nor an embodied soul (as Plato thought), but a pure transcendental ego, a consciousness that cannot be bracketed, but transcends its intentional object.

The main criticism of Husserl's program is that it entails solipsism, the idea that the only thing which really exists is the self or ego—all else being uncertain. Husserl tried to answer this objection by explaining how one transcendental ego can experience other such egos.

FOR FURTHER READING

Dreyfus, Hubert, ed. *Husserl, Intentionality and Cognitive Science*. (MIT Press, 1982).

Husserl, Edmund. *Ideas: General Introduction to Pure Phenomenology*, tr. W. R. Gibson. (Allen & Unwin, 1931).

Kockelman, Joseph. *Edmund Husserl's Phenomenology*. (Humanities Press, 1978).

Kolakowski, Leszek. *Husserl and the Search for Certitude*. (University of Chicago Press, 1987).

Solomon, Robert, ed. *Phenomenology and Existentialism*. (Harper & Row, 1972).

Speigelberg, Herbert. *The Phenomenological Movement*, 2 vol. (Martinus Nijhoff, 1960).

Stapleton, Timothy J. *Husserl and Heidegger*. (SUNY Press, 1983).

Ideas: General Introduction to Pure Phenomenology

THE THESIS OF THE NATURAL STANDPOINT AND ITS SUSPENSION

The Word of the Natural Standpoint: I and My World About Me

Our first outlook upon life is that of natural human beings, imagining, judging, feeling, willing, "*from the natural standpoint*." Let us make clear to ourselves what this means in the form of simple meditations which we can best carry on in the first person.

I am aware of a world, spread out in space endlessly, and in time becoming and become, without end. I am aware of it, that means, first of all, I discover it immediately, intuitively, I experience it. Through sight, touch, hearing, etc., in the different ways of sensory perception, corporeal things somehow spatially distributed are *for me simply there*, in verbal or figurative sense "present," whether or not I pay them special attention by busying myself with them, considering, thinking, feeling, willing. Animal beings also, perhaps men, are immediately there for me; I look up, I see them, I hear them coming towards me, I grasp them by the hand; speaking with them, I understand immediately what they are sensing and thinking, the feelings that stir them, what they wish or will. They too are present as realities in my field of intuition, even when I pay them no attention. But it is not necessary that they and other objects likewise should be present precisely in my *field of perception*. For me real objects are there, definite, more or less familiar, agreeing with what is actually perceived without being themselves perceived or even intuitively present. I can let my attention wander from the writing-table I have just seen and observed, through the unseen portions of the room behind my back to the verandah, into the garden, to the children in the summer-house, and so forth, to all the objects concerning which I precisely "know" that they are there and yonder in my immediate co-perceived surroundings—a knowledge which has nothing of conceptual thinking in it, and first changes into clear intuiting with the bestowing of attention, and even then only partially and for the most part very imperfectly.

But not even with the added reach of this intuitively clear or dark, distinct or indistinct *co-present* margin, which forms a continuous ring around the actual field of perception, does that world exhaust itself which in every waking moment is in some conscious measure "present" before me. It reaches rather in a fixed order of being the limitless behond. What is actually perceived, and what is more or less clearly co-present and determinate (to some extent at least), is partly pervaded, partly girt about with a *dimly apprehended depth or fringe of indeterminate reality*. I can pierce it with rays from the illuminating focus of attention with varying success. Determining representations, dim at first, then livelier, fetch me something out, a chain of such recollections takes shape, the circle of determinacy extends ever farther, and eventually so far that the connexion with the actual field of perception as the *immediate* environment is established. But in general the issue is a different one: an empty mist of dim indeterminacy gets studded over with intuitive possibilities or presumptions, and only the "form" of the world as "world" is foretokened. Moreover, the zone of indeterminacy is infinite. The misty horizon that can never be completely outlined remains necessarily there.

As it is with the world in its ordered being as a spatial present—the aspect I have so far been considering—so likewise is it with the world in respect to its *ordered being in the succession of time*. This world now present to me, and in every waking "now" obviously so, has its temporal horizon, infinite in both direction, its known and unknown, its intimately alive and its unalive past and future. Moving freely within the moment of experience which brings what is present into my intuitional grasp, I can follow up these connexions of the reality which immediately surrounds me. I can shift my standpoint in space and time, look this way and that, turn temporally forwards and backwards; I can provide for myself constantly new and more or less clear and meaningful perceptions and representations, and images also more or less clear, in which I make intuitable to myself whatever can possibly exist really or supposedly in the steadfast order of space and time.

In this way, when consciously awake, I find myself at all times, and without my ever being able to change this, set in relation to a world which, through its constant changes, remains one and ever the same. It is continually "present" for me, and I myself am a member of it. Therefore this world is not there for me as a mere *world of facts and affairs*, but, with the same immediacy, as a *world of values, a world of goods*, a *practical world*. Without further effort on my part I find the things before me furnished not only with the qualities that befit their positive nature, but with value-characters such as beautiful or ugly, agreeable or disagreeable, pleasant or unpleasant, and so forth. Things in their immediacy stand there as objects to be used, the "table" with its "books," the "glass to drink from," the "vase," the "piano," and so forth. These values and practicalities, they too belong to *the constitution of the "actually present" objects as such*, irrespective of my turning or not turning to consider them or indeed any other objects. The same considerations apply of course just as well to the men and beasts in my surroundings as to "mere things." They are my "friends" or my "foes," my "servants" or "superiors," "strangers" or "relatives," and so forth.

The "Cogito." My Natural World-about-me and the Ideal Worlds-about-me

It is then to this world, *the world in which I find myself and which is also my world-about-me*, that the complex forms of my manifold and shifting *spontaneities* of consciousness stand related: observing in the interests of research the bringing of meaning into conceptual form through description; comparing and distinguishing, collecting and counting, presupposing and inferring, the theorizing activity of consciousness, in short, in its different forms and stages. Related to it likewise are the diverse acts and states of sentiment and disapproval, joy and sorrow, desire and aversion, hope and fear, decision and action. All these, together with the sheer acts of the Ego, in which I become acquainted with the world as *immediately* given me, through spontaneous tendencies to turn towards it and to grasp it, are included under the one Cartesian expression: *Cogito*. In the natural urge of life I live continually in *this fundamental form of all "wakeful" living*, whether in addition I do or do not assert the *cogito*, and whether I am or am not "reflectively" concerned with the Ego and the *cogitare*. If I am so concerned, a new *cogito* has become livingly active, which for its part is not reflected upon, and so not objective for me.

I am present to myself continually as someone who perceives, represents, thinks, feels, desires, and so forth; and *for the most part* herein I find myself related in present experience to the fact-world which is constantly about me. But I am not always so related, not every *cogito* in which I live has for its *cogitatum* things, men, objects or contents of one kind or another. Perhaps I am busied with pure numbers and the laws they symbolize: nothing of this sort is present in the world about me, this world of "real fact." And yet the world of numbers also is there for me, as the field of objects with which I am arithmetically busied; while I am thus occupied some numbers or constructions of a numerical kind will be at the focus of vision, girt by an arithmetical horizon partly defined, partly not; but obviously this being-there-for-me, like the being there at all, is something very different from this. *The arithmetical world is there for me only when and so long as I occupy the arithmetical standpoint*. But the *natural* world, the world in the ordinary sense of the word, is *constantly there for me*, so long as I live naturally and look in its direction. I am then at the "*natural standpoint*," which is just another way of stating the same thing. And there is no need to modify these conclusions when I proceed to appropriate to myself the arithmetical world, and other similar "worlds," by adopting the corresponding standpoint. The natural world *still remains "present*," I am at the natural standpoint after as well as before, and in this respect *undisturbed by the adoption of new standpoints*. If my *cogito* is active *only* in the worlds proper to the new standpoints, the natural world remains unconsidered; it is now the background for my consciousness as act, but it is *not the encircling sphere within which an arithmetical world finds its true and proper place*. The two worlds are present together but *disconnected*, apart, that is, from their relation to the Ego, in virtue of which I can freely direct my glance or my acts to the one or to the other.

The "Other" Ego-subject and the Intersubjective Natural World-about-me

Whatever holds good for me personally, also holds good, as I know, for all other men whom I find present in my world-about-me. Experiencing them as men, I understand and take them as Ego-subjects, units like myself, and related to their natural surroundings. But this in such wise that I apprehend the world-about-them and the world-about-me objectively as one and the same world, which differs in each case only through affecting consciousness differently. Each has his place whence he sees the things that are present, and each enjoys accordingly different appearances of the things. For each, again, the fields of perception and memory actually present are different, quite apart from the fact that even that which is here intersubjectively known in common is known in different ways, is differently apprehended, shows different grades of clearness, and so forth. Despite all this, we come to understandings with our neighbours, and set up in common an objective spatio-temporal fact-world as *the world about us that is there for us all, and to which we ourselves none the less belong.*

The General Thesis of the Natural Standpoint

That which we have submitted towards the characterization of what is given to us from the natural standpoint, and thereby of the natural standpoint itself, was a piece of pure description *prior to all "theory."* In these studies we stand bodily aloof from all theories, and by "theories" we here mean anticipatory ideas of every kind. Only as facts of our environment, not as agencies for uniting facts validly together, do theories concern us at all. But we do not set ourselves the task of continuing the pure description and raising it to a systematically inclusive and exhaustive characterization of the data, in their full length and breadth, discoverable from the natural standpoint (or from any standpoint, we might add, that can be knit up with the same in a common consent). A task such as this can and must—as scientific—be undertaken, and it is one of extraordinary importance, although so far scarcely noticed. Here it is not ours to attempt. For us who are striving towards the entrance-gate of phenomenology all the necessary work in this direction has already been carried out; the few features pertaining to the natural standpoint which we need are of a quite general character, and have already figured in our descriptions, and been sufficiently *and fully clarified.* We even made a special point of securing this full measure of clearness.

We emphasize a most important point once again in the sentences that follow: I find continually present and standing over against me the one spatio-temporal fact-world to which I myself belong, as do all other men found in it and related in the same way to it. This "fact-world," as the world already tells us, I find to *be out there,* and also *take it just as it gives itself to me as something that exists out there.* All doubting and rejecting of the data of the natural world leaves standing the *general thesis of the natural standpoint.* "The" world is as fact-world always there; at the most it is at odd points "other" than I supposed, this or that under such names as "illusion," "hallucination," and the like, must be struck *out of it,* so to speak; but the "it" remains ever, in the sense of the general thesis, a world that has its being out there. To know it more comprehensively, more trustworthily, more perfectly than the naïve lore of experience is able to do, and to solve all the problems of scientific knowledge which offer themselves upon its ground, that is the goal of the *sciences of the natural standpoint.*

Radical Alteration of the Natural Thesis "Disconnexion," "Bracketing"

Instead now of remaining at this standpoint, we propose to alter it radically. Our aim must be to convince ourselves of the possibility of this alteration on grounds of principle.

The General Thesis according to which the real world about me is at all times known not merely in a general way as something apprehended, but as a fact-world *that has its being out there,* does *not* consist of course *in an act proper,* in an articulated judgment *about existence.* It is and remains something all the time the standpoint is adopted, that is, it endures persistently during the whole course of our life of natural endeavour. What has been at any time perceived clearly, or obscurely made present, in short everything out of the world of nature through experience and prior to any thinking, bears in its totality and in all its articulated sections the character "present" "out there," a character which can function essentially as the ground of support for an explicit (predicative) existential judgment which is in agreement with the character it is grounded upon. If we express that same judgment, we know quite well that in so doing we have simply put into the form of a statement and grasped as a predication what already lay somehow in the original experience, or lay there as the character of something "present to one's hand."

We can treat the potential and unexpressed thesis exactly as we do the thesis of the explicit judgment. A procedure of this sort, *possible at any time*, is, for instance, *the attempt to doubt everything* which *Descartes*, with an entirely different end in view, with the purpose of setting up an absolutely indubitable sphere of Being, undertook to carry through. We link on here, but add directly and emphatically that this attempt to doubt everything should serve us *only as a device of method*, helping us to stress certain points which by its means, as though secluded in its essence, must be brought clearly to light.

The attempt to doubt everything has its place in the realm of our *perfect freedom*. We can *attempt to doubt* anything and everything, however convinced we may be concerning what we doubt, even though the evidence which seals our assurance is completely adequate.

Let us consider what is essentially involved in an act of this kind. He who attempts to doubt is attempting to doubt "Being" of some form or other, or it may be Being expanded into such predicative forms as "It is," "It is this or thus," and the like. The attempt does not affect the form of Being itself. He who doubts, for instance, whether an object, whose Being he does not doubt, is constituted in such and such a way doubts *the way it is constituted*. We can obviously transfer this way of speaking from the doubting to the *attempt* at doubting. It is clear that we cannot doubt the Being of anything, and in the same act of consciousness (under the unifying form of simultaneity) bring what is substantive to this Being under the terms of the Natural Thesis, and so confer upon it the character of "being actually there" (*vorhanden*). Or to put the same in another way: we cannot at once doubt and hold for certain one and the same quality of Being. It is likewise clear that the *attempt* to doubt any object of awareness in respect of it *being actually there necessarily conditions a certain suspension (Aufhebung) of the thesis*; and it is precisely this that interests us. It is not a transformation of the thesis into its antithesis, of positive into negative; it is also not a transformation into presumption, suggestion, indecision, doubt (in one or another sense of the word); each shifting indeed is not at our free pleasure. *Rather is it something quite unique. We do not abandon the thesis we have adopted, we make no change in our conviction*, which remains in itself what it is so long as we do not introduce new motives of judgment, which we precisely refrain from doing. And yet the thesis undergoes a modification—whilst remaining in itself what it is, *we set it as it were "out of action,"* we *"disconnect it," "bracket it."* it still remains there like the bracketed in the bracket, like the disconnected outside the connexional system. We can also say: The thesis is experience as lived (*Erlebnis*), *but we make "no use" of it*, and by that, of course, we do not indicate privation (as when we say of the ignorant that he makes no use of a certain thesis); in this case rather, as with all parallel expressions, we are dealing with indicators that point to a definite but *unique form of consciousness*, which clamps on to the original simple thesis (whether it actually or even predicatively *posits* existence or not), and transvalues it in a quite peculiar way. *This transvaluing is a concern of our full freedom, and is opposed to all cognitive attitudes* that would set themselves up as coordinate with the *thesis*, and yet within the unity of "simultaneity" remain incompatible with it, as indeed it is in general with all attitudes whatsoever in the strict sense of the word.

In *the attempt to doubt* applied to a thesis which, as we presuppose, is certain and tenaciously held, the "disconnexion" takes place in and with a modification of the antithesis, namely with hte "*supposition*" (*Ansetzung*) *of Non-Being*, which is thus the partial basis of the attempt to doubt. With Descartes this is so markedly the case that one can say that his universal attempt at doubt is just an attempt at universal denial. We disregard this possibility here, we are not interested in every analytical component of the attempt to doubt, nor therefore in its exact and completely sufficing analysis. *We extract only the phenomenon of "bracketing" or "disconnection,"* which is obviously not limited to that of the attempt to doubt, although it can be detached from it with special ease, but can appear *in other contexts also*, and with no less ease *independently*. In relation to every thesis and wholly uncoerced we can use this *peculiar* ἐποχή, (*epokhe*—abstention), *a certain refraining from judgment which is compatible with the unshaken and unshakable because self-evidencing conviction of Truth*. The thesis is "put out of action," bracketed, it passes off into the modified status of a "bracketed thesis," and the judgment *simpliciter* into "*bracketed judgment*."

Naturally one should not simply identify this consciousness with that of "mere supposal," that nymphs, for instance, are dancing in a ring; for thereby *no disconnecting* of a living conviction that goes on living takes place, although from another side the close relation of the two forms of consciousness lies clear. Again, we are not concerned here with supposal in the sense of "*assuming*" or *taking for granted*, which in the equivocal speech of current usage may also be expressed in the words: "I suppose (I make the assumption) that it is so and so."

Let us add further that nothing hinders us *from speaking bracketing correlatively* also, in respect of *an objectivity to be posited*, what ever be the region or category to which it belongs. What is meant in this case is that *every thesis related to this objectivity* must be *disconnected* and changed into its bracketed counterpart. On closer view, moreover, the "bracketing" image is from the outset better suited to the sphere of the object, just as the expression "to put out of action" better suits the sphere of the Act or of Consciousness.

The Phenomenological ἐποχή

We can now let the universal ἐποχή, (*epokhe*—abstention) in the sharply defined and novel sense we have given to it step into the place of the Cartesian attempt at universal doubt. But on good grounds we *limit* the universality of this ϵποχη. For were it as inclusive as it is in general capable of being, then since every thesis and every judgment can be modified freely to any extent, and every objectivity that we can judge or criticize can be bracketed, no field would be left over for unmodified judgments, to say nothing of a science. But our design is just to discover a new scientific domain, such as might be won precisely *through the method of bracketing*, though only through a definitely limited form of it.

The limiting consideration can be indicated in a word.

We put out of action the general thesis which belongs to the essence of the natural standpoint, we place in brackets whatever it includes respecting the nature of Being: *this entire natural world therefore* which is continually "there for us," "present to our hand," and will ever remain there, is a "fact-world" of which we continue to be conscious, even though it pleases us to put it in brackets.

If I do this, as I am fully free to do, I do *not* then *deny* this "world," as though I were a sophist, *I do not doubt that it is there* as though I were a sceptic; but I use the "phenomenological" ἐποχή, which *completely bars me from using any judgment that concerns spatio-temporal existence* (*Dasein*).

Thus *all sciences which relate to this natural world*, though they stand never so firm to me, though they fill me with wondering admiration, though I am far from any thought of objecting to them in the least degree, *I disconnect them all, I make absolutely no use of their standards, I do not appropriate a single one of the propositions that enter into their systems, even though their evidential value is perfect, I take none of them, no one of them serves me for a foundation*—so long, that is, as it is understood, in the way these sciences themselves understand it, as a truth *concerning the realities* of this world. *I may accept it only after I have placed it in the bracket.* That means: only in the modified consciousness of the judgment as it appears in disconnexion, and *not as it figures within the science as its proposition, a proposition which claims to be valid and whose validity I recognize and make use of.*

The ἐποχή here in question will not be confined with that which positivism demands, and against which, as we were compelled to admit, it is itself an offender. We are not concerned at present with removing the preconceptions which trouble the pure positivity (*Sachlichkeit*) of research, with the constituting of a science "free from theory" and "free from metaphysics" by bringing all the grounding back to the immediate data, nor with the means of reaching such ends, concerning whose value there is indeed no question. What *we* demand lies along another line. The whole world as placed within the nature-setting and presented in experience as real, taken completely "free from all theory," just as it is in reality experienced, and made clearly manifest in and through the linkings of our experiences, has now no validity for us, it must be set in brackets, untested indeed but also uncontested. Similarly all theories and sciences, positivistic or otherwise, which relate to this world, however good they may be, succumb to the same fate.

CONSCIOUSNESS AND NATURAL REALITY

Intimation Concerning "Pure" or "Transcendential Consciousness" as Phenomenological Residuum

We have learnt to understand the meaning of the phenomenological ἐποχή (*epokhe*—abstention), but we are still quite in the dark as to its serviceability. In the first place it is not clear to what extent the limitation of the total field of the εποχη, as discussed in the previous pages, involves a real narrowing of its general scope. *For what can remain over when the whole world is bracketed, including ourselves and all our thinking* (*cogitare*)?

Since the reader already knows that the interest which governs these "Meditations" concerns a new eidetic science, he will indeed at first expect the world as fact to succumb to the disconnexion, but not *the world as Eidos*, nor any other sphere of Essential Being. The disconnecting of the world does not as a matter of fact mean the disconnecting of the number series, for instance, and the arithmetic relative to it.

However, we do not take this path, nor does our goal lie in its direction. That goal we could also refer to as *the winning of a new region of Being, the distinctive character of which has not yet been defined*, a region of *individual* Being, like every genuine region. We must leave the sequel to teach us what that more precisely means.

We proceed in the first instance by showing up simply and directly what we see; and since the Being to be thus shown up is neither more nor less than that which we refer to on essential grounds as "pure experiences (*Erlebnisse*)" "pure consciousness" with its pure "correlates of consciousness," and on the other side its "pure Ego," we observe that it is from *the Ego, the* consciousness, *the* experience as given to us from the natural standpoint, that we take our start.

I, the real human being, am a real object like others in the natural world. I carry out *cogitationes*, "acts of consciousness" in both a narrower and a wider sense, and these acts, as belonging to this human subject, are events of the same natural world. And all my remaining experiences (*Erlebnisse*) likewise, out of whose changing stream the specific acts of the Ego shine forth in so distinctive a way, glide into one another, enter into combinations, and are being incessantly modified. Now in its *widest connotation* the expression "*consciousness*" (then indeed less suited for its purpose) includes *all* experiences (*Erlebnisse*), and entrenched in the natural standpoint as we are even in our scientific thinking, grounded there in habits that are most firmly established since they have never misled us, we take all these data of psychological reflexion as real world-events, as the experiences (*Erlebnisse*) of animal beings. So natural is it to us to see them only in this light that, though acquainted already with the possibility of a change of standpoint, and on the search for the new domain of objects, we fail to notice that it is from out these centres of experience (*Erlebnisse*) themselves that through the adoption of the new standpoint the new domain emerges. Connected with this is the fact that instead of keeping our eyes turned towards these centres of experience, we turned them away and sought the new objects in the ontological realms of arithmetic, geometry, and the like, whereby indeed nothing truly new has to be won.

Thus we fix our eyes steadily upon the sphere of Consciousness and study what it is that we find immanent in *it*. At first, without having yet carried out the phenomenological suspensions of the element of judgment, we subject this sphere of Consciousness in its essential nature to a systematic though in no sense exhaustive analysis. What we lack above all is a certain general insight into the essence of *consciousness in general*, and quite specially also of consciousness, so far as in and through its essential Being, the "natural" fact-world comes to be known. In these studies we go so far as is needed to furnish the full insight at which we have been aiming, to wit, *that Consciousness in itself has a being of its own which in its absolute uniqueness of nature remains unaffected by the phenomenological disconnexion*. It therefore remains over as a "*phenomenological residuum*," as a region of Being which is in principle unique, and can become in fact the field of a new science—the science of Phenomenology.

Through this insight the "phenomenological" ἐποχή will for the first time deserve its name; to exercise it in full consciousness of its import will turn out to be the necessary operation which *renders "pure" consciousness accessible to us, and subsequently the whole phenomenological region*. And thus we shall be able to understand why this region and the new science attached to it was fated to remain unknown. From the natural standpoint nothing can be seen except the natural world. So long as the possibility of the phenomenological standpoint was not grasped, and the method of relating the objectivities which emerge therewith to a primordial form of apprehension had not been devised, the phenomenological world must needs have remained unknown, and indeed barely divined at all.

We would add yet the following to our terminology: Important motives which have their ground in epistemological requirements justify us in referring to "pure" consciousness, of which much is yet to be said, also as *transcendental consciousness*, and the operation through which it is acquired as *transcendental ἐποχή*. On grounds of method this operation will split up into different steps of "disconnexion" or "bracketing," and thus our method will assume the character of a graded reduction. For this reason we propose to speak, and even preponderatingly, of *phenomenological reductions* (though, in respect of their unity as a whole, we would speak in unitary form of *the* phenomenological reduction). From the epistemological viewpoint we would also speak of transcendental reductions. Moreover, these and *all* our terms must be understood exclusively in accordance with the sense which *our* presentations indicate for them, but not in any other one which history or the terminological habits of the reader may favour.

The Essence of Consciousness as Theme of Inquiry

We start with a series of observations within which we are not troubled with any phenomenological ἐποχή. We are directed to an "outer world," and, without forsaking the natural standpoint, reflect psychologically on our Ego and its experience (*Erleben*). We busy ourselves, precisely as we have done if we had never heard of the new viewpoint, with *the essential nature of "the consciousness of something,"* following, for instance, our consciousness of the existence of material things, living bodies and men, or that of technical and literary works, and so forth. We adhere to our general principle that each individual event has its essence that can be grasped in its eiditic purity, and in this purity must belong to a field available to eidetic inquiry. In accordance herewith the universal fact of nature conveyed by the words "I am," "I think," "I have a world over against me," and the like, has also its essential content, and it is on this exclusively that we now intend to concentrate. Thus we rehearse to ourselves by way of illustration certain conscious experiences chosen at random, and in their individuality just as they are in their natural setting as real facts of human life, and we make these present to ourselves through memory or in the free play of fancy. On the ground of illustrations such as these, which we assume to be presented with perfect clearness, we grasp and fix in adequate ideation the pure essences that interest us. The individual facts, the fact-character of the natural world in general, thereby escapes our theoretical scrutiny—as in all cases where our inquiry is purely eidetic.

We limit still further the theme of our inquiry. Its title ran: Consciousness, or more distinctly *Conscious experience* (*Erlebnis*) *in general*, to be taken in an extremely wide sense about whose exact definition we are fortunately not concerned. Exact definitions do not lie at the threshold of analysis of the kind we are here making, but are a later result involving great labour. As starting-point we take consciousness in a pregnant sense which suggests itself at once, most simply indicated through the Cartesian *cogito*, "I think." As is known Descartes understood this in a sense so wide as to include every case of "I perceive, I remember, I fancy, I judge, feel, desire, will," and all experiences of the Ego that in any way resemble the foregoing, in all the countless fluctuations of their special patterns. The Ego itself to which they are all related, spontaneous, in receptive or any other "attitude," and indeed the Ego in any and every sense, we leave at first out of consideration. We shall be concerned with it later, and fundamentally. For the present there is sufficient other material to serve as support for our analysis and grasp of the essential. And we shall find ourselves forthwith referred thereby to enveloping connexions of experience which compel us to widen our conception of a conscious experience beyond this circle of specific *cogitationes*.

We shall consider conscious experiences *in the concrete fullness and entirety* with which they figure in their concrete context—the *stream of experience*—and to which they are closely attached through their own proper essence. It then becomes evident that every experience in the stream which our reflexion can lay hold on has *its own essence open to intuition*, a "content" which can be considered in its *singularity in and for itself*. We shall be concerned to grasp this individual content of the *cogitatio* in its *pure* singularity, and to describe it in its general features, excluding everything which is not to be found in the *cogitatio* as it is in itself. We must likewise describe the *unity of consciousness* which is demanded *by the intrinsic nature of the cogitationes*, and so necessarily demanded that they could not be without this unity.

The Cogito as "Act." The Modal Form of Marginal Actuality

Let us start with an example. In front of me, in the dim light, lies this white paper. I see it, touch it. This perceptual seeing and touching of the paper as the full concrete experience *of* the paper that lies here as given in truth precisely with this relative lack of clearness, with this imperfect definition, appearing to me from this particular angle—is a *cogitatio*, a conscious experience. The paper itself with its objective qualities, its extension in space, its objective position in regard to that spatial thing I call my body, is not *cogitatio*, but *cogitatum*, not perceptual experience, but something perceived. Now that which is perceived can itself very well be a conscious experience; but it is evident that an object such as a material thing, this paper, for instance, as given in perceptual exerience, is in principle other than an experience, a being of a completely different kind.

Before pursuing this point farther, let us amplify the illustration. In perception properly so-called, as an explicit awareness (*Gewahren*), I am turned towards the object, to the paper, for instance, I apprehend it as being this here and now. The apprehension is a singling out, every perceived object having a background in experience. Around and about the paper lie books, pencils, ink-well, and so forth, and these in a certain sense are also "perceived," perceptually there, in the "field of intuition"; but whilst I was turned towards the paper there was no turning in their direction, nor any apprehending of them, not even in a secondary sense. They appeared and yet were not singled out, were not posited on their own account. Every perception of a thing has such a zone of *background intuitions* (or background awarenesses, if "intuiting" already includes the state of being turned towards), and this also is a "*conscious experience*," or more briefly a "consciousness *of*" all indeed that in point of fact lies in the co-perceived objective "background." We are not talking here of course of that which is to be found as an "objective" element in the objective space to which the background in question may belong, of all the things and thing-like events which a valid and progressive experience may establish there. What we say applies exclusively to that zone of consciousness which belongs to the model essence of a perception as "being turned towards an object," and further to that which belongs to the proper essence of this zone itself. But it is here implied that certain modifications of the original experience are possible, which we refer to as a free turning of the "look"—not precisely nor merely of the physical but of the "*mental look*"—from the paper at first *descried* to objects which had already appeared before of which we had been "implicitly" aware, and whereof *subsequent* to the directing of one's look thither we are explicitly aware, perceiving them "attentitively," or "noticing them near by."

We are aware of things not only in perception, but also consciously in recollections, in representations similar to recollections, and also in the free play of fancy, and this in "clear intuition" it may be, or without noticeable perceptibility after the manner of "dim" presentations; they float past us in different "characterizations" as real, possible, fancied, and so forth. All that we have stated concerning perceptual experiences holds good, obviously, of these other experiences, essentially different as they are. We shall not think of confusing the *objects of which we are aware* under these forms of consciousness (the fancy-shaped nymphs, for instance) with the conscious experiences themselves which are a consciousness *of* them. Then, again, we know that it is the essence of all such experiences—taking the same, as always, in their concrete fullness—to show that remarkable modification which transfers consciousness in the *mode of actual orientation* to consciousness in the *mode of non-actuality* and conversely. At the one time the experience is, so to speak "*explicitly*" aware of its objective content, at the other implicitly and merely *potentially*. The objective factor, whether in perception, memory, or fancy, may already be appearing to us, but *our mental gaze is not yet "directed" towards it*, not even in a secondary sense, to say nothing of being "busied" with it in some special way.

Similar remarks apply to all and any of the *cogitationes* in the sense illustrated by Descartes' use of the term, to all experiences of thought, feeling and will, except that, as will be emphasized (in the next paragraph), the "directedness towards," the "being turned towards," which is the distinctive mark of focal actuality, does not coincide, as in the favourite because simplest examples of sensory presentations, with singling out and noting the objects we are aware of. It is also obviously true of all such experiences that the focal is girt about with a "zone" of the marginal; *the stream of experience can never consist wholly of focal actualities*. These indeed determine, in a very general sense which must be extended beyond the circle of our illustrations, and through the contrast with marginal actualities already drawn, the *pregnant* meaning of the expression "cogito," "I have *consciousness* of something," "I perform an *act* of consciousness." In order to keep this well-established concept purely separate, we propose to reserve for it exclusively the Cartesian expressions *cogito* and *cogitationes*, unless through some addition, such as "marginal" or the like, we expressly indicate the modified use we are making of the term.

We can define a *"wakeful" Ego* as one that within its stream of experience is continually conscious in the specific form of the *cogito*; which, of course, does not mean that it can and does bring these experiences persistently or in general to predicative expression. Ego-subjects include animals. But, according to what we have said above, it belongs to the essence of the stream of experience of a wakeful Self that the continuously prolonged chain of *cogitationes* is constantly enveloped in a medium of dormant actuality (*Inaktualität*), which is ever prepared to pass off into the wakeful mode (*Aktualität*), as conversely the wakeful into the dormant.

Intentional Experience. Experience in General

However drastic the change which the experiences of a wakeful Consciousness undergo in their transition into the dormant state, the experiences as modified share the essential nature of the original experiences in an important respect. It belongs as a general feature to the essence of every actual *cogito* to be a consciousness *of* something. But according to what we have already said, the *modified cogitatio is likewise and in its own way Consciousness*, and *of the same* something as with the corresponding unmodified consciousness. Thus the essential property of Consciousness in its general form is preserved in the modification. All experiences which have these essential properties in common are also called *"internal experiences"* (acts in the *very wide sense* of the *Logical Studies*); in so far as they are a consciousness of something they are said to be *"intentionally related"* to this something.

We must, however, be quite clear on this point that *there is no question here of a relation between a psychological event—called experience (Erlebnis)—and some other real existent (Dasein)—called Object*—or of a *psychological connexion* obtaining between the one and the other *in objective reality*. On the contrary, we are concerned with experiences in their essential purity, with *pure essences*, and with that which is *involved in* the essence *"a priori," in unconditioned necessity*.

That an experience is the consciousness of something: a fiction, for instance, the fiction of this or that centaur; a perception, the perception of its "real" object; a judgment, the judgment concerning it subject-matter, and so forth, this does not relate to the experimental fact as lived within the world, more specifically within some given psychological context, but to the pure essence grasped ideationally as pure idea. In the very essence of an experience lies determined not only *that*, but also *whereof* it is a consciousness, and in what determinate or indeterminate sense it is this. So too in the essence of consciousness as dormant lies included the variety of wakeful *cogitationes*, into which it can be differentiated through the modification we have already referred to as "the noticing of what was previously unnoticed."

Under *experiences* in the *widest sense* we understand whatever is to be found in the stream of experience, not only therefore intentional experiences, *cogitationes* actual and potential taken in their full concreteness, but all the real (*reellen*) phases to be found in this stream and in its concrete sections.

For it is easily seen that *not every real phase* of the concrete unity of an intentional experience has itself the *basic character of intentionality*, the property of being a "consciousness of something." This is the case, for instance, with all sensory data, which play so great a part in the perceptive intuitions of things. In the experience of the perception of this white paper, more closely in those components of it related to the paper's quality of whiteness, we discover through properly directed noticing the sensory datum "white." This "whiteness" is something that belongs inseparably to the essence of the concrete perception, as a *real* (*reelles*) concrete constitutive portion of it. As the content which presents the whiteness of the paper as it appears to us it is the *bearer of* an intentionality, but not itself a consciousness of something. The same holds good of other data of experience, of the so-called *sensory feelings*, for instance. We shall be speaking of these at greater length in a later context.

The "Directedness" of the Pure Ego in the *Cogito*, and the Noticing that Apprehends

Though we are unable at this point to proceed farther with our descriptive analysis of intentional experiences in their essential nature, we would single out certain aspects as noteworthy in relation to further developments. If an intentional experience is actual, carried out, that is, after the manner of the *cogito*, the subject "directs" itself within it towards the intentional object. To the *cogito* itself belongs an immanent "glancing-towards" the object, a directedness which from another side springs forth from the "Ego," which can therefore never be absent. This glancing of the Ego towards something is in harmony with the act involved, perceptive in perception, fanciful in fancy, approving in approval, volitional in will, and so forth. This means, therefore, that this having in one's glance, in one's mental eye, which belongs to the *essence* of the *cogito*, to the act as such, is not in itself in turn a proper act, and in particular should not be confused with a perceiving (in however wide a sense this term be used), or with any other types of act related to perceptions. It should be noticed that *intentional* object of a consciousness (understood as the latter's full correlate) is by no means to be identified with *apprehended* object. We are accustomed without further thought to include the being apprehended in the concept of the object (of that generally which stands over against the subject), since in so far as we think of it and say something *about* it, we have made it into an object in the sense of something apprehended. In the widest sense of the world, apprehending an object (*Erfassen*) coincides with mindfully heeding it (*achten*), and noting its nature (*bemerken*), whether attentively as a special case, or cursorily, provided at least that these expressions are used in their customary sense. *This heeding or apprehending is not to be identified with the modus of "cogito" in general*, that of actuality, but seen more closely, with a *special act-modus* which every consciousness or every act which does not yet possess it can assume. Should it do this, its intentional object is not only known in a general way and brought within the directed glance of the mind, but is an apprehended and noted object. A turning towards a Thing, to be sure, cannot take place otherwise than in the way of apprehension, and the same holds good of all *objectivities that are "plainly presentable"*: here a turning towards (be it even in fancy) is *eo ipso* an "apprehending" and a "heeding." But in the act of valuation we are turned towards values, in acts of joy to the enjoyed, in acts of love to the beloved, in acting to the action, and *without* apprehending all this. The intentional object rather, that which is valued, enjoyed, beloved, hoped as such, the action as action, first becomes an apprehended object through a distinctively "*objectifying*" *turn of thought*. If one is turned towards some matter absorbed in appreciation, the apprehension of the matter is no doubt included in the total attitude; but it is not the *mere* matter in general, but the matter *values* or the *value* which is (and the point will concern us more in detail later on) *the complete intentional correlate of the act of valuation*. Thus "*to be turned in appreciation* towards some matter" does not already imply "*having*" the value "*for object*" in the special sense of object apprehended, as indeed we must have the object if we are to predicate anything of it; and similarly in regard to all logical acts which are related to it.

Thus in acts like those of appreciation we have an *intentional object in a double sense*: we must distinguish between the "*subject matter*" *pure and simple* and the *full intentional object*, and corresponding to this, a *double intentio*, a two-fold directedness. If we are directed towards some matter in an act of appreciation, the direction towards the matter in question is a noting and apprehending of it; but we are "directed"—only not in an apprehending way—also to the value. Not merely the *representing of the matter* in question, but also the *appreciating* which includes this representing, has the modus of actuality.

But we must hasten to add that it is only in respect of simple acts of valuation that the matter stands so simply. In general, acts of sentiment and will are consolidated upon a higher level, and the intentional objectivity also differentiates itself accordingly: there is also a complicating of the ways in which the objects included in the unitary total objectivity come under the directed mental glance. But in any case the following main propositions hold good:

In every act some mode of heeding (Achtsamkeit) holds sway. But wherever it is not the plain consciousness of a subject-matter, wherever some further "attitude towards" the subject-matter is grounded in such consciousness, *subject-matter and full intentional object* ("subject-matter" and "value," for instance), likewise *heeding the object and mentally scrutinizing it, separate out the one from the other*. But at the same time the possibility of a modification remains an essential property of these grounded acts, a modification whereby their full intentional objects become noticed, and in this sense "*represented*" objects, which now, from their side, become capable of serving as bases for explanations, relations, conceptual renderings, and predications. Thanks to this objectification we find facing us in natural setting, and therefore *as members of the natural world*, not natural things merely, but values and practical objects of every kind, cities, streets with street-lighting arrangements, dwellings, furniture, works of art, books, tools and so forth. . . .

Consciousness and Natural Reality. The View of The "Man in the Street"

All the essential characteristics of experience and consciousness which we have reached are for us necessary steps towards the attainment of the end which is unceasingly drawing us on, the discovery, namely, of the essence of that *"pure" consciousness* which is to fix the limits of the phenomenological field. Our inquiries were eidetic; but the individual instances of the essences we have referred to as experience, stream of experience, "consciousness" in all its senses, belonged as real events to the natural world. To that extent we have not abandoned the ground of the natural standpoint. Individual consciousness is interwoven with the *natural world* in a *twofold* way: it is some *man's* consciousness, or that of some *man* or *beast*, and in a large number at least of its particularizations it is a consciousness of this world. *In respect now of this intimate attachment with the real world, what is meant by saying that consciousness has an essence "of its own,"* that with other consciousness it constitutes a self-contained *connexion determined purely through this, its own essence,* the connexion, namely, of the stream of consciousness? Moreover, since we can interpret consciousness in the widest sense to cover eventually whatever the concept of experience includes, the question concerns the experience-stream's own essential nature and that of all its components. To what extent, in the first place, must the *material world* be fundamentally different in kind, *excluded from the experience's own essential nature*? And if it is this, if over against all consciousness and the essential being proper to it, it is that which is "*foreign*" and "*other*," how can consciousness be *interwoven* with it, and consequently with the whole world that is alien to consciousness? For it is easy to convince oneself that the material world is not just any portion of the natural world, but its fundamental stratum to which all other real being is *essentially* related. It still fails to include the souls of men and animals; and the new factor which these introduce is first and foremost their "experiencing" together with their conscious relationship to the world surrounding them. *But here consciousness and thinghood form a connected whole*, connected within the particular psychological unities which we call *animalia*, and in the last resort within the *real unity of the world as a whole*. Can the unity of a whole be other than made one through the essential proper nature of its parts, which must therefore have some *community of essence* instead of a fundamental heterogeneity?

To be clear, let us seek out the ultimate sources whence the general thesis of the world which I adopt when taking up the natural standpoint draws its nourishment, thereby enabling me as a conscious being to discover over against me an existing world of things, to ascribe to myself in this world a body, and to find for myself within this world a proper place. This ultimate source is obviously *sensory experience*. For our purpose, however, it is sufficient to consider *sensory perception*, which in a certain proper sense plays among experiencing acts the part of an original experience, whence all other experiencing acts draw a chief part of their power to serve as a ground. Every perceiving consciousness has this peculiarity, that it is the consciousness of *the embodied (leibhaftigen) self-presence of an individual object*, which on its own side and in a pure logical sense of the term is an individual or some logico-categorical modification of the same. In our own instance, that of sensory perception, or, in distincter terms, perception of a world of things, the logical individual is the Thing; and it is sufficient for us to treat the perception of things as representing all other perceptions (of properties, processes, and the like).

The natural wakeful life of our Ego is a continuous perceiving, actual or potential. The world of things and our body within it are continuously present to our perception. How then does and can *Consciousness itself* separate out as a *concrete thing in itself*, from that within it, of which we are conscious, namely, the *perceived being, "standing over against"* consciousness *"in and for itself"*?

I meditate first as would the man "in the street." I see and grasp the thing itself in its bodily reality. It is true that I sometimes deceive myself, and not only in respect of the perceived constitution of the thing, but also in respect of its being there at all. I am subject to an illusion or hallucination. The perception is not then "genuine." But if it is, if, that is, we can "confirm" its presence in the actual context of experience, eventually with the help of correct empirical thinking, then the perceived thing *is real* and itself really given, and that bodily in perception. Here perceiving considered simply as consciousness, and apart from the body and the bodily organs, appears as something in itself essenceless, an empty looking of an empty "Ego" towards the object itself which comes into contact with it in some astonishing way.

"Primary" and "Secondary" Qualities. The Bodily Given Thing "Mere Appearance" of the "Physically True"

If as a "man in the street" misled by sensibility I have indulged the inclination to spin out such thoughts as these, now, as a "man of science," I call to mind the familiar distinction between *secondary* and *primary* qualities, according to which the specific qualities of sense should be "merely subjective" and only the geometrico-physical qualities "objective." The colour and sound of a thing, its smell, its taste, and so forth, though they appear to cleave to the thing "bodily" as though belonging to its essence, are not themselves and as they appear to be, real, but mere "signs" of certain primary qualities. But if I recall familiar theories of Physics, I see at once that the meaning of such much-beloved propositions can hardly be the one which the words warrant: as though really only the "specific" sensory qualities of the perceived thing were mere appearance; which would come to saying that the "primary" qualities which remain after the *subtraction* of these same sensory qualities belonged to the same thing as it objectively and truly is, together with other such qualities which did not show forth as appearance. So understood, the old Berkeleian objection would hold good, namely, that extension, this essential nucleus of corporeality and all primary qualities, is unthinkable apart from the secondary qualities. Rather *the whole essential content of the perceived thing*, all that is present in the body, with all its qualities and all that can ever be perceived, *is "mere appearance,"* and the *"true thing" is that of physical science*. When the latter defines the given thing exclusively through concepts such as atoms, ions, energies, and so forth, and in every case as space-filling processes whose sole *characteristica* are mathematical expressions, its reference is to *something that transcends the whole content of the thing as present to us in bodily form*. It cannot therefore mean even the thing as lying in natural sensible space; in other words, its physical space cannot be the space of the world of bodily perception: otherwise it would also fall under the Berkeleian objection.

The "*true Being*" would therefore be entirely and *fundamentally something that is defined otherwise than as that which is given in perception as corporeal reality*, which is given exclusively through its sensory determinations, among which must also be reckoned the sensori-spatial. *The thing as strictly experienced gives the mere "this," an empty X which becomes the bearer of mathematical determinations, and of the corresponding mathematical formulae* and exists not in perceptual space, but in an "*objective space*," of which the former is the mere "symbol," *a Euclidean manifold of three dimensions that can be only symbolically represented.*

Let us then accept this. Let that which is given bodily in any perception be, as is taught there, "mere appearance," in principle "merely subjective," and yet no empty illusion. Yet that which is given in perception serves in the rigorous method of natural science for the valid determination, open to anyone to carry out and to verify through his own insight of that transcendent being whose "symbol" it is. The sensory content of that which is given in perception itself continues indeed to be reckoned as other than the true thing as it is in itself, but the *substratum*, the bearer (the empty X) of the perceived determinations still continues to count as that which is determined through exact method in the form of physical predicates. *All physical knowledge serves accordingly, and in the reverse sense, as an indicator of the course of possible experiences with the sensory things found in them and the occurrences in which they figure*. Thus it helps us to find our way about in the world of actual experience in which we all live and act.

The Real Nature of Perception and Its Transcendent Object

All this being presupposed, *what is it, we ask, that belongs to the concrete real nature (reellen Bestande) of the perception itself, as cogitatio*? Not the physical thing, as is obvious: radically transcendent as it is, transcendent over against the whole "world of appearance." But *even the latter*, though we refer to it habitually as "merely subjective," does not belong in all its detail of things and events to the real nature of perception, but is opposed to it as "transcendent." Let us consider this more closely. We have indeed already spoken of the transcendence of the thing, but only in passing. It concerns us now to win a deeper insight into *the relation of the transcendent to the Consciousness* that knows it, and to see how this mutual connexion, which has its own riddles, is to be understood.

We shut off the whole of physics and the whole domain of theoretical thought. We remain within the framework of plain intuition and the syntheses that belong to it, including perception. It is then evident that intuition and the intuited, perception and the thing perceived, though essentially related to each other, are in principle and of necessity *not really (reell) and essentially one and united.*

We start by taking an example. Keeping this table steadily in view as I go round it, changing my position in space all the time, I have continually the consciousness of the bodily presence out there of this one and self-same table, which in itself remains unchanged throughout. But the perception of the table is one that changes continuously, it is a continuum of changing perceptions. I close my eyes. My other senses are inactive in relation to the table. I have now no perception of it. I open my eyes, and the perception returns. The perception? Let us be more accurate. Under no circumstances does it return to me individually the same. Only the table is the same, known as identical through the synthetic consciousness which connects the new perception with the recollection. The perceived thing can be, without being perceived, without my being aware of it even as potential only (in the way of inactuality, as previously described), and perhaps without itself changing at all. But the perception itself is what it is within the steady flow of consciousness, and is itself constantly in flux; the perceptual now is ever passing over into the adjacent consciousness of the just-past, a new now simultaneously gleams forth, and so on. The perceived thing in general, and all its parts, aspects, and phases, whether the quality be primary or secondary, are necessarily transcendent to the perception, and on the same grounds everywhere. The colour of the thing seen is not in principle a real phase of the consciousness of colour; it appears, but even while it is appearing the appearance can and *must* be continually changing, as experience shows. The *same* colour appears "in" continuously varying patterns of *perspective colour-variations*. Similarly for every sensory quality and likewise for every spatial shape! One and the same shape (given *as* bodily the same) appears continuously ever again "in another way," in ever-differing perspective variations of shape. That is a necessary state of things, and it has obviously a more general bearing. For it is only in the interests of simplicity that we have illustrated our point by reference to a thing that appears unchanged in perception. The transfer to changes of any other sort is a perfectly simple proceeding.

An empirical consciousness of a self-same thing that looks "all-round" its object, and in so doing is continually confirming the unity of its own nature, essentially and necessarily possesses a manifold system of continuous patterns of appearance and perspective variations, in and through which all objective phases of the bodily self-given which appear in perception manifest themselves perspectively in definite continua. Every determinate feature has *its own* system of perspective variations; and for each of these features, as for the thing as a whole, the following holds good, namely, that it remains one and the same for the consciousness that in grasping it unites recollection and fresh perception synthetically together, despite interruption in the continuity of the course of actual perception. . . .

Indubitability of Immanent, Dubitability of Transcendent Perception

From all this important consequences follow. Every immanent perception necessarily guarantees the existence (*Existenz*) of its object. If reflective apprehension is directed to my experience, I apprehend an absolute Self whose existence (*Dasein*) is, in principle, undeniable, that is, the insight that it does not exist is, in principle, impossible; it would be nonsense to maintain the possibility of an experience *given in such a way not* truly existing. The stream of experience which is mine, namely, of the one who is thinking, may be to ever so great an extent uncomprehended, unknown in its past and future reaches, yet so soon as I glance towards the flowing life and into the real present it flows through, and in so doing grasp myself as the pure subject of this life (what that means will expressly concern us at a later stage), I say forthwith and because I must: *I am*, this life is, I live: *cogito*.

To every stream of experience, and to every Ego as such, there belongs, in principle, the possibility of securing this self-evidence: each of us bears in himself the warrant of this absolute existence (*Daseins*) as a fundamental possibility. But is it not conceivable, one might ask, that an Ego might have only fancies in its stream of experience, that the latter might consist of nothing beyond fictive intuitions? Such an Ego would thus discover only fictive *cogitationes*; its reflexions, by the very nature of this experiential medium, would be exclusively reflexions within the imagination. But that is obvious nonsense. That which floats before the mind may be a mere fiction; the floating itself, the fiction-producing consciousness, is not itself imagined, and the possibility of a perceiving reflexion which lays hold on absolute existence belongs to its essence as it does to every experience. No nonsense lies in the possibility that all alien consciousness which I posit in the experience of empathy does not exist. But *my* empathy and my consciousness in general is given in a primordial and absolute sense, not only essentially but existentially. This privileged position holds only for oneself and for the stream of experience to which the self is related; here only is there, and must there be, anything of the nature of immanent perception.

In contrast to this, it is, as we know, an essential feature of the thing-world that no perception, however perfect it may be, gives us anything absolute within its domain; and with this the following is essentially connected, namely, that every experience (*Erfahrung*), however far it extends, leaves open the possibility that what is given, despite the persistent consciousness of its bodily self-presence, does *not* exist. It is an essentially valid law that *existence in the form of a thing is never demanded as necessary by virtue of its givenness*, but in a certain way is always *contingent*. That means: It can always happen that the further course of experience will compel us to abandon what has already been set down and justified *in the light of empirical canons of rightness*. It was, so we afterwards say, mere illusion, hallucination, merely a coherent dream, and the like. Moreover, in this sphere of given data the open possibility remains of changes in apprehension, the turning of an appearance over into one which cannot unite with it harmoniously, and therewith an influence of later empirical positions on early ones whereby the intentional objects of these earlier positings suffer, so to speak, a posthumous reconstruction—eventualities which in the sphere of subject-experience (*Erlebnis*) are essentially excluded. In the absolute sphere, opposition, illusion, and being-otherwise have no place. It is a sphere of the absolutely established (*absoluter Position*).

In every way, then, it is clear that everything which is there for me in the world of things is on grounds of principle *only a presumptive reality*; that *I myself*, on the contrary, for whom it is there (excluding that which is imputed to the thing-world "by me"), I myself or my experience in its actuality am *absolute* Reality (*Wirklichkeit*), given through a positing that is unconditioned and simply indissoluble.

The thesis of my pure Ego and its personal life, which is "necessary" and plainly indubitable, thus stands opposed to the thesis of the world which is "contingent." All corporeally given thing-like entities can also not be, no corporeally given experiencing can also not be: that is the essential law, which defines this necessity and that contingency.

Obviously then the ontic necessity of the actual present experiencing is no pure essential necessity, that is, no pure eidetic specification of an essential law; it is the necessity of a fact (*Faktum*), and called "necessity" because an essential law is involved in the fact, and here indeed in its existence as such. The ideal possibility of a reflexion which has the essential character of a self-evident unshakeable *existential* thesis has its ground in the essential nature of a pure Ego *in general* and of an experiencing *in general.*

The reflexions in which we have been indulging also make it clear that no proofs drawn from the empirical consideration of the world can be conceived which could assure us with absolute certainty of the world's existence. The world is not doubtful in the sense that there are rational grounds which might be pitted against the tremendous force of unanimous experiences, but in the sense that a doubt is *thinkable*, and this is so because the possibility of non-Being is in principle never excluded. Every empirical power, be it ever so great, can be gradually outweighed and overcome. Nothing is thereby altered in the absolute Being of experiences, indeed these remain presupposed in all this all the time.

With this conclusion our study has reached its climax. We have won the knowledge we needed. In the essential connexions it has revealed to us already involved the most important of the premises on which depend those inferences we would draw concerning the detachability in principle of the whole natural world from the domain of consciousness, the sphere in which experiences have their being; inferences in which, as we can readily convince ourselves, a central, though not fully developed, thought of the quite otherwise oriented meditations of Descartes comes at last to its own. To reach our final goal we shall need indeed to add in the sequel a few supplementary discussions, which for the rest will not trouble us too much. Meanwhile let us draw our conclusions provisionally within a compass of limited bearing.

Chapter 38

MARTIN HEIDEGGER

Martin Heidegger (1889–1976) was born in Messkirch, an agricultural community in southwest Germany. He entered the seminary to become a Jesuit priest, but was soon attracted to philosophy and transferred to the University of Freiburg. There he studied under Edmund Husserl (see chapter 37). After graduation he became a professor at the University of Marburg, where he wrote his famous *Being and Time* (1927) and became a colleague of two of the leading Protestant theologians of the twentieth century, Rudolf Bultmann and Paul Tillich, both of whom he significantly influenced. In 1928 he was chosen as Husserl's successor at the University of Freiburg and was elected Rector of the University in 1933. For a brief period he was a member of the Nazi party, believing that it offered the best hope for the renewal of the nation. Although his reputation has been sullied by his brief support of the Nazis, there is no evidence that he shared Nazi fanatical beliefs. To his credit, he became disillusioned with the party and resigned the Rectorship and his party membership. After the war, he retired to the Black Forest where he spent his days writing. Meantime, his work had attracted worldwide attention and philosophers came from many countries to visit him in his mountain home.

Heidegger's thought is concerned with the question of the meaning of *being*, the question which he claims motivated the inquiries of the first philosophers but which had become neglected by subsequent philosophers. Some, such as Gilbert Ryle, would say it is a "pseudo question," for being is not a thing but a word referring to concepts that are instantiated. Heidegger disagrees and holds that we intuitively realize that there is something in the idea that a common reality underlies all reality. He then asks, Is there a particular being that is particularly suited to inquire into the meaning of being? His existential philosophy is a response to that question. Since human beings experience openness to the future and have a measure of freedom and responsibility, the question of who he is, is inescapable for him; but this question, if pursued in a correct manner, leads with equal inescapability into the question of Being in general. As Heidegger says in our reading, "Each of us is grazed at least once, perhaps more than once, by the hidden power of this question, even if he is not aware of what is happening to him."

The central question in the essay before us, "The Fundamental Question of Metaphysics," is "Why is there anything at all, rather than nothing?" Some may dismiss this as a nonsensical question, but that only shows that it is so primordial and, perhaps, unanswerable, that it seems pointless to raise it. Yet it leads us to wonder—What is the explanation of reality, of the universe, of our being here? According to Heidegger, wondering about this basic ontological question opens oneself up to the presence of Being. Heidegger traces the quest for Being back to the ancient Greeks, especially Parmenides.

Following his teacher Husserl, Heidegger uses the phenomenological method of drawing attention to salient features of experience (the phenomena), awakening us to patterns of reality that we have ignored.

FOR FURTHER READING

Guignon, C., ed. *The Cambridge Companion to Heidegger.* (Cambridge University Press, 1993).

Heidegger, Martin. *Being and Time,* trans. Edward Robinson and John Macquarrie. (Harper & Row, 1962).

Macquarrie, John. *Martin Heidegger.* (Lutterworth Press, 1968).

Olafson, Frederick. *Heidegger and the Philosophy of Mind.* (Yale University Press, 1987).

Richardson, J. *Existential Phenomenology: A Heideggerian Critique of the Cartesian Project.* (Oxford University Press, 1986).

Shahan, Robert and J. N. Mohanty, eds. *Thinking About Being: Aspects of Heidegger's Thought.* (Oklahoma University Press, 1984).

Solomon, Robert, ed. *Phenomenology and Existentialism.* (Harper & Row, 1972).

Speigelberg, Herbert. *The Pheomenological Movement,* 2 vol. (Martinus Nijhoff, 1960).

Stapleton, Timothy J. *Husserl and Heidegger.* (SUNY Press, 1983).

The Fundamental Question of Metaphysics

Why are there essents[1] rather than nothing? That is the question. Clearly it is no ordinary question. "Why are there essents, why is there anything at all, rather than nothing?"—obviously this is the first of all questions, though not in a chronological sense. Individuals and peoples ask a good many questions in the course of their historical passage through time. They examine, explore, and test a good many things before they run into the question "Why are there essents rather than nothing?" Many men never encounter this question, if by encounter we mean not merely to hear and read about it as an interrogative formulation but to ask the question, that is, to bring it about, to raise it, to feel its inevitability.

And yet each of us is grazed at least once, perhaps more than once, by the hidden power of this question, even if he is not aware of what is happening to him. The question looms in moments of great despair, when things tend to lose all their weight and all meaning becomes obscured. Perhaps it will strike but once like a muffled bell that rings into our life and gradually dies away. It is present in moments of rejoicing, when all the things around us are transfigured and seem to be there for the first time, as if it might be easier to think they are not than to understand that they are and are as they are. The question is upon us in boredom, when we are equally removed from despair and joy, and everything about us seems so hopelessly commonplace that we no longer care whether anything is or is not—and with this the question "Why are there essents rather than nothing?" is evoked in a particular form.

But this question may be asked expressly, or, unrecognized as a question, it may merely pass through our lives like a brief gust of wind; it may press hard upon us, or, under one pretext or another, we may thrust it away from us and silence it. In any case it is never the question that we ask first in point of time.

But it is the first question in another sense—in regard to rank. This may be clarified in three ways. The question "Why are there essents rather than nothing?" is first in rank for us first because it is the most far reaching, second because it is the deepest, and finally because it is the most fundamental of all questions.

1. "Essents" = "existents," "things that are."

It is the widest of all questions. It confines itself to no particular essent of whatever kind. The question takes in everything, and this means not only everything that is present in the broadest sense but also everything that ever was or will be. The range of this question finds its limit only in nothing, in that which simply is not and never was. Everything that is not nothing is covered by this question, and ultimately even nothing itself; not because it is *something*, since after all we speak of it, but because it *is* nothing. Our question reaches out so far that we can never go further. We do not inquire into this and that, or into each essent in turn, but from the very outset into the essent as a whole, or, as we say for reasons to be discussed below: into the essent as such in its entirety.

This broadest of questions is also the deepest: Why are there essents . . . ? Why, that is to say, on what ground? from what source does the essent derive? on what ground does it stand? The question is not concerned with particulars, with what essents are and of what nature at any time, here and there, with how they can be changed, what they can be used for, and so on. The question aims at the ground of what is insofar as it is. To seek the ground is to try to get to the bottom; what is put in question is thus related to the ground. However, since the question is a question, it remains to be seen whether the ground arrived at is really a ground, that is, whether it provides a foundation; whether it is a primal ground ⟨Ur-grund⟩; or whether it fails to provide a foundation and is an abyss ⟨Ab-grund⟩; or whether the ground is neither one nor the other but presents only a perhaps necessary appearance of foundation—in other words, it is a nonground ⟨Un-grund⟩. Be that as it may, the ground in question must account for the being of the essent as such. This question "why" does not look for causes that are of the same kind and on the same level as the essent itself. This "why" does not move on any one plane but penetrates to the "underlying" ⟨"zu-grunde" liegend⟩ realms and indeed to the very last of them, to the limit; turning away from the surface, from all shallowness, it strives toward the depths; this broadest of all questions is also the deepest.

Finally, this broadest and deepest question is also the most fundamental. What do we mean by this? If we take the question in its full scope, namely the essent as such in its entirety, it readily follows that in asking this question we keep our distance from every particular and individual essent, from every this and that. For we mean the essent as a whole, without any special preference. Still, it is noteworthy that in this questioning *one* kind of essent persists in coming to the fore, namely the men who ask the question. But the question should not concern itself with any particular essent. In the spirit of its unrestricted scope, all essents are of equal value. An elephant in an Indian jungle "is" just as much as some chemical combustion process at work on the planet Mars, and so on.

Accordingly, if our question "Why are there essents rather than nothing?" is taken in its fullest sense, we must avoid singling out any special, particular essent, including man. For what indeed is man? Consider the earth within the endless darkness of space in the universe. By way of comparison it is a tiny grain of sand; between it and the next grain of its own size there extends a mile or more of emptiness; on the surface of this grain of sand there lives a crawling, bewildered swarm of supposedly intelligent animals, who for a moment have discovered knowledge.[2] And what is the temporal extension of a human life amid all the millions of years? Scarcely a move of the second hand, a breath. Within the essent as a whole there is no legitimate ground for singling out this essent which is called mankind and to which we ourselves happen to belong.

But whenever the essent as a whole enters into this question, a privileged, unique relation arises between it and the act of questioning. For through this questioning the essent as a whole is for the first time opened up *as such* with a view to its possible ground, and in the act of questioning it is kept open. In relation to the essent as such in its entirety the asking of the question is not just any occurrence within the realm of the essent, like the falling of raindrops for example. The question "why" may be said to confront the essent as a whole, to break out of it, though never completely. But that is exactly why the act of questioning is privileged. Because it confronts the essent as a whole, but does not break loose from it, the content of the question reacts upon the questioning itself. Why the why? What is the ground of this question "why" which presumes to ask after the ground of the essent as a whole? Is the ground asked for in *this* why not merely a foreground—which would imply that the sought-for ground is again an essent? Does not the "first" question nevertheless

2. Cf. Nietzsche, *Über Wahrheit und Lüge im aussermoralischen Sinne*. 1873 *Nachlass*.

come first in view of the intrinsic rank of the question of being and its modulations?

To be sure, the things in the world, the essents, are in no way affected by our asking of the question "Why are there essents rather than nothing?" Whether we ask it or not, the planets move in their orbits, the sap of life flows through plant and animal.

But *if* this question is asked and if the act of questioning is really carried out, the content and the object of the question react inevitably on the act of questioning. Accordingly this questioning is not just any occurrence but a privileged happening that we call an *event*.

This question and all the questions immediately rooted in it, the questions in which this one question unfolds—this question "why" is incommensurable with any other. It encounters the search for its own why. At first sight the question "Why the why?" looks like a frivolous repetition and infinitum of the same interrogative formulation, like an empty and unwarranted brooding over words. Yes, beyond a doubt, that is how it looks. The question is only whether we wish to be taken in by this superficial look and so regard the whole matter as settled, or whether we are capable of finding a significant event in this recoil of the question "why" upon itself.

But if we decline to be taken in by surface appearances we shall see that this question "why," this question as to the essent as such in its entirety, goes beyond any mere playing with words, provided we possess sufficient intellectual energy to make the question actually recoil into its "why"—for it will not do so of its own accord. In so doing we find out that this privileged question "why" has its ground in a leap through which man thrusts away all the previous security, whether real or imagined, of his life. The question is asked only in this leap; it *is* the leap; without it there is no asking. What "leap" means here will be elucidated later. Our questioning is not yet the leap; for this it must undergo a transformation; it still stands perplexed in the face of the essent. Here it may suffice to say that the leap in this questioning opens up its own source—with this leap the question arrives at its own ground. We call such a leap, which opens up its own source, the original source or origin ⟨Ur-sprung⟩, the finding of one's own ground. It is because the question "Why are there essents rather than nothing?" breaks open the ground for all authentic questions and is thus at the origin ⟨Ursprung⟩ of them all that we must recognize it as the most fundamental of all questions.

It is the most fundamental of questions because it is the broadest and deepest, and conversely.

In this threefold sense the question is the first in rank—first, that is, in the order of questioning within the domain which this first question opens, defining its scope and thus founding it. Our question is the *question* of all authentic questions, i.e. of all self-questioning questions, and whether consciously or not it is necessarily implicit in every question. No questioning and accordingly no single scientific "problem" can be fully intelligible if it does not include, i.e. ask, the question of all questions. Let us be clear about this from the start: it can never be objectively determined whether anyone, whether we, really ask this question, that is whether we make the leap, or never get beyond a verbal formula. In a historical setting that does not recognize questioning as a fundamental human force, the question immediately loses its rank.

Anyone for whom the Bible is divine revelation and truth has the answer to the question "Why are there essents rather than nothing?" even before it is asked: everything that is, except God himself, has been created by Him. God himself, the increate creator, "is." One who holds to such faith can in a way participate in the asking of our question, but he cannot really question without ceasing to be a believer and taking all the consequences of such a step. He will only be able to act "as if" . . . On the other hand a faith that does not perpetually expose itself to the possibility of unfaith is no faith but merely a convenience: the believer simply makes up his mind to adhere to the traditional doctrine. This is neither faith nor questioning, but the indifference of those who can busy themselves with everything, sometimes even displaying a keen interest in faith as well as questioning.

What we have said about security in faith as one position in regard to the truth does not imply that the biblical "In the beginning God created heaven and earth" is an answer to our question. Quite aside from whether these words from the Bible are true or false for faith, they can supply no answer to our question because they are in no way related to it. Indeed, they cannot even be brought into relation with our question. From the standpoint of faith our question is "foolishness."

Philosophy is this very foolishness. A "Christian philosophy" is a round square and a misunderstanding. There is, to be sure, a thinking and questioning elaboration of the world of Christian experience, i.e. of faith. That is theology. Only epochs which no longer fully believe in the true greatness of the task of theology arrive at the disastrous notion that philosophy can help to provide a refurbished theology if not a substitute for theology, which will satisfy the needs and tastes of the time. For the original Christian faith philosophy is foolishness. To philosophize is to ask "Why are there essents rather than nothing?" Really to ask the question signifies: a daring attempt to fathom this unfathomable question by disclosing what it summons us to ask, to push our questioning to the very end. Where such an attempt occurs there is philosophy.

It would not serve our purpose to begin our discussion with a detailed report on philosophy. But there are a few things that all must know who wish to concern themselves with philosophy. They can be briefly stated.

All essential philosophical questioning is necessarily untimely. This is so because philosophy is always projected far in advance of its time, or because it connects the present with its antecedent, with what *initially* was. Philosophy always remains a knowledge which not only cannot be adjusted to a given epoch but on the contrary imposes its measure upon its epoch.

Philosophy is essentially untimely because it is one of those few things that can never find an immediate echo in the present. When such an echo seems to occur, when a philosophy becomes fashionable, either it is no real philosophy or it has been misinterpreted and misused for ephemeral and extraneous purposes.

Accordingly, philosophy cannot be directly learned like manual and technical skills; it cannot be directly applied, or judged by its usefulness in the manner of economic or other professional knowledge.

But what is useless can still be a force, perhaps the only real force. What has no immediate echo in everyday life can be intimately bound up with a nation's profound historical development, and can even anticipate it. What is untimely will have its own times. This is true of philosophy. Consequently there is no way of determining once and for all what the task of philosophy is, and accordingly what must be expected of it. Every state and every beginning of its development bears within it its own law. All that can be said is what philosophy cannot be and cannot accomplish.

A question has been stated: "Why are there essents rather than nothing?" We have claimed first place for this question and explained in what sense it is regarded as first.

We have not even begun to ask the question itself, but have digressed into a discussion about it. Such a digression is indispensable. For this question has nothing in common with our habitual concerns. There is no way of familiarizing ourselves with this question by a gradual transition from the things to which we are accustomed. Hence it must, as it were, be singled out in advance, presented. Yet in introducing the question and speaking of it, we must not postpone, let alone forget, the questioning itself.

Here then let us conclude our preliminary remarks.

Every essential form of spiritual life is marked by ambiguity. The less commensurate it is with other forms, the more it is misinterpreted.

Philosophy is one of the few autonomous creative possibilities and at times necessities of man's historical being-there.[3] The current misinterpretations of philosophy, all of which have some truth about them, are legion. Here we shall mention only two, which are important because of the light they throw on the present and future situation of philosophy. The first misinterpretation asks too much of philosophy. The second distorts its function.

Roughly speaking, philosophy always aims at the first and last grounds of the essent, with particular emphasis on man himself and on the meaning and goals of human being-there. This might suggest that philosophy can and must provide a foundation on which a nation will build its historical life and culture. But this is beyond the power of philosophy. As a rule such excessive demands take the form of a belittling of philosophy. It is said, for example: Because metaphysics did nothing to pave the way for the revolution it should be rejected. This is no cleverer than saying that because the carpenter's bench is useless for flying it should be abolished. Philosophy can never *directly* supply the energies and cre-

3. The word "Dasein" is ordinarily translated as "existence." It is used in "normal," popular discourse. But Heidegger breaks it into its components "Da" "there" and "Sein" "being," and puts his own definition on it. In general he means man's conscious, historical existence in the world, which is always projected into a there beyond its here. The German word Dasein has often been carried over into translations; the English strikes me as preferable.

ate the opportunities and methods that bring about a historical change; for one thing, because philosophy is always the concern of the few. Which few? The creators, those who initiate profound transformations. It spreads only indirectly, by devious paths that can never be laid out in advance, until at last, at some future date, it sinks to the level of a commonplace; but by then it has long been forgotten as original philosophy.

What philosophy essentially can and must be is this: a thinking that breaks the paths and opens the perspectives of the knowledge that sets the norms and hierarchies, of the knowledge in which and by which a people fulfills itself historically and culturally, the knowledge that kindles and necessitates all inquiries and thereby threatens all values.

The second misinterpretation involves a distortion of the function of philosophy. Even if philosophy can provide no foundation for a culture, the argument goes, it is nevertheless a cultural force, whether because it gives us an over-all, systematic view of what is, supplying a useful chart by which we may find our way amid the various possible things and realms of things, or because it relieves the sciences of their work by reflecting on their premises, basic concepts, and principles. Philosophy is expected to promote and even to accelerate—to make easier as it were—the practical and technical business of culture.

But—it is in the very nature of philosophy never to make things easier but only more difficult. And this not merely because its language strikes the everyday understanding as strange if not insane. Rather, it is the authentic function of philosophy to challenge historical being-there and hence, in the last analysis, being pure and simple. It restores to things, to the essents, their weight (being). How so? Because the challenge is one of the essential prerequisites for the birth of all greatness, and in speaking of greatness we are referring primarily to the works and destinies of nations. We can speak of historical destiny only where an authentic knowledge of things dominates man's being-there. And it is philosophy that opens up the paths and perspectives of such knowledge.

The misinterpretations with which philosophy is perpetually beset are promoted most of all by people of our kind, that is, by professors of philosophy. It is our customary business—which may be said to be justified and even useful—to transmit a certain knowledge of the philosophy of the past, as part of a general education. Many people suppose that this is philosophy itself, whereas at best it is the technique of philosophy.

In correcting these two misinterpretations I cannot hope to give you at one stroke a clear conception of philosophy. But I do hope that you will be on your guard when the most current judgments and even supposed observations assail you unawares. Such judgments are often disarming, precisely because they seem so natural. You hear remarks such as "Philosophy leads to nothing," "You can't do anything with philosophy," and readily imagine that they confirm an experience of your own. There is no denying the soundness of these two phrases, particularly common among scientists and teachers of science. Any attempt to refute them by proving that after all it does "lead to something" merely strengthens the prevailing misinterpretation to the effect that the everyday standards by which we judge bicycles or sulphur baths are applicable to philosophy.

It is absolutely correct and proper to say that "You can't do anything with philosophy." It is only wrong to suppose that this it the last word on philosophy. For the rejoinder imposes itself: granted that *we* cannot do anything with philosophy, might not philosophy, if we concern ourselves with it, do something *with us*? So much for what philosophy is not.

At the outset we stated a question: "Why are there essents rather than nothing?" We have maintained that to ask this question is to philosophize. When in our thinking we open our minds to this question, we first of all cease to dwell in any of the familiar realms. We set aside everything that is on the order of the day. Our question goes beyond the familiar and the things that have their place in everyday life. Nietzsche once said (*Werke, 7,* 269): "A philosopher is a man who never ceases to experience, see, hear, suspect, hope, and dream extraordinary things . . ."

To philosophize is to inquire into the *extra*-ordinary. But because, as we have just suggested, this questioning recoils upon itself, not only what is asked after is extraordinary but also the asking itself. In other words: this questioning does not lie along the way so that we bump into it one day unexpectedly. Nor is it part of everyday life: there is no requirement or regulation that forces us into it; it gratifies no urgent or prevailing need. The questioning itself is "out of order." It is entirely voluntary, based wholly and uniquely on the mystery of freedom, on what we have called the leap. The same Nietzsche said: "Philosophy . . . is a voluntary living amid ice and mountain heights" (*Werke, 15,* 2). To philosophize, we may now say, is an extra-ordinary inquiry into the extra-ordinary.

In the age of the earliest and crucial unfolding of Western philosophy among the Greeks, who first raised the authentic question of the essent as such in its entirety, the essent was called *physis*. This basic Greek word for the essent is customarily translated as "nature." This derives from the Latin translation, *natura*, which properly means "to be born," "birth." But with this Latin translation the original meaning of the Greek word *physis* is thrust aside, the actual philosophical force of the Greek word is destroyed. This is true not only of the Latin translation of *this* word but of all other Roman translations of the Greek philosophical language. What happened in this translation from the Greek into the Latin is not accidental and harmless; it marks the first stage in the process by which we cut ourselves off and alienated ourselves from the original essence of Greek philosophy. The Roman translation was later taken over by Christianity and the Christian Middle Ages. And the Christian Middle Ages were prolonged in modern philosophy, which, moving in the conceptual world of the Middle Ages, coined those representations and terms by means of which we still try to understand the beginnings of Western philosophy. These beginnings are regarded as something that present-day philosophers have supposedly transcended and long since left behind them.

But now let us skip over this whole process of deformation and decay and attempt to regain the unimpaired strength of language and words; for words and language are not wrappings in which things are packed for the commerce of those who write and speak. It is in words and language that things first come into being and are. For this reason the misuse of language in idle talk, in slogans and phrases, destroys our authentic relation to things. What does the word *physis* denote? It denotes self-blossoming emergence (e.g. the blossoming of a rose), opening up, unfolding, that which manifests itself in such unfolding and perseveres and endures in it; in short, the realm of things that emerge and linger on. According to the dictionary *phyein* means to grow or make to grow. But what does growing mean? Does it imply only to increase quantitatively, to become more and larger?

Physis as emergence can be observed everywhere, e.g. in celestial phenomena (the rising of the sun), in the rolling of the sea, in the growth of plants, in the coming forth of man and animal from the womb. But *physis*, the realm of that which arises, is not synonymous with these phenomena, which today we regard as part of "nature." This opening up and inward-jutting-beyond-itself ⟨in-sich-aus-sich-hinausstehen⟩ must not be taken as a process among other processes that we observe in the realm of the essent. *Physis* is being itself, by virtue of which essents become and remain observable.

The Greeks did not learn what *physis* is through natural phenomena, but the other way around: it was through a fundamental poetic and intellectual experience of being that they discovered what they had to call *physis*. It was this discovery that enabled them to gain a glimpse into nature in the restricted sense. Hence *physis* originally encompassed heaven as well as earth, the stone as well as the plant, the animal as well as man, and it encompassed human history as a work of men and the gods; and ultimately and first of all, it meant the gods themselves as subordinated to destiny. *Physis* means the power that emerges and the enduring realm under its sway. This power of emerging and enduring includes "becoming" as well as "being" in the restricted sense of inert duration. *Physis* is the process of a-rising, of emerging from the hidden, whereby the hidden is first made to stand.

But if, as is usually done, *physis* is taken not in the original sense of the power to emerge and endure, but in the later and present signification of nature; and if moreover the motion of material things, of the atoms and electrons, of what modern physics investigates as *physis*, is taken to be the fundamental manifestation of nature, then the first philosophy of the Greeks becomes a nature philosophy, in which all things are held to be of a material nature. In this case the beginning of Greek philosophy, as is perfectly proper for a beginning according to the common-sense view, gives the impression of what we, once again in Latin, designate as primitive. Thus the Greeks become essentially a higher type of Hottentot, whom modern science has left far behind. Disregarding the lesser absurdities involved in this view of the beginning of Western philosophy as something primitive, we need only say this: those who put forward such an interpretation forget that what is under discussion is philosophy, one of man's few great achievements. But what is great can only begin great. Its beginning is in fact that greatest thing of all. A small beginning belongs only to the small, whose dubious greatness it is to diminish all things;

small are the beginning of decay, though it may later become great in the sense of the enormity of total annihilation.

The great begins great, maintains itself only through the free recurrence of greatness within it, and if it is great ends also in greatness. So it is with the philosophy of the Greeks. It ended in greatness with Aristotle. Only prosaic common sense and the little man imagine that the great must endure forever, and equate this duration with eternity.

The Greeks called the essent as a whole *physis*. But it should be said in passing that even within Greek philosophy a narrowing of the word set in forthwith, although the original meaning did not vanish from the experience, knowledge, and orientation of Greek philosophy. Knowledge of its original meaning still lives on in Aristotle, when he speaks of the grounds of the essent as such (see *Metaphysics*, I, 1003 a 27).

But this narrowing of *physis* in the direction of "physics" did not occur in the way that we imagine today. We oppose the psychic, the animated, the living, to the "physical." But for the Greeks all this belonged to *physis* and continued to do so even after Aristotle. They contrasted it with what they called *thesis*, thesis, ordinance, or *nomos*, law, rule in the sense of *ethos*. This, however, denotes not mere norms but mores, based on freely accepted obligations and traditions; it is that which concerns free behavior and attitudes, the shaping of man's historical being, the *ethos* which under the influence of morality was later degraded to the ethical.

The meaning of *physis* is further restricted by contrast with *technē*—which denotes neither art nor technology but a knowledge, the ability to plan and organize freely, to master institutions (cf. Plato's *Phaedrus*). *Technē* is creating, building in the sense of a deliberate pro-ducing. (It would require a special study to explain what is essentially the same in *physis* and *technē*). The physical was opposed to the historical, a domain which for the Greeks was part of the originally broader concept of *physis*. But this has nothing whatever to do with a naturalistic interpretation of history. The realm of being as such and as a whole is *physis*—i.e. its essence and character are defined as that which emerges and endures. It is experienced primarily through what in a way imposes itself most immediately on our attention, and this was the later, narrower sense of *physis: ta physei onta, ta physika,* nature. If the question concerning *physis* in general was asked at all, i.e. if it was asked: What is the realm of being as such? it was primarily *ta physei onta* that gave the point of departure. Yet from the very outset the question could not dwell in this or that realm of nature, inanimate bodies, plants, animals, but had to reach out beyond *ta physika*.

In Greek, "beyond something" is expressed by the word *meta*. Philosophical inquiry into the realm of being as such is *meta ta physika*; this inquiry goes beyond the essent, it is metaphysics. Here it is not important to follow the genesis and history of this term in detail.

Accordingly, the question to which we have given first rank, "Why are there essents rather than nothing?" is the fundamental question of metaphysics. Metaphysics is a name for the pivotal point and core of all philosophy.

[In this introduction our treatment of the entire subject has been intentionally superficial and hence essentially vague. According to our explanation of the word *physis*, it signifies the being of the essent. If the questioning is *peri physeōs*, if it concerns the being of the essent, then the discussion has gone beyond *physis*, beyond "physics" in the ancient sense, and essentially beyond *ta physika*, beyond essents, and deals with being. From the very first "physics" has determined the essence and history of metaphysics. Even in the doctrines of being as pure act (Thomas Aquinas), as absolute concept (Hegel), as eternal recurrence of the identical will to power (Nietzsche), metaphysics has remained unalterably "physics."]

But the inquiry into being as such is of a different nature and origin.

Within the purview of metaphysics and thinking on its level, we can, to be sure, consider the question about being as such as merely a mechanical repetition of the question about the essent as such. In this case the question about being as such is just another transcendental question, though one of a higher order. But this reinterpretation of the question about being as such bars the road to its appropriate unfolding.

However, this new interpretation comes readily to mind; it is bound to suggest itself, particularly as we have spoken in *Sein und Zeit* of a "transcendental horizon." But the "transcendental" there intended is not that of the subjective consciousness; rather, it defines itself in terms of the existential-ecstatic temporality of human being-there. Yet the reinterpretation of the question of being as such tends to take the same form as the question of the essent as such, chiefly because the essential origin of the question of the existent as such and with it the essence of metaphysics remain obscure. And this draws all questions that are in any way concerned with being into the indeterminate.

In the present attempt at an "introduction to metaphysics" I shall keep this confused state of affairs in mind.

In the current interpretation the "question of being" signifies the inquiry into the essent as such (metaphysics). But from the standpoint of *Sein und Zeit*, the "question of being" means the inquiry into being as such. This signification of the title is also the appropriate one from the standpoint of the subject matter and of linguistics; for the "question of being" in the sense of the metaphysical question regarding the essent as such does *not inquire* thematically into being. In this way of asking, being remains forgotten.

But just as ambiguous as the "question of being" referred to in the title is what is said about "forgetfulness of being." It is pointed out—quite correctly—that metaphysics inquires into the being of the essent and that it is therefore an obvious absurdity to impute a forgetfulness of being to metaphysics.

But if we consider the question of being in the sense of an inquiry into being as such, it becomes clear to anyone who follows our thinking that being *as such* is precisely hidden from metaphysics, and remains forgotten—and so radically that the forgetfulness of being, which itself falls into forgetfulness, is the unknown but enduring impetus to metaphysical questioning.

If for the treatment of the "question of being" in the indeterminate sense we choose the name "metaphysics," then the title of the present work is ambiguous. For at first sight the questioning seems to remain within the sphere of the assent as such, yet at the very first sentence it strives to depart from this sphere in order to consider and inquire into another realm. Actually the title of the work is deliberately ambiguous.

The fundamental question of this work is of a different kind from the leading question of metaphysics. Taking what was said in *Sein und Zeit* (pp. 21 f. and 37 f.) as a starting point, we inquired into the *"disclosure of being."* "Disclosure of being" means the unlocking of what forgetfulness of being closes and hides. And it is through this questioning that a light first falls on the *essence* of metaphysics that had hitherto also been hidden.]

"Introduction to metaphysics" means accordingly: an introduction to the asking of the fundamental question. But questions and particularly fundamental questions do not just occur like stones and water. Questions are not found ready-made like shoes and clothes and books. Questions *are*, and are only as they are actually asked. A leading into the asking of the fundamental questions is consequently not a going to something that lies and stands somewhere; no, this leading-to must first awaken and create the questioning. The leading is itself a questioning advance, a preliminary questioning. It is a leading for which in the very nature of things there can be no following. When we hear of disciples, "followers," as in a school of philosophy for example, it means that the nature of questioning is misunderstood. Such schools can exist only in the domain of scientific and technical work. Here everything has its definite hierarchical order. This work is also an indispensable part of philosophy and has today been lost. But the best technical ability can never replace the actual power of seeing and inquiring and speaking.

"Why are there essents rather than nothing?" That is the question. To state the interrogative sentence, even in a tone of questioning, is not yet to question. To repeat the interrogative sentence several times in succession does not necessarily breathe life into the questioning; on the contrary, saying the sentence over and over may well dull the questioning.

But even though the interrogative sentence is not the question and not the questioning, it must not be taken as a mere linguistic form of communication, as though, for example, the interrogative sentence were only a statement "about" a question. When I say to you "Why are these essents rather than nothing?" the purpose of my speaking and questioning is not to communicate to you the fact that a process of questioning is now at work within me. The spoken interrogative sentence can of course be interpreted in this way, but this means precisely that the questioning has not been heard. In this case you do not join me in questioning, nor do you question yourself. No sign of a questioning attitude or state of mind is awakened. Such a state of mind consists in a *willing* to know. Willing—that is no mere wishing or striving. Those who wish to know also seem to question; but they do not go beyond the stating of the question; they stop precisely where the question begins. To question is to will to know. He who wills, he who puts his whole existence into a will, *is* resolved. Resolve does not shift about; it does not shirk, but acts from out of the moment and never stops. Re-solve is no mere decision to act, but the crucial beginning of action that anticipates and reaches through all action. To will is to be resolved. [The essence of willing is here carried back to determination ⟨Ent-schlossen-heit, unclosedness⟩. But the essence of resolve lies in the opening, the coming-out-of-cover ⟨Ent-borgenheit⟩ of human being-there into the clearing of being, and not in a storing up of energy for "action." See *Sein und Zeit*, § 44 and § 60. But its relation to being is of letting-be. The idea that all willing should be grounded in letting-be offends the understanding. See my lecture *Vom Wesen der Wahrheit*, 1930.]

But to know means: to be able to stand in the truth. Truth is the manifestness of the essent. To know is accordingly the ability to stand ⟨stehen⟩ in the manifestness of the essent, to endure ⟨bestehen⟩ it. Merely to have information, however abundant, is not to know. Even if curricula and examination requirements concentrate this information into what is of the greatest practical importance, it still does not amount to knowledge. Even if this information, pruned down to the most indispensable needs, is "close to life," is possession is not knowledge. The man who possesses such information and has learned a few practical tricks, will still be perplexed in the presence of real reality, which is always different from what the philistine means by down-to-earth; he will always be a bungler. Why? Because he has no knowledge, for to know means *to be able to learn.*

In the common-sense view, to be sure, knowledge belongs to the man who has no further need to learn because he has finished learning. No, only that man is knowing who understands that he must keep learning over and over again and who above all, on the basis of this understanding, has attained to the point where he is always *able to learn.* This is much more difficult than to possess information.

Ability to learn presupposes ability to inquire. Inquiry is the willing-to-know analyzed above: the resolve to be able to stand in the openness of the essent. Since we are concerned with the asking of the question that is first in rank, clearly the willing as well as the knowing is of a very special kind. So much the less will the interrogative sentence, even if it is uttered in an authentically questioning tone and even if the listener joins in the questioning, exhaustively reproduce the question. The questioning, which indeed is sounded in the interrogative sentence but which is still enclosed, wrapped up in the words, remains to be unwrapped. The questioning attitude must clarify and secure itself in this process, it must be consolidated by training.

Our next task lies in the development of the question "Why are there essents rather than nothing?" In what direction can it be asked? First of all the question is accessible in the interrogative sentence, which gives a kind of approximation of it. Hence its linguistic formulation must be correspondingly broad and loose. Let us consider our sentence in this respect. "Why are there essents rather than nothing?" The sentence has a caesura. "Why are there essents?" With these words the question is actually asked. The formulation of the question includes: 1) a definite indication of what is put into question, of what is *questioned*: 2) an indication of what the question is about, of what is asked. For it is clearly indicated what the question is about, namely the essent. What is asked after, that which is asked, is the why, i.e. the ground. What follows in the interrogative sentence, "rather than nothing," is only an appendage, which may be said to turn up of its own accord if for purposes of introduction we permit ourselves to speak loosely, a turn of phrase that says nothing further about the question or the object of questioning, an ornamental flourish. Actually the question is far more unambiguous and definite without such an appendage, which springs only from the prolixity of loose discourse. "Why are there essents?" The addition "rather than nothing" is dropped not only because we are striving for a strict formulation of the question but even more because it says nothing. For why should we go on to ask about nothing? Nothing is simply nothing. Here there is nothing more to inquire about. And above all, in talking about nothing or nothingness, we are not making the slightest advance toward the knowledge of the essent.

He who speaks of nothing does not know what he is doing. In speaking of nothing he makes it into a something. In speaking he speaks against what he intended. He contradicts himself. But discourse that contradicts itself offends against the fundamental rule of discourse (*logos*), against "logic." To speak of nothing is illogical. He who speaks and thinks illogically is unscientific. But he who goes so far as to speak of nothing in the realm of philosophy, where logic has its very home, exposes himself most particularly to the accusation of offending against the fundamental rule of all thinking. Such a speaking about nothing consists entirely of meaningless propositions. Moreover: he who takes the nothing seriously is allying himself with nothingness. He is patently promoting the spirit of negation and serving the cause of disintegration. Not only is speaking of nothing utterly repellent to thought; it also undermines all culture and all faith. What disregards the fundamental law of thought and also destroys faith and the will to build is pure nihilism.

On the basis of such considerations we shall do well, in our interrogative sentence, to cross out the superfluous words "rather than nothing" and limit the sentence to the simple and strict form: "Why are there essents?"

To this there would be no objection if . . . if in formulating our question, if altogether, in the asking of this question, we were as free as it may have seemed to us up to this point. But in asking this question we stand in a tradition. For philosophy has always, from time immemorial, asked about the ground of what is. With this question it began and with this question it will end, provided that it ends in greatness and not in an impotent decline. Ever since the question about the essent began, the question about the nonessent, about nothing, has gone side by side with it. And not only outwardly, in the manner of a by-product. Rather, the question about nothing has been asked with the same breadth, depth, and originality as the question about the essent. The manner of asking about nothing may be regarded as a gauge and hallmark for the manner of asking about the essent.

If we bear this in mind, the interrogative sentence uttered in the beginning, "Why are there essents rather than nothing?" seems to express the question about the essent far more adequately than the abbreviated version. It is not looseness of speech or prolixity that leads us to mention nothing. Nor is it an invention of ours; no, it is only strict observance of the original tradition regarding the meaning of the fundamental question.

Still, this speaking of nothing remains in general repellent to thought and in particular demoralizing. But what if both our concern for the fundamental rules of thought and our fear of nihilism, which both seem to counsel against speaking of nothing, should be based on a misunderstanding? And this indeed is the case. True, this misunderstanding is not accidental. It is rooted in long years of failure to understand the question about the essent. And this failure to understand arises from an increasingly hardened forgetfulness of being.

For it cannot be decided out of hand whether logic and its fundamental rules can, altogether, provide a standard for dealing with the question about the essent as such. It might be the other way around. Perhaps the whole body of logic as it is known to us, perhaps all the logic that we treat as a gift from heaven, is grounded in a very definite answer to the question about the essent; perhaps, in consequence, all thinking which solely follows the laws of thought prescribed by traditional logic is incapable from the very start of even understanding the question about the essent by its own resources, let alone actually unfolding the question and guiding it toward an answer. Actually it is only an appearance of strict, scientific method when we invoke the principle of contradiction and logic in general, in order to prove that all thinking and speaking about nothing are contradictory and therefore meaningless. In such a contention "logic" is regarded as a court of justice, established for all eternity, whose rights as first and last authority no rational man will impugn. Anyone who speaks against logic is therefore tacitly or explicitly accused of irresponsibility. And the mere accusation is taken as a proof and an argument relieving one of the need for any further, genuine reflection.

It is perfectly true that we cannot talk about nothing, as though it were a thing like the rain outside or a mountain or any object whatsoever. In principle, nothingness remains inaccessible to science. The man who wishes truly to speak about nothing must of necessity become unscientific. But this is a misfortune only so long as one supposes that scientific thinking is the only authentic rigorous thought, and that it alone can and must be made into the standard of philosophical thinking. But the reverse is true. All scientific thought is merely a derived form of philosophical thinking, which proceeded to freeze into its scientific cast. Philosophy never arises out of science or through science and it can never be accorded equal rank with the sciences. No, it is prior in rank, and not only "logically" or in a table representing the system of the sciences. Philosophy stands in a totally different realm and order. Only poetry stands in the same order as philosophy and its thinking, though poetry and thought are not the same thing. To speak of nothing will always remain a horror and an absurdity for science. But aside from the philosopher, the poet can do so—and not because, as common sense supposes, poetry is without strict rules, but because the spirit of poetry (only authentic and great poetry is meant) is essentially superior to the spirit that prevails in all mere science. By virtue of this superiority the poet always speaks as though the essent were being expressed and invoked for the first time. Poetry, like the thinking of the philosopher, has always so much world space to spare that in it each thing—a tree, a mountain, a house, the cry of a bird—loses all indifference and commonplaceness.

Authentic speaking about nothing always remains extraordinary. It cannot be vulgarized. It dissolves if it is placed in the cheap acid of a merely logical intelligence. Consequently true discourse about nothing can never be immediate like the description of a picture for example. Here I should like to cite a passage from one of Knut Hamsun's last works, *The Road Leads On*. The work forms a whole with *Vagabonds* and *August*. It describes the last years and end of this August, who embodies the uprooted modern man who can do everything equally well yet who cannot lose his ties with the extraordinary, because even in his weakness and despair he remains authentic and superior. In his last days August is alone in the high mountains. And the poet says: "Here he sits between his ears and all he hears is emptiness. An amusing conception, indeed. On the sea there were both motion and sound, something for the ear to feed upon, a chorus of waters. Here nothingness meets nothingness and the result is zero, not even a hole. Enough to make one shake one's head, utterly at a loss."[4]

We see that there is something very interesting about nothing. Let us then go back to our interrogative sentence; let us ask it through, and see whether this "rather than nothing" is merely a meaningless appendage or whether it does not have an essential meaning even in our provisional statement of the question.

Let us begin with the abbreviated, seemingly simpler, and ostensibly stricter form of the question: "Why are there essents?" When we inquire in this way, we start from the essent. The essent *is*. It is given, it confronts us; accordingly, it is to be found at any time, and it is, in certain realms, known to us. Now this essent, from which we start, is immediately questioned as to its ground. The questioning advances immediately toward a ground. Such a method is only an extension and enlargement, so to speak, of a method practiced in everyday life. Somewhere in the vineyard, for example, the vine-disease occurs; something incontestably present. We ask: where does it come from, where and what is the reason for it, the ground? Similarly the essent as a whole is present. We ask: where and what is the ground? This manner of questioning is represented in the simple formula: Why are there essents? Where and what is their ground? Tacitly we are asking after another and higher kind of essent. But here the question is not by any means concerned with the essent as such and as a whole.

But if we put the question in the form of our original interrogative sentence: "Why are there essents rather than nothing?" this addition prevents us in our questioning from beginning directly with an unquestionably given essent and, having scarcely begun, from continuing on to another expected essent as a ground. Instead this essent, through questioning, is held out into the possibility of nonbeing. Thereby the why takes on a very different power and penetration. Why is the essent torn away from the possibility of nonbeing? Why does it not simply keep falling back into nonbeing? Now the essent is no longer that which just happens to be present; it begins to waver and oscillate, regardless of whether or not we recognize the essent in all certainty, regardless of whether or not we apprehend it in its full scope. Henceforth the essent as such oscillates, insofar as we draw it into the question. The swing of the pendulum extends to the extreme and sharpest contrary possibility, to nonbeing and nothingness. And the search for the why undergoes a parallel change. It does not aim simply at providing an also present ground and explanation for what is present; now a ground is sought which will explain the emergence of the essent as an overcoming of nothingness. The ground that is now asked after is the ground of the decision for the essent over against nothingness, or more precisely, the ground for the oscillation of the essent, which sustains and unbinds us, half being, half not being, which is also why we can belong entirely to no thing, not even to ourselves; yet being-there ⟨Dasein⟩ is in every case mine.

[The qualification "in every case mine" means that being-there is allotted to me in order that my self should be being-there. But being-there signifies:

4. Knut Hamsun, *The Road Leads On* (Coward-McCann, 1934), p. 508. Trans. Eugene Gay-Tifft.

care of the ecstatically manifested being of the essent as such, not only of human being. Being-there is "in every case mine"; this means neither "posited through me" nor "apportioned to an individual ego." Being-there is *itself* by virtue of its essential relation to being in general. That is the meaning of the sentence that occurs frequently in *Sein und Zeit*: Being-there implies awareness of being.]

It is already becoming clearer that this "rather than nothing" is no superfluous appendage to the real question, but is an essential component of the whole interrogative sentence, which as a whole states an entirely different question from that intended in the question "Why are there essents?" With our question we place ourselves in the essent in such a way that it loses its self-evident character *as the essent*. The essent begins to waver between the broadest and most drastic extremes: "either essents—or nothing"—and thereby the questioning itself loses all solid foundation. Our questioning being-there is suspended, and in this suspense is nevertheless self-sustained.

But the essent is not changed by our questioning. It remains what it is and as it is. Our questioning is after all only a psycho-spiritual process in us which, whatever course it may take, cannot in any way affect the essent itself. True, the essent remains as it is manifested to us. But it cannot slough off the problematic fact that it might also *not* be what it is and as it is. We do not experience this possibility as something that we add to the essent by thinking; rather, the essent itself elicits this possibility, and in this possibility reveals itself. Our questioning only opens up the horizon, in order that the essent may dawn in such questionableness.

We still know far too little about the process of such questioning, and what we do know is far too crude. In this questioning we seem to belong entirely to ourselves. Yet it is this questioning that moves us into the open, provided that in questioning it transform itself (which all true questioning does), and cast a new space over everything and into everything.

The main thing is not to let ourselves be led astray by over-hasty theories, but to experience things as they are on the basis of the first thing that comes to hand. This piece of chalk has extension; it is a relatively solid, grayish white thing with a definite shape, and apart from all that, it is a thing to write with. This particular thing has the attribute of lying here; but just as surely, it has the attitude of potentially not lying here and not being so large. The possibility of being guided along the blackboard and of being used up is not something that we add to the thing by thought. Itself, as this essent, is in this possibility; otherwise it would not be chalk as a writing material. Correspondingly, every essent has in it this potentiality in a different way. This potentiality belongs to the chalk. It has in itself a definite aptitude for a definite use. True, we are accustomed and inclined, in seeking this potentiality in the chalk, to say that we cannot see or touch it. But that is a prejudice, the elimination of which is part of the unfolding of our question. For the present our question is only to open up the essent in its wavering between nonbeing and being. Insofar as the essent resists the extreme possibility of nonbeing, it stands in being, but it has never caught up with or overcome the possibility of nonbeing.

We suddenly find ourselves speaking of the nonbeing and being of the essent, without saying how this being or nonbeing is related to the essent. Are the two terms the same? The essent and its being? What, for example, is "the essent" in this piece of chalk? The very question is ambiguous, because the word "the essent" can be understood in two respects, like the Greek *to on*. The essent means first *that* which is at any time, in particular this grayish white, so-and-so-shaped, light, brittle mass. But "the essent" also means that which "brings it about," so to speak, that this thing is an essent rather than a nonessent, that which constitutes its being if it *is*. In accordance with this twofold meaning of the word "the essent," the Greek *to on* often has the second significance, not the essent itself, not that which is, but "is-ness," essentness, being. Over against this, "the essent" in the first sense signifies all or particular essent things themselves, in respect to themselves and not to their is-ness, their *ousia*.

The first meaning of *to on* refers to *ta onta* (entia), the second to *to einai* (esse). We have listed what the essent is in the piece of chalk. This was relatively easy to do. It was also easy to see that the object named can also *not* be, that this chalk need ultimately not be here and not be. What then is being in distinction to what can stand in being or fall back into nonbeing—what is being in distinction to the essent? Is it the same as the essent? We ask the question once again. But in the foregoing we did not list being; we listed only material mass, grayish-white light, so-and-so-shaped, brittle. But where is the being situated? It must belong to the chalk, for this chalk *is*.

We encounter the essent everywhere; it sustains and drives us, enhances and fills us, elevates and disappoints us; but with all this, where is, and wherein consists, the being of the essent? One might reply: this distinction between the essent and its being may occasionally have an importance from the standpoint of language and even of meaning; this distinction can be effected in mere thought, i.e. in ideas and opinions, but is it certain that anything essent in the essent corresponds to the distinction? And even this merely cogitated distinction is questionable; for it remains unclear *what* is to be thought under the name of "being." Meanwhile it suffices to know the essent and secure our mastery over it. To go further and introduce being as distinct from it is artificial and leads to nothing.

We have already said a certain amount about this frequent question: What comes of such distinctions? Here we are going to concentrate on our undertaking. We ask: "Why are there essents rather than nothing?" And in this question we seemingly stick to the essent and avoid all empty brooding about being. But what really are we asking? Why the essent as such is. We are asking for the ground of the essent: that it is and is what it is, and that there is not rather nothing. Fundamentally we are asking about being. But how? We are asking about the being of the essent. We are questioning the essent in regard to its being.

But if we persevere in our questioning we shall actually be questioning forward, asking about being in respect to its ground, even if this question remains undeveloped and it remains undecided whether being itself is not in itself a ground and a sufficient ground. If we regard this question of being as the first question in order of rank, should we ask it without knowing how it stands with being and how being stands in its distinction to the essent? How shall we inquire into, not to say find, the ground for the being of the essent, if we have not adequately considered and understood being itself? This undertaking would be just as hopeless as if someone were to try to bring out the cause and ground of a fire, and yet claim that he need not worry about the actual course of the fire or examine the scene of it.

Thus it transpires that the question "Why are there essents rather than nothing?" compels us to ask the preliminary question: "How does it stand with being?"

Here we are asking about something which we barely grasp, which is scarcely more than the sound of a word for us, and which puts us in danger of serving a mere word idol when we proceed with our questioning. Hence it is all the more indispensable that we make it clear from the very outset how it stands at present with being and with our understanding of being. And in this connection the main thing is to impress it on our experience that we cannot immediately grasp the being of the essent itself, either through the essent or in the essent—or anywhere else.

A few examples may be helpful. Over there, across the street, stands the high school building. An essent. We can look over the building from all sides, we can go in and explore it from cellar to attic, and note everything we encounter in that building: corridors, staircases, schoolrooms, and their equipment. Everywhere we find essents and we even find them in a very definite arrangement. Now where is the being of this high school? For after all it *is*. The building *is*. If anything belongs to this essent, it is its being; yet we do not find the being inside it.

Nor does the being consist in the fact that we look at the essent. The building stands there even if we do not look at it. We can find it only because it already *is*. Moreover, this building's being does not by any means seem to be the same for everyone. For us, who look at it or ride by, it is different than for the pupils who sit in it; not because they see it only from within but because for them this building really is what it is and as it is. You can, as it were, smell the being of this building in your nostrils. The smell communicates the being of this essent far more immediately and truly than any description or inspection could ever do. But on the other hand the building's being is not based on this odor that is somewhere in the air.

How does it stand with being? Can you see being? We see essents; this chalk for example. But do we see being as we see color and light and shade? Or do we hear, smell, taste, feel being? We hear the motorcycle racing through the street. We hear the grouse gliding through the forest. But actually we hear only the whirring of the motor, the sound the grouse makes. As a matter of fact it is difficult to describe even the pure sound, and we do not ordinarily do so, because it is *not* what we commonly hear. [From the standpoint of sheer sound] we always hear *more*. We hear the flying bird, even though strictly speaking we should say: a grouse is nothing audible, it is no manner of tone that fits into a scale. And so it is with the other senses. We touch velvet, silk; we see them directly as this and that kind of essent, the one different from the other. Wherein lies and wherein consists being?

But we must take a wider look around us and consider the lesser and greater circle within which we spend our days and hours, wittingly and wittingly, a circle whose limits shift continuously and which is suddenly broken through.

A heavy storm coming up in the mountains "is," or what here amounts to the same thing, "was" during the night. Wherein consists its being?

A distant mountain range under a broad sky . . . It "is." Wherein consists the being? When and to whom does it reveal itself? To the traveler who enjoys the landscape, or to the peasant who makes his living in it and from it, or to the meteorologist who is preparing a weather report? Who of these apprehends being? All and none. Or is what these men apprehend of the mountain range under the great sky only certain aspects of it, not the mountain range itself as it "is" as such, not that wherein its actual being consists? Who may be expected to apprehend this being? Or is it a non-sense, contrary to the sense of being, to inquire after what is in itself, behind those aspects? Does the being lie in the aspects?

The door of an early romanesque church is an essent. How and to whom is its being revealed? To the connoisseur of art, who examines it and photographs it on an excursion, or to the abbot who on a holiday passes through this door with his monks, or to the children who play in its shadow on a summer's day? How does it stand with the being of this essent?

A state—*is*. By virtue of the fact that the state police arrest a suspect, or that so-and-so-many typewriters are clattering in a government building, taking down the words of ministers and state secretaries? Or "is" the state in a conversation between the chancellor and the British foreign minister? The state *is*. But where is being situated? Is it situated anywhere at all?

A painting by Van Gogh. A pair of rough peasant shoes, nothing else. Actually the painting represents nothing. But as to what *is* in that picture, you are immediately alone with it as though you yourself were making your way wearily homeward with your hoe on an evening in late fall after the last potato fires have died down. What *is* here? The canvas? The brush strokes? The spots of color?

What in all these things we have just mentioned is the being of the essent? We run (or stand) around in the world with our silly subtleties and conceit. But where in all this is being?

All the things we have named *are* and yet—when we wish to apprehend being, it is always as though we were reaching into the void. The being after which we inquire is almost like nothing, and yet we have always rejected the contention that the essent in its entirety *is not.*

But being remains unfindable, almost like nothing, or ultimately *quite* so. Then, in the end, the word "being" is no more than an empty word. It means nothing real, tangible, material. Its meaning is an unreal vapor. Thus in the last analysis Nietzsche was perfectly right in calling such "highest concepts" as being "the last cloudy streak of evaporating reality." Who would want to chase after such a vapor, when the very term is merely a name for a great fallacy! "Nothing indeed has exercised a more simple power of persuasion hitherto than the error of Being . . ."[5]

"Being"—a vapor and a fallacy? What Nietzsche says here of being is no random remark thrown out in the frenzy of preparation for his central, never finished work. No, this was his guiding view of being from the earliest days of his philosophical effort. It is the fundamental support and determinant of his philosophy. Yet even now this philosophy holds its ground against all the crude importunities of the scribblers who cluster round him more numerous with each passing day. And so far there seems to be no end in sight to this abuse of Nietzche's work. In speaking here of Nietzsche, we mean to have nothing to do with all that—or with blind hero worship for that matter. The task in hand is too crucial and at the same time too sobering. It consists first of all, if we are to gain a true grasp of Nietzsche, in bringing his accomplishment to a full unfolding. Being a vapor, a fallacy? If this were so, the only possible consequence would be to abandon the question "Why are there essents as such and as a whole, rather than nothing?" For what good is the question if what it inquires into is only a vapor and a fallacy?

Does Nietzsche speak the truth? Or was he himself only the last victim of a long process of error and neglect, but as such the unrecognized witness to a new necessity?

Is it the fault of being that it is so involved? is it the fault of the word that it remains so empty? or are we to blame that with all our effort, with all our chasing after the essent, we have fallen out of be-

5. *The Twilight of Idols*, Nietzsche's Complete Works, Edinburgh and London, *16* (1911), 19, 22.

ing? And should we not say that the fault did not begin with us, or with our immediate or more remote ancestors, but lies in something that runs through Western history from the very beginning, a happening which the eyes of all the historians in the world will never perceive, but which nevertheless happens, which happened in the past and will happen in the future? What if it were possible that man, that nations in their greatest movements and traditions, are linked to being and yet had long fallen out of being, without knowing it, and that this was the most powerful and most central cause of their decline? (See *Sein und Zeit*, § 38, in particular pp. 179 f.)

We do not ask these questions incidentally, and still less do they spring from any particular outlook or state of mind; no, they are questions to which we are driven by that preliminary question which sprang necessarily from our main question "How does it stand with being?"—a sober question perhaps, but assuredly a very useless one. And yet a *question, the* question: is "being" a mere word and its meaning a vapor or is it the spiritual destiny of the Western world?

This Europe, in its ruinous blindness forever on the point of cutting its own throat, lies today in a great pincers, squeezed between Russia on one side and America on the other. From a metaphysical point of view, Russia and America are the same; the same dreary technological frenzy, the same unrestricted organization of the average man. At a time when the farthermost corner of the globe has been conquered by technology and opened to economic exploitation; when any incident whatever, regardless of where or when it occurs, can be communicated to the rest of the world at any desired speed; when the assassination of a king in France and a symphony concert in Tokyo can be "experienced" simultaneously; when time has ceased to be anything other than velocity, instantaneousness, and simultaneity, and time as history has vanished from the lives of all peoples; when a boxer is regarded as a nation's great man; when mass meetings attended by millions are looked on as a triumph—then, yes then, through all this turmoil a question still haunts us like a specter: What for?—Whither?—And what then?

The spiritual decline of the earth is so far advanced that the nations are in danger of losing the last bit of spiritual energy that makes it possible to see the decline (taken in relation to the history of "being"), and to appraise it as such. This simple observation has nothing to do with *Kulturpessimismus*, and of course it has nothing to do with any sort of optimism either; for the darkening of the world, the flight of the gods, the destruction of the earth, the transformation of men into a mass, the hatred and suspicion of everything free and creative, have assumed such proportions throughout the earth that such childish categories as pessimism and optimism have long since become absurd.

We are caught in a pincers. Situated in the center, our nation incurs the severest pressure. It is the nation with the most neighbors and hence the most endangered. With all this, it is the most metaphysical of nations. We are certain of this vocation, but our people will only be able to wrest a destiny from it if *within itself* it creates a resonance, a possibility of resonance for this vocation, and takes a creative view of its tradition. All this implies that this nation, as a historical nation, must move itself and thereby the history of the West beyond the center of their future "happening" and into the primordial realm of the powers of being. If the great decision regarding Europe is not to bring annihilation, that decision must be made in terms of new spiritual energies unfolding historically from out of the center.

To ask "How does it stand with being"? means nothing less than to recapture, to repeat ⟨wiederholen⟩, the beginning of our historical-spiritual existence, in order to transform it into a new beginning. This is possible. It is indeed the crucial form of history, because it begins in the fundamental event. But we do not repeat a beginning by reducing it to something past and now known, which need merely be imitated; no, the beginning must be begun again, more radically, with all the strangeness, darkness, insecurity that attend a true beginning. Repetition as we understand it is anything but an improved continuation with the old methods of what has been up to now.

The question "How is it with being?" is included as a preliminary question in our central question "Why are there essents rather than nothing?" If we now begin to look into that which is questioned in our preliminary question, namely being, the full truth of Nietzsche's dictum is at once apparent. For if we look closely, what more is "being" to us than a mere word, an indeterminate meaning, intangible as a vapor? Nietzsche's judgment, to be sure, was meant in a purely disparaging sense. For him "being" is a delusion that should never have come about. Is "being," then, indeterminate, vague as a vapor? It is indeed. But we do not mean to sidestep this fact. On the contrary, we must see how much of a fact it is if we are to perceive its full implication.

Our questioning brings us into the landscape we must inhabit as a basic prerequisite, if we are to win back our roots in history. We shall have to ask why this fact, that for us "being" is no more than a word and a vapor, should have arisen precisely today, or whether and why it has existed for a long time. We must learn to see that this fact is not as harmless as it seems at first sight. For ultimately what matters is not that the word "being" remains a mere sound and its meaning a vapor, but that we have fallen away from what this word says and for the moment cannot find our way back; that it is for this and no other reason that the word "being" no longer applies to anything, that everything, if we merely take hold of it, dissolves like a tatter of cloud in the sunlight. Because this is so—that is why we ask about being. And we *ask* because we know that truths have never fallen into any nation's lap. The fact that people still cannot and do not wish to understand this question, even if it is asked in a still more fundamental form, deprives the question of none of its cogency.

Of course we can, seemingly with great astuteness and perspicacity, revive the old familiar argument to the effect that "being" is the most universal of concepts, that it covers anything and everything, even the nothing which also, in the sense that it is thought or spoken, "is" something. Beyond the domain of this most universal concept "being," there is, in the strictest sense of the word, nothing more, on the basis of which being itself could be more closely determined. The concept of being is an ultimate. Moreover, there is a law of logic that says: the more comprehensive a concept is—and what could be more comprehensive than the concept of "being"?—the more indeterminate and empty is its content.

For every normally thinking man—and we all should like to be normal men—this reasoning is immediately and wholly convincing. But the question now arises: does the designation of being as the most universal concept strike the essence of being, or is it not from the very outset such a misinterpretation that all questioning becomes hopeless? This then is the question: can being be regarded only as the most universal concept which inevitably occurs in all special concepts, or is being of an entirely different essence, and hence anything but an object of "ontology," provided we take this word in its traditional sense?

The word "ontology" was first coined in the seventeenth century. It marks the development of the traditional doctrine of the essent into a discipline of philosophy and a branch of the philosophical system. But the traditional doctrine was an academic classification and ordering of what for Plato and Aristotle and again for Kant was a question, though no longer to be sure a primordial one. And it is in this sense that the word "ontology" is used today. Under this title each school of philosophy has set up and described a branch within its system. But we can also take the word "ontology" in the "broadest sense," "without reference to ontological directions and tendencies" (cf. *Sein und Zeit*, p. 11 top). In this case "ontology" signifies the endeavor to make being manifest itself, and to do so by way of the question "how does it stand with being?" (and not only with the essent as such). But since thus far this question has not even been heard, let alone echoed; since it has been expressly rejected by the various schools of academic philosophy, which strive for an "ontology" in the traditional sense, it may be preferable to dispense in the future with the terms "ontology" and "ontological." Two modes of questioning which, as we now see clearly, are worlds apart, should not bear the same name.

We ask the questions "how does it stand with being?" "What is the meaning of being?" *not* in order to set up an ontology on the traditional style, much less to criticize the past mistakes of ontology. We are concerned with something totally different: to restore man's historical being-there—and that always includes our own future being-there in the totality of the history allotted to us—to the domain of being, which it was originally incumbent on man to open up for himself. All this, to be sure, in the limits within which philosophy can accomplish anything.

Out of the fundamental question of metaphysics, "Why are there essents rather than nothing?" we have separated the preliminary question, "How does it stand with being?" The relation between the two questions requires clarification, for it is of a special kind. Ordinarily a preliminary question is dealt with before and outside the main question, though in reference to it. But, in principle, philosophical questions are never dealt with as though we might some day cast them aside. Here the preliminary question is not by any means outside of the main question; rather, it is the flame which burns as it were in the asking of the fundamental question; it is the flaming center of all questioning. That is to say: it is crucial for the first asking of the fundamental question that in asking its *preliminary* question we derive the decisive fundamental attitude that is here essential. That is why we have related the question of being to the destiny of Europe, where the destiny of the earth is being decided—while our own historic being there proves to be the center for Europe itself.

The question is:

Is being a mere word and its meaning a vapor, or does what is designated by the word "being" hold within it the historical destiny of the West?

To many ears the question may sound violent and exaggerated: for one might in a pinch suppose that a discussion of the question of being might be related in some very remote and indirect way to the decisive historical question of the earth, but assuredly not that the basic position and attitude of our questioning might be directly determined by the history of the human spirit on earth. And yet this relationship exists. Since our purpose is to set in motion the asking of the preliminary question, we must now show that, and to what extent, the asking of this question is an immediate and fundamental factor in the crucial historical question. For this demonstration it is necessary to anticipate an essential insight in the form of an assertion.

We maintain that this preliminary question and with it the fundamental question of metaphysics are historical questions through and through. But do not metaphysics and philosophy thereby become a historical science? Historical science after all investigates the temporal, while philosophy investigates the timeless. Philosophy is historical only insofar as it—like every work of the spirit—realizes itself in time. But in this sense the designation of metaphysical questioning as historical cannot characterize metaphysics, but merely expresses something obvious. Accordingly, the assertion is either meaningless and superfluous or else impossible, because it creates an amalgam of two fundamentally different kinds of science: philosophy and historical science.

In answer to this it must be said:

1. Metaphysics and philosophy are not sciences at all, and the fact that their questioning is basically historical cannot make them so.

2. Historical science does not determine a fundamental relation to history, but always presupposes such a relation. It is only for this reason that historical science can distort men's relation to history, which itself is always historical; or misinterpret it and degrade it to a mere knowledge of antiquities; or else deal with crucial fields in the light of this once established relation to history, and so produce cogent history. A historical relation between our historical being-there and history may become an object of knowledge and mark an advanced state of knowledge; but it need not. Moreover, all relations to history cannot be scientifically objectified and given a place in science, and it is precisely the essential ones that cannot. Historical science can never produce the historical relation to history. It can only illuminate a relation once supplied, ground it in knowledge, which is indeed an absolute necessity for the historical being-there of a wise people, and not either an "advantage" or a "disadvantage." Because it is only in philosophy—*as distinguished from all science*—that essential relations to the realm of what is take shape, this relation *can*, indeed *must*, for us today be a fundamentally historical one.

But for an understanding of our assertion that the "metaphysical" asking of the preliminary question is historical through and through, it is above all necessary to consider this: for us history is not synonymous with the past; for the past is precisely what is no longer happening. And much less is history the merely contemporary, which never happens but merely "passes," comes and goes by. History as happening is an acting and being acted upon which pass through the *present*, which are determined from out of the future, and which take over the past. It is precisely the present that vanishes in happening.

Our asking of the fundamental question of metaphysics is historical because it opens up the process of human being-there in its essential relations—i.e. its relations to the essent as such and as a whole—opens it up to unasked possibilities, futures, and at the same time binds it back to its past beginning, so sharpening it and giving it weight in its present. In this questioning our being-there is summoned to its history in the full sense of the word, called to history and to a decision in history. And this not after the fact, in the sense that we draw ethical, ideological lessons from it. No, the basic attitude of the questioning is in itself historical; it stands and maintains itself in happening, inquiring out of happening for the sake of happening.

But we have not yet come to the essential reason why this inherently historical asking of the question about being is actually an integral part of history on earth. We have said that the world is darkening. The essential episodes of this darkening are: the flight of the gods, the destruction of the earth, the standardization of man, the pre-eminence of the mediocre.

What do we mean by world when we speak of a darkening of the world? World is always world of the *spirit*. The animal has no world nor any environment ⟨Umwelt⟩. Darkening of the world means emasculation of the spirit, the disintegration, wasting away, repression, and misinterpretation of the spirit. We shall attempt to explain the emasculation of the spirit in one respect, that of misinterpretation. We have said: Europe lies in a pincers between Russia and America, which are metaphysically the same, namely in regard to their world character and their relation to the spirit. What makes the situation of Europe all the more catastrophic is that this enfeeblement of the spirit originated in Europe itself and—though prepared by earlier factors—was definitively determined by its own spiritual situation in the first half of the nineteenth century. It was then that occurred what is popularly and succinctly called the "collapse of German idealism." This formula is a kind of shield behind which the already dawning spiritlessness, the dissolution of the spiritual energies, the rejection of all original inquiry into grounds and men's bond with the grounds, are hidden and masked. It was not German idealism that collapsed; rather, the age was no longer strong enough to stand up to the greatness, breadth, and originality of that spiritual world, i.e. truly to realize it, for to realize a philosophy means something very different from applying theorems and insights. The lives of men began to slide into a world which lacked that depth from out of which the essential always comes to man and comes back to man, so compelling him to become superior and making him act in conformity to a rank. All things sank to the same level, a surface resembling a blind mirror that no longer reflects, that casts nothing back. The prevailing dimension became that of extension and number. Intelligence no longer meant a wealth of talent, lavishly spent, and the command of energies, but only what could be learned by everyone, the practice of a routine, always associated with a certain amount of sweat and a certain amount of show. In America and in Russia this development grew into a boundless etcetera of indifference and always-the-sameness—so much so that the quantity took on a quality of its own. Since then the domination in those countries of a cross section of the indifferent mass has become something more than a dreary accident. It has become an active onslaught that destroys all rank and every world-creating impulse of the spirit, and calls it a lie. This is the onslaught of what we call the demonic (in the sense of destructive evil). There are many indications of the emergence of this demonism, identical with the increasing helplessness and uncertainty of Europe against it and within itself. One of these signs is the emasculation of the spirit through misinterpretation; we are still in the midst of this process. This misinterpretation of the spirit may be described briefly in four aspects.

1. The crux of the matter is the reinterpretation of the spirit as *intelligence*, or mere cleverness in examining and calculating given things and the possibility of changing them and complementing them to make new things. This cleverness is a matter of mere talent and practice and mass division of labor. The cleverness itself is subject to the possibility of organization, which is never true of the spirit. The attitude of the littérateur and esthete is merely a late consequence and variation of the spirit falsified into intelligence. Mere intelligence is a semblance of spirit, masking its absence.

2. The spirit falsified into intelligence thus falls to the level of a tool in the service of others, a tool the manipulation of which can be taught and learned. Whether this use of intelligence relates to the regulation and domination of the material conditions of production (as in Marxism) or in general to the intelligent ordering and explanation of everything that is present and already posited at any time (as in positivism), or whether it is applied to the organization and regulation of a nation's vital resources and race—in any case the spirit as intelligence becomes the impotent superstructure of something else, which, because it is without spirit or even opposed to the spirit, is taken for the actual reality. If the spirit is taken as intelligence, as is done in the most extreme form of Marxism, then it is perfectly correct to say, in defense against it, that in the order of the effective forces of human being-there, the spirit, i.e. intelligence, must always be ranked below healthy physical activity and character. But this order becomes false once we understand the true essence of the spirit. For all true power and beauty of the body, all sureness and boldness in combat, all authenticity and inventiveness of the understanding, are grounded in the spirit and rise or fall only through the power or impotence of the spirit. The spirit is the sustaining, dominating principle, the first and the last, not merely an indispensable third factor.

3. As soon as the misinterpretation sets in that degrades the spirit to a tool, the energies of the spiritual process, poetry and art, statesmanship and religion, become subject to *conscious* cultivation and planning. They are split into branches. The spiritual world becomes culture and the individual strives to perfect himself in the creation and preservation of this culture. These branches become fields of free endeavor, which sets its own standards and barely manages to live up to them. These standards of production and consumption are called values. The cultural values preserve their meaning only by restricting themselves to an autonomous field: poetry for the sake of poetry, art for the sake of art, science for the sake of science.

Let us consider the example of science, which is of particular concern to us here at the university. The state of science since the turn of the century—it has remained unchanged despite a certain amount of house cleaning—is easy to see. Though today two seemingly different conceptions of science seem to combat one another—science as technical, practical, professional knowledge and science as cultural value per se—both are moving along the same downgrade of misinterpretation and emasculation of the spirit. They differ only in this: in the present situation the technical, practical conception of science as specialization can at least lay claim to frank and clear consistency, while the reactionary interpretation of science as a culture value, now making its reappearance, seeks to conceal the impotence of the spirit behind an unconscious lie. The confusion of spiritlessness can even go so far as to lead the upholders of the technical, practical view of science to profess their belief in science as a cultural value; then the two understand each other perfectly in the same spiritlessness. We may choose to call the institution where the specialized sciences are grouped together for purposes of teaching and research a university, but this is no more than a name; the "university" has ceased to be a fundamental force for unity and responsibility. What I said here in 1929, in my inaugural address, is still true of the German university: "The scientific fields are still far apart. Their subjects are treated in fundamentally different ways. Today this hodgepodge of disciplines is held together only by the technical organization of the universities and faculties and preserves what meaning it has only through the practical aims of the different branches. The sciences have lost their roots in their essential ground." (*Was ist Metaphysik*? 1929, p. 8.) Science today in all its branches is a technical, practical business of gaining and transmitting information. An awakening of the spirit cannot take its departure from such science. It it itself in need of an awakening.

4. The last misinterpretation of the spirit is based on the above-mentioned falsifications which represent the spirit as intelligence, and intelligence as a serviceable tool which, along with its product, is situated in the realm of culture. In the end the spirit as utilitarian intelligence and the spirit as culture become holiday ornaments cultivated along with many other things. They are brought out and exhibited as a proof that there is *no* intention to combat culture or favor barbarism. In the beginning Russian Communism took a purely negative attitude but soon went over to propagandist tactics of this kind.

In opposition to this multiple misinterpretation of the spirit, we define the essence of the spirit briefly as follows (I shall quote from the address I delivered on the occasion of my appointment as rector, because of its succinct formulation): "Spirit is neither empty cleverness nor the irresponsible play of the wit, nor the boundless work of dismemberment carried on by the practical intelligence; much less is it world-reason; no, spirit is a fundamental, knowing resolve toward the essence of being." (Rektoratsrede, p. 13.) Spirit is the mobilization of the powers of the essent as such and as a whole. Where spirit prevails, the essent as such becomes always and at all times more essent. Thus the inquiry into the essent as such and as a whole, the asking of the question of being, is one of the essential and fundamental conditions for an awakening of the spirit and hence for an original world of historical being-there. It is indispensable if the peril of world darkening is to be forestalled and if our nation in the center of the Western world is to take on its historical mission. Here we can explain only in these broad outlines why the asking of the question of being is in itself through and through historical, and why, accordingly, our question as to whether being will remain a mere vapor for us or become the destiny of the West is anything but an exaggeration and a rhetorical figure.

But if our question about being has this essential and decisive character, we must above all take an absolutely serious view of *the fact* that gives the question its immediate necessity, the fact that for us being has become little more than a mere word and its meaning an evanescent vapor. This is not the kind of fact which merely confronts us as something alien and other, which we need merely note as an occurrence. It is a fact in which we stand. It is a state of our being-there. And by state, of course, I do not mean a quality that can be demonstrated only psychologically. Here state means our entire constitution, the way in which we ourselves are constituted in regard to being. Here we are not concerned with psychology but with our history in an essential respect. When we call it a "fact" that being for us is a mere word and vapor, we are speaking very provisionally. We are merely holding fast, establishing something which has not yet been thought through, for which we still have no locus, even if it looks as though this something were an occurrence among us, here and now, or "in" us, as we like to say.

One would like to integrate the individual fact that for us being remains no more than an empty word and an evanescent vapor with the more general fact that many words, and precisely the essential ones, are in the same situation; that the language in general is worn out and used up—an indispensable but masterless means of communication that may be used as one pleases, as indifferent as a means of public transport, as a street car which everyone rides in. Everyone speaks and writes away in the language, without hindrance and above all *without danger*. That is certainly true. And only a very few are capable of thinking through the full implications of this misrelation and unrelation of present-day being-there to language.

But the emptiness of the word "being," the total disappearance of its appellative force, is not merely a particular instance of the general exhaustion of language; rather, the destroyed relation to being as such is the actual reason for the general misrelation to language.

The organizations for the purification of the language and defense against its progressive barbarization are deserving of respect. But such efforts merely demonstrate all the more clearly that we no longer know what is at stake in language. Because the destiny of language is grounded in a nation's *relation* to *being*, the question of being will involve us deeply in the question of language. It is more than an outward accident that now, as we prepare to set forth, in all its implication, the fact of the evaporation of being, we find ourselves compelled to take linguistic considerations as our starting point.

Chapter 39

JEAN-PAUL SARTRE

Jean-Paul Sartre (1905–1980) was born in Paris and was a teacher in a French high school. He served in the French army during World War II, was captured by the Germans, and spent time in a prison camp reading German philosophers (especially Hegel, Husserl, and Heidegger). After the war, Sartre's plays, novels, and philosophical work, especially *Being and Nothingness* (1943), set him apart as Europe's premier existentialist. Later he combined existentialism with Marxism, though he never joined the Communist party.

Here is Paul Johnson's description of the impact of Sartre and the essay we are about to reach on French society:

> [On October 29, 1945 shortly after the end of the war], at the Club Maintenant, Jean-Paul Sartre delivered a lecture, "Existentialism is a Humanism." Here was the new Paris. This occasion . . . was packed. Men and women fainted, fought for chairs, smashing thirty of them, shouted and barracked. It coincided with the launching of Sartre's new review, *Les Temps Modernes,* in which he argued that literary culture, plus the haute couture of the fashion shops, were the only things France now had left—a symbol of Europe, really—and he produced Existentialism to give people a bit of dignity and to preserve their individuality in the midst of degradation and absurdity. The response was overwhelming. As his consort, Simone de Beauvoir, put it, "We were astounded by the furore we caused." Existentialism was remarkably un-Gallic; hence perhaps, its attractiveness. Sartre was half-Alsacian (Albert Schweitzer was his cousin) and he was brought up in the house of his grandfather, Karl Schweitzer. His culture was as much German as French. He was essentially a product of the Berlin school and especially Heidegger, from whom most of his ideas derived. . . . Thus Existentialism was a French cultural import, which Paris then re-exported to Germany, its country of origin, in a sophisticated and vastly more attractive guise. (Paul Johnson *Modern Times,* Harper & Row, 1983, p. 575f)

In our first selection, "Bad Faith," from *Being and Nothingness,* Sartre contrasts "bad faith" with authenticity (good faith). He argues that any attempt to deny our freedom, to identify ourselves with our roles in society, our gender, race, or religion, is to act in bad faith. Authenticity is to acknowledge one's freedom at every moment of existence.

In our second selection, "Existentialism and Humanism," Sartre sets forth the broader principles of atheistic existentialism: that we are completely free; that since there is no God to give us an essence, we must create our own essence; that we are completely responsible for our actions, and are responsible for everyone else too; that because of the death of God and the human predicament, which leaves us totally free to create our values and our world, we must exist in anguish, forlornness, and despair. Yet there is a certain celebration and optimism in knowing that we are creators of our own values.

In this essay you will come across Sartre's notion that "existence precedes essence." This is a difficult idea, but he seems to mean something like the following. If you have an idea of something in your mind first and then create it, we would say that the idea (essence) of the thing precedes the actuality or existence of it. But if the thing existed before any idea of it, then its existence precedes its essence. If there were a God who created us, who had us in mind, we would have an essence (in terms of a function or purpose) and our existence would succeed our essence, but since, according to Sartre, there is no God to create us, we simply find ourselves existing and must create our own essence (i.e., give ourselves a function or purpose).

FOR FURTHER READING

Barrett, William. *Irrational Man.* (Doubleday, 1958).
Caws, Peter. *Sartre.* (Routledge, Chapman and Hall, 1984).
Kaufmann, Walter, ed. *Existentialism for Dostoevsky to Sartre.* (New American Library, 1975).
Murdoch, Iris. *Sartre, Romantic Rationalist.* (Viking Penguin, 1987).
Sartre, Jean Paul. *Being and Nothingness,* trans. H. Barnes. (Philosophical Library, 1956).
Sartre, Jean Paul, *Existentialism and Human Emotions*, trans. B. Frechtman (Philosophical Library, 1947).
Schilpp, P. A. *The Philosophy of Jean-Paul Sartre.* (Open Court, 1981).
Silverman, Hugh and Frederick Elliston, eds. *Jean-Paul Sartre: Contemporary Approaches to His Philosophy.* (Duquesne University Press, 1980).

Being and Nothingness

BAD FAITH

I. Bad Faith and Falsehood

The human being is not only the being by whom *négattés* are disclosed in the world; he is also the one who can take negative attitudes with respect to himself. In our Introduction we defined consciousness as "a being such that in its being, its being is in question in so far as this being implies a being other than itself." But now that we have examined the meaning of "the question," we can at present also write the formula thus: "Consciousness is a being, the nature of which is to be conscious of the nothingness of its being." In a prohibition or a veto, for example, the human being denies a future transcendence. But this negation is not explicative. My consciousness is not restricted to *envisioning a négatité*. It constitutes itself in its own flesh as the nihilation of a possibility. For that reason it must arise in the world as a *No*; it is as a No that the slave first apprehends the master, or that the prisoner who is trying to escape sees the guard who is watching him. There are even men (*e.g.*, caretakers, overseers, gaolers), whose social reality is uniquely that of the No, who will live and die, having forever been only a No upon the earth. Others, so as to make the No a part of their very subjectivity, establish their human personality as a perpetual negation. This is the meaning and function of what Scheler calls "the man of resentment"—in reality, the No. But there exist more subtle behaviors, the description of which will lead us further into the inwardness of consciousness. Irony is one of these. In irony a man annihilates what he posits within one and the same act; he leads us to believe in order not to be believed; he affirms to deny and denies to affirm; he creates a positive object but it has no being other than its nothingness. Thus attitudes of negation toward the self permit us to raise a new question: What are we to say is the being of man who has the possibility of denying himself? But it is out of the question to discuss the attitude of "self-negation" in its universality. The kinds of behavior which can be ranked under this heading are too diverse; we risk retaining only the abstract form of them. It is best to choose and to examine one determined attitude which is essential to human reality and which is such that consciousness instead of directing its negation outward turns it toward itself. This attitude, it seems to me, is *bad faith* (*mauvaise foi*).

Frequently this is identified with falsehood. We say indifferently of a person that he shows signs of bad faith or that he lies to himself. We shall willingly grant that bad faith is a lie to oneself, on condition that we distinguish the lie to oneself from lying in general. Lying is a negative attitude, we will agree to that. But this negation does not bear on consciousness itself; it aims only at the transcendent. The essence of the lie implies in fact that the liar actually is in complete possession of the truth which he is hiding. A man does not lie about what he is ignorant of; he does not lie when he spreads an error of which he himself is the dupe; he does not lie when he is mistaken. The ideal description of the liar would be a cynical consciousness, affirming truth within himself, denying it in his words, and denying that negation as such. Now this double negative attitude rests on the transcendent; the fact expressed is transcendent since it does not exist, and the original negation rests on a *truth*; that is, on a particular type of transcendence. As for the inner negation which I effect correlatively with the affirmation for myself of the truth, this rests on *words*; that is, on an event in the world. Furthermore the inner disposition of the liar is positive; it could be the object of an affirmative judgment. The liar intends to deceive and he does not seek to hide this intention from himself nor to disguise the translucency of consciousness; on the contrary, he has recourse to it when there is a question of deciding secondary behavior. It explicitly exercises a regulatory control over all attitudes. As for his flaunted intention of telling the truth ("I'd never want to deceive you! This is true! I swear it!")—all this, of course, is the object of an inner negation, but also it is not recognized by the liar as *his* intention. It is played, imitated, it is the intention of the character which he plays in the eyes of his questioner, but this character, precisely because he *does not exist*, is a transcendent. Thus the lie does not put into the play the inner structure of present consciousness; all the negations which constitute it bear on objects which by this fact are removed from consciousness. The lie then does not require special ontological foundation, and the explanations which the existence of negation in general requires are valid without change in the case of deceit. Of course we have described the ideal lie; doubtless it happens often enough that the liar is more or less the victim of his lie, that he half persuades himself of it. But these common, popular forms of the lie are also degenerate aspects of it; they represent intermediaries between falsehood and bad faith. The lie is a behavior of transcendence.

The lie is also a normal phenomenon of what Heidegger calls the "*mit-sein*."[1] It presupposes my existence, the existence of the *Other*, my existence *for* the Other, and the existence of the Other *for* me. Thus there is no difficulty in holding that the liar must make the project of the lie in entire clarity and that he must possess a complete comprehension of the lie and of the truth which he is altering. It is sufficient that an overall opacity hide his intentions from the *Other*; it is sufficient that the Other can take the lie for truth. By the lie consciousness affirms that it exists by nature as *hidden from the Other*; it utilizes for its own profit the ontological duality of myself and myself in the eyes of the Other.

The situation can not be the same for bad faith if this, as we have said, is indeed a lie to oneself. To be sure, the one who practices bad faith is hiding a displeasing truth or presenting as truth a pleasing untruth. Bad faith then has in appearance the structure of falsehood. Only what changes everything is the fact that in bad faith it is from myself that I am hiding the truth. Thus the duality of the deceiver and the deceived does not exist here. Bad faith on the contrary implies in essence the unity of a *single* consciousness. This does not mean that it can not be conditioned by the *mit-sein* like all other phenomena of human reality, but the *mit-sein* can call forth bad faith only by presenting itself as *a situation* which bad faith permits surpassing; bad faith does not come from outside to human reality. One does not undergo his bad faith; one is not infected with it; it is not a *state*. But consciousness affects itself

1. Tr. A "being-with" others in the world.

with bad faith. There must be an original intention and a project of bad faith; this project implies a comprehension of bad faith as such and a pre-reflective apprehension (of) consciousness as affecting itself with bad faith. It follows first that the one to whom the lie is told and the one who lies are one and the same person, which means that I must know in my capacity as deceiver the truth which is hidden from me in my capacity as the one deceived. Better yet I must know the truth very exactly *in order* to conceal it more carefully—and this not at two different moments, which at a pinch would allow us to re-establish a semblance of duality—but in the unitary structure of a single project. How then can the lie subsist if the duality which conditions it is suppressed?

To this difficulty is added another which is derived from the total translucency of consciousness. That which affects itself with bad faith must be conscious (of) its bad faith since the being of consciousness is consciousness of being. It appears then that I must be in good faith, at least to the extent that I am conscious of my bad faith. But then this whole psychic system is annihilated. We must agree in fact that if I deliberately and cynically attempt to lie to myself, I fail completely in this undertaking; the lie falls back and collapses beneath my look; it is ruined *from behind* by the very consciousness of lying to myself which pitilessly constitutes itself well within my project as its very condition. We have here an *evanescent* phenomenon which exists only in and through its own differentiation. To be sure, these phenomena are frequent and we shall see that there is in fact an "evanescence" of bad faith, which, it is evident, vacillates continually between good faith and cynicism: Even though the existence of bad faith is very precarious, and though it belongs to the kind of psychic structures which we might call *metastable,* it presents nonetheless an autonomous and durable form. It can even be the normal aspect of life for a very great number of people. A person can *live* in bad faith, which does not mean that he does not have abrupt awakenings to cynicism or to good faith, but which implies a constant and particular style of life. Our embarrassment then appears extreme since we can neither reject nor comprehend bad faith.

II. Patterns of Bad Faith

If we wish to get out of this difficulty, we should examine more closely the patterns of bad faith and attempt a description of them. This description will permit us perhaps to fix more exactly the conditions for the possibility of bad faith; that is, to reply to the questions we raised at the outset: "What must be the being of man if he is to be capable of bad faith?"

Take the example of a woman who has consented to go out with a particular man for the first time. She knows very well the intentions which the man who is speaking to her cherishes regarding her. She knows also that it will be necessary sooner or later for her to make a decision. But she does not want to realize the urgency; she concerns herself only with what is respectful and discreet in the attitude of her companion. She does not apprehend this conduct as an attempt to achieve what we call "the first approach"; that is, she does not want to see possibilities of temporal development which his conduct presents. She restricts this behavior to what is in the present; she does not wish to read in the phrases which he addresses to her anything other than their explicit meaning. If he says to her, "I find you so attractive!" she disarms this phrase of its sexual background; she attaches to the conversation and to the behavior of the speaker, the immediate meanings, which she images as objective qualities. The man who is speaking to her appears to her sincere and respectful as the table is round or square, as the wall coloring is blue or gray. The qualities thus attached to the person she is listening to are in this way fixed in a permanence like that of things, which is no other than the projection of the strict present of the qualities into the temporal flux. This is because she does not quite know what she wants. She is profoundly aware of the desire which she inspires, but the desire cruel and naked would humiliate and horrify her. Yet she would find no charm in a respect which would be only respect. In order to satisfy her, there must be a feeling which is addressed wholly to her *personality—i.e.,* to her full freedom—and which would be a recognition of her freedom. But at the same time this feeling must be wholly desire; that is, it must address itself to her body as object. This time then she refuses to apprehend the desire for what it is; she does not even give it a name; she recognizes it only to the extent that it transcends itself toward admiration, esteem, respect and that it is wholly absorbed in the more refined forms which it produces, to the extent of no longer figuring anymore as a sort of warmth and density. But then suppose he takes her hand. This act of her companion risks changing the situation by calling for an immediate decision. To leave the hand there is to consent in herself to flirt, to engage herself. To withdraw it is to break the troubled and unstable harmony which gives the hour its charm. The aim is to postpone the moment of decision as long as possible. We know what happens next; the young woman leaves her hand there, but she *does not notice* that she is leaving it. She does not notice because it happens by chance that she is at this moment all intellect. She draws her companion up to the most lofty regions of sentimental speculation; she speaks of Life, of her life, she shows herself in her essential aspect—a personality, a consciousness. And during this time the divorce of the body from the soul is accomplished; the hand rests inert between the warm hands of her companion—neither consenting nor resisting—a thing.

We shall say that this woman is in bad faith. But we see immediately that she uses various procedures in order to maintain herself in this bad faith. She has disarmed the actions of her companion by reducing them to being only what they are; that is, to existing in the mode of the in-itself. But she permits herself to enjoy his desire, to the extent that she will apprehend it as not being what it is, will recognize its transcendence. Finally while sensing profoundly the presence of her own body—to the point of being aroused, perhaps—she realized herself as *not being* her own body, and she contemplates it as though from above as a passive object to which events can *happen* but which can neither provoke them nor avoid them because all its possibilities are outside of it. What unity do we find in these various aspects of bad faith? It is a certain art of forming contradictory concepts which unite in themselves both an idea and the negation of that idea. The basic concept which is thus engendered utilizes the double property of the human being, who is at once a *facticity* and a *transcendence*. These two aspects of human reality are and ought to be capable of a valid coordination. But bad faith does not wish either to coordinate them or to surmount them in a synthesis. Bad faith seeks to affirm their identity while preserving their differences. It must affirm facticity as *being* transcendence and transcendence as *being* facticity, in such a way that at the instant when a person apprehends the one, he can find himself abruptly faced with the other.

We can find the prototype of formulae of bad faith in certain famous expressions which have been rightly conceived to produce their whole effect in a spirit of bad faith. Take for example the title of a work by Jacques Chardonne, *Love Is Much More than Love*. We see here how unity is established between *present* love in its facticity—"the contact of two skins," sensuality, egoism, Proust's mechanism of jealousy, Adler's battle of the *sexes, etc.*—and love as transcendence—Mauriac's "river of fire," the longing for the infinite, Plato's *eros*, Lawrence's deep cosmic intuition, *etc*. Here we leave facticity to find ourselves suddenly beyond the present and the factual condition of man, beyond the psychological, in the heart of metaphysics. On the other hand, the title of a play by Sarment, *I Am Too Great for Myself*, which also presents characters in bad faith, throws us first into full transcendence in order suddenly to imprison us within the narrow limits of our factual essence. We will discover this structure again in the famous sentence: "He has become what he was" or in its no less famous opposite: "Eternity at last changes each man into himself." It is well understood that these various formulae have only the appearance of bad faith; they have been conceived in this paradoxical form explicitly to shock the mind and discountenance it by an enigma. But it is precisely this appearance which is of concern to us. What counts here is that the formulae do not constitute new, solidly structured ideas; on the contrary, they are formed so as to remain in perpetual disintegration and so that we may slide at any time from naturalistic present to transcendence and *vice versa*.

We can see the use which bad faith can make of these judgments which all aim at establishing that I am not what I am. If I were only what I *am*, I could, for example, seriously consider an adverse criticism which someone makes of me, question myself scrupulously, and perhaps be compelled to recognize the truth in it. But thanks to transcendence, I am not subject to all that I am. I do not even have to discuss the justice of the reproach. As Suzanne says to Figaro, "To prove that I am right would be to recognize that I can be wrong." I am on a plane where no reproach can touch me since what I really am is my transcendence. I flee from myself, I escape myself, I leave my tattered garment in the hands of the fault-finder. But the ambiguity necessary for bad faith comes from the fact that I affirm here that I *am* my transcendence in the mode of being of a thing. It is only thus, in fact, that I can feel that I escape all reproaches. It is in the sense that our young woman purifies the desire of anything humiliating by being willing to consider it only as pure transcendence, which she avoids even naming. But inversely "I Am Too Great for Myself," while showing our transcendence changed into facticity, is the source of an infinity of excuses for our failures or our weaknesses. Similarly the young coquette maintains transcendence to the extent that the respect, the esteem manifested by the actions of her admirer are already on the plane of the transcendent. But she arrests this transcendence, she glues it down with all the facticity of the present; respect is nothing other than respect, it is an arrested surpassing which no longer surpasses itself toward anything.

But although this *metastable* concept of "transcendence-facticity" is one of the most basic instruments of bad faith, it is not the only one of its kind. We can equally well use another kind of duplicity derived from human reality which we will express roughly by saying that its being-for-itself implies complementarily a being-for-others. Upon any one of my conducts it is always possible to converge two looks, mine and that of the Other. The conduct will not present exactly the same structure in each case. But as we shall see later, as each look perceives it, there is between these two aspects of my being, no difference between appearance and being—as if I were to my self the truth of myself and as if the Other possessed only a deformed image of me. The equal dignity of being, possessed by my being-for-others and by my being-for-myself, permits a perpetually disintegrating synthesis and a perpetual game of escape from the for-itself to the for-others and from the for-others to the for-itself. We have seen also the use which our young lady made of our being-in-the-midst-of-the-world—*i.e.*, of our inert presence as a passive object among other objects—in order to relieve herself suddenly from the functions of her being-in-the-world—that is, from the being which causes there to be a world by projecting itself beyond the world towards its own possibilities. Let us note finally the confusing syntheses which play on the nihilating ambiguity of these temporal ekstases, affirming at once that I am what I have been (the man who deliberately *arrests himself* at one period in his life and refuses to take into consideration the later changes) and that I am not what I have been (the man who in the face of reproaches or rancor dissociates himself from his past by insisting on his freedom and on his perpetual re-creation). In all these concepts, which have only a transitive role in the reasoning and which are eliminated from the conclusion (like the imaginaries in the computations of physicists), we find again the same structure. We have to deal with human reality as a being which is what it is not and which is not what it is.

But what exactly is necessary in order for these concepts of disintegration to be able to receive even a pretence of existence, in order for them to be able to appear for an instant to consciousness, even in a process of evanescence? A quick examination of the idea of sincerity, the antithesis of bad faith, will be very instructive in this connection. Actually sincerity presents itself as a demand and consequently is not a *state*. Now what is the ideal to be attained in this case? It is necessary that a man be *for himself* only what he *is*. But is this not precisely the definition of the in-itself—or if you prefer—the principle of identity? To posit as an ideal the being of things, is this not to assert by the same stroke that this being does not belong to human reality and that the principle of identity, far from being a universal axiom universally applied, is only a synthetic principle enjoying a merely regional universality? Thus in order that the concepts of bad faith can put us under illusion at least for an instant, in order that the candor of "pure hearts" (*cf.* Gide, Kessel) can have validity for human reality as an ideal, the principle of identity must not represent a constitutive principle of human reality and human reality must not be necessarily what it is but must be able to be what it is not. What does this mean?

If man is what he is, bad faith is forever impossible and candor ceases to be his ideal and becomes instead his being. But is man what he is? And more generally, how can he *be* what he is when he exists as consciousness of being? If candor or sincerity is a universal value, it is evident that the maxim "one must be what one is" does not serve solely as a regulating principle for judgments and concepts by which I express what I am. It posits not merely an ideal of knowing but an ideal of *being*; it proposes for us an absolute equivalent of being with itself as a prototype of being. In this sense it is necessary that we *make ourselves* what we are. But what *are we* then if we have the constant obligations to make ourselves what we are, if our mode of being is having the obligation to be what we are?

Let us consider this waiter in the café. His movement is quick and forward, a little too precise, a little too rapid. He comes toward the patrons with a step a little too quick. He bends forward a little too eagerly; his voice, his eyes express an interest a little too solicitous for the order of the customer. Finally there he returns, trying to imitate in his walk the inflexible stiffness of some kind of automaton while carrying his tray with the recklessness of a tight-rope-walker by putting it in a perpetually unstable, perpetually broken equilibrium which he perpetually re-establishes by a light movement of the arm and hand. All his behavior seems to us a game. He applies himself to chaining his movements as if they were mechanisms, the one regulating the other; his gestures and even his voice seem to be mechanisms; he gives himself the quickness and pitiless rapidity of things. He is playing, he is amusing himself. But what is he playing? We need not watch long before we can explain it: he is playing at *being* a waiter in a café. There is nothing there to surprise us. The game is a kind of marking out and investigation. The child plays with his body in order to explore it, to take inventory of it; the waiter in the café plays with his condition in order to *realize* it. This obligation is not different from that which is imposed on all tradesmen. Their condition is wholly one of ceremony. The public demands of them that they realize it as a ceremony; there is the dance of the grocer, of the tailor, of the auctioneer, by which they endeavor to persuade their clientele that they are nothing but a grocer, an auctioneer, a tailor. A grocer who dreams is offensive to the buyer, because such a grocer is not wholly a grocer. Society demands that he limit himself to his function as a grocer, just as the soldier at attention makes himself into a soldier-thing with a direct regard which does not see at all, which is no longer meant to see, since it is the rule and not the interest of the moment which determines the point he must fix his eyes on (the sight "fixed at ten paces"). There are indeed many precautions to imprison a man in what he is, as if we lived in perpetual fear that he might escape from it, that he might break away and suddenly elude his condition.

In a parallel situation, from within, the waiter in the café can not be immediately a café waiter in the sense that this inkwell *is* an inkwell, or the glass is a glass. It is by no means that he can not form reflective judgments or concepts concerning his condition. He knows well what it "means": the obligation of getting up at five o'clock, of sweeping the floor of the shop before the restaurant opens, of starting the coffee pot going, *etc*. He knows the rights which it allows: the right to the tips, the right to belong to a union, *etc*. But all these concepts, all these judgments refer to the transcendent. It is a matter of abstract possibilities, of rights and duties conferred on a "person possessing rights." And it is precisely this person *who I have to be* (if I am the waiter in question) and who I am not. I is not that I do not wish to be this person or that I want this person to be different. But rather there is no common measure between his being and mine. It is a "representation" for others and for myself, which means that I can be he only in *representation*. But if I represent myself as him, I am not he; I am separated from him as the object from the subject, separated *by nothing*, but this nothing isolates me from him. I can not be he, I can only play *at being* him; that is, imagine to myself that I am he. And thereby I affect him with nothingness. In vain do I fulfill the functions of a café waiter. I can be he only in the neutralized mode, as the actor is Hamlet, by mechanically making the *typical gestures* of my state and by aiming at myself as an imaginary café waiter through those gestures taken as an "analogue." What I attempt to realize is a being-in-itself of the café waiter, as if it were not just in my power to confer their value and their urgency upon my duties and the rights of my position, as if it were not my free choice to get up each morning at five o'clock or to remain in bed, even though it meant getting fired. As if from the very fact that I sustain this role in existence I did not transcend it on every side, as if I did not constitute myself as one *beyond* my condition. Yet there is no doubt that I *am* in a sense a café waiter—otherwise could I not just as well call myself a diplomat or a reporter? But if I am one, this can not be in the mode of being in-itself. I am a waiter in the mode of *being what I am not*.

Furthermore we are dealing with more than mere social positions; I am never any one of my attitudes, any one of my actions. The good speaker is the one who *plays* at speaking, because he can not *be speaking*. The attentive pupil who wishes to *be* attentive, his eyes riveted on the teacher, his ears wide open, so exhausts himself in playing the attentive role that he ends up by no longer hearing anything. Perpetually absent to my body, to my acts, I am despite myself that "divine absence" of which Valéry speaks. I can not say either that I *am* here or that I *am* not here, in the sense that we say "that box of matches *is* on the table"; this would be to confuse my "being-in-the-world" with a "being-in-the-midst-of-the-world." Nor that I *am* standing, nor that I *am* seated; this would be to confuse my body with the idiosyncratic totality of which it is only one of the structures. On all sides I escape being and yet—I am. . . .

Consciousness of the Other is what it is not.

Furthermore the being of my own consciousness does not appear to be as the consciousness of the Other. It *is* because it makes itself, since its being is consciousness of being. But this means that making sustains being; consciousness has to be its own being, it is never sustained by being; it sustains being in the heart of subjectivity, which means once again that it is inhabited by being but that it is not being: *consciousness is not what it is.*

Under these conditions what can be the significance of the ideal of sincerity except as a task impossible to achieve, of which the very meaning is in contradiction with the structure of my consciousness. To be sincere, we said, is to be what one is. That supposes that I am not originally what I am. But here naturally Kant's "You ought, therefore you can" is implicitly understood. I can *become* sincere; this is what my duty and my effort to achieve sincerity imply. But we definitely establish that the original structure of "not being what one is" renders impossible in advance all movement toward being in itself or "being what one is." And this impossibility is not hidden from consciousness; on the contrary, it is the very stuff of consciousness; it is the embarrassing constraint which we constantly experience; it is our very incapacity to recognize ourselves, to constitute ourselves as being what we are. It is this necessity which means that, as soon as we posit ourselves as a certain being, by a legitimate judgment, based on inner experience or correctly deduced from a *priori* or empirical premises, then by that very positing we surpass this being—and that not toward another being but toward emptiness, toward *nothing*.

How then can we blame another for not being sincere or rejoice in our own sincerity since this sincerity appears to us at the same time to be impossible? How can we in conversation, in confession, in introspection, even attempt sincerity since the effort will be by its very nature be doomed to failure and since at the very time when we announce it we have a prejudicative comprehension of its futility? In introspection I try to determine exactly what I am, to make up my mind to be my true self without delay—even though it means consequently to set about searching for ways to change myself. But what does this mean if not that I am constituting myself as a thing? Shall I determine the ensemble of purposes and motivations which have pushed me to do this or that action? But this is already to postulate a causal determinism which constitutes the flow of my states of consciousness as a succession of physical states. Shall I uncover in myself "drives," even though it be to affirm them in shame? But is this not deliberately to forget that these drives are realized with my consent, that they are not forces of nature but that I lend them their efficacy by a perpetually renewed decision concerning their value. Shall I pass judgment on my character, on my nature? Is this not to veil from myself at that moment what I know only too well, that I thus judge a past to which by definition my present is not subject? The proof of this is that the same man who in sincerity posits that he is what in actuality he was, is indignant at the reproach of another and tries to disarm it by asserting that he can no longer be what he was. We are readily astonished and upset when the penalties of the court affect a man who in his new freedom *is no longer* the guilty person he was. But at the same time we require of this man that he recognize himself as *being* this guilty one. What then is sincerity except precisely a phenomenon of bad faith? Have we not shown indeed that in bad faith human reality is constituted as a being which is what it is not and which is not what it is?

Let us take an example: A homosexual frequently has an intolerable feeling of guilt, and his whole existence is determined in relation to this feeling. One will readily foresee that he is in bad faith. In fact it frequently happens that this man, while recognizing his homosexual inclination, while avowing each and every particular misdeed which he has committed, refuses with all his strength to consider himself "*a paederast*." His case is always "different," peculiar; there enters into it something of a game, of chance, of bad luck; the mistakes are all in the past; they are explained by a certain conception of the beautiful which women can not satisfy; we should see in them the results of a restless search, rather than the manifestations of a deeply rooted tendency, etc., etc. Here is assuredly a man in bad faith who borders on the comic since, acknowledging all the facts which are imputed to him, he refuses to draw from them the conclusion which they impose. His friend, who is his most severe critic, becomes irritated with this duplicity. The critic asks only one thing—and perhaps then he will show himself indulgent: that the guilty one recognize himself as guilty, that the homosexual declare frankly—whether humbly or boastfully matters little—"I am a paederast." We ask here: Who is in bad faith? The homosexual or the champion of sincerity?

The homosexual recognizes his faults, but he struggles with all his strength against the crushing view that his mistakes constitute for him a *destiny*. He does not wish to let himself be considered as a thing. He has an obscure but strong feeling that an homosexual is not an homosexual as this table is a table or as this red-haired man is red-haired. It seems to him that he has escaped from each mistake as soon as he has posited it and recognized it; he even feels that the psychic duration by itself cleanses him from each misdeed, constitutes for him an undetermined future, causes him to be born anew. Is he wrong? Does he not recognize in himself the peculiar, irreducible character of human reality? His attitude includes then an undeniable comprehension of truth. But at the same time he needs this perpetual rebirth, this constant escape in order to live; he must constantly put himself beyond reach in order to avoid the terrible judgment of collectivity. Thus he plays on the word *being*. He would be right actually if he understood the phrase, "I am not a paederast" in the sense of "I am not what I am." That is, if he declared to himself, "To the extent that a pattern of conduct is defined as the conduct of a paederast and to the extent that I have adopted this conduct, I am a paederast. But to the extent that human reality can not be finally defined by patterns of conduct, I am not one." But instead he slides surreptitiously towards a different connotation of the word "being." He understands "not being" in the sense of "not-being-in-itself." He lays claim to "not being a paederast" in the sense in which this table *is not* an inkwell.He is in bad faith.

But the champion of sincerity is not ignorant of the transcendence of human reality, and he knows how at need to appeal to it for his own advantage. He makes use of it even and brings it up in the present argument. Does he not wish, first in the name of sincerity, then of freedom, that the homosexual reflect on himself and acknowledge himself as an homosexual? Does he not let the other understand that such a confession will win indulgence for him? What does this mean if not that the man who will acknowledge himself as an homosexual will no longer be the same as the homosexual whom he acknowledges being and that he will escape into the region of freedom and of good will? The critic asks the man then to be what he is in order no longer to be what he is. It is the profound meaning of the saying, "A sin confessed is half pardoned." The critic demands of the guilty one that he constitute himself as a thing, precisely in order no longer to treat him as a thing. And this contradiction is constitutive of the demand of sincerity. Who can not see how offensive to the Other and how reassuring for me is a statement such as, "He's just a paederast," which removes a disturbing freedom from a trait and which aims at henceforth constituting all the acts of the Other as consequences following strictly from his essence. That is actually what the critic is demanding of his victim—that he constitute himself as a thing, that he should entrust his freedom to his friend as a fief, in order that the friend should return it to him subsequently—like a suzerain to his vassal. The champion of sincerity is in bad faith to the degree that in order to reassure himself, he pretends to judge, to the extent that he demands that freedom as freedom constitute itself as a thing. We have here only one episode in that battle to the death of consciousnesses which Hegel calls "the relation of the master and the slave." A person appeals to another and demands that in the name of his nature as consciousness he should radically destroy himself as consciousness, but while making this appeal he leads the other to hope for a rebirth beyond this destruction.

Very well, someone will say, but our man is abusing sincerity, playing one side against the other. We should not look for sincerity in the relation of the *Mit-sein* but rather where it is pure—in the relations of a person with himself. But who can not see that objective sincerity is constituted in the same way? Who can not see that the sincere man constitutes himself as a thing in order to escape the condition of a thing by the same act of sincerity? The man who confesses that he is evil has exchanged his disturbing "freedom-for-evil" for an inanimate character of evil; he *is* evil, he clings to himself, he is what he is. But by the same stroke, he escapes from that *thing*, since it is he who contemplates it, since it depends on him to maintain it under his glance or to let it collapse in an infinity of particular acts. He derives a *merit* from his sincerity, and the deserving man is not the evil man as he is evil but as he is beyond his evilness. At the same time the evil is disarmed since it is nothing, save on the plane of determinism, and since in confessing it, I posit my freedom in respect to it; my future is virgin; everything is allowed to me.

Thus the essential structure of sincerity does not differ from that of bad faith since the sincere man constitutes himself as what he is *in order not to be it.* This explains the truth recognized by all that one can fall into bad faith through being sincere. As Valéry pointed out, this is the case with Stendhal. Total, constant sincerity as a constant effort to adhere to oneself is by nature a constant effort to dissociate oneself from oneself. A person frees himself from himself by the very act by which he makes himself an object for himself. To draw up a perpetual inventory of what one is means constantly to redeny oneself and to take refuge in a sphere where one is no longer anything but a pure, free regard. The goal of bad faith, as we said, is to put oneself out of reach; it is an escape. Now we see that we must use the same terms to define sincerity. What does this mean?

In the final analysis the goal of sincerity and the goal of bad faith are not so different. To be sure, there is a sincerity which bears on the past and which does not concern us here; I am sincere if I confess *having had* this pleasure or that intention. We shall see that if this sincerity is possible, it is because in his fall into the past, the being of man is constituted as a being-in-itself. But here our concern is only with the sincerity which aims at itself in present immanence. What is its goal? To bring me to confess to myself what I am in order that I may finally coincide with my being; in a word, to cause myself to be, in the mode of the in-itself, what I am in the mode of "not being what I am." Its assumption is that fundamentally I am already, in the mode of the in-itself, what I have to be. Thus we find at the base of sincerity a continual game of mirror and reflection, a perpetual passage from the being which is what it is, to the being which is not what it is and inversely from the being which is not what it is to the being which is what it is. And what is the goal of bad faith? To cause me to be what I am, in the mode of "not being what one is," or not to be what I am in the mode of "being what one is." We find here the same game of mirrors. In fact in order for me to have an intention of sincerity, I must at the outset simultaneously be and not be what I am. Sincerity does not assign to me a mode of being or a particular quality, but in relation to that quality it aims at making me pass from one mode of being to another mode of being. This second mode of being, the ideal of sincerity, I am prevented by nature from attaining; and at the very moment when I struggle to attain it, I have a vague prejudicative comprehension that I shall not attain it. But all the same, in order for me to be able to conceive an intention in bad faith, I must have such a nature that within my being I escape from my being. If I were sad or cowardly in the way in which this inkwell is an inkwell, the possibility of bad faith could not even be conceived. Not only should I be unable to escape from my being; I could not even imagine that I could escape from it. But if bad faith is possible by virtue of a simple project, it is because so far as my being is concerned, there is no difference between being and non-being if I am cut off from my project.

Bad faith is possible only because sincerity is conscious of missing its goal inevitably, due to its very nature. I can try to apprehend myself as "*not being cowardly,*" when I am so, only on condition that the "being cowardly" is itself "in question" at the very moment when it exists, on condition that it is itself *one* question, that at the very moment when I wish to apprehend it, it escapes me on all sides and annihilates itself. The condition under which I can attempt an effort in bad faith is that in one sense, I am not this coward which I do not wish to be. But if I were not cowardly in the simple mode of not-being-what-one-is-not, I would be "in good faith" by declaring that I am not cowardly. Thus this inapprehensible coward is evanescent; in order for me not to be cowardly, I must in some way also be cowardly. That does not mean that I must be "a little" cowardly, in the sense that "a little" signifies "to a certain degree cowardly—and not cowardly to a certain degree." No. I must at once both be and not be totally and in all respects a coward. Thus in this case bad faith requires that I should not be what I am; that is, that there be an imponderable difference separating being from non-being in the mode of being of human reality.

But bad faith is not restricted to denying the qualities which I possess, to not seeing the being which I am. It attempts also to constitute myself as being what I am not. It apprehends me positively as courageous when I am not so. And that is possible, once again, only if I am what I am not; that is, if non-being in me does not have being even as non-being. Of course necessarily I *am not* courageous; otherwise bad faith would not be *bad* faith. But in addition my effort in bad faith must include the ontological comprehension that even in my usual being what I *am*, I am not it really and that there is no such difference between the being of "being-sad," for example—which I am in the mode of not being what I am—and the "non-being" of not-being-courageous which I wish to hide from myself. Moreover it is particularly requisite that the very negation of being should be itself the object of a perpetual nihilation, that the very meaning of "non-being" be perpetually in question in human reality. If I were not courageous in the way in which this inkwell is not a table; that is, if I were isolated in my cowardice, propped firmly against it, incapable of putting it in relation to its opposite, if I were not capable of *determining* myself as cowardly—that is, to deny courage to myself and thereby to escape my cowardice in the very moment that I posit it—if it were not on principle *impossible* for me to coincide with my *not-being-courageous* as well as with my being-courageous—then any project of bad faith would be prohibited me. Thus in order for bad faith to be possible, sincerity itself must be in bad faith. The condition of the possibility for bad faith is that human reality, in its most immediate being, in the intrastructure of the pre-reflective *cogito,* must be what it is not and not be what it is.

III. The "Faith" of Bad Faith

We have indicated for the moment only those conditions which render bad faith conceivable, the structures of being which permit us to form concepts of bad faith. We can not limit ourselves to these considerations; we have not yet distinguished bad faith from falsehood. The two-faced concepts which we have described would without a doubt be utilized by a liar to discountenance his questioner, although their two-faced quality being established on the being of a man and not on some empirical circumstance, can and ought to be evident to all. The true problem of bad faith stems evidently from the fact that bad faith is *faith.* It can not be either a cynical lie or certainty—if certainty is the intuitive possession of the object. But if we take belief as meaning the adherence of being to its object when the object is not given or is given indistinctly, then bad faith is belief; and the essential problem of bad faith is a problem of belief.

How can we believe by bad faith in the concepts which we forge expressly to persuade ourselves? We must note in fact that the project of bad faith must be itself in bad faith. I am not only in bad faith at the end of my effort when I have constructed my two-faced concepts and when I have persuaded myself. In truth, I have not persuaded myself; to the extent that I could be so persuaded, I have always been so. And at the very moment when I was disposed to put myself in bad faith, I of necessity was in bad faith with respect to this same disposition. For me to have represented it to myself as bad faith would have been cynicism; to believe it sincerely innocent would have been in good faith. The decision to be in bad faith does not dare to speak its name; it believes itself and does not believe itself in bad faith; it believes itself and does not believe itself in good faith. It is this which from the upsurge of bad faith, determines the later attitude and, as it were, the *Weltanschauung* of bad faith.

Bad faith does not hold the norms and criteria of truth as they are accepted by the critical thought of good faith. What it decides first, in fact, is the nature of truth. With bad faith a truth appears, a method of thinking, a type of being which is like that of objects; the ontological characteristic of the world of bad faith with which the subject suddenly surrounds himself is this: that here being is what it is not, and is not what it is. Consequently a peculiar type of evidence appears; *non-persuasive* evidence. Bad faith apprehends evidence but it is resigned in advance to not being fulfilled by this evidence, to not being persuaded and transformed into good faith. It makes itself humble and modest; it is not ignorant, it says, that faith is decision and that after each intuition, it must decide and *will what it is.* Thus bad faith in its primitive project and in its coming into the world decides on the exact nature of its requirement. It stands forth in the firm resolution *not to demand too much,* to count itself satisfied when it is barely persuaded, to force itself in decisions to adhere to uncertain truths. This original project of bad faith is a decision in bad faith on the nature of faith. Let us understand clearly that there is no question of a reflective, voluntary decision, but of a spontaneous determination of our being. One *puts oneself* in bad faith as one goes to sleep and one is in bad faith as one dreams. Once this mode of being has been realized, it is as difficult to get out of it as to wake oneself up; bad faith is a type of being in the world, like waking or dreaming, which by itself tends to perpetuate itself, although its structure is of the *metastable* type. But bad faith is conscious of its structure, and it has taken precautions by deciding that the metastable structure is the structure of being and that non-persuasion is the structure of all convictions. It follows that if bad faith is faith and if it includes in its original project its own negation (it determines itself to be not quite convinced in order to convince itself that I am what I am not), then to start with, a faith which wishes itself to be not quite convinced must be possible. What are the conditions for the possibility of such a faith?

I believe that my friend Pierre feels friendship for me. I believe it in *good faith*. I believe it but I do not have for it any self-evident intuition, for the nature of the object does not lend itself to intuition. I *believe it*; that is, I allow myself to give into all impulses to trust it; I decide to believe in it, and to maintain myself in this decision; I conduct myself, finally, as if I were certain of it—and all this in the synthetic unity of one and the same attitude. This which I define as good faith is what Hegel would call the *immediate*. It is simple faith. Hegel would demonstrate at once that the immediate calls for mediation and that belief by becoming *belief for itself*, passes to the state of non-belief. If I *believe* that my friend Pierre likes me, this means that his friendship appears to me as the meaning of all his acts. Belief is a particular consciousness of *the meaning* of Pierre's acts. But if I know that I believe, the belief appears to me as pure subjective determination without external correlative. This is what makes the very word "to believe" a term utilized indifferently to indicate the unwavering firmness of belief ("My God, I believe in you") and its character as disarmed and strictly subjective ("Is Pierre my friend? I do not know; I believe so.") But the nature of consciousness is such that in it the mediate and the immediate are one and the same being. To believe is to know that one believes, and to know that one believes is no longer to believe. Thus to believe is not to believe any longer because that is only to believe—this in the unity of one and the same non-thetic self-consciousness. To be sure, we have here forced the description of the phenomenon by designating it with the word to *know*; non-thetic consciousness is not to *know*. But it is in its very translucency at the origin of all knowing. Thus the non-thetic consciousness (of) believing is destructive of belief. But at the same time the very law of the pre-reflective *cogito* implies that the being of believing ought to be the consciousness of believing.

Thus belief is a being which questions its own being, which can realize itself only in its destruction, which can manifest itself to itself only by denying itself. It is a being for which to be is to appear and to appear is to deny itself. To believe is not-to-believe. We see that reason for it; the being of consciousness is to exist by itself, then to make itself be and thereby to pass beyond itself. In this sense consciousness is perpetually escaping itself, belief becomes non-belief, the immediate becomes mediation, the absolute becomes relative, and the relative becomes absolute. The ideal of good faith (to believe what one believes) is, like that of sincerity (to be what one is), an ideal of being-in-itself. Every belief is a belief that falls short; one never wholly believes what one believes. Consequently the primitive project of bad faith is only the utilization of this self-destruction of the fact or consciousness. If every belief in good faith is an impossible belief, then there is a place for every impossible belief. My inability to *believe* that I am courageous will not discourage me since every belief involves not quite believing. I shall define this impossible belief as *my* belief. To be sure, I shall not be able to hide from myself that I believe in order not to believe and that I do not believe *in order to* believe. But the subtle, total annihilation of bad faith by itself can not surprise me; it exists at the basis of all faith. What is it then? At the moment when I wish to believe myself courageous I *know* that I am a coward. And this certainly would come to destroy my belief. But *first*, I *am* not any more courageous than cowardly, if we are to understand this in the mode of being of the-in-itself. In the second place, I do not *know* that I am courageous; such a view of myself can be accompanied only by *belief*, for it surpasses pure reflective certitude. In the third place, it is very true that bad faith does not succeed in believing what it wishes to believe. But it is precisely as the acceptance of not believing what it believes that it is bad faith. Good faith wishes to flee the "not-believing-what-one-believes" by finding refuge in being. Bad faith flees being by taking refuse in "not-believing-what-one-believes." It has disarmed all beliefs in advance—those which it would like to take hold of and, by the same stroke, the others, those which it wishes to flee. In *willing* this self-destruction of belief, from which science escapes by searching for evidence, it ruins the beliefs which are opposed to it, which reveal themselves as *being only* belief. Thus we can better understand the original phenomenon of bad faith.

In bad faith there is no cynical lie nor knowing preparation for deceitful concepts. But the first act of bad faith is to flee what it can not flee, to flee what it is. The very project of flight reveals to bad faith an inner disintegration in the heart of being, and it is this disintegration which bad faith wishes to be. In truth, the two immediate attitudes which we can take in the face of our being are conditioned by the very nature of this being and its immediate relation with the in-itself. Good faith seeks to flee the inner disintegration of my being in the direction of the in-itself which it should be and is not. Bad faith seeks to flee the in-itself by means of the inner disintegration of my being. But it denies this very disintegration as it denies that it is itself bad faith. Bad faith seeks by means of "not-being-what-one is" to escape from the in-itself which I am not in the mode of being what one is not. It denies itself as bad faith and aims at the in-itself which I am not in the mode of "not-being-what-one-is not."[2] If bad faith is possible, it is because it is an immediate, permanent threat to every project of the human being; it is because consciousness conceals in its being a permanent risk of bad faith. The origin of this risk is the fact that the nature of conscious simultaneously is to be what it is not and not to be what it is. In the light of these remarks we can now approach the ontological study of consciousness, not as the totality of the human being, but as the instantaneous nucleus of this being.

2. If it is indifferent whether one is in good or in bad faith, because bad faith reapprehends good faith and slides to the very origin of the project of good faith, that does not mean that we can not radically escape bad faith. But this supposes a self-recovery of being which was previously corrupted. This self-recovery we shall call authenticity, the description of which has no place here.

Existentialism and Humanism

What is meant by the term *existentialism*?

Most people who use the word would be rather embarrassed if they had to explain it, since, now that the word is all the rage, even the work of a musician or painter is being called existentialist. . . . It seems that for want of an advance-guard doctrine analogous to surrealism, the kind of people who are eager for scandal and flurry turn to this philosophy which in other respects does not at all serve their purposes in this sphere.

Actually, it is the least scandalous, the most austere of doctrines. It is intended strictly for specialists and philosophers. Yet it can be defined easily. What complicates matters is that there are two kinds of existentialists; first, those who are Christian, among whom I would include Jaspers and Gabriel Marcel, both Catholic; and on the other hand, the atheistic existentialists, among whom I class Heidegger, and then the French existentialists and myself. What they have in common is that they think that existence precedes essence, or, if you prefer, that subjectivity must be the starting point.

Just what does that mean? Let us consider some object that is manufactured, for example, a book or paper-cutter: here is an object which has been made by an artisan whose inspiration came from a concept. He referred to the concept of what a paper-cutter is and likewise to a known method of production, which is part of the concept, something which is, by and large, a routine. Thus, the paper-cutter is at once an object produced in a certain way and, on the other hand, one having a specific use; and one cannot postulate a man who produces a paper-cutter but does not know what it is used for. Therefore, let us say that, for the paper-cutter, essence—that is, the ensemble of both the production routines and the properties which enable it to be both produced and defined—precedes existence. Thus, the presence of the paper-cutter or book in front of me is determined. Therefore, we have here a technical view of the world whereby it can be said that production precedes existence.

When we conceive God as the Creator, He is generally thought of as a superior sort of artisan. Whatever doctrine we may be considering, whether one like that of Descartes or that of Leibnitz, we always

Reprinted from Jean Paul Sartre, *Existentialism,* translated by Bernard Frechtman (1947) by permission of Philosophical Library.

grant that will more or less follows understanding or, at the very least, accompanies it, and that when God creates He knows exactly what He is creating. Thus, the concept of man in the mind of God is comparable to the concept of paper-cutter in the mind of the manufacturer, and, following certain techniques and a conception, God produces man, just as the artisan, following a definition and a technique, makes a paper-cutter. Thus, the individual man is the realization of a certain concept in the divine intelligence.

In the eighteenth century, the atheism of the *philosophes* discarded the idea of God, but not so much for the notion that essence precedes existence. To a certain extent, this idea is found everywhere; we find it in Diderot, in Voltaire, and even in Kant. Man has a human nature; this human nature, which is the concept of the human, is found in all men, which means that each man is a particular example of a universal concept, man. In Kant, the result of this universality is that the wild-man, the natural man, as well as the bourgeois, are circumscribed by the same definition and have the same basic qualities. Thus, here too the essence of man precedes the historical existence that we find in nature.

Atheistic existentialism, which I represent, is more coherent. It states that if God does not exist, there is at least one being in whom existence precedes essence, a being who exists before he can be defined by any concept, and that this being is man, or, as Heidegger says, human reality. What is meant here by saying that existence precedes essence? It means that, first of all, man exists, turns up, appears on the scene, and, only afterwards, defines himself. If man, as the existentialist conceives him, is indefinable, it is because at first he is nothing. Only afterward will he be something, and he himself will have made what he will be. Thus, there is no human nature, since there is no God to conceive it. Not only is man what he conceives himself to be, but he is also only what he wills himself to be after this thrust toward existence.

Man is nothing else but what he makes of himself. Such is the first principle of existentialism. It is also what is called subjectivity, the name we are labeled with when charges are brought against us. But what do we mean by this, if not that man has a greater dignity than a stone or table? For we mean that man first exists, that is, that man first of all is the being in the future. Man is at the start a plan which is aware of itself, rather than a patch of moss, a piece of garbage, or a cauliflower; nothing exists prior to this plan; there is nothing in heaven; man will be what he will have planned to be. Not what he will want to be. Because by the word "will" we generally mean a conscious decision, which is subsequent to what we have already made of ourselves. I may want to belong to a political party, write a book, get married; but all that is only a manifestation of an earlier, more spontaneous choice that is called "will." But if existence really does precede essence, man is responsible for what he is. Thus, existentialism's first move is to make every man aware of what he is and to make the full responsibility of his existence rest on him. And when we say that a man is responsible for himself, we do not only mean that he is responsible for his own individuality, but that he is responsible for all men.

The word subjectivism has two meanings, and our opponents play on the two. Subjectivism means, on the one hand, that an individual chooses and makes himself; and, on the other, that it is impossible for man to transcend human subjectivity. The second of these is the essential meaning of existentialism. When we say that man chooses his own self, we mean that every one of us does likewise; but we also mean by that that in making this choice he also chooses all men. In fact, in creating the man that we want to be, there is not a single one of our acts which does not at the same time create an image of man as we think he ought to be. To choose to be this or that is to affirm at the same time the value of what we choose, because we can never choose evil. We always choose the good, and nothing can be good for us without being good for all.

If, on the other hand, existence precedes essence, and if we grant that we exist and fashion our image at one and the same time, the image is valid for everybody and for our whole age. Thus, our responsibility is much greater than we might have supposed, because it involves all mankind. If I am a workingman and choose to join a Christian trade-union rather than be a communist, and if by being a member I want to show that the best thing for man is resignation, that the kingdom of man is not of this world, I am not only involving my own case—I want to be resigned for everyone. As a result, my action has involved all humanity. To take a more individual matter, if I want to marry, to have children; even if this marriage depends solely on my own circumstances or passion or wish, I am involving all humanity in monogamy and not merely myself. Therefore, I an responsible for myself and for everyone else. I am creating a certain image of man of my own choosing. In choosing myself, I choose man.

This helps us understand what the actual content is of such rather grandiloquent words as anguish, forlornness, despair. As you will see, it's all quite simple.

First, what is meant by anguish? The existentialists say at once that man is anguish. What that means is this: the man who involves himself and who realizes that he is not only the person he chooses to be, but also a law-maker who is, at the same time, choosing all mankind as well as himself, cannot help escape the feeling of his total and deep responsibility. Of course, there are many people who are not anxious; but we claim that they are hiding their anxiety, that they are fleeing from it. Certainly, many people believe that when they do something, they themselves are the only ones involved, and when someone says to them, "What if everyone acted that way?" they shrug their shoulders and answer, "Everyone doesn't act that way." But really, one should always ask himself, "What would happen if everybody looked at things that way?" There is no escaping this disturbing thought except by a kind of double-dealing. A man who lies and makes excuses for himself by saying "not everybody does that," is someone with an uneasy conscience, because the act of lying implies that a universal value is conferred upon the lie.

Anguish is evident even when it conceals itself. This is the anguish that Kierkegaard called the anguish of Abraham. You know the story: an angel has ordered Abraham to sacrifice his son; if it really were an angel who has come and said, "You are Abraham, you shall sacrifice your son," everything would be all right. But everyone might first wonder, "Is it really an angel, and am I really Abraham? What proof do I have?" . . .

Now, I'm not being singled out as an Abraham, and yet at every moment I'm obliged to perform exemplary acts. For every man, everything happens as if all mankind had its eyes fixed on him and were guiding itself by what he does. And every man ought to say to himself, "Am I really the kind of man who has the right to act in such a way that humanity might guide itself by my actions?" And if he does not say that to himself, he is masking his anguish.

There is no question here of the kind of anguish which would lead to quietism, to inaction. It is a matter of a simple sort of anguish that anybody who has had responsibilities is familiar with. For example, when a military officer takes the responsibility for an attack and sends a certain number of men to death, he chooses to do so, and in the main he alone makes the choice. Doubtless, orders come from above, but they are too broad; he interprets them, and on this interpretation depend the lives of ten or fourteen or twenty men. In making a decision he cannot help having a certain anguish. All leaders know this anguish. That doesn't keep them from acting; on the contrary, it is the very condition of their action. For it implies that they envisage a number of possibilities, and when they choose one, they realize that it has value only because it is chosen. We shall see that this kind of anguish, which is the kind that existentialism describes, is explained, in addition, by a direct responsibility to the other men whom it involves. It is not a curtain separating us from action, but is part of action itself.

When we speak of forlornness, a term Heidegger was fond of, we mean only that God does not exist and that we have to face all the consequences of this. The existentialist is strongly opposed to a certain kind of secular ethics which would like to abolish God with the least possible expense. About 1880, some French teachers tried to set up a secular ethics which went something like this: God is a useless and costly hypothesis; we are discarding it, but meanwhile, in order for there to be an ethics, a society, a civilization, it is essential that certain values be taken seriously and that they be considered as having an *a priori* existence. It must be obligatory, *a priori,* to be honest, not to lie, not to beat your wife, to have children, etc., etc. So we're going to try a little device which will make it possible to show that values exist all the same, inscribed in a heaven of ideas, though otherwise God does not exist. In other words—and this, I believe, is the tendency of everything called reformism in France—nothing will be changed if God does not exist. We shall find ourselves with the same norms of honesty, progress, and humanism, and we shall have made of God an outdated hypothesis which will peacefully die off by itself.

The existentialist, on the contrary, thinks it very distressing that God does not exist, because all possibility of finding values in a heaven of ideas disappears along with Him; there can be no longer an *a priori* Good, since there is no infinite and perfect consciousness to think it. Nowhere is it written that the Good exists, that we must be honest, that we must not lie; because the fact is we are on a plane where there are only men. Dostoievsky said, "If God didn't exist, everything would be possible." That is the very starting point of existentialism. Indeed, everything is permissible if God does not exist, and as a result man is forlorn, because neither within him nor without does he find anything to cling to. He can't start making excuses for himself.

If existence really does precede essence, there is no explaining things away by reference to a fixed and given human nature. In other words, there is no determinism, man is free, man is freedom. On the other hand, if God does not exist, we find no values or commands to turn to which legitimize our conduct. So, in the bright realm of values, we have no excuse behind us, no justification before us. We are alone, with no excuses.

That is the idea I shall try to convey when I say that man is condemned to be free. Condemned, because he did not create himself, yet, in other respects is free; because, once thrown into the world, he is responsible for everything he does. The existentialist does not believe in the power of passion. He will never agree that a sweeping passion is a ravaging torrent which fatally leads a man to certain acts and is therefore an excuse. He thinks that man is responsible for his passion.

The existentialist does not think that man is going to help himself by finding in the world some omen by which to orient himself. Because he thinks that man will interpret the omen to suit himself. Therefore, he thinks that man, with no support and no aid, is condemned every moment to invent man. Ponge, in a very fine article, has said, "Man is the future of man." That's exactly it. But if it is taken to mean that this future is recorded in heaven, that God sees it, then it is false, because it would really no longer be a future. If it is taken to mean that, whatever a man may be, there is a future to be forged, a virgin future before him, then this remark is sound. But then we are forlorn.

To give you an example which will enable you to understand forlornness better, I shall cite the case of one of my students who came to see me under the following circumstances: his father was on bad terms with his mother, and, moreover, was inclined to be a collaborationist; his older brother had been killed in the German offensive of 1940, and the young man, with somewhat immature but generous feelings, wanted to avenge him. His mother lived alone with him, very much upset by the half-treason of her husband and the death of her older son; the boy was her only consolation.

The boy was faced with the choice of leaving for England and joining the Free French Forces—that is, leaving his mother behind—or remaining with his mother and helping her to carry on. He was fully aware that the woman lived only for him and that his going-off—and perhaps his death—would plunge her into despair. He was also aware that every act that he did for his mother's sake was a sure thing, in the sense that it was helping her to carry on, whereas every effort he made toward going off and fighting was an uncertain move which might run aground and prove completely useless; for example, on his way to England he might, while passing though Spain, be detained indefinitely in a Spanish camp; he might reach England or Algiers and be stuck in an office at a desk job. As a result, he was faced with two very different kinds of action: one, concrete, immediate, but concerning only one individual; the other concerned an incomparably vaster group, a national collectivity, but for that very reason was dubious, and might be interrupted en route. And, at the same time, he was wavering between two kinds of ethics. On the one hand, an ethics of sympathy, of personal devotion; on the other, a broader ethics, but one whose efficacy was more dubious. He had to choose between the two.

Who could help him choose? Christian doctrine? No. Christian doctrine says, "Be charitable, love your neighbor, take the more rugged path, etc., etc." But which is the more rugged path? Whom should he love as a brother? The fighting man or his mother? Which does the greater good, the vague act of fighting in a group, or the concrete one of helping a particular human being to go on living? Who can decide *a priori*? Nobody. No book of ethics can tell him. The Kantian ethics says, "Never treat any person as a means, but as an end." Very well, if I stay with my mother, I'll treat her as an end and not as a means; but by virtue of this very fact, I'm running the risk of treating the people around me who are fighting, as means; and, conversely, if I go to join those who are fighting, I'll be treating them as an end, and, by doing that, I run the risk of treating my mother as a means.

If values are vague, and if they are always too broad for the concrete and specific case that we are considering, the only thing left for us is to trust our instincts. That's what this young man tried to do; and when I saw him, he said, "In the end, feeling is what counts. I ought to choose whichever pushes me in one direction. If I feel that I love my mother enough to sacrifice everything else for her—my desire for vengeance, for action, for adventure—then I'll stay with her. If, on the contrary, I feel that my love for my mother isn't enough, I'll leave."

But how is the value of a feeling determined? What gives his feeling for his mother value? Precisely the fact that he remained with her. I may say that I like so-and-so well enough to sacrifice a certain amount of money for him, but I may say so only if I've done it. I may say, "I love my mother well enough to remain with her" if I have remained with her. The only way to determine the value of this affection is, precisely, to perform an act which confirms and defines it. But, since I require this affection to justify my act, I find myself caught in a vicious circle. . . .

As for despair, the term has a very simple meaning. It means that we shall confine ourselves to reckoning only with what depends upon our will, or on the ensemble of probabilities which make our action possible. When we want something, we always have to reckon with probabilities. I may be counting on the arrival of a friend. The friend is coming by rail or street-car; this supposes that the train will arrive on schedule, or that the street-car will not jump the track. I am left in the realm of possibility; but possibilities are to be reckoned with only to the point where my action comports with the ensemble of these possibilities, and no further. The moment the possibilities I am considering are not rigorously involved by my action, I ought to disengage myself from them, because no God, no scheme, can adapt the world and its possibilities to my will. When Descartes said, "Conquer yourself rather than the world," he meant essentially the same thing.

The Marxists to whom I have spoken reply, "You can rely on the support of others in your action, which obviously has certain limits because you're not going to live forever. That means: rely on both what others are doing elsewhere to help you, in China, in Russia, and what they will do later on, after your death, to carry on the action and lead it to its fulfillment, which will be the revolution. You even *have* to rely upon that, otherwise you're immortal." I reply at once that I will always rely on fellow fighters insofar as these comrades are involved with me in a common struggle, in the unity of a party or a group in which I can more or less make my weight felt; that is, one whose ranks I am in as a fighter and whose movements I am aware of at every moment. In such a situation, relying on the unity and will of the party is exactly like counting on the fact that the train will arrive on time or that the car won't jump the track. But, given that man is free and that there is no human nature for me to depend on, I cannot count on men whom I do not know by relying on human goodness or man's concern for the good of society. I don't know what will become of the Russian revolution; I may make an example of it to the extent that at the present time it is apparent that the proletariat plays a part in Russia that it plays in no other nation. But I can't swear that this will inevitably lead to a triumph of the proletariat. I've got to limit myself to what I see.

Given that men are free, and that tomorrow they will freely decide what man will be, I cannot be sure that, after my death, fellow fighters will carry on my work to bring it to its maximum perfection. Tomorrow, after my death, some men may decide to set up Facism, and the others may be cowardly and muddled enough to let them do it. Fascism will then be the human reality, so much the worse for us.

Actually, things will be as man will have decided they are to be. Does that mean that I should abandon myself to quietism? No. First, I should involve myself; then, act on the old saying, "Nothing ventured, nothing gained." Nor does it mean that I shouldn't belong to a party, but rather that I shall have no illusions and shall do what I can. For example, suppose I ask myself, "Will socialization, as such, ever come about?" I know nothing about it. All I know is that I'm going to do everything in my power to bring it about. Beyond that, I can't count on anything. Quietism is the attitude of people who say, "Let others do what I can't do." The doctrine I am presenting is the very opposite of quietism, since it declares, "There is no reality except in action." Moreover, it goes further, since it adds, "Man is nothing else than his plan; he exists only to the extent that he fulfills himself; he is, therefore, nothing else than the ensemble of his acts, nothing else than his life."

Chapter 40

A. J. AYER

Alfred Jules Ayer (1910–1989) was born in London, the son of immigrant parents. He attended Eton and Christ Church, Oxford University, where he studied under Gilbert Ryle. When he was twenty-six he traveled to Vienna to meet Moritz Schlick, the leader of the Vienna Circle, a group of Logical Positivits. On his return to Oxford he wrote his most famous book, *Language, Truth and Logic,* a selection of which is reprinted here. He later became a professor at University College, London University, before returning to Oxford in 1960 to take up the Wykeham Professorship of Logic, where he taught until a short time before his death in 1989. A lifelong atheist, he astounded the public several months before his death with a report of a mystical experience. His heart had stopped for four minutes, during which time "I was confronted by a red light, exceedingly bright, and also very painful, even when I turned away from it. I was aware that this light was responsible for the government of the universe."[1]

Ayer was England's most prominent Logical Positivist. That philosophy, which had its roots in Hume's empiricism, like Hume, rejected metaphysics as nonsense. Its driving idea was that for a sentence to be meaningful, it must be verifiable in principle by experience. So my statement that atoms exist, though not observable by human senses, could conceivably be, if we had instruments to bring them to human consciousness. We must be able somehow to point to it. But moral and theological statements cannot be verified. Statements such as "Telling the truth is good" or "Killing innocents is bad" can't be observed. That is, we can observe a lie or a killing, but we can't observe the "goodness" or "badness" which are predicated of these subject terms. Ayer would reduce the value sentences to emotive expressions, such as "Telling the truth—Hurrah!" and "Killing Innocents—Boo!" Theological assertions such as"God exists" are simply nonsense, since they fail to express the conditions under which one could verify such claims. In the selection given below Ayer sets forth to eliminate all metaphysical discourse.

FOR FURTHER READING

Achinstein, Peter and Stephen Barker. *The Legacy of Logical Positivism.* (Johns Hopkins Press, 1969).

Ashby, R. W. "Logical Positivism" in D. J. O'Connor, ed. *A Critical History of Western Philosophy.* (Free Press, 1964).

Ayer, A. J., ed. *Logical Positivism.* (Free Press, 1959).

Ayer, A. J. *Language, Truth and Logic.* (Dover, 1936).

Gower, Barry, ed. *Logical Positivism in Perspective: Essays on "Language, Truth and Logic."* (Croom Helm, 1987).

1. "What I Saw When I Was Dead . . ." *Spectator* July 16, 1988, reprinted in *The Philosophy of A. J. Ayer,* ed. L. E. Hahn (Open Court, 1992), p. 48.

Hahn, Lewis, ed. *The Philosophy of A. J. Ayer.* (Open Court, 1992).
Macdonald, Graham and Crispin Wright, eds. *Fact, Science and Morality: Essays on A. J. Ayer's "Language, Truth and Logic"* (Blackwell, 1987).

Language, Truth and Logic

PREFACE TO FIRST EDITION

The views which are put forward in this treatise derive from the doctrines of Bertrand Russell and Wittgenstein, which are themselves the logical outcome of the empiricism of Berkeley and David Hume. Like Hume, I divide all genuine propositions into two classes: those which, in his terminology, concern "relations of ideas," and those which concern "matters of fact." The former class comprises the *a priori* propositions of logic and pure mathematics, and these I allow to be necessary and certain only because they are analytic. That is, I maintain that the reason why these propositions cannot be confuted in experience is that they do not make any assertion about the empirical world, but simply record our determination to use symbols in a certain fashion. Propositions concerning empirical matters of fact, on the other hand, I hold to be hypotheses, which can be probable but never certain. And in giving an account of the method of their validation I claim also to have explained the nature of truth.

To test whether a sentence expresses a genuine empirical hypothesis, I adopt what may be called a modified verification principle. For I require of an empirical hypothesis, not indeed that it should be conclusively verifiable, but that some possible sense-experience should be relevant to the determination of its truth or falsehood. If a putative proposition fails to satisfy this principle, and is not a tautology, then I hold that it is metaphysical, and that, being metaphysical, it is neither true nor false but literally senseless. It will be found that much of what ordinarily passes for philosophy is metaphysical according to this criterion, and, in particular, that it can not be significantly assert that there is a non-empirical world of values, or that men have immortal souls, or that there is a transcendent God.

As for the propositions of philosophy themselves, they are held to be linguistically necessary, and so analytic. And with regard to the relationship of philosophy and empirical science, it is shown that the philosopher is not in a position to furnish speculative truths, which would, as it were, compete with the hypotheses of science, nor yet to pass *a priori* judgements upon the validity of scientific theories, but that his function is to clarify the propositions of science by exhibiting their logical relationships, and by defining the symbols which occur in them. Consequently I maintain that there is nothing in the nature of philosophy to warrant the existence of conflicting philosophical "schools." And I attempt to substantiate this by providing a definitive solution of the problems which have been the chief sources of controversy between philosophers in the past.

The view that philosophizing is an activity of analysis is associated in England with the work of G.E. Moore and his disciples. But while I have learned a great deal from Professor Moore, I have reason to believe that he and his followers are not prepared to adopt such a thoroughgoing phenomenalism as I do, and that they take a rather different view of the nature of philosophical analysis. The philosophers with whom I am in the closest agreement are those who compose the "Viennese circle," under the leadership of Moritz Schlick, and are commonly known as logical positivists. And of these I owe most to Rudolf Carnap. Further, I wish to acknowledge my indebtedness to Gilbert Ryle, my original tutor in philosophy, and to Isaiah Berlin, who have discussed with me every point in the argument of this treatise, and made many valuable suggestions, although they both disagree with much of what I assert. . . .

Reprinted from A. J. Ayer, *Language, Truth and Logic* (Dover Press, 1952) by permission of Dover Publications.

CHAPTER 1: THE ELIMINATION OF METAPHYSICS

The traditional disputes of philosophers are, for the most part, as unwarranted as they are unfruitful. The surest way to end them is to establish beyond question what should be the purpose and method of a philosophical enquiry. And this is by no means so difficult a task as the history of philosophy would lead one to suppose. For if there are any questions which science leaves it to philosophy to answer, a straightforward process of elimination must lead to their discovery.

We may begin by criticising the metaphysical thesis that philosophy affords us knowledge of a reality transcending the world of science and common sense. Later on, when we come to define metaphysics and account for its existence, we shall find that it is possible to be a metaphysician without believing in a transcendent reality; for we shall see that many metaphysical utterances are due to the commission of logical errors, rather than to a conscious desire on the part of their authors to go beyond the limits of experience. But it is convenient for us to take the case of those who believe that it is possible to have knowledge of a transcendent reality as a starting-point for our discussion. The arguments which we use to refute them will subsequently be found to apply to the whole of metaphysics.

One way of attacking a metaphysician who claimed to have knowledge of a reality which transcended the phenomenal world would be to enquire from what premises his propositions were deduced. Must he not begin, as other men do, with the evidence of his senses? And if so, what valid process of reasoning can possibly lead him to the conception of a transcendent reality? Surely from empirical premises nothing whatsoever concerning the properties, or even the existence, of anything super-empirical can legitimately be inferred. But this objection would be met by a denial on the part of the metaphysician that his assertions were ultimately based on the evidence of his senses. He would say that he was endowed with a faculty of intellectual intuition which enabled him to know facts that could not be known through sense-experience. And even if it could be shown that he was relying on empirical premises, and that his venture into a non-empirical world was therefore logically unjustified, it would not follow that the assertions which he made concerning this non-empirical world could not be true. For the fact that a conclusion does not follow from its putative premise is not sufficient to show that it is false. Consequently one cannot overthrow a system of transcendent metaphysics merely by criticising the way in which it comes into being. What is required is rather a criticism of the nature of the actual statements which comprise it. And this is the line of argument which we shall, in fact, pursue. For we shall maintain that no statement which refers to a "reality" transcending the limits of all possible sense-experience can possibly have any literal significance; from which it must follow that the labours of those who have striven to describe such a reality have all been devoted to the production of nonsense.

It may be suggested that this is a proposition which has already been proved by Kant. But although Kant also condemned transcendent metaphysics, he did so on different grounds. For he said that the human understanding was so constituted that it lost itself in contradictions when it ventured out beyond the limits of possible experience and attempted to deal with things in themselves. And thus he made the impossibility of a transcendent metaphysic not, as we do, a matter of logic, but a matter of fact. He asserted, not that our minds could not conceivably have had the power of penetrating beyond the phenomenal world, but merely that they were in fact devoid of it. And this leads the critic to ask how, if it is possible to know only what lies within the bounds of sense-experience, the author can be justified in asserting that real things do exist beyond, and how he can tell what are the boundaries beyond which the human understanding may not venture, unless he succeeds in passing them himself. As Wittgenstein says, "in order to draw a limit to thinking, we should have to think both sides of this limit,"[1] a truth to which Bradley gives a special twist in maintaining that the man who is ready to prove that metaphysics is impossible is a brother metaphysician with a rival theory of his own.[2]

Whatever force these objections may have against the Kantian doctrine, they have none whatsoever against the thesis that I am about to set forth. It cannot here be said that the author is himself overstepping the barrier he maintains to be impassable. For the fruitlessness of attempting to transcend the limits of possible sense-experience will be deduced, not

1. *Tractatus Logico-Philosophicus*, Preface.

2. Bradley, *Appearance and Reality*, 2nd ed., p. 1.

from a psychological hypothesis concerning the actual constitution of the human mind, but from the rule which determines the literal significance of language. Our charge against the metaphysician is not that he attempts to employ the understanding in a field where it cannot profitably venture, but that he produces sentences which fail to conform to the conditions under which alone a sentence can be literally significant. Nor are we ourselves obliged to talk nonsense in order to show that all sentences of a certain type are necessarily devoid of literal significance. We need only formulate the criterion which enables us to test whether a sentence expresses a genuine proposition about a matter of fact, and then point out that the sentences under consideration fail to satisfy it. And this we shall now proceed to do. We shall first of all formulate the criterion in somewhat vague terms, and then give the explanations which are necessary to render it precise.

The criterion which we use to test the genuineness of apparent statements of fact is the criterion of verifiability. We say that a sentence is factually significant to any given person, if, and only if, he knows how to verify the proposition which it purports to express—that is, if he knows what observations would lead them, under certain conditions, to accept the proposition as being true, or reject it as being false. If, on the other hand, the putative proposition is of such a character that the assumption of its truth, or falsehood, is consistent with any assumption whatsoever concerning the nature of his future experience, then, as far as he is concerned, it is, if not a tautology, a mere pseudoproposition. The sentence expressing it may be emotionally significant to him; but it is not literally significant. And with regard to questions the procedure is the same. We enquire in every case what observations would lead us to answer the question, one way or the other; and, if none can be discovered, we must conclude that the sentence under consideration does not, as far as we are concerned, express a genuine question, however strongly its grammatical appearance may suggest that it does.

As the adoption of this procedure is an essential factor in the argument of this book, it needs to be examined in detail.

In the first place, it is necessary to draw a distinction between practical verifiability, and verifiability in principle. Plainly we all understand, in many cases believe, propositions which we have not in fact taken steps to verify. Many of these are propositions which we could verify if we took enough trouble. But there remain a number of significant propositions, concerning matters of fact, which we could not verify even if we chose; simply because we lack the practical means of placing ourselves in the situation where the relevant observations could be made. A simple and familiar example of such a proposition is the proposition is the proposition that there are mountains on the farther side of the moon. No rocket has yet been invented which would enable me to go and look at the farther side of the moon, so that I am unable to decide the matter by actual observation. But I do know what observations would decide it for me, if, as is theoretically conceivable, I were once in a position to make them. And therefore I say that the proposition is verifiable in principle, if not in practice, and is accordingly significant. On the other hand, such a metaphysical pseudo-proposition as "the Absolute enters into, but is itself incapable of, evolution and progress," is not even in principle verifiable. For one cannot conceive of an observation which would enable one to determine whether the Absolute did, or did not, enter into evolution and progress. Of course it is possible that the author of such a remark is using English words in a way in which they are not commonly used by English-speaking people, and that he does, in fact, intend to assert something which could be empirically verified. But until he makes us understand how the proposition that he wishes to express would be verified, he fails to communicate anything to us. And if he admits, as I think the author of the remark in question would have admitted, that his words were not intended to express either a tautology or a proposition which was capable, at least in principle, of being verified, then it follows that he has made an utterance which has no literal significance even for himself.

A further distinction which we must make is the distinction between the "strong" and the "weak" sense of the term "verifiable." A proposition is said to be verifiable, in the strong sense of the term, if, and only if, its truth could be conclusively established in experience. But it is verifiable, in the weak sense, if it is possible for experience to render it probable. In which sense are we using the term when we say that a putative proposition is genuine only if it is verifiable?

It seems to me that if we adopt conclusive verifiability as our criterion of significance, as some positivists have proposed, our argument will prove too much. Consider, for example, the case of general propositions of law—such propositions, namely, as "arsenic is poisonous"; "all men are mortal"; "a body tends to expand when it is heated." It is of the very nature of these propositions that their truth cannot be established with certainty by any finite series of observations. But if it is recognised that such general propositions of law are designed to cover an infinite number of cases, then it must be admitted that they cannot, even in principle, be verified conclusively. And then, if we adopt conclusive verifiability as our criterion of significance, we are logically obligated to treat these general propositions of law in the same fashion as we treat the statements of the metaphysician.

In face of this difficulty, some positivists have adopted the heroic course of saying that these general propositions are indeed pieces of nonsense, albeit an essentially important type of nonsense. But here the introduction of the term "important" is simply an attempt to hedge. It serves only to mark the authors' recognition that their view is somewhat too paradoxical, without in any way removing the paradox. Besides, the difficulty is not confined to the case of general propositions of law, though it is there revealed most plainly. It is hardly less obvious in the case of propositions about the remote past. For it must surely be admitted that, however strong the evidence in favour of historical statements may be, their truth can never become more than highly probable. And to maintain that they also constituted an important, or unimportant, type of nonsense would be unplausible, to say the very least. Indeed, it will be our contention that no proposition, other than a tautology, can possibly be anything more than a probable hypothesis. And if this is correct, the principle that a sentence can be factually significant only if it expresses what is conclusively verifiable is self-stultifying as a criterion of significance. For it leads to the conclusion that it is impossible to make a significant statement of fact at all.

Nor can we accept the suggestion that a sentence should be allowed to be factually significant if, and only if, it expresses something which is definitely confutable by experience. Those who adopt this course assume that, although no finite series of observations is ever sufficient to establish the truth of a hypothesis beyond all possibility of doubt, there are crucial cases in which a single observation, or series of observations, can definitely confute it. But, as we shall show later on, this assumption is false. A hypothesis cannot be conclusively confuted any more than it can be conclusively verified. For when we take the occurrence of certain observation as proof that a given hypothesis is false, we presuppose the existence of certain conditions. And though, in any given case, it may be extremely improbable that this assumption is false, it is not logically impossible. We shall see that there need be no self-contradiction in holding that some of the relevant circumstances are other than we have taken them to be, and consequently that the hypothesis has not really broken down. And if it is not the case that any hypothesis can be definitely confuted, we cannot hold that the genuineness of a proposition depends on the possibility of its definite confutation.

Accordingly, we fall back on the weaker sense of verification. We say that the question that must be asked about any putative statement of fact is not, Would any observations make its truth or falsehood logically certain? but simply, Would any observations be relevant to the determination of its truth or falsehood? And it is only if a negative answer is given to this second question that we conclude that the statement under consideration is nonsensical.

To make our position clearer, we may formulate it in another way. Let us call a proposition which records an actual or possible observation an experiential proposition. Then we may say that it is the mark of a genuine factual proposition, not that it should be equivalent to an experiential proposition, or any finite number of experiential propositions, but simply that some experiential propositions can be deduced from it in conjunction with certain other premises without being deducible from those other premises alone.

This criterion seems liberal enough. In contrast to the principle of conclusive verifiability, it clearly does not deny significance to general propositions or to propositions about the past. Let us see what kinds of assertion it rules out.

A good example of the kind of utterance that is condemned by our criterion as being not even false but nonsensical would be the assertion that the world of sense-experience was altogether unreal. It must, of course, be admitted that our senses do sometimes deceive us. We may, as the result of having certain sensations, expect certain other sensations to be obtainable which are, in fact, not obtainable. But, in all such cases, it is further sense-experience that informs us of the mistakes that arise out of sense-experience. We say that the senses sometimes deceive us, just because the expectations to which our sense-experiences give rise do not always accord with what we subsequently experience. That is, we rely on our senses to substantiate or confute the judgements which are based on our sensations. And therefore the fact that our perceptual judgements are sometimes found to be erroneous has not the slightest tendency to show that the world of sense-experience is unreal. And, indeed, it is plain that no conceivable observation, or series of observations, could have any tendency to show that the world revealed to us by sense-experience was unreal. Consequently, anyone who condemns the sensible world as a world of mere appearance, as opposed to reality, is saying something which, according to our criterion of significance, is literally nonsensical.

An example of a controversy which the application of our criterion obliges us to condemn as fictitious is provided by those who dispute concerning the number of substances that there are in the world. For it is admitted both by monists, who maintain that reality is one substance, and by pluralists, who maintain that reality is many, that it is impossible to imagine any empirical situation which would be relevant to the solution of their dispute. But if we are told that no possible observation could give any probability either to the assertion that reality was one substance or to the assertion that it was many, then we must conclude that neither assertion is significant. We shall see later on that there are genuine logical and empirical questions involved in the dispute between monists and pluralists. But the metaphysical question concerning "substance" is ruled out by our criterion as spurious.

A similar treatment must be accorded to the controversy between realists and idealists, in its metaphysical aspect. A simple illustration, which I have made us of in a similar argument elsewhere, will help to demonstrate this. Let us suppose that a picture is discovered and the suggestion made that it was painted by Goya. There is a definite procedure for dealing with such a question. The experts examine the picture to see in what way it resembles the accredited works of Goya, and to see if it bears any marks which are characteristic of a forgery; they look up contemporary records for evidence of the existence of such a picture, and so on. In the end, they may still disagree, but each one knows what empirical evidence would go to confirm or discredit his opinion. Suppose, now, that these men have studied philosophy, and some of them proceed to maintain that this picture is a set of ideas in the perceiver's mind, or in God's mind, others that it is objectively real. What possible experience could any of them have which would be relevant to the solution of this dispute one way or the other? In the ordinary sense of the term "real," in which it is opposed to "illusory," the reality of the picture is not in doubt. The disputants have satisfied themselves that the picture is real, in this sense, by obtaining a correlated series of sensations of sight and sensations of touch. Is there any similar process by which they could discover whether the picture was real, in the sense in which the term "real" is opposed to "ideal"? Clearly there is none. But, if that is so, the problem is fictitious according to our criterion. This does not mean that the realist-idealist controversy may be dismissed without further ado. For it can legitimately be regarded as a dispute concerning the analysis of existential propositions, and so as involving a logical problem which, as we shall see, can be definitively solved. What we have just shown is that the question at issue between idealists and realists becomes fictitious when, as is often the case, it is given a metaphysical interpretation.

There is no need for us to give further examples of the operation of our criterion of significance. For our object is merely to show that philosophy, as a genuine branch of knowledge, must be distinguished from metaphysics. We are not now concerned with the historical question how much of what has traditionally passed for philosophy is actually metaphysical. We shall, however, point out later on that the majority of the "great philosophers" of the past were not essentially metaphysicians, and thus reassure those who would otherwise be prevented from adopting our criterion by considerations of piety.

As to the validity of the verification principle . . . it will be shown that all propositions which have factual content are empirical hypotheses; and that the function of an empirical hypothesis is to provide a rule for the anticipation of experience. And this means that every empirical hypothesis must be relevant to some actual, or possible, experience, so that a statement which is not relevant to any experience is not an empirical hypothesis, and accordingly has no factual content. But this is precisely what the principle of verifiability asserts.

It should be mentioned here that the fact that the utterances of the metaphysician are nonsensical does not follow simply from the fact that they are devoid of factual content. It follows from that fact, together with the fact that they are not *a priori* propositions. . . . *a priori* propositions, which have always been attractive to philosophers on account of their certainty, owe this certainty to the fact that they are tautologies. We may accordingly define a metaphysical sentence as a sentence which purports to express a genuine proposition, but does, in fact, express neither a tautology nor an empirical hypothesis. And as tautologies and empirical hypotheses form the entire class of significant propositions, we are justified in concluding that all metaphysical assertions are nonsensical. Our next task is to show how they come to be made.

The use of the term "substance," to which we have already referred, provides us with a good example of the way in which metaphysics mostly comes to be written. It happens to be the case that we cannot, in our language, refer to the sensible properties of a thing without introducing a word or phrase which appears to stand for the thing itself as opposed to anything which may be said about it. And, as a result of this, those who are infected by the primitive superstition that to every name a single real entity must correspond assume that it is necessary to distinguish logically between the thing itself and any, or all, of its sensible properties. And so they employ the term "substance" to refer to the thing itself. But from the fact that we happen to employ a single word to refer to a thing, and make that word the grammatical subject of the sentences in which we refer to the sensible appearances of the thing, it does not by any means follow that the thing itself is a "simple entity," or that it cannot be defined in terms of the totality of its appearances. It is true that in talking of "its" appearances we appear to distinguish the thing from the appearances, but that is simply an accident of linguistic usage. Logical analysis shows that what makes these "appearances" the "appearances of" the same thing is not their relationship to an entity other than themselves, but their relationship to one another. The metaphysician fails to see this because he is misled by a superficial grammatical feature of his language.

A simpler and clearer instance of the way in which a consideration of grammar leads to metaphysics is the case of the metaphysical concept of Being. The origin of our temptation to raise questions about Being, which no conceivable experience would enable us to answer, lies in the fact that, in our language, sentences which express existential propositions and sentences which express attributive propositions may be of the same grammatical form. For instance, the sentences "Martyrs exist" and "Martyrs suffer" both consist of a noun followed by an intransitive verb, and the fact that they have grammatically the same appearance leads one to assume that they are of the same logical type. It is seen that in the proposition "Martyrs suffer," the members of a certain species are credited with a certain attribute, and it is sometimes assumed that the same thing is true of such a proposition as "Martyrs exist." If this were actually the case, it would, indeed, be as legitimate to speculate about the Being of martyrs as it is to speculate about their suffering. But, as Kant pointed out, existence is not an attribute. For, when we ascribe an attribute to a thing, we covertly assert that it exists: so that if existence were itself an attribute, it would follow that all positive existential propositions were tautologies, and all negative existential propositions self-contradictory; and this is not the case. So that those who raise questions about Being which are based on the assumption that existence is an attribute are guilty of following grammar beyond the boundaries of sense.

A similar mistake has been made in connection with such propositions as "Unicorns are fictitious." Here again the fact that there is a superficial grammatical resemblance between the English sentences "Dogs are faithful" and "Unicorns are fictitious," and between the corresponding sentences in other languages, creates the assumption that they are of the same logical type. Dogs must exist in order to have the property of being faithful, and so it is held that unless unicorns in some way existed they could not have the property of being fictitious. But, as it is plainly self-contradictory to say that fictitious objects exist, the device is adopted of saying that they are real in some nonempirical sense—that they have a mode of real being which is different from the mode of being of existent things. But since there is no way of testing whether an object is real in this sense, as there is for testing whether it is real in the ordinary sense, the assertion that fictitious objects have a special non-empirical mode of real being is devoid of all literal significance. It comes to be made as a result of the assumption that being fictitious is an attribute. And this is a fallacy of the same order as the fallacy of supposing that existence is an attribute, and it can be exposed in the same way.

In general, the postulation of real non-existent entities results from the superstition, just now referred to, that, to every word or phrase that can be the grammatical subject of a sentence, there must somewhere be a real entity corresponding. For as there is no place in the empirical world for many of these "entities," a special non-empirical world is invoked to house them. To this error must be attributed, not only the utterances of a Heidegger, who bases his metaphysics on the assumption that "Nothing" is a name which is used to denote something peculiarly mysterious, but also the prevalence of such problems as those concerning the reality of propositions and universals whose senselessness, though less obvious, is no less complete.

These few examples afford a sufficient indication of the way in which most metaphysical assertions come to be formulated. They show how easy it is to write sentences which are literally nonsensical without seeing that they are nonsensical. And thus we see that the view that a number of the traditional "problems of philosophy" are metaphysical, and consequently fictitious, does not involve any incredible assumptions about the psychology of philosophers.

Among those who recognise that if philosophy is to be accounted a genuine branch of knowledge it must be defined in such a way as to distinguish it from metaphysics, it is fashionable to speak of the metaphysician as a kind of misplaced poet. As his statements have no literal meaning, they are not subject to any criteria of truth or falsehood: but they may still serve to express, or arouse, emotion, and thus be subject to ethical or aesthetic standards. And it is suggested that they may have considerable value, as means of moral inspiration, or even as works of art. In this way, an attempt is made to compensate the metaphysician for his extrusion from philosophy.

I am afraid that this compensation is hardly in accordance with his deserts. The view that the metaphysician is to be reckoned among the poets appears to rest on the assumption that both talk nonsense. But this assumption is false. In the vast majority of cases the sentences which are produced by poets do have literal meaning. The difference between the man who uses language scientifically and the man who uses it emotively is not that the one produces sentences which are incapable of arousing emotion, and the other sentences which have no sense, but that the one is primarily concerned with the expression of true propositions, the other with the creation of a work of art. Thus, if a work of science contains true and important propositions, its value as a work of science will hardly be diminished by the fact that they are inelegantly expressed. And similarly, a work of art is not necessarily the worse for the fact that all the propositions comprising it are literally false. But to say that many literary works are largely composed of falsehoods is not to say that they are composed of pseudo-propositions. It is, in fact, very rare for a literary artist to produce sentences which have no literal meaning. And where this does occur, the sentences are carefully chosen for their rhythm and balance. If the author writes nonsense, it is because he considers it most suitable for bringing about the effects for which his writing is designed.

The metaphysician, on the other hand, does not intend to write nonsense. He lapses into it through being deceived by grammar, or through committing errors of reasoning, such as that which leads the view that the sensible world is unreal. But it is not the mark of a poet simply to make mistakes of this sort. There are some, indeed, who would see in the fact that the metaphysician's utterances are senseless a reason against the view that they have aesthetic value. And, without going so far as this, we may safely say that it does not constitute a reason for it.

It is true, however, that although the greater part of metaphysics is merely the embodiment of humdrum errors, there remain a number of metaphysical passages which are the work of genuine mystical feeling; and they may more plausibly be held to have moral or aesthetic value. But, as far as we are concerned, the distinction between the kind of metaphysics that is produced by a philosopher who has been duped by grammar, and the kind that is produced by a mystic who is trying to express the inexpressible, is of no great importance: what is important to us is to realise that even the utterances of the metaphysician who is attempting to expound a vision are literally senseless; so that henceforth we may pursue our philosophical researches with as little regard for them as for the more inglorious kind of metaphysics which comes from a failure to understand the workings of our language.

Chapter 41

W. V. O. QUINE

Willard van Orman Quine was born in Akron, Ohio, in 1908, and attended Oberlin College, where he studied mathematics and philosophy. He did graduate work at Harvard University, receiving his PhD in 1934 at the age of twenty-five. Upon graduating he traveled to Austria, visited members of the Vienna Circle and came under the influence of Rudolf Carnap. Returning to the United States a year later, he began teaching at Harvard which he continued for over forty years until his retirement in 1978.

Quine argues against two fundamental theses of empiricism: the analytic—synthetic distinction and the belief that individual observation statements are the fundamental unit of meaning. In the first part of this essay, he seeks to undermine the distinction between analytic and synthetic statements that underlies both the Kantian project and contemporary empiricism. One version of the argument appeals to the notion of *containment*: the predicate term is contained in the subject. Quine contends that the notion of *containment* is a vague metaphor and that its vagueness spreads over the entire analytic—synthetic distinction. Furthermore, the concept of analyticity rests on the concept of synonymy, on having the same meaning. That is, if it is analytic that "A bachelor is an unmarried male" this is because the terms "bachelor" and "unmarried male" are already synonymous. But, Quine argues, to say that these terms are synonymous is to presuppose that they are analytic. Hence the argument is circular.

In the second part of this essay, Quine attacks the notion of radical reductionism, which is tied to the verification theory of meaning and assumes that individual observation statements are the basic unit of meaning. Quine rejects this atomistic view, holding instead a "pragmatic coherentism." That is, all our beliefs form a holistic web, so that individual statements are never confirmed or falsified in isolation but only with reference to the holistic web. The most successful system of beliefs is that of science because it allows us to make correct predictions. This workability of our belief system is the pragmatic aspect of epistemology.

FOR FURTHER READING

Davidson, Donald and Jaakko Hintikka, eds. *Words and Objections: Essays on the Work of W. V. Quine*. (Reidel, 1969).

Gibson, Roger. *The Philosophy of W. V. Quine*. (University of Florida, 1982).

Hahn, Lewis and P. A. Schilpp, eds. *The Philosophy of W. V. Quine*. (Open Court, 1986).

Hookway, Christopher. *Quine: Language, Experience, and Reality*. (Stanford University Press, 1988).

Orenstein, Alex. *Willard van Orman Quine*. (Twayne Publishers, 1977).

Quine, W. V. *From a Logical Point of View*. (Harvard University, 1958).

Quine, W. V. *Ontological Relativity*. (Columbia University Press, 0000).

Romanas, George. *Quine and Analytic Philosophy*. (MIT Press, 1983).

Two Dogmas of Empiricism

Modern empiricism has been conditioned in large part by two dogmas. One is a belief in some fundamental cleavage between truths which are *analytic*, or grounded in meanings independently of matters of fact, and truths which are *synthetic*, or grounded in fact. The other dogma is *reductionism*: the belief that each meaningful statement is equivalent to some logical construct upon terms which refer to immediate experience. Both dogmas, I shall argue, are ill-founded. One effect of abandoning them is, as we shall see, a blurring of the supposed boundary between speculative metaphysics and natural science. Another effect is a shift toward pragmatism.

I. BACKGROUND FOR ANALYTICITY

Kant's cleavage between analytic and synthetic truths was foreshadowed in Hume's distinction between relations of ideas and matters of fact, and in Leibniz's distinction between truths of reason and truths of fact. Leibniz spoke of the truths of reason as true in all possible worlds. Picturesqueness aside, this is to say that the truths of reason are those which could not possibly be false. In the same vein we hear analytic statements defined as statements whose denials are self-contradictory. But this definition has small explanatory value; for the notion of self-contradictoriness, in the quite broad sense needed for this definition of analyticity, stands in exactly the same need of clarification as does the notion of analyticity itself. The two notions are the two sides of a single dubious coin.

Kant conceived of an analytic statement as one that attributes to its subject no more than is already conceptually contained in the subject. This formulation has two shortcomings: it limits itself to statements of subject-predicate form, and it appeals to a notion of containment which is left at a metaphorical level. But Kant's intent, evident more from the use he makes of the notion of analyticity than from his definition of it, can be restated thus: a statement is analytic when it is true by virtue of meanings and independently of fact. Pursuing this line, let us examine the concept of *meaning* which is presupposed.

Meaning, let us remember, is not to be identified with naming. Frege's example of 'Evening Star' and 'Morning Star', and Russell's of 'Scott' and 'the author of *Waverley*', illustrate that terms can name the same thing but differ in meaning. The distinction between meaning and naming is no less important at the level of abstract terms. The terms '9' and 'the number of the planets' name one and the same abstract entity but presumably must be regarded as unlike in meaning; for astronomical observation was needed, and not mere reflection on meanings, to determine the sameness of the entity in question.

The above examples consist of singular terms, concrete and abstract. With general terms, or predicates, the situation is somewhat different but parallel. Whereas a singular term purports to name an entity, abstract or concrete, a general term does not; but a general term is *true* of an entity, or of each of many, or of none. The class of all entities of which a general term is true is called the *extension* of the term. Now paralleling the contrast between the meaning of a singular term and the entity named, we must distinguish equally between the meaning of a general term and its extension. The general terms 'creature with a heart' and 'creature with kidneys', for example, are perhaps alike in extension but unlike in meaning.

Confusion of meaning with extension, in the case of general terms, is less common than confusion of meaning with naming in the case of singular terms. It is indeed a commonplace in philosophy to oppose intension (or meaning) to extension, or, in a variant vocabulary, connotation or denotation.

The Aristotelian notion of essence was the forerunner, no doubt, of the modern notion of intension or meaning. For Aristotle it was essential in men to be rational, accidental to be two-legged. But there is an important difference between this attitude and the doctrine of meaning. From the latter point of view it may indeed be conceded (if only for the sake of argument) that rationality is involved in the meaning of the word 'man' while two-leggedness is not; but two-leggedness may at the same time be viewed as involved in the meaning of 'biped' while rationality is not. Thus from the point of view of the doctrine of meaning it makes no sense to say of the actual individual, who is at once a man and a biped, that his rationality is essential and his two-leggedness accidental or vice versa. Things had essences, for Aristotle, but only linguistic forms have meanings. Meaning is what essence becomes when it is divorced from the object of reference and wedded to the word.

For the theory of meaning a conspicuous question is the nature of its objects: what sort of things are meanings? A felt need for meant entities may derive from an earlier failure to appreciate that meaning and reference are distinct. Once the theory of meaning is sharply separated from the theory of reference, it is a short step to recognizing as the primary business of the theory of meaning simply the synonymy of linguistic forms and the analyticity of statements; meanings themselves, as obscure intermediary entities, may well be abandoned.

The problem of analyticity then confronts us anew. Statements which are analytic by general philosophical acclaim are not, indeed, far to seek. They fall into two classes. Those of the first class, which may be called *logically true*, are typified by:

(1) No unmarried man is married.

The relevant feature of this example is that it not merely is true as it stands, but remains true under any and all reinterpretations of 'man' and 'married.' If we suppose a prior inventory of *logical* particles, comprising 'no', 'un-', 'not', 'if', 'then', 'and', etc., then in general a logical truth is a statement which is true and remains true under all reinterpretations of its components other than the logical particles.

But there is also a second class of analytic statements, typified by:

(2) No bachelor is married.

The characteristic of such a statement is that it can be turned into a logical truth by putting synonyms for synonyms; thus (2) can be turned into (1) by putting 'unmarried man' for its synonym 'bachelor'. We still lack a proper characterization of this second class of analytic statements, and therewith of analyticity generally, inasmuch as we have had in the above description to lean on a notion of 'synonymy' which is no less in need of clarification than analyticity itself.

In recent years Carnap has tended to explain analyticity by appeal to what he calls state-descriptions.[1] A state-description is any exhaustive assignment of truth values to the atomic, or noncompound, statements of the language. All other statements of the language are, Carnap assumes, built up of their component clauses by means of the familiar logical devices, in such a way that the truth value of any complex statement is fixed for each state-description by specifiable logical laws. A statement is then explained as analytic when it comes out true under every state-description. This account is an adaptation of Leibniz's 'true in all possible worlds'. But note that this version of analyticity serves its purpose only if the atomic statements of the language are, unlike 'John is a bachelor' and 'John is married', mutually independent. Otherwise there would be a state-description which assigned truth to 'John is a bachelor' and to 'John is married', and consequently 'No bachelors are married' would turn out synthetic rather than analytic under the proposed criterion. Thus the criterion of analyticity in terms of state-descriptions serves only for languages devoid of extra-logical synonym-pairs, such as 'bachelor' and 'unmarried man'—synonym-pairs of the type which give rise to the 'second class' of analytic statements. The criterion in terms of state-descriptions is a reconstruction at best of logical truth, not of analyticity.

I do not mean to suggest that Carnap is under any illusions on this point. His simplified model language with its state-descriptions is aimed primarily not at the general problem of analyticity but at another purpose, the clarification of probability and induction. Our problem, however, is analyticity; and here the major difficulty lies not in the first class of analytic statements, the logical truths, but rather in the second class, which depends on the notion of synonymy.

2. DEFINITION

There are those who find it soothing to say that the analytic statements of the second class reduce to those of the first class, the logical truths, by *definition*; 'bachelor', for example, is *defined* as 'unmar-

1. Carnap (3), pp. 9 ff; (4), pp. 70 ff.

ried man'. But how do we find that 'bachelor' is defined as 'unmarried man'? Who defined it thus, and when? Are we to appeal to the nearest dictionary, and accept the lexicographer's formulation as law? Clearly this would be to put the cart before the horse. The lexicographer is an empirical scientist, whose business is the recording of antecedent facts; and if he glosses 'bachelor' as 'unmarried man' it is because of his belief that there is a relation of synonymy between those forms, implicit in general or preferred usage prior to his own work. The notion of synonymy presupposed here has still to be clarified, presumably in terms relating to linguistic behaviour. Certainly the 'definition' which is the lexicographer's report of an observed synonymy cannot be taken as the ground of the synonymy.

Definition is not, indeed, an activity exclusively of philologists. Philosophers and scientists frequently have occasion to 'define' a recondite term by paraphrasing it into terms of a more familiar vocabulary. But ordinarily such a definition, like the philologist's, is pure lexicography, affirming a relation of synonymy antecedent to the exposition in hand.

Just what it means to affirm synonymy, just what the interconnections may be which are necessary and sufficient in order that two linguistic forms be properly describable as synonymous, is far from clear; but, whatever these interconnections may be, ordinarily they are grounded in usage. Definitions reporting selected instances of synonymy come then as reports upon usage.

There is also, however, a variant type of definitional activity which does not limit itself to the reporting of pre-existing synonymies. I have in mind what Carnap calls *explication*—an activity to which philosophers are given, and scientists also in their more philosophical moments. In explication the purpose is not merely to paraphrase the definiendum into an outright synonym, but actually to improve upon the definiendum by refining or supplementing its meaning. But even explication, though not merely reporting a pre-existing synonymy between definiendum and definiens, does rest, nevertheless, on *other* pre-existing synonymies. The matter may be viewed as follows. Any word worth explicating has some contexts which, as wholes, are clear and precise enough to be useful; and the purpose of explication is to preserve the usage of these favoured contexts while sharpening the usage of other contexts. In order that a given definition be suitable for purposes of explication, therefore, what is required is not that the definiendum in its antecedent usage be synonymous with the definiens, but just that each of these favoured contexts of the definiendum, taken as a whole in its antecendent usage, be synonymous with the corresponding context of the definiens.

Two alternative definientia may be equally appropriate for the purposes of a given task of explication and yet not be synonymous with each other; for they may serve interchangeably within the favoured contexts but diverge elsewhere. By cleaving to one of these definientia rather than the other, a definition of explicative kind generates, by fiat, a relation of synonymy between definiendum and definiens which did not hold before. But such a definition still owes its explicative function, as seen, to pre-existing synonymies.

There does, however, remain still an extreme sort of definition which does not hark back to prior synonymies at all: namely, the explicitly conventional introduction of novel notations for purposes of sheer abbreviation. Here the definiendum becomes synonymous with the definiens simply because it has been created expressly for the purpose of being synonymous with the definiens. Here we have a really transparent case of synonymy created by definition; would that all species of synonymy were as intelligible. For the rest, definition rests on synonymy rather than explaining it.

The word 'definition' has come to have a dangerously reassuring sound, owing no doubt to its frequent occurrence in logical and mathematical writings. We shall do well to digress now into a brief appraisal of the role of definition in formal work.

In logical and mathematical systems either of two mutually antagonistic types of economy may be striven for, and each has its peculiar practical utility. On the one hand, we may seek economy of practical expression—ease and brevity in the statement of multifarious relations. This sort of economy calls usually for distinctive concise notations for a wealth of concepts. Second, however, and oppositely, we may seek economy in grammar and vocabulary; we may try to find a minimum of basic concepts such that, once a distinctive notation has been appropriated to each of them, it becomes possible to express any desired further concept by mere combination and iteration of our basic notations. This second sort of economy is impractical in one way, since a poverty in basic idioms tends to a necessary lengthening of discourse. But it is practical in another way:

it greatly simplifies theoretical discourse *about* the language, through minimizing the terms and the forms of construction wherein the language consists.

Both sorts of economy, through prima facie incompatible, are valuable in their separate ways. The custom has consequently arisen of combining both sorts of economy by forging in effect two languages, the one a part of the other. The inclusive language, though redundant in grammar and vocabulary, is economical in message lengths, while the part, called primitive notation, is economical in grammar and vocabulary. Whole and part are correlated by rules of translation whereby each idiom not in primitive notation is equated to some complex built up of primitive notation. These rules of translation are the so-called *definitions* which appear in formalized systems. They are best viewed not as adjuncts to one language but as correlations between two languages, the one a part of the other.

But these correlations are not arbitrary. They are supposed to show how the primitive notations can accomplish all purposes, save brevity and convenience, of the redundant language. Hence the definiendum and its definiens may be expected, in each case, to be related in one or another of the three ways lately noted. The definiens may be a faithful paraphrase of the definiendum into the narrower notation, preserving a direct synonymy[2] as of antecedent usage; or the definiens may, in the spirit of explication, improve upon the antecedent usage of the definiendum; or finally, the definiendum may be a newly created notation, newly endowed with meaning here and now.

In formal and informal work alike, thus, we find that definition—except in the extreme case of the explicitly conventional introduction of new notations—hinges on prior relations of synonymy. Recognizing then that the notion of definition does not hold the key to synonymy and analyticity, let us look further into synonymy and say no more of definition.

3. INTERCHANGEABILITY

A natural suggestion, deserving close examination, is that the synonymy of two linguistic forms consists simply in their interchangeability in all contexts without change of truth value—interchangeability, in Leibniz's phrase, *salva veritate*.[3] Note that synonyms so conceived need not even be free from vagueness, as long as the vaguenesses match.

But it is not quite true that the synonyms 'bachelor' and 'unmarried man' are everywhere interchangeable *salva veritate*. Truths which become false under substitution of 'unmarried man' for 'bachelor' are easily constructed with the help of 'bachelor of arts' or 'bachelor's buttons'; also with the help of quotation, thus:

'Bachelor' has less than ten letters.

Such counter-instances can, however, perhaps be set aside by treating the phrases 'bachelor of arts' and 'bachelor's buttons' and the quotation ' "bachelor" ' each as a single indivisible word and then stipulating that the interchangeability *salva veritate* which is to be the touchstone of synonymy is not supposed to apply to fragmentary occurrences inside of a word. This account of synonymy, supposing it acceptable on other counts, has indeed the drawback of appealing to a prior conception of 'word' which can be counted on to present difficulties of formulation in its turn. Nevertheless, some progress might be claimed in having reduced the problem of synonymy to a problem of wordhood. Let us pursue this line a bit, taking 'word' for granted.

The question remains whether interchangeability *salva veritate* (apart from occurrences within words) is a strong enough condition for synonymy, or whether, on the contrary, some heteronymous expressions might be thus interchangeable. Now let us be clear that we are not concerned here with synonymy in the sense of complete identity in psychological associations or poetic quality; indeed no two expressions are synonymous in such a sense. We are concerned only with what may be called *cognitive* synonym. Just what this is cannot be said without successfully finishing the present study; but we know something about it from the need which arose for it in connection with analyticity in §1. The sort of synonymy needed there was merely such that any analytic statement could be turned into a logical truth by putting synonyms for synonyms. Turning the tables and assuming analyticity, indeed, we could explain cognitive synonymy of terms as follows (keeping to the familiar example): to say that 'bachelor'

2. According to an important variant sense of 'definition', the relation preserved may be the weaker relation of mere agreement in reference. But definition in this sense is better ignored in the present connection, being irrelevant to the question of synonymy.

3. Cf. Lewis (1), p. 373.

and 'unmarried man' are cognitively synonymous is to say no more nor less than that the statement:

(3) All and only bachelors are unmarried men

is analytic.[4]

What we need is an account of cognitive synonymy not presupposing analyticity—if we are to explain analyticity conversely with help of cognitive synonymy as undertaken in §1. And indeed such an independent account of cognitive synonymy is at present up for consideration, namely, interchangeability *salva veritate* everywhere except within words. The question before us, to resume the thread at last, is whether such interchangeability is a sufficient condition for cognitive synonymy. We can quickly assure ourselves that it is, by examples of the following sort. The statement:

(4) Necessarily all and only bachelors are bachelors

is evidently true, even supposing 'necessarily' so narrowly construed as to be truly applicable only to analytic statements. Then, if 'bachelor' and 'unmarried man' are interchangeable *salva veritate*, the result:

(5) Necessarily all and only bachelors are unmarried men

of putting 'unmarried man' for an occurrence of 'bachelor' in (4) must, like (4), be true. But to say that (5) is true is to say that (3) is analytic, and hence that 'bachelor' and 'unmarried man' are cognitively synonymous.

Let us see what there is about the above argument that gives it its air of hocus-pocus. The condition of interchangeability *salva veritate* varies in its force with variations in the richness of the language at hand. The above argument supposes we are working with a language rich enough to contain the adverb 'necessarily', this adverb being so construed as to yield truth when and only when applied to an analytic statement. But can we condone a language which contains such an adverb? Does the adverb really make sense? To suppose that it does is to suppose that we have already made satisfactory sense of 'analytic'. Then what are we so hard at work on right now?

Our argument is not flatly circular, but something like it. It has the form, figuratively speaking, of a closed curve in space.

Interchangeability *salva veritate* is meaningless until relativized to a language whose extent is specified in relevant respects. Suppose now we consider a language containing just the following materials. There is an indefinitely large stock of one-place predicates (for example, 'F' where 'Fx' means that x is a man) and many-place predicates (for example, 'G' where 'Gxy' means that x loves y), mostly having to do with extra-logical subject-matter. The rest of the language is logical. The atomic sentences consist each of a predicate followed by one or more variables 'x,' 'y', etc,.; and the complex sentences are built up of the atomic ones by truth functions ('not', 'and', 'or', etc.) and quantification. In effect such a language enjoys the benefits also of descriptions and indeed singular terms generally, these being contextually definable in known ways. Even abstract singular terms naming classes, classes of classes, etc., are contextually definable in case the assumed stock of predicates includes the two-place predicate of class membership. Such a language can be adequate to classical mathematics and indeed to scientific discourse generally, except in so far as the latter involves debatable devices such as contrary-to-fact conditionals or modal adverbs like 'necessarily'. Now a language of this type is extensional, in this sense: any two predicates which agree extensionally (that is, are true of the same objects) are interchangeable *salva veritate*.[5]

In an extensional language, therefore, interchangeability *salva veritate* is no assurance of cognitive synonymy of the desired type. That 'bachelor' and 'unmarried man' are interchangeable *salva veritate* in an extensional language assures us of no more than that (3) is true. There is no assurance here that the extensional agreement of 'bachelor' and 'unmarried man' rests on meaning rather than merely on accidental matters of fact, a does the extensional agreement of 'creature with a heart' and 'creature with kidneys'.

For most purposes extensional agreement is the nearest approximation to synonymy we need care about. But the fact remains that extensional agree-

4. This is cognitive synonymy in a primary, broad sense. Carnap ((3), pp. 56 ff.) and Lewis ((2), pp. 83 ff.) have suggested how, once this notion is at hand, a narrower sense of cognitive synonymy which is preferable for some purposes can in turn be derived. But this special ramification of concept-building lies aside from the present purposes and must not be confused with the broad sort of cognitive synonymy here concerned.

5. This is the substance of Quine (1), *121.

ment falls far short of cognitive synonymy of the type required for explaining analyticity in the manner of §1. The type of cognitive synonymy required there is such as to equate the synonymy of 'bachelor' and 'unmarried man' with the analyticity of (3), not merely with the truth of (3).

So we must recognize that interchangeability *salva veritate*, if construed in relation to an extensional language, is not a sufficient condition of cognitive synonymy in the sense needed for deriving analyticity in the manner of §1. If a language contains an intensional adverb 'necessarily' in the sense lately noted, or other particles to the same effect, then interchangeability *salva veritate* in such a language does afford a sufficient condition of cognitive synonymy; but such a language is intelligible only in so far as the notion of analyticity is already understood in advance.

The effort to explain cognitive synonymy first, for the sake of deriving analyticity from it afterward as in §1, is perhaps the wrong approach. Instead we might try explaining analyticity somehow without appeal to cognitive synonymy. Afterward we could doubtless derive cognitive synonymy from analyticity satisfactorily enough if desired. We have seen that cognitive synonymy of 'bachelor' and 'unmarried man' can be explained as analyticity of (3). The same explanation works for any pair of one-place predicates, of course, and it can be extended in obvious fashion to many-place predicates. Other syntactical categories can also be accommodated in fairly parallel fashion. Singular terms may be said to be cognitively synonymous when the statement of identity formed by putting '=' between them is analytic. Statements may be said simply to be cognitively synonymous when their biconditional (the result of joining them by 'if and only if') is analytic.[6] If we care to lump all categories into a single formulation, at the expense of assuming again the notion of 'word' which was appealed to early in this section, we can describe any two linguistic forms as cognitively synonymous when the two forms are interchangeable (apart from occurrences within 'words') *salva* (no longer *veritate* but) *analyticitate*. Certain technical questions arise, indeed, over cases of ambiguity or homonymy; let us not pause for them, however, for we are already digressing. Let us rather turn our backs on the problem of synonymy and address ourselves anew to that of analyticity.

6. The 'if and only if' itself is intended in the truth functional sense. See Carnap (3), p. 14.

4. SEMANTICAL RULES

Analyticity at first seemed most naturally definable by appeal to a realm of meanings. On refinement, the appeal to meanings gave way to an appeal to synonymy or definition. But definition turned out to be a will-o'-the-wisp, and synonymy turned out to be best understood only by dint of a prior appeal to analyticity itself. So we are back at the problem of analyticity.

I do not know whether the statement 'Everything green is extended' is analytic. Now does my indecision over this example really betray an incomplete understanding, an incomplete grasp of the 'meanings', of 'green' and 'extended'? I think not. The trouble is not with 'green' or 'extended', but with 'analytic'.

It is often hinted that the difficulty in separating analytic statements from synthetic ones in ordinary language is due to the vagueness of ordinary language and that the distinction is clear when we have a precise artificial language with explicit 'semantical rules'. This, however, as I shall now attempt to show, is a confusion.

The notion of analyticity about which we are worrying is a purported relation between statements and languages: a statement S is said to be *analytic* for a language L, and the problem is to make sense of this relation generally, that is, for variable 'S' and 'L'. The gravity of this problem is not perceptibly less for artificial languages than for natural ones. The problem of making sense of the idiom 'S is analytic for L', with variable 'S' and 'L', retains its stubbornness even if we limit the range of the variable 'L' to artificial languages. Let me now try to make this point evident.

For artificial languages and semantical rules we look naturally to the writings of Carnap. His semantical rules take various forms, and to make my point I shall have to distinguish certain of the forms. Let us suppose, to begin with, an artificial language L_0 whose semantical rules have the form explicitly of a specification, by recursion or otherwise, of all the analytic statements of L_0. The rules tell us that such and such statements, and only those, are the analytic statements of L_0. Now here the difficulty is simply that the rules contain the word 'analytic', which we do not understand! We understand what expressions the rules attribute analyticity to, but we do not understand what the rules attribute to those expressions. In short, before we can understand a rule which begins 'A statement S is analytic for language L_0 if and only if . . .', we must understand the general relative term 'analytic for'; we must understand 'S is analytic for L' where 'S' and 'L' are variables.

Alternatively we may, indeed, view the so-called rule as a conventional definition of a new simple symbol 'analytic-for-L_0', which might better be written untendentiously as 'K' so as not to seem to throw light on the interesting word 'analytic'. Obviously any number of classes K, M, N, etc. of statements of L_0 can be specified for various purposes or for no purpose; what does it mean to say that K, as against M, N, etc., is the class of the 'analytic' statements of L_0?

By saying what statements are analytic for L_0 we explain 'analytic-for-L_0' but not 'analytic', not 'analytic for'. We do not begin to explain the idiom 'S is analytic for L' with variable 'S' and 'L' even if we are content to limit the range of 'L' to the realm of artificial languages.

Actually we do know enough about the intended significance of 'analytic' to know that analytic statements are supposed to be true. Let us then turn to a second form of semantical rule, which says not that such and such statements are analytic but simply that such and such statements are included among the truths. Such a rule is not subject to the criticism of containing the un-understood word 'analytic'; and we may grant for the sake of argument that there is no difficulty over the broader term 'true'. A semantical rule of this second type, a rule of truth, is not supposed to specify all the truths of the language; it merely stipulates, recursively or otherwise, a certain multitude of statements which, along with others unspecified, are to count as true. Such a rule may be conceded to be quite clear. Derivatively, afterward, analyticity can be demarcated thus: a statement is analytic if it is (not merely true blue) true according to the semantical rule.

Still there is really no progress. Instead of appealing to an unexplained word 'analytic', we are now appealing to an unexplained phrase 'semantical rule'. Not every true statement which says that the statements of some class are true can count as a semantical rule—otherwise *all* truths would be 'analytic' in the sense of being true according to semantical rules. Semantical rules are distinguishable, apparently, only by the fact of appearing on a page under the heading 'Semantical Rules'; and this heading is itself then meaningless.

We can say indeed that a statement is *analytic-for-L_0* if and only if it is true according to such and such specifically appended 'semantical rules', but then we find ourselves back at essentially the same case which was originally discussed: 'S is analytic-for-L_0 if and only if. . . .' Once we seek to explain 'S is analytic for L' generally for variable 'L' (even allowing limitation of 'L' to artificial languages), the explanation 'true according to the semantical rules of L' is unavailing; for the relative term 'semantical rule of' is as much in need of clarification, at least, as 'analytic for'.

It may be instructive to compare the notion of semantical rule with that of postulate. Relative to a given set of postulates, it is easy to say what a postulate is: it is a member of the set. Relative to a given set of semantical rules, it is equally easy to say what a semantical rule is. But given simply a notation, mathematical or otherwise, and indeed as thoroughly understood a notation as you please in point of the translations or truth conditions of its statements, who can say which of its true statements rank as postulates? Obviously the question is meaningless—as meaningless as asking which points in Ohio are starting-points. Any finite (or effectively specifiable infinite) selection of statements (preferably true ones, perhaps) is as much *a* set of postulates as any other. The word 'postulate' is significant only relative to an act of enquiry; we apply the word to a set of statements just in so far as we happen, for the year or the moment, to be thinking of those statements in relation to the statements which can be reached from them by some set of transformations to which we have seen fit to direct our attention. Now the notion of semantical rule is as sensible and meaningful as that of postulate, if conceived in a similarly relative spirit—relative, this time, to one or another particular enterprise of schooling unconversant persons in sufficient conditions for truth of statements of some natural or artificial language L. But from this point of view no one signalization of a subclass of the truths of L is intrinsically more a semantical rule than another; and, if 'analytic' means 'true by semantical rules', no one truth of L is analytic to the exclusion of another.[7]

7. The foregoing paragraph was not part of the present essay as originally published; it was prompted by Martin (see Bibliography).

It might conceivably be protested that an artificial language L (unlike a natural one) is a language in the ordinary sense *plus* a set of explicit semantical rules—the whole constituting, let us say, an ordered pair; and that the semantical rules of L then are specifiable simply as the second component of the pair L. But, by the same token and more simply, we might construe an artificial language L outright as an ordered pair whose second component is the class of its analytic statements; and then the analytic statements of L become specifiable simply as the statements in the second component of L. Or better still, we might just stop tugging at our bootstraps altogether.

Not all the explanations of analyticity known to Carnap and his readers have been covered explicitly in the above considerations, but the extension to other forms is not hard to see. Just one additional factor should be mentioned which sometimes enters: sometimes the semantical rules are in effect rules of translation into ordinary language, in which case the analytic statements of the artificial language are in effect recognized as such from the analyticity of their specified translations in ordinary language. Here certainly there can be no thought of an illumination of the problem of analyticity from the side of the artificial language.

From the point of view of the problem of analyticity the notion of an artificial language with semantical rules is a *feu follet par excellence*. Semantical rules determining the analytic statements of an artificial language are of interest only in so far as we already understand the notion of analyticity; they are of no help in gaining this understanding.

Appeal to hypothetical languages of an artificially simple kind could conceivably be useful in clarifying analyticity, if the mental or behavioural or cultural factors relevant to analyticity—whatever they may be—were somehow sketched into the simplified model. But a model which takes analyticity merely as an irreducible character is unlikely to throw light on the problem of explicating analyticity.

It is obvious that truth in general depends on both language and extra-linguistic fact. The statement 'Brutus killed Caesar' would be false if the world had been different in certain ways, but it would also be false if the word 'killed' happened rather to have the sense of 'begat'. Thus one is tempted to suppose in general that the truth of a statement is somehow analysable into a linguistic component and a factual component. Given this supposition, it next seems reasonable that in some statements the factual component should be null; and these are the analytic statements. But, for all its a priori reasonableness, a boundary between analytic and synthetic statements simply has not been drawn. That there is such a distinction to be drawn at all is an unempirical dogma of empiricists, a metaphysical article of faith.

5. THE VERIFICATION THEORY AND REDUCTIONISM

In the course of these sombre reflections we have taken a dim view first of the notion of meaning, then of the notion of cognitive synonymy, and finally of the notion of analyticity. But what, it may be asked, of the verification theory of meaning? This phrase has established itself so firmly as a catchword of empiricism that we should be very unscientific indeed not to look beneath it for a possible key to the problem of meaning and the associated problems.

The verification theory of meaning, which has been conspicuous in the literature from Peirce onward, is that the meaning of a statement is the method of empirically confirming or infirming it. An analytic statement is that limiting case which is confirmed no matter what.

As urged in §1, we can as well pass over the question of meanings as entities and move straight to sameness of meaning, or synonymy. Then what the verification theory says is that statements are synonymous if and only if they are alike in point of method of empirical confirmation or infirmation.

This is an account of cognitive synonymy not of linguistic forms generally, but of statements.[8] However, from the concept of synonymy of statements we could derive the concept of synonymy for other linguistic forms, by considerations somewhat similar to those at the end of §3. Assuming the notion of 'word', indeed, we could explain any two forms as synonymous when the putting of the one form for an occurrence of the other in any statement (apart from occurrences within 'words') yields a synony-

8. The doctrine can indeed be formulated with terms rather than statements as the units. Thus Lewis describes the meaning of a term as '*a criterion in mind*, by reference to which one is able to apply or refuse to apply the expression in question in the case of presented, or imagined, things or situations' ((2), p. 133). For an instructive account of the vicissitudes of the verification theory of meaning, centered however on the question of meaning*fulness* rather than synonymy and analyticity, see Hempel.

mous statement. Finally, given the concept of synonymy thus for linguistic forms generally, we could define analyticity in terms of synonymy and logical truth as in §1. For that matter, we could define analyticity more simply in terms of just synonymy of statements together with logical truth; it is not necessary to appeal to synonymy of linguistic forms other than statements. For a statement may be described as analytic simply when it is synonymous with a logically true statement.

So if the verification theory can be accepted as an adequate account of statement synonymy, the notion of analyticity is saved after all. However, let us reflect. Statement synonymy is said to be likeness of method of empirical confirmation or infirmation. Just what are these methods which are to be compared for likeness? What, in other words, in the nature of the relation between a statement and the experiences which contribute to or detract from its confirmation?

The most naive view of the relation is that it is one of direct report. This is *radical reductionism.* Every meaningful statement is held to be translatable into a statement (true or false) about immediate experience. Radical reductionism, in one form or another, well antedates the verification theory of meaning explicitly so called. Thus Locke and Hume held that every idea must either originate directly in sense experience or else be compounded of ideas thus originating; and taking a hint from Tooke we might rephrase this doctrine in semantical jargon by saying that a term, to be significant at all, must be either a name of a sense datum or a compound of such names or an abbreviation of such a compound. So stated, the doctrine remains ambiguous as between sense data as sensory events and sense data as sensory qualities; and it remains vague as to the admissible ways of compounding. Moreover, the doctrine is unnecessarily and intolerably restrictive in the term-by-term critique which it imposes. More reasonably, and without yet exceeding the limits of what I have called radical reductionism, we may take full statements as our significant units—thus demanding that our statements as wholes be translatable into sense-datum language, but not that they be translatable term by term.

This emendation would unquestionably have been welcome to Locke and Hume and Tooke, but historically it had to await an important reorientation in semantics—the reorientation whereby the primary vehicle of meaning came to be seen no longer in the term but in the statement. This reorientation, explicit in Frege ((1), §60), underlies Russell's concept of incomplete symbols defined in use; also it is implicit in the verification theory of meaning, since the objects of verification are statements.

Radical reductionism, conceived now with statements as units, set itself the task of specifying a sense-datum language and showing how to translate the rest of significant discourse, statement by statement, into it. Carnap embarked on this project in the *Aufbau.*

The language which Carnap adopted as his starting-point was not a sense-datum language in the narrowest conceivable sense, for it included also the notations of logic, up through higher set theory. In effect, it included the whole language of pure mathematics. The ontology implicit in it (that is, the range of values of its variables) embraced not only sensory events but classes, classes of classes, and so on. Empiricists there are who would boggle at such prodigality. Carnap's starting-point is very parsimonious, however, in its extra-logical or sensory part. In a series of constructions in which he exploits the resources of modern logic with much ingenuity, Carnap succeeds in defining a wide array of important additional sensory concepts which, but for his constructions, one would not have dreamed were definable on so slender a basis. He was the first empiricist who, not content with asserting the reducibility of science to terms of immediate experience, took serious steps toward carrying out the reduction.

If Carnap's starting-point is satisfactory, still his constructions were, as he himself stressed, only a fragment of the full programme. The construction of even the simplest statements about the physical world was left in a sketchy state. Carnap's suggestions on this subject were, despite their sketchiness, very suggestive. He explained spatio-temporal point-instants as quadruples of real numbers and envisaged assignment of sense qualities to point-instants according to certain canons. Roughly summarized, the plan was that qualities should be assigned to point-instants in such a way as to achieve the laziest world compatible with our experience. The principle of least action was to be our guide in constructing a world from experience.

Carnap did not seem to recognize, however, that his treatment of physical objects fell short of reduction not merely through sketchiness, but in principle. Statements of the form 'Quality q is at point-instant *x;y;z;t*' were, according to this canons, to be apportioned truth values in such a way as to maximize and minimize certain overall features, and with growth of experience the truth values were to be progressively revised in the same spirit. I think this is a good schematization (deliberately over-simplified, to be sure) of what science really does; but it provides no indication, not even the sketchiest, of how a statement of the form 'Quality *q* is at *x;y;z;t*' could ever be translated into Carnap's initial language of sense data and logic. The connective 'is at' remains an added undefined connective; the canons counsel us in its use but not in its elimination.

Carnap seems to have appreciated this point afterward; for in his later writings he abandoned all notion of the translatability of statements about the physical world into statements about immediate experience. Reductionism in its radical form has long since ceased to figure in Carnap's philosophy.

But the dogma of reductionism has, in a subtler and more tenuous form, continued to influence the thought of empiricists. The notion lingers that to each statement, or each synthetic statement, there is associated a unique range of possible sensory events such that the occurrence of any of them would add to the likelihood of truth of the statement, and that there is associated also another unique range of possible sensory events whose occurrence would detract from that likelihood. This notion is of course implicit in the verification theory of meaning.

The dogma of reductionism survives in the supposition that each statement, taken in isolation from its fellows, can admit of confirmation or information at all. My counter-suggestion, issuing essentially from Carnap's doctrine of the physical world in the *Aufbau*, is that our statements about the external world face the tribunal of sense experience not individually but only as a corporate body.[9]

The dogma of reductionism, even in its attenuated form, is intimately connected with the other dogma—that there is a cleavage between the analytic and the synthetic. We have found ourselves led, indeed, from the latter problem to the former through the verification theory of meaning. More directly, the one dogma clearly supports the other in this way: as long as it is taken to be significant in general to speak of the confirmation and information of a statement, it seems significant to speak also of a limiting kind of statement which is vacuously confirmed, *ipso facto*, come what may; and such a statement is analytic.

The two dogmas are, indeed, at root identical. We lately reflected that in general the truth of statements does obviously depend both upon language and upon extra-linguistic fact; and we noted that this obvious circumstance carries in its train, not logically but all too naturally, a feeling that the truth of a statement is somehow analysable into a linguistic component and a factual component. The factual component must, if we are empiricists, boil down to a range of confirmatory experiences. In the extreme case where the linguistic component is all that matters, a true statement is analytic. But I hope we are now impressed with how stubbornly the distinction between analytic and synthetic has resisted any straightforward drawing. I am impressed also, apart from prefabricated examples of black and white balls in an urn, with how baffling the problem has always been of arriving at any explicit theory of the empirical confirmation of a synthetic statement. My present suggestion is that it is nonsense, and the root of much nonsense, to speak of a linguistic component and a factual component in the truth of any individual statement. Taken collectively, science has its double dependence upon language and experience; but this duality is not significantly traceable into the statements of science taken one by one.

The idea of defining a symbol in use was, as remarked, an advance over the impossible term-by-term empiricism of Locke and Hume. The statement, rather than the term, came with Frege to be recognized as the unit accountable to an empiricist critique. But what I am now urging is that even in taking the statement as unit we have drawn our grid too finely. The unit of empirical significance is the whole of science.

6. EMPIRICISM WITHOUT THE DOGMAS

The totality of our so-called knowledge or beliefs, from the most casual matters of geography and history to the profoundest laws of atomic physics or even of pure mathematics and logic, is a manmade fabric which impinges on experience only along the edges. Or, to change the figure, total science is like a field of force whose boundary conditions are experience. A conflict with experience at the periph-

9. This doctrine was well argued by Duhem, pp. 303–28. Or see Lowinger, pp. 132–40.

ery occasions readjustments in the interior of the field. Truth values have to be redistributed over some of our statements. Re-evaluation of some statements entails re-evaluation of others, because of their logical interconnections—the logical laws being in turn simply certain further statements of the system, certain further elements of the field. Having re-evaluated one statement we must re-evaluate some others, which may be statements logically connected with the first or may be the statements of logical connections themselves. But the total field is so underdetermined by its boundary conditions, experience, that there is much latitude of choice as to what statements to re-evaluate in the light of any single contrary experience. No particular experiences are linked with any particular statements in the interior of the field, except indirectly through considerations of equilibrium affecting the field as a whole.

If this view is right, it is misleading to speak of the empirical content of an individual statement—especially if it is a statement at all remote from the experiential periphery of the field. Furthermore, it becomes folly to seek a boundary between synthetic statements, which hold contingently on experience, and analytic statements, which hold come what may. Any statement can be held true come what may, if we make drastic enough adjustments elsewhere in the system. Even a statement very close to the periphery can be held true in the face of recalcitrant experience by pleading hallucination or by amending certain statements of the kind called logical laws. Conversely, by the same token, no statement is immune to revision. Revision even of the logical law of the excluded middle has been proposed as a means of simplifying quantum mechanics; and what difference is there in principle between such a shift and the shift whereby Kepler superseded Ptolemy, or Einstein Newton, or Darwin Aristotle?

For vividness I have been speaking in terms of varying distances from a sensory periphery. Let me try now to clarify this notion without metaphor. Certain statements, though *about* physical objects and not sense experience, seem peculiarly germane to sense experience—and in a selective way: some statements to some experiences, others to others. Such statements, especially germane to particular experiences, I picture as near the periphery. But in this relation of 'germaneness' I envisage nothing more than a loose association reflecting the relative likelihood, in practice, of our choosing one statement rather than another for revision in the event of recalcitrant experience. For example, we can imagine recalcitrant experiences to which we would surely be inclined to accommodate our system by re-evaluating just the statement that there are brick houses on Elm Street, together with related statements on the same topic. We can imagine other recalcitrant experiences to which we would be inclined to accommodate our system by re-evaluating just the statement that there are no centaurs, along with kindred statements. A recalcitrant experience can, I have urged, be accommodated by any of various alternative re-evaluations in various alternative quarters of the total system; but, in the cases which we are now imaging, our natural tendency to disturb the total system as little as possible would lead us to focus our revisions upon these specific statements concerning brick houses or centaurs. These statements are felt, therefore, to have a sharper empirical reference than highly theoretical statements of physics or logic or ontology. The latter statements may be thought of as relatively centrally located within the total network, meaning merely that little preferential connection with any particular sense data obtrudes itself.

As an empiricist I continue to think of the conceptual scheme of science as a tool, ultimately, for predicting future experience in the light of past experience. Physical objects are conceptually imported into the situation as convenient intermediaries—not by definition in terms of experience, but simply as irreducible posits comparable, epistemologically, to the gods of Homer. For my part I do, *qua* lay physicist, believe in physical objects and not in Homer's gods; and I consider it a scientific error to believe otherwise. But in point of epistemological footing the physical objects and the gods differ only in degree and not in kind. Both sorts of entities enter our conception only as cultural posits. The myth of physical objects is epistemologically superior to most in that it has proved more efficacious than other myths as a device for working a manageable structure into the flux of experience.

Positing does not stop with macroscopic physical objects. Objects at the atomic level are posited to make the laws of macroscopic objects, and ultimately the laws of experience, simpler and more manageable; and we need not expect or demand full definition of atomic and subatomic entities in terms of macroscopic ones, any more than definition of macroscopic things in terms of sense data. Science is a continuation of common sense, and it continues the common-sense expedient of swelling ontology to simplify theory.

Physical objects, small and large, are not the only posits. Forces are another example; and indeed we are told nowadays that the boundary between energy and matter is obsolete. Moreover, the abstract entities which are the substance of mathematics—ultimately classes and classes of classes and so on up—are another posit in the same spirit. Epistemologically these are myths on the same footing with physical objects and gods, neither better nor worse except for differences in the degree to which they expedite our dealings with sense experiences.

The overall algebra of rational and irrational numbers is underdetermined by the algebra of rational numbers, but is smoother and more convenient; and it includes the algebra of rational numbers as a jagged or gerrymandered part. Total science, mathematical and natural and human, is similarly but more extremely underdetermined by experience. The edge of the system must be kept squared with experience; the rest, with all its elaborate myths or fictions, has as its objective the simplicity of laws.

Ontological questions, under this view, are on a par with questions of natural science.[10] Consider the question whether to countenance classes as entities. This, as I have argued elsewhere,[11] is the question whether to quantify with respect to variables which take classes as values. Now Carnap (6) has maintained that this is a question not of matters of fact but of choosing a convenient language form, a convenient conceptual scheme or framework for science. With this I agree, but only on the proviso that the same be conceded regarding scientific hypotheses generally. Carnap ((6), p. 32 n) has recognized that he is able to preserve a double standard for ontological questions and scientific hypotheses only by assuming an absolute distinction between the analytic and the synthetic; and I need not say again that this is a distinction which I reject.[12]

The issue over there being classes seems more a question of convenient conceptual scheme; the issue over there being centaurs, or brick houses on Elm Street, seems more a question of fact. But I have been urging that this difference is only one of degree, and that it turns upon our vaguely pragmatic inclination to adjust one strand of the fabric of science rather than another in accommodating some particular recalcitrant experience. Conservatism figures in such choices, and so does the quest for simplicity.

Carnap, Lewis, and others take a pragmatic stand on the question of choosing between language forms, scientific frameworks; but their pragmatism leaves off at the imagined boundary between the analytic and the synthetic. In repudiating such a boundary I espouse a more thorough pragmatism. Each man is given a scientific heritage plus a continuing barrage of sensory stimulation; and the considerations which guide him in warping his scientific heritage to fit his continuing sensory promptings are, where rational, pragmatic.

10. 'L'ontologie fait corps avec la science elle-même et ne peut en être separée.' Meyerson, p. 439.

11. See Quine, *From a Logical Point of View*, 2nd edn. (Cambridge: Harvard University Press, 1961), p. 12 f., 102 ff.

12. For an effective expression of further misgivings over this distinction, see White (1).

BIBLIOGRAPHICAL REFERENCES

Carnap, Rudolf (1), *Der logische Aufbau der Welt* (Berlin, 1928).

—— (2), *The Logical Syntax of Language* (New York: Harcourt Brace, and London: Kegal Paul, 1937). Translation, with extensions, of *Logische Syntax der Sprache* (Vienna: Springer, 1934).

—— (3), *Meaning and Necessity* (Chicago: University of Chicago Press, 1947).

—— (4), *Logical Foundations of Probability* (Chicago: University of Chicago Press, 1950).

—— (5), 'Testability and Meaning', *Philosophy of Science,* 3 (1936), 419–71; 4 (1937), 1–40 (reprinted, New Haven: Graduate Philosophy Club, Yale University, 1950).

—— (6), 'Empiricism, Semantics, and Ontology', *Revue internationale de philosophie,* 4 (1950), 20–40. Reprinted in Linsky.

Duhem, Pierre, *La Théorie physique: son objet et sa structure* (Paris, 1906).

Frege, Gottlob (1), *Foundations of Arithmetic* (New York:

Philosophical Library, 1950). Reprint of *Grundlagen der Arithmetik* (Breslau, 1884) with English translation in parallel.

Hempel, C. G. (1), 'Problems and Changes in the Empiricist Criterion of Meaning', *Revue internationale de philosophie,* 4 (1950), 41–63. Reprinted in Linsky.

—— (2), 'The Concept of Cognitive Significance: A Reconsideration', *Proceedings of American Academy of Arts and Sciences,* 80 (1951), 61–77.

Lewis, C. I. (1), *A Survey of Symbolic Logic* (Berkeley, 1918).

—— (2), *An Analysis of Knowledge and Valuation* (La Salle, Ill.: Open Court, 1946).

Linsky, Leonard (ed.), *Semantics and the Philosophy of Language* (Urbana: University of Illinois Press, 1952).

Lowinger, Armand, *The Methodology of Pierre Duhem* (New York: Columbia University Press, 1941).

Martin, R. M., 'On "analytic" ', *Philosophical Studies,* 3 (1952), 42–7.

Meyerson, Émile, *Identité et realité.* (Paris, 1908; 4th edn., 1932).

Quine, W. V. (1), *Mathematical Logic* (New York: Norton, 1940; Cambridge: Harvard University Press, 1947; rev. edn., Cambridge: Harvard University Press, 1951).

Tooke, J. H., '*Έπεα πτεοόεντα; or, The Diversions of Purley.* 2 vols. (London, 1786, 1805, 1829; Boston, 1806).

White, Morton (1), 'The Analytic and the Synthetic: an Untenable Dualism', in Sidney Hook (ed.), *John Dewey: Philosopher of Science and Freedom* (New York: Dial Press, 1950), pp. 316–30. Reprinted in Linsky.

Chapter 42

Nelson Goodman

Nelson Goodman (1906–   ) until his retirement was Professor of Philosophy at Harvard University. In this selection, taken from his book *Fact, Fiction and Forecast,* Goodman argues that beside Hume's puzzle over induction, there is a second problem: what are the rules for deciding which properties are projectable into the future? Why does seeing another black raven confirm our hypothesis that all ravens are black or that the next raven we see will be black but the seeing of three bachelors in a room not count as evidence that tomorrow we will see three bachelors in this room? Inventing a new color term *grue*, made up from our color terms *green* and *blue*, Goodman illustrates the problem of projectability.

FOR FURTHER READING

Elgin, Catherine. *With Reference to Reference* (Hackett Publishing Co., 1983).

Goodman, Nelson. *Fact, Fiction and Forecast* (Harvard University Press, 1983).

Goodman, Nelson. *Problems and Projects.* (Hackett Publishing Co., 1972).

Goodman, Nelson. *Ways of Worldmaking.* (Hackett Publishing Co., 1978).

Mitchell, W.J.T. *Iconology* (University of Chicago Press, 1986).

Scheffler, I. *The Anatomy of Inquiry* (Hackett Publishing Co., 1981).

Fact, Fiction and Forecast

THE NEW RIDDLE OF INDUCTION

Confirmation of a hypothesis by an instance depends rather heavily upon features of the hypothesis other than its syntactical form. That a given piece of copper conducts electricity increases the credibility of statements asserting that other pieces of copper conduct electricity, and thus confirms the hypothesis that all copper conducts electricity. But the fact that a given man now in this room is a third son does not increase the credibility of statements asserting that other men now in this room are third sons, and so does not confirm the hypothesis that all men now in this room are third sons. Yet in both cases our hypothesis is a generalization of the evidence statement. The difference is that in the former case the hypothesis is a *lawlike* statement;

while in the latter case, the hypothesis is a merely contingent or accidental generality. Only a statement that is *lawlike*—regardless of its truth or falsity or its scientific importance—is capable of receiving confirmation from an instance of it; accidental statements are not. Plainly, then, we must look for a way of distinguishing lawlike from accidental statements.

So long as what seems to be needed is merely a way of excluding a few odd and unwanted cases that are inadvertently admitted by our definition of confirmation, the problem may not seem very hard or very pressing. We fully expect that minor defects will be found in our definition and that the necessary refinements will have to be worked out patiently one after another. But some further examples will show that our present difficulty is of a much graver kind.

Suppose that all emeralds examined before a certain time *t* are green.[1] At time *t*, then, our observations support the hypothesis that all emeralds are green; and this is in accord with our definition of confirmation. Our evidence statements assert that emerald *a* is green, that emerald *b* is green, and so on; and each confirms the general hypothesis that all emeralds are green. So far, so good.

Now let me introduce another predicate less familiar than "green". It is the predicate "grue" and it applies to all things examined before *t* just in case they are green but to other things just in case they are blue. Then at time *t* we have, for each evidence statement asserting that a given emerald is green, a parallel evidence statement asserting that that emerald is grue. And that statements that emerald *a* is grue, that emerald *b* is grue, and so on, will each confirm the general hypothesis that all emeralds are grue. Thus according to our definition, the prediction that all emeralds subsequently examined will be green and the prediction that all will be grue are alike confirmed by evidence statements describing the same observations. But if an emerald subsequently examined is grue, it is blue and hence not green. Thus although we are well aware which of the two incompatible predictions is genuinely confirmed, they are equally well confirmed according to our present definition. Moreover, it is clear that if we simply choose an appropriate predicate, then on the basis of these same observations we shall have equal confirmation, by our definition, for any prediction whatever about other emeralds—or indeed about anything else.[2] As in our earlier example, only the predictions subsumed under lawlike hypotheses are genuinely confirmed; but we have no criterion as yet for determining lawlikeness. And now we see that without some criterion, our definition not merely includes a few unwanted cases, but is so completely ineffectual that it virtually excludes nothing. We are left once again with the intolerable result that anything confirms anything. This difficulty cannot be set aside as an annoying detail to be taken care of in due course. It has to be met before our definition will work at all.

Nevertheless, the difficulty is often slighted because on the surface there seem to be easy ways of dealing with it. Sometimes, for example, the problem is thought to be much like the paradox of the ravens. We are here again, it is pointed out, making tacit and illegitimate use of information outside the stated evidence: the information, for example, that different samples of one material are usually alike in conductivity, and the information that different men in a lecture audience are usually not alike in the number of their older brothers. But while it is true that such information is being smuggled in, this does not by itself settle the matter as it settles the matter of the ravens. There the point was that when the smuggled information is forthrightly declared, its effect upon the confirmation of the hypothesis in question is immediately and properly registered by the definition we are using. On the other hand, if to our initial evidence we add statements concerning the conductivity of pieces of other materials or concerning the number of older brothers of members of other lecture audiences, this will not in the least affect the confirmation, according to our definition, of the hypothesis concerning copper or of that concerning other lecture audiences. Since our definition is insensitive to the bearing upon hypotheses of evidence so related to them, even when the evidence is fully declared, the difficulty about accidental hypotheses cannot be explained away on the ground that such evidence is being surreptitiously taken into account.

1. Although the example used is different, the argument to follow is substantially the same as that set forth in my note 'A Query on Confirmation' [*Journal of Philosophy*, XLIII (1946), 383–385.]

2. For instance, we shall have equal confirmation, by our present definition, for the prediction that roses subsequently examined will be blue. Let "emerose" apply just to emeralds examined before time *t*, and to roses examined later. Then all emeroses so far examined are grue, and this confirms the hypothesis that all emeroses are grue and hence the prediction that roses subsequently examined will be blue. The problem raised by such antecedents has been little noticed, but is no easier to meet than that raised by similarly perverse consequents.

A more promising suggestion is to explain the matter in terms of the effect of this other evidence not directly upon the hypothesis in question but *indirectly* through other hypotheses that *are* confirmed, according to our definition, by such evidence. Our information about other materials does by our definition confirm such hypotheses as that all pieces of iron conduct electricity, that no pieces of rubber do, and so on; and these hypotheses, the explanation runs, impart to the hypothesis that all pieces of copper conduct electricity (and also to the hypothesis that none do) the character of lawlikeness—that is, amenability to confirmation by direct positive instances when found. On the other hand, our information about other lecture audiences *disconfirms* many hypotheses to the effect that all the men in one audience are third sons, or that none are; and this strips any character of lawlikeness from the hypothesis that all (or the hypothesis that none) of the men in *this* audience are third sons. But clearly if this course is to be followed, the circumstances under which hypotheses are thus related to one another will have to be precisely articulated.

The problem, then, is to define the relevant ways in which such hypotheses must be alike. Evidence for the hypothesis that all iron conducts electricity enhances the lawlikeness of the hypothesis that all zirconium conducts electricity, but does not similarly affect the hypothesis that all the objects on my desk conduct electricity. Wherein lies the difference? The first two hypotheses fall under the broader hypothesis—call it "*H*"—that every class of things of the same material is uniform in conductivity; the first and third fall only under some such hypothesis as—call it "*K*"—that every class of things that are either all of the same material or all on a desk is uniform in conductivity. Clearly the important difference here is that evidence for a statement affirming that one of the classes covered by *H* has the property in question increases the credibility of any statement affirming that another such class has this property; while nothing of the sort holds true with respect to *K*. But this is only to say that *H* is lawlike and *K* is not. We are faced anew with the very problem we are trying to solve: the problem of distinguishing between lawlike and accidental hypotheses.

The most popular way of attacking the problem takes its cue from the fact that accidental hypotheses seem typically to involve some spatial or temporal restriction, or reference to some particular individual. They seem to concern the people in some particular room, or the objects on some particular person's desk; while lawlike hypotheses characteristically concern all ravens or all pieces of copper whatsoever. Complete generality is thus very often supposed to be a sufficient condition of lawlikeness; but to define this complete generality is by no means easy. Merely to require that the hypothesis contain no term naming, describing, or indicating a particular thing or location will obviously not be enough. The troublesome hypothesis that all emeralds are grue contains no such term; and where such a term does occur, as in hypotheses about men in *this room*, it can be suppressed in favor of some predicate (short or long, new or old) that contains no such term but applies only to exactly the same things. One might think, then, of excluding not only hypotheses that actually contain terms for specific individuals but also all hypotheses that are equivalent to others that do contain such terms. But, as we have just seen, to exclude only hypotheses of which *all* equivalents contain such terms is to exclude nothing. On the other hand, to exclude all hypotheses that have *some* equivalent containing such a term is to exclude everything; for even the hypothesis

All grass is green

has as an equivalent

All grass in London or elsewhere is green.

The next step, therefore, has been to consider ruling out predicates of certain kinds. A syntactically universal hypothesis is lawlike, the proposal runs, if its predicates are 'purely qualitative' or 'nonpositional'.[3] This will obviously accomplish nothing if a purely qualitative predicate is then conceived either as one that is equivalent to some expression free of terms for specific individuals, or as one that is equivalent to no expression that contains such a term; for this only raises again the difficulties just pointed out. The claim appears to be rather that at least in the case of a simple enough predicate we can readily determine by direct inspection of its meaning whether or not it is purely qualitative. But

3. Carnap took this course in his paper 'On the Application of Inductive Logic', *Philosophy and Phenomenological Research*, vol. 8 (1947), pp. 133–47, which is in part a reply to my 'A Query on Confirmation'. The discussion was continued in my note 'On Infirmities of Confirmation Theory', *Philosophy and Phenomenological Research*, vol. 8 (1947), pp. 149–51; and in Carnap's 'Reply to Nelson Goodman', same journal, same volume, pp. 461–2.

even aside from obscurities in the notion of 'the meaning' of a predicate, this claim seems to me wrong. I simply do not know how to tell whether a predicate is qualitative or positional, except perhaps by completely begging the question at issue and asking whether the predicate is 'well-behaved'—that is, whether simple syntactically universal hypotheses applying it are lawlike.

This statement will not go unprotested. "Consider", it will be argued, "the predicates 'blue' and 'green' and the predicate 'grue' introduced earlier, and also the predicate 'bleen' that applies to emeralds examined before time *t* just in case they are blue and to other emeralds just in case they are green. Surely it is clear", the argument runs, "that the first two are purely qualitative and the second two are not; for the meaning of each of the latter two plainly involves reference to a specific temporal position." To this I reply that indeed I do recognize the first two as well-behaved predicates admissible in lawlike hypotheses, and the second two as ill-behaved predicates. But the argument that the former but not the latter are purely qualitative seems to me quite unsound. True enough, if we start with "blue" and "green," then "grue" and "bleen" will be explained in terms of "blue" and "green" and a temporal term. But equally truly, if we start with "grue" and "bleen," then "blue" and "green" will be explained in terms of "grue" and "bleen" and a temporal term; "green", for example, applies to emeralds examined before time *t* just in case they are grue, and to other emeralds just in case they are bleen. Thus qualitativeness is an entirely relative matter and does not by itself establish any dichotomy of predicates. This relativity seems to be completely overlooked by those who contend that the qualitative character of a predicate is a criterion for its good behavior.

Of course, one may ask why we need worry about such unfamiliar predicates as "grue" or about accidental hypotheses in general, since we are unlikely to use them in making predictions. If our definition works for such hypotheses as are normally employed, isn't that all we need? In a sense, yes; but only in the sense that we need no definition, no theory of induction, and no philosophy of knowledge at all. We get along well enough without them in daily life and in scientific research. But if we seek a theory at all, we cannot excuse gross anomalies resulting from a proposed theory by pleading that we can avoid them in practice. The odd cases we have been considering are clinically pure cases that, though seldom encountered in practice, nevertheless display to best advantage the symptoms of a widespread and destructive malady.

We have so far neither any answer nor any promising clue to an answer to the question what distinguishes lawlike or confirmable hypotheses from accidental or non-confirmable ones; and what may at first have seemed a minor technical difficulty has taken on the stature of a major obstacle to the development of a satisfactory theory of confirmation. It is this problem that I call the new riddle of induction.

At the beginning of this lecture, I expressed the opinion that the problem of induction is still unsolved, but that the difficulties that face us today are not the old ones; and I have tried to outline the changes that have taken place. The problem of justifying induction has been displaced by the problem of defining confirmation, and our work upon this has left us with the residual problem of distinguishing between confirmable and non-confirmable hypotheses. One might say roughly that the first question was "Why does a positive instance of a hypothesis give any grounds for predicting further instances?"; that the newer question was "What is a positive instance of a hypothesis?"; and that the crucial remaining question is "What hypotheses are confirmed by their positive instances?"

The vast amount of effort expended on the problem of induction in modern times has thus altered our afflictions but hardly relieved them. The original difficulty about induction arose from the recognition that anything may follow upon anything. Then, in attempting to define confirmation in terms of the converse of the consequence relation, we found ourselves with the distressingly similar difficulty that our definition would make any statement confirm any other. And now, after modifying our definition drastically, we still get the old devastating result that any statement will confirm any statement. Until we find a way of exercising some control over the hypotheses to be admitted, our definition makes no distinction whatsoever between valid and invalid inductive inferences.

The real inadequacy of Hume's account lay not in his descriptive approach but in the imprecision of his description. Regularities inexperience, according to him, give rise to habits of expectation; and thus it is predictions conforming to past regularities that are normal or valid. But Hume overlooks the fact that some regularities do and some do not establish such habits; that predictions based on some regularities are valid while predictions based on other regularities are not. Every word you have heard me say has occurred prior to the final sentence of this lecture; but that does not, I hope, create any expectation that every word you will hear me say will be prior to that sentence. Again, consider our case of emeralds. All those examined before time *t* are green; and this leads us to expect, and confirms the prediction, that the next one will be green. But also, all those examined are grue; and this does not lead us to expect, and does not confirm the prediction, that the next one will be grue. Regularity in greenness confirms the prediction of further cases; regularity in grueness does not. To say that valid predictions are those based on past regularities, without being able to say *which* regularities, is thus quite pointless. Regularities are where you find them, and you can find them anywhere. As we have seen, Hume's failure to recognize and deal with this problem has been shared even by his most recent successors.

As a result, what we have in current confirmation theory is a definition that is adequate for certain cases that so far can be described only as those for which it is adequate. The theory works where it works. A hypothesis is confirmed by statements related to it in the prescribed way provided it is so confirmed. This is a good deal like having a theory that tells us that the area of a plane figure is one-half the base times the altitude, without telling us for what figures this holds. We must somehow find a way of distinguishing lawlike hypotheses, to which our definition of confirmation applies, from accidental hypotheses, to which it does not.

Today I have been speaking solely of the problem of induction, but what has been said applies equally to the more general problem of projection. As pointed out earlier, the problem of prediction from past to future cases is but a narrower version of the problem of projecting from any set of cases to others. We saw that a whole cluster of troublesome problems concerning dispositions and possibility can be reduced to this problem of projection. That is why the new riddle of induction, which is more broadly the problem of distinguishing between projectible and non-projectible hypotheses, is as important as it is exasperating.

Our failures teach us, I think, that lawlike or projectible hypotheses cannot be distinguished on any merely syntactical grounds or even on the ground that these hypotheses are somehow purely general in meaning.

Chapter 43

JOHN RAWLS

John Rawls (1921–), perhaps the most important political philosopher in the twentieth century, was educated at Princeton University and taught at Cornell and Harvard Universities. The author of several important works in philosophy, no twentieth century work in moral and political philosophy has had greater influence on our generation than Rawls's *A Theory of Justice* (1971). Robert Nisbett calls it the "long awaited successor to Rousseau's *Social Contract,* the Rock on which the Church of Equality can properly be founded in our time." In scope and power it rivals the classics of Hobbes, Locke, and Rousseau. Fundamentally a strong form of liberal egalitarianism, it seeks to justify the welfare state. We have included, as our final reading in this book of classics, Rawl's earlier essay, "Justice as Fairness" (1955), which outline the central ideas later to become developed in *A Theory of Justice.*

In "Justice as Fairness," Rawls sets forth a hypothetical contract theory in which participants decide on practices acknowledged "to be fair [and] bind themselves by the duty of fair play to follow the rules when it comes their turn to do so, and this implies a limitation on their pursuit of self-interest in particular cases." Parties to the contract are to act as rationally self-interested agents, and choose the basic principles which will govern their society. Rawls thinks that these conditions insure objectivity and impartiality of judgment. He calls the system "Justice As Fairness," because he seeks a contract on whose fairness all parties will agree. In effect, the parties to the contract should choose the kind of principles they could live with if their enemies were assigning them positions in society. Rawls argues that they would choose the following two principles:

1. Everyone will have an equal right to the most extensive liberty compatible with similar liberty for others.

2. "Inequalities are arbitrary unless it is reasonable to expect that they will work out for everyone's advantage, and provided the positions and offices to which they attach, or from which they may be gained, are open to all. These principles express justice as a complex of three ideas: liberty, equality and reward for services contributing to the common good."

It might be pointed out that this two-part second principle will be transformed in *A Theory of Justice,* where Rawls introduces the *difference* principle. The second principle will become:

2. Social and economic inequalities must satisfy two conditions:

a. They are to the greatest benefit of the least advantaged ("the difference principle").

b. They are attached to positions open to all under conditions of fair equality of opportunity.

Rawls's egalitarianism is more fully developed in *A Theory of Justice,* but it is present in the article, at least in outline. He believes that each minimally rational human being, who has a conception of the good (a value system), and is able to act justly, is valuable and equally so. He now states the main idea of his theory. Yet inequalities are justified if they work for the good of all. In his book, of course, that is not sufficient. They must aid the least well off in order to be justified.

Here is how Rawls states his aim in *A Theory of Justice*.

> My aim is to present a conception of justice which generalizes and carries to a higher level of abstraction the familiar theory of the social contrast as found, say, in Locke, Rousseau, and Kant. In order to do this we are not to think of the original contract as one to enter a particular society or to set up a particular form of government. Rather, the guiding idea is that the principles of justice for the basic structure of society are the object of the original agreement. They are the principles that free and rational persons concerned to further their own interests would accept in an initial position of equality as defining the fundamental terms of their association. These principles are to regulate all further agreements; they specify the kinds of social cooperation that can be entered into and the forms of government that can be established. This way of regarding the principles of justice I shall call *justice as fairness.*
>
> Thus we are to imagine that those who engage in social cooperation choose together, in one joint act, the principles which are to assign basic rights and duties and to determine the division of social benefits. Men are to decide in advance how they are to regulate their claims against one another and what is to be the foundation charter of their society. Just as each person must decide by rational reflection what constitutes his good, that is, the system of ends which it is rational for him to pursue, so a group of persons must decide once and for all what is to count among them as just and unjust. The choice which rational men would make in this hypothetical situation of equal liberty, assuming for the present that this choice problem has a solution, determines the principle of justice.
>
> In *justice as fairness* the original position of equality corresponds to the state of nature in the traditional theory of the social contract. This original position is not, of course, thought of as an actual historical state of affairs, much less as a primitive condition of culture. It is understood as a purely hypothetical situation characterized so as to lead to a certain conception of justice. Among the essential features of this situation is that no one knows his place in society, his class position or social status, nor does any one know his fortune in the distribution of natural assets and abilities, his intelligence, strength, and the like. I shall even assume that the parties do not know their conceptions of the good or their special psychological propensities. The principles of justice are chosen behind the *veil of ignorance*. This ensures that no one is advantaged or disadvantaged in the choice of principles by the outcome of natural chance or the contingency of social circumstances. Since all are similarly situated and no one is able to design principles to favor his particular condition, the principles of justice are the result of a fair agreement or bargain. For given the circumstances of the original position, the symmetry of everyone's relations to each other, this initial situation is fair between individuals as moral persons, that is, as rational beings with their own ends and capable, I shall assume, of a sense of justice. The *original position* is, one might say, the appropriate initial status quo, and thus the fundamental agreements reached in it are fair. This explains the propriety of the name "justice as fairness": it conveys the idea that the principles of justice are agreed to in an initial situation that is fair. . . .

Finally, Rawls argues that not only is the principle of fairness not a utilitarian principle but it is opposed to utilitarianism, because maximal utility may not be sought if it imposes unfair burdens on the less well off. Persons have rights which even the good of the society may not override.

FOR FURTHER READING

Barry, Brian. *Theories of Justice.* (University of California Press, 1989).
Daniels, Norman, ed. *Reading Rawls: Critical Studies of A Theory of Justice.* (Basil Blackwell, 1975).
Kukathas, Chandran and Philip Pettit. *Rawls: A Theory of Justice and its Critics.* (Stanford University Press, 1990).
Kymlicka, Will. *Contemporary Political Theory: An Introduction.* (Oxford University Press, 1990).
Nozick, Robert. *Anarchy, State and Utopia.* (Basic Books, 1974). A Libertarian critique of Rawls.
Pogge, Thomas. *Realizing Rawls.* (Cornell University Press, 1989).
Rawls, John. *A Theory of Justice.* (Harvard University Press, 1971).
Rawls, John. *Political Liberalism.* (Columbia University Press, 1994).
Sandel, Michael. *Liberalism and the Limits of Justice.* (Cambridge University Press, 1982).
Sterba, James, ed. *Justice: Alternative Political Perspectives,* 2nd ed. (Wadsworth Publishing Company, 1992). Contains a useful set of readings.
Wolff, Robert Paul. *Understanding Rawls.* (Princeton University Press, 1977).

Justice as Fairness

1. It might seem at first sight that the concepts of justice and fairness are the same, and that there is no reason to distinguish them, or to say that one is more fundamental than the other. I think that this impression is mistaken. In this paper I wish to show that the fundamental idea in the concept of justice is fairness; and I wish to offer an analysis of the concept of justice from this point of view. To bring out the force of this claim, and the analysis based upon it, I shall then argue that it is this aspect of justice for which utilitarianism, in its classical form, is unable to account, but which is expressed, even if misleadingly, by the ideas of the social contract.

To start with I shall develop a particular conception of justice by stating and commenting upon two principles which specify it, and by considering the circumstances and conditions under which they may be thought to arise. The principles defining this conception, and the conception itself are, of course, familiar. It may be possible, however, by using the notion of fairness as a framework, to assemble and to look at them in a new way. Before stating this conception, however, the following preliminary matters should be kept in mind.

Throughout I consider justice only as a virtue of social institutions, or what I shall call practices.[1] The principles of justice are regarded as formulating restrictions as to how practices may define positions and offices, and assign thereto powers and liabilities, rights and duties. Justice as a virtue of particular actions or of persons I do not take up at all. It is important to distinguish these various subjects of justice, since the meaning of the concept varies according to whether it is applied to practices, particular actions, or persons. These meanings are, indeed, connected, but they are not identical. I shall confine my discussion to the sense of justice as applied to practices, since this sense is the basic one. Once it is understood, the other senses should go quite easily.

Justice is to be understood in its customary sense as representing but *one* of the many virtues of so-

1. I use the word "practice" throughout as a sort of technical term meaning any form of activity specified by a system of rules which defines offices, roles, moves, penalties, defenses, and so on, and which gives the activity its structure. As examples one may think of games and rituals, trials and parliaments, markets and systems of property. I have attempted a partial analysis of the notion of a practice in a paper "Two Concepts of Rules" *Philosophical Review* LXIV (1955) 3–32.

cial institutions, for these may be antiquated, inefficient, degrading, or any number of other things, without being unjust. Justice is not to be confused with an all-inclusive vision of a good society; it is only one part of any such conception. It is important, for example, to distinguish that sense of equality which is an aspect of the concept of justice from that sense of equality which belongs to a more comprehensive social ideal. There may well be inequalities which one concedes are just, or at least not unjust, but which, nevertheless, one wishes, on other grounds, to do away with. I shall focus attention, then, on the usual sense of justice in which it is essentially the elimination of arbitrary distinctions and the establishment, within the structure of a practice, of a proper balance between competing claims.

Finally, there is no need to consider the principles discussed below as *the* principles of justice. For the moment it is sufficient that they are typical of a family of principles normally associated with the concept of justice. The way in which the principles of this family resemble one another, as shown by the background against which they may be thought to arise, will be made clear by the whole of the subsequent argument.

2. The conception of justice which I want to develop may be stated in the form of two principles as follows: first, each person participating in a practice, or affected by it, has an equal right to the most extensive liberty compatible with a like liberty for all; and second, inequalities are arbitrary unless it is reasonable to expect that they will work out for everyone's advantage, and provided the positions and offices to which they attach, or from which they may be gained, are open to all. These principles express justice as a complex of three ideas: liberty, equality, and reward for services contributing to the common good.[2]

The term "person" is to be construed variously depending on the circumstances. On some occasions it will mean human individuals, but in others it may refer to nations, provinces, business firms, churches, teams, and so on. The principles of justice apply in all these instances, although there is a certain logical priority to the case of human individuals. As I shall use the term "person," it will be ambiguous in the manner indicated.

The first principle holds, of course, only if other things are equal: that is, while there must always be a justification for departing from the initial position of equal liberty (which is defined by the pattern of rights and duties, powers and liabilities, established by a practice), and the burden of proof is placed on him who would depart from it, nevertheless, there can be, and often there is, a justification for doing so. Now, that similar particular cases, as defined by a practice, should be treated similarly as they arise, is part of the very concept of a practice; it is involved in the notion of an activity in accordance with rules.[3] The first principle expresses an analogous conception, but as applied to the structure of practices themselves. It holds, for example, that there is a presumption against the distinctions and classifications made by legal systems and other practices to the extent that they infringe on the original and equal liberty of the persons participating in them. The second principle defines how this presumption may be rebutted.

It might be argued at this point that justice requires only an equal liberty. If, however, a greater liberty were possible for all without loss or conflict, then it would be irrational to settle on a lesser liberty. There is no reason for circumscribing rights unless their exercise would be incompatible, or would render the practice defining them less effective. Therefore no serious distortion of the concept of justice is likely to follow from including within it the concept of the greatest equal liberty.

The second principle defines what sorts of inequalities are permissible; it specifies how the presumption laid down by the first principle may be put aside. Now by inequalities it is best to understand not *any* differences between offices and positions, but differences in the benefits and burdens attached

2. These principles are of course well-known in one form or another and appear in many analyses of justice even where the writers differ widely on other matters. Thus if the principle of equal liberty is commonly associated with Kant (see *The Philosophy of Law*, tr. by W. Hastie, Edinburgh, 1887, pp. 56 f.), it may be claimed that it can also be found in J. S. Mill's *On Liberty* and elsewhere, and in many other liberal writers. Recently H. L. A. Hart has argued for something like it in his paper "Are There Any Natural Rights?," *Philosophical Review*, LXIV (1955), 175–191. The injustice of inequalities which are not won in return for a contribution to the common advantage is, of course, widespread in political writings of all sorts. The conception of justice here discussed is distinctive, if at all, only in selecting these two principle in this form; but for another similar analysis, see the discussion by W. D. Lamont, *The Principles of Moral Judgment* (Oxford, 1946), ch. v.

3. This point was made by Sidgwick, *Methods of Ethics*, 6th ed. (London, 1901), Bk. III, ch. v, sec. 1. It has recently been emphasized by Sir Isaiah Berlin in a symposium, "Equality," *Proceedings of the Aristotelian Society*, n.s. LVI (1955–56), 305 f.

to them either directly or indirectly, such as prestige and wealth, or liability to taxation and compulsory services. Players in a game do not protest against there being different positions, such as batter, pitcher, catcher, and the like, nor to there being various privileges and powers as specified by the rules; nor do the citizens of a country object to there being the different offices of government such as president, senator, governor, judge, and so on, each with their special rights and duties. It is not differences of this kind that are normally thought of as inequalities, but differences in the resulting distribution established by a practice, or made possible by it, of the things men strive to attain or avoid. Thus they may complain about the pattern of honors and rewards set up by a practice (e.g., the privileges and salaries of government officials) or they may object to the distribution of power and wealth which results from the various ways in which men avail themselves of the opportunities allowed by it (e.g., the concentration of wealth which may develop in a free price system allowing large entrepreneurial or speculative gains).

It should be noted that the second principle holds that an inequality is allowed only if there is reason to believe that the practice with the inequality, or resulting in it, will work for the advantage of *every* party engaging in it. Here it is important to stress that *every* party must gain from the inequality. Since the principle applies to practices, it implies that the representative man in every office or position defined by a practice, when he views it as a going concern, must find it reasonable to prefer his condition and prospects with the inequality to what they would be under the practice without it. The principle excludes, therefore, the justification of inequalities on the grounds that the disadvantages of those in one position are outweighed by the greater advantages of those in another position. This rather simple restriction is the main modification I wish to make in the utilitarian principle as usually understood. When coupled with the notion of a practice, it is a restriction of consequence,[4] and one which some utilitarians, e.g., Hume and Mill, have used in their discussions of justice without realizing apparently its significance, or at least without calling attention to it.[5] Why it is a significant modification of principle, changing one's conception of justice entirely, the whole of my argument will show.

Further, it is also necessary that the various offices to which special benefits or burdens attach are open to all. It may be, for example, to the common advantage, as just defined, to attach special benefits to certain offices. Perhaps by doing so the requisite talent can be attracted to them and encouraged to give its best efforts. But any offices having special benefits must be won in a fair competition in which contestants are judged on their merits. If some offices were not open, those excluded would normally be justified in feeling unjustly treated, even if they benefited from the greater efforts of those who were allowed to compete for them. Now if one can assume that offices are open, it is necessary only to consider the design of practices themselves and how they jointly, as a system, work together. It will be a mistake to focus attention on the varying relative positions of particular persons, who may be known to us by their proper names, and to require that each such change, as a once for all transaction viewed in

4. In the paper referred to above, footnote 2, I have tried to show the importance of taking practices as the proper subject of the utilitarian principle. The criticisms of so-called "restricted utilitarianism" by J. J. C. Smart, "Extreme and Restricted Utilitarianism," *Philosophical Quarterly,* VI (1956), 344–354, and by H. J. McCloskey, "An Examination of Restricted Utilitarianism," *Philosophical Review,* LXVI (1957), 466–485, do not affect my argument. These papers are concerned with the very general proposition, which is attributed (with what justice I shall not consider) to S. E. Toulmin and P. H. Nowell-Smith (and in the case of the latter paper, also, apparently, to me); namely, the proposition that particular moral actions are justified by appealing to moral rules, and moral rules in turn by reference to utility. But clearly I meant to defend no such view. My discussion of the concept of rules as maxims is an explicit rejection of it. What I did argue was that, in the *logically special* case of practices (although actually quite a common case) where the rules have special features and are not moral rules at all but legal rules or rules of games and the like (except, perhaps, in the case of promises), there is a peculiar force to the distinction between justifying particular actions and justifying the system of rules themselves. Even then I claimed only that restricting the utilitarian principle to practices as defined strengthened it. I did not argue for the position that this amendment alone is sufficient for a complete defense of utilitarianism as a general theory of morals. In this paper I take up the question as to how the utilitarian principle itself must be modified, but here, too, the subject of inquiry is not all of morality at once, but a limited topic, the concept of justice.

5. It might seem as if J. S. Mill, in paragraph 36 of Chapter v of *Utilitarianism,* expressed the utilitarian principle in this modified form,but in the remaining two paragraphs of the chapter, and elsewhere, he would appear not to grasp the significance of the change. Hume often emphasizes that *every* man must benefit. For example, in discussing the utility of general rules, he holds that they are requisite to the "well-being of every individual"; from a stable system of property "every individual person must find himself a gainer in balancing the account. . . ." "Every member of society is sensible of this interest; everyone expresses this sense to his fellows along with the resolution he has taken of squaring his actions by it on the conditions that others will do the same." *A Treatise of Human Nature,* Bk. III, Pt. II, Section II, paragraph 22.

isolation, must be in itself just. It is the system of practices which is to be judged, and judged from a general point of view: unless one is prepared to criticize it from the standpoint of a representative man holding some particular office, one has no complaint against it.

3. Given these principles one might try to derive them from a priori principles of reason, or claim that they were known by intuition. These are familiar enough steps and, at least in the case of the first principle, might be made with some success. Usually, however, such arguments, made at this point, are unconvincing. They are not likely to lead to an understanding of the basis of the principles of justice, not at least as principles of justice. I wish, therefore, to look at the principles in a different way.

Imagine a society of persons amongst whom a certain system of practices is *already* well established. Now suppose that by and large they are mutually self-interested; their allegiance to their established practice is normally founded on the prospect of self-advantage. One need not assume that, in all senses of the term "person," the persons in this society are mutually self-interested. If the characterization as mutually self-interested applies when the line of division is the family, it may still be true that members of families are bound by ties of sentiment and affection and willingly acknowledge duties in contradiction to self-interest. Mutual self-interestedness in the relations between families, nations, churches, and the like, is commonly associated with intense loyalty and devotion on the part of individual members. Therefore, one can form a more realistic conception of this society if one thinks of it as consisting of mutually self-interested families, or some other association. Further, it is not necessary to suppose that these persons are mutually self-interested under all circumstances, but only in the usual situations in which they participate in their common practices.

Now suppose also that these persons are rational: they know their own interests more or less accurately; they are capable of tracing out the likely consequences of adopting one practice rather than another; they are capable of adhering to a course of action once they have decided upon it; they can resist present temptations and the enticements of immediate gain; and the bare knowledge or perception of the difference between their condition and that of others is not, within certain limits and in itself, a source of great dissatisfaction. Only the last point adds anything to the usual definition of rationality. This definition should allow, I think, for the idea that a rational man would not be greatly downcast from knowing, or seeing, that others are in a better position than himself, unless he thought their being so was the result of injustice, or the consequence of letting chance work itself out for no useful common purpose, and so on. So if these persons strike us as unpleasantly egoistic, they are at least free in some degree from the fault of envy.[6]

Finally, assume that these persons have roughly similar needs and interests, or needs and interests in various ways complementary, so that fruitful cooperation amongst them is possible; and suppose that they are sufficiently equal in power and ability to guarantee that in normal circumstances none is able to dominate the others. This condition (as well as the other) may seem excessively vague; but in view of the conception of justice to which the argument leads, there seems no reason for making it more exact here.

Since these persons are conceived as engaging in their common practices, which are already established, there is no question of our supposing them to come together to deliberate as to how they will set these practices up for the first time. Yet we can imagine that from time to time they discuss with one another whether any of them has a legitimate complaint against their established institutions. Such discussions are perfectly natural in any normal society. Now suppose that they have settled on doing this in the following way. They first try to arrive at the principles by which complaints, and so practices themselves, are to be judged. Their procedure for this is to let each person propose that principles upon which he wishes this complaints to be tried with the understanding that, if acknowledged, the complains of others will be similarly tried, and that no complaints will be heard at all until everyone is roughly of one mind as to how complaints are to be judged. They each understand further that the principles proposed and acknowledged on this occasion are binding on future occasions. Thus each will be wary of proposing a principle which would give him a peculiar ad-

6. It is not possible to discuss here this addition to the usual conception of rationality. If it seems peculiar, it may be worth remarking that it is analogous to the modification of the utilitarian principle which the argument as a whole is designed to explain and justify. In the same way that the satisfaction of interests, the representative claims of which violate the principles of justice, is not reason for having a practice (see sec. 7), unfounded envy, within limits, need not to be taken into account.

vantage, in his present circumstances, supposing it to be accepted. Each person knows that he will be bound by it in future circumstances the peculiarities of which cannot be known and which might well be such that the principle is then to his disadvantage. The idea is that everyone should be required to make *in advance* a firm commitment which others also may reasonably be expected to make, and that no one be given the opportunity to tailor the canons of a legitimate complaint to fit his own special condition, and then to discard them when they no longer suit his purpose. Hence each person will propose principles of a general kind which will, to a large degree, gain their sense from the various applications to be made of them, the particular circumstances of which being as yet unknown. These principles will express the conditions in accordance with which each is the least unwilling to have his interests limited in the design of practices, given the competing interests of the others, on the supposition that the interests of others will be limited likewise. The restrictions which would so arise might be thought of as those a person would keep in mind if he were designing a practice in which his enemy were to assign him his place.

The two main parts of this conjectural account have a definite significance. The character and respective situations of the parties reflect the typical circumstances in which questions of justice arise. The procedure whereby principles are proposed and acknowledged represents constraints, analogous to those of having a morality, whereby rational and mutually self-interested persons are brought to act reasonably. Thus the first part reflects the fact that questions of justice arise when conflicting claims are made upon the design of a practice and where it is taken for granted that each person will insist, as far as possible, on what he considers his rights. It is typical of cases of justice to involve persons who are pressing on one another their claims, between which a fair balance or equilibrium must be found. On the other hand, as expressed by the second part, having a morality must at least imply the acknowledgment of principles as impartially applying to one's own conduct as well as to another's, and moreover principles which may constitute a constraint, or limitation, upon the pursuit of one's own interests. There are, of course, other aspects of having a morality: the acknowledgment of moral principles must show itself in accepting a reference to them as reasons for limiting one's claims, in acknowledging the burden of providing a special explanation, or excuse, when one acts contrary to them, or else in showing shame and remorse and a desire to make amends, and so on. It is sufficient to remark here that having a morality is analogous to having made a firm commitment in advance; for one must acknowledge the principles of morality even when to one's disadvantage.[7] A man whose moral judgments always coincided with his interests could be suspected of having no morality at all.

Thus the two parts of the foregoing account are intended to mirror the kinds of circumstances in which questions of justice arise and the constraints which having a morality would impose upon persons so situated. In this way one can see how the acceptance of the principles of justice might come about, for given all these conditions as described, it would be natural if the two principles of justice were to be acknowledged. Since there is no way for anyone to win special advantages for himself, each might consider it reasonable to acknowledge equality as an initial principle. There is, however, no reason why they should regard this position as final; for if there are inequalities which satisfy the second principle, the immediate gain which equality would allow can be considered as intelligently invested in view of its future return. If, as is quite likely, these inequalities work as incentives to draw out better efforts, the members of this society may look upon them as concessions to human nature: they, like us, may think that people ideally should want to serve one another. But as they are mutually self-interested, their acceptance of these inequalities is merely the acceptance of the relations in which they actually stand, and a recognition of the motives which lead them to engage in their common practices. *They* have no title to complain of one another. And so provided that the conditions of the principle are met, there is no reason why they should not allow such inequalities. Indeed, it would be short-sighted of them not to do so, and could result, in most cases, only from their being dejected by the bare knowledge, or perception, that others are better situated.

7. The idea that accepting a principle as a moral principle implies that one generally acts on it, failing a special explanation, has been stressed by R. M. Hare, *The Language of Morals* (Oxford, 1952). His formulation of it needs to be modified, however, along the lines suggested by P. L. Gardiner, "On Assenting to a Moral Principle," *Proceedings of the Aristotelian Society*, n.s. LV (1955), 23–44. See also C. K. Grant, "Akrasia and the Criteria of Assent to Practical Principles," *Mind*, LXV (1956), 400–407, where the complexity of the criteria for assent is discussed.

Each person will, however, insist on an advantage to himself, and so on a common advantage, for none is willing to sacrifice anything for the others.

These remarks are not offered as a proof that persons so conceived and circumstanced would settle on the two principles, but only to show that these principles could have such a background, and so can be viewed as those principles which mutually self-interested and rational persons, when similarly situated and required to make in advance a firm commitment, could acknowledge as restrictions governing the assignment of rights and duties in their common practices, and thereby accept as limiting their rights against on another. The principles of justice may, then, be regarded as those principles which arise when the constraints of having a morality are imposed upon parties in the typical circumstances of justice.

4. These ideas are, of course, connected with a familiar way of thinking about justice which goes back at least to the Greek Sophists, and which regards the acceptance of the principles of justice as a compromise between persons of roughly equal power who would enforce their will on each other if they could, but who, in view of the equality of forces amongst them and for the sake of their own peace and security, acknowledge certain forms of conduct insofar as prudence seems to require. Justice is thought of as a pact between rational egoists the stability of which is dependent on a balance of power and a similarity of circumstances.[8] While the previous account is connected with this tradition, and with its most recent variant, the theory of games,[9] it differs from it in several important respects which, to forestall misinterpretations, I will set out here.

First, I wish to use the previous conjectural account of the background of justice as a way of analyzing the concept. I do not want, therefore, to be interpreted as assuming a general theory of human motivation: when I suppose that the parties are mutually self-interested, and are not willing to have their (substantial) interests sacrificed to others, I am referring to their conduct and motives as they are taken for granted in cases where questions of justice ordinarily arise. Justice is the virtue of practices where there are assumed to be competing interests and conflicting claims, and where it is supposed that persons will press their rights on each other. That persons are mutually self-interested in certain situations and for certain purposes is what gives rise to the question of justice in practices covering those circumstances. Amongst an association of saints, if such a community could really exist, the disputes about justice could hardly occur; for they would all work selflessly together for one end, the glory of God as defined by their common religion, and reference to this end would settle every question of right. The justice of practices does not come up until there are several different parties (whether we think of these as individuals, associations, or nations and so on, is irrelevant) who do press their claims on one another, and who do regard themselves as representatives of interests which deserve to be considered. Thus the previous account involves no general theory of human motivation. Its intent is simply to incorporate into the conception of justice the relations of men to one another which set the stage for questions of justice. It makes no difference how wide or general these relations are, as this matter does not bear on the analysis of the concept.

Again, in contrast to the various conceptions of the social contract, the several parties do not establish any particular society or practice; they do not covenant to obey a particular sovereign body or to accept a given constitution.[10] Nor do they, as in the

8. Perhaps the best known statement of this conception is that given by Glaucon at the beginning of Book II of Plato's *Republic*. Presumably it was, in various forms, a common view among the Sophists; but that Plato gives a fair representation of it is doubtful. See K. R. Popper, *The Open Society and Its Enemies*, rev. ed. (Princeton, 1950), pp. 112–118. Certainly Plato usually attributes to it a quality of manic egoism which one feels must be an exaggeration; on the other hand, see the Melian Debate in Thucydides, *The Peloponnesian War*, Book V, ch. VII, although it is impossible to say to what extent the views expressed there reveal any current philosophical opinion. Also in this tradition are the remarks of Epicurus on justice in *Principal Doctrines*, XXXI–XXXVIII. In modern times elements of the conception appear in a more sophisticated form in Hobbes *The Leviathan* and in Hume *A Treatise of Human Nature*, Book III, Pt. II, as well as in the writings of the school of natural law such as Pufendorf's *De jure naturae et gentium*. Hobbes and Hume are especially instructive. For Hobbes's argument see Howard Warrender's *The Political Philosophy of Hobbes* (Oxford, 1957). W. J. Baumol's *Welfare Economics and the Theory of the State* (London, 1952), is valuable in showing the wide applicability of Hobbes's fundamental idea (interpreting his natural law as principles of prudence), although in this book it is traced back only to Hume's *Treatise*.

9. See J. von Neumann and O. Morgenstern, *The Theory of Games and Economic Behavior*, 2nd ed. (Princeton, 1947). For a comprehensive and not too technical discussion of the developments since, see R. Duncan Luce and Howard Raiffa, *Games and Decisions: Introduction and Critical Survey* (New York, 1957). Chs. VI and XIV discuss the developments most obviously related to the analysis of justice.

10. For a general survey see J. W. Gough, *The Social Contract*, 2nd ed. (Oxford, 1957), and Otto von Gierke, *The Development of Political Theory*, tr. by B. Freyd (London, 1939), Pt. II, ch. 11.

theory of games (in certain respects a marvelously sophisticated development of this tradition), decide on individual strategies adjusted to their respective circumstances in the game. What the parties do is to *jointly* acknowledge certain *principles* of appraisal relating to their common *practices* either as already established or merely proposed. They accede to standards of judgment, not to a given practice; they do not make any specific agreement, or bargain, or adopt a particular strategy. The subject of their acknowledgment is, therefore, very general indeed; it is simply the acknowledgment of certain principles of judgment, fulfilling certain general conditions, to be used in criticizing the arrangement of their common affairs. The relations of mutual self-interest between the parties who are similarly circumstanced mirror the conditions under which questions of justice arise, and the procedure by which the principles of judgment are proposed and acknowledged reflects the constraints of having a morality. Each aspect, then, of the preceding hypothetical account serves the purpose of bringing out a feature of the notion of justice. One could, if one liked, view the principles of justice as the "solution" of this highest order "game" of adopting, subject to the procedure described, principles of argument for all coming particular "games" whose peculiarities one can in no way foresee. But this comparison, while no doubt helpful, must not obscure the fact that this highest order "game" is of a special sort.[11] Its significance is that its various pieces represent aspects of the concept of justice.

Finally, I do not, of course, conceive the several parties as necessarily coming together to establish their common practices for the first time. Some institutions may, indeed, be set up *de novo*; but I have framed the preceding account so that it will apply when the full complement of social institutions already exists and represents the result of a long period of development. Nor is the account in any way fictitious. In any society where people reflect on their institutions they will have an idea of what principles of justice would be acknowledged under the conditions described, and there will be occasions when questions of justice are actually discussed in this way. Therefore if their practices do not accord with these principles, this will affect the quality of their social relations. For in this case there will be some recognized situations wherein the parties are mutually aware that one of them is being forced to accept what the other would concede is unjust. The foregoing analysis may then be thought of as representing the actual quality of relations between persons as defined by practices accepted as just. In such practices the parties will acknowledge the principles on which it is constructed, and the general recognition of this fact shows itself in the absence of resentment and in the sense of being justly treated. Thus one common objection to the theory of the social contract, its apparently historical and fictitious character, is avoided.

5. That the principles of justice may be regarded as arising in the manner described illustrates an important fact about them. Not only does it bring out the idea that justice is a primitive moral notion in that it arises once the concept of morality is imposed on mutually self-interested agents similarly circumstanced, but it emphasizes that, fundamental to justice, is the concept of fairness which relates to right dealing between persons who are cooperating with or competing against one another, as when one speaks of fair games, fair competition, and fair bar-

11. The difficulty one gets into by a mechanical application of the theory of games to moral philosophy can be brought out by considering among several possible examples, R. B. Braithwaite's study, *Theory of Games as a Tool for the Moral Philosopher* (Cambridge, 1955). On the analysis there given, it turns out that the fair division of playing time between Matthew and Luke depends on their preferences, and these in turn are connected with the instruments they wish to play. Since Matthew has a threat advantage over Luke, arising purely from the fact that Matthew, the trumpeter, prefers both of them playing at once to neither of them playing, whereas Luke, the pianist, prefers silence to cacophony, Matthew is allotted 26 evenings of play to Luke's 17. If the situation were reversed, the threat advantage would be with Luke. See p. 36 f. But now we have only to suppose that Matthew is a jazz enthusiast who plays the drums, and Luke a violinist who plays sonatas, in which case it will be fair, on this analysis, for Matthew to play whenever and as often as he likes, assuming, of course, as it is plausible to assume, that he does not care whether Luke plays or not. Certainly something has gone wrong. To each according to his threat advantage is hardly the principle of fairness. What is lacking is the concept of morality, and it must be brought into the conjectural account in some way or other. In the text this is one by the form of the procedure whereby principles are proposed and acknowledged (Section 3). If one starts directly with the particular case as known, and if one accepts as given and definitive the preferences and relative positions of the parties, whatever they are, it is impossible to give an analysis of the moral concept of fairness. Braithwaite's use of the theory of games, insofar as it is intended to analyze the concept of fairness, is, I think, mistaken. This is not, of course, to criticize in any way the theory of games as a mathematical theory, to which Braithwaite's book certainly contributes, nor as an analysis of how rational (and amoral) egoists might behave (and so as an analysis of how people sometimes actually do behave). But it is to say that if the theory of games is to be used to analyze moral concepts, its formal structure must be interpreted in a special and general manner as indicted in the text. Once we do this, though, we are in touch again with a much older tradition.

gains. The question of fairness arises when free persons, who have no authority over one another, are engaging in a joint activity and amongst themselves settling or acknowledging the rules which define it and which determine the respective shares in its benefits and burdens. A practice will strike the parties as fair if none feels that, by participating in it, they or any of the others are taken advantage of, or forced to give in to claims which they do not regard as legitimate. This implies that each has a conception of legitimate claims which he thinks it reasonable for others as well as himself to acknowledge. If one thinks of the principles of justice as arising in the manner described, then they do define this sort of conception. A practice is just or fair, then, when it satisfies the principles which those who participate in it could propose to one another for mutual acceptance under the afore-mentioned circumstances. Persons engaged in a just, or fair, practice can face one another openly and support their respective positions, should they appear questionable, by reference to principles which it is reasonable to expect each to accept.

It is this notion of the possibility of mutual acknowledgment of principles by free persons who have no authority over one another which makes the concept of fairness fundamental to justice. Only if such acknowledgment is possible can there be true community between persons in their common practices; otherwise their relations will appear to them as founded to some extent on force. If, in ordinary speech, fairness applies more particularly to practices in which there is a choice whether to engage or not (e.g., in games, business competition), and justice to practices in which there is no choice (e.g., in slavery), the element of necessity does not render the conception of mutual acknowledgment inapplicable, although it may make it much more urgent to change unjust than unfair institutions. For one activity in which one can always engage is that of proposing and acknowledging principles to one another supposing each to be similarly circumstanced; and to judge practices by the principles so arrived at is to apply the standard of fairness to them.

Now if the participants in a practice accept its rules as fair, and so have no complaint to lodge against it, there arises a prima facie duty (and a corresponding prima facie right) of the parties to each other to act in accordance with the practice when it falls upon them to comply. When any number of persons engage in a practice, or conduct a joint undertaking according to rules, and thus restrict their liberty, those who have submitted to these restrictions when required have the right to a similar acquiescence on the part of those who have benefited by their submission. These conditions will obtain if a practice is correctly acknowledged to be fair, for in this case all who participate in it will benefit from it. The rights and duties so arising are special rights and duties in that they depend on previous actions voluntarily undertaken, in this case on the parties having engaged in a common practice and knowingly accepted its benefits.[12] It is not, however, an obligation which presupposes a deliberate performative act in the sense of a promise, or contract, and the like.[13] An unfortunate mistake of proponents of the idea of the social contract was to suppose that political obligation does require some such act, or at least to use language which suggests it. It is sufficient that one has knowingly participated in and accepted the benefits of a practice acknowledged to be fair. This prima facie obligation may, of course, be overridden: it may happen, when it comes one's turn to follow a rule, that other considerations will justify not doing so. But one cannot, in general, be released from this obligation by denying the justice of the practice only when it falls on one to obey. If a person rejects a practice, he should, so far as possible, declare his intention in advance, and avoid participating in it or enjoying its benefits.

This duty I have called that of fair play, but it should be admitted that to refer to it in this way is, perhaps, to extend the ordinary notion of fairness. Usually acting unfairly is not so much the breaking of any particular rule, even if the infraction is difficult to detect (cheating), but taking advantage of loop-holes or ambiguities in rules, availing oneself of unexpected or special circumstances which make it impossible to enforce them, insisting that rules be enforced to one's advantage when they should be suspended, and more generally, acting contrary to the intention of a practice. It is for this reason that one speaks of the sense of fair play: acting fairly requires more than simply being able to follow rules; what is fair must often be felt, or perceived, one wants to say. It is not, however, an unnatural ex-

12. For the definition of this prima facie duty, and the idea that it is a special duty, I am indebted to H. L. A. Hart. See this paper "Are There Any Natural Rights?," *Philosophical Review*, LXIV (1955), 185 f.

13. The sense of "performative" here is to be derived from J. L. Austin's paper in the symposium, "Other Minds," *Proceedings of the Aristotelian Society*, Supplementary Volume (1946), pp. 170–174.

tension of the duty of fair play to have it include the obligation which participants who have knowingly accepted the benefits of their common practice owe to each other to act in accordance with it when their performance falls due; for it is usually considered unfair if someone accepts the benefits of a practice but refuses to do his part in maintaining it. Thus one might say of the tax-dodger that he violates the duty of fair play: he accepts the benefits of government but will not do his part in releasing resources to it; and members of labor unions often say that fellow workers who refuse to join are being unfair: they refer to them as "free riders," as persons who enjoy what are the supposed benefits of unionism, higher wages, shorter hours, job security, and the like, but who refuse to share in its burdens in the form of paying dues, and so on.

The duty of fair play stands beside other prima facie duties such as fidelity and gratitude as a basic moral notion; yet it is not to be confused with them.[14] These duties are all clearly distinct, as would be obvious from their definitions. As with any moral duty, that of fair play implies a constraint on self-interest in particular cases; on occasion it enjoins conduct which a rational egoist strictly defined would not decide upon. So while justice does not require of anyone that he sacrifice his interests in that *general position* and procedure whereby the principles of justice are proposed and acknowledged, it may happen that in particular situations, arising in the context of engaging in a practice, the duty of fair play will often cross his interests in the sense that he will be required to forego particular advantages which the peculiarities of his circumstances might permit him to take. There is, of course, nothing surprising in this. It is simply the consequence of the firm commitment which the parties may be supposed to have made, or which they would make, in the general position, together with the fact that they have participated in and accepted the benefits of a practice which they regard as fair.

Now the acknowledgment of this constraint in particular cases, which is manifested in acting fairly or wishing to make amends, feeling ashamed, and the like, when one has evaded it, is one of the forms of conduct by which participants in a common practice exhibit their recognition of each other as persons with similar interests and capacities. In the same way that, failing a special explanation, the criterion for the recognition of suffering is helping one who suffers, acknowledging the duty of fair play is a necessary part of the criterion for recognizing another as a person with similar interests and feelings as oneself.[15] A person who never under any circumstances showed a wish to help others in pain would show, at the same time, that he did not recognize that they were in pain; nor could he have any feelings of affection or friendship for anyone; for having these feelings implies, failing special circumstances, that he comes to their aid when they are suffering. Recognition that another is a person in pain shows itself in sympathetic action; this primitive natural response of compassion is one of those responses upon which the various forms of moral conduct are built.

Similarly, the acceptance of the duty of fair play by participants in a common practice is a reflection in each person of the recognition of the aspirations and interests of the others to be realized by their joint activity. Failing a special explanation, their acceptance of it is a necessary part of the criterion for their recognizing one another as persons with similar interests and capacities, as the conception of their relations in the general position supposes them to be. Otherwise they would show no recognition of one another as persons with similar capacities and interests, and indeed, in some cases perhaps hypothetical, they would not recognize one another as persons at all, but as complicated objects involved in a complicated activity. To recognize another as a person one must respond to him and act towards him in certain ways; and these ways are intimately connected with the various prima facie duties. Ac-

14. This, however, commonly happens. Hobbes, for example, when invoking the notion of a "tacit covenant," appeals not to the natural law that promises should be kept but to his fourth law of nature, that of gratitude. On Hobbes's shift from fidelity to gratitude, see Warrender, *op. cit.*, pp. 51–52, 233–237. While it is not serious criticism of Hobbes, it would have improved his argument had he appealed to the duty of fair play. On his premises he is perfectly entitled to do so. Similarly, Sidgwick thought that a principle of justice, such as every man ought to receive adequate requital for his labor, is like gratitude universalized. See *Methods of Ethics*, Bk. III, ch. v, Sec. 5. There is a gap in the stock of moral concepts used by philosophers into which the concept of the duty of fair play fits quite naturally.

15. I am using the concept of criterion here in what I take to be Wittgenstein's sense. See *Philosophical Investigations* (Oxford, 1953); and Norman Malcolm's review, "Wittgenstein's *Philosophical Investigations*," *Philosophical Review*, LXIII (1954), 543–547. That the response of compassion, under appropriate circumstances, is part of the criterion for whether or not a person understands what "pain" means, is, I think, in the *Philosophical Investigations*. The view in the text is simply an extension of this idea. I cannot, however, attempt to justify it here. Similar thoughts are to be found, I think, in Max Schelere, *The Nature of Sympathy*, tr. by Peter Heath (New Haven, 1954). His way of writing is often so obscure that I cannot be certain.

knowledging these duties in *some* degree, and so having the elements of morality, is not a matter of choice, or of intuiting moral qualities, or a matter of expression of feelings or attitudes (the three interpretations between which philosophical opinion frequently oscillates); it is simply the possession of one of the forms of conduct in which the recognition of others as persons is manifested.

These remarks are unhappily obscure. Their main purpose here, however, is to forestall, together with the remarks in Section 4, the misinterpretation that, on the view presented, the acceptance of justice and the acknowledgment of the duty of fair play depends in every day life solely on there being a *de facto* balance of forces between the parties. It would indeed be foolish to underestimate the importance of such a balance in securing justice; but it is not the only basis thereof. The recognition of one another as persons with similar interests and capacities engaged in a common practice must, failing a special explanation, show itself in the acceptance of the principles of justice and the acknowledgment of the duty of fair play.

The conception at which we have arrived, then, is that the principles of justice may be thought of as arising once the constraints of having a morality are imposed upon rational and mutually self-interested parties who are related and situated in a special way. A practice is just if it is in accordance with the principles which all who participate in it might reasonably be expected to propose or to acknowledge before one another when they are similarly circumstanced and required to make a firm commitment in advance without knowledge of what will be their peculiar condition, and thus when it meets standards which the parties could accept as fair should occasion arise for them to debate its merits. Regarding the participants themselves, once persons knowingly engage in a practice which they acknowledge to be fair and accept the benefits of doing so, they are bound by the duty of fair play to follow the rules when it comes their turn to do so, and this implies a limitation on their pursuit of self-interest in particular cases.

Now one consequence of this conception is that, where it applies, there is no moral value in the satisfaction of a claim incompatible with it. Such a claim violates the conditions of reciprocity and community amongst persons, and he who presses it, not being willing to acknowledge it when pressed by another, has no grounds for complaint when it is denied; whereas he against whom it is pressed can complain. As it cannot be mutually acknowledged it is a resort to coercion; granting the claim is possible only if the party can compel acceptance of what the other will not admit. But it makes no sense to concede claims the denial of which cannot be complained of in preference to claims the denial of which can be objected to. Thus in deciding on the justice of a practice it is not enough to ascertain that it answers to wants and interests in the fullest and most effective manner. For if any of these conflict with justice, they should not be counted, as their satisfaction is no reason at all for having a practice. It would be irrelevant to say, even if true, that it resulted in the greatest satisfaction of desire. In tallying up the merits of a practice one must toss out the satisfaction of interests the claims of which are incompatible with the principles of justice.

6. The discussion so far has been excessively abstract. While this is perhaps unavoidable, I should now like to bring out some of the features of the conception of justice as fairness by comparing it with the conception of justice in classical utilitarianism as represented by Bentham and Sidgwick, and its counterpart in welfare economics. This conception assimilates justice to benevolence and the latter in turn to the most efficient design of institutions to promote the general welfare. Justice is a kind of efficiency.[16]

Now it is said occasionally that this form of utilitarianism puts no restrictions on what might be a just assignment of rights and duties in that there might be circumstances which, on utilitarian

16. While this assimilation is implicit in Bentham's and Sidgwick's moral theory, explicit statements of it as applied to justice are relatively rare. One clear instance in *The Principles of Morals and Legislation* occurs in ch. x, footnote 2 to section XL: ". . . justice, in the only sense in which it has a meaning, is an imaginary personage, feigned for the convenience of discourse, whose dictators are the dictates of utility, applied to certain particular cases. Justice, then, is nothing more than an imaginary instrument, employed to forward on certain occasions,and by certain means, the purposes of benevolence. The dictates of justice are nothing more than a part of the dictates of benevolence, which, on certain occasions, are applied to certain subjects. . . ." Likewise in *The Limits of Jurisprudence Refined,* ed. by C. W. Everett (New York, 1945), pp. 117 f., Bentham criticizes Grotius for denying that justice derives from utility; and in *The Theory of Legislation,* ed. by C. K. Ogden (London, 1931), p. 3, he says that he uses the words "just" and "unjust" along with other words "simply as collective terms including the ideas of certain pains or pleasures." That Sidgwick's conception of justice is similar to Bentham's is admittedly not evident from his discussion of justice in Book III, ch. v. of *Methods of Ethics.* But it follows, I think, from the moral theory he accepts. Hence C. D. Broad's criticisms of Sidgwick in the matter of distributive justice in *Five Types of Ethical Theory* (London, 1930), pp. 249–253, do not rest on a misinterpretation.

grounds, would justify institutions highly offensive to our ordinary sense of justice. But the classical utilitarian conception is not totally unprepared for this objection. Beginning with the notion that the general happiness can be represented by a social utility function consisting of a sum of individual utility functions with identical weights (this being the meaning of the maxim that each counts for one and no more than one),[17] it is commonly assumed that the utility functions of individuals are similar in all essential respects. Differences between individuals are ascribed to accidents of education and upbringing, and they should not be taken into account. This assumption, coupled with that of diminishing marginal utility, results in a prima facie case for equality, e.g., of equality in the distribution of income during any given period of time, laying aside indirect effects on the future. But even if utilitarianism is interpreted as having such restrictions built into the utility function, and even it it is supposed that these restrictions have in practice much the same result as the application of the principles of justice (and appear, perhaps, to be ways of expressing these principles in the language of mathematics and psychology), the fundamental idea is very different from the conception of justice as fairness. For one thing, that the principles of justice should be accepted is interpreted as the contingent result of a higher order administrative decision. The form of this decision is regarded as being similar to that of an entrepreneur deciding how much to produce of this or that commodity in view of its marginal revenue, or to that of someone distributing goods to needy persons according to the relative urgency of their wants. The choice between practices is thought of as being made on the basis of the allocation of benefits and burdens to individuals (these being measured by the present capitalized value of their utility over the full period of the practice's existence), which results from the distribution of rights and duties established by a practice.

Moreover, the individuals receiving these benefits are not conceived as being related in any way: they represent so many different directions in which limited resources may be allocated. The value of assigning resources to one direction rather than another depends solely on the preferences and interests of individuals as individuals. The satisfaction of desire has its value irrespective of the moral relations between persons, say as members of a joint undertaking, and of the claims which, in the name of these interests, they are prepared to make on one another;[18] and it is this value which is to be taken into account by the (ideal) legislator who is conceived as adjusting the rules of the system from the center so as to maximize the value of the social utility function.

It is thought that the principles of justice will not be violated by a legal system so conceived provided these executive decisions are correctly made. In this fact the principles of justice are said to have their derivation and explanation; they simply express the most important general features of social institutions in which the administrative problem is solved in the best way. These principles have, indeed, a special urgency because, given the facts of human nature, so much depends on them; and this explains the peculiar quality of the moral feelings associated with justice.[19] This assimilation of justice to a higher order executive decision, certainly a striking conception, is central to classical utilitarianism; and it also

17. This maxim is attributed to Bentham by J. S. Mill in *Utilitarianism,* ch. v, paragraph 36. I have not found it in Bentham's writings, nor seen such a reference. Similarly James Bonar, *Philosophy and Political Economy* (London, 1893), p. 234 n. But it accords perfectly with Bentham's ideas. See the hitherto unpublished manuscript in David Baumgardt, *Bentham and the Ethics of Today* (Princeton, 1952), Appendix IV. For example, "the total value of the stock of pleasure belonging to the whole community is to be obtained by multiplying the number expressing the value of it as respecting any one person, by the number expressing the multitude of such individuals" (p. 556).

18. An idea essential to the classical utilitarian conception of justice. Bentham is firm in his statement of it: "It is only upon that principle [the principle of asceticism], and not from the principle of utility, that the most abominable pleasure which the vilest of malefactors ever reaped from his crime would be reprobed, if it stood alone. The case is, that it never does stand alone; but is necessarily followed by such a quantity of pain (or, what comes to the same thing, such a chance for a certain quantity of pain) that the pleasure in comparison of it, is as nothing: and this is true and sole, but perfectly sufficient, reason for making it a ground for punishment" (*The Principles of Morals and Legislation,* ch. 11, sec. iv. See also ch. x, sec. x, footnote 1). The same point is made in *The Limits of Jurisprudence Defined,* pp. 115 f. Although much recent welfare economics, as found in such important works as I. M. D. Little, *A Critique of Welfare Economics,* 2nd ed. (Oxford, 1957) and K. J. Arrow, *Social Choice and Individual Values* (New York, 1951), dispenses with the idea of cardinal utility, and uses instead the theory of ordinal utility as stated by J. R. Hicks, *Value and Capital,* 2nd ed. (Oxford, 1946), Pt. I, it assumes with utilitarianism that individual preferences have value as such, and so accepts the idea being criticized here. I hasten to add, however, that this is no objection to it as a means of analyzing economic policy, and for that purpose it may, indeed, be a necessary simplifying assumption. Nevertheless it is an assumption which cannot be made in so far as one is trying to analyze moral concepts, especially the concept of justice, as economists would, I think, agree. Justice is usually regarded as a separate and distinct part of any comprehensive criterion of economic policy. See, for example, Tibor Scitovsky, *Welfare and Competition* (London, 1952), pp. 59–69, and Little, *op. cit.,* cs. vii.

19. See J. S. Mill's argument in *Utilitarianism,* ch. v, pars. 16–25.

brings out its profound individualism, in one sense of this ambiguous word. It regards persons as so many *separate* directions in which benefits and burdens may be assigned; and the value of the satisfaction or dissatisfaction of desire is not thought to depend in any way on the moral relations in which individuals stand, or on the kinds of claims which they are willing, in the pursuit of their interests, to press on each other.

7. Many social decisions are, of course, of an administrative nature. Certainly this is so when it is a matter of social utility in what one may call its ordinary sense: that is, when it is a question of the efficient design of social institutions for the use of common means to achieve common ends. In this case either the benefits and burdens may be assumed to be impartially distributed, or the question of distribution is misplaced, as in the instance of maintaining public order and security or national defense. But as an interpretation of the basis of the principles of justice, classical utilitarianism is mistaken. It *permits* one to argue, for example, that slavery is unjust on the grounds that the advantages to the slaveholder as slaveholder do not counterbalance the disadvantages to the slave and to society at large burdened by comparatively inefficient system of labor. Now the conception of justice as fairness, when applied to the practice of slavery with its offices of slaveholder and slave, would not allow one to consider the advantages of the slaveholder in the first place. As that office is not in accordance with principles which could be mutually acknowledged, the gains accruing to the slaveholder, assuming them to exist, cannot be counted as in *any* way mitigating the injustice of the practice. The question whether these gains outweigh the disadvantages to the slave and to society cannot arise, since in considering the justice of slavery these gains have no weight at all which requires that they be overridden. Where the conception of justice as fairness applies, slavery is *always* unjust.

I am not, of course, suggesting the absurdity that the classical utilitarians approved of slavery. I am only rejecting a type of argument which their view allows them to use in support of their disapproval of it. The conception of justice as derivative from efficiency implies that judging the justice of a practice is always, in principle at least, a matter of weighing up advantages and disadvantages, each having an intrinsic value or disvalue as the satisfaction of interests, irrespective of whether or not these interests necessarily involve acquiescence in principles which could not be mutually acknowledged. Utilitarianism cannot account for the fact that slavery is always unjust, nor for the fact that it would be recognized as irrelevant in defeating the accusation of injustice for one person to say to another, engaged with him in a common practice and debating its merits, that nevertheless it allowed of the greatest satisfaction of desire. The charge of injustice cannot be rebutted in this way. If justice were derivative from a higher order executive efficiency, this would not be so.

But now, even if it is taken as established that, so far as the ordinary conception of justice goes, slavery is always unjust (that is, slavery by definition violates commonly recognized principles of justice), the classical utilitarian would surely reply that these principles, as other moral principles subordinate to that of utility, are only generally correct. It is simply for the most part true that slavery is less efficient than other institutions; and while common sense may define the concept of justice so that slavery is unjust, nevertheless, where slavery would lead to the greatest satisfaction of desire, it is not wrong. Indeed, it is then right, and for the very same reason that justice, a ordinarily understood, is usually right. If, as ordinarily understood, slavery is always unjust, to this extent the utilitarian conception of justice might be admitted to differ from that of common moral opinion. Still the utilitarian would want to hold that, as a matter of moral principle, his view is correct in giving no special weight to considerations of justice beyond that allowed for by the general presumption of effectiveness. And this, he claims, is as it should be. The every day opinion is morally in error, although, indeed, it is a useful error, since it protects rules of generally high utility.

The question, then, relates not simply to the analysis of the concept of justice as common sense defines it, but the analysis of it in the wider sense as to how much weight considerations of justice, as defined, are to have when laid against other kinds of moral considerations. Here again I wish to argue that reasons of justice have a *special* weight for which only the conception of justice as fairness can account. Moreover, it belongs to the concept of justice that they do have this special weight. While Mill recognized that this was so, he thought that it could be accounted for by the special urgency of the moral feelings which naturally support principles of such high utility. But it is a mistake to resort to the urgency of feeling; as with the appeal to intuition, it manifests a failure to pursue the question far enough. The special weight of considerations of justice can be explained from the conception of justice as fairness. It is only necessary to elaborate a bit what has already been said as follows.

If one examines the circumstances in which a certain tolerance of slavery is justified, or perhaps better, excused, it turns out that these are of a rather special sort. Perhaps slavery exists as an inheritance from the past and it proves necessary to dismantle it piece by piece; at times slavery may conceivably be an advance on previous institutions. Now while there may be some excuse for slavery in special conditions, it is never an excuse for it that it is sufficiently advantageous to the slaveholder to outweigh the disadvantages to the slave and to society. A person who argues in this way is not perhaps making a wildly irrelevant remark; but he is guilty of a moral fallacy. There is disorder in his conception of the ranking of moral principles. For the slaveholder, by his own admission, has no moral title to the advantages which he receives as a slaveholder. He is no more prepared than the slave to acknowledge the principle upon which is founded the respective positions in which they both stand. Since slavery does not accord with principles which they could mutually acknowledge, they each may be supposed to agree that it is unjust: it grants claims which it ought not to grant and in doing so denies claims which it ought not to deny. Amongst persons in a general position who are debating the form of their common practices, it cannot, therefore, be offered as a reason for a practice that, in conceding these very claims that ought to be denied, it nevertheless meets existing interests more effectively. By their very nature the satisfaction of these claims is without weight and cannot enter into any tabulation of advantages and disadvantages.

Furthermore, it follows from the concept of morality that, to the extent that the slaveholder recognizes his position via-à-vis the slave to be unjust, he would not choose to press his claims. His not wanting to receive his special advantages is one of the ways in which he shows that he thinks slavery is unjust. It would be fallacious for the legislator to suppose, then, that it is a ground for having a practice that it brings advantages greater than disadvantages, if those for whom the practice is designed, and to whom the advantages flow, acknowledge that they have no moral title to them and do not wish to receive them.

For these reasons the principles of justice have a special weight; and with respect to the principle of the greatest satisfaction of desire, as cited in the general position amongst those discussing the merits of their common practices, the principles of justice have an absolute weight. In this sense they are not contingent; and this is why their force is greater than can be accounted for by the general presumption (assuming that there is one) of the effectiveness, in the utilitarian sense, of practices which in fact satisfy them.

If one wants to continue using the concepts of classical utilitarianism, one will have to say, to meet this criticism, that at least the individual or social utility functions must be so defined that no value is given to the satisfaction of interests the representative claims of which violate the principles of justice. In this way it is no doubt possible to include these principles within the form of the utilitarian conception; but to do so is, of course, to change its inspiration altogether as a moral conception. For it is to incorporate within it principles which cannot be understood on the basis of a higher order executive decision aiming at the greatest satisfaction of desire.

It is worth remarking, perhaps, that this criticism of utilitarianism does not depend on whether or not the two assumptions, that of individuals having similar utility functions and that of diminishing marginal utility, are interpreted as psychological propositions to be supported or refuted by experience, or as moral and political principles expressed in a somewhat technical language. There are, certainly, several advantages in taking them in the latter fashion.[20] For one thing, one might say that this is what Bentham and others really meant by them, at least as shown by how they were used in arguments for social reform. More importantly, one could hold that the best way to defend the classical utilitarian view is to interpret these assumptions as moral and political principles. It is doubtful whether, taken as psychological propositions, they are true of men in general as we know them under normal conditions. On the other hand, utilitarians would not have wanted to propose them merely as practical working prin-

20. See D. G. Ritchie, *Natural Rights* (London, 1894), pp. 95 ff., 249 ff. Lionel Robbins has insisted on this point on several occasions. See *An Essay on the Nature and Significance of Economic Science,* 2nd ed. (London, 1935), pp. 134–43, "Interpersonal Comparisons of Utility: A Comment," *Economic Journal,* XLVIII (1938), 635–41, and more recently, "Robertson on Utility and Scope," *Economica,* n.s. XX (1953), 108 f.

ciples of legislation, or as expedient maxims to guide reform, given the egalitarian sentiments of modern society.[21] When pressed they might well have invoked the idea of a more or less equal capacity of men in relevant respects if given an equal chance in a just society. But if the argument above regarding slavery is correct, then granting these assumptions as moral and political principles makes no difference. To view individuals as equally fruitful lines for the allocation of benefits, even as a matter of moral principle, still leaves the mistaken notion that the satisfaction of desire has value in itself irrespective of the relations between persons as members of a common practice, and irrespective of the claims upon one another which the satisfaction of interests represents. To see the error of this idea one must give up the conception of justice as an executive decision altogether and refer to the notion of justice as fairness: that participants in a common practice be regarded as having an original and equal liberty and that their common practices be considered unjust unless they accord with principles which persons so circumstanced and related could freely acknowledge before one another, and so could accept as fair. Once the emphasis is put upon the concept of the mutual recognition of principles by participants in a common practice the rules of which are to define their several relations and give form to their claims on one another, then it is clear that the granting of a claim the principle of which could not be acknowledged by each in the general position (that is, in the position in which the parties propose and acknowledge principles before one another) is not a reason for adopting a practice. Viewed in this way, the background of the claim is seen to exclude it from consideration; that it can represent a value in itself arises from the conception of individuals as separate lines for the assignment of benefits, as isolated persons who stand as claimants on an administrative or benevolent largesse. Occasionally persons do so stand to one another; but this is not the general case, nor, more importantly, is it the case when it is a matter of the justice of practices themselves in which participants stand in various relations to be appraised in accordance with standards which they may be expected to acknowledge before one another. Thus however mistaken the notion of the social contract may be as history, and however far it may overreach itself as a general theory of social and political obligation, it does express, suitably interpreted, an essential part of the concept of justice.[22]

8. By way of conclusion I should like to make two remarks: first, the original modification of the utilitarian principle (that it require of practices that the offices and positions defined by them be equal unless it is reasonable to suppose that the representative man in *every* office would find the inequality to his advantage), slight as it may appear at first sight, actually has a different conception of justice standing behind it. I have tried to show how this is so by developing the concept of justice as fairness and by indicating how this notion involves the mutual acceptance, from a general position, of the principles on which a practice is founded, and how this in turn requires the exclusion from consideration of claims violating the principles of justice. Thus the slight alteration of principle reveals another family of notions, another way of looking at the concept of justice.

Second, I should like to remark also that I have been dealing with the *concept* of justice. I have tried to set out the kinds of principles upon which judgments concerning the justice of practices may be said to stand. The analysis will be successful to the degree that it expresses the principles involved in these judgments when made by competent persons upon deliberation and reflection.[23] Now every people may be supposed to have the concept of justice, since in

21. As Sir Henry Maine suggested Bentham may have regarded them. See *The Early History of Institutions* (London, 1875), pp. 398 ff.

22. Thus Kant was not far wrong when he interpreted the original contract merely as an "Idea of Reason"; yet he still thought of it as a *general* criterion of right and as providing a general theory of political obligation. See the second part of the essay, "On the Saying 'That may be right in theory but has no value in practice' " (1793), in *Kant's Principles of Politics*, tr. by W. Hastie (Edinburgh, 1891). I have drawn on the contractarian tradition not for a general theory of political obligation but to clarify the concept of justice.

23. For a further discussion of the idea expressed here, see my paper, "Outline of a Decision Procedure for Ethics," in the *Philosophical Review*, LX (1951), 177–197. For an analysis, similar in many respects but using the notion of the ideal observer instead of that of the considered judgment of a competent person, see Roderick Firth, "Ethical Absolutism and the Ideal Observer," *Philosophy and Phenomenological Research*, XII (1952), 317–345. While the similarities between these two discussions are more important than the differences, an analysis based on the notion of a considered judgment of a competent person, as it is based on a kind of judgment, may prove more helpful in understanding the features of moral judgment than an analysis based on the notion of an ideal observer, although this remains to be shown. A man who rejects the conditions imposed on a considered judgment of a competent person could no longer profess to *judge* at all. This seems more fundamental than his rejecting the conditions of observation, for these do not seem to apply, in an ordinary sense, to making a moral judgment.

the life of every society there must be at least some relations in which the parties consider themselves to be circumstanced and related as the concept of justice as fairness requires. Societies will differ from one another not in having or in failing to have this notion but in the range of cases to which they apply it and in the emphasis which they give to it as compared with other moral concepts.

A firm grasp of the concept of justice itself is necessary if these variations, and the reasons for them, are to be understood. No study of the development of moral ideas and of the differences between them is more sound than the analysis of the fundamental moral concepts upon which it must depend. I have tried, therefore, to give an analysis of the concept of justice which should apply generally, however large a part the concept may have in a given morality, and which can be used in explaining the course of men's thoughts about justice and its relations to other moral concepts. How it is to be used for this purpose is a large topic which I cannot, of course, take up here. I mention it only to emphasize that I have been dealing with the concept of justice itself and to indicate what use I consider such an analysis to have.